W9-BCI-318

How to Design and Evaluate Research in Education

NINTH EDITION

Jack R. Fraenkel
San Francisco State University

Norman E. Wallen
San Francisco State University

Helen H. Hyun
San Francisco State University

HOW TO DESIGN AND EVALUATE RESEARCH IN EDUCATION, NINTH EDITION

Published by McGraw-Hill Education, 2 Penn Plaza, New York, NY 10121.

Some ancillaries, including electronic and print components, may not be available to customers outside the United States.

This book is printed on acid-free paper.

1 2 3 4 5 6 7 8 9 0 DOW/DOW 1 0 9 8 7 6 5 4

ISBN 978-0-07-811039-9
MHID 0-07-811039-4

Senior Vice President, Products & Markets: *Kurt L. Strand*
Vice President, Content Production & Technology Services: *Kimberly Meriwether David*
Managing Director: *William R. Glass*
Brand Manager & Managing Editor: *Penina Braffman*
Executive Director of Development: *Lisa Pinto*
Development Editor: *Vicki Malinee, Van Brien & Associates*
Associate Marketing Manager: *Alexandra Schultz*
Content Project Manager: *Mary Jane Lampe*
Buyer: *Jennifer Pickel*
Cover Designer: *Studio Montage*
Cover Image: *Group of students in anatomy class: © Creatas/PunchStock; Teacher observing: © 2007 Keith Eng*
Compositor: *MPS Limited*
Typeface: *10/12 Times*
Printer: *R. R. Donnelley*

Library of Congress Cataloging-in-Publication Data

Fraenkel, Jack R., 1932–
How to design and evaluate research in education / Jack R. Fraenkel,
Norman E. Wallen, Helen H. Hyun.—Ninth edition.
pages cm.
ISBN 978-0-07-811039-9 (alk. paper)
1. Education—Research—Methodology. 2. Education—Research—Evaluation.
3. Proposal writing in educational research. I. Title.
LB1028.F665 2015
370.72—dc23

2013042978

The Internet addresses listed in the text were accurate at the time of publication. The inclusion of a website does not indicate an endorsement by the authors or McGraw-Hill Education, and McGraw-Hill Education does not guarantee the accuracy of the information presented at these sites.

www.mhhe.com

ABOUT THE AUTHORS

Jack R. Fraenkel is Professor Emeritus of Interdisciplinary Studies in Education, and previously Director of the Research and Development Center, College of Education, San Francisco State University. He received his PhD from Stanford University and has taught courses in research methodology for more than 30 years. In 1997, he received the James A. Michener prize in writing for his writings about the social studies and the social sciences. His current work centers on advising and assisting faculty and students in generating and developing research endeavors.

Norman E. Wallen is Professor Emeritus of Interdisciplinary Studies in Education at San Francisco State University, where he taught from 1966 to 1992. An experienced researcher, he received his PhD from Syracuse University and taught courses in statistics and research design to master's and doctoral students for many years. He is a former member of the City Council of Flagstaff, Arizona, and the Executive Committee, Grand Canyon Chapter of the Sierra Club.

Helen H. Hyun is currently Associate Professor of Interdisciplinary Studies in Education at San Francisco State University. She received her EdD from Harvard University and has taught courses in research design and methodology to master's and doctoral students at both San Francisco State and the University of California at Berkeley. Her teaching and research interests include higher education policy, mixed methods research, and equity issues in education.

To Marge, Lina, and Jeff for all their support

CONTENTS IN BRIEF

Preface *xix*

PART 1

Introduction to Research *1*

1 The Nature of Research *2*

PART 2

The Basics of Educational Research *25*

2 The Research Problem *26*
3 Locating and Reviewing the Literature *37*
4 Ethics and Research *60*
5 Variables and Hypotheses *76*
6 Sampling *91*
7 Instrumentation *111*
8 Validity and Reliability *147*
9 Internal Validity *166*

PART 3

Data Analysis *185*

10 Descriptive Statistics *186*
11 Inferential Statistics *219*
12 Statistics in Perspective *245*

PART 4

Quantitative Research Methodologies *263*

13 Experimental Research *264*
14 Single-Subject Research *301*
15 Correlational Research *331*
16 Causal-Comparative Research *363*
17 Survey Research *390*

PART 5

Introduction to Qualitative Research *421*

18 The Nature of Qualitative Research *422*
19 Observation and Interviewing *442*
20 Content Analysis *475*

PART 6

Qualitative Research Methodologies *503*

21 Ethnographic Research *504*
22 Historical Research *532*

PART 7

Mixed-Methods Studies *553*

23 Mixed-Methods Research *554*

PART 8

Research by Practitioners *585*

24 Action Research *586*

PART 9

Writing Research Proposals and Reports *613*

25 Preparing Research Proposals and Reports *614*

Appendixes *A-1*

APPENDIX A Portion of a Table of Random Numbers *A-2*
APPENDIX B Selected Values from a Normal Curve Table *A-3*
APPENDIX C Chi-Square Distribution *A-4*
APPENDIX D Using Microsoft Excel *A-5*

Glossary *G-1*
Credits *C-1*
Index *I-1*

CONTENTS

Preface *xix*

PART 1 Introduction to Research *1*

1 The Nature of Research *2*

Interactive and Applied Learning *3* 

Some Examples of Educational Concerns *3*
Why Research Is of Value *4*
Ways of Knowing *4*
Types of Research *7*
General Research Types *15*
Critical Analysis of Research *16*
A Brief Overview of the Research Process *19*
Main Points *21*
Key Terms *22*
For Discussion *23*
References *23*
Research Exercise 1 *24*
Problem Sheet 1 *24*

PART 2 The Basics of Educational Research *25*

2 The Research Problem *26*

Interactive and Applied Learning *27* 

What Is a Research Problem? *27*
Research Questions *27*
Characteristics of Good Research Questions *28*
Main Points *35*
Key Terms *35*
For Discussion *35*
Research Exercise 2 *36*
Problem Sheet 2 *36*

3 Locating and Reviewing the Literature *37*

Interactive and Applied Learning *38* 

The Definition and Value of a Literature Review *38*
Types of Sources *38*
Steps Involved in a Literature Search *39*
Doing a Computer Search *44*
Writing the Literature Review Report *51*
Main Points *56*
Key Terms *58*
For Discussion *58*
References *58*
Research Exercise 3 *59*
Problem Sheet 3 *59*

4 Ethics and Research *60*

Interactive and Applied Learning *61* 

Some Examples of Unethical Practice *61*
A Statement of Ethical Principles *61*
Protecting Participants from Harm *63*
Ensuring Confidentiality of Research Data *64*
When (If Ever) Is Deception of Subjects Justified? *64*
Three Examples Involving Ethical Concerns *65*
Research with Children *67*
Regulation of Research *69*
Academic Cheating and Plagiarism *72*
Main Points *72*
Key Terms *73*
For Discussion *73*
References *74*
Research Exercise 4 *75*
Problem Sheet 4 *75*

5 Variables and Hypotheses *76*

Interactive and Applied Learning *77* 

The Importance of Studying Relationships *77*
Variables *78*
Hypotheses *84*
Main Points *88*
Key Terms *89*
For Discussion *89*
References *89*
Research Exercise 5 *90*
Problem Sheet 5 *90*

6 Sampling *91*

Interactive and Applied Learning *92* 

What Is a Sample? *92*
Random Sampling Methods *95*
Nonrandom Sampling Methods *98*
A Review of Sampling Methods *101*
Sample Size *103*
External Validity: Generalizing from a Sample *104*
Main Points *107*
Key Terms *108*
For Discussion *108*
Research Exercise 6 *110*
Problem Sheet 6 *110*

7 Instrumentation *111*

Interactive and Applied Learning *112* 

What Are Data? *112*
Means of Classifying Data-Collection Instruments *114*
Examples of Data-Collection Instruments *117*
Norm-Referenced Versus Criterion-Referenced Instruments *137*
Measurement Scales *138*
Preparing Data for Analysis *141*
Main Points *142*
Key Terms *144*
For Discussion *144*
References *144*
Research Exercise 7 *146*
Problem Sheet 7 *146*

8 Validity and Reliability *147*

Interactive and Applied Learning *148* 

The Importance of Valid Instrumentation *148*
Validity *148*
Reliability *155*
Main Points *163*
Key Terms *163*
For Discussion *164*
References *164*
Research Exercise 8 *165*
Problem Sheet 8 *165*

9 Internal Validity *166*

Interactive and Applied Learning *167* 

What Is Internal Validity? *167*
Threats to Internal Validity *168*
How Can a Researcher Minimize These Threats to Internal Validity? *180*

Main Points 181
Key Terms 182
For Discussion 183
Reference 183
Research Exercise 9 184
Problem Sheet 9 184

PART 3 Data Analysis 185

10 Descriptive Statistics 186

Interactive and Applied Learning 187

Statistics Versus Parameters 187
Two Fundamental Types of Numerical Data 187
Types of Scores 189
Techniques for Summarizing Quantitative Data 190
Techniques for Summarizing Categorical Data 209
Main Points 215
Key Terms 216
For Discussion 217
Research Exercise 10 218
Problem Sheet 10 218

11 Inferential Statistics 219

Interactive and Applied Learning 220

What Are Inferential Statistics? 220
The Logic of Inferential Statistics 221
Hypothesis Testing 228
Practical Versus Statistical Significance 230
Inference Techniques 233
Main Points 241
Key Terms 243
For Discussion 243
Research Exercise 11 244
Problem Sheet 11 244

12 Statistics in Perspective 245

Interactive and Applied Learning 246

Approaches to Research 246
Comparing Groups: Quantitative Data 247
Relating Variables Within a Group: Quantitative Data 251
Comparing Groups: Categorical Data 255
Relating Variables Within a Group: Categorical Data 257
A Recap of Recommendations 259
Main Points 259
Key Terms 260
For Discussion 260
Research Exercise 12 261
Problem Sheet 12 261

PART 4 Quantitative Research Methodologies 263

13 Experimental Research 264

Interactive and Applied Learning 265

The Uniqueness of Experimental Research 265
Essential Characteristics of Experimental Research 266
Control of Extraneous Variables 268
Group Designs in Experimental Research 268
Control of Threats to Internal Validity: A Summary 279
Evaluating the Likelihood of a Threat to Internal Validity in Experimental Studies 281
Control of Experimental Treatments 284
An Example of Experimental Research 285
Analysis of the Study 294
Main Points 296
Key Terms 297
For Discussion 298
References 299
Research Exercise 13 300
Problem Sheet 13 300

14 Single-Subject Research *301*

Interactive and Applied Learning *302*

Essential Characteristics of Single-Subject Research *302*

Single-Subject Designs *303*

Threats to Internal Validity in Single-Subject Research *309*

An Example of Single-Subject Research *314*

Analysis of the Study *327*

Main Points *328*

Key Terms *329*

For Discussion *329*

References *330*

15 Correlational Research *331*

Interactive and Applied Learning *332* 

The Nature of Correlational Research *332*

Purposes of Correlational Research *333*

Basic Steps in Correlational Research *339*

What Do Correlation Coefficients Tell Us? *341*

Threats to Internal Validity in Correlational Research *341*

Evaluating Threats to Internal Validity in Correlational Studies *345*

An Example of Correlational Research *347*

Analysis of the Study *358*

Main Points *360*

Key Terms *361*

For Discussion *361*

References *362*

16 Causal-Comparative Research *363*

Interactive and Applied Learning *364* 

What Is Causal-Comparative Research? *364*

Steps Involved in Causal-Comparative Research *367*

Threats to Internal Validity in Causal-Comparative Research *368*

Evaluating Threats to Internal Validity in Causal-Comparative Studies *370*

Data Analysis *371*

Associations Between Categorical Variables *373*

An Example of Causal-Comparative Research *374*

Analysis of the Study *386*

Main Points *387*

For Discussion *389*

Reference *389*

17 Survey Research *390*

Interactive and Applied Learning *391* 

What Is a Survey? *391*

Why Are Surveys Conducted? *391*

Types of Surveys *392*

Survey Research and Correlational Research *393*

Steps in Survey Research *393*

Nonresponse *404*

Problems in the Instrumentation Process in Survey Research *407*

Evaluating Threats to Internal Validity in Survey Research *407*

Data Analysis in Survey Research *407*

An Example of Survey Research *408*

Analysis of the Study *416*

Main Points *417*

Key Terms *419*

For Discussion *419*

References *420*

PART 5 Introduction to Qualitative Research 421

18 The Nature of Qualitative Research 422

Interactive and Applied Learning 423 

What Is Qualitative Research? 423
General Characteristics of Qualitative Research 424
Philosophical Assumptions Underlying Qualitative as Opposed to Quantitative Research 425
Postmodernism 427
Steps in Qualitative Research 427
Approaches to Qualitative Research 430
Qualitative Data Analysis 434
Generalization in Qualitative Research 434
Internal Validity in Qualitative Research 436
Ethics and Qualitative Research 436
Qualitative and Quantitative Research Reconsidered 437
Main Points 438
Key Terms 439
For Discussion 439
References 440

19 Observation and Interviewing 442

Interactive and Applied Learning 443 

Observation 443
Interviewing 448
Validity and Reliability in Qualitative Research 456
An Example of Qualitative Research 458
Analysis of the Study 469
Main Points 471
Key Terms 472
For Discussion 473
References 473

20 Content Analysis 475

Interactive and Applied Learning 476 

What Is Content Analysis? 476
Some Applications 477
Categorization in Content Analysis 478
Steps Involved in Content Analysis 478
An Illustration of Content Analysis 484
Using a Computer in Content Analysis 486
Advantages of Content Analysis 487
Disadvantages of Content Analysis 487
An Example of a Content Analysis Study 488
Analysis of the Study 499
Main Points 500
Key Terms 501
For Discussion 502
References 502

PART 6 Qualitative Research Methodologies 503

21 Ethnographic Research 504

Interactive and Applied Learning 505 

What Is Ethnographic Research? 505
The Unique Value of Ethnographic Research 506
Ethnographic Concepts 507
Sampling in Ethnographic Research 509
Do Ethnographic Researchers Use Hypotheses? 509
Data Collection in Ethnographic Research 510
Data Analysis in Ethnographic Research 514
Roger Harker and His Fifth-Grade Classroom 516
Advantages and Disadvantages of Ethnographic Research 518
An Example of Ethnographic Research 518
Analysis of the Study 528
Main Points 529
Key Terms 530
For Discussion 530
References 531

22 Historical Research 532

Interactive and Applied Learning 533 

What Is Historical Research? 533
Steps Involved in Historical Research? 534
Data Analysis in Historical Research 539
Generalization in Historical Research 539
Advantages and Disadvantages of Historical Research 540
An Example of Historical Research 541
Analysis of the Study 549
Main Points 550
Key Terms 551
For Discussion 552
References 552

PART 7 Mixed-Methods Studies 553

23 Mixed-Methods Research 554

Interactive and Applied Learning 555 

What Is Mixed-Methods Research? 555
Why Do Mixed-Methods Research? 556
Drawbacks of Mixed-Methods Studies 556
A (Very) Brief History 557
Types of Mixed-Methods Designs 558
Other Mixed-Methods Research Design Issues 560
Steps in Conducting a Mixed-Methods Study 561
Evaluating a Mixed-Methods Study 563
Ethics in Mixed-Methods Research 563
Summary 563
An Example of Mixed-Methods Research 563
Analysis of the Study 578
Main Points 581
Key Terms 582
For Discussion 583
References 583

PART 8 Research by Practitioners 585

24 Action Research 586

Interactive and Applied Learning 587 

What Is Action Research? 587
Types of Action Research 588
Steps in Action Research 591
Similarities and Differences Between Action Research and Formal Quantitative and Qualitative Research 593
The Advantages of Action Research 594
Hypothetical Examples of Practical Action Research 595
An Example of Action Research 600
A Published Example of Action Research 601
Analysis of the Study 608
Main Points 609
Key Terms 610
For Discussion 610
References 611

PART 9 Writing Research Proposals and Reports *613*

25 Preparing Research Proposals and Reports *614*

Interactive and Applied Learning *615* 

The Research Proposal *615*

The Major Sections of a Research Proposal or Report *615*

Sections Unique to Research Reports *622*

A Sample Research Proposal *626*

Main Points *638*

For Review *638*

Key Terms *639*

For Discussion *639*

References *639*

Appendixes *A-1*

APPENDIX A Portion of a Table of Random Numbers *A-2*

APPENDIX B Selected Values from a Normal Curve Table *A-3*

APPENDIX C Chi-Square Distribution *A-4*

APPENDIX D Using Microsoft Excel *A-5*

Glossary *G-1*

Credits *C-1*

Index *I-1*

LIST OF FEATURES

RESEARCH REPORTS

Cognitive Effects of Chess Instruction on Students at Risk for Academic Failure *286*

Implementation of the Guided Reading Approach With Elementary School Deaf Students *315*

Physical Education in Urban High School Class Settings: Features and Correlations between Teaching Behaviors and Learning Activities *348*

Internet Use, Abuse, and Dependence Among Students at a Southeastern Regional University *374*

Teaching Social Studies in the 21st Century: A Research Study of Secondary Social Studies Teachers' Instructional Methods and Practices *408*

Walk and Talk: An Intervention for Behaviorally Challenged Youths *458*

The "Nuts and Dolts" of Teacher Images in Children's Picture Storybooks: A Content Analysis *488*

Lessons on Effective Teaching from Middle School ESL Students *519*

Lydia Ann Stow: Self-Actualization in a Period of Transition *542*

Perceived Family Support, Acculturation, and Life Satisfaction in Mexican American Youth: A Mixed-Methods Exploration *564*

An Action Research Exploration Integrating Student Choice and Arts Activities in a Sixth Grade Social Studies Classroom *601*

RESEARCH TIPS

Key Terms to Define in a Research Study *31*

What a Good Summary of a Journal Article Should Contain *50*

Some Tips About Developing Your Own Instrument *115*

Sample Size *234*

How Not to Interview *455*

What to Do About Contradictory Findings *562*

Things to Consider When Doing In-School Research *598*

Questions to Ask When Evaluating a Research Report *622*

MORE ABOUT RESEARCH

Chaos Theory *8*

The Importance of a Rationale *33*

Patients Given Fake Blood Without Their Knowledge *65*

An Example of Unethical Research *67*

Department of Health and Human Services Revised Regulations for Research with Human Subjects *71*

Some Important Relationships That Have Been Clarified by Educational Research *80*

The Difficulty in Generalizing from a Sample *104*

Checking Reliability and Validity—An Example *158*

Threats to Internal Validity in Everyday Life *176*

Some Thoughts About Meta-Analysis *178*
Correlation in Everyday Life *213*
Interpreting Statistics *258*
Significant Findings in Experimental Research *283*
Important Findings in Single-Subject Research *303*
Examples of Studies Conducted Using Single-Subject Designs *313*
Important Findings in Correlational Research *334*
Significant Findings in Causal-Comparative Research *373*
Important Findings in Survey Research *397*
Important Findings in Content Analysis Research *479*
Important Findings in Ethnographic Research *506*
Important Findings in Historical Research *540*
An Important Example of Action Research *595*

CONTROVERSIES IN RESEARCH

Should Some Research Methods Be Preferred over Others? *15*
Clinical Trials—Desirable or Not? *63*
Ethical or Not? *70*
Sample or Census? *103*
Which Statistical Index Is Valid? *140*
High-Stakes Testing *151*
Is Consequential Validity a Useful Concept? *161*
Can Statistical Power Analysis Be Misleading? *240*
Statistical Inference Tests—Good or Bad? *249*
Do Placebos Work? *281*
How Should Research Methodologies Be Classified? *366*
Is Low Response Rate Necessarily a Bad Thing? *406*
Clarity and Postmodernism *428*
Portraiture: Art, Science, or Both? *431*
Should Historians Influence Policy? *538*
Are Some Methods Incompatible with Others? *558*
How Much Should Participants Be Involved in Research? *591*

TABLES

Table 4.1 Criteria for IRB Approval *69*
Table 6.1 Part of a Table of Random Numbers *96*
Table 7.1 Characteristics of the Four Types of Measurement Scales *140*
Table 7.2 Hypothetical Results of Study Involving a Comparison of Two Counseling Methods *141*
Table 8.1 Example of an Expectancy Table *154*
Table 8.2 Methods of Checking Validity and Reliability *159*
TABLE 9.1 Threats to the Internal Validity of a Study *180*
Table 9.2 General Techniques for Controlling Threats to Internal Validity *181*
Table 10.1 Hypothetical Examples of Raw Scores and Accompanying Percentile Ranks *190*
Table 10.2 Example of a Frequency Distribution *191*
Table 10.3 Example of a Grouped Frequency Distribution *191*
Table 10.4 Example of the Mode, Median, and Mean in a Distribution *196*
Table 10.5 Yearly Salaries of Workers in a Small Business *197*
Table 10.6 Calculation of the Standard Deviation of a Distribution *199*
Table 10.7 Comparisons of Raw Scores and z Scores on Two Tests *202*
Table 10.8 Data Used to Construct Scatterplot in Figure 10.17 *206*
Table 10.9 Frequency and Percentage of Total of Responses to Questionnaire *211*
Table 10.10 Grade Level and Gender of Teachers (Hypothetical Data) *212*
Table 10.11 Repeat of Table 10.10 *with* Expected Frequencies (in Parentheses) 212
Table 10.12 Position, Gender, and Ethnicity of School Leaders (Hypothetical Data) *212*
Table 10.13 Position and Ethnicity of School Leaders with Expected Frequencies (Derived from Table 10.12) *213*
Table 10.14 Position and Gender of School Leaders with Expected Frequencies (Derived from Table 10.12) *213*

Table 10.15 Gender and Ethnicity of School Leaders with Expected Frequencies (Derived from Table 10.12) *213*

Table 10.16 Total of Discrepancies Between Expected and Observed Frequencies in Tables 10.13 Through 10.15 214

Table 10.17 Crossbreak Table Showing Relationship Between Self-Esteem and Gender (Hypothetical Data) *214*

Table 11.1 Contingency Coefficient Values for Different-Sized Crossbreak Tables 238

Table 11.2 Commonly Used Inferential Techniques *239*

Table 12.1 Gain Scores on Test of Ability to Explain: Inquiry and Lecture Groups *250*

Table 12.2 Calculations from Table 12.1 *252*

Table 12.3 Interpretation of Correlation Coefficients When Testing Research Hypotheses *253*

Table 12.4 Self-Esteem Scores and Gains in Marital Satisfaction *254*

Table 12.5 Gender and Political Preference (Percentages) *256*

Table 12.6 Gender and Political Preference (Numbers) *256*

Table 12.7 Teacher Gender and Grade Level Taught: Case *1* 256

Table 12.8 Teacher Gender and Grade Level Taught: Case 2 256

Table 12.9 Crossbreak Table Showing Teacher Gender and Grade Level with Expected Frequencies Added (Data from Table 12.7) *257*

Table 12.10 Summary of Commonly Used Statistical Techniques *258*

Table 13.1 Effectiveness of Experimental Designs in Controlling Threats to Internal Validity *280*

Table 15.1 Three Sets of Data Showing Different Directions and Degrees of Correlation *333*

Table 15.2 Teacher Expectation of Failure and Amount of Disruptive Behavior for a Sample of *12* Classes 335

Table 15.3 Correlation Matrix for Variables in Student Alienation Study *338*

Table 15.4 Example of Data Obtained in a Correlational Design *340*

Table 16.1 Grade Level and Gender of Teachers (Hypothetical Data) *373*

Table 17.1 Advantages and Disadvantages of Survey Data Collection Methods *394*

Table 17.2 Advantages and Disadvantages of Closed-Ended Versus Open-Ended Questions *399*

Table 18.1 Quantitative Versus Qualitative Research *424*

Table 18.2 Major Characteristics of Qualitative Research *426*

Table 18.3 Differing Philosophical Assumptions of Quantitative and Qualitative Researchers *427*

Table 19.1 Interviewing Strategies Used in Educational Research *450*

Table 19.2 Qualitative Research Questions, Strategies, and Data Collection Techniques *457*

Table 20.1 Coding Categories for Women in Social Studies Textbooks *481*

Table 20.2 Sample Tally Sheet (Newspaper Editorials) *484*

Table 20.3 Clarity of Studies *484*

Table 20.4 Type of Sample *484*

Table 20.5 Threats to Internal Validity *486*

Table 24.1 Basic Assumptions Underlying Action Research *588*

Table 24.2 Similarities and Differences Between Action Research and Formal Quantitative and Qualitative Research *594*

Table 25.1 References APA Style *623*

FIGURES

Figure 1.1 Ways of Knowing *10*

Figure 1.2 Example of Results of Experimental Research: Effect of Method of Instruction on History Test Scores *11*

Figure 1.3 Is the Teacher's Assumption Correct? *18*

Figure 1.4 The Research Process *20*

Figure 2.1 Researchable Versus Nonresearchable Questions *29*

Figure 2.2 Some Times When Operational Definitions Would Be Helpful *32*

Figure 2.3 Relationship Between Voter Gender and Party Affiliation *34*

Figure 3.1 Excerpt from ERIC Journal Article *42*

Figure 3.2 Excerpt from ERIC Document *43*

Figure 3.3 Excerpt from ProQuest Dissertations and Theses *44*

Figure 3.4 Excerpt from Education Full Text *45*

Figure 3.5 Venn Diagrams Showing the Boolean Operators AND and OR *46*

Figure 3.6 Summary of Search Results *47*

Figure 3.7 Prompts for Evaluating Research Studies *51*

Figure 3.8 Example of an Annotated Table *52*

Figure 4.1 Example of a Consent Form *64*

Figure 4.2 Examples of Unethical Research Practices *66*

Figure 4.3 Example of a Consent Form for a Minor to Participate in a Research Study *68*

Figure 5.1 Quantitative Variables Compared with Categorical Variables *79*

Figure 5.2 Relationship Between Instructional Approach (Independent Variable) and Achievement (Dependent Variable), as Moderated by Gender of Students *82*

Figure 5.3 Examples of Extraneous Variables *83*

Figure 5.4 A Single Research Problem Can Suggest Several Hypotheses *85*

Figure 5.5 Directional Versus Nondirectional Hypotheses *87*

Figure 6.1 Representative Versus Nonrepresentative Samples *94*

Figure 6.2 Selecting a Stratified Sample *97*

Figure 6.3 Cluster Random Sampling *98*

Figure 6.4 Random Sampling Methods *99*

Figure 6.5 Convenience Sampling *100*

Figure 6.6 Nonrandom Sampling Methods *102*

Figure 6.7 Population as Opposed to Ecological Generalizing *106*

Figure 7.1 ERIC Database of Tests and Assessments *116*

Figure 7.2 Search Results for Social Studies Competency-Based Instruments *117*

Figure 7.3 Abstract from the ERIC Database *118*

Figure 7.4 Excerpt from a Behavior Rating Scale for Teachers *119*

Figure 7.5 Excerpt from a Graphic Rating Scale *119*

Figure 7.6 Example of a Product Rating Scale *120*

Figure 7.7 Interview Schedule (for Teachers) Designed to Assess the Effects of a Competency-Based Curriculum in Inner-City Schools *121*

Figure 7.8 Semi-Structured Interview Protocol *122*

Figure 7.9 Sample Observation Form *122*

Figure 7.10 Discussion-Analysis Tally Sheet *123*

Figure 7.11 Participation Flowchart *124*

Figure 7.12 Performance Checklist Noting Student Actions *125*

Figure 7.13 Time-and-Motion Log *126*

Figure 7.14 Example of a Self-Checklist *127*

Figure 7.15 Examples of Items from a Likert Scale Measuring Attitude Toward Teacher Empowerment *128*

Figure 7.16 Example of the Semantic Differential *129*

Figure 7.17 Pictorial Attitude Scale for Use with Young Children *129*

Figure 7.18 Sample Items from a Personality Inventory *130*

Figure 7.19 Sample Items from an Achievement Test *130*

Figure 7.20 Sample Item from an Aptitude Test *131*

Figure 7.21 Sample Items from an Intelligence Test *131*

Figure 7.22 Example from the Blum Sewing Machine Test *132*

Figure 7.23 Sample Items from the Picture Situation Inventory *133*

Figure 7.24 Example of a Sociogram *134*

Figure 7.25 Example of a Group Play *135*

Figure 7.26 Four Types of Measurement Scales *138*

Figure 7.27 A Nominal Scale of Measurement *138*

Figure 7.28 An Ordinal Scale: The Outcome of a Horse Race *139*

Figure 8.1 Types of Evidence of Validity *150*

Figure 8.2 Reliability and Validity *156*

Figure 8.3 Reliability of a Measurement *156*
Figure 8.4 Standard Error of Measurement *159*
Figure 8.5 The "Quick and Easy" Intelligence Test *160*
Figure 8.6 Reliability Worksheet *161*
Figure 9.1 A Mortality Threat to Internal Validity *169*
Figure 9.2 Location Might Make a Difference *170*
Figure 9.3 An Example of Instrument Decay *171*
Figure 9.4 A Data Collector Characteristics Threat *171*
Figure 9.5 A Testing Threat to Internal Validity *172*
Figure 9.6 A History Threat to Internal Validity *173*
Figure 9.7 Could Maturation Be at Work Here? *174*
Figure 9.8 The Attitude of Subjects Can Make a Difference *175*
Figure 9.9 Regression Rears Its Head *177*
Figure 9.10 Illustration of Threats to Internal Validity *179*
Figure 10.1 Example of a Frequency Polygon *192*
Figure 10.2 Example of a Positively Skewed Polygon *193*
Figure 10.3 Example of a Negatively Skewed Polygon *193*
Figure 10.4 Two Frequency Polygons Compared *193*
Figure 10.5 Histogram of Data in Table 10.3 *194*
Figure 10.6 The Normal Curve *195*
Figure 10.7 Averages Can Be Misleading! *197*
Figure 10.8 Different Distributions Compared with Respect to Averages and Spreads *198*
Figure 10.9 Boxplots *198*
Figure 10.10 Standard Deviations for Boys' and Men's Basketball Teams *200*
Figure 10.11 Fifty Percent of All Scores in a Normal Curve Fall on Each Side of the Mean *200*
Figure 10.12 Percentages Under the Normal Curve *200*
Figure 10.13 z Scores Associated with the Normal Curve *201*
Figure 10.14 Probabilities Under the Normal Curve *203*
Figure 10.15 Table Showing Probability Areas Between the Mean and Different z Scores *203*
Figure 10.16 Examples of Standard Scores *204*
Figure 10.17 Scatterplot of Data from Table 10.8 *206*
Figure 10.18 Relationship Between Family Cohesiveness and School Achievement in a Hypothetical Group of Students *208*
Figure 10.19 Further Examples of Scatterplots *209*
Figure 10.20 A Perfect Negative Correlation! *210*
Figure 10.21 Positive and Negative Correlations *210*
Figure 10.22 Examples of Nonlinear (Curvilinear) Relationships *210*
Figure 10.23 Example of a Bar Graph *211*
Figure 10.24 Example of a Pie Chart *212*
Figure 11.1 Selection of Two Samples from Two Distinct Populations *221*
Figure 11.2 Sampling Error *222*
Figure 11.3 A Sampling Distribution of Means *223*
Figure 11.4 Distribution of Sample Means *224*
Figure 11.5 The 95 Percent Confidence Interval *225*
Figure 11.6 The 99 Percent Confidence Interval *225*
Figure 11.7 We Can Be 99 Percent Confident *226*
Figure 11.8 Does a Sample Difference Reflect a Population Difference? *226*
Figure 11.9 Distribution of the Difference Between Sample Means *227*
Figure 11.10 Confidence Intervals *227*
Figure 11.11 Null and Research Hypotheses *229*
Figure 11.12 Illustration of When a Researcher Would Reject the Null Hypothesis *230*
Figure 11.13 How Much Is Enough? *231*
Figure 11.14 Significance Area for a One-Tailed Test *231*
Figure 11.15 One-Tailed Test Using a Distribution of Differences Between Sample Means *232*
Figure 11.16 Two-Tailed Test Using a Distribution of Differences Between Sample Means *232*
Figure 11.17 A Hypothetical Example of Type I and Type II Errors *233*
Figure 11.18 Rejecting the Null Hypothesis *239*

Figure 11.19 Power Under an Assumed Population Value *239*

Figure 11.20 A Power Curve *240*

Figure 12.1 Combinations of Data and Approaches to Research *247*

Figure 12.2 A Difference That Doesn't Make a Difference! *250*

Figure 12.3 Frequency Polygons of Gain Scores on Test of Ability to Explain: Inquiry and Lecture Groups *250*

Figure 12.4 90 Percent Confidence Interval for a Difference of 1.2 Between Sample Means *251*

Figure 12.5 Scatterplots with a Pearson *r* of .50 *253*

Figure 12.6 Scatterplot Illustrating the Relationship Between Initial Self-Esteem and Gain in Marital Satisfaction Among Counseling Clients *255*

Figure 12.7 95 Percent Confidence Interval for $r = .42$ *255*

Figure 13.1 Example of a One-Shot Case Study Design *269*

Figure 13.2 Example of a One-Group Pretest-Posttest Design *269*

Figure 13.3 Example of a Static-Group Comparison Design *270*

Figure 13.4 Example of a Randomized Posttest-Only Control Group Design *271*

Figure 13.5 Example of a Randomized Pretest-Posttest Control Group Design *272*

Figure 13.6 Example of a Randomized Solomon Four-Group Design *273*

Figure 13.7 A Randomized Posttest-Only Control Group Design, Using Matched Subjects *274*

Figure 13.8 Results (Means) from a Study Using a Counterbalanced Design *276*

Figure 13.9 Possible Outcome Patterns in a Time-Series Design *277*

Figure 13.10 Using a Factorial Design to Study Effects of Method and Class Size on Achievement *278*

Figure 13.11 Illustration of Interaction and No Interaction in a 2 by 2 Factorial Design *278*

Figure 13.12 Example of a 4 by 2 Factorial Design *279*

Figure 13.13 Guidelines for Handling Internal Validity in Comparison Group Studies *282*

Figure 14.1 Single-Subject Graph *303*

Figure 14.2 A-B Design *304*

Figure 14.3 A-B-A Design *305*

Figure 14.4 A-B-A-B Design *306*

Figure 14.5 B-A-B Design *307*

Figure 14.6 A-B-C-B Design *308*

Figure 14.7 Multiple-Baseline Design *308*

Figure 14.8 Multiple-Baseline Design *309*

Figure 14.9 Multiple-Baseline Design Applied to Different Settings *310*

Figure 14.10 Variations in Baseline Stability *311*

Figure 14.11 Differences in Degree and Speed of Change *312*

Figure 14.12 Differences in Return to Baseline Conditions *313*

Figure 15.1 Scatterplot Illustrating a Correlation of +1.00 *333*

Figure 15.2 Prediction Using a Scatterplot *334*

Figure 15.3 Multiple Correlation *336*

Figure 15.4 Discriminant Function Analysis *337*

Figure 15.5 Path Analysis Diagram *339*

Figure 15.6 Scatterplots for Combinations of Variables *343*

Figure 15.7 Eliminating the Effects of Age Through Partial Correlation *344*

Figure 15.8 Scatterplots Illustrating How a Factor (C) May Not Be a Threat to Internal Validity *347*

Figure 15.9 Circle Diagrams Illustrating Relationships Among Variables *347*

Figure 16.1 Examples of the Basic Causal-Comparative Design *368*

Figure 16.2 A Subject Characteristics Threat *369*

Figure 16.3 Does a Threat to Internal Validity Exist? *372*

Figure 17.1 Example of an Ideal Versus an Actual Telephone Sample for a Specific Question *395*

Figure 17.2 Example of an Internet Survey Created on SurveyMonkey *396*

Figure 17.3 Example of SurveyMonkey Data Results *397*

Figure 17.4 Example of Several Contingency Questions in an Interview Schedule *402*

Figure 17.5 Sample Cover Letter for a Mail Survey *403*

Figure 17.6 Demographic Data and Representativeness *405*

Figure 18.1 How Qualitative and Quantitative Researchers See the World *429*

Figure 19.1 Variations in Approaches to Observation *445*

Figure 19.2 The Importance of a Second Observer as a Check on One's Conclusions *447*

Figure 19.3 The Amidon/Flanders Scheme for Coding Categories of Interaction in the Classroom *448*

Figure 19.4 An Interview of Dubious Validity *453*

Figure 19.5 Don't Ask More Than One Question at a Time *454*

Figure 20.1 TV Violence and Public Viewing Patterns *477*

Figure 20.2 What Categories Should I Use? *481*

Figure 20.3 An Example of Coding an Interview *482*

Figure 20.4 Categories Used to Evaluate Social Studies Research *485*

Figure 21.1 Triangulation and Politics *515*

Figure 22.1 What Really Happened? *539*

Figure 22.2 Historical Research Is Not as Easy as You May Think! *541*

Figure 23.1 Exploratory Design *558*

Figure 23.2 Explanatory Design *559*

Figure 23.3 Triangulation Design *559*

Figure 24.1 Stakeholders *589*

Figure 24.2 The Role of the "Expert" in Action Research *590*

Figure 24.3 Levels of Participation in Action Research *591*

Figure 24.4 Participation in Action Research *593*

Figure 24.5 Experimental Design for the DeMaria Study *600*

Figure 25.1 Organization of a Research Report *624*

PREFACE

How to Design and Evaluate Research in Education is directed to students taking their first course in educational research. Because this field continues to grow so rapidly with regard to both the knowledge it contains and the methodologies it employs, the authors of any introductory text are forced to carefully define their goals as a first step in deciding what to include in their book. In our case, we continually kept three main goals in mind. We wanted to produce a text that would:

1. Provide students with the basic information needed to understand the research process, from idea formulation through data analysis and interpretation.
2. Enable students to use this knowledge to design their own research investigation on a topic of personal interest.
3. Permit students to read and understand the literature of educational research.

The first two goals are intended to satisfy the needs of those students who must plan and carry out a research project as part of their course requirements. The third goal is aimed at students whose course requirements include learning how to read and understand the research of others. Many instructors, ourselves included, build all three goals into their courses, since each one seems to reinforce the others. It is hard to read and fully comprehend the research of others if you have not yourself gone through the process of designing and evaluating a research project. Similarly, the more you read and evaluate the research of others, the better equipped you will be to design your own meaningful and creative research. In order to achieve the above goals, we have developed a book with the following characteristics.

CONTENT COVERAGE

Goal one, to provide students with the basic information needed to understand the research process, has resulted in a nine-part book plan. Part 1 (Chapter 1) introduces students to the nature of educational research, briefly overviews each of the seven methodologies discussed later in the text, and presents an overview of the research process as well as criticisms of it.

Part 2 (Chapters 2 through 9) discusses the basic concepts and procedures that must be understood before one can engage in research intelligently or critique it meaningfully. These chapters explain variables, definitions, ethics, sampling, instrumentation, validity, reliability, and internal validity. These and other concepts are covered thoroughly, clearly, and relatively simply. Our emphasis throughout is to show students, by means of clear and appropriate examples, how to set up a research study in an educational setting on a question of interest and importance.

Part 3 (Chapters 10 through 12) describes in some detail the processes involved in collecting and analyzing data.

Part 4 (Chapters 13 through 17) describes and illustrates the methodologies most commonly used in quantitative educational research. Many key concepts presented in Part 2 are considered again in these chapters in order to illustrate their application to each methodology. Finally, each methodology chapter concludes with a carefully chosen study from the published research literature. Each study is analyzed by the authors with regard to both its strengths and weaknesses. Students are shown how to read and critically analyze a study they might find in the literature.

Part 5 (Chapters 18 through 20) and Part 6 (Chapters 21 through 22) discuss qualitative research. Part 5 begins the coverage by describing qualitative research, its philosophy, and essential features. It has been expanded to include various types of qualitative research. This is followed by an expanded treatment of both data collection and analysis methods. Part 6 presents the qualitative methodologies of ethnography and historical research. As with the quantitative methodology chapters, all but one of these is followed by a carefully chosen research report from the published research literature, along with our analysis and critique.

Part 7 (Chapter 23) discusses Mixed-Methods Studies, which combine quantitative and qualitative methods. Again, as in other chapters, the discussion is followed by our analysis and critique of a research report we have chosen from the published research literature.

Part 8 (Chapter 24) describes the assumptions, characteristics, and steps of action research. Classroom examples of action research questions bring the subject to life, as does the addition of a critique of a published study.

Part 9 (Chapter 25) shows how to prepare a research proposal or report (involving a methodology of choice) that builds on the concepts and examples developed and illustrated in previous chapters.

RESEARCH EXERCISES

To achieve our second goal of helping students learn to apply their knowledge of basic processes and methodologies, we organized the first 12 chapters in the same order that students normally follow in developing a research proposal or conducting a research project. Then we concluded each of these chapters with a research exercise that includes a fill-in problem sheet. These exercises allow students to apply their understanding of the major concepts of each chapter. When completed, these accumulated problem sheets will have led students through the step-by-step processes involved in designing their own research projects. Although this step-by-step development requires some revision of their work as they learn more about the research process, the gain in understanding that results as they slowly see their proposal develop "before their eyes" justifies the extra time and effort involved.

Problem Sheet templates are available electronically at the Online Learning Center Web site, www.mhhe.com/fraenkel9e.

ACTUAL RESEARCH STUDIES

Our third goal, to enable students to read and understand the literature of educational research, has led us to conclude each of the methodology chapters in Parts 4, 5, 6, 7, and 8, with an annotated study that illustrates a particular research method. At the end of each study we analyze its strengths and weaknesses and offer suggestions as to how it might be improved. Similarly, at the end of our chapter on writing research proposals and reports, we include a student research proposal that we have critiqued with marginal comments. This annotated proposal has proved an effective means of helping students understand both sound and questionable research practices.

STYLE OF PRESENTATION

Because students are typically anxious regarding the content of research courses, we have taken extraordinary care not to overwhelm them with dry, abstract discussions, and we have adopted an informal writing style. More than in any text to date, our presentations are laced with clarifying examples and with summarizing charts, tables, and diagrams. Our experience in teaching research courses for more than 30 years has convinced us that there is no such thing as having "too many" examples in a basic text.

In addition to the many examples and illustrations that are embedded in the text, we have built the following pedagogical features into the book: (1) a graphic organizer for each chapter, (2) chapter objectives, (3) chapter-opening examples, (4) end-of-chapter summaries, (5) key terms with page references, (6) discussion questions, and (7) an extensive end-of-book glossary.

CHANGES IN THE NINTH EDITION

A number of key additions, new illustrations, and improved or refined examples, terminology, and definitions have been incorporated in this edition to further meet the goals of the text. The References have been updated throughout to include the latest research and have been reformatted to reflect use of APA style, Research Exercises and Problem Sheets have been revised with more effective questions.

Following is a sampling of chapter-by-chapter changes:

Chapter 1: The Nature of Educational Research
- New discussion on education research in the digital age

Chapter 3: Locating and Reviewing the Literature
- How to annotate sources prior to preparation of a literature review
- New example of an annotated bibliography in tabular form
- Updated screen shots of ERIC and other useful databases
- Updated image and text for acquiring survey results
- Tips for avoiding plagiarism when summarizing sources
- New set of prompts for evaluating published sources
- New section on academic style manuals (e.g., APA) with links to website and online tutorials

Chapter 4: Ethics and Research
- New information about online plagiarism checking tools
- Updated More About Research box with the latest Department of Health and Human Services regulations for research with human subjects

Chapter 5: Variables and Hypotheses
- New information on using propositions in qualitative research

Chapter 6: Sampling
- New material on "transferability" and how generalizing can be enhanced in qualitative studies

Chapter 7: Instrumentation
- New content on the use of data collection tools in qualitative research

Chapter 14: Single-Subject Research
- New annotated Research Report and Analysis on the effects of guiding reading with deaf students

Chapter 15: Correlational Research
- New annotated Research Report and Analysis on the features and correlations between teaching behaviors and learning activities in urban high school physical education

Chapter 17: Survey Research
- New information on polls and polling
- Discussion of SurveyMonkey and Qualtrics, the web-based survey tools most commonly used by academic institutions
- New annotated Research Report and Analysis on teaching secondary social studies

Chapter 24: Action Research
- New information on reflective practice in teacher research using self-study

New Annotated and Analyzed Research Reports: Three new Research Reports have been added to the text, introducing more research involving qualitative research as well as urban and secondary settings, helping the student apply the text's concepts and also practice evaluating published studies.

- Implementation of the Guided Reading Approach with Elementary School Deaf Students
- Physical Education in Urban High School Class Settings: Features and Correlations Between Teaching Behaviors and Learning Activities
- Teaching Social Studies in the 21st Century: A Research Study of Secondary Social Studies Teachers Instructional Methods and Practices

SPECIAL FEATURES

Support for Student Learning

How to Design and Evaluate Research in Education helps students become critical consumers of research and prepares them to conduct and report their own research.

Chapter-opening Features: Each chapter begins with an illustration that visually introduces a topic or issues related to the chapter. This is followed by an outline of chapter content, chapter learning objectives, the *Interactive and Applied Learning* feature that lists related supplementary material, and a related vignette.

More About Research, Research Tips,* and *Controversies in Research: These informative sections help students to think critically about research while illustrating important techniques in educational research.

End-of-Chapter Learning Supports: The chapters conclude with a reminder of the supplementary resources available, a detailed Main Points section, a listing of Key Terms, and Questions for Discussion.

Chapters 1–12 include a **Research Exercise** and a **Problem Sheet** to aid students in the construction of a research project.

Chapters 13–17 and 19–24 include an actual **Research Report** that has been annotated to highlight concepts discussed in the chapter.

Practical Resources and Examples for Doing and Reading Research

How to Design and Evaluate Research in Education provides a comprehensive introduction to research that is brought to life through practical resources and examples for doing and reading research.

- ***Research Tips* boxes** provide practical suggestions for doing research.
- The **Annotated Research Reports** at the conclusion of Chapters 13–17 and 19–24 present students with research reports and author commentary on how the study authors have approached and supported their research.
- **Research Exercises** and **Problems Sheets** at the conclusion of Chapters 1–13 are tools for students to use when creating their own research projects.
- ***Using Excel* boxes** show how these software programs can be used to calculate various statistics.
- Chapter 24: ***Action Research*** details how classroom teachers can and should do research to improve their teaching.
- Chapter 25: ***Preparing Research Proposals and Reports*** walks the reader through proposal and report preparation.
- **Resources on the Online Learning Center Web site** (see listing below) provide students with a place to start when gathering research tools.

SUPPLEMENTS THAT SUPPORT STUDENT LEARNING

Online Learning Center Web Site at www.mhhe.com/fraenkel9e

The Online Learning Center Web site offers tools for study, practice, and application including:

Study Resources

- Multiple quizzes and flashcards for testing content knowledge

Practice Resources

- Student Mastery Activities that provide students extra practice with specific concepts
- Data Analysis Examples and Exercises

Research Resources

- Statistics Program
- Correlation Coefficient Applet
- Chi Square Applet
- Research Wizard, a wizard version of the Problem Sheets
- Forms, including a Research Worksheet, Sample Consent Forms, Research Checklists, electronic versions of the Problem Sheets
- A Listing of Professional Journals
- *Bibliography Builder,* an electronic reference builder
- The McGraw-Hill Guide to Electronic Research

SUPPLEMENTS THAT SUPPORT INSTRUCTORS

Online Learning Center Web Site at www.mhhe.com/fraenkel9e

The Instructor's portion of the Online Learning Center offers a number of useful resources for classroom instruction, including an Instructor's Manual, Test Bank, Computerized Test Bank, chapter-by-chapter PowerPoint presentations, and additional resources.

ACKNOWLEDGMENTS

Directly and indirectly, many people have contributed to the preparation of this text. We will begin by acknowledging the students in our research classes, who, over the years, have taught us much. Also, we wish to thank the reviewers of this edition, whose generous comments have guided the preparation of this edition. They include:

Tom Kennedy, Nova Southeastern University

Reenay Rogers, University of West Alabama

Graham Stead, Cleveland State University

Andrew Topper, Grand Valley State University

Brenda Walling, East Central University

We would also like to thank Vicki Malinee of Van Brien and Associates and the editors and staff at McGraw-Hill for their efforts in turning the manuscript into the finished book before you.

Finally, we would like to thank our spouses for their unflagging support during the highs and lows that inevitably accompany the preparation of a text of this magnitude.

Jack R. Fraenkel
Norman E. Wallen
Helen H. Hyun

A Guided Tour of *How to Design and Evaluate Research in Education*

Welcome to *How to Design and Evaluate Research in Education*.

This comprehensive introduction to research methods was designed to present the basics of educational research in as interesting and understandable a way as possible. To accomplish this, we've created the following features for each chapter.

Opening Illustration

Each chapter opens with an illustrative depiction of a key concept that will be covered in the chapter.

Chapter Outline

Next, a chapter outline lists the topics to follow.

Interactive and Applied Learning Tools

This special feature lists the practice activities and resources related to the chapter that are available in the student supplements.

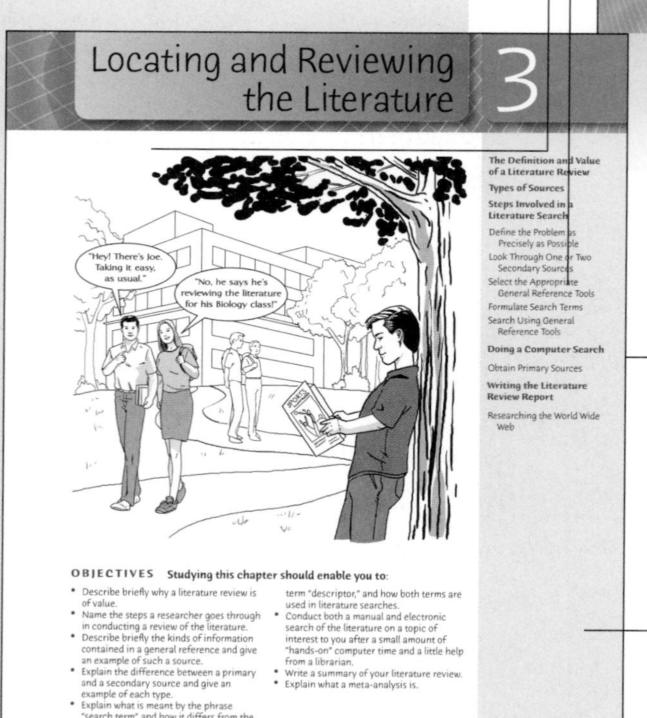

Locating and Reviewing the Literature 3

"Hey! There's Joe. Taking it easy, as usual."
"No, he says he's reviewing the literature for his Biology class!"
SPORTS

The Definition and Value of a Literature Review
Types of Sources
Steps Involved in a Literature Search
Define the Problem as Precisely as Possible
Look Through One or Two Secondary Sources
Select the Appropriate General Reference Tools
Formulate Search Terms
Search Using General Reference Tools
Doing a Computer Search
Obtain Primary Sources
Writing the Literature Review Report
Researching the World Wide Web

OBJECTIVES **Studying this chapter should enable you to:**

- Describe briefly why a literature review is of value.
- Name the steps a researcher goes through in conducting a review of the literature.
- Describe briefly the kinds of information contained in a general reference and give an example of such a source.
- Explain the difference between a primary and a secondary source and give an example of each type.
- Explain what is meant by the phrase "search term" and how it differs from the term "descriptor," and how both terms are used in literature searches.
- Conduct both a manual and electronic search of the literature on a topic of interest to you after a small amount of "hands-on" computer time and a little help from a librarian.
- Write a summary of your literature review.
- Explain what a meta-analysis is.

INTERACTIVE AND APPLIED LEARNING After, or while, reading this chapter:

Go to the Online Learning Center at www.mhhe.com/fraenkel9e to:

- Read the Guide to Electronic Research

Go to your online Student Mastery Activities book to do the following activities:

- Activity 3.1: Library Worksheet
- Activity 3.2: Where Would You Look?
- Activity 3.3: Do a Computer Search of the Literature

After a career in the military, Phil Gomez is in his first year as a teacher at an adult school in Logan, Utah. He teaches U.S. history to students who did not graduate from high school but who now are trying to obtain a diploma. He has learned the hard way, through trial and error, that there are a number of techniques that simply put students to sleep. He sincerely wants to be a good teacher, but he is having trouble getting his students interested in the subject. As he is the only history teacher in the school, the other teachers are not of much help.

He wants to get some ideas, therefore, about other approaches, strategies, and techniques that he might use. He decides to do an Internet search to see what he can find out about effective strategies for teaching high school history. His first search yields 12,847 hits! Phil is overwhelmed and at a loss for which sources to view. Should he look at books? Journal articles? Websites? Government documents? Unpublished reports? Where should he look for the most valid resources? And how could his searching be done more systematically?

Chapter-Opening Example

The chapter text begins with a practical example—a dialogue between researchers or a peek into a classroom—related to the content to follow.

Objectives

Chapter objectives prepare the student for the chapter ahead.

MORE ABOUT RESEARCH

Department of Health and Human Services Revised Regulations for Research with Human Subjects

The following HHS guidelines currently allow for exemption from IRB review for certain projects. However, please make sure to check with your IRB for their exempt research guidelines.

1. Research conducted in established or commonly accepted educational settings, involving normal educational practices, such as (i) research on regular and special education instructional strategies, or (ii) research on the effectiveness of or the comparison among instructional techniques, curricula, or classroom management methods.
2. Research involving the use of educational tests (cognitive, diagnostic, aptitude, achievement), survey procedures, interview procedures or observation of public behavior, unless: (i) information obtained is recorded in such a manner that human subjects can be identified, directly or through identifiers linked to the subjects; and (ii) any disclosure of the human subjects' responses outside the research could reasonably place the subjects at risk of criminal or civil liability or be damaging to the subjects' financial standing, employability, or reputation.
3. Research involving the use of educational tests (cognitive, diagnostic, aptitude, achievement), survey procedures, interview procedures, or observation of public behavior that is not exempt under paragraph (b)(2) of this section, if: (i) the human subjects are elected or appointed public officials or candidates for public office; or (ii) federal statute(s) require(s) without exception that the confidentiality of the personally identifiable information will be maintained throughout the research and thereafter.
4. Research involving the collection or study of existing data, documents, records, pathological specimens, or diagnostic specimens, if these sources are publicly available or if the information is recorded by the investigator in such a manner that subjects cannot be identified, directly or through identifiers linked to the subjects.
5. Research and demonstration projects which are conducted by or subject to the approval of department or agency heads, and which are designed to study, evaluate, or otherwise examine: (i) Public benefit or service programs; (ii) procedures for obtaining benefits or services under those programs; (iii) possible changes in or alternatives to those programs or procedures; or (iv) possible changes in methods or levels of payment for benefits or services under those programs.
6. Taste and food quality evaluation and consumer acceptance studies, (i) if wholesome foods without additives are consumed or (ii) if a food is consumed that contains a food ingredient at or below the level and for a use found to be safe, or agricultural chemical or environmental contaminant at or below the level found to be safe, by the Food and Drug Administration or approved by the Environmental Protection Agency or the Food Safety and Inspection Service of the U.S. Department of Agriculture.

U.S. Department of Health and Human Services, 45CFR 46.101(b)(1)–(6).

Research activities involving human subjects that are **exempt** from IRB review are identified in 45CFR 46.101(b)(1)–(6). (Institutions and IRBs may not create new categories of exempt research under 45 CFR Part 46.) Institutions should have a clear policy in place on who shall determine what research is exempt under .46.101(b).

*www.hhs.gov/ohrp/policy/hsdc95-02.html

More About Research

These boxes take a closer look at important topics in educational research. See a full listing of these boxes, starting on page xii.

RESEARCH TIPS

Key Terms to Define in a Research Study

- Terms necessary to ensure that the research question is sharply focused
- Terms that individuals outside the field of study may not understand
- Terms that have multiple meanings
- Terms that are essential to understanding what the study is about
- Terms to provide precision in specifications for instruments to be developed or located

Another important point to remember is that often it is a compound term or phrase that needs to be defined rather than only a single word. For example, the term *nondirective therapy* will surely not be clarified by precise definitions of *nondirective* and *therapy,* since it has a more specific meaning than the two words defined separately would convey. Similarly, such terms as *learning disability, bilingual education, interactive video,* and *home-centered health care* need to be defined as linguistic wholes.

Here are three definitions of the term *motivated to learn.* Which do you think is the clearest?

1. Works hard

2. Any classroom *judged* (by an observer spending at least one day per week for four to five weeks) to possess all the following characteristics:
   a. No more than three children working with the same materials at the same time
   b. The teacher never spending more than 20 minutes per day addressing the class as a group
   c. At least half of every class period open for students to work on projects of their own choosing at their own pace
   d. Several (more than three) sets of different kinds of educational materials available for every student in the class to use

Research Tips

These boxes provide practical pointers for doing research. See a full listing of these boxes on page xii.

CONTROVERSIES IN RESEARCH

High-Stakes Testing

High-stakes testing refers to the use of tests (often only a single achievement test) as the primary, or only, basis for decisions having major consequences. For students, such consequences include retention in grade and/or the denial of diplomas and awards. For schools, they include public praise or condemnation, sanctions, and financial rewards or punishments. "In state after state, legislatures, governors, and state boards, supported by business leaders, have imposed tougher requirements in mathematics, English, science, and other fields, together with new tests by which the performance of both students and schools is to be judged."*

For years, tests had been used as one indicator of performance; what was new was exclusive reliance on them. "The backlash, touching virtually every state that has instituted high-stakes testing, arises from a spectrum of complaints. A major complaint is that the focus on testing and obsessive test preparation, sometimes beginning in kindergarten, is killing innovative teaching and curricula and driving out good teachers. Other complaints are that (conversely) the standards on which the tests are based are too vague and that students have not been taught the material on which the tests are based; or that the tests are unfair to poor and minority students or to those who lack test-taking skills; or that the tests put too much stress on young children. And some argue that they are too long (in Massachusetts they can take up to 13 hours!) or too tough or simply not good enough."*

In response, the American Educational Research Association developed a position statement of "conditions essential to sound implementation of high-stakes educational testing programs."† It contained 14 specific points, 4 of the most important being that (1) such decisions about students should not be based on test scores alone; (2) tests should be made fairer to all students; (3) tests should match the curriculum; and (4) the reliability and validity of tests should continually be evaluated.

Two examples of responses to the guidelines were the following:

- "In the face of too much testing with far too severe consequences, the AERA positions, if implemented, would be a step forward relative to current practice."‡
- "The statement reflects what is desired for all state tests and assessments. But, just as all students have not yet met the standards, not all state tests and assessments will immediately meet the goals contained in this statement."§

What do you think? Are the complaints about high-stakes tests warranted?

*Schrag, P. (2000, August). High stakes are for tomatoes. *Atlantic Monthly, 286,* 19.

†American Educational Research Association. (2000). Position statement of the American Educational Research Association concerning high-stakes testing in pre-12 education. *Educational Researcher, 29* (11), 24–35.

‡Neill, M. (2000). Quoted in Initial responses to AERA's position statement concerning high-stakes testing. *Educational Researcher, 29* (11), 28.

§Martin, W. (2000). Quoted in Initial responses to AERA's position statement concerning high-stakes testing. *Educational Researcher, 29* (11), 27.

ones, or only problems involving subtraction, the test will be unrepresentative and hence not provide information from which valid inferences can be made.

One key element in **content-related evidence of validity,** then, concerns the adequacy of the sampling of directions, and so on. Regardless of the adequacy of the questions in an instrument, if they are presented in an inappropriate format (such as giving a test written in English to children whose English is minimal), valid results cannot be obtained. For this reason, it is important

Controversies in Research

These boxes highlight a controversy in research to provide you with a greater understanding of the issue. See a full listing of these boxes on page xiii.

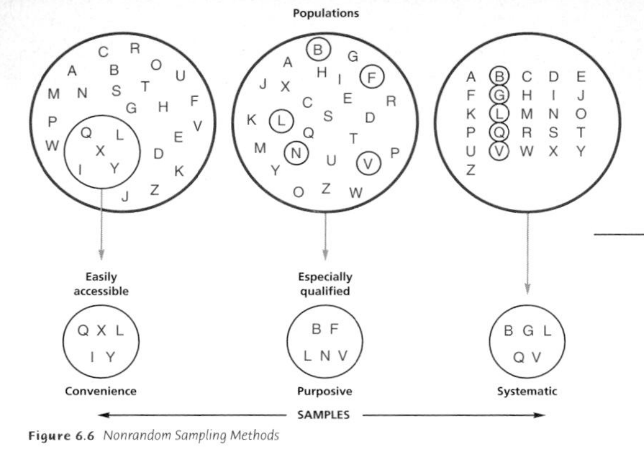

Figure 6.6 *Nonrandom Sampling Methods*

Figures and Tables

Numerous figures and tables explain or extend concepts presented in the text.

Research Reports

Published research reports are included at the conclusion of methodology chapters. The reports have been annotated to illustrate important points.

RESEARCH REPORT

Physical Education in Urban High School Class Settings: Features and Correlations between Teaching Behaviors and Learning Activities

Howard Z. Zeng, Raymond Leung, and Michael Hipscher
The City University of New York, Brooklyn College

Wenhao Liu
Slippery Rock University (PA)

Abstract

This study examined the features and correlations between teaching behaviors and learning activities in urban high school physical education (PE) class settings using direct instruction model. Participants were sixteen urban high school PE teachers and their students. Results indicated that the teachers spent their class times on the major teaching behaviors were: Informing 28.8%, Structuring 25.4%, Observing 17.0%, and Feedback 9.2%. The students spent their class times on the major learning activities were: Motor Engaged 56.2%, Cognitive Engaged 20.7%, and Waiting for a Turn 9.7%. Correlation analyses revealed that Informing, Questioning, and Feedback teaching behaviors were positively associated with Motor Engaged and Cognitive Engaged learning activities. When the teachers exhibited the behavior category of None of the Above, their students showed no motor and cognitive learning activities engagements. Findings suggested that, PE teachers should develop and employ teaching behaviors that promote and demonstrate physical skills and fitness because those teaching behaviors are positively associated with students' physical activity levels.

"As follows"

Prior research

Research on teaching in physical education (RT-PE) has accomplished remarkably with respect to how teaching behaviors are related to learning outcomes (Brophy & Good, 1986; Graham & Heimerer, 1981; Keating, Kulinna & Silverman, 1999; Martin & Kulinna, 2004; Silverman, Tyson & Morford, 1988). Silverman (1991) defined RT-PE as "research on what teachers and students do and how this affects or relates to learning and to the social dynamics of the class." (p. 352). This definition is broad and tells us that, when a study is conducted on teaching in physical education, both teacher's teaching behaviors and student's learning activities should be included in the parameters of a study.

Constitutive definition

Recently, research studies have provided sufficient information regarding the characteristics of effective teaching (Pangrazi, 2007; Kulinna, Cothran & Regualos, 2006; Siedentop & Tannehill, 2000). Based on the work done by previous researchers, the following characteristics were described as effective teaching/learning environments: (a) clear objectives and content covered; (b) well-organized and appropriate expectations; (c) meaningful task and high rates of success; (d) smooth transition and low rates of management time; (e) appropriate guidance and active supervision; (f) high rates in student-engaged time and low rates in student waiting time; and (g) teacher's enthusiasm and equitable support. The characteristics stated above have become important

348

CHAPTER 15 Correlational Research 349

guidelines for training novice teachers to grow to be an effective teacher (Pangrazi, 2007; Kulinna, Cothran & Regualos, 2006; Siedentop & Tannehill, 2000).

A number of previous studies in RT-PE focused on how teacher and student behaviors were associated with direct instruction, and eventually the direct instruction model in physical education was developed (Anderson, Evertson, & Brophy, 1979; Graber, 2001; Rosenshine, 1979; Rosenshine & Stevens, 1986; Sweeting & Rink, 1999). Rosenshine (1979) illustrated that direct instruction model in physical education possesses clear learning goals, adequate time for instruction and practice which is characterized by appropriate subject matters for students' abilities, low-level cognitive questions but meaningful task and high success by monitoring student performance and providing immediate and specific feedback.

Silverman, Tyson, and Morford (1988) found that students spending their class time on motor skill practice with teacher's feedback was positively associated with their motor learning achievement. Furthermore, regarding how time is spent in physical education classes, Silverman (1991) summarized that most students spent less than 30% of the class time on motor activities but the majority of the time on waiting, explanation/demonstration, and/or receiving information.

Good review

Faucette and Patterson (1990) compared teaching behaviors and students' activity levels taught by specialists versus non-specialists in elementary physical education class settings. The researchers found that specialists employed informing, structuring, questioning, feedback, and reward teaching behaviors whereas non-specialists utilized silent monitoring and attending teaching behaviors, thereby suggesting that different teaching behaviors caused different students' activity levels. The rates of students' activity levels were 35.0% and 16.5% taught by specialists and non-specialists respectively (Faucette & Patterson, 1990).

Potentially useful

Small

More recently, researchers have used different observation instruments to investigate, describe, and compare the differences and similarities of teaching behaviors and student learning activities in physical education classes (Banville, 2006; Banville & Rikard, 2001; Keating et al., 1999; Martin & Kulinna, 2005; Mitcell & Castelli, 2003). Significant linear correlations between teaching behaviors and learning activities with correlation coefficients ranging from .26 to .42 have been found (Martin & Kulinna, 2004, 2005; Mitcell & Castelli, 2003).

Martin and Kulinna's study (2005) involved 43 physical education teachers (20 from elementary school, 11 from middle school, and 12 from high school). The main purposes of their study were: (a) to determine whether teachers' intentions to teach lessons more active physically were related to teaching behaviors (e.g., demonstrating and promoting fitness); and (b) whether teacher behaviors were associated with how much time their students spent on various activities. They found that general instruction and management behaviors were negatively related to students' moderate to vigorous physical activities; general instruction behaviors, however, were positively associated with students' sitting and standing behaviors.

Justification

Although RT-PE have accomplished plentifully, Silverman (1991) pointed out that the majority of studies in teaching physical education were conducted at the K-8 levels using preservice teachers as participants (even though 17 years after Dr. Silverman's famous general review for the accomplishments in the field of research in teaching physical education). Studies at the high school level were very limited, and the features of teaching behaviors and learning activities at the high school level were not well-documented. Hence, the relationship between teachers' teaching behaviors and students' learning activities in high school physical education classes remained unanswered. As a result, the present study was designed to extend previous research (K-8) by not only employing high

Analysis of the Study

PURPOSE/JUSTIFICATION

The purpose was "to examine the features and correlations between teaching behaviors and learning activities in urban high school physical education classes" that used direct instruction (p. 350). The main justification was to address a gap in the research literature on the relationship between physical education instructors' teaching behaviors and students' learning activities in secondary schools. The researchers sought "to extend previous research (K–8) by not only employing high school (9–12) physical education teachers as participants but also examining the characteristics of effective teaching in high school physical education classes" (p. 350).

Teachers and students (we assume their parents) provided informed consent prior to data collection. There appear to be no concerns regarding harm, confidentiality, or deception although the researchers noted they did not disclose to teachers the true nature of their class observations so as not to influence their normal teaching behavior.

DEFINITIONS

Formal definitions are not provided for the primary terms in the study: *teaching behaviors* and *learning activities*. Both terms are operationally defined by observational data collected from the Direct Instruction Behavior Analysis (DIBA) system. The DIBA included 14 categories, 8 relating to teaching behaviors and 6 assessing learning activities. These observational data were coded to produce the quantitative indicators "percentage of time" spent on specified behaviors and "rate per minute" (RPM) used to measure frequency for the 14 predefined categories. We think the study would have been improved by clarifying two DIBA definitions: (1) cognitively engaged—"listens to" and "gains information" and (2) response preparing—students "get ready" (see also Instrumentation).

Other key terms include *direct instruction*, *physical education classes*, and *urban high school*. The researchers provide a constitutive definition for "direct instruction model," which they describe as possessing "clear learning goals, adequate time for instruction and practice which is characterized by appropriate subject matters for students' abilities, low-level cognitive questions but meaningful task and high success by monitoring student performance and providing immediate and specific feedback" (p. 350). Definitions are not provided for *physical education classes* although the researchers list the type and duration of classes observed: basketball/fitness, volleyball/fitness, yoga, dance, soccer/fitness, weight lifting/fitness, and tennis. Similarly, *urban high school* is not defined but the researchers provide demographic information about each school site in terms of total student enrollment and racial/ethnic breakdown.

PRIOR RESEARCH

An extensive review of the research literature is provided to support the design and justification for the study. Citing both older and more recent research (studies published within five years from their study), the researchers do well in summarizing the major theoretical and empirical findings related to their research question. Moreover, they revisit their literature review findings in the discussion section. For example, the authors state that "the findings of this study were quite different from those of the Martin and Kulinna's study (2005)" (p. 354). In doing so, the authors situate their study within the context of the research literature.

HYPOTHESES

The hypothesis is not stated explicitly, but clearly implied. The authors' implied hypothesis is that teaching behaviors linked to direct instruction in physical education are correlated with student learning behaviors.

SAMPLE

The sample included 16 physical education teachers and their students from three urban high schools located in New York City, New York. Demographic information about the teachers was limited to gender and number of years teaching. The authors do not describe the student sample other than a narrative account of the pooled demographics of each of the three schools. This demographic information could have been presented more clearly for the reader had the authors included it in a separate table. Moreover, the authors neglected to include standard measures of socioeconomic status about the high schools such as the percentage of students receiving free/reduced lunch, and the percentage who are English language learners. The implied population is all high school physical education teachers and their students in the United States. Generalizing beyond the sample is limited as participating teachers were not

Each research report is critiqued by the authors, with both its strengths and weaknesses discussed.

Chapter Review

The chapter ends with a listing of the review resources available for students on the Online Learning Center Web site at www.mhhe.com/fraenkel9e.

Go back to the **INTERACTIVE AND APPLIED LEARNING** feature at the beginning of the chapter for a listing of interactive and applied activities. Go to the **Online Learning Center** at **www.mhhe.com/fraenkel9e** to take quizzes, practice with key terms, and review chapter content.

Main Points

THE NATURE OF QUALITATIVE RESEARCH

- The term *qualitative research* refers to studies that investigate the *quality* of relationships, activities, situations, or materials.
- The natural setting is a direct source of data, and the researcher is a key part of the instrumentation process in qualitative research.
- Qualitative data are collected mainly in the form of words or pictures and seldom involve numbers. Coding is the primary technique used in data analysis.
- Qualitative researchers are especially interested in how things occur and particularly in the perspectives of the subjects of a study.
- Qualitative researchers do not, usually, formulate a hypothesis beforehand and then seek to test it. Rather, they allow hypotheses to emerge as a study develops.
- Qualitative and quantitative research differ in the philosophical assumptions that underlie the two approaches.

STEPS INVOLVED IN QUALITATIVE RESEARCH

- The steps involved in conducting a qualitative study are not as distinct as they are in quantitative studies. They often overlap and sometimes are even conducted concurrently.
- All qualitative studies begin with a foreshadowed problem, the particular phenomenon the researcher is interested in investigating. Some qualitative researchers state propositions to help their data collection and also analysis.
- Researchers who engage in a qualitative study of some type usually select a purposive sample. Several types of purposive samples exist.
- There is no treatment in a qualitative study, nor is there any manipulation of variables.
- The collection of data in a qualitative study is ongoing.
- Conclusions are drawn continuously throughout the course of a qualitative study.

APPROACHES TO QUALITATIVE RESEARCH

- A biographical study tells the story of the special events in the life of a single individual.

Main Points

Bulleted main points highlight the key concepts of the chapter.

GENERALIZATION IN QUALITATIVE RESEARCH

- Generalizing is possible in qualitative research, but it is of a type different from that found in quantitative studies. Most likely it will be done by interested practitioners.

ETHICS AND QUALITATIVE RESEARCH

- The identities of all participants in a qualitative study should be protected, and they should be treated with respect.

RECONSIDERING QUALITATIVE AND QUANTITATIVE RESEARCH

- Aspects of both qualitative and quantitative research often are used together in a study. Increased attention is being given to such mixed-methods studies.
- Whether qualitative or quantitative research is the most appropriate boils down to what the researcher wants to find out.

Key Terms

autobiography 430
biographical study 430
case study 432
coding 434
confirming sample 434
critical sample 434
extreme case sample 434
foreshadowed problem 428
generalization in qualitative research 434
grounded theory study 431
homogeneous sample 434
instrumental case study 433
intrinsic case study 433
life history 430
maximal variation sample 434
multiple- (collective) case study 433
narrative research 430
opportunistic sample 434
oral history 430
phenomenological study 430
portraiture 431
positivism 425
postmodernist 427
purposive sample 428
qualitative research 424
replication 435
snowball sample 434
theoretical framework 425
theoretical sample 434
typical sample 434

For Discussion

1. What do you see as the greatest strength of qualitative research? the biggest weakness?
2. Are there any topics or questions that could *not* be studied using a qualitative approach? If so, give an example. Is there any type of information that qualitative research cannot provide? If so, what might it be?
3. Qualitative researchers are sometimes accused of being too subjective. What do you think a qualitative researcher might say in response to such an accusation?
4. Qualitative researchers say that "complete" objectivity is impossible. Would you agree? Explain your reasoning.
5. "The essence of all good research is understanding, rather than an attempt to prove something." What does this statement mean?

Key Terms

Key terms are listed with page references.

For Discussion

End-of-chapter questions are designed for in-class discussion.

Research Exercises

The research exercise explains how to fill in the Problem Sheet that follows.

Research Exercise 13: Research Methodology

Using Problem Sheet 13, describe in as much detail as you can the procedures of your study, including analysis of results—that is, *what* you intend to do, *when, where,* and *how.* Lastly, indicate any unresolved problems you see at this point in your planning.

Problem Sheet 13

Research Methodology

You should complete Problem Sheet 13 once you have decided which of the methodologies described in Chapters 13–17 and 19–24 you plan to use. You might wish to consider, however, whether your research question could be investigated by other methodologies.

1. The question or hypothesis of my study is: ______
2. The methodology I intend to use is: ______
3. Describe how you will conduct the study, that is, the data collection process. When, where, and how will you collect the data? Over what time span will the data be gathered, and in what types of situations? Can you foresee any limitations or problems? ______
4. If you are planning an intervention study (e.g., an experiment), please discuss in detail the intervention or treatment planned. ______
5. The major problems I foresee at this point include the following: ______

OLC An electronic version of this Problem Sheet that you can fill in and print, save, or e-mail is available on the Online Learning Center at www.mhhe.com/fraenkel9e.

Problem Sheets

Individually, the problem sheets allow students to apply their understanding of the major concepts of each chapter. As a whole, they walk students through each step of the research process.

PART 1

Introduction to Research

Research takes many forms. In Part 1, we introduce you to the subject of educational research and explain why knowledge of the various types of research is of value to educators. Because research is but one way to obtain knowledge, we also describe several other ways and compare the strengths and weaknesses of each. We give a brief overview of educational research methodologies to set the stage for a more extensive discussion in later chapters. Lastly, we discuss criticisms of the research process.

1 The Nature of Research

Some Examples of Educational Concerns

Why Research Is of Value

Ways of Knowing

Sensory Experience
Agreement with Others
Expert Opinion
Logic
The Scientific Method

Types of Research

Quantitative and Qualitative Research
Experimental Research
Correlational Research
Causal-Comparative Research
Survey Research
Ethnographic Research
Historical Research
Action Research
Evaluation Research
All Have Value
Education Research in the Digital Age

General Research Types

Descriptive Studies
Associational Research
Intervention Studies
Meta-Analysis

Critical Analysis of Research

A Brief Overview of the Research Process

"It seems pretty obvious to me that the more you know about a subject, the better you can teach it!"
"Right! Just like we know that evidence is overwhelmingly in favor of phonics as the best way to teach reading!"
"Well, you both may be in for a surprise!"

OBJECTIVES Studying this chapter should enable you to:

- Explain what is meant by the term "educational research" and give two examples of the kinds of topics educational researchers might investigate.
- Explain why a knowledge of scientific research methodology can be of value to educators.
- Name and give an example of four ways of knowing other than the method used by scientists.
- Explain what is meant by the term "scientific method."
- Give an example of six different types of research methodologies used by educational researchers.
- Describe briefly what is meant by critical research.
- Describe the differences among descriptive, associational, and intervention-type studies.
- Describe briefly the difference between basic and applied research.
- Describe briefly the difference between quantitative and qualitative research.
- Describe briefly what is meant by mixed-methods research.
- Describe briefly the basic components involved in the research process.

INTERACTIVE AND APPLIED LEARNING After, or while, reading this chapter:

Go to the Online Learning Center at www.mhhe.com/fraenkel9e to:

- Learn More About Why Research Is of Value

Go to your online Student Mastery Activities book to do the following activities:

- Activity 1.1: Empirical vs. Nonempirical Research
- Activity 1.2: Basic vs. Applied Research
- Activity 1.3: Types of Research
- Activity 1.4: Assumptions
- Activity 1.5: General Research Types

"Dr. Hunter? I'm Molly Levine. I called you about getting some advice about the master's degree program in your department."

"Hello, Molly. Pleased to meet you. Come on in. How can I be of help?"

"Well, I'm thinking about enrolling in the master's degree program in marriage and family counseling, but first I want to know what the requirements are."

"I don't blame you. It's always wise to know what you are getting into. To obtain the degree, you'll need to take a number of courses, and there is also an oral exam once you have completed them. You also will have to complete a small-scale study."

"What do you mean?"

"You actually will have to do some research."

"Wow! What does that involve? What do you mean by research, anyway? And how does one do it? What kinds of research are there?"

To find out the answers to Molly's questions, as well as a few others, read this chapter.

Some Examples of Educational Concerns

- A high school principal in San Francisco wants to improve the morale of her faculty.
- The director of the gifted student program in Denver would like to know what happens during a typical week in an English class for advanced placement students.
- An elementary school counselor in Boise wishes he could get more students to open up to him about their worries and problems.
- A tenth-grade biology teacher in Atlanta wonders if discussions are more effective than lectures in motivating students to learn biological concepts.
- A physical education teacher in Tulsa wonders if ability in one sport correlates with ability in other sports.
- A seventh-grade student in Philadelphia asks her counselor what she can do to improve her study habits.
- The president of the local PTA in Little Rock, parent of a sixth-grader at Cabrillo School, wonders how he can get more parents involved in school-related activities.

Each of these examples, although fictional, represents a typical question or concern facing many of us in education today. Together, these examples suggest that teachers, counselors, administrators, parents, and students continually need information to do their jobs. Teachers need to know what kinds of materials, strategies, and activities best help students learn. Counselors need to know what problems hinder or prevent students from learning and how to help them with these problems. Administrators need to know how to provide an environment for happy and productive learning. Parents need to know how to help their children succeed in school. Students need to know how to study to learn as much as they can.

Why Research Is of Value

How can educators, parents, and students obtain the information they need? Many ways of obtaining information, of course, exist. One can consult experts, review books and articles, question or observe colleagues with relevant experience, examine one's own past experience, or even rely on intuition. All these approaches suggest possible ways to proceed, but the answers they provide are not always reliable. Experts may be mistaken; source documents may contain no insights of value; colleagues may have no experience in the matter; and one's own experience or intuition may be irrelevant or misunderstood.

This is why a knowledge of scientific research methodology can be of value. The scientific method provides us with another way of obtaining information—information that is as accurate and reliable as we can get. Let us compare it, therefore, with some of the other ways of knowing.

Ways of Knowing

SENSORY EXPERIENCE

We see, we hear, we smell, we taste, we touch. Most of us have seen fireworks on the Fourth of July, heard the whine of a jet airplane's engines overhead, smelled a rose, tasted chocolate ice cream, and felt the wetness of a rainy day. The information we take in from the world through our senses is the most immediate way we have of knowing something. Using sensory experience as a means of obtaining information, the director of the gifted-student program mentioned at the start of this chapter, for example, might visit an advanced placement English class to see and hear what happens during a week or two of the semester.

Sensory data, to be sure, can be refined. Seeing the temperature on an outdoor thermometer can refine our knowledge of how cold it is; a top-quality stereo system can help us hear Beethoven's Fifth Symphony with greater clarity; similarly, smell, taste, and touch can all be enhanced, and usually need to be. Many experiments in sensory perception have revealed that we are not always wise to trust our senses too completely. Our senses can (and often do) deceive us: The gunshot we hear becomes a car backfiring; the water we see in the road ahead is but a mirage; the chicken we thought we tasted turns out to be rabbit.

Sensory knowledge is undependable; it is also incomplete. The data we take in through our senses do not account for all (or even most) of what we seem to feel is the range of human knowing. To obtain reliable knowledge, therefore, we cannot rely on our senses alone but must check what we think we know with other sources.

AGREEMENT WITH OTHERS

One such source is the opinions of others. Not only can we share our sensations with others, we can also check on the accuracy and authenticity of these sensations: Does this soup taste salty to you? Isn't that John over there? Did you hear someone cry for help? Smells like mustard, doesn't it?

Obviously, there is a great advantage to checking with others about whether they see or hear what we do. It can help us discard what is untrue and manage our lives more intelligently by focusing on what is true. If, while hiking in the country, I do not hear the sound of an approaching automobile but several of my companions do and alert me to it, I can proceed with caution. All of us frequently discount our own sensations when others report that we are missing something or "seeing" things incorrectly. Using agreement with others as a means of obtaining information, the tenth-grade biology teacher in Atlanta, for example, might check with her colleagues to see if they find discussions more effective than lectures in motivating their students to learn.

The problem with such common knowledge is that it, too, can be wrong. A majority vote of a committee is no guarantee of the truth. My friends might be wrong about the presence of an approaching automobile, or the automobile they hear may be moving away from rather than toward us. Two groups of eyewitnesses to an accident may disagree as to which driver was at fault. Hence, we need to consider some additional ways to obtain reliable knowledge.

EXPERT OPINION

Perhaps there are particular individuals we should consult—experts in their field, people who know a great deal about what we are interested in finding out. We are likely to believe a noted heart specialist, for example, if he says that Uncle Charlie has a bad heart. Surely, a person with a PhD in economics knows more than most of us do about what makes the economy tick. And shouldn't we believe our family dentist if she tells us that back molar has to be pulled? To use expert opinion as a means of obtaining information, perhaps the physical education teacher in Tulsa should ask a noted authority in the physical education field whether ability in one sport correlates with ability in another.

Well, maybe. It depends on the credentials of the experts and the nature of the question about which they are being consulted. Experts, like all of us, can be mistaken. For all their study and training, what experts know is still based primarily on what they have learned from reading and thinking, from listening to and observing others, and from their own experience. No expert, however, has studied or experienced all there is to know in a given field, and thus even an expert can never be totally sure. All any expert can do is give us an opinion based on what he or she knows, and no matter how much this is, it is never all there is to know. Let us consider, then, another way of knowing: logic.

LOGIC

We also know things logically. Our intellect—our capability to reason things out—allows us to use sensory data to develop a new kind of knowledge. Consider the famous syllogism:

All human beings are mortal.
Sally is a human being.
Therefore, Sally is mortal.

To assert the first statement (called the *major premise*), we need only generalize from our experience about the mortality of individuals. We have never experienced anyone who was not mortal, so we state that all human beings are. The second statement (called the *minor premise*) is based entirely on sensory experience. We come in contact with Sally and classify her as a human being. We don't have to rely on our senses, then, to know that the third statement (called the *conclusion*) must be true. Logic tells us it is. As long as the first two statements are true, the third statement must be true.

Take the case of the counselor in Philadelphia who is asked to advise a student on how to improve her study habits. Using logic, she might present the following argument: Students who take notes on a regular basis in class find that their grades improve. If you take notes on a regular basis, then your grades should improve as well.

This is not all there is to logical reasoning, of course, but it is enough to give you an idea of another way of knowing. There is a fundamental danger in logical reasoning, however: It is only when the major and minor premises of a syllogism are *both* true that the conclusion is guaranteed to be true. If either of the premises is false, the conclusion may or may not be true.*

*In the note-taking example, the major premise (all students who take notes on a regular basis in class improve their grades) is probably *not* true.

There is still another way of knowing to consider: the method of science.

THE SCIENTIFIC METHOD

When many people hear the word *science,* they think of things like white lab coats, laboratories, test tubes, or space exploration. Scientists are people who know a lot, and the term *science* suggests a tremendous body of knowledge. What we are interested in here, however, is science as a method of knowing. It is the **scientific method** that is important to researchers.

What is this method? Essentially it involves testing ideas in the public arena. Almost all of us humans are capable of making connections—of seeing relationships and associations—among the sensory information we experience. Most of us then identify these connections as "facts"—items of knowledge about the world in which we live. We may speculate, for example, that our students may be less attentive in class when we lecture than when we engage them in discussion. A physician may guess that people who sleep between six and eight hours each night will be less anxious than those who sleep more or less than that amount. A counselor may feel that students read less than they used to because they spend most of their free time watching television. But in each of these cases, we do not really know if our belief is true. What we are dealing with are only guesses or hunches, or as scientists would say, hypotheses.

What we must do now is put each of these guesses or hunches to a rigorous test to see if it holds up under more controlled conditions. To investigate our speculation on attentiveness scientifically, we can observe carefully and systematically how attentive our students are when we lecture and when we hold a class discussion. The physician can count the number of hours individuals sleep, then measure and compare their anxiety levels. The counselor can compare the reading habits of students who watch different amounts of television.

Such investigations, however, do not constitute science unless they are made public. This means that all aspects of the investigation are described in sufficient detail so that the study can be repeated by anyone who questions the results—provided, of course, that those interested possess the necessary competence and resources. Private procedures, speculations, and conclusions are not scientific until they are made public.

There is nothing very mysterious, then, about how scientists work in their quest for reliable knowledge. In reality, many of us proceed this way when we try to reach an intelligent decision about a problem that is bothering us. These procedures can be boiled down to five distinct steps.

1. First, there is a problem of some sort—some disturbance in our lives that disrupts the normal or desirable state of affairs. Something is bothering us. For most of us who are not scientists, it may be a tension of some sort, a disruption in our normal routine. Examples would be if our students are not as attentive as we wish or if we have difficulty making friends. To the professional scientist, it may be an unexplained discrepancy in one's field of knowledge, a gap to be closed. Or it could be that we want to understand the practice of human sacrifice in terms of its historical significance.
2. Second, steps are taken to define more precisely the problem or the questions to be answered, to become clearer about exactly what the purpose of the study is. For example, we must think through what we mean by *student attentiveness* and why we consider it insufficient; the scientist must clarify what is meant by *human sacrifice* (e.g., how does it differ from murder?).
3. Third, we attempt to determine what kinds of information would solve the problem. Generally speaking, there are two possibilities: study what is already known or carry out a piece of research. As you will see, the first is a prerequisite for the second; the second is a major focus of this text. In preparation, we must be familiar with a wide range of possibilities for obtaining information, so as to get firsthand information on the problem. For example, the teacher might consider giving a questionnaire to students or having someone observe during class. The scientist might decide to examine historical accounts or spend time in societies where the practice of human sacrifice exists (or has until recently). Spelling out the details of information gathering is a major aspect of planning a research study.
4. Fourth, we must decide, as far as it is possible, how we will organize the information that we obtain. It is not uncommon, in both daily life and research, to discover that we cannot make sense of all the information we possess (sometimes referred to as *information overload*). Anyone attempting to understand another society while living in it has probably experienced this phenomenon. Our scientist will surely encounter this problem, but so will our teacher unless she has figured out how to handle the questionnaire and/or observational information that is obtained.
5. Fifth, after the information has been collected and analyzed, it must be interpreted. While this step may seem straightforward at first, this is seldom the case. As you will see, one of the most important parts of research is to avoid kidding ourselves. The teacher may conclude that her students are inattentive because they dislike lectures, but she may be misinterpreting the information. The scientist may conclude that human sacrifice is or was a means of trying to control nature, but this also may be incorrect.

In many studies, there are several possible explanations for a problem or phenomenon. These are called *hypotheses* and may occur at any stage of an investigation. Some researchers state a hypothesis (e.g., "Students are less attentive during lectures than during discussions") right at the beginning of a study. In other cases, hypotheses emerge as a study progresses, sometimes even when the information that has been collected is being analyzed and interpreted. The scientist might find that instances of sacrifice seemed to be more common after such societies made contact with other cultures, suggesting a hypothesis such as: "Sacrifice is more likely when traditional practices are threatened."

We want to stress two crucial features of scientific research: freedom of thought and public procedures. At every step, it is crucial that the researcher be as open as humanly possible to alternative ways of focusing and clarifying the problem, collecting and analyzing information, and interpreting results. Further, the process must be as public as possible. It is not a private game to be played by a group of insiders. The value of scientific research is that it can be *replicated* (i.e., repeated) by anyone interested in doing so.*

The general order of the scientific method, then, is as follows:

Identifying a problem or question
Clarifying the problem
Determining the information needed and how to obtain it
Organizing the information
Interpreting the results

In short, the essence of all research originates in curiosity—a desire to find out how and why things

*This is not to imply that replicating a study is a simple matter. It may require resources and training—and it may be impossible to repeat any study in exactly the same way it was done originally. The important principle, however, is that public evidence (as opposed to private experience) is the criterion for belief.

happen, including why people do the things they do, as well as whether or not certain ways of doing things work better than others.

A common misperception of science fosters the idea that there are fixed, once-and-for-all answers to particular questions. This contributes to a common, but unfortunate, tendency to accept, and rigidly adhere to, oversimplified solutions to very complex problems. While certainty is appealing, it is contradictory to a fundamental premise of science: All conclusions are to be viewed as tentative and subject to change, should new ideas and new evidence warrant revision. It is particularly important for educational researchers to keep this in mind, since the demand for final answers from parents, administrators, teachers, and politicians can often be intense. An example of how science changes is shown in the More About Research box on page 8.

For many years, there has been a strong tendency in Western culture to value scientific information over all other kinds. In recent years, the limitations of this view have become increasingly recognized and discussed. In education, we would argue that other ways of knowing, in addition to the scientific, should at least be considered.

As we have seen, there are many ways to collect information about the world around us. Figure 1.1 on page 10 illustrates some of these ways of knowing.

Types of Research

All of us engage in actions that have some of the characteristics of formal research, although perhaps we do not realize this at the time. We try out new methods of teaching, new materials, new textbooks. We compare what we did this year with what we did last year. Teachers frequently ask students and colleagues their opinions about school and classroom activities. Counselors interview students, faculty, and parents about school activities. Administrators hold regular meetings to gauge how faculty members feel about various issues. School boards query administrators, administrators query teachers, teachers query students and each other.

We observe, we analyze, we question, we hypothesize, we evaluate. But rarely do we do these things systematically. Rarely do we observe under controlled conditions. Rarely are our instruments as accurate and reliable as they might be. Rarely do we use the variety of research techniques and methodologies at our disposal.

The term **research** can mean any sort of "careful, systematic, patient study and investigation in some field of knowledge."[1] **Basic research** is concerned with clarifying underlying processes, with the hypothesis usually expressed as a theory. Researchers engaged in basic research studies are not particularly interested in examining the effectiveness of specific educational practices. An example of basic research might be an attempt to refine one or more stages of Erickson's psychological theory of development. **Applied research**, on the other hand, *is* interested in examining the effectiveness of particular educational practices. Researchers engaged in applied research studies *may or may not* want to investigate the degree to which certain theories are useful in practical settings. An example might be an attempt by a researcher to find out whether a particular theory of how children learn to read can be applied to first graders who are non readers. Many studies combine the two types of research. An example would be a study that examines the effects of particular teacher behaviors on students while also testing a theory of personality.

Many methodologies fit within the framework of research. If we learn how to use more of these methodologies where they are appropriate and if we can become more knowledgeable in our research efforts, we can obtain more reliable information upon which to base our educational decisions. Let us look, therefore, at some of the research methodologies we might use. We shall return to each of them in greater detail in Parts 4 and 5.

QUANTITATIVE AND QUALITATIVE RESEARCH

Another distinction involves the difference between **quantitative** and **qualitative research**. Although we shall discuss the basic differences between these two types of research more fully in Chapter 18, we will provide a brief overview here. In the simplest sense, quantitative data deal primarily with numbers, whereas qualitative data primarily involve words. But this is too simple and too brief. Quantitative and qualitative methods differ in their assumptions about the purpose of research itself, methods utilized by researchers, kinds of studies undertaken, role of the researcher, and degree to which generalization is possible.

Quantitative researchers usually base their work on the belief that the world is a *single reality* that can be approximated by careful study. Qualitative researchers,

MORE ABOUT RESEARCH

Chaos Theory

The origins of what is now known as **chaos theory** are usually traced to the 1970s. Since then, it has come to occupy a prominent place in mathematics and the natural sciences and, to a lesser extent, in the social sciences.

Although the physical sciences have primarily been known for their basic laws, or "first principles," it has long been known by scientists that most of these laws hold precisely only under ideal conditions that are not found in the "real" world. Many phenomena, such as cloud formations, waterfall patterns, and even the weather, elude precise prediction. Chaos theorists argue that the natural laws that are so useful in science may, in themselves, be the exception rather than the rule.

Although precise prediction of such phenomena as the swing of a pendulum or what the weather will be at a particular time is in most cases impossible, repeated patterns, according to a major principle of chaos theory, can be discovered and used, even when the content of the phenomena is chaotic. Developments in computer technology, for example, have made it possible to translate an extremely long sequence of "data points," such as the test scores of a large group of individuals, into colored visual pictures of fascinating complexity and beauty. Surprisingly, these pictures show distinct patterns that are often quite similar across different content areas, such as physics, biology, economics, astronomy, and geography. Even more surprising is the finding that certain patterns recur as these pictures are enlarged. The most famous example is the "Mandlebrot Bug," shown in Photographs 1.1 and 1.2. Note that Photograph 1.2 is simply a magnification of a portion of Photograph 1.1. The tiny box in the lower left corner of Photograph 1.1 is magnified to produce the box in the upper left-hand corner of Photograph 1.2. The tiny box within this box is then, in turn, magnified to produce the larger portion of Photograph 1.2, including the reappearance of the "bug" in the lower right corner. The conclusion is that even with highly complex data (think of trying to predict the changes that might occur in a cloud formation), predictability exists if patterns can be found across time or when the scale of a phenomenon is increased.

IMPLICATIONS FOR EDUCATIONAL RESEARCH

We hope that this brief introduction has not only stimulated your interest in what has been called, by some, the third revolution in science during the twentieth century (the theory of relativity and the discovery of quantum mechanics being the first two), but that it helps to make sense out of what we view as some implications for educational research. What are these implications?*

If chaos theory is correct, the difficulty in discovering widely generalizable rules or laws in education, let alone the social sciences in general, may not be due to inadequate concepts and theories or to insufficiently precise measurement and methodology, but may simply be an unavoidable fact about the world. Another implication is that whatever "laws" we do discover may be seriously limited in their applicability—across geography, across individual and/or group differences, and across time. If this is so, chaos theory provides support for researchers to concentrate on studying topics at the local level—classroom, school, agency—and for repeated studies over time to see if such laws hold up.

Another implication is that educators should pay more attention to the intensive study of the exceptional or the unusual, rather than treating such instances as trivial, incidental, or "errors." Yet another implication is that researchers should focus on predictability on a larger scale—that is, looking for patterns in individuals or groups over larger units of time. This would suggest a greater emphasis on long-term studies rather than the easier-to-conduct (and cheaper) short-time investigations that are currently the norm.

Not surprisingly, chaos theory has its critics. In education, the criticism is not of the theory itself, but more with misinterpretations and/or misapplications of it.† Chaos theorists do not say that all is chaos; quite the contrary, they say that we must pay more attention to chaotic phenomena and revise our conceptions of predictability. At the same time, the laws of gravity still hold, as, with less certainty, do many generalizations in education.

*For more extensive implications in the field of psychology, see Duke, M. P. (1994). Chaos theory and psychology: Seven propositions. *Genetic, Social and General Psychology Monographs, 120,* 267–286.

†See Hunter, W., Benson, J., & Garth, D. (1997). Arrows in time: The misapplication of chaos theory to education. *Journal of Curriculum Studies, 29,* 87–100.

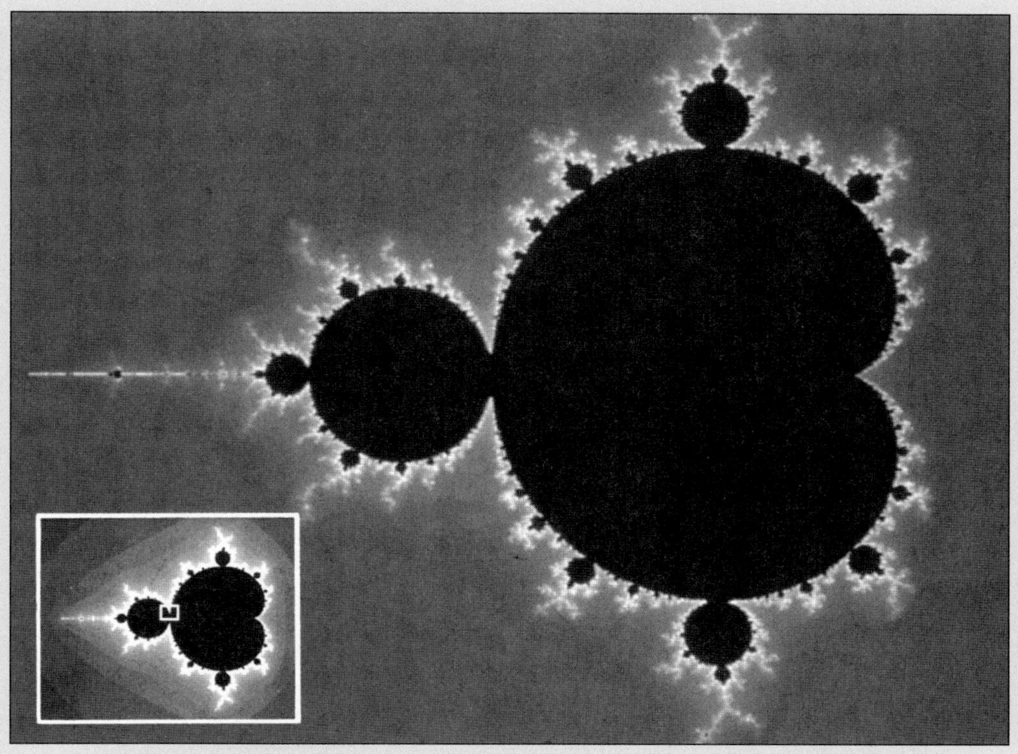

Photographs 1.1 and 1.2 *The Mandlebrot Bug*

Source: Peitgen, H-O, & Richter, P. H. (1986). *The beauty of fractals.* Berlin: Springer-Verlag.

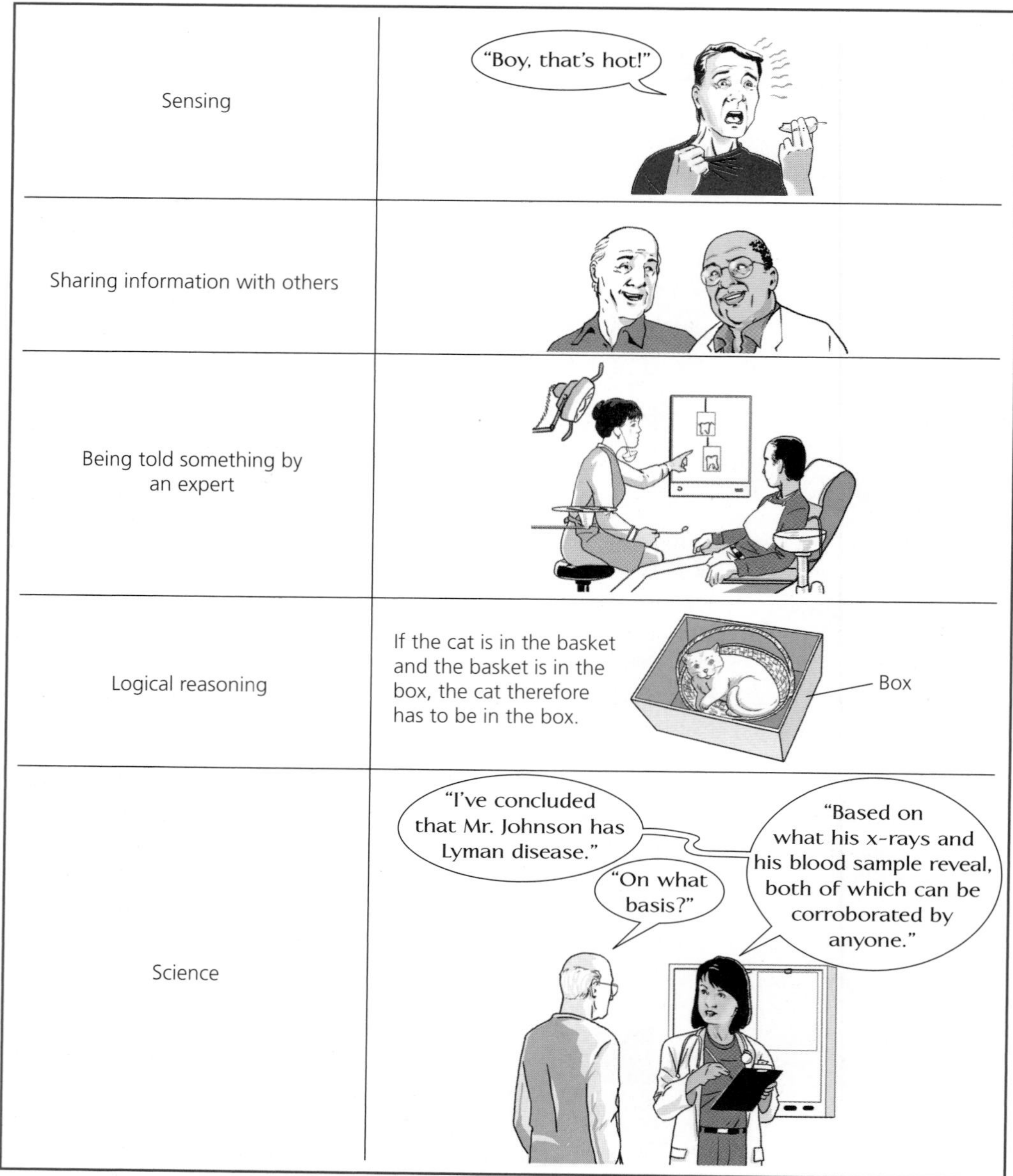

Figure 1.1 *Ways of Knowing*

on the other hand, are likely to assume that the world is made up of *multiple realities,* socially constructed by different individual views of the same situation.

When it comes to the purpose of research, quantitative researchers seek to establish relationships between variables and look for and sometimes explain the *causes* of such relationships. Qualitative researchers, on the other hand, are more concerned with understanding situations and events from the viewpoint of the participants. Accordingly, the participants often tend to be directly involved in the research process itself.

Quantitative research has established widely agreed-on general formulations of steps that guide researchers in their work. Quantitative research designs tend to be *preestablished.* Qualitative researchers have a much greater flexibility in both the strategies and techniques they use and the overall research process itself. Their designs tend to *emerge* during the course of the research.

The ideal researcher role in quantitative research is that of a *detached* observer, whereas qualitative researchers tend to become *immersed* in the situations in which they do their research. The prototypical study in the quantitative tradition is the experiment; for qualitative researchers, it is an ethnography.

Lastly, most quantitative researchers want to establish generalizations that transcend the immediate situation or particular setting. Qualitative researchers, on the other hand, often do not even try to generalize beyond the particular situation, but may leave it to the reader to assess applicability. When they do generalize, their generalizations are usually very limited in scope.

Many of the distinctions just described, of course, are not absolute. Sometimes researchers will use both qualitative and quantitative approaches in the same study. This kind of research is referred to as **mixed-methods research**. Its advantage is that by using multiple methods, researchers are better able to gather and analyze considerably more and different kinds of data than they would be able to using just one approach. Mixed-methods studies can emphasize one approach over the other or give each approach roughly equal weight.

Consider an example. It is often common in surveys to use closed-ended questions that lend themselves to quantitative analysis (such as through the calculation of percentages of different types of responses), but also open-ended questions that permit qualitative analysis (such as following up a response that interviewees give to a particular question with further questions by the researcher to encourage them to elaborate and explain their thinking).

Studies in which researchers use both quantitative and qualitative methods are becoming more common, as we will see in Chapter 23.

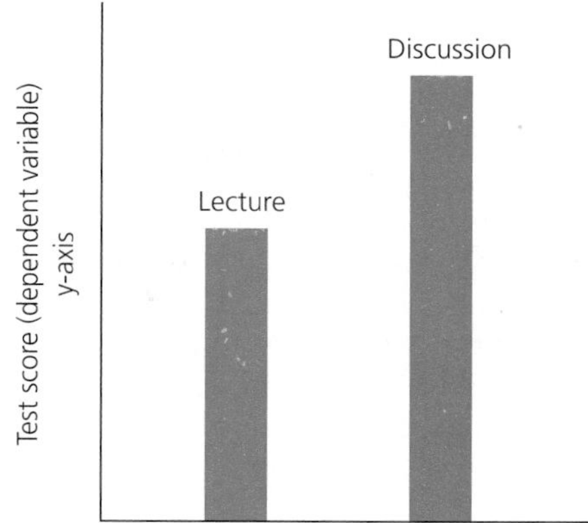

Figure 1.2 *Example of Results of Experimental Research: Effect of Method of Instruction on History Test Scores*[a]

[a]Many of the examples of data presented throughout this text, including that shown in Figure 1.2, are hypothetical. When actual data are shown, the source is indicated.

EXPERIMENTAL RESEARCH

Experimental research is the most conclusive of scientific methods. Because the researcher actually establishes different treatments and then studies their effects, results from this type of research are likely to lead to the most clear-cut interpretations.

Suppose a history teacher is interested in the following question: How can I most effectively teach important concepts (such as democracy or colonialism) to my students? The teacher might compare the effectiveness of two or more methods of instruction (usually called the *independent variable*) in promoting the learning of historical concepts. After systematically assigning students to contrasting forms of history instruction (such as inquiry versus programmed units), the teacher could compare the effects of these contrasting methods by testing students' conceptual knowledge. Student learning in each group could be assessed by an objective test or some other measuring device. If the average scores on the test (usually called the *dependent variable*) differed, they would give some idea of the effectiveness of the various methods. A simple graph could be plotted to show the results, as illustrated in Figure 1.2.

In the simplest sort of experiment, two contrasting methods are compared and an attempt is made to control for all other (extraneous) variables—such as student ability level, age, grade level, time, materials, and teacher characteristics—that might affect the outcome under investigation. Methods of such control could include holding the classes during the same or closely related periods of time, using the same materials in both groups, comparing students of the same age and grade level, and so on.

Of course, we want to have as much control as possible over the assignment of individuals to the various treatment groups, to ensure that the groups are similar. But in most schools, systematic assignment of students to treatment groups is difficult, if not impossible, to achieve. Nevertheless, useful comparisons are still possible. You might wish to compare the effect of different teaching methods (e.g., lectures versus discussion) on student achievement or attitudes in two or more *intact* history classes in the same school. If a difference exists between the classes in terms of what is being measured, this result can suggest how the two methods compare, even though the exact causes of the difference would be somewhat in doubt. We discuss this type of experimental research in Chapter 13.

Another form of experimental research, **single-subject research**, involves the intensive study of a single individual (or sometimes a single group) over time. These designs are particularly appropriate when studying individuals with special characteristics by means of direct observation. We discuss this type of research in Chapter 14.

CORRELATIONAL RESEARCH

Another type of research is done to determine relationships among two or more variables and to explore their implications for cause and effect; this is called **correlational research**. This type of research can help us make more intelligent predictions.

For instance, could a math teacher predict which sorts of individuals are likely to have trouble learning the subject matter of algebra? If we could make fairly accurate predictions in this regard, then perhaps we could suggest some corrective measures for teachers to use to help such individuals so that large numbers of "algebra-haters" are not produced.

How do we do this? First, we need to collect various kinds of information on students that we think is related to their achievement in algebra. Such information might include their performance on a number of tasks logically related to the learning of algebra (such as computational skills, ability to solve word problems, and understanding of math concepts), their verbal abilities, their study habits, aspects of their backgrounds, their early experiences with math courses and math teachers, the number and kinds of math courses they've taken, and anything else that might conceivably point to how those students who do well in math differ from those who do poorly.

We then examine the data to see if any relationships exist between some or all of these characteristics and subsequent success in algebra. Perhaps those who perform better in algebra have better computational skills or higher self-esteem or receive more attention from the teacher. Such information can help us predict more accurately the likelihood of learning difficulties for certain types of students in algebra courses. It may even suggest specific ways to help students learn better.

In short, correlational research seeks to investigate the extent to which one or more relationships of some type exist. The approach requires no manipulation or intervention on the part of the researcher other than administering the instrument(s) necessary to collect the data desired. In general, one would undertake this type of research to look for and describe relationships that may exist among naturally occurring phenomena, without trying in any way to alter these phenomena. We talk more about correlational research in Chapter 15.

CAUSAL-COMPARATIVE RESEARCH

Another type of research is intended to determine the cause for or the consequences of differences between groups of people; this is called **causal-comparative research**. Suppose a teacher wants to determine whether students from single-parent families do more poorly in her course than students from two-parent families. To investigate this question experimentally, the teacher would systematically select two groups of students and then assign each to a single- or two-parent family—which is clearly impossible (not to mention unethical!).

To test this question using a causal-comparative design, the teacher might compare two groups of students who already belong to one or the other type of family to see if they differ in their achievement. Suppose the groups do differ. Can the teacher definitely conclude that the difference in family situation produced the difference in achievement? Alas, no. The teacher can conclude that a difference does exist but cannot say for sure what caused the difference.

Interpretations of causal-comparative research are limited, therefore, because the researcher cannot say conclusively whether a particular factor is a cause or a result of the behavior(s) observed. In the example presented here, the teacher cannot be certain whether (1) any perceived difference in achievement between the two groups is due to the difference in home situation, (2) the parent status is due to the difference in achievement between the two groups (although this seems unlikely), or (3) some unidentified factor is at work. Nevertheless, despite problems of interpretation, causal-comparative studies are of value in identifying *possible* causes of observed variations in the behavior patterns of students. In this respect, they are very similar to correlational studies. We discuss causal-comparative research in Chapter 16.

SURVEY RESEARCH

Another type of research obtains data to determine specific characteristics of a group. This is called

survey research. Take the case of a high school principal who wants to find out how his faculty feels about his administrative policies. What do they like about his policies? What do they dislike? Why? Which policies do they like the best or least?

These sorts of questions can best be answered through a variety of survey techniques that measure faculty attitudes toward the policies of the administration. A *descriptive survey* involves asking the same set of questions (often prepared in the form of a written questionnaire or ability test) of a large number of individuals either by mail, by telephone, or in person. When answers to a set of questions are solicited in person, the research is called an *interview.* Responses are then tabulated and reported, usually in the form of frequencies or percentages of those who answer in a particular way to each of the questions.

The difficulties involved in survey research are mainly threefold: (1) ensuring that the questions are clear and not misleading, (2) getting respondents to answer questions thoughtfully and honestly, and (3) getting a sufficient number of the questionnaires completed and returned to enable making meaningful analyses. The big advantage of survey research is that it has the potential to provide us with a lot of information obtained from quite a large sample of individuals.

If more details about particular survey questions are desired, the principal (or someone else) can conduct personal interviews with faculty. The advantages of an interview (over a questionnaire) are that open-ended questions (those requiring a response of some length) can be used with greater confidence, particular questions of special interest or value can be pursued in depth, follow-up questions can be asked, and items that are unclear can be explained. We discuss survey research in Chapter 17.

ETHNOGRAPHIC RESEARCH

In all the examples presented so far, the questions being asked involve *how well, how much,* or *how efficiently* knowledge, attitudes, or opinions and the like exist or are being developed. Sometimes, however, researchers may wish to obtain a more complete picture of the educational process than answers to these questions provide. When they do, some form of *qualitative research* is called for. Qualitative research differs from the previous (quantitative) methodologies in both its methods and its underlying philosophy. In Chapter 18, we discuss these differences, along with recent efforts to reconcile the two approaches.

Consider the subject of physical education. Just how do physical education teachers teach their subject? What kinds of things do they do as they go about their daily routine? What sorts of things do students do? In what kinds of activities do they engage? What explicit and implicit rules of games in PE classes seem to help or hinder the process of learning?

To gain some insight into such concerns, an **ethnographic study** can be conducted. The emphasis in this type of research is on documenting or portraying the everyday experiences of individuals by observing and interviewing them and relevant others. An elementary classroom, for example, might be observed on as regular a basis as possible, and the students and teacher involved might be interviewed in an attempt to describe, as fully and as richly as possible, what goes on in that classroom. Descriptions (a better word might be *portrayals*) might depict the social atmosphere of the classroom; the intellectual and emotional experiences of students; the manner in which the teacher acts toward and reacts to students of different ethnicities, sexes, or abilities; how the "rules" of the class are learned, modified, and enforced; the kinds of questions asked by the teacher and students; and so forth. The data could include detailed prose descriptions by students of classroom activities, audio of teacher-student conferences, video of classroom discussions, examples of teacher lesson plans and student work, sociograms depicting "power" relationships in the classroom, and flowcharts illustrating the direction and frequency of certain types of comments (e.g., the kinds of questions asked by teacher and students of one another and the responses that different kinds produce).

In addition to ethnographic research, qualitative research includes *historical research* (see Chapter 22) and several other, less commonly used approaches. Casey,[2] for example, has identified 18 types of "narrative" methods. In Chapter 18, we discuss four of the most distinctive of these. These include *biography,* where the researcher focuses on important experiences in the life of an individual and interacts with the person to clarify meanings and interpretations (e.g., a study of the career of a high school principal). In *phenomenology,* the researcher focuses on a particular phenomenon (such as school board conflict), collects data through in-depth interviews with participants, and then identifies what is common to their perceptions. A third approach is the *case study,* in which a single individual, group, or important example is studied extensively and varied data are collected and used to formulate interpretations applicable to the specific case (e.g., a particular school board) or to provide useful generalizations. Lastly, *grounded theory* emphasizes continual interplay between raw data and the researcher's interpretations that emerge from the data. Its central purpose is to inductively develop a theory from data (e.g., a study of teacher morale in a particular school beginning with interviews and other types of data).

HISTORICAL RESEARCH

You are probably already familiar with **historical research**. In this type of research, some aspect of the past is studied, either by perusing documents of the period or by interviewing individuals who lived during the time. The researcher then attempts to reconstruct as accurately as possible what happened during that time and to explain why it did.

For example, a curriculum coordinator in a large urban school district might want to know what sorts of arguments have been made in the past as to what should be included in the social studies curriculum for grades K–12. She could read what various social studies and other curriculum theorists have written on the topic and then compare their positions. The major problems in historical research are making sure that the documents or individuals really did come from (or live during) the period under study and, once this is established, ascertaining that what the documents or individuals say is true. We discuss historical research in more detail in Chapter 22.

ACTION RESEARCH

Action research differs from all the preceding methodologies in two fundamental ways. The first is that generalization to other persons, settings, or situations is of minimal importance. Instead of searching for powerful generalizations, action researchers (often teachers or other education professionals, rather than professional researchers) focus on getting information that will enable them to change conditions in a particular situation in which they are personally involved. Examples would include improving the reading capabilities of students in a specific classroom, reducing tensions between ethnic groups in the lunchroom at a particular middle school, or identifying better ways to serve special education students in a specified school district. Accordingly, any of the methodologies discussed earlier may be appropriate.

The second difference involves the attention paid to the active involvement of the subjects* in a study (i.e., those on whom data is collected), as well as those likely to be affected by the study's outcomes. Commonly used terms in action research, therefore, are *participants* or *stakeholders,* reflecting an intent to involve them directly in the research process as part of "the research team." The extent of participation varies from just helping to select instruments and/or collect data to helping to formulate the research purpose and question to actually participating in all aspects of the research investigation from start to finish. We discuss action research in some detail in Chapter 24.

EVALUATION RESEARCH

There are many different kinds of evaluations depending on the object being evaluated and the purpose of the evaluation. **Evaluation research** is usually described as either *formative* or *summative*. **Formative evaluations** are intended to improve the object being evaluated; they help to form or strengthen it by examining the delivery of the program or technology and the quality of its implementation. In contrast, **summative evaluations** seek to examine the effects or outcomes of an object by describing what happens after the delivery of the program or technology in order to assess whether the object caused the outcome.

An example of a formative evaluation product is a needs assessment report. A needs assessment determines the appropriate audience for the program, as well as the extent of the need and what might work to meet the need. Summative evaluations can be thought of as either (a) outcome evaluations, which investigate whether the program or technology appeared to have caused demonstrable effects on specifically defined target outcomes, or (b) impact evaluations, which are broader and attempt to assess the overall effects (intended or unintended) of the program or technology as a whole.

Evaluators ask many different kinds of questions and often use a variety of methods to address them. For example, in summative evaluations, evaluators often use quasi-experimental research designs to assess the hypothesized causal effects of a program. Formative evaluations that examine program implementation may also include analysis of existing data sources, surveys, interviews, observational data, and focus groups.†

*"Participant" is also readily used now instead of "subject."

† For foundational readings on evaluation research, see: Patton, M. Q. (1982). *Practical evaluation.* Beverly Hills, CA: Sage; also, Patton, M. Q. (2002). *Qualitative research and evaluation methods* (3rd ed.). Thousand Oaks, CA: Sage.

Should Some Research Methods Be Preferred over Others?

Several researchers* have expressed their concern that the U.S. Department of Education is showing favoritism toward the narrow view that experimental research is, if not the only, at least the most respectable form of research and the only one worthy of being called scientific. Such a preference has implications for both the funding of school programs and educational research. As one writer commented, "How scared should we be when the federal government endorses a particular view of science and rejects others?"†

*Berliner, D. C. (2002). Educational research: The hardest science of all. *Educational Researcher, 31* (8), 18–20; Erickson, F. E., & Gutierrez, K. (2002). Culture, rigor, and science in educational research. *Educational Researcher, 31*(8), 21–24.

† St. Pierre, E. A. (2002). Science rejects postmodernism. *Educational Researcher, 31* (8), 25.

ALL HAVE VALUE

It must be stressed that each of the research methodologies described so briefly here has value for us in education. Each constitutes a different way of inquiring into the realities that exist within our classrooms and schools and into the minds and emotions of teachers, counselors, administrators, parents, and students. Each represents a different tool for trying to understand what goes on, and what works, in schools. It is inappropriate to consider any one or two of these approaches as superior to any of the others. The effectiveness of a particular methodology depends in large part on the nature of the research question one wants to ask and the specific context within which the particular investigation is to take place. We need to gain insights into what goes on in education from as many perspectives as possible, and hence we need to construe research in broad rather than narrow terms.

As far as we are concerned, research in education should ask a variety of questions, move in a variety of directions, encompass a variety of methodologies, and use a variety of tools. Different research orientations, perspectives, and goals should be not only allowed but also encouraged. The intent of this book is to help you learn how and when to use several of these methodologies.

EDUCATION RESEARCH IN THE DIGITAL AGE

Advances in communication and digital technology have affected education researchers both in terms of subject matter and access to information. From studying the effects of computer-assisted instruction and distance learning to using Internet-based surveys for data collection, technology continues to have a major impact on educational research. Along with these dynamic changes are important learning and teaching issues for students and faculty alike. Some examples include developing electronic information retrieval skills and critical evaluation strategies for assessing online resources. In Chapter 3, we discuss approaches for conducting electronic, manual, or hybrid searches to locate relevant sources in electronic or paper/print format, and provide guidelines for critically evaluating different types of sources. In Chapter 17, we discuss the advantages and disadvantages of Internet-based survey research, an increasingly popular data collection mode among researchers and students.

General Research Types

It is useful to consider the various research methodologies we have described as falling within one or more general research categories: descriptive, associational, or intervention-type studies.

DESCRIPTIVE STUDIES

Descriptive studies describe a given state of affairs as fully and carefully as possible. One of the best examples of descriptive research is found in botany and zoology, where each variety of plant and animal species is meticulously described and information is organized into useful taxonomic categories.

In educational research, the most common descriptive methodology is the survey, as when researchers summarize the characteristics (abilities, preferences, behaviors, and so on) of individuals or groups or (sometimes) physical environments (such as schools). Qualitative approaches, such as ethnographic and historical methodologies are also primarily descriptive in nature. Examples of descriptive studies in education include identifying the achievements of various groups of students; describing the behaviors of teachers, administrators, or counselors; describing the attitudes of parents; and describing the physical capabilities of schools. The description of phenomena is the starting point for all research endeavors.

Descriptive research in and of itself, however, is not very satisfying, since most researchers want to have a more complete understanding of people and things. This requires a more detailed analysis of the various aspects of phenomena and their interrelationships. Advances in biology, for example, have come about, in large part, as a result of the categorization of descriptions and the subsequent determination of relationships among these categories.

ASSOCIATIONAL RESEARCH

Educational researchers also want to do more than simply describe situations or events. They want to know how (or if), for example, differences in achievement are related to such things as teacher behavior, student diet, student interests, or parental attitudes. By investigating such possible relationships, researchers are able to understand phenomena more completely. Furthermore, the identification of relationships enables one to make predictions. If researchers know that student interest is related to achievement, for example, they can predict that students who are more interested in a subject will demonstrate higher achievement in that subject than students who are less interested. Research that investigates relationships is often referred to as **associational research**. Correlational and causal-comparative methodologies are the principal examples of associational research. Other examples include studying relationships (1) between achievement and attitude, between childhood experiences and adult characteristics, or between teacher characteristics and student achievement—all of which are correlational studies—and (2) between methods of instruction and achievement (comparing students who have been taught by each method) or between gender and attitude (comparing attitudes of males and females)—both of which are causal-comparative studies.

As useful as associational studies are, they too are ultimately unsatisfying because they do not permit researchers to "do something" to influence or change outcomes. Simply determining that student interest is predictive of achievement does not tell us how to change or improve either interest or achievement, although it does suggest that increasing interest would increase achievement. To find out whether one thing will have an effect on something else, researchers need to conduct some form of intervention study.

INTERVENTION STUDIES

In **intervention studies**, a particular method or treatment is expected to influence one or more outcomes. Such studies enable researchers to assess, for example, the effectiveness of various teaching methods, curriculum models, classroom arrangements, and other efforts to influence the characteristics of individuals or groups. Intervention studies can also contribute to general knowledge by confirming (or failing to confirm) theoretical predictions (for instance, that abstract concepts can be taught to young children). The primary methodology used in intervention research is the experiment.

Some types of educational research may combine these three general approaches. Although historical, ethnographic, and other qualitative research methodologies are primarily descriptive in nature, at times they may be associational if the investigator examines relationships. A descriptive historical study of college entrance requirements over time that examines the relationship between those requirements and achievement in mathematics is also associational. An ethnographic study that describes in detail the daily activities of an inner-city high school and also finds a relationship between media attention and teacher morale in the school is both descriptive and associational. An investigation of the effects of different teaching methods on concept learning that also reports the relationship between concept learning and gender is an example of a study that is both an intervention and an associational-type study.

META-ANALYSIS

Meta-analysis is an attempt to reduce the limitations of individual studies by trying to locate all of the studies on a particular topic and then using statistical means to synthesize the results of these studies. In Chapter 3, we discuss meta-analysis in more detail. In subsequent chapters, we examine in detail the limitations that are likely to be found in various types of research. Some apply to all types, while others are more likely to apply to particular types.

Critical Analysis of Research

There are some who feel that researchers who engage in the kinds of research we have just described take a bit too much for granted—indeed, that they make a number of unwarranted (and usually unstated) assumptions about the nature of the world in which we live. These critics (usually referred to as **critical researchers**) raise a number of philosophical, linguistic, ethical, and political questions not only about educational research as it is usually conducted but also about all fields of inquiry, ranging from the physical sciences to literature.

In an introductory text, we cannot hope to do justice to the many arguments and concerns these critics have raised over the years. What we can do is provide an introduction to some of the major questions they have repeatedly asked.

The first issue is *the question of reality:* As any beginning student of philosophy is well aware, there is no way to demonstrate whether anything "really exists." There is, for example, no way to prove conclusively to others that I am looking at what I call a *pencil* (e.g., others may not be able to see it; they may not be able to tell where I am looking; I may be dreaming). Further, it is easily demonstrated that different individuals may describe the same individual, action, or event quite differently—leading some critics to the conclusion that there is no such thing as reality, only individual (and different) perceptions of it. One implication of this view is that any search for knowledge about the "real" world is doomed to failure.

We would acknowledge that what the critics say is correct: We cannot, once and for all, "prove" anything, and there is no denying that perceptions differ. We would argue, however, that our commonsense notion of reality (that what most knowledgeable persons agree exists is what is real) has enabled humankind to solve many problems—even the question of how to put a man on the moon.

The second issue is *the question of communication.* Let us assume that we can agree that some things are "real." Even so, the critics argue that it is virtually impossible to show that we use the same terms to identify these things. For example, it is well known that the Inuit have many different words (and meanings) for the English word *snow.* To put it differently, no matter how carefully we define even a simple term such as *shoe,* the possibility always remains that one person's shoe is not another's. (Is a slipper a shoe? Is a shower clog a shoe?) If so much of language is imprecise, how then can relationships or laws—which try to indicate how various terms, things, or ideas are connected—be precise?

Again, we would agree. People often do not agree on the meaning of a word or phrase. We would argue, however (as we think would most researchers), that we can define terms clearly enough to enable different people to agree sufficiently about what words mean that they can communicate and thus get on with the acquisition of useful knowledge.

The third issue is *the question of values.* Historically, scientists have often claimed to be value free, that is, "objective," in their conduct of research. Critics have argued, however, that what is studied in the social sciences, including the topics and questions with which educational researchers are concerned, is never objective but rather socially constructed. Such things as teacher-student interaction in classrooms, the performance of students on examinations, the questions teachers ask, and a host of other issues and topics of concern to educators do not exist in a vacuum. They are influenced by the society and times in which people live. As a result, such topics and concerns, as well as how they are defined, inevitably reflect the *values* of that society. Further, even in the physical sciences, the choice of problems to study and the means of doing so reflect the values of the researchers involved.

Here, too, we would agree. We think that most researchers in education would acknowledge the validity of the critics' position. Many critical researchers charge, however, that such agreement is not sufficiently reflected in research reports. They say that many researchers fail to admit or identify "where they are coming from," especially in their discussions of the findings of their research.

The fourth issue is *the question of unstated assumptions.* An **assumption** is anything that is taken for granted rather than tested or checked. Although this issue is similar to the previous issue, it is not limited to values but applies to both general and specific assumptions that researchers make with regard to a particular study. Some assumptions are so generally accepted that they are taken for granted by practically all social researchers (e.g., the sun will come out; the earth will continue to rotate). Other assumptions are more questionable. An example given by Krathwohl[3] clarifies this. He points out that if researchers change the assumptions under which they operate, this may lead to different consequences. If we assume, for example, that mentally limited students learn in the same way as other students but more slowly, then it follows that given sufficient time and motivation, they can achieve as well as other students. The consequences of this view are to give these individuals more time, to place them in classes where the competition is less intense, and to motivate them to achieve. If, on the other hand, we assume that they use different conceptual structures into which they fit what they learn, this

Figure 1.3 *Is the Teacher's Assumption Correct?*

assumption leads to a search for simplified conceptual structures they can learn that will result in learning that approximates that of other students. Frequently authors do not make such assumptions clear.

In many studies, researchers implicitly assume that the terms they use are clear, that their samples are appropriate, and that their measurements are accurate. Designing a good study can be seen as trying to reduce these kinds of assumptions to a minimum. Readers should always be given enough information so that they do not have to make such assumptions. Figure 1.3 illustrates how an assumption can often be incorrect.

The fifth issue is *the question of societal consequences.* Critical theorists argue that traditional research efforts (including those in education) predominantly serve political interests that are, at best, conservative or, at worst, oppressive. They point out that such research is almost always focused on improving existing practices rather than raising questions about the practices themselves. They argue that, intentional or not, the efforts of most educational researchers have served essentially to reinforce the status quo. A more extreme position alleges that educational institutions (including research), rather than enlightening the citizenry, have served instead to prepare them to be uncritical functionaries in an industrialized society.

We would agree with this general criticism but note that there have been a number of investigations of the status quo itself, followed by suggestions for improvement, that have been conducted and offered by researchers of a variety of political persuasions.

Let us examine each of these issues in relation to a hypothetical example. Suppose a researcher decides to study the effectiveness of a course in formal logic in improving the ability of high school students to analyze arguments and arrive at defensible conclusions from data. The researcher accordingly designs a study that is sound enough in terms of design to provide at least a partial answer as to the effectiveness of the course. Let us address the five issues presented in relation to this study.

1. *The question of reality:* The abilities in question (analyzing arguments and reaching accurate conclusions) clearly are abstractions. They have no physical reality per se. But does this mean that such abilities do not "exist" in any way whatsoever? Are they nothing more than artificial by-products of our conceptual language system? Clearly, this is not the case. Such abilities do indeed exist in a somewhat limited sense, as when we talk about the "ability" of a person to do well on tests. But is test performance indicative of how well a student can perform in real life? If it is not, is the performance of students on such tests important? A critic might allege that the ability to analyze, for example, is situation specific: Some people are good analyzers on tests; others, in public forums; others, of written materials; and so forth. If this is so, then the concept of a general ability to "analyze arguments" would be an illusion. We think a good argument can be made that this is not the case—based on commonsense experience and on some research findings. We must admit, however, that the critic has a

point (we don't know for sure how general this ability is), and one that should not be overlooked.

2. *The question of communication:* Assuming that these abilities do exist, can we define them well enough so that meaningful communication can result? We think so, but it is true that even the clearest definition does not always guarantee meaningful communication. This is often revealed when we discover that the way we use a term differs from how someone else uses the same term, despite previous agreement on a definition. We may agree, for example, that a "defensible conclusion" is one that does not contradict the data and that follows logically from the data, yet still find ourselves disagreeing as to whether or not a particular conclusion is a defensible one. Debates among scientists often boil down to differences as to what constitutes a defensible conclusion from data.
3. *The question of values:* Researchers who decide to investigate outcomes such as the ones in this study make the assumption that the outcomes are either desirable (and thus to be enhanced) or undesirable (and thus to be diminished), and they usually point out why this is so. Seldom, however, are the values (of the researchers) that led to the study of a particular outcome discussed. Are these outcomes studied because they are considered of highest priority? because they are traditional? socially acceptable? easier to study? financially rewarding?

   The researcher's decision to study whether a course in logic will affect the ability of students to analyze arguments reflects his or her values. Both the outcomes and the method studied reflect Eurocentric ideas of value; the Aristotelian notion of the "rational man" (or woman) is not dominant in all cultures. Might some not claim, in fact, that we need people in our society who will question basic assumptions more than we need people who can argue well from these assumptions? While researchers probably cannot be expected to discuss such complex issues in every study, these critics render a service by urging all of us interested in research to think about how our values may affect our research endeavors.
4. *The question of unstated assumptions:* In carrying out such a study, the researcher is assuming not only that the outcome is desirable but that the findings of the study will have some influence on educational practice. Otherwise, the study is nothing more than an academic exercise. Educational methods research has been often criticized for leading to suggested practices that, for various reasons, are unlikely to be implemented. While we believe that such studies should still be done, researchers have an obligation to make such assumptions clear and to discuss their reasonableness.
5. *The question of societal consequences:* Finally, let us consider the societal implications of a study such as this. Critics might allege that this study, while perhaps defensible as a scientific endeavor, will have a negative overall impact. How so? First by fostering the idea that the outcome being studied (the ability to analyze arguments) is more important than other outcomes (e.g., the ability to see novel or unusual relationships). This allegation has, in fact, been made for many years in education—that researchers have overemphasized the study of some outcomes at the expense of others.

   A second allegation might be that such research serves to perpetuate discrimination against the less privileged segments of society. If it is true, as some contend, that some cultures are more "linear" and others more "global," then a course in formal logic (being primarily linear) may increase the advantage already held by students from the dominant linear culture.[4] It can be argued that a fairer approach would teach a variety of argumentative methods, thereby capitalizing on the strengths of all cultural groups.

To summarize, we have attempted to present the major issues raised by an increasingly vocal part of the research community. These issues involve the nature of reality, the difficulty of communication, the recognition that values always affect research, unstated assumptions, and the consequences of research for society as a whole. While we do not agree with some of the specific criticisms raised by these writers, we believe the research enterprise is the better for their efforts.

A Brief Overview of the Research Process

Regardless of methodology, all researchers engage in a number of similar activities. Almost all research plans include, for example, a problem statement, a hypothesis, definitions, a literature review, a sample of subjects, tests or other measuring instruments, a description of procedures to be followed, including a time schedule, and a description of intended data analyses. We deal with each of these components in some detail throughout this book, but we want to give you a brief overview of them before we proceed.

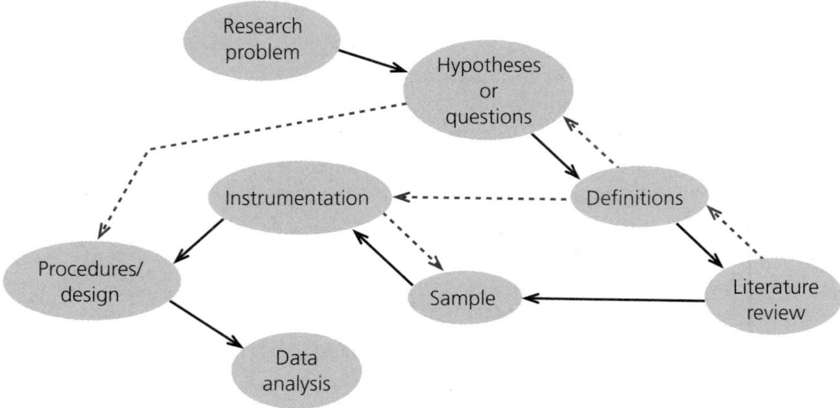

Figure 1.4 *The Research Process*

Figure 1.4 presents a schematic of the research components. The solid-line arrows indicate the sequence in which the components are usually presented and described in research proposals and reports. They also indicate a useful sequence for planning a study (i.e., thinking about the research problem, followed by the hypothesis, followed by the definitions, and so forth). The broken-line arrows indicate the most likely departures from this sequence (e.g., consideration of instrumentation sometimes results in changes in the sample; clarifying the question may suggest which type of design is most appropriate). The nonlinear pattern is intended to point out that, in practice, the process does not necessarily follow a precise sequence. In fact, experienced researchers often consider many of these components simultaneously as they develop their research plan.

Statement of the research problem: The problem of a study sets the stage for everything else. The **problem statement** should be accompanied by a description of the background of the problem (what factors caused it to be a problem in the first place) and a rationale or justification for studying it. Any legal or ethical ramifications related to the problem should be discussed and resolved.

Formulation of an exploratory question or a hypothesis: Research problems are usually stated as questions, and often as hypotheses. A **hypothesis** is a prediction, a statement of what specific results or outcomes are expected to occur. The hypotheses of a study should clearly indicate any relationships expected between the **variables** (the factors, characteristics, or conditions) being investigated and be so stated that they can be tested within a reasonable period of time. Not all studies are hypothesis-testing studies, but many are.

Definitions: All key terms in the problem statement and hypothesis should be defined as clearly as possible.

Review of the related literature: Other studies related to the research problem should be located and their results briefly summarized. The **literature review** (of appropriate journals, reports, monographs, etc.) should shed light on what is already known about the problem and should indicate logically why the proposed study would result in an extension of this prior knowledge.

Sample: The **subjects*** (the **sample**) of the study and the larger group, or **population** (to whom results are to be generalized), should be clearly identified. The sampling plan (the procedures by which the subjects will be selected) should be described.

Instrumentation: Each of the measuring **instruments** that will be used to collect data from the subjects should be described in detail, and a rationale should be given for its use.

Procedures: The actual **procedures** of the study—what the researcher will do (what, when, where, how, and with whom) from beginning to end, in the order in which they will occur—should be spelled out in detail (although this is not written in stone). This, of course, is much less feasible and appropriate in a qualitative study. A realistic

*The term *subjects* is offensive to some because it can imply that those being studied are deprived of dignity. We use it because we know of no other term of comparable clarity in this context.

time schedule outlining when various tasks are to be started, along with expected completion dates, should also be provided. All materials (e.g., textbooks) and/or equipment (e.g., computers) that will be used in the study should also be described. The general design or methodology (e.g., an experiment or a survey) to be used should be stated. In addition, possible sources of bias should be identified, and how they will be controlled should be explained.

Data analysis: Any statistical techniques, both descriptive and inferential, to be used in the **data analysis** should be described. The comparisons to be made to answer the research question should be made clear.

Go back to the **INTERACTIVE AND APPLIED LEARNING** feature at the beginning of the chapter for a listing of interactive and applied activities. Go to the **Online Learning Center** at **www.mhhe.com/fraenkel9e** to take quizzes, practice with key terms, and review chapter content.

Main Points

WHY RESEARCH IS OF VALUE

- The scientific method provides an important way to obtain accurate and reliable information.

WAYS OF KNOWING

- There are many ways to obtain information, including sensory experience, agreement with others, expert opinion, logic, and the scientific method.
- The scientific method is considered by researchers the most likely way to produce reliable and accurate knowledge.
- The scientific method involves answering questions through systematic and public data collection and analysis.

TYPES OF RESEARCH

- Some of the most commonly used research methodologies in education are experimental research, correlational research, causal-comparative research, survey research, ethnographic research, historical research, and action research.
- Experimental research involves manipulating conditions and studying effects.
- Correlational research involves studying relationships among variables within a single group and frequently suggests the possibility of cause and effect.
- Causal-comparative research involves comparing known groups that have had different experiences to determine possible causes or consequences of group membership.
- Survey research involves describing the characteristics of a group by means of such instruments as interview questions, questionnaires, and tests.
- Ethnographic research concentrates on documenting or portraying the everyday experiences of people, using observation and interviews.
- Ethnographic research is one form of qualitative research. Other common forms of qualitative research include the case study, biography, phenomenology, and grounded theory.
- A case study is a detailed analysis of one or a few individuals.
- Historical research involves studying some aspect of the past.

- Action research is a type of research by practitioners designed to help improve their practice.
- Evaluation research aims to improve the object or program being evaluated, usually by strengthening its delivery, implementation, and outcomes.
- Each of the research methodologies described constitutes a different way of inquiring into reality and is thus a different tool for understanding what goes on in education.

GENERAL RESEARCH TYPES

- Individual research methodologies can be classified into general research types. Descriptive studies describe a given state of affairs. Associational studies investigate relationships. Intervention studies assess the effects of a treatment or method on outcomes.
- Quantitative and qualitative research methodologies are based on different assumptions; they also differ on the purpose of research, the methods used by researchers, the kinds of studies undertaken, the researcher's role, and the degree to which generalization is possible.
- Mixed-methods research incorporates both quantitative and qualitative approaches.
- Meta-analysis attempts to synthesize the results of all the individual studies on a given topic by statistical means.

CRITICAL ANALYSIS OF RESEARCH

- Critical analysis of research raises basic questions about the assumptions and implications of educational research.

THE RESEARCH PROCESS

- Almost all research plans include a problem statement, an exploratory question or hypothesis, definitions, a literature review, a sample of subjects, instrumentation, a description of procedures to be followed, a time schedule, and a description of intended data analyses.

Key Terms

action research 14
applied research 7
associational research 16
assumption 17
basic research 7
causal-comparative research 12
chaos theory 8
correlational research 12
critical researcher 16
data analysis 21
descriptive studies 15
ethnographic study 13
evaluation research 14
experimental research 11
formative evaluation 14
historical research 14
hypothesis 20
instrument 20
intervention studies 16
literature review 20
meta-analysis 16
mixed-methods research 11
population 20
problem statement 20
procedure 20
qualitative research 7
quantitative research 7
research 7
sample 20
scientific method 5
single-subject research 12
subject 20
summative evaluation 14
survey research 13
variable 20

For Discussion

1. "Speculation, procedures, and conclusions are not scientific unless they are made public." Is this true? Discuss.
2. Most quantitative researchers believe that the world is a single reality, whereas most qualitative researchers believe that the world is made up of multiple realities. Which position would you support? Why?
3. Can you think of some other ways of knowing besides those mentioned in this chapter? What are they? What, if any, are the limitations of these methods?
4. "While certainty is appealing, it is contradictory to a fundamental premise of science." What does this mean? Discuss.
5. Is there such a thing as private knowledge? If so, can you give an example?
6. Many people seem to be uneasy about the idea of research, particularly research in schools. How would you explain this?

References

1. Research. (1984). *Webster's new world dictionary of the American language* (2nd ed., p. 1208). New York: Simon and Schuster.

2. Casey, K. (1995, 1996). The new narrative research in education. *Review of Research in Education, 21,* 211–253.

3. Krathwohl, D. R. (2009). *Methods of educational and social science research* (3rd ed., p. 91). Long Grove, IL: Waveland Press.

4. Ramirez, M., & Casteneda, A. (1974). *Cultural democracy, biocognitive development and education.* New York: Academic Press.

Research Exercise 1: What Kind of Research?

Think of a research idea or problem you would like to investigate. Using Problem Sheet 1, briefly describe the problem in a sentence or two. Then indicate the type of research methodology you would use to investigate this problem. Finally, explain briefly your reasons for choosing this approach.

Problem Sheet 1

Research Method

1. A possible topic or problem I am thinking of researching is: ______________________
____
____
2. The specific method(s) that seem(s) most appropriate for me to use at this time is/are (*circle all you think are appropriate*):
   a. an experiment
   b. a survey
   c. an ethnography
   d. a correlational study
   e. a causal-comparative study
   f. a case study
   g. a content analysis
   h. a historical study
   i. an action research or teacher research study
   j. a program evaluation
3. The overall research approach I am planning to use is (*circle one*):
   a. Qualitative b. Quantitative c. Mixed Methods
4. My reason(s) for using this approach is/are as follows:
____
____
____
____
____
____

An electronic version of this Problem Sheet that you can fill in and print, save, or e-mail is available on the Online Learning Center at www.mhhe.com/fraenkel9e.

PART 2

The Basics of Educational Research

In Part 2, we introduce or expand on many of the basic ideas involved in educational research. These include concepts such as hypotheses, variables, sampling, measurement, validity, reliability, and many others. We also begin to supply you with certain skills that will enhance your ability to understand the research process. These include how to select a research problem, formulate a hypothesis, conduct a literature search, choose a sample, define words and phrases clearly, develop a valid instrument, plus many others. Regardless of the methodology a researcher uses, all of these skills are important to learn.

2 The Research Problem

What Is a Research Problem?

Research Questions

Characteristics of Good Research Questions

Research Questions Should Be Feasible

Research Questions Should Be Clear

Research Questions Should Be Significant

Research Questions Often Investigate Relationships

"My research question is: 'What's the absolute best way to teach history to ninth-graders?'"
"Sorry, Suzy, but that question, as stated, isn't researchable."

OBJECTIVES **Studying this chapter should enable you to:**

- Give some examples of potential research problems in education.
- Formulate a research question.
- Distinguish between researchable and nonresearchable questions.
- Name five characteristics that good research questions possess.
- Describe three ways to clarify unclear research questions.
- Give an example of an operational definition and explain how such definitions differ from other kinds of definitions.
- Explain what is meant, in research, by the term "relationship" and give an example of a research question that involves a relationship.

INTERACTIVE AND APPLIED LEARNING After, or while, reading this chapter:

Go to the Online Learning Center at www.mhhe.com/fraenkel9e to:

- Learn More About What Makes a Question Researchable

Go to your online Student Mastery Activities book to do the following activities:

- Activity 2.1: Research Questions and Related Designs
- Activity 2.2: Changing General Topics into Research Questions
- Activity 2.3: Operational Definitions
- Activity 2.4: Justification
- Activity 2.5: Evaluating Research Questions

Robert Adams, a high school teacher in Omaha, Nebraska, wants to investigate whether the inquiry method will increase the interest of his eleventh-grade students in history. Phyllis Gomez, a physical education teacher in an elementary school in Phoenix, Arizona, wants to find out how her sixth-grade students feel about the new exercise program recently mandated by the school district. Tami Mendoza, a counselor in a large inner-city high school in San Francisco, wonders whether a client-centered approach might help ease the hostility that many of her students display during counseling sessions. Each of these examples presents a problem that could serve as a basis for research. Research problems—the focus of a research investigation—are what this chapter is about.

What Is a Research Problem?

A research problem is exactly that—a problem that someone would like to research. A problem can be anything that a person finds unsatisfactory or unsettling, a difficulty of some sort, a state of affairs that needs to be changed, anything that is not working as well as it might. Problems involve areas of concern to researchers, conditions they want to improve, difficulties they want to eliminate, questions for which they seek answers.

For researchers and students alike, research problems are usually identified from several sources including (1) the research literature—see detailed discussion in Chapter 3 on the role of the literature review in formulating research questions; (2) problems in practice or work-related contexts; and (3) personal biography or history (such as current or past personal experiences or identities, race, ethnicity, gender, class background, family customs, religion, and so forth).

Research Questions

Usually a research problem is initially posed as a question, which serves as the focus of the researcher's investigation. In our view, the research question should dictate the research type and paradigm (qualitative, quantitative, or mixed methods) used to conduct the study rather than the other way around, that is, the methodology determining the question. The following examples of initial research questions in education are not sufficiently developed for actual use in a research project but would be suitable during the early stage of formulating a research question. An appropriate methodology and research paradigm (in parentheses) are provided for each question. Although there are other possible methodologies that might be used, we consider those given here as particularly suitable.

- Does client-centered therapy produce more satisfaction in clients than traditional therapy? (experimental research; quantitative)
- What goes on in after-school programs during an average week? (ethnographic research; qualitative)
- Does behavior modification reduce aggression in autistic children? (single-subject experimental research; quantitative)
- Do teachers behave differently toward students of different genders? (causal-comparative research; quantitative or mixed methods)
- How can we predict which students might have trouble learning certain kinds of subject matter? (correlational research; quantitative)

- How do parents feel about the school counseling program? (survey research; quantitative)
- Why do first-generation college students have a lower graduation rate at San Simeon University? (case study; mixed methods)
- How can principals improve faculty morale at low-performing middle schools? (interview research; qualitative)

What all these questions have in common is that we can collect data of some sort to answer them (at least in part). That's what makes them researchable. For example, a researcher can measure the satisfaction levels of clients who receive different methods of therapy. Or researchers can observe and interview to describe the functioning of an elementary school classroom. To repeat, then, what makes these questions researchable is that some sort of information *can* be collected to answer them.

Other kinds of questions, however, *cannot* be answered by collecting and analyzing data. Here are two examples:

1. Should philosophy be included in the high school curriculum?
2. What is the meaning of life?

Why can't these questions be researched? What about them prevents us from collecting information to answer them? The reason is both simple and straightforward: There is no way to collect information to answer either question. Both questions are, in the final analysis, not researchable.

The first question is a question of *value*—it implies notions of right and wrong, proper and improper—and therefore does not have any **empirical** (or observable) **referents**. There is no way to deal, empirically, with the verb *should*. How can we empirically determine whether or not something "should" be done? What data could we collect? There is no way for us to proceed. However, if the question is changed to "Do people *think* philosophy should be included in the high school curriculum?" it becomes researchable. Why? Because now we can collect data to help us answer the question.

The second question is *metaphysical* in nature—that is, transcendental, beyond the physical. Answers to this sort of question lie beyond the accumulation of information.

Here are more ideas for research questions. Which ones (if any) do you think are researchable?

1. Is God good?
2. Are children more engaged when taught by a teacher of the same gender?
3. Does high school achievement influence the academic achievement of university students?
4. What is the best way to teach grammar?
5. What would schools be like today if World War II had not occurred?

We hope you identified questions 2 and 3 as the two that are researchable. Questions 1, 4, and 5, as stated, cannot be researched. Question 1 is another metaphysical question and, as such, does not lend itself to empirical research (we could ask people if they *believe* God is good, but that would be another question). Question 4 asks for the "best" way to do something. Think about this one for a moment. Is there any way we can determine the best way to do anything? To be able to determine this, we must examine every possible alternative, and a moment's reflection brings us to the realization that this can never be accomplished. How would we ever be sure that all possible alternatives have been examined? Question 5 requires the creation of impossible conditions. We can, of course, investigate what people *think* schools would be like. Figure 2.1 illustrates the difference between researchable and nonresearchable questions.

Characteristics of Good Research Questions

Once a research question has been formulated, researchers want to turn it into as good a question as possible. Good research questions possess four essential characteristics.

1. The question is *feasible* (i.e., it can be investigated without expending an undue amount of time, energy, or money).
2. The question is *clear* (i.e., most people would agree as to what the key words in the question mean).
3. The question is *significant* (i.e., it is worth investigating because it will contribute important knowledge about the human condition).
4. The question is *ethical* (i.e., it will not involve physical or psychological harm or damage to human beings or to the natural or social environment of which they are a part). We will discuss the subject of ethics in detail in Chapter 4.

Let us discuss some of these characteristics in more detail.

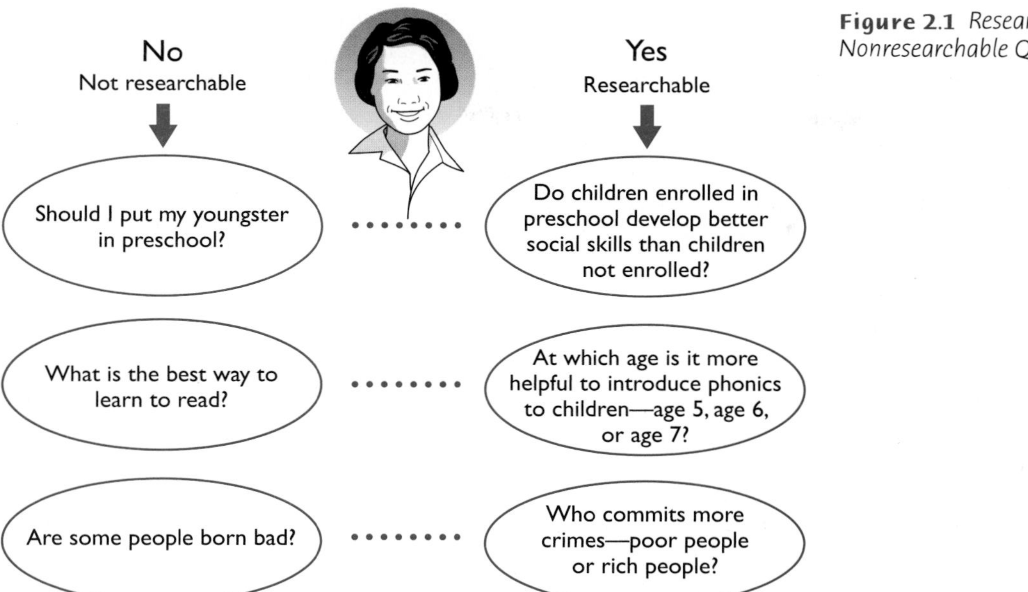

Figure 2.1 *Researchable Versus Nonresearchable Questions*

RESEARCH QUESTIONS SHOULD BE FEASIBLE

Feasibility is an important issue in designing research studies. A feasible question is one that can be investigated with available resources. Some questions (such as those involving space exploration, e.g., or the study of the long-term effects of special programs, such as Head Start) require a great deal of time and money; others require much less. Unfortunately, the field of education, unlike medicine, business, law, agriculture, pharmacology, or the military, has never established an ongoing research effort tied closely to practice. Most of the research that is done in schools or other educational institutions is likely to be done by "outsiders"—often university professors and their students—and usually is funded by temporary grants. Thus, lack of feasibility often seriously limits research efforts. Following are two examples of research questions, one feasible and one not so feasible.

Feasible: How do the students at Oceana High School feel about the new guidance program recently instituted in the district?

Not so feasible: How would achievement be affected by giving each student his or her own laptop computer to use for a semester?

RESEARCH QUESTIONS SHOULD BE CLEAR

Because the research question is the focus of a research investigation, it is particularly important that the question be clear. What exactly is being investigated? Let us consider two examples of research questions that are not clear enough.

Example 1. *"Is a humanistically oriented classroom effective?"* Although the phrase *humanistically oriented classroom* may seem quite clear, many people may not be sure exactly what it means. If we ask, What *is* a humanistically oriented classroom? we begin to discover that it is not as easy as we might have thought to describe its essential characteristics. What happens in such classrooms that is different from what happens in other classrooms? Do teachers use certain kinds of strategies? Do they lecture? In what sorts of activities do students participate? What do such classrooms look like—how is the seating arranged, for example? What kinds of materials are used? Is there much variation to be found from classroom to classroom in the strategies employed by the teacher or in the sorts of activities in which students engage? Do the kinds of materials available and/or used vary?

Another term in this question is also ambiguous. What does the term *effective* mean? Does it mean "results in increased academic proficiency," "results in happier children," "makes life easier for teachers," or "costs less money"? Maybe it means all these things and more.

Example 2. *"How do teachers feel about mainstreaming students with learning disabilities?"* The first term that needs clarification is *teachers.* What age group does this involve? What level of experience (are probationary teachers, e.g., included)? Are teachers in both public and private schools included? Are teachers throughout the nation included, or only those in a specific locality? Does the term refer to teachers who do not teach special classes as well as those who do?

The phrase *feel about* is also ambiguous. Does it mean opinions? emotional reactions? Does it suggest actions? or what? The terms *mainstreaming* and *students with learning disabilities* also need to be clarified. An example of a legal definition of "learning disabled" is:

> A disorder in one or more of the basic psychological processes involved in understanding or in using language, spoken or written, which disorder may manifest itself in imperfect ability to listen, think, speak, read, write, spell, or do mathematical calculations. Such term includes such conditions as perceptual disabilities, brain injury, minimal brain dysfunction, dyslexia, and developmental aphasia. Such term does not include a learning problem that is primarily the result of visual, hearing or motor disabilities, of mental retardation, of emotional disturbance, or of environmental, cultural, or economic disadvantage.*

Note that this definition itself contains some ambiguous words, such as *imperfect ability,* which lend themselves to a wide variety of interpretations.

As we begin to think about these (or other) questions, it appears that terms which seemed at first glance to be words or phrases that everyone would easily understand are really quite complex and far more difficult to define than we might originally have thought.

This is true of many current educational concepts and methodologies. Consider such terms as *core curriculum, client-centered counseling, active learning,* and *quality management.* What do such terms mean? If you were to ask a sample of five or six teachers, counselors, or administrators, you probably would get several different definitions. Although such ambiguity is valuable in some circumstances and for certain purposes, it represents a problem to investigators of a research question. Researchers have no choice but to be specific about the terms used in a research question, to define precisely what is to be studied. In making this effort, researchers gain a clearer picture of how to proceed with an investigation and, in fact, sometimes decide to change the very nature of the research. How, then, might the clarity of a research question be improved?

*Legal definition from The Individuals with Disabilities Education Act cited in **U.S.C.** § 1401(26) (2000).

Defining Terms. There are essentially three ways to clarify important terms in a research question. The first is to use a **constitutive definition**—that is, to use what is often referred to as the *dictionary approach.* Researchers simply use other words to say more clearly what is meant. Thus, the term *humanistic classroom* might be defined as

> A classroom in which: (1) the needs and interests of students have the highest priority; (2) students work on their own for a considerable amount of time in each class period; and (3) the teacher acts as a guide and a resource person rather than an informant.

Notice, however, that this definition is still somewhat unclear, since the words being used to explain the term *humanistic* are themselves ambiguous. What does it mean to say that the "needs and interests of students have the highest priority" or that "students work on their own"? What is a "considerable amount" of each class period? What does a teacher do when acting as a "guide" or a "resource person"? Further clarification is needed.

Students of communication have demonstrated just how difficult it is to be sure that the message sent is the message received. It is probably true that no one ever completely understands the meaning of terms that are used to communicate. That is, we can never be certain that the message we receive is the one the sender intended. Some years ago, one of the leaders in our field was said to have become so depressed by this idea that he quit talking to his colleagues for several weeks. A more constructive approach is simply to do the best we can. We must try to explain our terms to others. While most researchers try to be clear, there is no question that some do a much better job than others.

"It all depends on how you define 'chop.'"

RESEARCH TIPS

Key Terms to Define in a Research Study

- Terms necessary to ensure that the research question is sharply focused
- Terms that individuals outside the field of study may not understand
- Terms that have multiple meanings
- Terms that are essential to understanding what the study is about
- Terms to provide precision in specifications for instruments to be developed or located

Another important point to remember is that often it is a compound term or phrase that needs to be defined rather than only a single word. For example, the term *nondirective therapy* will surely not be clarified by precise definitions of *nondirective* and *therapy,* since it has a more specific meaning than the two words defined separately would convey. Similarly, such terms as *learning disability, bilingual education, interactive video,* and *home-centered health care* need to be defined as linguistic wholes.

Here are three definitions of the term *motivated to learn.* Which do you think is the clearest?

1. Works hard
2. Is eager and enthusiastic
3. Sustains attention to a task*

As you have seen, the dictionary approach to clarifying terms has its limitations. A second possibility is **clarification by example**. Researchers might think of a few humanistic classrooms with which they are familiar and then try to describe as fully as possible what happens in these classrooms. Usually we suggest that people observe such classrooms to see for themselves how they differ from other classrooms. This approach also has its problems, however, since our descriptions may still not be as clear to others as they would like.

Thus, a third method of clarification is to define important terms operationally. **Operational definitions** require that researchers specify the actions or operations necessary to measure or identify the term. For example, here are two possible operational definitions of the term *humanistic classroom.*

1. Any classroom *identified* by specified experts as constituting an example of a humanistic classroom
2. Any classroom *judged* (by an observer spending at least one day per week for four to five weeks) to possess all the following characteristics:
   a. No more than three children working with the same materials at the same time
   b. The teacher never spending more than 20 minutes per day addressing the class as a group
   c. At least half of every class period open for students to work on projects of their own choosing at their own pace
   d. Several (more than three) sets of different kinds of educational materials available for every student in the class to use
   e. Nontraditional seating—students sit in circles, small groupings of seats, or even on the floor to work on their projects
   f. Frequent (at least two per week) discussions in which students are encouraged to give their opinions and ideas on topics being read about in their textbooks

This listing of characteristics and behaviors may be a quite unsatisfactory definition of a humanistic classroom to many people (and perhaps to you). But it is considerably more specific (and thus clearer) than the definition with which we began.† Armed with this definition (and the necessary facilities), researchers could decide quickly whether or not a particular classroom qualified as an example of a humanistic classroom.

Defining terms operationally is a helpful way to clarify their meaning. Operational definitions are useful tools and should be learned by all students of research.

*We judge 3 to be the clearest, followed by 1 and then 2.

†This is not to say that this list would not be improved by making the guidelines even more specific. These characteristics, however, do meet the criterion for an operational definition—they specify the actions researchers need to take to measure or identify the variable being defined.

Figure 2.2 *Some Times When Operational Definitions Would Be Helpful*

Lastly, students should take care to reference any sources that directly informed their definitions. Remember that the operations or activities necessary to measure or identify the term must be specified. Which of the following possible definitions of the term *motivated to learn mathematics* do you think are operational?

1. As shown by enthusiasm in class
2. As judged by the student's math teacher using a rating scale she developed
3. As measured by the "Math Interest" questionnaire
4. As shown by attention to math tasks in class
5. As reflected by achievement in mathematics
6. As indicated by records showing enrollment in mathematics electives
7. As shown by effort expended in class
8. As demonstrated by number of optional assignments completed
9. As demonstrated by reading math books outside class
10. As observed by teacher aides using the "Mathematics Interest" observation record*

In addition to their value in helping readers understand how researchers actually obtain the information they need, operational definitions are often helpful in clarifying terms. Thinking about how to measure *job satisfaction,* for example, is likely to force a researcher to clarify, in his or her own mind, what he or she means by the term. (For everyday examples of times when operational definitions are needed, see Figure 2.2.)

Despite their virtues, however, operational definitions in and of themselves are often not illuminating. Reading that "language proficiency is (operationally) defined as the student's score on the TOLD test" is not very helpful

*The operational definitions are 2, 3, 6, 8, and 10. The nonoperational definitions are 1, 4, 5, 7, and 9, because the activities or operations necessary for identifying the behavior have not been specified.

MORE ABOUT RESEARCH

The Importance of a Rationale

Research in education, as in all of social science, has sometimes been criticized as trivial. Some years ago, Senator William Proxmire gained considerable publicity for his "golden fleece" awards, which he bestowed on government-funded studies that he considered particularly worthless or trivial. Some recipients complained of "cheap shots," arguing that their research had not received a complete or fair hearing. While it is doubtless true that research is often specialized in nature and not easily communicated to persons outside the field, we believe more attention should be paid to:

- Avoiding esoteric terminology
- Defining key terms clearly and, when feasible, both constitutively and operationally
- Making a clear and persuasive case for the importance of a study

unless the reader is familiar with this particular test. Even when this is the case, it is more satisfactory to be informed of what the researcher means by the term. For these reasons we believe that an operational definition should always be accompanied by a constitutive one.

The importance of researchers being clear about the terms in their research questions cannot be overstated. Researchers will have difficulty proceeding with plans for the collection and analysis of data if they do not know exactly what kind of data to look for. And they will not know what data to look for if they are unclear about the meaning of the key terms in the research question.

RESEARCH QUESTIONS SHOULD BE SIGNIFICANT

Research questions also should be *worth* investigating. In essence, we need to consider whether getting the answer to a question is worth the time and energy (and often money). What, we might ask, is the value of investigating a particular question? In what ways will it contribute to our knowledge about education? to our knowledge of human beings? Is such knowledge important in some way? If so, how? These questions ask researchers to think about why a research question is worthwhile—that is, important or significant.

It probably goes without saying that a research question is of interest to the person who asks it. But is interest alone sufficient justification for an investigation? For some people, the answer is a clear yes. They say that any question that someone sincerely wants an answer to is worth investigating. Others, however, say that personal interest, in and of itself, is an insufficient reason. Too often, they point out, personal interest can result in the pursuit of trivial or insignificant questions. Because most research efforts require some (and often a considerable) expenditure of time, energy, materials, money, and/or other resources, it is easy to appreciate the point of view that some useful outcome or payoff should result from the research. The investment of oneself and others in a research enterprise should contribute some knowledge of value to the field of education.

Generally speaking, most researchers do not believe that research efforts based primarily on personal interest alone warrant investigation. Furthermore, there is some reason to question a "purely curious" motive on psychological grounds. Most questions probably have some degree of hidden motivation behind them, and for the sake of credibility, these reasons should be made explicit.

One of the most important tasks for any researcher, therefore, is to think through the value of the intended research before too much preliminary work is done. Three important questions should be asked:

1. How might answers to this research question advance knowledge in my field?
2. How might answers to this research question improve educational practice?
3. How might answers to this research question improve the human condition?

As you think about possible research questions, ask yourself: Why would it be important to answer this question? Does the question have implications for the improvement of practice? for administrative decision making? for program planning? Is there an important issue that can be illuminated to some degree by a study of this question? Is it related to a current theory that I have doubts about or would like to substantiate? Thinking through possible answers to these questions can help you judge the significance of a potential research question.

In our experience, student justifications for a proposed study are likely to have two weaknesses. First,

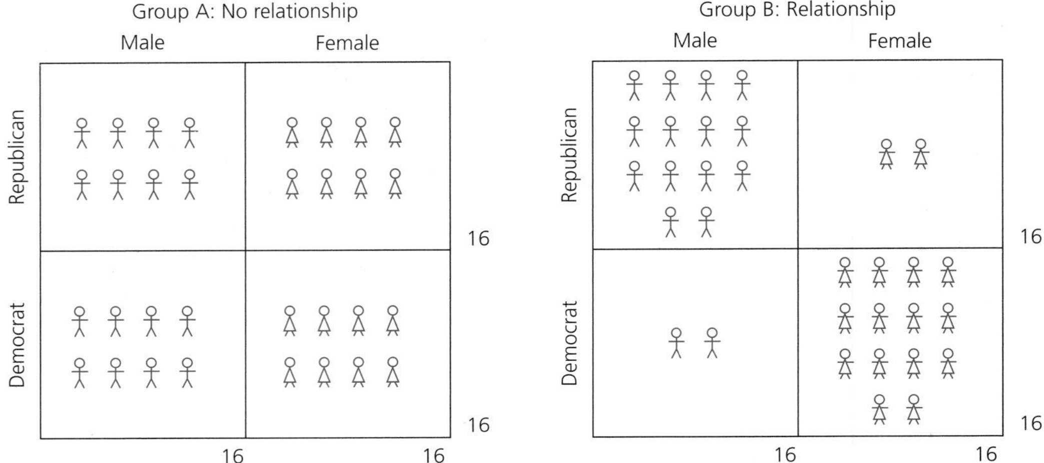

Figure 2.3 *Relationship Between Voter Gender and Party Affiliation*

they assume too much—for example, that everyone would agree with them (i.e., it is self-evident) that it is important to study something like self-esteem or ability to read. In point of fact, not everyone does agree that these are important topics to study; nonetheless, it is still the researcher's job to make the case that they *are* important rather than merely assuming that they are.

Second, students often overstate the implications of a study. Evidence of the effectiveness of a particular teaching method does *not,* for example, imply that the method will be generally adopted or that improvement in student achievement will automatically result. It *would* imply, for example, that more attention should be given to the method in teacher-training programs.

RESEARCH QUESTIONS OFTEN INVESTIGATE RELATIONSHIPS

There is an additional characteristic that good research questions often possess. They frequently (but not always) suggest a relationship of some sort to be investigated. (We discuss the reasons for this in Chapter 5.) A suggested relationship means that two qualities or characteristics are tied together or connected in some way. Are motivation and learning related? If so, how? What about age and attractiveness? speed and weight? height and strength? a principal's administrative policies and faculty morale?

It is important to understand how the term *relationship* is used in research, since the term has other meanings in everyday life. When researchers use the term *relationship,* they are not referring to the nature or quality of an association between people, for example. What we and other researchers mean is perhaps best clarified visually. Look, for example, at the data for groups A and B in Figure 2.3. What do you notice?

The hypothetical data for group A show that out of a total of 32 individuals, 16 are Republicans and 16 are Democrats. It also shows that half are male and half are female. Group B shows the same breakdown by party affiliation and gender. What is different between the two groups is that there is no association or relationship between gender and political party in group A, whereas there is a very strong relationship between these two factors in group B. We can express the relationship in group B by saying that males tend to be Republicans while females tend to be Democrats. We can also express this relationship in terms of a prediction. Should another female join group B, we would predict she would be a Democrat since 14 of the previous 16 females are Democrats.

Go back to the **INTERACTIVE AND APPLIED LEARNING** feature at the beginning of the chapter for a listing of interactive and applied activities. Go to the **Online Learning Center** at **www.mhhe.com/fraenkel9e** to take quizzes, practice with key terms, and review chapter content.

Main Points

RESEARCH PROBLEM

- A research problem is the focus of a research investigation.

RESEARCH QUESTIONS

- Many research problems are stated as questions.
- The essential characteristic of a researchable question is that there be some sort of information that can be collected in an attempt to answer the question.

CHARACTERISTICS OF GOOD RESEARCH QUESTIONS

- Research questions should be feasible—that is, capable of being investigated with available resources.
- Research questions should be clear—that is, unambiguous.
- Research questions should be significant—that is, worthy of investigation.
- Research questions should be ethical—that is, their investigation should not involve physical or psychological harm or damage to human beings or to the natural or social environment of which they are a part.
- Research questions often (although not always) suggest a relationship to be investigated. The term *relationship,* as used in research, refers to a connection or association between two or more characteristics or qualities.

DEFINING TERMS IN RESEARCH

- Three common ways to clarify ambiguous or unclear terms in a research question involve the use of constitutive (dictionary-type) definitions, definition by example, and operational definitions.
- A constitutive definition uses additional terms to clarify meaning.
- An operational definition describes how examples of a term are to be measured or identified.

Key Terms

clarification by example 31
constitutive definition 30
empirical referent 28
operational definition 31

For Discussion

1. Here are three examples of research questions. How would you rank them on a scale of 1 to 5 (5 = highest, 1 = lowest) for clarity? for significance? Why?
   a. How many students in the sophomore class signed up for a course in driver training this semester?
   b. Why do so many students in the district say they dislike English?
   c. Is inquiry or lecture more effective in teaching social studies?
2. How would you define *humanistically oriented classroom?*
3. Some terms used frequently in education, such as *motivation, achievement,* and even *learning,* are very hard to define clearly. Why do you suppose this is so?
4. How might the term *excellence* be defined operationally? Give an example.
5. "Even the clearest of definitions does not always guarantee meaningful communication." Is this really true? Why or why not?
6. We would argue that operational definitions should always be accompanied by constitutive definitions. Would you agree? Can you think of an instance when this might not be necessary?
7. Most researchers do not believe that research efforts based primarily on personal interest warrant investigation. Do you agree in all cases? Can you think of a possible exception?

Research Exercise 2: The Research Question

Using Problem Sheet 2, restate the research problem you listed in Research Exercise 1 in a sentence or two, and then formulate a research question related to this problem. Now list all the key terms in the question that you think are not clear and need to be defined. Define each of these terms both constitutively and operationally, and then state why you think your question is an important one to study.

Problem Sheet 2

The Research Question

1. My (restated) research problem is: ______________________________
____
2. My research question(s) is/are: ______________________________
____
3. The following are key terms in the problem or question that are not clear and thus need to be defined:

a. ____________ d. ____________
b. ____________ e. ____________
c. ____________ f. ____________

4. Here are my constitutive definitions for these terms: ______________
____
____
____
5. Here are my operational definitions for these terms: ______________
____
____
____
6. My rationale for investigating this question/problem (why I would argue that it is an important question to investigate) is as follows: ______________
____
____

An electronic version of this Problem Sheet that you can fill in and print, save, or e-mail is available on the Online Learning Center at www.mhhe.com/fraenkel9e.

Locating and Reviewing the Literature

3

The Definition and Value of a Literature Review

Types of Sources

Steps Involved in a Literature Search

Define the Problem as Precisely as Possible

Look Through One or Two Secondary Sources

Select the Appropriate General Reference Tools

Formulate Search Terms

Search Using General Reference Tools

Doing a Computer Search

Obtain Primary Sources

Writing the Literature Review Report

Researching the World Wide Web

"Hey! There's Joe. Taking it easy, as usual."
"No, he says he's reviewing the literature for his Biology class!"
SPORTS ILLUSTRATED

OBJECTIVES **Studying this chapter should enable you to:**

- Describe briefly why a literature review is of value.
- Name the steps a researcher goes through in conducting a review of the literature.
- Describe briefly the kinds of information contained in a general reference and give an example of such a source.
- Explain the difference between a primary and a secondary source and give an example of each type.
- Explain what is meant by the phrase "search term" and how it differs from the term "descriptor," and how both terms are used in literature searches.
- Conduct both a manual and electronic search of the literature on a topic of interest to you after a small amount of "hands-on" computer time and a little help from a librarian.
- Write a summary of your literature review.
- Explain what a meta-analysis is.

INTERACTIVE AND APPLIED LEARNING After, or while, reading this chapter:

Go to the Online Learning Center at www.mhhe.com/fraenkel9e to:

- Read the Guide to Electronic Research

Go to your online Student Mastery Activities book to do the following activities:

- Activity 3.1: Library Worksheet
- Activity 3.2: Where Would You Look?
- Activity 3.3: Do a Computer Search of the Literature

After a career in the military, Phil Gomez is in his first year as a teacher at an adult school in Logan, Utah. He teaches U.S. history to students who did not graduate from high school but who now are trying to obtain a diploma. He has learned the hard way, through trial and error, that there are a number of techniques that simply put students to sleep. He sincerely wants to be a good teacher, but he is having trouble getting his students interested in the subject. As he is the only history teacher in the school, the other teachers are not of much help.

He wants to get some ideas, therefore, about other approaches, strategies, and techniques that he might use. He decides to do an Internet search to see what he can find out about effective strategies for teaching high school history. His first search yields 12,847 hits! Phil is overwhelmed and at a loss for which sources to view. Should he look at books? Journal articles? Websites? Government documents? Unpublished reports? Where should he look for the most valid resources? And how could his searching be done more systematically?

In this chapter, you will learn some answers to these (and related) questions. When you have finished reading, you should have a number of ideas about how to conduct a systematic or "planned" search of the educational literature.

The Definition and Value of a Literature Review

A **literature review** is an assessment of a body (or bodies) of literature that pertains to a specific question. A literature review is helpful in several ways. It not only helps researchers glean the ideas of others interested in a particular research question (through important research findings and theories), but it also lets them read about the results of similar or related studies. Literature reviews also give researchers ideas about areas where more research needs to be done. They refer to these as "gaps" in the literature. In fact, a detailed literature review is usually required of master's and doctoral students when they design a thesis. In some graduate programs, students must propose theses or dissertations that address gaps in the existing literature. Thus researchers often weigh information from a literature review in light of their own interests and situation. There are two important points here: Researchers need to be able not only to locate other work dealing with their intended area of study but also to evaluate this work in terms of its relevance to the research question of interest.

Types of Sources

A researcher needs to be familiar with three basic types of sources as he or she begins to search for information related to the research question. These terms apply both to computerized searching (online or electronic) as well as manual searching (using print/paper tools to locate print/paper sources). Regardless of the tools involved, the search process is similar.

1. **General reference tools** are the sources researchers often refer to first. In effect, they tell where to look to locate other sources—such as articles, books, reports, and other documents—that deal directly with the research question. General reference tools are usually either *indexes,* which list the author, title, and place of publication of articles and other materials, or **abstracts**, which give a brief summary or

annotation of various publications, as well as their author, title, and place of publication. Historically, indexes and abstracts were only available in paper format, but since the advent of computers and the Internet, most libraries have access to indexes and abstracts through online databases containing electronic indexes, abstracts, dictionaries, and encyclopedias. For example, the *Current Index to Journals in Education* (CIJE) and *Resources in Education* (RIE), the indexes most frequently used by researchers in education, are no longer available as distinct publications in paper format. Instead, since 2002 the information they contain is now only available electronically in ERIC (Education Resources Information Center), an online database of education research and information sponsored by the U.S. Department of Education and the Institute of Education Sciences. (We'll show you how to do an ERIC search of the literature later in this chapter.) Similarly, *Psychological Abstracts,* the general reference most commonly used by researchers in psychology, is now only available through PsycINFO, a computer database compiled by the American Psychological Association (APA) that includes abstracts and bibliographic citations for journal articles, evaluation reports, conference papers and proceedings, speeches, and the like.

2. **Primary sources** are publications in which researchers report the results of their studies directly to the reader. Most primary sources in education are journals, such as the *Journal of Educational Research* or the *Journal of Research in Science Teaching*. These journals are usually published monthly or quarterly, and the articles in them typically report on a particular research study. Most college libraries pay for subscriptions to online collections that provide registered students free access to a wide array of online databases, including electronic journals that allow users to download full text articles on demand.
3. **Secondary sources** refer to publications in which authors describe the work of others. The most common secondary sources in education are textbooks. A textbook in educational psychology, for example, may describe several studies as a way to illustrate various ideas and concepts in psychology. Other commonly used secondary sources include educational encyclopedias, research reviews (usually peer-reviewed journals that publish literature reviews on specific topics), and yearbooks.

Researchers who seek information systematically on a given topic would refer first to one or more general reference tools to locate primary and secondary sources of value. For a quick overview of the problem at hand, secondary sources are probably the best bet. For detailed information about the research that others have done, primary sources should be consulted.

Today, most researchers search the literature electronically by means of a personal computer. In the past, before the rise of the Internet and the World Wide Web, most searches were done manually. Manual searching (using print/paper tools to locate print/paper sources) is now used primarily by library users interested in locating rare or historical sources. However, some professors also require students to conduct manual searches because not all sources are available electronically. Although the interface may be different, both processes are the same in terms of the steps involved.

Steps Involved in a Literature Search

The following steps are involved in a literature search:

1. Define the research problem as precisely as possible.
2. Look at relevant secondary sources (these can include research reviews).
3. Select and peruse one or two appropriate general reference works.
4. Formulate search terms (key words or phrases) pertinent to the problem or question of interest.
5. Search for relevant primary sources using appropriate general reference tools.
6. Obtain and read relevant primary sources, and note and summarize key points in the sources.

Let us consider each of these steps in some detail.

DEFINE THE PROBLEM AS PRECISELY AS POSSIBLE

The first thing a researcher needs to do is to state the research question as specifically as possible. General questions such as "What sorts of teaching methods work well in urban classrooms?" or "How can a principal be a more effective leader?" are too fuzzy to be of much help when looking through a general reference. The question of interest should be narrowed down to a specific area of concern. More specific questions, therefore, might be, "Is discussion more effective than showing a video clip in motivating students to learn social studies concepts?" or "What sorts of strategies do principals at high-performing elementary schools use to improve faculty and staff morale?" A serious effort should be made to state the question so that it focuses on the specific issue for investigation.

LOOK THROUGH ONE OR TWO SECONDARY SOURCES

Once the research question has been stated in specific terms, it is a good idea to look through one or two secondary sources to get an overview of previous work that has been done on the problem. This needn't be a monumental chore or take an overly long time to complete. The main intent is to get some idea of what is already known about the problem and of some of the other questions that are being asked. Researchers may also get an idea or two about how to revise or improve the research question. Here are some of the most commonly used secondary sources in educational research:

Encyclopedia of Educational Research (current edition online only): Contains brief summaries of over 300 topics in education. Excellent source for getting a brief overview of the problem. The last print edition was published in 2004.

Handbook of Research on Teaching (latest edition published in 2001): Contains longer articles on various aspects of teaching. Most are written by educational researchers who specialize in the topic on which they are writing.

National Society for the Study of Education (NSSE) Yearbooks: Published every year, these yearbooks deal with recent research on various topics. Each book usually contains from 10 to 12 chapters dealing with various aspects of the topic. The society, which was founded in 1901 and dissolved in 2008, has continued to publish its yearbooks without interruption as part of the *Teachers College Record* at Columbia University.

Review of Educational Research: Published four times a year by the American Educational Research Association (AERA), this journal contains reviews of research and extensive bibliographies on various topics in education and is available online through ERIC.

Review of Research in Education: Published yearly, each volume contains surveys and syntheses of research on important topics written by leading educational researchers. RRE is currently available online in ERIC.

Subject Guide to Books in Print (current edition): Each of the preceding sources contains reviews of research on various topics of importance in education. There are many topics, however, that have not been treated in a recent review. If a research question deals with such a topic, the best chance for locating information discussing research on the topic lies in recent books on the subject. The best source for identifying books that might discuss research on a topic is the current edition of *Books in Print,* available in both print and electronic formats.

In addition, many professional associations and organizations have published handbooks of research in their fields. These include:

- *Handbook of Reading Research*
- *Handbook of Research on Curriculum*
- *Handbook of Research on Educational Administration*
- *Handbook of Research on Mathematics Teaching and Learning*
- *Handbook of Research on School Supervision*
- *Handbook of Research on Multicultural Education*
- *Handbook of Research on Music Teaching and Learning*
- *Handbook of Research on Social Studies Teaching and Learning*
- *Handbook of Research on Teacher Education*
- *Handbook of Research on the Teaching of English*
- *Handbook of Research on the Education of Young Children*

Each of these handbooks includes a current summary of research dealing with important topics related to its particular field of study. To locate a handbook in paper format, use your library catalog; to locate a handbook in electronic format, use your library catalog, database list, and/or electronic journal list. Other places to look for books on a topic of interest are the library catalog and the curriculum department (for textbooks) in the library. Education Index and PsycINFO also list newly published professional books in their fields.

SELECT THE APPROPRIATE GENERAL REFERENCE TOOLS

After reviewing a secondary source to get a more informed overview of the problem, researchers should have a clearer idea of exactly what to investigate. At this point, it is a good idea to look again at the research question to see if it needs to be rewritten in any way to make it more focused. Once satisfied, researchers can select one or two general references to help identify particular journals or other primary sources related to the question. Of the many general reference tools a researcher can consult, here is a list of the ones most commonly used:

Education Index: Since 2004, this online-only publication indexes articles from more than 300 educational publications. This electronic index includes three separate databases: (1) Education Index Retrospective, which covers the period 1929–1982; (2) Education Index, which contains sources from 1983 to the present; and, (3) Education Full Text, which has abstracts and full-text articles dating back to 1983.

Education Resources Information Center (ERIC): ERIC is an online database of education research and information sponsored by the U.S. Department of Education and the Institute of Education Sciences. It includes indexes and abstracts, journal articles, reports, and other documents in education, counseling, and related social science disciplines. In 2002, after the major education indexes formerly known as the Current Index to Journals in Education (CIJE) and Resources in Education (RIE) merged and ceased print publication, ERIC began to offer access to their content electronically. Today, ERIC provides citations and direct access to more than 1.3 million bibliographic sources, including citations to articles from more than 750 journals, as well as unpublished documents including curriculum guides, conference papers, and research reports. Although full-text access to all *current* education-related sources is not yet possible, ERIC provides users with abstracts and exact citation information about the source. Publication information usually includes the following: article title, author, journal name, page, and volume and issue numbers, as well as an ERIC identifying number. For ERIC journal articles (EJs), the number is EJ + a six-digit number (Figure 3.1); for nonjournal article documents in ERIC, the number is ED + a six-digit number (Figure 3.2). ERIC documents (EDs) are documents produced by state departments of education, final reports of federally funded research projects, reports from school districts, commissioned papers written for government agencies, and other published and unpublished documents. Abstracts and bibliographic information are usually provided on all documents. Many reports that would otherwise never be published are reported in ERIC, which makes this an especially valuable resource to use.

PsycINFO: PsycINFO, the electronic version of the now-ceased *Psychological Abstracts*, is a database containing summaries and citations of literature in the field of psychology dating back to the 1800s (and even some records from the 1700s and 1600s). Produced by the American Psychological Association (APA), the largest and most distinguished professional association of psychologists and scientists in the world, PsycINFO contains abstracts and bibliographic data of journal articles, book chapters, books, technical reports, and dissertations in the social and behavioral sciences, and is available on the association's APA PsycNET.

Two additional general reference tools that sometimes provide information about educational research are the following:

Exceptional Child Education Resources (ECER) online database: ECER is a bibliographic database produced by the Council for Exceptional Children (its print publication ceased in 2004). ECER provides information about exceptional children from more than 200 journals. Using a format similar to ERIC, it provides author, subject, and title indexes. It is worth consulting if a research topic deals with exceptional children, since it covers several journals not searched for in ERIC.

Social Science Citation Index (SSCI): Another type of citation and indexing service, SSCI offers the forward search, a unique feature that can be helpful to researchers. When a researcher has found an article that contains information of interest, he or she can locate the author's name in the SSCI to find out the names of other authors

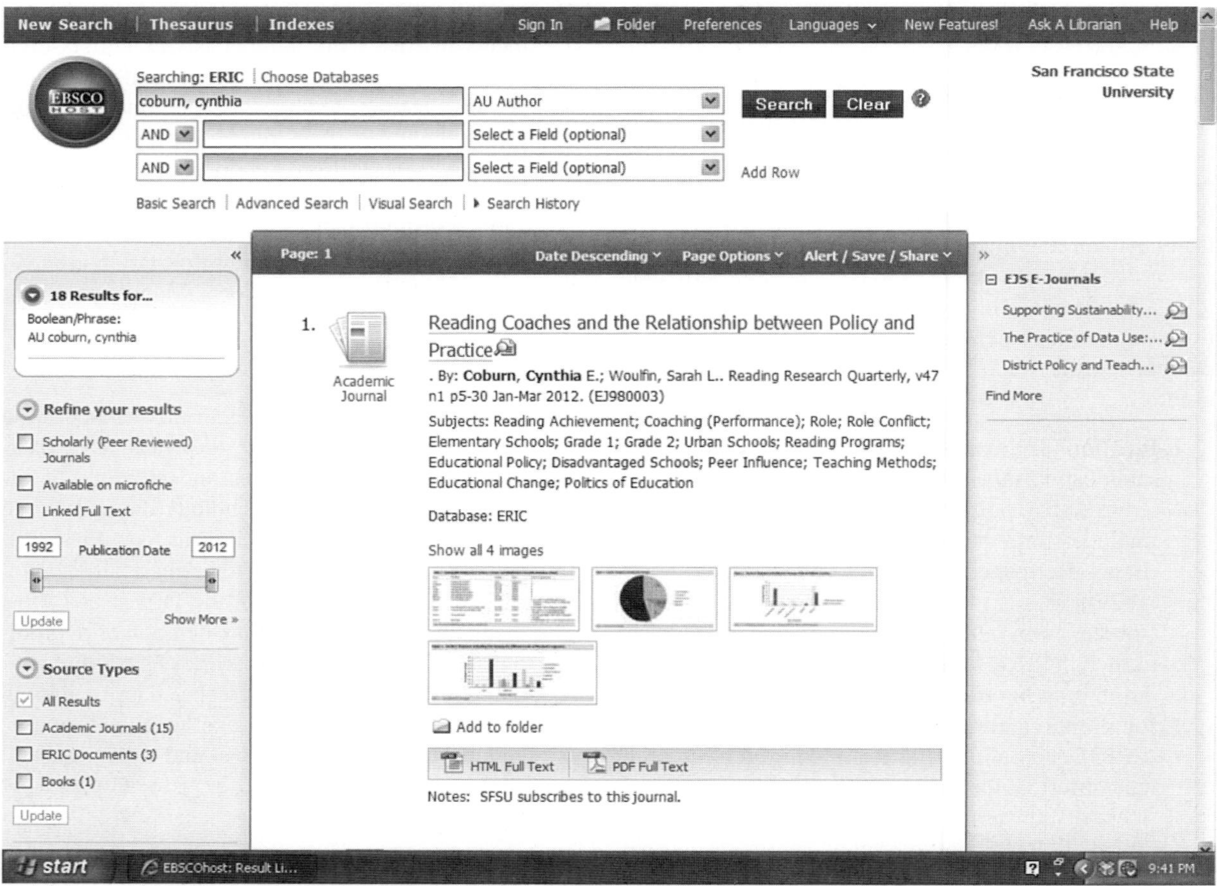

Figure 3.1 *Excerpt from ERIC Journal Article*

who have cited this same article and the journals in which their articles appeared. These additional articles may also be of interest to the researcher, particularly in compiling a references list for an *annotated bibliography* (a list of sources on a topic with brief summaries) or a literature review. The researcher can determine what additional books and articles were cited by these other authors and thus conceivably obtain information that otherwise might be missed. Most libraries offer SSCI online searching since it is available as part of the Web of Science database (currently published by Thomson Scientific). Most doctoral dissertations and many master's theses in education report on original research and hence are valuable sources for literature reviews.

ProQuest Dissertations and Theses: ProQuest maintains a digital library that has more than 1.4 million titles, including abstracts and full text files of doctoral dissertations and master's theses submitted by more than 1,000 graduate schools and universities in North America, Europe, and Asia. Coverage includes the complete text of most dissertations and theses completed from 1988 to the present, in addition to abstracts of theses and dissertations dating back to 1861 (Figure 3.3).

FORMULATE SEARCH TERMS

Once a general reference work has been selected, researchers need to formulate **search terms**—words or phrases they can use to locate primary sources. Search terms are the most important words in the problem

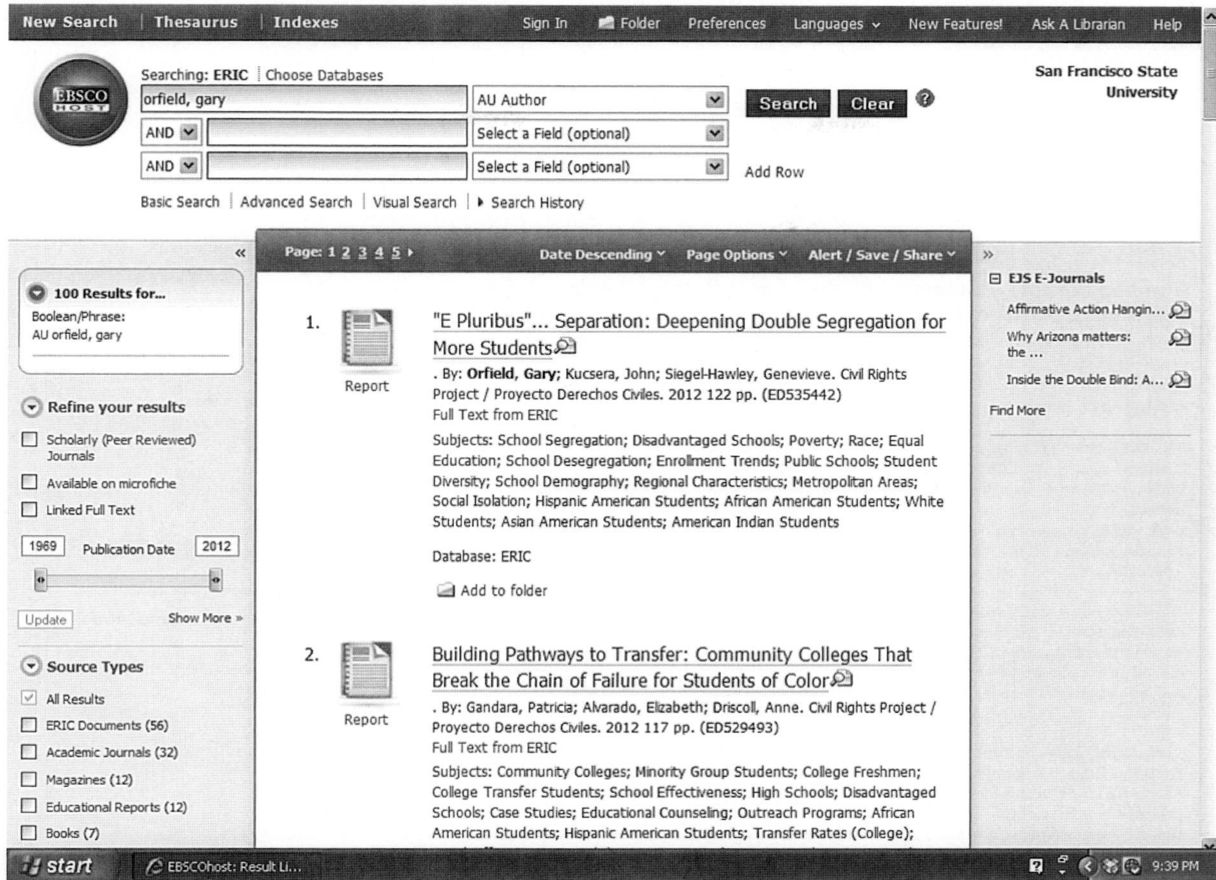

Figure 3.2 *Excerpt from ERIC Document*

statement. Take, for example, the research question, "Do students taught by a teaching team learn more than students taught by an individual teacher?" What are the most important words—the key terms—in this question? Remember that a researcher conducts a literature search to find out what other research has been done with regard to—and what others think about—the research question of interest. The key term in this question, therefore, is *teaching team.* This term, plus other similar or synonymous terms, should be listed. Possibilities here might include *team teaching, joint teaching, cooperative teaching, collaboration and teaching,* and the like. The researcher would then select the appropriate general reference tool.

Indexes and abstracts, whether in electronic or print/paper format, are designed to present uniform access to citation information. Each citation—whether in a database, index, or abstract—contains information unique to the citation (i.e., author, title, publication date, etc.). In addition, each citation is assigned vocabulary words that help categorize related articles. In most databases the assigned vocabulary words are referred to as **subject terms** or **subject headings**, and in ERIC these terms are referred to specifically as **descriptors**. Learning which subject terms, subject headings, or descriptors are used in a specific system can help researchers more easily identify all related articles on a particular subject or topic.

If using an online database to search the literature, to retrieve results the researcher would enter search terms in the search boxes provided (Figure 3.4). Using a paper/print tool, the user would look at a list of subject terms

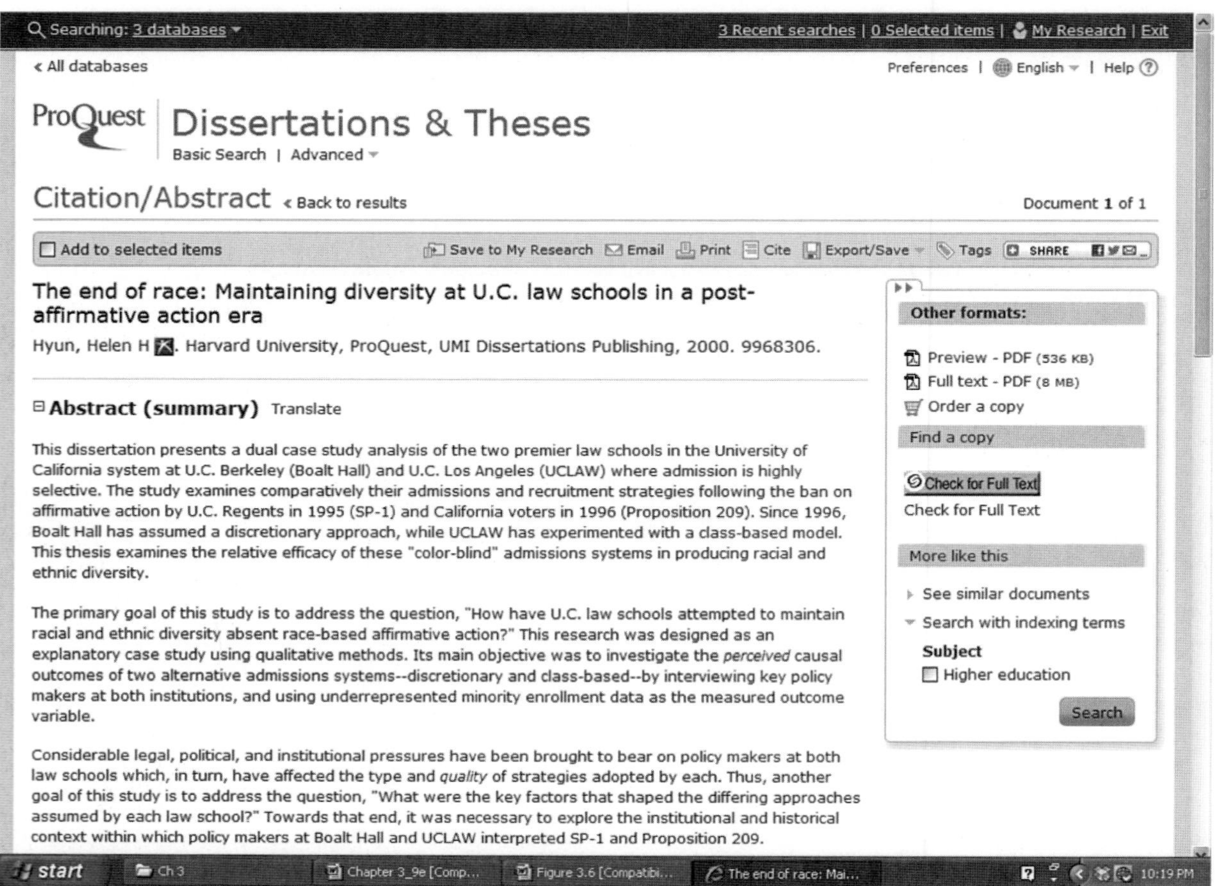

Figure 3.3 *Excerpt from ProQuest Dissertations and Theses*

that match the search terms listed in the resource to find a list of relevant citations. He or she would then select the articles that seem to bear on the research topic.

SEARCH USING GENERAL REFERENCE TOOLS

Although there is no magic formula to follow, many researchers in education turn to library resources and other information resources available online. An online search of the literature can be performed in databases available through the websites of almost all university libraries and most public libraries. Many state departments of education also provide access to online education databases, as do some county offices of education and some large school systems. The database most commonly used by educational researchers is ERIC, which can be searched electronically back to 1966. Other databases include PsycINFO, Exceptional Child Education Resources, and ProQuest Dissertations and Theses. More than 200 other specialized databases in other subject areas exist; to find out more about them, contact a nearby college or university library and ask for assistance from a reference librarian.

Doing a Computer Search

To illustrate the steps involved in online searching, we will next describe an actual search conducted using the ERIC database.

Define the Problem as Precisely as Possible. The research problem should be stated as specifically as possible so that relevant descriptors can

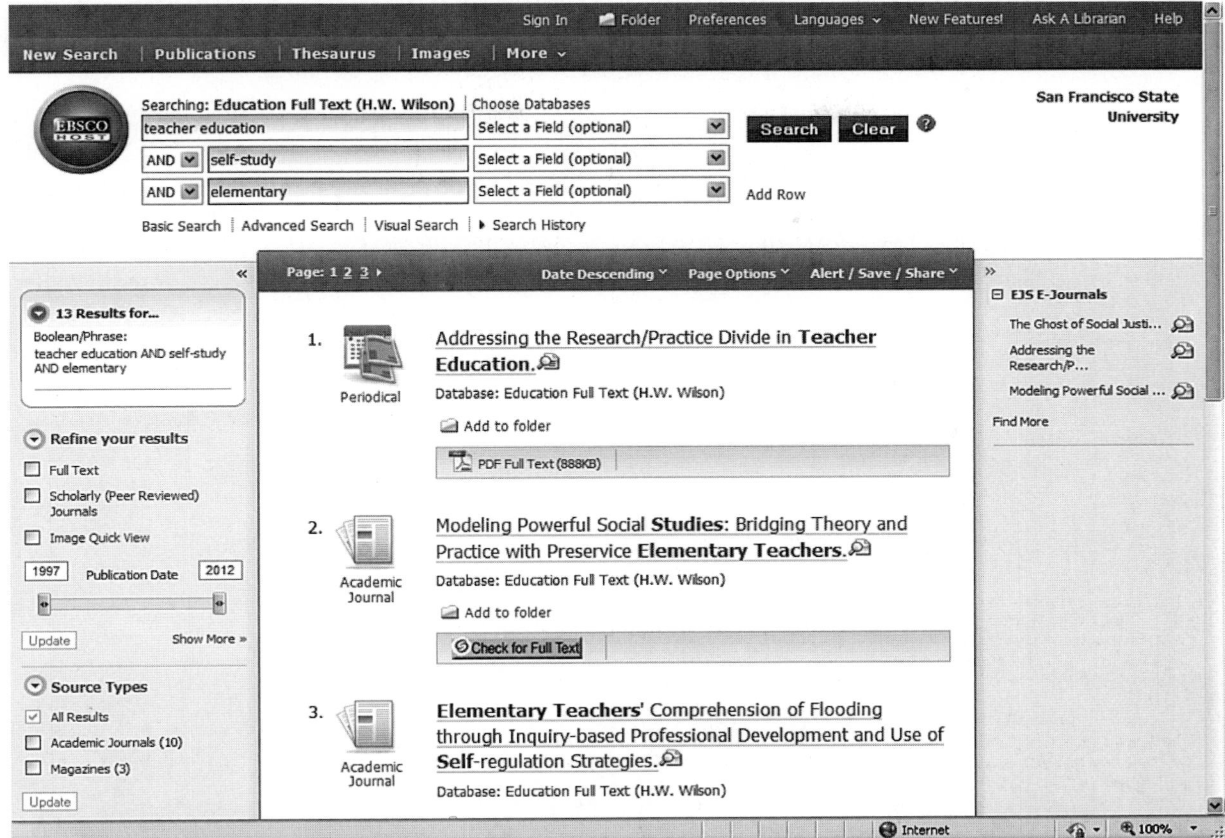

Figure 3.4 *Excerpt from Education Full Text*

be identified. A broad statement of a problem such as, "How effective are questioning techniques?" is much too general. It is liable to produce an extremely large number of references, many of which probably will be irrelevant to the researcher's question of interest. For the purposes of our search, therefore, we posed the following research question: "What sorts of questioning techniques help students understand historical concepts most effectively?"

Decide on the Extent of the Search. The researcher must now decide how many references to obtain. For a review for a journal article, a researcher might decide to review only 20 to 25 fairly recent references. For a more detailed review, such as a master's thesis, perhaps 30 or 40 might be reviewed. For a very exhaustive review, as for a doctoral dissertation, as many as 100 or more references might be searched.

Decide on the Database. As we mentioned earlier, many databases are available, but the one most commonly used is ERIC. Subject terms or headings may not be applicable to different databases, although many do overlap. In ERIC, as noted earlier, subject terms are referred to as "descriptors." We used the ERIC database in this example, as it is still the best for searches involving educational topics.

Select Search Words and Discover Descriptors. Researchers often begin a search in ERIC using keywords they use to describe their topic. The researcher types these keywords in ERIC to tell the computer what to search for. The selection of keywords is somewhat of an art form. If the keyword is too general, too many references may be located, many of which are likely to be irrelevant. If the keyword is too narrow, too few references will be located, and many of those

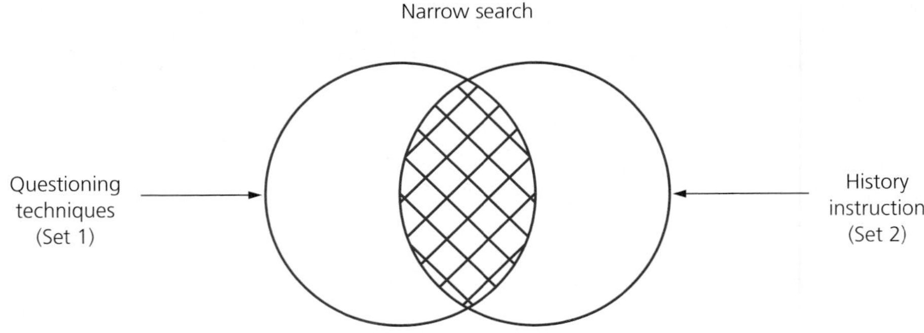

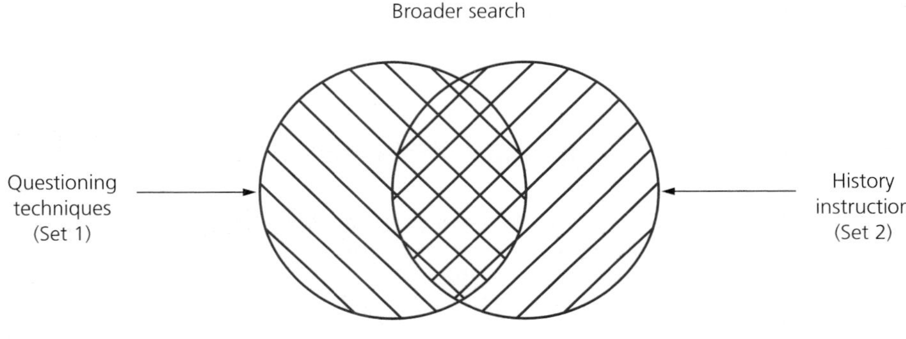

Figure 3.5 *Venn Diagrams Showing the Boolean Operators* AND *and* OR

applicable to the research question may be missed. Furthermore, if the keyword used is not the same or similar to the descriptors used by the system to describe the topic, then few or no search results will be found. For ERIC users, the ERIC thesaurus provides a list of descriptors commonly used in their databases. Search results in ERIC also list descriptors and subject terms associated with individual citations.

Keywords and descriptors can be used singly or in various combinations to locate references. Certain key words, called **Boolean operators**, enable the retrieval of terms in various combinations. The most commonly used Boolean operators are *and* and *or.* For example, by asking a computer to search for a single keyword or descriptor such as *inquiry,* all references containing this term would be selected. By connecting two keywords or descriptors with the word *and,* however, researchers can narrow the search to locate only the references that contain *both* of the descriptors. Asking the computer to search for *questioning techniques and history instruction* would narrow the search because only references containing both keywords or descriptors would be located. On the other hand, by using the word *or,* a search can be broadened, since any references with *either* one of the keywords or descriptors would be located. Thus, asking the computer to search for *questioning techniques or history instruction* would broaden the search because references containing either one of these terms would be located. Figure 3.5 illustrates the results of using these Boolean operators.

All sorts of combinations are possible. For example, a researcher might ask the computer to search for *questioning techniques or inquiry and history instruction or civics instruction.* For a reference to be selected, it would have to contain either the descriptor term *questioning techniques* or the descriptor term *inquiry,* as well as either the descriptor term *history instruction* or the descriptor term *civics instruction.*

For our search, we chose the following descriptors: *questioning techniques, concept teaching,* and *history instruction.* We also considered using a number of related terms. These included *inquiry, teaching methods,* and *learning processes* under *questioning techniques,* and *concept formation* and *cognitive development* under *concept teaching.* Upon reflection, however, we decided not to include *teaching methods* or *learning processes,* as we felt these terms were too broad to apply specifically to our research question. We also decided not to include *cognitive development* for the same reason.

Conduct the Search. After determining which descriptors to use, the next step is to enter them into the database and let it do its work. Figure 3.6 presents a summary of the search results. As you can see, we asked the database first to search for *questioning techniques* (search no. 1), followed by *history instruction* (search no. 2), followed by a combination (search no. 3) of these two descriptors (note the use of the Boolean operator *and*). This resulted in a total of 5,124 references for *questioning techniques,* 6,891 references for *history instruction,* and 65 for a combination of these two descriptors. We then asked the database to search just for the descriptors *concept* and *teaching* (search no. 4). This produced a total of 41,159 references. Because we were particularly interested in concept teaching as applied to questioning techniques and history instruction, however, we asked the database to search for a combination (search no. 5) of these three descriptors (again note the use of the operator *and*). This produced two references. If full text is available, the two

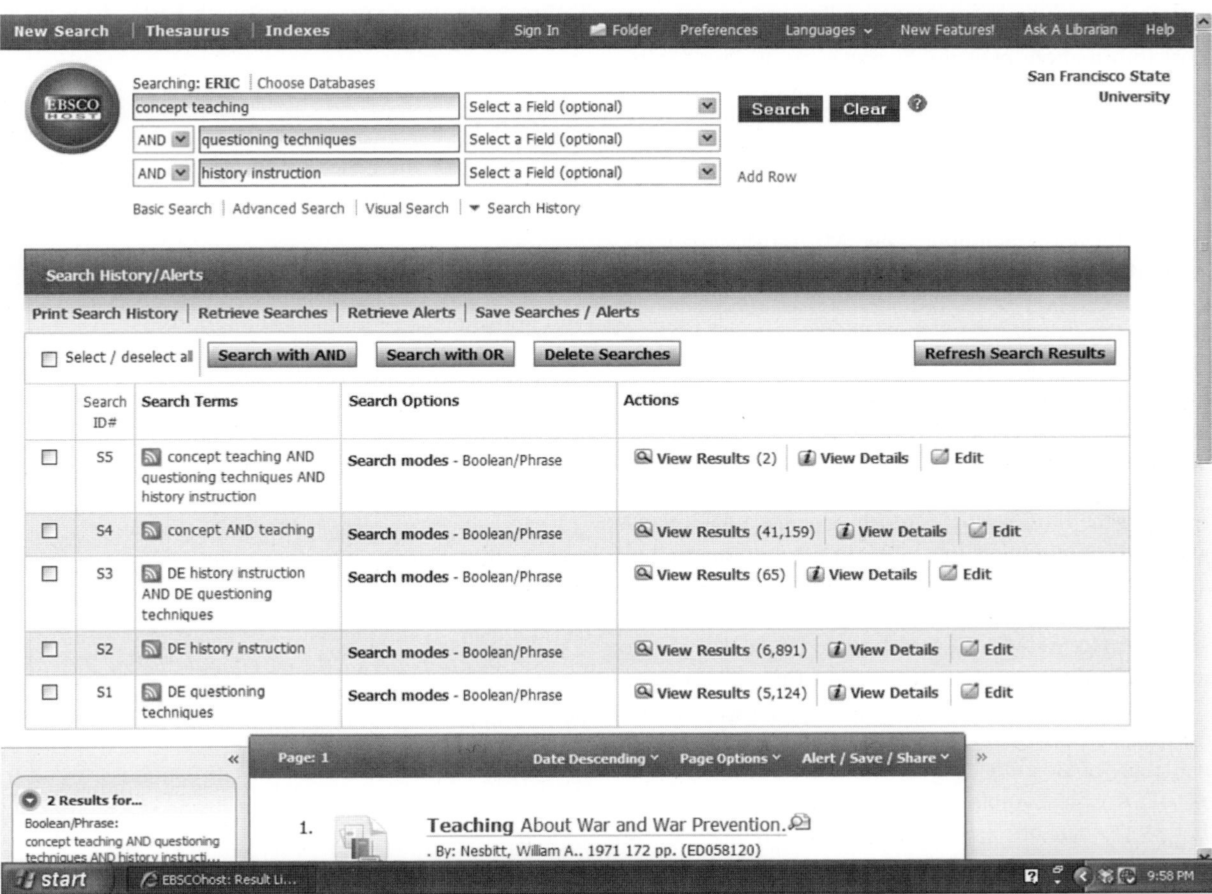

Figure 3.6 *Summary of Search Results*

references can usually be downloaded immediately, printed, saved, or e-mailed.

If the initial effort of a search produces too few references, the search can be broadened by using more general descriptors. Thus, we might have used the term *social studies instruction* rather than *history instruction* had we not obtained enough references in our search. Similarly, a search can be narrowed by using more specific descriptors. For example, we might have used the specific descriptor *North American history* rather than the inclusive term *history.*

Documenting Citation Information. Once a researcher has located references, he or she needs to document the information found and prepare it for later use. If any articles are found that deal with some aspect of the researcher's topic, the author, title, page, publication date, and publication source should be recorded. Several output options are available, including saving, e-mailing, printing, and exporting references. Researchers should choose the option that contains the most information, as it might prove useful later. Standard information would include citation information, the abstract, and in some cases the complete full text of the document.

Many databases, including some versions of ERIC provide options to save, e-mail, or print citations in specific formats, including APA, MLA (Modern Language Association), University of Chicago, and other academic citation styles used to cite references in the literature. Researchers must develop their own process for saving and documenting information found while completing their research. Whether using classic tools (like index cards) or newer tools (like EndNote, RefWorks, and Zotero) to take notes and record and organize your citations, the important thing is to take care to record the bibliographic information completely and accurately. Nothing is more annoying than trying to find an incorrect reference listed in a bibliography.

Searching ERIC. Researchers today find it easier and quicker to search reference tools (as well as most other references) online. In addition to compiling abstracts and citations, many articles are now instantly available for downloading as Portable Document Format (PDF) files. Another important feature of ERIC is that more than one descriptor can be searched at the same time.

Suppose a researcher were interested in finding information on the use of questioning in teaching science. A search of the ERIC database using the descriptors *questioning techniques* and *science* would reveal the abstracts and citations of several articles. Notice that the word *source* indicates where to find the articles if the researcher wants to read all or part of them—one is in the journal *Research in Science and Technological Education* and the other in *International Journal of Science Education.*

Searching PsycINFO. Searching through PsycINFO is similar to searching through ERIC. As in ERIC, key words or subject terms and descriptors can be used singularly or in various combinations to locate references. All articles of interest can then be located in the identified journals. The best strategy for a thorough search is probably as follows.

1. Before 1965: Search Education Index.
2. From 1966 to 1968: Search ERIC and Education Index.
3. From 1969 to the present: Search ERIC, Education Index, and other education databases.

OBTAIN PRIMARY SOURCES

After searching the general references, researchers will have a list of bibliographic citations. The next step is to locate each of the sources listed, then read and take notes on those relevant to the research problem. There are two major types of primary sources to be familiar with in this regard—journals and reports.*

Professional Journals. Many journals in education publish reports of research. Some publish articles on a wide range of educational topics, while others limit what they print to a particular specialization, such as social studies education. Most researchers become familiar with the journals in their field of interest and look them over from time to time. Examples include the *American Educational Research Journal, Child Development, Educational Administration Quarterly, Journal of Educational Research, Journal of Research in Science Teaching, Reading Research Quarterly,* and *Theory and Research in Social Education.*

Reports. Many important research findings are first published as reports. Almost all funded research

*Students should reference primary sources and avoid citing secondary sources in their papers.

projects produce a final report of their activities and findings when research is completed. In addition, each year many reports on research activities are published by the U.S. government, by state departments of education, by private organizations and agencies, by local school districts, and by professional associations. Furthermore, many individual researchers report on their recent work at professional meetings and conferences.

Most reports are abstracted in ERIC and are available as PDF files. Many papers, such as the reports of presidential task forces, national conferences, or specially called professional meetings, are published only as reports. They are usually far more detailed than journal articles and much more up-to-date. Also, they are not copyrighted. Reports are a very valuable source of up-to-date information that could not be obtained anywhere else.

Locating Primary Sources. Most primary source material is located in academic journals, since that is where most of the research findings in education are published. Although more and more journals are available online through library websites, to conduct a thorough search of relevant primary sources, it may be necessary to search manually for sources only available in print/paper format. Depending on the layout of the library, users can often go right to the stacks where print/paper journals are shelved alphabetically. In some libraries, however, only the librarian can retrieve the journals.

A problem that every researcher faces at one time or another is that a needed book or journal is not available in the library. When this is the case, it can usually be obtained directly from the author. Addresses of authors (e-mail and conventional) are often listed in education databases. An author's address can sometimes be found in the directory of a professional association, such as the *American Educational Research Association Biographical Membership Directory* or *Who's Who in American Education.* If a reprint or book cannot be obtained directly from the author, it may be possible to obtain it from another library in the area through **interlibrary loan**, a service that nearly all libraries provide. By entering information into a database, a library user can find out within seconds which libraries within a designated area have a particular book or journal.

Using Secondary Sources to Locate Primary Sources. Although the principal goal of a literature review is to assess original reports of empirical research that have been published mainly in academic journals, secondary sources can be useful. Locating published review articles—either literature reviews or *meta-analyses,* which we describe in the next section—can give students a sense of the depth and breadth of the literature related to a topic. They only need to add the keyword "review" to the list of search terms or descriptors used in their initial search of the literature to produce extensive reference lists (or bibliographies) contained in research reviews—a technique called "branching." In addition, *landmark studies* are considered highly significant by experts for understanding a topic. While reading a review, a student may come across the name of a researcher repeatedly and/or an explicit statement by the author that a study is especially important. In this case, the student should add the landmark source(s) to his or her reading list for inclusion in the literature review.

Researchers often discuss the findings of their empirical studies in terms of the theoretical literature. Understanding the major theories and theorists—particularly landmark theorists—that have contributed to the literature on a topic is paramount for preparing a comprehensive review. This can be done by adding the term "theory" as a keyword or descriptor in an electronic database search. In general, major theorists conduct research studies themselves, some of which are considered landmark studies. Including a discussion of the major theories and theorists in a literature review provides important contextual information for the review reader to better understand the empirical research findings to be evaluated.

Meta-Analysis. In academic journals, the literature reviews accompanying research reports are usually required to be brief. Unfortunately, this largely prevents much in the way of critical analysis of individual studies. Furthermore, traditional literature reviews basically depend on the judgment of the reviewer and hence are prone to subjectivity.

In an effort to moderate this subjective tendency and reduce the time required in reviewing many studies on the same topic, the concept of **meta-analysis** has been developed. In the simplest terms, when a researcher does a meta-analysis, he or she averages the results of the selected studies to get an overall index of outcome or relationship. The first requirement is that results be described statistically, most commonly through the calculation of effect sizes and correlation coefficients (we explain both later in the text). In one of the earliest

RESEARCH TIPS

What a Good Summary of a Journal Article Should Contain

- The problem being addressed
- The purpose of the study
- The hypotheses of the study (if there are any)
- The methodology the researcher used
- A description of the subjects involved
- The results
- The conclusions

studies using meta-analysis,[1] 375 studies on the effectiveness of psychotherapy were analyzed, leading to the conclusion that the average client was, after therapy, appreciably better off than the average person not in therapy.

As you might expect, this methodology has had widespread appeal in many disciplines—to date, hundreds of meta-analyses have been done. Critics raise a number of objections, some of which have been at least partly remedied by statistical adjustments. We think the most serious criticisms are that a poorly designed study counts as much as one that has been carefully designed and executed and that the evaluation of the meaning of the final index remains a judgment call, although an informed one. The former objection can be remedied by deleting "poor" studies, but this brings back the subjectivity meta-analysis was designed to mitigate. It is clear that meta-analysis is here to stay; we agree with those who argue that it cannot replace an informed, careful review of individual studies, however. In any event, the literature review should include a search for relevant meta-analysis reports, as well as individual studies.

Evaluating Primary Sources. When all the desired journal articles and documents are gathered together, the review can begin. It is a good idea to begin with the most recent articles and work backward. The reason for this is that most of the more recent articles will cite the earlier articles and thus provide a quick overview of previous work. How should an article be read? While there is no one perfect way to do this, here are some helpful suggestions:

Read the abstract or the summary first. This will tell whether the article is worth reading in its entirety. Record the bibliographic data and take notes on the article using your preferred note-keeping tool (electronic, manual, or a hybrid). Almost all research articles follow approximately the same format. They usually include an abstract; an introductory section that presents the research problem or question and reviews other related studies; the objectives of the study or the hypotheses to be tested; a description of the research procedures, including the subjects studied, the research design, and the data collection instruments and tools used; the results or findings of the study; a summary (if there is no abstract); and the researcher's conclusions. Also, make sure to use the branching technique discussed earlier by perusing the references (or bibliography) listed at the end of the article to help you locate other relevant sources.

Be as brief as possible in taking notes, yet do not exclude anything that might be important to describe later in the full review. For each of these steps, the following should be noted:

1. *Problem:* State it clearly.
2. *Hypotheses or objectives:* List them exactly as stated in the article.
3. *Procedures:* List the research methodology used (experiment, case study, and so on), the number of subjects and how they were selected, and the kind of instrument (questionnaire, tally sheet, and so on) used. Make note of any unusual techniques employed.
4. *Findings:* List the major findings. Indicate whether the objectives of the study were attained and whether the hypotheses were supported. Often the findings are summarized in a table.
5. *Conclusions:* Record or summarize the author's conclusions. Note your disagreements with the author and the reasons for such disagreement. Note strengths or weaknesses of the study that make the results particularly applicable or limited with regard to your research question. See Figure 3.7 for general prompts aimed at critically analyzing research articles.

- Introduction: Is the research problem clearly described? (Did the researcher convince you the problem area is significant?) Is the purpose of the study clearly stated? Is the scope of the study defined too narrowly? Is it too broad? Are key research terms clearly explained and defined?
- Literature Review: Does the literature review presented help you understand the problem? Does the researcher explain how the study differs from earlier ones reported in the literature? Does the researcher describe related theories? Identify gaps in the literature?
- Design and Methodology: Were the research setting and sample described in sufficient detail? Are there any obvious flaws or weaknesses in the researcher's methods of observation or instruments used? Are there any obvious sampling flaws? (e.g., were appropriate participants selected?) Were the descriptions of procedures and methods of observation sufficiently detailed? Were any important details missing?
- Findings and Conclusions: Was the description of results clearly communicated? Did the conclusion(s) seem justified? Did the report lack any information important for evaluating its findings? Overall, did the study make an important contribution to advancing knowledge?

Figure 3.7 *Prompts for Evaluating Research Studies*

Tips for Avoiding Unintentional Plagiarism. What is plagiarism? Simply put, it is the act of misrepresenting someone else's ideas as your own. One of the most challenging tasks of preparing a literature review is to paraphrase primary sources in your own words. This can be especially difficult when the study authors already provide a summary or abstract of their study. In many cases, students commit plagiarism unintentionally when they misuse or under-cite sources in their written work. Whether unintentional or not, plagiarism is a serious offense that can lead to dismissal at many U.S. colleges and universities. Some general tips to use when summarizing sources are: (1) do not use someone else's words or ideas without referencing the source or including the information in quotation marks; (2) refer to an academic style manual to credit or cite the source correctly (improper citation may also be considered plagiarism); (3) use quotations sparingly; (4) while it's better to over-cite than to under-cite, don't go overboard!

Writing the Literature Review Report

Once you have located and evaluated the sources relevant to your topic, you are ready for the final steps in preparing your review of the literature. In addition to locating and evaluating your sources, the next steps involve organizing, integrating, and synthesizing these sources. This process is inductive and often leads students to believe they are regressing, rather than progressing. As researchers and professors who have written and supervised many student literature reviews, our advice to you is to be patient and flexible! The process may appear as if you are going backward (not forward), but this is part of the larger process of discovery involved in doing research. *Part of this process involves reformulating the main question that guides your literature review oftentimes in the process of reviewing the research.* For example, let's say you begin your literature search interested in the topic of mixed-ability grouping in elementary school classrooms. Your initial query is "What do we know about heterogeneous grouping in elementary schools?" After reviewing the research and familiarizing yourself with the vocabulary and background related to the topic, your revised question becomes "What are the effects of inclusion practices on elementary school student achievement?" This restated question is much improved because it (1) includes key terms or vocabulary currently used by researchers in the field; (2) helps to clarify the purpose and scope of the literature review; and (3) examines the topic more deeply by exploring a possible relationship between inclusion practices (the presumed cause) and student achievement (the presumed outcome).

Study	Definition/measure	Sample	Method	Key findings
Alexander, Entwisle, & Horsey (1997)	Academic engagement; behavioral measure (marks for work habits from report cards and teachers' report of externalizing behavior).	Random sample of 1st-grade students in Baltimore; collected school completion data.	Survey; longitudinal design; logistic regression.	The study found a strong relationship between behavioral disengagement in the early years and dropping out of high school.
Battistich, Solomon, Watson, & Schaps (1997)	Academic engagement; classroom observation (participation, on-task behavior).	24 ethnically diverse elementary schools that were participating in the intervention program entitled Caring School Communities.	Multi-method study: classroom observation, student and teacher survey.	Students' sense of community was positively associated with academic engagement.
Birch & Ladd (1997)	Engagement/school adjustment; scales for liking, avoidance, cooperative participation, and self-directedness.	Kindergarten students; primarily White.	Survey; cross-sectional design; regression analyses.	Dependency in teacher-child relations was correlated with less positive school engagement.
Blumenfeld & Meece (1988)	Cognitive engagement; self-reports of learning strategies; distinction made between superficial and higher-level learning strategies.	4th-to-6th-grade students in science classes; middle-class schools	Multi-method-surveys, interviews, and classroom observations; cross-sectional design; quantitative and qualitative analysis of lessons where cognitive engagement scores differed substantially.	Procedural complexity of task was negatively related to use of high-level cognitive strategies; teachers who pressed students for understanding and communicated high expectations had students with higher cognitive engagement.

Figure 3.8 *Example of an Annotated Table*

Source: Fredricks, J.A., Blumenfeld, P.C., & Paris, A.H. (2004). School engagement: Potential of the concept, state of the evidence. *Review of Educational Research, 74* (1), 59–109. Reprinted with permission.

The process of evaluating, integrating, and synthesizing relevant sources in a literature review involves analyzing and categorizing the literature into major topics and subtopics. There are many strategies for organizing the structure of a review. A common one is to include summary tables to provide readers with an overview of the research related to, for example: (1) definitions of key constructs and measures; (2) differing research methods used in studies examining the same research question or phenomenon; and (3) key study characteristics and findings.

Creating tables to summarize relevant sources is helpful for providing readers with an overview of the literature. These summary or *annotated tables* are particularly useful for presenting complex topics, but they should not be used in place of text when the topics found in the literature are straightforward. In other words, summary tables should be included judiciously. An example of an annotated table describing empirical research on key study characteristics and findings related to school engagement is seen in Figure 3.8. Note that the studies are listed in alphabetical order by researchers' last names.

Literature reviews may differ in format, but they typically consist of the following five parts:

1. The *introduction* briefly describes the nature of the research problem and states the research question. The researcher also explains in this section what led him or her to investigate the question and why it is an important question to investigate.
2. The *body* of the review briefly reports what others have found or thought about the research problem. Related studies are usually discussed together, grouped under subheadings (to make the review easier to read). Major studies are described in more detail, while less important work can be referred to in just a line or two. Often this is done by referring to several studies that reported similar results in a single sentence, somewhat like this: "Several other small-scale studies reported similar results (Avila, 2009; Brown, 2006; Cartwright, 2009; Davis & Lim, 2008; Martinez, 2007)."
3. The *summary* of the review ties together the main threads revealed in the literature reviewed and presents a composite picture of what is—and is not—known or thought to date. Findings may be tabulated to give readers some idea of how many other researchers have reported identical or similar findings or have similar recommendations.
4. Any *conclusions* the researcher feels are justified based on the state of knowledge revealed in the literature should be included. What does the literature suggest are appropriate courses of action to take to try to solve the problem? And what are other important research questions that should be examined?
5. A *reference list* (or bibliography) with full bibliographic data for all sources mentioned in the review is essential. There are many ways to format reference lists, but the one outlined in the *Publication Manual of the American Psychological Association* (2009) is particularly easy to use.

A Note on APA Style. Several academic style manuals are currently used in higher education (e.g., *MLA Handbook for Writers of Research Papers*, *University of Chicago Manual of Style*, and Turabian's *A Manual for Writers of Term Papers, Theses, and Dissertations*). Most instructors require students to adopt a discipline-specific style guide for writing and formatting research papers. In the field of educational research, the *Publication Manual of the American Psychological Association,* or APA Style Manual, is most widely used. Dating back to the 1950s, APA style was initially conceived as a set of standards (guidelines and rules) promoting consistency for manuscripts submitted to academic journals. Now in its sixth edition (published in 2009), the APA manual covers other types of documents including theses, dissertations, and general term papers. The manual itself is over 400 pages long, contains more than 200 rules, and is organized around three major categories: page formatting, text rules, and documentation. *Page formatting* includes rules about margins, indents, spacing, tables, figures, and general paper organization. *Text rules* include guidelines for the presentation of quotations, and *documentation* refers to citations and references. There are many Internet sites that have truncated versions of APA rules. While some of these can be helpful, they should not be used as a replacement for the text, which can be found in most campus or online bookstores. We also encourage students to peruse the APA website (www.apa.org) and download the free online tutorial on the basics of APA style: www.apastyle.org/learn/tutorials/basics-tutorial.aspx.

RESEARCHING THE WORLD WIDE WEB

The **World Wide Web (WWW)** is part of the Internet, a vast reservoir of information on all sorts of topics in a wide variety of areas. Prior to 1993, the Internet was barely mentioned in the research literature. Today, it cannot be ignored. Despite the fact that ERIC and (on occasion) PsycINFO remain the databases of choice when it comes to research involving most educational topics, researching the Internet should also be considered. Space prevents us from describing the Internet in detail, but we do wish to point out some of its important features.

Using a **Web browser** (the computer program that lets you gain access to the Internet), a researcher can find information on almost any topic with just a few clicks of the mouse button. Some of the information on the Internet has been classified into **indexes,** which can be easily searched by going from one category to another. In addition, several **search engines** are available that are similar in many respects to those we used in our search of the ERIC database. Let us consider both indexes and search engines in a bit more detail.

Indexes. Indexes group websites together under similar *categories,* such as *Australian universities, London art galleries,* and *science laboratories.* This is similar to what libraries do when they group similar kinds of information resources together. The results of an index search will be a list of websites related to the topic being searched. If a researcher is interested in finding the site for a particular university in Australia, for example, he or she should try using an index.

Indexes often provide an excellent starting point for a review of the literature. This is especially true when a researcher does not have a clear idea for a research question or topic to investigate. Browsing through an index can be a profitable source of ideas. Felden offers an illustration:

> For a real-world comparison, suppose I need some household hardware of some sort to perform a repair; I may not always know exactly what is necessary to do the job. I may have a broken part, which I can diligently carry to a hardware store to try to match. Luckily, most hardware stores are fairly well organized and have an assortment of aisles, some with plumbing supplies, others with nails and other fasteners, and others with rope, twine, and other materials for tying things together. Proceeding by general category (i.e., electrical, plumbing, woodworking, etc.), I can go to approximately the right place and browse the shelves for items that may fit my repair need. I can examine the materials, think over their potential utility, and make my choice.[2]

Search Engines. If one wants more specific information, such as biographical information about George Orwell, however, one should use a search engine, because it will search *all* of the contents of a website. Search engines such as Google Scholar or the Librarians' Index to the Internet use software programs (sometimes called *spiders* or *Web crawlers*) that search the entire Internet, looking at millions of websites and then indexing all of the words on them. The search results obtained are usually ranked in order of relevancy (i.e., the number of times the researcher's search terms appear in a document or how closely the document appears to match one of the *key words* submitted as query terms by the researcher).

A search engine like Google Scholar will search for and find the individual pages of a website that match a researcher's search, even if the site itself has nothing to do with what the researcher is looking for. As a result, one usually has to wade through an awful lot of irrelevant information. Felden gives us an example:

> Returning to the hardware store analogy, if I went to the store in search of some screws for my household project and employed an automatic robot instead of using my native cunning to browse the (well-arranged) aisles, the robot could conceivably return (after perusing the entire store) with everything that had a screw in it somewhere. The set of things would be a wildly disparate collection. It would include all sorts of boxes of screws, some of them maybe even the kind I was looking for, but also a wide array of other material, much of it of no use for my project. There might be birdhouses of wood held together with screws, tools assembled with screws, a rake with a screw fastening its handle to its prongs. The robot would have done its job properly. It had been given something to match, in this case a screw, and it went out and did its work efficiently and thoroughly, although without much intelligence.[3]

To be satisfied with the results of a search, therefore, one needs to know what to ask for and how to phrase the request to increase the chances of getting what is desired. If a researcher wants to find out information about universities, but not English universities, for example, he or she should ask specifically in that way.

Thus, although it would be a mistake to search only the Internet when doing a literature search (thereby ignoring a plethora of other material that often is so much better organized), it has some definite advantages for some kinds of research. Unfortunately, it also has some disadvantages. Here are some of each:

Advantages of Searching the Internet

- *Currency:* Many resources on the Internet are updated very rapidly; often they represent the very latest information about a given topic.
- *Access to a wide variety of materials:* Many resources, including works of art, manuscripts, even entire library collections, can be reviewed at leisure using a personal computer.
- *Varied formats:* Material can be sent over the Internet in different formats, including text, video, sound, and animation.
- *Immediacy:* The Internet is "open" 24 hours a day. Information can be viewed on one's own computer and can be examined as desired or saved to a hard drive or disk for later examination and study.

Disadvantages of Searching the Internet

- *Disorganization:* Unfortunately, much of the information on the Internet is not well organized. It employs few of the well-developed classification systems used by libraries and archives. This disorganization makes it an absolute necessity for researchers to have good online searching skills.

- *Time commitment:* There is always a need to search continually for new and more complete information. Doing a search on the Internet often (if not usually) can be quite time-consuming and (regretfully) sometimes less productive than doing a search using more traditional sources.
- *Lack (sometimes) of credibility:* Anyone can publish something on the Internet. As a result, much of the material one finds there may have little, if any, credibility.
- *Uncertain reliability:* It is so easy to publish information on the Internet that it often is difficult to judge its worth. One of the most valuable aspects of a library collection is that most of its material has been collected carefully. Librarians make it a point to identify and select important works that will stand the test of time. Much of the information one finds on the Internet is ill-conceived or trivial.
- *Ethical violations:* Because material on the Internet is so easy to obtain, there is a greater temptation for researchers to use the material without citation or permission. Copyright violation is much more likely than with traditional material.
- *Undue reliance:* The amount of information available on the Internet has grown so rapidly in the last few years that some researchers may be misled to think they can find everything they need on the Internet, thereby causing them to ignore other, more traditional sources of information.

In searching the Internet, then, here are a few tips to get the best search results.[4] Many of these would apply to searching ERIC or PsycINFO as well.

- *Use the most specific keyword you can think of.* Take some time to list several of the words that are likely to appear on the kind of website you have in mind. Then pick the most unusual word from your list. For example, if you're looking for information about efforts to save tiger populations in Asia, don't use *tigers* as your search term. You'll be swamped with sites about the Detroit *Tigers,* the Princeton *Tigers,* and every other sports team that uses the word *tigers* in its name. Instead, try searching for a particular tiger species that you know to be on the endangered list—*Bengal tiger* or *Sumatran tiger* or *Siberian tiger.*[5]
- *Make it a multistep process.* Don't assume that you will find what you want on the first try. Review the first couple of pages of your results. Look particularly at the sites that contain the kind of information you want. What unique words appear on those pages? Now do another search using just those words.
- *Narrow the field by using just your previous results.* If the keywords you choose return too much information, try a second search of just the results you obtained in your first search. This is sometimes referred to as *set searching*. Here's a tip we think you'll find extremely helpful: Simply add another keyword to your search request and submit it again.
- *Look for your keyword in the website title.* Frequently, the best strategy is to look for your unique keyword in the title of websites. If you are looking for information about inquiry teaching in secondary school history classes, for example, begin with a search of sites that have *inquiry teaching* in the title. Then do a second search of just those results, looking for *secondary school history classes.*
- *Find out if case counts.* Check to find out if the search engine you are using pays any attention to upper- and lowercase letters in your keywords. "Will a search for java, a microsystems program, for example, also find sites that refer to the program as JAVA?"[5]
- *Check your spelling.* If you have used the best keywords that you can think of and the search engine reports "No results found" (or something similar), check your spelling before you do anything else. Usually, the fact that a search engine does not come up with any results is due to a spelling or typing error.
- *Assess the credibility and reliability of Internet sources.* One quick way to evaluate the accuracy and objectivity of information published on the Internet is to check the URL or domain address extension. Web addresses ending in .gov, .edu, and .org are sponsored, respectively, by the federal government, higher education institutions, and nonprofit organizations. Although these resources are not necessarily free of error and bias, compare them to URL extensions ending in .com, which represent commercial vendors that often use website advertising to generate revenue for profit. In addition, scan the site for the organization's purpose statement as well as the author's credentials (and contact information), then judge for yourself.

Public Internet websites that provide educational resources and information include:

The National Center for Education Statistics (http://nces.ed.gov): NCES is located in the U.S. Department of Education and the Institute of Education Sciences and serves as the primary federal entity for collecting and analyzing data related to education.

California Department of Education (www.cde.ca.gov): Includes information collected by

California schools on testing and accountability, curriculum and instruction, finance and grants, and data and statistics that assess needs and measure performance. (*Note:* Also, check the departments of education websites of other states.)

RAND Education (www.rand.org/education): RAND Education is an education "think tank," a nonprofit organization that conducts policy-based research and analysis to address major problems in the educational system. The website provides free access to recent reports and literature reviews, as well as links to other RAND publications and books.

The Urban Institute (www.urban.org): A nonpartisan think tank that conducts economic and social policy research affecting urban areas, including an Education Policy Center with a strong emphasis on immigrant children, poverty, and health care. Publishes books, as well as studies and reports, that are often available on the website.

Google Scholar (http://scholar.google.com): Provides a simple way to do a broad search for scholarly literature, including peer-reviewed papers, theses, books, abstracts, and articles. Google Scholar should be used as a supplement to, not as a substitute for, searching through academic databases.

Other education databases, available through most libraries, include:

ProQuest Education Journals: Offers access to more than 745 top educational publications, including nearly 600 titles in full text.

Education Research Complete: Topics covered include all levels of education from early childhood to higher education, and all educational specialties, such as multilingual education, health education, and testing.

Education Full Text: A bibliographic database produced by the H. W. Wilson Company that lists indexes, abstracts, and full-text articles from more than 350 journals dating back to 1996.

ERIC (EBSCO): References articles in more than 750 professional journals, thousands of unpublished research reports, conference papers, and curriculum guides in all areas of education.

Academic Search Premier: Provides full-text access to nearly 1,560 academic journals in education, humanities, and the social and physical sciences.

JSTOR: Contains the full text of more than 169 national and international journals available from JSTOR, an organization founded in 1995 to promote global scholarship using its digital archives.

ProQuest Dissertations and Theses: With more than 2 million entries, PQD&T is the single, central, authoritative resource for information about doctoral dissertations and master's theses.

Web of Science: The ISI Web of Science is the interface for institutional access to the ISI Citation Databases, which cover over 10,000 leading journals and over 100,000 book-based and journal conference proceedings.

Go back to the **INTERACTIVE AND APPLIED LEARNING** feature at the beginning of the chapter for a listing of interactive and applied activities. Go to the **Online Learning Center** at **www.mhhe.com/fraenkel9e** to take quizzes, practice with key terms, and review chapter content.

Main Points

THE VALUE OF A LITERATURE REVIEW

- A literature review helps researchers learn what others have written about a topic. It also lets researchers see the results of other related studies.
- A detailed literature review is often required of master's and doctoral students when they design a thesis.

TYPES OF SOURCES FOR A LITERATURE REVIEW

- Researchers need to be familiar with three basic types of sources (general references, primary sources, and secondary sources) in doing a literature review.
- General reference tools are sources a researcher consults to locate other sources.
- Primary sources are publications in which researchers report the results of their investigations. Most primary source material is located in journal articles.
- Secondary sources refer to publications in which authors describe the work of others.
- The most common secondary sources in education are textbooks.
- Search terms are keywords or phrases researchers use to help locate relevant primary sources.

STEPS INVOLVED IN A LITERATURE SEARCH

- The essential steps involved in a review of the literature include: (1) defining the research problem as precisely as possible; (2) deciding on the extent of the search; (3) deciding on the data base(s) to be searched; (4) formulating search terms; (5) searching general reference tools for relevant primary sources; (6) obtaining and reading the primary sources, and noting and summarizing key points in the sources.

WAYS TO DO A LITERATURE SEARCH

- Today, there are two ways to do a literature search—manually, using print/paper tools to locate print/paper sources; and electronically, by means of a computer. The most common and frequently used method, however, is to search online, via computer. Regardless of the tools involved, the search process is similar.
- There are five essential points (problem, hypotheses, procedures, findings, and conclusions) that researchers should record when taking notes on a study.

DOING A COMPUTER SEARCH

- Computer searches of the literature have a number of advantages—they are fast, are fairly inexpensive, provide printouts, and enable researchers to search using more than one descriptor at a time.
- The steps in a traditional manual search are similar to those in a computer search, though computer searches are usually the norm.
- Researching the Internet should be considered, in addition to ERIC and PsycINFO, in doing a literature search.
- Some of the information on the Internet is classified into indexes, which group websites together under similar categories.
- To obtain more specific information, search engines should be used, because they search all of the contents of a website.

THE LITERATURE REVIEW REPORT

- The literature review report consists of an introduction, the body of the review, a summary, the researcher's conclusions, and a bibliography.

- A literature review should include a search for relevant meta-analysis reports, as well as individual studies.
- When a researcher does a meta-analysis, he or she averages the results of a group of selected studies to get an overall index of outcome or relationship.

Key Terms

abstract 38
Boolean operator 46
descriptor 43
general reference tool 38
index 53
interlibrary loan 49
literature review 38
meta-analysis 49
primary source 39
search engine 53
search term 42
secondary source 39
subject heading 43
subject term 43
Web browser 53
World Wide Web (WWW) 53

For Discussion

1. Why might it be unwise for a researcher not to do a review of the literature before planning a study?
2. Many published research articles include only a few references to related studies. How would you explain this? Is this justified?
3. Which do you think are more important to emphasize in a literature review—the opinions of experts in the field or related studies? Why?
4. One rarely finds books referred to in literature reviews. Why do you suppose this is so? Is it a good idea to refer to books?
5. Can you think of any type of information that should *not* be included in a literature review? If so, give an example.
6. Professor Jones states that he does not have his students do a literature review before planning their master's theses because they "take too much time," and he wants them to get started collecting their data as quickly as possible. In light of the information we have provided in this chapter, what would you say to him? Why?
7. Can you think of any sorts of studies that would *not* benefit from having the researcher conduct a literature review? If so, what might they be?

References

1. Smith, M. L., Glass, G. V., & Miller, T. I. (1980). Primary, secondary, and meta-analysis research. *Educational Researcher, 5* (10), 3–8.
2. Felden, N. (2000). *Internet research: Theory and practice* (2nd ed., pp. 124–125). London: McFarland.
3. Felden, N. (2000). *Internet research: Theory and practice* (2nd ed., p. 127). London: McFarland.
4. Glossbrenner, A., & Glossbrenner, E. (1998, pp. 11–13). *Search engines.* San Francisco: San Francisco State University Press.
5. Glossbrenner, A., & Glossbrenner, E. (1998, p. 12). *Search engines.* San Francisco: San Francisco State University Press.

Research Exercise 3: Review of the Literature

Using Problem Sheet 3, list the specific problem(s) and/or question(s) you will address in a brief review of the literature related to your study. Indicate what types of sources you did and did not include and why. Then summarize the conclusions you arrived at based on what you found in your review.

Problem Sheet 3

Review of the Literature

1. What are the specific problem(s) or question(s) to be addressed in your literature review?
____
____
____
2. What general reference tools did you use to conduct your search? (List specific electronic databases consulted.)
____
____
3. What search terms did you use?
a. _______________ d. _______________
b. _______________ e. _______________
c. _______________ f. _______________
4. Specify the scope of the review and explain your inclusion/exclusion criteria (i.e., what was and was not included and why?).
____
____
5. What topics and subtopics emerged about your problem and question as you conducted your search?
____
____
____
6. What are your conclusions based on the findings of your review?
____
____
____
____

An electronic version of this Problem Sheet that you can fill in and print, save, or e-mail is available on the Online Learning Center at www.mhhe.com/fraenkel9e.

4 Ethics and Research

Some Examples of Unethical Practice

A Statement of Ethical Principles

Protecting Participants from Harm

Ensuring Confidentiality of Research Data

When (If Ever) Is Deception of Subjects Justified?

Three Examples Involving Ethical Concerns

Research with Children

Regulation of Research

Academic Cheating and Plagiarism

OBJECTIVES **Studying this chapter should enable you to:**

- Describe briefly what is meant by "ethical" research.
- Describe briefly three important ethical principles recommended for researchers to follow.
- State the basic question with regard to ethics that researchers need to ask before beginning a study.
- State the three questions researchers need to address to protect research participants from harm.
- Describe the procedures researchers must follow to ensure confidentiality of data collected in a research investigation.
- Describe when it might be appropriate to deceive participants in a research investigation and the researcher's responsibilities in such a case.
- Describe the special considerations involved when doing research with children.

INTERACTIVE AND APPLIED LEARNING After, or while, reading this chapter:

Go to the Online Learning Center at www.mhhe.com/fraenkel9e to:

- Learn More About What Constitutes Ethical Research

Go to your online Student Mastery Activities book to do the following activities:

- Activity 4.1: Ethical or Not?
- Activity 4.2: Some Ethical Dilemmas
- Activity 4.3: Violations of Ethical Practice
- Activity 4.4: Why Would These Research Practices Be Unethical?

Mary Abrams and Lamar Harris, both juniors at a large midwestern university, meet weekly for lunch. "I can't believe it," Mary says.

"What's the matter?" asks Lamar.

"Professor Thomas says that we have to participate in one of his research projects if we want to pass his course. He says it is a course requirement. I don't think that's right, and I'm pretty upset about it. Can you believe it?"

"Wow. Can he do that? I mean, is that ethical?"

No, it's not! Mary has a legitimate (and ethical) complaint here. This issue—whether professors can require students to participate in research projects to pass a course—is one example of an unethical practice that sometimes occurs.

The whole question of what is—and what isn't—ethical is the focus of this chapter.

Some Examples of Unethical Practice

The term *ethics* refers to questions of right and wrong. When researchers think about ethics, they must ask themselves if it is "right" to conduct a particular study or carry out certain procedures—that is, whether they are doing **ethical research**. Are there some kinds of studies that should *not* be conducted? You bet! For example, it is unethical when a researcher

- requires a group of high school sophomores to sign a form in which they agree to participate in a research study.
- asks first-graders sensitive questions without obtaining the consent of their parents to question them.
- deletes data that do not support the hypothesis.
- requires university students to fill out a questionnaire about their sexual practices.
- involves a group of eighth-graders in a research study that may harm them psychologically without informing them or their parents of this fact.

Each of these examples involves one or more violations of ethical practice. When researchers think about ethics, the basic question to ask in this regard is, Will any physical or psychological harm come to anyone as a result of my research? Naturally, no researcher wants this to happen to any of the subjects in a research study. Because this is such an important (and often overlooked) issue, we need to discuss it in some detail.

In a somewhat larger sense, ethics also refers to questions of right and wrong. By behaving ethically, a person is doing what is right. But what does it mean to be "right" as far as research is concerned?

A Statement of Ethical Principles

Webster's New World Dictionary defines *ethical* (behavior) as "conforming to the standards of conduct of a given profession or group." What researchers consider to be ethical, therefore, is largely a matter of agreement among them. Some years ago, the Committee on Scientific and Professional Ethics of the American Psychological Association published a list of ethical principles for the conduct of research with human subjects. We have adapted many of these principles so they apply to educational research. Please read the following statement and think carefully about what it means.

> The decision to undertake research rests upon a considered judgment by the individual educator about how best to contribute to science and human welfare. Once one decides to conduct research, the educator considers various ways by which he might invest his talents and resources. Keeping this in mind, the educator carries out the research with respect and concern for the dignity and welfare of the people who participate and with cognizance of federal and state regulations and professional standards governing the conduct of research with human participants.
>
> *a.* In planning a study, researchers have the responsibility to evaluate carefully any ethical concerns. Should any of the ethical principles listed below be compromised, the educator has a correspondingly serious obligation to observe stringent safeguards to protect the rights of human participants.
>
> *b.* Considering whether a participant in a planned study will be a "subject at risk" or a "subject at minimal risk," according to recognized standards, is of primary ethical concern to the researcher.
>
> *c.* The researcher always retains the responsibility for ensuring that a study is conducted ethically. The researcher is also responsible for the ethical treatment of research participants by collaborators, assistants, students, and employees, all of whom, however, incur similar obligations.
>
> *d.* Except in minimal-risk research, the researcher establishes a clear and fair agreement with research participants, before they participate, that clarifies the obligations and responsibilities of each. The researcher has the obligation to honor all promises and commitments included in that agreement. The researcher informs the participants of all aspects of the research that might reasonably be expected to influence their willingness to participate in the study and answers honestly any questions they may have about the research. Failure by the researcher to make full disclosure prior to obtaining informed consent requires additional safeguards to protect the welfare and dignity of the research participants. Furthermore, research with children or with participants who have impairments that would limit understanding and/or communication requires special safeguarding procedures.
>
> *e.* Sometimes the design of a study makes necessary the use of concealment or deception. When this is the case, the researcher has a special responsibility to: (i) determine whether the use of such techniques is justified by the study's prospective scientific or educational value; (ii) determine whether alternative procedures are available that do not use concealment or deception; and (iii) ensure that the participants are provided with sufficient explanation as soon as possible.
>
> *f.* The researcher respects the right of any individual to refuse to participate in the study or to withdraw from participating at any time. The researcher's obligation in this regard is especially important when he or she is in a position of authority or influence over the participants in a study. Such positions of authority include, but are not limited to, situations in which research participation is required as part of employment or in which the participant is a student, client, or employee of the investigator.
>
> *g.* The researcher protects all participants from physical and mental discomfort, harm, and danger that may arise from participating in a study. If risks of such consequences exist, the investigator informs the participant of that fact. Research procedures likely to cause serious or lasting harm to a participant are not used unless the failure to use these procedures might expose the participant to risk of greater harm, or unless the research has great potential benefit and fully informed and voluntary consent is obtained from each participant. All participants must be informed as to how they can contact the researcher within a reasonable time period following their participation should stress or potential harm arise.
>
> *h.* After the data are collected, the researcher provides all participants with information about the nature of the study and does his or her best to clear up any misconceptions that may have developed. Where scientific or humane values justify delaying or withholding this information, the researcher has a special responsibility to carefully supervise the research and to ensure that there are no damaging consequences for the participant.
>
> *i.* Where the procedures of a study result in undesirable consequences for any participant, the researcher has the responsibility to detect and remove or correct these consequences, including long-term effects.
>
> *j.* Information obtained about a research participant during the course of an investigation is confidential unless otherwise agreed upon in advance. When the possibility exists that others may obtain access to such information,

Clinical Trials—Desirable or Not?

Clinical trials are the final test of a new drug. They offer an opportunity for drug companies to prove that new and previously unused medicines are safe and effective to use by giving such medicines to volunteers. However, there has been an increase in the number of complaints against such trials. A flagrant example of this was cited in the *San Francisco Chronicle*.* A scientist gave a volunteer participant in one such trial what turned out to be a lethal dose of an experimental drug.

There has been an increase in the number of clinical trials, as well as a corresponding increase in the number of volunteers involved in such trials. In 1995 about 500,000 volunteers participated; by 1999 the number had jumped to 700,000.† Another concern is that some of the physicians who conduct such trials may have a financial stake in the outcome. No uniform policy currently exists on the disclosure of investigators' financial interests to patients who participate in such trials.

Proponents of clinical trials argue that, when properly conducted, clinical trials have paved the way for new medicines and procedures that have saved many lives. Volunteers can gain access to promising drugs long before they are available to the general public. And patients usually get excellent care from physicians and nurses while they are undergoing such trials. Last, but not least, such care often is free.

What do you think? Are clinical trials justified?

*Abate, T. (2001, May 28). Maybe conflicts of interest are scaring clinical trial patients. *San Francisco Chronicle*.

†Report issued at the Association of Clinical Research Professionals Convention, San Francisco, California, May 20, 2001.

> this possibility, together with the plans for protecting confidentiality, is explained to the participant as part of the procedure for obtaining informed consent.[1]

This statement of ethical principles suggests three very important issues that every researcher should address: protecting participants from harm, ensuring confidentiality of research data, and the question of deception of subjects. How can these issues be addressed, and how can the interests of the subjects involved in research be protected?

Protecting Participants from Harm

It is a fundamental responsibility of every researcher to do all in his or her power to ensure that participants in a research study are protected from physical or psychological harm, discomfort, or danger that may arise due to research procedures. This is perhaps the most important ethical decision of all. Any sort of study that is likely to cause lasting, or even serious, harm or discomfort to any participant should not be conducted, unless the research has the potential to provide information of extreme benefit to human beings. Even when this may be the case, participants should be fully informed of the dangers involved and in no way required to participate.

A further responsibility in protecting individuals from harm is obtaining their **informed consent** if they may be exposed to any risk. (Figure 4.1 shows an example of a consent form.) Fortunately, almost all educational research involves activities that are within the customary, usual procedures of schools or other agencies and as such involve little or no risk. Legislation recognizes this by specifically exempting most categories of educational research from formal review processes. Nevertheless, researchers should carefully consider whether there is any likelihood of risk involved and, if there is, provide full information followed by formal consent by participants (or their guardians). Three important ethical questions to ask about harm in any study are:

1. Could people be harmed (physically or psychologically) during the study?
2. If so, could the study be conducted in another way to find out what the researcher wants to know?
3. Is the information that may be obtained from this study so important that it warrants possible harm to the participants?

These are difficult questions, and they deserve discussion and consideration by all researchers.

Figure 4.1 *Example of a Consent Form*

CONSENT TO SERVE AS A SUBJECT IN RESEARCH

I consent to serve as a subject in the research investigation entitled: ________

____

____

The nature and general purpose of the research procedure and the known risks involved have been explained to me by ______________________.
The investigator is authorized to proceed on the understanding that I may terminate my service as a subject at any time I so desire.

I understand the known risks are: ______________________

____

____

I understand also that it is not possible to identify all potential risks in an experimental procedure, and I believe that reasonable safeguards have been taken to minimize both the known and the potentially unknown risks.

Witness ______________________ Signed ______________________
(subject)

Date ______________________

To be retained by the principal investigator.

Ensuring Confidentiality of Research Data

Once the data in a study have been collected, researchers should make sure that no one else (other than perhaps a few key research assistants) has access to the data. Whenever possible, the names of the subjects should be removed from all data collection forms. This can be done by assigning a number or letter to each form, or subjects can be asked to furnish information anonymously. When this is done, not even the researcher can link the data to a particular subject. Sometimes, however, it is important in a study to identify individual subjects. When this is the case, the linkage system should be carefully guarded.

All subjects should be assured that any data collected from or about them will be held in confidence. The names of individual subjects should never be used in any publications that describe the research. And all participants in a study should always have the right to withdraw from the study or to request that data collected about them not be used.

When (If Ever) Is Deception of Subjects Justified?

The issue of deception is particularly troublesome. Many studies cannot be carried out unless some deception of subjects takes place. It is often difficult to find naturalistic situations in which certain behaviors occur frequently. For example, a researcher may have to wait a long time for a teacher to reinforce students in a certain way. It may be much easier for the researcher to observe the effects of such reinforcement by employing the teacher as a confederate.

Sometimes it is better to deceive subjects than to cause them pain or trauma, as investigating a particular research question might require. The famous Milgram study of obedience is a good example.[2] In this study, subjects were ordered to give increasingly severe electric shocks to another subject whom they could not see sitting behind a screen. What they did not know was that the individual to whom they thought they were administering the shocks was a confederate of the experimenter, and no shocks were actually being administered. The

Patients Given Fake Blood Without Their Knowledge*

Failed Study Used Change in FDA Rules

ASSOCIATED PRESS

Chicago—A company conducted an ill-fated blood substitute trial without the informed consent of patients in the study—some of whom died, federal officials say.

Baxter International Inc. was able to test the substitute, known as HemAssist, without consent because of a 1996 change in federal Food and Drug Administration regulations.

The changes, which broke a 50-year standard to get consent for nearly all experiments on humans, were designed to help research in emergency medicine that could not happen if doctors took the time to get consent.

But the problems with the HemAssist trial are prompting some medical ethicists to question the rule change.

"People get involved in something to their detriment without any knowledge of it," George Annas, a professor of health law at the Boston University School of Public Health, told the *Chicago Tribune*. "We use people. What's the justification for that?"

No other company has conducted a no-consent experiment under the rule, FDA officials said.

Baxter officials halted their clinical trial of HemAssist last spring after reviewing data on the first 100 trauma patients placed in the nationwide study.

Of the 52 critically ill patients given the substitute, 24 died, representing a 46.2 percent mortality rate. The Deerfield, Ill.-based company had projected 42.6 percent mortality for critically ill patients seeking emergency treatment.

There has been an intense push to find a blood substitute to ease the effects of whole-blood shortages.

Researchers say artificial blood lasts longer than conventional blood, eliminates the time-consuming need to match blood types and wipes out the risk of contamination from such viruses as HIV and hepatitis.

The 1996 regulations require a level of community notification that is not used in most scientific studies, including community meetings, news releases and post-study follow-up.

No lawsuits have arisen from the blood substitute trial, Baxter officials said.

**San Francisco Chronicle.* (1999, January 18).

dependent variable was the level of shock subjects administered before they refused to administer any more. Out of a total of 40 subjects who participated in the study, 26 followed the "orders" of the experimenter and (so they thought) administered the maximum shock possible of 450 volts! Even though no shocks were actually administered, publication of the study results produced widespread controversy. Many people felt the study was unethical. Others argued that the importance of the study and its results justified the deception. Notice that the study raises questions about not only deception but also harm, since some participants could have suffered emotionally from later consideration of their actions.

Current professional guidelines are as follows:

- Whenever possible, a researcher should conduct the study using methods that do not require deception.
- If alternative methods cannot be devised, the researcher should determine whether the use of deception is justified by the prospective study's scientific, educational, or applied value.
- If the participants are deceived, the researcher must ensure that they are provided with sufficient explanation as soon as possible.

Perhaps the most serious problem involving deception is what it has done to the reputation of the scientific community. In general when people begin to think of scientists and researchers as liars, or as individuals who misrepresent what they are about, the overall image of science suffers. Fewer and fewer people are willing to participate in research investigations today because of this perception. As a result, the search for reliable knowledge about our world may be impeded.

Three Examples Involving Ethical Concerns

Here are brief descriptions of three research studies. Let us consider each in terms of (1) presenting possible harm to the participants, (2) ensuring the confidentiality of the research data, and (3) knowingly practicing deception. (Figure 4.2 illustrates some examples of unethical research practices.)

Study 1. The researcher plans to observe (unobtrusively) students in each of 40 classrooms—eight visits

Figure 4.2 *Examples of Unethical Research Practices*

each of 40 minutes' duration. The purpose of these observations is to look for relationships between the behavior of students and certain teacher behavior patterns.

Possibility of Harm to the Participants. This study would fall within the exempt category regarding the possibility of harm to the participants. Neither teachers nor students are placed under any risk, and observation is an accepted part of school practice.

Confidentiality of the Research Data. The only issue that is likely to arise in this regard is the possible but unlikely observation of a teacher behaving in an illegal or unethical way (e.g., physically or verbally abusing a student). In the former case, the researcher is legally required to report the incident. In the latter case, the researcher must weigh the ethical dilemma involved in not reporting the incident against that of violating assurances of confidentiality.

Deception. Although no outright deception is involved, the researcher is going to have to give the teachers a rationale for observing them. If the specific teacher characteristic being observed (e.g., need to control) is given, the behavior in question is likely to be affected. To avoid this, the researcher might explain that the purpose of the study is to investigate different teaching styles—without divulging the specifics. To us, this does not seem to be unethical. An alternative is to tell the teachers that specific details cannot be divulged until after data have been collected for fear of changing their behavior. If this alternative is pursued, some teachers might refuse to participate.

Study 2. The researcher wishes to study the value of a workshop on suicide prevention for high school students. The workshop is to consist of three two-hour meetings in which danger signals, causes of suicide, and community resources that provide counseling will be discussed. Students will volunteer, and half will be assigned to a comparison group that will not participate in the workshop. Outcomes will be assessed by comparing the information learned and attitudes of those attending the meetings with those who do not attend.

Possibility of Harm to the Participants. Whether this study fits the exempt category with regard to any possibility of risk for the participants depends on the extent to which it is atypical for the school in question. We think that in most schools, this study would probably be considered atypical. In addition, it is conceivable that the material presented could place a student at risk by stirring up emotional reactions. In any case, the researcher should inform parents as to the nature of the study and the possible risks involved and obtain their consent for their children to participate.

Confidentiality of the Research Data. No problems are foreseen in this regard, although confidentiality as to what will occur during the workshop cannot, of course, be guaranteed.

Deception. No problems are foreseen.

Study 3. The researcher wishes to study the effects of "failure" versus "success" by teaching junior high

An Example of Unethical Research

A series of studies reported in the 1950s and 1960s received widespread attention in psychology and education and earned their author much fame, including a knighthood. They addressed the question of how much of one's performance on IQ tests was likely to be hereditary and how much was due to environmental factors.

Several groups of children were studied over time, including identical twins raised together and apart, fraternal twins raised together and apart, and same-family siblings. The results were widely cited to support the conclusion that IQ is about 80 percent hereditary and 20 percent environmental.

Some initial questions were raised when another researcher found a considerably lower hereditary percentage. Subsequent detailed investigation of the initial studies* revealed highly suspicious statistical treatment of data, inadequate specification of procedures, and questionable adjustment of scores, all suggesting unethical massaging of data. Such instances, which are reported occasionally, underscore the importance of repeating studies, as well as the essential requirement that all procedures and data be available for public scrutiny.

*Kamin, L. (1974). *The science and politics of I.Q.* New York: John Wiley.

students a motor skill during a series of six 10-minute instructional periods. After each training period, the students will be given feedback on their performance as compared with that of other students. To control extraneous variables (such as coordination), the researcher plans to randomly divide the students into two groups—half will be told that their performance was "relatively poor" and the other half will be told that they are "doing well." Their actual performance will be ignored.

Possibility of Harm to the Participants. This study presents several problems. Some students in the "failure" group may well suffer emotional distress. Although students are normally given similar feedback on their performance in most schools, feedback in this study (being arbitrary) may conflict dramatically with their prior experience. The researcher cannot properly inform students, or their parents, about the deceptive nature of the study, since to do so would in effect destroy the study.

Confidentiality of the Research Data. Confidentiality does not appear to be an issue in this study.

Deception. The deception of participants is clearly an issue. One alternative is to base feedback on actual performance. The difficulty here is that each student's extensive prior history will affect both individual performance and interpretation of feedback, thus confounding the results. Some, but not all, of these extraneous variables can be controlled (perhaps by examining school records for data on past history or by pretesting students). Another alternative is to weaken the experimental treatment by trying to lessen the possibility of emotional distress (e.g., by saying to participants in the failure group, "You did not do quite as well as most") and confining the training to one time period. Both of these alternatives, however, would lessen the chances of any relationship emerging.

Research with Children

Studies using children as participants present special issues for researchers. The young are more vulnerable in some respects, have fewer legal rights, and may not understand the language of informed consent. Therefore, the following specific guidelines need to be considered:

- Informed consent of parents or of those legally designated as caretakers is required for participants defined as minors. Signers must be provided all necessary information in appropriate language and must have the opportunity to refuse. (Figure 4.3 shows an example of a consent form for a minor.)
- Researchers do not present themselves as diagnosticians or counselors in reporting results to parents, nor do they report information given by a child in confidence.
- Children may never be coerced into participation in a study.
- Any form of remuneration for the child's services does not affect the application of these (and other) ethical principles.

San Francisco State University
Parental Permission for a Minor to Participate in Research
Research Title

A. PURPOSE AND BACKGROUND
My name is ________. I am a (*graduate student/faculty member*) at San Francisco State University and I am conducting a research study about ________. I am inviting your child to take part in the research because he/she ________________.

(State the purpose of the research; the purpose must be the same as stated in the protocol. In fact, sections throughout this form should mirror the protocol statement. State why the prospective subject is being invited to participate in this study, e.g. "he/she is in the after school program I am studying.")

B. PROCEDURES
If you agree to let your child participate in this research study, the following will occur:

- Your child will be asked to *(play math games and take a test)*
- This will take place in their regular classroom as part of my scheduled curriculum.
- Your child will participate in a group discussion in social studies class about their attitudes about extracurricular activities. The discussions will be audiotaped. *(OR///)*
- Your child will be invited to participate in an after school tutoring project. The tutoring sessions will take place between 3:45 and 4:45 PM on five Tuesdays and Thursdays during the spring semester.

(State where the research will take place, how long it will take, and at what time of day it will occur. State the time each procedure will take, and also state the total time it will take.)

C. RISKS
There is a risk of loss of privacy, which the researcher will reduce by not using any real names or other identifiers in the written report. The researcher will also keep all data in a locked file cabinet in a secure location. Only the researcher will have access to the data. At the end of the study, data will be (see "Guidelines for Data Retention.")

There may be some discomfort for your child at being asked some of the questions. Your child may answer only those questions he or she wants to, or he or she may stop the entire process at any time, without penalty.

(State the risks involved, and how the researcher will reduce them. If the questions are very sensitive and may cause anxiety or other negative emotions, researcher should include a brief list of counseling contacts they may consult.)

D. CONFIDENTIALITY
State how you will protect the confidentiality of the data collected. Where will you store it, will it be password-protected if stored on a computer, or in a locked office if it's paper data. How long will the data be kept, what will happen to it when the project is over? (Will it be destroyed, kept for future research—if so the research must be consistent with the original purpose.)

E. DIRECT BENEFITS

F. COSTS

G. COMPENSATION

H. QUESTIONS
Questions about your child's rights as a study participant, or comments or complaints about the study also may be addressed to the Office for the Protection of Human Subjects at Your University.

J. CONSENT
You have been given a copy of this consent form to keep. PARTICIPATION IN THIS RESEARCH STUDY IS VOLUNTARY. You are free to decline to have your child participate in this research study. You may withdraw your child's participation at any point without penalty. Your decision whether or not to participate in this research study will have no influence on your or your child's present or future status at your university

Child's Name ____

Signature ______________________________ Date ______________
Parent

Signature ______________________________ Date ______________
Researcher

Figure 4.3 *Example of a Consent Form for a Minor to Participate in a Research Study*

Regulation of Research

The regulation most directly affecting researchers is the National Research Act of 1974. It requires that all research institutions receiving federal funds establish what are known as **institutional review boards (IRBs)** to review and approve research projects. Such a review must take place whether the research is to be done by a single researcher or a group of researchers. In the case of federally funded investigations, failure to comply can mean that the entire institution (e.g., a university) will lose all of its federal support (e.g., veterans' benefits, scholarship money). Needless to say, this is a severe penalty. The federal agency that has the major responsibility for establishing the guidelines for research involving human subjects is the Department of Health and Human Services (HHS).

At institutions receiving federal funding, any affiliated researchers (including co-researchers, research technicians, and student assistants) planning to use human subjects are currently required to pass an online research training course administered by the National Institutes of Health (NIH) or the Collaborative Institutional Training Initiative (CITI). Once the course is completed successfully, a course completion report is issued that is valid for three years. (The NIH course can be found at http://phrp.nihtraining.com/users/login.php and the CITI course at www.citiprogram.org/.) Both courses take approximately two to three hours to complete and can be bookmarked so that the course does not have to be taken during one sitting. The CITI course takes a little longer to complete but is recommended for social, behavioral, and educational researchers because of the elective modules that can be tailored to a particular field of study. Researchers and students should check with their own institutions about specific policies and procedures regarding the research training course. Usually, the report of completion must be submitted along with any research protocol materials to the IRB for approval.

An IRB must have at least five members, consist of both men and women, and include at least one nonscientist. It must include one person not affiliated with the institution. Individuals competent in a particularly relevant area may be invited to assist in a review but may not vote. Furthermore, individuals with a conflict of interest must be excluded, although they may provide information.

If the IRB regularly reviews research involving a vulnerable category of subjects (e.g., such as studies involving the developmentally disabled), the board must include one or more individuals who are primarily concerned with the welfare of these subjects.

The IRB examines all proposed research with respect to certain basic criteria. Sometimes the criteria used by an IRB to determine whether a study is "exempt," for example, may differ from those specified by the HHS (see the More About Research box on HHS revised regulations). Oftentimes, the criteria set forth by an institutional IRB are more conservative than those stipulated by the federal government because of risk management related to litigation liability and funding withdrawal. Researchers and students are advised to consult with their own institution's IRB policies and procedures. The IRB board can request that a study be modified to meet their criteria before it will be approved. If a proposed study fails to satisfy any one of these criteria, the study will not be approved (Table 4.1).

TABLE 4.1 ***Criteria for IRB Approval***

- Minimization of risk to participants (e.g., by using procedures that do not unnecessarily expose subjects to risk).
- Risks that may occur are reasonable in relation to benefits that are anticipated.
- Equitable selection (i.e., the proposed research does not discriminate among individuals in the population).
- Protection of vulnerable individuals (e.g., children, pregnant women, prisoners, mentally disabled or economically disadvantaged persons).
- Informed consent—researchers must provide complete information about all aspects of the proposed study that might be of interest or concern to a potential participant, and this must be presented in a form that participants can easily understand.
- Participants have the right to withdraw from the study at any time without penalty.
- Informed consent will be appropriately documented.
- Monitoring of the data being collected to ensure the safety of the participants.
- Privacy and confidentiality—ensuring that any and all information obtained during a study is not released to outside individuals where it might have embarrassing or damaging consequences.

Ethical or Not?

In September 1998, a U.S. District Court judge halted a study begun in 1994 to evaluate the effectiveness of the U.S. Job Corps program. For two years, the researchers had randomly assigned 1 out of every 12 eligible applicants to a control group that was denied service for three years—a total of 6,000 applicants. If applicants refused to sign a waiver agreeing to participate in the study, they were told to reapply two years later. The class action lawsuit alleged psychological, emotional, and economic harm to the control subjects. The basis for the judge's decision was a failure to follow the federal law that required the methodology to be subject to public review. A preliminary settlement pledged to locate all of the control subjects by the year 2000, invite them into the Job Corps (if still eligible), and pay each person $1,000.*

In a letter to the editor† of *Mother Jones* in April 1999, however, Judith M. Gueron, the President of Manpower Demonstration Research Corporation (*not* the company awarded the evaluation grant) defended the study on two grounds: (1) since there were only limited available openings for the program, random selection of qualified applicants "is arguably fairer" than first-come, first-served; and (2) the alleged harm to those rejected is unknown, since they were free to seek other employment or training.

What do you think?

*Price, J. (1999, January/February). Job Corps lottery. *Mother Jones*, 21–22.
†Backtalk. (1999, April). *Mother Jones,* 13.

IRB Boards classify research proposals in three categories:

Category I (Exempt Review)—the proposed study presents no possible risk to adult participants (e.g., an anonymous mailed survey on innocuous topics or an anonymous observation of public behavior). This type of study is exempt from the requirement of informed consent.

Category II (Expedited Review)—the proposed study presents no more than minimal risk to participants. A typical example would be a study of individual or group behavior of adults where there is no psychological intervention or deception involved. This category of research does not require written documentation of informed consent, although oral consent is required. Most classroom research projects fall in this category.

Category III (Full Review)—the proposed study includes questionable elements, such as research involving special populations, vulnerable individuals, unusual equipment or procedures, deception, intervention, or some form of invasive measurement. A meeting of all IRB members is required, and the researcher must appear in person to discuss and answer questions about the research.

The question of risk for participants is of particular interest to the IRB. The board may terminate a study if it appears that serious harm to subjects is likely to occur. Any and all potential risk(s) to subjects must be minimized. What this means is that any risk should not be any greater than those ordinarily encountered in daily life or during the performance of routine physical or psychological examinations or tests.

Some researchers were unhappy with the regulations that were issued in 1974 by HHS because they felt that the rules interfered unnecessarily with projects that posed minimal risk. Their opposition resulted in a 1981 set of revised guidelines, amended most recently in 2005, as shown in the More About Research box on page 71. These guidelines apply to all research funded by HHS. As mentioned, Institutional Review Boards determine which studies qualify to be exempt from the guidelines, so check with your IRB prior to assuming your proposed research project does not require review.

Another law affecting research is the Family Privacy Act of 1974, also known as the Buckley Amendment. It is intended to protect the privacy of students' educational records. One of its provisions is that data that identify students may not, with some exceptions, be made available without permission from the student or, if under legal age, parents or legal guardians. Consent forms must specify what data will be disclosed, for what purposes, and to whom.

The relationship between the current guidelines and qualitative research is not as clear as it is for quantitative research. In recent years, therefore, there have been a number of suggestions for a specific code of ethics for qualitative research.[3] In quantitative studies, subjects can be told the content and the possible dangers involved in

MORE ABOUT RESEARCH

Department of Health and Human Services Revised Regulations for Research with Human Subjects

The following HHS guidelines currently allow for exemption from IRB review for certain projects. However, please make sure to check with your IRB for their exempt research guidelines.

1. Research conducted in established or commonly accepted educational settings, involving normal educational practices, such as (i) research on regular and special education instructional strategies, or (ii) research on the effectiveness of or the comparison among instructional techniques, curricula, or classroom management methods.
2. Research involving the use of educational tests (cognitive, diagnostic, aptitude, achievement), survey procedures, interview procedures or observation of public behavior, unless: (i) information obtained is recorded in such a manner that human subjects can be identified, directly or through identifiers linked to the subjects; and (ii) any disclosure of the human subjects' responses outside the research could reasonably place the subjects at risk of criminal or civil liability or be damaging to the subjects' financial standing, employability, or reputation.
3. Research involving the use of educational tests (cognitive, diagnostic, aptitude, achievement), survey procedures, interview procedures, or observation of public behavior that is not exempt under paragraph (b)(2) of this section, if: (i) the human subjects are elected or appointed public officials or candidates for public office; or (ii) federal statute(s) require(s) without exception that the confidentiality of the personally identifiable information will be maintained throughout the research and thereafter.
4. Research involving the collection or study of existing data, documents, records, pathological specimens, or diagnostic specimens, if these sources are publicly available or if the information is recorded by the investigator in such a manner that subjects cannot be identified, directly or through identifiers linked to the subjects.
5. Research and demonstration projects which are conducted by or subject to the approval of department or agency heads, and which are designed to study, evaluate, or otherwise examine: (i) Public benefit or service programs; (ii) procedures for obtaining benefits or services under those programs; (iii) possible changes in or alternatives to those programs or procedures; or (iv) possible changes in methods or levels of payment for benefits or services under those programs.
6. Taste and food quality evaluation and consumer acceptance studies, (i) if wholesome foods without additives are consumed or (ii) if a food is consumed that contains a food ingredient at or below the level and for a use found to be safe, or agricultural chemical or environmental contaminant at or below the level found to be safe, by the Food and Drug Administration or approved by the Environmental Protection Agency or the Food Safety and Inspection Service of the U.S. Department of Agriculture.

U.S. Department of Health and Human Services, 45CFR 46.101(b)(1)–(6).

Research activities involving human subjects that are **exempt** from IRB review are identified in 45CFR 46.101(b)(1)–(6). (Institutions and IRBs may not create new categories of exempt research under 45 CFR Part 46.) Institutions should have a clear policy in place on who shall determine what research is exempt under .46.101(b).

*www.hhs.gov/ohrp/policy/hsdc95-02.html

a study. In qualitative studies, however, the relationship between research and participant evolves over time. As Bogdan and Biklen suggest, doing qualitative research with informants can be "more like having a friendship than a contract. The people who are studied have a say in regulating the relationship and they continuously make decisions about their participation."[4] As a result, Bogdan and Biklen offer the following suggestions for qualitative researchers that might be considered when the criteria used by an IRB may not apply:[5]

1. Avoid research sites where informants may feel coerced to participate in the research.
2. Honor the privacy of informants—find a way to recruit informants so that they may choose to participate in the study.
3. Tell participants who are being interviewed how long the interview will take.
4. Unless otherwise agreed to, the identities of informants should be protected so that the information collected does not embarrass or otherwise harm them. Anonymity should extend not only to written reports but also to the verbal reporting of information.
5. Treat informants with respect and seek their cooperation in the research. Informants should be told of

the researcher's interest and they should give their permission for the researcher to proceed. Written consent should always be obtained.

6. Make it clear to all participants in a study the terms of any agreement negotiated with them.
7. Tell the truth when findings are written up and reported. Mail in a separate card indicating that they completed the questionnaire.

One further legal matter should be mentioned. Attorneys, physicians, and members of the clergy are protected by laws concerning privileged communications (i.e., they are protected by law from having to reveal information given to them in confidence). Researchers do not have this protection. It is possible, therefore, that any subjects who admit, on a questionnaire, to having committed a crime could be arrested and prosecuted. As you can see, it would be a risk therefore for the participants in a research study to admit to a researcher that they had participated in a crime. If such information is required to attain the goals of a study, a researcher can avoid the problem by omitting all forms of identification from the questionnaire. When mailed questionnaires are used, the researcher can keep track of nonrespondents by having each participant mail in a separate card indicating that they completed the questionnaire.

Academic Cheating and Plagiarism

A chapter on ethics and research would not be complete without some mention of academic dishonesty. Many educators believe the Internet has facilitated student cheating and plagiarism through easy access to electronic papers and resources. Prior to the Internet, **plagiarism**—the act of misrepresenting someone else's work as one's own—was more difficult to commit and get away with. Today, online plagiarism-checking tools like Turnitin are available for faculty and students to identify possible instances of plagiarism. The tool compares a student's assignment against an electronic database of publications for possible plagiarism as well as improper citation of text-based sources. As we discussed in Chapter 3, most colleges and universities have academic dishonesty policies in place and severe consequences for students who get caught, for example, a failing course grade or even academic dismissal. In our experience teaching undergraduate and graduate students, we believe a good number of students engage in plagiarism *unintentionally*. We think many students are unaware of attribution rules related to the proper use and citation of published and unpublished sources. As such, please refer to page 51 for tips on avoiding unintentional plagiarism.

Go back to the **INTERACTIVE AND APPLIED LEARNING** feature at the beginning of the chapter for a listing of interactive and applied activities. Go to the **Online Learning Center** at **www.mhhe.com/fraenkel9e** to take quizzes, practice with key terms, and review chapter content.

Main Points

BASIC ETHICAL PRINCIPLES

- *Ethics* refers to questions of right and wrong.
- There are a number of ethical principles that all researchers should be aware of and apply to their investigations.
- The basic ethical question for all researchers to consider is whether any physical or psychological harm could come to anyone as a result of the research.
- All subjects in a research study should be assured that any data collected from or about them will be held in confidence.
- The term *deception,* as used in research, refers to intentionally misinforming the subjects of a study as to some or all aspects of the research topic.

- Plagiarism is the act of misrepresenting someone else's work as one's own.
- Unintentional plagiarism can be avoided through the proper use and citation of published and unlisted sources.

RESEARCH WITH CHILDREN

- Children as research subjects present problems for researchers that are different from those of adult subjects. Children are more vulnerable, have fewer legal rights, and often do not understand the meaning of *informed consent.*

REGULATION OF RESEARCH

- Before any research involving human beings can be conducted at an institution that receives federal funds, it must be reviewed by an institutional review board (IRB) at the institution.
- The federal agency that has the major responsibility for establishing the guidelines for research studies that involve human subjects is the Department of Health and Human Services.

Key Terms

ethical research 61
informed consent 63
institutional review board (IRB) 69
plagiarism 72

For Discussion

1. Here are three descriptions of ideas for research. Which (if any) might have some ethical problems? Why?
   a. A researcher is interested in investigating the effects of diet on physical development. He designs a study in which two groups are to be compared. Both groups are composed of 11-year-olds. One group is to be given an enriched diet, high in vitamins, that has been shown to have a strengthening effect on laboratory animals. A second group is not to be given this diet. The groups are to be selected from all the 11-year-olds in an elementary school near the university where the researcher teaches.
   b. A researcher is interested in the effects of music on attention span. She designs an experimental study in which two similar high school government classes are to be compared. For a five-week period, one class has classical music played softly in the background as the teacher lectures and holds class discussions on the current unit of study. The other class studies the same material and participates in the same activities as the first class but does not have any music played during the five weeks.
   c. A researcher is interested in the effects of drugs on human beings. He asks the warden of the local penitentiary for subjects to participate in an experiment. The warden assigns several prisoners to participate in the experiment but does not tell them what it is about. The prisoners are injected with a number of drugs whose effects are unknown. Their reactions to the drugs are then described in detail by the researcher.
2. Which, if any, of the preceding studies would be exempt under the revised guidelines shown in the More About Research box on page 71?
3. Can you suggest a research study that would present ethical problems if done with children but not if done with adults?
4. Are there any research questions that should *not* be investigated in schools? If so, why not?

5. "Sometimes the design of a study makes necessary the use of concealment or deception." Discuss. Can you describe a study in which deception might be justified?
6. "Any sort of study that is likely to cause lasting, or even serious, harm or discomfort to any participant should not be conducted, unless the research has the potential to provide information of extreme benefit to human beings." Would you agree? If so, why? What might be an example of such information?

References

1. Adapted from the Committee on Scientific and Professional Ethics and Conduct. (1981). Ethical principles of psychologists. *American Psychologist, 36,* 633–638. Copyright 1981 by the American Psychological Association. Reprinted by permission.

2. Milgram, S. (1967). Behavioral study of obedience. *Journal of Abnormal and Social Psychology, 67,* 371–378.

3. For example, see Cassell, J., & Wax, M. (Eds.). (1980). Ethical problems in fieldwork. *Social Problems 27* (3); Curry, B. K., & Davis, J. E. (1995, Sept.–Oct.). Representing: The obligations of faculty as researchers. *Academe,* 40–43; Lincoln, Y. (1995). Emerging criteria for quality in qualitative and interpretive research. *Qualitative Inquiry 1* (3), 275–289.

4. Bogdan, R. C., & Biklen, S. K. (2007). *Qualitative research for education: An introduction to theory and methods* (5th ed.). Boston: Allyn & Bacon.

5. Bogdan, R. C., & Biklen, S. K. (2007). *Qualitative research for education: An introduction to theory and methods* (5th ed., pp. 49–50). Boston: Allyn & Bacon.

Research Exercise 4: Ethics and Research

Using Problem Sheet 4, restate the research question you developed in Problem Sheet 3. Identify any possible ethical problems in carrying out such a study. How might such problems be remedied?

Problem Sheet 4

Ethics and Research

1. My research question is: ______________________________

____

2. The possibilities of harm to participants (if any) are as follows: ______________________________

____

____

____

I would handle these problems as follows: ______________________________

____

3. The possibilities of problems of confidentiality (if any) are as follows: ______________________________

____

____

____

I would handle these problems as follows: ______________________________

____

4. The possibilities of problems of deception (if any) are as follows: ______________________________

____

____

____

I would handle these problems as follows: ______________________________

____

5. In which IRB category (I, II, or III) do you think your proposed study should be considered? State why. ______________________________

____

____

____

An electronic version of this Problem Sheet that you can fill in and print, save, or e-mail is available on the Online Learning Center at www.mhhe.com/fraenkel9e.

5 Variables and Hypotheses

The Importance of Studying Relationships

Variables

What Is a Variable?

Quantitative Versus Categorical Variables

Independent Versus Dependent Variables

Moderator Variables

Mediator Variables

Extraneous Variables

Hypotheses

What Is a Hypothesis?

Advantages of Stating Hypotheses in Addition to Research Questions

Disadvantages of Stating Hypotheses

Important Hypotheses

Directional Versus Nondirectional Hypotheses

Hypotheses and Qualitative Research

How many variables can you identify?

OBJECTIVES **Studying this chapter should enable you to:**

- Explain what is meant by the term "variable" and name five variables that might be investigated by educational researchers.
- Explain how a variable differs from a constant.
- Distinguish between a quantitative and a categorical variable.
- Explain how independent and dependent variables are related.
- Give an example of a moderator variable.
- Explain what a hypothesis is and formulate two hypotheses that might be investigated in education.
- Name two advantages and two disadvantages of stating research questions as hypotheses.
- Distinguish between directional and nondirectional hypotheses and give an example of each.

INTERACTIVE AND APPLIED LEARNING After, or while, reading this chapter:

Go to the Online Learning Center at www.mhhe.com/fraenkel9e to:

- Learn More About Hypotheses: To State or Not to State

Go to your online Student Mastery Activities book to do the following activities:

- Activity 5.1: Directional vs. Nondirectional Hypotheses
- Activity 5.2: Testing Hypotheses
- Activity 5.3: Categorical vs. Quantitative Variables
- Activity 5.4: Independent and Dependent Variables
- Activity 5.5: Formulating a Hypothesis
- Activity 5.6: Moderator Variables

Marge Jenkins and Jenna Rodriguez are having coffee following a meeting of their graduate seminar in educational research. Both are puzzled by some of the ideas that came up in today's meeting of the class.

"I'm not sure I agree with Ms. Naser" (their instructor), says Jenna. "She said that there are a lot of advantages to predicting how you think a study will come out."

"Yeah, I know," replies Marge. "But formulating a hypothesis seems like a good idea to me."

"Well, perhaps, but there are some disadvantages, too."

"Really? I can't think of any."

"Well, what about . . . ?"

Actually, both Jenna and Marge are correct. There are both advantages and disadvantages to stating a hypothesis in addition to one's research question. We'll discuss examples of both in this chapter.

The Importance of Studying Relationships

We mentioned in Chapter 2 that an important characteristic of many research questions is that they suggest a relationship of some sort to be investigated. Not all research questions, however, suggest relationships. Sometimes researchers are interested only in obtaining descriptive information to find out how people think or feel or to describe how they behave in a particular situation. Other times the intent is to describe a particular program or activity. Such questions also are worthy of investigation. As a result, researchers may ask questions like the following:

- How do the parents of the sophomore class feel about the counseling program?
- What changes would the staff like to see instituted in the curriculum?
- Has the number of students enrolling in college preparatory as compared to noncollege preparatory courses changed over the last four years?
- How does the new reading program differ from the one used in this district in the past?
- What does an inquiry-oriented social studies teacher do?

Notice that no relationship is suggested in these questions. The researcher simply wants to identify characteristics, behaviors, feelings, or thoughts. It is often necessary to obtain such information as a first step in designing other research or making educational decisions of some sort.

The problem with purely descriptive research questions is that answers to them do not help us understand why people feel or think or behave a certain way, why programs possess certain characteristics, why a particular strategy is to be used at a certain time, and so forth. We may learn what happened, or where or when (and even how) something happened, but not why it happened. As a result, our understanding of a situation, group, or phenomenon is limited. For this reason, scientists highly value research questions that suggest relationships to be investigated, because the answers to them help explain the nature of the world in which we live. We learn to understand the world by learning to explain how parts of it are related. We begin to detect *patterns* or connections between the parts.

We believe that understanding is generally enhanced by the demonstration of relationships or connections. It is for this reason that we favor the formation of a hypothesis that predicts the existence of a relationship. There may be times, however, when a researcher wants to hypothesize that a relationship does *not* exist. Why so? The only persuasive argument we know of is that of contradicting an existing widespread (but perhaps erroneous) belief. For example, if it can be shown that a great many people believe, in the absence of adequate evidence, that young boys are less sympathetic than young girls, a study in which a researcher finds no difference between boys and girls (i.e., *no* relationship between gender and sympathy) might be of value (such a study may have been done, although we are not aware of one). Unfortunately, most (but by no means all) of the methodological mistakes made in research (such as using inadequate instruments or too small a sample of participants) increase the chance of finding no relationship between variables. (We shall discuss several such mistakes in later chapters.)

Variables

WHAT IS A VARIABLE?

At this point, it is important to introduce the idea of variables, since a relationship is a statement about variables. What is a variable? A **variable** is a concept—a noun that stands for variation within a class of objects, such as *chair, gender, eye color, achievement, motivation,* or *running speed.* Even *spunk, style,* and *lust for life* are variables. Notice that the individual members in the class of objects, however, must differ—or vary—to qualify the class as a variable. If all members of a class are identical, we do not have a variable. Such characteristics are called **constants**, since the individual members of the class are not allowed to vary, but rather are held constant. In any study, some characteristics will be variables, while others will be constants.

An example may make this distinction clearer. Suppose a researcher is interested in studying the effects of reinforcement on student achievement. The researcher systematically divides a large group of students, all of whom are ninth-graders, into three smaller subgroups. She then trains the teachers of these subgroups to reinforce their students in different ways (one gives verbal praise, the second gives monetary rewards, the third gives extra points) for various tasks the students perform. In this study, *reinforcement* would be a variable (it contains three variations), while the grade level of the students would be a constant.

Notice that it is easier to see what some of these concepts stand for than others. The concept of *chair,* for example, stands for the many different objects that we sit on that possess legs, a seat, and a back. Furthermore, different observers would probably agree as to how particular chairs differ. It is not so easy, however, to see what a concept like *motivation* stands for, or to agree on what it means. The researchers must be specific here—they must define *motivation* as clearly as possible. They must do this so that it can be measured or manipulated. We cannot meaningfully measure or manipulate a variable if we cannot define it. As we mentioned, much educational research involves looking for a relationship among variables. But what variables?

There are many variables "out there" in the world that can be investigated. Obviously, we can't investigate them all, so we must choose. Researchers choose certain variables to investigate because they suspect that these variables are somehow related and believe that discovering the nature of this relationship, if possible, can help us make more sense out of the world in which we live.

QUANTITATIVE VERSUS CATEGORICAL VARIABLES

Variables can be classified in several ways. One way is to distinguish between quantitative and categorical variables. **Quantitative variables** exist in some degree (rather than all or none) along a continuum from less to more, and we can assign numbers to different individuals or objects to indicate how much of the variable they possess. Two obvious examples are height (John is six feet tall and Sally is five feet four inches) and weight (Mr. Adams weighs only 150 pounds and his wife 140 pounds, but their son tips the scales at an even 200 pounds). We can also assign numbers to various individuals to indicate how much "interest" they have in a subject, with a 5 indicating very much interest, a 4 much interest, a 3 some interest, a 2 little interest, a 1 very little interest, down to a 0 indicating no interest. If we can assign numbers in this way, we have the variable *interest.*

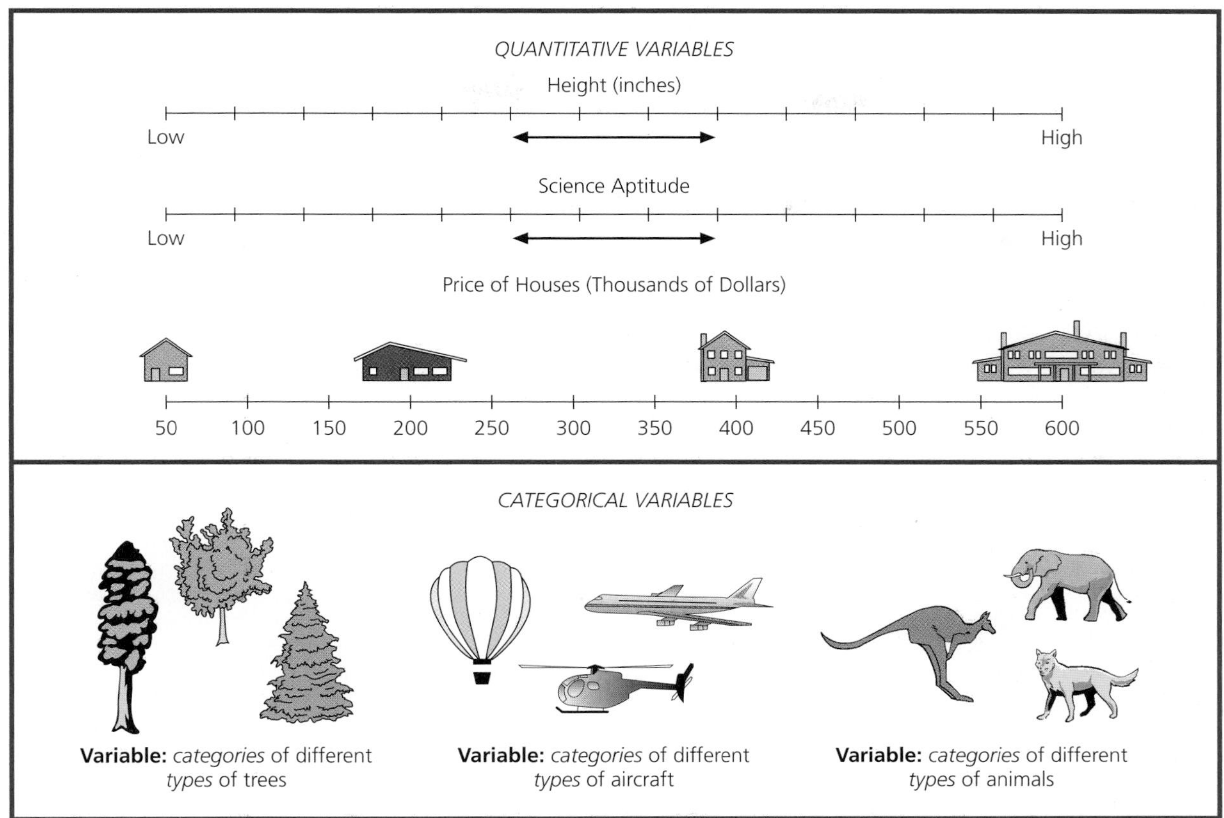

Figure 5.1 *Quantitative Variables Compared with Categorical Variables*

Quantitative variables can often (but not always) be subdivided into smaller and smaller units. Length, for example, can be measured in miles, yards, feet, inches, or in whatever subdivision of an inch is needed. By way of contrast, **categorical variables** do not vary in degree, amount, or quantity but are qualitatively different. Examples include eye color, gender, religious preference, occupation, position on a baseball team, and most kinds of research "treatments" or "methods." For example, suppose a researcher wishes to compare certain attitudes in two different groups of voters, one in which each individual is registered as a member of one political party and the other in which individuals are members of another party. The variable involved would be *political party.* This is a categorical variable—a person is either in one or the other category, not somewhere in between being a registered member of one party and being a registered member of another party. All members within each category of this variable are considered the same as far as party membership is concerned (Figure 5.1).

Can *teaching method* be considered a variable? Yes, it can. Suppose a researcher is interested in studying teachers who use different methods in teaching. The researcher locates one teacher who lectures exclusively, another who buttresses her lectures with slides, films, and computer images, and a third who uses the case-study method and lectures not at all. Does the teaching method "vary"? It does. You may need to practice thinking of differences in methods or in groups of people (teachers compared to administrators, for example) as variables, but acquiring proficiency in this idea is extremely useful in learning about research.

MORE ABOUT RESEARCH

Some Important Relationships That Have Been Clarified by Educational Research

1. "The more time beginning readers spend on phonics, the better readers they become." (Despite a great deal of research on the topic, this statement can neither be clearly supported nor refuted. It is clear that phonic instruction is an important ingredient; what is not clear is how much time should be devoted to it.)*
2. "The use of manipulatives in elementary grades results in better math performance." (The evidence is quite supportive of this method of teaching mathematics.)†
3. "Behavior modification is an effective way to teach simple skills to very slow learners." (There is a great deal of evidence to support this statement.)‡
4. "The more teachers know about specific subject matter, the better they teach it." (The evidence is inconclusive despite the seemingly obvious fact that teachers must know more than their students.)§
5. "Among children who become deaf before language has developed, those with hearing parents become better readers than those with deaf parents." (The findings of many studies *refute* this statement.)||

*Calfee, R., & Drum, P. (1986). Research on teaching reading. In Wittrock, M. C. (Ed.), *Handbook of research on teaching* (3rd ed., pp. 804–849). New York: Macmillan.

†Suydam, M. N. (1986, February). Research report: Manipulative materials and achievement. *Arithmetic Teacher, 10,* 32.

‡Deno, S. L. (1982). Behavioral treatment methods. In H. E. Mitzel (Ed.), *Encyclopedia of educational research* (5th ed., pp. 199–202). New York: Macmillan.

§Shulman, L. (1986). Paradigms and research programs in the study of teaching. In M. C. Wittrock (Ed.), *Handbook of research on teaching* (3rd ed., pp. 3–36). New York: Macmillan.

||Kampfe, C. M., & Turecheck, A. G. (1987, March). Reading achievement of prelingually deaf students and its relationship to parental method of communication: A review of the literature. *American Annals of the Deaf, 10,* 11–15.

Now, here are several variables. Which ones are quantitative variables and which ones are categorical variables?

1. Make of automobile
2. Learning ability
3. Ethnicity
4. Cohesiveness
5. Heartbeat rate
6. Gender*

Researchers in education often study the relationship between (or among) either (1) two (or more) quantitative variables; (2) one categorical and one quantitative variable; or (3) two or more categorical variables. Here are some examples of each:

1. *Two quantitative variables*
   - Age and amount of interest in school
   - Reading achievement and mathematics achievement
   - Classroom humanism and student motivation
   - Amount of time watching television and aggressiveness of behavior
2. *One categorical and one quantitative variable*
   - Method used to teach reading and reading achievement
   - Counseling approach and level of anxiety
   - Nationality and liking for school
   - Student gender and amount of praise given by teachers
3. *Two categorical variables*
   - Ethnicity and father's occupation
   - Gender of teacher and subject taught
   - Administrative style and college major
   - Religious affiliation and political party membership

Sometimes researchers have a choice of whether to treat a variable as quantitative or categorical. It is not uncommon, for example, to find studies in which a variable such as *anxiety* is studied by comparing a group of "high-anxiety" students to a group of "low-anxiety" students. This treats anxiety as though it were a categorical variable. While there is nothing really wrong with doing this, there are three reasons why it is preferable in such situations to treat the variable as quantitative.

1. Conceptually, we consider variables such as anxiety in people to be a matter of degree, not a matter of either-or.

*1, 3, and 6 represent categorical variables; 2, 4, and 5 represent quantitative variables.

2. Collapsing the variable into two (or even several) categories eliminates the possibility of using more detailed information about the variable, since differences among individuals within a category are ignored.
3. The dividing line between groups (e.g., between individuals of high, middle, and low anxiety) is almost always arbitrary (i.e., lacking in any defensible rationale).

INDEPENDENT VERSUS DEPENDENT VARIABLES

A common and useful way to think about variables is to classify them as *independent* or *dependent.* **Independent variables** are those that the researcher chooses to study to assess their possible effect(s) on one or more other variables. An independent variable is presumed to affect (at least partly cause) or somehow influence at least one other variable. The variable that the independent variable is presumed to affect is called a **dependent variable**. In commonsense terms, the dependent variable "depends on" what the independent variable does to it, how it affects it. For example, a researcher studying the relationship between *childhood success in mathematics* and *adult career choice* is likely to refer to the former as the independent variable and subsequent career choice as the dependent variable.

It is possible to investigate more than one independent (and also more than one dependent) variable in a study. For simplicity's sake, however, we present examples in which only one independent and one dependent variable are involved.

The relationship between independent and dependent variables can be portrayed graphically as follows:

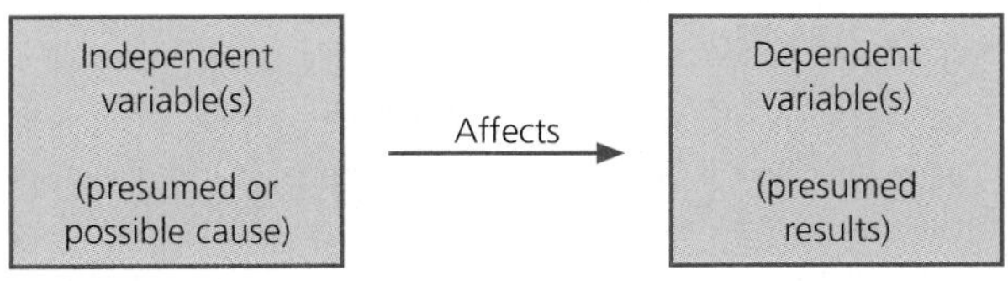

At this point, let's check your understanding. Suppose a researcher plans to investigate the following question: "Will students who are taught by a team of three teachers learn more science than students taught by one individual teacher?" What are the independent and dependent variables in this question?*

Notice that there are two conditions (sometimes called *levels*) in the independent variable—"three teachers" and "one teacher." Also notice that the dependent variable is not "science learning" but "*amount* of science learning." Can you see why?

At this point, things begin to get a bit complicated. Independent variables may be either *manipulated* or *selected.* A **manipulated variable** is one that the researcher *creates.* Such variables are typically found in experimental studies (see Chapter 13). Suppose, for example, that a researcher decides to investigate the effect of different amounts of reinforcement on reading achievement and systematically assigns students to three different groups. One group is praised continuously every day during their reading session; the second group is told simply to "keep up the good work"; the third group is told nothing at all. The researcher, in effect, manipulates the conditions in this experiment, thereby creating the variable *amount of reinforcement.* Whenever a researcher sets up experimental conditions, one or more variables are created. Such variables are called manipulated variables, **experimental variables**, or **treatment variables**.

Sometimes researchers *select* an independent variable that already exists. In this case, the researcher must locate and select examples of it, rather than creating it. In our earlier example of reading methods, the researcher would have to locate and select existing examples of each reading method, rather than arranging for them to happen. Selected independent variables are not limited to studies that compare different treatments; they are found in both correlational and causal-comparative studies (see Chapters 15 and 16). They can be either categorical or quantitative. The key idea here, however, is that the independent variable (either created or selected) is thought to affect the dependent variable. Here are a few examples of possible relationships between a selected independent variable and a dependent variable:

Independent Variable	Dependent Variable
Gender (categorical)	Musical aptitude (quantitative)
Mathematical ability (quantitative)	Career choice (categorical)
Gang membership (categorical)	Subsequent marital status (categorical)
Test anxiety (quantitative)	Test performance (quantitative)

Notice that none of the independent variables in these pairs could be directly manipulated by the researcher. Notice also that, in some instances, the independent/dependent relationship might be reversed, depending on

*The independent (categorical) variable is the *number of teachers,* and the dependent (quantitative) variable is the *amount of science learning*

which one the researcher thought might be the cause of the other. For example, the researcher might think that test performance causes anxiety, not the reverse.

Generally speaking, most studies in education that have one quantitative and one categorical variable are studies comparing different methods or treatments. As we indicated, the independent variable in such studies (the different methods or treatments) represents a categorical variable. Often the other (dependent) variable is quantitative and is referred to as an **outcome variable**.* The reason is rather clear-cut. The investigator, after all, is interested in the effect(s) of the differences in method on one or more outcomes (student achievement, their motivation, interest, and so on).

Again, let's check your understanding. Suppose a researcher plans to investigate the following question: "Will students like history more if taught by the inquiry method than if taught by the case-study method?" What is the outcome variable in this question?†

MODERATOR VARIABLES

A **moderator variable** is a special type of independent variable. It is a secondary independent variable that has been selected for study to determine if it affects or *modifies* the basic relationship between the primary independent variable and the dependent variable. Thus, if an experimenter thinks that the relationship between variables X and Y might be altered in some way by a third variable Z, then Z could be included in the study as a moderator variable.

Consider an example. Suppose a researcher is interested in comparing the effectiveness of a discussion- oriented approach to a more visually oriented approach for teaching a unit in a U.S. history class. Suppose further that the researcher suspects that the discussion approach may be superior for the girls in the class (who appear to be more verbal and to learn better through conversing with others) and that the visual approach may be more effective for boys (who seem to perk up every time a DVD is shown). When the students are tested together at the end of the unit, the overall results of the two approaches may show no difference, but when the results of the girls are separated from those of the boys, the two approaches may reveal different results for each subgroup. If so, then the gender variable *moderates* the relationship between

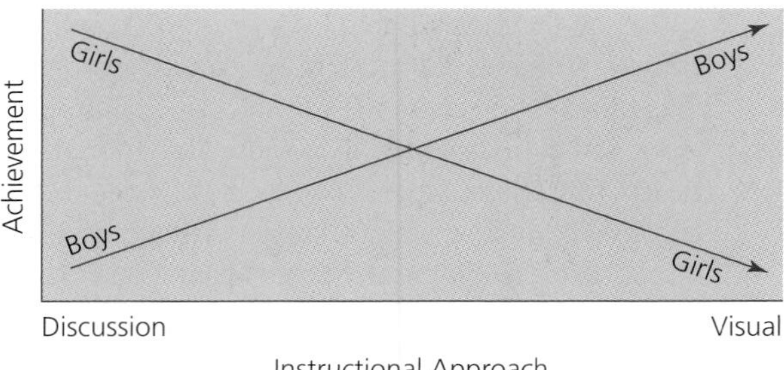

Figure 5.2 *Relationship Between Instructional Approach (Independent Variable) and Achievement (Dependent Variable), as Moderated by Gender of Students*

the *instructional approach* (the independent variable) and *effectiveness* (the dependent variable). The influence of this moderator variable can be seen in Figure 5.2.

Here are two examples of research questions that contain moderator variables:

Research Question 1: "Does anxiety affect test performance and, if so, does it depend on test-taking experience?"

- Independent variable: *anxiety level*
- Moderator variable: *test-taking experience*
- Dependent variable: *test performance*

Research Question 2: "Do high school students taught primarily by the inquiry method perform better on tests of critical thinking than high school students taught primarily by the demonstration method and, if so, does it vary with grade level?"

- Independent variable: *instructional method*
- Moderator variable: *grade level*
- Dependent variable: *performance on critical thinking tests*

As you can see, the inclusion of a moderator variable (or even two or three) in a study can provide considerably more information than just studying a single independent variable alone. We recommend their inclusion whenever appropriate.

MEDIATOR VARIABLES

While a moderator variable can modify or influence the strength of a relationship between two other variables, a **mediator variable** is one that attempts to explain the relationship between the two other variables. Let us reexamine the relationship in hypothesis 1 between anxiety level (AL) and test performance (TP) on a high-stakes test like the SAT exam. The moderator variable in this case is test-taking experience (TTE) because the

*It is also possible for an outcome variable to be categorical. For example, the variable *college completion* could be divided into the categories of *dropouts* and *college graduates*.

†*Liking for history* is the outcome variable.

The principal of a high school compares the final examination scores of two history classes taught by teachers who use different methods, not realizing that they are also different in many other ways because of *extraneous variables.* The classes differ in:

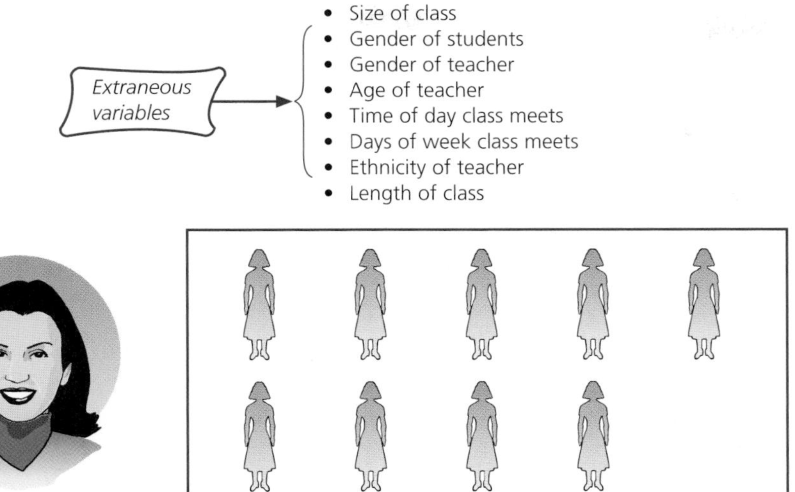

Ms. Brown's (age 31) history class meets from 9:00 to 9:50 A.M., Tuesdays and Thursdays. The class contains 9 students, all girls.

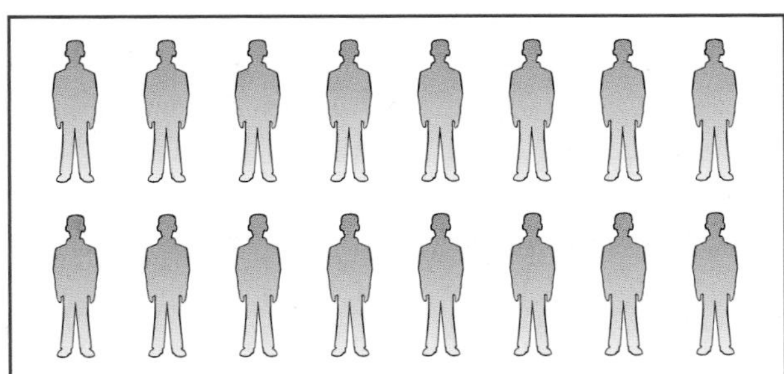

Mr. Thompson's (age 54) history class meets from 2:00 to 3:00 P.M., Mondays and Wednesdays. The class contains 16 students, all boys.

Figure 5.3 *Examples of Extraneous Variables*

relationship between AL and TP is stronger for students with prior experience taking the SAT. A possible mediator variable in this case could be socioeconomic status (SES) because it could explain why there is a relationship between AL and TP.

EXTRANEOUS VARIABLES

A basic problem in research is that there are many possible independent variables that could have an effect on the dependent variables. Once researchers have decided which variables to study, they must be concerned about the influence or effect of other variables that exist. Such variables are usually called **extraneous variables**. The task is to control these extraneous variables somehow to eliminate or minimize their effect.

Look again at the research question about team teaching on page 81. What are some other variables that could have an effect on the learning of students in a classroom situation?

There are many possible extraneous variables. The personality of the teachers involved, the experience level of the students, the time of day the classes are taught, the nature of the subject taught, the textbooks used, the type of learning activities the teachers employ, and the teaching methods—all are possible extraneous variables that could affect learning in this study. Figure 5.3 illustrates the importance of identifying extraneous variables.

One way to control extraneous variables is to hold them constant. For example, if a researcher includes only boys as the subjects of a study, she is controlling the variable of *gender.* We would say that the gender of the subjects does not vary; it is a constant in this study.

Researchers must continually think about how they might control the possible effect(s) of extraneous variables. We will discuss how to do this in some detail in Chapter 9, but for now you need to make sure you understand the difference between independent and dependent variables and to be aware of extraneous variables. Try your hand at the following question: "Will female students who are taught history by a teacher of the same gender like the subject more than female students taught by a teacher of a different gender?" What are the variables?*

Hypotheses

WHAT IS A HYPOTHESIS?

A **hypothesis** is, simply put, a prediction of the possible outcomes of a study. For example, here is a research question followed by its restatement in the form of a possible hypothesis:

Question: Will students who are taught history by a teacher of the same gender like the subject more than students taught by a teacher of a different gender?

Hypothesis: Students taught history by a teacher of the same gender will like the subject more than students taught history by a teacher of a different gender.

Here are two more examples of research questions followed by the restatement of each as a possible hypothesis:

Question: Is rapport with clients of counselors using client-centered therapy different from that of counselors using behavior-modification therapy?

Hypothesis: Counselors who use a client-centered therapy approach will have a greater rapport with their clients than counselors who use a behavior-modification approach.

Question: How do teachers feel about special classes for the educationally handicapped?

Hypothesis: Teachers in XYZ School District believe that students attending special classes for the educationally handicapped will be stigmatized.

or

Teachers in XYZ School District believe that special classes for the educationally handicapped will help such students improve their academic skills.

Many different hypotheses can come from a single research problem, as illustrated in Figure 5.4.

ADVANTAGES OF STATING HYPOTHESES IN ADDITION TO RESEARCH QUESTIONS

Stating hypotheses has both advantages and disadvantages. What are some of the advantages? First, a hypothesis forces us to think more deeply and specifically about the possible outcomes of a study. Elaborating on a question by formulating a hypothesis can lead to a more sophisticated understanding of what the question implies and exactly what variables are involved. Often, as in the case of the third example, when more than one hypothesis seems to suggest itself, we are forced to think more carefully about what we really want to investigate.

A second advantage of restating questions as hypotheses involves a philosophy of science. The rationale underlying this philosophy is as follows: If one is attempting to build a body of knowledge in addition to answering a specific question, then stating hypotheses is a good strategy because it enables one to make specific predictions based on prior evidence or theoretical argument. If these predictions are borne out by subsequent research, the entire procedure gains both in persuasiveness and efficiency. A classic example is Albert Einstein's theory of relativity. Many hypotheses were formulated as a result of Einstein's theory, which were later verified through research. As more and more of these predictions were shown to be fact, not only did they become useful in their own right, they also provided increasing support for the original ideas in Einstein's theory, which generated the hypotheses in the first place.

Lastly, stating a hypothesis helps us see if we are, or are not, investigating a relationship. If not, we may be prompted to formulate one.

*The dependent variable is *liking for history,* the independent variable is the *gender of the teacher.* Possible extraneous variables include the *personality* and *ability of the teacher(s)* involved; the *personality* and *ability level of the students;* the *materials used,* such as textbooks; the *style of teaching; ethnicity* and/or *age of the teacher and students;* and others. The researcher would want to control as many of these variables as possible.

Figure 5.4 *A Single Research Problem Can Suggest Several Hypotheses*

DISADVANTAGES OF STATING HYPOTHESES

Essentially, the disadvantages of stating hypotheses are threefold. First, stating a hypothesis may lead to a **bias**, either conscious or unconscious, on the part of the researcher. Once investigators state a hypothesis, they may be tempted to arrange the procedures or manipulate the data in such a way as to bring about a desired outcome.

This is probably more the exception than the rule. Researchers are assumed to be intellectually honest—although there are some famous exceptions. All studies should be subject to peer review; in the past, a review of suspect research has, on occasion, revealed such inadequacies of method that the reported results were cast into doubt. Furthermore, any particular study can be replicated to verify the findings of the study. Unfortunately, few educational research studies are repeated, so this "protection" is somewhat of an illusion. A dishonest investigator stands a fair chance of getting away with falsifying results. Why would a person deliberately distort his or her findings? Probably because professional recognition and financial reward accrue to those who publish important results.

Even for the great majority of researchers who are honest, however, commitment to a hypothesis may lead to distortions that are unintentional and unconscious. But it is probably unlikely that any researcher in the field of education is ever totally disinterested in the outcomes of a study; therefore, his or her attitudes and/or knowledge may favor a particular result. For this reason, we think it is desirable for researchers to make known their predilections regarding a hypothesis so that they are clear to others interested in their research. This also allows investigators to take steps to guard (as much as possible) against their personal biases.

The second disadvantage of stating hypotheses at the outset is that it may sometimes be unnecessary, or even inappropriate, in research projects of certain types, such as descriptive surveys and ethnographic studies. In many such studies, it would be unduly presumptuous, as well as futile, to predict what the findings of the inquiry will be.

The third disadvantage of stating hypotheses is that focusing attention on a hypothesis may prevent researchers from noticing other phenomena that might be important to study. For example, deciding to study the effect of a "humanistic" classroom on student motivation might lead a researcher to overlook its effect on such characteristics as sex-typing or decision making, which would be quite noticeable to another researcher who was not focusing solely on motivation. This seems to be a good argument against all research being directed toward hypothesis testing.

Consider the example of a research question presented earlier in this chapter: "How do teachers feel about special classes for the educationally handicapped?" We offered two (of many possible) hypotheses that might arise out of this question: (1) "Teachers believe that students attending special classes for the educationally handicapped will be stigmatized" and (2) "Teachers believe that special classes for the educationally handicapped will help such students improve their academic skills." Both of these hypotheses implicitly suggest a comparison between special classes for the educationally handicapped and some other kind of arrangement. Thus, the relationship to be investigated is between teacher beliefs and type of class. Notice that it is important to compare what teachers think about special classes with their beliefs about other kinds of arrangements. If researchers looked only at teacher opinions about special classes without also identifying their views about other kinds of arrangements, they would not know if their beliefs about special classes were in any way unique or different.

IMPORTANT HYPOTHESES

As we think about possible hypotheses suggested by a research question, we begin to see that some of them are more important than others. What do we mean by *important?* Simply that some may lead to more useful knowledge. Compare, for example, the following pairs of hypotheses. Which hypothesis in each pair would you say is more important?

Pair 1

a. Second-graders like school less than they like watching television.
b. Second-graders like school less than first-graders but more than third-graders.

Pair 2

a. Most students with academic disabilities prefer being in regular classes rather than in special classes.
b. Students with academic disabilities will have more negative attitudes about themselves if they are placed in special classes than if they are placed in regular classes.

Pair 3

a. Counselors who use client-centered therapy procedures get different reactions from counselees than do counselors who use traditional therapy procedures.
b. Counselees who receive client-centered therapy express more satisfaction with the counseling process than do counselees who receive traditional therapy.

In each of the three pairs, we think that the second hypothesis is more important than the first, since in each case (in our judgment) not only is the relationship to be investigated clearer and more specific but also investigation of the hypothesis seems more likely to lead to a greater amount of knowledge. It also seems to us that the information to be obtained will be of more use to people interested in the research question.

DIRECTIONAL VERSUS NONDIRECTIONAL HYPOTHESES

Let us make a distinction between directional and nondirectional hypotheses. A **directional hypothesis** indicates the specific direction (such as higher, lower, more, or less) that a researcher expects to emerge in a relationship. The particular direction expected is based on what the researcher has found in the literature, in theory, or from personal experience. The second hypothesis in each of the three pairs is a directional hypothesis.

Sometimes it is difficult to make specific predictions. If a researcher suspects that a relationship exists but has no basis for predicting the direction of the relationship, she cannot make a directional hypothesis. A **nondirectional hypothesis** does not make a specific prediction about what direction the outcome of a study will take. In nondirectional form, the second hypotheses of the three pairs would be stated as follows:

1. First-, second-, and third-graders will feel differently toward school.
2. There will be a difference between the scores on an attitude measure of students with academic disabilities placed in special classes and such students placed in regular classes.
3. There will be a difference in expression of satisfaction with the counseling process between counselees who receive client-centered therapy and counselees who receive traditional therapy.

Figure 5.5 illustrates the difference between a directional and a nondirectional hypothesis. If the person

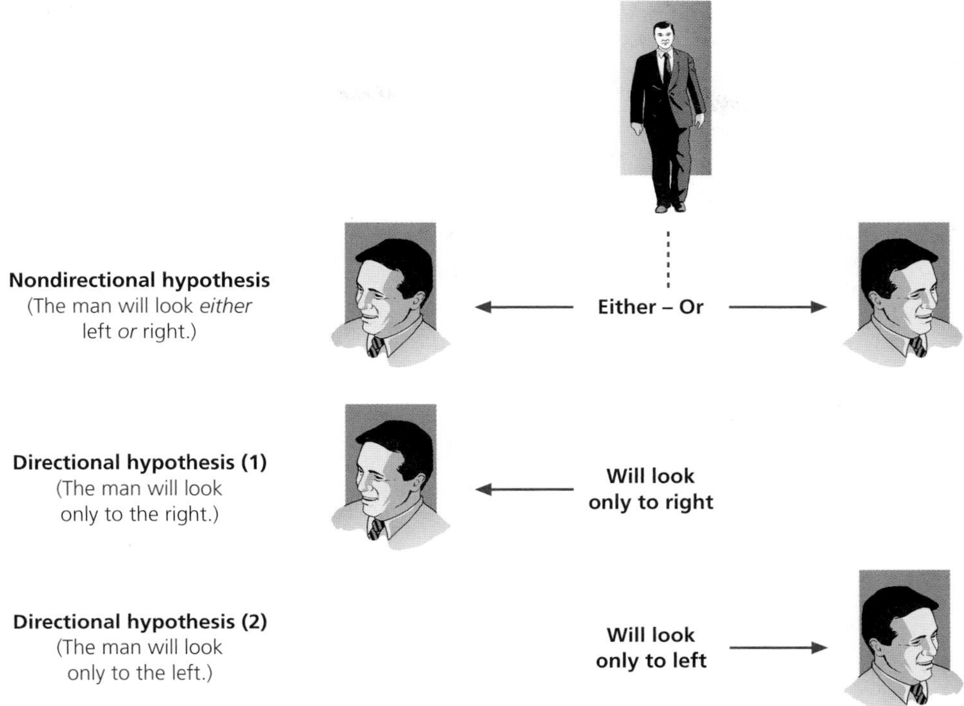

Figure 5.5 *Directional Versus Nondirectional Hypotheses*

pictured is approaching a street corner, three possibilities exist when he reaches the corner:

- He will continue to look straight ahead.
- He will look to his right.
- He will look to his left.

A nondirectional hypothesis would predict that he will look one way *or* the other. A directional hypothesis would predict that he will look in a particular direction (e.g., to his right). Since a directional hypothesis is riskier (because it is less likely to occur), it is more convincing when confirmed.*

Both directional and nondirectional hypotheses appear in the literature of research, and you should learn to recognize each.

HYPOTHESES AND QUALITATIVE RESEARCH

What is notable about the formation of hypotheses in qualitative research is that they are typically *not* stated at the beginning of a study, but rather they *emerge* as a study progresses. Rather than testing hypotheses as in quantitative studies, qualitative researchers are more likely to generate new hypotheses as a result of what they find as they go about their work—as they observe patterns and relationships in the natural setting rather than hypothesizing what such patterns and relationships might be beforehand. Many qualitative researchers *do* state some of their ideas before they begin a study, but these are usually called **propositions** rather than hypotheses.[1] Propositions differ from hypotheses in that they are not intended to be tested against the data (as in quantitative research) but rather are viewed as flexible tools intended to help guide researchers in their collection and analysis of qualitative data. The reluctance of qualitative researchers to formulate hypotheses at the beginning of a study is based on their conviction that participants and situations often differ widely and must first be understood before any hypotheses can be suggested.

Be that as it may, propositions can help qualitative researchers by creating areas of focus or foci for their data collection, thus making the process more manageable. Propositions can come from a range of sources

*If he looks straight ahead, neither a directional nor a nondirectional hypothesis is confirmed.

including theoretical and empirical research literature, but also professional and experiential knowledge. The following is an example of a theoretical proposition used by a doctoral student researcher to guide a qualitative study that explored how first-generation college (FGC) students of color successfully negotiate academic and social challenges at elite universities: "This phenomenological study explores the proposition that FGC students of color persist at highly selective four-year institutions by seeking counterspaces or 'third spaces' that sustain their motivation to succeed in college."* After interviewing several participants, the use of Bhabha's[2] sociocultural third space theory turned out to be less applicable than other psychological theories related to identity change. Since propositions are intended as flexible tools to help focus data collection, the researcher was able to discard her first proposition and restate it as one that examined the role of transformational resistance theory[3] in college persistence.

*The proposition was taken from a doctoral dissertation proposal submitted for a research design class taught by one of the authors at San Francisco State University.

Go back to the **INTERACTIVE AND APPLIED LEARNING** feature at the beginning of the chapter for a listing of interactive and applied activities. Go to the **Online Learning Center** at **www.mhhe.com/fraenkel9e** to take quizzes, practice with key terms, and review chapter content.

Main Points

THE IMPORTANCE OF STUDYING RELATIONSHIPS

- Identifying relationships among variables enhances understanding.
- Understanding relationships helps us to explain the nature of our world.

VARIABLES

- A variable is any characteristic or quality that varies among the members of a particular group.
- A constant is any characteristic or quality that is the same for all members of a particular group.
- A quantitative variable varies in amount or degree, but not in kind.
- A categorical variable varies only in kind, not in degree or amount.
- Several kinds of variables are studied in educational research, the most common being independent and dependent variables.
- An independent variable is presumed to affect or influence other variables.
- Independent variables are sometimes called *experimental variables* or *manipulated variables*.
- A dependent (or outcome) variable is presumed to be affected by one or more independent variables.
- Independent variables may be either manipulated or selected. A manipulated variable is created by the researcher. A selected variable is one that already exists that the researcher locates and then chooses to study.
- A moderator variable is a secondary independent variable that the researcher selects to study because he or she thinks it may affect the basic relationship between the primary independent variable and the dependent variable.
- An extraneous variable is an independent variable that may have unintended effects on a dependent variable in a particular study.
- A *proposition* is a tentative, flexible statement used sometimes by qualitative researchers to help guide their data collection and analysis.

HYPOTHESES

- The term *hypothesis,* as used in research, refers to a prediction of results usually made before a study commences.
- Stating a research question as a hypothesis has both advantages and disadvantages.
- An important hypothesis is one that is likely to lead, if it is supported, to a greater amount of important knowledge than a nonimportant hypothesis.
- A directional hypothesis is a prediction about the specific nature of a relationship—for example, method A is more effective than method B.
- A nondirectional hypothesis is a prediction that a relationship exists without specifying its exact nature—for example, there will be a difference between method A and method B (without saying which will be more effective).

Key Terms

bias 85
categorical variable 79
constant 78
dependent variable 81
directional hypothesis 86
experimental variable 81
extraneous variable 83
hypothesis 84
independent variable 81
manipulated variable 81
mediator variable 82
moderator variable 82
nondirectional hypothesis 86
outcome variable 82
proposition 87
quantitative variable 78
treatment variable 81
variable 78

For Discussion

1. Here are several research questions. Which ones suggest relationships?
   a. How many students are enrolled in the sophomore class this year?
   b. As the reading level of a text passage increases, does the number of errors students make in pronouncing words in the passage increase?
   c. Do individuals who see themselves as socially "attractive" expect their romantic partners also to be (as judged by others) socially attractive?
   d. What does the faculty dislike about the new English curriculum?
   e. Who is the brightest student in the senior class?
   f. Will students who score above the 90th percentile on a standardized reading test also score above the 90th percentile on a standardized writing test?
   g. Which political party contains the most Protestants—Democratic or Republican?
2. How would you rank the questions in item 1 in terms of significance? Why?
3. What might cause a researcher to state a directional hypothesis rather than a nondirectional hypothesis? What about the reverse?
4. Are there any variables that researchers should *not* study? Explain.
5. It is often argued that we cannot meaningfully measure a variable if we cannot define it. Is this true? always? Discuss.
6. "Commitment to a hypothesis may lead to distortions that are unintentional and unconscious." Would you agree? If so, can you give an example of such a hypothesis?
7. Can you think of a possible study for which it would be presumptuous to predict the outcome?

References

1. Maxwell, J. A. (2005). *Qualitative research design: An interactive approach* (2nd ed., p. 69). Thousand Oaks, CA: Sage.

2. Bhabha, H. K. (1994). *The location of culture*. New York, NY: Routledge.

3. Solorzano, D., & Delgado Bernal, D. (2001). Examining transformational resistance through a Critical Race and LatCrit Theory Framework: Chicana and Chicano students in an urban context. *Urban Education, 36,* 308–342.

Research Exercise 5: Variables, Hypotheses, and Propositions

If you are planning a quantitative study, try to formulate a testable hypothesis that is related to the research question you developed in Research Exercise 2. Using Problem Sheet 5, state the hypothesis in a sentence or two and check to see if it suggests a relationship between at least two variables. If it does not, revise it so that it does. Now indicate which is the independent and which is the dependent variable. Next, list as many extraneous variables as you can think of that might affect the results of your study. On the other hand, if you are planning a qualitative or mixed-methods study, state your proposition(s).

Problem Sheet 5

Variables, Hypotheses, and Propositions

1. My research question is: ______________________________
2. For a *quantitative* study, my hypothesis is:

   ____

   ____

   ____
3. This hypothesis suggests a relationship between at least two variables:

   a. ______________________________

   b. ______________________________

   c. ______________________________
4. More specifically, the variables in my study are:

   a. Dependent ________________ *(Is it categorical or quantitative?—circle one.)*

   b. Independent ________________ *(Is it categorical or quantitative?—circle one.)*
5. Possible extraneous variables that might affect my results include:

   a. ______________________________

   b. ______________________________

   c. ______________________________
6. I am planning a *qualitative or mixed-methods study*. The proposition(s) is/are:

   ____

   ____

   ____

An electronic version of this Problem Sheet that you can fill in and print, save, or e-mail is available on the Online Learning Center at www.mhhe.com/fraenkel9e.

Sampling 6

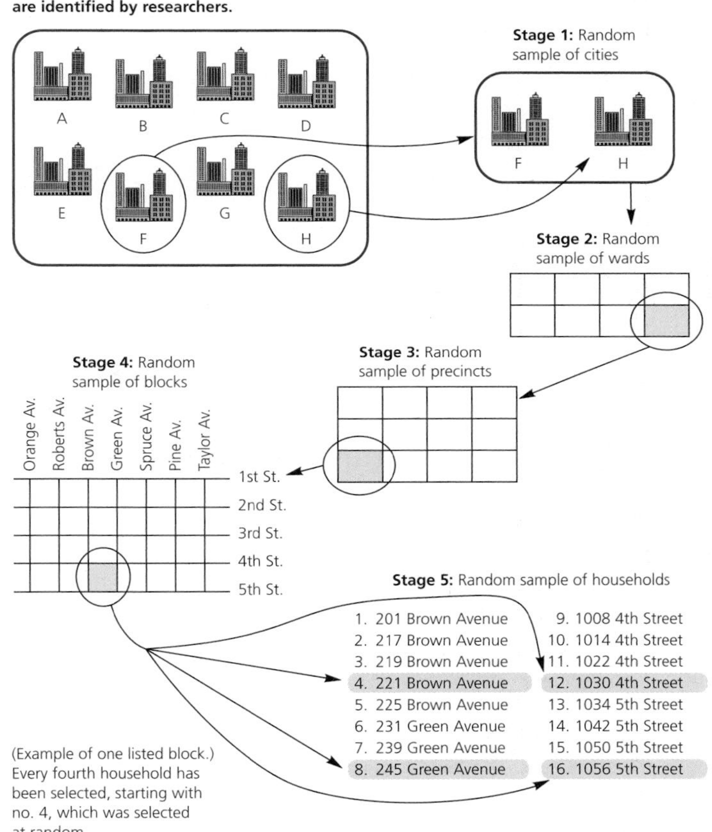

MULTISTAGE SAMPLING

What Is a Sample?

Samples and Populations

Defining the Population

Target Versus Accessible Populations

Random Versus Nonrandom Sampling

Random Sampling Methods

Simple Random Sampling

Stratified Random Sampling

Cluster Random Sampling

Two-Stage Random Sampling

Nonrandom Sampling Methods

Systematic Sampling

Convenience Sampling

Purposive Sampling

A Review of Sampling Methods

Sample Size

External Validity: Generalizing from a Sample

Population Generalizability

When Random Sampling Is Not Feasible

Ecological Generalizability

OBJECTIVES Studying this chapter should enable you to:

- Distinguish between a sample and a population.
- Explain what is meant by the term "representative sample."
- Explain how a target population differs from an accessible population.
- Explain what is meant by "random sampling," and describe briefly three ways of obtaining a random sample.
- Use a table of random numbers to select a random sample from a population.
- Explain how stratified random sampling differs from cluster random sampling.
- Explain what is meant by "systematic sampling," "convenience sampling," and "purposive sampling."
- Explain how the size of a sample can make a difference in terms of representativeness of the sample.
- Explain what is meant by the term "external validity."
- Distinguish between population generalizability and ecological generalizability and discuss when it is (and when it is not) appropriate to generalize the results of a study.

INTERACTIVE AND APPLIED LEARNING After, or while, reading this chapter:

Go to the Online Learning Center at www.mhhe.com/fraenkel9e to:

- Learn More About Sampling and Representativeness

Go to your online Student Mastery Activities book to do the following activities:

- Activity 6.1: Identifying Types of Sampling
- Activity 6.2: Drawing a Random Sample
- Activity 6.3: When Is It Appropriate to Generalize?
- Activity 6.4: True or False?
- Activity 6.5: Stratified Sampling
- Activity 6.6: Designing a Sampling Plan

Rosa Pak, a research professor at a large eastern university, wishes to study the effect of a new mathematics program on the mathematics achievement of students who are performing poorly in math in elementary schools throughout the United States. Because of a number of factors, of which time and money are only two, it is impossible for Rosa and her colleagues to try out the new program with the entire population of such students. They must select a *sample*. What is a sample anyway? Are there different kinds of samples? Are some kinds better than others to study? And just how does one go about obtaining a sample in the first place? Answers to questions like these are some of what you will learn in this chapter.

When we want to know something about a certain group of people, we usually find a few members of the group whom we know—or don't know—and study them. After we have finished "studying" these individuals, we usually come to some conclusions about the larger group of which they are a part. Many "commonsense" observations, in fact, are based on observations of relatively few people. It is not uncommon, for example, to hear statements such as: "Most female students don't like math"; "You won't find very many teachers voting Republican"; and "Most school superintendents are men."

What Is a Sample?

Most people, we think, base their conclusions about a group of people (students, Republicans, football players, actors, and so on) on the experiences they have with a fairly small number, or **sample**, of individual members. Sometimes such conclusions are an accurate representation of how the larger group of people acts or what they believe, but often they are not. It all depends on how representative (i.e., how similar) the sample is of the larger group.

One of the most important steps in the research process is the selection of the sample of individuals who will participate (be observed or questioned). **Sampling** refers to the process of selecting these individuals.

SAMPLES AND POPULATIONS

A sample in a research study is the group on which information is obtained. The larger group to which one hopes to apply the results is called the **population**.* All 700 (or whatever total number of) students at State University who are majoring in mathematics, for example, constitute a population; 50 of those students constitute a sample. Students who own automobiles make up another population, as do students who live in the campus dormitories. Notice that a group may be both a sample in one context and a population in another context. All State University students who own automobiles constitute the population of automobile owners at State, yet they also constitute a sample of all automobile owners at state universities across the United States.

When it is possible, researchers would prefer to study the entire population of interest. Usually, however, this is difficult to do. Most populations of interest are large, diverse, and scattered over a large geographic area. Finding, let alone contacting, all the members can be time-consuming and expensive. For that reason, of necessity,

*In some instances the sample and population may be identical.

researchers often select a sample to study. Some examples of samples selected from populations follow:

- A researcher is interested in studying the effects of diet on the attention span of third-grade students in a large city. There are 1,500 third-graders attending the elementary schools in the city. The researcher selects 150 of these third-graders, 30 each in five different schools, as a sample for study.
- An administrator in a large urban high school is interested in student opinions on a new counseling program in the district. There are six high schools and some 14,000 students in the district. From a list of all students enrolled in the district schools, the administrator selects a sample of 1,400 students (350 from each of the four grades, 9–12) to whom he plans to mail a questionnaire asking their opinion of the program.
- The principal of an elementary school wants to investigate the effectiveness of a new U.S. history textbook used by some of the teachers in the district. Out of a total of 22 teachers who are using the text, she selects a sample of 6. She plans to compare the achievement of the students in these teachers' classes with those of another 6 teachers who are not using the text.

DEFINING THE POPULATION

The first task in selecting a sample is to define the population of interest. In what group, exactly, is the researcher interested? To whom does he or she want the results of the study to apply? The population, in other words, is the group of interest to the researcher, the group to whom the researcher would like to generalize the results of the study. Here are some examples of populations:

- All high school principals in the United States
- All elementary school counselors in the state of California
- All students attending Central High School in Omaha, Nebraska, during the academic year 2005–2006
- All students in Ms. Brown's third-grade class at Wharton Elementary School

These examples reveal that a population can be any size and that it will have at least one (and sometimes several) characteristic(s) that sets it off from any other population. Notice that a population is always *all* of the individuals who possess a certain characteristic (or set of characteristics).

In educational research, the population of interest is usually a group of persons (students, teachers, or other individuals) who possess certain characteristics. In some cases, however, the population may be defined as a group of classrooms, schools, or even facilities. For example:

- All fifth-grade classrooms in Delaware (the hypothesis might be that classrooms in which teachers display a greater number and variety of student products have higher achievement)
- All high school gymnasiums in Nevada (the hypothesis might be that schools with "better" physical facilities produce more winning teams)

TARGET VERSUS ACCESSIBLE POPULATIONS

Unfortunately, the actual population (called the **target population**) to which a researcher would really like to generalize is rarely available. The population to which a researcher is *able* to generalize, therefore, is the **accessible population**. The former is the researcher's ideal choice; the latter, his or her realistic choice. Consider these examples:

Research problem to be investigated: The effects of computer-assisted instruction on the reading achievement of first- and second-graders in California.

Target population: All first- and second-grade children in California.

Accessible population: All first- and second-grade children in the Laguna Salada elementary school district of Pacifica, California.

Sample: Ten percent of the first- and second-grade children in the Laguna Salada district in Pacifica, California.

Research problem to be investigated: The attitudes of fifth-year teachers-in-training toward their student-teaching experience.

Target population: All fifth-year students enrolled in teacher-training programs in the United States.

Accessible population: All fifth-year students enrolled in teacher-training programs in the State University of New York.

Sample: Two hundred fifth-year students selected from those enrolled in the teacher-training programs in the State University of New York.

The more narrowly researchers define the population, the more they save on time, effort, and (probably) money, but the more they limit generalizability. It is essential that researchers describe the population and the sample in sufficient detail so that interested individuals

Figure 6.1
Representative Versus Nonrepresentative Samples

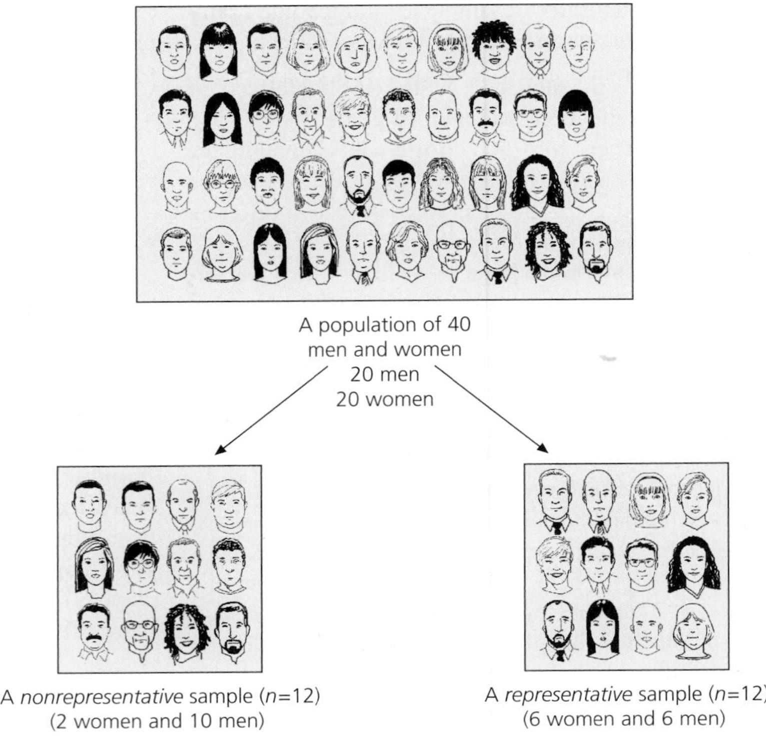

can determine the applicability of the findings to their own situations. Failure to define in detail the population of interest, and the sample studied, is one of the most common weaknesses of published research reports. It is important to note that the actual sample may be different from the sample originally selected because some subjects may refuse to participate, some subjects may drop out, data may be lost, and the like. We repeat, therefore, that it is very important to describe the characteristics of the actual sample studied in some detail.

RANDOM VERSUS NONRANDOM SAMPLING

Following is an example of each of the two main types of sampling.

Random sampling: The dean of a school of education in a large midwestern university wishes to find out how her faculty feel about the current sabbatical leave requirements at the university. She places all 150 names of the faculty in a hat, mixes them thoroughly, and then draws out the names of 25 individuals to interview.*

*A better way to do this will be discussed shortly, but this gives you the idea.

Nonrandom sampling: The president of the same university wants to know how his junior faculty feel about a promotion policy that he has recently introduced (with the advice of a faculty committee). He selects a sample of 30 from the total faculty of 1,000 to talk with. Five faculty members from each of the six schools that make up the university are chosen on the basis of the following criteria: They have taught at the university for less than five years, they are nontenured, they belong to one of the faculty associations on campus, and they have not been a member of the committee that helped the president draft the new policy.

In the first example, 25 names were selected from a hat after all the names had been mixed thoroughly. This is called **random sampling** because every member of the population (the 150 faculty members in the school) presumably had an equal chance of being selected. There are more sophisticated ways of drawing a random sample, but they all have the same intent—to select a *representative* sample from the population (Figure 6.1). The basic idea is that the group of individuals selected is very much like the entire population.

One can never be sure of this, of course, but if the sample is selected randomly and is sufficiently large, a researcher should get an accurate view of the larger group. The best way to ensure this is to see that no bias enters the selection process—that the researcher (or other factors) cannot consciously or unconsciously influence who gets chosen to be in the sample. We explain more about how to minimize bias later in this chapter.

In the second example, the president wants representativeness, but not as much as he wants to make sure there are certain kinds of faculty in his sample. Thus, he has stipulated that each of the individuals selected must possess all the criteria mentioned. Each member of the population (the entire faculty of the university) does *not* have an equal chance of being selected; some, in fact, have *no* chance. Hence, this is an example of **nonrandom sampling**, sometimes called purposive sampling (see p. 101). Here is another example of a random sample contrasted with a nonrandom sample.

Random: A researcher wishes to conduct a survey of all social studies teachers in a midwestern state to determine their attitudes toward the new state guidelines for teaching history in the secondary schools. There are a total of 725 social studies teachers in the state. The names of these teachers are obtained and listed alphabetically. The researcher then numbers the names on the list from 001 to 725. Using a table of random numbers, which he finds in a statistics textbook, he selects 100 teachers for the sample.

Nonrandom: The manager of the campus bookstore at a local university wants to find out how students feel about the services the bookstore provides. Every day for two weeks during her lunch hour, she asks every person who enters the bookstore to fill out a short questionnaire she has prepared and drop it in a box near the entrance before leaving. At the end of the two-week period, she has a total of 235 completed questionnaires.

In the second example, notice that all bookstore users did not have an equal chance of being included in the sample, which included only those who visited during the lunch hour. That is why the sample is not random. Notice also that some may not have completed the questionnaire.

Random Sampling Methods

After making a decision to sample, researchers try hard, in most instances, to obtain a sample that is representative of the population of interest—that means they prefer random sampling. The three most common ways of obtaining this type of sample are simple random sampling, stratified random sampling, and cluster sampling. A less common method is two-stage random sampling.

SIMPLE RANDOM SAMPLING

A **simple random sample** is one in which each and every member of the population has an equal and independent chance of being selected. If the sample is large, this method is the best way yet devised to obtain a sample representative of the population of interest. Let's take an example: Define a population as all eighth-grade students in school district Y. Imagine there are 500 students. If you were one of these students, your chance of being selected would be 1 in 500, if the sampling procedure were indeed random. Everyone would have the same chance of being selected.

The larger a random sample is in size, the more likely it is to represent the population. Although there is no guarantee of representativeness, of course, the likelihood of it is greater with large random samples than with any other method. Any differences between the sample and the population should be small and unsystematic. Any differences that do occur are the result of chance, rather than bias on the part of the researcher.

The key to obtaining a random sample is to ensure that each and every member of the population has an equal and independent chance of being selected. This can be done by using what is known as a **table of random numbers**—an extremely large list of numbers that has no order or pattern. Such lists can be found in the back of most statistics books. Table 6.1 illustrates part of a typical table of random numbers.

For example, to obtain a sample of 200 from a population of 2,000 individuals, using such a table, select a column of numbers, start anywhere in the column, and begin reading four-digit numbers. (Why four digits? Because the final number, 2,000, consists of four digits, and we must always use the same number of digits for each person. Person 1 would be identified as 0001; person 2, as 0002; person 635, as 0635; and so forth.) Then proceed to write down the first 200 numbers in the column that have a value of 2,000 or less.

TABLE 6.1 *Part of a Table of Random Numbers*

011723	223456	222167	032762	062281	565451
912334	379156	233989	109238	934128	987678
086401	016265	411148	251287	602345	659080
059397	022334	080675	454555	011563	237873
666278	106590	879809	899030	909876	198905
051965	004571	036900	037700	500098	046660
063045	786326	098000	510379	024358	145678
560132	345678	356789	033460	050521	342021
727009	344870	889567	324588	400567	989657
000037	121191	258700	088909	015460	223350
667899	234345	076567	090076	345121	121348
042397	045645	030032	657112	675897	079326
987650	568799	070070	143188	198789	097451
091126	021557	102322	209312	909036	342045

Let us take the first column of four numbers in Table 6.1 as an example. Reading only the first four digits, look at the first number in the column: It is 0117, so number 117 in the list of individuals in the population would be selected for the sample. Look at the second number: It is 9123. There is no 9123 in the population (because there are only 2,000 individuals in the entire population). So go on to the third number: It is 0864, hence number 864 in the list of individuals in the population would be chosen. The fourth number is 0593, so number 593 gets selected. The fifth number is 6662. There is no 6662 in the population, so go on to the next number, and so on, until reaching a total of 200 numbers, each representing an individual in the population who will be selected for the sample. Most researchers use computer-generated lists to obtain their samples randomly. This can be done quite easily using Excel software (see the box entitled "Using Excel to Draw a Random Sample" in Chapter 11 on p. 235).

The advantage of random sampling is that, if large enough, it is very likely to produce a representative sample. Its biggest disadvantage is that it is not easy to do. Each and every member of the population must be identified. In most cases, we must be able to contact the individuals selected. In all cases, we must know *who* 117 (for example) is.

Furthermore, simple random sampling is not used if researchers wish to *ensure* that certain subgroups are present in the sample in the same proportion as they are in the population. To do this, researchers must engage in what is known as stratified sampling.

STRATIFIED RANDOM SAMPLING

Stratified random sampling is a process in which certain subgroups, or *strata,* are selected for the sample in the same proportion as they exist in the population. Suppose the director of research for a large school district wants to find out student response to a new twelfth-grade American government textbook the district is considering adopting. She intends to compare the achievement of students using the new book with that of students using the more traditional text the district has purchased in the past. Since she has reason to believe that gender is an important variable that may affect the outcomes of her study, she decides to ensure that the proportion of males and females in the study is the same as in the population. The steps in the sampling process would be as follows:

1. She identifies the target (and accessible) population: all 365 twelfth-grade students enrolled in American government courses in the district.
2. She finds that there are 219 females (60 percent) and 146 males (40 percent) in the population. She decides to have a sample made up of 30 percent of the target population.
3. Using a table of random numbers, she then randomly selects 30 percent *from each stratum* of the population, which results in 66 female (30 percent of 219) and 44 male (30 percent of 146) students being selected from these subgroups. The proportion of males and females is the same in both the population and sample—40 and 60 percent (Figure 6.2).

The advantage of stratified random sampling is that it increases the likelihood of representativeness, especially if one's sample is not very large. It virtually ensures that key characteristics of individuals in the population are included in the same proportions in the sample. The disadvantage is that it requires more effort on the part of the researcher.

CLUSTER RANDOM SAMPLING

In both random and stratified random sampling, researchers want to make sure that certain kinds of individuals are included in the sample. But there are times when it is not possible to select a sample of individuals from a population. Sometimes, for example, a list of all members of the population of interest is not available. Obviously, then, simple random or stratified random sampling cannot be used. Frequently, researchers cannot select a sample of individuals due to administrative or other restrictions. This is especially true in schools. For example, if a target population were all

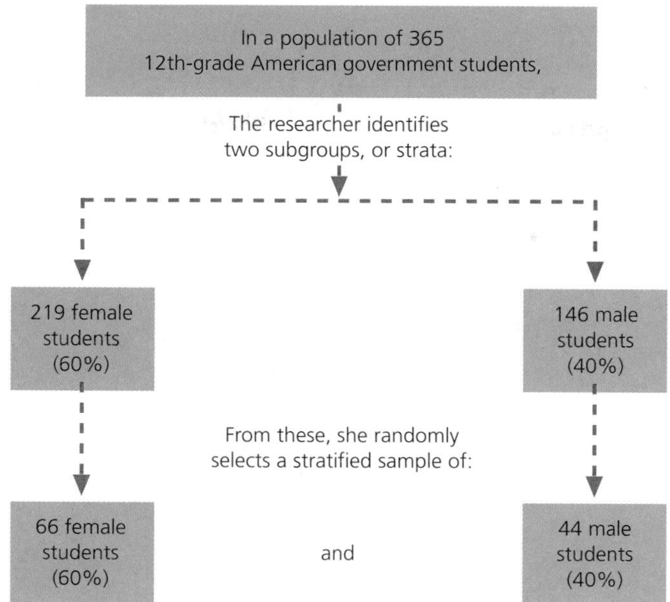

Figure 6.2 *Selecting a Stratified Sample*

eleventh-grade students within a district enrolled in U.S. history courses, it would be unlikely that the researcher could pull out randomly selected students to participate in an experimental curriculum. Even if it could be done, the time and effort required would make such selection difficult. About the best the researcher could hope for would be to study a number of intact classes—that is, classes already in existence. The selection of groups, or clusters, of subjects rather than individuals is known as **cluster random sampling**. Just as simple random sampling is more effective with larger numbers of individuals, cluster random sampling is more effective with larger numbers of clusters.

Let us consider another example of cluster random sampling. The superintendent of a large unified school district in a city on the East Coast wants to obtain some idea of how teachers in the district feel about merit pay. There are 10,000 teachers in all the elementary and secondary schools of the district, and there are 50 schools distributed over a large area. The superintendent does not have the funds to survey all teachers in the district, and he needs the information about merit pay quickly. Instead of randomly selecting a sample of teachers from every school, therefore, he decides to interview all the teachers in selected schools. The teachers in each school, then, constitute a cluster. The superintendent assigns a number to each school and then uses a table of random numbers to select 10 schools (20 percent of the population). All the teachers in the selected schools then constitute the sample. The interviewer questions all the teachers at each of these 10 schools, rather than having to travel to all the schools in the district. If these teachers do represent the remaining teachers in the district, then the superintendent is justified in drawing conclusions about the feelings of the entire population of teachers in his district about merit pay. It is possible that this sample is not representative, of course. Because the teachers to be interviewed all come from a small number of schools in the district, it might be the case that these schools differ in some ways from the other schools in the district, thereby influencing the views of the teachers in those schools with regard to merit pay. The more schools selected, the more likely the findings will be applicable to the population of teachers (Figure 6.3).

Cluster random sampling is similar to simple random sampling except that groups rather than individuals are randomly selected (i.e., the sampling unit is a group rather than an individual). The advantages of cluster random sampling are that it can be used when it is difficult or impossible to select a random sample of individuals, it is often far easier to implement in schools, and it is frequently less time-consuming. Its disadvantage is that there is a far greater chance of selecting a sample that is not representative of the population.

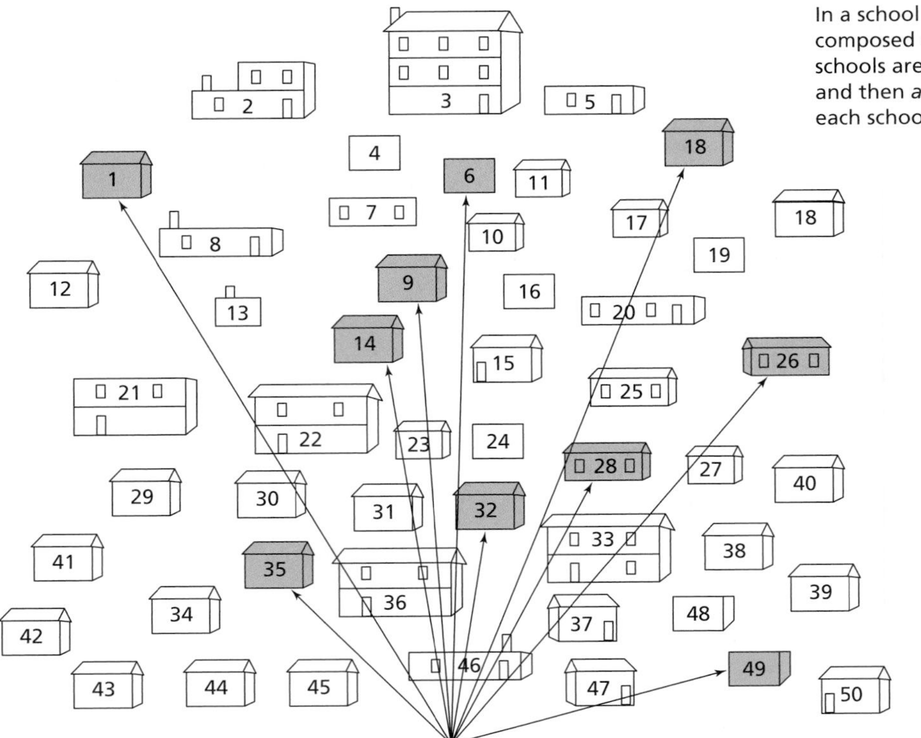

In a school district (population) composed of 50 schools, 10 schools are randomly selected, and then *all* of the teachers in each school are selected.
All teachers in the selected schools are interviewed

Figure 6.3 *Cluster Random Sampling*

Many beginning researchers make a common error with regard to cluster random sampling: randomly selecting only *one* cluster as a sample and then observing or interviewing all individuals within that cluster. Even if there are a large number of individuals within the cluster, it is the cluster that has been randomly selected, rather than individuals; hence the researcher is not entitled to draw conclusions about a target population of such individuals. Yet some researchers do draw such conclusions. We repeat, they should not.

TWO-STAGE RANDOM SAMPLING

It is often useful to combine cluster random sampling with individual random sampling. This is accomplished by **two-stage random sampling**. Rather than randomly selecting 100 students from a population of 3,000 ninth-graders located in 100 classes, the researcher might decide to select 25 classes randomly from the population of 100 classes and then randomly select 4 students from each class. This is much less time-consuming than visiting most of the 100 classes. Why would this be better than using all the students in four randomly selected classes? Because four classes would be too few to ensure representativeness, even though they were selected randomly.

Figure 6.4 illustrates the different random sampling methods we have discussed.

Nonrandom Sampling Methods

SYSTEMATIC SAMPLING

In **systematic sampling**, every *n*th individual in the population list is selected for inclusion in the sample. For example, in a population list of 5,000 names, to select a sample of 500, a researcher would select every tenth name on the list until reaching a total of 500 names. Here is an example of this type of sampling: The principal of a large middle school (grades 6–8) with 1,000 students wants to know how students feel about the new menu in the school cafeteria. She obtains an alphabetical list of all students in the school and selects every tenth student on the list to be in the sample. To guard against bias, she puts the numbers 1 to 10 into a hat and draws one out.

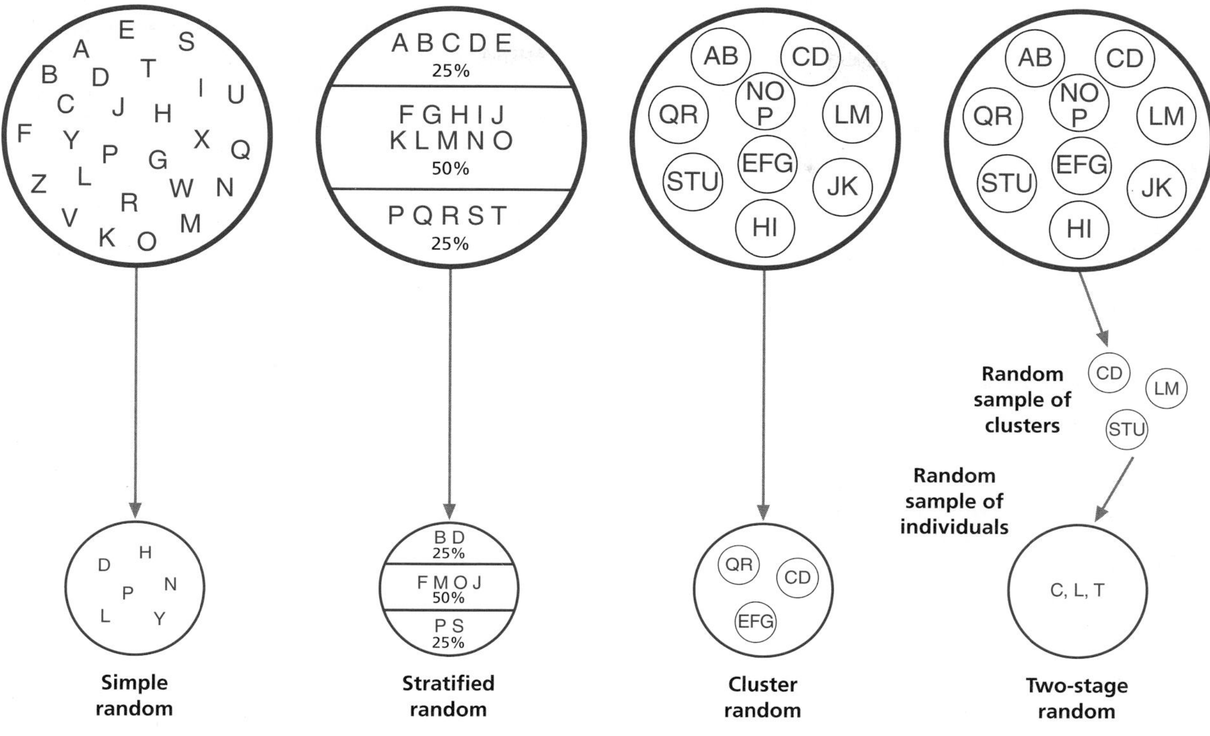

Figure 6.4 *Random Sampling Methods*

It is a 3. So she selects the students numbered 3, 13, 23, 33, 43, and so on until she has a sample of 100 students to be interviewed.

This method is technically known as systematic sampling with a **random start**. In addition, there are two terms that are frequently used when referring to systematic sampling. The **sampling interval** is the distance in the list between each of the individuals selected for the sample. In the example given, it was 10. A simple formula to determine it is:

$$\frac{\text{Population size}}{\text{Desired sample size}}$$

The **sampling ratio** is the proportion of individuals in the population that is selected for the sample. In the example, it was .10, or 10 percent. A simple way to determine the sampling ratio is:

$$\frac{\text{Sample size}}{\text{Population size}}$$

There is a danger in systematic sampling that is sometimes overlooked. If the population has been ordered systematically—that is, if the arrangement of individuals on the list is in some sort of pattern that accidentally coincides with the sampling interval—a markedly biased sample can result. This is sometimes called **periodicity**. Suppose that the middle school students in the preceding example had not been listed alphabetically but rather by homeroom and that the homeroom teachers had previously listed the students in their rooms by grade point average, high to low. That would mean that the better students would be at the top of each homeroom list. Suppose also that each homeroom had 30 students. If the principal began her selection of every tenth student with the first or second or third student on the list, her sample would consist of the better students in the school rather than a representation of the entire student body. (Do you see why? Because in each homeroom, the poorest students would be those who were numbered between 24 and 30, and they would never get chosen.)

When planning to select a sample from a list of some sort, therefore, researchers should carefully examine the list to make sure there is no cyclical pattern present. If the list has been arranged in a particular order, researchers should make sure the arrangement will not bias the sample in some way that could distort the results. If such seems to be the case, steps should be taken to ensure representativeness—for example, by randomly selecting individuals from each of the cyclical portions. In fact, if a population list is randomly ordered, a systematic sample drawn from the list is a random sample.

CONVENIENCE SAMPLING

Many times it is extremely difficult (sometimes even impossible) to select either a random or a systematic nonrandom sample. At such times, a researcher may use **convenience sampling**. A convenience sample is a group of individuals who (conveniently) are available for study (Figure 6.5). Thus, a researcher might decide to study two third-grade classes at a nearby elementary school because the principal asks for help in evaluating the effectiveness of a new spelling textbook. Here are examples of convenience samples:

- To find out how students feel about food service in the student union at an East Coast university, the manager stands outside the main door of the cafeteria one Monday morning and interviews the first 50 students who walk out of the cafeteria.
- A high school counselor interviews all the students who come to him for counseling about their career plans.
- A news reporter for a local television station asks passersby on a downtown street corner their opinions about plans to build a new baseball stadium in a nearby suburb.
- A university professor compares student reactions to two different textbooks in her statistics classes.

In each of these examples, a certain group of people was chosen for study because they were available. The obvious advantage of this type of sampling is convenience. But just as obviously, it has a major disadvantage in that the sample will quite likely be biased. Take the case of the TV reporter who is interviewing passersby on a downtown street corner. Many possible sources of bias

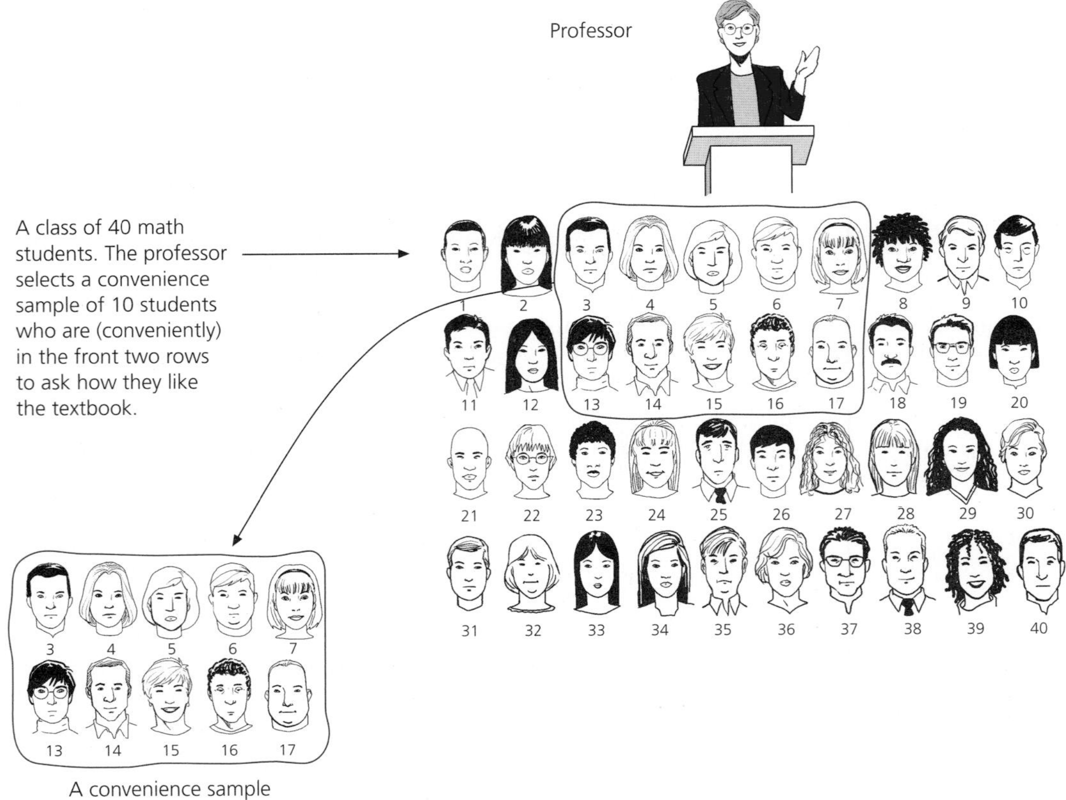

Figure 6.5 *Convenience Sampling*

exist. First of all, of course, anyone who is not downtown that day has no chance to be interviewed. Second, those individuals who are unwilling to give their views will not be interviewed. Third, those who agree to be interviewed will probably be individuals who hold strong opinions one way or the other about the stadium. Fourth, depending on the time of day, those who are interviewed quite possibly will be unemployed or have jobs that do not require them to be indoors. And so forth.

In general, convenience samples cannot be considered representative of any population and should be avoided if at all possible. Unfortunately, sometimes they are the only option a researcher has. When such is the case, the researcher should be especially careful to include information on demographic and other characteristics of the sample studied. The study should also be *replicated,* that is, repeated, with a number of similar samples to decrease the likelihood that the results obtained were simply a one-time occurrence. We will discuss replication in more depth later in the chapter.

PURPOSIVE SAMPLING

On occasion, based on previous knowledge of a population and the specific purpose of the research, investigators use personal judgment to select a sample. Researchers assume they can use their knowledge of the population to judge whether or not a particular sample will be representative. Here are some examples:

- An eighth-grade social studies teacher chooses the two students with the highest grade point averages in her class, the two whose grade point averages fall in the middle of the class, and the two with the lowest grade point averages to find out how her class feels about including a discussion of current events as a regular part of classroom activity. Similar samples in the past have represented the viewpoints of the total class quite accurately.
- A graduate student wants to know how retired people age 65 and over feel about their "golden years." He has been told by one of his professors, an expert on aging and the aged population, that the local Association of Retired Workers is a representative cross section of retired people age 65 and over. He decides to interview a sample of 50 people who are members of the association to get their views.

In both of these examples, previous information led the researcher to believe that the sample selected would be representative of the population. There is a second form of purposive sampling in which it is not expected that the persons chosen are themselves representative of the population, but rather that they possess the necessary information *about* the population. For example:

- A researcher is asked to identify the unofficial power hierarchy in a particular high school. She decides to interview the principal, the union representative, the principal's secretary, and the school custodian because she has prior information that leads her to believe they are the people who possess the information she needs.
- For the past five years, the leaders of the teachers' association in a midwestern school district have represented the views of three-fourths of the teachers in the district on most major issues. This year, therefore, the district administration decides to interview just the leaders of the association rather than select a sample from all the district's teachers.

Purposive sampling is different from convenience sampling in that researchers do not simply study whoever is available but rather use their judgment to select a sample that they believe, based on prior information, will provide the data they need. The major disadvantage of purposive sampling is that the researcher's judgment may be in error—he or she may not be correct in estimating the representativeness of a sample or their expertise regarding the information needed. In the second example, this year's leaders of the teachers' association may hold views markedly different from those of their members. Figure 6.6 illustrates the methods of convenience, purposive, and systematic sampling.

A Review of Sampling Methods

Let us illustrate each of the previous sampling methods using the same hypothesis: "Students with low self-esteem demonstrate lower achievement in school subjects."

Target population: All eighth-graders in California.

Accessible population: All eighth-graders in the San Francisco Bay Area (seven counties).

Feasible sample size: $n = 200$–250.

Simple random sampling: Identify all eighth-graders in all public and private schools in the seven counties (estimated number of eighth-grade students = 9,000). Assign each student a number, and then use a table of random numbers to select a sample of 200. The difficulty here is that it is time-consuming to identify every eighth-grader in the Bay Area and to contact (probably) about 200 different schools in order to administer instruments to one or two students in those schools.

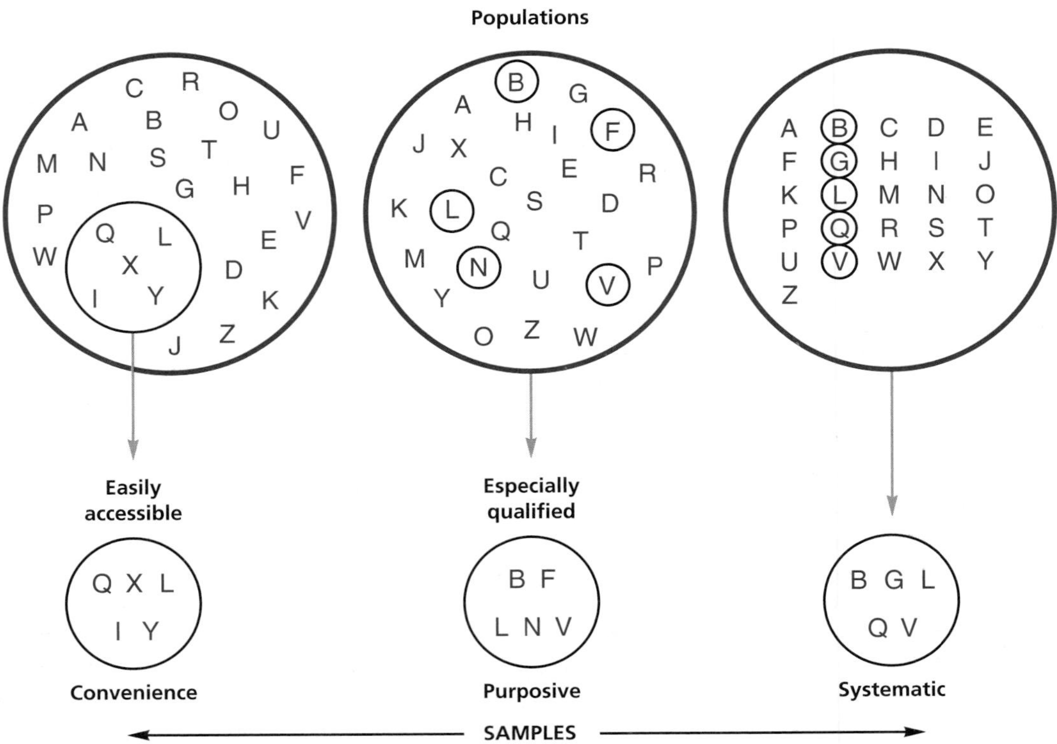

Figure 6.6 *Nonrandom Sampling Methods*

Cluster random sampling: Identify all public and private schools having an eighth grade in the seven counties. Assign each of the schools a number, and then randomly select four schools and include all eighth-grade classes in each school. (We would estimate 2 classes per school $\times$ 30 students per class $\times$ 4 schools = a total of 240 students.) Cluster random sampling is much more feasible than simple random sampling to implement, but it is limited because of the use of only four schools, even though they are to be selected randomly. For example, the selection of only four schools may exclude the selection of private-school students.

Stratified random sampling: Obtain data on the number of eighth-grade students in public versus private schools and determine the proportion of each type (e.g., 80 percent public, 20 percent private). Determine the number from each type to be sampled: public = 80 percent of 200 = 160; private = 20 percent of 200 = 40. Randomly select samples of 160 and 40 students from respective subpopulations of public and private students. Stratification may be used to ensure that the sample is representative on other variables as well. The difficulty with this method is that stratification requires that the researcher know the proportions in each stratum of the population, and it also becomes increasingly difficult as more variables are added. Imagine trying to stratify not only on the public-private variable but also (for example) on student ethnicity, gender, and socioeconomic status, and on teacher gender and experience.

Two-stage random sampling: Randomly select 25 schools from the accessible population of schools, and then randomly select eight eighth-grade students from each school ($n = 8 \times 25 = 200$). This method is much more feasible than simple random sampling and more representative than cluster sampling. It may well be the best choice in this example, but it still requires permission from 25 schools and the resources to collect data from each.

Convenience sampling: Select all eighth-graders in four schools to which the researcher has access (again, we estimate two classes of 30 students per school, so $n = 30 \times 4 \times 2 = 240$). This method precludes generalizing beyond these four schools,

CONTROVERSIES IN RESEARCH

Sample or Census?

Samples look at only part of the population. A *census* tries to look at the entire population. The U.S. Census Bureau, charged with conducting the U.S. Census every 10 years, estimated that the 2010 census missed 1.5 million minorities, most of whom are African Americans and Hispanics living in low-income, urban neighborhoods. The procedure for taking a census consists of sending out mailings and following up with door-to-door canvassing of nonrespondents.

Some statisticians have proposed augmenting the head-count by surveying a separate representative sample and using these data to estimate the size and demographics of nonrespondents. Supporters of the idea argue that this would provide a better picture of the population; opponents say that the assumptions involved, along with processing errors, would produce more error.

It can be argued that a sizable random sample of the entire population accompanied by more extensive follow-up would provide more accurate data than the current procedure at no greater expense, but this is precluded by the Constitution. (For more on this topic, search the Internet for national census sampling.)

unless a strong argument with supporting data can be made for their similarity to the entire group of accessible schools.

Purposive sampling: Select eight classes from throughout the seven counties on the basis of demographic data showing that they are representative of all eighth-graders. Particular attention must be paid to self-esteem and achievement scores. The problem is that such data are unlikely to be available and, in any case, cannot eliminate possible differences between the sample and the population on other variables—such as teacher attitude and available resources.

Systematic sampling: Select every 45th student from an alphabetical list for each school.

$$\frac{200 \text{ students in sample}}{9{,}000 \text{ students in population}} = \frac{1}{45}$$

This method is almost as inconvenient as simple random sampling and is likely to result in a biased sample, since the 45th name in each school is apt to be in the last third of the alphabet (remember there are an estimated 60 eighth-graders in each school), introducing probable ethnic or cultural bias.

Sample Size

Drawing conclusions about a population after studying a sample is never totally satisfactory, since researchers can never be sure that their sample is perfectly representative of the population. Some differences between the sample and the population are bound to exist, but if the sample is randomly selected and of sufficient size, these differences are likely to be relatively insignificant and incidental. The question remains, therefore, as to what constitutes an adequate, or sufficient, size for a sample.

Unfortunately, there is no clear-cut answer to this question. Suppose a target population consists of 1,000 eighth-graders in a given school district. Some sample sizes, of course, are obviously too small. Samples with 1 or 2 or 3 individuals, for example, are so small that they cannot possibly be representative. Probably any sample that has less than 20 to 30 individuals is too small, since that would only be 2 or 3 percent of the population. On the other hand, a sample can be too large, given the amount of time and effort the researcher must put into obtaining it. In this example, a sample of 250 or more individuals would probably be needlessly large, as that would constitute a quarter of the population. But what about samples of 50 or 100? Would these be sufficiently large? Would a sample of 200 be too large? At what point, exactly, does a sample stop being too small and become sufficiently large? The best answer is that a sample should be as large as the researcher can obtain with a reasonable expenditure of time and energy. This, of course, is not as much help as one would like, but it suggests that researchers should try to obtain as large a sample as they reasonably can.

There are a few guidelines that we would suggest with regard to the *minimum* number of subjects needed. For descriptive studies, we think a sample with a minimum number of 100 is essential. For correlational studies, a sample of at least 50 is deemed necessary to establish the existence of a relationship. For experimental and causal-comparative studies, we recommend a minimum of 30 individuals per group, although sometimes experimental studies with only 15 individuals in each group can

MORE ABOUT RESEARCH

The Difficulty in Generalizing from a Sample

In 1936 the *Literary Digest,* a popular magazine of the time, selected a sample of voters in the United States and asked them for whom they would vote in the upcoming presidential election—Alf Landon (Republican) or Franklin Roosevelt (Democrat). The magazine editors obtained a sample of 2,375,000 individuals from lists of automobile and telephone owners in the United States (about 20 percent returned the mailed postcards). On the basis of their findings, the editors predicted that Landon would win by a landslide. In fact, it was Roosevelt who won the landslide victory. What was wrong with the study?

Certainly not the size of the sample. The most frequent explanations have been that the data were collected too far ahead of the election and that *a lot* of people changed their minds, and/or that the sample of voters was heavily biased in favor of the more affluent, and/or that the 20 percent return rate introduced a major bias. What do you think?

A common misconception among beginning researchers is illustrated by the following statement: "Although I obtained a random sample only from schools in San Francisco, I am entitled to generalize my findings to the entire state of California because the San Francisco schools (and hence my sample) reflect a wide variety of socioeconomic levels, ethnic groups, and teaching styles." The statement is incorrect because variety is not the same thing as representativeness. For the San Francisco schools to be representative of all the schools in California, they must be very similar (ideally, identical) with respect to characteristics such as the ones mentioned. Ask yourself: Are the San Francisco schools representative of the entire state with regard to ethnic composition of students? The answer, of course, is that they are not.

be defended if they are very tightly controlled; studies using only 15 subjects per group should probably be replicated, however, before too much is made of any findings.* In qualitative studies, the number of participants in a sample is usually somewhere between 1 and 20.

External Validity: Generalizing from a Sample

As indicated earlier in this chapter, researchers generalize when they apply the findings of a particular study to people or settings that go beyond the particular people or settings used in the study. The whole notion of science is built on the idea of **generalizing**. Every science seeks to find basic principles or laws that can be applied to a great variety of situations and, in the case of the social sciences, to a great many people. Most researchers wish to generalize their findings to appropriate populations. But when is generalizing warranted? When can researchers say with confidence that what they have learned about a sample is also true of the population? Both the nature of the sample and the environmental conditions—the setting—within which a study takes place must be considered in thinking about generalizability. The extent to which the results of a study can be generalized determines the **external validity** of the study. In the next two chapters, we also discuss how the concept of validity is applied to instruments (instrument validity) and to the internal design of a study.

POPULATION GENERALIZABILITY

Population generalizability refers to the degree to which a sample represents the population of interest. If the results of a study only apply to the group being studied and if that group is fairly small or is narrowly defined, the usefulness of any findings is seriously limited. This is why trying to obtain a representative sample is so important. Because conducting a study takes a considerable amount of time, energy, and (frequently) money, researchers usually want the results of an investigation to be as widely applicable as possible.

When we speak of **representativeness**, however, we are referring only to the essential, or relevant, characteristics of a population. What do we mean by *relevant?* Only that the characteristics referred to might possibly be a contributing factor to any results that are obtained. For example, if a researcher wished to select a sample of first- and second-graders to study the effect of reading method on pupil achievement, such characteristics as height, eye color, or jumping ability would be judged to be irrelevant—that is, we would not expect any variation in them to have an effect on how easily a child learns to read, and hence we would not be overly concerned if those characteristics were not adequately represented in the sample.

*More specific guidelines are provided in the Research Tips box on page 234 in Chapter 11.

Other characteristics, such as age, gender, or visual acuity, on the other hand, might (logically) have an effect and hence should be appropriately represented in the sample.

Whenever purposive or convenience samples are used, generalization is made more plausible if data are presented to show that the sample is representative of the intended population on at least some relevant variables. This procedure, however, can never guarantee representativeness on all relevant variables.

One aspect of generalizability that is often overlooked in "methods" or "treatment" studies pertains to the teachers, counselors, administrators, or others who administer the various treatments. We must remember that such studies involve not only a sample of students, clients, or other recipients of the treatments but also a sample of those who implement the various treatments. Thus, a study that randomly selects students but not teachers is only entitled to generalize the outcomes to the population of students—*if* they are taught by the same teachers. To generalize the results to other teachers, the sample of teachers must also be selected randomly and must be sufficiently large.

Finally, we must remember that the sample in any study is the group about whom data are actually obtained. The best sampling plan is of no value if information is missing on a sizable portion of the initial sample. Once the sample has been selected, every effort must be made to ensure that the necessary data are obtained on each person in the sample. This is often difficult to do, particularly with questionnaire-type survey studies, but the results are well worth the time and energy expended. Unfortunately, there are no clear guidelines as to how many subjects can be lost before representativeness is seriously impaired. Any researchers who lose over 10 percent of the originally selected sample would be well advised to acknowledge this limitation and qualify their conclusions accordingly.

While most researchers seek to generalize their findings beyond the sample they have studied, qualitative researchers are unlikely to engage in statistical generalization in ways quantitative researchers try to do using randomly selected, representative samples. This process, also referred to as probability sampling, is uncommon in qualitative research, which relies more on nonrandom techniques such as purposive sampling (see Chapter 18 under "Sampling in Qualitative Research"). Rather than generalize from sample to population using statistical methods, qualitative researchers attempt to build theoretical claims through a process called *transferability*. Transferability refers to the generalization of a study's findings by the consumer—rather than the producer—of the research. In other words, the reader makes the transfer of information possible but only if the researcher provides ample details about the study participant(s) and setting. For more information on transferability, see Chapter 18 under "Generalization in Qualitative Research."

Do researchers always want to generalize? The only time researchers are not interested in generalizing beyond the confines of a particular study is when the results of an investigation are of interest only as applied to a particular group of people at a particular time, and where all of the members of the group are included in the study. An example might be the opinions of an elementary school faculty on a specific issue such as whether to implement a new math program. This might be of value to that faculty for decision making or program planning, but not to anyone else.

WHEN RANDOM SAMPLING IS NOT FEASIBLE

As we have shown, sometimes it is not feasible or even possible to obtain a random sample. When this is the case, researchers should describe the sample as thoroughly as possible (detailing, e.g., age, gender, ethnicity, and socioeconomic status) so that interested others can judge for themselves the degree to which any findings apply, and to whom and where. This is clearly an inferior procedure compared to random sampling, but sometimes it is the only alternative one has.

There is another possibility when a random sample is impossible to obtain: It is called **replication**. The researcher (or other researchers) repeats the study using different groups of subjects in different situations. If a study is repeated several times, using different groups of subjects and under different conditions of geography, socioeconomic level, ability, and so on, and if the results obtained are essentially the same in each case, a researcher may have additional confidence about generalizing the findings.

In the vast majority of studies that have been done in education, random samples have not been used. There seem to be two reasons for this. First, educational researchers may be unaware of the hazards involved in generalizing when one does not have a random sample. Second, in many studies it is simply not feasible for a researcher to invest the time, money, or other resources necessary to obtain a random sample. For the results of a particular study to be applicable to a larger group, then, the researcher must argue convincingly that the sample employed, even though not chosen randomly, is in fact representative of the target population. This is difficult, however, and always subject to contrary arguments.

ECOLOGICAL GENERALIZABILITY

Ecological generalizability refers to the degree to which the results of a study can be extended to other settings or conditions. Researchers must make clear the nature of the environmental conditions—the setting—under which a study takes place. These conditions must be the same in all important respects in any new situation in which researchers wish to assert that their findings apply. For example, it is not justifiable to generalize from studies on the effects of a new reading program on third-graders in a large urban school system to teaching mathematics, even to those students in that system. Research results from urban school environments may not apply to suburban or rural school environments; results obtained with transparencies may not apply to those with textbooks. What holds true for one subject, or with certain materials, or under certain conditions, or at certain times may not generalize to other subjects, materials, conditions, or times.

An example of inappropriate ecological generalizing would be in a study that found that a particular method of instruction applied to map reading resulted in greater transfer to general map interpretation on the part of fifth-graders in several schools. The researcher accordingly might recommend that the method of instruction be used in other content areas, such as mathematics and science, overlooking differences in content, materials, and skills involved, in addition to probable differences in resources, teacher experience, and the like. Improper ecological generalizing such as this remains the bane of much educational research.

Unfortunately, application of the powerful technique of random sampling is virtually never possible with respect to ecological generalizing. While it is conceivable that a researcher could identify "populations" of organization patterns, materials, classroom conditions, and so on, and then randomly select a sizable number of combinations from all possible combinations, the logistics of doing so boggle the mind. Therefore, researchers must be cautious about generalizing the results from any one study. Only when outcomes have been shown to be similar through replication across specific environmental conditions can we generalize across those conditions. Figure 6.7 illustrates the difference between population and ecological generalizing.

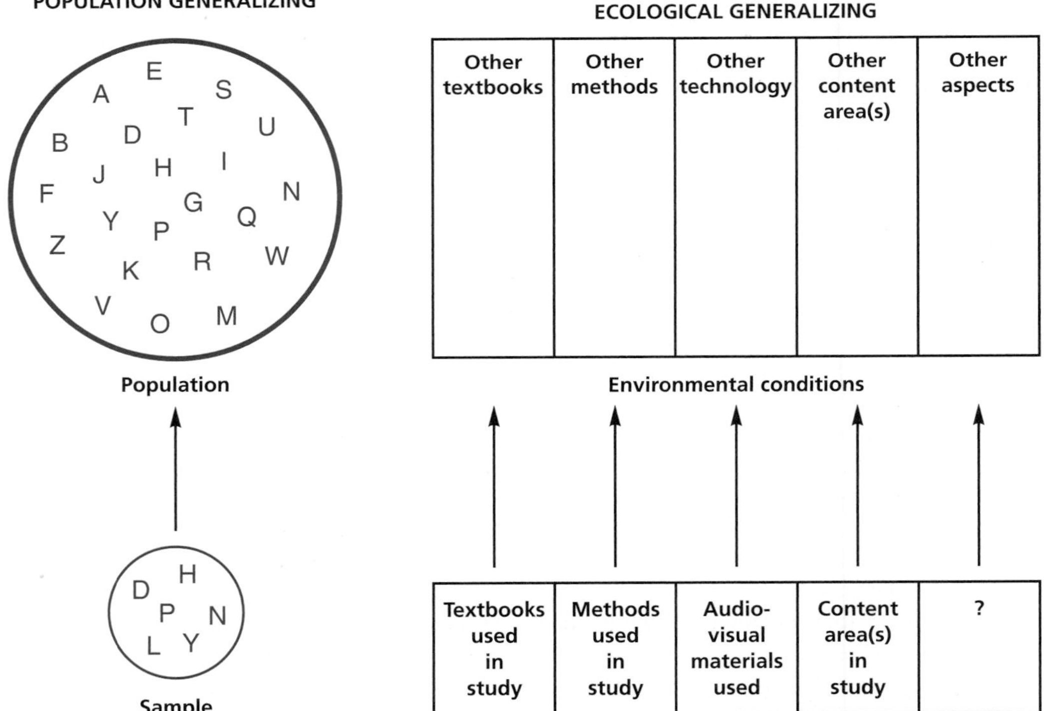

Figure 6.7 *Population as Opposed to Ecological Generalizing*

Go back to the **INTERACTIVE AND APPLIED LEARNING** feature at the beginning of the chapter for a listing of interactive and applied activities. Go to the **Online Learning Center** at **www.mhhe.com/fraenkel9e** to take quizzes, practice with key terms, and review chapter content.

Main Points

SAMPLES AND SAMPLING

- The term *sampling,* as used in research, refers to the process of selecting the individuals who will participate (e.g., be observed or questioned) in a research study.
- A sample is any part of a population of individuals on whom information is obtained. It may, for a variety of reasons, be different from the sample originally selected.

SAMPLES AND POPULATIONS

- The term *population,* as used in research, refers to all the members of a particular group. It is the group of interest to the researcher, the group to whom the researcher would like to generalize the results of a study.
- A target population is the actual population to whom the researcher would like to generalize; the accessible population is the population to whom the researcher is entitled to generalize.
- A representative sample is a sample that is similar to the population on all characteristics.

RANDOM VERSUS NONRANDOM SAMPLING

- Sampling may be either random or nonrandom. Random sampling methods include simple random sampling, stratified random sampling, cluster random sampling, and two-stage random sampling. Nonrandom sampling methods include systematic sampling, convenience sampling, and purposive sampling.

RANDOM SAMPLING METHODS

- A simple random sample is a sample selected from a population in such a manner that all members of the population have an equal chance of being selected.
- A stratified random sample is a sample selected so that certain characteristics are represented in the sample in the same proportion as they occur in the population.
- A cluster random sample is one obtained by using groups as the sampling unit rather than individuals.
- A two-stage random sample selects groups randomly and then chooses individuals randomly from these groups.
- A table of random numbers lists and arranges numbers in no particular order and can be used to select a random sample.

NONRANDOM SAMPLING METHODS

- A systematic sample is obtained by selecting every *n*th name in a population.
- A convenience sample is any group of individuals that is conveniently available to be studied.
- A purposive sample consists of individuals who have special qualifications of some sort or are deemed representative on the basis of prior evidence.

SAMPLE SIZE

- Samples should be as large as a researcher can obtain with a reasonable expenditure of time and energy. A recommended minimum number of subjects is 100 for a descriptive study, 50 for a correlational study, and 30 in each group for experimental and causal-comparative studies.

EXTERNAL VALIDITY (GENERALIZABILITY)

- The term *external validity,* as used in research, refers to the extent that the results of a study can be generalized from a sample to a population.
- The term *population generalizability* refers to the extent to which the results of a study can be generalized to the intended population.
- The term *ecological generalizability* refers to the extent to which the results of a study can be generalized to conditions or settings other than those that prevailed in a particular study.

REPLICATION

- When a study is replicated, it is repeated with a new sample and sometimes under new conditions.

Key Terms

accessible population 93
cluster random sampling 97
convenience sampling 100
ecological generalizability 106
external validity 104
generalizing 104
nonrandom sampling 95
periodicity 99
population 92
population generalizability 104
purposive sampling 101
random sampling 94
random start 99
replication 105
representativeness 104
sample 92
sampling 92
sampling interval 99
sampling ratio 99
simple random sample 95
stratified random sampling 96
systematic sampling 98
table of random numbers 95
target population 93
two-stage random sampling 98

For Discussion

1. A team of researchers wants to determine student attitudes about the recreational services available in the student union on campus. The team stops the first 100 students it meets on a street in the middle of the campus and asks each of them questions about the union. What are some possible ways that this sample might be biased?

2. Suppose a researcher is interested in studying the effects of music on learning. He obtains permission from a nearby elementary school principal to use the two third-grade classes in the school. The ability level of the two classes, as shown by standardized tests, grade point averages, and faculty opinion, is quite similar. In one class, the researcher plays classical music softly every day for a semester. In the other class, no music is played. At the end of the semester, he finds that the class in which the music was played has a markedly higher average in arithmetic than the other class, although they do not differ in any other respect. To what population (if any) might the results of this study be generalized? What, exactly, could the researcher say about the effects of music on learning?
3. When, if ever, might a researcher not be interested in generalizing the results of a study? Explain.
4. "The larger a sample, the more justified a researcher is in generalizing from it to a population." Is this statement true? Why or why not?
5. Some people have argued that no population can ever be studied in its entirety. Would you agree? Why or why not?
6. "The more narrowly researchers define the population, the more they limit generalizability." Is this always true? Discuss.
7. "The best sampling plan is of no value if information is missing on a sizable proportion of the initial sample." Why is this so? Discuss.
8. "The use of random sampling is almost never possible with respect to ecological generalizing." Why is this so? Can you think of a possible study for which ecological generalizing would be possible? If so, give an example.

Research Exercise 6: Sampling Plan

Use Problem Sheet 6 to describe, as fully as you can, your sample—that is, the subjects you will include in your study. Describe the type of sample you plan to use and how you will obtain the sample. Indicate whether you expect your study to have population generalizability. If so, to what population? if not, why not? Then indicate whether the study would have ecological generalizability. If so, to what settings? if not, why would it not?

Problem Sheet 6

Sampling Plan

1. My research question is: ______________________________

____

2. My intended sample (participants in your study) consists of (*state who and how many*): ______________________________

____

3. Key demographics (characteristics of the sample) are as follows (e.g., age range, sex distribution, ethnic breakdown, socioeconomic status, location [where are these subjects located?]): ______________________________

____

4. State what type of sample you plan to use (i.e., convenience, purposive, simple random, stratified random, cluster, systematic). ______________________________

____

5. I will gain access to and/or get contact information for my sample through the following steps: ______________________________

____

6. What, if any, are the inclusion/exclusion criteria for participation in your study?

____

7. External validity:

   a. To whom do you think you can generalize the results of your study? Explain.

   ____

   b. If applicable, to what settings/conditions could you generalize the results of your study (ecological validity)?

   ____

   c. If results are not generalizable, why not?

   ____

An electronic version of this Problem Sheet that you can fill in and print, save, or e-mail is available on the Online Learning Center at www.mhhe.com/fraenkel9e.

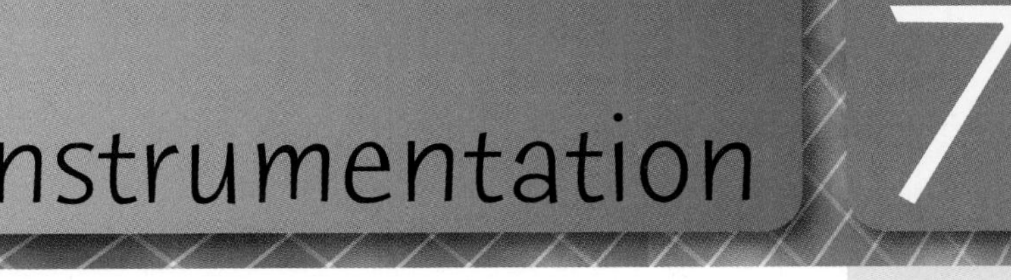

7 Instrumentation

What Are Data?

Key Questions

Validity, Reliability, and Objectivity

Usability

Means of Classifying Data-Collection Instruments

Who Provides the Information?

Where Did the Instrument Come From?

Written Response Versus Performance

Examples of Data-Collection Instruments

Researcher-Completed Instruments

Subject-Completed Instruments

Unobtrusive Measures

Norm-Referenced Versus Criterion-Referenced Instruments

Norm-Referenced Instruments

Criterion-Referenced Instruments

Measurement Scales

Nominal Scales

Ordinal Scales

Interval Scales

Ratio Scales

Measurement Scales Reconsidered

Preparing Data for Analysis

Scoring the Data

Tabulating and Coding the Data

OBJECTIVES Studying this chapter should enable you to:

- Explain what is meant by the term "data."
- Explain what is meant by the term "instrumentation."
- Name three ways in which data can be collected by researchers.
- Explain what is meant by the term "data-collection instrument."
- Describe five types of researcher-completed instruments used in educational research.
- Describe five types of subject-completed instruments used in educational research.
- Explain what is meant by the term "unobtrusive measures" and give two examples of such measures.
- Name four types of measurement scales and give an example of each.
- Name three different types of scores used in educational research and give an example of each.
- Describe briefly the difference between norm-referenced and criterion-referenced instruments.
- Describe briefly how to score, tabulate, and code data for analysis.

INTERACTIVE AND APPLIED LEARNING After, or while, reading this chapter:

Go to the Online Learning Center at www.mhhe.com/fraenkel9e to:

- Learn More About Developing Instruments

Go to your online Student Mastery Activities book to do the following activities:

- Activity 7.1: Major Categories of Instruments and Their Uses
- Activity 7.2: Which Type of Instrument Is Most Appropriate?
- Activity 7.3: Types of Scales
- Activity 7.4: Norm-Referenced vs. Criterion-Referenced Instruments
- Activity 7.5: Developing a Rating Scale
- Activity 7.6: Design an Instrument

Monica Stuart and Ben Colen are discussing last night's lecture in their educational research class.

"I must admit that I was pretty impressed," says Monica.

"How come?"

"That list of measuring instruments Professor Fraenkel described last night. Questionnaires, rating scales, true-false tests, sociograms, logs, anecdotal records, tally sheets, . . . It just went on and on. I never knew there were so many ways to measure something—so many measuring devices. And what he said about measurement—that really impressed me! Remember? He said that if something exists, you can measure it!"

"Yeah, it was quite a feat," says Ben. "I have to admit that. I don't know about the idea that everything can be measured, though. What about something that is very abstract?"

"Like what?"

"Well, how about, say, alienation? or motivation? How would you measure them? I'm not sure they even *can* be measured!"

"Well, here's what I'd do," says Monica. "I would . . ."

How would *you* measure motivation? Do instruments exist that could measure something this abstract? To get some ideas, read this chapter.

What Are Data?

The term **data** refers to the kinds of information researchers obtain on the subjects of their research. Demographic information, such as age, gender, ethnicity, religion, and so on, is one kind of data; scores from a commercially available or researcher-prepared test are another. Responses to the researcher's questions in an oral interview or written replies to a survey questionnaire are other kinds. Essays written by students, grade-point averages obtained from school records, performance logs kept by coaches, anecdotal records maintained by teachers or counselors—all constitute various kinds of data that researchers might want to collect as part of a research investigation. An important decision for every researcher to make during the planning phase of an investigation, therefore, is what kind(s) of data he or she intends to collect. The device (such as a pencil-and-paper test, a questionnaire, or a rating scale) the researcher uses to collect data is called an *instrument.**

KEY QUESTIONS

Generally, the whole process of preparing to collect data is called **instrumentation**. It involves not only

*Most, but not all, research requires the use of an instrument. In studies where data are obtained exclusively from existing records (grades, attendance, etc.), no instrument is needed.

the selection or design of the instruments but also the *procedures and the conditions* under which the instruments will be administered. Several questions arise:

1. *Where* will the data be collected? This question refers to the *location* of the data collection. Where will it be? in a classroom? a schoolyard? a private home? on the street?
2. *When* will the data be collected? This question refers to the *time* of collection. When is it to take place? in the morning? afternoon? evening? over a weekend?
3. *How often* are the data to be collected? This question refers to the *frequency* of collection. How many times are the data to be collected? only once? twice? more than twice?
4. *Who* is to collect the data? This question refers to the *administration* of the instruments. Who is to do this? the researcher? someone selected and trained by the researcher?

These questions are important because how researchers answer them may affect the data obtained. It is a mistake to think that researchers need only locate or develop a "good" instrument. The data provided by any instrument may be affected by any or all of the preceding considerations. The most highly regarded of instruments will provide useless data, for instance, if administered incorrectly; by someone disliked by respondents; under noisy, inhospitable conditions; or when subjects are exhausted.

All these questions are important for researchers to answer, therefore, *before* they begin to collect the data they need. A researcher's decisions about location, time, frequency, and administration are always affected by the kind(s) of instrument to be used. And for it to be of any value, every instrument, no matter what kind, must allow researchers to draw accurate conclusions about the capabilities or other characteristics of the people being studied.

VALIDITY, RELIABILITY, AND OBJECTIVITY

A frequently used (but somewhat old-fashioned) definition of a valid instrument is that it measures what it is supposed to measure. A more accurate definition of **validity** revolves around the defensibility of the inferences researchers make from the data collected through the use of an instrument. An instrument, after all, is a device used to gather data. Researchers then use these data to make inferences about the characteristics of certain individuals.* But to be of any use, these inferences must be correct. All researchers, therefore, want instruments that permit them to draw warranted, or valid, conclusions about the characteristics (ability, achievement, attitudes, and so on) of the individuals they study.

To measure math achievement, for example, a researcher needs to have some assurance that the instrument she intends to use actually does measure such achievement. Another researcher who wants to know what people think or how they feel about a particular topic needs assurance that the instrument used will allow him to make accurate inferences. There are various ways to obtain such assurance, and we discuss them in Chapter 8.

A second consideration is **reliability**. A reliable instrument is one that gives consistent results. If a researcher tested the math achievement of a group of individuals at two or more different times, for example, he or she should expect to obtain close to the same results each time. This consistency would give the researcher confidence that the results actually represented the achievement of the individuals involved. As with validity, a number of procedures can be used to determine the reliability of an instrument. We discuss several of them in Chapter 8.

A final consideration is objectivity. **Objectivity** refers to the absence of subjective judgments. Whenever possible, researchers should try to eliminate subjectivity from the judgments they make about the achievement, performance, or characteristics of subjects. Unfortunately, complete objectivity is probably never attained. Acknowledging this, qualitative researchers openly seek ways to address subjectivity in their research studies to minimize bias and maximize validity.

We discuss each of these concepts in much more detail in Chapter 8. In this chapter, we look at some of the various kinds of instruments that can be (and often are) used in research and discuss how to find and select them.

USABILITY

A number of practical considerations face every researcher. One of these is how easy it will be to use any instrument he or she designs or selects. How long will it take to administer? Are the directions clear? Is it appropriate for the ethnic or other groups to whom

*Sometimes instruments are used to collect data on something other than individuals (such as groups, programs, and environments), but since most of the time we are concerned with individuals in educational research, we use this terminology throughout our discussion.

it will be administered? How easy is it to score? Are the results easy to interpret? How much does it cost? Do equivalent forms exist? Have any problems been reported by others who used it? Does evidence of its reliability and validity exist? Getting satisfactory answers to such questions can save a researcher a lot of time and energy and can prevent a lot of headaches.

Means of Classifying Data-Collection Instruments

Instruments can be classified in a number of ways. Here are some of the most useful.

WHO PROVIDES THE INFORMATION?

In educational research, three general methods are available for obtaining information. Researchers can get the information (1) themselves, with little or no involvement of other people; (2) directly from the subjects of the study; or (3) from others, frequently referred to as **informants**, who are knowledgeable about the subjects. Let us follow a specific example. A researcher wishes to test the hypothesis that inquiry teaching in history classes results in higher-level thinking than does the lecture method. The researcher may elect option 1, in which case she may observe students in the classroom, noting the frequency of oral statements indicative of higher-level thinking. Or, she may examine existing student records that may include test results and/or anecdotal material she considers indicative of higher-level thinking. If she elects option 2, the researcher is likely to administer tests or request student products (essays, problem sheets) for evidence. She may also decide to interview students using questions designed to reveal their thinking about history (or other topics). Finally, if the researcher chooses option 3, she is likely to interview persons (teachers, other students) or ask them to fill out rating scales in which the interviewees assess each student's thinking skills based on their prior experience with the student. Examples of each type of method are:

1. *Researcher instruments*
   - A researcher interested in learning and memory development counts the number of times it takes different nursery school children to learn to navigate their way correctly through a maze located in their school playground. He records his findings on a **tally sheet**.
   - A researcher interested in the concept of mutual attraction describes in ongoing *field notes* how the behaviors of people who work together in various settings have been observed to differ on this variable.
2. *Subject instruments*
   - A researcher in an elementary school administers a *weekly spelling* test that requires students to spell correctly the new words learned in class during the week.
   - At a researcher's request, an administrator passes out a **questionnaire** during a faculty meeting that asks the faculty's opinions about the new mathematics curriculum recently instituted in the district.
   - A researcher asks high school English teachers to have their students keep a *daily log* in which they record their reactions to the plays they read each week.
3. *Informant instruments*
   - A researcher asks teachers to use a *rating scale* to rate each of their students on their phonic reading skills.
   - A researcher asks parents to keep *anecdotal records* describing the TV characters their preschoolers spontaneously role-play.
   - A researcher interviews the president of the student council about student views on the school's disciplinary code. Her responses are recorded on an *interview schedule*.

WHERE DID THE INSTRUMENT COME FROM?

There are essentially two basic ways for a researcher to acquire an instrument: (1) find and administer a previously existing instrument of some sort or (2) administer an instrument the researcher personally developed or had developed by someone else.

Developing an instrument has its problems. Primarily, it is not easy to do. Developing a "good" instrument usually takes a fair amount of time and effort, not to mention a considerable amount of skill.

Selecting an already developed instrument when appropriate, therefore, is preferred. Such instruments are usually developed by experts who possess the necessary skills. Choosing an instrument that has already been developed takes far less time than developing a new instrument to measure the same thing.

Designing one's own instrument is time-consuming, and we do not recommend it for those without a considerable amount of time, energy, and money to invest in the

RESEARCH TIPS

Some Tips About Developing Your Own Instrument

1. Be sure you are clear about what variables are to be assessed. Much time and effort can be wasted by definitions that are too ambiguous. If more than one variable is involved, be sure that both the meaning and the items for each variable are kept distinct. In general, a particular item or question should be used for only one variable.
2. Review existing instruments that measure similar variables to decide upon a format and to obtain ideas on specific items.
3. Decide on a format for each variable. Although it is sometimes appropriate to mix multiple-choice, true-false, matching, rating, and open-ended items, doing so complicates scoring and is usually undesirable. Remember: Different variables often require different formats.
4. Begin compiling and/or writing items. Be sure that, in your judgment, each is logically valid—that is, that the item is consistent with the definition of the variable. Try to ensure that the vocabulary is appropriate for the intended respondents.
5. Have colleagues review the items for logical validity. Supply colleagues with a copy of your definitions and a description of the intended respondents. Be sure to have them evaluate format as well as content.
6. Revise items based on colleague feedback. At this point, try to have about twice as many items as you intend to use in the final form (generally at least 20). Remember that more items generally provide higher reliability.
7. Locate a group of people with experience appropriate to your study. Have them review your items for logical validity. Make any revisions needed, and complete your items. You should have half again as many items as intended in the final form.
8. Try out your instrument with a group of respondents who are as similar as possible to your study respondents. Have them complete the instrument, and then discuss it with them, to the extent that this is feasible, given their age, sophistication, and so forth.
9. If feasible, conduct a statistical item analysis with your tryout data (at least 20 respondents are necessary). Such analyses are not difficult to carry out, especially if you have a computer. The information provided on each item indicates how effective it is and sometimes even suggests how to improve it. See, for example, Murphy, K. R., & Davidshofer, C. O. (1991). *Psychological testing: Principles and applications.* Englewood Cliffs, NJ: Prentice Hall.
10. Select and revise items as necessary until you have the number you want.

endeavor. Fortunately, a number of already developed, useful instruments exist, and they can be located quite easily online. A comprehensive listing of testing resources can be found by accessing the ERIC database: http://eric.ed.gov (Figure 7.1).

As an example, we typed the phrase (using quotes) "social studies" and the word *instruments* in the box labeled "Search Terms." This produced a list of 765 documents. As this was far too many to peruse, we changed the search terms to "social studies" *competency-based instruments.* This produced a much more manageable list of five references as shown in Figure 7.2. We clicked #1 "Social Studies. Competency-Based Education Assessment Series" to obtain a description of the instrument (Figure 7.3), as well as a full-text PDF file of the document including the instrument itself and scoring guide.

Almost any topic can be searched in this way to obtain a list of instruments that measure or assess some aspect of the topic. In general, an electronic file containing the instrument can be downloaded immediately or obtained from the ERIC Document Reproduction Service.

ERIC's test collection currently includes more than 9,000 instruments of various types. Several years ago ERIC underwent considerable changes. The clearinghouses were closed in early 2004, and in September 2004 a new website was introduced that provides users with markedly improved search capabilities that utilize more efficient retrieval methods to access the ERIC database (1966–present). In October 2004 free full-text nonjournal ERIC resources were introduced, including over 100,000 full-text documents. Users can now refine their search results through the use of the ERIC thesaurus and various ERIC identifiers. For example, search results in ERIC can now be limited to publications that contain instruments like tests and questionnaires (check it out!).

To get information on a preexisting instrument's use, validity, and reliability, reviews are available through

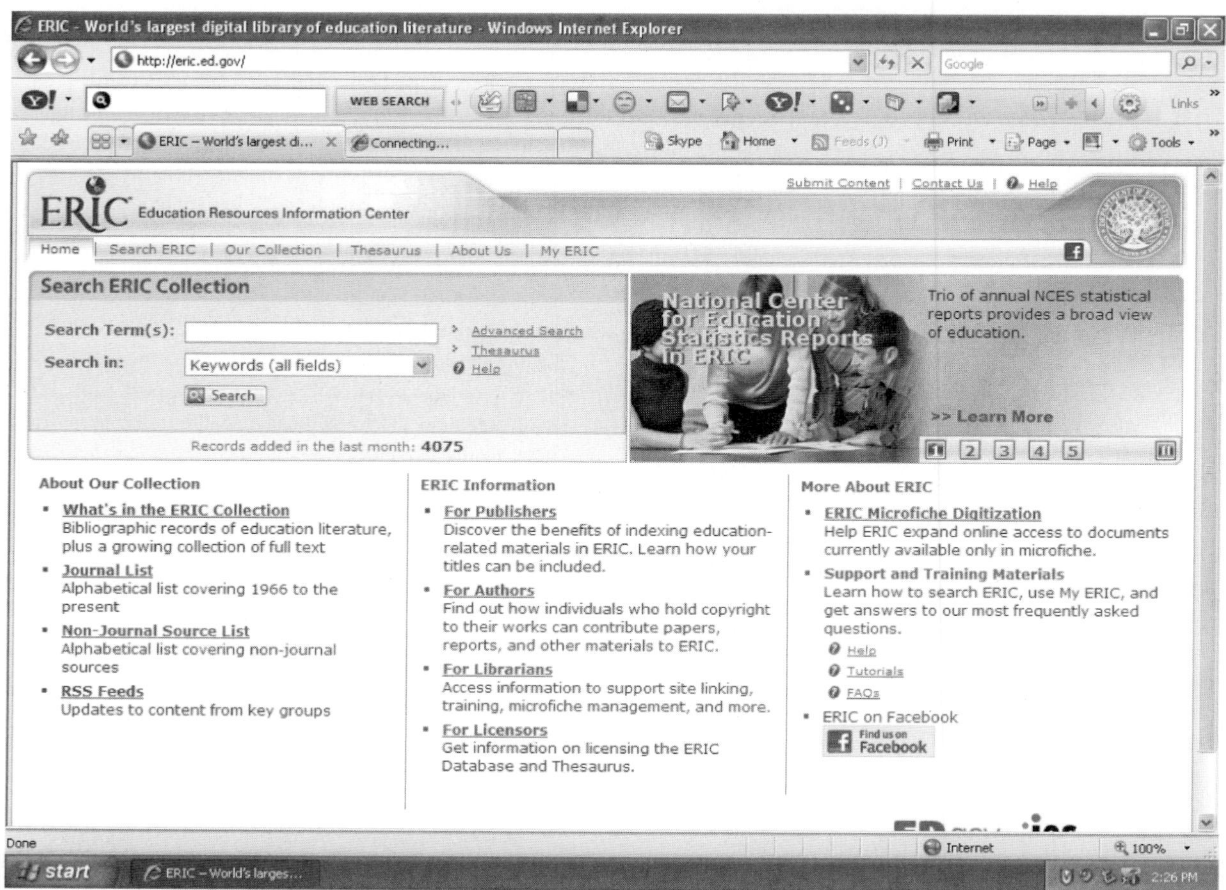

Figure 7.1 *ERIC Database of Tests and Assessments*

The Mental Measurements Yearbooks and *Tests in Print,* both produced by the Buros Institute at the University of Nebraska.* The yearbooks are published periodically with supplements produced between issues. Each yearbook provides reviews of the standardized tests that have been published since the last issue. The institute's *Tests in Print* is a comprehensive bibliography of commercial tests. Unfortunately, only the references to the instruments and reviews of them are available online; the actual instruments themselves are available only in print/paper form from the publisher.

With so many instruments now available to the research community, we recommend that, except in unusual cases, researchers devote their energies to adapting (and/or improving) those that now exist rather than trying to start from scratch to develop entire new measures.

*So named for Oscar Buros, who started the yearbooks back in 1938.

Here are some useful Internet resources that include test locator services, advice on how to select and evaluate a test, published instrument reviews, information on fair testing practices, and connections to several searchable databases that may be useful to researchers looking for specific test information.

The ERIC Clearinghouse on Assessment and Evaluation (http://ericae.net): ERIC/AE is an Internet test locator service provided collaboratively by ERIC, the Educational Testing Service (ETS), the Buros Institute, and Pro-Ed Publishing.

ERIC/ETS Test Collection Test File (www.ets.org/testcoll): The ERIC/ETS Test Collection Test File, a joint project of ERIC and the ETS, contains records on over 9,500 tests and research instruments.

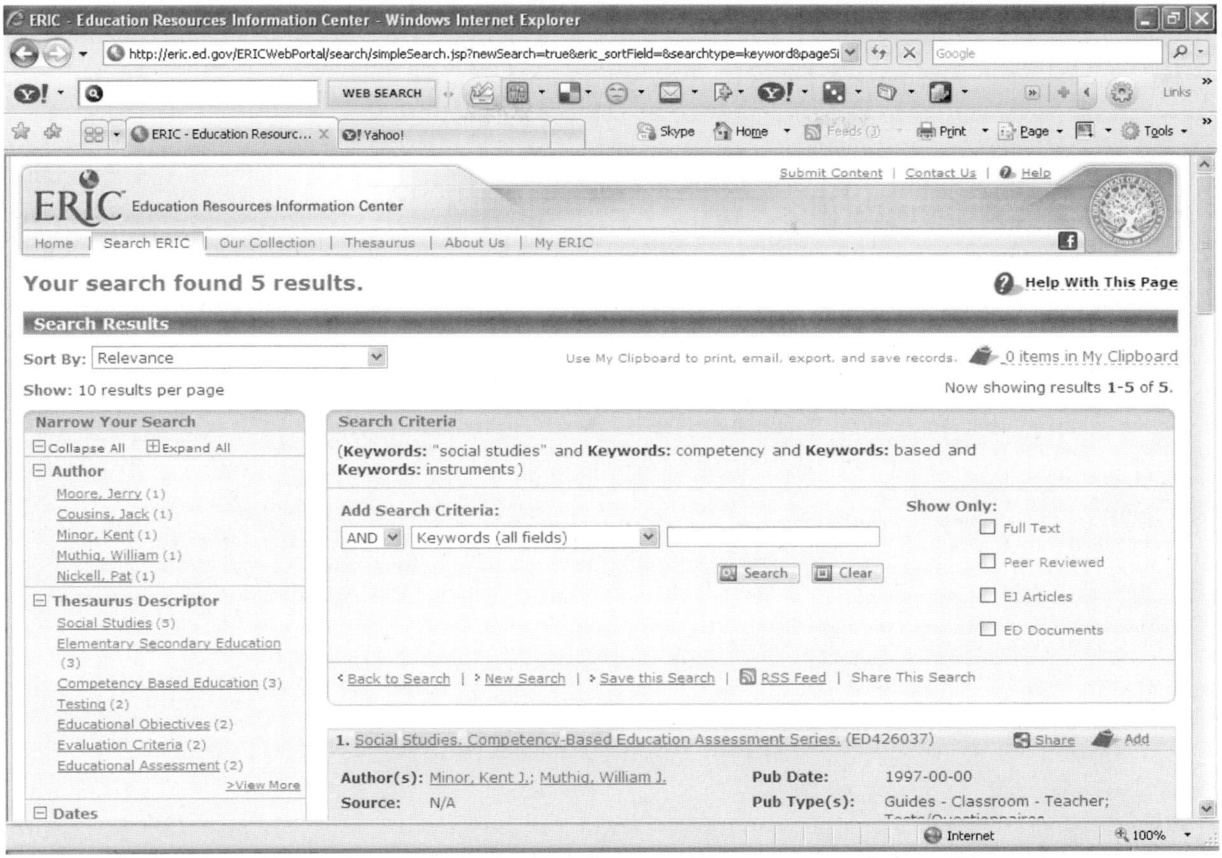

Figure 7.2 *Search Results for Social Studies Competency-Based Instruments*

The Buros Test Review Locator (http://buros.unl.edu/buros/jsp/search.jsp): Provides evaluations of tests and over 4,000 commercially available instruments.

WRITTEN RESPONSE VERSUS PERFORMANCE

Another way to classify instruments is in terms of whether they require a written or marked response from subjects or a more general evaluation of subjects' performance. **Written-response instruments** include objective (e.g., multiple-choice, true-false, matching, or short-answer) tests, short-essay examinations, questionnaires, interview schedules, rating scales, and checklists. **Performance instruments** include any device designed to measure either a procedure or a product. *Procedures* are ways of doing things, such as mixing a chemical solution, diagnosing a problem in an automobile, writing a letter, solving a puzzle, or setting the margins on a typewriter. *Products* are the end results of procedures, such as the correct chemical solution, the correct diagnosis of auto malfunction, or a properly typed letter. Performance instruments are designed to see whether and how well procedures can be followed and to assess the quality of products.

Written-response instruments are generally preferred over performance instruments, since the use of the latter is frequently quite time-consuming and often requires equipment or other resources that are not readily available. A large amount of time would be required to have even a fairly small sample of students (imagine 35!) complete the steps involved in a high school science experiment.

Examples of Data-Collection Instruments

When it comes to *administering* the instruments to be used in a study, either the researchers (or their assistants or other informants) must do it themselves, or they must

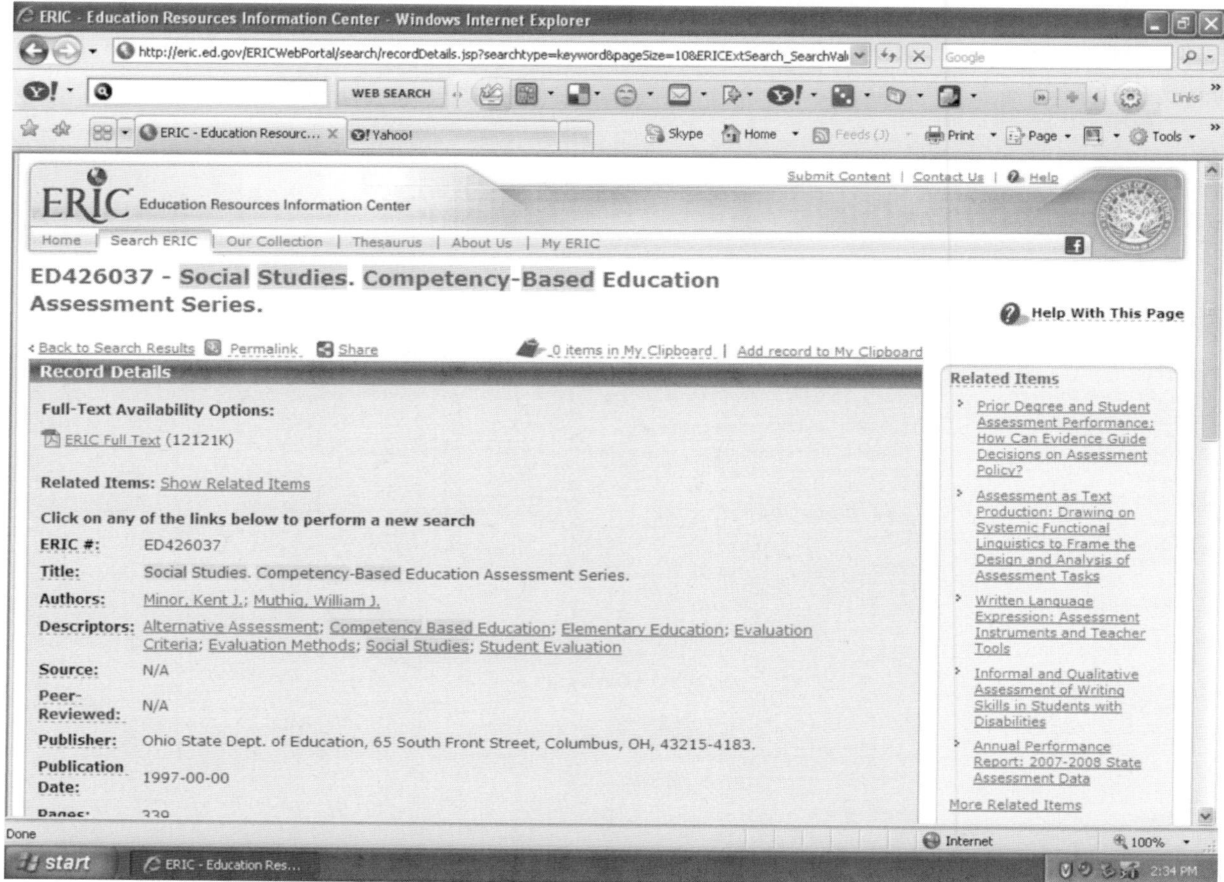

Figure 7.3 *Abstract from the ERIC Database*

Source: From ERIC (Educator Resources Information Center). Reprinted by permission of the U.S. Department of Education, operated by Computer Sciences Corporation. www.eric.ed.gov

ask the subjects of the study to provide the information desired. Therefore, we group the instruments in the following discussion according to whether they are completed by researchers or by subjects. Examples of these instruments include:

Researcher completes:	**Subject completes:**
Rating scales	Questionnaires
Interview schedules	Self-checklists
Observation forms	Attitude scales
Tally sheets	Personality (or character) inventories
Flowcharts	Achievement/aptitude tests
Performance checklists	Performance tests
Anecdotal records	Projective devices
Time-and-motion logs	Sociometric devices

This distinction, of course, is by no means absolute. Many of the instruments we list might, on a given occasion, be completed by either the researcher(s) or subjects in a particular study.

In most qualitative studies, however, the researcher serves as the primary data collection instrument (we discuss this idea in Chapter 18 under "Generalization in Qualitative Research" and also Chapter 19, "Observation and Interviewing"). Qualitative data collection tools that use open-ended items such as interview, focus group, and observational protocol yield data that are interpreted by the researcher, making them researcher-completed instruments. In general, qualitative researchers believe a researcher's worldview, or theoretical framework, greatly influences how research studies are designed and their results interpreted (see Chapter 18, "Philosophical Assumptions Underlying Qualitative as Opposed to Quantitative Research").

RESEARCHER-COMPLETED INSTRUMENTS

Rating Scales. A rating is a measured judgment of some sort. When we rate people, we make a judgment about their behavior or something they have produced. Thus, both behaviors (such as how well a person gives an oral report) and products (such as a written copy of a report) of individuals can be rated.

Notice that the terms *observations* and *ratings* are not synonymous. A rating is intended to convey the rater's judgment about an individual's behavior or product. An observation is intended merely to indicate whether a particular behavior is present or absent (see the time-and-motion log in Figure 7.13 on p. 126). Sometimes, of course, researchers may do both. The activities of a small group engaging in a discussion, for example, can be both observed and rated.

Behavior Rating Scales. Behavior rating scales appear in several forms, but those most commonly used ask the observer to circle or mark a point on a continuum to indicate the rating. The simplest of these to construct is a *numerical rating scale,* which provides a series of numbers, each representing a particular rating.

Figure 7.4 shows such a scale designed to rate teachers. The problem with this rating scale is that different observers are quite likely to have different ideas about the meaning of the terms that the numbers represent (*excellent, average,* etc.). In other words, the different rating points on the scale are not described fully enough. The same individual, therefore, might be rated quite differently by two different observers. One way to address this problem is to give additional meaning to each number by describing it more fully. For example, in Figure 7.4, the rating 5 could be defined as "among the top 5 percent of all teachers you have had." In the absence of such definitions, the researcher must either rely on the training of the respondents or treat the ratings as subjective opinions.

Instructions: For each of the behaviors listed below, circle the appropriate number, using the following key: 5 = Excellent, 4 = Above Average, 3 = Average, 2 = Below Average, 1 = Poor.

A. Explains course material clearly

1 2 3 4 5

B. Establishes rapport with students

1 2 3 4 5

C. Asks high-level questions

1 2 3 4 5

D. Varies class activities

1 2 3 4 5

Figure 7.4 *Excerpt from a Behavior Rating Scale for Teachers*

The *graphic rating scale* is an attempt to improve on the vagueness of numerical rating scales. It describes each of the characteristics to be rated and places them on a horizontal line on which the observer is to place a check mark. Figure 7.5 presents an example of a graphic rating scale. Here again, this scale would be improved by adding definitions, such as defining *always* as "95 to 100 percent of the time," and *frequently* as "70 to 94 percent of the time."

Product Rating Scales. As we mentioned earlier, researchers may wish to rate products. Examples of products that are frequently rated in education are book reports, maps and charts, diagrams, drawings, notebooks,

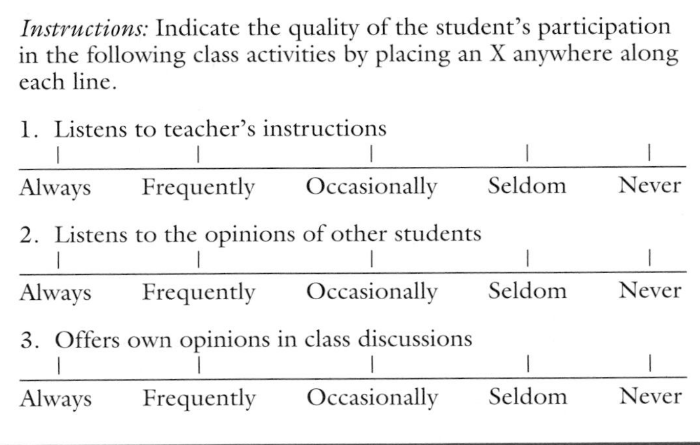
Instructions: Indicate the quality of the student's participation in the following class activities by placing an X anywhere along each line.

1. Listens to teacher's instructions

Always | Frequently | Occasionally | Seldom | Never

2. Listens to the opinions of other students

Always | Frequently | Occasionally | Seldom | Never

3. Offers own opinions in class discussions

Always | Frequently | Occasionally | Seldom | Never

Figure 7.5 *Excerpt from a Graphic Rating Scale*

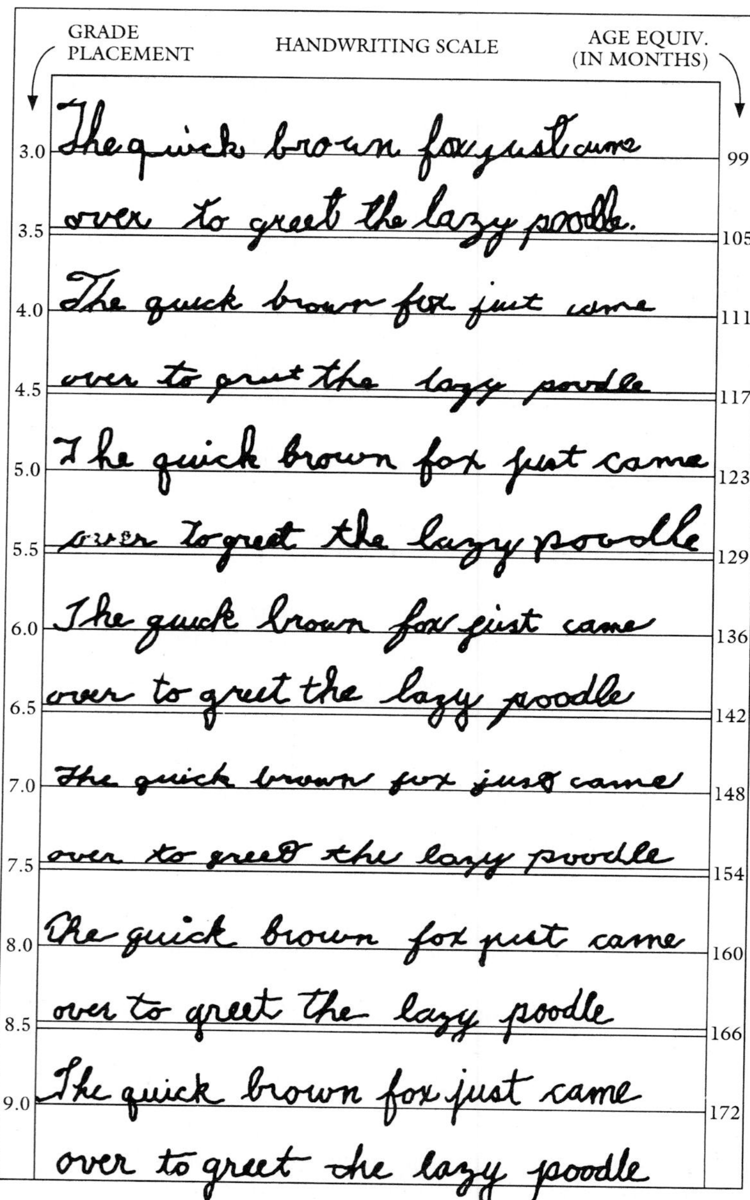

Figure 7.6 *Example of a Product Rating Scale*

Source: Handwriting scale used in the California Achievement Tests, Form W (1957), CTB/McGraw-Hill, Monterey, CA. Copyright © 1957 by McGraw-Hill.

essays, and creative endeavors of all sorts. Whereas behavior ratings must be done at a particular time (when the researcher can observe the behavior), a big advantage of product ratings is that they can be done at any time.* Figure 7.6 presents an example of a scale rating the product "handwriting." To use this scale, an actual sample of the student's handwriting is obtained. It is then moved along the scale until the quality of the handwriting in the sample is most similar to the example shown on the scale. Although nearly 60 years old, it remains a classic example of this type of instrument.

*Some behavior rating scales are designed to assess behavior over a period of time—for example, how frequently a teacher asks high-level thought questions.

Interview Protocol. **Interview protocol** involves basically the same kind of instrument as a questionnaire—a set of questions to be answered by the subjects of the study. There are some important differences in how interviews and questionnaires are administered, however. Interviews are conducted orally, either in person or over the phone, and the answers to the questions are recorded by the researcher (or someone he or she has trained). The advantages of this instrument are that the interviewer can clarify any questions that are obscure and also can ask the respondent to expand on answers that are particularly important or revealing. A big disadvantage, however, is that it takes much longer than the questionnaire to complete. Furthermore, the presence of the researcher may inhibit respondents from saying what they really think. Establishing a comfortable rapport with participants is an important first step in the interview process.

Figure 7.7 illustrates a structured interview schedule. Notice that this interview schedule requires the interviewers to do considerable writing, unless the interview is taped. Some interview schedules phrase questions so that the responses are likely to fall in certain categories. This is sometimes call *precoding.* Precoding enables the interviewer to check appropriate items rather than transcribe responses, thus preventing the respondent from having to wait while the interviewer records a response.

Figure 7.8 shows an example of a semi-structured, qualitative interview protocol used in a dissertation study of African American community college students who transferred successfully to a four-year institution. Notice how the interviewer uses "probes" throughout

1. Would you rate pupil academic learning as excellent, good, fair, or poor?
   a. If you were here last year, how would you compare pupil academic learning to previous years?
   b. Please give specific examples.
2. Would you rate pupil attitude toward school generally as excellent, good, fair, or poor?
   a. If you were here last year, how would you compare pupil attitude toward school generally to previous years?
   b. Please give specific examples.
3. Would you rate pupil attitude toward learning as excellent, good, fair, or poor?
   a. If you were here last year, how would you compare attitude toward learning to previous years?
   b. Please give specific examples.
4. Would you rate pupil attitude toward self as excellent, good, fair, or poor?
   a. If you were here last year, how would you compare pupil attitude toward self to previous years?
   b. Please give specific examples.
5. Would you rate pupil attitude toward other students as excellent, good, fair, or poor?
   a. If you were here last year, how would you compare attitude toward other students to previous years?
   b. Please give specific examples.
6. Would you rate pupil attitude toward you as excellent, good, fair, or poor?
   a. If you were here last year, how would you compare pupil attitude toward you to previous years?
   b. Please give specific examples.
7. Would you rate pupil creativity–self-expression as excellent, good, fair, or poor?
   a. If you were here last year, how would you compare pupil creativity–self-expression to previous years?
   b. Please give specific examples.

Figure 7.7 *Interview Schedule (for Teachers) Designed to Assess the Effects of a Competency-Based Curriculum in Inner-City Schools*

Figure 7.8 *Semi-Structured Interview Protocol*

1. What people or services were the most beneficial to you for transferring to State University (SU) from your Community College (CC)?
2. Why do you think you were successful? (*Probe*: Tell me how you achieved your goal.)
3. Did anyone give you personal support or strength at your CC that helped you to transfer to SU? (*Probe*: Can you tell me about the person you think helped you the most to achieve your goal of transferring to SU? What did that person say or do that helped you?)
4. What did you struggle with as you prepared to transfer? What were some of the major obstacles? (*Probe*: Thinking back, can you recall a really tough experience or day you had when you thought you weren't going to succeed? Tell me about it.)
5. If you could talk to an administrator or faculty member at the CC you attended, what would you say to them about your transfer process, and how could it be improved to help other African American students like you?

the interview protocol to draw out the participant. *Probes* are improvised questions that depend on the answer given by the interviewee.

Observation Forms. Paper-and-pencil observation forms (sometimes called *observation schedules*) are fairly easy to construct. A sample of such a form is shown in Figure 7.9. As you can see, the form requires the observer not only to record certain behaviors but also to evaluate some as they occur.

Initially, observation forms should always be used on a trial basis in situations similar to those to be observed in order to work out any bugs or ambiguities. A frequent weakness in many observation forms is that they ask the observer to record more behaviors than can be done accurately (or to watch too many individuals at the same time). As is frequently the case, the simpler the instrument, the better.

Tally Sheets. A tally sheet is a device often used by researchers to record the frequency of student behaviors, activities, or remarks. How many high school students follow instructions during fire drills, for example? How many instances of aggression or helpfulness do elementary students exhibit on the playground? How often do students in Mr. Jordan's fifth-period U.S. history class

Figure 7.9 *Sample Observation Form*

Directions:

1. Place a check mark each time the teacher:

		Frequency
a. asks individual students a question	✓ ✓ ✓ ✓ ✓ ✓	6
b. asks questions to the class as a whole	✓ ✓	2
c. disciplines students	✓	1
d. asks for quiet	✓ ✓ ✓	3
e. asks students if they have any questions	✓	1
f. sends students to the chalkboard	✓ ✓	2

2. Place a check mark each time the teacher asks a question that requires:

		Frequency
a. memory or recall of information	✓ ✓ ✓ ✓ ✓	5
b. comparison	✓ ✓	2
c. an inference	✓ ✓ ✓	3
d. a generalization		0
e. specific application	✓	1

ask questions? How often do they ask inferential questions? Tally sheets can help researchers record answers to these kinds of questions efficiently.

A tally sheet is simply a listing of various categories of activities or behaviors on a piece of paper. Every time a subject is observed engaging in one of these activities or behaviors, the researcher places a tally in the appropriate category. The kinds of statements that students make in class, for example, often indicate the degree to which they understand various concepts and ideas. The possible category systems that might be devised are probably endless, but Figure 7.10 presents one example.

Flowcharts. A particular type of tally sheet is the participation flowchart. Flowcharts are particularly helpful in analyzing class discussions. Both the number and direction of student remarks can be charted to gain some idea of the quantity and focus of students' verbal participation in class.

One of the easiest ways to do this is to prepare a seating chart on which a box is drawn for each student in the class being observed. A tally is then placed in the box of a particular student each time he or she makes a verbal comment. To indicate the direction of individual student comments, arrows can be drawn from the box of a student making a comment to the box of the student to whom the comment is directed. Figure 7.11 illustrates what such a flowchart might look like. This chart suggests that Robert, Felix, and Mercedes dominated the discussion, with contributions from Al, Gail, Jack, and Sam. Joe and Nancy said nothing. Note that a subsequent discussion, or a different topic, however, might reveal a quite different pattern.

Performance Checklists. One of the most frequently used of all measuring instruments is the checklist. A performance checklist consists of a list of behaviors that make up a certain type of performance (using a microscope, typing a letter, solving a mathematics problem, and so on). It is used to determine whether an individual behaves in a certain (usually desired) way when asked to complete a particular task.

Type of Remark		
1. Asks question calling for factual information	Related to lesson	𝍸
	Not related to lesson	𝍷
2. Asks question calling for clarification	Related to lesson	𝍸 𝍷𝍷
	Not related to lesson	
3. Asks question calling for explanation	Related to lesson	𝍸 𝍷𝍷𝍷
	Not related to lesson	
4. Asks question calling for speculation	Related to lesson	𝍷
	Not related to lesson	
5. Asks question of another student	Related to lesson	𝍷
	Not related to lesson	𝍷𝍷
6. Gives own opinion on issue	Related to lesson	𝍷
	Not related to lesson	𝍷𝍷𝍷
7. Responds to another student	Related to lesson	
	Not related to lesson	𝍷𝍷𝍷𝍷
8. Summarizes remarks of another student	Related to lesson	
	Not related to lesson	
9. Does not respond when addressed by teacher	Related to lesson	
	Not related to lesson	𝍷𝍷
10. Does not respond when addressed by another student	Related to lesson	𝍷
	Not related to lesson	

Figure 7.10 *Discussion-Analysis Tally Sheet*

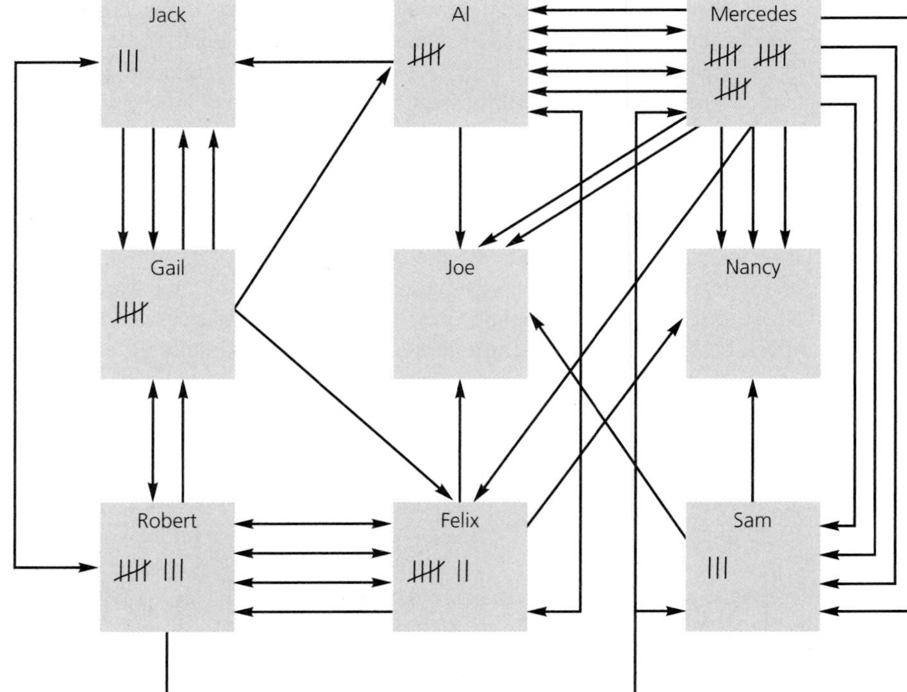

Figure 7.11 *Participation Flowchart*

Source: Adapted from Sawin, E. I. (1969, p. 179). *Evaluation and the work of the teacher.* Belmont, CA: Wadsworth. Reprinted by permission of Sage Publishers, Inc.

If a particular behavior is present when an individual is observed, the researcher places a check mark opposite it on the list.

Figure 7.12 presents part of a performance checklist developed more than 80 years ago to assess a student's skill in using a microscope. Note that the items on this checklist (as any well-constructed checklist should) ask the observer to indicate only *if* the desired behaviors take place. No subjective judgments are called for on the part of the observer as to how well the individual performs. Items that call for such judgments are best left to rating scales.

Anecdotal Records. Another way of recording the behavior of individuals is the anecdotal record. It is just what its name implies—a record of observed behaviors written down in the form of anecdotes. There is no set format; rather, observers are free to record any behavior they think is important and need not focus on the same behavior for all subjects. To produce the most useful records, however, observers should try to be as specific and as factual as possible and to avoid evaluative, interpretive, or overly generalized remarks. The American Council on Education describes four types of anecdotes, stating that the first three are to be avoided. Only the fourth type is desired.

1. Anecdotes that evaluate or judge the behavior of the child as good or bad, desirable or undesirable, acceptable or unacceptable . . . *evaluative statements* (to be avoided).
2. Anecdotes that account for or explain the child's behavior, usually on the basis of a single fact or thesis . . . *interpretive statements* (to be avoided).
3. Anecdotes that describe certain behavior in general terms, as happening frequently, or as characterizing the child . . . *generalized statements* (to be avoided).
4. Anecdotes that tell exactly what the child did or said, that describe concretely the situation in which the action or comment occurred, and that tell clearly what other persons also did or said . . . *specific or concrete descriptive statements* (the type desired).[1]

Here are examples of each of the four types:

Evaluative: Julius talked loud and much during poetry; wanted to do and say just what he wanted and didn't consider the right working out of things. Had to ask him to sit by me. Showed a bad attitude about it.

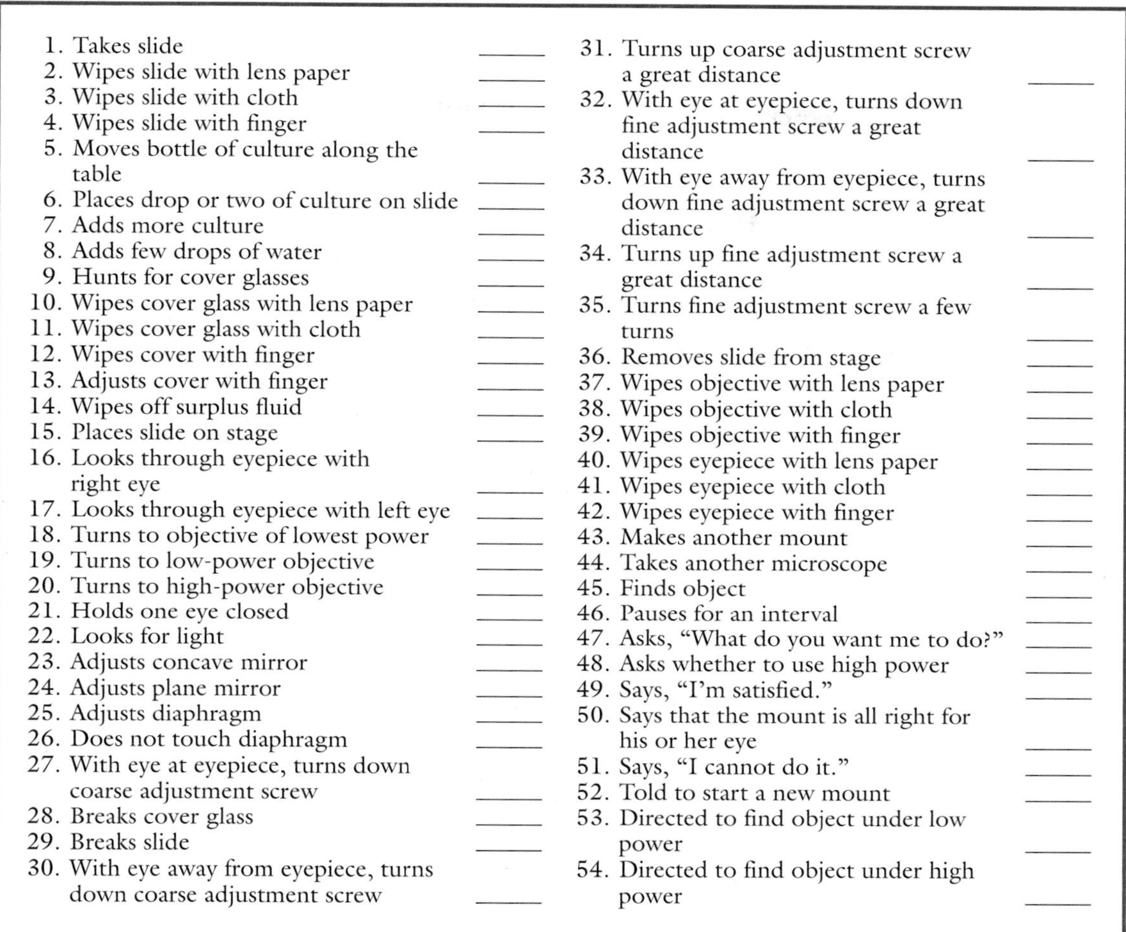

1. Takes slide	______	31. Turns up coarse adjustment screw a great distance	______
2. Wipes slide with lens paper	______	32. With eye at eyepiece, turns down fine adjustment screw a great distance	______
3. Wipes slide with cloth	______	33. With eye away from eyepiece, turns down fine adjustment screw a great distance	______
4. Wipes slide with finger	______	34. Turns up fine adjustment screw a great distance	______
5. Moves bottle of culture along the table	______	35. Turns fine adjustment screw a few turns	______
6. Places drop or two of culture on slide	______	36. Removes slide from stage	______
7. Adds more culture	______	37. Wipes objective with lens paper	______
8. Adds few drops of water	______	38. Wipes objective with cloth	______
9. Hunts for cover glasses	______	39. Wipes objective with finger	______
10. Wipes cover glass with lens paper	______	40. Wipes eyepiece with lens paper	______
11. Wipes cover glass with cloth	______	41. Wipes eyepiece with cloth	______
12. Wipes cover with finger	______	42. Wipes eyepiece with finger	______
13. Adjusts cover with finger	______	43. Makes another mount	______
14. Wipes off surplus fluid	______	44. Takes another microscope	______
15. Places slide on stage	______	45. Finds object	______
16. Looks through eyepiece with right eye	______	46. Pauses for an interval	______
17. Looks through eyepiece with left eye	______	47. Asks, "What do you want me to do?"	______
18. Turns to objective of lowest power	______	48. Asks whether to use high power	______
19. Turns to low-power objective	______	49. Says, "I'm satisfied."	______
20. Turns to high-power objective	______	50. Says that the mount is all right for his or her eye	______
21. Holds one eye closed	______	51. Says, "I cannot do it."	______
22. Looks for light	______	52. Told to start a new mount	______
23. Adjusts concave mirror	______	53. Directed to find object under low power	______
24. Adjusts plane mirror	______	54. Directed to find object under high power	______
25. Adjusts diaphragm	______		
26. Does not touch diaphragm	______		
27. With eye at eyepiece, turns down coarse adjustment screw	______		
28. Breaks cover glass	______		
29. Breaks slide	______		
30. With eye away from eyepiece, turns down coarse adjustment screw	______		

Figure 7.12 *Performance Checklist Noting Student Actions*

Source: Educational Research Bulletin (1922–61) by R. W. Tyler. Copyright 1930 by Ohio State University, College of Education. Reproduced with permission of Ohio State University, College of Education in the format Textbook via Copyright Clearance Center.

Interpretive: For the last week Sammy has been a perfect wiggle-tail. He is growing so fast he cannot be settled. . . . Of course the inward change that is taking place causes the restlessness.

Generalized: Sammy is awfully restless these days. He is whispering most of the time he is not kept busy. In the circle, during various discussions, even though he is interested, his arms are moving or he is punching the one sitting next to him. He smiles when I speak to him.

Specific (the type desired): The weather was so bitterly cold that we did not go on the playground today. The children played games in the room during the regular recess period. Andrew and Larry chose sides for a game which is known as stealing the bacon. I was talking to a group of children in the front of the room while the choosing was in process and in a moment I heard a loud altercation. Larry said that all the children wanted to be on Andrew's side rather than on his. Andrew remarked, "I can't help it if they all want to be on my side."[1]

Time-and-Motion Logs. There are occasions when researchers want to make a very detailed observation of an individual or a group. This is often the case, for example, when trying to identify the reasons underlying a particular problem or difficulty that an individual

Time	Activity
11:32	Stacked paper
	Picked up pencil
	Wrote name
	Moved paper closer
	Continued with reading
	Rubbed nose
	Looked at Art's paper
	Started to work . . .
11:45	Worked and watched
	Made funny faces
	Giggled. Looked at Lorrie and smiled
	Borrowed Art's paper
	Erased
	Stacked paper
	Read
	Slid paper around
	Worked briefly
	Picked up paper and read
	Thumb in mouth, watched Miss D
11:47	Worked and watched
	Made funny face
	Giggled. Looked and smiled at Lorrie
	Paper up—read
	Picked eye
	Studied bulletin board
	Paper down—read again
	Fidgeted with paper
	Played with pencil and fingers
	Watched me
	Watched L.
	Laughed at her
	Erased
	Hand up
	Laughed. Watched D.
	Got help
11:50	Looked at Lorrie
	Tapped fingers on desk
	Wrote
	Slid down in desk
	Hand to head, listened to D. helping Lorrie
	Blew breath out hard
	Fidgeted with paper
	Looked at other group
	Held chin
	Watched Charles
	Read, hands holding head
	Erased
	Watched other group, chin on hand
	Made faces—yawned—fidgeted
	Held head
	Read, pointing to words
	Wrote
	Put head on arm on desk
	Held chin
	Read
	Rubbed eye
11:55	Wrote

Figure 7.13 *Time-and-Motion Log*

Source: Hilda Taba (1957). Problem identification. In ASCD 1957 Yearbook: *Research for Curriculum Improvement,* pp. 60–61. © 1957 ASCD. Used with permission. The Association for Supervision and Curriculum Development is a worldwide community of educators advocating sound policies and sharing best practices to achieve the success of each learner. To learn more, visit ASCD at www.ascd.org.

or class is having (working very slowly, failing to complete assigned tasks, inattentiveness, and so on).

A time-and-motion study is the observation and detailed recording over a given period of time of the activities of one or more individuals (e.g., during a 15-minute laboratory demonstration). Observers try to record everything an individual does as objectively as possible and at brief, regular intervals (such as every 3 minutes, with a 1-minute break interspersed between intervals).

The late Hilda Taba, a pioneer in educational evaluation, once cited an example of a fourth-grade teacher who believed that her class's considerable slowness was due to the fact that they were extremely meticulous in their work. To check this out, she decided to conduct a detailed time-and-motion study of one typical student. The results of her study indicated that this student, rather than being overly meticulous, was actually unable to focus his attention on a particular task for any concerted period of time. Figure 7.13 illustrates what she observed.

SUBJECT-COMPLETED INSTRUMENTS

Questionnaires. The interview schedule shown in Figure 7.7 on page 121 could be used as a questionnaire. In a questionnaire, the subjects respond to the questions by writing or, more commonly, by marking an answer sheet. Advantages of questionnaires are that they can be mailed or given to large numbers of people at the same time. The disadvantages are that unclear or seemingly ambiguous questions cannot be clarified, and the respondent has no chance to expand on or react verbally to a question of particular interest or importance. For more information on electronic questionnaires and Web-based survey providers like SurveyMonkey, see Chapter 17.

Selection items on questionnaires include multiple-choice, true-false, matching, or interpretive-exercise questions. Supply items include short-answer or essay questions. We'll give some examples of each of these types of items when we discuss achievement tests later in the chapter.

Self-Checklists. A self-checklist is a list of several characteristics or activities presented to the subjects of a study. The individuals are asked to study the list and then to place a mark opposite the characteristics they possess or the activities in which they have engaged for a particular length of time. Self-checklists are often used when researchers want students to diagnose or to appraise their own performance. One example of a self-checklist for use with elementary school students is shown in Figure 7.14.

Attitude Scales. The basic assumption that underlies all attitude scales is that it is possible to discover attitudes by asking individuals to respond to a series of statements of preference. Thus, if individuals agree with the statement, "A course in philosophy should be required of all candidates for a teaching credential," researchers infer that these students have a positive attitude toward such a course (assuming students understand the meaning of the statement and are sincere in their responses). An attitude scale, therefore, consists of a set of statements to which an individual responds. The pattern of responses is then viewed as evidence of one or more underlying attitudes.

Attitude scales are often similar to rating scales in form, with words and numbers placed on a continuum. Subjects circle the word or number that best represents how they feel about the topics included in the questions or statements in the scale. A commonly used attitude scale in educational research is the **Likert scale**, named

Date ________________ Name ______________________________

Instructions: Place a check (✓) in the space provided for those days, during the past week, when you have participated in the activity listed. Circle the activity if you feel you need to participate in it more frequently in the weeks to come.

	Mon	Tues	Wed	Thurs	Fri
1. I participated in class discussions.	✓	✓	✓		
2. I did not interrupt others while they were speaking.	✓	✓	✓	✓	✓
3. I encouraged others to offer their opinions.		✓			✓
4. I listened to what others had to say.	✓	✓	✓		✓
5. I helped others when asked.				✓	
6. I asked questions when I was unclear about what had been said.		✓		✓	
7. I looked up words in the dictionary that I did not know how to spell.					✓
8. I considered the suggestions of others.	✓	✓	✓		
9. I tried to be helpful in my remarks.	✓	✓		✓	
10. I praised others when I thought they did a good job.					✓

Figure 7.14 *Example of a Self-Checklist*

Figure 7.15 *Examples of Items from a Likert Scale Measuring Attitude Toward Teacher Empowerment*

Instructions: Circle the choice after each statement that indicates your opinion.

1. All professors of education should be required to spend at least six months teaching at the elementary or secondary level every five years.

Strongly agree	Agree	Undecided	Disagree	Strongly disagree
(5)	(4)	(3)	(2)	(1)

2. Teachers' unions should be abolished.

Strongly agree	Agree	Undecided	Disagree	Strongly disagree
(1)	(2)	(3)	(4)	(5)

3. All school administrators should be required by law to teach at least one class in a public school classroom every year.

Strongly agree	Agree	Undecided	Disagree	Strongly disagree
(5)	(4)	(3)	(2)	(1)

after the man who designed it.[2] Figure 7.15 presents a few examples from a Likert scale. On some items, a 5 (strongly agree) will indicate a positive attitude and be scored 5. On other items, a 1 (strongly disagree) will indicate a positive attitude and be scored 5 (thus, the ends of the scale are reversed when scoring), as shown in item 2 in Figure 7.15.

A unique sort of attitude scale that is especially useful for classroom research is the **semantic differential**.[3] It allows a researcher to measure a subject's attitude toward a particular concept. Subjects are presented with a continuum of several pairs of adjectives (*good-bad, cold-hot, priceless-worthless,* and so on) and asked to place a check mark between each pair to indicate their attitudes. Figure 7.16 presents an example.

A scale that has particular value for determining the attitudes of young children uses simply drawn faces. When the subjects of an attitude study are primary school children or younger, they can be asked to place an X under a face, such as the ones shown in Figure 7.17, to indicate how they feel about a topic.

The subject of attitude scales is discussed rather extensively in the literature on evaluation and test development, and students interested in a more extended treatment should consult a standard textbook on these subjects.[4]

Personality (or Character) Inventories. Personality inventories are designed to measure certain traits of individuals or to assess their feelings about themselves. Examples of such inventories include the Minnesota Multiphasic Personality Inventory, the IPAT Anxiety Scale, the Piers-Harris Children's Self-Concept Scale (How I Feel About Myself), and the Kuder Preference Record. Figure 7.18 lists some typical items from this type of test. The specific items, of course, reflect the variable(s) the inventory addresses.

Achievement Tests. **Achievement**, or ability, **tests** measure an individual's knowledge or skill in a given area or subject. They are mostly used in schools to measure learning or the effectiveness of instruction. The California Achievement Test, for example, measures achievement in reading, language, and arithmetic. The Stanford Achievement Test measures a variety of areas, such as language usage, word meaning, spelling, arithmetic computation, social studies, and science. Other commonly used achievement tests include the Comprehensive Tests of Basic Skills, the Iowa Tests of Basic Skills, the Metropolitan Achievement Test, and the Sequential Tests of Educational Progress (STEP). In research that involves comparing instructional methods, achievement is frequently the dependent variable.

Achievement tests can be classified in several ways. General achievement tests are usually batteries of tests (such as the STEP tests) that measure such things as vocabulary, reading ability, language usage, math, and social studies. One of the most common general achievement tests is the Graduate Record Examination, which

Instructions: Listed below are several pairs of adjectives. Place a check mark (✓) on the line between each pair to indicate how you feel. Example: Hockey:

exciting :___:___:___:___:___:___:___: dull

If you feel that hockey is very exciting, you would place a check mark in the first space next to the word *exciting*. If you feel that hockey is very dull, you would place a check mark in the space nearest the word *dull*. If you are sort of undecided, you would place a check mark in the middle space between the two words. Now rate each of the activities that follow [*only one is listed*]:

Working with other students in small groups

friendly :___:___:___:___:___:___:___: unfriendly
happy :___:___:___:___:___:___:___: sad
easy :___:___:___:___:___:___:___: hard
fun :___:___:___:___:___:___:___: work
hot :___:___:___:___:___:___:___: cold
good :___:___:___:___:___:___:___: bad
laugh :___:___:___:___:___:___:___: cry
beautiful :___:___:___:___:___:___:___: ugly

Figure 7.16 *Example of the Semantic Differential*

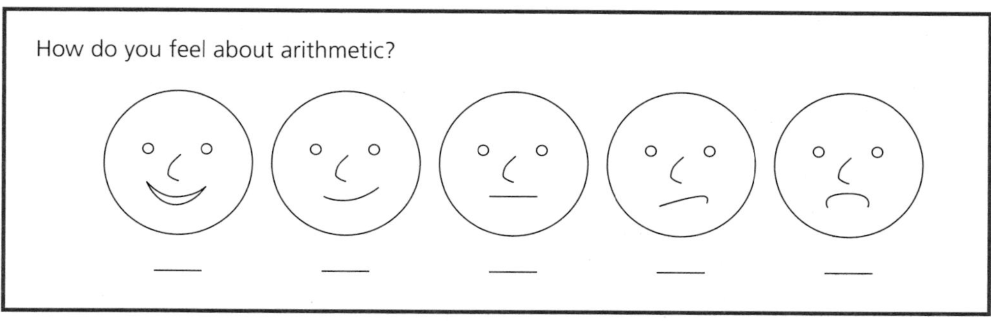

Figure 7.17 *Pictorial Attitude Scale for Use with Young Children*

students must pass before they can be admitted to most graduate programs. Specific achievement tests, on the other hand, are tests that measure an individual's ability in a specific subject, such as English, world history, or biology. Figure 7.19 illustrates the kinds of items found on an achievement test.

Aptitude Tests. Another well-known type of ability test is the so-called general **aptitude**, or intelligence, **test**, which assesses intellectual abilities that are not, in most cases, specifically taught in school. Some measure of general ability is frequently used as either an independent or a dependent variable in research. In attempting to assess the effects of different instructional programs, for example, it is often necessary (and very important) to control this variable so that groups exposed to the different programs are not markedly different in general ability.

Aptitude tests are intended to measure an individual's potential to achieve; in actuality, they measure present skills or abilities. They differ from achievement tests in their purpose and often in content, usually including a wider variety of skills or knowledge. The same test may be either an aptitude or an achievement test, depending on

Instructions: Check the option that most correctly describes you.

SELF-ESTEEM	Quite often	Sometimes	Almost never
1. Do you think your friends are smarter than you?	___	___	___
2. Do you feel good about your appearance?	___	___	___
3. Do you avoid meeting new people?	___	___	___

STRESS	Quite often	Sometimes	Almost never
1. Do you have trouble sleeping?	___	___	___
2. Do you feel on top of things?	___	___	___
3. Do you feel you have too much to do?	___	___	___

Figure 7.18 *Sample Items from a Personality Inventory*

Figure 7.19 *Sample Items from an Achievement Test*

Instructions: Use the map to answer questions 1 and 2. Circle the correct answer.

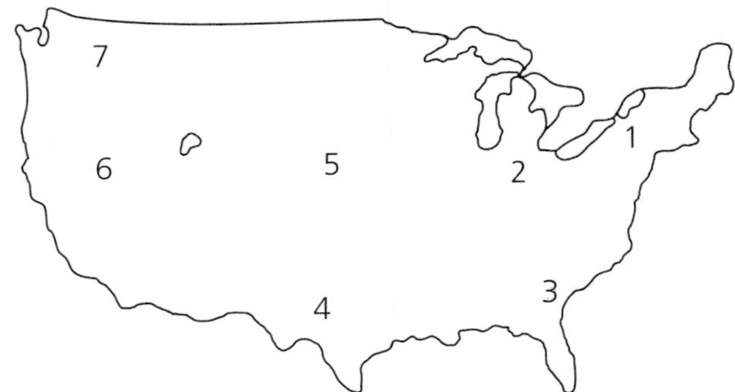

1. Which number shows an area declining in population?
   - A 1
   - B 3
   - C 5
   - D 7

2. Which number shows an area that once belonged to Mexico?
   - A 3
   - B 5
   - C 6
   - D None of the above

the purpose for which it is used. A mathematics achievement test, for example, may also measure aptitude for additional mathematics. Although such tests are used primarily by counselors to help individuals identify areas in which they may have potential, they also can be used in research. In this regard, they are particularly useful for purposes of control. For example, to measure the effectiveness of an instructional program designed to increase problem-solving ability in mathematics, a researcher might decide to use an aptitude test to adjust for initial differences in ability. Figure 7.20 presents an example of one kind of item found on an aptitude test.

Aptitude tests may be administered to individuals or groups. Each method has both advantages and disadvantages. The big advantage of group tests is that they are more convenient to administer and hence save considerable time. One disadvantage is that they require a great deal of reading, and students who are low in reading

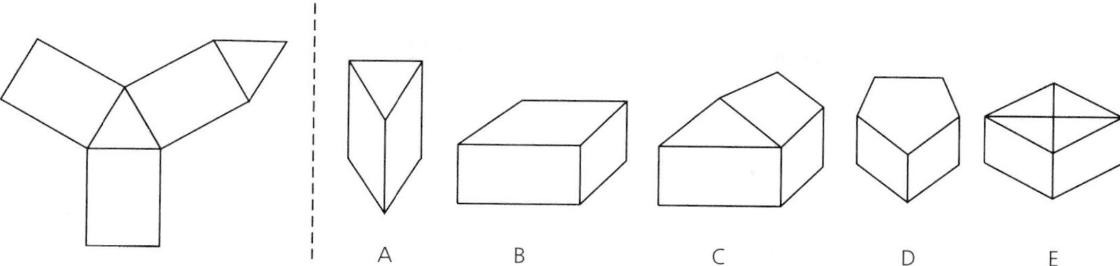

Figure 7.20 *Sample Item from an Aptitude Test*

ability are thus at a disadvantage. Furthermore, it is difficult for those taking the test to have test instructions clarified or to have any interaction with the examiner (which sometimes can raise scores). Lastly, the range of possible tasks on which the student can be examined is much less with a group-administered test than with an individually administered test.

The California Test of Mental Maturity (CTMM) and the Otis-Lennon are examples of group tests. The best-known of the individual aptitude tests is the Stanford-Binet Intelligence Scale, although the Wechsler scales are used more widely. Whereas the Stanford-Binet gives only one IQ score, the Wechsler scales also yield a number of subscores. The two Wechsler scales are the Wechsler Intelligence Scale for Children (WISC-III) for ages 5 to 15 and the Wechsler Adult Intelligence Scale (WAIS-III) for older adolescents and adults.

Many intelligence tests provide reliable and valid evidence when used with certain kinds of individuals and for certain purposes (e.g., predicting the college grades of middle-class Caucasians). On the other hand, they have increasingly come under attack when used with other persons or for other purposes (such as identifying members of certain minority groups to be placed in special classes). Furthermore, there is increasing recognition that most intelligence tests fail to measure many important abilities, including the ability to identify or conceptualize unusual sorts of relationships. As a result, the researcher must be especially careful in evaluating any such test before using it and must determine whether it is appropriate for the purpose of the study. (We discuss some ways to do this when we consider validity in Chapter 8.) Figure 7.21 presents examples of the kinds of items on an intelligence test.

Performance Tests. As we have mentioned, a performance test measures an individual's performance on a particular task. An example would be a typing test, in which individual scores are determined by how accurately and how rapidly people type.

As Sawin has suggested, it is not always easy to determine whether a particular instrument should be called a *performance test,* a *performance checklist,* or a performance *rating scale.*[5] A performance test is the most objective of the three. When a considerable amount of judgment is required to determine if the various aspects of a performance were done correctly, the device is likely to be classified as either a checklist or rating scale. Figure 7.22 illustrates a performance test developed more than 70 years ago to measure sewing ability. In this test, the individual is requested to sew *on* the line in part A of the test, and *between* the lines on part B of the test.[6]

Projective Devices. A **projective device** is any sort of instrument with a vague stimulus that allows individuals to project their interests, preferences, anxieties, prejudices, needs, and so, on through their responses

1. How are *frog* and *toy* alike and how are they different?
2. Here is a sequence of pictures.

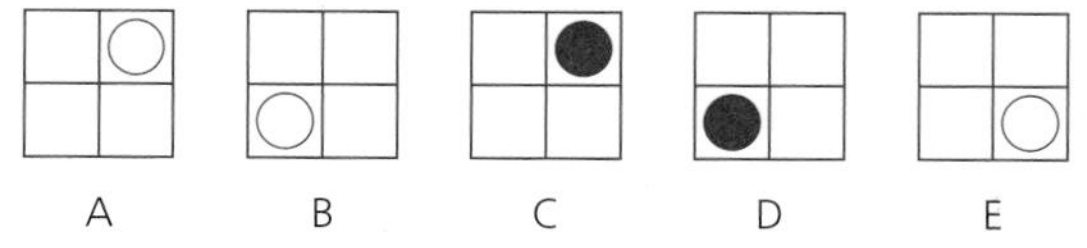

Which of the following would come next in the sequence?

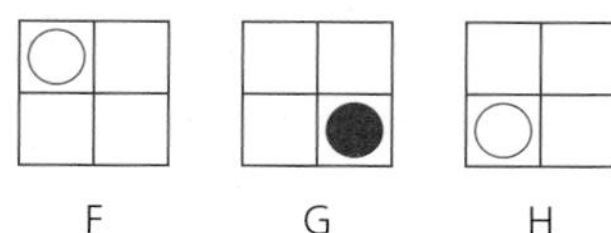

Figure 7.21 *Sample Items from an Intelligence Test*

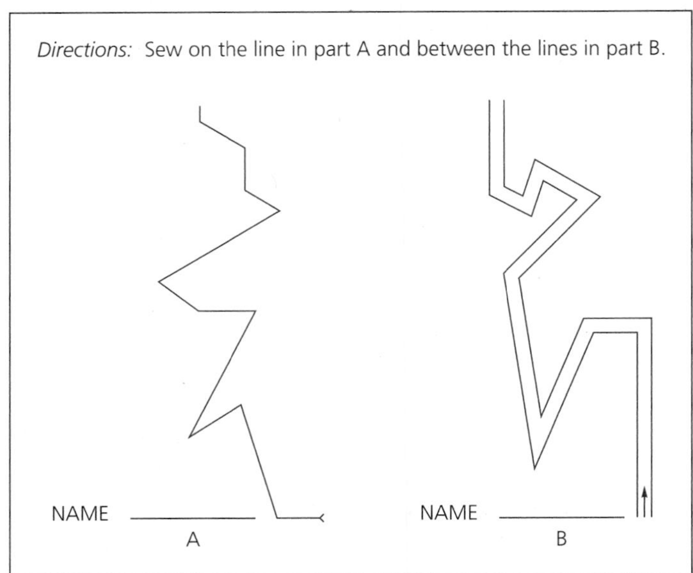

Figure 7.22 *Example from the Blum Sewing Machine Test*

Source: Blum, M. L. Selection of sewing machine operators. *Journal of Applied Psychology, 27* (1), 36. Copyright 1943 by the American Psychological Association. Reproduced with permission.

to it. This kind of device has no "right" answers (or any clear-cut answers of any sort), and its format allows an individual to express something of his or her own personality. There is room for a wide variety of responses.

Perhaps the best-known example of a projective device is the Rorschach Ink Blot Test, in which individuals are presented with a series of ambiguously shaped ink blots and asked to describe what the blots look like. Another well-known projective test is the Thematic Apperception Test (TAT), in which pictures of events are presented and individuals are asked to make up a story about each picture. One application of the projective approach to a classroom setting is the Picture Situation Inventory, one of the few examples especially adapted to classroom situations. This instrument consists of a series of cartoonlike drawings, each portraying a classroom situation in which a child is saying something. Students taking the test are to enter the response of the teacher, thereby presumably indicating something of their own tendencies in the situation. Two of the pictures in this test are reproduced in Figure 7.23.

Sociometric Devices. **Sociometric devices** ask individuals to rate their peers in some way. Two examples include the sociogram and the "group play." A *sociogram* is a visual representation, usually by means of arrows, of the choices people make about other individuals with whom they interact. It is frequently used to assess the climate and structure of interpersonal relationships within a classroom, but it is by no means limited to such an environment. Each student is usually represented by a circle (if female) or a triangle (if male), and arrows are then drawn to indicate different student choices with regard to a particular question. Students may be asked, for example, to list three students whom they consider leaders of the class; admire the most; find especially helpful; would like to have for a friend; would like to have as a partner in a research project; and so forth. The responses students give are then used to construct the sociogram. Figure 7.24 illustrates a sociogram.

Another version of a sociometric device is the *group play.* Students are asked to cast different members of their group in various roles in a play to illustrate their interpersonal relationships. The roles are listed on a piece of paper, and then the members of the group are asked to write in the name of the student they think each role best describes. Almost any type of role can be suggested. The casting choices that individuals make often shed considerable light on how some individuals are viewed by others. Figure 7.25 presents an example of this device.

Item Formats. Although the types of items or questions used in different instruments can take many forms, each item can be classified as either a selection item or a supply item. A *selection item* presents a set of possible responses from which respondents are to select the most appropriate answer. A *supply item,* on the other hand, asks respondents to formulate and then supply their own answers. Here are examples of each type.

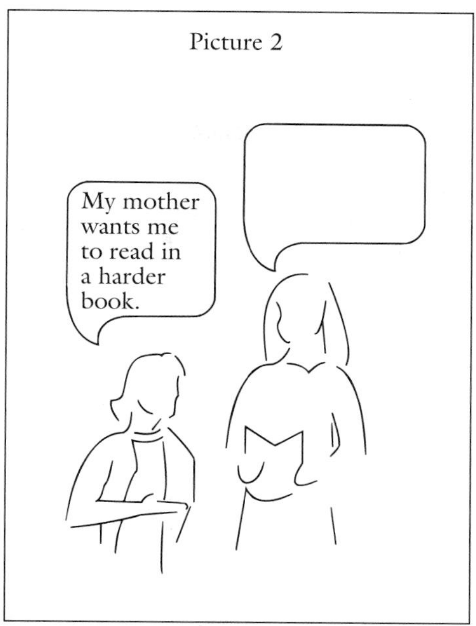

Figure 7.23 *Sample Items from the Picture Situation Inventory*

Source: Rowan, N. T. (1967, p. 68). The relationship of teacher interaction in classroom situations to teacher personality variables. Unpublished doctoral dissertation. Salt Lake City: University of Utah.

Selection Items. *True-false items:* True-false items present either a true or a false statement, and the respondent has to mark either true (T) or false (F). Frequently used variations of the words *true* and *false* are *yes-no* or *right-wrong,* which often are more useful when attempting to question or interview young children. Here is an example of a true-false item:

T F I get very nervous whenever I have to speak in public.

Multiple-choice items: Multiple-choice items consist of two parts: the stem, which contains the question, and several (usually four) possible choices. Here is an example:

Which of the following expresses your opinion on abortion?

a. It is immoral and should be prohibited.
b. It should be discouraged but permitted under unusual circumstances.
c. It should be available under a wide range of conditions.
d. It is entirely a matter of individual choice.

Matching items: Matching items are variations of the multiple-choice format. They consist of two groups listed in columns—the left-hand column containing the questions or items to be thought about and the right-hand column containing the possible responses to the questions. The respondent pairs the choice from the right-hand column with the corresponding question or item in the left-hand column. Here is an example:

Instructions: For each item in the left-hand column, select the item in the right-hand column that represents your first reaction. Place the appropriate letter in the blank. Each lettered item may be used more than once or not at all.

Column A	**Column B**
Special classes for the:	
___ 1. severely disabled	a. should be increased
___ 2. mildly disabled	b. should be maintained
___ 3. hard of hearing	c. should be decreased
___ 4. visually impaired	d. should be eliminated
___ 5. learning disabled	
___ 6. emotionally disturbed	

Interpretive exercises: One difficulty with using true-false, multiple-choice, and matching items to measure achievement is that these items often do not measure complex learning outcomes. One way to get at more

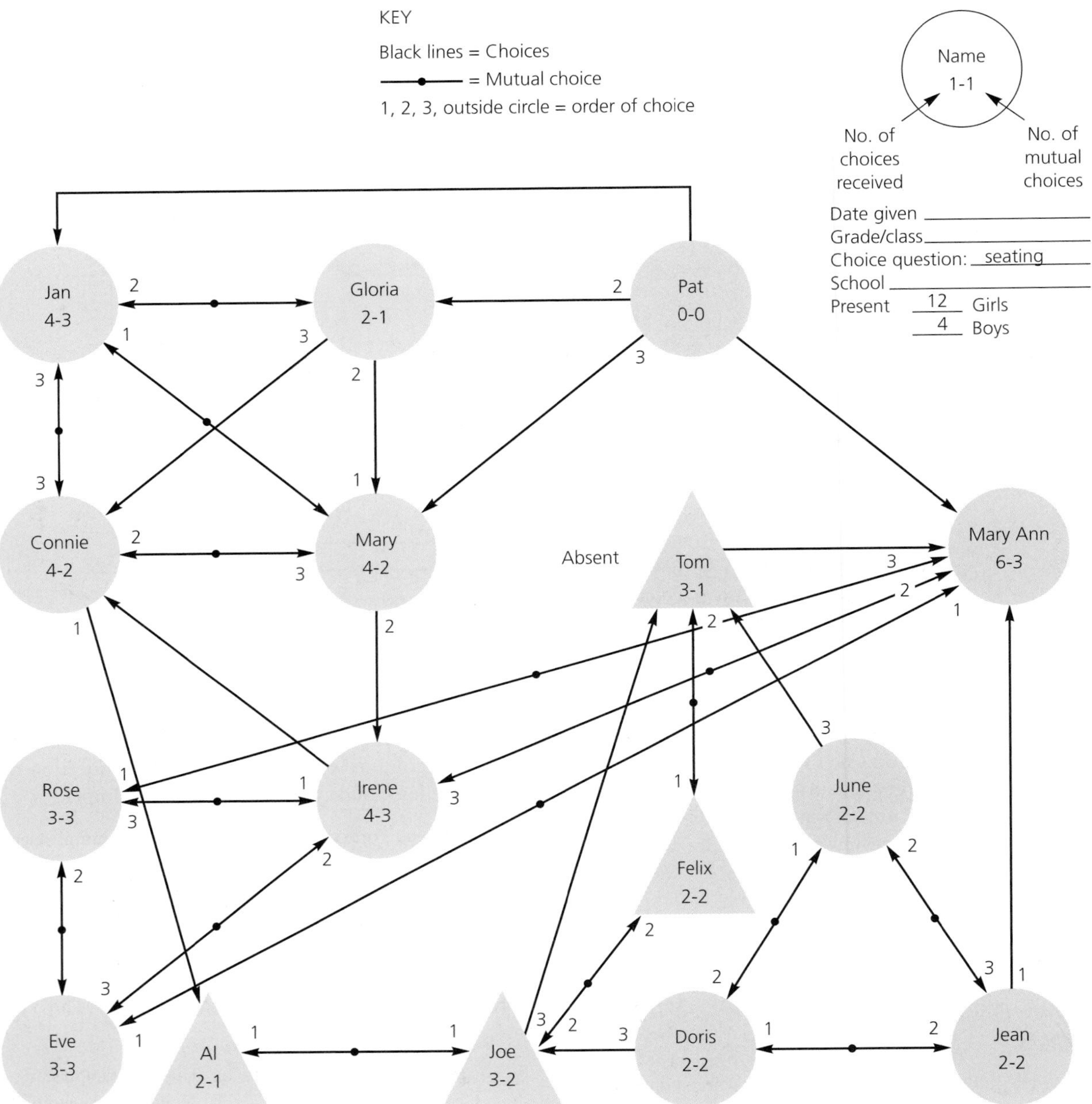

Figure 7.24 *Example of a Sociogram*

complex learning outcomes is to use what is called an *interpretive exercise.* An interpretive exercise consists of a selection of introductory material (this may be a paragraph, map, diagram, picture, chart) followed by one or more selection items that ask a respondent to interpret this material. Two examples of interpretive exercises follow.

Example 1.

Directions: Read the following comments a teacher made about testing. Then answer the question that follows the comments by circling the letter of the best answer.

"Students go to school to learn, not to take tests. In addition, tests cannot be used to indicate a student's absolute

Directions: Imagine you are the casting director for a large play. Your job is to choose the individuals who will take the various parts (listed below) in the play. Since some of the parts are rather small, you may select the same individual to play more than one part. Choose individuals you think would be the most *natural* for the part, that is, those who are most like the role in real life.

1. The parts

Part 1—someone who is well liked by all members of the group ______

Part 2—someone who is disliked by many people ______

Part 3—someone who always gets angry about things of little consequence ______

Part 4—someone who has wit and a good sense of humor ______

Part 5—someone who is very quiet and rarely says anything ______

Part 6—someone who does not contribute much to the group ______

Part 7—someone who is angry a lot of the time ______

2. Your role

Which part do you think you could play best? ______

Which part would other members of the group ask you to play? ______

Figure 7.25 *Example of a Group Play*

level of learning. All tests can do is rank students in order of achievement, and this relative ranking is influenced by guessing, bluffing, and the subjective opinions of the teacher doing the scoring. The teaching-learning process would benefit if we did away with tests and depended on student self-evaluation."

1. Which one of the following unstated assumptions is this teacher making?
   a. Students go to school to learn.
   b. Teachers use essay tests primarily.
   c. Tests make no contribution to learning.
   d. Tests do not indicate a student's absolute level of learning.

Example 2.

Directions: Paragraph A contains a description of the testing practices of Mr. Smith, a high school teacher. Read the description and each of the statements that follow it. Mark each statement to indicate the type of *inference* that can be drawn about it from the material in the paragraph. Place the appropriate letter in front of each statement using the following key:

T—if the statement may be *inferred as true.*

F—if the statement may be *inferred as untrue.*

N—if *no inference* may be drawn about it from the paragraph.

Paragraph A

Approximately one week before a test is to be given, Mr. Smith carefully goes through the textbook and constructs multiple-choice items based on the material in the book. He always uses the exact wording of the textbook for the correct answer so that there will be no question concerning its correctness. He is careful to include some test items from each chapter. After the test is given, he lists the scores from high to low on the blackboard and tells each student his or her score. He does not return the test papers to the students, but he offers to answer any questions they might have about the test. He puts the items from each test into a test file, which he is building for future use.

(T) 1. Mr. Smith's tests measure a limited range of learning outcomes.

(F) 2. Some of Mr. Smith's test items measure at the understanding level.

(N) 3. Mr. Smith's tests measure a balanced sample of subject matter.

(N) 4. Mr. Smith uses the type of test item that is best for his purpose.

(T) 5. Students can determine where they rank in the distribution of scores on Mr. Smith's tests.

(F) 6. Mr. Smith's testing practices are likely to motivate students to overcome their weaknesses.[7]

Supply Items. *Short-answer items:* A short-answer item requires the respondent to supply a word, phrase, number, or symbol that is necessary to complete a statement or answer a question. Here is an example:

> *Directions:* In the space provided, write the word that best completes the sentence.
>
> When the number of items in a test is increased, the ____of the scores on the test is likely to increase. (Answer: reliability.)

Short-answer items have one major disadvantage: It is usually difficult to write a short-answer item so only one word completes it correctly. In the first question under paragraph 1, for example, many students might argue that the word *range* would also be correct.

Essay questions: An essay question is one that respondents are asked to write about at length. As with short-answer questions, subjects must produce their own answers. Generally, however, they are free to determine how to answer the question, what facts to present, which to emphasize, what interpretations to make, and the like. For these reasons, the essay question is a particularly useful device for assessing an individual's ability to organize, integrate, analyze, and synthesize information. It is especially useful in measuring the so-called higher-level learning outcomes, such as analysis, synthesis, and evaluation. Here are two examples of essay questions:

Example 1

Mr. Rogers, a ninth-grade science teacher, wants to measure his students' "ability to interpret scientific data" with a paper-and-pencil test.

1. Describe the steps that Mr. Rogers should follow.
2. Give reasons to justify each step.

Example 2

For a course that you are teaching or expect to teach, prepare a complete plan for evaluating student achievement. Be sure to include the procedures you would follow, the instruments you would use, and the reasons for your choices.[8]

UNOBTRUSIVE MEASURES

Many instruments require the cooperation of the respondent in one way or another and involve some kind of intrusion into ongoing activities. On occasion, respondents will dislike or even resent being tested, observed, or interviewed. Furthermore, the reaction of respondents to the instrumentation process—that is, to being tested, observed, or interviewed—often will, to some degree, affect the nature of the information researchers obtain.

To eliminate this reactive effect, researchers at times attempt to use what are called **unobtrusive measures,**[9] which are data-collection procedures that involve no intrusion into the naturally occurring course of events. In most instances, no instrument is required, only some form of record keeping. Here are examples of such procedures:

- The degree of fear induced by a ghost-story-telling session can be measured by noting the shrinking diameter of a circle of seated children.
- Library withdrawals could be used to demonstrate the effect of the introduction of a new unit on Chinese history in a social studies curriculum.
- The interest of children in Christmas or other holidays might be demonstrated by the amount of distortion in the size of their drawings of Santa Claus or other holiday figures.
- Racial attitudes in two elementary schools might be compared by noting the degree of clustering of members of different ethnic groups in the lunchroom and on the playground.
- The values held by people of different countries might be compared through analyzing different types of published materials, such as textbooks, plays, handbooks for youth organizations, magazine advertisements, and newspaper headlines.
- Some idea of the attention paid to patients in a hospital might be determined by observing the frequency of notes, both informal and required, made by attending nurses to patients' bedside records.
- The degree of stress felt by college students might be assessed by noting the nature and frequency of sick-call visits to the college health center.
- Student attitudes toward, and interest in, various topics can be noted by observing the amount of graffiti about those topics written on school walls.

Many variables of interest can be assessed, at least to some degree, through the use of unobtrusive measures. The reliability and validity of inferences based on such measures will vary depending on the procedure used. Nevertheless, unobtrusive measures add an important and useful dimension to the array of possible data sources available to researchers. They are particularly valuable as supplements to interviews and questionnaires, often providing a useful way to corroborate (or contradict) what these more traditional data sources reveal.[10]

Norm-Referenced Versus Criterion-Referenced Instruments

NORM-REFERENCED INSTRUMENTS

All individual scores derive meaning by comparing them to the scores of a particular group. This means that the nature of the group is extremely important. Whenever this is done, researchers must be sure that the reference group makes sense. Comparing a boy's score on a grammar test to a group of girls' scores on that test, for example, may be quite misleading since girls usually score higher in grammar. The group to which the comparison is made is called the **norm group**, and instruments that provide such information are referred to as **norm-referenced instruments**.

CRITERION-REFERENCED INSTRUMENTS

An alternative to the use of customary achievement or performance instruments, most of which are norm-referenced, is to use a **criterion-referenced instrument**—usually a test.

The intent of such tests is somewhat different from that of norm-referenced tests; criterion-referenced tests focus more directly on instruction. Rather than evaluating learner progress through gain in scores (e.g., from 40 to 70 on an achievement test), a criterion-referenced test is based on a specific goal, or target (called a *criterion*), for each learner to achieve. This criterion for excellence, or "pass," is usually stated as a fairly high percentage of correctly answered questions (such as 80 or 90 percent). Examples of criterion-referenced and norm-referenced evaluation statements are as follows:

Criterion-referenced: A student . . .

- spelled every word in the weekly spelling list correctly.
- solved at least 75 percent of the assigned problems.
- achieved a score of at least 80 out of 100 on the final exam.
- did at least 25 push-ups within a five-minute period.
- read a minimum of one nonfiction book a week.

Norm-referenced: A student . . .

- scored at the 50th percentile in his group.
- scored above 90 percent of all the students in the class.
- received a higher grade point average in English literature than any other student in the school.
- ran faster than all but one other student on the team.
- and one other in the class were the only ones to receive As on the midterm.

The advantage of a criterion-referenced instrument is that it gives both teacher and students a clear-cut goal to work toward. As a result, it has considerable appeal as a means of improving instruction. In practice, however, several problems arise. First, teachers seldom set or reach the ideal of individualized student goals. Rather, class goals are more the rule, the idea being that all students will reach the criterion—though, of course, some may not and many will exceed it. The second problem is that it is difficult to establish even class criteria that are meaningful. What, precisely, should a class of fifth-graders be able to do in mathematics? Solve story problems, many would say. We would agree, but of what complexity? and requiring which mathematics subskills? In the absence of independent criteria, we have little choice but to fall back on existing expectations, and this is typically (though not necessarily) done by examining existing texts and tests. As a result, the specific items in a criterion-referenced test often turn out to be indistinguishable from those in the usual norm-referenced test, with one important difference: A criterion-referenced test at any grade level will almost certainly be easier than a norm-referenced test. It *must* be easier if most students are to get 80 or 90 percent of the items correct. In preparing such tests, researchers must try to write items that will be answered correctly by 80 percent of the students—after all, they don't want 50 percent of their students to fail. The desired difficulty level for norm-referenced items, however, is at or about 50 percent, in order to provide the maximum opportunity for the scores to distinguish the ability of one student from another.

While a criterion-referenced test *may* be more useful at times and in certain circumstances than the more customary norm-referenced test (this issue is still being debated), it is often inferior for research purposes. Why? Because, in general, a criterion-referenced test will provide much less variability of scores, because it is easier. Whereas the usual norm-referenced test will provide a range of scores somewhat less than the possible range (i.e., from zero to the total number of items in the test), a criterion-referenced test, if it is true to its rationale, will have most of the students (surely at least half) getting a

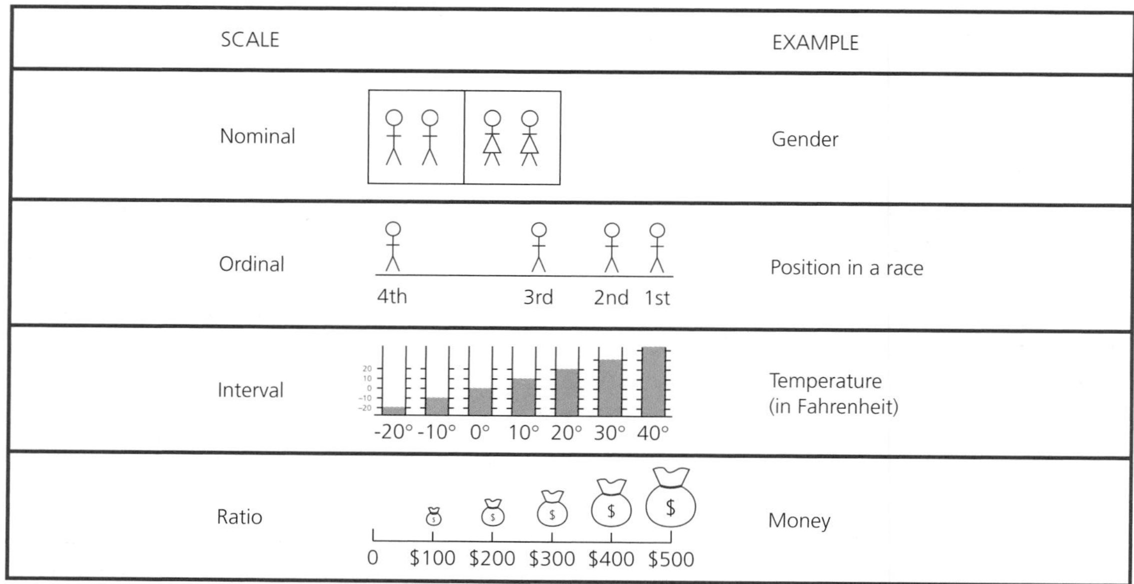

SCALE
EXAMPLE
Nominal
Gender
Ordinal
4th
3rd
2nd
1st
Position in a race
Interval
-20° -10° 0° 10° 20° 30° 40°
Temperature
(in Fahrenheit)
Ratio
0 $100 $200 $300 $400 $500
Money

Figure 7.26 *Four Types of Measurement Scales*

high score. Because, in research, we usually want maximum variability to have any hope of finding relationships with other variables, the use of criterion-referenced tests is often self-defeating.*

Measurement Scales

You will recall from Chapter 5 that there are two basic types of variables—quantitative and categorical. Each uses a different type of analysis and measurement, requiring the use of different measurement scales. There are four types of measurement scales: nominal, ordinal, interval, and ratio (Figure 7.26).

NOMINAL SCALES

A **nominal scale** is the simplest form of measurement researchers can use. When using a nominal scale, researchers simply assign numbers to different categories in order to show differences (Figure 7.27). For example, a researcher concerned with the variable of gender might group data into two categories, male and female, and assign the number 1 to females and the number 2 to males. Another researcher, interested in studying methods of teaching reading, might assign the number 1 to the whole-word method, the number 2 to the phonics method, and the number 3 to the "mixed" method. In most cases, the advantage to assigning numbers to the categories is to facilitate computer analysis. There is no

*An exception is in program evaluation, where some researchers advocate the use of criterion-referenced tests because they want to determine how many students reach a predetermined standard (criterion).

Figure 7.27 *A Nominal Scale of Measurement*

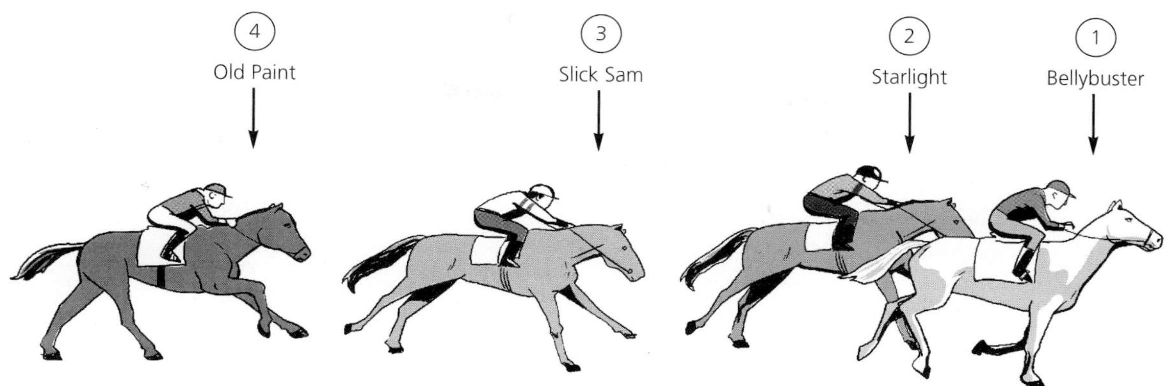

Figure 7.28 *An Ordinal Scale: The Outcome of a Horse Race*

implication that the phonics method (assigned number 2) is "more" of anything than the whole-word method (assigned number 1).

ORDINAL SCALES

An **ordinal scale** is one in which data may be ordered in some way—high to low or least to most. For example, a researcher might rank-order student scores on a biology test from high to low. Notice, however, that the difference in scores or in actual ability between the first- and second-ranked students and between the fifth- and sixth-ranked students would not necessarily be the same. Ordinal scales indicate relative standing among individuals, as Figure 7.28 demonstrates.

INTERVAL SCALES

An **interval scale** possesses all the characteristics of an ordinal scale with one additional feature: The distances between the points on the scale are equal. For example, the distances between scores on most commercially available mathematics achievement tests are usually considered equal. Thus, the distance between scores of 70 and 80 is considered to be the same as the distance between scores of 80 and 90. Notice, however, that the zero point on an interval scale does not indicate a total absence of what is being measured. Thus, 0° (zero degrees) on the Fahrenheit scale, which measures temperature, does not indicate *no* temperature.

To illustrate further, consider the commonly used IQ score. Is the difference between an IQ of 90 and one of 100 (10 points) the same as the difference between an IQ of 40 and one of 50 (also 10 points)? or between an IQ of 120 and one of 130? If we believe that the scores constitute an interval scale, we *must* assume that 10 points has the same meaning at different points on the scale. Do we know whether this is true? No, we do not, as we shall now explain.

With respect to some measurements, we can demonstrate equal intervals. We do so by having an agreed-on standard unit. This is one reason why we have a Bureau of Standards, located in Washington, DC. You could, if you wished to do so, go to the bureau and actually "see" a standard inch, foot, ounce, and so on, that defines these units. While it might not be easy, you could conceivably check your carpenter's rule using the "standard inch" to see if an inch is an inch all along your rule. You literally could place the "standard inch" at various points along your rule.

There is no such standard unit for IQ or for virtually any variable commonly used in educational research. Over the years, sophisticated and clever techniques have been developed to create interval scales for use by researchers. The details are beyond the scope of this text, but you should know that they all are based on highly questionable assumptions.

In actual practice, most researchers prefer to "act as if" they have an interval scale, because it permits the use of more sensitive data analysis procedures and because, over the years, the results of doing so make sense. Nevertheless, acting as if we have interval scales requires an assumption that (at least to date) cannot be proved.

RATIO SCALES

An interval scale that does possess an actual, or true, zero point is called a **ratio scale**. For example, a scale

CONTROVERSIES IN RESEARCH

Which Statistical Index Is Valid?

Measurements, of course, are not limited to test scores and the like. For example, a widely used measurement is the "index of unemployment" provided by the Bureau of Labor Statistics. One of its many uses is to study the relationship between unemployment and crime. Its validity for this purpose has been questioned by the author of a study who found that while this index showed no relationship to property crimes, two different indexes that reflected long-term (rather than temporary) unemployment did show substantial relationships. The author concluded, "Clearly, we need to become as interested in the selection of appropriate indicators as we are with the specification of appropriate models and the selection of statistical techniques."*

What do you think? Why did the different indexes give different results?

*Chamlin, M. B. (2000). Unemployment, economic theory, and property crime: A note on measurement. *Journal of Quantitative Criminology, 16* (4), 454.

designed to measure height would be a ratio scale, because the zero point on the scale represents the absence of height (i.e., *no* height). Similarly, the zero on a bathroom weight scale represents zero, or no, weight. Ratio scales are almost never encountered in educational research, since rarely do researchers engage in measurement involving a true zero point (even on those rare occasions when a student receives a zero on a test of some sort, this does not mean that whatever is being measured is totally absent in the student). Some other variables that *do* have ratio scales are income, time on task, and age.

MEASUREMENT SCALES RECONSIDERED

At this point, you may be saying, Well, okay, but so what? Why are these distinctions important? There are two reasons why you should have at least a rudimentary understanding of the differences between these four types of scales. First, they convey different amounts of information. Ratio scales provide more information than do interval scales; interval, more than ordinal; and ordinal, more than nominal. Hence, if possible, researchers should use the type of measurement that will provide them with the maximum amount of information needed to answer their research question. Second, some types of statistical procedures are inappropriate for the different scales. The way in which the data in a research study are organized dictates the use of certain types of statistical analyses, but not others (we shall discuss this point in more detail in Chapter 11). Table 7.1 presents a summary of the four types of measurement scales.

TABLE 7.1 ***Characteristics of the Four Types of Measurement Scales***

Measurement Scale	Characteristics
Nominal	Groups and labels data only; reports frequencies or percentages.
Ordinal	Ranks data; uses numbers only to indicate ranking.
Interval	Assumes that equal differences between scores really mean equal differences in the variable measured.
Ratio	All of the above, plus a true zero point.

Often researchers have a choice to make. They must decide whether to consider data as ordinal or interval. For example, suppose a researcher uses a self-report questionnaire to measure self-esteem. The questionnaire is scored for the number of items answered (yes or no) in the direction indicating high self-esteem. For a given sample of 60, the researcher finds that the scores range from 30 to 75.

The researcher may now decide to treat scores as interval data, in which case she assumes that equal distances (e.g., 30–34, 35–39, 40–44) in score represent equal differences in self-esteem.* If the researcher is uncomfortable with this assumption, she could use the scores to rank the individuals in her sample from highest (rank 1) to lowest (rank 60). If she were then to use only these rankings

*Notice that she cannot treat the scores as ratio data, since a score of zero cannot be assumed to represent zero (i.e., no) self-esteem.

in subsequent analysis, she would now be assuming that her instrument provides only ordinal data.

Fortunately, researchers can avoid this choice. They have another option—to treat the data separately according to both assumptions (i.e., to treat the scores as ordinal data, and then again as interval data). The important thing to realize is that a researcher must be prepared to defend the assumptions underlying her choice of a measurement scale used in the collection and organization of data.

Preparing Data for Analysis

Once the instruments being used in a study have been administered, the researcher must score the data that have been collected and then organize it to facilitate analysis.

SCORING THE DATA

Collected data must be scored accurately and consistently. If they are not, any conclusions a researcher draws from the data may be erroneous or misleading. Each individual's test (questionnaire, essay, etc.) should be scored using exactly the same procedures and criteria. When a commercially purchased instrument is used, the scoring procedures are made much easier. Usually the instrument developer will provide a scoring manual that lists the steps to follow in scoring the instrument, along with a scoring key. It is a good idea to double-check one's scoring to ensure that no mistakes have been made.

The scoring of a self-developed test can produce difficulties, and hence researchers have to take special care to ensure that scoring is accurate and consistent. Essay examinations, in particular, are often very difficult to score in a consistent manner. For this reason, it is usually advisable to have a second person also score the results. Researchers should carefully prepare their scoring plans, in writing, ahead of time and then try out their instrument by administering and scoring it with a group of individuals similar to the population they intend to sample in their study. Problems with administration and scoring can thus be identified early and corrected before it is too late.

TABULATING AND CODING THE DATA

When the data have been scored, the researcher must tally or tabulate them in some way. Usually this is done by transferring the data to some sort of summary data sheet or card. The important thing is to record one's data accurately and systematically. If categorical data are being recorded, the number of individuals scoring in each category are tallied. If quantitative data are being recorded, the data are usually listed in one or more columns, depending on the number of groups involved in the study. For example, if the data analysis is to consist simply of a comparison of the scores of two groups on a posttest, the data would most likely be placed in two columns, one for each group, in descending order. Table 7.2, for example, presents some hypothetical results of a study involving a comparison of two counseling methods with an instrument measuring rapport. If pre and posttest scores are to be compared, additional columns could be added. Subgroup scores could also be indicated.

When different kinds of data are collected (i.e., scores on several different instruments) in addition to biographical information (gender, age, ethnicity, etc.), they are usually recorded in a computer or on data cards, one card for each individual from whom data were collected. This facilitates easy comparison and grouping (and regrouping) of data for purposes of analysis. In addition, the data are coded. In other words, some type of code is used to protect the privacy of the

TABLE 7.2 *Hypothetical Results of Study Involving a Comparison of Two Counseling Methods*

Score for "Rapport"	Method A	Method B
96–100	0	0
91–95	0	2
86–90	0	3
81–85	2	3
76–80	2	4
71–75	5	3
66–70	6	4
61–65	9	4
56–60	4	5
51–55	5	3
46–50	2	2
41–45	0	1
36–40	0	1
	N = 35	35

individuals in the study. Thus, the names of males and females might be coded as 1 and 2. Coding of data is especially important when data are analyzed by computer, since any data not in numerical form must be coded in some systematic way before they can be entered into the computer. Thus, categorical data, to be analyzed on a computer, are often coded numerically (e.g., pretest scores 1, and posttest scores 2).

The first step in coding data is often to assign an ID number to every individual from whom data has been collected. If there were 100 individuals in a study, for example, the researcher would number them from 001 to 100. If the highest value for any variable being analyzed involves three digits (e.g., 100), then every individual code number must have three digits (e.g., the first individual to be numbered must be 001, not 1).

The next step would be to decide how any categorical data being analyzed are to be coded. Suppose a researcher wished to analyze certain demographic information obtained from 100 subjects who answered a questionnaire. If his study included juniors and seniors in a high school, he might code the juniors as 11 and the seniors as 12. Or, if respondents were asked to indicate which of four choices they preferred (as in certain multiple-choice questions), the researcher might code each of the choices [e.g., (*a*), (*b*), (*c*), (*d*) as 1, 2, 3, or 4, respectively]. The important thing to remember is that the coding must be consistent—that is, once a decision is made about how to code someone, all others must be coded the same way, and this (and any other) coding rule must be communicated to everyone involved in coding the data.

Go back to the **INTERACTIVE AND APPLIED LEARNING** feature at the beginning of the chapter for a listing of interactive and applied activities. Go to the **Online Learning Center** at **www.mhhe.com/fraenkel9e** to take quizzes, practice with key terms, and review chapter content.

Main Points

WHAT ARE DATA?

- The term *data* refers to the kinds of information researchers obtain on the subjects of their research.

INSTRUMENTATION

- The term *instrumentation* refers to the entire process of collecting data in a research investigation.

VALIDITY AND RELIABILITY

- An important consideration in the choice of a research instrument is validity: the extent to which results from it permit researchers to draw warranted conclusions about the characteristics of the individuals studied.
- A reliable instrument is one that gives consistent results.

OBJECTIVITY AND USABILITY

- Whenever possible, researchers try to eliminate subjectivity from the judgments they make about the achievement, performance, or characteristics of subjects.
- An important consideration for any researcher in choosing or designing an instrument is its ease of use.

WAYS TO CLASSIFY INSTRUMENTS

- Research instruments can be classified in many ways. Some of the more common are in terms of who provides the data, the method of data collection, who collects the data, and what kind of response they require from the subjects.
- Research data are obtained by directly or indirectly assessing the subjects of a study.
- Self-report data are provided by the subjects of a study themselves.
- Informant data are provided by other people about the subjects of a study.

TYPES OF INSTRUMENTS

- There are many types of researcher-completed instruments. Some of the more commonly used are rating scales, interview schedules, observation forms, tally sheets, flowcharts, performance checklists, anecdotal records, and time-and-motion logs.
- Many types of instruments are completed by the subjects of a study rather than the researcher. Some of the more commonly used of this type are questionnaires; self-checklists; attitude scales; personality inventories; achievement, aptitude, and performance tests; and projective and sociometric devices.
- The types of items or questions used in subject-completed instruments can take many forms, but they all can be classified as either selection or supply items. Examples of selection items include true-false items, multiple-choice items, matching items, and interpretive exercises. Examples of supply items include short-answer items and essay questions.
- An excellent source for locating already available tests is the ERIC database.
- Unobtrusive measures require no intrusion into the normal course of affairs.

NORM-REFERENCED VERSUS CRITERION-REFERENCED INSTRUMENTS

- Instruments that provide scores that compare individual scores to the scores of an appropriate reference group are called *norm-referenced instruments.*
- Instruments that are based on a specific target for each learner to achieve are called *criterion-referenced instruments.*

MEASUREMENT SCALES

- Four types of measurement scales—nominal, ordinal, interval, and ratio—are used in educational research.
- A nominal scale uses numbers to indicate membership in one or more categories.
- An ordinal scale uses numbers to rank or order scores from high to low.
- An interval scale uses numbers to represent equal intervals in different segments on a continuum.
- A ratio scale uses numbers to represent equal distances from a known zero point.

PREPARING DATA FOR ANALYSIS

- Collected data must be scored accurately and consistently.
- Once scored, data must be tabulated and coded.

Key Terms

achievement test 128
aptitude test 129
criterion-referenced instrument 137
data 112
informant 114
instrumentation 112
interval scale 139
interview protocol 120
Likert scale 127
nominal scale 138
norm group 137
norm-referenced instrument 137
objectivity 113
ordinal scale 139
performance instrument 117
projective device 131
questionnaire 114
ratio scale 139
reliability 113
semantic differential 128
sociometric device 132
tally sheet 114
unobtrusive measure 136
validity 113
written-response instrument 117

For Discussion

1. What type of instrument do you think would be best suited to obtain data about each of the following?
   a. The free-throw shooting ability of a tenth-grade basketball team
   b. How nurses feel about a new management policy recently instituted in their hospital
   c. Parental reactions to a proposed campaign to raise money for an addition to the school library
   d. The "best-liked" boy and girl in the senior class
   e. The "best" administrator in a particular school district
   f. How well students in a food management class can prepare a balanced meal
   g. Characteristics of all students who are biology majors at a midwestern university
   h. How students at one school compare to students at another school in mathematics ability
   i. The potential of various high school seniors for college work
   j. What the members of a kindergarten class like and dislike about school
2. Which do you think would be the easiest to measure—the attention level of a class, student interest in a poem, or participation in a class discussion? Why? Which would be the hardest to measure?
3. Is it possible to measure a person's self-concept? If so, how? What about his or her body image?
4. Are there any things (ideas, objects, etc.) that cannot be measured? If so, give an example.
5. Of all the instruments presented in this chapter, which one(s) do you think would be the hardest to use? the easiest? Why? Which one(s) do you think would provide the most dependable information? Why?
6. It sometimes would not be fair to compare an individual's score on a test to the scores of other individuals taking the same test. Why?

References

1. American Council on Education. (1945, pp. 32–33). *Helping teachers understand children.* Washington, DC: American Council on Education.

2. Likert, A. (1932). A technique for the measurement of attitudes. *Archives de Psychologie, 6* (140), 173–177.

3. Osgood, C., Suci, G., & Tannenbaum, P. (1962). *The measurement of meaning.* Urbana, IL: University of Illinois Press.

4. See, for example, Popham, W. J. (1992). *Educational evaluation* (3rd ed., pp. 150–173). Englewood Cliffs, NJ: Prentice Hall.

5. Sawin, E. I. (1969, p. 176). *Evaluation and the work of the teacher.* Belmont, CA: Wadsworth.

6. Blum, M. L. (1943). Selection of sewing machine operators. *Journal of Applied Psychology, 27* (2), 35–40.

7. Gronlund, N. E. (1988). *How to construct achievement tests* (4th ed., pp. 66–67). Englewood Cliffs, NJ: Prentice Hall. Reprinted by permission of Prentice Hall, Inc. Also see Gronlund's (1997) *Assessment of student achievement* (6th ed.). Boston: Allyn & Bacon.

8. Gronlund, N. E. (1988). *How to construct achievement tests* (4th ed., pp. 76–77). Englewood Cliffs, NJ: Prentice Hall. Reprinted by permission of Prentice Hall, Inc.

9. Webb, E. J., Campbell, D. T., Schwartz, R. D., & Sechrest, L. (1966). *Unobtrusive measures: Nonreactive research in the social sciences.* Chicago: Rand McNally.

10. The use of unobtrusive measures is an art in itself. We can only scratch the surface of the topic here. For a more extended discussion, along with many interesting examples, the reader is referred to Webb, E. J., Campbell, D. T., Schwartz, R. D., & Sechrest, L. (1966). *Unobtrusive measures: Nonreactive research in the social sciences.* Chicago: Rand McNally.

Research Exercise 7: Instrumentation

Name all of the instrument(s) you intend to use in your study, and whether they are preexisting or if you will need to develop them yourself. Describe how you will use the instrument(s) (i.e., where, when, and how you will collect the data you will need) and how many items each instrument will contain. Then explain how the instrument is to be scored or how it can be interpreted.

Problem Sheet 7

Instrumentation

1. My research question is:

____

____

2. Describe the type(s) of instrument(s) you plan to use for your study (e.g., interview protocol, attitudinal survey, achievement test, observation scale, questionnaire, focus group protocol).

____

____

3. Is it a preexisting instrument or one you plan to develop?

____

____

4. If preexisting, state the name of the instrument. Also, why did you decide to use this particular instrument?

____

____

5. What is the instrument supposed to measure or assess?

____

____

6. How many items will the instrument contain?

____

____

7. How will the instrument be scored or interpreted?

____

____

An electronic version of this Problem Sheet that you can fill in and print, save, or e-mail is available on the Online Learning Center at www.mhhe.com/fraenkel9e.

Validity and Reliability

8

The Importance of Valid Instrumentation

Validity

Content-Related Evidence
Criterion-Related Evidence
Construct-Related Evidence

Reliability

Errors of Measurement
Test-Retest Method
Equivalent-Forms Method
Internal-Consistency Methods
The Standard Error of Measurement (SEMeas)
Scoring Agreement
Validity and Reliability in Qualitative Research

"I've failed Mr. Johnson's test three times. But he keeps giving me problems that he has never taught or told us about."
"Sounds to me like an invalid test."
"But he says it's very reliable."
"Can a test be reliable but not valid?"

OBJECTIVES **Studying this chapter should enable you to:**

- Explain what is meant by the term "validity" as it applies to the use of instruments in educational research.
- Name three types of evidence of validity that can be obtained, and give an example of each type.
- Explain what is meant by the term "correlation coefficient" and describe briefly the difference between positive and negative correlation coefficients.
- Explain what is meant by the terms "validity coefficient" and "reliability coefficient."
- Explain what is meant by the term "reliability" as it applies to the use of instruments in educational research.
- Explain what is meant by the term "errors of measurement."
- Explain briefly the meaning and use of the term "standard error of measurement."
- Describe briefly three ways to estimate the reliability of the scores obtained using a particular instrument.
- Describe how to obtain and evaluate scoring agreement.

INTERACTIVE AND APPLIED LEARNING After, or while, reading this chapter:

Go to the Online Learning Center at www.mhhe.com/fraenkel9e to:

- Learn More About Validity and Reliability

Go to your online Student Mastery Activities book to do the following activities:

- Activity 8.1: Instrument Validity
- Activity 8.2: Instrument Reliability (1)
- Activity 8.3: Instrument Reliability (2)
- Activity 8.4: What Kind of Evidence: Content-Related, Criterion-Related, or Construct-Related?
- Activity 8.5: What Constitutes Construct-Related Evidence of Validity?

"It isn't fair, Tony!"

"What isn't, Lily?"

"Those tests that Ms. Leonard gives. Grrr!"

"What about them?"

"Well, take this last test we had on the Civil War. All during her lectures and the class discussions over the last few weeks, we've been talking about the causes and effects of the war."

"So?"

"Well, then on this test, she asked a lot about battles and generals and other stuff that we didn't study."

"Did you ask her how come?"

"Yeah, I did. She said she wanted to test our thinking ability. But she was asking us to think about material she hadn't even gone over or discussed in class. That's why I think she isn't fair."

Lily is correct. Her teacher, in this instance, isn't being fair. Although she isn't using the term, what Lily is talking about is a matter of *validity*. It appears Ms. Leonard is giving an *invalid* test. What this means, and why it isn't a good thing for a teacher (or any researcher) to do, is largely what this chapter is about.

The Importance of Valid Instrumentation

The quality of the instruments used in research is very important, for the conclusions researchers draw are based on the information they obtain using these instruments. Accordingly, researchers use a number of procedures to ensure that the inferences they draw, based on the data they collect, are valid and reliable.

Validity refers to the appropriateness, meaningfulness, correctness, and usefulness of the inferences a researcher makes. *Reliability* refers to the consistency of scores or answers from one administration of an instrument to another, and from one set of items to another. Both concepts are important to consider when it comes to the selection or design of the instruments a researcher intends to use. In this chapter, therefore, we shall discuss both validity and reliability in some detail.

Validity

Validity is the most important idea to consider when preparing or selecting an instrument for use. More than anything else, researchers want the information they obtain through the use of an instrument to serve their purposes. For example, to find out what teachers in a particular school district think about a recent policy passed by the school board, researchers need both an instrument to record the data and some sort of assurance that the information obtained will enable them to *draw correct conclusions* about teacher opinions. The drawing of correct conclusions based on the data obtained from an assessment is what validity is all about. Though not essential, some kind of score that summarizes the information for each person greatly simplifies the comprehension and use of data, and because most instruments provide such scores, we present the following discussion in this context.

In recent years, **validity** has been defined as referring to the *appropriateness, correctness, meaningfulness,* and *usefulness* of the specific *inferences* researchers make based on the data they collect. *Validation* is the process of collecting and analyzing evidence to support such inferences. There are many ways to collect evidence, and we will discuss some of them shortly. The important point here is to realize that validity refers to the degree to which evidence supports any inferences a researcher makes based on the data he or she collects using a particular instrument. It is the inferences about the specific uses of an instrument that are validated, not the instrument itself.* These inferences should be appropriate, meaningful, correct, and useful.

One interpretation of this conceptualization of validity has been that test publishers no longer have a responsibility to provide evidence of validity. We do not agree; publishers have an obligation to state what an instrument is intended to measure and to provide evidence that it does. Nonetheless, researchers must still give attention to the way in which *they* intend to interpret the information.

An appropriate inference would be one that is relevant—that is, related—to the purposes of the study. If the purpose of a study was to determine what students know about African culture, for example, it would make no sense to make inferences about this from their scores on a test about the physical geography of Africa.

A meaningful inference is one that says something about the *meaning* of the information (such as test scores) obtained through the use of an instrument. What exactly does a high score on a particular test mean? What does such a score allow us to say about the individual who received it? In what way is an individual who receives a high score different from one who receives a low score? And so forth. It is one thing to collect information from people. We do this all the time—names, addresses, birth dates, shoe sizes, car license numbers, and so on. But unless we can make inferences that mean something from the information we obtain, it is of little use. The purpose of research is not merely to collect data but to use such data to draw warranted conclusions about the people (and others like them) on whom the data were collected.

A useful inference is one that helps researchers make a decision related to what they were trying to find out. Researchers interested in the effects of inquiry-related teaching materials on student achievement, for example, need information that will enable them to infer whether achievement is affected by such materials and, if so, how.

Validity, therefore, depends on the amount and type of evidence there is to support the interpretations researchers wish to make concerning data they have collected. The crucial question is: Do the results of the assessment provide useful information about the topic or variable being measured?

What kinds of evidence might a researcher collect? Essentially, there are three main types.

Content-related evidence of validity refers to the content and format of the instrument. How appropriate is the content? How comprehensive? Does it logically get at the intended variable? How adequately does the sample of items or questions represent the content to be assessed? Is the format appropriate? The content and format must be consistent with the definition of the variable and the sample of subjects to be measured.

Criterion-related evidence of validity refers to the relationship between scores obtained using the instrument and scores obtained using one or more other instruments or measures (often called a *criterion*). How strong is this relationship? How well do such scores estimate, present, or predict future performance of a certain type?

Construct-related evidence of validity refers to the nature of the psychological construct or characteristic being measured by the instrument. How well does a measure of the construct explain differences in the behavior of individuals or their performance on certain tasks? We provide further explanation of this rather complex concept later in the chapter.

Figure 8.1 illustrates these three types of evidence.

*This is somewhat of a change from past interpretations. It is based on the set of standards prepared by a joint committee consisting of members of the American Educational Research Association, the American Psychological Association, and the National Council on Measurement in Education. See American Psychological Association. (1985, pp. 9–18; 19–23). *Standards for educational and psychological testing*. Washington, DC: American Psychological Association.

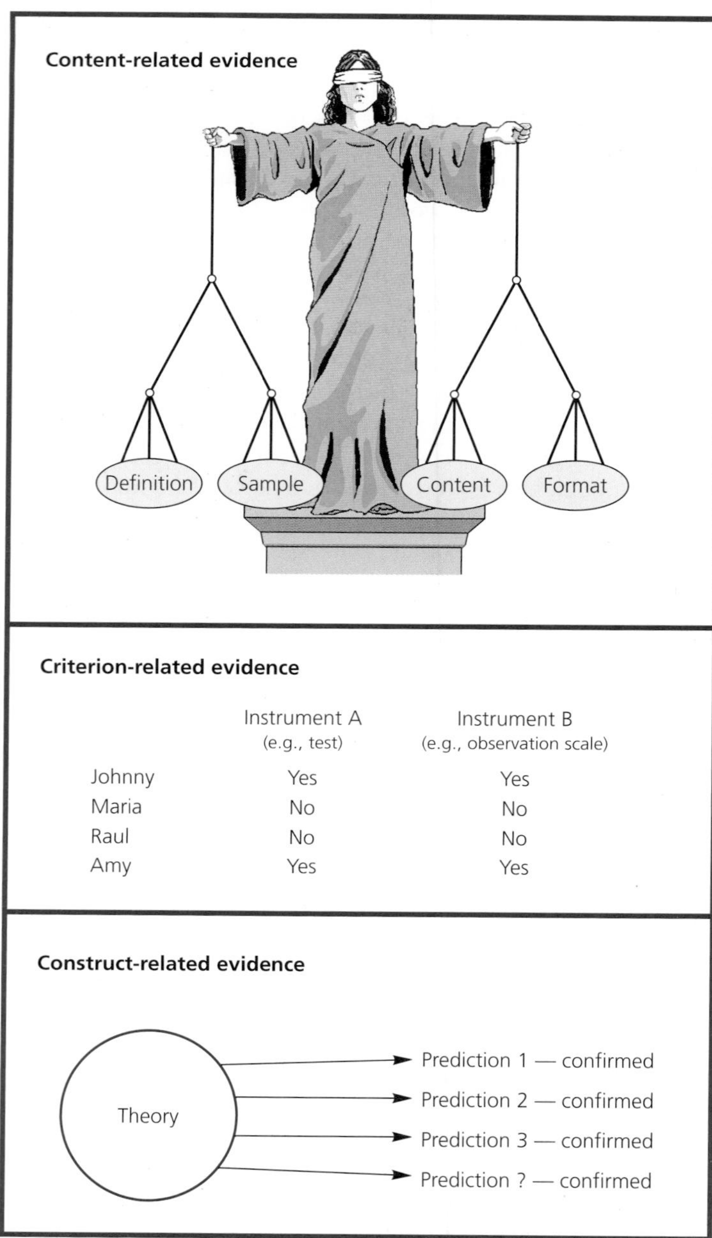

Figure 8.1 *Types of Evidence of Validity*

CONTENT-RELATED EVIDENCE

Suppose a researcher is interested in the effects of a new math program on the mathematics ability of fifth-graders. The researcher expects that students who complete the program will be able to solve a number of different types of word problems correctly. To assess their mathematics ability, the researcher plans to give them a math test containing about 15 such problems. The performance of the students on this test is important only to the degree that it provides evidence of their ability to solve these kinds of problems. Hence, performance on the instrument in this case (the math test) will provide valid evidence of the mathematics ability of these students *if* the instrument provides an adequate sample of the types of word problems covered in the program. If only easy problems are included on the test, or only very difficult or lengthy

High-Stakes Testing

High-stakes testing refers to the use of tests (often only a single achievement test) as the primary, or only, basis for decisions having major consequences. For students, such consequences include retention in grade and/or the denial of diplomas and awards. For schools, they include public praise or condemnation, sanctions, and financial rewards or punishments. "In state after state, legislatures, governors, and state boards, supported by business leaders, have imposed tougher requirements in mathematics, English, science, and other fields, together with new tests by which the performance of both students and schools is to be judged."*

For years, tests had been used as one indicator of performance; what was new was exclusive reliance on them. "The backlash, touching virtually every state that has instituted high-stakes testing, arises from a spectrum of complaints. A major complaint is that the focus on testing and obsessive test preparation, sometimes beginning in kindergarten, is killing innovative teaching and curricula and driving out good teachers. Other complaints are that (conversely) the standards on which the tests are based are too vague and that students have not been taught the material on which the tests are based; or that the tests are unfair to poor and minority students or to those who lack test-taking skills; or that the tests put too much stress on young children. And some argue that they are too long (in Massachusetts they can take up to 13 hours!) or too tough or simply not good enough."*

In response, the American Educational Research Association developed a position statement of "conditions essential to sound implementation of high-stakes educational testing programs."† It contained 14 specific points, 4 of the most important being that (1) such decisions about students should not be based on test scores alone; (2) tests should be made fairer to all students; (3) tests should match the curriculum; and (4) the reliability and validity of tests should continually be evaluated.

Two examples of responses to the guidelines were the following:

- "In the face of too much testing with far too severe consequences, the AERA positions, if implemented, would be a step forward relative to current practice."‡
- "The statement reflects what is desired for all state tests and assessments. But, just as all students have not yet met the standards, not all state tests and assessments will immediately meet the goals contained in this statement."§

What do you think? Are the complaints about high-stakes tests warranted?

*Schrag, P. (2000, August). High stakes are for tomatoes. *Atlantic Monthly, 286*, 19.

†American Educational Research Association. (2000). Position statement of the American Educational Research Association concerning high-stakes testing in pre-12 education. *Educational Researcher, 29* (11), 24–35.

‡Neill, M. (2000). Quoted in Initial responses to AERA's position statement concerning high-stakes testing. *Educational Researcher, 29* (11), 28.

§Martin, W. (2000). Quoted in Initial responses to AERA's position statement concerning high-stakes testing. *Educational Researcher, 29* (11), 27.

ones, or only problems involving subtraction, the test will be unrepresentative and hence not provide information from which valid inferences can be made.

One key element in **content-related evidence of validity**, then, concerns the adequacy of the sampling. Most instruments (and especially achievement tests) provide only a sample of the kinds of problems that might be solved or questions that might be asked. Content validation, therefore, is partly a matter of determining if the content that the instrument contains is an adequate sample of the domain of content it is supposed to represent.

The other aspect of content validation has to do with the format of the instrument. This includes such things as the clarity of printing, size of type, adequacy of work space (if needed), appropriateness of language, clarity of directions, and so on. Regardless of the adequacy of the questions in an instrument, if they are presented in an inappropriate format (such as giving a test written in English to children whose English is minimal), valid results cannot be obtained. For this reason, it is important that the characteristics of the intended sample be kept in mind.

How does one obtain content-related evidence of validity? A common way to do this is to have someone look at the content and format of the instrument and judge whether or not it is appropriate. The "someone," of course, should not be just anyone, but rather an individual who can be expected to render an intelligent judgment about the adequacy of the instrument—in other words, someone who knows enough about what is to be measured to be a competent judge.

The usual procedure is somewhat as follows. The researcher writes out the definition of what he or she wants to measure and then gives this definition, along with the instrument and a description of the intended sample, to one or more judges. The judges look at the definition, read over the items or questions in the instrument, and place a check mark in front of each question or item that they feel does not measure one or more aspects of the definition (e.g., objectives) or other criteria. They also place a check mark in front of each aspect not assessed by any of the items. In addition, the judges evaluate the appropriateness of the instrument format. The researcher then rewrites any item or question so checked and resubmits it to the judges, and/or writes new items for criteria not adequately covered. This continues until the judges approve all the items or questions in the instrument and also indicate that they feel the total number of items is an adequate representation of the total domain of content covered by the variable being measured.

To illustrate how a researcher might go about trying to establish content-related validity, let us consider two examples.

Example 1. Suppose a researcher desires to measure students' ability to *use information that they have previously acquired.* When asked what she means by this phrase, she offers the following definition.

As evidence that students can use previously acquired information, they should be able to:

1. Draw a correct conclusion (verbally or in writing) that is based on information they are given.
2. Identify one or more logical implications that follow from a given point of view.
3. State (orally or in writing) whether two ideas are identical, similar, unrelated, or contradictory.

How might the researcher obtain such evidence? She decides to prepare a written test that will contain various questions. Students' answers will constitute the evidence she seeks. Here are three examples of the kinds of questions she has in mind, designed to produce each of the three types of evidence listed.

1. If A is greater than B, and B is greater than C, then:
   a. A must be greater than C.
   b. C must be smaller than A.
   c. B must be smaller than A.
   d. All of the above are true.
2. Those who believe that increasing consumer expenditures would be the best way to stimulate the economy would advocate
   a. an increase in interest rates.
   b. an increase in depletion allowances.
   c. tax reductions in the lower income brackets.
   d. a reduction in government expenditures.
3. Compare the dollar amounts spent by the U.S. government during the past 10 years for (*a*) debt payments, (*b*) defense, and (*c*) social services.

Now, look at each of the questions and the corresponding objective they are supposed to measure. Do you think each question measures the objective it was designed for? If not, why not?*

Example 2. Here is what another researcher designed as an attempt to measure (at least in part) the ability of students to *explain why events occur.*

Read the directions that follow, and then answer the question.

Directions: Here are some facts.

Fact W: A camper started a fire to cook food on a windy day in a forest.

Fact X: A fire started in some dry grass near a campfire in a forest.

Here is another fact that happened later the same day in the same forest.

Fact Y: A house in the forest burned down.

You are to explain what might have caused the house to burn down (Fact Y). Would Fact W and X be useful as parts of your explanation?

a. Yes, both W and X and the possible cause-and-effect relationship between them would be useful.

b. Yes, both W and X would be useful, even though neither was likely a cause of the other.

c. No, because only one of Facts W and X was likely a cause of Y.

d. No, because neither W or X was likely a cause of Y.[1]

*We would rate correct answers to questions 1 (choice *d*) and 2 (choice *c*) as valid evidence, although 1 could be considered questionable, since students might view it as somewhat tricky. We would not rate the answers to 3 as valid, since students are not asked to contrast ideas, only facts.

Once again, look at the question and the objective it was designed to measure. Does it measure this objective? If not, why not?*

Attempts like these to obtain evidence of some sort (in the previous instances, the support of independent judges that the items measure what they are supposed to measure) typify the process of obtaining content-related evidence of validity. As we mentioned previously, however, the qualifications of the judges are always an important consideration, and the judges must keep in mind the characteristics of the intended sample.

CRITERION-RELATED EVIDENCE

To obtain **criterion-related evidence of validity**, researchers usually compare performance on one instrument (the one being validated) with performance on some other, independent criterion. A **criterion** is a second test or other assessment procedure presumed to measure the same variable. For example, if an instrument has been designed to measure academic ability, student scores on the instrument might be compared with their grade-point averages (the external criterion). If the instrument does indeed measure academic ability, then students who score high on the test would also be expected to have high grade-point averages. Can you see why?

There are two forms of criterion-related validity—predictive and concurrent. To obtain evidence of **predictive validity**, researchers allow a time interval to elapse between administration of the instrument and obtaining the criterion scores. For example, a researcher might administer a science aptitude test to a group of high school students and later compare their scores on the test with their end-of-semester grades in science courses.

On the other hand, when instrument data and criterion data are gathered at nearly the same time, and the results are compared, this is an attempt by researchers to obtain evidence of **concurrent validity**. An example is when a researcher administers a self-esteem inventory to a group of eighth-graders and compares their scores on it with their teachers' ratings of student self-esteem obtained at about the same time.

A key index in both forms of criterion-related validity is the correlation coefficient.† A **correlation coefficient**, symbolized by the letter *r*, indicates the degree of relationship that exists between the scores individuals obtain on two instruments. A positive relationship is indicated when a high score on one of the instruments is accompanied by a high score on the other or when a low score on one is accompanied by a low score on the other. A negative relationship is indicated when a high score on one instrument is accompanied by a low score on the other, and vice versa. All correlation coefficients fall somewhere between +1.00 and −1.00. An *r* of .00 indicates that no relationship exists.

"He looks very promising—but let's see how he does on the written test."

When a correlation coefficient is used to describe the relationship between a set of scores obtained by the same group of individuals on a particular instrument and their scores on some criterion measure, it is called a **validity coefficient**. For example, a validity coefficient of +1.00 obtained by correlating a set of scores on a mathematics aptitude test (the predictor) and another set of scores, this time on a mathematics achievement test (the criterion), for the same individuals would indicate that each individual in the group had exactly the same relative standing on both measures. Such a correlation, if obtained, would allow the researcher to predict perfectly math achievement based on aptitude test scores. Although this correlation coefficient would be very unlikely, it illustrates what such coefficients mean. The higher the validity coefficient obtained, the more accurate a researcher's predictions are likely to be.

*We would rate a correct answer to this question as valid evidence of student ability to explain why events occur.

†The correlation coefficient, explained in detail in Chapter 10, is an extremely useful statistic. This is one of its many applications or uses.

Gronlund suggests the use of an expectancy table as another way to depict criterion-related evidence.[2] An **expectancy table** is nothing more than a two-way chart, with the predictor categories listed down the left-hand side of the chart and the criterion categories listed horizontally along the top of the chart. For each category of scores on the predictor, the researcher then indicates the percentage of individuals who fall within each of the categories on the criterion.

Table 8.1 presents an example. As you can see from the table, 51 percent of the students who were classified outstanding by these judges received a grade of A in orchestra, 35 percent received a B, and 14 percent received a C. Although this table refers only to this particular group, it could be used to predict the scores of other aspiring music students who were evaluated by these same judges. If a student obtained an evaluation of "outstanding," we might predict (approximately) that he or she would have a 51 percent chance of receiving an A, a 35 percent chance of receiving a B, and a 14 percent chance of receiving a C.

Expectancy tables are particularly useful devices for researchers to use with data collected in schools. They are simple to construct, easily understood, and clearly show the relationship between two measures.

It is important to realize that the nature of the criterion is the most important factor in gathering criterion-related evidence. High positive correlations do not mean much if the criterion measure does not make logical sense. For example, a high correlation between scores on an instrument designed to measure aptitude for science and scores on a physical fitness test would not be relevant criterion-related evidence for either instrument. Think back to the example we presented earlier of the questions designed to measure student ability to explain why events occur. What sort of criteria could be used to establish criterion-referenced validity for those items?

TABLE 8.1 *Example of an Expectancy Table*

Judges' Classification of Music Aptitude	Course Grades in Orchestra (Percentage Receiving Each Grade)			
	A	B	C	D
Outstanding	51	35	14	0
Above average	20	43	37	0
Average	0	6	83	11
Below average	0	0	13	87

CONSTRUCT-RELATED EVIDENCE

Construct-related evidence of validity is the broadest of the three categories of evidence for validity that we are considering. There is no single piece of evidence that satisfies construct-related validity. Rather, researchers attempt to collect a variety of *different* types of evidence (the more and the more varied the better) that will allow them to make warranted inferences—to assert, for example, that the scores obtained from administering a self-esteem inventory permit accurate inferences about the degree of self-esteem that people who receive those scores possess.

Usually, there are three steps involved in obtaining construct-related evidence of validity: (1) the variable being measured is clearly defined; (2) hypotheses, based on a theory underlying the variable, are formed about how people who possess a lot versus a little of the variable will behave in a particular situation; and (3) the hypotheses are tested both logically and empirically.

To make the process clearer, let us consider an example. Suppose a researcher interested in developing a pencil-and-paper test to measure honesty wants to use a construct-validity approach. First, he defines *honesty*. Next he formulates a theory about how "honest" people behave as compared to "dishonest" people. For example, he might theorize that honest individuals, if they find an object that does not belong to them, will make a reasonable effort to locate the individual to whom the object belongs. Based on this theory, the researcher might hypothesize that individuals who score high on his honesty test will be more likely to attempt to locate the owner of an object they find than individuals who score low on the test. The researcher then administers the honesty test, separates the names of those who score high and those who score low, and gives all of them an opportunity to be honest. He might, for example, leave a wallet with $5 in it lying just outside the test-taking room so that the individuals taking the test can easily see it and pick it up. The wallet displays the name and phone number of the owner in plain view. If the researcher's hypothesis is substantiated, more of the high scorers than the low scorers on the honesty test will attempt to call the owner of the wallet. (This could be checked by having the number answered by a recording machine asking the caller to leave his or her name and number.) This is one piece of evidence that could be used to support inferences about the honesty of individuals, based on the scores they receive on this test.

We must stress, however, that a researcher must carry out a series of studies to obtain a *variety* of evidence suggesting that the scores from a particular instrument can be used to draw correct inferences about the variable that the instrument purports to measure. It is a broad array of evidence, rather than any one particular type of evidence, that is desired.

Consider a second example. Some evidence that might be considered to support a claim for construct validity in connection with a test designed to measure mathematical reasoning ability might be as follows:

- Independent judges all indicate that all items on the test require mathematical reasoning.
- Independent judges all indicate that the features of the test itself (such as test format, directions, scoring, and reading level) would not in any way prevent students from engaging in mathematical reasoning.
- Independent judges all indicate that the sample of tasks included in the test is relevant and representative of mathematical reasoning tasks.
- A high correlation exists between scores on the test and grades in mathematics.
- High scores have been made on the test by students who have had specific training in mathematical reasoning.
- Students actually engage in mathematical reasoning when they are asked to "think aloud" as they go about trying to solve the problems on the test.
- A high correlation exists between scores on the test and teacher ratings of competence in mathematical reasoning.
- Higher scores are obtained on the test by mathematics majors than by general science majors.

Other types of evidence might be listed for the preceding task (perhaps you can think of some), but we hope this is enough to make clear that it is not just one type, but many types, of evidence that a researcher seeks to obtain. Determining whether the scores obtained through the use of a particular instrument measure a particular variable involves a study of how the test was developed, the theory underlying the test, how the test functions with a variety of people and in a variety of situations, and how scores on the test relate to scores on other appropriate instruments. Construct validation involves, then, a wide variety of procedures and many different types of evidence, including both content-related and criterion-related evidence. The more evidence researchers have from many different sources, the more confident they become about interpreting the scores obtained from a particular instrument.

Reliability

Reliability refers to the consistency of the scores obtained—how consistent they are for each individual from one administration of an instrument to another and from one set of items to another. Consider, for example, a test designed to measure typing ability. If the test is reliable, we would expect a student who receives a high score the first time he takes the test to receive a high score the next time he takes the test. The scores would probably not be identical, but they should be close.

The scores obtained from an instrument can be quite reliable but not valid. Suppose a researcher gave a group of eighth-graders two forms of a test designed to measure their knowledge of the Constitution of the United States and found their scores to be consistent: those who scored high on form A also scored high on form B; those who scored low on A scored low on B; and so on. We would say that the scores were reliable. But if the researcher then used these same test scores to predict the success of these students in their physical education classes, she would probably be looked at in amazement. Any inferences about success in physical education based on scores on a Constitution test would have no validity. Now, what about the reverse? Can an instrument that yields unreliable scores permit valid inferences? No! If scores are completely inconsistent for a person, they provide no useful information. We have no way of knowing which score to use to infer an individual's ability, attitude, or other characteristic.

The distinction between reliability and validity is shown in Figure 8.2. Reliability and validity always depend on the context in which an instrument is used. Depending on the context, an instrument may or may not yield reliable (consistent) scores. If the data are unreliable, they cannot lead to valid (legitimate) inferences—as shown in target (*a*). As reliability improves, validity may improve, as shown in target (*b*), or it may not, as shown in target (*c*). An instrument may have good reliability but low validity, as shown in target (*d*). What is desired, of course, is both high reliability and high validity, as target (*e*) shows.

ERRORS OF MEASUREMENT

Whenever people take the same test twice, they will seldom perform exactly the same—that is, their scores or answers will not usually be identical. This may be due to a variety of factors (differences in motivation,

Figure 8.2 *Reliability and Validity*

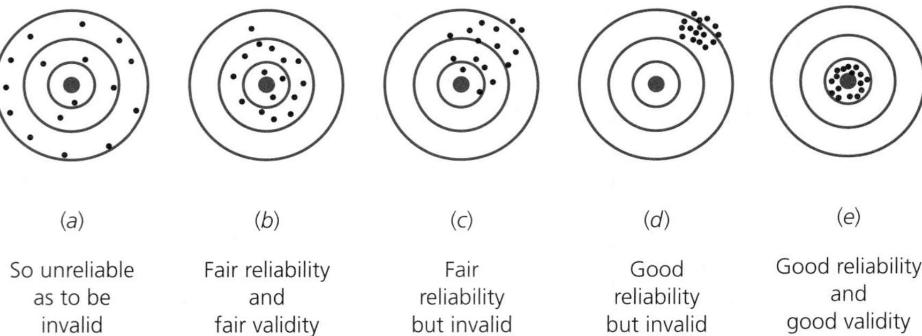

The bull's-eye in each target represents the information that is desired. Each dot represents a separate score obtained with the instrument. A dot in the bull's-eye indicates that the information obtained (the score) is the information the researcher desires.

energy, anxiety, a different testing situation, and so on), and it is inevitable. Such factors result in **errors of measurement** (Figure 8.3).

Because errors of measurement are always present to some degree, researchers expect some variation in test scores (e.g., in answers or ratings) when an instrument is administered to the same group more than once, when two different forms of an instrument are used, or even from one part of an instrument to another. Reliability estimates provide researchers with an idea of how much variation to expect. Such estimates are usually expressed as another application of the correlation coefficient known as a **reliability coefficient**.

As we mentioned earlier, a validity coefficient expresses the relationship between scores of the same individuals on two *different* instruments. A reliability coefficient also expresses a relationship, but this time it is between scores of the same individuals on the same instrument at two different times, or on two parts of the *same* instrument. The three best-known ways to obtain a reliability coefficient are the test-retest method, the equivalent-forms method; and the internal-consistency methods. Unlike other uses of the correlation coefficient, reliability coefficients must range from .00 to 1.00—that is, have no negative values.

"I can't believe that my blood pressure is 170 over 110!"

"Maybe it's due to poor reliability of the measurement. Let's wait a few minutes, and check it again."

Figure 8.3 *Reliability of a Measurement*

TEST-RETEST METHOD

The **test-retest method** involves administering the same test twice to the *same* group after a certain time interval has elapsed. A reliability coefficient is then calculated to indicate the relationship between the two sets of scores obtained.

Reliability coefficients will be affected by the length of time that elapses between the two administrations of the test. The longer the time interval, the lower the reliability coefficient is likely to be, since there is a greater likelihood of changes in the individuals taking the test. In checking for evidence of test-retest reliability, an appropriate time interval should be selected. This interval should be that during which individuals would be assumed to retain their relative position in a meaningful group.

There is no point in studying, or even conceptualizing, a variable that fluctuates wildly in individuals for whom it is measured. When researchers assess someone as academically talented, for example, or skilled in typing or as having a poor self-concept, they assume that this characteristic will continue to differentiate individuals for some period of time. It is impossible to study a variable that has no stability in the individual.

Researchers do not expect all variables to be equally stable. Experience has shown that some abilities (such as writing) are more subject to change than others (such as abstract reasoning). Some personal characteristics (such as self-esteem) are considered to be more stable than others (such as teenage vocational interests). Mood is a variable that, by definition, is considered to be stable for short periods of time—a matter of minutes or hours. But even here, unless the instrumentation used is reliable, meaningful relationships with other (perhaps causal) variables will not be found. For most educational research, stability of scores over a two- to three-month period is usually viewed as sufficient evidence of test-retest reliability. In reporting test-retest reliability coefficients, therefore, the time interval between the two testings should always be reported.

EQUIVALENT-FORMS METHOD

When the **equivalent-forms method** is used, two different but equivalent (also called *alternate* or *parallel*) forms of an instrument are administered to the *same* group of individuals during the same time period. Although the questions are different, they should sample the same content and they should be constructed separately from each other. A reliability coefficient is then calculated between the two sets of scores obtained. A high coefficient would indicate strong evidence of reliability—that the two forms are measuring the same thing.

It is possible to combine the test-retest and equivalent- forms methods by giving two different forms of the same test with a time interval between the two administrations. A high reliability coefficient would indicate not only that the two forms are measuring the same sort of performance but also what we might expect with regard to consistency over time.

INTERNAL-CONSISTENCY METHODS

The methods mentioned so far all require two administration or testing sessions. There are several **internal-consistency methods** of estimating reliability, however, that require only a single administration of an instrument.

Split-half Procedure. The **split-half procedure** involves scoring two halves (usually odd items versus even items) of a test separately for each person and then calculating a correlation coefficient for the two sets of scores. The coefficient indicates the degree to which the two halves of the test provide the same results and hence describes the internal consistency of the test.

The reliability coefficient is calculated using what is known as the *Spearman-Brown prophecy formula*. A simplified version of this formula is:

$$\text{Reliability of scores on total test} = \frac{2 \times \text{reliability for } \frac{1}{2} \text{ test}}{1 + \text{reliability for } \frac{1}{2} \text{ test}}$$

Thus, if we obtained a correlation coefficient of .56 by comparing one-half of the test items to the other half, the reliability of scores for the total test would be:

$$\text{Reliability of scores on total test} = \frac{2 \times .56}{1 + .56} = \frac{1.12}{1.56} = .72$$

This illustrates an important characteristic of reliability. The reliability of a test (or any instrument) can generally be increased by the addition of more items, provided they are similar to the original ones.

Kuder-Richardson Approaches. Perhaps the most frequently employed method for determining internal consistency is the **Kuder-Richardson approach**, particularly formulas KR20 and KR21. The latter formula requires only three pieces of information—the number of items on the test, the mean, and the standard deviation. Note, however, that formula KR21 can be used only if it can be assumed that the items are of equal difficulty.* A frequently used version of the KR21 formula is:

$$\text{KR21 reliability coefficient} = \frac{K}{K-1}\left[1 - \frac{M(K-M)}{K(SD^2)}\right]$$

where K = number of items on the test, M = mean of the set of test scores, and SD = standard deviation of the set of test scores.†

Although this formula may look somewhat intimidating, its use is actually quite simple. For example, if

*Formula KR20 does not require the assumption that all items are of equal difficulty, although it is harder to calculate. Computer programs for doing so are commonly available, however, and should be used whenever a researcher cannot assume that all items are of equal difficulty.

†See Chapter 10 for an explanation of standard deviation.

Checking Reliability and Validity—An Example

The projective device (Picture Situation Inventory) described on pages 132 and 133 consists of 20 pictures, each scored on the variables *control need* and *communication* according to a point system. For example, here are some illustrative responses to picture 1 of Figure 7.23. The control need variable, defined as "motivated to control moment-to-moment activities of their students," is scored as follows:

- "I thought you would enjoy something special." (1 point)
- "I'd like to see how well you can do it." (2 points)
- "You and Tom are two different children." (3 points)
- "Yes, I would appreciate it if you would finish it." (4 points)
- "Do it quickly please." (5 points)

In addition to the appeal to content validity, there is some evidence in support of these two measures (control and communication).

Rowan studied relationships between the two scores and several other measures with a group of elementary school teachers.* She found that teachers scoring high on control need were more likely to (1) be seen by classroom observers as imposing themselves on situations and having a higher content emphasis, (2) be judged by interviewers as having more rigid attitudes of right and wrong, and (3) score higher on a test of authoritarian tendencies.

In a study of ability to predict success in a program preparing teachers for inner-city classrooms, evidence was found that the Picture Situation Inventory control score had predictive value.†

Correlations existed between the control score obtained on entrance to the program and a variety of measures subsequently obtained through classroom observation in student teaching and subsequent first-year teaching assignments. The most clear-cut finding was that those scoring higher in control need had classrooms observed as less noisy. The finding adds somewhat to the validity of the measurement, since a teacher with higher control need would be expected to have a quieter room.

The reliability of both measures was found to be adequate (.74 and .81) when assessed by the split-half procedure. When assessed by follow-up over a period of eight years, the consistency over time was considerably lower (.61 and .53), as would be expected.

*Rowan, N. T. (1967). The relationship of teacher interaction in classroom situations to teacher personality variables. Unpublished doctoral dissertation. Salt Lake City: University of Utah.

†Wallen, N. E. (1971). *Evaluation report to Step-TTT Project.* San Francisco, CA: San Francisco State University.

$K = 50$, $M = 40$, and $SD = 4$, the reliability coefficient would be calculated as:

$$\begin{aligned}\text{Reliability} &= \frac{50}{49}\left[1 - \frac{40(50-40)}{50(4^2)}\right]\\ &= 1.02\left[1 - \frac{40(10)}{50(16)}\right]\\ &= 1.02\left[1 - \frac{400}{800}\right]\\ &= (1.02)(1 - .50)\\ &= (1.02)(.50)\\ &= .51\end{aligned}$$

Thus, the reliability estimate for scores on this test is .51.

Is a reliability estimate of .51 good or bad? high or low? As is frequently the case, there are some benchmarks we can use to evaluate reliability coefficients. First, we can compare a given coefficient with the extremes that are possible. As you will recall, a coefficient of .00 indicates a complete absence of a relationship, hence no reliability at all, whereas 1.00 is the maximum possible coefficient that can be obtained. Second, we can compare a given reliability coefficient with the sorts of coefficients that are usually obtained for measures of the same type. The reported reliability coefficients for many commercially available achievement tests, for example, are typically .90 or higher when Kuder-Richardson formulas are used. Many classroom tests report reliability coefficients of .70 and higher. Compared to these figures, our obtained coefficient must be judged rather low. For research purposes, a useful rule of thumb is that reliability should be at least .70 and preferably higher.

Alpha Coefficient. Another check on the internal consistency of an instrument is to calculate an

TABLE 8.2 *Methods of Checking Validity and Reliability*

Validity ("Truthfulness")			
Method			**Procedure**
Content-related evidence			Obtain expert judgment
Criterion-related evidence			Relate to another measure of the same variable
Construct-related evidence			Assess evidence on predictions made from theory
Reliability ("Consistency")			
Method	**Content**	**Time Interval**	**Procedure**
Test-retest	Identical	Varies	Give identical instrument twice
Equivalent forms	Different	None	Give two forms of instrument
Equivalent forms/ retest	Different	Varies	Give two forms of instrument, with time interval between
Internal consistency	Different	None	Divide instrument into halves and score each or use Kuder-Richardson approach
Scoring observer agreement	Identical	None	Compare scores obtained by two or more observers or scorers

alpha coefficient (frequently called **Cronbach alpha** after the man who developed it). This coefficient (α) is a general form of the KR20 formula to be used in calculating the reliability of items that are not scored right versus wrong, as in some essay tests where more than one answer is possible.[3]

Table 8.2 summarizes the methods used in checking the validity and reliability of an instrument.

THE STANDARD ERROR OF MEASUREMENT (SEMeas)

The **standard error of measurement (SEMeas)** is an index that shows the extent to which a measurement would vary under changed circumstances (i.e., the amount of *measurement error*). Because there are many ways in which circumstances can vary, there are many possible standard errors for a given score. For example, the standard error will be smaller if it includes only error due to different content (internal-consistency or equivalent-forms reliability) than if it also includes error due to the passage of time (test-retest reliability). Under the assumption that errors of measurement are normally distributed (see p. 195 in Chapter 10), a range of scores can be determined that shows the amount of error to be expected.

For many IQ tests, the standard error of measurement over a one-year period and with different specific content is about 5 points. Over a 10-year period, it is about 8 points. This means that a score fluctuates considerably more the longer the time between measurements. Thus, a person scoring 110 can expect to have a score between 100 and 120 one year later; five years later, the score can be expected to be between 94 and 126 (Figure 8.4). Note that we doubled the standard errors of measurement in computing the ranges within which the second score is expected to fall. This was done so we could be 95 percent sure that our estimates were correct.

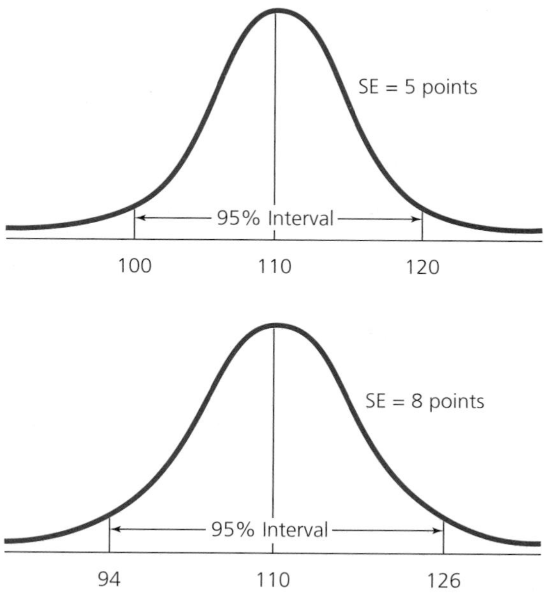

Figure 8.4 *Standard Error of Measurement*

The formula for the standard error of measurement is $SD\sqrt{1 - r_{11}}$ where SD = the standard deviation of scores and r_{11} = the reliability coefficient appropriate to the conditions that vary. In the preceding example, the standard error (SEMeas) of 5 in the first example was obtained as follows:

$$SD = 16, r_{11} = .90$$

$$SEM = 16\sqrt{1 - .90} = 16\sqrt{.10} = 16(.32) = 5.1$$

SCORING AGREEMENT

Most tests and many other instruments are administered with specific directions and are scored objectively, that is, with a key that requires no judgment on the part of the scorer. Although differences in the resulting scores with different administrators or scorers are still possible, it is generally considered highly unlikely that they would occur. This is not the case with instruments that are susceptible to differences in administration, scoring, or both, such as essay evaluations. In particular, instruments that use direct observation are highly vulnerable to observer differences. Researchers who use such instruments are obliged to investigate and report the degree of **scoring agreement**. Such agreement is enhanced by training the observers and by increasing the number of observation periods.

Instruments differ in the amount of training required for their use. In general, observation techniques require considerable training for optimum use. Such training usually consists of explaining and discussing the procedures involved, followed by trainees using the instruments as they observe video or live situations. All trainees observe the same behaviors and then discuss any differences in scoring. This process, or some variation thereon, is repeated until independent observers reach an acceptable level of agreement. What is desired is a correlation of at least .90 among scorers or agreement of at least 80 percent. Usually, even after such training, 8 to 12 observation periods are required to get evidence of adequate reliability over time.

To further illustrate the concept of reliability, let's take an actual test and calculate the internal consistency of its items. Figure 8.5 presents an example of a

Figure 8.5 *The "Quick and Easy" Intelligence Test*

Directions: Read each of the following questions and write your answers on a separate sheet of paper. Suggested time to take the test is 10 minutes.

1. There are two people in a room. The first is the son of the second person, but the second person is not the first person's father. How are the two people related?
2. Who is buried in Grant's tomb?
3. Some months have 30 days, some have 31. How many have 28 days?
4. If you had only one match and entered a dark room in which there was an oil lamp, an oil heater, and some firewood, which would you light first?
5. If a physician gave you three pills and told you to take one every half hour, how long would they last?
6. A person builds a house with four sides to it, a rectangular structure, with each side having a southern exposure. A big bear comes wandering by. What color is the bear?
7. A farmer has 17 sheep. All but 9 died. How many did he have left?
8. Divide 30 by $\frac{1}{2}$. Add 10. What is the correct answer?
9. Take two apples from three apples. What do you have?
10. How many animals of each species did Moses take aboard the Ark?

Is Consequential Validity a Useful Concept?

In recent years, increased attention has been given to a concept called *consequential validity,* originally proposed by Samuel Messick in 1989.* He intended not to change the core meaning of *validity* but to expand it to include two new ideas: "value implications" and "social consequences."

Paying attention to value implications requires the "appraisal of the value implications of the construct label, of the theory underlying test interpretation, and the ideologies in which the theory is imbedded."† This involves expanding the idea of construct-related evidence of validity that we discussed on pages 154–155. *Social consequences* refers to "the appraisal of both potential and actual social consequences of applied testing."

Disagreement with Messick has been primarily with regard to applying his proposal. Using his experience as a developer of a widely used college admissions test battery (ACT) as an example, Reckase systematically analyzed the feasibility of using this concept. He concluded that, although difficult, the critical analysis of value implications is both feasible and useful.‡

However, he argued that assessing the cause-and-effect relationships implied in determining potential and actual social consequences of the use of a test is difficult or impossible, even with a clear intended use such as determining college admissions. Citing the concern of the National Commission on Testing and Public Policy that such tests often undermine vital social policies,§ he argues that obtaining the necessary data seems unlikely and that, by definition, appraising unintended consequences is not possible ahead of time, because one does not know what they are.

What do you think of Messick's proposal?

*Messick, S. (1989). Consequential validity. In R. L. Linn (Ed.). *Educational measurement* (3rd ed., pp. 13–103). New York: American Council on Education.

†Messick, S. (1989). Consequential validity. In R. L. Linn (Ed.). *Educational measurement* (3rd ed., p. 20). New York: American Council on Education.

‡Reckase, M. D. (1998). Consequential validity from the test developer's perspective. *Educational Measurement Issues and Practice, 17* (2), 13–16.

§National Commission on Testing and Public Policy. *From gatekeeper to gateway: Transforming testing in America* (Technical report). Chestnut Hill, MA: Boston College.

nontypical intelligence test that we have adapted. Follow the directions and take the test. Then we will calculate the split-half reliability.

Now look at the answer key in the footnote at the bottom of page 162. Give yourself one point for each correct answer. Assume, for the moment, that a score on this test provides an indication of intelligence. If so, each item on the test should be a partial measure of intelligence. We could, therefore, divide the 10-item test into two 5-item tests. One of these 5-item tests can consist of all the odd-numbered items, and the other 5-item test can consist of all the even-numbered items. Now, record your score on the odd-numbered items and also on the even-numbered items.

We now want to see if the odd-numbered items provide a measure of intelligence similar to that provided by the even-numbered items. If they do, your scores on the odd-numbered items and the even-numbered items should be pretty close. If they are not, then the two 5-item tests do not give consistent results. If this is the case, then the total test (the 10 items) probably does not give consistent results either, in which case the score could not be considered a reliable measure.

Ask five other people to take the test. Record their scores on the odd and even sets of items, using the worksheet shown in Figure 8.6.

Take a look at the scores on each of the five-item sets for each of the five individuals, and compare them with your own. What would you conclude about the reliability of the scores? What would you say about any

Person	Score on five-item test 1 (#1, 3, 5, 7, 9)	Score on five-item test 2 (#2, 4, 6, 8, 10)
You	________	________
#1	________	________
#2	________	________
#3	________	________
#4	________	________
#5	________	________

Figure 8.6 *Reliability Worksheet*

inferences about intelligence a researcher might make based on scores on this test? Could they be valid?*

Note that we have examined only one aspect of reliability (internal consistency) for results of this test. We still do not know how much a person's score might change if we gave the test at two different times (test-retest reliability). We could get a different indication of reliability if we gave one of the five-item tests at one time and the other five-item test at another time to the same people (equivalent-forms/retest reliability). Try to do this with a few individuals, using a worksheet like the one shown in Figure 8.6.

Researchers typically use the procedures just described to establish reliability. Normally, however, they test many more people (at least 100). You should also realize that most tests would have many more than 10 items, since longer tests are usually more reliable than short ones, presumably because they provide a larger sampling of a person's behavior.

In sum, we hope it is clear that a major aspect of research design is the obtaining of reliable and valid information. Because both reliability and validity depend on the way in which instruments are used and on the inferences researchers wish to make from them, researchers can never simply assume that their instrumentation will provide satisfactory information. They can have more confidence if they use instruments on which there is previous evidence of reliability and validity, provided they use the instruments in the same way—that is, under the same conditions as existed previously. Even then, researchers cannot be sure; even when all else remains the same, the mere passage of time may have impaired the instrument in some way.

What this means is that there is no substitute for checking reliability and validity as a part of the research procedure. There is seldom any excuse for failing to check internal consistency, since the necessary information is at hand and no additional data collection is required. Reliability over time does, in most cases, require an additional administration of an instrument, but this can often be done. In considering this option, it should be noted that not all members of the sample need be retested, though this is desirable. It is better to retest a randomly selected subsample, or even a convenience subsample, than to have no evidence of retest reliability at all. Another option is to test and retest a different, though very similar, sample.

Obtaining evidence on validity is more difficult but seldom prohibitive. Content-related evidence can usually be obtained, since it requires only a few knowledgeable and available judges. It is unreasonable to expect a great deal of construct-related evidence to be obtained, but, in many studies, criterion-related evidence can be obtained. At a minimum, a second instrument should be administered. Locating or developing an additional means of instrumentation is sometimes difficult and occasionally impossible (e.g., there is probably no way to validate a self-report questionnaire on sexual behavior), but the results are well worth the time and energy involved. As with retest reliability, a subsample can be used, or both instruments can be given to a different, but similar, sample.

VALIDITY AND RELIABILITY IN QUALITATIVE RESEARCH

While many qualitative researchers use many of the procedures we have described, some take the position that validity and reliability, as we have discussed them, are either irrelevant or not suited to their research efforts because they are attempting to describe a specific situation or event as viewed by a particular individual. They emphasize instead the honesty, believability, expertise, and integrity of the researcher. We maintain that all researchers should ensure that any inferences they draw that are based on data obtained through the use of an instrument are appropriate, credible, and backed up by evidence of the sort we have described in this chapter.

Specific methods for enhancing the validity and reliability of qualitative studies are discussed in Chapters 18, 19, and 21. Moreover, in the next chapter, we discuss the concept of *internal validity* and how it applies both to quantitative and qualitative research.

*You might want to assess the content validity of this test. How would you define *intelligence?* As you define the term, how would you evaluate this test as a measure of intelligence?

Answer Key for Q-E Intelligence Test on page 160. 1. Mother and son; 2. Ulysses S. Grant; 3. All of them; 4. The match; 5. One hour; 6. White; 7. Nine; 8. 70; 9. Two; 10. None. (It wasn't Moses, but Noah who took the animals on the Ark.)

Go back to the **INTERACTIVE AND APPLIED LEARNING** feature at the beginning of the chapter for a listing of interactive and applied activities. Go to the **Online Learning Center** at **www.mhhe.com/fraenkel9e** to take quizzes, practice with key terms, and review chapter content.

Main Points

VALIDITY

- It is important for researchers to use valid instruments, for the conclusions they draw are based on the information they obtain using these instruments.
- The term *validity,* as used in research, refers to the appropriateness, meaningfulness, correctness, and usefulness of any inferences a researcher draws based on data obtained through the use of an instrument.
- Content-related evidence of validity refers to judgments on the content and logical structure of an instrument as it is to be used in a particular study.
- Criterion-related evidence of validity refers to the degree to which information provided by an instrument agrees with information obtained on other, independent instruments.
- A criterion is a standard for judging; with reference to validity, it is a second instrument against which scores on an instrument can be checked.
- Construct-related evidence of validity refers to the degree to which the totality of evidence obtained is consistent with theoretical expectations.
- A validity coefficient is a numerical index representing the degree of correspondence between scores on an instrument and a criterion measure.
- An expectancy table is a two-way chart used to evaluate criterion-related evidence of validity.

RELIABILITY

- The term *reliability,* as used in research, refers to the consistency of scores or answers provided by an instrument.
- Errors of measurement refer to variations in scores obtained by the same individuals on the same instrument.
- The test-retest method of estimating reliability involves administering the same instrument twice to the same group of individuals after a certain time interval has elapsed.
- The equivalent-forms method of estimating reliability involves administering two different, but equivalent, forms of an instrument to the same group of individuals at the same time.
- The internal-consistency method of estimating reliability involves comparing responses to different sets of items that are part of an instrument.
- Scoring agreement requires a demonstration that independent scorers can achieve satisfactory agreement in their scoring.
- The standard error of measurement is a numerical index of measurement error.

Key Terms

alpha coefficient 159
concurrent validity 153
construct-related evidence of validity 154
content-related evidence of validity 151
correlation coefficient 153
criterion 153
criterion-related evidence of validity 153
Cronbach alpha 159
equivalent-forms method 157
errors of measurement 156
expectancy table 154
internal-consistency methods 157
Kuder-Richardson approach 157
predictive validity 153
reliability 155
reliability coefficient 156
scoring agreement 160
split-half procedure 157
standard error of measurement (SEMeas) 159
test-retest method 156
validity 149
validity coefficient 153

For Discussion

1. We point out in the chapter that scores from an instrument may be reliable but not valid, yet not the reverse. Why would this be so?
2. What type of evidence—content-related, criterion-related, or construct-related—do you think is the easiest to obtain? the hardest? Why?
3. In what way(s) might the format of an instrument affect its validity?
4. "There is no single piece of evidence that satisfies construct-related validity." Is this statement true? If so, explain why.
5. Which do you think is harder to obtain, validity or reliability? Why?
6. Might reliability ever be more important than validity? Explain.
7. How would you assess the Q-E Intelligence Test in Figure 8.5 with respect to validity? Explain.
8. The importance of using *valid* instruments in research cannot be overstated. Why?

References

1. Wallen, N. E., Durkin, M. C., Fraenkel, J. R., McNaughton, A. J., & Sawin, E. I. (1969, p. 307). *The Taba Curriculum Development Project in Social Studies: Development of a comprehensive curriculum model for social studies for grades one through eight, inclusive of procedures for implementation and dissemination.* Menlo Park, CA: Addison-Wesley.

2. Gronlund, N. E. (1988). *How to construct achievement tests* (4th ed., p. 140). Englewood Cliffs, NJ: Prentice Hall.

3. See Cronbach, L. J. (1951). Coefficient alpha and the internal structure of tests. *Psychometrika, 16,* 297–334.

Research Exercise 8: Validity and Reliability

Use Problem Sheet 8 to describe how you plan to check on the validity and reliability of scores obtained with your instruments. If you plan to use an existing instrument, summarize what you have been able to learn about the validity and reliability of results obtained with it. If you plan to develop an instrument, explain how you will attempt to ensure validity and reliability. In either case, explain how you will obtain evidence to check validity and reliability.

Problem Sheet 8

Validity and Reliability

1. My research question is: ______________________________

   ____

2. If you plan to use an *existing* instrument, describe what you have learned about the validity and reliability of scores obtained with this instrument.

   ____

   ____

3. If you plan to *develop* an instrument, explain how you will try to ensure the validity and reliability of results obtained with this instrument by using one or more of the tips described on page 115 (*specify which*).

   ____

   ____

4. If you have not already indicated so above for each instrument that you plan to use, tell specifically how you will check for:

   a. internal consistency ______________________________

   ____

   b. stability (reliability over time) ______________________________

   ____

   c. validity ______________________________

   ____

An electronic version of this Problem Sheet that you can fill in and print, save, or e-mail is available on the Online Learning Center at www.mhhe.com/fraenkel9e.

9 Internal Validity

What Is Internal Validity?

Threats to Internal Validity

Subject Characteristics
Loss of Subjects (Mortality)
Location
Instrumentation
Testing
History
Maturation
Attitude of Subjects
Regression
Implementation
Factors That Reduce the Likelihood of Finding a Relationship

How Can a Researcher Minimize These Threats to Internal Validity?

Two Points to Emphasize

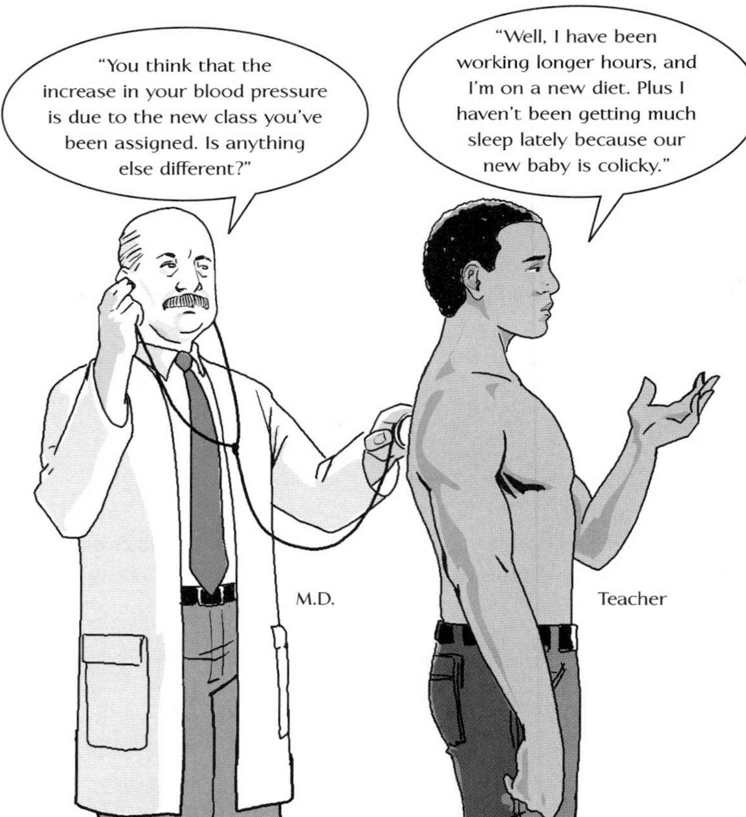

"You think that the increase in your blood pressure is due to the new class you've been assigned. Is anything else different?"
"Well, I have been working longer hours, and I'm on a new diet. Plus I haven't been getting much sleep lately because our new baby is colicky."
M.D.
Teacher

OBJECTIVES **Studying this chapter should enable you to:**

- Explain what is meant by the term "internal validity."
- Explain what is meant by each of the following threats to internal validity and give an example of each:
  - "subject characteristics" threat
  - "mortality" threat
  - "location" threat
  - "instrumentation" threat
  - "testing" threat
  - "history" threat
  - "maturation" threat
  - "subject attitude" threat
  - "regression" threat
  - "implementation" threat
- Identify various threats to internal validity in published research articles.
- Suggest possible remedies for specific examples of the various threats to internal validity.

INTERACTIVE AND APPLIED LEARNING After, or while, reading this chapter:

Go to the Online Learning Center at www.mhhe.com/fraenkel9e to:

- Learn More About Internal Validity

Go to your online Student Mastery Activities book to do the following activities:

- Activity 9.1: Threats to Internal Validity
- Activity 9.2: What Type of Threat?
- Activity 9.3: Controlling Threats to Internal Validity

Suppose the results of a study show that high school students taught by the inquiry method score higher on a test of critical thinking, on the average, than do students taught by the lecture method. Is this difference in scores due to the difference in methods—to the fact that the two groups have been taught differently? Surely, the researcher who is conducting the study would like to conclude this. Your first inclination may be to think the same. This may not be a legitimate interpretation, however.

What if the students who were taught using the inquiry method were better critical thinkers to begin with? What if some of the students in the inquiry group were also taking a related course during this time at a nearby university? What if the teachers of the inquiry group were simply better teachers? Any of these (or other) factors might explain why the inquiry group scored higher on the critical thinking test. Should this be the case, the researcher may be mistaken in concluding that there is a difference in effectiveness between the two methods, for the obtained difference in results may be due *not* to the difference in methods but to something else.

In any study that either describes or tests relationships, there is always the possibility that the relationship shown in the data is, in fact, due to or explained by something else. If so, the relationship observed is not at all what it seems and it may lose whatever meaning it appears to have. Many alternative hypotheses may exist, in other words, to explain the outcomes of a study. These alternative explanations are often referred to as *threats to internal validity,* and they are what this chapter is about.

What Is Internal Validity?

Perhaps unfortunately, the term *validity* is used in three different ways by researchers. In addition to internal validity, which we discuss in this chapter, you will see reference to instrument (or measurement) validity, as discussed in Chapter 8, and external (or generalization) validity, as discussed in Chapter 6.

When a study has **internal validity**, it means that any relationship observed between two or more variables should be unambiguous as to what it means rather than being due to "something else." The "something else" may, as we suggested, be any one (or more) of a number of factors, such as the age or ability of the subjects, the conditions under which the study is conducted, or the type of materials used. If these factors are not in some way or another controlled or accounted for, the researcher can never be sure that they are not the reason for any observed results. Stated differently, internal validity means that observed differences on the dependent variable are directly related to the independent variable, and not due to some other unintended variable.

In qualitative research, a study is said to have good internal validity if alternative explanations (the "something else") have been systematically ruled out. Toward that goal, qualitative researchers should have a plan for how they treat discrepant or disconfirming data. Regardless of whether a study is qualitative or quantitative, if these "rival hypotheses" are not controlled or accounted for in some way, the researcher can never be sure that they are not the reason for any observed results.

Consider this example. Suppose a researcher finds a correlation of .80 between height and mathematics test scores for a group of elementary school students (grades 1–5)—that is, the taller students have higher math scores. Such a result is quite misleading. Why? Because it is clearly a by-product of age. Fifth-graders are taller and better in math than first-graders simply because they are older and more developed. To explore this relationship further is pointless; to let it affect school practice would be absurd.

Or consider a study in which the researcher hypothesizes that, in classes for learning-disabled students, teacher expectation of student failure is related to amount of disruptive behavior. Suppose the researcher finds a high correlation between these two variables. Should he or she conclude that this is a meaningful relationship? Perhaps. But the correlation might also be explained by another variable, such as the ability level of the class (classes low in ability might be expected to have more disruptive behavior *and* higher teacher expectation of failure).*

In our experience, a systematic consideration of possible **threats to internal validity** receives the least attention of all the aspects of planning a study. Often, the possibility of such threats is not discussed at all. Probably this is because their consideration is not seen as an essential step in carrying out a study. Researchers cannot avoid deciding on what variables to study, or how the sample will be obtained, or how the data will be collected and analyzed. They can, however, ignore or simply not think about possible alternative explanations for the outcomes of a study until after the study is completed—at which point it is almost always too late to do anything about them. Identifying possible threats during the planning stage of a study, on the other hand, can often lead researchers to design ways of eliminating or at least minimizing these threats.

In recent years, many useful categories of possible threats to internal validity have been identified. Although most of these categories were originally designed for application to experimental studies, some apply to other types of methodologies as well. We discuss the most important of these possible threats in this chapter.

Various ways of controlling for these threats have also been identified. We discuss some of these in the remainder of this chapter and others in subsequent chapters.

Threats to Internal Validity

SUBJECT CHARACTERISTICS

The selection of people for a study may result in the individuals (or groups) differing from one another in unintended ways that are related to the variables to be studied. This is sometimes referred to as *selection bias,* or a **subject characteristics threat**. In our example of teacher expectations and class disruptive behavior, the ability level of the class fits this category. In studies that compare groups, subjects in the groups may differ on such variables as age, gender, ability, socioeconomic background, and the like. If not controlled, these variables may explain away whatever differences between groups are found. The list of such subject characteristics is virtually unlimited, but some examples that might affect the results of a study include:

- Age
- Strength
- Maturity
- Gender
- Ethnicity
- Coordination
- Speed
- Intelligence
- Vocabulary
- Attitude
- Reading ability
- Fluency
- Manual dexterity
- Socioeconomic status
- Religious beliefs
- Political beliefs

In a particular study, the researcher must decide, based on previous research or experience, which variables are most likely to create problems, and do his or her best to prevent or minimize their effects. In studies comparing groups, there are several methods of equating groups, which we discuss in Chapters 13 and 16. In correlational studies, there are certain statistical techniques that can be used to control such variables, provided information on each variable is obtained. We discuss these techniques in Chapter 15.

LOSS OF SUBJECTS (MORTALITY)

No matter how carefully the subjects of a study are selected, it is common to "lose" some as the study progresses (Figure 9.1). This is known as a **mortality threat**. For one reason or another (e.g., illness, family relocation, or the requirements of other activities), some individuals may drop out of the study. This is especially true in most intervention studies, since they take place over time.

Subjects may be absent during the collection of data or fail to complete tests, questionnaires, or other instruments. Failure to complete instruments is especially a problem in questionnaire studies. In such studies, it is not uncommon to find that 20 percent or more of the subjects involved do not return their forms. Remember, the actual sample in a study is not the total of those selected but only those from whom data are obtained.

Loss of subjects, of course, not only limits generalizability but also can introduce bias—*if* those subjects who are lost would have responded differently from those

*Can you suggest any other variables that would explain a high correlation (should it be found) between a teacher's expectation of failure and the amount of disruptive behavior that occurs in class?

Figure 9.1 *A Mortality Threat to Internal Validity*

from whom data were obtained. Many times this is quite likely, since those who do not respond or who are absent probably act this way for a reason. In the example we presented earlier in which the researcher was studying the possible relationship between amount of disruptive behavior by students in class and teacher expectations of student failure, it is likely that those teachers who failed to describe their expectations to the researcher (and who would therefore be "lost" for the purposes of the study) would differ from those who did provide this information in ways affecting disruptive behavior.

In studies comparing groups, loss of subjects probably will not be a problem if the loss is about the same in all groups. But if there are sizable differences between groups in terms of the numbers who drop out, this is certainly a conceivable alternative explanation for whatever findings appear. In comparing students taught by different methods (e.g., lecture versus discussion), one might expect the poorer students in each group to be more likely to drop out. If more of the poorer students drop out of either group, the other method may appear more effective than it actually is.

Of all the threats to internal validity, mortality is perhaps the most difficult to control. A common misconception is that the threat is eliminated simply by replacing the lost subjects. No matter how this is done—even if they are replaced by new subjects selected randomly—researchers can never be sure that the replacement subjects will respond as those who dropped out would have. It is more likely, in fact, that they will *not*. Can you see why?*

It is sometimes possible for a researcher to argue that the loss of subjects in a study is not a problem. This is done by exploring the reasons for such loss and then offering an argument as to why these reasons are not relevant to the particular study at hand. Absence from class on the day of testing, for example, probably would not in most cases favor a particular group, since it would be incidental rather than intentional—unless the day and time of the testing was announced beforehand.

Another attempt to eliminate the problem of mortality is to provide evidence that the subjects lost were similar to those remaining on pertinent characteristics such as age, gender, ethnicity, pretest scores, or other variables that presumably might be related to the study outcomes. While desirable, such evidence can never demonstrate conclusively that those subjects who were lost would not have responded differently from those who remained. When all is said and done, the best solution to the problem of mortality is to do one's best to prevent or minimize the loss of subjects.

Some examples of a mortality threat include the following:

- A high school teacher decides to teach his two English classes differently. His one o'clock class spends a large amount of time writing analyses of plays, whereas his two o'clock class spends much time acting out and discussing portions of the same plays. Halfway through the semester, several students in the two o'clock class are excused to participate in the annual school play—thus they are "lost" from the study. If they, as a group, are better students than the rest of their class, their loss will lower the performance of the two o'clock class.
- A researcher wishes to study the effects of a new diet on building endurance in long-distance runners. She receives a grant to study, over a two-year period, a group of such runners who are on the track team at several nearby high schools in a large urban school district. The study is designed to compare runners who are given the new diet with similar runners in the district who are not given the diet. About 5 percent of the runners who receive the diet and about 20 percent of those who do not receive the diet, however, are

*Since those who drop out have done so for a reason, their replacements will be different at least in this respect; thus, they may see things differently or feel differently, and their responses may accordingly be different.

seniors, and they graduate at the end of the first year of the study. Because seniors are probably better runners, this loss will cause the remaining no-diet group to appear weaker than the diet group.

LOCATION

The particular locations in which data are collected, or in which an intervention is carried out, may create alternative explanations for results. This is called a **location threat**. For example, classrooms in which students are taught by, say, the inquiry method may have more resources (texts and other supplies, equipment, parent support, and so on) available to them than classrooms in which students are taught by the lecture method. The classrooms themselves may be larger, have better lighting, or contain better-equipped workstations. Such variables may account for higher performance by students. In our disruptive behavior versus teacher expectations example, the availability of support (resources, aides, and parent assistance) might explain the correlation between the major variables of interest. Classes with fewer resources might be expected to have more disruptive behavior and higher teacher expectations of failure.

The location in which tests, interviews, or other instruments are administered may affect responses (Figure 9.2). Parent assessments of their children at home may be different from assessments of their children at school. Student performance on tests may be lower if tests are given in noisy or poorly lighted rooms. Observations of student interaction may be affected by the physical arrangement of certain classrooms. Such differences might provide defensible alternative explanations for the results in a particular study.

The best method of control for a location threat is to hold location constant—that is, keep it the same for all participants. When this is not feasible, the researcher should try to ensure that different locations do not systematically favor or jeopardize the hypothesis. This may require the collection of additional descriptions of the various locations.

Here are examples of a location threat:

- A researcher designs a study to compare the effects of team versus individual teaching of U.S. history on student attitudes toward history. The classrooms in which students are taught by a single teacher have fewer books and materials than the ones in which students are taught by a team of three teachers.
- A researcher decides to interview counseling and special education majors to compare their attitudes toward their respective master's degree programs. Over a three-week period, he manages to interview all of the students enrolled in the two programs. Although he is able to interview most of the students in one of the university classrooms, scheduling conflicts prevent this classroom from being available for him to interview the remainder. As a result, he interviews 20 of the counseling students in the coffee shop of the student union.

INSTRUMENTATION

The way in which instruments are used may also constitute a threat to the internal validity of a study. As discussed in Chapter 8, scores from the instruments used in a study can lack evidence of validity. Lack of this

Figure 9.2 *Location Might Make a Difference*

Figure 9.3 *An Example of Instrument Decay*

Figure 9.4 *A Data Collector Characteristics Threat*

kind of validity does not necessarily present a threat to *internal* validity—but it may.*

Instrument Decay. Instrumentation can create problems if the nature of the instrument (including the scoring procedure) is *changed* in some way or another. This is usually referred to as **instrument decay**. This is often the case when the instrument permits different interpretations of results (as in essay tests) or is especially long or difficult to score, thereby resulting in fatigue of the scorer (Figure 9.3). Fatigue often happens when a researcher scores a number of tests one after the other; he or she becomes tired and scores the tests differently (e.g., more rigorously at first, more generously later). The principal way to control instrument decay is to schedule data collection and/or scoring so as to minimize changes in any of the instruments or scoring procedures.

Here are examples of instrument decay:

- A professor grades 100 essay-type final examinations over a five-hour period without taking a break. Each essay encompasses between 10 and 12 pages. He grades the papers of each class in turn and then compares the results.
- The administration of a large school district changes its method of reporting absences. Only students who are considered truant (absence is unexcused) are reported as absent; students who have a written excuse (from parents or school officials) are not reported. The district reports a 55 percent decrease in absences since the new reporting system has been instituted.

Data Collector Characteristics. The characteristics of the data gatherers—an inevitable part of most instrumentation—can also affect results. Gender, age, ethnicity, language patterns, or other characteristics of the individuals who collect the data in a study may affect the nature of the data they obtain (Figure 9.4). If these characteristics are related to the variables being investigated, they may offer an alternative explanation for whatever findings appear. Suppose both male and female data gatherers were used in the prior example of a researcher wishing to study the relationship between disruptive behavior and teacher expectations. It might be that the female data collectors would elicit more confessions of an expectation of student failure on the part of teachers and generate more incidents of disruptive behavior on the part of students during classroom observations than would the males. If so, any correlation between teacher expectations of failure and the amount of disruptive behavior by students might be explained (at least partly) as an artifact of who collected the data.

The primary ways to control this threat include using the same data collector(s) throughout, analyzing data separately for each collector, and (in comparison-group studies) ensuring that each collector is used equally with all groups.

Data Collector Bias. There is also the possibility that the data collector(s) and/or scorer(s) may unconsciously distort the data in such a way as to make certain outcomes (such as support for the hypothesis)

*In general, we expect lack of validity of scores to make it *less* likely that any relationships will be found. There are times, however, when "poor" instrumentation can *increase* the chances of "phony" or "spurious" relationships emerging.

more likely. Examples include some classes being allowed more time on tests than other classes; interviewers asking "leading" questions of some interviewees; observer knowledge of teacher expectations affecting quantity and type of observed behaviors of a class; and judges of student essays favoring (unconsciously) one instructional method over another.

The two principal techniques for handling **data collector bias** are to standardize all procedures, which usually requires some sort of training of the data collectors, and to ensure that the data collectors lack the information they would need to distort results—also known as *planned ignorance.* Data collectors should be either unaware of the hypothesis or unable to identify the particular characteristics of the individuals or groups from whom the data are being collected. Data collectors do not need to be told which method group they are observing or testing or how the individuals they are testing performed on other tests.

Examples of data collector bias are:

- All teachers in a large school district are interviewed regarding their future goals and their views on faculty organizations. The hypothesis is that those planning a career in administration will be more negative in their views on faculty organizations than those planning to continue teaching. Interviews are conducted by the vice principal in each school. Teachers are likely to be influenced by the fact that the person interviewing them is the vice principal, and this may account for the hypothesis being supported.
- An interviewer unconsciously smiles at certain answers to certain questions during an interview.
- An observer with a preference for inquiry methods observes more "attending behavior" in inquiry-identified than noninquiry-identified classes.
- A researcher is aware, when scoring the end-of-study examinations, which students were exposed to which treatment in an intervention study.

TESTING

In intervention studies, where data are collected over a period of time, it is common to test subjects at the beginning of the intervention(s). By *testing,* we mean the use of any form of instrumentation, not just "tests." If substantial improvement is found in posttest (compared to pretest) scores, the researcher may conclude that this improvement is due to the intervention. An alternative explanation, however, may be that the improvement is due to the use of the pretest. Why is this? Let's look at the reasons.

Suppose the intervention in a particular study involves the use of a new textbook. The researcher wants to see if students score higher on an achievement test if they are taught the subject using this new text than did students who have used the regular text in the past. The researcher pretests the students before the new textbook is introduced and then posttests them at the end of a six-week period. The students may be "alerted" to what is being studied by the questions in the pretest, however, and accordingly make a greater effort to learn the material. This increased effort on the part of the students (rather than the new textbook) could account for the improvement. It may also be that "practice" on the pretest by itself is responsible for the improvement. This is known as a **testing threat** (Figure 9.5).

Consider another example. Suppose a counselor in a large high school is interested in finding out whether student attitudes toward mental health are affected by a special unit on the subject. He decides to administer an attitude questionnaire to the students before the unit is introduced

"How'd you do on the final?"
"I killed it! I remembered the questions on the 'diagnostic' test we took at the beginning of the semester."

Figure 9.5 *A Testing Threat to Internal Validity*

and then administer it again after the unit is completed. Any change in attitude scores may be due to the students thinking about and discussing their opinions as a result of the pretest rather than as a result of the intervention.

Notice that it is not always the administration of a pretest per se that creates a possible testing effect, but rather the "interaction" that occurs between taking the test and the intervention. A pretest sometimes can make students more alert to or aware of what may be about to take place, making them more sensitive to and responsive toward the treatment that subsequently occurs. In some studies, the possible effects of pretesting are considered so serious that such testing is eliminated.

A similar problem is created if the instrumentation process permits subjects to figure out the nature of the study. This is most likely to happen in single-group (correlational) studies of attitudes, opinions, or similar variables other than ability. Students might be asked their opinions, for example, about teachers and also about different subjects to test the hypothesis that student attitude toward teachers is related to student attitude toward the subjects taught. They may see a connection between the two sets of questions, especially if they are both included on the same form, and answer accordingly.

Examples of testing threats are:

- A researcher uses exactly the same set of problems to measure change over time in student ability to solve mathematics word problems. The first administration of the test is given at the beginning of a unit of instruction; the second administration is given at the end of the unit of instruction, three weeks later. If improvement in scores occurs, it may be due to sensitization to the problems produced by the first test and the practice effect rather than to any increase in problem-solving ability.
- A researcher incorporates items designed to measure self-esteem and achievement motivation in the same questionnaire. The respondents may figure out what the researcher is after and react accordingly.
- A researcher uses pre- and posttests of anxiety level to compare students given relaxation training with students in a control group. Lower scores for the relaxation group on the posttest may be due to the training, but they also may be due to sensitivity (created by the pretest) to the training.

HISTORY

On occasion, one or more unanticipated, and unplanned for, events may occur during the course of a study that can affect the responses of subjects (Figure 9.6). Such an event is referred to in educational research as a **history threat**. In the study we suggested of students being taught by the inquiry versus the lecture method, for example, a boring visitor who dropped in on and spoke to the lecture class just before an upcoming examination would be an illustration. If the visitor's remarks in some way discouraged or turned off students in the lecture class, they might have done less well on the examination than if the visitor had not appeared. Another example involves a personal experience of one of the authors of

Figure 9.6 *A History Threat to Internal Validity*

this text. He remembers clearly the day that President John F. Kennedy died, since he had scheduled an examination for that very day. The author's students at that time, stunned into shock by the announcement of the president's death, were unable to take the examination. Any comparison of examination results taken on this day with the examination results of other classes taken on other days would have been meaningless.

Researchers can never be certain that one group has not had experiences that differ from those of other groups. As a result, they should continually be alert to any such influences that may occur (e.g., in schools) during the course of a study. As you will see in Chapter 13, some research designs handle this threat better than others do.

Two examples of a history threat are:

- A researcher designs a study to investigate the effects of simulation games on ethnocentrism. She plans to select two high schools to participate in an experiment. Students in both schools will be given a pretest designed to measure their attitudes toward minority groups. School A will then be given the simulation games during their social studies classes over a three-day period, and school B will watch travel films. Both schools will then be given the same test to see if their attitude toward minority groups has changed. The researcher conducts the study as planned, but a special documentary on racial prejudice is shown in school A between the pretest and the posttest.
- The achievement scores of five elementary schools whose teachers use a cooperative learning approach are compared with those of five schools whose teachers do not use this approach. During the course of the study, the faculty of one of the schools where cooperative learning is not used is engaged in a disruptive conflict with the school principal.

MATURATION

Often, change during an intervention may be due to factors associated with the passing of time rather than to the intervention itself (Figure 9.7). This is known as a **maturation threat**. Over the course of a semester, for example, very young students, in particular, will change in many ways simply because of aging and experience. Suppose, for example, that a researcher is interested in studying the effect of special grasping exercises on the ability of two-year-olds to manipulate various objects. She finds that such exercises are associated with marked increases in the manipulative ability of the children over a six-month period. Two-year-olds mature very rapidly, however, and the improvement in their manipulative ability may be due simply to this fact rather than the grasping exercises. Maturation is a serious threat only in studies using pre-post data for the intervention group, or in studies that span a number of years. The best way to control for maturation is to include a well-selected comparison group in the study.

"I'm much more confident after a year in that self-esteem class."
"That's great!"

Figure 9.7 *Could Maturation Be at Work Here?*

Examples of a maturation threat are:

- A researcher reports that students in liberal arts colleges become less accepting of authority between their freshman and senior years and attributes this to the many "liberating" experiences they have undergone in college. This may be the reason, but it also may be because they simply have grown older.
- A researcher tests a group of students enrolled in a special class for "students with artistic potential" every year for six years, beginning when they are age five. She finds that their drawing ability improves markedly over the years.

ATTITUDE OF SUBJECTS

How subjects view a study and participate in it can also threaten internal validity. One example is the well-known **Hawthorne effect**, first observed in the Hawthorne plant of the Western Electric Company some years ago.[1] It was accidentally discovered that productivity increased not only when improvements were made in physical working conditions (such as an increase in the number of coffee breaks and better lighting) but also when such conditions were unintentionally made worse (for instance, the number of coffee breaks was reduced and the lighting was dimmed). The usual explanation for this is that the special attention and recognition received by the workers were responsible; they felt someone cared about them and was trying to help them. This positive effect, resulting from increased attention and recognition of subjects, has subsequently been referred to as the *Hawthorne effect.*

It has also been suggested that recipients of an experimental treatment may perform better because of the novelty of the treatment rather than the specific nature of the treatment. It might be expected, then, that subjects who know they are part of a study may show improvement as a result of a feeling that they are receiving some sort of special treatment—no matter what this treatment may be (Figure 9.8).

An opposite effect can occur whenever, in intervention studies, the members of the control group receive no treatment at all. As a result, they may become demoralized or resentful and hence perform more poorly than the treatment group. It may thus appear that the experimental group is performing better as a result of the treatment, when this is not the case.

One remedy for these **subject attitude threats** is to provide the control or comparison group(s) with a special or novel treatment comparable to that received by the experimental group. While simple in theory, this is not easy to do in most educational settings. Another possibility, in some cases, is to make it easy for students to believe that the treatment is just a regular part

Figure 9.8 *The Attitude of Subjects Can Make a Difference*

MORE ABOUT RESEARCH

Threats to Internal Validity in Everyday Life

Consider the following commonly held beliefs:

- Because failure often precedes suicide, it is therefore the cause of suicide. (probable history and mortality threats)
- Boys are genetically more talented in mathematics than are girls. (probable subject attitude and history threats)
- Girls are genetically more talented in language than are boys. (probable history and subject attitude threats)
- Minority students are less academically able than students from the dominant culture. (probable subject characteristics, subject attitude, location, instrumentation, and history threats)
- People on welfare are lazy. (probable subject characteristics, location, and history threats)
- Schooling makes students rebellious. (probable maturation and history threats)
- A policy of expelling students who don't "behave" improves a school's test scores. (probable mortality threat)
- Indoctrination changes attitude. (probable testing threat)
- So-called miracle drugs cure intellectual disability. (probable regression threat)
- Smoking marijuana leads eventually to using cocaine and heroin. (probable mortality threat)

of instruction—that is, not part of an experiment. For example, it is sometimes unnecessary to announce that an experiment is being conducted.

Here are examples of a subject attitude threat:

- A researcher decides to investigate the possible reduction of test anxiety by playing classical music during examinations. She randomly selects 10 freshman algebra classes from the five high schools in a large urban school district. In five of these classes, she plays classical music softly in the background during examinations. In the other five (the control group), she plays no music. The students in the control group, however, learn that music is being played in the other classes and express some resentment when their teachers tell them that the music cannot be played in their class. This resentment may actually cause them to be more anxious during exams or intentionally to inflate their anxiety scores.
- A researcher hypothesizes that critical thinking skill is correlated with attention to detail. He administers a somewhat novel test that provides a separate score for each variable (critical thinking and attention to detail) to a sample of eighth-graders. The novelty of the test may confuse some students, while others may think it is silly. In either case, the scores of these students are likely to be lower on *both* variables because of the format of the test, not because of any lack of ability. It may appear, therefore, that the hypothesis is supported. Neither score is a valid indicator of ability for such students, so this particular attitudinal reaction creates a threat to internal validity.

REGRESSION

A **regression threat** may be present whenever change is studied in a group that is extremely low or high in its preintervention performance (Figure 9.9). Studies in special education are particularly vulnerable to this threat, since the students in such studies are frequently selected on the basis of previous low performance. The regression phenomenon can be explained statistically, but for our purposes it simply describes the fact that a group selected because of unusually low (or high) performance will, on the average, score closer to the mean on subsequent testing, regardless of what transpires in the meantime. Thus, a class of students of markedly low ability may be expected to score higher on posttests regardless of the effect of any intervention to which they are exposed. Like maturation, the use of an equivalent control or comparison group handles this threat—and this seems to be understood as reflected in published research.

Examples of a possible regression threat are:

- An Olympic track coach selects the members of her team from those who have the fastest times during the final trials for various events. She finds that their average time increases the next time they run, however, which she perhaps erroneously attributes to poorer track conditions.
- Those students who score in the lowest 20 percent on a math test are given special help. Six months later their average score on a test involving similar problems has improved, but not necessarily because of the special help.

Figure 9.9 *Regression Rears Its Head*

IMPLEMENTATION

The treatment or method in any experimental study must be administered by someone—the researcher, the teachers involved in the study, a counselor, or some other person. This fact raises the possibility that the experimental group may be treated in ways that are unintended and not necessarily part of the method, yet which give them an advantage of one sort or another. This is known as an **implementation threat.** It can happen in either of two ways.

First, an implementation threat can occur when different individuals are assigned to implement different methods, and these individuals differ in ways related to the outcome. Consider our previous example in which two groups of students are taught by either an inquiry or a lecture method. The inquiry teachers may simply be better teachers than the lecture teachers.

There are a number of ways to control for this possibility. The researcher can attempt to evaluate the individuals who implement each method on pertinent characteristics (such as teaching ability) and then try to equate the treatment groups on these dimensions (e.g., by assigning teachers of equivalent ability to each group). Clearly, this is a difficult and time-consuming task. Another control is to require that each method be taught by all teachers in the study. Where feasible, this is a preferable solution, though it also is vulnerable to the possibility that some teachers may have different abilities to implement the different methods. Still another control is to use *several* different individuals to implement each method, thereby reducing the chances of an advantage to either method.

Second, an implementation threat can occur when some individuals have a personal bias in favor of one method over the other. Their preference for the method, rather than the method itself, may account for the superior performance of students taught by that method. This is a good reason why a researcher should, if at all possible, *not* be one of the individuals who implements a method in an intervention study. It is sometimes possible to keep individuals who are implementers ignorant of the nature of a study, but it is generally very difficult—in part because teachers or others involved in a study will usually need to be given a rationale for their participation. One solution for this is to allow individuals to choose the method they wish to implement, but this creates the possibility of differences in characteristics discussed previously. An alternative is to have all methods used by all implementers, but with their preferences known beforehand. Note that preference for a method as a *result* of using it does not constitute a threat—it is simply one of the by-products of the method itself.

MORE ABOUT RESEARCH

Some Thoughts About Meta-Analysis

As we mentioned in Chapter 3, the main argument in favor of doing a meta-analysis is that the weaknesses in individual studies should balance out or be reduced by combining the results of a series of studies. In short, researchers who do a meta-analysis attempt to remedy the shortcomings of any particular study by statistically combining the results of several (hopefully many) studies that were conducted on the same topic. Thus, the threats to internal validity that we discussed in this chapter should be reduced and generalizability should be enhanced.

How is this done? Essentially by calculating what is called *effect size* (see Chapter 12). Researchers conducting a meta-analysis do their best to locate all of the studies on a particular topic (i.e., all of the studies having the same independent variable). Once located, effect sizes and an overall average effect size for each dependent variable are calculated.* As an example, Vockell and Asher report an average delta (Δ) of .80 on the effectiveness of cooperative learning.†

*This is not always easy to do. Frequently, published reports lack the necessary information, although it can sometimes be deduced from what is reported.

†Vockell, E. L., & Asher, J. W. (1995). *Educational research* (2nd ed., p. 361). Englewood Cliffs, NJ: Prentice Hall.

As we have mentioned, meta-analysis is a way of quantifying replications of a study. It is important to note, however, that the term *replication* is used rather loosely in this context, since the studies that the researcher(s) has collected may have little in common except that they all have the same independent variable. Our concerns are twofold: Merely obtaining several studies, even if they all have the same independent variable, does not mean that they will necessarily balance out each other's weaknesses—they might all have the *same* weakness. Secondly, in doing a meta-analysis, equal weight is given to both good *and bad* studies—that is, no distinction is made between studies that have been well designed and conducted and those that have not been so well designed and/or conducted. Results of a well-designed study in which the researchers used a large random sample, for example, would count the same as results from a poorly controlled study in which researchers used a convenience or purposive sample.

A partial solution to these problems that we support is to combine meta-analysis with judgmental review. This has been done by judging studies as good or bad and comparing the results; sometimes they agree. If, however, there is a sufficient number of good studies (we would argue for a minimum of seven), we see little to be gained by including poor ones.

Meta-analyses are here to stay, and there is little question that they can provide the research community with valuable information. But we do not think excessive enthusiasm for the technique is warranted. Like many things, it is a tool, not a panacea.

This is also true of other by-products. If teacher skill or parent involvement, for example, improves as a *result* of the method, it would not constitute a threat. Finally, the researcher can observe in an attempt to see that the methods are administered as intended.

Examples of an implementation threat are:

- A researcher is interested in studying the effects of a new diet on the physical agility of young children. After obtaining the permission of the parents of the children to be involved, all of whom are first-graders, he randomly assigns the children to an experimental group and a control group. The experimental group is to try the new diet for three months, and the control group is to stay with its regular diet. The researcher overlooks the fact, however, that the teacher of the experimental group is an accomplished instructor of some five years' experience, while the instructor of the control group is a first-year teacher, newly appointed.
- A group of clients who stutter is given a relatively new method of therapy called *generalization training.* Both client and therapist interact with people in the "real world" as part of the therapy. After six months of receiving therapy, the fluency of these clients is compared with that of a group receiving traditional in-the-office therapy. Speech therapists who use new methods are likely to be more generally competent than those working with the comparison group. If so, greater improvement for the generalization group may be due not to the new method but rather to the skill of the therapist.

Figure 9.10 illustrates, and Table 9.1 briefly summarizes, each of the threats we have discussed.

*This seems unlikely.

†If these teacher characteristics are a *result* of the type of school, then they do not constitute a threat.

Figure 9.10 *Illustration of Threats to Internal Validity*

Note: We are not implying that any of these statements are necessarily true; our guess is that some are and some are not.

FACTORS THAT REDUCE THE LIKELIHOOD OF FINDING A RELATIONSHIP

In many studies, the various factors we have discussed could also serve to *reduce,* or even prevent, the chances of a relationship being found. For example, if the methods (the treatment) in a study are not adequately implemented—that is, adequately tried—the effect of actual differences between them on outcomes may be obscured. Similarly, if the members of a control or comparison group become "aware" of the experimental

TABLE 9.1 ***Threats to the Internal Validity of a Study***

Threat	Definition
Subject Characteristics	The selection of people for a study may result in the individuals or groups differing from one another in unintended ways that are related to the variables being studied. Also called "selection bias."
Mortality	The loss of subjects in a study due to attrition, withdrawal, or low participation rates may introduce bias and affect the outcome of a study.
Location	The particular locations in which data are collected, or in which an intervention is carried out, may create alternative explanations for results.
Instrumentation	The ways in which instruments are used may constitute an internal validity threat. Possible instrumentation threats include changes in the instrument and how it is scored, characteristics of the data collector, and/or bias on the part of the data collector.
Testing	The use of a pretest in intervention studies may create a "practice effect" that can affect the results of a study and/or how participants respond to an intervention.
History	A history threat is when an unforeseen or unplanned event occurs during the course of a study.
Maturation	Change during an intervention may be due sometimes to factors associated with the passing of time rather than the intervention.
Subject Attitude	The way subjects view a study and their participation in it can be considered a threat to internal validity; the positive impact of an intervention is known as the "Hawthorne effect."
Regression	A regression threat is possible when change is studied in a group with extreme low or high performances as determined by a pretest. On average, the group will score closer to the mean on subsequent testing regardless of the treatment or intervention.
Implementation	The experimental group may be treated in unintended ways that give them an undue advantage affecting results.

treatment, they may increase their efforts because they feel "left out," thereby reducing real differences in achievement between treatment groups that otherwise would be seen. Sometimes, teachers of a control group may unwittingly give some sort of "compensation" to motivate the members of their group, thereby lessening the impact of the experimental treatment. Finally, the use of instruments that produce unreliable scores and/or the use of small samples may result in a reduced likelihood of a relationship or relationships being observed.

How Can a Researcher Minimize These Threats to Internal Validity?

Throughout this chapter, we have suggested a number of techniques or procedures that researchers can employ to control or minimize the possible effects of threats to internal validity. Essentially, they boil down to four alternatives. A researcher can try to do any or all of the following.

1. Standardize the conditions under which the study occurs—such as the way(s) in which the treatment is implemented (in intervention studies), the way(s) in which the data are collected, and so on. This helps control for location, instrumentation, subject attitude, and implementation threats.
2. Obtain more information on the subjects of the study—that is, on relevant characteristics of the subjects—and use that information in analyzing and interpreting results. This helps control for a subject characteristics threat and (possibly) a mortality threat, as well as maturation and regression threats.
3. Obtain more information on the details of the study—that is, where and when it takes place, extraneous events that occur, and so on. This helps control for location, instrumentation, history, subject attitude, and implementation threats.

TABLE 9.2 ***General Techniques for Controlling Threats to Internal Validity***

	Technique			
Threat	**Standardize Conditions**	**Obtain More Information on Subjects**	**Obtain More Information on Details**	**Choose an Appropriate Design**
Subject characteristics		X		X
Mortality		X		X
Location	X		X	X
Instrumentation	X		X	
Testing				X
History			X	X
Maturation		X		X
Subject attitude	X		X	X
Regression		X		X
Implementation	X		X	X

4. Choose an appropriate design. The proper design can do much to control these threats to internal validity.

Because control by design applies primarily to experimental and causal-comparative studies, we shall discuss it in detail in Chapters 13 and 16. The four alternatives are summarized in Table 9.2.

TWO POINTS TO EMPHASIZE

We want to end this chapter by emphasizing two things. First, these various threats to internal validity can be greatly reduced by planning. Second, such planning often requires collecting additional information *before* a study begins (or while it is taking place). It is often too late to consider how to control these threats once the data have been collected.

Go back to the **INTERACTIVE AND APPLIED LEARNING** feature at the beginning of the chapter for a listing of interactive and applied activities. Go to the **Online Learning Center** at **www.mhhe.com/fraenkel9e** to take quizzes, practice with key terms, and review chapter content.

Main Points

THE MEANING OF INTERNAL VALIDITY

- When a study lacks internal validity, one or more alternative hypotheses exist to explain the outcomes. These alternative hypotheses are referred to by researchers as *threats to internal validity.*
- When a study has internal validity, it means that any relationship observed between two or more variables is unambiguous, rather than being due to something else.

THREATS TO INTERNAL VALIDITY

- Some of the more common threats to internal validity are differences in subject characteristics, mortality, location, instrumentation, testing, history, maturation, attitude of subjects, regression, and implementation.

- The selection of people for a study may result in the individuals or groups differing (i.e., the characteristics of the subjects may differ) from one another in unintended ways that are related to the variables to be studied.
- No matter how carefully the subjects of a study (the sample) are selected, it is common to lose some of them as the study progresses. This is known as *mortality.* Such a loss of subjects may affect the outcomes of a study.
- The particular locations in which data are collected, or in which an intervention is carried out, may create alternative explanations for any results that are obtained.
- The way in which instruments are used may also constitute a threat to the internal validity of a study. Possible instrumentation threats include changes in the instrument, characteristics of the data collector(s), and/or bias on the part of the data collectors.
- The use of a pretest in intervention studies sometimes may create a "practice effect" that can affect the results of a study. A pretest can also sometimes affect the way subjects respond to an intervention.
- On occasion, one or more unanticipated and unplanned for events may occur during the course of a study that can affect the responses of subjects. This is known as a *history threat.*
- Sometimes change during an intervention study may be due more to factors associated with the passing of time than to the intervention itself. This is known as a *maturation threat.*
- The attitude of subjects toward a study (and their participation in it) can create a threat to internal validity. This is known as *subject attitude threat.*
- When subjects are given increased attention and recognition because they are participating in a study, their responses may be affected. This is known as the *Hawthorne effect.*
- Whenever a group is selected because of unusually high or low performance on a pretest, it will, on average, score closer to the mean on subsequent testing, regardless of what transpires in the meantime. This is called a *regression threat.*
- Whenever an experimental group is treated in ways that are unintended and not a necessary part of the method being studied, an implementation threat can occur.

CONTROLLING THREATS TO INTERNAL VALIDITY

- Researchers can use a number of techniques or procedures to control or minimize threats to internal validity. Essentially they boil down to four alternatives: (1) standardizing the conditions under which the study occurs, (2) obtaining and using more information on the subjects of the study, (3) obtaining and using more information on the details of the study, and (4) choosing an appropriate design.

Key Terms

data collector bias 172
Hawthorne effect 175
history threat 173
implementation threat 177
instrument decay 171
internal validity 167
location threat 170
maturation threat 174
mortality threat 168
regression threat 176
subject attitude threat 175
subject characteristics threat 168
testing threat 172
threat to internal validity 168

For Discussion

1. Can a researcher prove conclusively that a study has internal validity? Explain.
2. In Chapter 6, we discussed the concept of external validity. In what ways, if any, are internal and external validity related? Can a study have internal validity but not external validity? If so, how? What about the reverse?
3. Students often confuse the concept of internal validity with the idea of instrument validity. How would you explain the difference between the two?
4. What threat (or threats) to internal validity might exist in each of the following?
   a. A researcher decides to try out a new mathematics curriculum in a nearby elementary school and to compare student achievement in math with that of students in another elementary school using the regular curriculum. The researcher is not aware, however, that the students in the new-curriculum school have computers to use in their classrooms.
   b. A researcher wishes to compare two different kinds of textbooks in two high school chemistry classes over a semester. She finds that 20 percent of one group and 10 percent of the other group are absent during the administration of unit tests.
   c. In a study investigating the possible relationship between marital status and perceived social changes during the last five years, men and women interviewers get different reactions from female respondents to the same questions.
   d. Teachers of an experimental English curriculum as well as teachers of the regular curriculum administer both pre- and posttests to their own students.
   e. Eighth-grade students who volunteer to tutor third-graders in reading show greater improvement in their own reading scores than a comparison group that does not participate in tutoring.
   f. A researcher compares the effects of weekly individual and group counseling on the improvement of study habits. Each week the students counseled as a group fill out questionnaires on their progress at the end of their meetings. The students counseled individually, however, fill out the questionnaires at home.
   g. Those students who score in the bottom 10 percent academically in a school in an economically depressed area are selected for a special program of enrichment. The program includes special games, extra and specially colored materials, special snacks, and new books. The students score substantially higher on achievement tests six months after the program is instituted.
   h. A group of older people are asked to fill out a questionnaire designed to investigate the possible relationship between activity level and sense of life satisfaction.
5. How could you determine whether the threats you identified in each of the situations in question 4 actually exist?
6. Which threats discussed in this chapter do you think are the most important for a researcher to consider? Why? Which do you think would be the most difficult to control? Explain.

Reference

1. Roethlisberger, F. J., & Dickson, W. J. (1939). *Management and the worker.* Cambridge, MA: Harvard University Press.

Research Exercise 9: Internal Validity

State the question or hypothesis of your study at the top of Problem Sheet 9. In the spaces indicated, place an X after each of the threats to internal validity that apply to your study, explain why they are threats, and describe how you intend to control for those most likely to occur (i.e., prevent them from affecting the outcome of your study). Finally, what can you say to convince others that the results of your study are credible and not due merely to coincidence or chance?

Problem Sheet 9

Internal Validity

1. My research question is: ______________________________

____

2. Place an *X* after any of the threats listed that you think might apply to your study:

Subject characteristics _____ Instrumentation _____ Maturation _____

Mortality _____ Testing _____ History _____ Subject attitude _____

Implementation _____ Location _____ Regression _____ Other

3. Please describe how you will attempt to control for those threats that you have marked:

Threat #1: ______________________________

____

Threat #2: ______________________________

____

Threat #3: ______________________________

____

Threat #4: ______________________________

____

4. What assurances can you provide (through your design, sampling procedure, etc.) to support the claims that your study findings are valid? In other words, how will you convince the reader that the findings or relationships resulting from the study are not due to or explained by something other than what you claim?

____

____

____

An electronic version of this Problem Sheet that you can fill in and print, save, or e-mail is available on the Online Learning Center at www.mhhe.com/fraenkel9e.

PART 3

Data Analysis

Part 3 introduces the subject of statistics—important tools that are frequently used by researchers in the analysis of their data. Chapter 10 presents a discussion of descriptive statistics and provides a number of techniques for summarizing both quantitative and categorical data. Chapter 11 deals with inferential statistics—how to determine whether an outcome can be generalized or not—and briefly discusses the most commonly used inferential statistics. Chapter 12 then places what we have presented in the previous two chapters in perspective. We provide examples of comparing groups and of relating variables within a group. We conclude the chapter with a summary of recommendations for using both descriptive and inferential statistics.

10 Descriptive Statistics

Statistics Versus Parameters

Two Fundamental Types of Numerical Data

Quantitative Data

Categorical Data

Types of Scores

Raw Scores

Derived Scores

Which Scores to Use?

Techniques for Summarizing Quantitative Data

Frequency Polygons

Skewed Polygons

Histograms and Stem-Leaf Plots

The Normal Curve

Averages

Spreads

Standard Scores and the Normal Curve

Correlation

Techniques for Summarizing Categorical Data

The Frequency Table

Bar Graphs and Pie Charts

The Crossbreak Table

A Normal Distribution?

OBJECTIVES **Reading this chapter should enable you to:**

- Explain the difference between a statistic and a parameter.
- Differentiate between categorical and quantitative data and give an example of each.
- Name three different types of scores used in educational research and give an example of each.
- Construct a frequency polygon from data.
- Construct a histogram and a stem-leaf plot from data.
- Explain what is meant by the terms "normal distribution" and "normal curve."
- Calculate the mean, median, and mode for a frequency distribution of data.
- Calculate the range and standard deviation for a frequency distribution of data.
- Explain what a five-number summary is.
- Explain what a boxplot displays.
- Explain how any particular score in a normal distribution can be interpreted in standard deviation units.
- Explain what a "*z* score" is and tell why it is advantageous to be able to express scores in *z* score terms.
- Explain how to interpret a normal distribution.
- Construct and interpret a scatterplot.
- Explain more fully what a correlation coefficient is.
- Calculate a Pearson correlation coefficient.
- Prepare and interpret a frequency table, a bar graph, and a pie chart.
- Prepare and interpret a crossbreak table.

INTERACTIVE AND APPLIED LEARNING After, or while, reading this chapter:

Go to the Online Learning Center at www.mhhe.com/fraenkel9e to:

- Review the Sample Statistics
- Learn More About Techniques for Summarizing Quantitative and Categorical Data

Go to your online Student Mastery Activities book to do the following activities:

- Activity 10.1: Construct a Frequency Polygon
- Activity 10.2: Compare Frequency Polygons
- Activity 10.3: Calculate Averages
- Activity 10.4: Calculate the Standard Deviation
- Activity 10.5: Calculate a Correlation Coefficient
- Activity 10.6: Analyze Crossbreak Tables
- Activity 10.7: Compare z Scores
- Activity 10.8: Prepare a Five-Number Summary
- Activity 10.9: Summarize Salaries
- Activity 10.10: Compare Scores
- Activity 10.11: Custodial Times
- Activity 10.12: Collect Data

Tim Williams, Juan Martinez, and Julia McNaughton have just come from their 9:00 A.M. statistics class. They are discussing some ideas over coffee in the student union.

Tim: "I just read in today's paper that the average salary per year for secondary school teachers is $52,000."

Juan: "Really? Dr. Wallen said its about $43,000."

Julia: "Well, one of them must be wrong!"

Tim: "Not necessarily, Julia. There are averages and then there are averages . . ."

Yes, Tim is correct. We'll explain how, and why, later in the chapter, as well as a lot more. Read on.

Statistics Versus Parameters

The major advantage of **descriptive statistics** is that they permit researchers to describe the information contained in many, many scores with just a few indices, such as the mean and median (more about these in a moment). When such indices are calculated for a sample drawn from a population, they are called **statistics**; when they are calculated from the entire population, they are called **parameters**. Because most educational research involves data from samples rather than from populations, we refer mainly to statistics in the remainder of this chapter. We present the most commonly used techniques for summarizing such data. Some form of summary is essential to interpret data collected on any variable—a long list of scores or categorical representations is simply unmanageable.

Two Fundamental Types of Numerical Data

In Chapter 7, we presented a number of instruments used in educational research. The researcher's intention in using these instruments is to collect information of some sort—measures of abilities, attitudes, beliefs, reactions, and so forth—that will enable him or her to draw some conclusions about the sample of individuals being studied.

As we have seen, such information can be collected in several ways, but it can be reported in only three ways: through words, through numbers, and sometimes through graphs or charts that show patterns or describe relationships. In certain types of research, such as interviews, ethnographic studies, or case studies, researchers often try to describe their findings through a narrative description of some sort. Their intent is not to reduce the information

Using Excel to Perform Statistical Calculations

Microsoft Office Excel, more commonly known as Excel, is a software program that can be used to analyze and manipulate data using tables and formulas. We do not have the space to present a complete explanation of how to use the program, but in this and the next chapter, we provide brief, step-by-step instructions on how to use Excel to calculate many of the descriptive statistics in the text including means, standard deviations, and correlations. Excel can also be used to conduct many hypothesis tests, including independent and repeated-measures *t*-tests, analysis of variance (ANOVA), and chi-square tests.

In Appendix D, we present a more detailed explanation of how to use Excel (for PC) that illustrates many of the steps we describe, including instructions about how to load the analysis ToolPak. (The ToolPak must be loaded in order to perform statistical functions in Excel). Note that Macintosh users should consult the Microsoft website (www.microsoft.com) for help on how to use Excel for Mac computers as the screen interface differs.

to numerical form but to present it in a descriptive form, and often as richly as possible. We give examples of this method of reporting information in Chapters 19, 20, and 21. In this chapter, however, we concentrate on numerical ways of reporting information.

Much of the information reported in educational research consists of numbers of some sort—test scores, percentages, grade point averages, ratings, frequencies, and the like. The reason is an obvious one—numbers are a useful way to simplify information. Numerical information, usually referred to as *data,* can be classified in one of two basic ways: as either categorical or quantitative data.

Just as there are categorical and quantitative variables (see Chapter 5), there are two types of numerical data. Categorical data differ in *kind,* but not in degree or amount. Quantitative data, on the other hand, differ in *degree* or *amount.*

QUANTITATIVE DATA

Quantitative data are obtained when the variable being studied is measured along a scale that indicates how much of the variable is present. Quantitative data are reported in terms of scores. Higher scores indicate that more of the variable (such as weight, academic ability, self-esteem, or interest in mathematics) is present than do lower scores. Examples of quantitative data are:

- The amount of money spent on sports equipment by various schools in a particular district in a semester (the variable is *amount of money spent on sports equipment*)
- SAT scores (the variable is *scholastic aptitude*)
- The temperatures recorded each day during the months of September through December in Omaha, Nebraska, in a given year (the variable is *temperature*)
- The anxiety scores of all first-year students enrolled at San Francisco State University in 2014 (the variable is *anxiety*)

CATEGORICAL DATA

Categorical data simply indicate the total number of objects, individuals, or events a researcher finds in a particular category. Thus, a researcher who reports the number of people for or against a particular government policy, or the number of students completing a program in successive years, is reporting categorical data. Notice that what the researcher is looking for is the frequency of certain characteristics, objects, individuals, or events. Many times it is useful, however, to convert these frequencies into percentages. Examples of categorical data follow:

- The representation of each ethnic group in a school (the variable is *ethnicity*); for example, Caucasian, 1,462 (41 percent); black, 853 (24 percent); Hispanic, 760 (21 percent); Asian, 530 (15 percent)
- The number of male and female students in a chemistry class (the variable is *gender*)
- The number of teachers in a large school district who use (1) the lecture and (2) the discussion method (the variable is *teaching method*)
- The number of each type of tool found in a workroom (the variable is *type of tool*)

- The number of each kind of merchandise found in a large department store (the variable is *type of merchandise*)

You may find it helpful at this point to refer back to Figure 7.26 in Chapter 7. The ordinal, interval, and ratio scales all pertain to quantitative data; the nominal scale pertains to categorical data.

Types of Scores

Quantitative data are usually reported in the form of scores. Scores can be reported in many ways, but an important distinction to understand is the difference between raw scores and derived scores.

RAW SCORES

Almost all measurement begins with what is called a **raw score**, which is the initial score obtained. It may be the total number of items an individual gets correct or answers in a certain way on a test, the number of times a certain behavior is tallied, the rating given by a teacher, and so forth. Examples include the number of questions answered correctly on a science test, the number of questions answered "positively" on an attitude scale, the number of times "aggressive" behavior is observed, a teacher's rating on a "self-esteem" measure, or the number of choices received on a sociogram.

Taken by itself, an individual raw score is difficult to interpret, since it has little meaning. What, for example, does it mean to say a student received a score of 62 on a test if that is all the information you have? Even if you know that there were 100 questions on the test, you don't know whether 62 is an extremely high (or extremely low) score, since the test may have been easy or difficult.

We often want to know how one individual's raw score compares to those of other individuals taking the same test, and (perhaps) how he or she has scored on similar tests taken at other times. This is true whenever we want to interpret an individual score. Because raw scores by themselves are difficult to interpret, they often are converted to what are called *derived scores*.

DERIVED SCORES

Derived scores are obtained by taking raw scores and converting them into more useful scores on some type of standardized basis. They indicate where a particular individual's raw score falls in relation to all other raw scores in the same distribution. They enable a researcher to say how well the individual has performed compared to all others taking the same test. Examples of derived scores are age- and grade-level equivalents, percentile ranks, and standard scores.

Age and Grade-level Equivalents. **Age-equivalent scores** and **grade-equivalent scores** tell us of what age or grade an individual score is typical. Suppose, for example, that the average score on a beginning-of-the-year arithmetic test for all eighth-graders in a certain state is 62 out of a possible 100. Students who score 62 will have a grade equivalent of 8.0 on the test regardless of their actual grade placement—whether in sixth, seventh, eighth, ninth, or tenth grade, the student's performance is typical of beginning eighth-graders. Similarly, a student who is 10 years and 6 months old may have an age-equivalent score of 12-2, meaning that his or her test performance is typical of students who are 12 years and 2 months old.

Percentile Ranks. A **percentile rank** refers to the percentage of individuals scoring at or below a given raw score. Percentile ranks are sometimes referred to as *percentiles,* although this term is not quite correct as a synonym.*

Percentile ranks are easy to calculate. A simple formula for converting raw scores to percentile ranks (PRs) is as follows:

$$\text{PR} = \frac{\underset{\text{below score}}{\text{number of students}} + \underset{\text{all score}}{\text{all students}}}{\text{total number in group}} \times 100$$

Suppose a total of 100 students took an examination, and 18 of them received a raw score above 85, while two students received a score of 85. Eighty students, then, scored somewhere below 85. What is the percentile rank of the two students who received the score of 85? Using the formula

$$\text{PR} = \frac{80 + 2}{100} \times 100 = 82$$

the percentile rank of these two students is 82.

*A percentile is the *point* below which a certain percentage of scores fall. The 70th percentile, for example, is the *point* below which 70 percent of the scores in a distribution fall. The 99th percentile is the *point* below which 99 percent of the scores fall, and so forth. Thus, if 20 percent of the students in a sample score below 40 on a test, then the 20th percentile is a score of 40. A person who obtains a score of 40 has a percentile rank of 20.

TABLE 10.1 *Hypothetical Examples of Raw Scores and Accompanying Percentile Ranks*

Raw Score	Cumulative Frequency	Percentile Frequency	Rank
95	1	25	100
93	1	24	96
88	2	23	92
85	3	21	84
79	1	18	72
75	4	17	68
70	6	13	52
65	2	7	28
62	1	5	20
58	1	4	16
54	2	3	12
50	1	1	4
	$N = 25$		

Often percentile ranks are calculated for each of the scores in a group. Table 10.1 presents a group of scores with the percentile rank of each score indicated.

Standard Scores. Standard scores provide another means of indicating how one individual compares to other individuals in a group. **Standard scores** indicate how far a given raw score is from a reference point. They are particularly helpful in comparing an individual's relative achievement on different types of instruments (such as comparing a person's performance on a chemistry achievement test with an instructor's rating of his work in a laboratory). Many different systems of standard scores exist, but the two most commonly used and reported in educational research are z scores and T scores. We shall discuss both types later in the chapter.

WHICH SCORES TO USE?

Given these various types of scores, how do researchers decide which to use? Recall that the usefulness of derived scores is primarily in making individual raw scores meaningful to students, parents, teachers, and others. Despite their value in this respect, some derived scores should *not* be used in research. This is the case if the researcher is assuming an interval scale, as is often done. Percentile ranks, for example, should never be used because they, almost certainly, do not constitute an interval scale. Age- and grade-equivalent scores likewise have serious limitations because of the way they are obtained. Usually the best scores to use are standard scores, which are sometimes provided in instrument manuals and, if not, can easily be calculated. If standard scores are not used, it is far preferable to use raw scores—converting derived scores, for example, back to the original raw scores, if necessary—rather than use percentile ranks or age/grade equivalents.

Techniques for Summarizing Quantitative Data

Note: None of the techniques in this section for summarizing quantitative data is appropriate for categorical data; they are for use only with quantitative data.

FREQUENCY POLYGONS

Listed here are the scores of a group of 50 students on a midsemester biology test.

64, 27, 61, 56, 52, 51, 3, 15, 6, 34, 6, 17, 27, 17, 24, 64, 31, 29, 31, 29, 31, 29, 29, 31, 31, 29, 61, 59, 56, 34, 59, 51, 38, 38, 38, 38, 34, 36, 36, 34, 34, 36, 21, 21, 24, 25, 27, 27, 27, 63

How many students received a score of 34? Did most of the students receive a score above 50? How many received a score below 30? As you can see, when the data are simply listed in no apparent order, as they are here, it is difficult to tell.

To make any sense out of these data, we must put the information into some sort of order. One of the most common ways to do this is to prepare a **frequency distribution**. This is done by listing the scores in rank order from high to low, with tallies to indicate the number of subjects receiving each score (Table 10.2). Often, the scores in a distribution are grouped into intervals. This results in a **grouped frequency distribution**, as shown in Table 10.3.

Although frequency distributions like the ones in Tables 10.2 and 10.3 can be quite informative, often the information they contain is hard to visualize. To further the understanding and interpretation of quantitative data, it is helpful to present it in a graph. One such graphical display is known as a **frequency polygon**. Figure 10.2 presents a frequency polygon of the data in Table 10.3.

TABLE 10.2 *Example of a Frequency Distribution*[a]

Raw Score	Frequency
64	2
63	1
61	2
59	2
56	2
52	1
51	2
38	4
36	3
34	5
31	5
29	5
27	5
25	1
24	2
21	2
17	2
15	1
6	2
3	1
	$n = 50$

[a]Technically, the table should include all scores, including those for which there are zero frequencies. We have eliminated those to simplify the presentation.

TABLE 10.3 *Example of a Grouped Frequency Distribution*

Raw Scores (Intervals of Five)	Frequency
60–64	5
55–59	4
50–54	3
45–49	0
40–44	0
35–39	7
30–34	10
25–29	11
20–24	4
15–19	3
10–14	0
5–9	2
0–4	1
	$n = 50$

The steps involved in constructing a frequency polygon are as follows:

1. List all scores in order of size, and tally how many students receive each score. Group scores, if necessary, into intervals.*
2. Label the horizontal axis by placing all of the possible scores (or groupings) on that axis, at equal intervals, starting with the lowest score on the left.
3. Label the vertical axis by indicating frequencies, at equal intervals, starting with zero.
4. For each score (or grouping of scores), find the point where it intersects with its frequency of occurrence, and place a dot at that point. Remember that each score (or grouping of scores) with zero frequency must still be plotted.
5. Connect all the dots with a straight line.

As you can see by looking at Figure 10.1, the fact that a large number of the students scored in the middle of this distribution is illustrated quite nicely.†

SKEWED POLYGONS

Data can be distributed in almost any shape. If a researcher obtains a set of data in which many individuals received low scores, for example, the shape of the distribution would look something like the frequency polygon shown in Figure 10.2. As you can see, in this particular distribution, only a few individuals received the higher scores. The frequency polygon in Figure 10.2 is said to be **positively skewed** because the tail of the distribution trails off to the right, in the direction of the higher (more *positive*) score values. Suppose the reverse were true. Imagine that a researcher obtained a set of data in which few individuals received relatively low scores. Then the shape of the distribution would look like the frequency polygon in Figure 10.3. This polygon is said to be **negatively skewed**, since the longer tail of the distribution goes off to the left.

*Grouping scores into intervals such as five or more is often necessary when there are many scores in the distribution. Generally, 12 to 15 intervals on the x-axis is recommended.

†A common mistake of students is to treat the vertical axis as if the numbers represented specific individuals. They do not. They represent *frequencies*. Each number on the vertical axis is used to plot the number of individuals at each score. In Figure 10.1, the dot above the interval 25–29 shows that 11 persons scored somewhere within the interval 25–29.

Using Excel to Construct Frequency Distributions and Histograms or Bar Graphs

In Excel, you can use the Histogram Data Analysis tool to create a frequency distribution table and draw an accompanying histogram or bar graph. First, to construct a frequency distribution table, choose the **Tools→Data Analysis** command, select **Histogram** from the Analysis Tools list, and click **OK.** In the Histogram dialog box that appears, use the input range box to identify the data you want to use to construct a frequency distribution and histogram. If your data ranges already include labels, check the Labels box. Next, use the **Output Options** button to tell Excel where to place your frequency distribution and histogram. If you want to put them in a new workbook, select the New Workbook button. To customize your histogram, make choices using Output Options. For example, checking the Cumulative Percentage creates a line showing cumulative percentages in your histogram. Finally, select the **Chart Output** check to tell Excel to include a histogram with the frequency distribution, and click **OK.** (Remember that the Analysis ToolPak must be installed first before any statistical operations can be performed. See Appendix D.)

Figure 10.1 *Example of a Frequency Polygon*

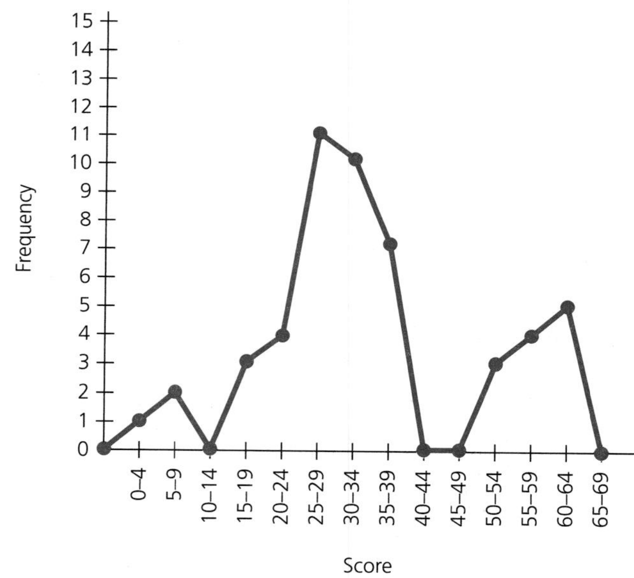

Frequency polygons are particularly useful in comparing two (or sometimes more) groups. In Chapter 7, Table 7.2, we presented hypothetical results of a study involving a comparison of two counseling methods. Figure 10.4 on page 193 shows the polygons constructed using the data from Table 7.2.

This figure reveals several important findings. First, it is evident that method B resulted in higher scores, overall, than did method A. Second, it is clear that the scores for method B are more spread out. Third, it is clear that the reason for method B being higher overall is not that there are fewer scores at the low end of the scale (although this might have happened, it did not). In fact, the groups are almost identical in the number of scores below 61: A=10, B=12. The reason method B is higher overall is that there were fewer cases in the

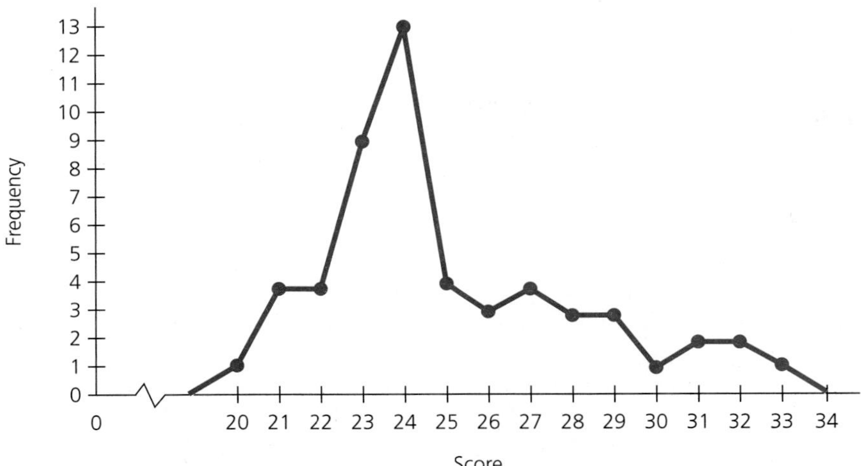

Figure 10.2 *Example of a Positively Skewed Polygon*

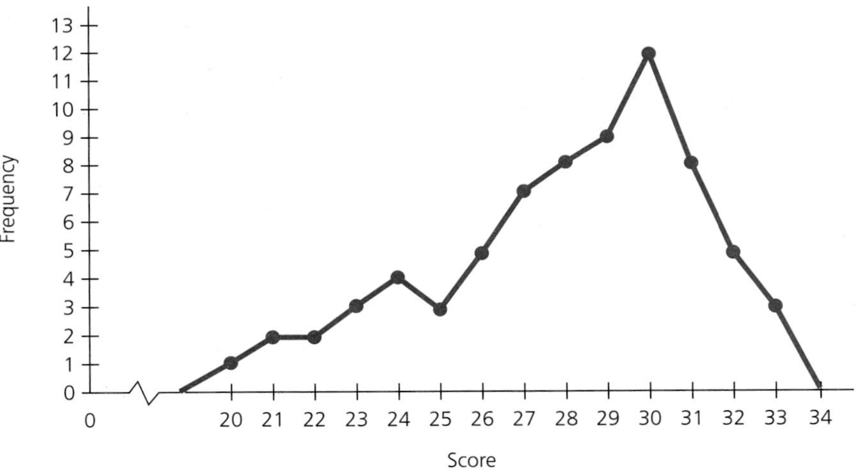

Figure 10.3 *Example of a Negatively Skewed Polygon*

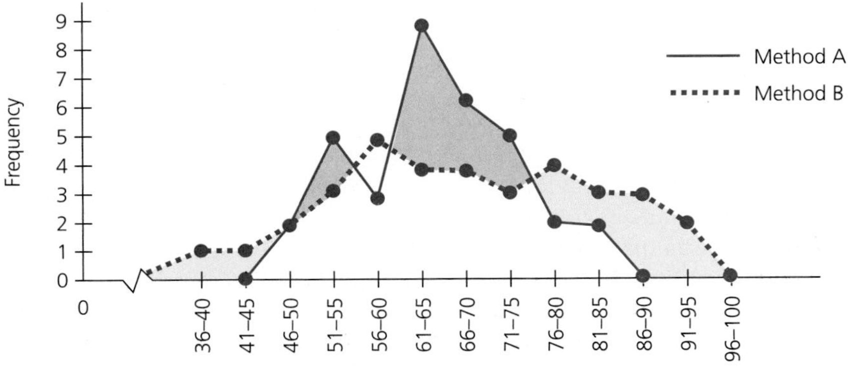

Figure 10.4 *Two Frequency Polygons Compared*

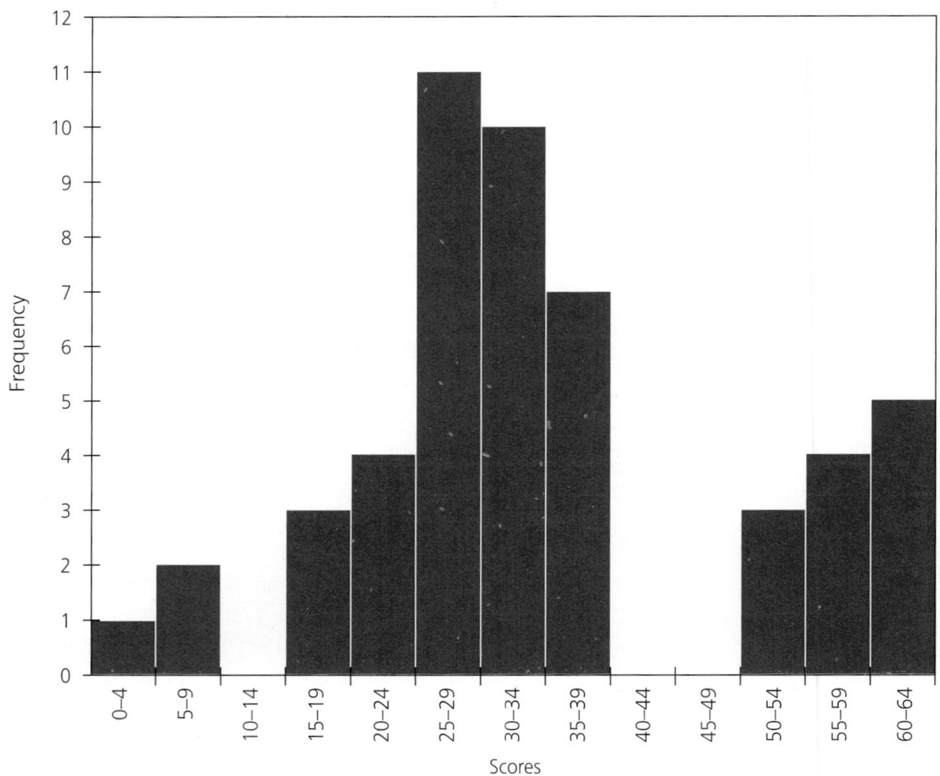

Figure 10.5 *Histogram of Data in Table 10.3*

middle range of the scores (between 60 and 75), and more cases above 75. If this is not clear to you, study the shaded areas in the figure. Many times we want to know not only which group is higher overall but also where the differences are. In this example we see that method B resulted in more variability and that it resulted in a substantial number of scores higher than those in method A.

HISTOGRAMS AND STEM-LEAF PLOTS

A **histogram** is a bar graph used to display quantitative data at the interval or ratio level of measurement. The bars are arranged in order from left to right on the horizontal axis, and the widths of the bars indicate the range of values that fall within each bar. Frequencies are shown on the vertical axis, and the point of intersection of the two axes is always zero. Furthermore, the bars in a histogram (in contrast to those in a bar graph) touch, indicating that they illustrate quantitative rather than categorical data. Figure 10.5 is a histogram of the data presented in the grouped frequency distribution shown in Table 10.3.

A **stem-leaf plot** is a display that organizes a set of data to show both its shape and its distribution. Each data value is split into a "stem" and a "leaf." The leaf is usually the last digit of the number, and the other digits to the left of the leaf form the stem. For example, the number 149 would be split

stem 14
leaf 9

Let us construct a stem-leaf plot for the following set of scores on a math quiz: 29, 37, 32, 46, 45, 45, 54, 51, 55, 55, 55, 60. First, separate each number into a stem and a leaf. Since these are two-digit numbers, the tens digit is the stem and the units digit is the leaf. Next, group the numbers with the same stems as shown next, listing them in numerical order:

Math Quiz Scores

Stem	Leaf
2	9
3	72
4	655
5	41555
6	0

Finally, reorder the leaf values in sequence:

Math Quiz Scores

Stem	Leaf
2	9
3	27
4	556
5	14555
6	0

One advantage that a stem-leaf plot has over a histogram is that it shows not only the frequency of values within each interval but also reveals all of the individual values within each interval.

Stem-leaf plots are particularly helpful in comparing and contrasting two distributions. For example, following is a back-to-back stem-leaf plot comparing the home runs hit by Babe Ruth during his years with the New York Yankees with those hit by Mark McGwire during his years with the St. Louis Cardinals.

Babe Ruth		Mark McGwire
	0	9,9
	1	
5,2	2	2
5,4	3	2,3,9,9
9,7,6,6,6,1,1	4	2,9
9,4,4	5	2,8
0	6	5
	7	0

Who do you think was the better home run hitter? How would Barry Bonds of the San Francisco Giants, who hit 73 home runs in 2003, compare?

THE NORMAL CURVE

Often researchers draw a smooth curve instead of the series of straight lines in a frequency polygon. The smooth curve suggests that we are not just connecting a series of dots (i.e., the actual frequencies of scores in a particular distribution), but rather showing a generalized distribution of scores that is not limited to one specific set of data. These smooth curves are known as **distribution curves.**

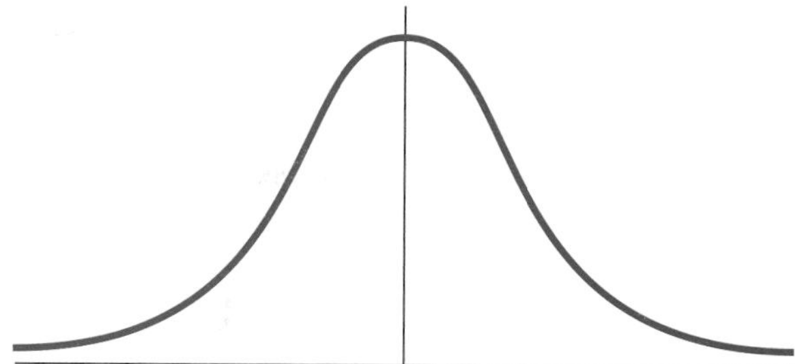

Figure 10.6 *The Normal Curve*

Many distributions of data tend to follow a certain specific shape of distribution curve called a **normal distribution.** When a distribution curve is normal, the large majority of the scores are concentrated in the middle of the distribution, and the scores decrease in frequency the farther away from the middle they are, as shown in Figure 10.6.

The **normal curve** is based on a precise mathematical equation. As you can see, it is symmetrical and bell shaped. The distribution of some human characteristics, such as height and weight, approximate such a curve, while many others, such as spatial ability, manual dexterity, and creativity, are often assumed to do so. The normal curve is very useful to researchers, and we shall discuss it in more detail later in the chapter.

AVERAGES

Averages, or **measures of central tendency,** enable a researcher to summarize the data in a frequency distribution with a single number. The three most commonly used averages are the mode, the median, and the mean. Each represents a type of average or typical score attained by a group of individuals on some measure.

The Mode.

The **mode** is the most frequent score in a distribution—that is, the score attained by more students than any other score. In the following distribution, what is the mode?

25, 20, 19, 17, 16, 16, 16,
14, 14, 11, 10, 9, 9

The mode is 16. What about this distribution?

25, 24, 24, 23, 22, 20, 19, 19, 18, 11, 10

This distribution (called a *bimodal distribution*) has two modes, 24 and 19. Because the mode really doesn't tell us very much about a distribution, however, it is not used very often in educational research.

The Median. The **median** is the point below and above which 50 percent of the scores in a distribution fall—in short, the midpoint. In a distribution that contains an uneven number of scores, the median is the middlemost score (provided that the scores are listed in order). Thus, in the distribution 5, 4, 3, 2, 1, the median is 3. In a distribution that contains an even number of scores, the median is the point halfway between the two middlemost scores. Thus, in the distribution 70, 74, 82, 86, 88, 90, the median is 84. Hence, the median is not necessarily one of the actual scores in the distribution being summarized.

Note that two very different distributions might have the same median:

Distribution A: 98, 90, 84, 82, 76

Distribution B: 90, 87, 84, 65, 41

In both distributions, the median is 84.

It may look like the median is fairly easy to determine. This is usually the case with ungrouped data. For grouped data, calculating the median requires somewhat more work. It can, however, be estimated by locating the score that has half of the area under the frequency polygon above it and half below it.

The median is the most appropriate average to calculate when the data result in skewed distributions.

The Mean. The **mean** is another average of all the scores in a distribution.* It is determined by adding up all of the scores and then dividing this sum by the total number of scores. The mean of a distribution containing scores of 52, 68, 74, 86, 95, and 105, therefore, is 80. How did we determine this? We simply added up all the scores, which came to 480, and then divided this sum by 6, the total number of scores. In symbolic form, the formula for computing the mean looks like this:

$$\overline{X} = \frac{\Sigma X}{n}$$

*Actually, there are several kinds of means (geometric, harmonic, etc.), but their use is specialized and infrequent. We refer here to the arithmetic mean.

TABLE 10.4 ***Example of the Mode, Median, and Mean in a Distribution***

Raw Score	Frequency
98	1
97	1
91	2
85	1
80	5
77	7
72	5
65	3
64	7
62	10
58	3
45	2
33	1
11	1
5	1
	$n = 50$

Mode = 62; median = 64.5; mean = 66.7

where Σ represents "sum of," X represents any raw score value, n represents the total number of scores, and $\overline{X}$ represents the mean.

Table 10.4 presents a frequency distribution of scores on a test and each of the preceding measures of central tendency. As you can see, each of these indices tells us something a little different. The most frequent score was 62, but would we want to say that this was the most typical score? Probably not. The median of the scores was 64.5. The mean was 66.7. Perhaps the mean is the best description of the distribution of scores, but it, too, is not totally satisfactory because the distribution is skewed. Table 10.4 shows that these indices are only *summaries* of all the scores in a distribution and often do not have the same value. They are not intended to show variation or spread (Figure 10.7).

Which of the three averages (measures of central tendency), then, is best? It depends. The mean is the only one of the three that uses all the information in a distribution, since every score is used in calculating it, and it is generally preferred over the other two measures. However, it tends to be unduly influenced by extreme scores. (Can you see why?) On occasion, therefore, the median gives a more accurate indication of the typical

Figure 10.7 *Averages Can Be Misleading!*

score in a distribution. Suppose, for example, that the yearly salaries earned by various workers in a small business were as shown in Table 10.5.

The mean of these salaries is $75,000. Would it be correct to say that this is the average yearly salary paid in this company? Obviously it would not. The extremely high salary paid to the owner of the company "inflates" the mean, so to speak. Using it as a summary figure to indicate the average yearly salary would give an erroneous impression. In this instance, the median would be the more appropriate average to calculate, since it would not be as affected by the owner's salary. The median is $27,000, a far more accurate indication of the typical salary for the year.

TABLE 10.5 ***Yearly Salaries of Workers in a Small Business***

Mr. Davis	$ 10,500
Mr. Thompson	20,000
Ms. Angelo	22,500
Mr. Schmidt	24,000
Ms. Wills	26,000
Ms. Brown	28,000
Mr. Greene	36,000
Mr. Adams	43,000
Ms. Franklin	65,000
Mr. Payson (owner)	475,000

SPREADS

While measures of central tendency are useful statistics for summarizing the scores in a distribution, they are not sufficient. Two distributions may have identical means and medians, for example, yet be quite different in other ways. For example, consider these two distributions:

Distribution A: 19, 20, 25, 32, 39

Distribution B: 2, 3, 25, 30, 75

The mean in both of these distributions is 27, and the median in both is 25. Yet you can see that the distributions differ considerably. In distribution A, the scores are closer together and tend to cluster around the mean. In distribution B, they are much more spread out. Hence the two distributions differ in what statisticians call **variability**. Figure 10.8 illustrates further examples.

Thus, measures of central tendency, when presented without any accompanying information of how spread out or dispersed the data are, can be misleading. To say that the average annual income of all the players in the National Basketball Association in 1998 was $275,000 hides the fact that some players earned far less, whereas someone like Michael Jordan earned more

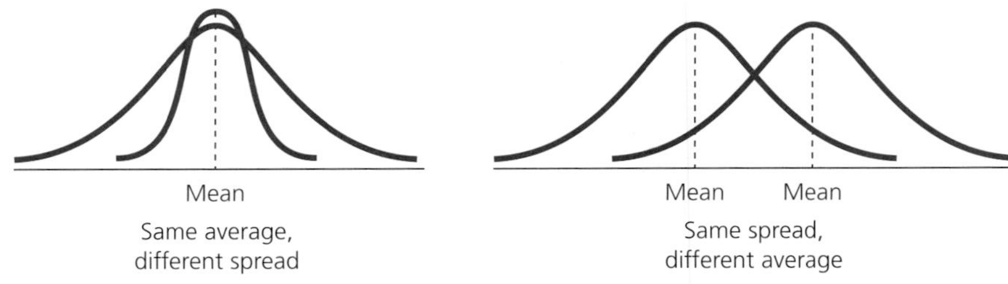

Figure 10.8 *Different Distributions Compared with Respect to Averages and Spreads*

than $5 million. The distribution of players' salaries was skewed to the right and very spread out. Knowing only the mean gives us an inadequate description of the distribution of salaries for players in the NBA.

There is a need, therefore, for measures researchers can use to describe the *spread,* or variability, that exists within a distribution. Let us consider three—the interquartile range, the overall range, and the standard deviation.

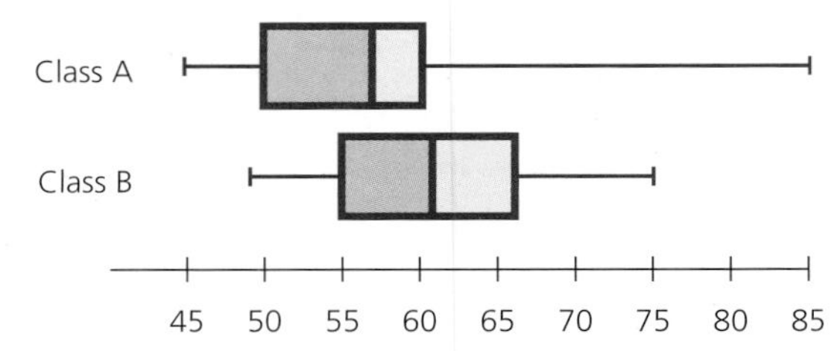

Figure 10.9 *Boxplots*

Quartiles and the Five-Number Summary. When a distribution is skewed, both the variability and the general shape of the distribution can be described by reporting several *percentiles.* A **percentile** in a set of numbers is a value below which a certain percentage of the numbers fall and above which the rest of the numbers fall.

You may have encountered percentiles if you have ever taken a standardized test such as the SAT and received a report saying "Raw score 630, percentile 84." You received a score of 630, but perhaps more useful is the fact that 84 percent of those who took the examination scored lower than you did.

The median is the 50th percentile. Other percentiles that are important are the 25th percentile, also known as the *first quartile* (Q_1), and the 75th percentile, the *third quartile* (Q_3). A useful way to describe a skewed distribution, therefore, is to give what is known as a **five-number summary**, consisting of the lowest score, Q_1, the median, Q_3, and the highest score. The interquartile range (IQR) is the difference between the third and first quartiles ($Q_3 - Q_1 = IQR$).

Boxplots. The five-number summary of a distribution can be graphically portrayed by means of a **boxplot.** Boxplots are especially useful in comparing two or more distributions. Figure 10.9 gives boxplots for the distributions of the midterm scores of two classes taking the same biology exam. Each central box has its ends at the quartiles, and the median is marked by the line within the box. The "whiskers" at either end extend to the lowest and highest scores.*

Figure 10.9 permits an immediate comparison between the two classes. Overall, class B did better, but the upper whiskers illustrate that class A had the student with the highest score. Figure 10.9 is but another example of how effectively graphs can convey information.

Though the five-number summary is an extremely useful numerical description of a distribution, it is not the most common. That accolade belongs to a combination of the mean (a measure of center) and the standard deviation (a measure of spread). The *standard deviation* and its brother, the *variance,* measure the spread of scores from the mean. They should only be used in conjunction with the mean.

The Range. The overall **range** represents the distance between the highest and lowest scores in a distribution. Thus, if the highest score in a distribution is 89 and the lowest is 11, the range would be 89 − 11, or 78. Because it involves only the two most extreme scores in a distribution, the range is but a crude indication of variability. Its main advantage is that it gives a quick (although rough) estimate of variability.

The Standard Deviation. The **standard deviation** (SD) is the most useful index of variability. It is a single number that represents the spread of a

*Boxplots are sometimes called *box-and-whiskers diagrams.*

"I don't think I can make it to class today, Dr. Roberts. I'm feeling a couple of standard deviations below the mean."

TABLE 10.6 ***Calculation of the Standard Deviation of a Distribution***

Raw Score	Mean	$X - \overline{X}$	$(X - \overline{X})^2$
85	54	31	961
80	54	26	676
70	54	16	256
60	54	6	36
55	54	1	1
50	54	−4	16
45	54	−9	81
40	54	−14	196
30	54	−24	576
25	54	−29	841
			$\Sigma = 3640$

$$\text{Variance (SD}^2) = \frac{\Sigma(X - X)^2}{n}$$

$$= \frac{3640}{10} = 364^{a}$$

$$\text{Standard deviation (SD)} = \sqrt{\frac{\Sigma(X - \overline{X})^2}{n}}$$

$$= \sqrt{364} = 19.08^{b}$$

[a]The symbol for the variance of a sample sometimes is shown as s^2; the symbol for the variance of a population is σ^2.

[b]The symbol for the standard deviation of a sample sometimes is shown as s; the symbol for the standard deviation of a population is σ.

distribution. As with the mean, every score in the distribution is used to calculate it. The steps involved in calculating the standard deviation are straightforward.

1. Calculate the mean of the distribution.

$$\overline{X} = \frac{\Sigma X}{n}$$

2. Subtract the mean from each score. Each result is symbolized $X - \overline{X}$.
3. Square each of these scores $(X - \overline{X})^2$
4. Add up all the squares of these scores:

$$\Sigma(X - \overline{X})^2$$

5. Divide the total by the number of scores. The result is called the **variance**.
6. Take the square root of the variance. This is the standard deviation.

These steps can be summarized as follows:

$$\text{SD} = \sqrt{\frac{\Sigma(X - \overline{X})^2}{n}}$$

where SD is the symbol for standard deviation, Σ is the symbol for "sum of," X is the symbol for a raw score, $\overline{X}$ is the symbol for the mean, and n represents the number of scores in the distribution.

This procedure sounds more complicated than it is. It really is not difficult to calculate. Table 10.6 illustrates the calculation of the standard deviation of a distribution of 10 scores.

You will notice that the more spread out scores are, the greater the deviation scores will be and hence the larger the standard deviation. The closer the scores are to the mean, the less spread out they are and hence the smaller the standard deviation. Thus, if we were describing two sets of scores on the same test and we stated that the standard deviation of the scores in set 1 was 2.7 and the standard deviation in set 2 was 8.3, we would know that there was much less variability in set 1—that is, the scores were closer together.

An important point involving the standard deviation is that if a distribution is normal, then the mean plus or minus three standard deviations will encompass about 99 percent of all the scores in the distribution. For example, if the mean of a distribution is 72 and the standard deviation is 3, then just about 99 percent of the scores in the distribution are somewhere between scores of 63 and 81. Figure 10.10 provides an illustration of standard deviation.

Figure 10.10 *Standard Deviations for Boys' and Men's Basketball Teams*

The Standard Deviation of a Normal Distribution. The total area under the normal curve represents all of the scores in a normal distribution. In such a curve, the mean, median, and mode are identical, so the mean falls at the exact center of the curve. It thus is also the most frequent score in the distribution. Because the curve is symmetrical, 50 percent of the scores must fall on each side of the mean.

Here are some important facts about the normal distribution:

- Fifty percent of all the observations (e.g., scores) fall on *each* side of the mean (Figure 10.11).
- In any normal distribution, 68 percent of the scores fall within one standard deviation of the mean. Half of these (34 percent) fall within one standard deviation above the mean and the other half within one standard deviation below the mean.
- Another 27 percent of the observations fall between one and two standard deviations away from the mean. Hence 95 percent (68 percent + 27 percent) fall within two standard deviations of the mean.
- In all, 99.7 percent of the observations fall within three standard deviations of the mean. Figure 10.12 illustrates all three of these facts, often referred to as the **68-95-99.7 rule**.

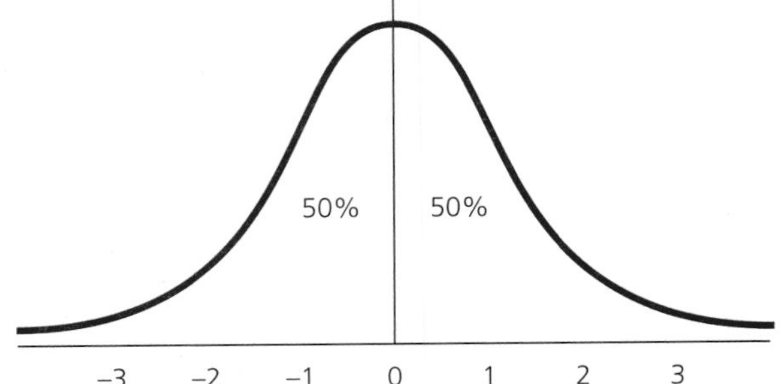

Figure 10.11 *Fifty Percent of All Scores in a Normal Curve Fall on Each Side of the Mean*

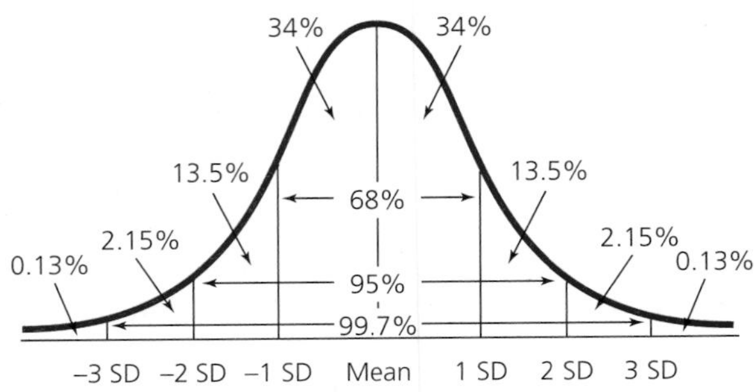

Figure 10.12 *Percentages Under the Normal Curve*

Hence we see that almost all of the scores in a normal distribution lie between the mean and plus or minus three standard deviations. Only .13 percent of all the scores fall above 3 SD, and .13 percent fall below −3 SD.

If a set of scores is normally distributed, we can interpret any particular score if we know how far, in standard deviation units, it is from the mean. Suppose, for example, the mean of a normal distribution is 100 and the standard deviation is 15. A score that lies one standard deviation above the mean, therefore, would equal 115. A score that lies one standard deviation below the mean would equal 85. What would a score that lies 1.5 standard deviations above the mean equal?*

We also can determine how a particular individual's score compares with all the other scores in a normal distribution. For example, if a person's score lies exactly one standard deviation above the mean, then we know that slightly more than 84 percent of all the other scores in the distribution lie below his or her score.† If a distribution is normal and we know the mean and the standard deviation of the distribution, we can determine the percentage of scores that lie above and below any given score (see Figure 10.12). This is one of the most useful characteristics of the normal distribution.

STANDARD SCORES AND THE NORMAL CURVE

Researchers often are interested in seeing how one person's score compares with another's. To determine this, researchers often convert raw scores to derived scores. Earlier we described two types of derived scores—age/grade equivalents and percentile ranks—but mentioned another type—standard scores—only briefly. We discuss them now in somewhat more detail, since they are very useful.

Standard scores use a common scale to indicate how an individual compares to other individuals in a group. These scores are particularly helpful in comparing an individual's relative position on different instruments. The two standard scores that are most frequently used in educational research are *z* scores and *T* scores.

*122.5

†Fifty percent of the scores in the distribution must lie below the mean; 34 percent must lie between the mean and +1 SD. Therefore 84 percent (50 percent + 34 percent) of the scores in the distribution must be below +1 SD.

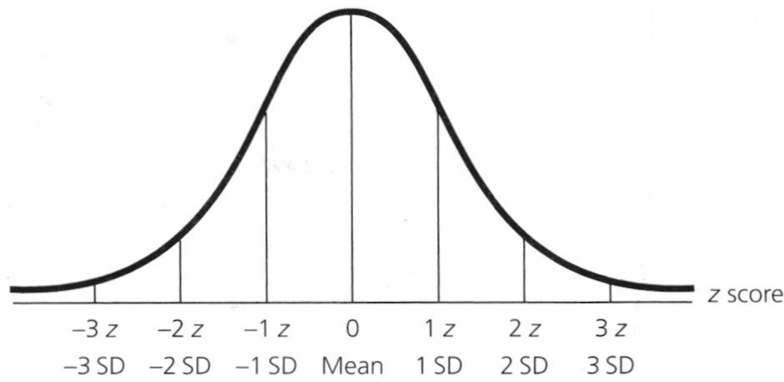

Figure 10.13 *z Scores Associated with the Normal Curve*

z Scores. The simplest form of standard score is the **z score**. It expresses how far a raw score is from the mean in standard deviation units. A raw score that is exactly on the mean corresponds to a *z* score of zero; a raw score that is exactly one standard deviation above the mean equals a *z* score of +1, while a raw score that is exactly one standard deviation below the mean equals a *z* score of −1. Similarly, a raw score that is exactly two standard deviations above the mean equals a *z* score of +2, and so forth. One *z*, therefore, equals one standard deviation (1 z = 1 SD), 2 z = 2 SD, −0.5 z = −0.5 SD, and so on (Figure 10.13). Thus, if the mean of a distribution was 50 and the standard deviation was 2, a raw score of 52 would equal a *z* score of +1, a raw score of 46 would equal a *z* score of −2, and so forth.

A big advantage of *z* scores is that they allow raw scores on different tests to be compared. For example, suppose a student received raw scores of 60 on a biology test and 80 on a chemistry test. A naive observer might be inclined to infer, at first glance, that the student was doing better in chemistry than in biology. But this might be unwise, for how "well" the student is doing comparatively cannot be determined until we know the mean and standard deviation for each distribution of scores. Let us further suppose that the mean on the biology test was 50, but on the chemistry test it was 90. Also assume that the standard deviation on the biology test was 5, but on the chemistry test it was 10. What does this tell us? The student's raw score in biology (60) is actually two standard deviations *above* the mean (a *z* score of +2), whereas his raw score in chemistry (80) is one standard deviation *below* the mean (a *z* score of −1). Rather than doing better in chemistry, as the raw scores by themselves suggest, the student is actually doing better in biology. Table 10.7 compares both the raw scores, the *z* scores, and the percentile rank of the student on both tests.

Using Excel to Calculate the Mean, Median, and Standard Deviation of a Distribution

	A	B	C
1	45		
2	56		
3	76		
4	87		
5	88		
6	61		
7	34		
8	67		
9	55		
10	88		
11	92		
12	85		
13	78		
14	84		
15	77		
16	71.53		
17	77		
18	17.7		

Excel can be used to calculate many descriptive statistics. Simply click on an empty cell, and then click on **Function** under the **Insert** menu. This will open a dialogue box. You can search for a function, such as **Average, Median,** or **Standard Deviation.** Enter the function you wish to search for in the **Search for a function** box, and click **Go.** Excel will present you with a number of possible matches from which to choose. You may have to access the help files to distinguish between similar functions (e.g., **STDEV** is the sample standard deviation, while **STDEVP** is the population standard deviation). Click on the function you wish to use, and then click **OK.** This will bring up the **Function Arguments** dialog box. In this box you can enter the individual cell numbers you wish to include in the calculation, or you can highlight a group of adjoining cells on the spreadsheet by clicking on the first cell and dragging to the last cell. Finally, click **OK** on the Function Argument dialogue box. Excel will calculate the result and enter it into the (formerly) empty cell on the spreadsheet that you began with.

As you learn the names of functions you commonly use, you can enter them directly, without resorting to the Insert and Function procedure described. We did this in the example to the left. First we opened an Excel spreadsheet and then listed the data in cells A1 through A15. We then clicked on the cells where we wanted the statistics to appear and typed in the following commands:

- To obtain the mean: =**AVERAGE(A1:A15)***
- To obtain the median: =**MEDIAN(A1:A15)**
- To obtain the standard deviation: =**STDEV(A1:A15)**

We typed in these commands in cells A16, A17, and A18, and hit "Return" each time. The corresponding values† then appeared in those cells: 71.53 (the mean), 77 (the median), and 17.7 (the standard deviation).

**Note:* All commands must always begin with an equal sign (=) *before* typing in the name of the formula and the list to which the formula is to be applied. You must then hit "Return," and the corresponding value will appear in the designated cell. See Appendix D.
†Shortened to two decimal points.

TABLE 10.7 *Comparisons of Raw Scores and z Scores on Two Tests*

Test	Raw Score	Mean	SD	z Score	Percentile Rank
Biology	60	50	5	+2	98
Chemistry	80	90	10	−1	16

Of course, z scores are not always exactly one or two standard deviations away from the mean. Actually, researchers apply the following formula to convert a raw score into a z score.

$$z \text{ score} = \frac{\text{raw score} - \text{mean}}{\text{standard deviation}}$$

Thus, for a raw score of 80, a mean of 65, and a standard deviation of 12, the z score will be:

$$z = \left(\frac{80 - 65}{12}\right) = 1.25$$

Probability and z Scores. Another important characteristic of the normal distribution is that the percentages associated with areas under the curve can be thought of as probabilities. A **probability** is a percent stated in decimal form and refers to the likelihood of an event occurring. For example, if there is a probability that an event will occur 25 percent of the time, this event can be said to have a probability of .25. Similarly, an event that will probably occur 90 percent of the time is

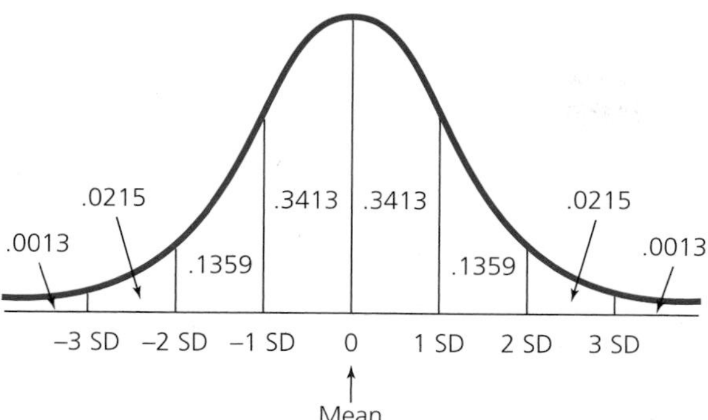

Figure 10.14 *Probabilities Under the Normal Curve*

said to have a probability of .90. All of the percentages associated with areas under a normal curve, therefore, can be expressed in decimal form and viewed as probability statements. Some of these probabilities are shown in Figure 10.14.

Considering the area under the normal curve in terms of probabilities is very helpful to a researcher. Let us consider an example. We have previously shown that approximately 34 percent of the scores in a normal distribution lie between the mean and 1 SD. Because 50 percent of the scores fall above the mean, roughly 16 percent of the scores must therefore lie above 1 SD ($50 - 34 = 16$). Now, if we express 16 percent in decimal form and interpret it as a probability, we can say that the probability of randomly selecting an individual from the population who has a score of 1 SD or more above the mean is .16. Usually this is written as $p = 16$, with the p meaning probability. Similarly, we can determine the probability of randomly selecting an individual who has a score lying at or below −2 SD or lower, or between +1 SD and −1 SD, and so on. Figure 10.14 shows that the probability of selecting an individual who has a score lower than −2 SD is $p = .0228$, or roughly 2 in 100. The probability of randomly selecting an individual who has a score between −1 SD and +1 SD is $p = .6826$, and so forth.

Statistical tables exist (see part of one in Appendix B) that give the proportion of scores associated with any particular z score in the normal distribution (e.g., for $z = 1.10$, the proportion [i.e., the probability] for the area between the mean of $z = 0$ and $z = 1.10$ is .3643, and for the area beyond z, it is .1357). Hence, a researcher can be very precise in describing the position of any particular score relative to other scores in a normal distribution. Figure 10.15 shows a portion of such a table.

T Scores. Raw scores that are below the mean of a distribution convert to negative z scores. This is somewhat awkward. One way to eliminate negative z scores is to convert them into T scores. ***T* scores** are simply z scores expressed in a different form. To change a z score to a T score, we simply multiply the z score by 10 and add 50. Thus, a z score of +1 equals a T score of 60 ($1 \times 10 = 10$; $10 + 50 = 60$). A z score of −2 equals a T score of 30 ($-2 = 10 = -20$; $-20 + 50 = 30$). A z score of zero (which is the equivalent of the mean of the raw scores) equals a T score of 50. You should see that a distribution of T scores has a mean of 50 and a standard deviation

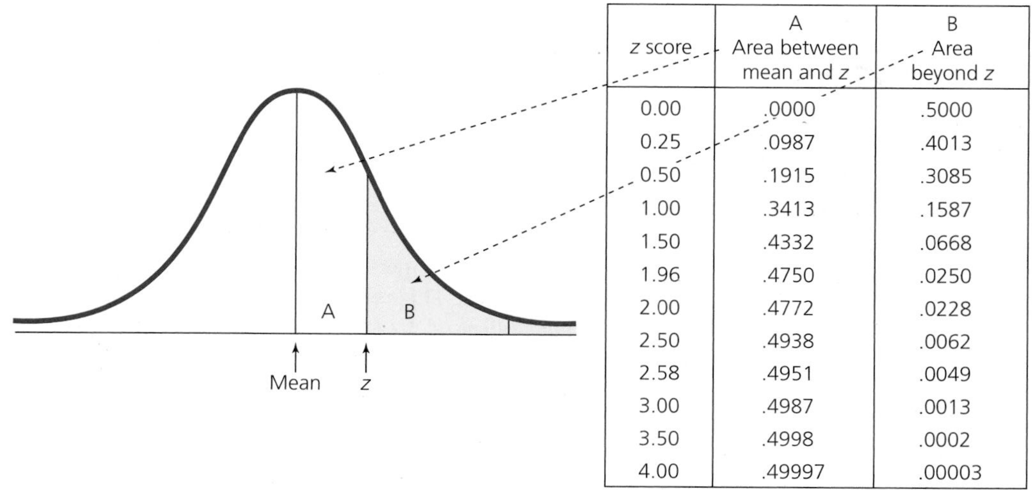

z score	A Area between mean and *z*	B Area beyond *z*
0.00	.0000	.5000
0.25	.0987	.4013
0.50	.1915	.3085
1.00	.3413	.1587
1.50	.4332	.0668
1.96	.4750	.0250
2.00	.4772	.0228
2.50	.4938	.0062
2.58	.4951	.0049
3.00	.4987	.0013
3.50	.4998	.0002
4.00	.49997	.00003

Figure 10.15 *Table Showing Probability Areas Between the Mean and Different z Scores*

Figure 10.16 *Examples of Standard Scores*

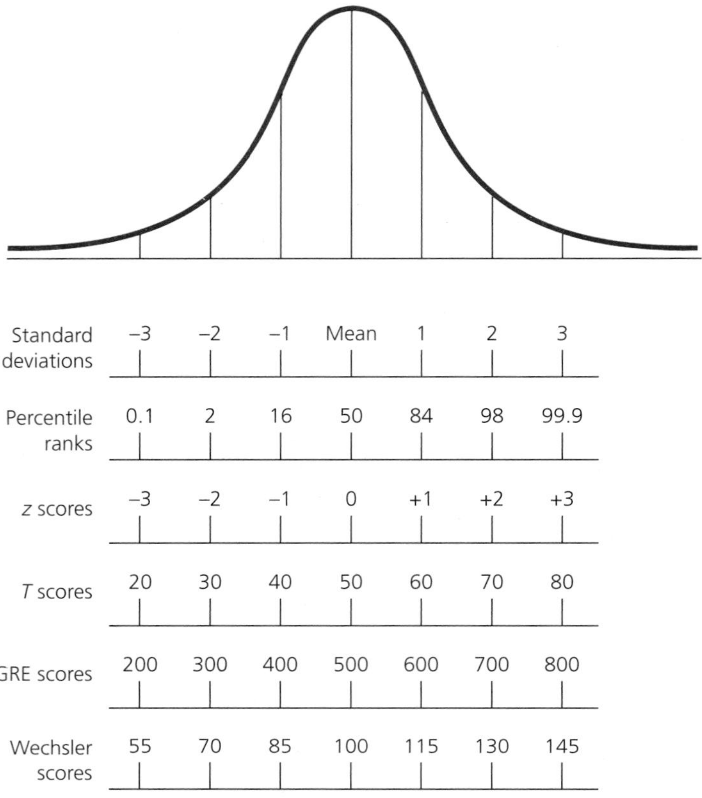

of 10. If you think about it, you should also see that a *T* score of 50 equals the 50th percentile.

When a researcher knows, or can assume, that a distribution of scores is normal, both *T* and *z* scores can be interpreted in terms of percentile ranks because there is then a direct relationship between the two. Figure 10.16 illustrates this relationship. There are other systems similar to *T* scores, which differ only in the choice of values for the mean and standard deviation. Two of the most common, those used with the Graduate Record Examination ($\overline{X}$ = 500, SD = 100) and the Wechsler Intelligence Scales ($\overline{X}$ = 100, SD = 15), are also illustrated in Figure 10.16.

The Importance of the Normal Curve and z Scores. You may have noticed that the preceding discussion of the use of *z* scores, percentages, and probabilities in relation to the normal curve was always qualified by the words "*if* or *when* the distribution of scores is normal." You should recall that *z* scores can be calculated regardless of the shape of the distribution of original scores. But it is *only* when the distribution is normal that the conversion to percentages or probabilities as described is legitimate. Fortunately, many distributions *do* approximate the normal curve. This is most likely when a sample is chosen randomly from a broadly defined population. (It would be very unlikely, e.g., with achievement scores in a sample that consisted only of gifted students.)

When actual data do not approximate the normal curve, they can be changed to do so. In other words, any distribution of scores can be "normalized." The procedure for doing so is not complicated, but it makes the assumption that the characteristic is "really" normally distributed. Most published tests that permit use of standard scores have normalized the score distributions in order to permit the translation of *z* scores to percentages. This relationship—between *z* scores and percentages of area under the normal curve—is also basic to many inferential statistics.

CORRELATION

In many places throughout this text we have stated that the most meaningful research is that which seeks to

Using Excel to Compute Correlations

To conduct correlational analysis using Excel, first enter your data into two columns in a worksheet with the *X* values in one column and the *Y* values in another column. Next, select **Tools→Data Analysis.** In the Data Analysis dialog box choose **Correlation** tool from the Analysis Tools list, and click OK. Identify the range of *X* and *Y* values you want to analyze by entering the worksheet range. If the input range includes labels, select the Labels in the First Row box. Confirm that the **Grouped By** button—either Columns or Rows—reflects how your data are organized. Next, use the **Output Options** button to tell Excel where to place your correlation results. For example, to place the results into a range in your existing worksheet, select the Output Range button and then indicate the range address in the Output Range text box. If you want to put them in a new workbook, select the New Workbook button. Then click **OK.** Excel calculates the correlation coefficient and significance results for the data you identified and puts it in the location you specified. (For an example, see Appendix D.)

find, or verify, relationships among variables. Comparing the performance of different groups is, as you have seen, one way to study relationships. In such studies one variable is categorical—the variable that defines the groups (e.g., method A versus method B). The other variable is most often quantitative, and groups are typically compared using frequency polygons, averages, and spreads.

In correlational research, researchers seek to determine whether a relationship exists between two (or more) quantitative variables, such as age and weight or reading and writing ability. Sometimes, such relationships are useful in prediction, but most often the eventual goal is to say something about causation. Although causal relationships cannot be proved through correlational studies, researchers hope eventually to make causal statements as an outgrowth of their work. The totality of studies showing a relationship between incidence of lung cancer and cigarette use is a current example. We will discuss correlational research in further detail in Chapter 15.

Scatterplots. What is needed is a means to determine whether relationships exist in data. A useful technique for representing relationships with quantitative data is the scatterplot. A **scatterplot** is a pictorial representation of the relationship between two quantitative variables.

Scatterplots are easy to construct, provided some common pitfalls are avoided. First, to be plotted, there must be a score on each variable for each individual; second, the grouping intervals (if any) within each variable (axis) must be of equal size; third, *each* individual must be represented by one, and only one, point of intersection. We used the data in Table 10.8 to construct the scatterplot in Figure 10.17. The steps involved are the following:

1. Decide which variable will be represented on each axis. It makes no difference which variable is placed on which axis. We have used the horizontal (x) axis for variable 1 and the vertical (y) axis for variable 2.
2. Divide each axis into about 12 to 15 sections. Each point on the axis will represent a particular score or group of scores. Be sure all scores can be included.
3. Group scores if desirable. It was not necessary for us to group scores for variable 1, since all of the scores fall within a 15-point range. For variable 2, however, representing *each* score on the axis would result in a great many points on the vertical axis. Therefore, we grouped them within *equal sized* intervals of five points each.
4. Plot, for each person, the point where the vertical and horizontal lines for his or her scores on the two variables intersect. For example, Pedro had a score of 12 on variable 1, so we locate 12 on the horizontal axis. He had a score of 41 on variable 2, so we locate that score (in the 40–44 grouping) on the vertical axis. We then draw imaginary lines from each of these points until they intersect, and mark an X or a dot at that point.

TABLE 10.8 *Data Used to Construct Scatterplot in Figure 10.17*

Individual	Scores Variable 1	Scores Variable 2	Grouped Scores Variable 2	Frequency of Grouped Scores Variable 2
Pedro	12	41	75–79	1
John	21	76	70–74	0
Alicia	9	29	65–69	0
Charles	7	21	60–64	1
Bonnie	13	43	55–59	0
Phil	11	37	50–54	1
Sue	7	14	45–49	0
Oscar	18	63	40–44	2
Jean	15	54	35–39	2
Dave	14	39	30–34	0
			25–29	1
			20–24	1
			15–19	0
			10–14	1

Figure 10.17 *Scatterplot of Data from Table 10.8*

Using Excel to Draw a Scatterplot

Excel can also be used to draw a scatterplot to illustrate the relationship between two quantitative variables. The dataset to be illustrated must be entered into two columns in an Excel worksheet, with the *X* variable in one column and the *Y* variable in another. Once the data are entered, pull down the **Insert** menu, then click on **Chart.** When the chart window opens, click on **Scatter.** Then click on **Next** at the bottom of the dialogue box. Another dialogue box will open. Click on the first cell in the upper left of the two columns of data, and drag down to the last cell in the lower right. Click on **Finish** at the bottom of the dialogue box to display the finished chart. Shown here is an example of the relationship between two quizzes for a hypothetical class of 15 high school chemistry students. Note that the correlation coefficient is shown to the left of the scatterplot. In this instance, $r = .97$, indicating a very strong, positive relationship between the two sets of quiz scores for this group of students.

X	Y
27	32
24	27
34	33
36	38
18	21
16	15
13	17
25	28
10	12
15	16
19	18
14	14
27	29
7	8
24	22

$r = .97$

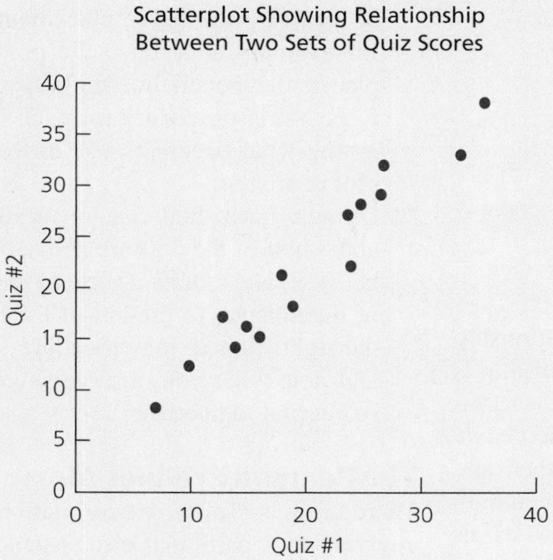

Scatterplot Showing Relationship Between Two Sets of Quiz Scores

5. In the same way, plot the scores of all 10 students on both variables. The completed result is a scatterplot.

Interpreting a Scatterplot. How do researchers interpret scatterplots? What are they intended to reveal? Researchers want to know not only *if* a relationship exists between variables but also *to what degree.* The degree of relationship, if one exists, is what a scatterplot illustrates.

Consider Figure 10.17. What does it tell us about the relationship between variable 1 and variable 2? This question can be answered in several ways.

1. We might say that high scores on variable 1 go with high scores on variable 2 (as in John's case) and that low scores also tend to go together (as in Sue's case).
2. We might say that by knowing a student's score on one variable, we can estimate his or her score on the other variable fairly closely. Suppose, for example, a new student attains a score of 16 on variable 1. What would you predict his or her score would be on variable 2? You probably would *not* predict a score of 75 or one of 25 (we would predict a score somewhere from 45 to 59).
3. The customary interpretation of a scatterplot that looks like this would be that there is a strong or high degree of relationship between the two variables.

Outliers. Outliers are scores or measurements that differ by such large amounts from those of other individuals in a group that they must be given careful consideration as special cases. They indicate an unusual exception to a general pattern. They occur in scatterplots, as well as frequency distribution tables, histograms, and frequency polygons. Figure 10.18 shows the relationship between family cohesiveness and school achievement. Notice the lonely individual near the lower right corner with a high score in family cohesiveness but a low score in achievement. Why? The answer should be of interest to the student's teacher.

Correlation Coefficients and Scatterplots.

Figure 10.19 presents several other examples of scatterplots. Studying them will help you understand the notion of a relationship and also further your understanding of the correlation coefficient. As we mentioned in Chapter 8, a **correlation coefficient**, designated

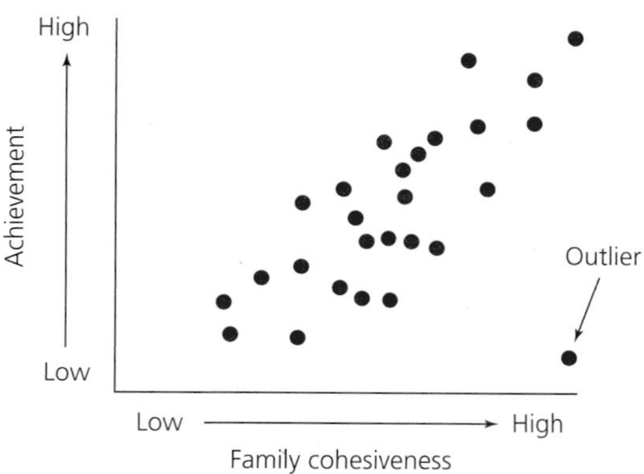

Figure 10.18 *Relationship Between Family Cohesiveness and School Achievement in a Hypothetical Group of Students*

by the symbol *r*, expresses the degree of relationship between two sets of scores.* A positive relationship is indicated when high scores on one variable are accompanied by high scores on the other, when low scores on one are accompanied by low scores on the other, and so forth. A negative relationship is indicated when high scores on one variable are accompanied by low scores on the other, and vice versa (Figure 10.20).

You should recall that correlation coefficients are never more than +1.00, indicating a perfect positive relationship, or −1.00, indicating a perfect negative relationship. Perfect positive or negative correlations, however, are rarely, if ever, achieved (Figure 10.21). If the two variables are highly related, a coefficient somewhat close to +1.00 or −1.00 will be obtained (such as .85 or −.93). The closer the coefficient is to either of these extremes, the greater the degree of the relationship. If there is no or hardly any relationship, a coefficient of .00 or close to it will be obtained. The coefficient is calculated directly from the same scores used to construct the scatterplot.

The scatterplots in Figure 10.19 illustrate different degrees of correlation. Both positive and negative correlations are shown. Scatterplots (*a*), (*b*), and (*c*) illustrate different degrees of positive correlation, while scatterplots (*e*), (*f*), (*g*), and (*h*) illustrate different degrees of negative correlation. Scatterplot (*d*) indicates no relationship between the two variables involved.

*In this context, the correlation coefficient indicates the degree of relationship between two *variables*. You will recall from Chapter 8 that it is also used to assess the reliability and validity of measurements.

To better understand the meaning of different values of the correlation coefficient, we suggest that you try the following two exercises with Figure 10.19.

1. Lay a pencil flat on the paper on scatterplot (*a*) so that the entire length of the pencil is touching the paper. Place it in such a way that it touches or covers as many dots as possible. Take note that there is clearly one "best" placement. You would not, for example, maximize the points covered if you placed the pencil horizontally on the scatterplot. Repeat this procedure for each of the scatterplots, noting what occurs as you move from one scatterplot to another.
2. Draw a horizontal line on scatterplot (*a*) so that about half of the dots are above the line and half are below it. Next, draw a vertical line so that about half of the dots are to the left of the line and half are to the right. Repeat the procedure for each scatterplot and note what you observe as you move from one scatterplot to another.

The Pearson Product-Moment Coefficient. There are many different correlation coefficients, each applying to a particular circumstance and each calculated by means of a different computational formula. The one we have been illustrating is the one most frequently used: the **Pearson product-moment coefficient** of correlation (also known as the **Pearson *r***). It is symbolized by the lowercase letter *r*. When the data for both variables are expressed in terms of quantitative scores, the Pearson *r* is the appropriate correlation coefficient to use. It assumes that the relationship is best described by a straight line. (It is not difficult to calculate, and we'll show you how in Chapter 12.) It is designed for use with interval or ratio data.

Eta. Another index of correlation that you should become familiar with is called **eta** (symbolized as η). We shall not illustrate how to calculate eta (since it requires computational methods beyond the scope of this text), but you should know that it is used when a scatterplot shows that a straight line is not the best fit for the plotted points. In the examples shown in Figure 10.22, for example, you can see that a curved line provides a much better fit to the data than would a straight line.

Eta is interpreted in much the same way as the Pearson *r*, except that it ranges from .00 to 1.00, rather than from −1.00 to +1.00. Higher values, as with the other correlation coefficients, indicate higher degrees of relationship.

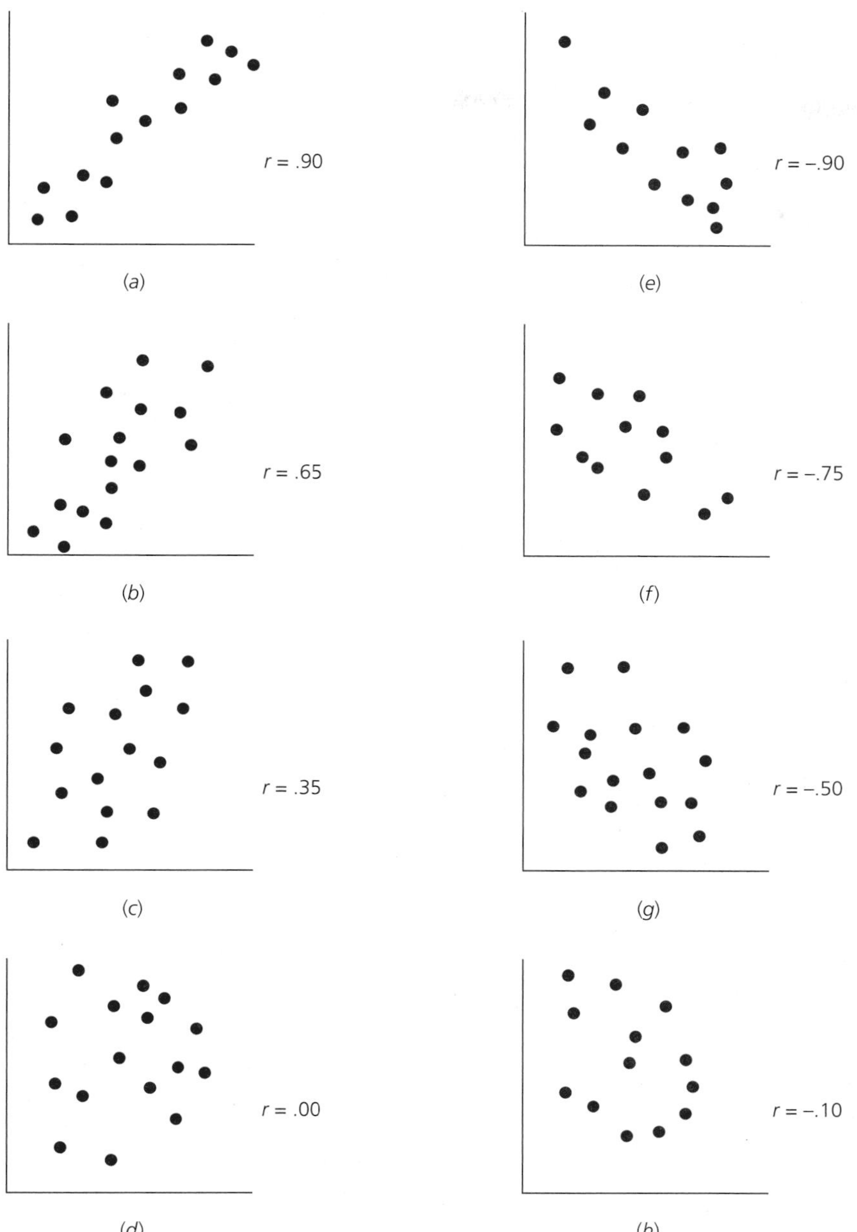

Figure 10.19 *Further Examples of Scatterplots*

Techniques for Summarizing Categorical Data

THE FREQUENCY TABLE

Suppose a researcher, using a questionnaire, has been collecting data from a random sample of 50 teachers in a large urban school district. The questionnaire covers many variables related to their activities and interests. One of the variables is *learning activity I use most frequently in my classroom.* The researcher arranges the data on this variable (and others) in the form of a frequency table, which shows the frequency with which each type, or category, of learning activity is mentioned. The researcher simply places a tally mark for each individual in the sample alongside the activity mentioned.

Figure 10.20 *A Perfect Negative Correlation!*

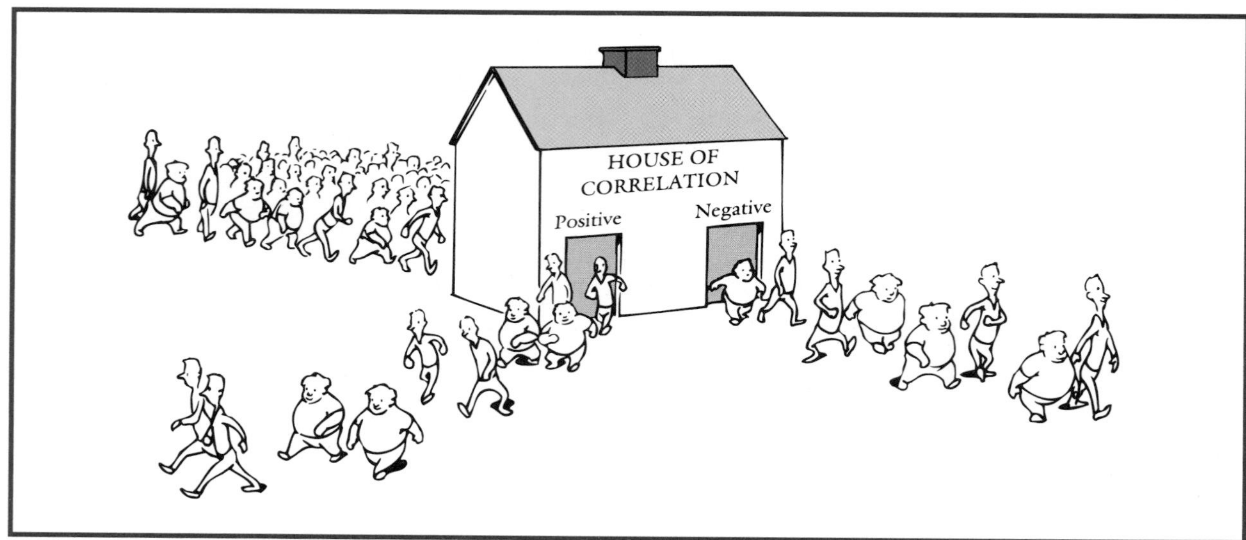

Figure 10.21 *Positive and Negative Correlations*

Figure 10.22 *Examples of Nonlinear (Curvilinear) Relationships*

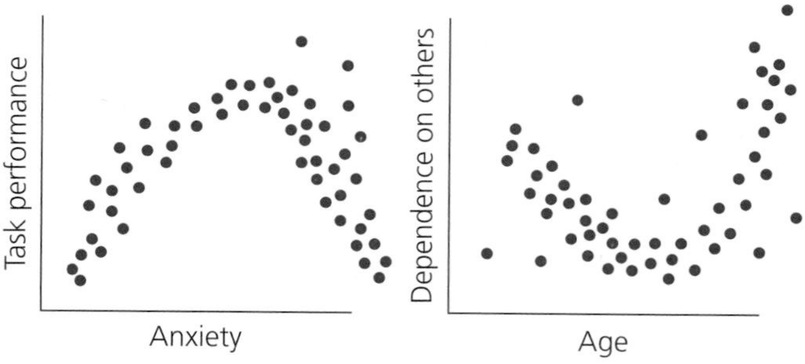

When all 50 individuals are tallied, the results look like the following frequency listing:

Response	Tally	Frequency
Lectures	𝍸 𝍸 𝍸	15
Class discussions	𝍸 𝍸	10
Oral reports	IIII	4
Library research	II	2
Seatwork	𝍸	5
Demonstrations	𝍸 III	8
Audiovisual presentations	𝍸 I	6
		$n = 50$

The tally marks have been added up at the end of each row to show the total number of individuals who listed that activity. Often with categorical data, researchers are interested in proportions, because they wish to make an estimate (if their sample is random) about the proportions in the total population from which the sample was selected. Thus, the total numbers in each category are often changed to percentages. This has been done in Table 10.9, with the categories arranged in descending order of frequency.

TABLE 10.9 *Frequency and Percentage of Total of Responses to Questionnaire*

Response	Frequency	Percentage of Total (%)
Lectures	15	30
Class discussions	10	20
Demonstrations	8	16
Audiovisual presentations	6	12
Seatwork	5	10
Oral reports	4	8
Library research	2	4
Total	50	100

BAR GRAPHS AND PIE CHARTS

There are two other ways to illustrate a difference in proportions. One is a **bar graph** portrayal, as shown in Figure 10.23; another is a **pie chart**, as shown in Figure 10.24.

THE CROSSBREAK TABLE

When a relationship between two categorical variables is of interest, it is usually reported in the form of a **crossbreak table** (sometimes called a **contingency table**). The simplest crossbreak is a 2 by 2 table, as shown in Table 10.10. Each individual is tallied in one, and only one, cell that corresponds to the combination of gender and grade level. You will notice that the numbers in each of the cells in Table 10.10 represent totals—the total number of individuals who fit the characteristics of the cell (e.g., junior high male teachers). Although percentages and proportions are sometimes calculated for cells, we do not recommend it, as this is often misleading.

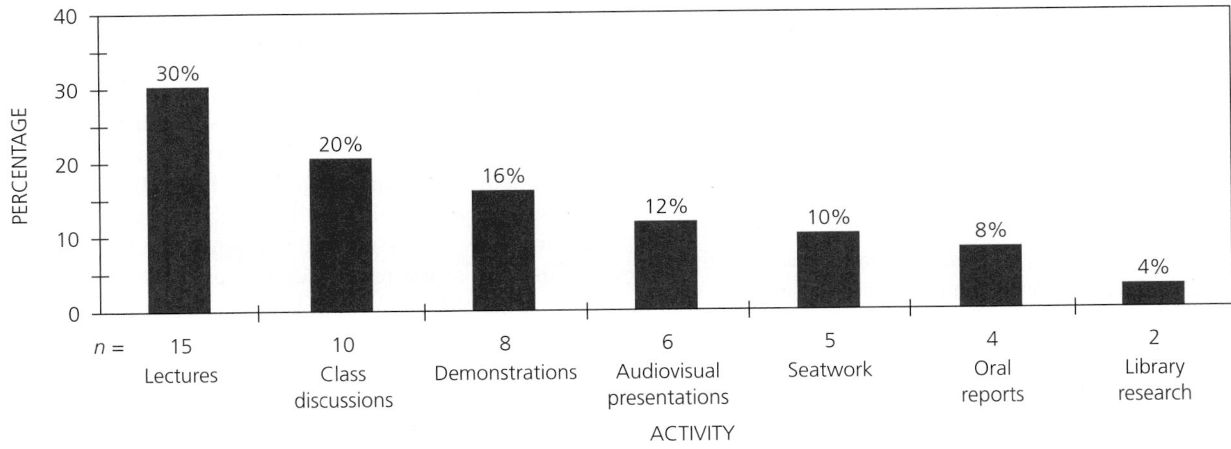

Figure 10.23 *Example of a Bar Graph*

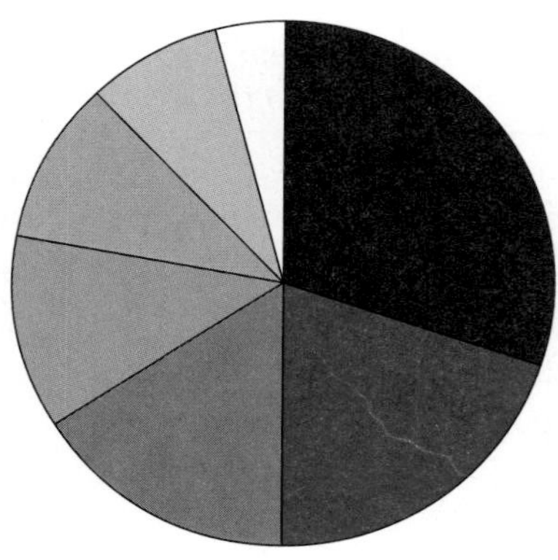

Figure 10.24 *Example of a Pie Chart*

TABLE 10.10 ***Grade Level and Gender of Teachers (Hypothetical Data)***

	Male	Female	Total
Junior high school teachers	40	60	100
High school teachers	60	40	100
Total	100	100	200

It probably seems obvious that Table 10.10 reveals a relationship between teacher gender and grade level. A junior high school teacher is more likely to be female; a high school teacher is more likely to be male. Often, however, it is useful to calculate "expected" frequencies to see results more clearly. What do we mean by "expected"? If there is no relationship between variables, we would "expect" the proportion of cases within each cell of the table corresponding to a category of a variable to be identical to the proportion within that category in the entire group. Look, for example, at Table 10.11. Exactly one-half (50 percent) of the total group of teachers in this table are female. If gender is unrelated to grade level, we would "expect" that the same proportion (exactly one-half) of the junior high school teachers would be female. Similarly, we would "expect" that one-half of the high school teachers would be female. The "expected" frequencies, in other words, would be 50 female junior high school teachers and 50 female high school teachers, rather than the 60 female junior high school and 40 female high school teachers that were actually obtained. These expected and actual, or "observed," frequencies are shown in each box (or "cell") in Table 10.11. The expected frequencies are shown in parentheses.*

TABLE 10.11 ***Repeat of Table 10.10 with Expected Frequencies (in Parentheses)***

	Male	Female	Total
Junior high school teachers	40 (50)	60 (50)	100
High school teachers	60 (50)	40 (50)	100
Total	100	100	200

TABLE 10.12 ***Position, Gender, and Ethnicity of School Leaders (Hypothetical Data)***

	Administrators		Teachers		
	White	Nonwhite	White	Nonwhite	Total
Male	50	20	150	80	300
Female	20	10	150	120	300
Total	70	30	300	200	600

Comparing expected and actual frequencies makes the degree and direction of the relationship clearer. This is particularly helpful with more complex tables. Look, for example, at Table 10.12. This table contains not two, but three, variables.

The researcher who collected and summarized these data hypothesized that appointment to administrative (or other nonteaching) positions rather than teaching positions is related to (1) gender and (2) ethnicity. While it is possible to examine Table 10.12 in its entirety to evaluate these hypotheses, it is much easier to see the relationships by extracting components of the table. Let us look at the relationship of each variable in the table to the other two variables. By taking two variables at a time, we can compare (1) position and ethnicity;

*Expected frequencies can also be provided ahead of time, based on theory or prior experience. In this example, the researcher might have wanted to know whether the characteristics of junior high school teachers in a particular school fit the national pattern. National percentages would then be used to determine expected frequencies.

MORE ABOUT RESEARCH

Correlation in Everyday Life

Many commonplace relationships (true or not) can be expressed as correlations. For example, Boyle's law states that the volume and pressure of a gas vary inversely if kept at a constant temperature. Another way to express this is that the correlation between volume and pressure is -1.00. This relationship, however, is only theoretically true—that is, it exists only for a perfect gas in a perfect vacuum. In real life, the correlation is lower.

Consider the following sayings:

1. "Spare the rod and spoil the child" implies a negative correlation between punishment and spoiled behavior.
2. "Idle hands are the devil's workplace" implies a positive correlation between idleness and mischief.
3. "There's no fool like an old fool" suggests a positive correlation between foolishness and age.
4. "A stitch in time saves nine" suggests a positive correlation between how long one waits to begin a corrective action and the amount of time (and effort) required to fix the problem.
5. "The early bird catches the worm" suggests a positive correlation between early rising and success.
6. "You can't teach an old dog new tricks" implies a negative correlation between age of adults and ability to learn.
7. "An apple a day keeps the doctor away" suggests a negative correlation between the consumption of apples and illness.
8. "Faint heart never won fair maiden" suggests a negative correlation between timidity and female receptivity.

TABLE 10.13 *Position and Ethnicity of School Leaders with Expected Frequencies (Derived from Table 10.12)*

	Administrators	Teachers	Total
White	70 (62)	300 (308)	370
Nonwhite	30 (38)	200 (192)	230
Total	100	500	600

TABLE 10.14 *Position and Gender of School Leaders with Expected Frequencies (Derived from Table 10.12)*

	Administrators	Teachers	Total
Male	70 (50)	230 (250)	300
Female	30 (50)	270 (250)	300
Total	100	500	600

(2) position and gender; and (3) gender and ethnicity. Table 10.13 presents the data for position and ethnicity, Table 10.14 presents the data for position and gender, and Table 10.15 presents the data for gender and ethnicity.

Let us review the calculation of expected frequencies by referring to Table 10.13. This table shows the relationship between ethnicity and position. Since one-sixth of the total group (100/600) are administrators, we would expect 62 whites to be administrators ($\frac{1}{6}$ of 370). Likewise, we would expect 38 of the nonwhites to be administrators ($\frac{1}{6}$ of 230). Since five-sixths of the total group are teachers, we would expect 308 of the whites ($\frac{5}{6}$ of 370) and 192 of the nonwhites ($\frac{5}{6}$ of 230) to be teachers. As you can see, however, the actual frequencies for administrators were 70 (rather than 62) whites, and 30 (rather than 38) nonwhites, and the actual frequencies for teachers were 300 (rather than 308) whites, and 200 (rather than 192) nonwhites. This tells us that there is a discrepancy between what we would expect (if there is no relationship) and what we actually obtained. Discrepancies between the frequencies expected and those actually obtained can also be seen in Tables 10.14 and 10.15.

TABLE 10.15 *Gender and Ethnicity of School Leaders with Expected Frequencies (Derived from Table 10.12)*

	Administrators	Teachers	Total
Male	200 (185)	100 (115)	300
Female	170 (185)	130 (115)	300
Total	370	230	600

An index of the strength of the relationships can be obtained by summing the discrepancies in each table. In Table 10.13, the sum equals 32, in Table 10.14, it equals 80, and in Table 10.15 it equals 60. The calculation of these sums is shown in Table 10.16. The discrepancy between expected and observed frequencies is greatest

TABLE 10.16 *Total of Discrepancies Between Expected and Observed Frequencies in Tables 10.13 Through 10.15*

Table 10.13	Table 10.14	Table 10.15
(70 vs. 62) = 8	(70 vs. 50) = 20	(200 vs. 185) = 15
(30 vs. 38) = 8	(30 vs. 50) = 20	(170 vs. 185) = 15
(300 vs. 308) = 8	(230 vs. 250) = 20	(100 vs. 115) = 15
(200 vs. 192) = 8	(270 vs. 250) = 20	(130 vs. 115) = 15
Total 32	80	60

in Table 10.14, position and gender; less in Table 10.15, gender and ethnicity; and least in Table 10.13, position and ethnicity. A numerical index showing degree of relationship—the contingency coefficient—will be discussed in Chapter 11.

Thus, the data in the crossbreak tables reveal that there is a slight tendency for there to be more white administrators and more nonwhite teachers than would be expected (Table 10.13). There is a stronger tendency toward more white males and nonwhite females than would be expected (Table 10.15). The strongest relationship indicates more male administrators and more female teachers than would be expected (Table 10.14). In sum, the chances of having an administrative position appear to be considerably greater if one is male, and slightly enhanced if one is white.

In contrast to the preceding example, where each variable (ethnicity, gender, role) is clearly categorical, a researcher sometimes has a choice whether to treat data as quantitative or as categorical. Take the case of a researcher who measures self-esteem by a self-report questionnaire scored for number of items answered (yes or no) in the direction indicating high self-esteem. The researcher might decide to use these scores to divide the sample ($n = 60$) into high, middle, and low thirds. The researcher might use only this information for each individual and subsequently treat the data as categorical, as is shown, for example, in Table 10.17. Most researchers would advise against treating the data this way, however, since it "wastes" so much information—for example, differences in scores within each category are ignored. A quantitative analysis, by way of contrast, would compare the mean self-esteem scores of males and females.

TABLE 10.17 *Crossbreak Table Showing Relationship Between Self-Esteem and Gender (Hypothetical Data)*

	Self Esteem		
Gender	**Low**	**Middle**	**High**
Male	10	15	5
Female	5	10	15

In such situations (i.e., when one variable is quantitative and the other is treated as categorical), correlation is another option. When data on a variable assumed to be quantitative have been divided into two categories, a biserial correlation coefficient can be calculated and interpreted the same as a Pearson r coefficient.* If the categories are assumed to reflect a true division, calculation of a point biserial coefficient is an option, but must be interpreted with caution.

*A detailed explanation of these statistics is beyond the scope of this text. For further details, consult any statistics text.

Go back to the **INTERACTIVE AND APPLIED LEARNING** feature at the beginning of the chapter for a listing of interactive and applied activities. Go to the **Online Learning Center** at **www.mhhe.com/fraenkel9e** to take quizzes, practice with key terms, and review chapter content.

Main Points

STATISTICS VERSUS PARAMETERS

- A parameter is a characteristic of a population. It is a numerical or graphic way to summarize data obtained from the population.
- A statistic, on the other hand, is a characteristic of a sample. It is a numerical or graphic way to summarize data obtained from a sample.

TYPES OF NUMERICAL DATA

- There are two fundamental types of numerical data a researcher can collect. Quantitative data are obtained by determining placement on a scale that indicates amount or degree. Categorical data are obtained by determining the frequency of occurrences in each of several categories.

TYPES OF SCORES

- A raw score is the initial score obtained when using an instrument; a derived score is a raw score that has been translated into a more useful score on some type of standardized basis to aid in interpretation.
- Age/grade equivalents are derived scores that indicate the typical age or grade associated with an individual raw score.
- A percentile rank is the percentage of a specific group scoring at or below a given raw score.
- A standard score is a mathematically derived score having comparable meaning on different instruments.

TECHNIQUES FOR SUMMARIZING QUANTITATIVE DATA

- A frequency distribution is a two-column listing, from high to low, of all the scores along with their frequencies. In a grouped frequency distribution, the scores have been grouped into equal intervals.
- A frequency polygon is a graphic display of a frequency distribution. It is a graphic way to summarize quantitative data for one variable.
- A graphic distribution of scores in which only a few individuals receive high scores is called a *positively skewed polygon;* one in which only a few individuals receive low scores is called a *negatively skewed polygon.*
- A histogram is a bar graph used to display quantitative data at the interval or ratio level of measurement.
- A stem-leaf plot is similar to a histogram, except it lists specific values instead of bars.
- The normal distribution is a theoretical distribution that is symmetrical and in which a large proportion of the scores are concentrated in the middle.
- A distribution curve is a smoothed-out frequency polygon.
- The distribution curve of a normal distribution is called a *normal curve.* It is bell shaped, and its mean, median, and mode are identical.
- There are several measures of central tendency (averages) that are used to summarize quantitative data. The two most common are the mean and the median.
- The mean of a distribution is determined by adding up all of the scores and dividing this sum by the total number of scores.

- The median of a distribution marks the point above and below which half of the scores in the distribution lie.
- The mode is the most frequent score in a distribution.
- The term *variability,* as used in research, refers to the extent to which the scores on a quantitative variable in a distribution are spread out.
- The most common measure of variability used in educational research is the standard deviation.
- The range, another measure of variability, represents the difference between the highest and lowest scores in a distribution.
- A five-number summary of a distribution reports the lowest score, the first quartile, the median, the third quartile, and the highest score.
- Five-number summaries of distributions are often portrayed graphically by the use of boxplots.

STANDARD SCORES AND THE NORMAL CURVE

- Standard scores use a common scale to indicate how an individual compares to other individuals in a group. The simplest form of standard score is a z score. A z score expresses how far a raw score is from the mean in standard deviation units.
- The major advantage of standard scores is that they provide a better basis for comparing performance on different measures than do raw scores.
- The term *probability,* as used in research, refers to a prediction of how often a particular event will occur. Probabilities are usually expressed in decimal form.

CORRELATION

- A correlation coefficient is a numerical index expressing the degree of relationship between two quantitative variables. The one most commonly used in educational research is the Pearson r.
- A scatterplot is a graphic way to describe a relationship between two quantitative variables.

TECHNIQUES FOR SUMMARIZING CATEGORICAL DATA

- Researchers use various graphic techniques to summarize categorical data, including frequency tables, bar graphs, and pie charts.
- A crossbreak table is a graphic way to report a relationship between two or more categorical variables.

Key Terms

68-95-99.7 rule 200
age-equivalent score 189
average 195
bar graph 211
boxplot 198
correlation coefficient 207
crossbreak table/contingency table 211
derived score 189
descriptive statistic 187
distribution curve 195
eta (η) 208
five-number summary 198
frequency distribution 190
frequency polygon 190
grade-equivalent score 189
grouped frequency distribution 190
histogram 194

mean 196
measures of central tendency 195
median 196
mode 195
negatively skewed 191
normal curve 195
normal distribution 195
outlier 207
parameter 187
Pearson product-moment coefficient/Pearson *r* 208
percentile 198
percentile rank 189
pie chart 211
positively skewed 191
probability 202
quantitative data 188
range 198
raw score 189
scatterplot 205
standard deviation 198
standard score 190
statistic 187
stem-leaf plot 194
***T* score 203**
variability 197
variance 199
***z* score 201**

For Discussion

1. Would you expect the following correlations to be positive or negative? Why?
   a. Bowling scores and golf scores
   b. Reading scores and arithmetic scores for sixth-graders
   c. Age and weight for a group of 5-year-olds; for a group of people over 70
   d. Life expectancy at age 40 and frequency of smoking
   e. Size and strength for junior high students
2. Why do you think so many people mistrust statistics? How might such mistrust be alleviated?
3. Would it be possible for two different distributions to have the same standard deviation but different means? What about the reverse? Explain.
4. "The larger the standard deviation of a distribution, the more heterogeneous the scores in that distribution." Is this statement true? Explain.
5. "The most complete information about a distribution of scores is provided by a frequency polygon." Is this statement true? Explain.
6. Grouping scores in a frequency distribution has its advantages but also its disadvantages. What might be some examples of each?
7. "Any single raw score, in and of itself, tells us nothing." Would you agree? Explain.
8. The relationship between age and strength is said to be curvilinear. What does this mean? Might there be exceptions to this relationship? What might cause such an exception?

Research Exercise 10: Descriptive Statistics

If you are planning a quantitative study, indicate the descriptive statistics you would use to summarize the data you intend to collect. Even if you are planning a qualitative or mixed-methods study, in some cases including descriptive statistics and data analysis strategies may be appropriate and useful. Finally, discuss your procedures for dealing with discrepant cases or outliers.

Problem Sheet 10

Descriptive Statistics

1. My research question is: ____

____

2. If you are designing a quantitative study, place an *X* after each of the descriptive statistics listed that you will use to summarize your data.

   Frequency polygon _____ Five-number summary _____ Box plot _____ Percentages _____

   Mean _____ Median _____ Standard deviation _____ Frequency table _____ Bar graph _____

   Pie chart _____ Correlation coefficient _____ Scatterplot _____

3. Place an *X* after the technique(s) you would use to describe any relationships found in your study.

   a. Comparison of frequency polygons ______

   b. Comparison of averages ______

   c. Crossbreak table(s) ______

   d. Correlation coefficient ______

   e. Scatterplot ______

   f. Reporting of percentages ______

4. How will you deal with discrepant cases or outliers in your data analysis?

An electronic version of this Problem Sheet that you can fill in and print, save, or e-mail is available on the Online Learning Center at www.mhhe.com/fraenkel9e.

Inferential Statistics 11

What Are Inferential Statistics?

The Logic of Inferential Statistics

Sampling Error
Distribution of Sample Means
Standard Error of the Mean
Confidence Intervals
Confidence Intervals and Probability
Comparing More Than One Sample
The Standard Error of the Difference Between Sample Means

Hypothesis Testing

The Null Hypothesis
Hypothesis Testing: A Review

Practical Versus Statistical Significance

One- and Two-Tailed Tests
Use of the Null Hypothesis: An Evaluation

Inference Techniques

Parametric Techniques for Analyzing Quantitative Data
Nonparametric Techniques for Analyzing Quantitative Data
Parametric Techniques for Analyzing Categorical Data
Nonparametric Techniques for Analyzing Categorical Data
Summary of Techniques
Power of a Statistical Test

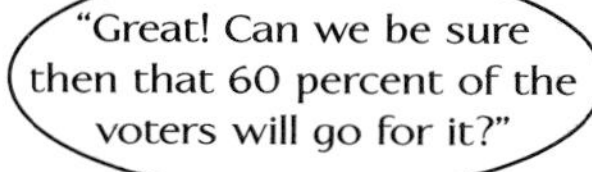
"Survey results show that 60 percent of those we interviewed support our bond issue."
"Great! Can we be sure then that 60 percent of the voters will go for it?"
"No, not exactly. But it is very likely that between 55 percent and 65 percent will!"

OBJECTIVES **Studying this chapter should enable you to:**

- Explain what is meant by the term "inferential statistics."
- Explain the concept of sampling error.
- Describe briefly how to calculate a confidence interval.
- State the difference between a research hypothesis and a null hypothesis.
- Describe briefly the logic underlying hypothesis testing.
- State what is meant by the terms "significance level" and "statistically significant."
- Explain the difference between a one- and a two-tailed test of significance.
- Explain the difference between parametric and nonparametric tests of significance.
- Name three examples of parametric tests used by educational researchers.
- Name three examples of nonparametric tests used by educational researchers.
- Describe what is meant by the term "power" with regard to statistical tests.
- Explain the importance of random sampling with regard to the use of inferential statistics.

INTERACTIVE AND APPLIED LEARNING After, or while, reading this chapter:

Go to the Online Learning Center at www.mhhe.com/fraenkel9e to:

- Practice with Sample Graphs
- Learn More About the Purpose of Inferential Statistics

Go to your online Student Mastery Activities book to do the following activities:

- Activity 11.1: Probability
- Activity 11.2: Learn to Read a *t*-Table
- Activity 11.3: Calculate a *t*-Test
- Activity 11.4: Perform a Chi-Square Test
- Activity 11.5: Conduct a *t*-Test
- Activity 11.6: The Big Game

"Paulo, I'm worried."

"Why, Julie?"

"Well, in my job as director of the new elementary math program for the district, I have to find out how well the students in the program are doing. This year, we're testing the fifth-graders."

"Yeah, so? What's to worry about?"

"Well, I gave the end-of-the-semester exam to one of the fifth-grade classes at Hoover Elementary last week. I got the results back just today."

"And?"

"Get this. Their average score was only 65 out of a possible 100 points! Of course this is just one class, but still . . . I'm afraid that it may be true of all the fifth-grade classes."

"Not necessarily, Julie. That would depend on how similar the Hoover kids are to the other fifth-graders in the district. What you need is some way to estimate the average score of all of the district's fifth-graders—but you can't do it from that class."

"I assume you're thinking about some sort of inferential test, eh?"

"Yep, you got it."

How might Julie make such an estimate? To find out, read this chapter.

What Are Inferential Statistics?

Descriptive statistics are but one type of statistic that researchers use to analyze their data. Many times they wish to make inferences about a population based on data they have obtained from a sample. To do this, they use inferential statistics. Let us consider how.

Suppose a researcher administers a commercially available IQ test to a sample of 65 students selected from a particular elementary school district and finds their average score is 85. What does this tell her about the IQ scores of the entire population of students in the district? Does the average IQ score of students in the district also equal 85? Or is this sample of students different, on the average, from other students in the district? If these students are different, how are they different? Are their IQ scores higher—or lower?

What the researcher needs is some way to estimate how closely statistics, such as the mean of the IQ scores, obtained on a sample agree with the corresponding parameters of the population without actually obtaining data on the entire population. Inferential statistics provide such a way.

Inferential statistics are certain types of procedures that allow researchers to make inferences about a population based on findings from a sample. In Chapter 6, we discussed the concept of a random sample and pointed out that obtaining a random sample is desirable because it helps ensure that one's sample is representative of a larger population. When a sample is representative, all the characteristics of the population are assumed to be present in the sample in the same degree. No sampling procedure, not even random sampling, guarantees a totally representative sample, but the chance of obtaining one is greater with random sampling than with any other method. And the more a sample represents a population, the more researchers are entitled to assume that what they find out about the sample will also be true of that population. Making inferences about populations on the basis of random samples is what inferential statistics is all about.

As with descriptive statistics, the techniques of inferential statistics differ depending on which type of data—categorical or quantitative—a researcher wishes to analyze. This chapter begins with techniques applicable to quantitative data, because they provide the best introduction to the logic behind inference techniques and because most educational research involves such data. Some techniques for the analysis of categorical data are presented at the end of the chapter.

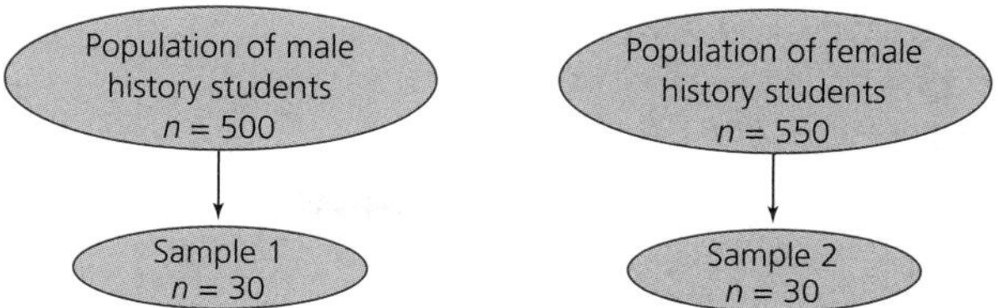

Figure 11.1 *Selection of Two Samples from Two Distinct Populations*

The Logic of Inferential Statistics

Suppose a researcher is interested in the difference between males and females with respect to interest in history. He hypothesizes that female students find history more interesting than do male students. To test the hypothesis, he decides to perform the following study. He obtains one random sample of 30 male history students from the population of 500 male tenth-grade students taking history in a nearby school district and another random sample of 30 female history students from the female population of 550 female tenth-grade history students in the district. All students are given an attitude scale to complete. The researcher now has two sets of data: the attitude scores for the male group and the attitude scores for the female group. The design of the study is shown in Figure 11.1. The researcher wants to know whether the male population is different from the female population—that is, will the mean score of the male group on the attitude test differ from the mean score of the female group? But the researcher does not know the means of the two populations. All he has are the means of the two samples. He has to rely on the two samples to provide information about the populations.

Is it reasonable to assume that each sample will give a fairly accurate picture of its population? It certainly is possible, since each sample was randomly selected from its population. On the other hand, the students in each sample are only a small portion of their population, and only rarely is a sample absolutely identical to its parent population on a given characteristic. The data the researcher obtains from the two samples will depend on the individual students selected to be in each sample. If another two samples were randomly selected, their makeup would differ from the original two, their means on the attitude scale would be different, and the researcher would end up with a different set of data. How can the researcher be sure that any particular sample he has selected is, indeed, a representative one? He cannot. Maybe another sample would be better.

SAMPLING ERROR

This is the basic difficulty that confronts us when we work with samples: Samples are not likely to be identical to their parent populations. This difference between a sample and its population is referred to as **sampling error** (Figure 11.2). Furthermore, no two samples will be the same in all their characteristics. Two different samples from the same population will not be identical: They will be composed of different individuals, they will have different scores on a test (or other measure), and they will probably have different sample means.

Consider the population of high school students in the United States. It would be possible to select literally thousands of different samples from this population. Suppose we took two samples of 25 students each from this population and measured their heights. What would you estimate our chances would be of finding exactly the same mean height in both samples? Very, very unlikely. In fact, we could probably take sample after sample and very seldom obtain two sets of people having exactly the same mean height.

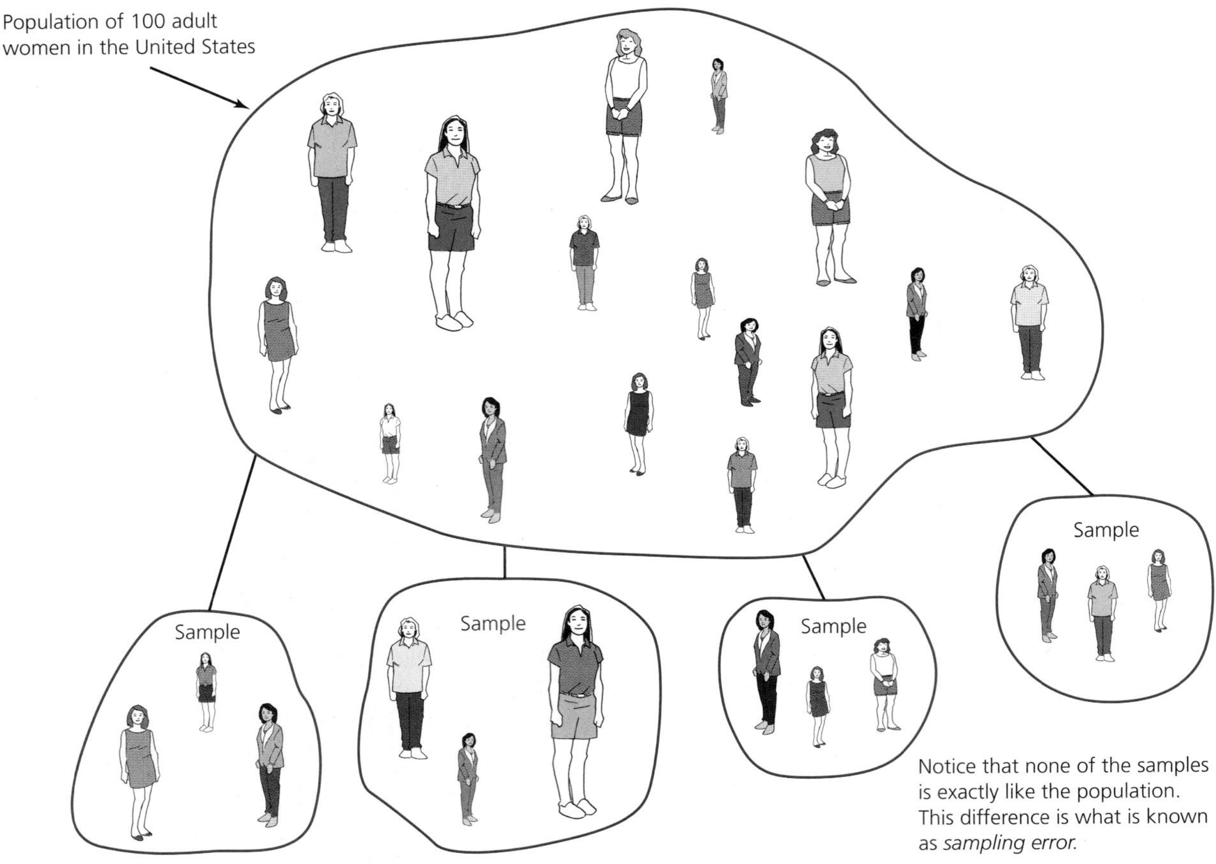
Population of 100 adult women in the United States
Sample
Sample
Sample
Sample
Notice that none of the samples is exactly like the population. This difference is what is known as *sampling error.*

Figure 11.2 *Sampling Error*

DISTRIBUTION OF SAMPLE MEANS

All of this might suggest that it is impossible to formulate any rules that researchers can use to determine similarities between samples and populations. Not so. Fortunately, large collections of random samples do pattern themselves in such a way that it is possible for researchers to predict accurately some characteristics of the population from which the sample was selected.

Were we able to select an infinite number of random samples (all of the same size) from a population, calculate the mean of each, and then arrange these means into a frequency polygon, we would find that they shaped themselves into a familiar pattern. The means of a large number of random samples tend to be normally distributed, unless the size of each of the samples is small (less than 30) *and* the scores in the population are *not* normally distributed. Once sample size reaches 30, however, the *distribution of sample means* is very nearly normal, even if the population is not normally distributed. (We realize that this is not immediately obvious; should you wish more explanation of why this is true, consult any introductory statistics text.)

Like all normal distributions, a distribution of sample means (called a **sampling distribution**) has its own mean and standard deviation. The mean of a sampling distribution (the "mean of the means") is equal to the mean of the population. In an infinite number of samples, some will have means larger than the population mean and some will have means smaller than the population mean (Figure 11.3). These data tend to neutralize each other, resulting in an overall average that is equal to the mean of the population. Consider an example. Suppose you have a population of only three scores—1, 2, 3. The mean of this population

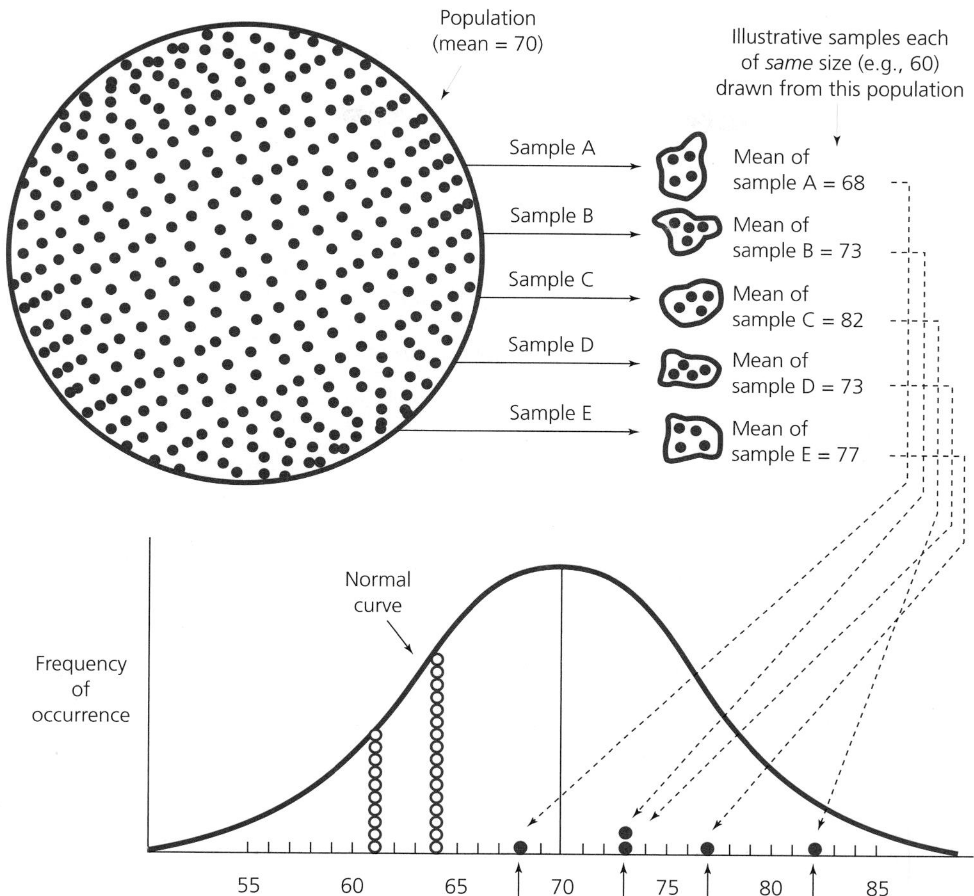

Figure 11.3 *A Sampling Distribution of Means*

is 2. Now, take all of the possible types of samples of size two. How many would there be? Nine—(1, 1); (1, 2); (1, 3); (2, 1); (2, 2); (2, 3); (3, 1); (3, 2); (3, 3). The means of these samples are 1, 1.5, 2, 1.5, 2, 2.5, 2, 2.5, and 3, respectively. Add up all these means and divide by nine (i.e., 18 ÷ 9), and you see that the mean of these means equals 2, the same as the population mean.

STANDARD ERROR OF THE MEAN

The standard deviation of a sampling distribution of means is called the **standard error of the mean (SEM)**. As in all normal distributions, therefore, the 68-95-99.7 rule holds: approximately 68 percent of the sample means fall between ±1 SEM; approximately 95 percent fall between ±2 SEM; and 99.7 percent fall between ±3 SEM (Figure 11.4).

Thus, if we know or can accurately estimate the mean and the standard deviation of the sampling distribution, we can determine whether it is likely or unlikely that a particular sample mean could be obtained from that population. Suppose the mean of a population is 100, for example, and the standard error of the mean is 10. A sample mean of 110 would fall at +1 SEM, a sample mean of 120 would fall at +2 SEM, a sample mean of 130 would fall at +3 SEM; and so forth.

It would be very unlikely to draw a sample from the population whose mean fell above +3 SEM. Why? Because, as in all normal distributions (and remember, the sampling distribution is a normal distribution—of *means*), only 0.0013 of all values (in this case, sample

Figure 11.4 *Distribution of Sample Means*

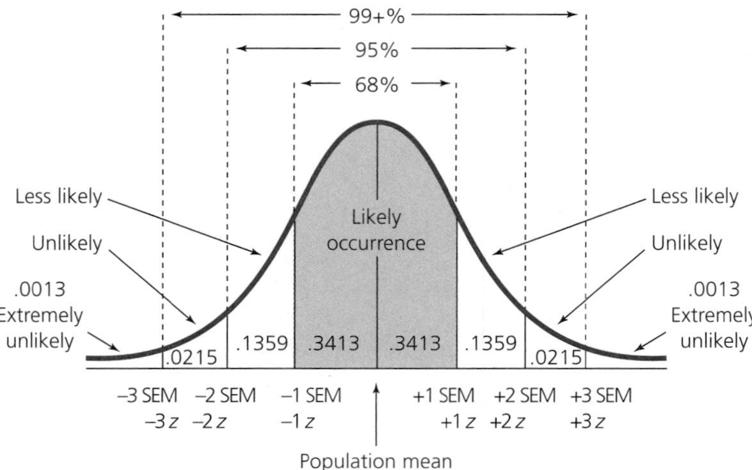

means) fall above +3 SEM. It would not be unusual to select a sample from this population and find that its mean is 105, but selecting a sample with a mean of 130 would be unlikely—very unlikely!

It is possible to use *z* scores to describe the position of any particular sample mean within a distribution of sample means. We discussed *z* scores in Chapter 10. We now want to express means as *z* scores. Remember that a *z* score simply states how far a score (or mean) differs from the mean of scores (or means) in standard deviation units. The *z* score tells a researcher exactly where a particular sample mean is located relative to all other sample means that could have been obtained. For example, a *z* score of +2 would indicate that a particular sample mean is two standard errors above the population mean. Only about 2 percent of all sample means fall above a *z* score of +2. Hence, a sample with such a mean would be unusual.

Estimating the Standard Error of the Mean. How do we obtain the standard error of the mean? Clearly, we cannot calculate it directly, since we would need, literally, to obtain a huge number of samples and their means.* Statisticians have shown, however, that the standard error can be calculated using a simple formula requiring the standard deviation of the population and the size of the sample. Although we seldom know the standard deviation of the population, fortunately it can be *estimated*† using the standard deviation of the sample. To calculate the SEM, then, simply divide the standard deviation of the sample by the square root of the sample size minus one:

$$\text{SEM} = \frac{\text{SD}}{\sqrt{n-1}}$$

Let's review the basic ideas we have presented so far.

1. The sampling distribution of the mean (or any descriptive statistic) is the distribution of the means (or other statistic) obtained (theoretically) from an infinitely large number of samples of the same size.
2. The shape of the sampling distribution in many (but not all) cases is the shape of the normal distribution.
3. The SEM (standard error of the mean)—that is, the standard deviation of a sampling distribution of means—can be estimated by dividing the standard deviation of the sample by the square root of the sample size minus one.
4. The frequency with which a particular sample mean will occur can be estimated by using *z* scores based on sample data to indicate its position in the sampling distribution.

CONFIDENCE INTERVALS

We now can use the SEM to indicate boundaries, or limits, within which the population mean lies. Such boundaries are called **confidence intervals**. How are they determined?

Let us return to the example of the researcher who administered an IQ test to a sample of 65 elementary

*If we did have these means, we would calculate the standard error just like any other standard deviation, treating each mean as a score.

†The fact that the standard error is based on an estimated value rather than a known value does introduce an unknown degree of imprecision into this process.

school students. You will recall that she obtained a sample mean of 85 and wanted to know how much the population mean might differ from this value. We are now in a position to give her some help in this regard.

Let us assume that we have calculated the estimated standard error of the mean for her sample and found it to equal 2.0. Applying this to a sampling distribution of means, we can say that 95 percent of the time the population mean will be between $85 \pm 1.96\ (2) = 85 \pm 3.92 = 81.08$ to 88.92. Why $\pm$ 1.96? Because the area between $\pm 1.96\ z$ equals 95 percent (.95) of the total area under the normal curve.* This is shown in Figure 11.5.†

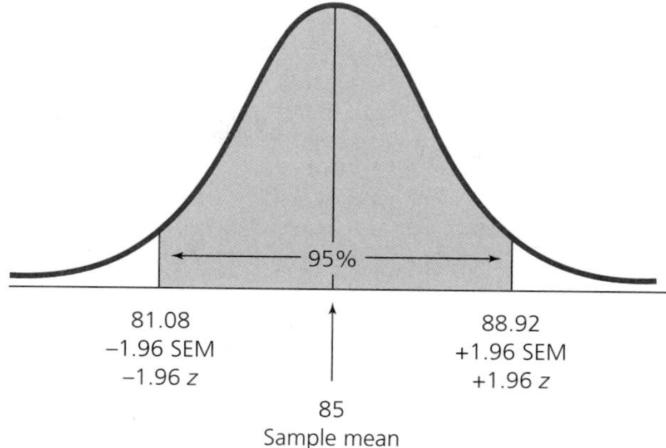

Figure 11.5 *The 95 Percent Confidence Interval*

Suppose this researcher then wished to establish an interval that would give her more confidence than $p = .95$ in making a statement about the population mean. This can be done by calculating the 99 percent confidence interval. The 99 percent confidence interval is determined in a manner similar to that for determining the 95 percent confidence interval. Given the characteristics of a normal distribution, we know that 0.5 percent of the sample means will lie below −2.58 SEM and another 0.5 percent will lie above +2.58 SEM (see Figure 10.12 in Chapter 10). Using the previous example, in which the mean of the sample was 85 and the SEM was 2, we calculate the interval as follows: $85 \pm 2.58\ (\text{SEM}) = 85 \pm 2.58(2.0) = 85 \pm 5.16 = 79.84$ to 90.16. Thus the 99 confidence interval lies between 79.84 and 90.16, as shown in Figure 11.6.

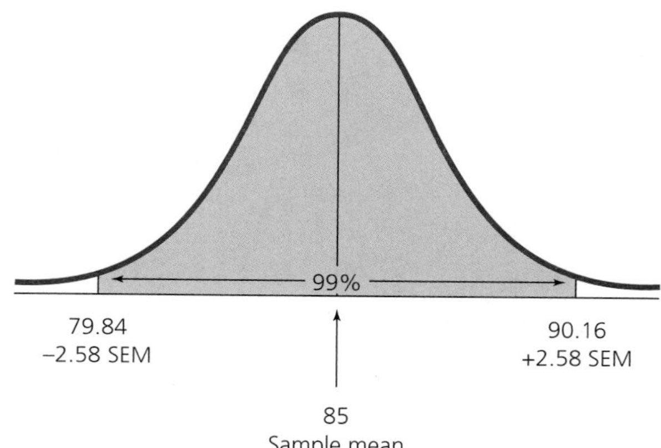

Figure 11.6 *The 99 Percent Confidence Interval*

Our researcher can now answer her question about approximately how much the population mean differs from the sample mean. While she cannot know exactly what the population mean is, she can indicate the "boundaries" or limits within which it is likely to fall (Figure 11.7). To repeat, these limits are called *confidence intervals.* The 95 percent confidence interval spans a segment on the horizontal axis that we are 95 percent certain contains the population mean. The 99 percent confidence interval spans a segment on the horizontal axis within which we are even more certain (99 percent certain) that the population mean falls.‡ We could be mistaken, of course—the population mean could lie outside these intervals—but it is not very likely.§

*By looking at the normal curve table in Appendix B, we see that the area between the mean and $1.96\ z = .4750$. Multiplied by 2, this equals .95, or 95 percent, of the total area under the curve.

†Strictly speaking, it is not proper to consider a distribution of population means around the sample mean. In practice, we interpret confidence intervals in this way. The legitimacy of doing so requires a demonstration beyond the level of an introductory text.

‡Notice that it is *not* correct to say that the population mean falls within the 95 percent confidence interval 95 times out of 100. The population mean is a fixed value, and it either does or does not fall within this interval. The correct way to think of a confidence interval is to view it in terms of replicating the study. Suppose we replicated the study with another sample and calculated the 95 percent confidence interval for that sample. Suppose we then replicated the study once again with a third sample and calculated the 95 percent confidence interval for this third sample. We would continue until we had drawn 100 samples and calculated the 95 percent confidence interval for each of these 100 samples. We would find that the population mean lay within 95 percent of these intervals.

§The likelihood of the population mean being outside the 95 percent confidence interval is only 5 percent, and that of being outside the 99 percent confidence interval only 1 percent. Analogous reasoning and procedures can be used with sample sizes less than 30.

Figure 11.7 *We Can Be 99 Percent Confident*

CONFIDENCE INTERVALS AND PROBABILITY

Let us return to the concept of probability introduced in Chapter 10. As we use the term here, **probability** is nothing more than predicted relative occurrence, or relative frequency. When we say that something would occur 5 times in 100, we are expressing a probability. We could just as well say the probability is 5 in 100. In our earlier example, we can say, therefore, that the probability of the population mean being *outside* the 81.08–88.92 limits (the 95 percent confidence interval) is only 5 in 100. The probability of it being *outside* the 79.84–90.16 limits (the 99 percent confidence interval) is even less—only 1 in 100. Remember that it is customary to express probabilities in decimal form, for example, $p = .05$ or $p = .01$. What would $p = .10$ signify? *

COMPARING MORE THAN ONE SAMPLE

Up to this point, we have been explaining how to make inferences about the population mean using data from just one sample. More typically, however, researchers want to compare two or more samples. For example, a researcher might want to determine if there is a difference in attitude between fourth-grade boys and girls in mathematics; whether there is a difference in achievement between students taught by the discussion method as compared to the lecture method; and so forth.

Our previous logic also applies to a difference between means. For example, if a difference between means is found between the test scores of two samples in a study, a researcher wants to know if a difference exists in the populations from which the two samples were selected (Figure 11.8). In essence, we ask the same

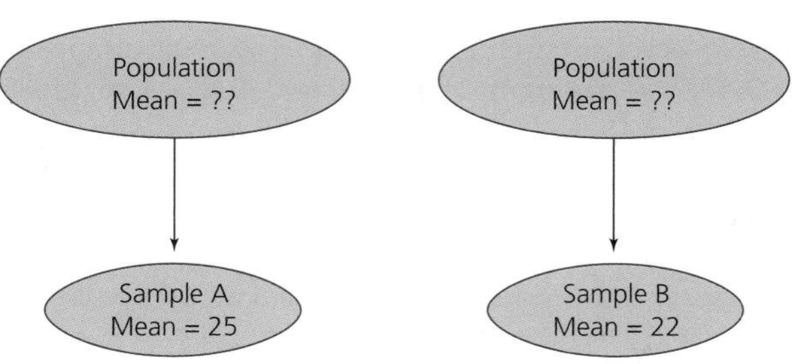

Figure 11.8 *Does a Sample Difference Reflect a Population Difference?*[a]

[a]Question: Does the three-point difference between the means of sample A and sample B reflect a difference between the means of population A and population B?

*A probability of 10 in 100.

question we asked about one mean, only this time we ask it about a difference *between* means. Hence we ask, "Is the difference we have found a likely or an unlikely occurrence?" It is possible that the difference can be attributed simply to sampling error—to the fact that certain samples, rather than others, were selected (the "luck of the draw," so to speak). Once again, inferential statistics help us out.

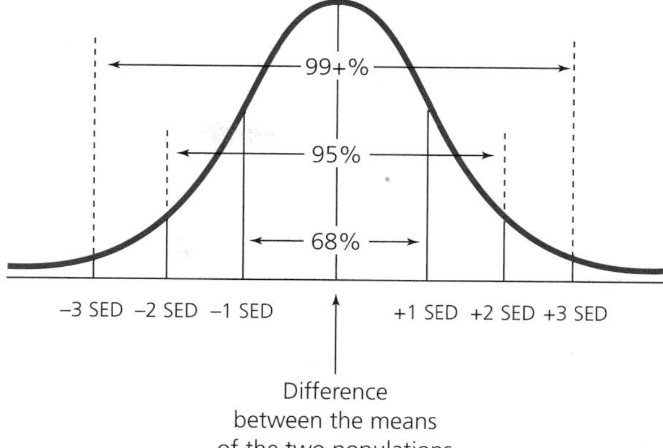

Figure 11.9 *Distribution of the Difference Between Sample Means*

THE STANDARD ERROR OF THE DIFFERENCE BETWEEN SAMPLE MEANS

Fortunately, differences between sample means are also likely to be normally distributed. The distribution of differences between sample means also has its own mean and standard deviation. The mean of the sampling distribution of differences between sample means is equal to the difference between the means of the two populations. The standard deviation of this distribution is called the **standard error of the difference (SED).** The formula for computing the SED is:

$$SED = \sqrt{(SEM_1)^2 + (SEM_2)^2}$$

where $_1$ and $_2$ refer to the respective samples.

Because the distribution is normal, slightly more than 68 percent of the differences between sample means will fall between ±1 SED (again, remember that the standard error of the difference is a standard deviation); about 95 percent of the differences between sample means will fall between ±2 SED, and 99+ percent of these differences will fall between ±3 SED (Figure 11.9).

Now we can proceed similarly to the way we did with individual sample means. A researcher estimates the standard error of the difference between means and then uses it, along with the difference between the two sample means and the normal curve, to estimate probable limits (confidence intervals) within which the difference between the means of the two populations is likely to fall.

Let us consider an example. Imagine that the difference between two sample means is 14 raw score points and the calculated SED is 3. Just as we did with one sample population mean, we can now indicate limits within which the difference between the means of the two populations is likely to fall. If we say that the difference between the means of the two populations is between 11 and 17 (±1 SED), we have slightly more than a 68 percent chance of being right. We have somewhat more than a 95 percent chance of being right if we say the difference between the means of the two populations is between 8 and 20 (±2 SED), and better than a 99 percent chance of being right if we say the difference between the means of the two populations is between 5 and 23 (±3 SED). Figure 11.10 illustrates these confidence intervals.

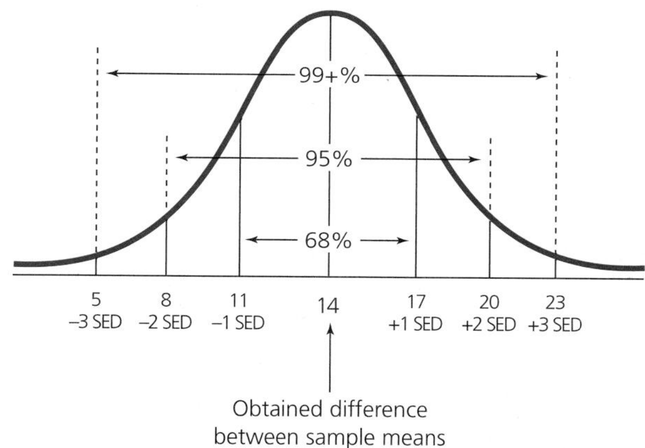

Figure 11.10 *Confidence Intervals*

Suppose the difference between two other sample means is 12. If we calculated the SED to be 2, would it be likely or unlikely for the difference between population means to fall between 10 and 14?*

*Likely, since 68 percent of the differences between population means fall between these values.

Hypothesis Testing

How does all this apply to research questions and research hypotheses? You will recall that many hypotheses predict a relationship. In Chapter 10, we presented techniques for examining data for the existence of relationships. We pointed out in previous chapters that virtually all relationships in data can be examined through one (or more) of three procedures: a comparison of means, a correlation, or a crossbreak table. In each instance, some degree of relationship may be found. If a relationship is found in the data, is there likely to be a similar relationship in the population, or is it simply due to sampling error—to the fact that a particular sample, rather than another, was selected for study? Once again, inferential statistics can help.

The logic discussed earlier applies to any particular form of a hypothesis and to many procedures used to examine data. Thus, correlation coefficients and differences between them can be evaluated in essentially the same way as means and differences between means; we just need to obtain the standard error of the correlation coefficient(s). The procedure used with crossbreak tables differs in technique, but the logic is the same. We will discuss it later in the chapter.

When testing hypotheses, it is customary to proceed in a slightly different way. Instead of determining the boundaries within which the population mean (or other parameter) can be said to fall, a researcher determines the likelihood of obtaining a sample value (e.g., a difference between two sample means) if there is *no* relationship (i.e., no difference between the means of the two populations) in the populations from which the samples were drawn. The researcher formulates both a research hypothesis and a null hypothesis. To test the research hypothesis, the researcher must formulate a null hypothesis.

THE NULL HYPOTHESIS

As you will recall, the **research hypothesis** specifies the predicted outcome of a study. Many research hypotheses predict the nature of the relationship the researcher thinks exists in the population; for example: "The population mean of students using method A is greater than the population mean of students using method B."

The **null hypothesis** most commonly used specifies there is no relationship in the population; for example: "There is *no* difference between the population mean of students using method A and the population mean of students using method B." (This is the same thing as saying the difference between the means of the two populations is zero.) Figure 11.11 offers a comparison of research and null hypotheses.

The researcher then proceeds to test the null hypothesis. The same information is needed as before: the knowledge that the sampling distribution is normal, and the calculated standard error of the difference (SED). What is different in a hypothesis test is that instead of using the obtained sample value (e.g., the obtained difference between sample means) as the mean of the sampling distribution (as we did with confidence intervals), we use zero.*

We then can determine the probability of obtaining a particular sample value (such as an obtained difference between sample means) by seeing where such a value falls on the sampling distribution. If the probability is small, the null hypothesis is rejected, thereby providing support for the research hypothesis. The results are said to be *statistically significant.*

What counts as "small"? In other words, what constitutes an unlikely outcome? Probably you have guessed. It is customary in educational research to view as unlikely any outcome that has a probability of .05 ($p = .05$) or less. This is referred to as the .05 **level of significance**. When we reject a null hypothesis at the .05 level, we are saying that the probability of obtaining such an outcome is only 5 times (or less) in 100. Some researchers prefer to be even more stringent and choose a .01 level of significance. When a null hypothesis is rejected at the .01 level, it means that the likelihood of obtaining the outcome is only 1 time (or less) in 100.

HYPOTHESIS TESTING: A REVIEW

Let us review what we have said. The logical sequence for a researcher who wishes to engage in hypothesis testing is as follows:

1. State the research hypothesis (e.g., "There is a difference between the population mean of students using method A and the population mean of students using method B").
2. State the null hypothesis (e.g., "There is no difference between the population mean of students using

*Actually, any value could be used, but zero is used in virtually all educational research.

(Null Hypothesis)
"You know, I read recently that most researchers believe there really is no difference between the average score of students taught mathematics by the 'new' math and the average score of those students taught by the traditional lecture/discussion approach."

(Research Hypothesis)
"I don't believe it. Let's compare a sample of our students this year and see. I bet that the students taught by the new math will do better."

Figure 11.11 *Null and Research Hypotheses*

method A and the population mean of students using method B," or "The difference between the two population means is zero").

3. Determine the sample statistics pertinent to the hypothesis (e.g., the mean of sample A and the mean of sample B).
4. Determine the probability of obtaining the sample results (i.e., the difference between the mean of sample A and the mean of sample B) if the null hypothesis is true.
5. If the probability is small, reject the null hypothesis, thus affirming the research hypothesis.
6. If the probability is large, do not reject the null hypothesis, which means you cannot affirm the research hypothesis.

Let us use our previous example in which the difference between sample means was 14 points and the SED was 3 (see Figure 11.10). In Figure 11.12 we see that the sample difference of 14 falls far beyond +3 SED; in fact, it exceeds 4 SED. Thus, the probability of obtaining such a sample result is considerably less than .01, and as a result, the null hypothesis is rejected. If the difference in sample means had been 4 instead of 14, would the null hypothesis be rejected?*

*No. The probability of a difference of 4 is too high—much larger than .05.

Figure 11.12 *Illustration of When a Researcher Would Reject the Null Hypothesis*

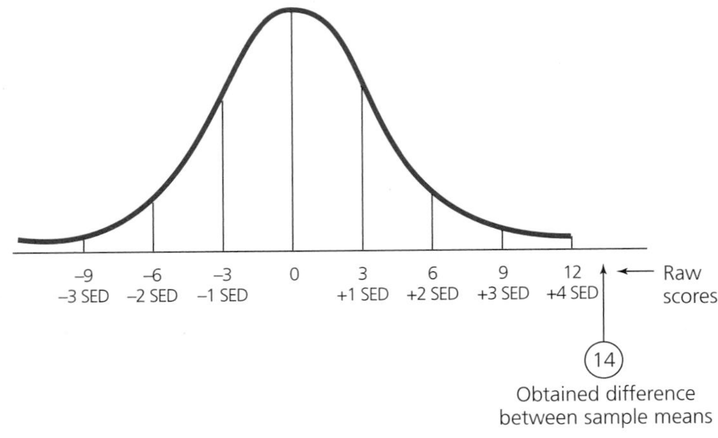

Practical Versus Statistical Significance

The fact that a result is statistically significant (not due to chance) does not mean that it has any practical or educational value in the real world in which we all work and live. **Statistical significance** only means that one's results are likely to occur by chance less than a certain percentage of the time, say 5 percent. So what? Remember that this only means the observed relationship most likely would not be zero in the population. But it does not mean necessarily that it is *important!* Whenever we have a large enough random sample, almost any result will turn out to be statistically significant. Thus, a very small correlation coefficient, for example, may turn out to be statistically significant but have little (if any) **practical significance**. In a similar sense, a very small difference in means may yield a statistically significant result but have little educational import.

Consider a few examples. Suppose a random sample of 1,000 high school baseball pitchers on the East Coast reveals an average fastball speed of 75 mph, while a second random sample of 1,000 high school pitchers in the Midwest shows an average fastball speed of 71 mph. Now this difference of 4 mph might be statistically significant (due to the large sample size), but we doubt that baseball fans would say that it is of any practical importance (Figure 11.13). Or suppose that a researcher tries out a new method of teaching mathematics to high school juniors. She finds that those students exposed to method A (the new method) score, on the average, two points higher on the final examination than the students exposed to method B (the older, more traditional method), and that this difference is statistically significant. We doubt that the mathematics department would immediately encourage all of its members to adopt method A on the basis of this two-point difference. Would you?

Ironically, the fact that most educational studies involve smaller samples may actually be an advantage when it comes to practical significance. Because smaller sample size makes it harder to detect a difference even when there is one in the population, a larger difference in means is therefore required to reject the null hypothesis. This is so because a smaller sample results in a larger standard error of the difference in means (SED). Therefore, a larger difference in means is required to reach the significance level (see Figure 11.10). It is also possible that relationships of potential practical significance may be overlooked or dismissed because they are not statistically significant (more on this in the next chapter).

One should always take care in interpreting results—just because one brand of radios is significantly more powerful than another brand statistically does not mean that those looking for a radio should rush to buy the first brand.

ONE- AND TWO-TAILED TESTS

In Chapter 5, we made a distinction between directional and nondirectional hypotheses. There is sometimes an advantage to stating hypotheses in directional form that is related to significance testing. We refer again to a hypothetical example of a sampling distribution of

Figure 11.13 *How Much Is Enough?*

differences between means in which the calculated SED equals 3. Previously, we interpreted the statistical significance of an obtained difference between sample means of 14 points. The statistical significance of this difference was quite clear-cut, since it was so large. Suppose, however, that the obtained difference was not 14, but 5.5 points. To determine the probability associated with this outcome, we must know whether the researcher's hypothesis was a directional or a nondirectional one. If the hypothesis was directional, the researcher specified ahead of time (before collecting any data) which group would have the higher mean (e.g., "The mean score of students using method A will be higher than the mean score of students using method B.").

If this had been the case, the researcher's hypothesis would be supported only if the mean of sample A was higher than the mean of sample B. The researcher must decide beforehand that he or she will subtract the mean of sample B from the mean of sample A. A large difference between sample means in the opposite direction would not support the research hypothesis. A difference between sample means of +2 is in the hypothesized direction, therefore, but a difference of −2 (should the mean of sample B be higher than the mean of sample A) is not. Because the researcher's hypothesis can be supported only if he or she obtains a positive difference between the sample means, the researcher is justified in using only the positive tail of the sampling distribution to locate the obtained difference. This is referred to as a **one-tailed test** of statistical significance (Figure 11.14).

At the 5 percent level of significance ($p = .05$), the null hypothesis may be rejected only if the obtained difference between sample means reaches or exceeds

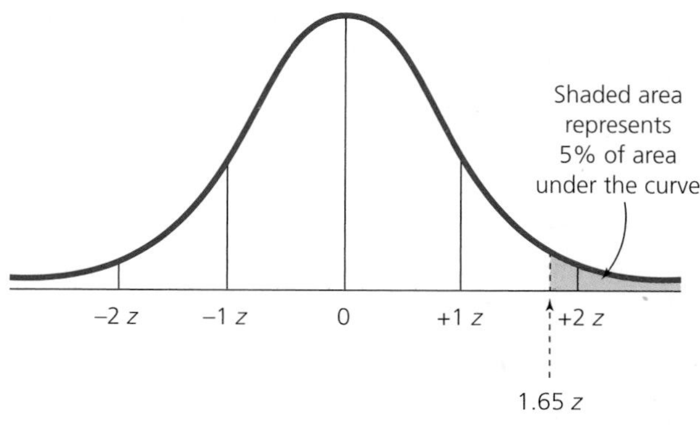

Figure 11.14 *Significance Area for a One-Tailed Test*

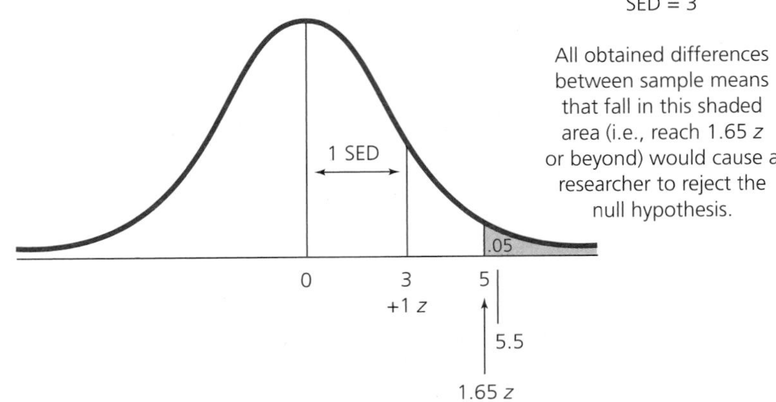
SED = 3
All obtained differences between sample means that fall in this shaded area (i.e., reach 1.65 z or beyond) would cause a researcher to reject the null hypothesis.
1 SED
.05
0
3
+1 z
5
5.5
1.65 z

Figure 11.15 *One-Tailed Test Using a Distribution of Differences Between Sample Means*

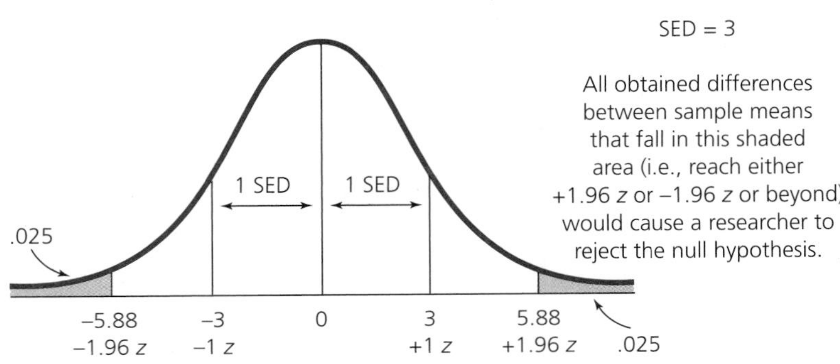
SED = 3
All obtained differences between sample means that fall in this shaded area (i.e., reach either +1.96 z or −1.96 z or beyond) would cause a researcher to reject the null hypothesis.
.025
1 SED
1 SED
−5.88
−1.96 z
−3
−1 z
0
3
+1 z
5.88
+1.96 z
.025

Figure 11.16 *Two-Tailed Test Using a Distribution of Differences Between Sample Means*

1.65 SED* in the one tail. As shown in Figure 11.15, this requires a difference between sample means of 5 points or more.† Our previously obtained difference of 5.5 would be significant at this level, therefore, since it not only reaches, but exceeds, 1.65 SED.

What if the hypothesis was nondirectional? If this was the case, the researcher would not have specified beforehand which group would have the higher mean. The hypothesis would then be supported by a suitable difference in *either* tail. This is called a **two-tailed test** of statistical significance. If a researcher uses the .05 level of significance, this requires that the 5 percent of the total area must include both tails—that is, there is 2.5 percent in each tail. As a result, a difference in sample means of almost 6 points (either +5.88 or −5.88) is required to reject the null hypothesis (Figure 11.16), since 1.96(3) = 5.88.

*By looking in the normal curve table in Appendix B, we see that the area beyond 1.65 *z* equals .05, or 5 percent of the area under the curve.

†Since an area of .05 in one tail equals a *z* of 1.65, and the SED is 3, we multiply 1.65(3) to find the score value at this point: 1.65(3) = 4.95, or 5 points.

USE OF THE NULL HYPOTHESIS: AN EVALUATION

There appears to be much misunderstanding regarding the use of the null hypothesis. First, it often is stated in place of a research hypothesis. While it is easy to replace a research hypothesis (which predicts a relationship) with a null hypothesis (which predicts no relationship), there is no good reason for doing so. As we have seen, the null hypothesis is merely a useful methodological device.

Second, there is nothing sacred about the customary .05 and .01 significance levels—they are merely conventions. It is a little ridiculous, for example, to fail to reject the null hypothesis with a sample value that has a probability of .06. To do so might very well result in what is known as a **Type II error**—this error results when a researcher fails to reject a null hypothesis that is false. A **Type I error**, on the other hand, results when a researcher rejects a null hypothesis that is true. In our example in which there was a 14-point difference between sample means, for example, we rejected the null hypothesis at the .05 level. In doing so, we realized that a 5 percent chance remained of being wrong—that is, a 5 percent chance that

	Susie has pneumonia.	Susie does not have pneumonia.
Doctor says that symptoms like Susie's occur only 5 percent of the time in healthy people. To be safe, however, he decides to treat Susie for pneumonia.	Doctor is correct. Susie does have pneumonia and the treatment cures her.	Doctor is wrong. Susie's treatment was unnecessary and possibly unpleasant and expensive. **Type I error** (α)
Doctor says that symptoms like Susie's occur 95 percent of the time in healthy people. In his judgment, therefore, her symptoms are a false alarm and do not warrant treatment, and he decides not to treat Susie for pneumonia.	Doctor is wrong. Susie is not treated and may suffer serious consequences. **Type II error** (β)	Doctor is correct. Unnecessary treatment is avoided.

Figure 11.17 *A Hypothetical Example of Type I and Type II Errors*

the null hypothesis was true. Figure 11.17 provides an example of Type I and Type II errors.

Finally, there is also nothing sacrosanct about testing an obtained result against zero. In our previous example, for instance, why not test the obtained value of 14 (or 5.5, etc.) against a hypothetical population difference of 1 (or 3, etc.)? Testing only against zero can mislead one into exaggerating the importance of the obtained relationship. We believe the reporting of inferential statistics should rely more on confidence intervals and less on whether a particular level of significance has been attained.

Inference Techniques

It is beyond the scope of this text to treat in detail each of the many techniques that exist for answering inference questions about data. We shall, however, present a brief summary of the more commonly used tests of statistical significance that researchers employ and then illustrate how to do one such test.

In Chapter 10, we made a distinction between quantitative and categorical data. We pointed out that the type of data a researcher collects often influences the type of statistical analysis required. A statistical technique appropriate for quantitative data, for example, will generally be inappropriate for categorical data.

There are two basic types of inference techniques that researchers use. **Parametric techniques** make various kinds of assumptions about the nature of the population from which the sample(s) involved in the research study are drawn. **Nonparametric techniques**, on the other hand, make few (if any) assumptions about the nature of the population from which the samples are taken. An advantage of parametric techniques is that they are generally more powerful* than nonparametric techniques and hence much more likely to reveal a true difference or relationship if one really exists. Their disadvantage is that often a researcher cannot satisfy the assumptions they require (e.g., that the population is normally distributed on the characteristic of interest). The advantage of nonparametric techniques is that they are safer to use when a researcher cannot satisfy the assumptions underlying the use of parametric techniques.

PARAMETRIC TECHNIQUES FOR ANALYZING QUANTITATIVE DATA†

The *t*-Test for Means. The *t*-test is a parametric statistical test used to see whether a difference between the means of two samples is significant. The test

*We discuss the power of a statistical test later in this chapter.

†Many texts distinguish between techniques appropriate for nominal, ordinal, and interval scales of measurement (see Chapter 7). It turns out that in most cases parametric techniques are most appropriate for interval data, while nonparametric techniques are more appropriate for ordinal and nominal data. Researchers rarely know for certain whether their data justify the assumption that interval scales have actually been used.

RESEARCH TIPS

Sample Size

Students frequently ask for more specific rules on sample size. Unfortunately, there are no simple answers. However, under certain conditions, some guidelines are available. The most important condition is random sampling, but there are other specific requirements that are discussed in statistics texts. Assuming these assumptions are met, the following apply:

Top table: Sample size required for concluding that a sample *correlation coefficient* is statistically significant (i.e., different from zero in the population) at the .05 level of confidence.

Bottom table: Sample size required for concluding that a *difference in sample means* is statistically significant (i.e., the difference between the means of the two populations is not zero) at the .05 level of confidence. These calculations require that the population standard deviation be known or estimated from the sample standard deviations. Let us assume, for example, that the standard deviation in both populations is 15 and each of the samples is the same size.

Value of sample *r*	.05	.10	.15	.20	.25	.30	.40	.50
Sample size required	1,539	400	177	100	64	49	25	16

Difference between the sample means	2 points	5 points	10 points	15 points
Required size of each sample	434	71	18	8

produces a value for *t* (called an obtained *t*), which the researcher then checks in a statistical table (similar to the one shown in Appendix B) to determine the level of significance that has been reached. As we mentioned earlier, if the .05 level of significance is reached, the researcher customarily rejects the null hypothesis and concludes that a real difference does exist.

There are two forms of this *t*-test, a *t*-test for independent means and a *t*-test for correlated means. The ***t*-test for independent means** is used to compare the mean scores of two *different,* or independent, groups. For example, if two randomly selected groups of eighth-graders (31 in each group) were exposed to two different methods of teaching for a semester and then given the same achievement test at the end of the semester, their achievement scores could be compared using a *t*-test. Let us assume that the researcher suspected that those students exposed to method A would score significantly higher on the end-of-semester achievement test. Accordingly, she formulated the following null and alternative hypotheses:

Null hypothesis: population mean of method A = population mean of method B

Research hypothesis: population mean of method A > population mean of method B

She finds that the mean score on the achievement test of the students who were taught by method A equals 85 and that the mean score of the students taught by method B equals 80. Obviously, these two sample means are different. However, this difference could be due to chance (i.e., sampling error). The key question is whether these means are different *enough* that our researcher can conclude that the difference is most likely not due to chance but actually to the difference between the two teaching methods.

To evaluate her research hypothesis, our researcher conducts a one-tailed *t*-test for independent samples and finds that the *t*-value (the test statistic) is 2.18. To be statistically significant at the .05 level, with 60 degrees of freedom (*df*), a *t*-value of at least 1.67 is required, since the test is a one-tailed test. Because the obtained *t*-value of 2.18 is beyond 1.67, it is an unlikely value, and hence the null hypothesis is rejected. Our researcher concludes that the difference between the two means is statistically significant—that is, it was not merely a chance occurrence but indeed represents a real difference between the achievement scores of the two groups.

Let us say a word about the concept **degrees of freedom (df)**, which we referred to in the preceding

Using Excel to Draw a Random Sample

Excel can also be used to draw a random sample from a population. Here is how to do it. First, list your dataset in any of the columns on an Excel worksheet. Under the **Tools** menu, click on **Data Analysis,** and then on **Sampling.** In the sampling dialogue box, indicate the array of cells from which you wish to draw the sample. Under "Type of Sample," click **Random,** and under "Number of Samples," type in how many numbers you wish to have in the sample. Then click on the cells where you want the numbers in the random sample to appear.

Here is an example. Following the steps described, we asked for a random sample of 15 numbers to be selected from the list of 100 numbers we had listed in cells A1:E20. The numbers shown in cells G1:G15 were selected.

Population of 100 Scores

Row	A	B	C	D	E	F	G
1	67	65	33	98	9		55
2	74	71	36	87	14		67
3	92	92	69	85	51		85
4	77	80	65	57	32		32
5	88	86	58	59	87		73
6	81	78	57	94	98		9
7	73	70	45	91	68		57
8	72	70	45	28	52		65
9	71	78	41	27	21		11
10	90	89	12	65	30		55
11	89	93	11	38	38		67
12	95	96	10	55	37		92
13	80	82	9	56	59		7
14	70	73	58	66	58		46
15	84	85	57	88	46		37
16	67	65	41	71	60		
17	45	73	12	7	80		
18	55	26	13	40	11		
19	62	33	28	32	12		
20	12	11	29	31	29		

Random sample (G1:G15)

example. This concept is quite important in many inferential statistics tests. In essence, it refers to the number of scores in a frequency distribution that are "free to vary"—that is, that are not fixed. For example, suppose you had a distribution of only three scores, *a*, *b*, and *c*, that must add up to 10. It is apparent that *a*, *b*, and *c* can have a number of different values (such as 3, 5, and 2; or 1, 6, and 3; or 2, 2, and 6) and still add up to 10. But once any two of these values are fixed, or set, the third value is also set; it cannot vary.

Thus, should $a = 3$ and $b = 5$, *c must* equal 2. Hence, we say that there are two degrees of freedom in this distribution; any two of the values are "free to vary," so to speak, but once they are set, the third is also fixed. Degrees of freedom are calculated in an independent samples *t*-test by subtracting 2 from the total number of values in *both* groups.* In this example, there are

*In a study with only one group, you would subtract 1 from the total value of the group.

two groups, with 31 students in each group; hence there are 30 values in each group that are free to vary, resulting in a total of 60 degrees of freedom.

The ***t*-test for correlated means** is used to compare the mean scores of the *same* group before and after a treatment of some sort is given, to see if any observed gain is significant, or when the research design involves two matched groups. It is also used when the *same* subjects receive two different treatments in a study.

Consider an example. Suppose a sports psychologist believes that anxiety often makes basketball players perform poorly when shooting free throws in close games. She decides to investigate the effectiveness of relaxation training for reducing the level of anxiety such athletes experience and thus improving their performance at the free throw line. She formulates these hypotheses:

Null hypothesis: There will be no change in performance at the free throw line.

Research hypothesis: Performance at the free throw line will improve.

She randomly selects a sample of 15 athletes to undergo the training. During the week before the training sessions (the treatment), she measures the athletes' level of anxiety. She then exposes the athletes to the treatment. For a week afterward, she again measures the athletes' level of anxiety.

She finds that the mean number of free throws completed equals five per game before the training and seven after the training has been completed. She conducts a *t*-test for repeated measures and obtains a *t*-statistic of 2.43. Statistical significance at the .05 level, for a one-tailed test, with 14 degrees of freedom, requires a *t*-statistic of at least 1.76. Since the obtained *t*-value is more than that, the researcher concludes that such a result is unusual (i.e., unlikely to be a chance result); therefore, she rejects the null hypothesis. She concludes that relaxation therapy can reduce the anxiety level of these athletes.

Analysis of Variance. When researchers desire to find out whether there are significant differences between the means of *more than* two groups, they commonly use a technique called **analysis of variance (ANOVA)**, which is actually a more general form of the *t*-test that is appropriate to use with three or more groups. (It can also be used with two groups.) In brief, variation both within and between each of the groups is analyzed statistically, yielding what is known as an *F* value. As in a *t*-test, this *F* value is then checked in a statistical table to see if it is statistically significant. It is interpreted quite similarly to the *t*-value, in that the larger the obtained value of *F*, the greater the likelihood that statistical significance exists.

For example, imagine that a researcher wishes to investigate the effectiveness of three drugs used to relieve headaches. She randomly selects three groups of individuals who routinely suffer from headaches (with 20 in each group) and formulates the following hypotheses:

Null hypothesis: There is no difference between groups.

Research hypothesis: There is a difference between groups.

The researcher obtains an *F* value of 3.95. The critical region for the corresponding degrees of freedom at the .05 level, for a two-tailed test, is 3.17. Therefore, she would reject the null hypothesis and conclude that the effectiveness of the three drugs is not the same.

When only two groups are being compared, the *F* test is sufficient to tell the researcher whether significance has been achieved. When more than two groups are being compared, the *F* test will not, by itself, tell us which of the means are different. A further (but quite simple) procedure, called a *post hoc analysis,* is required to find this out. ANOVA is also used when more than one independent variable is investigated, as in *factorial designs,* which we discuss in Chapter 13.

Analysis of Covariance. **Analysis of covariance (ANCOVA)** is a variation of ANOVA used when, for example, groups are given a pretest related in some way to the dependent variable and their mean scores on this pretest are found to differ. ANCOVA enables the researcher to adjust the posttest mean scores on the dependent variable for each group to compensate for the initial differences between the groups on the pretest. The pretest is called the *covariate.* How much the posttest mean scores must be adjusted depends on how large the difference between the pretest means is and the degree of relationship between the covariate and the dependent variable. Several covariates can be used in an ANCOVA test, so in addition to (or instead of) adjusting for a pretest, the researcher can adjust for the effect of other variables. (We discuss this further in Chapter 13). Like ANOVA, ANCOVA produces an *F* value, which is then looked up in a statistical table to determine whether it is statistically significant.

Multivariate Analysis of Variance. **Multivariate analysis of variance (MANOVA)** differs from ANOVA in only one respect: It incorporates two or more dependent variables in the same analysis, thus permitting a more powerful test of differences among means. It is justified only when the researcher has reason to believe correlations exist among the dependent variables. Similarly, **multivariate analysis of covariance (MANCOVA)** extends ANCOVA to include two or more dependent variables in the same analysis. The specific value that is calculated is **Wilk's lambda**, a number analogous to F in analysis of variance.

The *t*-Test for *r*. The ***t*-test for *r*** is used to see whether a correlation coefficient calculated on sample data is significant—that is, whether it represents a nonzero correlation in the population from which the sample was drawn. It is similar to the t-test for means, except that here the statistic being dealt with is a correlation coefficient (r) rather than a difference between means. The test produces a value for t (again called an obtained t), which the researcher checks in a statistical probability table to see whether it is statistically significant. As with the other parametric tests, the larger the obtained value for t, the greater the likelihood that significance has been achieved.

For example, a researcher is using a regular two-tailed test, with alpha = .05, to determine if a nonzero correlation exists in a particular population. He randomly selects a sample of 30 individuals. Checking the appropriate statistical table (critical values for the Pearson correlation), he finds that with $\alpha = .05$ and $n = 30$ (28 *df*), the table lists a critical value of 0.361. The sample correlation, therefore (independent of sign) must have a value equal to or greater than 0.361 for the researcher to reject the null hypothesis and conclude that there is a significant correlation in the population. Any sample correlation between 0.361 and −0.361 would be considered likely (i.e., due to sampling error) and hence *not* statistically significant.

NONPARAMETRIC TECHNIQUES FOR ANALYZING QUANTITATIVE DATA

The Mann-Whitney *U* Test. The **Mann-Whitney *U* test** is a nonparametric alternative to the t-test used when a researcher wishes to analyze ranked data. The researcher intermingles the scores of the two groups and then ranks them as if they were all from just one group. The test produces a value (U), whose probability of occurrence is then checked by the researcher in the appropriate statistical table. The logic of the test is as follows: If the parent populations are identical, then the sum of the pooled rankings for *each* group should be about the same. If the summed ranks are markedly different, on the other hand, then this difference is likely to be statistically significant.

The Kruskal-Wallis One-Way Analysis of Variance. The **Kruskal-Wallis one-way analysis of variance** is used when researchers have more than two independent groups to compare. The procedure is quite similar to the Mann-Whitney U test. The scores of the individuals in the several groups are pooled and then ranked as though they all came from one group. The sums of the ranks added together for each of the separate groups are then compared. This analysis produces a value (H), whose probability of occurrence is checked by the researcher in the appropriate statistical table.

The Sign Test. The **sign test** is used when a researcher wants to analyze two related (as opposed to independent) samples. Related samples are connected in some way. For example, often a researcher will try to equalize groups on IQ, gender, age, or some other variable. The groups are *matched,* so to speak, on these variables. Another example of a related sample is when the same group is both pre- and posttested (i.e., tested twice). Each individual, in other words, is tested on two different occasions (as with the t-test for correlated means).

This test is very easy to use. The researcher simply lines up the pairs of related subjects and then determines how many times the paired subjects in one group scored higher than those in the other group. If the groups do not differ significantly, the totals for the two groups should be about equal. If there is a marked difference in scoring (such as many more in one group scoring higher), the difference may be statistically significant. Again, the probability of this occurrence can be determined by consulting the appropriate statistical table.

The Friedman Two-Way Analysis of Variance. If more than two related groups are involved, then the **Friedman two-way analysis of variance** test can be used. For example, if a researcher employs four matched groups, this test would be appropriate.

PARAMETRIC TECHNIQUES FOR ANALYZING CATEGORICAL DATA

***t*-Test For Proportions.** The most commonly used parametric tests for analyzing categorical data are the ***t*-tests for a difference in proportions**—that is, whether the proportion in one category (e.g., males) is different from the proportion in another category (e.g., females). As is the case with the *t*-tests for means, there are two forms: one ***t*-test for independent proportions** and one ***t*-test for correlated proportions**. The latter is used primarily when the same group is being compared, as in the proportion of individuals agreeing with a statement before and after receiving an intervention of some sort.

NONPARAMETRIC TECHNIQUES FOR ANALYZING CATEGORICAL DATA

The Chi-Square Test. The **chi-square test** is used to analyze data that are reported in categories. For example, a researcher might want to compare how many male and female teachers favor a new curriculum to be instituted in a particular school district. He asks a sample of 50 teachers if they favor or oppose the new curriculum. If they do not differ significantly in their responses, he would expect that about the same proportion of males and females would be in favor of (or opposed to) instituting the curriculum.

The chi-square test is based on a comparison between expected frequencies and actual, obtained frequencies. If the obtained frequencies are similar to the expected frequencies, then researchers conclude that the groups do not differ (in our example, they do not differ in their attitude toward the new curriculum). If there are considerable differences between the expected and obtained frequencies, on the other hand, then researchers conclude that there is a significant difference in attitude between the two groups.

As with all of these inference techniques, the chi-square test yields a value (χ^2). The chi-square test is not limited to comparing expected and obtained frequencies for only two variables. See Table 10.11 for an example.

After the value for χ^2 has been calculated, we want to determine how likely it is that such a result could occur if there were no relationship in the population—that is, whether the obtained pattern of results does not exist in the population but occurred because of the particular sample that was selected. As with all inferential tests, we determine this by consulting a probability table (Appendix C).

You will notice that the chi-square table in Appendix C also has a column headed "degrees of freedom." Degrees of freedom are calculated in crossbreak tables as follows, using an example of a table with three rows and two columns.

Step 1: Subtract 1 from the number of rows: $3 - 1 = 2$
Step 2: Subtract 1 from the number of columns: $2 - 1 = 1$
Step 3: Multiply step 1 by step 2: $(2)(1) = 2$

TABLE 11.1 *Contingency Coefficient Values for Different-Sized Crossbreak Tables*

Size of Table (No. of Cells)	Upper Limit[a] for C Calculated
2 by 2	.71
3 by 3	.82
4 by 4	.87
5 by 5	.89
6 by 6	.91

[a]The upper limits for unequal-sized tables (such as 2 by 3 or 3 by 4) are unknown but can be estimated from the values given. Thus, the upper limit for a 3 by 4 table would approximate .85.

Thus, in this example, there are two degrees of freedom.

Contingency Coefficient. The final step in the chi-square test process is to calculate the **contingency coefficient**, symbolized by the letter *C*, to which we referred in Chapter 10. It is a measure of the degree of association in a contingency table. We show how to calculate both the chi-square test and the contingency coefficient in Chapter 12.

The contingency coefficient cannot be interpreted in exactly the same way as the correlation coefficient. It must be interpreted by using Table 11.1. This table gives the upper limit for *C*, depending on the number of cells in the crossbreak table.

SUMMARY OF TECHNIQUES

The names of the most commonly used inferential procedures and the data type appropriate to their use are summarized in Table 11.2.

This summary should be useful to you whenever you encounter these terms in your reading. While the details of both mathematical rationale and calculation differ greatly among these techniques, the most important things to remember are as follows:

1. The end product of all inference procedures is the same: a statement of probability relating the sample data to hypothesized population characteristics.
2. All inference techniques assume random sampling. Without random sampling, the resulting probabilities are in error—to an unknown degree.
3. Inference techniques are intended to answer only one question: Given the sample data, what are probable population characteristics? These techniques do

TABLE 11.2 *Commonly Used Inferential Techniques*

	Parametric	Nonparametric
Quantitative	*t*-test for independent means	Mann-Whitney *U* test
	t-test for correlated means	Kruskal-Wallis one-way analysis of variance
	Analysis of variance (ANOVA)	Sign test
	Analysis of covariance (ANCOVA)	Friedman two-way analysis of variance
	Multivariate analysis of variance (MANOVA)	
	t-test for *r*	
Categorical	*t*-test for difference in proportions	Chi square

not help decide whether the data show results that are meaningful or useful—they indicate only the extent to which they may be generalizable.

POWER OF A STATISTICAL TEST

The **power of a statistical test** is similar to the power of a telescope. Astronomers looking at Mars or Venus with a low-power telescope probably can see that these planets look like spheres, but it is unlikely that they can see much by way of differences. With high-power telescopes, however, they can see such differences as moons and mountains. When the purpose of a statistical test is to assess differences, power is the probability that the test will correctly lead to the conclusion that there *is* a difference when, in fact, a difference exists.

Suppose a football coach wants to study a new technique for kicking field goals. He asks a (random) sample of 30 high school players to each kick 30 goals. They take the same "test" after being coached in the new technique. The mean number of goals is 11.2 before coaching and 18.8 after coaching—a difference of 7.6. The null hypothesis is that any positive difference (i.e., the number of goals after coaching minus the number of goals before coaching) is a chance difference from the true population difference of zero. A one-tailed *t*-test is the technique used to test for statistical significance.

In this example, the critical value for rejecting the null hypothesis at the .05 level is calculated. Assume the critical value turns out to be 5.8. Any difference in means that is larger than +5.8 would result in rejection of the null hypothesis. Since our difference is 7.6, we therefore reject the null hypothesis. Figure 11.18 illustrates this condition.

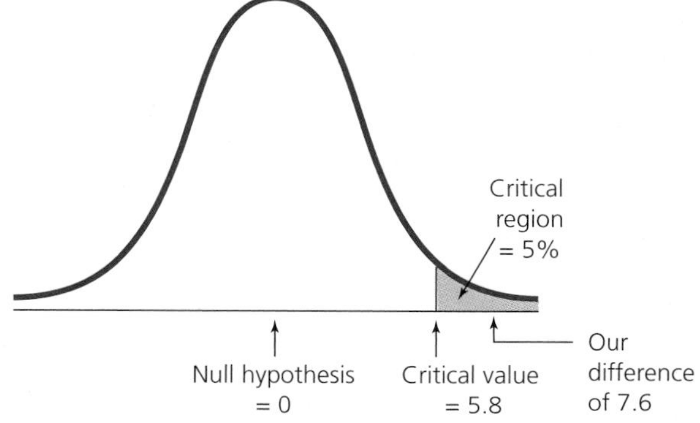

Figure 11.18 *Rejecting the Null Hypothesis*

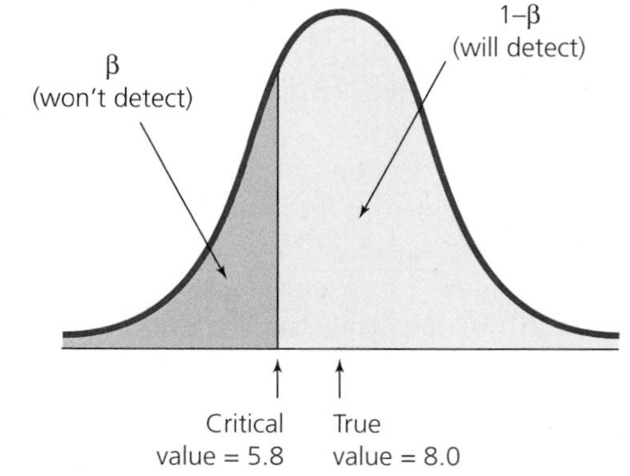

Figure 11.19 *Power Under an Assumed Population Value*

Now assume that we somehow know that the real difference in the population is actually 8.0. This is shown in Figure 11.19. The dark-shaded part shows the probability that the null hypothesis (which we now "know" to be wrong) will not be rejected by using the critical

Can Statistical Power Analysis Be Misleading?

Can statistical power analysis mislead researchers? An example is provided by a study that found that in the year following the 1994 federal ban on assault weapons, gun homicides declined 6.7 percent more than would have been expected, based on preexisting trends. This difference was not statistically significant. The authors carried out a statistical power analysis and concluded that a larger sample and longer time period were needed to have a sufficiently powerful statistical test that could detect an effect if any truly existed.*

*Koper, C. S., & Roth, J. A. (2001). The impact of the 1994 assault weapon ban on gun violence outcomes: An assessment of multiple outcome measures and some lessons for policy evaluation. *Journal of Quantitative Criminology, 17*(1), 33–74.

Kleck argued that even with a much longer time frame and larger sample (and therefore greater statistical power), the possible impact of the ban was so slight (because assault weapons comprised only 2 percent of the guns used in crime) that "we could not reliably detect so minuscule an impact."† He agreed with the study's authors that the observed decline may well have been due to other factors, such as reduced crack use in high-crime neighborhoods (uncontrolled variables). He asked, in light of such known limitations, whether such studies are worth doing. Koper and Roth argued that they are because of the importance of decisions regarding such social policy issues.‡

What do you think? Are such studies worth doing?

†Kleck, G. (2001). Impossible policy evaluations and impossible conclusions: A comment on Koper and Roth. *Journal of Quantitative Criminology, 17*(1), 80.

‡Koper, C. S., & Roth, J. A. (2001). A priori assertions versus empirical inquiry: A reply to Kleck. *Journal of Quantitative Criminology, 17*(1), 81–88.

value of 5.8—that is, it shows how often one would get a value of 5.8 or less, which is not sufficient to cause the null hypothesis to be rejected. This area is beta, and is determined from a *t*-table. The power under this particular "known" value of the population difference is the lightly shaded area $1 - \beta$. You can see, then, that in this instance, if the real value is 8, a *t*-test using $p = .05$ will very often fail to detect it.

The power $(1 - \beta)$ for a series of assumed "true" values can be obtained in the same way. When power is plotted against assumed "real" values, the result is called a *power curve* and looks something like Figure 11.20. Comparing such power curves for different techniques (e.g., a *t*-test versus the Mann-Whitney *U* test) indicates their relative efficiency for use in a particular circumstance. Parametric tests (e.g., ANOVA, *t*-tests) are generally, but not always, more powerful than nonparametric tests (e.g., chi square, Mann-Whitney *U* test).

Clearly, researchers want to use a powerful statistical test—one that can detect a relationship if one exists in the population—if they possibly can. If at all possible, therefore, power should be increased. How might this be done?

There are at least four ways to increase power in addition to the use of parametric tests when appropriate:

1. Decrease sampling error by:
   a. Increasing sample size. An estimate of the necessary sample size can be obtained by doing a statistical power analysis. This requires an estimation of all of the values (except n = sample size) used

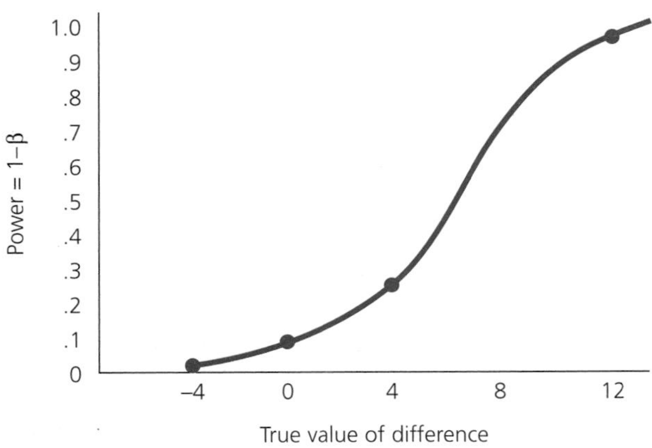

Figure 11.20 *A Power Curve*

in calculating the statistic you plan to use and solving for n (see, e.g., Table 12.2 on p. 252 for the formulas used to calculate the t-test).*

b. Using reliable measures to decrease measurement error.

*Tables are available for estimating sample size based on a combination of desired effect size (see p. 248) and desired level of power. See also Lipsey, M. W. (1990). *Design sensitivity: Statistical power for experimental research.* Newbury Park, CA: Sage.

c. Decreasing variability in the sample by restricting demographics (e.g., "ninth-graders" instead of "high schoolers"). However, this reduces generalizability.

2. Controlling for extraneous variables, as these may obscure the relationship being studied.
3. Increasing the strength of the treatment (if there is one), perhaps by using a larger time period.
4. Using a one-tailed test, when such is justifiable.

Go back to the **INTERACTIVE AND APPLIED LEARNING** feature at the beginning of the chapter for a listing of interactive and applied activities. Go to the **Online Learning Center** at **www.mhhe.com/fraenkel9e** to take quizzes, practice with key terms, and review chapter content.

Main Points

WHAT ARE INFERENTIAL STATISTICS?

- Inferential statistics refer to certain procedures that allow researchers to make inferences about a population based on data obtained from a sample.
- The term *probability,* as used in research, refers to the predicted relative frequency with which a given event will occur.

SAMPLING ERROR

- The term *sampling error* refers to the variations in sample statistics that occur as a result of repeated sampling from the same population.

THE DISTRIBUTION OF SAMPLE MEANS

- A sampling distribution of means is a frequency distribution resulting from plotting the means of a very large number of samples from the same population.
- The standard error of the mean is the standard deviation of a sampling distribution of means. The standard error of the difference between means is the standard deviation of a sampling distribution of *differences* between sample means.

CONFIDENCE INTERVALS

- A confidence interval is a region extending both above and below a sample statistic (such as a sample mean) within which a population parameter (such as the population mean) may be said to fall with a specified probability of being wrong.

HYPOTHESIS TESTING

- Statistical hypothesis testing is a way of determining the probability that an obtained sample statistic will occur, given a hypothetical population parameter.
- A research hypothesis specifies the nature of the relationship the researcher thinks exists in the population.
- The null hypothesis typically specifies that there is no relationship in the population.

SIGNIFICANCE LEVELS

- The term *significance level* (or *level of significance*), as used in research, refers to the probability of a sample statistic occurring as a result of sampling error.
- The significance levels most commonly used in educational research are the .05 and .01 levels.
- Statistical significance and practical significance are not necessarily the same. Even if a result is statistically significant, it may not be practically (i.e., educationally) significant.

TESTS OF STATISTICAL SIGNIFICANCE

- A one-tailed test of significance involves the use of probabilities based on one-half of a sampling distribution because the research hypothesis is a directional hypothesis.
- A two-tailed test, on the other hand, involves the use of probabilities based on both sides of a sampling distribution because the research hypothesis is a nondirectional hypothesis.

PARAMETRIC TESTS FOR QUANTITATIVE DATA

- A parametric statistical test requires various kinds of assumptions about the nature of the population from which the samples involved in the research study were taken.
- Some of the commonly used parametric techniques for analyzing quantitative data include the *t*-test for means, ANOVA, ANCOVA, MANOVA, MANCOVA, and the *t*-test for *r*.

PARAMETRIC TESTS FOR CATEGORICAL DATA

- The most common parametric technique for analyzing categorical data is the *t*-test for differences in proportions.

NONPARAMETRIC TESTS FOR QUANTITATIVE DATA

- A nonparametric statistical technique makes few, if any, assumptions about the nature of the population from which the samples in the study were taken.
- Some of the commonly used nonparametric techniques for analyzing quantitative data are the Mann-Whitney *U* test, the Kruskal-Wallis one-way analysis of variance, the sign test, and the Friedman two-way analysis of variance.

NONPARAMETRIC TESTS FOR CATEGORICAL DATA

- The chi-square test is the nonparametric technique most commonly used to analyze categorical data.
- The contingency coefficient is a descriptive statistic indicating the degree of relationship between two categorical variables.

POWER OF A STATISTICAL TEST

- The power of a statistical test for a particular set of data is the likelihood of identifying a difference, when in fact it exists, between population parameters.
- Parametric tests are generally, but not always, more powerful than nonparametric tests.

Key Terms

analysis of covariance (ANCOVA) 236
analysis of variance (ANOVA) 236
chi-square test 238
confidence interval 224
contingency coefficient 238
degrees of freedom (df) 234
Friedman two-way analysis of variance 237
inferential statistics 220
Kruskal-Wallis one-way analysis of variance 237
level of significance 228
Mann-Whitney *U* test 237
multivariate analysis of covariance (MANCOVA) 237
multivariate analysis of variance (MANOVA) 237
nonparametric technique 233
null hypothesis 228
one-tailed test 231
parametric technique 233
power of a statistical test 239
practical significance 230
probability 226
research hypothesis 228
sampling distribution 222
sampling error 221
sign test 237
standard error of the difference (SED) 227
standard error of the mean (SEM) 223
statistical significance 230
***t*-test for a difference in proportions 237**
***t*-test for correlated means 236**
***t*-test for correlated proportions 238**
***t*-test for independent means 234**
***t*-test for independent proportions 238**
***t*-test for *r* 237**
two-tailed test 232
Type I error 232
Type II error 232
Wilk's lambda 237

For Discussion

1. "Hypotheses can never be proven, only supported." Is this statement true or not? Explain.
2. No two samples will be the same in all of their characteristics. Why won't they?
3. When might a researcher not need to use inferential statistics to analyze his or her data?
4. "No sampling procedure, not even random sampling, guarantees a totally representative sample." Is this true? Discuss.
5. Could a relationship that is practically significant be ignored because it is not statistically significant? What about the reverse? Can you suggest an example of each?

Research Exercise 11: Inferential Statistics

Using Problem Sheet 11, indicate which inference technique(s), if any, are appropriate for your study. Indicate whether you would or would not do a significance test and/or calculate a confidence interval, and if not, explain why. If you do not intend to use any inference techniques in your study, explain why.

Problem Sheet 11

Inferential Statistics

1. My research question is: ______________________________
   ____
2. An appropriate inferential technique for my study would be:
   ____
   ____
3. Indicate whether you would use a *parametric* or *nonparametric* technique and why.
   ____
   ____
4. Indicate whether you would or would not do a *significance test* and why.
   ____
   ____
5. Indicate whether you would or would not calculate a *confidence interval* because:
   ____
   ____
6. I would not use any inferential techniques in my study because:
   ____
   ____
7. The type of sample used in my sample is:
   ____
   ____
8. The use of this type of sample in my study places the following limitation(s) on my use of inferential statistics:
   ____
   ____

An electronic version of this Problem Sheet that you can fill in and print, save, or e-mail is available on the Online Learning Center at www.mhhe.com/fraenkel9e.

Statistics in Perspective 12

Approaches to Research
Comparing Groups: Quantitative Data
Techniques
Interpretation
Relating Variables Within a Group: Quantitative Data
Techniques
Interpretation
Comparing Groups: Categorical Data
Techniques
Interpretation
Relating Variables Within a Group: Categorical Data
A Recap of Recommendations

OBJECTIVES **Studying this chapter should enable you to:**

- Apply several recommendations when comparing data obtained from two or more groups.
- Apply several recommendations when relating variables within a single group.
- Explain what is meant by the term "effect size."
- Describe briefly how to use frequency polygons, scatterplots, and crossbreak tables to interpret data.
- Differentiate between statistically significant and practically significant research results.

INTERACTIVE AND APPLIED LEARNING After, or while, reading this chapter:

Go to the Online Learning Center at www.mhhe.com/fraenkel9e to:

- Learn More About Statistical Versus Practical Significance

Go to your online Student Mastery Activities book to do the following activities:

- Activity 12.1: Statistical vs. Practical Significance
- Activity 12.2: Appropriate Techniques
- Activity 12.3: Interpret the Data
- Activity 12.4: Collect Some Data

"Well, the results are in," says Tamara Phillips. "I got the consultant's report about that study we did last semester."

"What study was that?" asks Felicia Lee, as the two carpool to Eisenhower Middle School, where they both teach eighth-grade social studies.

"Don't you remember? That guy from the university came down and asked some of us who taught social studies to try an inquiry approach?"

"Oh, yeah, I remember. I was in the experimental group—we used a series of inquiry-oriented lessons that they designed. They compared the results of our students with those of students who were similar in ability whose teachers did not use those lessons. What did they find out?"

"Well, the report states that those students whose teachers used the inquiry lessons had significantly higher test scores. But I'm not quite sure what that suggests."

"It means that the inquiry method is superior to whatever method the teachers of the other group used, doesn't it?" asks Felicia.

"I'm not sure. It depends on whether the significance they're talking about refers to practical or only statistical significance," replies Tamara.

"What's the difference?"

This difference—between statistical and practical significance—is an important one when it comes to talking about the results of a study. It is one of the things you will learn about in this chapter.

Now that you are somewhat familiar with both descriptive and inferential statistics, we want to relate them more specifically to practice. What are appropriate uses of these statistics? What are appropriate interpretations of them? What are the common errors or mistakes you should watch out for as either a participant in or consumer of research?

There are appropriate uses for both descriptive and inferential statistics. Sometimes, however, either or both types can be used inappropriately. In this chapter, therefore, we want to discuss the appropriate use of the descriptive and inferential statistics described in the previous two chapters. We will present a number of recommendations that we believe all researchers should consider when they use either type of statistics.*

*We acknowledge that not all researchers would agree with these recommendations.

Approaches to Research

Much research in education is done in one of two ways: either two or more groups are compared or variables within one group are related. Furthermore, as you have seen, the data in a study may be either quantitative or categorical. Thus, four different combinations of research are possible, as shown in Figure 12.1.

Remember that all groups are made up of individual units. In most cases, the unit is one person and the group is a group of people. Sometimes, however, the unit is itself a group (e.g., a class of students). In such cases, the "group" would be a collection of classes. This is illustrated by the following hypothesis: "Teacher friendliness is related to student learning." This hypothesis could be studied with a group of classes and a measure of both teacher "friendliness" and average student learning for each *class*.

	Data	
	Quantitative	Categorical
Two or more groups are compared		
Variables within one group are related		

Figure 12.1 *Combinations of Data and Approaches to Research*

Another complication arises in studies in which the same individuals receive two or more different treatments or methods. In comparing treatments, we are not then comparing different groups of people but different groups of scores obtained by the same group at different times. Nevertheless, the statistical analysis fits the comparison group model. We discuss this point further in Chapter 13.

Comparing Groups: Quantitative Data

TECHNIQUES

Whenever two or more groups are compared using quantitative data, the comparisons can be made in a variety of ways: through frequency polygons, calculation of one or more measures of central tendency (averages), and/or calculation of one or more measures of variability (spreads). Frequency polygons provide the most information; averages are useful summaries of each group's performance; and spreads provide information about the degree of variability in each group.

When analyzing data obtained from two groups, therefore, the first thing researchers should do is construct a frequency polygon of each group's scores. This will show all the information available about each group and also help researchers decide which of the shorter and more convenient indices to calculate. For example, examination of the frequency polygon of a group's scores can indicate whether the median or the mean is the most appropriate measure of central tendency to use. When comparing quantitative data from two groups, therefore, we recommend the following:

Recommendation 1: As a first step, prepare a frequency polygon of each group's scores.

Recommendation 2: Use these polygons to decide which measure of central tendency is appropriate to calculate. If any polygon shows extreme scores at one end, use medians for all groups rather than, or in addition to, means.

INTERPRETATION

Once the descriptive statistics have been calculated, they must be interpreted. At this point, the task is to describe, in words, what the polygons and averages tell researchers about the question or hypothesis being investigated. A key question arises: How large does a difference in means between two groups have to be in order to be important? When will this difference *make a difference?* How does one decide? You will recall that this is the issue of practical versus statistical significance that we discussed in Chapter 11.

Use Information About Known Groups. Unfortunately, in most educational research, this information is difficult to obtain. Sometimes, prior experience can be helpful. One of the advantages of IQ scores is that, over the years, many educators have had enough experience with them to make differences between them meaningful. Most experienced counselors, administrators, and teachers realize, for example, that a difference in means of less than 5 points between two groups has little useful meaning, no matter how statistically significant the difference may be. They also know that a difference between means of 10 points is enough to have important implications. At other times, a researcher may have available a frame of reference, or standard, to use in interpreting the magnitude of a difference between means. One such standard consists of the mean scores of *known groups*. In a study of critical thinking in which one of the present authors participated, for example, the end-of-year mean score for a group of eleventh-graders who received a special curriculum was higher than is typical of the mean scores of

"That's the gist of what I want to say. Now get me some statistics to base it on."

eleventh-graders in general *and* close to the mean score of a group of college students, whereas a comparison group scored lower than both. Because the special-curriculum group also demonstrated a fall-to-spring mean gain that was twice that of the comparison group, the total evidence obtained through comparing their performance with other groups indicated that the gains made by the special-curriculum group were important.

Calculate the Effect Size. Another technique for assessing the magnitude of a difference between the means of two groups is to calculate what is known as **effect size (ES)**.*

Effect size takes into account the size of the difference between means that is obtained, regardless of whether it is statistically significant. One of the most commonly used indexes of effect size is called delta (Δ) and is obtained by dividing the difference between the means of the two groups being compared by the standard deviation of the comparison group. Thus:

$$\Delta = \frac{\text{mean of experimental group} - \text{mean of comparison group}}{\text{standard deviation of comparison group}}$$

When pre-to-post gains in the mean scores of two groups are compared, the formula is modified as follows:

$$\Delta = \frac{\text{mean experimental gain} - \text{mean comparison gain}}{\text{standard deviation of gain of comparison group}}$$

The standard deviation of gain score is obtained by first getting the gain (post-to-pre) score for each individual and then calculating the standard deviation as usual.†

While effect size is a useful tool for assessing the magnitude of a difference between the means of two groups, it does not, in and of itself, answer the question of how large it must be for researchers to consider an obtained difference important. As is the case with significance levels, this is essentially an arbitrary decision. Most researchers consider that any effect size of .50 (i.e., half a standard deviation of the comparison group's scores) or larger is an important finding. If the scores fit the normal distribution, such a value indicates that the difference in means between the two groups is about one-twelfth the distance between the highest and lowest scores of the comparison group. When assessing the magnitude of a difference between the means of two groups, therefore, we recommend the following:

Recommendation 3: Compare obtained results with data on the means of known groups, if possible.

Recommendation 4: Calculate an effect size. Interpret an ES of .50 or larger as important. (Smaller values of ES may have theoretical, as opposed to practical, importance.)

Use Inferential Statistics. A third method for judging the importance of a difference between the means of two groups is by the use of **inferential statistics**. It is common to find, even before examining polygons or differences in means, that a researcher has applied an inference technique (a *t*-test, an analysis of variance, and so on) and then used the results as the *only* criterion for evaluating the importance of the results. This practice has come under increasing attack for the following reasons:

1. Unless the groups compared are random samples from specified populations (which is unusual), the results (probabilities, significance levels, and confidence intervals) are to an unknown degree in error and hence misleading.

*The term *effect size* is used to identify a group of statistical indices, all of which have the common purpose of clarifying the magnitude of relationship.

†There are more effective ways to obtain gain scores, but we will delay a discussion until subsequent chapters.

Statistical Inference Tests—Good or Bad?

Our recommendations regarding statistical inference are not free of controversy. At one extreme are the views of Carver* and Schmidt,† who argue that the use of statistical inference tests in educational research should be banned. And in 2000 a survey of AERA members (American Educational Research Association) indicated that 19 percent agreed.‡

At the other extreme are those who agree with Robinson and Levin that "authors should *first* indicate whether the observed effect is a statistically improbable one, and *only if* it is should they indicate how *large or important* it is (is it a difference that *makes* a difference)."§

Cahan argued, to the contrary, that the way to avoid misleading conclusions regarding effects is not by using significance tests, but rather using confidence intervals accompanied by increased sample size.||

In 1999 the American Psychological Association Task Force on Statistical Inference recommended that inference tests not be banned, but that researchers should "always provide some effect size estimate when reporting a p value," and further that "reporting and interpreting effect sizes in the context of previously reported research is *essential* to good research."#

What do you think? Should significance tests be banned in educational research?

*Carver, R. P. (1993). The case against statistical significance testing revisited. *Journal of Experimental Education, 61,* 287–292.
†Schmidt, F. L. (1996). Statistical significance testing and cumulative knowledge in psychology: Implications for training of researchers. *Psychological Methods, 1,* 115–129.
‡Mittag, K. C., & Thompson, B. (2000). A national survey of AERA members' perceptions of statistical significance tests and other statistical issues. *Educational Researcher, 29*(3), 14–19.
§Robinson, D. H., & Levin, J. R. (January/February 1997). Reflections on statistical and substantive significance, with a slice of replication. *Educational Researcher, 26,* 22.
||Cahan, S. (2000). Statistical significance is not a "Kosher Certificate" for observed effects: A critical analysis of the two-step approach to the evaluation of empirical results. *Educational Researcher, 29*(5), 34.
#Wilkinson, L., & the APA Task Force on Statistical Inference (1999). Statistical methods in psychology journals: Guidelines and explanations. *American Psychologist, 54,* 599.

2. The outcome is greatly affected by sample size. With 100 cases in each of two groups, a mean difference in IQ score of 4.2 points is statistically significant at the .05 level (assuming the standard deviation is 15, as is typical with most IQ tests). Although statistically significant, this difference is so small as to be meaningless in any practical sense.
3. The actual magnitude of difference is minimized or sometimes overlooked.
4. The purpose of inferential statistics is to provide information pertinent to generalizing sample results to populations, not to evaluate sample results.

With regard to the use of inferential statistics, therefore, we recommend the following:

Recommendation 5: Consider using inferential statistics only if you can make a convincing argument that a difference between means of the magnitude obtained is important (Figure 12.2).

Recommendation 6: Do not use tests of statistical significance to evaluate the magnitude of a difference between sample means. Use them only as they were intended: to judge the generalizability of results.

Recommendation 7: Unless random samples were used, interpret probabilities and/or significance levels as crude indices, not as precise values.

Recommendation 8: Report the results of inference techniques as confidence intervals rather than (or in addition to) significance levels.

Example. Let us give an example to illustrate this type of analysis. We shall present the appropriate calculations in detail and then interpret the results. Imagine that we have two groups of eighth-grade students, 60 in each group, who receive different methods of social studies instruction for one semester. The teacher of one group uses an inquiry method of instruction, while the teacher of the other group uses the lecture method. The researcher's hypothesis is that the inquiry method will result in greater improvement than the lecture method in explaining skills as measured by the "test of ability to explain" (see p. 152) in Chapter 8. Each student is tested at the beginning

Figure 12.2 *A Difference That Doesn't Make a Difference!*

and at the end of the semester. The test consists of 40 items; the range of scores on the pretest is from 3 to 32, or 29 points. A gain score (posttest-pretest) is obtained. These gain scores are shown in the frequency distributions in Table 12.1 and the frequency polygons in Figure 12.3.

TABLE 12.1 *Gain Scores on Test of Ability to Explain: Inquiry and Lecture Groups*

	Inquiry		Lecture	
Gain Scores[a]	Frequency	Cumulative Frequency	Frequency	Cumulative Frequency
11	1	60	0	60
10	3	59	2	60
9	5	56	3	58
8	7	51	4	55
7	9	44	4	51
6	9	35	7	47
5	6	26	9	40
4	6	20	8	31
3	5	14	7	23
2	4	9	6	16
1	2	5	4	10
0	3	3	5	6
−1	0	0	1	1

[a]A negative score indicates the pretest was higher than the posttest.

These polygons indicate that a comparison of means is appropriate. Why?* The mean of the inquiry group is 5.6 compared to the mean of 4.4 for the lecture group. The difference between means is 1.2. In this instance, a comparison with the means of known groups is not possible, since such data are not available. A calculation of effect size results in an ES of .44, somewhat below the .50 that most researchers recommend for significance. Inspection of Figure 12.3, however, suggests that the difference between the means of the two groups should

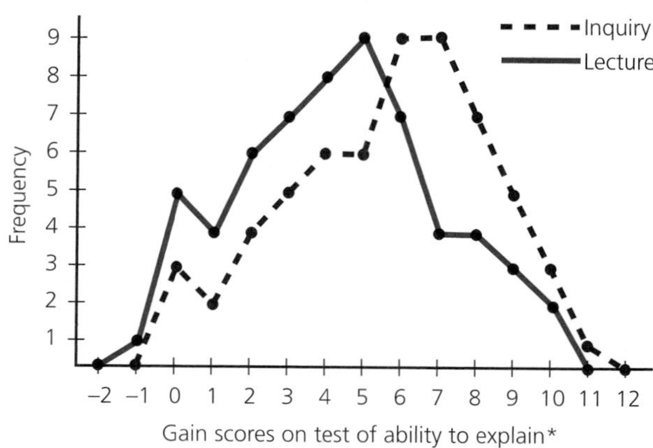

Figure 12.3 *Frequency Polygons of Gain Scores on Test of Ability to Explain: Inquiry and Lecture Groups*

*A negative score indicates the pretest was higher than the posttest.

*The polygons are nearly symmetrical without extreme scores at either end.

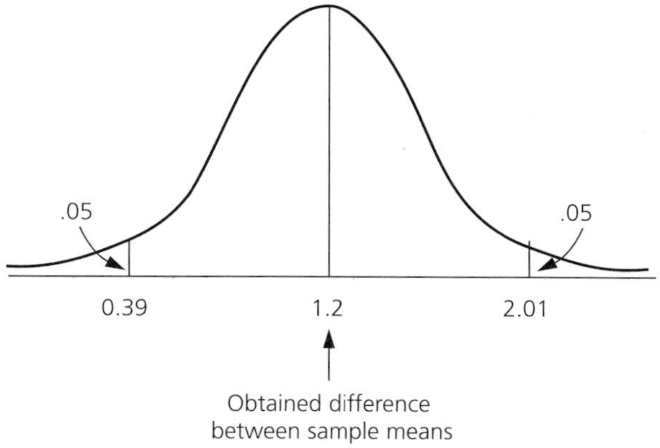

Figure 12.4 *90 Percent Confidence Interval for a Difference of 1.2 Between Sample Means*

not be discounted. Figure 12.4 and Table 12.2 show that the number of students gaining 7 or more points is 25 in the inquiry group and 13 (about half as many) in the lecture group. A gain of 7 points on a 40-item test can be considered substantial, even more so when it is recalled that the range was 29 points (3–32) on the pretest. If a gain of 8 points is used, the numbers are 16 in the inquiry group and 9 in the lecture group. If a gain of 6 points is used, the numbers become 34 and 20. We would argue that these discrepancies are large enough, in context, to recommend the inquiry method over the lecture method.

The use of an inference technique (a *t*-test for independent means) indicates that $p < .05$ in one tail (Table 12.2).* This leads the researcher to conclude that the observed difference between means of 1.2 points probably is not due to the particular samples used. Whether this probability can be taken as exact depends primarily on whether the samples were randomly selected. The 90 percent confidence interval is shown in Figure 12.4.† Notice that a difference of zero between the population means is not within the confidence interval.

*A directional hypothesis indicates use of a one-tailed test (see p. 230).

†1.65 SED gives .05 in one tail of the normal curve. 1.65 (SED) = 1.65(.49) = .81. 1.2 ± .81 equals .39 to 2.01. This is the 90 percent confidence interval. Use of 1.65 rather than 1.96 is justified because the researcher's hypothesis is concerned *only* with a *positive* gain (a one-tailed test). The 95 percent or any other confidence interval could, of course, have been used.

Relating Variables Within a Group: Quantitative Data

TECHNIQUES

Whenever a relationship between quantitative variables within a single group is examined, the appropriate techniques are the **scatterplot** and the **correlation coefficient**. The scatterplot illustrates all the data visually, while the correlation coefficient provides a numerical summary of the data. When analyzing data obtained from a single group, therefore, researchers should begin by constructing a scatterplot. Not only will it provide all the information available, but it will help them judge which correlation coefficient to calculate (the choice usually will be between the Pearson *r*, which assumes a **linear**, or **straight-line**, **relationship**, and eta, which describes a **curvilinear**, or curved, **relationship**).‡

Consider Figure 12.5. All of the five scatterplots shown represent a Pearson correlation of about .50. Only in (*a*), however, does this coefficient (.50) completely convey the nature of the relationship. In (*b*) the relationship is understated, since it is a curvilinear one, and eta would give a higher coefficient. In (*c*) the coefficient does not reflect the fan-shaped nature of the relationship. In (*d*) the coefficient does not reveal that there are two distinct subgroups. In (*e*) the coefficient is greatly inflated by a few unusual cases. While these illustrations are a bit exaggerated, similar results are often found in real data.

When examining relationships within a single group, therefore, we recommend the following:

Recommendation 9: Begin by constructing a scatterplot.

Recommendation 10: Use the scatterplot to determine which correlation coefficient is appropriate to calculate.

Recommendation 11: Use *both* the scatterplot and the correlation coefficient to interpret results.

INTERPRETATION

Interpreting scatterplots and correlations presents problems similar to those we discussed in relation to

‡Because both of these correlations describe the magnitude of relationship, they are also examples of effect size (see footnote, p. 248).

TABLE 12.2 *Calculations from Table 12.1*

Inquiry Group						Lecture Group					
Gain Score	f[a]	fX[b]	$X-\overline{X}$[c]	$(X-\overline{X})^2$[d]	$f(X-\overline{X})^2$[e]	Gain Score	f	fX	$X-\overline{X}$	$(X-\overline{X})^2$	$f(X-\overline{X})^2$
11	1	11	5.4	29.2	29.2	11	0	0	6.6	43.6	0.0
10	3	30	4.4	19.4	58.2	10	2	20	5.6	31.4	62.8
9	5	45	3.4	11.6	58.0	9	3	27	4.6	21.2	63.6
8	7	56	2.4	5.8	40.6	8	4	32	3.6	13.0	52.0
7	9	63	1.4	2.0	18.0	7	4	28	2.6	6.8	27.2
6	9	54	0.4	0.2	1.8	6	7	42	1.6	2.6	18.2
5	6	30	−0.6	0.4	2.4	5	9	45	0.6	0.4	3.6
4	6	24	−1.6	2.6	15.6	4	8	32	−0.4	0.2	1.6
3	5	15	−2.6	6.8	34.0	3	7	21	−1.4	2.0	14.0
2	4	8	−3.6	13.0	52.0	2	6	12	−2.4	5.8	34.8
1	2	2	−4.6	21.2	42.4	1	4	4	−3.4	11.6	46.4
0	3	0	−5.6	31.4	94.2	0	5	0	−4.4	19.4	97.0
−1	0	0	−6.6	43.6	0.0	−1	1	−1	−5.4	29.2	29.2
−2	0	0	−7.6	57.8	0.0	−2	0	0	−6.4	41.0	0.0
Total		Σ=338			Σ=446.4			Σ =262			Σ= 450.4

$$\overline{X}_1 = \frac{\Sigma fX}{n} = \frac{338}{60} = 5.6 \qquad \overline{X}_2 = \frac{\Sigma fX}{n} = \frac{262}{60} = 4.4$$

$$\text{SD}_1 = \sqrt{\frac{f(X - \overline{X})^2}{n}} = \sqrt{\frac{446.4}{60}} = \sqrt{7.4} = 2.7 \qquad \text{SD}_2 = \sqrt{\frac{f(X - \overline{X})^2}{n}} = \sqrt{\frac{450.4}{60}} = \sqrt{7.5} = 2.7$$

$$\text{SEM}_1 = \frac{\text{SD}}{\sqrt{n-1}} = \frac{2.7}{\sqrt{59}} = \frac{2.7}{7.7} = .35 \qquad \text{SEM}_2 = \frac{\text{SD}}{\sqrt{n-1}} = \frac{2.7}{\sqrt{59}} = \frac{2.7}{7.7} = .35$$

$$\text{SED} = \sqrt{(\text{SEM}_1)^2 + (\text{SEM}_2)^2} = \sqrt{.35^2 + .35^2} = \sqrt{.12 + .12} = \sqrt{.24} = .49$$

$$t = \frac{\overline{X}_1 - \overline{X}_2}{\text{SED}} = \frac{1.2}{.49} = 2.45 \qquad p < .05$$

$$\text{ES}(\Delta) = \frac{\overline{X}_1 - \overline{X}_2}{\text{SD}_2} = \frac{1.2}{2.4} = .44$$

[a] f = frequency

[b] fX = frequency × score

[c] $X - \overline{X}$ = score − mean

[d] $(X - \overline{X})^2$ = (score − mean)^2

[e] $f(X - \overline{X})^2$ = frequency × (score − mean)^2

differences in means. How large must a correlation coefficient be to suggest an *important* relationship? What does an important relationship look like on a scatterplot?

As you can see, doing or evaluating research is not cut-and-dried; it is not a matter of following a set of rules, but rather requires informed judgment. In judging correlation coefficients, one must first assess their appropriateness, as was done with those in Figure 12.5. If the Pearson correlation coefficient is an adequate summary (and we have shown in Figure 12.5 that this is not always the case), most researchers would agree to the interpretations shown in Table 12.3 when testing a research hypothesis.

As with a comparison of means, the use of inferential statistics to judge the importance of the magnitude of a relationship is both common and often misleading. With a sample of 100, a correlation of only .20 is statistically

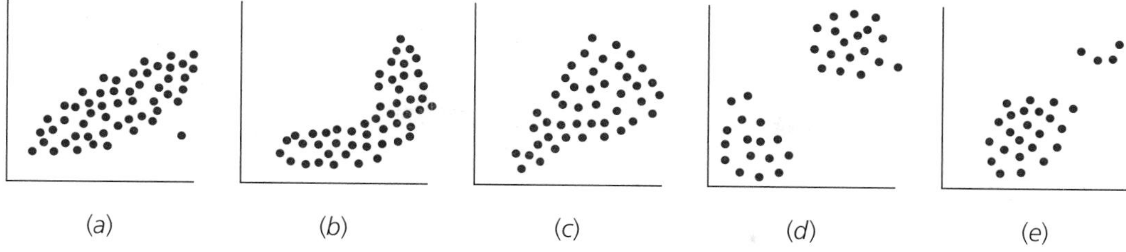

Figure 12.5 *Scatterplots with a Pearson r of .50*

significant at the .05 level with a two-tailed test. Accordingly, we recommend the following when interpreting scatterplots and correlation coefficients:

Recommendation 12: Draw a line that best fits all points in a scatterplot, and note the extent of deviations from it. The smaller the deviations all along the line, the more useful the relationship.*

Recommendation 13: Consider using inferential statistics only if you can give a convincing argument for the importance of the size of the relationship found in the sample.

Recommendation 14: Do not use tests of statistical significance to evaluate the magnitude of a relationship. Use them, as they were intended, to judge generalizability.

Recommendation 15: Unless a random sample was used, interpret probabilities and/or significance levels as crude indices, not as precise values.

Recommendation 16: Report the results of inference techniques as confidence intervals rather than as significance levels.

*Try this with Figure 12.5.

TABLE 12.3 ***Interpretation of Correlation Coefficients When Testing Research Hypotheses***

Magnitude of r	Interpretation
.00 to .40	Of little practical importance except in unusual circumstances; perhaps of theoretical value.*
.41 to .60	Large enough to be of practical as well as theoretical use.
.61 to .80	Very important, but rarely obtained in educational research.
.81 or above	Possibly an error in calculation; if not, a very sizable relationship.

*When selecting a very few people from a large group, even correlations this small may have predictive value.

Example. Let us now consider an example to illustrate the analysis of a suspected relationship between variables. Suppose a researcher wishes to test the hypothesis that, among counseling clients, improvement in marital satisfaction after six months of counseling is related to self-esteem at the beginning of counseling. In other words, people with higher self-esteem would be expected to show more improvement in marital satisfaction after undergoing therapy for a period of six months than people with lower self-esteem. The researcher obtains a group of 30 clients, each of whom takes a self-esteem inventory and a marital satisfaction inventory prior to counseling. The marital satisfaction inventory is taken again at the end of six months of counseling. The data are shown in Table 12.4.

The calculations shown in Table 12.4 are not as hard as they look. Here are the steps that we followed to obtain $r = .42$:

1. Multiply n by ΣXY: 30(7,023) = 210,690
2. Multiply ΣX by ΣY: (1,007)(192) = 193,344
3. Subtract step 2 from step 1: 210,690 − 193,344 = 17,346
4. Multiply n by ΣX^2: 30(35,507) = 1,065,210
5. Square ΣX: $(1,007)^2$ = 1,014,049
6. Subtract step 5 from step 4: 1,065,210 − 1,014,049 = 51,161
7. Multiply n by ΣY^2: 30(2,354) = 70,620
8. Square ΣY: $(192)^2$ = 36,864
9. Subtract step 8 from step 7: 70,620 − 36,864 = 33,756
10. Multiply step 6 by step 9: (51,161)(33,756) = 1,726,990,716
11. Take the square root of step 10: $\sqrt{1,726,990,716}$ = 41,557
12. Divide step 3 by step 11: 17,346/41,557 = .42

Using the data presented in Table 12.4, the researcher plots a scatterplot and finds that it reveals two things. First, there is a tendency for individuals with higher initial self-esteem scores to show greater improvement in marital satisfaction than those with lower initial self-esteem scores.

TABLE 12.4 *Self-Esteem Scores and Gains in Marital Satisfaction*

Client	Self-Esteem Score Before Counseling (X)	X^2	Gain in Marital Satisfaction After Counseling (Y)	Y^2	XY
1	20	400	−4	16	−80
2	21	441	−2	4	−42
3	22	484	−7	49	−154
4	24	576	1	1	24
5	24	576	4	16	96
6	25	625	5	25	125
7	26	676	−1	1	−26
8	27	729	8	64	216
9	29	841	2	4	58
10	28	784	5	25	140
11	30	900	5	25	150
12	30	900	14	196	420
13	32	1024	7	49	219
14	33	1089	15	225	495
15	35	1225	6	36	210
16	35	1225	16	256	560
17	36	1269	11	121	396
18	37	1396	14	196	518
19	36	1296	18	324	648
20	38	1444	9	81	342
21	39	1527	14	196	546
22	39	1527	15	225	585
23	40	1600	4	16	160
24	41	1681	8	64	328
25	42	1764	0	0	0
26	43	1849	3	9	129
27	43	1849	5	25	215
28	43	1849	8	64	344
29	44	1936	4	16	176
30	45	2025	5	25	225
Total (Σ)	$\Sigma = 1{,}007$	$\Sigma = 35{,}507$	$\Sigma = 192$	$\Sigma = 2{,}354$	$\Sigma = 7{,}023$

$$r = \frac{n\Sigma XY - \Sigma X \Sigma Y}{\sqrt{[n\Sigma X^2 - (\Sigma X)^2][n\Sigma Y^2 - (\Sigma Y^2)]}} = \frac{30(7023) - (1007)(192)}{\sqrt{[30(35507) - (1007)^2][30(2354) - (192)^2]}}$$

$$= \frac{210690 - 193344}{\sqrt{(1065210 - 1014049)(70620 - 36864)}} = \frac{17346}{\sqrt{(51161)(33756)}}$$

$$= \frac{17346}{\sqrt{1726990716}} = \frac{17346}{41557} = .42$$

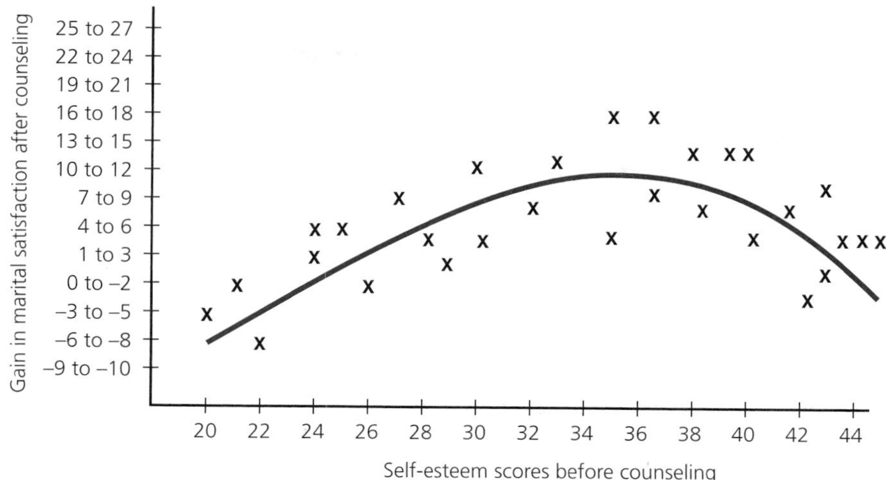

Figure 12.6 *Scatterplot Illustrating the Relationship Between Initial Self-Esteem and Gain in Marital Satisfaction Among Counseling Clients*

Second, it also shows that the relationship is more correctly described as curvilinear—that is, clients with low *or* high self-esteem show less improvement than those with a moderate level of self-esteem (remember, these data are fictional). Pearson r equals .42. The value of eta obtained for these same data is .82, indicating a substantial degree of relationship between the two variables. We have not shown the calculations for eta since they are somewhat more complicated than those for r. The relationship is illustrated by the smoothed curve shown in Figure 12.6.

The researcher calculates the appropriate inference statistic (a t-test for r), as shown, to determine whether $r = .42$ is significant.

$$\text{Standard error of } r = \text{SE}_r = \frac{1}{\sqrt{n-1}}$$

$$= \frac{1}{\sqrt{29}} = .185$$

$$t_r = \frac{r - .00}{\text{SE}_r} = \frac{.42 - .00}{.185}$$

$$= 2.3; p < .01$$

As you can see, it results in an obtained value of 2.3 and a probability of $p < .01$, using a one-tailed test. A one-tailed test is appropriate for r if the direction of the relationship was predicted before examining the data. The probability associated with eta would (presumably) be obtained using a two-tailed test (unless the researcher predicted the shape of the curve from Figure 12.6 before examining the data). An eta of .82 is also statistically significant at $p = .01$, indicating that the relationship is unlikely to be due to the particular sample studied. Whether or not these probabilities are correct depends on whether or not the sample was randomly selected. The 95 percent confidence interval around the obtained value for r is shown in Figure 12.7.

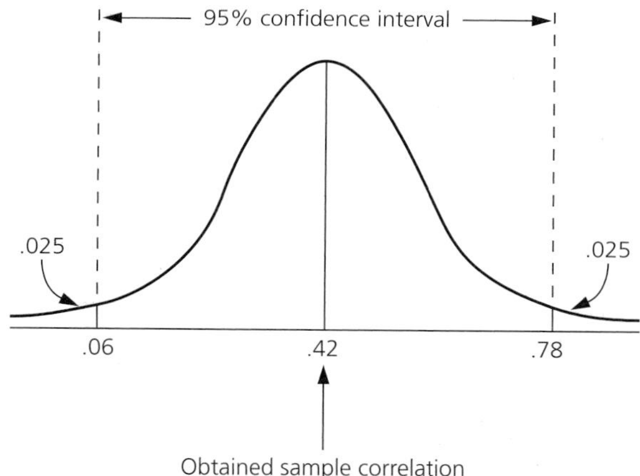

Figure 12.7 *95 Percent Confidence Interval for* $r = .42$

Comparing Groups: Categorical Data

TECHNIQUES

When the data involved are categorical data, groups may be compared by reporting either percentages (or proportions) or frequencies in crossbreak tables. Table 12.5 gives a fictitious example.

TABLE 12.5 *Gender and Political Preference (Percentages)*

	Percentage of Males	Percentage of Females
Democrat	20	50
Republican	70	45
Other	10	5
Total	100	100

TABLE 12.6 *Gender and Political Preference (Numbers)*

	Males	Females
Democrat	2	30
Republican	7	27
Other	1	3

TABLE 12.7 *Teacher Gender and Grade Level Taught: Case 1*

	Grade 4	Grade 5	Grade 6	Grade 7	Total
Male	10	20	20	30	80
Female	40	30	30	20	120
Total	50	50	50	50	200

INTERPRETATION

Once again, we must look at summary statistics—even percentages—carefully. Percentages can be misleading unless the number of cases is also given. At first glance, Table 12.5 may look impressive—until one discovers that the data in it represent 60 females and only 10 males. In crossbreak form, Table 12.6 represents the actual *numbers,* as opposed to percentages, of individuals.

Table 12.7 illustrates a fictitious relationship between teacher gender and grade level taught. As you can see, the largest number of male teachers is to be found in grade 7, and the largest number of female teachers is to be found in grade 4. Here, too, however, we must ask: How much difference must there be between these frequencies for us to consider them important? One of the limitations of categorical data is that such evaluations are even harder than with quantitative data. One possible approach is to examine prior experience or knowledge. Table 12.7 does suggest a trend toward an increasingly larger proportion of male teachers in the higher grades—but, again, is the trend substantial enough to be considered important?

TABLE 12.8 *Teacher Gender and Grade Level Taught: Case 2*

	Grade 4	Grade 5	Grade 6	Grade 7	Total
Male	22	22	25	28	97
Female	28	28	25	22	103
Total	50	50	50	50	200

The data in Table 12.8 show the same trend, but the pattern is much less striking. Perhaps prior experience or research shows (somehow) that gender differences become important whenever the within-grade difference is more than 10 percent (or a frequency of 5 in these data). Such knowledge is seldom available, however, which leads us to consider the summary statistic (similar to the correlation coefficient) known as the *contingency coefficient* (see Chapter 11). To use it, however, remember that the data *must* be presented in crossbreak tables. Calculating the contingency coefficient is easily done by hand or by computer. You will recall that this statistic is not as straightforward in interpretation as the correlation coefficient, since its interpretation depends on the number of cells in the crossbreak table. Nevertheless, we recommend its use.

Perhaps because of the difficulties mentioned, most research reports using percentages or crossbreaks rely on inference techniques to evaluate the magnitude of relationships. In the absence of random sampling, their use suffers from the same liabilities as with quantitative data. When analyzing categorical data, therefore, we recommend the following:

Recommendation 17: Whenever possible, place all data into crossbreak tables.

Recommendation 18: To clarify the importance of relationships, patterns, or trends, calculate a contingency coefficient.

Recommendation 19: Do not use tests of statistical significance to evaluate the magnitude of relationships. Use them, as intended, to judge generalizability.

Recommendation 20: Unless a random sample was used, interpret probabilities and/or significance levels as crude indices, not as precise values.

Example. Once again, let us consider an example to illustrate an analysis, this time involving categorical data when comparing groups. Let us return to Tables 12.7 and 12.8 to illustrate the major recommendations for analyzing categorical data. We shall consider Table 12.7 first. Because there are 50 teachers, or 25 percent, of the total

TABLE 12.9 ***Crossbreak Table Showing Teacher Gender and Grade Level with Expected Frequencies Added (Data from Table 12.7)***

	Grade 4	Grade 5	Grade 6	Grade 7	Total
Male	10 (20)	20 (20)	20 (20)	30 (20)	80
Female	40 (30)	30 (30)	30 (30)	20 (30)	120
Total	50	50	50	50	200

of 200 teachers at each grade level (4–7), we would expect that there would be 25 percent of the total number of male teachers and 25 percent of the total number of female teachers at *each* grade level as well. Out of the total of 200 teachers, 80 are male and 120 are female. Hence, the expected frequency for male teachers at each of the grade levels would be 20 (25 percent of 80), and for female teachers 30 (25 percent of 120). These expected frequencies are shown in parentheses in Table 12.9. We then calculate the contingency coefficient, which equals .28.

By referring to Table 11.1 in Chapter 11, we estimate that the upper limit for a 2 by 4 table (which we have here) is approximately .80. Accordingly, a contingency coefficient of .28 indicates only a slight degree of relationship. As a result, we would not recommend testing for significance. Were we to do so, however, we would find by looking in a chi-square probability table that three degrees of freedom requires a chi-square value of 7.81 to be considered significant at the .05 level. Our obtained value for chi square was 16.66, indicating that the small relationship we have discovered probably does exist in the population from which the sample was drawn.* This is a good example of the difference between statistical and practical significance. Our obtained correlation of .28 is statistically significant but practically insignificant. A correlation of .28 would be considered by most researchers as having little practical importance.

If we carry out the same analysis for Table 12.8, the resulting contingency coefficient is .10. Such a correlation is, for all practical purposes, meaningless, but should we (for some reason) wish to see if it was statistically significant, we would find that it is not significant at the .05 level (the chi-square value = 1.98, far below the 7.82 needed for significance).

Again, the calculations from Table 12.9 are not difficult. Here are the steps we followed:

1. For the first cell (Grade 4, male), subtract E from O: $= 10 - 20 = -10$
2. Square the result: $(O - E)^2 = (-10)^2 = 100$
3. Divide the result by E:

$$\Sigma \frac{(O - E)^2}{E} = \frac{100}{20} = 5.00$$

O	E	O − E	(O − E)²	(O − E)²/E	
10	20	−10	100	100/20	= 5.00
40	30	10	100	100/30	= 3.33
20	20	0	0	0	= 0
30	30	0	0	0	= 0
20	20	0	0	0	= 0
30	30	0	0	0	= 0
30	20	10	100	100/20	= 5.00
20	30	−10	100	100/30	= 3.33

4. Repeat this process for each cell. (Be sure to include *all* cells.)
5. Add the results of all cells:

$$5.00 + 3.33 + 5.00 + 3.33 = 16.66 = \chi^2$$

6. To calculate the contingency coefficient, we used the formula:

$$C = \sqrt{\frac{\chi^2}{\chi^2 + n}} = \sqrt{\frac{16.66}{16.66 + 200}} = .28$$

*Assuming the sample is random.

Relating Variables Within a Group: Categorical Data

Although the preceding section involves comparing groups, the reasoning also applies to hypotheses that examine relationships among categorical variables within just one group. A moment's thought shows why. The procedures available to us are the same—percentages or crossbreak tables. Suppose our hypothesis is that among college students, gender is related to political preference. To test this we must divide the data we obtain from this group by gender and political preference. This gives us the crossbreak in Table 12.6. Because all such hypotheses must be tested by dividing people into groups, the statistical analysis is the same whether seen as one group, subdivided, or as two or more different groups.

A summary of the most commonly used statistical techniques, both descriptive and inferential, as used with quantitative and categorical data, is shown in Table 12.10.

MORE ABOUT RESEARCH

Interpreting Statistics

- Suppose a researcher found a correlation of .08 between drinking grapefruit juice and subsequent incidence of arthritis to be statistically significant. Is that possible? (Yes, it is quite possible. If the sample had been randomly selected, and the sample size was around 500, a correlation of .08 would be statistically significant at the .05 level. But because of the small relationship—and many uncontrolled variables—we would not stop drinking grapefruit juice based on an *r* of only .08!)
- Suppose an early intervention program was found to increase IQ scores on average by 12 points, but that this was not statistically significant at the .05 level. How much attention would you give to this report? (We would pay considerable attention; 12 IQ points is a lot and could be very important if confirmed in replications. Evidently the sample size was rather small.)
- Suppose the difference in polling preference for a particular candidate was found to be 52 percent for the Democrat as opposed to 48 percent for the Republican, with a margin of error of 2 percent at the .05 level. Would you consider this difference important? (One way of reporting such results is that the probability of the difference being due to chance is less than .01.* In addition, a difference of only 4 points is of great practical importance since the winner in a two-person election needs only 51 percent of the vote to win. A very similar prediction proved wrong in the 1948 presidential election, when Truman defeated Dewey. The usual explanations are that the sample was not random and thus not representative, and/or that a lot of people changed their minds before they entered the voting booth.)

*The SE of each percentage must be 2.00 (the margin of error) divided by 1.96 (the number of standard deviations required at the 5 percent level), or approximately 1.00. The standard error of the difference (SED) equals the square root of $(1^2 + 1^2)$ or 1.4. The difference between 48 percent and 52 percent—4 percent—divided by 1.4 (the SED) equals 2.86, which yields a probability of less than .01.

TABLE 12.10 ***Summary of Commonly Used Statistical Techniques***

	DATA	
	Quantitative	**Categorical**
Two or more groups are compared:		
Descriptive Statistics	• Frequency polygons • Averages • Spreads • Effect size	• Percentages • Bar graphs • Pie charts • Crossbreak (contingency) tables
Inferential Statistics	• *t*-test for means • ANOVA • ANCOVA • MANOVA • MANCOVA • Confidence intervals • Mann-Whitney *U* test • Kruskal-Wallis ANOVA • Sign test • Friedman two-way ANOVA	• chi square • *t*-test for proportions
Relationships among variables are studied within one group:		
Descriptive Statistics	• Scatterplot • Correlation coefficient (*r*) • eta	• Crossbreak (contingency) tables • Contingency coefficient
Inferential Statistics	• *t*-test for *r* • Confidence intervals	• chi square • *t*-test for proportions

A Recap of Recommendations

You may have noticed that many of our recommendations are essentially the same, regardless of the method of statistical analysis involved. To stress their importance, we want to state them again here, all together, phrased more generally.

We recommend that researchers:

- Use graphic techniques before calculating numerical summary indices. Pay particular attention to outliers.
- Use both graphs and summary indices to interpret results of a study.
- Make use of external criteria (such as prior experience or scores of known groups) to assess the magnitude of a relationship whenever such criteria are available.
- Use professional consensus when evaluating the magnitude of an effect size (including correlation coefficients).
- Consider using inferential statistics only if you can make a convincing case for the importance of the size of the relationship found in the sample.
- Use tests of statistical significance only to evaluate generalizability, not to evaluate the magnitude of relationships.
- When random sampling has not occurred, treat probabilities as approximations or crude indices rather than as precise values.
- Report confidence intervals rather than, or in addition to, significance levels whenever possible.

We also want to make a final recommendation involving the distinction between parametric and nonparametric statistics. Since the calculation of statistics has now become rather easy and quick owing to the availability of many computer programs, we conclude with the following suggestion to researchers:

- Use *both* parametric and nonparametric techniques to analyze data. When the results are consistent, interpretation will thereby be strengthened. When the results are not consistent, discuss possible reasons.

Go back to the **INTERACTIVE AND APPLIED LEARNING** feature at the beginning of the chapter for a listing of interactive and applied activities. Go to the **Online Learning Center** at **www.mhhe.com/fraenkel9e** to take quizzes, practice with key terms, and review chapter content.

Main Points

APPROACHES TO RESEARCH

- A good deal of educational research is done in one of two ways: either two or more groups are compared, or variables within one group are related.
- The data in a study may be either quantitative or categorical.

COMPARING GROUPS USING QUANTITATIVE DATA

- When comparing two or more groups using quantitative data, researchers can compare them through frequency polygons, calculation of averages, and calculation of spreads.
- We recommend, therefore, constructing frequency polygons, using data on the means of known groups, calculating effect sizes, and reporting confidence intervals when comparing quantitative data from two or more groups.

RELATING VARIABLES WITHIN A GROUP USING QUANTITATIVE DATA

- When researchers examine a relationship between quantitative variables within a single group, the appropriate techniques are the scatterplot and the correlation coefficient.

- Because a scatterplot illustrates all the data visually, researchers should begin their analysis of data obtained from a single group by constructing a scatterplot.
- Therefore, we recommend constructing scatterplots and using both scatterplots and correlation coefficients when relating variables involving quantitative data within a single group.

COMPARING GROUPS USING CATEGORICAL DATA

- When the data are categorical, groups can be compared by reporting either percentages or frequencies in crossbreak tables.
- It is a good idea to report *both* the percentage and the number of cases in a crossbreak table, as percentages alone can be misleading.
- Therefore, we recommend constructing crossbreak tables and calculating contingency coefficients when comparing categorical data involving two or more groups.

RELATING VARIABLES WITHIN A GROUP USING CATEGORICAL DATA

- When you are examining relationships among categorical data within one group, we again recommend constructing crossbreak tables and calculating contingency coefficients.

TWO FINAL RECOMMENDATIONS

- When tests of statistical significance can be applied, it is recommended that they be used to evaluate generalizability only, not to evaluate the magnitude of relationships. Confidence intervals should be reported in addition to significance levels.
- Both parametric and nonparametric techniques should be used to analyze data rather than either one alone.

Key Terms

correlation coefficient 251
curvilinear relationship 251
effect size (ES) 248
inferential statistics 248
linear relationship 251
scatterplot 251
straight-line relationship 251

For Discussion

1. Give some examples of how the results of a study might be significant statistically yet unimportant educationally. Could the reverse be true?
2. Are there times when a slight difference in means (e.g., an effect size of less than .50) might be important? Explain your answer.
3. When comparing groups, the use of frequency polygons helps us decide which measure of central tendency is the most appropriate to calculate. How so?
4. Why is it important to consider outliers in scatterplots?
5. "When analyzing data obtained from two groups, the first thing researchers should do is construct a frequency polygon of each group's scores." Why is this important—or is it?
6. Why is it important to use *both* graphs and summary indices (e.g., the means) to interpret the results of a study—or is it?
7. A picture, supposedly, is worth a thousand words. Would this statement also apply to analyzing the results of a study? Can numbers alone ever give a complete picture of a study's results? Why or why not?

Research Exercise 12: Statistics in Perspective

Using Problem Sheet 12, describe any change you would make in techniques to be used from those you described in Problem Sheets 10 and 11. Then tell how you would evaluate the magnitude of any relationship you might find.

Problem Sheet 12

Statistics in Perspective

1. My research question is:

   ____

   ____

   ____

   ____

2. Are there changes in the statistics you indicated on Problem Sheets 10 or 11? If so, explain:

   ____

   ____

   ____

   ____

   ____

3. I would evaluate the magnitude of any relationship(s) I find by:

   ____

   ____

   ____

   ____

An electronic version of this Problem Sheet that you can fill in and print, save, or e-mail is available on the Online Learning Center at www.mhhe.com/fraenkel9e.

PART 4

Quantitative Research Methodologies

In Part 4, we begin a more detailed discussion of some of the methodologies that educational researchers use. We concentrate here on quantitative research, with a separate chapter devoted to group-comparison experimental research, single-subject experimental research, correlational research, causal-comparative research, and survey research. In each chapter, we not only discuss the method in some detail, but we also provide examples of published studies in which the researchers used one of these methods. We conclude each chapter with an analysis of a particular study's strengths and weaknesses.

13 Experimental Research

The Uniqueness of Experimental Research

Essential Characteristics of Experimental Research

Comparison of Groups

Manipulation of the Independent Variable

Randomization

Control of Extraneous Variables

Group Designs in Experimental Research

Poor Experimental Designs

True Experimental Designs

Quasi-Experimental Designs

Factorial Designs

Control of Threats to Internal Validity: A Summary

Evaluating the Likelihood of a Threat to Internal Validity in Experimental Studies

Control of Experimental Treatments

An Example of Experimental Research

Analysis of the Study

Purpose/Justification

Prior Research

Definitions

Hypotheses

Sample

Instrumentation

Procedures/Internal Validity

Data Analysis and Results

Discussion/Interpretation

OBJECTIVES Studying this chapter should enable you to:

- Describe briefly the purpose of experimental research.
- Describe the basic steps involved in conducting an experiment.
- Describe two ways in which experimental research differs from other forms of educational research.
- Explain the difference between random assignment and random selection and the importance of each.
- Explain what is meant by the phrase "manipulation of variables" and describe three ways in which such manipulation can occur.
- Distinguish between examples of weak and strong experimental designs and draw diagrams of such designs.
- Identify various threats to internal validity associated with different experimental designs.
- Explain three ways in which various threats to internal validity in experimental research can be controlled.
- Explain how matching can be used to equate groups in experimental studies.
- Describe briefly the purpose of factorial and counterbalanced designs and draw diagrams of such designs.
- Describe briefly the purpose of a time-series design and draw a diagram of this design.
- Describe briefly how to assess probable threats to internal validity in an experimental study.
- Recognize an experimental study when you see one in the literature.

INTERACTIVE AND APPLIED LEARNING After, or while, reading this chapter:

Go to the Online Learning Center at www.mhhe.com/fraenkel9e to:

- Learn More About What Constitutes an Experiment

Go to your online Student Mastery Activities book to do the following activities:

- Activity 13.1: Group Experimental Research Questions
- Activity 13.2: Designing an Experiment
- Activity 13.3: Characteristics of Experimental Research
- Activity 13.4: Random Selections vs. Random Assignment

Does team-teaching improve the achievement of students in high school social studies classes? Abigail Johnson, the principal of a large high school in Minneapolis, Minnesota, having heard encouraging remarks about the idea at a recent educational conference, wants to find out. Accordingly, she asks some of her eleventh-grade world history teachers to participate in an experiment. Three teachers are to combine their classes into one large group. These teachers are to work as a team, sharing the planning, teaching, and evaluation of these students. Three other teachers are assigned to teach a class in the same subject individually, with the usual arrangement of one teacher per class. The students selected to participate are similar in ability, and the teachers will teach at the same time, using the same curriculum. All are to use the same standardized tests and other assessment instruments, including written tests prepared jointly by the six teachers. Periodically during the semester, Ms. Johnson will compare the scores of the two groups of students on these tests.

This is an example of an experiment—the comparison of a treatment group with a nontreatment group. In this chapter, you will learn about various procedures that researchers use to carry out such experiments, as well as how they try to ensure that it is the experimental treatment rather than some uncontrolled variable that causes the changes in achievement.

Experimental research is one of the most powerful research methodologies that researchers can use. Of the many types of research that might be used, the experiment is the best way to establish cause-and-effect relationships among variables. Yet experiments are not always easy to conduct. In this chapter, we will show you both the power of, and the problems involved in, conducting experiments.

The Uniqueness of Experimental Research

Of all the research methodologies described in this book, **experimental research** is unique in two very important respects: It is the only type of research that directly attempts to influence a particular variable, and when properly applied, it is the best type for testing hypotheses about cause-and-effect relationships. In an experimental study, researchers look at the effect(s) of at least one independent variable on one or more dependent variables. The **independent variable** in experimental research is also frequently referred to as the **experimental**, or **treatment**, **variable**. The **dependent variable**, also known as the **criterion**, or **outcome**, **variable**, refers to the results or outcomes of the study.

The major characteristic of experimental research that distinguishes it from all other types of research is that researchers *manipulate* the independent variable. They decide the nature of the treatment (i.e., what is going to happen to the subjects of the study), to whom it is to be applied, and to what extent. Independent variables frequently manipulated in educational research include methods of instruction, types of assignment, learning materials, rewards given to students, and types of questions asked by teachers. Dependent variables that are frequently studied include achievement, interest in a subject, attention span, motivation, and attitudes toward school.

After the treatment has been administered for an appropriate length of time, researchers observe or measure the groups receiving different treatments (by means of a posttest of some sort) to see if they differ. Another way of saying this is that researchers want to see whether the treatment made a difference. If the average scores of the groups on the posttest do differ and researchers cannot find any sensible alternative explanations for this difference, they can conclude that the treatment did have an effect and is likely the cause of the difference.

Experimental research, therefore, enables researchers to go beyond description and prediction, beyond the identification of relationships, to at least a partial determination of what causes them. Correlational studies may demonstrate a strong relationship between socioeconomic level and academic achievement, for instance, but they cannot demonstrate that improving socioeconomic level will necessarily improve achievement. Only experimental research has this capability. Some actual examples of the kinds of experimental studies that have been conducted by educational researchers are:

- The effect of small classes on instruction.[1]
- The effect of early reading instruction on growth rates of at-risk kindergarteners.[2]
- The use of intensive mentoring to help beginning teachers develop balanced instruction.[3]
- The effect of lotteries on Web survey response rates.[4]
- Introduction of a course on bullying into preservice teacher-training curriculum.[5]
- Using social stories to enhance the interpersonal conflict resolution skills of children with learning disabilities.[6]
- Improving the self-concept of students through the use of hypnosis.[7]

Essential Characteristics of Experimental Research

The word **experiment** has a long and illustrious history in the annals of research. It has often been hailed as the most powerful method that exists for studying cause and effect. Its origins go back to the very beginnings of history when, for example, primeval humans first experimented with ways to produce fire. One can imagine countless trial-and-error attempts on their part before achieving success by sparking rocks or by spinning wooden spindles in dry leaves. Much of the success of modern science is due to carefully designed and meticulously implemented experiments.

The basic idea underlying all experimental research is really quite simple: Try something and systematically observe what happens. Formal experiments consist of two basic conditions. First, at least two (but often more) conditions or methods are *compared* to assess the effect(s) of particular conditions or "treatments" (the independent variable). Second, the independent variable is directly *manipulated* by the researcher. Change is planned for and deliberately manipulated to study its effect(s) on one or more outcomes (the dependent variable). Let us discuss some important characteristics of experimental research in a bit more detail.

COMPARISON OF GROUPS

An experiment usually involves two groups of subjects, an experimental group and a control or a comparison group, although it is possible to conduct an experiment with only one group (by providing all treatments to the same subjects) or with three or more groups. The **experimental group** receives a treatment of some sort (such as a new textbook or a different method of teaching), while the **control group** receives no treatment (or the **comparison group** receives a different treatment). The control or the comparison group is crucially important in all experimental research, for it enables the researcher to determine whether the treatment has had an effect or whether one treatment is more effective than another.

Historically, a pure control group is one that receives no treatment at all. While this is often the case in medical or psychological research, it is rarely true in educational research. The control group almost always receives a different treatment of some sort. Some educational researchers, therefore, refer to comparison groups rather than to control groups.

Consider an example. Suppose a researcher wished to study the effectiveness of a new method of teaching science. He or she would have the students in the experimental group taught by the new method, but the students in the comparison group would continue to be taught by their teacher's usual method. The researcher would not administer the new method to the experimental group and have a control group *do nothing*. Any method of instruction would likely be more effective than no method at all!

MANIPULATION OF THE INDEPENDENT VARIABLE

The second essential characteristic of all experiments is that the researcher actively *manipulates* the independent variables. What does this mean? Simply put, it means that the researcher deliberately and directly determines what forms the independent variable will take and then which group will get which form. For example, if the independent variable in a study is the amount of enthusiasm an instructor displays, a researcher might train two teachers to display different amounts of enthusiasm as they teach their classes.

Although many independent variables in education can be manipulated, many others cannot. Examples of independent variables that can be manipulated include teaching method, type of counseling, learning activities, assignments given, and materials used; examples of independent variables that cannot be manipulated include gender, ethnicity, age, and religious preference. Researchers can manipulate the kinds of learning activities to which students are exposed in a classroom, but they cannot manipulate, say, religious preference—that is, students cannot be "made into" Protestants, Catholics, Jews, or Muslims, for example, to serve the purposes of a study. To manipulate a variable, researchers must decide who is to get something and when, where, and how they will get it.

The independent variable in an experimental study may be established in several ways—either (1) one form of the variable versus another; (2) presence versus absence of a particular form; or (3) varying degrees of the same form. An example of (1) would be a study comparing the inquiry method with the lecture method of instruction in teaching chemistry. An example of (2) would be a study comparing the use of PowerPoint slides versus no PowerPoint slides in teaching statistics. An example of (3) would be a study comparing the effects of different specified amounts of teacher enthusiasm on student attitudes toward mathematics. In both (1) and (2), the variable (method) is clearly categorical. In (3), a variable that in actuality is quantitative (*degree* of enthusiasm) is treated as categorical (the effects of only specified *amounts* of enthusiasm will be studied) in order for the researcher to manipulate (i.e., to control for) the amount of enthusiasm.

RANDOMIZATION

An important aspect of many experiments is the random assignment of subjects to groups. Although there are certain kinds of experiments in which random assignment is not possible, researchers try to use randomization whenever feasible. It is a crucial ingredient in the best kinds of experiments. Random assignment is similar, but not identical, to the concept of random selection we discussed in Chapter 6. **Random assignment** means that every individual who is participating in an experiment has an equal chance of being assigned to any of the experimental or control conditions being compared. **Random selection**, on the other hand, means that every member of a population has an equal chance of being selected to be a member of the sample. Under random assignment, each member of the sample is given a number (arbitrarily), and a table of random numbers (see Chapter 6) is then used to select the members of the experimental and control groups.

Three things should be noted about the random assignment of subjects to groups. First, it takes place before the experiment begins. Second, it is a *process* of assigning or distributing individuals to groups, not a result of such distribution. This means that you cannot look at two groups that have already been formed and be able to tell, just by looking, whether or not they were formed randomly. Third, the use of random assignment allows the researcher to form groups that, right at the beginning of the study, are *equivalent*—that is, they differ only by chance in any variables of interest. In other words, random assignment is intended to eliminate the threat of **extraneous**, or additional, **variables**—not only those of which researchers are aware but also those of which they are not aware—that might affect the outcome of the study. This is the beauty and the power of random assignment. It is one of the reasons why experiments are, in general, more effective than other types of research for assessing cause-and-effect relationships.

This last statement is tempered, of course, by the realization that groups formed through random assignment may still differ somewhat. Random assignment ensures only that groups are equivalent (or at least as equivalent as human beings can make them) at the beginning of an experiment.

Furthermore, random assignment is no guarantee of equivalent groups unless both groups are sufficiently large. No one would expect random assignment to result in equivalence if only five subjects were assigned to each group, for example. There are no rules for determining how large groups must be, but most researchers are uncomfortable relying on random assignment with fewer than 40 subjects in each group.

Control of Extraneous Variables

Researchers in an experimental study have an opportunity to exercise far more control than in most other forms of research. They determine the treatment (or treatments), select the sample, assign individuals to groups, decide which group will get the treatment, try to control other factors besides the treatment that might influence the outcome of the study, and then (finally) observe or measure the effect of the treatment on the groups when the treatment is completed.

In Chapter 9, we introduced the idea of internal validity and discussed several kinds of threats to internal validity. It is very important for researchers conducting an experimental study to do their best to **control** for—that is, to eliminate or to minimize the possible effect of—these threats. If researchers are unsure whether another variable might be the cause of a result observed in a study, they cannot be sure what the cause really is. For example, if a researcher attempted to compare the effects of two different methods of instruction on student attitudes toward history but did not make sure that the groups involved were equivalent in ability, then ability might be a possible alternative explanation (rather than the difference in methods) for any differences in attitudes of the groups found on a posttest.

In particular, researchers who conduct experimental studies try their best to control any and all subject characteristics that might affect the outcome of the study. They do this by ensuring that the two groups are as equivalent as possible on all variables other than the one or ones being studied (i.e., the independent variables).

How do researchers minimize or eliminate threats due to subject characteristics? Many ways exist. Here are some of the most common:

Randomization: As we mentioned before, if subjects can be randomly assigned to the various groups involved in an experimental study, researchers can assume that the groups are equivalent. This is the best way to ensure that the effects of one or more possible extraneous variables have been controlled.

Holding certain variables constant: The idea here is to eliminate the possible effects of a variable by removing it from the study. For example, if a researcher suspects that gender might influence the outcomes of a study, she could control for it by restricting the subjects of the study to females and by excluding all males. The variable of gender, in other words, is held constant. However, there is a cost involved (as there almost always is) for this control, as the generalizability of the results of the study are correspondingly reduced.

Building the variable into the design: This solution involves building the variable(s) into the study to assess their effects. It is the exact opposite of the previous idea. Using the preceding example, the researcher would include *both* females and males (as distinct groups) in the design of the study and then analyze the effects of *both* gender and method on outcomes.

Matching: Often pairs of subjects can be matched on certain variables of interest. If a researcher felt that age, for example, might affect the outcome of a study, he might endeavor to match students according to their ages and then assign one member of each pair (randomly if possible) to each of the comparison groups.

Using subjects as their own controls: When subjects are used as their own controls, their performance under both (or all) treatments is compared. Thus, the same students might be taught algebra units first by an inquiry method and later by a lecture method. Another example is the assessment of an individual's behavior during a period of time before and after a treatment is implemented to see whether changes in behavior occur.

Using analysis of covariance: As mentioned in Chapter 11, analysis of covariance can be used to equate groups statistically on the basis of a pretest or other variables. The posttest scores of the subjects in each group are then adjusted accordingly.

We will shortly show you a number of research designs that illustrate how several of these controls can be implemented in an experimental study.

Group Designs in Experimental Research

The **design** of an experiment can take a variety of forms. Some of the designs we present in this section are better than others, however. Why "better"? Because of the various threats to internal validity identified in Chapter 9: Good designs control many of these threats, while poor designs control only a few. The quality of an experiment depends on how well the various threats to internal validity are controlled.

POOR EXPERIMENTAL DESIGNS

Designs that are "weak" do not have built-in controls for threats to internal validity. In addition to the independent variable, there are a number of other plausible explanations for any outcomes that occur. As a result, any researcher who uses one of these designs has difficulty assessing the effectiveness of the independent variable.

The One-Shot Case Study. In the **one-shot case study design**, a single group is exposed to a treatment or event and a dependent variable is subsequently observed (measured) to assess the effect of the treatment. A diagram of this design is as follows:

The One-Shot Case Study Design

X	*O*
Treatment	Observation (Dependent variable)

The symbol *X* represents exposure of the group to the treatment of interest, while *O* refers to observation (measurement) of the dependent variable. The placement of the symbols from left to right indicates the order in time of *X* and *O*. As you can see, the treatment, *X*, comes before observation of the dependent variable, *O*.

Suppose a researcher wishes to see if a new textbook increases student interest in history. He uses the textbook (*X*) for a semester and then measures student interest (*O*) with an attitude scale. A diagram of this example is shown in Figure 13.1.

The most obvious weakness of this design is its absence of any control. The researcher has no way of knowing if the results obtained at *O* (as measured by the attitude scale) are due to treatment *X* (the textbook). The design does not provide for any comparison, so the researcher cannot compare the treatment results (as measured by the attitude scale) with the same group before using the new textbook, or with those of another group using a different textbook. Because the group has not been pretested in any way, the researcher knows nothing about what the group was like before using the text.

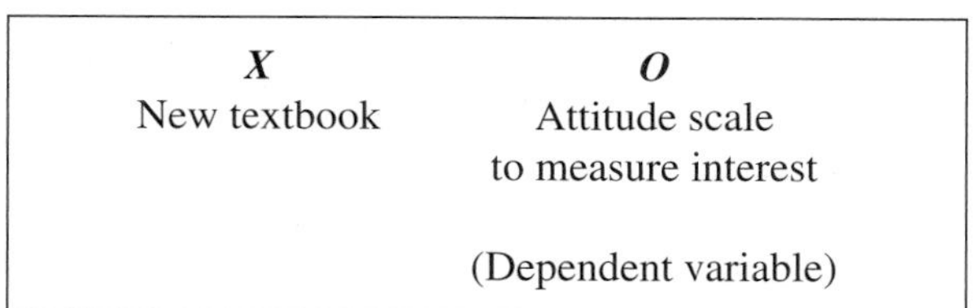

Figure 13.1 *Example of a One-Shot Case Study Design*

Thus, he does not know whether the treatment had *any* effect at all. It is quite possible that the students who use the new textbook *will* indicate very favorable attitudes toward history. But the question remains, were these attitudes produced by the new textbook? Unfortunately, the one-shot case study does not help us answer this question. To remedy this design, a comparison could be made with another group of students who had the same course content presented in the regular textbook. (We shall show you just such a design shortly.) Fortunately, the flaws in the one-shot design are so well known that it is seldom used in educational research.

The One-Group Pretest-Posttest Design. In the **one-group pretest-posttest design**, a single group is measured or observed not only after being exposed to a treatment of some sort, but also before. A diagram of this design is as follows:

The One-Group Pretest-Posttest Design

O	*X*	*O*
Pretest	Treatment	Posttest

Consider an example of this design. A principal wants to assess the effects of weekly counseling sessions on the attitudes of certain "hard-to-reach" students in her school. She asks the counselors in the program to meet once a week with these students for a period of 10 weeks, during which sessions the students are encouraged to express their feelings and concerns. She uses a 20-item scale to measure student attitudes toward school both immediately before and after the 10-week period. Figure 13.2 presents a diagram of the design of the study.

This design is better than the one-shot case study (the researcher at least knows whether any change occurred), but it is still weak. Nine uncontrolled-for threats to

O	*X*	*O*
Pretest: 20-item attitude scale completed by students (Dependent variable)	Treatment: 10 weeks of counseling	Posttest: 20-item attitude scale completed by students (Dependent variable)

Figure 13.2 *Example of a One-Group Pretest-Posttest Design*

internal validity exist that might also explain the results on the posttest. They are history, maturation, instrument decay, data collector characteristics, data collector bias, testing, statistical regression, attitude of subjects, and implementation. Any or all of these may influence the outcome of the study. The researcher would not know if any differences between the pretest and the posttest are due to the treatment or to one or more of these threats. To remedy this, a comparison group, which does not receive the treatment, could be added. Then if a change in attitude occurs between the pretest and the posttest, the researcher has reason to believe that it was caused by the treatment (symbolized by *X*).

The Static-Group Comparison Design.

In the **static-group comparison design**, two already existing, or intact, groups are used. These are sometimes referred to as *static groups,* hence the name for the design. This design is sometimes called a **nonequivalent control group design**. A diagram of this design is as follows:

The Static-Group Comparison Design

X	*O*
	O

The dashed line indicates that the two groups being compared are already formed—that is, the subjects are not randomly assigned to the two groups. *X* symbolizes the experimental treatment. The blank space in the design indicates that the "control" group does not receive the experimental treatment; it may receive a different treatment or no treatment at all. The two *O*s are placed exactly vertical to each other, indicating that the observation or measurement of the two groups occurs at the same time.

Consider again the example used to illustrate the one-shot case study design. We could apply the static-group comparison design to this example. The researcher would (1) find two intact groups (two classes), (2) assign the new textbook (*X*) to one of the classes but have the other class use the regular textbook, and then (3) measure the degree of interest of all students in both classes at the same time (e.g., at the end of the semester). Figure 13.3 presents a diagram of this example.

Although this design provides better control over history, maturation, testing, and regression threats,* it is more vulnerable not only to mortality and location,† but also, more importantly, to the possibility of differential subject characteristics.

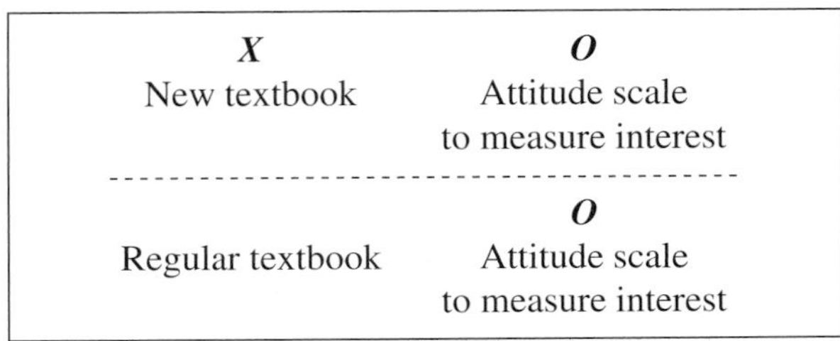

Figure 13.3 *Example of a Static-Group Comparison Design*

The Static-Group Pretest-Posttest Design.

The **static-group pretest-posttest design** differs from the static-group comparison design only in that a pretest is given to both groups. A diagram for this design is as follows:

The Static-Group Pretest-Posttest Design

O	*X*	*O*
O		*O*

In analyzing the data, each individual's pretest score is subtracted from his or her posttest score, thus permitting analysis of "gain" or "change." While this provides better control of the subject characteristics threat (since it is the *change* in each student that is analyzed), the amount of gain often depends on initial performance; that is, the group scoring higher on the pretest is likely to improve more (or in some cases less), and thus subject characteristics still remains somewhat of a threat. Further, administering a pretest raises the possibility of a testing threat. In the event that the pretest is used to match groups, this design becomes the matching-only pretest-posttest control group design (see p. 275), a much more effective design.

TRUE EXPERIMENTAL DESIGNS

The essential ingredient of a true experimental design is that subjects are randomly assigned to treatment groups. As discussed earlier, random assignment is a powerful technique for controlling the subject characteristics threat to internal validity, a major consideration in educational research.

*History and maturation remain possible threats because the researcher cannot be sure that the two groups have been exposed to the same extraneous events or have the same maturational processes.

†This is because the groups may differ in the number of subjects lost and/or in the kinds of resources provided.

The Randomized Posttest-Only Control Group Design. The **randomized posttest-only control group design** involves two groups, both of which are formed by random assignment. One group receives the experimental treatment while the other does not, and then both groups are posttested on the dependent variable. A diagram of this design is as follows:

The Randomized Posttest-Only Control Group Design

Treatment group	*R*	*X*	*O*
Control group	*R*	*C*	*O*

As before, the symbol *X* represents exposure to the treatment and *O* refers to the measurement of the dependent variable. *R* represents the random assignment of individuals to groups. *C* now represents the control group.

In this design, the control of certain threats is excellent. Through the use of random assignment, the threats of subject characteristics, maturation, and statistical regression are well controlled for. Because none of the subjects in the study are measured twice, testing is not a possible threat. This is perhaps the best of all designs to use in an experimental study, provided there are at least 40 subjects in each group.

There are, unfortunately, some threats to internal validity that are not controlled for by this design. The first is mortality. Because the two groups are similar, we might expect an equal dropout rate from each group. However, exposure to the treatment may cause more individuals in the experimental group to drop out (or stay in) than in the control group. This may result in the two groups becoming dissimilar in terms of their characteristics, which in turn may affect the results on the posttest. For this reason, researchers should always report how many subjects drop out of each group during an experiment. An attitudinal threat is possible. In addition, implementation, data collector bias, location, and history threats may exist. These threats can sometimes be controlled by appropriate modifications to this design.

As an example of this design, consider a hypothetical study in which a researcher investigates the effects of a series of sensitivity training workshops on faculty morale in a large high school district. The researcher randomly selects a sample of 100 teachers from all the teachers in the district. The researcher then (1) randomly assigns the teachers in the district to two groups; (2) exposes one group, but not the other, to the training; and then (3) measures the morale of each group using a questionnaire. Figure 13.4 presents a diagram of this hypothetical experiment.

Again we stress that it is important to keep clear the distinction between random selection and random assignment. Both involve the process of randomization, but for a different purpose. Random selection, you will recall, is intended to provide a representative sample. But it may or may not be accompanied by the random assignment of subjects to groups. Random assignment is intended to equate groups, and often is not accompanied by random selection.

The Randomized Pretest-Posttest Control Group Design. The **randomized pretest-posttest control group design** differs from the randomized posttest-only control group design solely in the use of a pretest. Two groups of subjects are used, with both groups being measured or observed twice. The first measurement serves as the pretest, the second as the posttest.

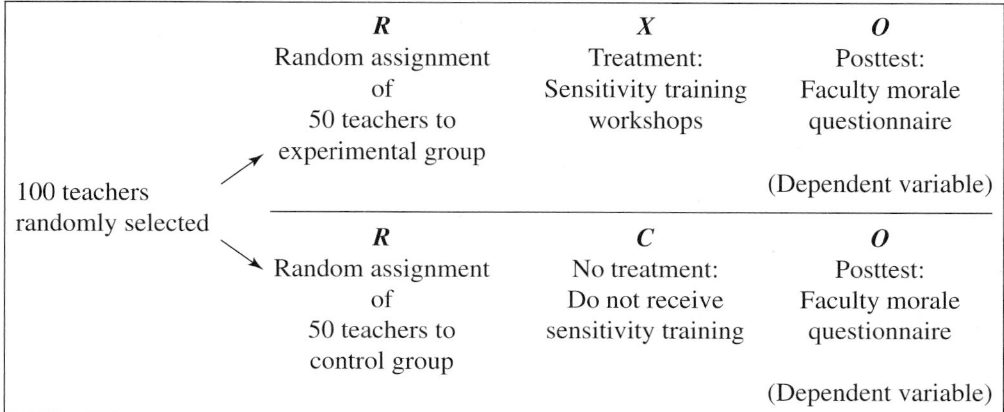

Figure 13.4 *Example of a Randomized Posttest-Only Control Group Design*

Random assignment is used to form the groups. The measurements or observations are collected at the same time for both groups. A diagram of this design follows:

The Randomized Pretest-Posttest Control Group Design

Treatment group	*R*	*O*	*X*	*O*
Control group	*R*	*O*	*C*	*O*

The use of the pretest raises the possibility of a **pretest treatment interaction** threat, since it may "alert" the members of the experimental group, thereby causing them to do better (or more poorly) on the posttest than the members of the control group. A trade-off is that it provides the researcher with a means of checking whether the two groups are really similar—that is, whether random assignment actually succeeded in making the groups equivalent. This is particularly desirable if the number in each group is small (less than 30). If the pretest shows that the groups are not equivalent, the researcher can seek to make them so by using one of the **matching designs** we will discuss shortly. A pretest is also necessary if the amount of change over time is to be assessed.

Let us illustrate this design by using our previous example involving the use of sensitivity workshops. Figure 13.5 presents a diagram of how this design would be used.

The Randomized Solomon Four-Group Design. The **randomized Solomon four-group design** is an attempt to eliminate the possible effect of a pretest. It involves random assignment of subjects to four groups, with two of the groups being pretested and two not. One of the pretested groups and one of the unpretested groups is exposed to the experimental treatment. All four groups are then posttested. A diagram of this design is as follows:

The Randomized Solomon Four-Group Design

Treatment group	*R*	*O*	*X*	*O*
Control group	*R*	*O*	*C*	*O*
Treatment group	*R*		*X*	*O*
Control group	*R*		*C*	*O*

The randomized Solomon four-group design combines the pretest-posttest control group and posttest-only control group designs. The first two groups represent the pretest-posttest control group design, while the last two groups represent the posttest-only control group design. Figure 13.6 presents an example of the randomized Solomon four-group design.

The randomized Solomon four-group design provides the best control of the threats to internal validity that we have discussed. A weakness, however, is that it requires a large sample because subjects must be assigned to four groups. Furthermore, conducting a study involving four groups at the same time requires a considerable amount of energy and effort on the part of the researcher.

Random Assignment with Matching. In an attempt to increase the likelihood that the groups of subjects in an experiment will be equivalent, pairs of individuals may be matched on certain variables.

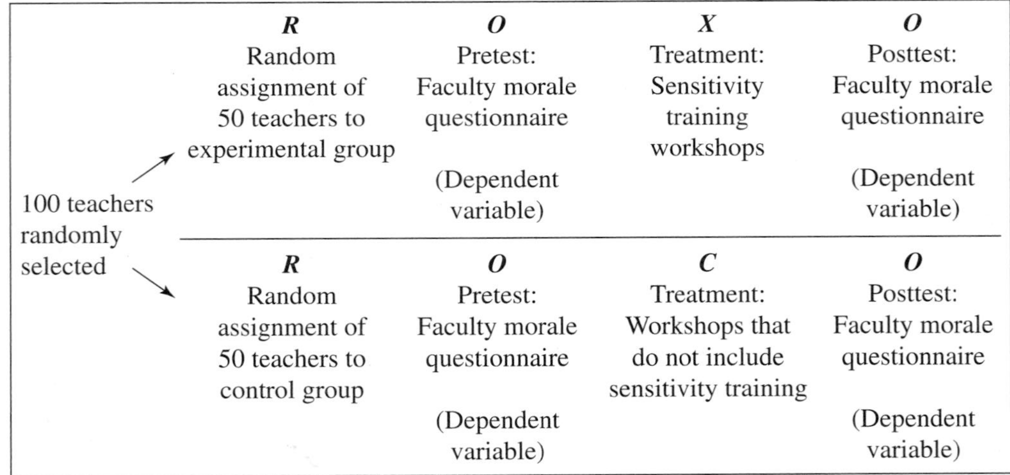

Figure 13.5 *Example of a Randomized Pretest-Posttest Control Group Design*

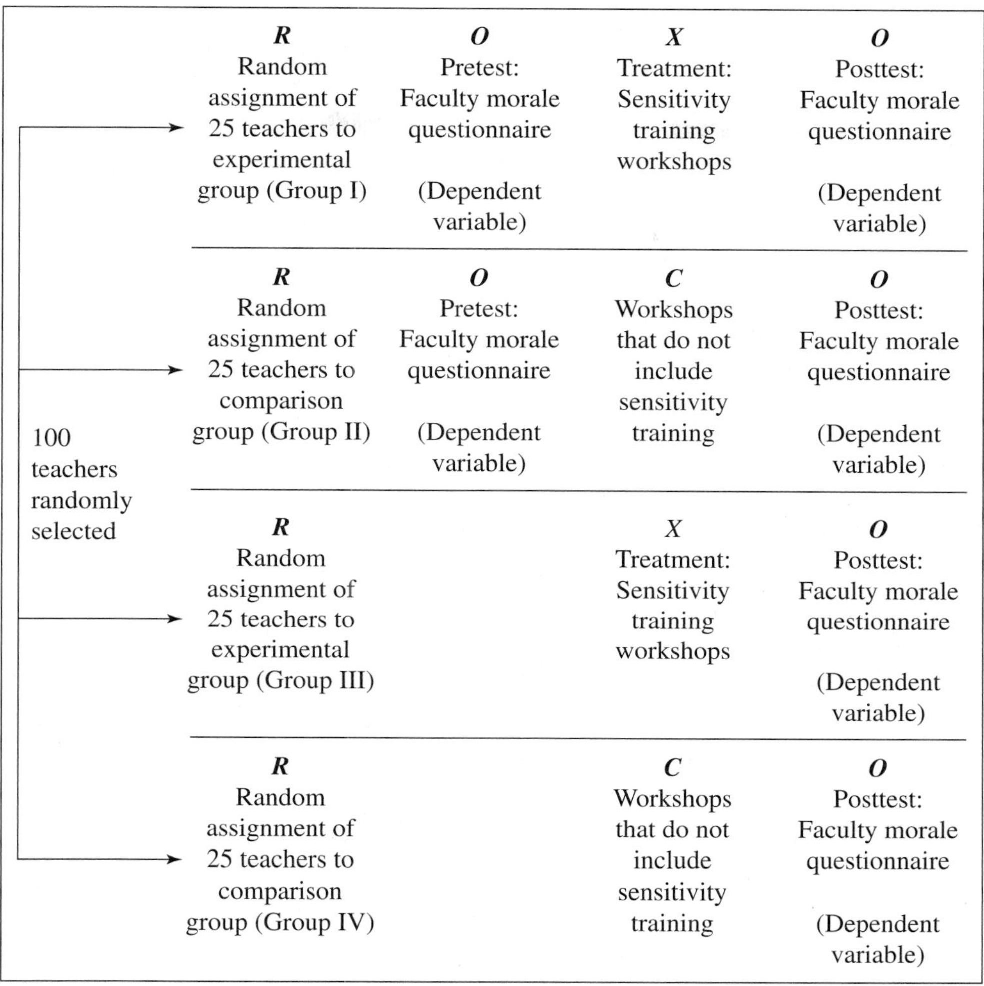

Figure 13.6 *Example of a Randomized Solomon Four-Group Design*

The choice of variables on which to match is based on previous research, theory, and/or the experience of the researcher. The members of each matched pair are then assigned to the experimental and control groups at random. This adaptation can be made to both the posttest-only control group design and the pretest-posttest control group design, although the latter is more common. Diagrams of these designs are:

The Randomized Posttest-Only Control Group Design, Using Matched Subjects

Treatment group	M_r	X	O
Control group	M_r	C	O

The Randomized Pretest-Posttest Control Group Design, Using Matched Subjects

Treatment group	M_r	O	X	O
Control group	M_r	O	C	O

The symbol M_r refers to the fact that the members of each matched pair are randomly assigned to the experimental and control groups.

Although a pretest of the dependent variable is commonly used to provide scores on which to match, a measurement of any variable that shows a substantial relationship to the dependent variable is appropriate. Matching may be done in either or both of two ways: mechanically or statistically. Both require a score for each subject on *each* variable on which subjects are to be matched.

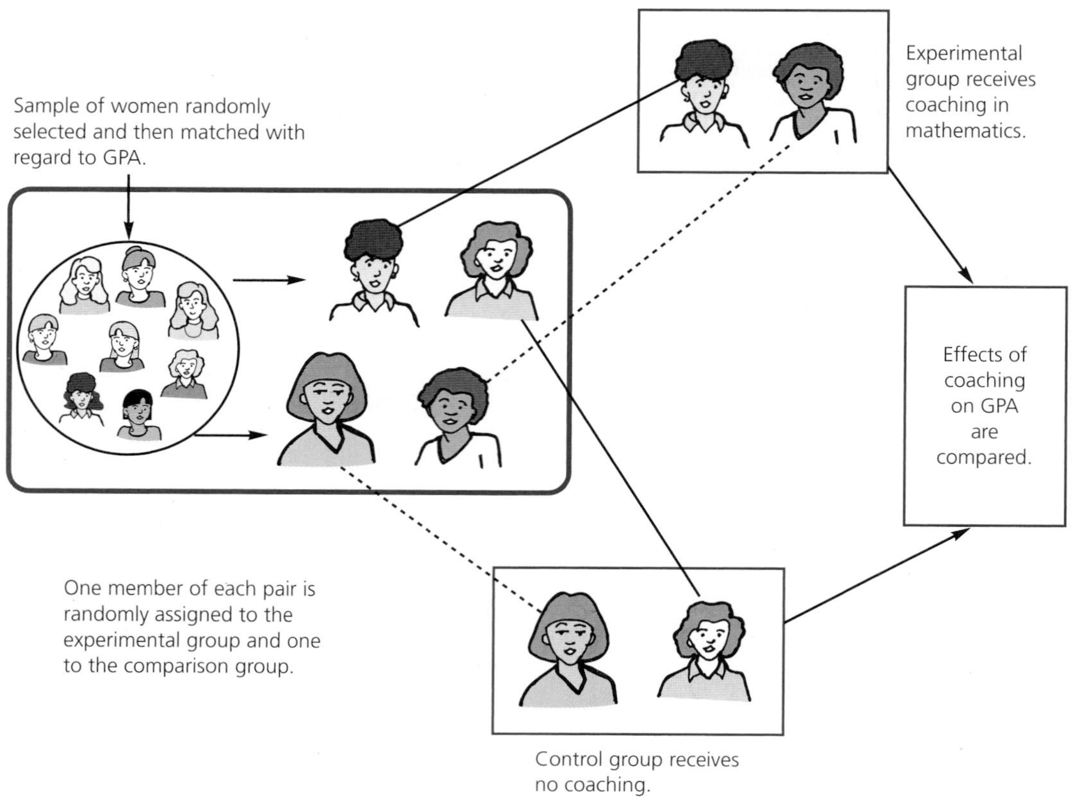
Sample of women randomly selected and then matched with regard to GPA.
Experimental group receives coaching in mathematics.
Effects of coaching on GPA are compared.
One member of each pair is randomly assigned to the experimental group and one to the comparison group.
Control group receives no coaching.

Figure 13.7 *A Randomized Posttest-Only Control Group Design, Using Matched Subjects*

Mechanical matching is a process of pairing two persons whose scores on a particular variable are similar. Two girls, for example, whose mathematics aptitude scores and test anxiety scores are similar might be matched on those variables. After the matching is completed for the entire sample, a check should be made (through the use of frequency polygons) to ensure that the two groups are indeed equivalent on each matching variable. Unfortunately, two problems limit the usefulness of mechanical matching. First, it is very difficult to match on more than two or three variables—people just don't pair up on more than a few characteristics, making it necessary to have a very large initial sample to draw from. Second, in order to match, it is almost inevitable that some subjects must be eliminated from the study because no "matches" for them can be found. Samples then are no longer random even though they may have been before matching occurred.

As an example of a mechanical matching design with random assignment, suppose a researcher is interested in the effects of academic coaching on the grade-point averages (GPA) of low-achieving students in science classes. The researcher randomly selects a sample of 60 students from a population of 125 such students in a local elementary school and matches them by pairs on GPA, finding that she can match 40 of the 60. She then randomly assigns each subject in the resulting 20 pairs to either the experimental or the control group. Figure 13.7 presents a similar example.

Statistical matching,* on the other hand, does not necessitate a loss of subjects, nor does it limit the number of matching variables. Each subject is given a "predicted" score on the dependent variable, based on the correlation between the dependent variable and the variable (or variables) on which the subjects are being matched. The difference between the predicted and actual scores for each individual is then used to compare experimental and control groups.

*__Statistical equating__ is a more common term than its synonym, *statistical matching*. We believe the meaning for the beginning student is better conveyed by the term *matching*.

When a pretest is used as the matching variable, the difference between the predicted and actual score is called a **regressed gain score**. This score is preferable to the more straightforward **gain scores** (posttest minus pretest score for each individual) primarily because it is more reliable. We discuss a similar procedure under partial correlation in Chapter 15.

If mechanical matching is used, one member of each matched pair is randomly assigned to the experimental group, the other to the control group. If statistical matching is used, the sample is divided randomly at the outset, and the statistical adjustments are made after all data have been collected. Although some researchers advocate the use of statistical over mechanical matching, statistical matching is not infallible. Its major weakness is that it assumes that the relationship between the dependent variable and each predictor variable can be properly described by a straight line rather than a curved line. Whichever procedure is used, the researcher must (in this design) rely on random assignment to equate groups on all other variables related to the dependent variable.

QUASI-EXPERIMENTAL DESIGNS

Quasi-experimental designs do not include the use of random assignment. Researchers who employ these designs rely instead on other techniques to control (or at least reduce) threats to internal validity. We shall describe some of these techniques as we discuss several quasi-experimental designs.

The Matching-Only Design. The **matching-only design** differs from random assignment with matching only in the fact that random assignment is not used. The researcher still matches the subjects in the experimental and control groups on certain variables, but he or she has no assurance that they are equivalent on others. Why? Because even though matched, subjects already are in intact groups. This is a serious limitation but often is unavoidable when random assignment is impossible—that is, when intact groups must be used. When several (say, 10 or more) groups are available for a method study and the groups can be randomly assigned to different treatments, this design offers an alternative to random assignment of subjects. After the groups have been randomly assigned to the different treatments, the individuals receiving one treatment are matched with individuals receiving the other treatments. The design shown in Figure 13.7 is still preferred, however.

It should be emphasized that matching (whether mechanical or statistical) is never a substitute for random assignment. Furthermore, the correlation between the matching variable(s) and the dependent variable should be fairly substantial. (We suggest at least .40.) Realize also that unless it is used in conjunction with random assignment, matching controls only for the variable(s) being matched. Diagrams of each of the matching-only control group designs follow:

The Matching-Only Posttest-Only Control Group Design

Treatment group	*M*	*X*	*O*
Control group	*M*	*C*	*O*

The Matching-Only Pretest-Posttest Control Group Design

Treatment group	*M*	*O*	*X*	*O*
Control group	*M*	*O*	*C*	*O*

The *M* in this design means that the subjects in each group have been matched (on certain variables) but not randomly assigned to the groups.

Counterbalanced Designs. **Counterbalanced designs** represent another technique for equating experimental and comparison groups. In this design, each group is exposed to all treatments, however many there are, but in a different order. Any number of treatments may be involved. An example of a diagram for a counterbalanced design involving three treatments is as follows:

A Three-Treatment Counterbalanced Design

Group I	X_1	*O*	X_2	*O*	X_3	*O*
Group II	X_2	*O*	X_3	*O*	X_1	*O*
Group III	X_3	*O*	X_1	*O*	X_2	*O*

This arrangement involves three groups. Group I receives treatment 1 and is posttested, then receives treatment 2 and is posttested, and last receives treatment 3 and is posttested. Group II receives treatment 2 first, then treatment 3, and then treatment 1, being posttested after each treatment. Group III receives treatment 3 first, then treatment 1, followed by treatment 2, also being posttested after each treatment. The order in which the groups receive the treatments should be determined randomly.

How do researchers determine the effectiveness of the various treatments? Simply by comparing the average scores for all groups on the posttest for each

	Study 1		Study 2	
	Weeks 1–4	*Weeks 5–8*	*Weeks 1–4*	*Weeks 5–8*
Group I	Method $X = 12$	Method $Y = 8$	Method $X = 10$	Method $Y = 6$
Group II	Method $Y = 8$	Method $X = 12$	Method $Y = 10$	Method $X = 14$
Overall Means:	Method $X = 12$; Method $Y = 8$		Method $X = 12$; Method $Y = 8$	

Figure 13.8 *Results (Means) from a Study Using a Counterbalanced Design*

treatment. In other words, the averaged posttest score for all groups for treatment 1 can be compared with the averaged posttest score for all groups for treatment 2, and so on, for however many treatments there are.

This design controls well for the subject characteristics threat to internal validity but is particularly vulnerable to multiple-treatment interference—that is, performance during a particular treatment may be affected by one or more of the previous treatments. Consequently, the results of any study in which the researcher has used a counterbalanced design must be examined carefully. Consider the two sets of hypothetical data shown in Figure 13.8.

The interpretation in study 1 is clear: Method *X* is superior for both groups regardless of sequence and to the same degree. The interpretation in study 2, however, is much more complex. Overall, method *X* appears superior, and by the same amount as in study 1. In both studies, the overall mean for *X* is 12, while for *Y* it is 8. In study 2, however, it appears that the difference between *X* and *Y* depends on previous exposure to the other method. Group I performed much worse on method *Y* when it was exposed to it following *X*, and group II performed much better on *X* when it was exposed to it after method *Y*. When either *X* or *Y* was given first in the sequence, there was no difference in performance. It is not clear that method *X* is superior in all conditions in study 2, whereas this is quite clear in study 1.

Time-Series Designs. The typical pre- and posttest designs examined up to now involve observations or measurements taken immediately before and after treatment. A **time-series design**, however, involves repeated measurements or observations over a period of time both before and after treatment. It is really an elaboration of the one-group pretest-posttest design presented in Figure 13.2. An extensive amount of data is collected on a single group. If the group scores essentially the same on the pretests and then considerably improves on the posttests, the researcher has more confidence that the treatment is causing the improvement than if just one pretest and one posttest were given. An example might be a teacher who gives a weekly test to her class for several weeks before giving them a new textbook to use, and then monitors how they score on a number of weekly tests after they have used the text. A diagram of the basic time-series design is as follows:

A Basic Time-Series Design

$O_1 \quad O_2 \quad O_3 \quad O_4 \quad O_5 \quad X \quad O_6 \quad O_7 \quad O_8 \quad O_9 \quad O_{10}$

The threats to internal validity that endanger use of this design include history (something could happen between the last pretest and the first posttest), instrumentation (if, for some reason, the test being used is changed at any time during the study), and testing (due to a practice effect). The possibility of a pretest-treatment interaction is also increased with the use of several pretests.

The effectiveness of the treatment in a time-series design is basically determined by analyzing the pattern of test scores that results from the several tests. Figure 13.9 illustrates several possible outcome patterns that might result from the introduction of an experimental variable (*X*). The vertical line indicates the point at which the experimental treatment is introduced. In this figure, the change between time periods 5 and 6 gives the same kind of data that would be obtained using a one-group pretest-posttest design. The collection of additional data before and after the introduction of the treatment, however, shows how misleading a one-group pretest-posttest design can be. In (A), the improvement is shown to be no more than that which occurs from one data collection period to another—regardless of method. You will notice that performance does improve from time to time, but no trend or overall increase is

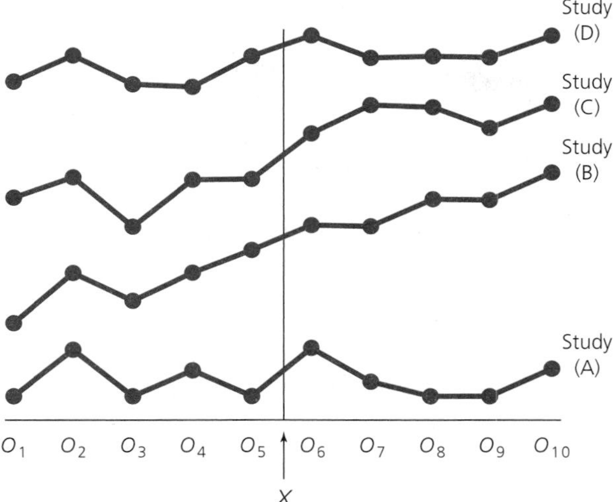

Figure 13.9 *Possible Outcome Patterns in a Time-Series Design*

apparent. In (B), the gain from periods 5 to 6 appears to be part of a trend already apparent before the treatment was begun (quite possibly an example of maturation). In (D) the higher score in period 6 is only temporary, as performance soon approaches what it was before the treatment was introduced (suggesting an extraneous event of transient impact). Only in (C) do we have evidence of a consistent effect of the treatment.

The time-series design is a strong design, although it is vulnerable to history (an extraneous event could occur after period 5) and instrumentation (owing to the several test administrations at different points in time). The extensive amount of data collection required, in fact, is a likely reason why this design is infrequently used in educational research. In many studies, especially in schools, it simply is not feasible to give the same instrument eight to ten times. Even when it is possible, serious questions are raised concerning the validity of instrument interpretation with so many administrations. An exception is the use of unobtrusive devices that can be applied over many occasions, since interpretations based on them should remain valid.

FACTORIAL DESIGNS

Factorial designs extend the number of relationships that may be examined in an experimental study. They are essentially modifications of either the posttest-only control group or pretest-posttest control group designs (with or without random assignment), which permit the investigation of additional independent variables. Another value of a factorial design is that it allows a researcher to study the **interaction** of an independent variable with one or more other variables, sometimes called *moderator variables.* **Moderator variables** may be either treatment variables or subject characteristic variables. A diagram of a factorial design is as follows:

Factorial Design

Treatment	R	O	X	Y_1	O
Control	R	O	C	Y_1	O
Treatment	R	O	X	Y_2	O
Control	R	O	C	Y_2	O

This design is a modification of the pretest-posttest control group design. It involves one treatment and one control group, and a moderator variable having two levels (Y_1 and Y_2). In this example, two groups would receive the treatment (X) and two would not (C). The groups receiving the treatment would differ on Y, however, as would the two groups not receiving the treatment. Because each variable, or factor, has two levels, the above design is called a 2 by 2 factorial design. This design can also be illustrated as follows:

Alternative Illustration of the Preceding Example

	X	C
Y_1		
Y_2		

A variation of this design uses two or more different treatment groups and no control groups. Consider the example we have used before of a researcher comparing the effectiveness of inquiry and lecture methods of instruction on achievement in history. The independent variable in this case (method of instruction) has two levels—inquiry (X_1) and lecture (X_2). Now imagine the researcher wants to see whether achievement is also influenced by class size. In that case, Y_1 might represent small classes and Y_2 might represent large classes.

As we suggest, it is possible using a factorial design to assess not only the separate effect of each independent variable but also their joint effect. In other words, the researcher is able to see how one of the variables might moderate the other (hence the reason for calling these variables *moderator variables*).

	Method	
Class size	**Inquiry (X_1)**	**Lecture (X_2)**
Small (Y_1)		
Large (Y_2)		

Figure 13.10 *Using a Factorial Design to Study Effects of Method and Class Size on Achievement*

Let us continue with the example of the researcher who wished to investigate the effects of method of instruction and class size on achievement in history. Figure 13.10 illustrates how various combinations of these variables could be studied in a factorial design.

Factorial designs, therefore, are an efficient way to study several relationships with one set of data. Let us emphasize again, however, that their greatest virtue lies in the fact that they enable a researcher to study interactions between variables.

Figure 13.11, for example, illustrates two possible outcomes for the 2 by 2 factorial design shown in Figure 13.10. The scores for each group on the posttest (a 50-item quiz on American history) are shown in the boxes (usually called *cells*) corresponding to each combination of method and class size.

In study (*a*) in Figure 13.11, the inquiry method was shown to be superior in both small and large classes, and small classes were superior to large classes for both methods. Hence no interaction effect is present. In study (*b*), students did better in small than in large classes with both methods; however, students in small classes did better when they were taught by the inquiry method, but students in large classes did better when they were taught by the lecture method. Thus, even though students did better in small than in large classes in general, how well they did depended on the teaching method. As a result, the researcher cannot say that either method was always better; it depended on the size of the class in which students were taught. There was an interaction,

(*a*) No interaction between class size and method

	Method		
Class size	Inquiry (X_1)	Lecture (X_2)	Mean
Small (Y_1)	46	38	42
Large (Y_2)	40	32	36
Mean =	43	35	

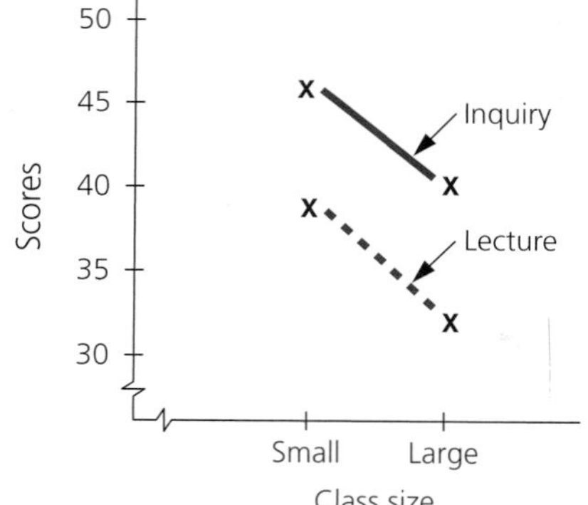

(*b*) Interaction between class size and method

	Method		
Class size	Inquiry (X_1)	Lecture (X_2)	Mean
Small (Y_1)	48	42	45
Large (Y_2)	32	38	35
Mean =	40	40	

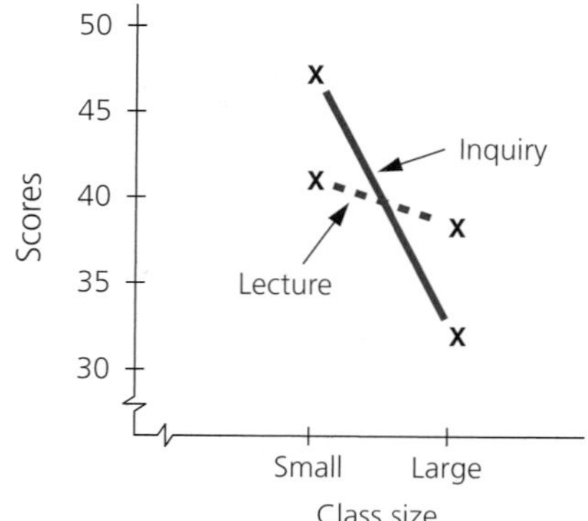

Figure 13.11 *Illustration of Interaction and No Interaction in a 2 by 2 Factorial Design*

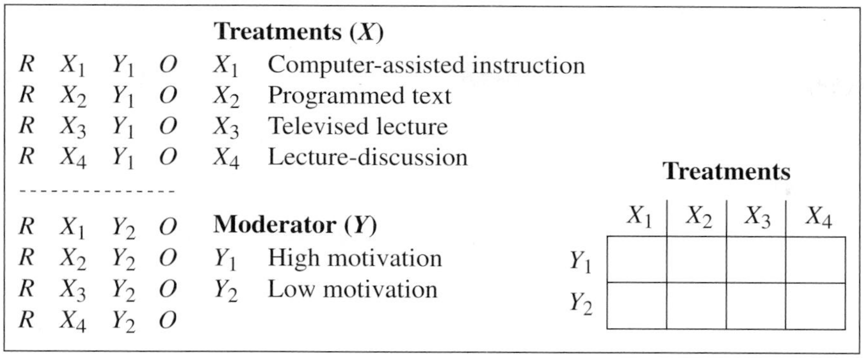

	Treatments (X)	
R X_1 Y_1 O	X_1	Computer-assisted instruction
R X_2 Y_1 O	X_2	Programmed text
R X_3 Y_1 O	X_3	Televised lecture
R X_4 Y_1 O	X_4	Lecture-discussion
- - - - - - - - - - - - - -		
R X_1 Y_2 O	**Moderator (Y)**	
R X_2 Y_2 O	Y_1	High motivation
R X_3 Y_2 O	Y_2	Low motivation
R X_4 Y_2 O		

	Treatments			
	X_1	X_2	X_3	X_4
Y_1				
Y_2				

Figure 13.12 *Example of a 4 by 2 Factorial Design*

in other words, between class size and method, and this in turn affected achievement.

Suppose a factorial design was *not* used in study (*b*). If the researcher simply compared the effect of the two methods, without taking class size into account, he would have concluded that there was no difference in their effect on achievement (notice that the means of both groups = 40). The use of a factorial design enables us to see that the effectiveness of the method, in this case, depended on the size of the class in which it was used. It appears that an interaction existed between method and class size.

A factorial design involving four levels of the independent variable and using a modification of the posttest-only control group design was employed by Tuckman.[8] In this study, the independent variable was type of instruction, and the moderator was amount of motivation. It is a 4 by 2 factorial design (Figure 13.12). Many additional variations are also possible, such as 3 by 3, 4 by 3, and 3 by 2 by 3 designs. Factorial designs can be used to investigate more than two variables, although rarely are more than three variables studied in one design.

Control of Threats to Internal Validity: A Summary

Table 13.1 presents our evaluation of the effectiveness of each of the preceding designs in controlling the threats to internal validity that we discussed in Chapter 9. You should remember that these assessments reflect our judgment; not all researchers would necessarily agree. We have assigned two pluses (+ +) to indicate a *strong* control (the threat is *unlikely* to occur); one plus (+) to indicate *some* control (the threat *might* occur); a minus (−) to indicate a *weak* control (the threat is *likely* to occur); and a question mark (?) to those threats whose likelihood, owing to the nature of the study, we cannot determine.

You will notice that these designs are most effective in controlling the threats of subject characteristics, mortality, history, maturation, and regression. Note that mortality is controlled in several designs because any subject lost is lost to both the experimental and control methods, thus introducing no advantage to either. A location threat is a minor problem in the time-series design because the location where the treatment is administered is usually constant throughout the study; the same is true for data collector characteristics, although such characteristics may be a problem in other designs if different collectors are used for different methods. This is usually easy to control, however. Unfortunately, time-series designs do suffer from a strong likelihood of instrument decay and data collector bias, since data (by means of observations) must be collected over many trials, and the data collector can hardly be kept in the dark as to the intent of the study.

Unconscious bias on the part of data collectors is not controlled by any of these designs, nor is an implementation effect. Either implementers or data collectors can, unintentionally, distort the results of a study. The data collector should be kept ignorant as to who received which treatment, if this is feasible. It should be verified that the treatment is administered and the data collected as the researcher intended.

As you can see in Table 13.1, a testing threat may be present in many of the designs, although its magnitude depends on the nature and frequency of the instrumentation involved. It can occur only when subjects respond to an instrument on more than one occasion.

TABLE 13.1 *Effectiveness of Experimental Designs in Controlling Threats to Internal Validity*

	Threat											
Design	**Subject Characteristics**	**Mortality**	**Location**	**Instrument Decay**	**Data Collector Characteristics**	**Data Collector Bias**	**Testing**	**History**	**Maturation**	**Attitude of Subjects**	**Regression**	**Implementation**
One-shot case study	−	−	−	(NA)	−	−	(NA)	−	−	−	−	−
One group pretest-posttest	−	?	−	−	−	−	−	−	−	−	−	−
Static-group comparison	−	−	−	+	−	−	+	?	+	−	−	−
Randomized posttest-only control group	++	+	−	+	−	−	++	+	++	−	++	−
Randomized pretest-posttest control group	++	+	−	+	−	−	+	+	++	−	++	−
Randomized Solomon four-group	++	++	−	+	−	−	++	+	++	−	++	−
Randomized posttest-only control group with matched subjects	++	+	−	+	−	−	++	+	++	−	++	−
Matching-only pretest-posttest control group	+	+	−	+	−	−	+	+	+	−	+	−
Counterbalanced	++	++	−	+	−	−	+	++	++	++	++	−
Time-series	++	−	+	−	+	+	−	−	+	−	++	−
Factorial with randomization	++	++	−	++	−	−	+	+	++	−	++	−
Factorial without randomization	?	?	−	++	−	−	+	+	+	−	?	−

Key: (++) = strong control, threat unlikely to occur; (+) = some control, threat may possibly occur; (-) = weak control, threat likely to occur; (?) = can't determine; (NA) = threat does not apply.

The attitudinal (or demoralization) effect is best controlled by the counterbalanced design since each subject receives both (or all) special treatments. In the remaining designs, it can be controlled by providing another "special" experience during the alternative treatment. Special mention should be made of the double-blind type of experiment. Such studies are common in medicine but hard to arrange in education. The key element is that neither the subjects nor the researcher knows the identity of those receiving each treatment. This is most easily accomplished in medical studies by means of a *placebo* (sometimes a sugar pill) that is indistinguishable from the actual medicine.

Regression is not likely to be a problem except in the one-group pretest-posttest design, since it should occur equally in experimental and control conditions if it

Do Placebos Work?

The placebo effect—the expectation that some patients will show improvement if they are given any kind of treatment at all, even a sugar pill—has long been acknowledged by physicians and others involved in clinical trials. But does this effect really exist?

Two researchers in Denmark suggested it often does not. They reviewed 114 clinical trials in which patients were given real medicine, a placebo, or no treatment at all. Their report, published in the *New England Journal of Medicine* in May 2001, showed that "placebos offer no significant advantage over "no treatment" for dozens of conditions ranging from colds and seasickness to hypertension and Alzheimer's disease. (The exception was pain relief, which sugar pills seem to bring to about 15 percent of patients.)"* The researchers speculated that one explanation of the placebo effect may simply have been an unconscious desire by patients to please their doctors.

What do you think? Do some patients try (unconsciously) to please their doctors?

*Reported in *Time,* June 4, 2001, p. 65.

occurs at all. It could, however, possibly occur in a static-group pretest-posttest control group design, if there are large initial differences between the two groups.

Evaluating the Likelihood of a Threat to Internal Validity in Experimental Studies

An important consideration in planning an experimental study or in evaluating the results of a reported study is the likelihood of threats to internal validity. As we have shown, a number of possible threats to internal validity may exist. The question that a researcher must ask is: How likely is it that any *particular* threat exists in *this* study?

To aid in assessing this likelihood, we suggest the following procedures.

Step 1: Ask: What specific factors either are known to affect the dependent variable or may logically be expected to affect this variable? (Note that researchers need *not* be concerned with factors unrelated to what they are studying.)

Step 2: Ask: What is the likelihood of the comparison groups differing on each of these factors? (A difference between groups cannot be explained away by a factor that is the same for all groups.)

Step 3: Evaluate the threats on the basis of how likely they are to have an effect, and plan to control for them. If a given threat cannot be controlled, acknowledge this.

The importance of step 2 is illustrated in Figure 13.13. In each diagram, the thermometers depict the performance of subjects receiving method A compared to those receiving method B. In diagram (*a*), subjects receiving method A performed higher on the posttest but *also* performed higher on the pretest; thus, the difference in pretest achievement accounts for the difference on the posttest. In diagram (*b*), subjects receiving method A performed higher on the posttest but did *not* perform higher on the pretest; thus, the posttest results *cannot* be explained by, or attributed to, different achievement levels prior to receiving the methods.

Let us consider an example to illustrate how these different steps might be employed. Suppose a researcher wishes to investigate the effects of two different teaching methods (e.g., lecture versus inquiry instruction) on critical thinking ability of students (as measured by scores on a critical thinking test). The researcher plans to compare two groups of eleventh-graders, one group being taught by an instructor who uses the lecture method, the other group being taught by an instructor who uses the inquiry method. Assume that intact classes will be used rather than random assignment to groups. Several of the threats to internal validity discussed in Chapter 9 are considered and evaluated using the steps just presented. We would argue that this is the kind of thinking researchers should engage in when planning a research project.

Subject Characteristics. Although many possible subject characteristics might affect critical thinking

Figure 13.13 *Guidelines for Handling Internal Validity in Comparison Group Studies*

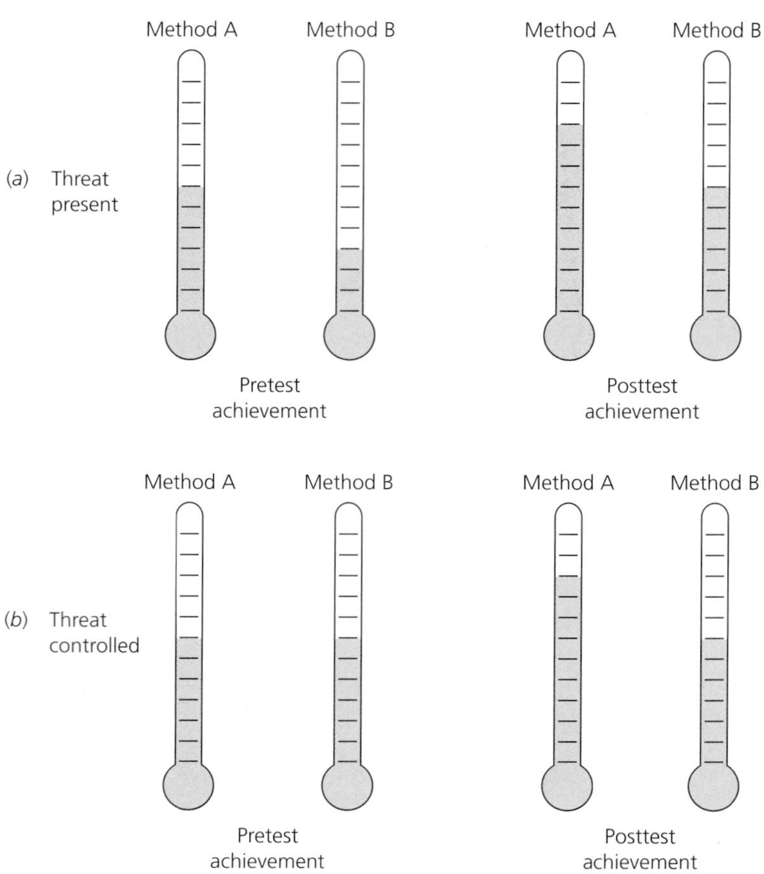

ability, we identify only two here—(1) initial critical thinking ability and (2) gender.

1. **Critical thinking ability.** *Step 1:* Posttreatment critical thinking ability of students in the two groups is almost certainly related to initial critical thinking ability. *Step 2:* Groups may well differ unless randomly assigned or matched. *Step 3:* Likelihood of having an effect unless controlled: high.
2. **Gender.** *Step 1:* Posttreatment critical ability may be related to gender. *Step 2:* Groups may differ in proportions of each gender unless controlled by matching. *Step 3:* Likelihood of having an effect unless controlled: moderate.

Mortality. *Step 1:* Mortality is likely to affect posttreatment scores on any measure of critical thinking since those subjects who drop out or are otherwise lost would likely have lower scores. *Step 2:* Groups probably would not differ in numbers lost, but this should be verified. *Step 3:* Likelihood of having an effect unless controlled: moderate.

Location. *Step 1:* If location of implementation of treatment and/or of data collection differs for the two groups, this could affect posttreatment scores on the critical thinking test. Posttreatment scores would be expected to be affected by such resources as class size, availability of reading materials, films, and so forth. *Step 2:* This threat may differ for groups unless controlled for by standardizing locations for implementation and data collection. The classrooms using each method may differ systematically unless steps are taken to ensure that resources are comparable. *Step 3:* Likelihood of having an effect unless controlled: moderate to high.

Significant Findings in Experimental Research

In our opinion, some of the most important research in social psychology, with obvious implications for education, has been that on the effects of cooperative social interaction on negative attitudes, or the tendency of people to dislike others. A series of experimental studies begun in the 1940s led to the generalization that liking for group members, including those of different backgrounds and ethnicity, is increased by cooperative activities that lead to a successful outcome.* An application of this finding is the "jigsaw technique," which requires each member of a group to teach other members a section of material to be learned.† Experimental studies generally support the effectiveness of this procedure.

*Stephan, W. G. (1985). Intergroup relations. In G. Lindzey and E. Aronson (Eds.), *Handbook of social psychology.* New York: Random House.
†Aronson, E., Stephan, C., Sikes, J., Blaney, N., & Snapp, M. (1978). *The jigsaw classroom.* Beverly Hills: Sage.

Instrumentation.

1. **Instrument decay.** *Step 1:* Instrument decay may affect any outcome. *Step 2:* Instrument decay could differ for groups. This should not be a major problem, provided all instruments used are carefully examined and any alterations found are corrected. *Step 3:* Likelihood of having an effect unless controlled: low.
2. **Data collector characteristics.** *Step 1:* Data collector characteristics might affect scores on critical thinking test. *Step 2:* This threat might differ for groups unless controlled by using the same data collector(s) for all groups. *Step 3:* Likelihood of having an effect unless controlled: moderate.
3. **Data collector bias.** *Step 1:* Bias could certainly affect scores on critical thinking test. *Step 2:* This threat might differ for groups unless controlled by training implementers in administration of the instrument and/or keeping them ignorant as to which treatment group is being tested. *Step 3:* Likelihood of having an effect unless controlled: high.

Testing. *Step 1:* Pretesting, if used, might well affect posttest scores on critical thinking test. *Step 2:* Presumably the pretest would affect both groups equally, however, and would not be likely to interact with method, since instructors using each method are teaching critical thinking skills. *Step 3:* Likelihood of having an effect unless controlled: low.

History. *Step 1:* Extraneous events that might affect critical thinking skills are difficult to conjecture, but they might include such things as a special TV series on thinking, attendance at a district workshop on critical thinking by some students, or participation in certain extracurricular activities (e.g., debates) that occur during the course of the study. *Step 2:* In most cases, these events would likely affect both groups equally and hence are not likely to constitute a threat. Such events should be noted and their impact on each group assessed to the degree possible. *Step 3:* Likelihood of having an effect unless controlled: low.

Maturation. *Step 1:* Maturation could affect outcome scores since critical thinking is presumably related to individual growth. *Step 2:* Presuming that the instructors teach each method over the same time period, maturation should not be a threat. *Step 3:* Likelihood of having an effect unless controlled: low.

Attitude of Subjects. *Step 1:* Subjects' attitudes could affect posttest scores. *Step 2:* If the members of either group perceive that they are receiving any sort of "special attention," this could be a threat. The extent to which either treatment is "novel" should be evaluated. *Step 3:* Likelihood of having an effect unless controlled: low to moderate.

Regression. *Step 1:* Regression is unlikely to affect posttest scores unless subjects are selected on the basis of extreme scores. *Step 2:* This threat is unlikely to affect groups differently, although it could do so. *Step 3:* Likelihood of having an effect unless controlled: low.

Implementation. *Step 1:* Instructor characteristics are likely to affect posttreatment scores. *Step 2:*

Because different instructors teach the methods, they may well differ. This could be controlled by having several instructors for each method, by having each instructor teach both methods, or by monitoring instruction. *Step 3:* Likelihood of having an effect unless controlled: high.

The trick, then, to identifying threats to internal validity is, first, to think of different variables (conditions, subject characteristics, and so on) that might affect the outcome variable of the study and, second, to decide, based on evidence and/or experience, whether these things would affect the comparison groups differently. If so, the influence of these factors may provide an alternative explanation for the results. If this seems likely, a threat to internal validity of the study may indeed be present and needs to be minimized or eliminated. It should then be discussed in the final report on the research project.

Control of Experimental Treatments

The designs discussed in this chapter are all intended to improve the internal validity of an experimental study. As you have seen, each has its advantages and disadvantages, and each provides a way of handling some threats but not others.

Another issue, however, cuts across all designs. While it has been touched on in earlier sections, particularly in connection with location and implementation threats, it deserves more attention than it customarily receives. The issue is that of researcher control over the experimental treatment(s). Of course, an essential requirement of a well-conducted experiment is that researchers have control over the treatment—that is, they control the what, who, when, and how of it. A clear example of researcher control is the testing of a new drug; clearly, the drug is the treatment and the researcher can control who administers it, under what conditions, when it is given, to whom, and how much. Unfortunately, researchers seldom have this degree of control in educational research.

In the ideal situation, a researcher can specify precisely the ingredients of the treatment; in actual practice, many treatments or methods are too complex to describe precisely. Consider the example we have previously given of a study comparing the effectiveness of inquiry and lecture methods of instruction. What, exactly, is the individual who implements each method to do? Researchers may differ greatly in their answers to this question. Ambiguity in specifying exactly what the implementer of the treatment is to do leads to major problems in implementation. How are researchers to train teachers to implement the methods involved in a study if they can't specify the essential characteristics of those methods? Even supposing that adequate specification can be achieved and training methods developed, how can researchers be sure the methods are implemented *correctly?* These problems must be faced by any researcher using any of the designs we have discussed.

A consideration of this issue frequently leads to consideration (and assessment) of possible tradeoffs. The greatest control is likely to occur when the researcher is the one implementing the treatment; this, however, also provides the greatest opportunity for an implementation threat to occur. The more the researcher diffuses implementation by adding other implementers in the interest of reducing threats, however, the more he or she risks distortion or dilution of the treatment. The extreme case is the use of existing treatment groups—that is, groups located by the researcher that already are receiving certain treatments. Most authors refer to these as causal-comparative or *ex post facto* studies (see Chapter 16), and do not consider them to fall under the category of experimental research. In such studies, the researcher must locate groups receiving the specified treatment(s) and then use a matching-only design or, if sufficient lead time exists before implementation of the treatment, a time-series design. We are not persuaded that such studies, if treatments are carefully identified, are necessarily inferior with respect to cause-effect conclusions compared with studies in which treatments are assigned to teachers (or others) by the researcher. Both are equally open to most of the threats we have discussed. The existing groups are more susceptible to subject characteristics, location, and regression threats than true experiments, but not necessarily more so than quasi-experiments. One would expect fewer problems with an attitudinal effect, since existing practice is not altered. Greater history and maturation threats exist because the researcher would have less control. Implementation is difficult to assess. Teachers who are already implementing a new method may be enthusiastic if they initially chose the method, but they also may be better teachers. On the other hand, teachers assigned to a method that is new to them may be either enthusiastic or resentful. We conclude that both types of study are legitimate.

An Example of Experimental Research

In the remainder of this chapter, we present a published example of experimental research. Along with a reprint of the actual study itself, we critique the study, identify its strengths, and discuss areas we think could be improved. We also do this at the end of Chapters 14 to 17 and 19 to 24, in each case analyzing the type of study discussed in the chapter. In selecting the studies for review, we used the following criteria:

- The study had to exemplify typical, but not outstanding, methodology and permit constructive criticism.
- The study had to have enough interest value to hold the attention of students, even though specific professional interests may not be directly addressed.
- The study had to be concisely reported.

In total, these studies represent the diversity of special interests in the field of education.

In critiquing each of these studies, we used a series of categories and questions that should, by now, be familiar to you. They are:

Purpose/justification: Is it logical? Is it convincing? Is it sufficient? Do the authors show how the results of the study have important implications for theory, practice, or both? Are assumptions made explicit?

Definitions: Are major terms clearly defined? If not, are they clear in context?

Prior research: Has previous work on the topic been covered adequately? Is it clearly connected to the present study?

Hypotheses: Are they stated? Implied? Appropriate for the study?

Sample: What type of sample is used? Is it a random sample? If not, is it adequately described? Do the authors recommend or imply generalizing to a population? If so, is the target population clearly indicated? Are possible limits to generalizing discussed?

Instrumentation: Is it adequately described? Is evidence of adequate reliability presented? Is evidence of validity provided? How persuasive is the evidence or the argument for validity of inferences made from the instruments?

Procedures/internal validity: What threats are evident? Were they controlled? If not, were they discussed?

Data analysis: Are data summarized and reported appropriately? Are descriptive and inferential statistics (if any) used appropriately? Are the statistics interpreted correctly? Are limitations discussed?

Results: Are they clearly presented? Is the written summary consistent with the data reported?

Discussion/interpretations: Do the authors place the study in a broader context? Do they recognize limitations of the study, especially with regard to population and ecological generalizing of results?

From: (2007). *International Journal of Special Education, 13*(2), 89–96.

Cognitive Effects of Chess Instruction on Students at Risk for Academic Failure

Saahoon Hong
and
William M. Bart
University of Minnesota

Cognitive effects of chess instruction on students at risk for academic failure was examined. Thirty-eight students, from three elementary schools, participated in this study. The experimental group received a ninety-minute chess lesson once per week over a three-month period; and the control group students regularly attended school activities after class. The experimental group performance on the test was not different from the control group performance. However, chess skill rating and TONI-3 posttest scores were significantly correlated when controlling for TONI-3 pretest score (d = 0.29). This suggests that chess skill rating is a key predictor for the improvement of student cognitive skills. Students at risk at beginning levels of competency in chess may be able to improve their cognitive skills and to improve their skill at chess.

unclear: $r = .52$

Justification

Chess playing is a strategy game that requires higher order cognitive skills. The acquisition of higher order cognitive skills plays a major role in enabling students to better establish and attain goals, identify potential responses when making decisions, and achieve self-regulated learning (Wehmeyer, Palmer, Agran, Mithaug, & Martin, 2000). As a result, investigators have examined the usefulness of chess playing to develop higher order cognitive skills (Horgan, 1987; Horgan & Morgan, 1990). Higher order cognitive skills such as analysis, evaluation, and logical thinking are prevalent in the game of chess (Grossen, 1991).

Chess playing involves the comprehension of chess positions, the analysis of moves and their sequences, and the evaluation of positions resulting from certain moves (Bart, 2004; Cleveland, 1907; Gobet & Simon, 1996; Holding, 1985). Since these processes are considered to be transferable skills (Ericsson & Staszewski, 1989; Ericsson & Kintsch, 1995; Gobet & Simon, 1996), chess playing receives considerable attention as a learning tool and part of the curriculum.

Justification
Prior research

Research on chess instruction has tended to provide empirical support for the beneficial effects of chess training on performance on cognitive tasks (Horgan, 1987; Smith & Cage, 2000; Christiaen & Verholfstadt 1978; Frank & D'Hondt, 1979). For example, in an experimental study, Frank & D'Hordt (1979) found that an experimental group of learners receiving chess instruction scored better on both numerical and verbal aptitude tests than did a control group of learners not receiving chess instruction. These findings lend credence to the application of chess instruction to students with cognitive challenges. Thus chess instruction may be a productive intervention for students at risk for academic failure.

Definition

Students at risk are defined as students who are one or more years behind their age or grade level in mathematics or reading skills (Sapp, 1993). Most of them require the same assistance as students with disabilities (Sapp & Farrell, 1994). Students at risk tend to rely on previously employed but unsuccessful responses, process information less effectively, and are often unable to solve problems in their lives (Agran & Wehmeyer, 1999; Swanson & Alexander, 1997; Wehmeyer & Kelchner, 1995). They have difficulties in utilizing higher order cognitive skills.

Feuerstein (1980) claimed that enriched environments could resolve these difficulties. Teaching and practicing these cognitive skills through chess playing to students at risk have produced better results in basic skills than over reliance on drilling, direct instruction, or other current school improvement methodologies (Pogrow, 1988). Pogrow even argued that the acquisition of higher order cognitive skills compensates students at risk who are deficient in basic skills, because higher order cognitive skills are considered as a knowledge base for all learning. In addition, Pogrow contended that students at risk have competencies to provide solutions on even difficult tasks requiring higher order thinking processes, when enough time and resources are given.

Prior research

However, this hardly occurs in education for students at risk, because they are provided with less opportunity to improve higher order cognitive skills (Allington & McGill-Branzen, 1989). This lack of instructional opportunities resulted from the view that students at risk could not benefit from instruction in higher order cognitive skills (Leshowitz, Jenkens, Heaton, & Bough, 1993).

A common approach for students at risk is to remedy their deficiencies in the basics, like reading, writing, and math. This approach mostly relies on repetitive drill. Knapp and Shields (1990) criticized the repetitive drill approach that tends to: (a) underestimate student competencies; (b) prevent students from accessing more challenging and interesting work; and (c) deprive students of a meaningful context for learning. Such criticism sheds light on the development of higher order cognitive skill instruction (Means & Knapp, 1991). Pogrow's model supports the view that teaching higher order cognitive skills provides students at risk with opportunities to use what they already know, in the form of encoding and retrieving processes. Consequently, these processes could lead students at risk to major gains in basic skills.

In conclusion, research on chess instruction for students at risk may likely provide both regular and special educators with practical suggestions on how to develop higher order cognitive skills and to improve scholastic achievement levels among learners. Furthermore, Storey (2000) suggested that chess instruction could also benefit children with disabilities, even though only anecdotal evidence is available for the effect of chess play on students with disabilities (Remsen, 1998; Wojcio, 1995). This study will examine this issue as it concerns students who are at risk for academic failure. The main purpose of this study is to examine cognitive effects of chess instruction on students at risk for academic failure.

Implied hypothesis

Purpose

METHOD

Participants

Thirty-eight students, ages 8 to 12, from three elementary schools participated in this study. The schools are located in Seoul, Korea. There were 20 students from one school, seven students from a second school, and eleven students from a third school.

Convenience Sample

The students were randomly placed into two groups: a control group and an experimental group. There were 15 males and 5 females in the control group with an average age of 9.74 years and 12 males and 6 females in the experimental group with an average age of 9.71 years. In the control group, there were 17 students at risk and 3 students with learning disabilities and, in the experimental group, there were 15 students at risk and 3 students with learning disabilities. As to the distribution of students by grade, the control group consisted of three students in third grade, nine students in fourth grade, seven students in fifth grade, and one student in sixth grade. The experimental group consisted of three students were in third grade, five students in fourth grade, six students in fifth grade, and four students in sixth grade.

True experiment

Demographics

Instruments

The Korean Basic Skills Test. The Korean Ministry of Education and Human Resource Development and the Korean Institute of Curriculum and Evaluation in 2002 collaboratively developed the Korean Basic Skills Test (KBST) in 2002. The KBST measures student basic abilities in mathematics, reading, and writing. For third grade students (Ministry of Education and Human Resource Development, 2003), the average KBST scores were 93.89 for reading, 94.88 for writing, and 92.28 for mathematics. The basic ability cutoff scores for students at risk were 75 for reading, 78 for writing, and 77 for math. The percentages of students below those cutoff scores were 3.45 percent for reading, 3.00 percent for writing, and 6.84 percent for mathematics. 1.34 percent of students were identified as student at risk in all reading, writing, and mathematics. Student at risk for academic failure lacked basic abilities in reading, mathematics, or writing.

Operational definition of "at risk"?

One investigator identified students at risk by using the KBST. Approximately 3–5% of the students per school fell into this category. The students at risk showed significant deficits in more than one area among the domains of reading, writing, and mathematics.

The Raven's Progressive Matrices Test. The Raven's Progressive Matrices Test (RPM) is designed to measure nonverbal abilities such as student perception of relationships in geometric figures and reasoning by analogy independent of language and formal schooling (Raven, Raven, & Court, 2000). The RPM is also considered to be a fine measure of logical ability and spatial ability (Raven, Court, and Raven, 1985). The RPM comes in three types: the Colored Progressive Matrices (CPM), the Standard Progressive Matrices (SPM), and the Advanced Progressive Matrices (APM). This study made use of the SPM consisting of five sets with 12 problems in each set. The test-retest reliabilities range from .83 to .93. In this study, the correlation between the RPM pretest scores and the posttest scores was .78.

Opinion

Acceptable

The SPM has fine concurrent validity. For example, correlations between the SPM and WISC-R ranged from .83 to .92 in a stratified sample of Canadian children ranging in age from seven to eleven years (Rogers & Holmes, 1987). Horgan and Morgan (1990) contended that the type of reasoning required to solve SPM items is similar to chess reasoning for a wide range of subjects, even though norms for children are limited.

Opinion

Good

Opinion

The Test of Nonverbal Intelligence—Third Edition. The Test of Nonverbal Intelligence-Third Edition (TONI-3) is a norm-referenced test and a language-free measure of cognitive ability (Brown, Sherbenou, & Johnsoen, 1997). In particular, the TONI-3 was designed to measure problem solving, aptitude, and reasoning skills. Two equivalent forms are available. Each form of the TONI-3 has 50 items. Converted scores from obtained raw scores are provided with a mean 100 and a standard deviation of 15. It is particularly useful for individuals who are believed to have difficulties in taking tests, disabilities, or lack of exposure to the British and United States cultures. In this study, students received two forms (A and B).

The TONI-3 has fine psychometric properties. For example, alternate forms reliability has ranged from .79 to .92. A correlation between TONI and SPM was .92. In this study, the correlation between the two forms of the TONI-3 tests was .69.

Opinion

A little low

Chess Quiz. Students in the experimental group received a Chess Quiz that was developed by the chess instructor. At the twentieth session of chess instruction, students in the experimental group completed the Chess Quiz with a score range of 0 to 40. For each item, each participant in the experimental group was asked to find all possible

20th or 12th? See following.

capture moves in a position. The Chess Quiz did not include any questions assessing the use of chess strategies. It simply measured student knowledge about chess pieces and their moves. The Pearson product-moment correlation between chess class attendance and the quiz was .80.

Construct validity

Chess Skill Rating. Chessmaster 9000 provided artificial opponents to participants in the experimental group. With each game of chess, a participant received a score of 1 for a win, a score of .5 for a draw or a stalemate, and a score of 0 for a loss. Each artificial player had an Elo rating that indicated the quality of its play. Elo ratings range from 0 for a beginner to approximately 2850 for a World Chess Champion. The Elo rating scale is the official scale of chess player skill for the United States Chess Federation.

On the basis of the Elo scale, players with ratings of 2500 and above are called grandmasters, and players with ratings of below 1200, Class E. Until the players complete 20 games, they are given a provisional rating. Each participant in the experimental group played against an initial artificial opponent provided by Chessmaster 9000 that had a chess rating of 300. The formula for chess skill rating presented by Fogel, Hays, Hahn, and Quon (2004) was used to determine the Elo rating of each participant.

Procedure. After each school identified the students at risk, the homeroom teacher sent consent forms to the students and their parents. The study began with administration of two pretests after the consent forms were returned. A researcher and a research assistant administered the TONI-3 and the RPM to the students in the first week of this study. The TONI-3 was administered individually and the RPM was administered in groups.

How were students identified? Did they use KBST?

The participants were then randomly assigned to an experimental group or a control group. The experimental group received a 90-minute chess lesson once per week and the control group students attended regular school activities after class. At the end of the chess intervention, the participants received the TONI-3 and the RPM. Students in the experimental group completed the Chess Quiz.

True experiment

Chess instruction consisted of 12 separate lessons over a 3-month period. Each lesson included three segments: reviewing, lecturing, and chess playing. The chess instructor developed and provided a set of quizzes. The quiz was used to identify student difficulty in understanding chess moves and rules. Each subsequent lesson started with reviewing a previous lesson and a quiz. The last six lessons were implemented in a computer lab with chess software and allowed students to practice higher order cognitive skills.

12 or 20?

Overall, the chess instructor asked the students to follow four steps to develop their chess skills: (1) understand chess rules; (2) think ahead for a plan; (3) implement the plan; and (4) seek feedback and rehearsal. The researcher and the chess instructor developed twelve sessions derived from the Comprehensive Chess Course (Pelts & Alburt, 1992). The chess software was used as a tool to practice and generalize the contents of each lesson.

Good description of instruction

Chess playing was new to most of the students. Although three students stated that they sometimes played chess with their brothers, their knowledge of basic chess rules was shallow.

RESULTS

Preliminary Analysis

Although students were assigned randomly to each group, the pre-test intelligence test means for the control and experimental groups were compared using a one-way analysis of variance (ANOVA). The groups appeared equivalent on gender, age, grade, school, and disabilities. The mean TONI-3 pretest scores of the control group (M = 85.60; SD = 20.48) and the experimental group (M = 96.50; SD = 17.12) were not significantly different, $F(1, 36) = 3.13$, $p > .05$. The mean Raven's Progressive Matrices (RPM) pretest scores of the control group (M = 26.20; SD = 10.96) and the experimental group (M = 29.39; SD = 8.56) were also not significantly different, $F(1, 36) = .98$, $p > .05$.

Large difference (10 points)

In addition, comparable KBST pretest mean scores for the two groups were not significantly different. For the reading KBST pretest scores, the means of the control group (M = 59.08; SD = 21.72, n = 12) and the experimental group (M = 66.71; SD = 15.68, n = 7) were not significantly different with $F(1, 17) = .66$, $p > .05$. For the mathematics KBST pretest scores, the means of the control group (M = 60.00; SD = 16,78, n = 11) and the experimental group (M = 64.29; SD = 9.27, n = 9) were not significantly different with $F(1, 16) = .38$, $p > .05$. For the writing KBST pretest scores, the means of the control group (M = 68.56; SD = 17.66, n = 9) and the experimental group (M = 62.20; SD = 21.95. n = 5) were also not significantly different with $F(1, 12) = .35$, $p > .05$.

Very small *n*'s

Some Descriptive and Inferential Statistical Analyses

Table 1 provides descriptive statistics for the intelligence test scores.

TABLE 1 *Means and Standard Deviations of Intelligence Test Scores*

		Pre-Test		Post-Test	
Instrument	**Group**	**M**	**SD**	**M**	**SD**
TONI-3	Control	85.60	20.49	97.25	13.18
	Experimental	96.50	17.12	100.83	11.78
RPM	Control	32.30	27.60	39.20	28.66
	Experimental	37.33	26.03	40.94	23.31

Inconsistent with previous text

A repeated measures ANOVA with a 2 × 2 factorial design was employed to determine whether chess instruction would influence the experimental group TONI-3 and RPM scores. The first factor related to treatment, i.e., the control and experimental groups. The second factor represented time, i.e., the pretest and the posttest. The repeated measures ANOVA examine the main effect and the interactive effect of treatment and time as independent variables on the TONI-3 and RPM scores as dependent variables.

See text pp. 236 and 237.

Tests hypothesis

Although the TONI-3 mean scores significantly increased from the pretest to the posttest, $F(1, 36) = 11.84$, $p < .001$, the main effect for chess instruction was not significant for the TONI-3 with $F(1, 36) = 2.40$, $p > .05$. The treatment X time interaction effect, reflecting differences among the groups in amount of change, was also not statistically significant for the TONI-3 with $F(1, 36) = 2.481$, $p > .05$. In other words, the changed scores of TONI-3 in the experimental chess group were similar to those in the control group. There was no significant difference between the two groups after the chess instruction. The effect size for the experimental group was 0.29 and the effect size for the control group was 0.68.

Misleading (see our analysis)

Sizeable difference

As to the results of the repeated measures ANOVA on the other intelligence test scores, the RPM mean scores significantly increased from the pretest to the posttest with $F(1, 36) = 4.20$, $p < .05$. But the results of repeated measures of ANOVA show that the main effect for treatment was not significant for the RPM with $F(1, 36) = .169$, $p > .05$

and the treatment × time interaction effect, reflecting differences among the groups in amount of change, was also not significant for the RPM with $F(1, 33) = .756, p > .05$. In other words, the score changes for the RPM in the chess group were similar to those of the control group. There was no significant difference between the two groups after the chess instruction. The effect size for the experimental group was 0.15 and the effect size for the control group was 0.25.

Tests hypothesis

Table 2 provides descriptive statistics for chess-related measures.

TABLE 2 *Means, Standard Deviations, Maxima, and Minima of Chess-Related Measures*

Measure	M	SD	Maximum	Minimum
Chess Skill Rating	131.39	84.94	441	101
Chess Quiz Score	22.83	11.29	39	4
Chess Practice in Minutes	620	194.97	900	270

Note: Highest Possible Chess Quiz Score = 40. Highest Possible Chess Practice Score = 1080 minutes.

Regarding the chess quiz with its score range of 0–40, some students scored very well on the chess quiz and other students scored rather poorly. The maximum chess quiz score that a student received was 39; whereas, the minimum was 4. The maximum minutes of chess practice was 900 minutes; whereas, the minimum was 270 minutes. Student practice length outside chess class was not counted in this study.

Partial Correlation Analysis

Partial correlation analysis was used to explore relationships among pre- and posttest scores, chess skill ratings, chess quiz scores, and chess practice for participants in the experimental group. Table 3 provides the partial correlations among those variables controlling for TONI-3 pretest scores.

TABLE 3 *Partial Correlations among Selected Variables Controlling for TONI-3 Pretest Scores*

Control Variable	Variable	1	2	3	4
TONI-3 Pretest	1. TONI-3 Posttest	1.00	.52*	.33	.23
	2. Chess Skill Rating		1.00	.42	.28
	3. Chess Quiz			1.00	.48
	4. Chess Practice				1.00

*$p < .05$

Among those partial correlations, only the partial correlation between the TONI-3 posttest score and chess skill rating controlling for TONI-3 pretest score was significant with $r = .52, p < .05$.

The median of TONI-3 pretest scores divided the TONI-3 pretest scores into a Low group and a High group. All students showing improvement in chess skill ratings were in the High group of TONI-3 pretest scores. Thus, student TONI-3 posttest scores in the High group are somewhat related to chess skill ratings. In the Low group of TONI-3 pretest, chess skill ratings remained the same.

A stepwise regression was conducted to evaluate whether variables, like TONI-3 pretest score, chess skill rating, chess quiz, and chess practice, were necessary to predict

TONI-3 posttest score. The stepwise regression analysis indicated a model that included two significant predictors, F (2, 15) = 12.25, $p < .001$. The two predictors, TONI-3 pretest score and chess skill rating, were positively associated with the TONI-3 posttest scores. The TONI-3 pretest score is a predictor for the TONI-3 post-test score ($R^2 = .480$). R^2 changes to .620 with the addition of the chess skill rating. They account for 62% of the variance among the TONI-3 posttest scores. Although the sample size is small, this result suggests that the chess skill rating was somewhat related to the increased posttest TONI-3 scores.

Right

In contrast, the partial correlation of the RPM posttest score and the chess skill rating with the RPM pretest score being held constant was not significant, $r = .11$. Table 4 provides the partial correlations among selected variables controlling for RPM pretest scores.

TABLE 4 ***Partial Correlations among Selected Variables Controlling for RPM Pretest Scores***

Control Variable	Variable	1	2	3	4
RPM Pretest	1. RPM Posttest	1.00	.11	.03	.17
	2. Chess Skill Rating		1.00	.31	.33
	3. Chess Quiz			1.00	.50*
	4. Chess Practice				1.00

*$p < .05$

DISCUSSION

The results of this study indicate a lack of cognitive effects of chess instruction. In the analysis of two cognitive tests, changes in experimental group performances were not different from changes in the control group performances. The results tend not to support the view that chess instruction for the beginner at risk for academic failure has salutary cognitive effects on such students. This finding is not consistent with the results of previous studies (Christiaen & Verholfstadt, 1978; Frank & D'Hondt, 1979; Smith & Cage, 2000) that showed improved cognitive skills after providing chess instruction.

We disagree (see our analysis)

Right

This inconsistent result could be explained by two interpretations: The first interpretation is that students at risk could require more time for chess instruction than a twelve-session chess instruction period for one semester. Pogrow (1988) held that time and resources are key factors in developing higher reasoning skills. Students at risk could require more sessions to develop their chess skill. Thus, the lack of cognitive effects of chess instruction might be explained by the limited number of chess instruction periods. Bart (2004) suggested at least one whole academic year and preferably two academic years as the duration for effective chess instruction. It is likely that more time on task learning chess and studying chess could facilitate the development of cognitive skills and capabilities among learners including students at risk.

Not clear to us

The second interpretation is that novice chess players at risk for academic failure could hardly develop their cognitive skills until they reach a certain level of chess skill. This interpretation is consistent with the results of Horgan and Morgan's (1990) study. To Horgan and Morgan, attaining certain levels of chess skill could be associated with improvement in higher order cognitive skills.

There was no correlation between chess skill rating and RPM score. That finding is not consistent with the findings of Horgan and Morgan (1990) and Frydman and Lynn (1992). This inconsistent result can be explained by different chess skill levels. In this study, the mean chess skill rating was 131.39 with a standard deviation of 84.94. The

may be

Horgan and Morgan study and the Frydman and Lynn study were conducted with club chess players with chess ratings greater than 1000.

One intriguing result in this study is that chess skill rating and TONI-3 posttest score were significantly correlated when controlling for TONI-3 pretest score. This suggests that chess skill rating is a key predictor for the improvement of student cognitive skills. Students at risk who are at beginning levels of competency in chess may be able to improve their cognitive skills and their skill at chess. **Questionable**

One limitation of this study is that the chess instruction suggested by Pelts and Alburt (1992) was not specifically developed for students at risk or with disabilities whose needs are individually different. A preferred model of chess instruction may focus on more opportunities for the students to acquire knowledge of strategies and tactics in chess. It is likely that the deeper levels of chess competency involving knowledge of strategies and tactics need to be acquired in order for higher levels of nonverbal intelligence and other cognitive capabilities to be attained. It is obvious that chess instruction should take the characteristics of students at risk into consideration and be reorganized for further studies. In addition, instructor knowledge of pedagogy for students at risk may contribute to effective chess instruction. **We agree**

In conclusion, we recommend that the cognitive effects of chess instruction on students at risk for academic failure continue to be studied. Chess instruction specially configured may prove to be very efficacious in producing salutary cognitive effects among students at risk for academic failure in the USA, and elsewhere in the world. **Need more here**

References

Agran, M., & Wehmeyer, M. (1999). *Teaching problem solving to students with mental retardation*. Washington, DC: American Association on Mental Retardation.

Allington, R., & McGill-Franzen, A. (1989). School response to reading failure: Chapter 1 and special education students in grades 2, 4, and 8. *Elementary School Journal*, *89*, 529–542.

Bart, W. (2004, May). *Cognitive enhancement: An approach to the development of intelligence*. Poster presentation at the annual meeting of the American Psychological Society, Chicago, Illinois.

Brown, L., Sherbenou, R., & Johnsoen, S. (1997). *Examiner's manual: Test of Nonverbal Intelligence* (3rd ed.). Austin, TX: PRO-ED.

Christiaen, J., & Verholfstadt, D. (1978). Chess and cognitive development. *Nederlandse Tydschrift voor de Psychologie en haar Grensbebieden*, *36*, 561–582.

Cleveland, A. (1907). The psychology of chess and of learning to play it. *American Journal of Psychology*, *18*, 269–308.

Ericsson, K., & Kintsch, W. (1995). Long-term working memory, *Psychological Review*, *102*, 211–245.

Ericsson, K. & Staszewski, J. (1989). Skilled memory and expertise: Mechanisms of exceptional performance. In D. Klahr and K. Kotovsky (Eds.), *Complex Information Processing: The Impact of Herbert A. Simon* (pp. 235–267). Hillsdale, NJ: Erlbaum.

Feuerstein, R. (1980). *Instrumental Enrichment*. Baltimore: University Park Press.

Fogel, D., Hays, T., Hahn, S., & Quon, J. (2004). A self-learning evolutionary chess program. *Proceedings of the IEEE*, *92*, 12, 1947–1954.

Frank, A., & D'Hondt, W. (1979). Aptitudes and learning chess in Zaire. *Psychopathologie Africane*, *15*, 81–98.

Frydman, M., & Lynn, R. (1992). The general intelligence and spatial abilities of gifted young Belgian chess players. *British Journal of Psychology*, *83*, 233–235.

Gobet, F., & Simon, H. (1996). The roles of recognition processes and look-ahead search in time-constrained expert problem solving: Evidence from grandmaster-level chess. *Psychological Science*, *7*, 52–55.

Grossen, B. (1991). The fundamental skills of higher order thinking. *Journal of Learning Disabilities*, *24*, 343–353.

Holding, D. (1985). *The psychology of chess skill*. Hillsdale, NJ: Erlbaum.

Horgan, D. (1987). Chess as a way to teach thinking. *Teaching, Thinking and Problem Solving*, *9*, 4–11.

Horgan, D., & Morgan, D. (1990). Chess expertise in children. *Applied Cognitive Psychology*, *4*, 109–128.

Knapp, M., & Shields, P. (1990). Reconceiving academic instruction for the children of poverty. *Phi Delta Kappan*, *71*, 753–58.

Leshowitz, B., Jenkens, K., Heaton, S., & Bough, T. (1993). Fostering critical thinking skills in students with learning disabilities: An instructional program. *Journal of Learning Disabilities*, *26*, 483–490.

Means, B., & Knapp, M. (1991). Cognitive approaches to teaching advanced skills to educationally disadvantaged students. *Phi Delta Kappan*, *73*, 282–289.

Ministry of Education & Human Resource Development. (2003). *2002 haknyoundo chodeunghakgyo 3 haknyoun gichohakruk jindanpyoungga gookasoojoon pyojip boonseok kyoulkwa.* [The analysis of third-grade Korean-version Basic Skill Test scores in 2002]. Seoul, Korea: The Ministry of Education & Human Resource Development.

Pelts, R., & Alburt, L. (1992). *Comprehensive chess course volume 1* (4th edition). NewYork, NY: Chess Information and Research Center.

Pogrow, S. (1988). Teaching thinking to at-risk elementary students. *Educational Leadership*, *45,* 7, 79–85.

Raven, J., Raven, J., & Court, J. (2000). *Manual for Raven's Progressive Matrices and Vocabulary Scales*. Oxford: Oxford Psychologists Press.

Remsen, D. (1998). Churchill school for learning disabilities wins three trophies at nationals. *Chess Life*, *53*, 622.

Rogers, W., & Holmes, B. (1987). Individually administered intelligence test scores: Equivalent or comparable? *Alberta Journal of Educational Research*, *33*, 2–20.

Sapp, M (1993). *Test anxiety: Applied research, assessment and treatment intervention*. Lanham, MD: University Press of America.

Sapp, M., & Farrell, W. (1994). Cognitive-behavioral interventions: Applications for academically at-risk and special education students. *Preventing School Failure*, *38,* 19–24.

Smith, J., & Cage, B. (2000). The effects of chess instruction on the mathematics achievement of Southern, rural, Black secondary students. *Research in the Schools*, *7,* 19–26.

Storey, K. (2000). Teaching beginning chess skills to students with disabilities. *Preventing School Failure*, *44,* 45–49.

Swanson, H., & Alexander, J. (1997). Cognitive processes as predictors of word recognition and reading comprehension in learning-disabled and skilled readers: Revisiting the specificity hypothesis. *Journal of Educational Psychology*, *89*, 128–158.

Wehmeyer, M., & Kelchner, K. (1995). Interpersonal cognitive problem solving skills of individuals with mental retardation. *Education and Training in Mental Retardation and Developmental Disabilities*, *29*, 265–278.

Wehmeyer, M., Palmer, S., Agran, M., Mithaug, D., & Martin, J. (2000). Teaching students to become causal agents in their lives: The self-determining learning model of instruction. *Exceptional Children*, *66*, 439–453.

Wojcio, M. (1995). Chess is very special. *Chess Life*, *50*, 767.

Analysis of the Study

PURPOSE/JUSTIFICATION

The purpose is clearly stated: to examine the cognitive effects of chess instruction on students at risk for academic failure. There appear to be no ethical problems re confidentiality, risk or deception.

The justification consists of (a) the need for students, particularly those "at risk," to acquire higher order cognitive skills and (b) the likely efficacy of chess playing for acquiring such skills.

PRIOR RESEARCH

Studies are cited in support of both (a) and (b). At present, only anecdotal evidence is said to be available regarding chess instruction with at-risk students.

DEFINITIONS

"At risk students" is defined as those one or more years below their age or grade level in mathematics or reading. However, it is not clear whether the reference to writing in the last paragraph under "Instruments" applies to the current study—if so it implies a different definition including writing performance. It is implied that the KBST, an achievement test, was used to select students—an operational definition. "Chess instruction" is not specifically defined but is made acceptably clear by the description of intervention procedures, though it is not clear whether it included 12 or 20 class sessions.

HYPOTHESES

None is stated, but the clearly implied hypothesis is that chess instruction will improve the cognitive test performance of at-risk students as compared to "regular class instruction."

SAMPLE

The convenience sample consisted of 38 students aged 8 to 12 identified as "at risk" by three elementary schools in Seoul, Korea. Some demographic data are provided but not on variables such as socioeconomic status that would help assess generalizability. We think more description of the 6 students with learning disabilities should have been given.

INSTRUMENTATION

The Korean Basic Skills Test was apparently used to select students, though no reliability or validity information is provided. All students were administered two tests before and after the 12(?)-lesson, three-month intervention period. The Test of Nonverbal Intelligence (TONI-3) is a "language-free measure of cognitive ability." Alternate forms reliability is cited and is acceptable. The Raven's Progressive Matrices Test (RPM) is also nonverbal and intended to get at cognitive abilities though they are described somewhat differently. Retest reliabilities are given and are acceptable. Correlations with WISC-R are cited and are good. We think more discussion of the validity of these tests for this sample should have been provided. In addition, the experimental group was given a chess quiz and a chess skill rating derived from 20 games played on Chessmaster 9000.

PROCEDURES/INTERNAL VALIDITY

The study is a true experiment in that the sample was randomly divided into experimental and control groups—chess instruction versus regular class activities. It is not clear why the groups were 20 and 18 in number rather than 19 each. With respect to "subject characteristics" the groups appear similar in age, learning disabilities, and gender. There are indications, discussed next, that the experimental group had higher initial cognitive ability. The experimental group had more students in sixth grade and fewer in fourth grade, which may be related to the higher cognitive skills in this group. Given more sixth-graders, it is unclear why the experimental group was (slightly) younger. Given the limitations of random assignment with small groups, a matched pairs followed by random assignment design would have been preferable. Location and history threats are possible. There apparently was no loss of subjects. Instrumentation, data collector characteristics, testing, maturation, and regression should have been controlled by the design. Data collector bias is possible because collectors obviously knew which group they were testing. Implementation was evidently done by one teacher, so teacher characteristics are inseparable from the chess method and may account for the outcomes.

DATA ANALYSIS AND RESULTS

Although ANOVA is a proper analysis for this study design, its use is misleading without recognition of the lack of random sampling (see pp. 248 and 249). Further, reliance on significance tests obscures the findings. The first instance of this is in the comparison of experimental and control groups on the pretests, presumably done in recognition that random assignment is no guarantee of equivalence with small groups (see text p. 267). On the TONI-3 we calculated an effect size (see p. 248) of .53 in favor of the experimental group. The data on the RPM are inconsistent between Table 1 and the accompanying text but also show a somewhat higher mean for the experimental group. The data for the KBST are of little value due to the (unexplained) small size of the groups ($n = 5$ to $n = 12$). The interaction term in the 2 by 2 design provides the test of the hypothesis. With respect to both tests, the lack of "significance" obscures the important differences in gain. The effect sizes for comparing group gains are not provided, but differences on both tests favor the control group and for TONI-3 the difference in effect size of gains is substantial (Ex =.29, vs. Con = .68). The correlation of .52 between chess skill rating and gain on TONI-3 indicates that skill did predict gain.

DISCUSSION/INTERPRETATION

We agree that the study did not support the implied hypothesis that chess instruction would improve cognitive skills. We do not agree that it indicated "a lack of cognitive effects." The experimental group showed less improvement on both tests, substantially so on TONI-3. This is particularly surprising because the experimental (chess) group scored higher on the pretests. We think possible explanations for this should have been explored. We think some discussion of results with the six students with learning disabilities should have been included.

The correlation between gain on TONI-3 and chess skill rating is of interest but not as a "key predictor for improvement of cognitive skills" because adding this variable to the multiple R only added 14 percent to the predictable variance and because of the limited, though important, cognitive abilities tested.

We agree that this topic deserves further study but wish the authors had offered suggestions reflecting these concerns.

Go back to the **INTERACTIVE AND APPLIED LEARNING** feature at the beginning of the chapter for a listing of interactive and applied activities. Go to the **Online Learning Center** at **www.mhhe.com/fraenkel9e** to take quizzes, practice with key terms, and review chapter content.

Main Points

THE UNIQUENESS OF EXPERIMENTAL RESEARCH

- Experimental research is unique in that it is the only type of research that directly attempts to influence a particular variable, and it is the only type that, when used properly, can really test hypotheses about cause-and-effect relationships. Experimental designs are some of the strongest available for educational researchers to use in determining cause and effect.

ESSENTIAL CHARACTERISTICS OF EXPERIMENTAL RESEARCH

- Experiments differ from other types of research in two basic ways—comparison of treatments and the direct manipulation of one or more independent variables by the researcher.

RANDOMIZATION

- Random assignment is an important ingredient in the best kinds of experiments. It means that every individual who is participating in the experiment has an equal chance of being assigned to any of the experimental or control conditions that are being compared.

CONTROL OF EXTRANEOUS VARIABLES

- The researcher in an experimental study has an opportunity to exercise far more control than in most other forms of research.
- Some of the most common ways to control for the possibility of differential subject characteristics (in the various groups being compared) are randomization, holding certain variables constant, building the variable into the design, matching, using subjects as their own controls, and using analysis of the covariance.

POOR EXPERIMENTAL DESIGNS

- Three weak designs that are occasionally used in experimental research are the one-shot case study design, the one-group pretest-posttest design, and the static-group comparison design. They are considered weak because they do not have built-in controls for threats to internal validity.
- In a one-shot case study, a single group is exposed to a treatment or event, and its effects are assessed.
- In the one-group pretest-posttest design, a single group is measured or observed both before and after exposure to a treatment.
- In the static-group comparison design, two intact groups receive different treatments.

TRUE EXPERIMENTAL DESIGNS

- The essential ingredient of a true experiment is random assignment of subjects to treatment groups.
- The randomized posttest-only control group design involves two groups formed by random assignment.
- The randomized pretest-posttest control group design differs from the randomized posttest-only control group only in the use of a pretest.
- The randomized Solomon four-group design involves random assignment of subjects to four groups, with two being pretested and two not.

MATCHING

- To increase the likelihood that groups of subjects will be equivalent, pairs of subjects may be matched on certain variables. The members of the matched groups are then assigned to the experimental and control groups.
- Matching may be either mechanical or statistical.
- Mechanical matching is a process of pairing two persons whose scores on a particular variable are similar.
- Two difficulties with mechanical matching are that it is very difficult to match on more than two or three variables, and that in order to match, some subjects must be eliminated from the study when no matches can be found.
- Statistical matching does not necessitate a loss of subjects.

QUASI-EXPERIMENTAL DESIGNS

- The matching-only design differs from random assignment with matching only in that random assignment is not used.
- In a counterbalanced design, all groups are exposed to all treatments, but in a different order.
- A time-series design involves repeated measurements or observations over time, both before and after treatment.

FACTORIAL DESIGNS

- Factorial designs extend the number of relationships that may be examined in an experimental study.

Key Terms

comparison group 266
control 268
control group 266
counterbalanced design 275
criterion variable 265
dependent variable 265
design 268
experiment 266
experimental group 266
experimental research 265
experimental variable 265
extraneous variable 267
factorial design 277
gain score 275
independent variable 265
interaction 277
matching design 272
matching-only design 275
mechanical matching 274
moderator variable 277
nonequivalent control group design 270
one-group pretest-posttest design 269

one-shot case study design 269

outcome variable 265

pretest treatment interaction 272

quasi-experimental design 275

random assignment 267

random selection 267

randomized posttest-only control group design 271

randomized pretest-posttest control group design 271

randomized Solomon four-group design 272

regressed gain score 275

static-group comparison design 270

static-group pretest-posttest design 270

statistical equating 274

statistical matching 274

time-series design 276

treatment variable 265

For Discussion

1. An occasional criticism of experimental research is that it is very difficult to conduct in schools. Would you agree? Why or why not?
2. Are there any cause-and-effect statements you can make that you believe would be true in most schools? Would you say, for example, that a sympathetic teacher "causes" elementary school students to like school more?
3. Are there any advantages to having more than one independent variable in an experimental design? If so, what are they? What about more than one dependent variable?
4. What designs could be used in each of the following studies? (*Note:* More than one design is possible in each instance.)
   a. A comparison of two different ways of teaching spelling to first-graders.
   b. An assessment of the effectiveness of weekly tutoring sessions on the reading ability of third-graders.
   c. A comparison of a third-period high school English class taught by the discussion method with a third-period (same high school) English class taught by the lecture method.
   d. The effectiveness of reinforcement in decreasing stuttering in students with this speech defect.
   e. The effects of a year-long weight-training program on a group of high school athletes.
   f. The possible effects of age, gender, and method on student liking for history.
5. What flaw can you find in each of the following studies?
   a. A teacher tries out a new mathematics textbook with her class for a semester. At the end of the semester, she reports that the class's interest in mathematics is markedly higher than she has ever seen it in the past with other classes using another text.
   b. A teacher divides his class into two subgroups, with each subgroup being taught spelling by a different method. Each group listens to the teacher instruct the other group while they wait their turn.
   c. A researcher calls for eighth-grade students to volunteer to tutor third-grade students who are having difficulty in reading. She compares their effectiveness as tutors with a control group of students who are assigned to be tutors (they do not volunteer). The students of the volunteers have a much greater level of improvement in reading than the students who were assigned to tutor.
   d. A teacher decides to try out a new textbook in one of her social studies classes. She uses it for four weeks and then compares this class's scores on a unit test with the scores of her previous classes. All classes are studying the same material.

During the unit test, however, a fire drill occurs, and the class loses about 10 minutes of the time allotted for the test.

e. Two groups of third-graders are compared with regard to running ability, subsequent to different training schedules. One group is tested during physical education class in the school gymnasium, while the other is tested after school on the football field.

f. A researcher compares a third-period English class with a fifth-period chemistry class in terms of student interest in the subject taught. The English class is taught by the discussion method, while the chemistry class is taught by the lecture method.

References

1. Nye, B., et al. (2001). Are effects of small classes cumulative? Evidence from a Tennessee experiment. *American Educational Research Journal, 37*(1), 123–151.

2. Lo, Y., et al. (2009). Examining the impacts of early reading intervention on the growth rates in basic literacy skills of at-risk urban kindergarteners. *Journal of Special Education, 43,* 12–28.

3. Stanulis, R. N., & Floden, R. E. (2009). Intensive mentoring as a way to help beginning teachers develop balanced instruction. *Journal of Teacher Education, 60*(3), 112–122.

4. Heerwegh, D. (2006). An investigation of the effect of lotteries on Web survey response rates. *Field Methods, 18*(5), 205–220.

5. Benitez, J. L. et al. (2009). The impact of a course on bullying within the pre-service teacher training curriculum. *Electronic Journal of Research in Educational Psychology, 7*(1), 191–207.

6. Kalyva, E., & Agaliotis, I. (2009). Can social stories enhance the interpersonal conflict resolution skills of children with LD? *Research in Developmental Disabilities: A Multidisciplinary Journal, 30*(7), 192–202.

7. DeVos, H. M., & Louw, D. A. (2009). Hypnosis-induced mental training programmes as a strategy to improve the self-concept of students. *Higher Education: The International Journal of Higher Education and Educational Planning, 57*(2), 141–154.

8. Tuckman, B. W. (1999). *Conducting Educational Research* (5th ed., p. 152). New York: College Publishers.

Research Exercise 13: Research Methodology

Using Problem Sheet 13, describe in as much detail as you can the procedures of your study, including analysis of results—that is, *what* you intend to do, *when, where,* and *how.* Lastly, indicate any unresolved problems you see at this point in your planning.

Problem Sheet 13

Research Methodology

You should complete Problem Sheet 13 once you have decided which of the methodologies described in Chapters 13–17 and 19–24 you plan to use. You might wish to consider, however, whether your research question could be investigated by other methodologies.

1. The question or hypothesis of my study is: ______________________________

____

____

____

2. The methodology I intend to use is: ______________________________

____

____

3. Describe how you will conduct the study, that is, the data collection process. When, where, and how will you collect the data? Over what time span will the data be gathered, and in what types of situations? Can you foresee any limitations or problems?

____

____

____

4. If you are planning an intervention study (e.g., an experiment), please discuss in detail the intervention or treatment planned. ______________________________

____

____

5. The major problems I foresee at this point include the following: ______________

____

____

____

____

An electronic version of this Problem Sheet that you can fill in and print, save, or e-mail is available on the Online Learning Center at www.mhhe.com/fraenkel9e.

Single-Subject Research 14

OBJECTIVES **Studying this chapter should enable you to:**

- Describe briefly the purpose of single-subject research.
- Describe the essential characteristics of such research.
- Describe two ways in which single-subject research differs from other forms of experimental research.
- Explain what a baseline is and why it is used.
- Explain what an A-B design is.
- Explain what a reversal (A-B-A) design is.
- Explain what an A-B-A-B design is.
- Explain what a B-A-B design is.
- Explain what an A-B-C-B design is.
- Explain what a multiple-baseline design is.
- Identify various threats to internal validity associated with single-subject studies.
- Explain three ways in which threats to internal validity in single-subject studies can be controlled.
- Discuss the external validity of single-subject research.
- Critique research articles that involve single-subject designs.

Essential Characteristics of Single-Subject Research

Single-Subject Designs

The Graphing of Single-Subject Designs
The A-B Design
The A-B-A Design
The A-B-A-B Design
The B-A-B Design
The A-B-C-B Design
Multiple-Baseline Designs

Threats to Internal Validity in Single-Subject Research

Control of Threats to Internal Validity in Single-Subject Research
External Validity in Single-Subject Research: The Importance of Replication
Other Single-Subject Designs

An Example of Single-Subject Research

Analysis of the Study

Purpose/Justification/Prior Research
Definitions
Hypotheses
Sample
Instrumentation
Procedures/Internal Validity
Data Analysis/Results/Discussion

INTERACTIVE AND APPLIED LEARNING After, or while, reading this chapter:

Go to the Online Learning Center at www.mhhe.com/fraenkel9e to:

- Learn More About Essential Characteristics of Single-Subject Research

Go to your online Student Mastery Activities book to do the following activities:

- Activity 14.1: Single-Subject Research Questions
- Activity 14.2: Characteristics of Single-Subject Research
- Activity 14.3: Analyze Some Single-Subject Data

Jasmin Wong, a third-grade teacher in a small elementary school in San Diego, California, finds her teaching continually interrupted by Alex, a student who can't seem to keep quiet. Distressed, she asks herself what she might do to control this student and wonders whether some kind of "time-out" activity might work. With this in mind, she asks some of the other teachers in the school whether brief periods of removing Alex from the class might decrease the frequency of his disruptive behavior.

This question is exactly the sort that can be answered best by means of a single-subject A-B-A-B design. In this chapter, you will learn what an A-B-A-B design involves and how it works, as well as some other ideas about single-subject research.

Essential Characteristics of Single-Subject Research

All of the designs described in the previous chapter on experimental research involve the study of groups. At times, however, group designs are not appropriate for a researcher to use, particularly when the usual instruments are not pertinent and observation must be the method of data collection. Sometimes there are just not enough subjects available to make the use of a group design practical. In other cases, intensive data collection on a few individuals makes more sense. Researchers who wish to study children who suffer from multiple disabilities (e.g., who are both deaf and blind) may have only a small number of children available to them, say six or less. It would make little sense to form two groups of three each in such an instance. Further, each child would probably need to be observed in great detail.

Single-subject designs are adaptations of the basic time-series design shown in Figure 13.9 in the previous chapter. The difference is that data are collected and analyzed for only one subject at a time. They are most commonly used to study the changes in behavior an individual exhibits after exposure to an intervention or treatment of some sort. Developed primarily in special education, where much of the usual instrumentation is inappropriate, single-subject designs have been used by researchers to demonstrate that children with Down syndrome, for example, are capable of far more complex learning than was previously believed.*

Following are the titles of some published reports of single-subject studies that have been conducted by educational researchers:

- "Systematic Instruction for Social-Pragmatic Language Skills in Lunchroom Settings"[1]
- "The Effect of a Self-Monitored Relaxation Breathing Exercise on Male Adolescent Aggressive Behavior"[2]
- "Effects of Ordinary and Adaptive Toys on Preschool Children with Developmental Disabilities"[3]
- "The Effects of Improvisational Music Therapy on Joint Attention Behaviors in Autistic Children: A Randomized Controlled Study"[4]
- "Decreasing Excessive Media Usage While Increasing Physical Activity"[5]
- "Effects of Assisted-Repeated Reading on Students of Varying Reading Ability"[6]
- "Enhancing Instructional Efficiency Through Generalization and Instructive Feedback"[7]

*Increasingly, single-subject designs are being used in certain kinds of studies where the unit of observation is a single group rather than a single individual.

MORE ABOUT RESEARCH

Important Findings in Single-Subject Research

For a long time, it was thought that there were many things, including independent living skills, that severely intellectually limited or emotionally disturbed children and adults could not be expected to learn. A series of studies in the 1960s, however, proved that they could learn a great deal through procedures known originally as *operant conditioning,* and subsequently as *behavior modification* or *applied behavioral analysis.** More recent studies refined these methods.†

*Bensberg, G. J., Colwell, C. N., & Cassel, R. H. (1965). Teaching the profoundly retarded self-help activities by behavior shaping techniques. *American Journal of Mental Deficiency, 69,* 674–679; Lovaas, O.I., Freitag, L., Nelson, K., & Whalen, C. (1967). The establishment of imitation and its use for the development of complex behavior in schizophrenic children. *Behavior Research and Therapy, 5,* 171–181.
†Wolery, M., Bailey, D. B., & Sugai, G. (1998). *Effective teaching principles and practices of applied behavior analysis with exceptional students.* Needham, MA: Allyn and Bacon.

Single-Subject Designs

THE GRAPHING OF SINGLE-SUBJECT DESIGNS

Single-subject researchers primarily use line graphs to present their data and to illustrate the effects of a particular intervention or treatment. Figure 14.1 presents an illustration of such a graph. The dependent (outcome) variable is displayed on the vertical axis (the *ordinate,* or *y*-axis). For example, if we were teaching a self-help skill to a severely disabled child, the number of correct responses would be shown on the vertical axis.

The horizontal axis (the *abscissa,* or *x*-axis) is used to indicate a sequence of time, such as sessions, days, weeks, trials, or months. As a rough rule of thumb, the horizontal axis should be anywhere from one and one-half to two times as long as the vertical axis.

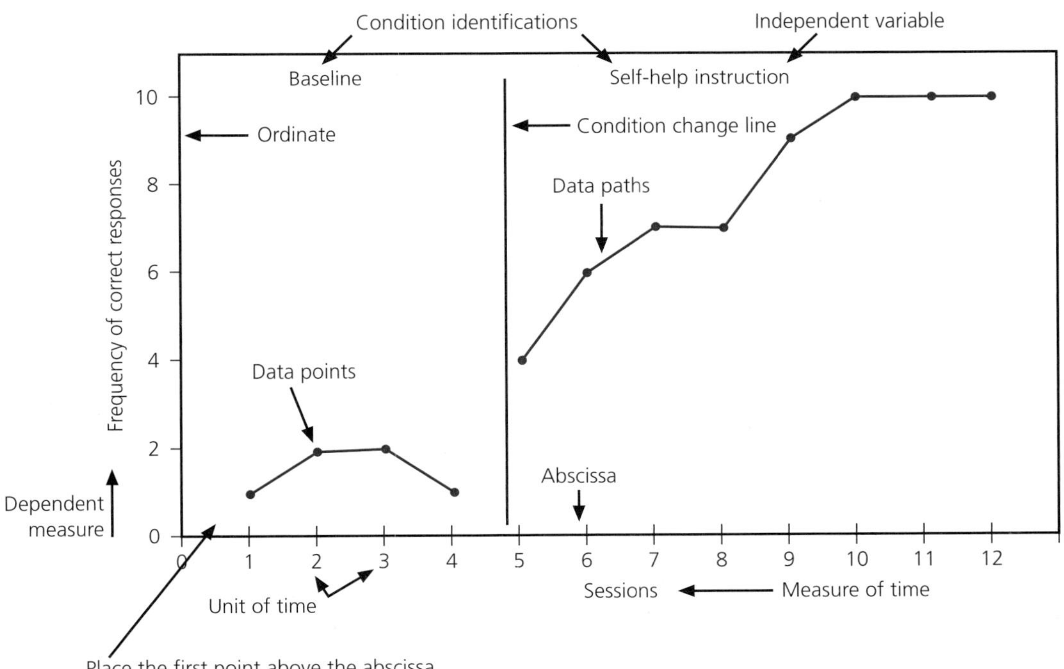

Figure 14.1 *Single-Subject Graph*

A description of the *conditions* involved in the study is listed just above the graph. The first condition is usually the **baseline**, followed by the intervention (the independent variable). *Condition lines*, indicating when the condition has changed, separate the conditions. The dots are *data points.* They represent the data collected at various times during the study. They are placed on the graph by finding the intersection of the time when the data point was collected (e.g., session 6) and the results at that time (six correct responses). These data points are then connected to illustrate trends in the data. Lastly, there is a figure caption near the bottom of the graph, which is a summary of the figure, usually listing both the independent and the dependent variables.

THE A-B DESIGN

The basic approach of researchers using an **A-B design** is to collect data on the same subject, operating as his or her own control, under two conditions or phases. The first condition is the pretreatment condition, typically called (as mentioned before) the *baseline period,* and identified as A. During the baseline period, the subject is assessed for several sessions until it appears that his or her typical behavior has been reliably determined. The baseline is extremely important in single-subject research since it is the best estimate of what would have occurred if the intervention were not applied. Enough data points must be obtained to determine a clear picture of the existing condition; certainly one should collect a minimum of three data points before implementing the intervention. The baseline, in effect, provides a comparison to the intervention condition.

Once the baseline condition has been established, a treatment or intervention condition, identified as B, is introduced and maintained for a period of time. Typically, though not necessarily, a highly specific behavior is taught during the intervention condition, with the instructor serving as the data collector—usually by recording the number of correct responses (e.g., answers to questions) or behaviors (e.g., looking at the teacher) given by the subject during a fixed number of trials.

As an example of an A-B design, consider a researcher interested in the effects of verbal praise on a particularly nonresponsive junior high school student during instruction in mathematics. The researcher could observe the student's behavior for, say, five days while instruction in math is occurring, then praise him verbally for five sessions and observe his behavior immediately after the praise. Figure 14.2 illustrates this A-B design.

As you can see, five measures were taken before the intervention and five more during the intervention. Looking at the data in Figure 14.2, the intervention

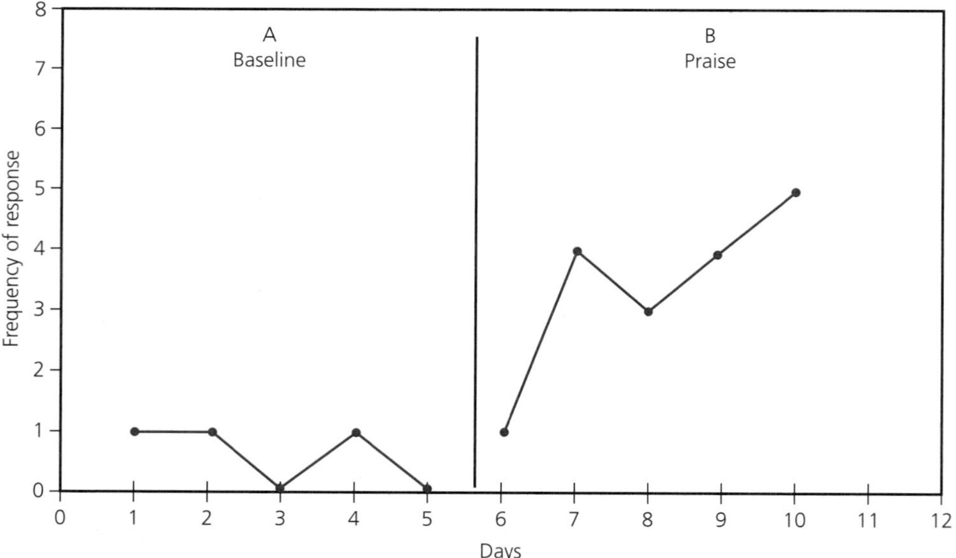

Frequency of response across baseline and praise conditions

Figure 14.2 *A-B Design*

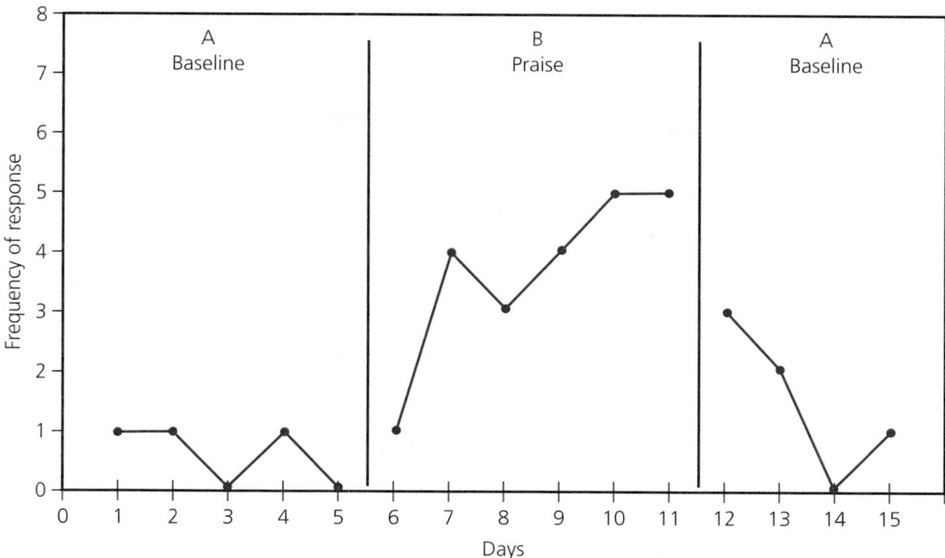

Frequency of response across baseline and praise conditions

Figure 14.3 *A-B-A Design*

appears to have been effective. The amount of responsiveness after the intervention (the praise) increased markedly. However, there is a major problem with the A-B design. Similar to the one-shot case study that it resembles, the researcher does not know whether any behavior change occurred *because* of the treatment. It is possible that some other variable (other than praise) actually caused the change, or even that the change would have occurred naturally, without any treatment at all. Thus the A-B design fails to control for various threats to internal validity; it does not determine the effect of the independent variable (praise) on the dependent variable (responsiveness) while ruling out the possible effect(s) of extraneous variables. As a result, researchers usually try to improve on the A-B design by using an A-B-A design.*

THE A-B-A DESIGN

When using an **A-B-A design** (sometimes called *reversal designs*), researchers simply add another baseline period. This improves the design considerably. If the behavior during the treatment period differs from the behavior during either baseline period, we have stronger evidence for the effectiveness of the intervention. In our previous example, the researcher, after praising the student for, say, five days could eliminate the praise and observe the student's behavior for another five days with no praise. This would reduce threats to internal validity, because it is unlikely that something would occur at the precise time the intervention is presented to cause an increase in the behavior and at the precise time the intervention is removed to cause a decrease in the behavior. Figure 14.3 illustrates the A-B-A design.

Although the decrease in threats to internal validity is a definite advantage of the A-B-A design, there is a significant ethical disadvantage to this design: It involves leaving the subjects in the A condition. Many researchers would feel uncomfortable about ending this type of study without some degree of final improvement being shown. As a result, an extension of this design—the A-B-A-B design, is frequently used.

THE A-B-A-B DESIGN

In the **A-B-A-B design**, two baseline periods are combined with two treatment periods. This further strengthens any conclusion about the effectiveness of the treatment, because it permits the effectiveness of the

*Another option is to replicate this design with additional individuals with treatment beginning at different times, thereby reducing the likelihood that the passage of time or other conditions are responsible for changes.

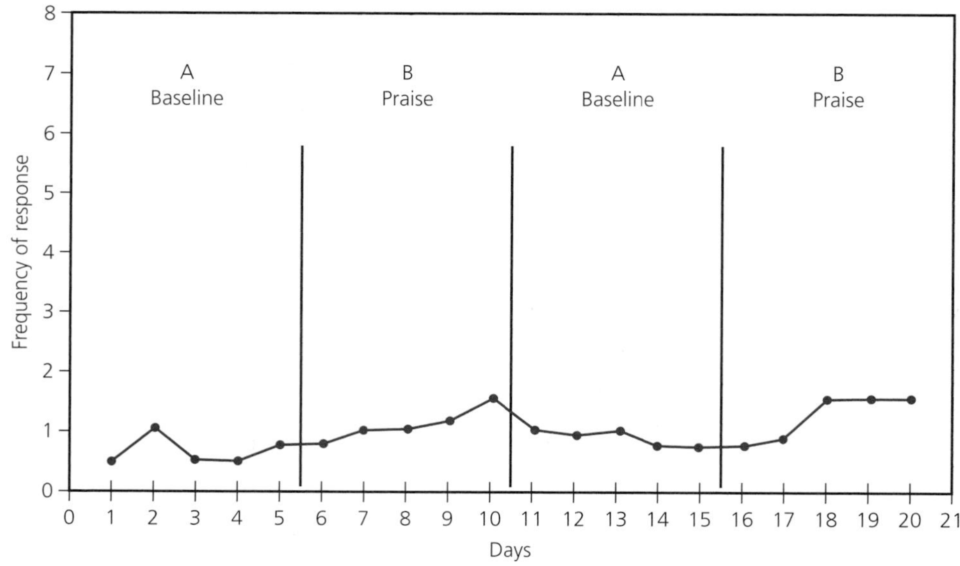

Frequency of response across baseline and praise conditions

Figure 14.4 *A-B-A-B Design*

treatment to be demonstrated *twice*. In fact, the second treatment can be extended indefinitely if a researcher so desires. If the behavior of the subject is essentially the same during both treatment phases and better (or worse) than both baseline periods, the likelihood of another variable being the cause of the change is decreased markedly. Another advantage here is evident—the ethical problem of leaving the subject(s) without an intervention is avoided.

To implement an A-B-A-B design in the previous example, the researcher would reinstate the experiment treatment, B (praise), for five days after the second baseline period and observe the subject's behavior. As with the A-B-A design, the researcher hopes to demonstrate that the dependent variable (responsiveness) changes whenever the independent variable (praise) is applied. If the subject's behavior changes from the first baseline to the first treatment period, from the first treatment to the second baseline, and so on, the researcher has evidence that praise is indeed the cause of the change. Figure 14.4 illustrates the results of a hypothetical study involving an A-B-A-B design.

Notice that a clear baseline is established, followed by an increase in response during treatment, followed by a decrease in response when treatment is stopped, followed by an increase in response once the treatment is instituted again. This pattern provides fairly strong evidence that it is the treatment, rather than history, maturation, or something else, that is responsible for the improvement.

Although evidence such as that shown in Figure 14.4 would be considered a strong argument for causation, you should be aware that the A-B-A and A-B-A-B designs suffer from limitations: The possibility of data-collector bias (the individual who is giving the treatment also usually collects the data) and an instrumentation effect (the need for an extensive number of data collection periods) can lead to changes in the conditions of data collection.

THE B-A-B DESIGN

Occasionally there are times when an individual's behavior is so severe or disturbing (e.g., excessive fighting both in and outside of class) that a researcher cannot wait for a baseline to be established. In such cases, a **B-A-B design** may be used. This design involves a treatment followed by a baseline followed by a return to the treatment. This design is also appropriate when there is a lack of behavior—for example, if the subjects have never exhibited the desired (e.g., paying attention) behaviors in the past—or when an intervention is already ongoing (e.g., an after-school detention program) and a researcher wishes to establish its effect. Figure 14.5 illustrates the B-A-B design.

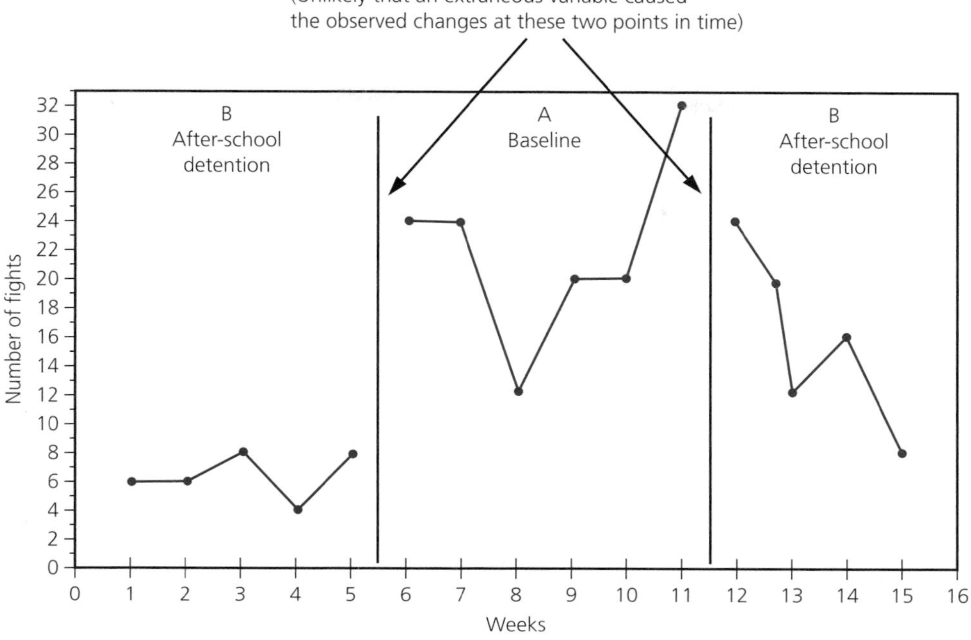

Figure 14.5 *B-A-B Design*

THE A-B-C-B DESIGN

The **A-B-C-B design** is a further modification of the A-B-A design. The C in this design refers to a variation of the intervention in the B condition. In the first two conditions, the baseline and intervention data are collected. During the C condition, the intervention is *changed* to control for any extra attention the subject may have received during the B phase. For example, in our earlier example, one might argue that it was not the praise that was responsible for any improved responsiveness (should that occur) on the part of the subject, but rather the extra attention that the subject received.

The C condition, therefore, might be praise given no matter how the subject responds (i.e., whether or not he or she offers responses). Thus, as shown in Figure 14.6, a conclusion could be reached that *contingent* (or *selective*) praise is critical for improved responsiveness, as compared to the mere increase in overall praise.

MULTIPLE-BASELINE DESIGNS

An alternative to the A-B-A-B design is the multiple-baseline design. **Multiple-baseline designs** are typically used when it is not possible or ethical to withdraw a treatment and return to the baseline condition. When using a multiple-baseline design, researchers do more than collect data on one behavior for one subject in one setting; they collect on several behaviors for one subject, obtaining a baseline for each during the *same* period of time.

When using a multiple-baseline design across behaviors, the researcher systematically applies the treatment at different times for each behavior until all of them are undergoing the treatment. If behavior changes in each case only after the treatment has been applied, the treatment is judged to be the cause of the change. It is important that the behaviors being treated, however, remain independent of each other. If behavior 2, for example, is affected by the introduction of the treatment to behavior 1, then the effectiveness of the treatment cannot be determined. A diagram of a multiple-baseline design involving three behaviors is shown in Figure 14.7.

In this design, treatment is applied first to change behavior 1, then behavior 2, and then behavior 3 until all three behaviors are undergoing the treatment. For example, a researcher might investigate the effects of

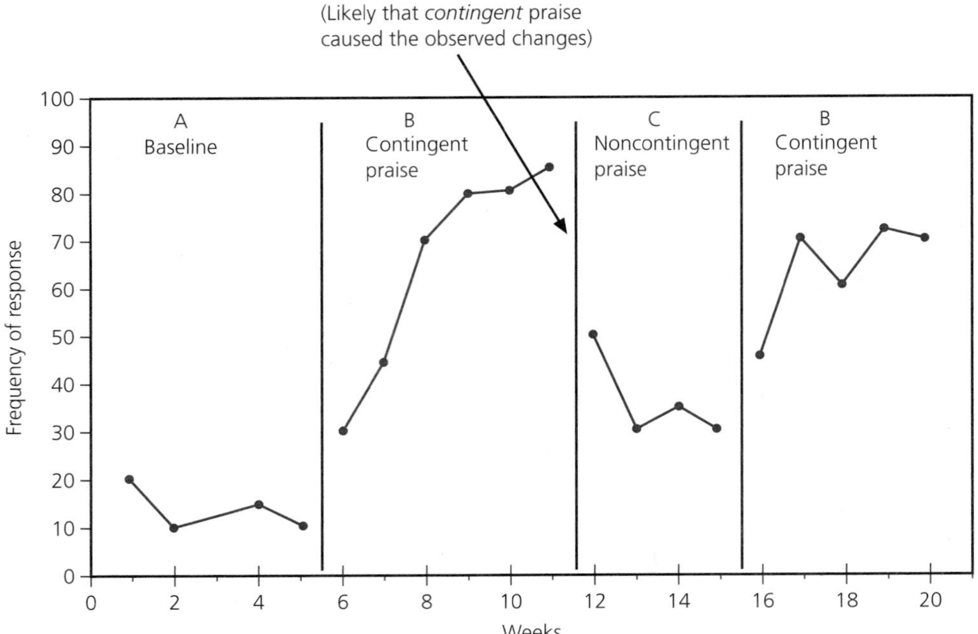

Frequency of response across baseline, contingent praise, and noncontingent praise conditions

Figure 14.6 *A-B-C-B Design*

Figure 14.7 *Multiple-Baseline Design*

Behavior 1	*O O O O X O X O X O X O X O X O X O X O X O*
Behavior 2	*O O O O O O O X O X O X O X O X O X O X O*
Behavior 3	*O O O O O O O O O O X O X O X O X O X O*

"time-out" (removing a student from class activities for a period of time) on decreasing various undesirable behaviors of a particular student. Suppose the behaviors are (1) talking out of turn; (2) tearing up worksheets; and (3) making derogatory remarks toward another student. The researcher begins by applying the time-out treatment first to behavior 1, then to behavior 2, and then to behavior 3. At that point, the treatment will have been applied to all three behaviors. The more behaviors that are eliminated or reduced, the more effective the treatment can be judged to be. How many times the researcher must apply the treatment is a matter of judgment and depends on the subjects involved, the setting, and the behaviors the researcher wishes to decrease or eliminate (or encourage). Multiple-baseline designs also are sometimes used to collect data on *several* subjects with regard to a *single* behavior, or to measure a subject's behavior in two or more *different* settings.

Figure 14.8 illustrates the effects of a treatment in a hypothetical study using a multiple-baseline design. Notice that each of the behaviors changed only when the treatment was introduced. Figure 14.9 illustrates the design applied to different settings.

In practice, the results of the studies described here rarely fit the ideal model in that the data points often show more fluctuation, making trends less clear-cut. This feature makes data collector bias even more of a problem, particularly when the behavior in question is more complex than just a simple response such as picking up an object. Data collector bias in multiple-baseline studies remains a serious concern.

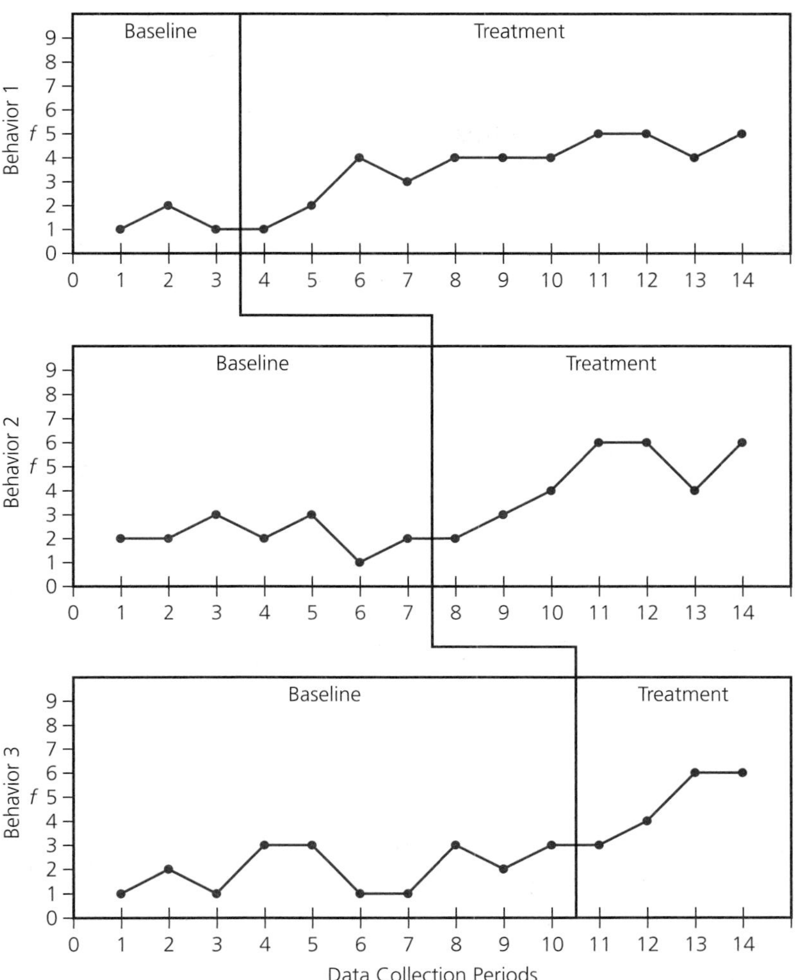

Figure 14.8 *Multiple-Baseline Design*

Threats to Internal Validity in Single-Subject Research

As we mentioned earlier, there are unfortunately several threats to the internal validity of single-subject studies. Some of the most important involve the length of the baseline and intervention conditions, the number of variables changed when moving from one condition to another, the degree and speed of any change that occurs, a return—or not—of the behavior to baseline levels, the independence of behaviors, and the number of baselines. Let us discuss each of these in more detail.

Condition Length. Condition length refers to how long the baseline and intervention conditions are in effect. It is essentially the number of data points gathered during a condition. A researcher must have enough data points (a minimum of three) to establish a clear pattern or trend. Take a look at Figure 14.10(*a*) on page 311. The data shown in the baseline condition appear to be stable, and hence it would be appropriate for the researcher to introduce the intervention. In Figure 14.10(*b*), the data points appear to be moving in a direction opposite to that which is desired, and hence here too it would be appropriate for the researcher to introduce the intervention. In Figure 14.10(*c*), the data points vary greatly; no trend has been established, and hence the researcher

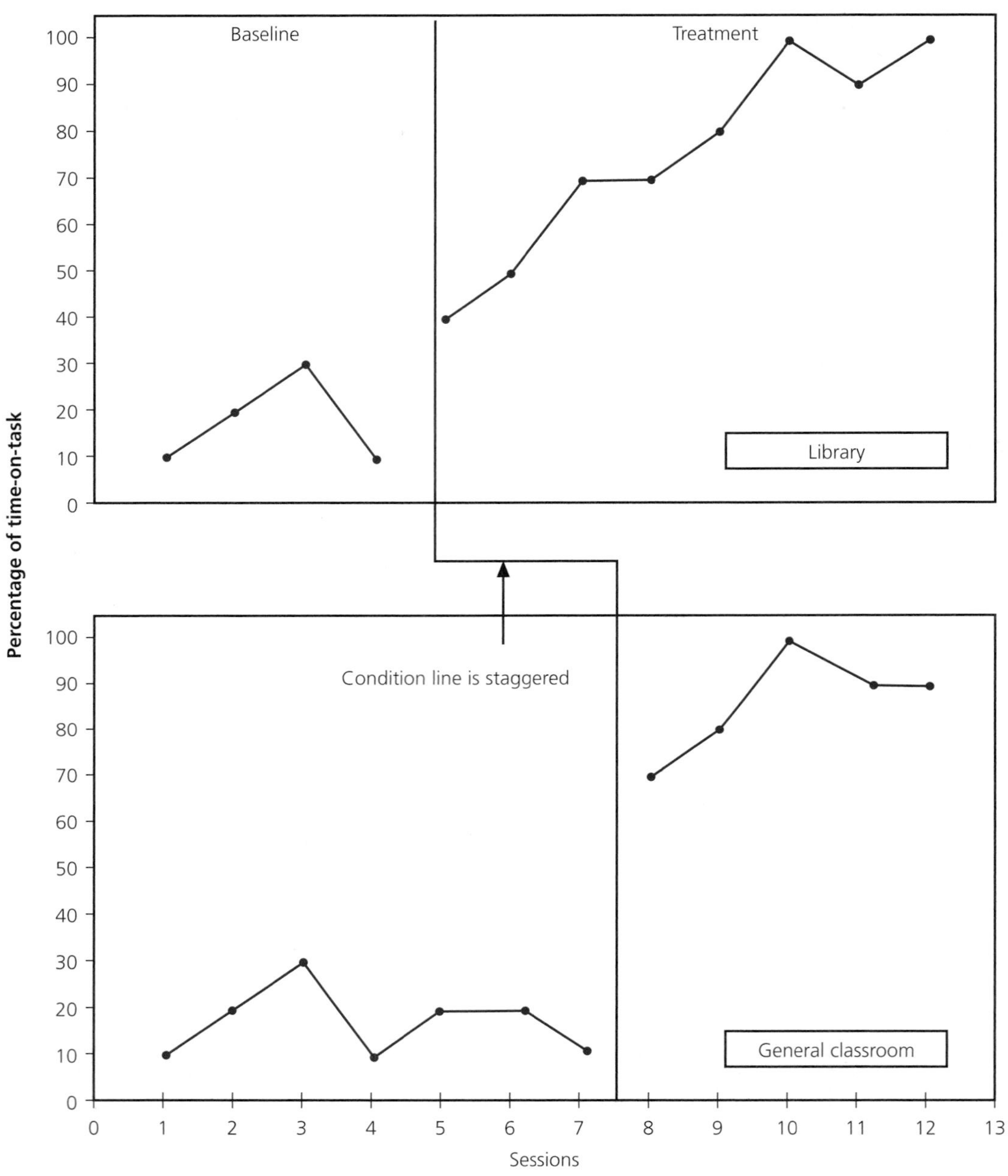

Figure 14.9 *Multiple-Baseline Design Applied to Different Settings*

should stay in the baseline condition for a longer period of time. Note that the data points in Figure 14.10(*d*) appear to be moving in the *same* direction as that which is desired. If the baseline condition were to be ended at this time and the intervention introduced, the effects of the intervention might be difficult to determine.

In the real world, of course, it is often difficult to obtain enough data points to see a clear trend. Often there are practical problems such as a need to begin the study due to a shortage of time or an ethical concern such as a subject displaying very dangerous behavior. Nevertheless, the stability of data points must always be taken

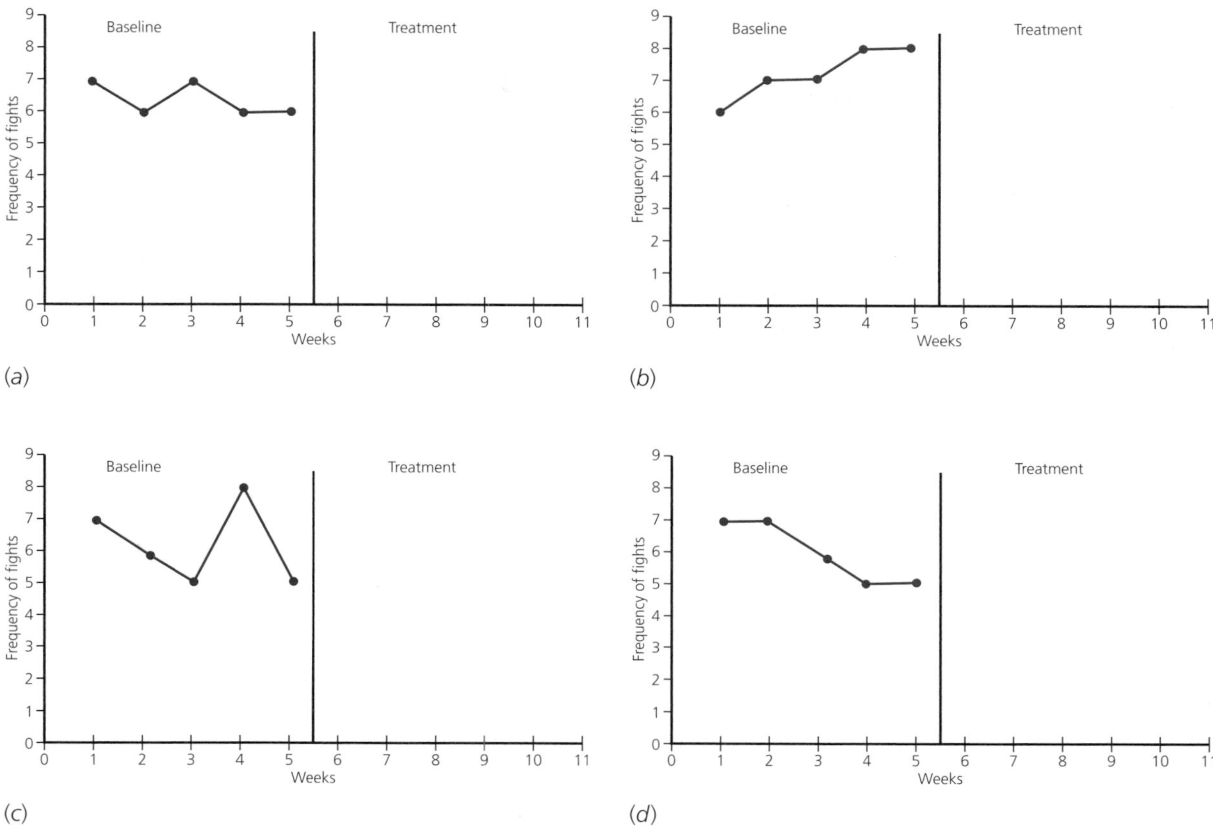

Figure 14.10 *Variations in Baseline Stability*

into account by those who conduct (and those who read) single-subject studies.

Number of Variables Changed When Moving from One Condition to Another. One of the most important considerations in single-subject research is the number of variables introduced: Only one variable should be changed at a time when moving from one condition to another. For instance, consider our previous example in which a researcher is interested in determining the effects of time-out on decreasing certain undesirable behaviors of a student. The researcher should take care that the only treatment she introduces during the intervention condition is the time-out experience. This step changes only one variable. If the researcher were to introduce not only the time-out experience *but also* another experience (e.g., counseling the student during the time-out), she would be changing *two* variables. In effect, the treatment would be confounded. The intervention would now consist of two variables mixed together. Unfortunately, the only thing the researcher could now conclude would be whether the combined treatment was or was not effective. He or she would not know if it was the counseling or the time-out that was the cause. Thus, when analyzing a single-subject design, it is always important to determine whether only one variable at a time has been changed. If this is not the case, any conclusions that are drawn may be erroneous.

Degree and Speed of Change. Researchers must also take into account the magnitude with which the data change at the time the intervention condition is implemented (i.e., when the independent variable is introduced or removed). Look, for example, at Figure 14.11(*a*). The baseline condition reveals that the data have stability. When the intervention is introduced, however, the

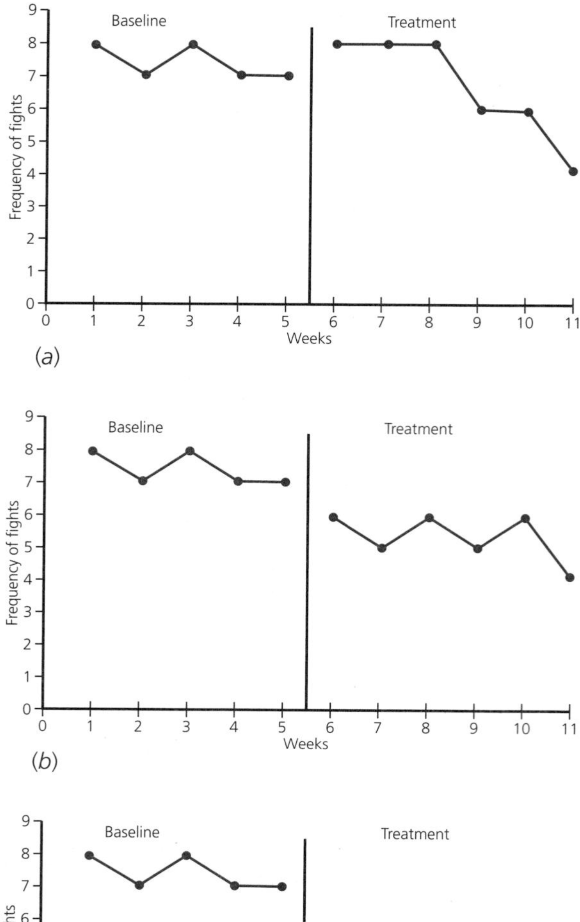

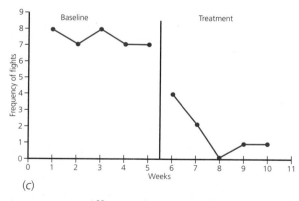

Figure 14.11 *Differences in Degree and Speed of Change*

subject's behavior does not change for a period of three sessions. This does not indicate a very strong experimental effect. If the independent variable (whatever it may be) were effective, one would assume that the subject's behavior would have changed more quickly. It is possible, of course, that the independent variable was effective, but not of sufficient strength to bring about an immediate change (or the behavior may have been resistant to change). Nevertheless, researchers must consider all such possibilities if there is a slow or delayed change once the intervention is introduced. Figure 14.11(*b*) indicates there was a fairly immediate change but that it was of small magnitude. Only in Figure 14.11(*c*) do we see a dramatic and rapid change once the intervention was introduced. A researcher would be more likely to conclude that the independent variable was effective in this case than he or she would in either of the other two.

Return to Baseline Level. Look at Figure 14.12(*a*). Notice that in returning to the baseline condition, there was not a rapid change in behavior. This suggests that something else may have occurred when the intervention condition was introduced. We would expect that the behavior of the subject would have returned to baseline levels fairly quickly if the intervention had been the causal factor in changing the subject's behavior. The fact that the subject's behavior did not return to the original baseline level suggests that one or more extraneous variables may have produced the effects observed during the intervention condition. On the other hand, look at Figure 14.12(*b*). Here we see that the change from intervention to baseline levels was abrupt and rapid. This suggests that the independent variable was likely the cause of the changes in the dependent variable. Note, however, that, because the treatment was intended to have a lasting impact, a slower return to baseline may have been desirable, though it would have complicated interpretation.

Independence of Behaviors. This concern is most applicable to multiple-baseline studies. Imagine for a moment that a researcher is investigating various methods of teaching history. The researcher defines two separate behaviors that she is going to measure. These include (1) ability to locate the central idea, and (2) ability to summarize the important points in various historical documents. The researcher obtains baseline data for each of these skills and then implements an intervention (providing worksheets that give clues about how to locate important ideas in historical documents). The subject's ability to locate the central idea in a document improves quickly and considerably. However, the subject's ability to summarize important points also improves. It is quite evident that these two skills are not independent. They appear to be related in some way, conceivably dependent on the same underlying cognitive ability, and hence they improve together.

MORE ABOUT RESEARCH

Examples of Studies Conducted Using Single-Subject Designs

- Determining the collateral effects of peer tutor-training on a student with severe disabilities (an A-B design).*
- Effects of training in rapid decoding on the reading comprehension of adult learners (an A-B-A design).†
- Effects of self-recording on reducing off-task behavior of a high school student with an attention-deficit hyperactivity disorder (an A-B-A-B design).‡
- Assessing the acquisition of first-aid treatments by elementary-aged children (a multiple-baseline across subjects design).§
- Effects of a self-management procedure on the classroom and academic behavior of students with mild handicaps (a multiple-baseline across settings design).||

*Martella, R. C., Marchand-Martella, N. E., Young, K. R., & McFarland, C. A. (1995). *Behavior Modification, 19,* 170–191.
†Tan, A., Moore, D. W., Dixon, R. S., & Nichelson, T. (1994). *Journal of Behavioral Education, 4,* 177–189.
‡Stewart, K. G., & McLaughlin, T. F. (1992). *Child and Family Behavior Therapy 14*(3), 53–59.
§Marchand-Martella, N. E., Martella, R. C., Agran, M., & Young, K. R. (1991). *Child and Family Behavior Therapy 13*(4), 29–43.
||Smith, D. J., Nelson, J. R., Young, K. R., & West, R. P. (1992). *School Psychology Review, 21,* 59–72.

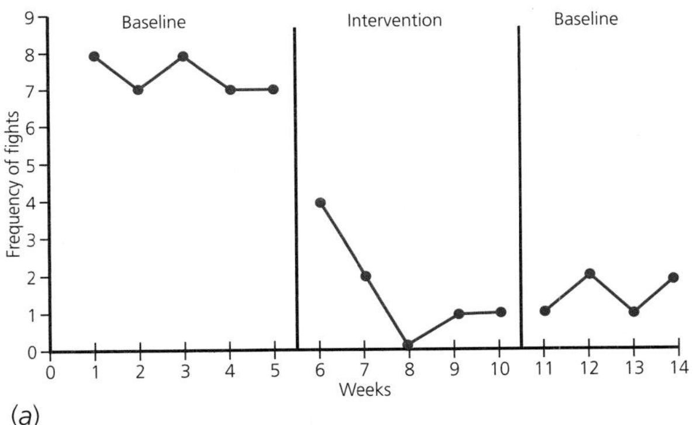

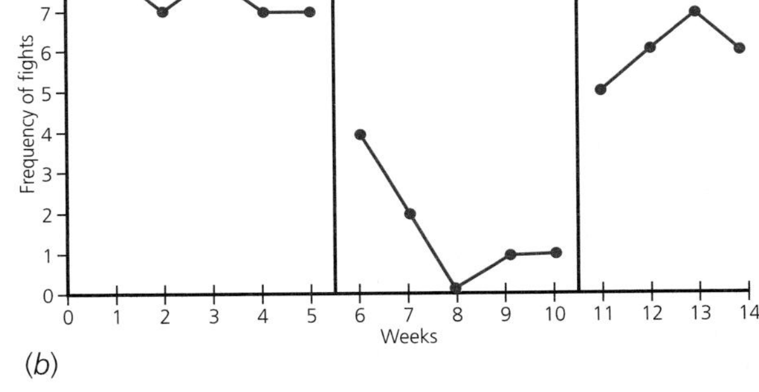

Figure 14.12 *Differences in Return to Baseline Conditions*

Number of Baselines. To have a multiple-baseline design, a researcher must have at least two baselines. Although the baselines begin at the same time, the interventions are introduced at different times. As we mentioned earlier, the chances that an extraneous variable caused the results when using a multiple-baseline design across two behaviors are lessened, since it is less likely that the same extraneous event caused the observed changes for both behaviors at different times. The probability that an extraneous event caused the changes in a multiple-baseline design across three behaviors, therefore, is even less.

Thus, the greater the number of baselines, the greater the probability that the intervention is the cause of any changes in behavior, since the likelihood that an extraneous variable caused the changes is correspondingly decreased the more behaviors we have.

There is a problem with a large number of baselines, however. The more baselines there are, the longer the later behaviors must remain in baseline—that is, are kept from receiving the intervention. For example, if we follow the recommendation mentioned earlier of establishing stable data points before we introduce the intervention condition, this would mean that the first behavior is in baseline for a minimum of three sessions, the second for six sessions, and the third for nine. Should we use four baselines, the fourth behavior would be in baseline condition for 12 sessions! This is a very long time for a behavior to be kept from receiving the intervention. As a general rule, however, it is important to remember that the fewer the number of baselines, the less likely we can conclude that it is the intervention rather than some other variable that causes any changes in behavior.

CONTROL OF THREATS TO INTERNAL VALIDITY IN SINGLE-SUBJECT RESEARCH

Single-subject designs are most effective in controlling for subject characteristics, mortality, testing, and history threats; they are less effective with location, data collector characteristics, maturation, and regression threats; and they are definitely weak when it comes to instrument decay, data collector bias, attitudinal, and implementation threats.

A location threat is most often only a minor threat in multiple-baseline studies, because the location where the treatment is administered is usually constant throughout the study. The same is true for data collector characteristics, although such characteristics can be a problem if the data collector is changed over the course of the study.

Single-subject designs unfortunately do suffer from a strong likelihood of instrument decay and data collector bias, since data must be collected (usually by means of observations) over many trials, and the data collector can hardly be kept in the dark as to the intent of the study.

Neither implementation nor attitudinal effect threats are well controlled for in single-subject research. Either implementers or data collectors can, unintentionally, distort the results of a study. Data collector bias is a particular problem when the same person is both implementer (e.g., acting as the teacher) and data collector. A second observer, recording independently, reduces this threat but increases the amount of staff needed to complete the study. A testing threat is usually not a threat, since presumably the subject cannot affect observational data.

EXTERNAL VALIDITY IN SINGLE-SUBJECT RESEARCH: THE IMPORTANCE OF REPLICATION

Single-subject studies are weak when it comes to **external validity**—that is, generalizability. One would hardly advocate use of a treatment shown to be effective with only one subject! As a result, studies involving single-subject designs that show a particular treatment to be effective in changing behaviors must rely on replications—across individuals rather than groups—if such results are to be found worthy of generalization.

OTHER SINGLE-SUBJECT DESIGNS

There are a variety of other, less used designs that fall within the single-subject category. One is the *multitreatment design,* which introduces a different treatment into an A-B-A-B design (i.e., A-B-A-C-A). The *alternating-treatments design* alternates two or more different treatments after an initial baseline period (e.g., A-B-C-B-C). A variation of this is illustrated in the study analysis in this chapter, which eliminates the baseline, becoming a B-C-B, B-C-B-C, or B-C-B-C-B design. The *multiprobe design* differs from a multiple-baseline design only in that fewer data points are used, in an attempt to reduce the data collection burden and avoid threats to internal validity. Finally, features of all these designs can be combined.*

An Example of Single-Subject Research

In the remainder of this chapter, we present a published example of single-subject research followed by a critique of its strengths and weaknesses. As we did in our critique of the group comparison experimental research study in Chapter 13, we use the concepts introduced in earlier parts of the book in our analysis.

*For a more detailed discussion of various types of single-subject designs, see Barlow, D. H., & Hersen, M. (1984). *Single-case experimental designs: Strategies for studying behavior change* (2nd ed.), New York: Pergamon Press.

RESEARCH REPORT

From: (2010). *American Annals of the Deaf 155*(3), 377–385. Reproduced with permission from Gallaudet University Press.

Implementation of the Guided Reading Approach With Elementary School Deaf Students

Barbara R. Schirmer
Department of Education,
University of Detroit

Laura Schaffer
Michigan School for the Deaf,
Flint, Michigan

The researchers investigated the effects of the Guided Reading approach (Fountas & Pinnell, 1996) on the reading development of elementary school deaf students over a period of 2 school years. A single-subject experimental research designed was used. Qualitative analyses of observations of instruction and interviews with the teachers were conducted to determine fidelity to the Guided Reading protocol. Visual display of graphed Running Records scores during the 2-year implementation showed that all students improved during intervention, all participants except the oldest group experienced a drop in scores from the end of one school year to the beginning of the next, and that it took months for most students to regain their previous year's scores; some had not done so even by the end of fall term.

Instructional practices for developing reading in deaf children were grounded historically in comprehension at the sentence level, so that instruction might be concentrated on English grammatical structures. This was done because it was believed that it was English grammar that presented the greatest barrier to proficient reading and writing. For example, *Reading Milestones* (Quigley, McAnally, King, & Rose, 1991), a basal reading series that was developed specifically for deaf readers, was based on research conducted by Quigley and associates in the 1970s (e.g., Quigley, Power, & Steinkamp, 1977; Quigley, Wilbur, & Montanelli, 1974) to highlight particular sentence structures that had been found to be most problematic for deaf readers. The series controls the appearance of language structures so that structures considered to be easier are presented in the earliest materials; as the child gains skill, stories with increasingly more complex sentence structures are presented (Quigley et al., 1991). When LaSasso (1987) conducted a survey of educational programs for deaf and hard of hearing students in the United States, she found that the majority used basal readers and the most popular was *Reading Milestones.*

Prior research

The general shift to whole language approaches in the 1990s was paralleled in deaf education. When LaSasso and Mobley (1997) replicated LaSasso's 1987 study a decade later, most educational programs characterized their reading program as whole language, though the majority reported using basal readers, the most popular still being *Reading Milestones.*

Within the past decade, there has been considerable research to support the importance of phonemic awareness and phonic analysis in learning to read (e.g., Allor, 2002; National Reading Panel, 2000; Snow, Burns, & Griffin, 1998). The result has been a shift to reading programs that emphasize developing these skills, and, indeed, federal Reading First grants were largely distributed to early reading instruction programs that incorporated direct and systematic instruction in phonemic awareness and phonic analysis (Office of the Inspector General, 2006; U.S. Department of Education, 2008). This particular shift in general education has not yet seen a parallel shift in deaf education, though one reason may be that in the past, practices in deaf education trailed practices in reading education; when particular approaches are at peak interest in deaf education, interest in applying the same approaches is waning in general education (Schirmer & Williams, 2010). Furthermore, this particular shift presents a dilemma in deaf education because phonemic awareness and phonic analysis are dependent on ability to hear, although approaches such as Visual Phonics are attempts to circumvent the auditory process (Narr, 2008; Trezak & Malmgren, 2005; Trezak & Wang, 2006; Trezak, Wang, Woods, Gampp, & Paul, 2007).

Prior research

Conclusions of the National Reading Panel (2000) emphasized the importance of five key areas for reading instruction: phonemic awareness, phonics, fluency, vocabulary, and text comprehension. When Schirmer and McGough (2005) conducted a synthetic review of the research literature on the reading development and reading instruction of deaf students, and compared findings to the review of research literature done by the National Reading Panel, they found that in the areas for which there was sufficient research with deaf readers, these same areas were important for deaf readers. However, they also found a very small body of research on instructional strategies identified by the panel as effective with normally developing readers and readers with disabilities. Schirmer and Williams (2010) similarly found little research on effective instructional strategies, and no research on effective instructional models (i.e., the framework for the reading program as a lesson structure).

Justification

In spite of the absence of research on instructional models for teaching reading to deaf readers and the limited research assessing the effectiveness of instructional strategies with this population, classroom instruction clearly cannot wait for the establishment of evidence-based models and strategies. In seeking a model for reading instruction at a school for the deaf in the Midwest, the literacy specialists and classroom teachers certainly needed one for which there was some evidence of effectiveness, but also they sought an approach that was likely to be accepted by the teachers for their instructional repertoire. In other words, they needed a model with the potential for social validity—that is, significance of goals, acceptability of instructional procedures, and importance of outcomes (Lane & Beebe-Frankenberger, 2004). The Guided Reading approach had been developed a decade earlier, by Fountas and Pinnell (1996), and it quickly become popular among general education teachers working with hearing readers. Indeed, during the previous several years, Fountas and Pinnell had developed lists of reading materials categorized across a range of difficulty levels to support reading instruction. This list of leveled books has grown continuously since it was first published (Fountas & Pinnell, 1996,1999), and it is now available on a website to accommodate the constant additions (Fountas & Pinnell, 2008). This list of leveled books serves to increase the ease of adoption and implementation by teachers. Guided Reading is recommended by the Laurent Clerc National Deaf Education Center (2009) for use with deaf students, though to date no research on efficacy has been published.

Though lacking a body of research on efficacy even with hearing readers (though it is included among effective instructional approaches, such as by Reutzel, 2007, and Cunningham and Allington, 2007), the Guided Reading approach incorporates the evidence-based practices for which there is current consensus. According to Gambrell, Malloy, and Mazzoni (2007), these practices include creating a classroom culture that fosters motivation to engage in literacy activities, teaching reading as an authentic activity (for pleasure, for information, for completing a task), providing students with scaffolded instruction in the five key areas of reading instruction (phonemic awareness, phonics, fluency, vocabulary, and text comprehension), giving students ample time to read in class, providing children with high-quality literature across a range of genres, using multiple texts that link and expand vocabulary and concepts, connecting new concepts to background knowledge, balancing student- and teacher-led discussions of texts, using the new literacies of the Internet and technology-based instruction, and using a variety of assessment strategies and techniques.

Guided Reading was thus selected as the main instructional model for teaching deaf students at the elementary level. The purpose of the present study was to investigate the effects of the Guided Reading approach on the reading development of students who were deaf in grades 1–5 over a period of 2 school years. The study was designed to answer the question, Does the Guided Reading approach improve the reading achievement of elementary school students who are deaf?

Purpose

Implied hypothesis

METHODOLOGY

Participants

The participants in the present study included a convenience sample of students who were deaf and enrolled in grades 1–5 at the outset of the study, plus these students' classroom teachers, who were certified as teachers of the deaf with a range of experience from 2 to 30 years. During the duration of the study, there were a few personnel changes among the teachers, with a teacher leaving in the fall during both school years and long-term substitutes hired.

Correct

How many?

The setting was a state school for the deaf. The school describes its curriculum as a regular public school curriculum with modifications in terms of presenting information via American Sign Language (ASL) and written English. Students, teachers, and staff are assessed regularly with the Sign Communication Proficiency Interview; teachers and staff are provided training as needed to ensure that the campus is barrier free in terms of communication. School size was approximately 180 students during the first year and 160 students during the second year of intervention; class sizes per grade at the elementary level ranged from 4 to 9 students. Besides the teacher of the deaf, most classes had at least one teacher aide.

Good description

ASL was the language of instruction, and so teachers and students communicated in ASL throughout the school day. Speech and language services were conducted in pull-out sessions with the speech-language clinician. Guided Reading instruction was conducted in ASL.

All of the students in the elementary school were instructed with the Guided Reading approach, but not all of the students were included in the study. We included only those students for whom we had baseline data and who had no concomitant disability that affected cognitive functioning. We also excluded one student for whom we had only one data point beyond baseline for the first school year. Demographic information on the 19 participants is provided in Table 1.

Instruction was done within each classroom, students were grouped by reading level, and the classroom teacher conducted the lessons. Guided Reading lessons were conducted three to four times each week during each academic year of the study.

TABLE 1 *Student Participant Demographics*

Student	Chronological age (years: months at start of Guided Reading instruction)	Grade year 1–year 2	Gender	Level of hearing loss	Parents' hearing status
BD	6:3	1–2	M	Profound	Deaf
CR	7:9	1–2	F	Profound	Hearing
DE	8:9	1–2	F	Profound	Hearing
JS	6:6	1–2	M	Profound	Deaf
CS	7:2	2–3	M	Profound	Hearing
MD	7:4	2–3	M	Mild mixed	Hearing
BR	9:0	3–4	F	Moderate/profound	Hearing
HY	9:9	3–4	M	Mild/severe	Hearing
LD	8:2	3–4	M	Mild/severe	Hearing
LE	8:2	3–4	F	Profound	Deaf
OL	9:3	3–3	F	Profound	Hearing
CE	10:0	3–4	M	Profound	Hearing
CI	9:0	4–5	F	Profound	Deaf
CN	9:3	4–5	M	Profound	Hearing
DN	11:10	5–6	F	Profound	Hearing
GS	10:5	5–6	M	Profound	Hearing
LI	10:4	5–6	M	Profound	Hearing
PR	12:5	5–6	M	Profound	Hearing
RT	11:0	5–6	M	Profound	Hearing

Design

Good

The study used a single-subject experimental research design. Qualitative analyses of observations of instruction and interviews with the teachers were conducted to determine idelity to the Guided Reading protocol.

Variables

The independent variable was the Guided Reading protocol, which has four steps: *selection of leveled books, introduction of the book, silent reading,* and *discussion.*

Step 1: Selection of Leveled Books The teacher selects a book that the students can read with greater than 90% accuracy but is not so easy that there is no opportunity to build problem-solving strategies. Guided Reading requires that a selection of books along a continuum of difficulty levels has been identified. Each student is provided with a copy of the book to be read.

Step 2: Introduction of the Book The teacher introduces the book by having the students look at the cover, read the title and the name of the author, and talk about the topic. Vocabulary words crucial to understanding the story are briefly discussed, but the teacher does not do vocabulary instruction per se and does not teach new sight words. We modified this step to involve the direct teaching of new words, as deaf students typically have smaller vocabularies than same-age hearing peers and the vocabulary load of reading material is based on vocabulary norms for hearing readers.

Step 3: Silent Reading The students read the book independently and silently. The teacher observes, notes student behaviors during reading, and provides support with word recognition, understanding unfamiliar sentence structures, and comprehension when needed. We made two modifications to this step. One modification, "interactive Guided Reading," is a technique in which "the teacher carefully guides, directs, or coaches students through the silent reading of a meaningful chunk of text by asking them a question, giving prompts, or helping them formulate a question that they then try to answer as they read the designated section of text. Sometimes the teacher helps students make predictions" (Cooper & Kiger, 2009, p. 35). The other modification was to have the students read aloud or in sign language (depending on individual preference) for the first reading of the story so that the teacher could notate problems with word recognition and assist when needed. (Because the school was bilingual, some students did use their oral skills routinely, though the teachers were expected to use ASL exclusively.)

Good description

Step 4: Discussion After reading, the students discuss the book. The teacher has the students revisit the text to find evidence of interpretations and to discuss strategies for problem solving. The students might also be asked to re-read a passage independently or with a partner. In the interactive Guided Reading modification we implemented, the "teacher encourages students to reflect on the strategies they have used and to discuss how those strategies have helped them construct meaning" (Cooper & Kiger, 2009, p. 35).

The dependent variable was reading achievement level as measured by Running Records (Clay, 2000). In carrying out Running Records assessment, the teacher asked the student to read aloud/in sign a new passage at the same reading level as the material used for instruction in sign. During reading, the teacher made a check mark for each word the student read correctly, notated when the student did not know a word, and wrote the word used by the student when it was a substitution, repetition, omission, or incorrect pronunciation. The teacher also notated the student's reading fluency. The student was then asked to retell the story, and the teacher appraised the student's inclusion of setting, characters, events, and important details.

Dependent variable

Instrumentation

Used in score?

Comprehension?

Running Records is a criterion-referenced assessment tool, and trustworthiness of scores depends on two key factors: (a) the teacher's skill in recording the student's reading errors (or miscues) and (b) materials that are accurately differentiated by difficulty level. Even when scores are trustworthy because the teacher's assessment is reliable from student to student and the materials are accurately graded, scores do not provide a comprehensive assessment of reading abilities, most particularly because word recognition is emphasized at the expense of comprehension. Recently, Denton, Ciancio, and Fletcher (2006) found support for the validity of Running Records, noting that it has practical usefulness as a progress-monitoring tool, but cautioned that it does not provide comprehensive information on reading ability.

Not clear to us

Need more here

Given the two key factors that influence trustworthiness, the issue of teacher skill in our study was mitigated by the training provided to the teachers in administering Running Records, the use of single-subject design which compares the student's performance only against himself or herself, and the consistency in having the same teacher assess the same students. The issue of accuracy in ascertaining the difficulty level of the reading materials was mitigated by using the same set of graded materials for assessment as were used for instruction, so variations between levels should be equivalent whether used for assessment or instruction.

Good

Procedure

In May of the year preceding implementation of the Guided Reading approach, the elementary-level students were assessed with Running Records by their respective classroom teachers.

During a teacher in-service day before the start of school in September, the first author, who is a university professor, presented a half-day workshop encompassing explanation and discussion of the essential reading tasks (i.e., word recognition, fluency, comprehension), how to determine the deaf student's reading level, how to select a reading lesson structure, and strategies to use before, during, and after reading. The second author, who was the school's literacy specialist, then presented a half-day workshop specifically on the Guided Reading approach with deaf students at the elementary level.

The teachers were then coached throughout each academic year to use the Guided Reading approach with their students and to conduct a Running Records assessment monthly to assess student progress and adjust instruction accordingly. When personnel changes occurred, the second author provided ad hoc training on Guided Reading. The second author observed the teachers periodically, offered feedback, provided reading materials as needed, and met informally with them on a recurring basis. The first author identified articles and books that provided the second author (i.e., the literacy specialist) with evidence-based strategies that were then shared with the classroom teachers. The first author also observed several teachers during the year and provided feedback to the classroom teachers and to the second author in her role as literacy specialist.

Measures

The measures included (a) Running Records, as described above, assessed monthly, with the first assessment taking place at the end of the previous school year to develop baseline, and (b) observation notes taken during formal observations in spring term of each of the 2 years and interviews conducted informally throughout the school year and formally once during spring term.

Qualitative data

The possible range of Running Records scores is 1–19, with the following breakdown by grade level: kindergarten (1–3), grade 1 (4-8), grade 2 (9–11), grades 2–3 (12), grade 3 (13–14), grade 3–4 (15-16), grade 4 (17–18), and grade 5 (19).

The teachers were asked to conduct a monthly Running Records assessment on each student. However, school events and student absences caused several months to be missing from the assessment data. For example, no Running Records data were collected in December of the first year.

It would have been preferable to conduct a more regular schedule of observations and interviews. However, the role of literacy specialist was not full-time, and therefore did not allow for such a schedule.

ANALYSIS AND RESULTS

The predominant feature of single-subject experimental research is its focus on intrasubject comparisons rather than the intersubject comparisons that characterize other quantitative designs. A visual analysis is employed rather than a statistical analysis for each participant's graphed data (Cooper, Heron, & Heward, 2007; Kazdin, 2010).

Figure 1 displays the Running Records scores for the 19 elementary-level student participants per grade level. Graphed results of the Running Records data show several major patterns.

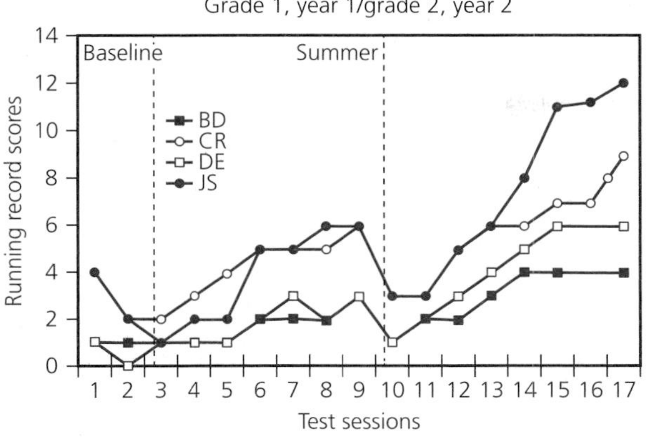

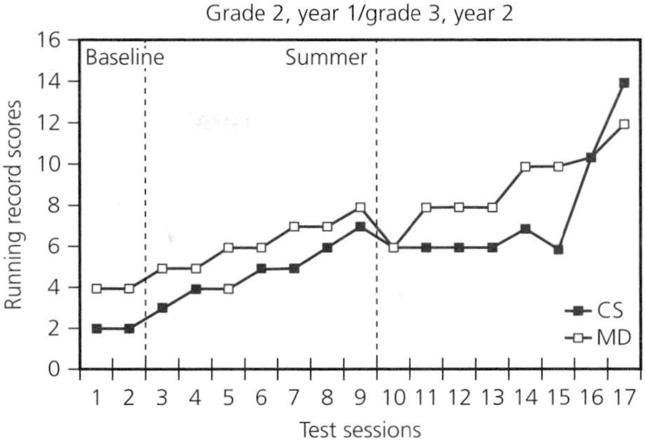

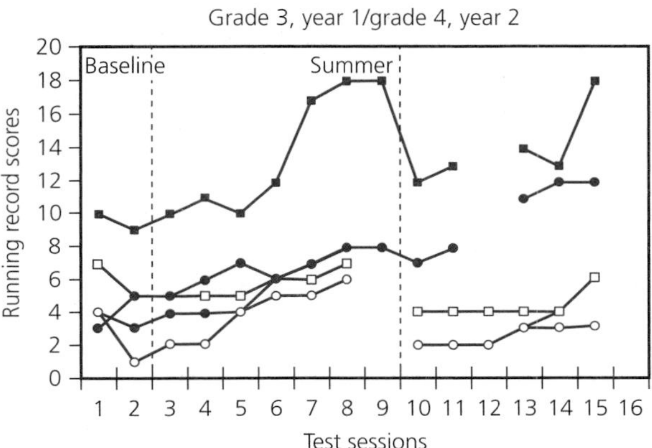

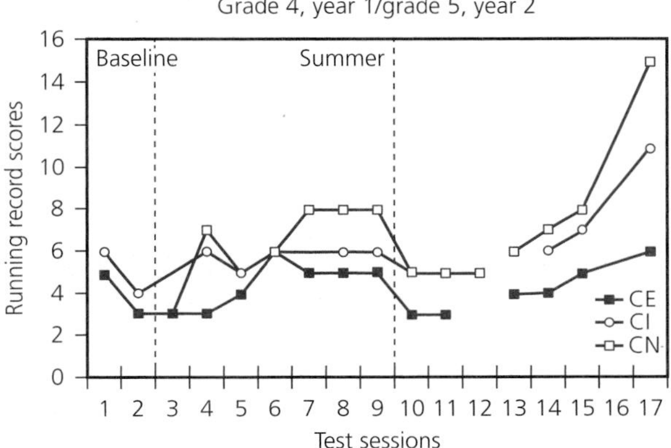

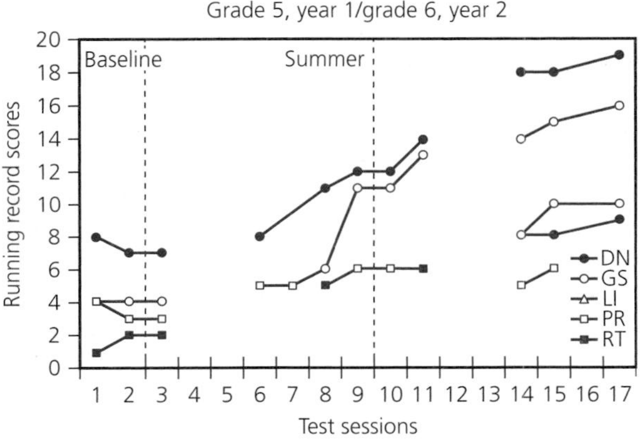

Note. Equivalent grade level scores are based on the leveled stories used as reading material for the present study. The leveling criteria used by Fountas and Pinnell (1996, 1999) result in broader spans (e.g., midgrade 1) than readability formulas typically provide (e.g., reading grade level 1.4, 1.5, and 1.6).

Running Records score	Equivalent grade level
1	Fall, kindergarten
2	Midyear, kindergarten
3	Spring, kindergarten
4	Early fall, 1
5	Late fall, 1
6	Midyear, 1
7	Early spring, 1
8	Late spring, 1
9	Fall, 2
10	Midyear, 2
11	Spring, 2
12	2–3 transition
13	Fall, 3
14	Midyear, 3
15	Spring, 3–4 transition
16	Fall, 3–4 transition
17	Midyear, 4
18	Spring, 4
19	5

Figure 1 *Changes in Running Records Scores, Grades 1–5, Years 1 and 2*

We disagree. See analysis

The first pattern is the improvement in scores during the Guided Reading instruction. As the graphs show, progress ranged from a half year to 1 year of progress for grade 1 students the first year, and half a year to 2 years of progress the following year, when they were second graders. Of the two students in grade 2 during the first year of intervention, one made almost 1 year of progress and the other half a year, but the following year both made almost 2 years of progress. Of the five students in grade 3 the first year, progress ranged from one quarter of a year to 2½ years, but the following year, when they were fourth graders, achievement was bifurcated, with three students making no progress and two making about 2 years of progress. Two of the students made approximately half a year of progress as fourth graders and, similarly, half a year of progress as fifth graders; a third student made half a year of progress in fourth grade but more than 1 year of progress in fifth grade. The fewest assessments were conducted with the students in grade 5, though even with these fewer data points, the pattern of improvement is fairly comparable to those of the other grade levels. Progress ranged from approximately half a year to more than 1 year when they were fifth graders, and half a year to 2 years when they were sixth graders.

A second pattern that is apparent in the visual display of graphed data is the drop in scores from the end of one school year and the beginning of another school year, particularly for students at the earlier grade levels and particularly between the end of the first year of Guided Reading instruction and the beginning of the second year. During baseline, this drop is demonstrated with the two data points to the left of the dotted line in Figure 1, the first of which is May and the second of which is September. The second line on the graph is meant to separate visually the data collected during the first year of intervention from fall of the second year. Though the second line does not represent an official second baseline phase, it could be argued that it represents a de facto baseline insofar as the students received no formal reading instruction during the summer months. As such, these two baseline phases demonstrate a lack of progress or a decline in performance during baseline versus improvement in performance during Guided Reading instruction for most of the participants. It is interesting that this holds for students in grades 1–4 during year 1 and 2–5 in the fall of year 2, but not for students in grade 5 during year 1 and grade 6 in the fall of year 2, whose performance declined slightly, remained stable, or improved slightly between May and September.

A third pattern is seen in the length of time it took in the new school year for the students to recapture the level they had achieved at the end of the previous school year. It took most or all of fall term for the grade 2 students to regain the level they had achieved at the end of grade 1 the previous May. One of the grade 3 students regained his May score by October, but the other student did not, even by December. Three of the grade 4 students either just regained or did not regain the scores they had achieved when they were third graders, and one took months to regain his May score. The one student who regained his May score fairly quickly also had a relatively low dip between May and September. It took at least 5 months for the grade 5 students to regain the scores they had achieved at the end of fourth grade. The only students who diverged from this pattern were those who were in grade 5 the first year of the study. There was no dip in their scores between testing at the end of grade 5 and the beginning of grade 6.

A fourth pattern is the low scores at the outset regardless of grade level. Of the 19 participants, none were at or close to grade level when Guided Reading instruction began. The disparity between reading level as assessed by Running Records and school grade level became increasingly greater from grade 1 through grade 5. At the end of the first school year, only three students had achieved scores higher than first-grade level—one student in grade 3 who attained a spring grade 4 level, one student in grade 5 who attained a spring grade 2 level, and one student in grade 5 who attained a grades 2–3 transition level. Only the latter two students maintained these gains by fall. The student who had achieved a spring grade 4 level at the end of grade 3 was assessed at a grades 2–3 transition level in September, and though she had progressed month by month, had not regained grade 4 by the end of fall term.

In order to determine fidelity, qualitative analysis of the data obtained from formal observations and interviews was carried out. We specifically conducted a content analysis, which involved coding the data based upon the components of the Guided Reading approach as a priori categories (in accordance with criteria for coding qualitative observational and interview data according to Patton, 2002). We found variation among teachers in fidelity to the Guided Reading Approach and changes in fidelity from year 1 to year 2. During both years, all of the teachers employed some features, but only one teacher employed all features of the approach.

Need more details

One component of Guided Reading is the selection of reading material that is at the student's instructional reading level (i.e., word recognition is better than 90% but the material is difficult enough to offer an opportunity for strategy instruction). Content analysis showed that all of the teachers (with the exception of the grade 2 teacher) selected material that was at the students' independent level rather than their instructional level during the first year. Given that the teachers themselves assessed the students monthly, it was clearly a concern that they selected material that was not at the students' appropriate level for instruction. During the second year of implementation, the teachers were more consistent in selecting instructional-level material.

A second component of Guided Reading is before-reading instruction that incorporates introduction of the book, discussion of the topic, and teaching of new vocabulary. We found that during the first year of instruction, all of the teachers incorporated introduction of the book in terms of topic. However, except for the grade 2 teacher, they commonly left out presentation of new vocabulary. During the second year of implementation, all but one of the teachers consistently included the preteaching of new vocabulary, and they all continued to employ the other before-reading activities.

All of the teachers employed oral/sign reading. However, during both years of implementation, they did not routinely chunk the material as the interactive Guided Reading modification would require. Because the students were reading aloud/in sign, teacher support with word recognition, sentence structures, vocabulary, and comprehension was fairly constant, providing little opportunity for the students to engage in extended reading of passages. Silent reading was rarely incorporated as a step after oral/sign reading. These patterns were noted in both years of implementation.

After-reading discussion, the fourth component of Guided Reading, was often left out of instruction during the first year of implementation. When it was included, teacher questions focused on comprehension at the detail and inferential levels, but questions did not encourage students to reflect on the strategies they used for problem solving and understanding. During the second year of implementation, the teachers usually incorporated after-reading activities, though they tended to focus on vocabulary more than comprehension.

DISCUSSION

Our findings indicate that the elementary-level deaf students, whose teachers used the Guided Reading approach as their regular classroom reading instruction model, made progress in reading achievement as measured by Running Records. For most of the students, progress was modest and inhibited by summer regressions.

In comparing our results to findings with deaf students during the past two decades, which have shown that the average deaf student gains one third of a grade equivalent change each school year (Holt, 1993; Trader, 2000; Wolk & Allen, 1984), we found that outcomes were better than this average for most of the students in our study. However, it is generally recognized that the goal for reading growth is 1 year of progress for each school year, and only a few students came close to this benchmark.

How?

The data indicate that three modifications are likely to strengthen outcomes. The first is to improve adherence to the steps of the Guided Reading approach by providing teachers with a greater amount of in-class coaching and offering regularized professional development sessions throughout the school year. The second modification is to add a summer reading program for the students. Research indicates that such programs are most effective when they involve parents, incorporate a well-defined reading curriculum as well as opportunities for recreational reading, and utilize a summer camp model as the context (Lauer, Akiba, & Wilkerson, 2006). Given that students attending a state school for the deaf do not live in proximity to one another, the summer reading program would need to be either residential for a 4- or 6-week period of perhaps 3 days per week, or involve web-based delivery. The third modification is to incorporate greater family involvement. One such program is the Shared Reading Project (Laurent Clerc National Deaf Education Center, 2010), in which parents are taught to read effectively to their deaf children, using ASL.

LIMITATIONS OF THE STUDY

It is important to note several limitations of the present study in the contextualizing of the outcomes. One of these is that baseline did not meet recognized standards for length, stability, and trend (Division 16, 2003; Horner et al., 2005). In order to conduct a field study that respected the integrity and autonomy of the educational setting, we needed to accommodate our methodological design to the decision made that all of the elementary school teachers would employ Guided Reading as their instructional approach and instruction would begin in the fall. We were therefore not able to withhold instruction from any student for any length of time, which a more extended baseline would have necessitated. Complicating the matter was that the teachers would only be assessing the students monthly, and the likelihood of the presence of intervening variables between monthly baseline assessment was high. Our selection of two data points for baseline represents recognition that such data might not represent stability of performance, as baseline is intended to show, but that it adequately measured performance prior to implementation of the instructional approach.

We disagree. See analysis

Another limitation is the teachers' fidelity to the Guided Reading approach. Our data on fidelity is narrow, as the lead teacher was only able to formally observe the teachers a few times during the 2 years of implementation, and the teachers' self-reported adherence to the Guided Reading protocol may not have fully reflected their actual instruction. Fidelity was undoubtedly further influenced by changes in teaching personnel, the concomitant training of new teachers, and the reality that their ability to fully implement the approach would undoubtedly take time. In spite of the limited data on fidelity, our qualitative analysis indicates that teachers did not regularly employ all components of the approach, with the exception of the grade 2 teacher.

Internal validity

Related to fidelity to Guided Reading is that the teachers may have used other approaches to reading instruction in addition to or in place of Guided Reading some of the time. These intervening variables could have affected results positively or negatively; that is, outcomes may have been inflated or deflated because of these other approaches being used. Certainly, in future research, more regularized observation and coaching should be incorporated in order to assure that the approach being investigated is indeed the approach being used in instruction.

CONCLUSION

The present study was designed to assess the effectiveness of Guided Reading as an instructional approach to improving the reading achievement of elementary-level students who are deaf. Given the low scores at the outset for most of the participants, and the dip that typically took place each summer, progress for most of the participants was far below the benchmark of 1 year of progress per each year of school. So though the approach appeared to be effective, outcomes were modest.

In carrying out this study, we learned as much about how messy it is to conduct classroom research, particularly as a schoolwide intervention, as we learned about implementing Guided Reading. The small body of classroom intervention research in deaf education clearly reflects the difficulties inherent in adhering to the standards of methodological design within the complex world of the school environment. Yet it is precisely this type of research that has social validity and, therefore, provides findings on approaches that are likely to be acceptable to teachers, because these approaches have been studied in settings just like their own classrooms. With this in mind, we suggest that future research be aimed at replicating the present study, with populations of deaf students in a range of educational settings and using different communication modes, but with better controls that would assure reliable student assessment at whatever schedule is established and teacher fidelity to the approach. Indeed, replication is the means by which single-subject experimental research demonstrates generalizability of findings.

References

Allor, J. H. (2002). The relationships of phonemic awareness and rapid naming to reading development. *Learning Disabilities Quarterly, 25,* 47–57.

Clay, M. M. (2000). *Running Records for classroom teachers.* Portsmouth, NH: Heinemann.

Cooper, J. D., & Kiger, N. D. (2009). *Literacy: Helping children construct meaning* (7th ed.). Boston: Houghton Mifflin.

Cooper, J. O., Heron, T. E., & Reward, W. L. (2007). *Applied behavior analysis* (2nd ed.). Upper Saddle River, NJ: Merrill/Prentice Hall.

Cunningham, P. M., & Allington, R. L. (2007). *Classrooms that work: They can all read and write* (4th ed.). Boston: Allyn & Bacon.

Denton, C. A., Ciancio, D. J., & Fletcher, J. M. (2006). Validity, reliability, and utility of the Observation Survey of Early Literacy Achievement. *Reading Research Quarterly, 41,* 8–34.

Division 16, American Psychological Association, and Society for the Study of School Psychology Task Force on Evidence-Based Interventions in School Psychology. (2003). *Procedural and coding manual for review of evidence-based interventions.* Washington, DC: American Psychological Association.

Fountas, I., & Pinnell, G. S. (1996). *Guided Reading: Good first teaching for all children.* Portsmouth, NH: Heinemann.

Fountas, I., & Pinnell, G. S. (1999). *Matching books to readers: Using leveled books in Guided Reading, K–3.* Portsmouth. NH: Heinemann.

Fountas, I., & Pinnell, G. S. (2008). *Leveled books: K–8.* Retrieved from http://www.fountasandpinnellleveledbooks.com/default.aspx

Gambrell, L. B., Malloy, J. A., & Mazzoni, S. A. (2007). Evidence-based practices for comprehensive literacy instruction. In L. B. Gambrell, L. M. Morrow, & M. Pressley (Eds.), *Best practices in literacy instruction* (pp. 11–29). New York: Guilford.

Holt, J. (1993). Stanford Achievement Test—eighth edition: Reading comprehension subgroup results. *American Annals of the Deaf, 138,* 172–175.

Horner, R. H., Carr, E. G., Halle, J., McGee, G., Odom, S., & Wolery, M. (2005). The use of single-subject research to identify evidence-based practice in special education. *Exceptional Children, 71,* 165–179.

Kazdin, A. E. (2010). *Single-case research designs: Methods for clinical and applied settings* (2nd ed.). New York: Oxford University Press.

Lane, K. L, & Beebe-Frankenberger, M. (2004). *School-based interventions.* Boston: Allyn & Bacon.

LaSasso, C. (1987). Survey of reading instruction for hearing-impaired students in the United States. *Volta Review, 89,* 85–98.

LaSasso, C. J., & Mobley, R. T. (1997). National survey of reading instruction for deaf or hard-of-hearing students in the U.S. *Volta Review, 99,* 31–58.

Lauer, P. A., Akiba, M., & Wilkerson, S. B. (2006). Out-of-school-time programs: A meta-analysis for at-risk students. *Review of Educational Research, 76,* 275–313.

Laurent Clerc National Deaf Education Center. (2009). *Guided reading and writing with deaf and hard of hearing children.* Retrieved from Gallaudet University website: http://clerccenter.gallaudet.edu/Clerc_Center/Information_and_Resources/Info_to_Go/Language_and_Literacy/Literacy_at_the_Clerc_Center/Literacy-It_All_Connects/Guided_Reading_and_Writing.html

Laurent Clerc National Deaf Education Center. (2010). *Shared reading project.* Retrieved from Gallaudet University website: http://clerccenter.gallaudet.edu/Clerc_Center/Information_and_Resources/Info_to_Go/Language_and_Literacy/Literacy_at_the_Clerc_Center/Welcome_to_Shared_Reading_Project.html

Narr, R. F. (2008). Phonological awareness and decoding in Deaf/hard of hearing students who use Visual Phonics. *Journal of Deaf Studies and Deaf Education, 13,* 405–416.

National Reading Panel. (2000). *Report of the National Reading Panel: Teaching children to read: An evidence-based assessment of the scientific research literature on reading and its implications for reading instruction.* Washington, DC: U.S. Department of Health and Human Services.

Office of the Inspector General. (2006). *The Reading First Program's grant application process: Final inspection report.* Retrieved from U.S. Department of Education website: http://www.ed.gov/about/offices/list/oig/aireports/i13f0017.pdf

Patton, M. Q. (2002). *Qualitative research and evaluation methods* (3rd ed.). Thousand Oaks, CA: Sage.

Quigley, S., McAnally, E, King, C., & Rose, S. (1991). *Reading milestones.* Austin, TX: PRO-ED.

Quigley, S., Power, D., & Steinkamp, M. (1977). The language structure of deaf children. *Volta Review, 79,* 73–84.

Quigley, S., Wilbur, R., & Montanelli, D. (1974). Question formation in the language of deaf students. *Journal of Speech and Hearing Research, 17,* 699–713.

Reutzel, D. R. (2007). Organizing effective literacy instruction: Differentiating instruction to meet the needs of all children. In L. B. Gambrell, L. M. Morrow, & M. Pressley (Eds.), *Best practices in literacy instruction* (pp. 313–343). New York: Guilford.

Schirmer, B. R., & McGough, S. M. (2005). Teaching reading to children who are deaf: Do the conclusions of the National Reading Panel apply? *Review of Educational Research, 75,* 83–117.

Schirmer, B. R., & Williams, C. (2010). Approaches to reading instruction. In M. Marschark & P. E. Spencer (Eds.), *Oxford handbook of deaf studies, language, and education* (2nd ed., pp. 115–129). Oxford, England: Oxford University Press.

Snow, C. E., Burns, M. S., & Griffin, P. (Eds.). (1998). *Preventing reading difficulties in young children.* Washington, DC: National Academy Press.

Traxler, C. B. (2000). The Stanford Achievement Test, ninth edition: National norming and performance standards for deaf and hard of hearing students. *Journal of Deaf Studies and Deaf Education, 5,* 337–348.

Trezek, B. J., & Malmgren, K. W. (2005). The efficacy of utilizing a phonics treatment package with middle school deaf and hard of hearing students. *Journal of Deaf Studies and Deaf Education, 10,* 256–271.

Trezek, B. J., & Wang, Y. (2006). Implications of utilizing a phonics-based reading curriculum with children who are deaf or hard of hearing. *Journal of Deaf Studies and Deaf Education, 11,* 202–213.

Trezek, B. J., Wang, Y, Woods, D. G., Gampp, T. L., & Paul, P. V. (2007). Using Visual Phonics to supplement reading instruction for students who are deaf or hard of hearing. *Journal of Deaf Studies and Deaf Education, 12,* 373–384.

U. S. Department of Education. (2007). *Reading first.* Retrieved from http://www.ed.gov/programs/readingfirst/index.html

Wolk, S., & Allen, T. E. (1984). A five-year follow-up of reading comprehension achievement of hearing-impaired students in special education programs. *Journal of Special Education. 18,* 161–176.

Analysis of the Study

PURPOSE/JUSTIFICATION/PRIOR RESEARCH

The purpose is clearly stated as: "To investigate the effects of the Guided Reading approach on the reading development of students who were deaf in grades 1–5 over a period of 2 school years." An extensive background is provided with respect to related research and curriculum. A strong justification is made based on the rationale and use of the teaching method and the lack of research evidence on effectiveness. There appear to be no problems of risk, confidentiality, or deception.

DEFINITIONS

A definition of reading development/reading achievement (they appear to be used as synonyms) is needed. The operational definition is "score on the monthly Running Records test." Unfortunately, it is not entirely clear what is assessed by this test—see "Instrumentation." The Guided Reading method is extensively and well described.

HYPOTHESES

None are stated. It is strongly implied that (all?) students will show gains in achievement over time—one and two years.

SAMPLE

The authors properly recognize that their sample is "convenience" and that replication is needed for this and other reasons. The sample of students is well described. The description of teachers is minimal but probably sufficient. The number of teachers should be given.

INSTRUMENTATION

This study used an A-B-A-B design with four phases: A1 = baseline; B1 = first-year treatment; A2 = summer; B2 = second-year treatment. The measure of reading achievement was scored on the monthly test—a teacher observation of the student signing a written passage. Presumably, passages were equated for word difficulty within each grade level. Data on observer agreement should be provided for at least a sample of testings. Because it is different phases that are compared, it is the overall student performance in each phase that must be reliable. This requires a sufficient number of scores within each phase. The study results (Figure 1) show that this is the case for all 19 students in phase B1. It is also the case for phase B2 for grades 1 and 2, less so for the other grades.

Use of observation and interviews to check the fidelity of instruction is commendable; however, more detail is needed especially with regard to the content analysis.

As is common with such designs, much reliance is placed on content (logical) validity and on the training of testers. This is persuasive provided that what is used as the score is the number of correct words—presumably adjusted if passages differed in number of words. However, it is not clear whether the tester notations of "fluency" and "inclusiveness" were included in the score; such variables are much more a matter of judgment. The authors report a finding of "support for validity" but give no further data or description. The statement that "scores do not provide a comprehensive assessment of reading abilities, most particularly because word recognition is emphasized (sic) at the expense of comprehension" is important but does not clarify what is measured.

PROCEDURES/INTERNAL VALIDITY

Procedures are clearly described. The A-B-A-B design provides good control of the internal validity threats of subject characteristics, maturation, loss of subjects, location, history, subject attitude, instrument decay, data collector characteristics, testing, and regression. As the authors note, an implementation threat is possible if the teachers use additional materials or methods but this seems unlikely to us. Data collector bias is a potential threat because the teacher/testers obviously knew which phase the student was in at the time of testing. This threat seems minimal to us if the score is simply number of words correct.

DATA ANALYSIS/RESULTS/DISCUSSION

Data are presented in graphic form as is typical with this design. We disagree with the statement that using only two data points for baseline is adequate to measure "performance prior to implementation." Better evidence of improvement is found in the trends for the two treatment phases. With reservations, we agree with the discussion of results, that is, improvement was shown. However, the use of grade levels is not clear or satisfactory. Statements such as "progress ranged from a half year to 1 year of progress for grade 1 students" imply differences between fixed points whereas the graphs rely on a series of points showing trend. Perhaps these statements are derived from a sort of visual average within phases, which is difficult for us to recap from the graphs. Our attempts support the discussion with respect to phase B1 but not in all cases for phase B2. For example, the data points for student CS in grade 2 do not justify the statement that in B2 "both (students) made almost 2 years of progress." Without the last two data points, CS shows virtually no gain during B2. The "thinness" of data for phase two should be acknowledged.

In general, the authors do a commendable job, both in the limitations section and throughout, of recognizing limitations of the study. A small point is that we do not see that the "three modifications are likely to strengthen outcomes," however appropriate, follows from "the data."

Go back to the **INTERACTIVE AND APPLIED LEARNING** feature at the beginning of the chapter for a listing of interactive and applied activities. Go to the **Online Learning Center** at **www.mhhe.com/fraenkel9e** to take quizzes, practice with key terms, and review chapter content.

Main Points

ESSENTIAL CHARACTERISTICS OF SINGLE-SUBJECT RESEARCH

- Single-subject research involves the extensive collection of data on one subject at a time.
- An advantage of single-subject designs is that they can be applied in settings where group designs are difficult to put into play.

SINGLE-SUBJECT DESIGNS

- Single-subject designs are most commonly used to study the changes in behavior an individual exhibits after exposure to a treatment or intervention of some sort.
- Single-subject researchers primarily use line graphs to present their data and to illustrate the effects of a particular intervention or treatment.
- The basic approach of researchers using an A-B design is to expose the same subject, operating as his or her own control, to two conditions or phases.
- When using an A-B-A design (sometimes called a *reversal design*), researchers simply add another baseline period to the A-B design.
- In the A-B-A-B design, two baseline periods are combined with two treatment periods.
- The B-A-B design is used when an individual's behavior is so severe or disturbing that a researcher cannot wait for a baseline to be established.
- In the A-B-C-B design, the C condition refers to a variation of the intervention in the B condition. The intervention is changed during the C phase typically to control for any extra attention the subject may have received during the B phase.

MULTIPLE-BASELINE DESIGNS

- Multiple-baseline designs are used when it is not possible or ethical to withdraw a treatment and return to baseline.
- When a multiple-baseline design is used, researchers do more than collect data on one behavior for one subject in one setting; they collect on several behaviors for one subject, obtaining a baseline for each during the same period of time.

- Multiple-baseline designs also are sometimes used to collect data on several subjects with regard to a single behavior, or to measure a subject's behavior in two or more different settings.

THREATS TO INTERNAL VALIDITY IN SINGLE-SUBJECT RESEARCH

- Several threats to internal validity exist with regard to single-subject designs. These include the length of the baseline and intervention conditions, the number of variables changed when moving from one condition to another, the degree and speed of any change that occurs, a return—or not—of the behavior to baseline levels, the independence of behaviors, and the number of baselines.

CONTROLLING THREATS IN SINGLE-SUBJECT STUDIES

- Single-subject designs are most effective in controlling for subject characteristics, mortality, testing, and history threats.
- They are less effective with location, data collector characteristics, maturation, and regression threats.
- They are especially weak when it comes to instrument decay, data collector bias, attitude, and implementation threats.

EXTERNAL VALIDITY AND SINGLE-SUBJECT RESEARCH

- Single-subject studies are weak when it comes to generalizability.
- It is particularly important to replicate single-subject studies to determine whether they are worthy of generalization.

OTHER SINGLE-SUBJECT DESIGNS

- Variations on the basic designs discussed in this chapter include the A-B-A-C-A design; the A-B-C-B-C design; and the multiprobe design.

Key Terms

A-B design 304
A-B-A design 305
A-B-A-B design 305
A-B-C-B design 307
B-A-B design 306
baseline 304
external validity 314
multiple-baseline design 307
single-subject design 302

For Discussion

1. Could single-subject designs be implemented in secondary schools? If so, what difficulties do you think one might encounter?
2. Professor Jones has a very difficult student in his introductory statistics class who keeps interrupting the other students when they attempt to answer the professor's questions. How might the professor use one of the designs described in this chapter to reduce the student's interruptions?
3. Can you suggest any instances where a B-A-B design might be required in a typical elementary school? What might they be?
4. Would random sampling be possible in single-subject research? Why or why not?
5. Which do you think is easier to conduct: single-subject or group comparison research? Why?

6. What sorts of questions lend themselves better to single-subject than to other kinds of research?
7. What sorts of behaviors might require only a few data points to establish a baseline? Give some examples.
8. When might it be unethical to stop the intervention to return to baseline in an A-B-A design? Give an example.
9. In terms of difficulty, how would you rate single-subject research on a scale of 1 to 10? What do you think is the most difficult aspect of this kind of research? Why?

References

1. Angell, M. et al. (2008). Systematic instruction for social-pragmatic language skills in lunchroom settings. *Education and Training in Developmental Disabilities, 43*(3), 342–359.

2. Gaines, T., & Barry, L. (2008). The effect of a self-monitored relaxation breathing exercise on male adolescent aggressive behavior. *Adolescence (San Diego): An international quarterly devoted to the physiological, psychological, psychiatric, sociological, and educational aspects of the second decade of human life, 43*(170), 291.

3. Hsieh, H. (2008). Effects of ordinary and adaptive toys on pre-school children with developmental disabilities. *Research in Developmental Disabilities: A Multidisciplinary Journal, 29*(5), 459–466.

4. Kim, J., et al. (2008). The effects of improvisational music therapy on joint attention behaviors in autistic children: A randomized controlled study. *Journal of Autism and Developmental Disorders, 38*(9), 1758–1766.

5. Larwin, K., & Larwin, D. (2008). Decreasing excessive media usage while increasing physical activity: A single-subject research study. *Behavior Modification, 32*(6), 938–956.

6. Hapstak, J., & Tracey, D. (2007). Effects of assisted-repeated reading on students of varying reading ability: A single-subject experimental research study. *Reading Horizons, 47*(4), 315–334.

7. Tekin-Iftar, E., et al. (2008). Enhancing instructional efficiency through generalization and instructive feedback: A single-subject study with children with mental retardation. *International Journal of Special Education, 23*(1), 147–158.

Correlational Research 15

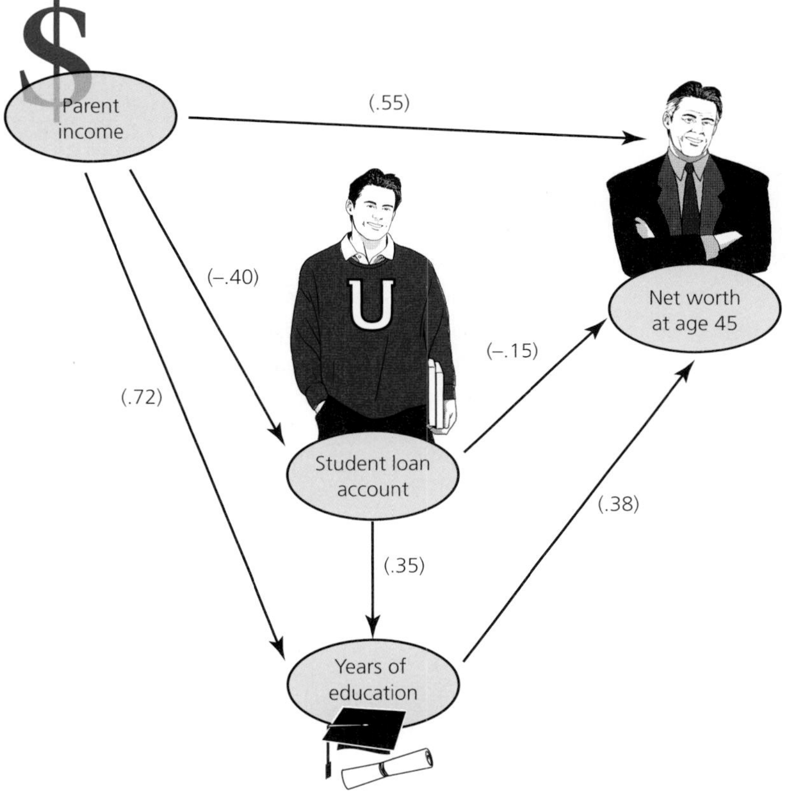

The Nature of Correlational Research

Purposes of Correlational Research

Explanatory Studies
Prediction Studies
More Complex Correlational Techniques

Basic Steps in Correlational Research

Problem Selection
Sample
Instruments
Design and Procedures
Data Collection
Data Analysis and Interpretation

What Do Correlation Coefficients Tell Us?

Threats to Internal Validity in Correlational Research

Subject Characteristics
Location
Instrumentation
Testing
Mortality

Evaluating Threats to Internal Validity in Correlational Studies

An Example of Correlational Research

Analysis of the Study

Purpose/Justification
Definitions
Prior Research
Hypotheses
Sample
Instrumentation
Procedures/Internal Validity
Data Analysis/Results
Discussion/Interpretation

OBJECTIVES **Studying this chapter should enable you to:**

- Describe briefly what is meant by associational research.
- State the two major purposes of correlational studies.
- Distinguish between predictor and criterion variables.
- Explain the role of correlational studies in exploring causation.
- Explain how a scatterplot can be used to predict an outcome.
- Describe what is meant by a prediction equation.
- Explain briefly the main ideas underlying multiple correlation, factor analysis, and path analysis.
- Identify and describe briefly the steps involved in conducting a correlational study.
- Interpret correlation coefficients of different magnitude.
- Explain the rationale underlying partial correlation.
- Describe some of the threats to internal validity that exist in correlation studies and explain how to identify them.
- Discuss how to control for these threats.
- Recognize a correlation study when you come across one in the educational research literature.

INTERACTIVE AND APPLIED LEARNING After, or while, reading this chapter:

Go to the Online Learning Center at www.mhhe.com/fraenkel9e to:

- Learn More About What Correlation Coefficients Tell Us

Go to your online Student Mastery Activities book to do the following activities:

- Activity 15.1: Correlational Research Questions
- Activity 15.2: What Kind of Correlation?
- Activity 15.3: Think Up an Example
- Activity 15.4: Match the Correlation Coefficient to Its Scatterplot
- Activity 15.5: Calculate a Correlation Coefficient
- Activity 15.6: Construct a Scatterplot
- Activity 15.7: Correlation in Everyday Life
- Activity 15.8: Regression

Justine Gibbs, a high school biology teacher, was bothered last year by the fact that many of her tenth-grade students had considerable difficulty learning many of the concepts in biology while some learned them rather easily. Before the semester begins this year, therefore, she would like to be able to predict which sorts of individuals are likely to have trouble learning these concepts. If she could make some fairly accurate predictions, she might be able to suggest corrective measures (e.g., special tutorial sessions) so that fewer students would have difficulty in her biology classes.

The appropriate methodology called for here is *correlational research*. What Ms. Gibbs might do is to collect different kinds of data on her students that might be related to the difficulties they do—or do not—have with biology. Any variables that might be related to success—or failure—in biology (e.g., their anxiety toward the subject, their previous knowledge, how well they understand abstractions, their performance in other science courses) would be useful. This might give her some ideas about how those students who learn biological concepts easily differ from those who find them difficult. This, in turn, might help her predict who might have trouble learning biology next semester. This chapter, therefore, describes for Ms. Gibbs (and you) what correlational research is all about.

The Nature of Correlational Research

Correlational research, like causal-comparative research (which we discuss in Chapter 16), is an example of what is sometimes called *associational research.* In associational research, the relationships among two or more variables are studied without any attempt to influence them. In their simplest form, correlational studies investigate the possibility of relationships between only two variables, although investigations of more than two variables are common. In contrast to experimental research, however, there is no manipulation of variables in correlational research.

Correlational research is also sometimes referred to as a form of descriptive research because it describes an existing relationship between variables. The way it describes this relationship, however, is quite different from the descriptions found in other types of studies. A correlational study describes the degree to which two or more quantitative variables are related, and it does so by using a correlation coefficient.*

When a correlation is found to exist between two variables, it means that scores within a certain range on one variable are associated with scores within a certain range on the other variable. You will recall that a positive correlation means high scores on one variable tend to be associated with high scores on the other variable, while low scores on one are associated with low scores on the other.

*Although associations among two or more categorical variables can also be studied, such studies are not usually referred to as *correlational.* They are similar with respect to overall design and threats to internal validity, however, and we discuss them further in Chapter 16.

TABLE 15.1 *Three Sets of Data Showing Different Directions and Degrees of Correlation*

(A) $r = +1.00$		(B) $r = -1.00$		(C) $r = 0$	
X	**Y**	**X**	**Y**	**X**	**Y**
5	5	5	1	2	1
4	4	4	2	5	4
3	3	3	3	3	4
2	2	2	4	1	5
1	1	1	5	4	2

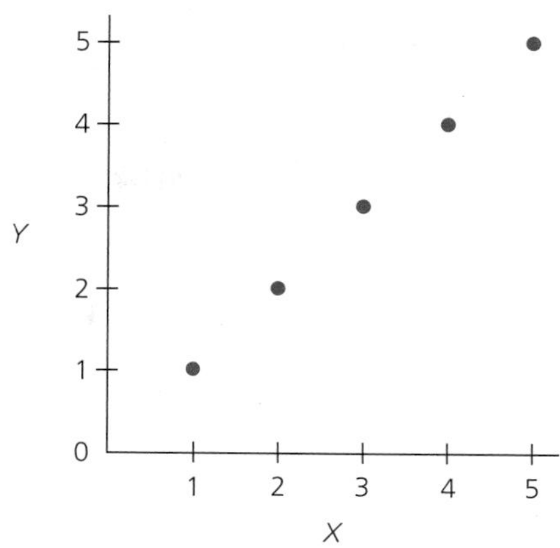

Figure 15.1 *Scatterplot Illustrating a Correlation of +1.00*

A negative correlation, on the other hand, means high scores on one variable are associated with low scores on the other variable, and low scores on one are associated with high scores on the other—Table 15.1(B). As we also have indicated before, relationships like those shown in Table 15.1 can be illustrated graphically through the use of scatterplots. Figure 15.1, for example, illustrates the relationship shown in Table 15.1(A).

Purposes of Correlational Research

Correlational research is carried out for one of two basic purposes—either to help explain important human behaviors or to predict likely outcomes.

EXPLANATORY STUDIES

A major purpose of correlational research is to clarify our understanding of important phenomena by identifying relationships among variables. Particularly in developmental psychology, where experimental studies are especially difficult to design, much has been learned by analyzing relationships among several variables. For example, correlations found between variables such as complexity of parent speech and rate of language acquisition have taught researchers much about how language is acquired. Similarly, the discovery that—among variables related to reading skill—auditory memory shows a substantial correlation with reading ability has expanded our understanding of the complex phenomenon of reading. The current belief that smoking causes lung cancer, although based in part on experimental studies of animals, rests heavily on correlational evidence of the relationship between frequency of smoking and incidence of lung cancer.

Researchers who conduct explanatory studies often investigate a number of variables they believe are related to a more complex variable, such as motivation or learning. Variables found not to be related or only slightly related (i.e., when correlations below .20 are obtained) are then dropped from further consideration, while those found to be more highly related (i.e., when correlations beyond +.40 or −.40 are obtained) often serve as the focus of additional research, using an experimental design, to see whether the relationships are indeed causal.

Let us say a bit more here about causation. Although the discovery of a correlational relationship does not establish a causal connection, most researchers who engage in correlational research are probably trying to gain some idea about cause and effect. A researcher who carried out the fictitious study whose results are illustrated in Figure 15.2, for example, would probably be inclined to conclude that a teacher's expectation of failure is a partial (or at least a contributing) cause of the amount of disruptive behavior his or her students display in class.

It must be stressed, however, that correlational studies *do not,* in and of themselves, establish cause and effect. In the previous example, one could just as well argue that the amount of disruptive behavior in a class causes a teacher's expectation of failure, or that *both* teacher expectation and disruptive behavior are caused by some third factor—such as the ability level of the class.

MORE ABOUT RESEARCH

Important Findings in Correlational Research

One of the most famous, and controversial, examples of correlational research is that relating frequency of tobacco smoking to incidence of lung cancer. When these studies began to appear, many argued for smoking as a major cause of lung cancer. Opponents did not argue for the reverse—that is, that cancer causes smoking—for the obvious reason that smoking occurs first. They did, however, argue that both smoking and lung cancer are caused by other factors such as genetic predisposition, lifestyle (sedentary occupations might result in more smoking and less exercise), and environment (smoking and lung cancer might be more prevalent in smoggy cities).

Despite a persuasive theory—smoking clearly could irritate lung tissue—the argument for causation was not sufficiently persuasive for the surgeon general to issue warnings until experimental studies showed that exposure to tobacco smoke did result in lung cancer in animals.

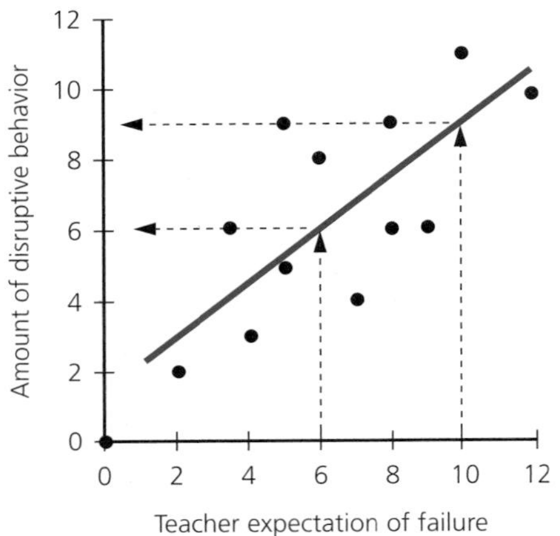

Figure 15.2 *Prediction Using a Scatterplot*

The possibility of causation is strengthened, however, if a time lapse occurs between measurement of the variables being studied. If the teacher's expectations of failure were measured before assigning students to classes, for example, it would seem unreasonable to assume that class behavior (or, likewise, the ability level of the class) would cause the teacher's failure expectations. The reverse, in fact, would make more sense. Certain other causal explanations, however, remain persuasive, such as the socioeconomic level of the students involved. Teachers might have higher expectations of failure for economically poor students. Such students also might exhibit a greater amount of disruptive behavior in class regardless of their teacher's expectations. The search for cause and effect in correlational studies, therefore, is fraught with difficulty. Nonetheless, it can be a fruitful step in the search for causes. We return to this matter later in the discussion of threats to internal validity in correlational research.

PREDICTION STUDIES

A second purpose of correlational research is **prediction**: If a relationship of sufficient magnitude exists between two variables, it becomes possible to predict a score on one variable if a score on the other variable is known. Researchers have found, for example, that high school grades are highly related to college grades. Hence, high school grades can be used to predict college grades. We would predict that a person with a high GPA in high school would be likely to have a high GPA in college. The variable that is used to make the prediction is called the **predictor variable**; the variable about which the prediction is made is called the **criterion variable**. Hence, in the preceding example, high school grades would be the predictor variable, and college grades would be the criterion variable. As we mentioned in Chapter 8, **prediction studies** are also used to determine the predictive validity of measuring instruments.

Using Scatterplots to Predict a Score. Prediction can be illustrated through the use of scatterplots. Suppose, for example, that we obtain the data shown in Table 15.2 from a sample of 12 classes. Using these data, we find a correlation of .71 between the variables teacher expectation of failure and amount of disruptive behavior.

Plotting the data in Table 15.2 produces the scatterplot shown in Figure 15.2. Once a scatterplot such as this has been constructed, a straight line, known as a **regression line**, can be calculated mathematically. The calculation of this line is beyond the scope of this text, but a general understanding of its use can be obtained by looking at Figure 15.2. The regression line comes the closest to all of the scores depicted on the scatterplot of any straight line that could be drawn. A

TABLE 15.2 *Teacher Expectation of Failure and Amount of Disruptive Behavior for a Sample of 12 Classes*

Class	Teacher Expectation of Failure (Ratings)	Amount of Disruptive Behavior (Ratings)
1	10	11
2	4	3
3	2	2
4	4	6
5	12	10
6	9	6
7	8	9
8	8	6
9	6	8
10	5	5
11	5	9
12	7	4

researcher can then use the line as a basis for prediction. Thus, as you can see, a teacher with a score of 10 on expectation of failure would be predicted to have a class with a score of 9 on amount of disruptive behavior, and a teacher with an expectation score of 6 would be predicted to have a class with a disruptive behavior score of 6. Similarly, a second regression line can be drawn to predict a score on teacher expectation of failure if we know his or her class's score on amount of disruptive behavior.

Being able to predict a score for an individual (or group) on one variable based on the individual's (or group's) score on another variable is extremely useful. A school administrator, for example, could use Figure 15.2 (if it were based on real data) to (1) identify and select teachers who are likely to have less disruptive classes; (2) provide training to those teachers who are predicted to have a large amount of disruptive behavior in their classes; or (3) plan for additional assistance for such teachers. Both the teachers and students involved would benefit accordingly.

A Simple Prediction Equation. Although scatterplots are fairly easy devices to use in making predictions, they are inefficient when pairs of scores from a large number of individuals have been collected. Fortunately, the regression line we just described can be expressed in the form of a **prediction equation**, which has the following form:

$$Y'_1 = a + bX_1$$

where Y'_1 = the predicted score on Y (the criterion variable) for individual i, X_1 = individual i's score on X (the predictor variable), and a and b are values calculated mathematically from the original scores. For any given set of data, a and b are constants.

We mentioned earlier that high school GPA has been found to be highly related to college GPA. In this example, therefore, the symbol Y' stands for the predicted first-semester college GPA (the criterion variable), and X_1 stands for the individual's high school GPA (the predictor variable). Let us assume that a = .18 and b = .73. By substituting in the equation, we can predict a student's first-semester college GPA. Thus, if an individual's high school GPA is 3.5, we would predict that his or her first-semester college GPA would be 2.735 (i.e., .18 + .73 (3.5) = 2.735). We later can compare the student's actual first-semester college GPA to the predicted GPA. If there is a close similarity between the two, we gain confidence in using the prediction equation to make future predictions.

This predicted score will not be exact, however, and hence researchers also calculate an index of prediction error, known as the **standard error of estimate**. This index gives an estimate of the degree to which the predicted score is likely to be incorrect. The smaller the standard error of estimate, the more accurate the prediction. This index of error, as you would expect, is much larger for small values of r than for large r's.*

Furthermore, if we have more information on the individuals about whom we wish to predict, we should be able to decrease our errors of prediction. This is what a technique known as multiple regression (or multiple correlation) is designed to do.

MORE COMPLEX CORRELATIONAL TECHNIQUES

Multiple Regression. **Multiple regression** is a technique that enables researchers to determine a correlation between a criterion variable and the best combination of *two or more* predictor variables. Let us return to our previous example involving the high positive correlation between high school GPA and first-semester

*If the reason for this is unclear to you, refer again to the scatterplots in Figures 10.19 and 15.2.

college GPA. Suppose it is also found that a high positive correlation (r = .68) exists between first-semester college GPA and the verbal scores on the SAT college entrance examination, and a moderately high positive correlation (r = .51) exists between the mathematics scores on the SAT and first-semester college GPA. It is possible, using a multiple regression prediction formula, to use *all three* of these variables to predict what a student's GPA will be during his or her first semester in college. The formula is similar to the simple prediction equation, except that it now includes more than one predictor variable and more than two constants. It takes the following form:

$$Y' = a + b_1X_1 + b_2X_2 + b_3X_3$$

where Y' once again stands for the predicted first-semester college GPA; a, b_1, b_2, and b_3 are constants; X_1 = the high school GPA; X_2 = the verbal SAT score; and X_3 = the mathematics SAT score. Let us imagine that a = .18, b_1 = .73, b_2 = .0005, and b_3 = .0002. We know that the student's high school GPA is 3.5. Suppose his or her SAT verbal and mathematics scores are 580 and 600, respectively. Substituting in the formula, we would predict that the student's first-semester GPA would be 3.15.

$$\begin{aligned} Y' &= .18 + .73(3.5) + .0005(580) \\ &\quad + .0002(600) \\ &= .18 + 2.56 + .29 + .12 \\ &= 3.15 \end{aligned}$$

Again, we could later compare the actual first-semester college GPA obtained by this student with the predicted score to determine the accuracy of our prediction.

The Coefficient of Multiple Correlation. The **coefficient of multiple correlation**, symbolized by R, indicates the strength of the correlation between the combination of the predictor variables and the criterion variable. It can be thought of as a simple Pearson correlation between the actual scores on the criterion variable and the predicted scores on that variable. In the previous example, we used a combination of high school GPA, SAT verbal score, and SAT mathematics score to predict that a particular student's first-semester college GPA would be 3.15. We then could obtain that same student's *actual* first-semester college GPA (e.g., it might be 2.95). If we did this for 100 students, we could then calculate the correlation (R) between predicted and actual GPA. If R turned out to be +1.00, for example, it would mean that the predicted scores correlated perfectly with the actual scores on the criterion variable. An R of +1.00, of course, would be most unusual to obtain. In actual practice, Rs of .70 or .80 are considered quite high. The higher R is, of course, the more reliable a prediction will be. Figure 15.3 illustrates the relationships among a criterion and two predictors. The amount of college GPA accounted for by high school GPA (about 36 percent) is increased by about 13 percent by adding test score as a second predictor.

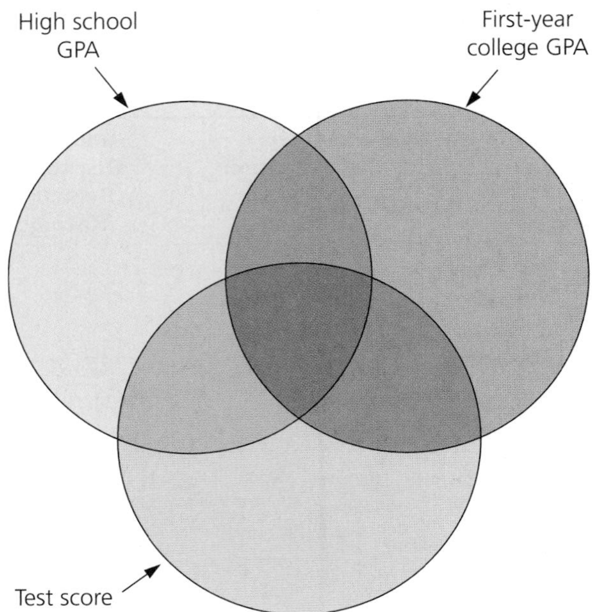

Figure 15.3 *Multiple Correlation*

The Coefficient of Determination. The square of the correlation between a predictor and a criterion variable is known as the **coefficient of determination**, symbolized by r^2. If the correlation between high school GPA and college GPA, for example, equals .60, then the coefficient of determination would equal .36. What does this mean? In short, the coefficient of determination indicates the percentage of the variability among the criterion scores that can be attributed to differences in the scores on the predictor variable. Thus, if the correlation between high school GPA and college GPA for a group of students is .60, 36 percent $(.60)^2$ of the differences in the college GPAs of those students can be attributed to differences in their high school GPAs.

The interpretation of R^2 (for multiple regression) is similar to that of r^2 (for simple regression). Suppose in our example that used three predictor variables that the multiple correlation coefficient is equal to .70. The coefficient of determination, then, is equal to $(.70)^2$, or .49. Thus, it would be appropriate to say that 49 percent of the variability in the criterion variable is predictable on the basis of the three predictor variables. Another way of saying this is that high school GPA, verbal SAT scores, and mathematics SAT scores (the three predictor variables), taken together, account for about 49 percent of the variability in college GPA (the criterion variable).

The value of a prediction equation depends on whether it can be used with a *new* group of individuals. Researchers can never be sure the prediction equation they develop will work successfully when it is used to predict criterion scores for a new group of persons. In fact, it is quite likely that it will be less accurate when so used, since the new group will not be identical to the one used to develop the prediction equation. The success of a particular prediction equation with a new group, therefore, usually depends on the group's similarity to the group used to develop the prediction equation originally.

Discriminant Function Analysis. In most prediction studies, the criterion variable is quantitative—that is, it involves scores that can fall anywhere along a continuum from low to high. Our previous example of college GPA is a quantitative variable, for scores on the variable can fall anywhere at or between 0.00 and 4.00. Sometimes, however, the criterion variable may be a categorical variable—that is, it involves membership in a group (or category) rather than scores along a continuum. For example, a researcher might be interested in predicting whether an individual is more like engineering majors or business majors. In this instance, the criterion variable is dichotomous—an individual is either in one group or the other. Of course, a categorical variable can have more than just two categories (e.g., engineering majors, business majors, education majors, science majors). The technique of multiple regression cannot be used when the criterion variable is categorical; instead, a technique known as **discriminant function analysis** is used. The purpose of the analysis and the form of the prediction equation, however, are similar to those for multiple regression. Figure 15.4 illustrates the logic; note that the scores of the individual represented by the six faces remain the same for both categories. The person's score is compared to the scores of both researchers and teachers. These hypothetical results show that "Me" is more similar to researchers on "A" and more similar to teachers on "B" and "C."

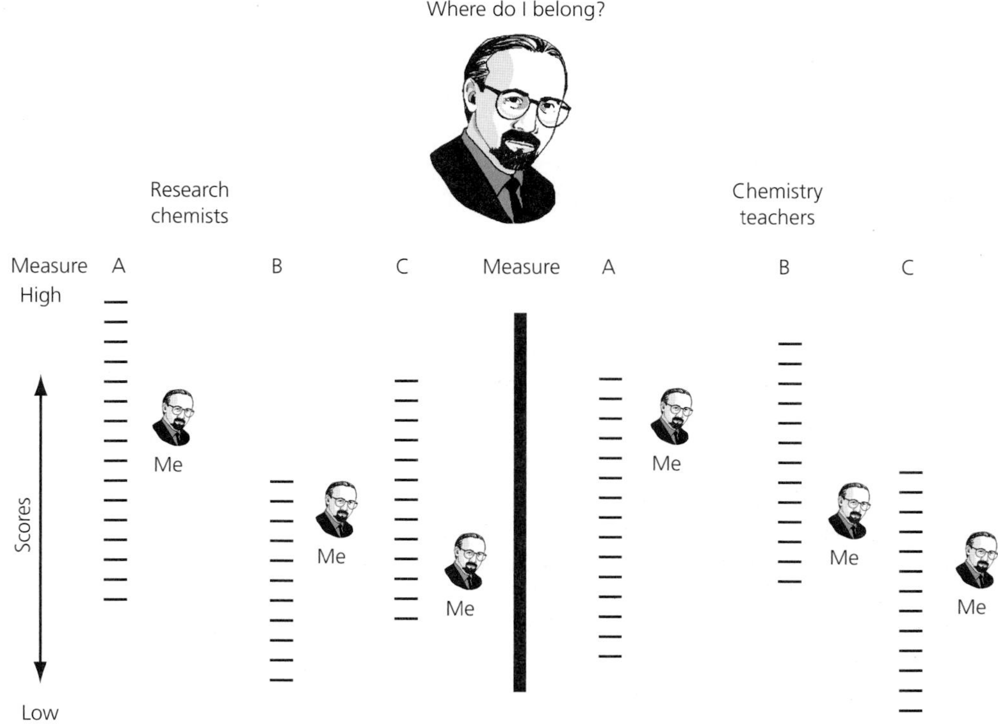

Figure 15.4 *Discriminant Function Analysis*

Factor Analysis. When a number of variables are investigated in a single study, analysis and interpretation of data can become rather cumbersome. It is often desirable, therefore, to reduce the number of variables by grouping those that are moderately or highly correlated with one another into *factors.*

Factor analysis is a technique that allows a researcher to determine if many variables can be described by a few factors. The mathematical calculations involved are beyond the scope of this book, but the technique essentially involves a search for "clusters" of variables, all of which are correlated with each other. Each cluster represents a factor. Studies of group IQ tests, for example, have suggested that the many specific scores used could be explained as a result of a relatively small number of factors. While controversial, these results did provide one means of comprehending the mental abilities required to perform well on such tests. They also led to new tests designed to test these identified abilities more effectively.

Path Analysis. **Path analysis** is used to test the likelihood of a causal connection among three or more variables. Some of the other techniques we have described can be used to explore theories about causality, but path analysis is far more powerful than the rest. Although a detailed explanation of this technique is too technical for inclusion here, the essential idea behind path analysis is to formulate a theory about the possible causes of a particular phenomenon (such as student alienation)—that is, to identify causal variables that could explain why the phenomenon occurs—and then to determine whether correlations among all the variables are consistent with the theory.

Suppose a researcher theorizes as follows: (1) Certain students are more alienated in school than others because they do not find school enjoyable and because they have few friends; (2) they do not find school enjoyable partly because they have few friends and partly because they do not perceive their courses as being in any way related to their needs; and (3) perceived relevance of courses is related slightly to number of friends. The researcher would then measure each of these variables (degree of alienation, personal relevance of courses, enjoyment in school, and number of friends) for a number of students. Correlations between pairs of each of the variables would then be calculated. Let us imagine that the researcher obtains the correlations shown in the correlation matrix in Table 15.3.

What does this table reveal about possible causes of student alienation? Two of the variables (relevance of courses at −.48 and school enjoyment at −.53) shown in the table are sizable predictors of such alienation. Nevertheless, to remind you again, just because these variables predict student alienation, you should not assume that they cause it. Furthermore, something of a problem exists in the fact that the two predictor variables correlate with *each other.* As you can see, school enjoyment and perceived relevance of courses not only predict student alienation, but they also correlate highly with each other ($r = .65$). Now, does perceived relevance of courses affect student alienation independently of school enjoyment? Does school enjoyment affect student alienation independently of perception of course relevance? Path analysis can help the researcher determine the answers to these questions.

TABLE 15.3 *Correlation Matrix for Variables in Student Alienation Study*

	School Enjoyment	Number of Friends	Alienation
Relevance of courses	.65	.24	−.48
School enjoyment		.58	−.53
Number of friends			−.27

Path analysis, then, involves four basic steps. First, a theory that links several variables is formulated to explain a particular phenomenon of interest. In our example, the researcher theorized the following causal connections: (1) When students perceive their courses as being unrelated to their needs, they will not enjoy school; (2) if they have few friends in school, this will contribute to their lack of enjoyment, and (3) the more a student dislikes school and the fewer friends he or she has, the more alienated he or she will be. Second, the variables specified by the theory are then measured in some way.* Third, correlation coefficients are computed to indicate the strength of the relationship between each of the pairs of variables postulated in the theory. And, fourth, relationships among the correlation coefficients are analyzed in relation to the theory.

Path analysis variables are typically shown in the type of diagram illustrated in Figure 15.5.† Each variable in the theory is shown in the figure. Each arrow indicates a

*Note that this step is very important. The measures must be valid representations of the variables. The results of the path analysis will be invalid if this is not the case.

†The process of path analysis and the diagrams drawn are, in practice, often more complex than the one shown here.

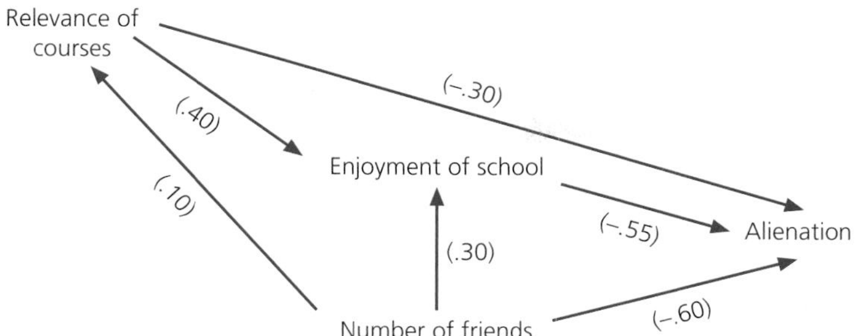

Figure 15.5 *Path Analysis Diagram*

hypothesized causal relationship in the direction of the arrow. Thus, liking for school is hypothesized to influence alienation; number of friends influences school enjoyment, and so on. Notice that in this example all of the arrows point in one direction only. This means that the first variable is hypothesized to influence the second variable, but not vice versa. Numbers similar (but not identical) to correlation coefficients are calculated for each pair of variables. If the results were as shown in Figure 15.5, the causal theory of the researcher would be supported. Do you see why?*

Structural Modeling. Structural modeling is a sophisticated method for exploring and possibly confirming causation among several variables. Its complexity is beyond the scope of this text. Suffice it to say that it combines multiple regression, path analysis, and factor analysis. The computations are greatly simplified by use of computer programs; the computer program most widely used is probably LISREL.[1]

Basic Steps in Correlational Research

PROBLEM SELECTION

The variables to be included in a correlational study should be based on a sound rationale growing out of experience or theory. The researcher should have some reason for thinking certain variables may be related. As always, clarity in defining variables will avoid many problems later on. In general, three major types of problems are the focus of correlational studies:

1. Is variable *X* related to variable *Y*?
2. How well does variable *P* predict variable *C*?
3. What are the relationships among a large number of variables, and what predictions can be made that are based on them?

Almost all correlational studies will revolve around one of these types of questions. Some examples of published correlational studies are:

- "What Makes Professional Development Effective?"[2]
- "Verbal Ability and Teacher Effectiveness"[3]
- "Bullying and Stress in Early Adolescence"[4]
- "An Investigation of the Relationship Between Health Literacy and Social Communication Skills in Older Adults"[5]
- "A Correlational Study of Art-Based Measures of Cognitive Development: Clinical and Research Implications for Art Therapists Working with Children"[6]
- "A Correlational Study of the Relationships Among Student Performance, Student Feelings, and Teacher Perceptions"[7]
- "Perfectionism and Peer Relations Among Children with Obsessive-Compulsive Disorder"[8]

SAMPLE

The sample for a correlational study, as in any type of study, should be selected carefully and, if possible, randomly. The first step in selecting a sample, of course, is to identify an appropriate population, one that is meaningful and from which data on *each* of the variables of interest can be collected. The minimum acceptable sample size for a correlational study is considered by most researchers to be no less than 30. Data obtained from a sample smaller than 30 may give an inaccurate estimate of the degree of relationship. Samples larger than 30 are much more likely to provide meaningful results.

*Because alienation is "caused" primarily by lack of enjoyment (−.55) and number of friends (−.60). The perceived lack of relevance of courses does contribute to degree of alienation, but primarily because relevance "causes" enjoyment. Enjoyment is partly caused by number of friends. Perceived relevance of courses is only slightly caused by number of friends.

INSTRUMENTS

The instruments used to measure the two (or more) variables involved in a correlational study may take any one of a number of forms (see Chapter 7), but they must yield quantitative data. Although data sometimes can be collected from records of one sort or another (e.g., grade transcripts), most correlational studies involve the administration of some type of instrument (tests, questionnaires, and so on) and sometimes observation. As with any study, whatever instruments are used must yield reliable scores. In an explanatory study, the instruments must also show evidence of validity. If they do not truly measure the intended variables, then any correlation that is obtained will not be an indication of the intended relationship. In a prediction study, it is not essential that we know what variable is actually being measured—if it works as a predictor, it is useful. However, prediction studies are most likely to be successful, and certainly more satisfying, when we know what we are measuring!

DESIGN AND PROCEDURES

The basic design used in a correlational study is quite straightforward. Using the symbols introduced in our discussion of experimental designs in Chapter 13, this design can be diagrammed as:

Design for a Correlational Study

	Observations	
Subjects	O_1	O_2
A	–	–
B	–	–
C	–	–
D	–	–
E	–	–
F	–	–
G	–	–
etc.		

As you can see, two (or more) scores are obtained from *each* individual in the sample, one score for each variable of interest. The pairs of scores are then correlated, and the resulting correlation coefficient indicates the degree of relationship between the variables.

Notice, again, that we cannot say that the variable being measured by the first instrument (O_1) is the cause of any differences in scores we may find in the variable being measured by the second instrument (O_2). As we have mentioned before, three possibilities exist:

1. The variable being measured by O_1 may cause the variable being measured by O_2.
2. The variable being measured by O_2 may cause the variable being measured by O_1.
3. Some third, perhaps unidentified and unmeasured, variable may cause both of the other variables.

Different numbers of variables can be investigated in correlational studies, and sometimes quite complex statistical procedures are used. The basic research design for all correlational studies, however, is similar to the one just shown. An example of data obtained with a correlational design is shown in Table 15.4.

TABLE 15.4 *Example of Data Obtained in a Correlational Design*

Student	(O_1) Self-Esteem	(O_2) Mathematics Achievement
José	25	95
Felix	23	88
Rosita	25	96
Phil	18	81
Jenny	12	65
Natty	23	73
Lina	22	92
Jill	15	71
Jack	24	93
James	17	78

DATA COLLECTION

In an explanatory study, all the data on both variables will usually be collected within a fairly short time. Often, the instruments used are administered in a single session, or in two sessions one immediately after the other. Thus, if a researcher were interested in measuring the relationship between verbal aptitude and memory, a test of verbal aptitude and another of memory would be administered closely together to the same group of subjects. In a prediction study, the measurement of the criterion variables often takes place sometime after the measurement of the predictor variables. If a researcher were interested in studying the predictive value of a mathematics aptitude test, the aptitude test might be administered just prior to the beginning of a course in mathematics. Success in the course (the criterion variable, as indicated by course grades) would then be measured at the end of the course.

DATA ANALYSIS AND INTERPRETATION

As we have mentioned previously, when variables are correlated, a **correlation coefficient** is produced. This coefficient will be a decimal, somewhere between 0.00 and +1.00 or −1.00. The closer the coefficient is to +1.00 or −1.00, the stronger the relationship. If the sign is positive, the relationship is positive, indicating that high scores on one variable tend to go with high scores on the other variable. If the sign is negative, the relationship is negative, indicating that high scores on one variable tend to go with low scores on the other variable. Coefficients that are at or near .00 indicate that no relationship exists between the variables involved.

What Do Correlation Coefficients Tell Us?

It is important to be able to interpret correlation coefficients sensibly since they appear so frequently in articles about education and educational research. Unfortunately, they are seldom accompanied by scatterplots, which usually help interpretation and understanding.

The meaning of a given correlation coefficient depends on how it is applied. It is generally agreed that correlation coefficients below .35 show only a slight relationship between variables. Such relationships have almost no value in any predictive sense. (It may, of course, be important to know that certain variables are not related. Thus we would expect to find a very low correlation, for instance, between years of teaching experience and number of students enrolled.) Correlations between .40 and .60 are often found in educational research and may have theoretical or practical value, depending on the context. A correlation of at least .50 must be obtained before any crude predictions can be made about individuals. Even then, such predictions will be subject to sizable errors. Only a correlation of .65 or higher will allow individual predictions that are reasonably accurate for most purposes. Correlations over .85 indicate a close relationship between the variables correlated and are useful in predicting individual performance, but correlations this high are rarely obtained in educational research, except when checking on reliability.

As we illustrated in Chapter 8, correlation coefficients are also used to check the reliability and validity of scores obtained from tests and other instruments used in research; when so used, they are called *reliability* and *validity coefficients.* When used to check reliability of scores, the coefficient should be at least .70, preferably higher; many tests achieve reliability coefficients of .90. The correlation between two different scorers, working independently, should be at least .90. When used to check validity of scores, the coefficient should be at least .50, and preferably higher.

Threats to Internal Validity in Correlational Research

Recall from Chapter 9 that a major concern to researchers is that extraneous variables may explain away any results that are obtained.* A similar concern applies to correlational studies. A researcher who conducts a correlational study should always be alert to alternative explanations for relationships found in the data. What might account for any correlations that are reported as existing between two or more variables?

Consider again the hypothesis that teacher expectation of failure is positively correlated with student disruptive behavior. A researcher conducting this study would almost certainly have a cause-and-effect sequence in mind, most likely that teacher expectation is a partial cause of disruptive behavior. Why? Because disruptive behavior is undesirable (because it clearly interferes with both academic learning and a desirable classroom climate). Thus, it would be helpful to know what might be done to reduce it. While teacher expectation of failure *might* be considered the dependent variable, it seems less likely since such expectations would be of little interest if they have no effect on students.

If, indeed, the researcher's intentions are as we have described, he might have carried out an experiment. However, it is difficult to see how teacher expectation could be experimentally manipulated. It might, however, be possible to study whether attempts to *change*

*It can be argued that such threats are irrelevant to the predictive use of correlational research. The argument is that one can predict even if the relationship is an artifact of other variables. Thus, predictions of college achievement can be made from high school grades even if both are highly related to socioeconomic status. While we agree with the practical utility of such predictions, we believe that research should seek to illuminate relationships that have at least the potential for explanation.

teacher expectations result in subsequent *changes* in amount of disruptive behavior, but such a study requires developing and implementing training methods. Before embarking on such development and implementation, therefore, one might well ask whether there is any relationship between the primary variables. This is why a correlational study is an appropriate first step.

A positive correlation resulting from such a study would most likely be viewed as at least some evidence to suggest that modifying teacher expectations would result in less disruptive behavior, thereby justifying further experimental efforts. (It may also be that some principals or teacher-trainers would wish to institute mechanisms for changing teacher expectations before waiting for experimental confirmation, just as the medical profession began warning about the effects of smoking in the absence of conclusive experimental evidence.) Before investing time and resources in developing training methods and carrying out an experiment, the researcher needs to be as confident as possible that he is not misinterpreting his correlation. If the relationship he has found really reflects the opposite cause-and-effect sequence (student behavior causing teacher expectations), or if *both* are a result of other causes, such as student ability or socioeconomic status, changes in teacher expectation are *not* likely to be accompanied by a reduction in disruptive behavior. The former problem (direction of cause and effect) can be largely eliminated by assessing teacher expectations *prior* to direct involvement with the student group. The latter problem—of other causes—is the one we turn to now.

Some of the threats we discussed in Chapter 9 do not apply to correlational studies. Implementation, history, maturation, attitude of subjects, and regression threats are not applicable since no intervention occurs. There are some threats, however, that do apply.

SUBJECT CHARACTERISTICS

Whenever two or more characteristics of individuals (or groups) are correlated, there exists the possibility that yet *other* characteristics can explain any relationships that are found. In such cases, the other characteristics can be controlled through a statistical technique known as **partial correlation**. Let us illustrate the logic involved by using the example of the relationship between teachers' expectations of failure and the amount of disruptive behavior by students in their classes. This relationship is shown in Figure 15.6(*a*).

The researcher desires to control, or "get rid of," the variable of "ability level" for the classes involved, since it is logical to assume that it might be a cause of variation in the other two variables. To control for this variable, the researcher needs to measure the ability level of each class. She can then construct scatterplots as shown in Figure 15.6(*b*) and (*c*). Scatterplot (*b*) shows the correlation between amount of disruptive behavior and class ability level; scatterplot (*c*) shows the correlation between teacher expectation of failure and class ability level.

The researcher can now use scatterplot (*b*) to predict the disruptive behavior score for class 1, based on the ability score for class 1. In doing so, the researcher would be assuming that the regression line shown in scatterplot (*b*) correctly represents the relationship between these variables (class ability level and amount of disruptive behavior) in the data. Next, the researcher subtracts the *predicted* disruptive behavior score from the *actual* disruptive behavior score. The result is called the *adjusted disruptive behavior score*—that is, the score has been "adjusted" by taking out the influence of ability level. For class 1, the predicted disruptive behavior score is 7 (based on a class ability score of 5). In actuality this class scored 11 (higher than expected), so the adjusted score for amount of disruptive behavior is $(11 - 7)$, or 4.

The same procedure is then followed to adjust teacher expectation scores for class ability level, as shown in scatterplot (*c*) $(10 - 7 = 3)$. After repeating this process for the entire sample of classes, the researcher is now in a position to determine the correlation between the *adjusted* disruptive behavior scores and the *adjusted* teacher expectation scores. The result is the correlation between the two major variables with the effect of class ability having been eliminated, and thus controlled. Methods of calculation, involving the use of relatively simple formulas are available to greatly simplify this procedure.[9] Figure 15.7 shows another way to think about partial correlation. The top circles illustrate (by amount of overlap) the correlation between *A* and *B*. The bottom circles show the same overlap but reduced by "taking out" the overlap of *C* with *A* and *B*. What remains (the diagonally lined section) illustrates the partial correlation of *A* and *B* with the effects of *C* removed.

LOCATION

A location threat is possible whenever all instruments are administered to each subject at a specified location, but the location is different for different subjects. It is not uncommon for researchers to encounter differences in testing conditions, particularly when individual tests are required. In one school, a comfortable, well-lit, and

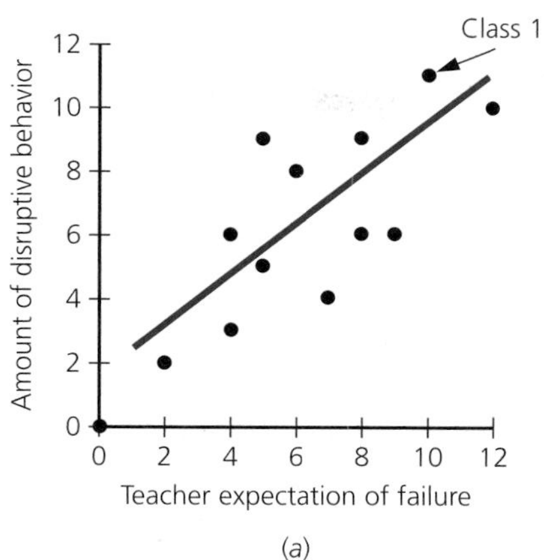

(a)

Amount of disruptive behavior in class as related to teacher expectation of failure

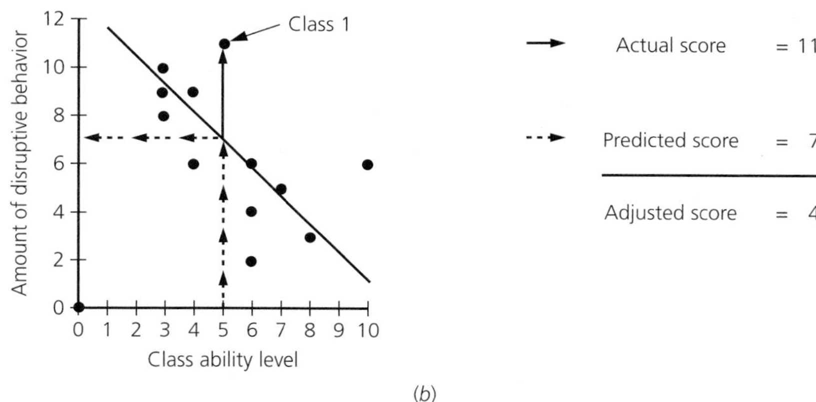

(b)

Amount of disruptive behavior as related to ability level of class

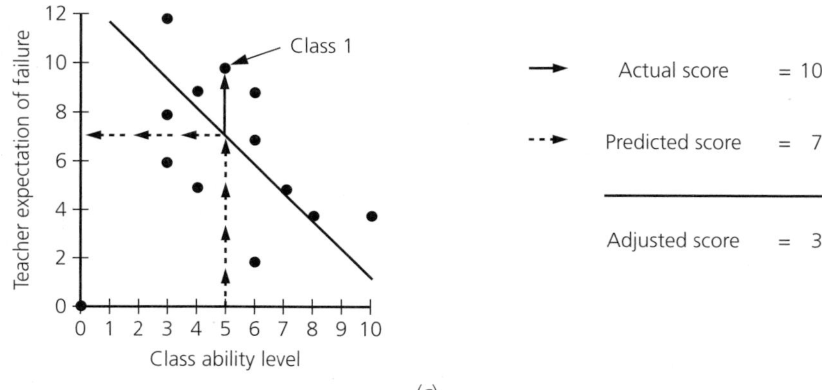

(c)

Teacher expectation of failure as related to ability level of class

Figure 15.6 *Scatterplots for Combinations of Variables*

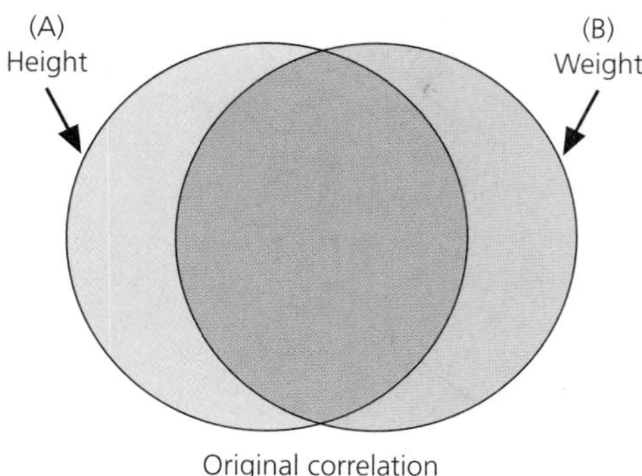

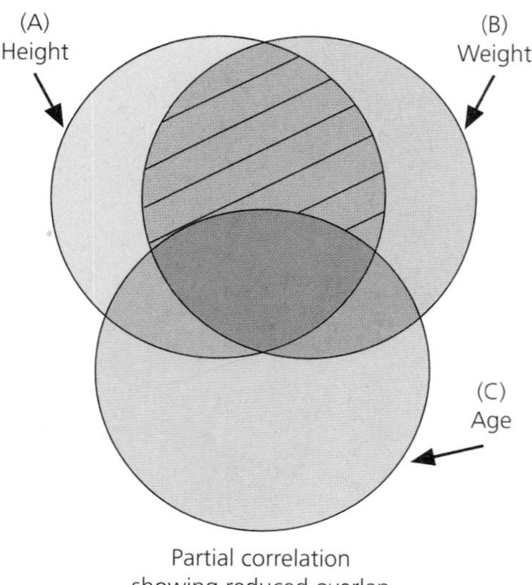

Figure 15.7 *Eliminating the Effects of Age Through Partial Correlation*

ventilated room may be available. In another, a custodian's closet may have to do. Such conditions can increase (or decrease) subject scores. If both measures are not administered to all subjects under the same conditions, the conditions rather than the variables being studied may account for the relationship. If only part of a group, for example, responds to instruments in an uncomfortable, poorly lit room, they might score lower on an achievement test and respond more negatively to a rating scale measuring student liking for school, thus producing a misleading correlation coefficient.

Similarly, conditions in different schools may account for observed relationships. A high negative correlation between amount of disruptive behavior in class and achievement may be simply a reflection of differing resources. Students in schools with few science materials can be expected to do poorly in science and also to be disruptive because of boredom or hostility. The only solutions to location problems such as these are either to measure the extraneous variables (such as resource level) and use partial correlation or to determine correlations separately for each location, provided the number of students at each location is sufficiently large (a minimum n of 30).

INSTRUMENTATION

Instrument Decay. In any study using a particular instrument many times, thought must be given to the possibility of instrument decay. This is most likely in observational studies since most other correlational studies do not use instruments many times (with the same subjects at least). When both variables are measured by an observational device at the same time, care must be taken to ensure that observers don't become tired, bored, or inattentive (this may require using additional observers). In a study in which observers are asked to record (during the same time period) both the number of "thought questions" asked by the teacher and the attentiveness of students, for example, a tired (or bored) observer might miss instances of each, resulting in low scores for the class on both variables, and thus distortion in the correlation.

Data Collector Characteristics. Characteristics of data collectors can create a threat if different persons administer both instruments. Gender, age, or ethnicity, for example, may affect specific responses, particularly with opinion or attitudinal instruments, as well as the seriousness with which respondents answer certain questions. One might expect an Air Force colonel in uniform, for example, to engender different scores on instruments measuring attitudes toward the military and (separately) toward the aerospace industry than a civilian data collector. If each data collector gives both instruments to several groups, the correlation between these scores will be higher as a result of the impact of the data collector. Fortunately, this threat is easily avoided by having each instrument administered by a different individual.

Data Collector Bias. Another instrumentation threat can result from unconscious bias on the part of the data gatherers whenever both instruments are given or scored by the same person. It is not uncommon, particularly with individually administered performance tests, for the same person to administer both tests to the same student, and even during the same time period. It is likely that the observed or scored performance on the first test will affect the way in which the second test is administered and/or scored. It is almost impossible to avoid expectations based on the first test, and these may well affect the examiner's behavior on the second testing. A high score on the first test, for example, may lead to examiner expectation of a high score on the second, resulting in students being given additional time or encouragement on the second test. While precise instructions for administering instruments are helpful, a better solution is to have different administrators for each test.

TESTING

The experience of responding to the first instrument that is administered in a correlational study may influence subject responses to the second instrument. Students asked to respond first to a "liking for teacher" scale, and then shortly thereafter to a "liking for social studies" scale are likely to see a connection. You can imagine them saying, perhaps, something like, "Oh, I see, if I don't like the teacher, I'm not supposed to like the subject." To the extent that this happens, the results obtained can be misleading. The solution is to administer instruments, if possible, at different times and in different contexts.

MORTALITY

Mortality, strictly speaking, is not a problem of internal validity in correlational studies since anyone "lost" must be excluded from the study—correlations cannot be obtained unless a researcher has a score for each person on *both* of the variables being measured.

There are times, however, when loss of subjects may make a relationship more (or less) likely in the remaining data, thus creating a threat to *external* validity. Why external validity? Because the sample actually studied is often not the sample initially selected, because of mortality. Let us refer again to the study hypothesizing that teacher expectation of failure would be positively correlated with amount of disruptive student behavior. It might be that those teachers who refused to participate in the study were those who had a very low expectation of failure—who, in fact, expected their students to achieve at unrealistically high levels. It also seems likely that the classes of those same teachers would exhibit a lot of disruptive behavior as a result of such unrealistic pressure from these teachers. Their loss would serve to *increase* the correlation obtained. Because there is no way to know whether this possibility is correct, the only thing the researcher can do is to try to avoid losing subjects.

Evaluating Threats to Internal Validity in Correlational Studies

The evaluation of specific threats to internal validity in correlational studies follows a procedure similar to that for experimental studies.

Step 1: Ask: What are the specific factors that are known to affect or could logically affect one of the variables being correlated? It does not matter which variable is selected.

Step 2: Ask: What is the likelihood of each of these factors also affecting the *other* variable being correlated with the first? We need not be concerned with any factor unrelated to either variable. A factor must be related to *both* variables to be a threat.*

Step 3: Evaluate the various threats in terms of their likelihood, and plan to control them. If a given threat cannot be controlled, this should be acknowledged and discussed.

As we did in Chapter 13, let us consider an example to show how these steps might be applied. Suppose a researcher wishes to study the relationship between social skills (as observed) and job success (as rated by supervisors) of a group of severely disabled young adults in a career education program. Listed here again are several threats to internal validity discussed in Chapter 9 and our evaluation of each.

Subject Characteristics. We consider here only four of many possible characteristics.

1. **Severity of disability.** *Step 1:* Rated job success can be expected to be related to severity of disability. *Step 2:* Severity of disability can also be expected to be related to social skills. Therefore, severity should be assessed and controlled (using partial correlation). *Step 3:* Likelihood of having an effect unless controlled: high.
2. **Socioeconomic level of parents.** *Step 1:* Parents' socioeconomic level is likely to be related to social skills. *Step 2:* Parental socioeconomic status is not likely to be related to job success for this group. While it is desirable to obtain socioeconomic data

*This rule must be modified with respect to data collector and testing threats, where knowledge about the first instrument (or scores on it) may influence performance or assessment on the second instrument.

(to find out more about the sample), it is not of high priority. *Step 3:* Likelihood of having an effect unless controlled: low.

3. **Physical strength and coordination.** *Step 1:* These characteristics may be related to job success. *Step 2:* Strength and coordination are not likely to be related to social skills. While it is desirable to obtain such information, it is not of high priority. *Step 3:* Likelihood of having an effect unless controlled: low.
4. **Physical appearance.** *Step 1:* Physical appearance is likely to be related to social skills. *Step 2:* It is also likely to be related to rated job success. Therefore, this variable should be assessed and controlled (again by using partial correlation). *Step 3:* Likelihood of having an effect unless controlled: high.

Mortality. *Step 1:* Subjects "lost" are likely to have poorer job performance. *Step 2:* Lost subjects are also more likely to have poorer social skills. Thus, loss of subjects can be expected to reduce magnitude of correlation. *Step 3:* Likelihood of having an effect unless controlled: moderate to high.

Location. *Step 1:* Because the subjects of the study would (inevitably) be working at different job sites and under different conditions, location may well be related to rated job success. *Step 2:* If social skill is observed on-site, it may be related to the specific site conditions. While it is possible that this threat could be controlled by independently assessing the job-site environments, a better solution would be to assess social skills at a common site such as that used for group training. *Step 3:* Likelihood of having an effect unless controlled: high.

Instrumentation.

1. **Instrument decay.** *Step 1:* Instrument decay, if it has occurred, is likely to be related to how accurately social skills are measured. Observations should be scheduled, therefore, to preclude this possibility. *Step 2:* Instrument decay would be unlikely to affect job ratings. Therefore, its occurrence would not be expected to account for any relationship found between the major variables. *Step 3:* Likelihood of having an effect unless controlled: low.
2. **Data collector characteristics.** *Step 1:* Data collector characteristics might well be related to job ratings since interaction of data collectors and supervisors is a necessary part of this study. *Step 2:* Characteristics of data collectors presumably would not be related to their observation of social skills; nevertheless, to be on the safe side, this possibility should be controlled by having the same data collectors observe all subjects. *Step 3:* Likelihood of having an effect unless controlled: moderate.
3. **Data collector bias.** *Step 1:* Ratings of job success should not be subject to data collector bias, since different supervisors will rate each subject. *Step 2:* Observations of social skills may be related to preconceptions of observers about the subjects, *especially* if they have prior knowledge of job success ratings. Therefore, observers should have no knowledge of job ratings. *Step 3:* Likelihood of having an effect unless controlled: high.

Testing. *Step 1:* In this example, performance on the first instrument administered cannot, of course, be affected by performance on the second. *Step 2:* In this study, scores on the second instrument cannot be affected by performance on the first, since the subjects are unaware of their performance on the first instrument. *Step 3:* Likelihood of having an effect unless controlled: zero.

Rationale for the Process of Evaluating Threats in Correlational Studies. We will try to demonstrate the logic behind the principle that a factor must be related to both correlated variables to explain a correlation between them. Consider the three scatterplots shown in Figure 15.8, which represent the scores of a group of individuals on three variables: *A*, *B*, and *C*. Scatterplot 1 shows a substantial correlation between *A* and *B*; scatterplot 2 shows a substantial correlation between *A* and *C*; scatterplot 3 shows a zero correlation between *B* and *C*.

Suppose the researcher is interested in determining whether the correlation between variables *A* and *B* can be "explained" by variable *C*. *A* and *B*, in other words, represent the variables being studied, while *C* represents a third variable being evaluated as a potential threat to internal validity. If the researcher tries to explain the correlation between *A* and *B* as due to *C*, he or she cannot. Here's why.

Suppose we say that person 1, shown in scatterplot 1, is high on *A* and *B because* he or she is high on *C*. Sure enough, being high on *C would* predict being high on *A*. You can see this in scatterplot 2. However, being high on *C* does *not* predict being high on *B*, because although some individuals who scored high on *C* did score high on *B*, others who scored high on *C* scored in the middle or low on *B*. You can see this in scatterplot 3.

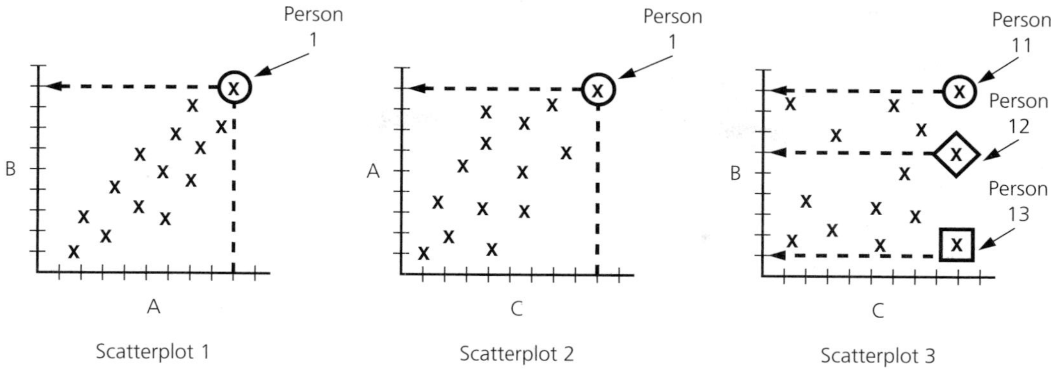

Figure 15.8 *Scatterplots Illustrating How a Factor (C) May Not Be a Threat to Internal Validity*

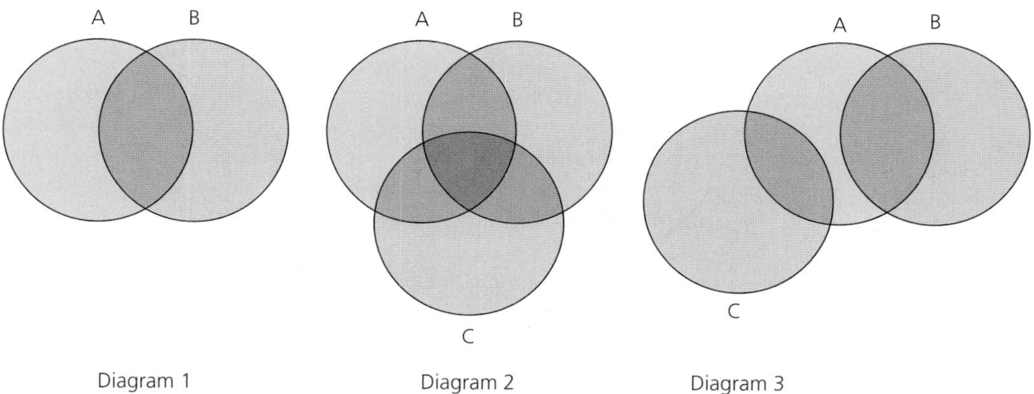

Figure 15.9 *Circle Diagrams Illustrating Relationships Among Variables*

Another way of portraying this logic is with circle diagrams, as shown in Figure 15.9.

Diagram 1 in Figure 15.9 illustrates a correlation between *A* and *B*. This is shown by the overlap in circles; the greater the overlap, the greater the correlation. Diagram 2 shows a third circle, *C*, which represents the additional variable that is being considered as a possible threat to internal validity. Because it is correlated with *both A* and *B*, it may be considered a possible explanation for at least part of the correlation between them. This is shown by the fact that circle *C* overlaps *both A* and *B*. By way of contrast, diagram 3 shows that whereas *C* is correlated with *A*, it is *not* correlated with *B* (there is no overlap). Because *C* overlaps only with *A* (i.e., it does not overlap with *both* variables), it *cannot* be considered a possible alternative explanation for the correlation between *A* and *B*. Diagram 3, in other words, shows what the three scatterplots in Figure 15.8 do, namely, that *A* is correlated with *B*, and that *A* is correlated with *C*, but that *B* is *not* correlated with *C*.

An Example of Correlational Research

In the remainder of this chapter, we present a published example of correlational research, followed by a critique of its strengths and weaknesses. As we did in our critique of the experimental and single-subject studies analyzed in Chapters 13 and 14, we use several of the concepts introduced in earlier parts of the book in our analysis.

Physical Education in Urban High School Class Settings: Features and Correlations between Teaching Behaviors and Learning Activities

Howard Z. Zeng, Raymond Leung, and Michael Hipscher
The City University of New York, Brooklyn College

Wenhao Liu
Slippery Rock University (PA)

Abstract

This study examined the features and correlations between teaching behaviors and learning activities in urban high school physical education (PE) class settings using direct instruction model. Participants were sixteen urban high school PE teachers and their students. Results indicated that the teachers spent their class times on the major teaching behaviors were: Informing 28.8%, Structuring 25.4%, Observing 17.0%, and Feedback 9.2%. The students spent their class times on the major learning activities were: Motor Engaged 56.2%, Cognitive Engaged 20.7%, and Waiting for a Turn 9.7%. Correlation analyses revealed that Informing, Questioning, and Feedback teaching behaviors were positively associated with Motor Engaged and Cognitive Engaged learning activities. When the teachers exhibited the behavior category of None of the Above, their students showed no motor and cognitive learning activities engagements. Findings suggested that, PE teachers should develop and employ teaching behaviors that promote and demonstrate physical skills and fitness because those teaching behaviors are positively associated with students' physical activity levels.

"As follows"

Prior research

Constitutive definition

Research on teaching in physical education (RT-PE) has accomplished remarkably with respect to how teaching behaviors are related to learning outcomes (Brophy & Good, 1986; Graham & Heimerer, 1981; Keating, Kulinna & Silverman, 1999; Martin & Kulinna, 2004; Silverman, Tyson & Morford, 1988). Silverman (1991) defined RT-PE as "research on what teachers and students do and how this affects or relates to learning and to the social dynamics of the class." (p. 352). This definition is broad and tells us that, when a study is conducted on teaching in physical education, both teacher's teaching behaviors and student's learning activities should be included in the parameters of a study.

Recently, research studies have provided sufficient information regarding the characteristics of effective teaching (Pangrazi, 2007; Kulinna, Cothran & Regualos, 2006; Siedentop & Tannehill, 2000). Based on the work done by previous researchers, the following characteristics were described as effective teaching/learning environments: (a) clear objectives and content covered; (b) well-organized and appropriate expectations; (c) meaningful task and high rates of success; (d) smooth transition and low rates of management time; (e) appropriate guidance and active supervision; (f) high rates in student-engaged time and low rates in student waiting time; and (g) teacher's enthusiasm and equitable support. The characteristics stated above have become important guidelines for training novice teachers to grow to be an effective teacher (Pangrazi, 2007; Kulinna, Cothran & Regualos, 2006; Siedentop & Tannehill, 2000).

A number of previous studies in RT-PE focused on how teacher and student behaviors were associated with direct instruction, and eventually the direct instruction model in physical education was developed (Anderson, Evertson, & Brophy, 1979; Graber, 2001; Rosenshine, 1979; Rosenshine & Stevens, 1986; Sweeting & Rink, 1999). Rosenshine (1979) illustrated that direct instruction model in physical education possesses clear learning goals, adequate time for instruction and practice which is characterized by appropriate subject matters for students' abilities, low-level cognitive questions but meaningful task and high success by monitoring student performance and providing immediate and specific feedback.

Silverman, Tyson, and Morford (1988) found that students spending their class time on motor skill practice with teacher's feedback was positively associated with their motor learning achievement. Furthermore, regarding how time is spent in physical education classes, Silverman (1991) summarized that most students spent less than 30% of the class time on motor activities but the majority of the time on waiting, explanation/demonstration, and/or receiving information.

Faucette and Patterson (1990) compared teaching behaviors and students' activity levels taught by specialists versus non-specialists in elementary physical education class settings. The researchers found that specialists employed informing, structuring, questioning, feedback, and reward teaching behaviors whereas non-specialists utilized silent monitoring and attending teaching behaviors, thereby suggesting that different teaching behaviors caused different students' activity levels. The rates of students' activity levels were 35.0% and 16.5% taught by specialists and non-specialists respectively (Faucette & Patterson, 1990).

Good review

More recently, researchers have used different observation instruments to investigate, describe, and compare the differences and similarities of teaching behaviors and student learning activities in physical education classes (Banville, 2006; Banville & Rikard, 2001; Keating et al., 1999; Martin & Kulinna, 2005; Mitcell & Castelli, 2003). Significant linear correlations between teaching behaviors and learning activities with correlation coefficients ranging from .26 to .42 have been found (Martin & Kulinna, 2004, 2005; Mitcell & Castelli, 2003).

Potentially useful

Small

Martin and Kulinna's study (2005) involved 43 physical education teachers (20 from elementary school, 11 from middle school, and 12 from high school). The main purposes of their study were: (a) to determine whether teachers' intentions to teach lessons more active physically were related to teaching behaviors (e.g., demonstrating and promoting fitness); and (b) whether teacher behaviors were associated with how much time their students spent on various activities. They found that general instruction and management behaviors were negatively related to students' moderate to vigorous physical activities; general instruction behaviors, however, were positively associated with students' sitting and standing behaviors.

Although RT-PE have accomplished plentifully, Silverman (1991) pointed out that the majority of studies in teaching physical education were conducted at the K-8 levels using preservice teachers as participants (even though 17 years after Dr. Silverman's famous general review for the accomplishments in the field of research in teaching physical education). Studies at the high school level were very limited, and the features of teaching behaviors and learning activities at the high school level were not well-documented. Hence, the relationship between teachers' teaching behaviors and students' learning activities in high school physical education classes remained unanswered. As a result, the present study was designed to extend previous research (K-8) by not only employing high

Justification

school (9-12) physical education teachers as participants but also examining the characteristics of effective teaching in high school physical education classes. The purpose of this study was to examine the features and correlations between teaching behaviors and learning activities in urban high school physical education classes.

Purpose

METHODS

Participants and Settings

Sixteen in-service physical education teachers (6 females and 10 males) from three urban high schools in the East Coast of the United States were observed during their regularly scheduled physical education classes. The teaching experiences of these teachers ranged from 5-25 years. They taught physical education skill/activities/fitness classes five days a week, 3-5 classes a day. These teachers and their students were selected because they were cooperating teachers in the physical education teacher education program of the principal investigator's university. Moreover, all the teachers and students in the current study were from the same school district, city, and state.

Convenience sample

The demographic information for the three high schools was: (a) school one: grade levels: 9 to 12, class size: 32-34, enrollment: 4,054, ethnicity %: 36 white, 29 black, 15 Hispanic, 22 Asian, (b) School two: grade levels: 9 to 12, class size: 31-34, enrollment: 3,500, ethnicity %: 25 white, 43 black 9 Hispanic, 25 Asian, (c) School three: grade levels: 9 to 12, class size: 32-35, enrollment: 3,024, ethnicity %: 37 white, 10 black, 29 Hispanic, 26 Asian (New York City Department of Education, 2007). The curricular requirements and standards as outlined by the state, district, and schools were: (a) basic motor and manipulative skills, cardiorespiratory endurance, flexibility, muscular strength, endurance, and body composition; (b) to participate in physical activities that develop physical fitness skills, demonstrate fundamental motor, non-loco-motor, and manipulative skills, understand the effects of activity on the body and the risks associated with inactivity, understand the relationship between physical activity and individual well being; (c) students will have the necessary knowledge and skills to establish and maintain physical fitness, participate in physical activity, and maintain personal health (New York State Education Department, 2007).

Use table to display demographics

Subject matters involved in the observed physical education classes were basketball/ fitness (8 lessons), volleyball/fitness (8 lessons), yoga (6 lessons), dance (4 lessons), soccer/ fitness (2 lessons), weight lifting/fitness (2 lessons), and tennis (2 lessons). In order to ensure that the teachers' behaviors were not being influenced, the behavioral categories of the observation instrument were not disclosed to the participants. The teachers were informed that, "We will come to your class videotaping your lesson as whatever it is supposed to be."

Instrumentation

The Direct Instruction Behavior Analysis (DIBA, Zakrajsek & Tannehill, 1989) was utilized to collect data. The DIBA system was a systematic observation instrument designed to collect data on teacher and student behaviors, and could be used for teaching performance analysis (Zakrajsek & Tannehill, 1989). The DIBA system characterized those behaviors identified by the researchers of the direct instruction model (Fielding, Kaneenui & Gersten, 1983; Graham & Heimerer, 1981; Rosenshine, 1979). In addition, there was a "Comments" section on the 'DIBA Recording Sheet', which allowed the recorder to write down his/her comments or note about the lesson. These comments or notes would be useful when the researchers explained and illustrated what were the reasons behind

Validity and reliability evidence?

the quantitative data. In brief, the DIBA was selected to be the instrument believing to be able to better fulfill the purpose of the current study although there were different instruments in the field of teaching physical education.

Weak rationale

The DIBA was composed of 14 categories. The first eight categories were used to determine the instructors' teaching behaviors and the last six categories were used to decide students' learning activities (Zakrajsek & Tannehill, 1989):

1. Teaching Information. Teacher tells, explains, demonstrates, reviews, or summarizes.
2. Teacher Observing. Teacher silently observes, watches, or monitors student performance.
3. Teacher Structuring. Teacher stresses objectives and important points, directs performance, or signals transitions.
4. Teacher Questioning. Teacher asks questions that are intended to evoke a verbal or motor response.
5. Teacher Praise/Encouragement. Teacher praises, commends, accepts, or encourages student performance or attempts.
6. Teacher Feedback. Teacher gives feedback that is immediate, specific, and task relevant (can include correct or incorrect responses).
7. Teacher Controlling. Teacher uses disciplinary comments or actions to criticize or to justify authority.
8. None of the Above. Teacher's behaviors are not related to the instructional process (but exhibited during the class).
9. Motor Engaged. Student is actively engaged in an appropriate motor task/activity.
10. Cognitive Engaged. Student listens to or reads about subject matter and gains information.
11. Response Preparing. Student gets ready to respond to a learning task.
12. Gets Equipment/Relocates. Student is following teacher's direction or information to get the equipment or move to a different location.
13. Waits for a Turn. Student is waiting in a line for his or her turn to practice a task.
14. Off-Task. Student is not engaged in an appropriate motor or cognitive task. (*pp.* 244-245)

How does this differ from (1) Teacher Information?

Procedures

After obtaining permission to conduct the study from the Institutional Review Board and the administrators of the high schools, the informed consent and cover letters were delivered to the participants. The purposes of the study were explained to the teachers. The informed consent forms were obtained from both the teachers and the students before the videotaping procedures took place. During the investigation, two lessons were videotaped for each teacher and his/her students. As a result, a total of 32 lessons were videotaped. Two digital camcorders (Sony DCR TRV 350 NTSC, Japan, 2003) were utilized to perform the videotaping tasks. Lessons were videotaped from the moment when the teachers officially started the lesson until the teachers dismissed the class. The time students were in the locker rooms was excluded from videotaping. During each videotaping session, the camcorder was placed in a non-obtrusive location to minimize the reactive effects.

Good description

Before data were collected, two observers underwent training with the observation instrument. After four practice coding sessions (120 minute per session) were conducted, the inter-observer agreement (IOA) exceeded 80%. Inter-observer

Adequate

reliabilities for the DIBA were calculated as suggested by "The general formula for computing reliability of interobserver" (Siedentop & Tannehill, 2000; p. 336). The inter-observer reliabilities were checked for each coding day (recording six lessons per coding day).

Operational definitions

After all the lessons were recorded, the following procedures were executed: (a) interval recording technique was used to code the videotaped lessons, producing percentage of time that participants and their students spent on the predefined behaviors categories; (b) event recording was also used to code the videotaped lessons, resulting in a frequency of the behavioral categories exhibited by the participants and their students. Rate per minute (RPM) was used as the measurement unit with the event recording to describe and compare the frequencies among the behavioral categories (Siedentop & Tannehill, 2000); (c) the "Recording Procedures" in the DIBA (Zakrajsek & Tannehill, 1989, pp. 245–248) were followed through the entire coding process.

Data Analyses

Descriptive statistics were computed on the 14 behavioral categories. Of these 14 behavioral categories, two categories (Teacher Controlling and Student Off-Task) had no or limited occurrence frequencies. As a result, correlation analyses were conducted between the teaching behaviors and learning activities among the 12 behavioral categories only.

RESULTS

The purpose of this study was to examine the features and correlations between teaching behaviors and learning activities in urban high school physical education class settings using the DIBA system. Fourteen categories in the DIBA were analyzed; wherein eight categories described teaching behaviors and six categories described students' learning activities. For the percentage data, the means and standard deviations were computed from the 32 observed lessons. The RPM data were analyzed using correlational analysis techniques. The general IOA values over the 14 behavioral from the DIBA for the percentage data and the RPM data were .91 and .89 respectively, thus meeting the criteria for systematic observational research (Siedentop & Tannehill, 2000). Based on the above mentioned conditions, the total time recorded on tapes was 1026 min for the 32 lessons. The average length of one lesson in this study was 32 min, which was 71% of a regular 45-min lesson.

The results of this study were summarized as follows. On average, the teachers spent their class time with 28.8% for Informing, 25.4% for Structuring, 17.0% for Observing, 9.2% for Feedback, 3.2% for Questioning, 1.9% for Praise/Encourage, .3% for Controlling, and 14.1% for None of the Above behaviors in a lesson. The students spent their class time with 56.2% on Motor Engaged, 20.7% on Cognitive Engaged, 6.8% on Response-Preparing, 6.4% on Get-Equipment/Relocation, and 9.7% on Waiting for a Turn in a lesson.

These features were confirmed by the RPM data. With respect to the teaching behavioral variables, the RPM for Informing was 3.29, for Structuring was 2.54, for Observing was 1.20, for Feedback was .71, for Praise/Encourage was .14, for Controlling was .01, and for None of the Above was 1.28. In regard to students' activity variables, the RPM for Motor Engaged was 5.3, for Cognitive Engaged was 1.90, for Response Preparing was .31, for Get-Equipment/Relocation was .68, and for Waiting for a Turn was .98. The descriptive statistics of the 13 behavioral categories are presented in Table 1.

TABLE 1 *Descriptive Statistics of Interval and Event Recording for Thirteen* Categories from Thirty-two Classes*

	Percentage (%)		RPM Data	
Variables	*M*	*SD*	*M*	*SD*
Teaching Behaviors				
Informing	28.828	14.788	3.294	2.251
Observing	16.984	12.258	1.197	.937
Structuring	25.401	14.065	2.536	1.524
Questioning	3.168	2.752	.363	.781
Praise/Encourage	1.897	2.578	.144	.246
Feedback	9.248	6.568	.712	.535
Controlling	.352	.926	.014	.036
None of the above	14.149	12.918	1.278	1.339
Learning Activities				
Motor-engaged	56.224	15.793	5.285	2.545
Cognitive-engaged	20.737	10.382	1.904	1.176
Response-preparing	6.769	4.389	.308	.296
Equipment/Relocating	6.396	4.663	.679	.458
Waiting for a Turn	9.745	11.897	.975	.887

*Students Off-Task category in the DIBA were not able to enter the Descriptive Statistics due to no occur frequency.

Furthermore, the correlation analysis revealed that the following five correlation coefficients (*rs*) were significant ($p < .05$) and meaningful: teacher Informing associate with students' Motor Engaged ($r = .558$), teacher Questioning associate with students' Cognitive Engaged ($r = .406$), and teacher Feedback vs. students' Cognitive Engaged ($r = .362$). It was noted that, when the teachers exhibited the behaviors of None of the Above, their students showed no motor and cognitive activities engagement (None of the Above associate with Motor Engaged, $r = -.510$; and None of the Above associate with Cognitive Engaged, $r = -.516$). The correlations between the teaching behaviors and the learning activities are presented in Table 2.

Table 2 says 'informing'

Moderate relationships

DISCUSSION

The objectives of this study were to examine the features and correlations between teaching behaviors and learning activities in urban high school physical education class settings. It was important to note that the results of this study were based upon and limited to the behavioral categories and the definitions of the DIBA instrument; and the results were also affected by the nature of the subject matters involved in the 32 observed lessons. We realized that the teachers in the current study spent their class time on the seven different teaching behaviors in different ways when comparing with the previous studies in the RT-PE literatures. The characteristics of effective teaching (e.g., clear objectives and content covered, well-organized and appropriate expectations, meaningful task and high rates of success, and smooth transition and low rates of management time) were found or identified through out the 32 lessons. We also realised that the students in the present study spent more class time on Motor Engaged (56.2%) and Cognitive Engaged (20.7%) than the previous studies in the RT-PE literatures. These two learning activities (Motor Engaged and Cognitive Engaged) were regarded as instructional products by the previous researchers (e.g., Martin & Kulinna, 2004; Rink, 2003; Silverman, 1991; Siedentop & Tannehill, 2000).

Study limitations

"Found"

TABLE 2 *Correlations among Teaching Behaviors and Students Activities by Event Recording for Twelve Variables from DIBA System (N = 32)*

Variable	1	2	3	4	5	6	7	8	9	10	11	12
Inform	–											
Observ	−.236	–										
Struct	.121	−.496**	–									
Quest	.100	−.204	−.156	–								
Pra/Enc	−.088	−.112	.011	−.050	–							
Feedba	.174	−.156	.028	−.143	.407*	–						
Nonabv	−.302	.297	−.084	.011	−.222	−.399*	–					
MotorE	.588**	.069	.249	−.285	−.128	.215	−.510**	–				
Cognit	.406*	−.295	.172	−.021	−.199	.362*	−.516**	.146	–			
RePrep	.204	−.044	.057	.266	−.079	.090	−.168	.296	.085	–		
EquiRe	−.378*	.058	−.306	.035	.186	.001	.036	.385*	.180	.021	–	
Waiting	−.663**	−.095	−.101	.175	.330	−.063	.115	−.409*	−.269	.015	.349*	–

Note. Two variables (Controlling and Off-Task) in the DIBA were not used for correlation analysis because the RPM were too low or no occur frequency. Inform = Informing, Observ = Observing, Struct = Structuring, Quest = Questioning, Pra/Enc = Praise/Encourage, Feedba = Feedback, Nonabv = None of the Above, MotorE = Motor-engaged, Cognit = Cognitive-engaged, RePrep = Response-preparing, EquiRe = Equipment/Relocating, Waiting = Waiting for a turn. * $P < .05$, ** $P < .01$.

Findings related to prior studies

Or .558? **see p. 355**

Specifically, the findings of this study were quite different from those of the Martin and Kulinna's study (2005), in which the researchers found that teachers spent their class time on Instructing (44%), Managing (28%), Observing (20%), and Demonstration (3%). Furthermore, the students in their study spent time on the five activities as follows: Standing (39%), Sitting (21%), Lying Down (1%), Walking (21%), and Motor Engaged (18%). Martin and Kulinna (2005) reported that only 4% of class time was spent on Motor Engaged activities and 61% of class time was spent on non-motor-engaged activities (e.g., sitting, standing, or lying down). On the contrary, the students in the current study spent 56.2% of class time on physical activities or Motor Engaged activities; 20.7% of class time on Cognitive Engaged; and only 23% of class time on other three non-motor-engaged activities. These findings reflected that the students in the current study had higher rates of academic learning time than that of the previous studies, thus demonstrating the characteristics of effective learning environment.

The national goal tor school physical education programs emphasized that 50% or more of class time should be spent with students being physically active [U.S. Department of Health and Human Services (USDHHS), 2000]. In order to meet the national goal. Martin and Kulinna (2005) suggested urgently, teachers in the field of physical education should possess knowledge and class management skills thai will enable them to provide physical activities for their students with maximizing opportunities for appropriate practices.

Obviously, the findings of the present study were different from those of Silverman (1991) who stated in his RT-PR review that the majority of the students engaging in motor activities were about 30% of their class time, and about 15% of which was spent on Motor Engaged at an appropriate level. Furthermore, most of those teachers spent about 25% of their class time on explanation/demonstration or informing.

With regard to the relationships between teaching behaviors and learning activities, the findings of this study were inconsistent with the findings of Martin and Kulinna (2005), in which the researchers reported that general instruction behaviors (Informing, Questioning, and Feedback) were negatively related to students' Motor Engaged activities. In contrast, the current study found that the general instruction behaviors (Informing, Questioning, and Feedback) were positively related to students' learning activities (e.g., Informing associated with Motor Engaged $r = .558$) Questioning associated with Cognitive Engaged $r = .406$, and Feedback associated with Cognitive Engaged $r = .362$).

Or .588 as Table 2?

Furthermore, in contrast with the findings from the previous studies (Faucette & Patterson, 1990; Martin & Kulinna, 2005; Mitcell & Castelli, 2003), we would like to conduct the following discussion in regard to the percentage of class time the teachers and students spent on each of the predefined 'Teaching Behaviors' and 'Learning Activities'. The above findings might be related to the following factors:

Subject Matters of the Physical Education Classes. The subject matters of the physical education classes included in this investigation were basketball/fitness (8 lessons), volleyball/ fitness (8 lessons), Yoga (6 lessons), dance (4 lessons), soccer/fitness (2 lessons), weight lift/ fitness (2 lessons), and tennis (2 lessons). Among the 32 physical education lessons, 12 lessons were individualized activities and 20 lessons were characterized by small group exercises. Teaching individualized activities, such as circulate fitness exercises, modem dances, martial arts, and yoga, demanded more instructional behaviors (e.g., informing, structuring, questioning, feedback, and reward); but students' Motor Engaged activities could significantly increase because teachers' instructional behaviors and students' activities occurred almost at the same time (Faucette & Patterson, 1990; Graber, 2001; Mitcell & Castelli, 2003: Rink, 2003). When applying the teaching-learning pattern in individual activities to teach general physical fitness for team sports (e.g., basketball, volleyball, and soccer), the activities become 'individualized'. This might explain why the teachers and students spent higher percentages of class time on teacher Informing (28.8%), teacher Structuring (25.4%), and students' Motor Engaged (56.2%). Hence, these findings demonstrated that the participants appeared to be practitioners who knew how to maximize activity-learning time of the students and they had the skills to motivate their students to participate in the activities they offered.

Internal validity threats

Impacts of National Physical Education Standards. Researchers (Banville, 2006; Mitcell & Castelli, 2003; Mozen, 2005) indicated that, in recent years, the six national standards for physical educated persons and the 10 beginning teacher standards established by the National Association for Sport and Physical Education (NASPE) have had great impact on physical education at all school levels. In regard to the characteristics and backgrounds of the participants, they all possessed teacher certificates, had bachelor or higher degrees, had five or more years of experiences in teaching physical education in public schools, were involved in academic activities in physical education teacher education programs at local universities by serving as cooperating teachers, and were familiar with and were carrying out the national standards in their daily teaching. These characteristics and background made them unique in the present study. These characteristics might also explain the higher percentage of time students were engaging in motor activities (56.2%) in the current study than that (18.0%) in the Martin and Kulinna's (2005) study.

Several factors might explain the current findings in that 14.1% of class time was on None of the Above teaching behaviors and 9.7% of class time was on Wait for a Turn activities. First, 18 out of 32 classes in this investigation had class rosters of over 60 students. Although the teachers were well-trained practitioners, they still could not overcome the class oversize issue. Second, the main reason causing the students to have higher waiting time was insufficient equipment and facilities. Third, it should be recognized that the None of the Above behaviors and the Waiting for a Turn activities were the two major areas requiring special attention if one wanted to improve the effectiveness of teaching in high school physical education.

The Correlations between Teaching Behaviors and Learning Activities. The findings showed that the following three correlations among teaching behaviors and learning activities were significant and had practical meaning to the physical education professionals: Teacher

Informing was associated with Students Motor Engaged; Teacher Questioning was associated with Students Cognitive Engage; and Teacher Feedback was associated with Students Cognitive Engaged. These findings suggested that teachers should carefully plan and implement their instructions with Informing (teacher tells, explains, demonstrates, reviews, or summarizes); Questioning (teacher asks questions that are intended to evoke a verbal or motor response); and Feedback (teacher gives feedback that is immediate, specific, and task relevant) to ensure the quality of physical education (Graham, Holt/Hale & Parker, 2006; Mohnsen, 2003; Pangrazi, 2007; Rink, 2003). When teachers were involved in none-instructional behaviors, their students would exhibit non-learning activities (e.g., None of the Above was associated with none Cognitive Engaged; and None of the Above was associated with none Motor Engaged). These findings suggested that, since the most important purpose of a physical education class was to maximize students' activity/academic learning time-physical education (ALT-PE) (Graham, Holt/Hale & Parker, 2006; Mohnsen, 2003; Parker, 1989; USDHHS, 2000), teachers should carefully choose their subject matters and employ teaching behaviors that would enable them to increase students' engagement in motor and cognitive learning activities (Culpepper & Tarr, 2007; Hagood, Lynn & *Ratliffe*, 2007; Mohnsen, 2003; Pangrazi, 2007; Siedentop & Tannehill, 2000).

In summary, the findings of this study provide a set of new data and information that describe the features and interrelationships between teaching behaviors and learning activities in urban high school physical education class settings. On average, high school students in the current study involved over 50% of class time in Motor Engaged activities, and they reached the national goal for school physical education programs recommended by the USDHHS (2000). The significant correlations between teaching behaviors and learning activities revealed that teaching behaviors of Informing, Questioning, and Feedback are positively associated with students' Motor Engaged and Cognitive Engaged learning activities. It is further suggested that physical education teachers should develop and employ teaching behaviors that promote and demonstrate physical skills, fitness and activities, because those teaching behaviors are positively associated with students' physical activity levels.

No—See Table 2

Unclear to us

Finally, the features summarized from the 32 observed physical education lessons in this study seem to imply that the major characteristics of effective teaching and learning environment, that is, "teachers who present a clear explanation and demonstration, allocate time for motor skill practice, and structure practice so that students are appropriately or successfully engaged will promote student learning," (Silverman, 1991, p. 357) do occur during the present investigation. Researchers should continue to inquire, to explore, and to conduct research in high school physical education settings; and share the findings to their colleagues. By doing so, our physical education profession will be able to stand out in the educational system.

"With"

REFERENCES

Anderson, L., Evertson, C., & Brophy, J. (1979). An experimental study of effective teaching in first-grade reading groups. *The Elementary School Journal, 79,* 193–223.

Banville, D. (2006). Analysis of exchanges between novice and cooperating teacher during internships using the NCATE/NASPE standards for teacher preparation in physical education as guidelines. *Research Quarterly for Exercise and Sport, 77,* 208–221.

Banville, D., & Rikard, L. (2001). Observational Toots for Teacher Reflection. *Journal of Physical Education, Recreation, and Dance, 72,* 46–49.

Brophy, J. E., & Good, T. L. (1986). Teacher behavior and student achievement. In M.C. Wittrock (Ed.), *Handbook of research on teaching* (3rd. ed., pp. 328–375). New York: Macmillan.

Culpepper, D., & Tarr, S. (2007). The role of specific curriculum model on overall physical activity in elementary, middle, and high school students. *Research Quarterly for Exercise and Sport, 78,* A-54–55.

Faucette, N., & Patterson, P. (1990). Comparing teaching behaviors and student activity levels in classes taught by

P. E. specialists versus nonspecialists. *Journal of Teaching Physical Education, 9,* 106–114.

Fielding, G., Kaneenui, E., & Gersten, R. (1983). A comparison of an inquiry and a direct instruction approach to teaching legal concepts and applications to secondary school students. *Journal of Educational Research, 76,* 288–292.

Graham, G., & Heimerer, E. (1981). Research on teacher effectiveness: A summary with implications for Teaching. *Quest, 33,* 14–25.

Graham, G., Holt/Hale, S. A., & Parker, M. (2006). *Children moving: A reflective approach to teaching physical education (7th ed.)* Mountain View, CA: Mayfield.

Graber, K. (2001). Research on teaching in physical education. In V. Richardson (Ed.), *Handbook of research on teaching* (4th ed., pp. 491–519). Washington, DC: American Educational Research Association.

Hagood, S., Lynn, S., & Ratliffe, T. (2007). Impact of teacher professional development on student activity level. *Research Quarterly for Exercise and Sport, 78,* A-58–59.

Keating, X.D., Kulinna, P. M., & Silverman, S. (1999). Measuring teaching behaviors, lesson context, and physical activity in school physical education programs: Comparing the SOFIT and the C-SOFIT instruments. *Measurement in Physical Education and Exercise Science, 3,* 207–220.

Kulinna, P. H., Cothran, D. J., & Regualos, R. (2006). Teacher's reports of student misbehaviors in physical education. *Research Quarterly for Exercise and Sport, 77,* 32–40.

Martin, J. J., & Kulinna, P. H. (2004). Self-efficacy theory and theory of planned behavior: Teaching physically active physical education classes. *Research Quarterly for Exercise and Sport, 75,* 288–297.

Martin, J. J., & Kulinna, P. H. (2005). A social cognitive perspective of physical activity related behavior in physical education. *Journal of Teaching in Physical Education, 24,* 265–281.

Mitcell, M., & Castelli, D. (2003). Student performance data, school attributes, and relationship. *Journal of Teaching in Physical Education, 22,* 494–511.

Mohnsen, B. S. (2003). Teaching middle school physical education. Champaign, IL: Human Kinetics.

Mozen, D. (2005). Best practices of effective student-teacher supervision based on NASPE standards: The NASPE standards for beginning teachers can help mentor teachers and college supervisors instill good practices in preservice teachers. *Journal of Physical Education, Recreation, and Dance, 76,* 40–42.

New York City Department of Education. (2007). *New York City DOE Region 8.* From http://en.wikipedia.org/w/index.php?title=New_York_City_DOE_Region8&redirect=no

New York State Education Department. (2007). *The New York State Education Department Physical Education Profile.* From http://www.emsc.nysed.gov/http://www.emsc.nysed.gov/ ciai/pe/profile.htm

Pangrazi, R. P. (2007). Dynamic physical education for elementary school children (15th ed.). San Francisco, CA: Benjamin Cummings.

Parker, M. (1989). Academic learning time-physical education (ALT-PE), 1982 Revision. In P. W. Darst, D. B. Zakrajsek, & V. H. Mancini (Eds.), *Analyzing physical education and sport instruction* (2nd ed.) (pp. 195–205). Champaign, IL: Human Kinetics.

Rink, J. (2003). Effective instruction in physical education. In S. J. Silverman, & C. D. Ennis (Eds.), *Student learning in physical education.* Champaign, IL: Human Kinetics.

Rosenshine, B. (1979). Content, time and direct instruction. In P. L. Peterson & H. J. Walberg (Eds.), *Research on Teaching: Concepts, findings, and implications* (pp. 57–74). Berkeley, CA: McCutchan.

Rosenshine, B. & Stevens, R. (1986). Teaching functions. In M. Wittrock (Ed.), *Handbook of research on teaching (3rd ed., pp. 376–391).* New York: MacMillan.

Siedentop, D. & Tannehill, D. (2000). *Developing teaching skills in physical education* (4th ed.). Mountain View, CA: Mayfield.

Silverman, S. (1991). Research in teaching in physical education. *Research Quarterly for Exercise and Sport, 62,* 352–364.

Silverman, S., Tyson, L. A., & Morford, L. M. (1988). Relationships of organization, time, and student achievement in physical education. *Teaching and Teacher Education, 4,* 247–257.

Sweeting, T., & Rink, J. (1999). Effects of direct instruction and environmentally designed instruction on the process and product characteristics of a fundamental skill. *Journal of Teaching in Physical Education, 18,* 216–233.

U.S. Department of Health and Human Services. (2000). *Healthy people 2010: understanding and improving health.* Washington, DC: U.S. Government Printing Office.

Zakrajasek, D. B., & Tannehill, D. (1989). Direct Instruction Behavior Analysis (DIBA) In P. W. Darst, D. B. Zakrajsek, & V. H. Mancini (Eds.) *Analyzing physical education and sport instruction* (2nd ed.) (pp. 243–248). Champaign, IL: Human Kinetics.

Zeng, H., Leung, R., Liu, W., & Hipscher, M. (2009). Physical education in urban high school class settings: Features and correlations between teaching behaviors and learning activities. *The Physical Educator*, *66*(4), 186–196.

Analysis of the Study

PURPOSE/JUSTIFICATION

The purpose was "to examine the features and correlations between teaching behaviors and learning activities in urban high school physical education classes" that used direct instruction (p. 350). The main justification was to address a gap in the research literature on the relationship between physical education instructors' teaching behaviors and students' learning activities in secondary schools. The researchers sought "to extend previous research (K–8) by not only employing high school (9–12) physical education teachers as participants but also examining the characteristics of effective teaching in high school physical education classes" (p. 350).

Teachers and students (we assume their parents) provided informed consent prior to data collection. There appear to be no concerns regarding harm, confidentiality, or deception although the researchers noted they did not disclose to teachers the true nature of their class observations so as not to influence their normal teaching behavior.

DEFINITIONS

Formal definitions are not provided for the primary terms in the study: *teaching behaviors* and *learning activities*. Both terms are operationally defined by observational data collected from the Direct Instruction Behavior Analysis (DIBA) system. The DIBA included 14 categories, 8 relating to teaching behaviors and 6 assessing learning activities. These observational data were coded to produce the quantitative indicators "percentage of time" spent on specified behaviors and "rate per minute" (RPM) used to measure frequency for the 14 predefined categories. We think the study would have been improved by clarifying two DIBA definitions: (1) cognitively engaged—"listens to" and "gains information" and (2) response preparing—students "get ready" (see also Instrumentation).

Other key terms include *direct instruction*, *physical education classes*, and *urban high school*. The researchers provide a constitutive definition for "direct instruction model," which they describe as possessing "clear learning goals, adequate time for instruction and practice which is characterized by appropriate subject matters for students' abilities, low-level cognitive questions but meaningful task and high success by monitoring student performance and providing immediate and specific feedback" (p. 350). Definitions are not provided for *physical education classes* although the researchers list the type and duration of classes observed: basketball/fitness, volleyball/fitness, yoga, dance, soccer/fitness, weight lifting/fitness, and tennis. Similarly, *urban high school* is not defined but the researchers provide demographic information about each school site in terms of total student enrollment and racial/ethnic breakdown.

PRIOR RESEARCH

An extensive review of the research literature is provided to support the design and justification for the study. Citing both older and more recent research (studies published within five years from their study), the researchers do well in summarizing the major theoretical and empirical findings related to their research question. Moreover, they revisit their literature review findings in the discussion section. For example, the authors state that "the findings of this study were quite different from those of the Martin and Kulinna's study (2005)" (p. 354). In doing so, the authors situate their study within the context of the research literature.

HYPOTHESES

The hypothesis is not stated explicitly, but clearly implied. The authors' implied hypothesis is that teaching behaviors linked to direct instruction in physical education are correlated with student learning behaviors.

SAMPLE

The sample included 16 physical education teachers and their students from three urban high schools located in New York City, New York. Demographic information about the teachers was limited to gender and number of years teaching. The authors do not describe the student sample other than a narrative account of the pooled demographics of each of the three schools. This demographic information could have been presented more clearly for the reader had the authors included it in a separate table. Moreover, the authors neglected to include standard measures of socioeconomic status about the high schools such as the percentage of students receiving free/reduced lunch, and the percentage who are English language learners. The implied population is all high school physical education teachers and their students in the United States. Generalizing beyond the sample is limited as participating teachers were not selected randomly but were all affiliated with the researchers' university. Thus, cooperating teachers in the study represented a convenience sample described by the authors as unique.

INSTRUMENTATION

The Direct Instruction Behavior Analysis (DIBA) is an observational data collection tool that includes 14 categories. The first eight categories assess teacher behaviors and include teacher: information, observing, structuring, questioning, praise-encouragement, feedback, controlling; and none of the above. The other six categories measure student learning activities including: motor engaged, cognitive engaged, response preparing, gets equipment/relocates, waits for turn, and off-task.

The validity of the DIBA was not discussed, which we think is a major flaw. The only rationale provided by the authors for selecting the DIBA was the following: "In brief, the DIBA was selected to be the instrument believing to be able [sic] to better fulfill the purpose of the current study although there were different instruments in the field of teaching physical education" (p. 350). Further, two of the teacher behavior categories—teaching information and teacher structuring—appear to include overlapping behaviors. The former is defined as "teacher tells, explains, demonstrates, reviews and summarizes," and the latter defined as "teacher stresses objectives and important points, directs performance, or signals transitions." It seems to us that stressing objectives and important points should be part of the "teaching information" category since it usually accompanies explaining, reviewing, and summarizing.

Instead of discussing the validity of the DIBA, the authors focus primarily on the inter-rater reliability of the instrument. They discuss in great detail the process by which two observers were trained to increase scoring agreement for specific DIBA behaviors and activities using videotaped footage of 32 PE classes that were 32 minutes long on average. The coders were trained during four practice sessions totaling 480 minutes, and reached above 80 percent agreement on their scoring, which was adequate (see text p. 160 for our discussion of scoring agreement for observational instruments). It is unclear whether this and the even higher agreements reported for the final data (.91 and .89) were obtained for each of the 14 scales or for all scales combined. Inasmuch as there is great variation from one scale to another (see Table 1), the latter gives misleadingly high indexes. It is the agreement for each scale that matters.

PROCEDURES/INTERNAL VALIDITY

The procedures, which consisted of collecting videotaped data from 32 physical education lessons as well as the scoring agreement and coding processes, are clearly described although there is no mention of how the 32 lessons were selected for coding. As we discuss in Chapter 15, correlational studies *do not*, in and of themselves, establish cause and effect. Nevertheless, the authors seek to examine the effects of teacher-directed learning on student engagement in PE classes in their explanatory study. While their implied hypothesis is supported, the authors raise two alternative explanations for the relationships found in their data. First, location is a possible internal validity threat because 12 out of 32 classes involved individualized instruction (such as modern dance, martial arts, and yoga), which could explain the greater amount of instructional time spent on teacher informing, teacher structuring, and student motor engagement. Additionally, 18 out of 32 classes had very high enrollments (over 60 students), as well as insufficient equipment and resources, which could explain the increased "waiting for a turn" activities and "none of the above" behaviors captured in the data. A statistical technique not used by the authors to address these location threats is to measure the extraneous variables (such as resource level) and use partial correlation or determine correlations separately for each location.

DATA ANALYSIS/RESULTS

The overall data analysis is appropriate and the results are reported descriptively by means and standard deviations calculated for percentage of time and RPM for 13 of the 14 DIBA variables. The authors omitted students "off-task" behavior from their analysis due to low or no occurrence. Bivariate correlations for 12 out of 14 variables are presented in a crossbreak table showing correlation coefficients and statistical significance. Statistical significance is misleading because of the lack of a random sample (see text pp. 248–249 and 253). The magnitude of correlation is the proper index of significance. A typographical error appears for a statistically significant correlation coefficient described in the results section between teacher informing and students motor engaged (r =.588 in Table 2 on p. 354 compared to .558 in text on p. 353 and p. 355). In either case, the magnitude of r as being between .41 and .60 is large enough to be of practical as well as theoretical use. The correlation coefficient tells us there is a positive relationship between the two variables and that almost 35 percent of the variation in students' observed motor engagement is related to teacher informing behavior. Teacher informing (not "questioning" as stated on p. 353) and teacher feedback were also positively correlated with students' cognitive engagement (r = .406 and r = .362, respectively). The results support the researchers' implied hypothesis that direct teaching behaviors are correlated with increased student motor and cognitive engagement. We do not understand the statement that "when the teachers exhibited the behaviors of None of the Above, their students showed no motor and cognitive activities engagement" (p. 353). The correlations that follow this statement show instead that teachers exhibiting more of this behavior had students showing less motor and cognitive engagement, not that they showed "no" such behavior.

DISCUSSION/INTERPRETATION

The study did a good job of describing characteristics of effective teaching using student-centered approaches to learning in high school physical education classes. We agree the study's implied hypothesis—relationships between teaching and learning behaviors in a direct instruction setting—was supported. However, generalizing beyond the three New York schools studied is unwarranted given the convenience nature of the sample. Standard demographic information about the students such as socioeconomic status was not provided, which would have been helpful. Furthermore, the authors neglected to include any evidence about the validity and reliability of the DIBA instrument on which their study is based. The researchers did a good job of discussing limitations and possible internal validity threats. The teachers in the study were atypical in their higher levels of education, training, and experience. In other words, those characteristics could explain increased student engagement behaviors compared to prior study findings. Furthermore, the age and grade level of students in the study are other variables that limit comparison with prior studies. Finally, we think the study would have benefitted greatly from another round of proofreading and editing.

Go back to the **INTERACTIVE AND APPLIED LEARNING** feature at the beginning of the chapter for a listing of interactive and applied activities. Go to the **Online Learning Center** at **www.mhhe.com/fraenkel9e** to take quizzes, practice with key terms, and review chapter content.

Main Points

THE NATURE OF CORRELATIONAL RESEARCH

- The major characteristic of correlational research is seeking out associations among variables.

PURPOSES OF CORRELATIONAL RESEARCH

- Correlational studies are carried out either to help explain important human behaviors or to predict likely outcomes.
- If a relationship of sufficient magnitude exists between two variables, it becomes possible to predict a score on one variable if a score on the other variable is known.
- The variable that is used to make the prediction is called the *predictor variable.*
- The variable about which the prediction is made is called the *criterion variable.*
- Both scatterplots and regression lines are used in correlational studies to predict a score on a criterion variable.
- A predicted score is never exact. As a result, researchers calculate an index of prediction error, which is known as the *standard error of estimate.*

COMPLEX CORRELATIONAL TECHNIQUES

- Multiple regression is a technique that enables a researcher to determine a correlation between a criterion variable and the best combination of two or more predictor variables.

- The coefficient of multiple correlation (R) indicates the strength of the correlation between the combination of the predictor variables and the criterion variable.
- The value of a prediction equation depends on whether it predicts successfully with a new group of individuals.
- When the criterion variable is categorical rather than quantitative, discriminant function analysis (rather than multiple regression) must be used.
- Factor analysis is a technique that allows a researcher to determine whether many variables can be described by a few factors.
- Path analysis is a technique used to test the likelihood of causal connections among three or more variables.

BASIC STEPS IN CORRELATIONAL RESEARCH

- These include, as in most research, selecting a problem, choosing a sample, selecting or developing instruments, determining procedures, collecting and analyzing data, and interpreting results.

CORRELATION COEFFICIENTS AND THEIR MEANING

- The meaning of a given correlation coefficient depends on how it is applied.
- Correlation coefficients below .35 show only a slight relationship between variables.
- Correlations between .40 and .60 may have theoretical and/or practical value depending on the context.
- Only when a correlation of .65 or higher is obtained can reasonably accurate predictions be made.
- Correlations over .85 indicate a very strong relationship between the variables correlated.

EVALUATING THREATS TO INTERNAL VALIDITY IN CORRELATIONAL RESEARCH

- Threats to the internal validity of correlational studies include subject characteristics, location, instrument decay, data collection, testing, and mortality.
- Results of correlational studies must always be interpreted with caution, because they may suggest, but they cannot establish, causation.

Key Terms

coefficient of determination 336
coefficient of multiple correlation 336
correlation coefficient 341
criterion variable 334
discriminant function analysis 337
factor analysis 338
multiple regression 335
partial correlation 342
path analysis 338
prediction 334
prediction equation 335
prediction study 334
predictor variable 334
regression line 334
standard error of estimate 335

For Discussion

1. Which type of relationship would a researcher be more pleased to have the results of a study reveal—positive or negative—or would it matter? Explain.
2. What is the difference between an effect and a relationship? Which is more important, or can this be determined?

3. Are there any types of instruments that could *not* be used in a correlational study? If so, why?
4. Would it be possible for a correlation to be statistically significant yet educationally insignificant? If so, give an example.
5. Why do you suppose people often interpret correlational results as proving causation?
6. What is the difference, if any, between the *sign* of a correlation and the *strength* of a correlation?
7. "Correlational studies, in and of themselves, do not establish cause and effect." Is this true? Why or why not?
8. "The possibility of causation (in a correlational study) is strengthened if a time lapse occurs between measurement of the variables being studied." Why?
9. To interpret correlation coefficients sensibly, it is a good idea to show the scatterplots on which they are based. Why is this true? Explain.

References

1. Joreskog, K. G., & Sorbom, D. (1988). LISREL VII. Analysis of linear structural relationships by maximum likelihood and least squares methods: Statistical package for the social sciences. New York: McGraw-Hill.

2. Garet, M. S., et al. (2001). What makes professional development effective? Results from a national sample of teachers. *American Educational Research Journal, 38*(1), 915–945.

3. Andrew, M. D., et al. (2005). Verbal ability and teacher effectiveness. *Journal of Teacher Education, 56*(9), 343–354.

4. Konishi, C., & Hymel, S. (2009). Bullying and stress in early adolescence: The role of coping and social support. *Journal of Early Adolescence, 29*(3), 333–356.

5. Hester, E. (2009). An investigation of the relationship between health literacy and social communication skills in older adults. *Communication Disorders Quarterly, 30*(2), 112–119.

6. Hagood, M. (2002). A correlational study of art-based measures of cognitive development: Clinical and research implications for art therapists working with children. *Art Therapy: Journal of the American Art Therapy Association, 19*(2), 63–68.

7. Schappe, J. (2005). Early childhood assessment: A correlational study of the relationships among student performance, student feelings, and teacher perceptions. *Early Childhood Education Journal, 33*(3), 187–193.

8. Ye, H. et al. (2008). Perfectionism and peer relations among children with obsessive-compulsive disorder. *Child Psychiatry and Human Development, 39*(4), 415–426.

9. Hinkle, D. E., Wiersma, W., & Jurs, S. G. (1981). *Applied statistics for the behavioral sciences.* Chicago: Rand McNally.

Causal-Comparative Research 16

Is there a difference between natural grass and Astro-turf?

What Is Causal-Comparative Research?

Similarities and Differences Between Causal-Comparative and Correlational Research

Similarities and Differences Between Causal-Comparative and Experimental Research

Steps Involved in Causal-Comparative Research

Problem Formulation

Sample

Instrumentation

Design

Threats to Internal Validity in Causal-Comparative Research

Subject Characteristics

Other Threats

Evaluating Threats to Internal Validity in Causal-Comparative Studies

Data Analysis

Associations Between Categorical Variables

An Example of Causal-Comparative Research

Analysis of the Study

Purpose

Justification/Prior Research

Definitions

Hypotheses

Sample

Instrumentation

Procedures/Results and Internal Validity

Data Analysis, Discussion, and Interpretation

OBJECTIVES **Studying this chapter should enable you to:**

- Explain what is meant by the term "causal-comparative research."
- Describe briefly how causal-comparative research is both similar to and different from both correlational and experimental research.
- Identify and describe briefly the steps involved in conducting a causal-comparative study.
- Draw a diagram of a design for a causal-comparative study.
- Describe how data are collected in causal-comparative research.
- Describe some of the threats to internal validity that exist in causal-comparative studies and discuss how to control for these threats.
- Recognize a causal-comparative study when you come across one in the educational research literature.

INTERACTIVE AND APPLIED LEARNING After, or while, reading this chapter:

Go to the Online Learning Center at www.mhhe.com/fraenkel9e to:

- Learn More About Important Causal-Comparative Research

Go to your online Student Mastery Activities book to do the following activities:

- Activity 16.1: Causal-Comparative Research Questions
- Activity 16.2: Experiment or Causal-Comparative Study
- Activity 16.3: Causal-Comparative vs. Experimental Hypotheses
- Activity 16.4: Analyze Some Causal-Comparative Data

Joseph Perea has just completed his first year of teaching chemistry in a small high school in rural Idaho. His method of teaching involved primarily lecturing to his students. At the end-of-the-year faculty party, he is discussing the year with Mary Roberts, one of the other teachers in the school.

"Ah, Mary, I'm a bit discouraged. Things did not turn out the way I had hoped."

"How come?"

"A lot of my students didn't seem to like my teaching very much. And they didn't do well on the final exam that I gave."

"You know, Joe, Bruce (Bruce Washington, who taught chemistry last year) used some inquiry science materials. I remember him saying that his students really liked them. Maybe you should try them next term."

"I wonder whether his approach would work for me?"

An appropriate method for this kind of question is a causal-comparative study. What that involves is the focus of this chapter.

What Is Causal-Comparative Research?

In causal-comparative research, investigators attempt to determine the cause *or* consequences of differences that *already exist* between or among groups of individuals. As a result, it is sometimes viewed, along with correlational research, as a form of associational research, since both describe conditions that already exist. A researcher might observe, for example, that two groups of individuals differ on some variable (such as teaching style) and then attempt to determine the *reason* for, or the *results* of, this difference. The difference between the groups, however, has *already occurred.* Because both the effect(s) and the alleged cause(s) have already occurred, and hence are studied in retrospect, causal-comparative research is also referred to sometimes as *ex post facto* (from the Latin for "after the fact") *research.* This is in contrast to an experimental study, in which a researcher *creates* a difference between or among groups and then compares their performance (on one or more dependent variables) to determine the effects of the created difference.

The group difference variable in a causal-comparative study is either a variable that cannot be manipulated (such as ethnicity) or one that might have been manipulated but for one reason or another has not been (such as teaching style). Sometimes ethical constraints prevent a variable from being manipulated, thus preventing the effects of variations in the variable from being examined by means of an experimental study. A researcher might be interested, for example, in the effects of a new diet on very young children. Ethical considerations, however, might prevent the researcher from deliberately varying the diet to which the children are exposed. Causal-comparative research, however, would allow the researcher to study the effects of the diet if he or she could find a group of children who *have already been exposed* to the diet. The researcher could then compare them with a similar group of children who had not been exposed to the diet. Much of the research in medicine and sociology is causal-comparative in nature.

Another example is the comparison of scientists and engineers in terms of their originality. As in correlational research, explanations or predictions can be made from either variable to the other: Originality could be predicted from group membership, or group membership could be predicted from originality. However, most such studies attempt to explore causation rather than to foster prediction. Are "original" individuals more likely to become scientists? Do scientists become more original as they become immersed in their work? And so forth. Notice that if it were possible, a correlational study might be preferable, but that it is not appropriate when one of the variables (in this case, the nature of the groups) is a categorical variable.

Following are examples of different types of causal-comparative research:

Type 1: Exploration of *effects* (dependent variable) caused by membership in a given group
Question: What differences in abilities are caused by gender?
Research hypothesis: Females have a greater amount of linguistic ability than males.

Type 2: Exploration of *causes* (independent variable) of group membership
Question: What causes individuals to join a gang?
Research hypothesis: Individuals who are members of gangs have more aggressive personalities than individuals who are not members of gangs.

Type 3: Exploration of the *consequences* (dependent variable) of an intervention
Question: How do students taught by the inquiry method react to propaganda?
Research hypothesis: Students who were taught by the inquiry method are more critical of propaganda than are those who were taught by the lecture method.

Causal-comparative studies have been used frequently to study the differences between males and females. They have demonstrated the superiority of girls in language and of boys in math at certain age levels. The attributing of these differences to gender—as cause—must be tentative. One could hardly view gender as being caused by ability, but there are many other probable links in the causal chain, including societal expectations of males and females.

The basic causal-comparative approach, therefore, is to begin with a noted difference between two groups and to look for possible causes for, or consequences of, this difference. A researcher might be interested, for example, in the reason(s) why some individuals become addicted to alcohol while others develop a dependence on pills. How can this be explained? Descriptions of the two groups (alcoholics and pill poppers) might be compared to see if their characteristics differ in ways that might account for the difference in choice of drug.

Sometimes causal-comparative studies are conducted solely as an alternative to experiments. Suppose, for example, that the curriculum director in a large, urban high school district is considering implementing a new English curriculum. The director might try out the curriculum experimentally, selecting a few classes at random throughout the district, and compare student performance in these classes with comparison groups who continue to experience the regular curriculum. This might take a considerable amount of time, however, and be quite costly in terms of materials, teacher preparation workshops, and so on. As an alternative, the director might consider a causal-comparative study and compare the achievement of students in school districts that are currently using this curriculum with the achievement of students in similar districts that do not use the new curriculum. If the results show that students in districts (similar to his) with the new curriculum are achieving higher scores in English, the director would have a basis for going ahead and implementing the new curriculum in his district. Like correlational studies, causal-comparative investigations often identify relationships that later are studied experimentally.

Despite their advantages, however, causal-comparative studies do have serious limitations. The most serious lie in the lack of control over threats to internal validity. Because the manipulation of the independent variable has already occurred, many of the controls we discussed in Chapter 13 cannot be applied. Thus, considerable caution must be expressed in interpreting the outcomes of a causal-comparative study. As with correlational studies, relationships can be identified, but causation cannot be fully established. As we have pointed out before, the alleged cause may really be an effect, the effect may be a cause, or there may be a third variable that produced both the alleged cause and effect.

SIMILARITIES AND DIFFERENCES BETWEEN CAUSAL-COMPARATIVE AND CORRELATIONAL RESEARCH

Causal-comparative research is sometimes confused with correlational research. Although similarities do exist, there are notable differences.

CONTROVERSIES IN RESEARCH

How Should Research Methodologies Be Classified?

Opinions differ as to how the different types of research methodology should be classified. No single system for classifying research methods has been widely accepted. To be sure, clear distinctions have been drawn between experimental and nonexperimental methods and between group-comparison and single-subject forms of experimental research. However, different authors use different categories to describe nonexperimental research, with the most common being the ones we use in this text (correlational, causal-comparative, and survey). These categories, however, are mostly a matter of convenience and custom rather than reflecting essential differences. Correlational and causal-comparative methods differ largely in the nature of the variables investigated (quantitative vs. categorical) and the methods of data analysis. Survey research differs from the other two primarily in its purpose. We must admit that such a system is not very satisfying.

Johnson has proposed a new means of classification.* He suggests using a combination of *purpose* (descriptive, predictive, or explanatory) and *time frame* (retrospective, cross-sectional, or longitudinal) to identify different methods. Such combinations produce a total of nine different types. While we would agree that his typology is logically more consistent, we do not find it useful nor appropriate for an introductory text. Why? Because the steps involved in correlational, causal-comparative, and survey research are quite different, and we believe strongly that students need to learn these steps. We see no reason to increase the complexity involved in doing so. We also note that a survey of teachers of educational research showed that 80 percent favored retaining the correlational versus causal-comparative distinction, apparently finding it useful despite its deficiencies.†

*Johnson, B. (2001). Towards a new classification of nonexperimental quantitative research. *Educational Researcher, 30*(2), 3–13.

†Allyn and Bacon. (1996). *Research methods survey.* Boston: Allyn & Bacon.

Similarities. Both causal-comparative and correlational studies are examples of associational research—that is, researchers who conduct them seek to explore relationships among variables. Both attempt to explain phenomena of interest. Both seek to identify variables that are worthy of later exploration through experimental research, and both often provide guidance for subsequent experimental studies. Neither permits the manipulation of variables by the researcher, however. Both attempt to explore causation, but, in both cases, causation must be argued; the methodology alone does not permit causal statements.

Differences. Causal-comparative studies typically compare two or more groups of subjects, while correlational studies require a score on each variable for each subject. Correlational studies investigate two (or more) quantitative variables, whereas causal-comparative studies typically involve at least one categorical variable (group membership). Correlational studies often analyze data using scatterplots and/or correlation coefficients, while causal-comparative studies often compare averages or use crossbreak tables.

SIMILARITIES AND DIFFERENCES BETWEEN CAUSAL-COMPARATIVE AND EXPERIMENTAL RESEARCH

Similarities. Both causal-comparative and experimental studies typically require at least one categorical variable (group membership). Both compare group performances (average scores) to determine relationships. Both typically compare separate groups of subjects.*

Differences. In experimental research, the independent variable is manipulated; in causal-comparative research, no manipulation takes place. Causal-comparative studies are likely to provide much weaker evidence for causation than do experimental studies. In experimental research, the researcher can sometimes assign subjects to treatment groups; in causal-comparative research, the groups are already formed—the researcher must locate them. In experimental studies, the researcher has much greater flexibility in formulating the structure of the design.

*Except in counterbalanced, time-series, or single-subject experimental designs (see Chapters 13 and 14).

Steps Involved in Causal-Comparative Research

PROBLEM FORMULATION

The first step in formulating a problem in causal-comparative research is usually to identify and define the particular phenomena of interest and then to consider possible causes for, or consequences of, these phenomena. Suppose, for example, that a researcher is interested in student creativity. What causes creativity? Why are a few students highly creative while most are not? Why do some students who initially appear to be creative seem to lose this characteristic? Why do others who at one time are not creative later become so? And so forth.

The researcher speculates, for example, that high-level creativity might be caused by a combination of social failure, on the one hand, and personal recognition for artistic or scientific achievement, on the other. The researcher also identifies a number of alternative hypotheses that might account for a difference between highly creative and noncreative students. Both the quantity and quality of a student's interests, for example, might account for differences in creativity. Highly creative students might tend to have many diverse interests. Parental encouragement to explore ideas might also account partly for creativity, as might some types of intellectual skills.

Once possible causes of the phenomena have been identified, they are (usually) incorporated into a more precise statement of the research problem the researcher wishes to investigate. In this instance, the researcher might state that the objective of his research is "to examine possible differences between students of high and low creativity." Note that differences in a number of variables can be investigated in a causal-comparative study to determine which variable (or combination of variables) seems most likely to cause the phenomenon (creativity, in this case) being studied. This testing of several alternative hypotheses is a basic characteristic of good causal-comparative research and, whenever possible, should be the basis for identifying the variables on which the comparison groups are to be contrasted. This provides a rational basis for selection of the variables to be investigated, rather than relying on what is often called the *shotgun approach,* in which a large number of measures are administered simply because they seem interesting or are available. They also serve to remind the researcher that the findings of a causal-comparative study are open to a variety of causal explanations.

SAMPLE

Once the researcher has formulated the problem statement (and hypotheses, if any) the next step is to select the sample of individuals to be studied. The most important task here is to define carefully the characteristic to be studied and then to select groups that differ in this characteristic. In the preceding example, this means defining as clearly as possible the term *creativity.* If possible, operational definitions should be employed. A highly creative student might be defined, for example, as one who "has developed an award-winning scientific or artistic product."

The researcher also needs to think about whether the group obtained using the operational definition is likely to be reasonably homogeneous in terms of factors causing creativity. For example, are students who are creative in science similar to students who are creative in art with respect to causation? This is a very important question to ask. If creativity has different "causes" in different fields, the search for causation is only confused by combining students from such fields. Do ethnic, age, or gender differences produce differences in creativity? The success of a causal-comparative study depends in large degree on how carefully the comparison groups are defined.

It is very important to select groups that are homogeneous with regard to at least some important variables. For example, if the researcher assumes that the same causes are operating for all creative students, regardless of gender, ethnicity, or age, he or she may find no differences between comparison groups simply because too many other variables are involved. If all creative students are treated as a homogeneous group, no differences may be found between highly creative and noncreative students, whereas if only creative and noncreative female art students are compared, differences may be found.

Once the defined groups have been selected, they can be matched on one or more variables. This process of matching controls certain variables, thereby eliminating any group differences on these variables. This is desirable in type 1 and type 3 studies (see p. 365), since the researcher wants the groups as similar as possible in order to explain differences on the dependent variable(s) as being due to group membership. Matching is not as appropriate in type 2 studies, because the researcher presumably knows little about the extraneous variables that might be related to group differences and as a result cannot match on them.

INSTRUMENTATION

There are no limits on the types of instruments that may be used in causal-comparative studies. Achievement tests, questionnaires, interview schedules, attitudinal measures, observational devices—any of the devices discussed in Chapter 7 can be used.

DESIGN

The basic causal-comparative design involves selecting two or more groups that differ on a particular variable of interest and comparing them on another variable or variables. No manipulation is involved. The groups differ in one of two ways: One group either possesses a characteristic (often called a *criterion*) that the other does not, or the groups differ on known characteristics. These two variations of the same basic design (sometimes called a *criterion-group design*) are as follows:

The Basic Causal-Comparative Designs

	Group	Independent variable	Dependent variable
(*a*)	I	C	O
		(Group possesses characteristic)	(Measurement)
	II	$-C$	O
		(Group does not possess characteristic)	(Measurement)
(*b*)	I	C_1	O
		(Group possesses characteristic 1)	(Measurement)
	II	C_2	O
		(Group possesses characteristic 2)	(Measurement)

The letter C is used in this design to represent the presence of the characteristic. The dashed line is used to show that intact groups are being compared. Examples of these causal-comparative designs are presented in Figure 16.1.

(a)	Group	Independent variable	Dependent variable
	I	C	O
		Dropouts	Level of self-esteem
	II	$(-C)$	O
		Nondropouts	Level of self-esteem
(b)	**Group**	**Independent variable**	**Dependent variable**
	I	C_1	O
		Counselors	Amount of job satisfaction
	II	C_2	O
		Teachers	Amount of job satisfaction

Figure 16.1 *Examples of the Basic Causal-Comparative Design*

Threats to Internal Validity in Causal-Comparative Research

Two weaknesses in causal-comparative research are lack of randomization and inability to manipulate an independent variable. As we have mentioned, random assignment of subjects to groups is not possible in causal-comparative research since the groups are already formed. Manipulation of the independent variable is not possible because the groups have already been exposed to the independent variable.

SUBJECT CHARACTERISTICS

The major threat to the internal validity of a causal-comparative study is the possibility of a subject characteristics threat. Because the researcher has had no say in either the selection or formation of the comparison groups, there is always the likelihood that the groups are not equivalent on one or more important variables other than the identified group membership variable (Figure 16.2). A group of girls, for example, might be older than a comparison group of boys.

There are a number of procedures that a researcher can use to reduce the chance of a subject characteristics threat in a causal-comparative study. Many of these are also used in experimental research (see Chapter 13).

Figure 16.2 *A Subject Characteristics Threat*

Matching of Subjects. One way to control for an extraneous variable is to match subjects from the comparison groups on that variable. In other words, pairs of subjects, one from each group, are found that are similar on that variable. Students might be matched on GPA, for example, in a study of attitudes. Individuals with similar GPAs would be matched. If a match cannot be found for a particular subject, he or she is then eliminated from the study. As you have probably realized, the problem with matching is that often matches cannot be found for many subjects, and hence the size of the sample is accordingly reduced. Matching becomes even more difficult when the researcher tries to match on two or more variables.

Finding or Creating Homogeneous Subgroups. Another way to control for an extraneous variable is either to find, or restrict one's comparison to, groups that are relatively homogeneous on that variable. In the attitude study, the researcher could either seek to find two groups that have similar GPAs (say, all 3.5 GPA or above) or form subgroups that represent various levels of the extraneous variable (e.g., divide the groups into high, middle, and low GPA subgroups), and then compare the comparable subgroups (low GPA subgroup with the other low GPA subgroup, and so on).

Statistical Matching. The third way to control for an important extraneous variable is to match the groups on that variable, using the technique of statistical matching. As described in Chapter 13, statistical matching adjusts scores on a posttest for initial differences on some other variable that is assumed to be related to performance on the dependent variable.

OTHER THREATS

The likelihood of the remaining threats to internal validity depends on the type of study being considered. In nonintervention studies, the main additional concerns are loss of subjects, location, instrumentation, and sometimes history and maturation. If the persons who are lost to data collection are different from those who remain (as is often probable) *and* if more are lost from one group than the other(s), internal validity is threatened. If unequal numbers are lost, an effort should be made to determine the probable reasons.

A location threat is possible if the data are collected under different conditions for different groups. Similarly, if different data collectors are used with different groups, an instrumentation threat is introduced. Fortunately, it is usually relatively easy to ensure that variations in location and data collectors do not exist.

The possibility of data collector bias can usually be controlled, as in experimental studies, by ensuring that whoever collects the data lacks any information that might bias results. Instrument decay may occur in observational studies and with repeated administration of the same test to the same group(s). It can be controlled as in experimental studies.

In intervention-type studies, in addition to the threats just discussed, all of the remaining threats that we discussed in Chapter 13 may be present. Unfortunately, most are harder to control in causal-comparative studies than in experimental research. The fact that the researcher does not directly manipulate the treatment variable makes it more likely that a history threat may exist. It may also mean that the length of the treatment time may have varied, thus creating a possible maturation threat. An attitude threat is less likely because nothing "special" is introduced. Regression may be a threat if one of the groups was initially selected on the basis of extreme scores. Finally, a pretest/treatment interaction effect, as in experimental studies, may exist if a pretest was used in the study. As we mentioned in Chapter 13 (see p. 284), we think both experimental and causal-comparative intervention studies are useful.

Evaluating Threats to Internal Validity in Causal-Comparative Studies

The evaluation of specific threats to internal validity in causal-comparative studies involves a set of steps similar to those presented in Chapter 13 for experimental studies.

Step 1: Ask: What specific factors either are known to affect or may logically be expected to affect the variable on which groups are being compared? Note that this is the dependent variable for type 1 and type 3 studies (see p. 284), but the independent variable for type 2 studies. As we mentioned with regard to experimental studies, the researcher need not be concerned with factors unrelated to what is being studied.

Step 2: Ask: What is the likelihood of the comparison groups differing on each of these factors? (Remember that a difference between groups cannot be explained away by a factor that is the same for all groups.)

Step 3: Evaluate the threats on the basis of how likely they are to have an effect, and plan to control for them. If a given threat cannot be controlled, this should be acknowledged.

Again, let us consider an example to illustrate how these steps might be employed. Suppose a researcher wishes to explore possible causes of students dropping out in inner-city high schools. He or she hypothesizes three possible causes: (1) family instability, (2) low student self-esteem, and (3) lack of a support system related to school and its requirements. The researcher compiles a list of recent dropouts and randomly selects a comparison group of students still in school. He then interviews students in both groups to obtain data on each of the three possible causal variables.

As we did in Chapters 13 and 15, we list here a number of the threats to internal validity discussed in Chapter 9, followed by our evaluation of each as they might apply to this study.

Subject Characteristics. Although many possible subject characteristics might be considered, we deal with only four here—socioeconomic level of the family, gender, ethnicity, and marketable job skills.

1. **Socioeconomic level of the family.** *Step 1:* Socioeconomic level may be related to all three of the hypothesized causal variables. *Step 2:* Socioeconomic level can be expected to be related to dropping out versus staying in school. It should therefore be controlled by some form of matching. *Step 3:* Likelihood of having an effect unless controlled: high.
2. **Gender.** *Step 1:* Gender may also be related to each of the three hypothesized causal variables. *Step 2:* It may well be related to dropping out. Accordingly, the researcher should either restrict this study only to males or females or ensure that the comparison group has the same gender proportions as the dropout group.* *Step 3:* Likelihood of having an effect unless controlled: high.
3. **Ethnicity.** *Step 1:* Ethnicity may also be related to all three of the hypothesized causal variables. *Step 2:* It may be related to dropping out. Therefore, the two groups should be matched with respect to ethnicity. *Step 3:* Likelihood of having an effect unless controlled: moderate to high.
4. **Marketable job skills.** *Step 1:* Job skills may be related to each of the three hypothesized causal variables. *Step 2:* They are likely to be related to dropping out, since students often drop out if they are able to make money working. It would be desirable,

*This is an example of stratifying a sample—in this case, the comparison group.

therefore, to assess job skills and then control by some form of matching. *Step 3:* Likelihood of having an effect unless controlled: moderate to high.

Mortality. *Step 1:* It is probable that refusing to be interviewed is related to each of the three hypothesized causal variables. *Step 2:* It is also probable that more students in the dropout group will refuse to be interviewed (since they may be working, it may be harder to arrange time for an interview) than will students in the comparison group. The only solution would be to make every effort to get cooperation for the interviews from all subjects in both groups. *Step 3:* Likelihood of having an effect unless controlled: high.

Location. *Step 1:* While it seems unlikely that the causal variables would differ for different schools, this might be the case. *Step 2:* It is quite likely that location (i.e., the specific high schools involved in the study) is related to dropping out. (Dropout rates typically differ across schools.) The best solution is to analyze the data separately for each school. *Step 3:* Likelihood of having an effect unless controlled: moderate.

Instrumentation.

1. **Instrument decay.** *Step 1:* Instrument decay in this study means interviewer fatigue. This certainly could affect the information obtained from students in both groups. *Step 2:* The fatigue factor could be different for the two groups, depending on how interviews are scheduled; the solution is to try to schedule interviews to prevent fatigue from occurring. *Step 3:* Likelihood of having an effect unless controlled: moderate.
2. **Data collector characteristics.** *Step 1:* Data collector characteristics can be expected to influence the information obtained on the three hypothesized causal variables; for this reason, training of interviewers to standardize the interview process is very important. *Step 2:* Despite such training, different interviewers might elicit different information. Therefore, interviewers should be balanced across the two groups; that is, each interviewer should be scheduled to do the same number of interviews with each group. *Step 3:* Likelihood of having an effect unless controlled: moderate.
3. **Data collector bias.** *Step 1:* Bias might well be related to information obtained on the three hypothesized causal variables. *Step 2:* Bias might differ for the two groups; for example, an interviewer might behave differently when interviewing dropouts. The solution is to keep interviewers ignorant as to which group subjects belong to. To do this, care has to be taken both with the questions to be asked and the training of interviewers. *Step 3:* Likelihood of having an effect unless controlled: high.

Other Threats. Implementation, history, maturation, attitudinal, and regression threats do not affect this kind (type 2) of causal-comparative study.

The trick to identifying threats to internal validity in causal-comparative studies (as in experimental studies) is, first, to think of various things (conditions, other variables, and so on) that might affect the outcome variable of the study. Then, second, to decide, based on evidence or experience, whether these things would be likely to affect the comparison groups differently. If so, this may provide an alternative explanation for the results. If this seems likely, a threat to the internal validity of the study may indeed be present and needs to be controlled. Many of these threats can be greatly reduced if causal-comparative studies are replicated. Figure 16.3 summarizes the process of evaluating the presence of threats to internal validity.

Data Analysis

The first step in analyzing data in a causal-comparative study is to construct frequency polygons and then calculate the mean and standard deviation of each group if the variable is quantitative. These descriptive statistics are then assessed for magnitude (see Chapter 12). A statistical inference test may or may not be appropriate, depending on whether random samples were used from identified populations (such as creative vs. noncreative high school seniors). The most commonly used test in causal-comparative studies is a *t*-test for differences between means. When more than two groups are used, then either an analysis of variance or an analysis of covariance is the appropriate test. Analysis of covariance is particularly helpful in causal-comparative research because a researcher cannot always match the comparison groups on all relevant variables other than the ones of primary interest. As mentioned in Chapter 11, analysis of covariance provides a way to match groups "after the fact" on such variables as age, socioeconomic status,

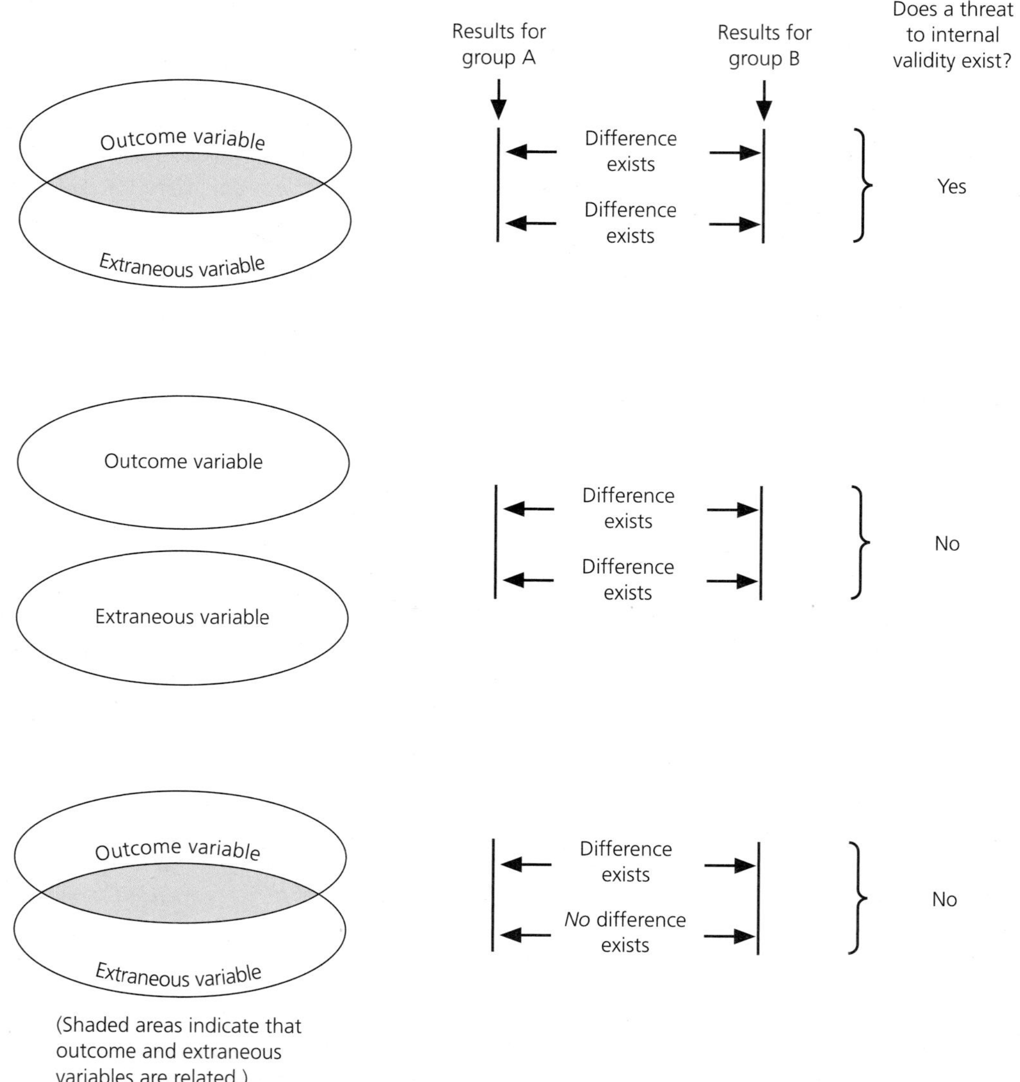

Figure 16.3 *Does a Threat to Internal Validity Exist?*

aptitude, and so on. Before analysis of covariance can be used, however, the data involved need to satisfy certain assumptions.[1]

The results of a causal-comparative study must be interpreted with caution. As with correlational studies, causal-comparative studies are good at identifying relationships between variables, but they do not demonstrate cause and effect.

There are two ways to strengthen the interpretability of causal-comparative studies. First, as we mentioned earlier, alternative hypotheses should be formulated and investigated whenever possible. Second, if the dependent variables involved are categorical, the relationships among all of the variables in the study should be examined using the technique of discriminant function analysis, which we briefly described in Chapter 15.

The most powerful way to check on the possible causes identified in a causal-comparative study, of course, is to perform an experiment. The presumed cause (or causes) identified can sometimes be manipulated.

MORE ABOUT RESEARCH

Significant Findings in Causal-Comparative Research

A widely cited causal-comparative study was conducted by two researchers in the 1940s.* They compared two groups of 500 boys, one group identified as juvenile delinquents based on their having been institutionalized (seven months on average), and a second group not so identified. Both groups were from the same "high risk" area of Boston. Pairs of boys, one from each group, were matched on ethnicity, IQ, and age. The major differences they found between the groups were that the boys in the delinquent group had more solid muscular bodies, were more energetic and extroverted, were more unconventional and defiant, were less methodical and abstract, and came from less cohesive, less affectionate families. Combining these characteristics resulted in a table for predicting probable delinquency that has received considerable validation in other settings over the years.† Nonetheless, argument continues as to the nature of cause and effect and as to the desirability of using such predictive information. It could be used either for benevolent intervention (as envisioned by the researchers who did the original study) or to stigmatize and coerce.

*Gluek, S., & Gluek, E. (1950). *Unraveling juvenile delinquency.* Cambridge, MA: Harvard University Press.

†Gluek, S., & Gluek, E. (1974). *Of delinquency and crime.* Springfield, IL: C. Thomas.

Should differences between experimental and control groups now be found, the researcher then has a much better reason for inferring causation.

Associations Between Categorical Variables

Up to this point, our discussion of associational methods has considered only the situations in which (1) one variable is categorical and the other(s) is(are) quantitative (causal-comparative), and (2) both variables are quantitative (correlational). It is also possible to investigate associations between categorical variables. Both crossbreak tables (see Chapter 10) and contingency coefficients are used. An example of a relationship between categorical variables is shown in Table 16.1.

TABLE 16.1 *Grade Level and Gender of Teachers (Hypothetical Data)*

Grade Level	Males	Females	Total
Elementary	40	70	110
Junior High	50	40	90
Senior High	80	60	140
Total	170	170	340

As was true with correlation, such data can be used for purposes of prediction and, with caution, in the search for cause and effect. Knowing that a person is a teacher and male, for example, we can predict, with some degree of confidence (on the basis of the data in Table 16.1), that he teaches either junior or senior high school, since 76 percent of males who are teachers do so. We can also estimate how much in error our prediction is likely to be. Based on the data in Table 16.1, the probability of our prediction being in error is 40/170, or .24. In this example, the possibility that gender is a major *cause* of teaching level seems quite remote—there are other variables, such as historical patterns of teacher preparation and hiring, that make more sense when one tries to explain the relationship.

There are no techniques analogous to partial correlation (see Chapter 15) or the other techniques that have evolved from correlational research that can be used with categorical variables. Further, prediction from crossbreak tables is much less precise than from scatterplots. Fortunately, there are relatively few questions of interest in education that involve two categorical variables. It is common, however, to find a researcher treating variables that are conceptually quantitative (and measured accordingly) as if they were categorical. For example, a researcher arbitrarily may divide a set of quantitative scores into high, middle, and low groups. Nothing is gained by this procedure, and it suffers from two serious defects: the loss of the precision that is acquired through the use of correlational techniques and the essential arbitrariness of the division into groups. How does one decide which score separates "high" scores from "middle" scores, for example? In general, therefore, such arbitrary division should be avoided.*

*There are times when a quantitative variable is justifiably treated as a categorical variable. For example, creativity is generally considered to be a quantitative variable. One might, however, establish criteria for dividing this continuum into only two categories—"highly creative" and "typically creative"—as a way of studying relationships with other variables more efficiently.

An Example of Causal-Comparative Research

In the remainder of this chapter, we present a published example of causal-comparative research, followed by a critique of its strengths and weaknesses. As we did in our critiques of the different types of research studies we analyzed in other chapters, we use concepts introduced in earlier parts of the book in our analysis. This study is an example of mixed-methods research.

RESEARCH REPORT

From: (2007). *Journal of American College Health, 56*(2), 137–143.

Internet Use, Abuse, and Dependence Among Students at a Southeastern Regional University

Beverly L. Fortson, PhD; Joseph R. Scotti, PhD; Yi-Chuen Chen, PhD; Judith Malone, BS; Kevin S. Del Ben, PhD

Abstract

Purpose

Objective: *To assess Internet use, abuse, and dependence.* ***Participants:*** *411 undergraduate students.* ***Results:*** *Ninety percent of participants reported daily Internet use. Approximately half of the sample met criteria for Internet abuse, and one-quarter met criteria for Internet dependence. Men and women did not differ on the mean amount of time accessing the Internet each day; however, the reasons for accessing the Internet differed between the 2 groups. Depression was correlated with more frequent use of the Internet to meet people, socially experiment, and participate in chat rooms, and with less frequent face-to-face socialization. In addition, individuals meeting criteria for Internet abuse and dependence endorsed more depressive symptoms, more time online, and less face-to-face socialization than did those not meeting the criteria.* ***Conclusions:*** *Mental health and student affairs professionals should be alert to the problems associated with Internet overuse, especially as computers become an integral part of college life.*

Keywords: dependence, depression, Internet abuse

Internet access has become easier and more affordable throughout the United States, especially on college campuses; an estimated 92% of college students have

At the time of the study, all authors were with West Virginia University.

computer access,[1] and approximately 86% of college students report having accessed the Internet for some purpose during their lives.[2] In a 2001 survey of 281,064 freshmen from 421 4-year colleges, 74% reported Internet use for research or homework, 19% participated in Internet chat rooms, 69% communicated via e-mail, and 58% reported use of the Internet for "other" purposes.[3] Scherer[4] found that 73% of college students accessed the Internet at least once a day and spent approximately 8.1 hours a week online. Anderson[5] found that students spent approximately 1.6 hours a day on the Internet. In a more recent study, Rotunda et al[6] found that students spent an average of 3.3 hours a day on the Internet. These studies, published over a 7-year period (1997 to 2003), suggest that college students are spending increasing amounts of time accessing the Internet. Thus, the question arises as to whether there may be associated detrimental effects.

Justification

Prior research

Justification

Sex Differences in Internet Use. Although researchers have shown little difference in the amount of time men and women spend online, they have consistently found that men and women differ in their reasons for accessing the Internet. Weiser[7] found that men were more likely than were women to use the Internet for purposes related to entertainment and leisure, whereas females used it primarily for interpersonal communication and educational assistance. Odell et al.[8] similarly found that men reported greater use of the Internet for visiting sex sites, researching purchases, checking the news, playing games, and listening to and copying music, whereas more women used the Internet for e-mail and school-related research. Researchers[9–11] have obtained many of these same results cross-culturally; however, results by Joiner et al.[12] were not entirely consistent with these previous studies. Joiner et al found that men were more likely than were women to use the Internet for leisure activities (e.g., downloading material from the Internet, using game Web sites), but women did not use the Internet for communication more than men did.

Prior research

Justification

Problems Related to Internet Use. A small percentage of college student Internet users develop problematic behaviors, such as cravings, sleep disturbance, depression, and withdrawal symptoms, as a result of their Internet use.[13, 14] From a sample of 531 college students, Scherer[4] found that 13% met criteria for Internet dependency and, as such, believed their Internet usage interfered with their daily functioning. The Internet-dependent students were predominantly male and reported more leisure-time Internet use than did nondependent students. Approximately 9% of the college students in Anderson's[5] study endorsed dependence on the Internet. Morahan-Martin and Schumacher[15] also found that 8.1% of college students met their criteria for pathological Internet use. Again, most of the pathological users were male and were more likely to use online games and *technologically sophisticated sites* (e.g., file-transfer protocols, remote support communication software, virtual reality). Morahan-Martin and Schumacher[15] also found that pathological Internet users reported being generally lonelier than others and more socially disinhibited online.

Justification

Prior research

In the research on problematic Internet use, experts have typically defined abuse and dependence using criteria similar to that for pathological gambling, suggesting that Internet addiction is considered a behavioral addiction. Such a definition is controversial, with opponents of the use of these criteria holding that Internet addiction (as well as sex or food addictions) is not based on empirical research, as is pathological gambling.[13] In addition, pathological gambling involves more serious financial issues (e.g., loss of large sums of money, illegal activities to repay losses, heavy borrowing from legal and illegal sources) than does pathological Internet use. In response to such issues, Anderson[5] used criteria modeled after the substance-related disorders from the *Diagnostic and Statistical*

Manual of Mental Disorders, 4th edition text revision (*DSM-IV-TR*[16]) to evaluate pathological Internet use.

Instrument

In the present study, we examined Internet use among college students using a questionnaire that we constructed primarily on the basis of the work of Scherer.[4] Like Scherer, we assessed social styles and preferences for the types of therapy one would choose if one were to seek professional help for a problem, such as Internet dependence. Unlike Scherer, we modeled our Internet abuse and dependence criteria after the *DSM-IV-TR*[16] criteria for substance abuse and dependence. We considered participants to abuse the Internet if they endorsed 1 or more symptoms supporting a maladaptive pattern of behavior that resulted in significant impairment or distress (e.g., failure to fulfill major roles, legal problems related to Internet use, continued use despite problems). We also considered them Internet dependent if they endorsed 3 or more symptoms of dependency (e.g., tolerance; withdrawal; being online for periods longer than intended; impairment in social, occupational, or recreational activities because of Internet use). In a departure from the previously cited studies, we gathered data via paper surveys and over a restricted-access Internet site.

Operational definitions

Part of purpose

METHODS

Participants

Volunteer

We recruited 485 (55% female) undergraduate students enrolled in an introductory psychology course at a large southeastern regional university. Of these, we deleted 74 from the final data set because of incomplete questionnaires; these students did not differ from the final sample on any available demographic variables.

Large *n*
Sample description

The final sample of 411 participants was 56% female, 91% Caucasian (4% African American, 2% Asian American, and 2% Hispanic), and primarily (50%) from West Virginia (Pennsylvania, 20%; Maryland, New Jersey, and Virginia, 6%–7% each; and the remaining 11% from 13 other states and 3 countries). Of the participants, 63.7% were freshmen; 22.6%, sophomores; 9.8%, juniors, and 3.9%, seniors. On average, participants were aged 20.4 years ($SD = 3.2$, range = 18–56). Men were slightly older ($M = 20.8$ years, $SD = 3.5$) than were women ($M = 20.1$ years, $SD = 2.9$), $t(406) = 2.0$, $p < .05$.

Materials

Demographics. We included questions, pertaining to sex, race and ethnicity, year of birth, year in college, and current state or country of permanent residence to describe the sample. Participants also answered questions about social style and preferences for therapy. The first item on social style was about perceived sociability (1 = *very sociable,* 2 = *sociable,* 3 = *sociable, but shy or introverted,* 4 = *not really sociable; somewhat of a loner*); the second item was about contexts for social interaction (1 = *more face-to-face than on the Internet,* 2 = *equally face-to-face and on the Internet,* 3 = *more on the Internet than face-to-face,* 4 = *seldom, I do not socialize much face-to-face or online*). We also assessed preferences for 7 therapy formats (from *face-to-face with an individual* to *online with a group*) if one were to ever seek psychological treatment (eg, for Internet abuse or dependence). Tables 1, 2, and 3 show all items and related rating scales.

The demographics questionnaire also contained 9 items to evaluate whether participants felt that their use of the Internet interfered with their daily functioning; that is, did they meet criteria for Internet abuse and dependence (on the basis of *DSM-IV-TR* criteria, as previously discussed).

TABLE 1 *Ratings of Sociability*

Social style	%
I consider myself to be . . .	
Very sociable	34
Sociable	46
Sociable but shy or introverted	19
Not really sociable; somewhat of a loner	1
I socialize . . .	
More face-to-face than on the Internet	74
Equally face-to-face and on the Internet	23
More on the Internet than face-to-face	3
Seldom; I do not socialize much face-to-face or online	I

TABLE 2 *Preferences for Therapy*

Preference for therapy	*M*	*SD*
Face-to-face with an individual	4.0	1.1
Face-to-face in a group	2.9	1.2
Face-to-face in a workshop	2.9	2.1
Telephone hotline	2.2	1.3
E-mail hotline	2.0	1.2
Online with an individual	2.5	1.3
Online with a group	1.9	1.1

Note. Scales are scored as follows: 1 = *very unlikely*, 2 = *somewhat likely*, 3 = *unsure*, 4 = *somewhat likely*, 5 = *very likely*.

Internet Use. The Internet Usage Questionnaire consisted of 17 items to determine how often the participants accessed the Internet and for what purposes they did so. We constructed these items on the basis of Scherer's[4] work and scored them from 0 to 4 (0 = *no;* 1 = *yes,* at least once per year; 2 = *yes, at least once per month;* 3 = *yes, at least once per week;* 4 = *yes, at least once per day*). Table 4 shows the questionnaire items. We obtained a Cronbach's alpha of .62, indicating an acceptable level of internal consistency for a short research survey with nonhomogenous items of this kind.[17,18]

Low

Still poor reliability

Depression. The Center for Epidemiological Studies Depression Scale (CES-D) is a 20-item questionnaire that we used to identify the presence and severity of depressive symptomatology. Higher scores on the measure indicate a higher frequency of occurrence of the symptoms, with a score of 16 or more suggesting clinical cases of depression. The CES-D has high internal consistency, moderate test-retest reliability, and concurrent and construct validity.[19]

Operational definition

Specific data needed

Procedure

We conducted this study, which the university's institutional review board approved, as a portion of a larger project[20] comparing the results of psychometric surveys completed

Purpose?

Why?

TABLE 3 *Reported Behaviors Related to Internet Abuse and Dependence*

Behavior (matching *DSM-IV* criteria)	Criterion	*M*	*SD*	% (yes, definitely)
Behavior related to Internet abuse				
Failure to fulfill major responsibilities at work, school, or home because of Internet use	1	1.6	0.8	
Legal problems related to Internet use	3	1.0	0.2	1
Continued to use Internet despite recurrent social problems caused or increased by Internet use	4	1.8	0.8	21
Behavior related to Internet dependence				
Developed tolerance symptoms, such as increased Internet use to get the same desired feeling or a decrease in desired feeling with the same amount of use	1	1.1	0.4	2
Experienced withdrawal symptoms in reaction to decreased Internet use that either interrupted important areas of life functioning or led to use of a similar object to relieve symptoms	2	1.1	0.4	2
Used Internet for longer periods than intended	3	3.1	0.8	
Consistent desire to, or unsuccessful efforts to, cut down or control use of the Internet	4	1.3	0.5	3
Social, occupational, or recreational activities reduced because of Internet use	6	1.9	0.8	
Continued use of the Internet despite knowledge of having a psychological or physical problem that is caused or worsened by use	7	1.4	0.7	12

Note. For abuse criterion 1 and dependence criteria 3 and 6, 1 = *never*, 2 = *rarely*, 3 = *sometimes*, 4 = *often*, 5 = *very frequently*. For criteria 2, 4, and 7, 1 = *definitely not*, 2 = *somewhat*, 3 = *yes, definitely*. DSM-IV = *Diagnostic and Statistical Manual of Mental Disorders*, 4th ed.[16]

Randomly?

via the Internet with those completed on paper. We entered participants into 1 of 2 conditions (paper or Internet) on the basis of the data collection session they attended; participants were unaware of the conditions prior to arrival. All participants completed informed consent agreements. Those in the Paper Condition completed the survey on paper immediately; we gave those assigned to the Internet Condition a slip of paper with the Web address to the restricted study site (along with a user name and password), asked them to complete the questionnaire within the next 24 hours, and dismissed them. Of the 411 participants in the final sample, 211 completed the survey on paper (51%), and 200 completed it via the Internet (49%). Participants in these 2 conditions did not differ on key demographic variables nor on the time they typically spent accessing the Internet each day. After survey completion, participants received extra credit for a course. (This research project was one of multiple opportunities for students to earn extra credit in their courses.) All participants also received a list of referrals in the event

Which ones?

Recruitment of students

TABLE 4 *Frequency of Internet Access, by Reasons and Services*

Variable	M	SD	% reporting daily use
Reason for accessing the Internet			
Academic	3.3	0.7	41
Relationship maintenance	3.1	1.3	57
Social experimentation	1.0	1.4	9
Meeting people	0.9	1.2	4
Sexual material	0.7	1.2	4
Illegal/immoral purpose	0.3	0.8	1
Other	1.1	1.0	1
Service used			
World Wide Web	3.7	0.5	78
Search	3.3	0.8	42
E-mail	3.7	0.7	80
Courses	2.6	0.9	12
Library	2.0	1.1	5
Newsgroup	1.2	1.4	9
Chat	0.9	1.2	6
Bulletin board	0.8	1.2	4
Shopping	1.2	1.0	1
Single-user game	1.5	1.4	9
Multiuser game	0.6	1.1	3
Other	0.4	0.9	1

Note. Scales are scored as follows: 0 = *no use*, 1= *once per year*, 2 = *once per month*, 3 = *once per week*, 4 = *once per day*.

that answering the questions led to psychological difficulties or if an individual wanted to follow up with psychological services after participating in the research.

Ethics

RESULTS

Paper Versus Internet Survey Completion

We conducted multivariate analyses of variance (MANOVAs) to examine whether differences existed in responding between those who completed the survey on paper versus the Internet. We analyzed each major variable category (e.g., frequency of accessing the Internet for different reasons and services, sociability, symptoms of Internet abuse and dependence, therapy preferences, and depressive symptoms) in separate MANOVAs. We found no differences between Internet and paper respondents for most categories and their component variables. The one exception was a significant effect for survey version: Internet and paper respondents differed in their reasons for accessing the Internet, Hotelling's T = .04, $F(6, 406) = 3.0$, $p < .01$; however, only 2 of the 6 variables in this category showed differences. Individuals completing the Internet version were more likely to report use of the Internet for academic purposes ($M = 3.4$, $SD = 0.6$; $M = 3.2$, $SD = 0.7$, for Internet and paper, respectively), $F(1, 409) = 7.0$, $p < .01$, and to access sexual

Hotelling's T is similar to "t" test

Small differences

See text, page 208

material ($M = 0.8$, $SD = 1.2$; $M = 0.6$, $SD = 1.2$, for Internet and paper respectively), $F(1, 409) = 4.2$, $p < .05$. The effect size for these variables was small ($\eta^2 < .05$) and represented only 2 of several dozen variables, suggesting these were spurious effects and that the survey results from the paper and Internet conditions did not differ in any consistent or meaningful way; thus, we present all further results collapsed across condition.

Depression, Sociability, and Therapy Options

On the CES-D, we obtained a mean score of 13.9 ($SD = 8.9$), with 33% of the sample exceeding the clinical cutoff score of 16 or above, suggesting the presence of clinical depression. Table 1 shows ratings of participants' levels of sociability and their preferences for modes of socialization. Most students described themselves as *very sociable* (34%) or *sociable* (46%) and reported that they socialized more *face-to-face* (74%) than they did by other means. Table 2 shows preferences for therapy options. If seeking treatment for psychological problems, most participants reported that they would prefer treatment to be face-to-face with an individual ($M = 4.0$; $SD = 1.1$).

Internet Use

On the Internet Usage Questionnaire, 90% of the participants reported daily use of the Internet for some activity (9.5% weekly use, 0.5% monthly use), such as e-mail, Web access, chat rooms, and shopping. Time accessing the Internet ranged from less than 30 minutes a day (20%), to 30–60 minutes (31%), 1–4 hours (37%), 4–8 hours (9%), 8–12 hours (1%), and 12–24 hours (1%). Table 4 provides descriptive data on reasons for using the Internet and the services accessed.

Internet Abuse and Dependence

We calculated Internet abuse and dependence by using a set of liberal (i.e., ratings at the midpoint or higher on each relevant item; *sometimes* to *very frequently* or *somewhat* to *yes definitely*) and conservative (i.e., ratings only at the high point on each relevant item; *very frequently* or *yes definitely*) criteria. More than half (57.2%, $n = 235$) of the sample reported a pattern of behavior sufficient to meet criteria for Internet abuse under the liberal criteria; 21.9% ($n = 90$) met the definition for abuse using the conservative criteria. In both cases, more than 95% of those meeting abuse criteria endorsed continued Internet use despite current social problems, and less than 5% reported legal problems related to Internet use.

One-quarter (26.3%, $n = 108$) of the sample reported a pattern of behavior sufficient to meet criteria for Internet dependence under the liberal criteria (60.2% of these indicating tolerance and/or withdrawal); 1.2% ($n = 5$) met the definition for dependence using the conservative criteria (80% of these indicating tolerance and/or withdrawal). Participants endorsed all the individual criteria for dependence at similarly high rates. Table 3 contains the statistics for each of the individual abuse and dependence items.

Sex Differences in Internet Use

A MANOVA indicated a sex difference in reasons for accessing the Internet, Hotelling's $T = .39$, $F(6, 404) = 26.3$, $p < .001$. We calculated univariate analyses of variance (ANOVAs) on each dependent variable as follow-up tests to the MANOVA. There were no reported sex differences in frequency of accessing the Internet for academic use, maintaining relationships, or socially experimenting. Sex differences (women < men) existed

Small differences [on meeting new people, $F(1, 409) = 8.0$, $p < .01$ ($M = 0.7$, SD = 1.1, $M = 1.0$, SD = 1.3);

seeking sexual material, $F(1, 409) = 150.2$, $p < .001$ (M = 0.2, SD = 0.6, M = 1.4, SD = 1.4); and seeking illegal or immoral material. $F(1, 409) = 42.4$, $p < .001$ (M = 0.1, SD = 0.4, M = 0.6, SD = 1.0). Each of these differences was for infrequently occurring activities, with men reporting higher access rates than did women.

Large differences

A MANOVA indicated a sex difference in frequency of accessing different Internet services, Hotelling's $T = .14$, $F(11, 399) = 5.0$, $p < .001$. We conducted ANOVAs on each dependent variable as follow-up tests to the MANOVA. There were no reported sex differences in use of the Internet for e-mail, library services, course access, shopping, or searching. Sex differences (women < men) existed on Web usage, $F(1, 409) = 10.4$, $p < .001$ (M = 3.7, SD = 0.6, M = 3.8, SD = 0.5); newsgroups, $F(1, 409) = 3.9$, $p < .05$ (M = 1.1, SD = 1.4, M = 1.4, SD = 1.5); chat rooms, $F(1, 409) = 31.9$, $p < .001$ (M = 0.6, SD = 1.0, M = 1.3, SD = 1.4); single-user games, $F(1, 409) = 6.6$, $p < .05$ (M = 1.3, SD = 1.4, M = 1.7, SD = 1.4); multi-user games, $F(1, 409) = 18.1$, $p < .001$ (M = 0.4, SD = 0.9, M = 0.9, SD = 1.3); and bulletin boards. $F(1, 409) = 6.0$, $p < .05$ (M = 0.6, SD = 1.1, M = 0.9, SD = 1.3). Again, on items with sex differences, men reported higher access rates than did women.

Some differences are large, some are small

We did not find sex differences on perceived sociability and social behavior or on the mean amount of time accessing the Internet each day. In addition, there were no sex differences on individual questions regarding symptoms of Internet abuse and dependence or on mean CES-D symptoms. There were no sex differences in meeting criteria (liberal or conservative) for Internet abuse or dependence, except that men (62.8%) were more likely than were women (52.8%) to meet the liberal criteria for Internet abuse, $\chi^2(1, N = 411) = 4.1$, $p < .05$.

Large difference

Relations of Internet Use and Psychological Symptoms

We conducted chi-square analyses to examine whether participants meeting the liberal criteria for Internet abuse or dependence reported different reasons for accessing the Internet or used different services than did those participants not meeting the liberal criteria. (Analyses using the conservative criteria were highly similar or could not be calculated because of the small sample sizes.) Participants meeting, versus not meeting, the liberal criteria for Internet abuse were more likely to report accessing the Internet to maintain relationships, meet people, socially experiment, and seek illegal/immoral material, as well as to use the Web, conduct searches, use chat rooms, and play single- and multi-user games, minimum $\chi^2(4, N = 411) = 11.2$, $p < .05$. Participants meeting the liberal criteria for Internet dependence were more likely to report accessing the Internet for these same reasons and to use these same services, minimum $\chi^2(4, N = 411) = 10.8$, $p < .05$, with several exceptions. Dependent individuals were more likely to access the Internet for sexual material, but not for illegal/immoral purposes, and were more likely to use e-mail, library resources, newsgroups, and shopping services, but not multi-user games, minimum $\chi^2(4, N = 411) = 10.0$, $p < .05$. Last, participants meeting the liberal criteria for Internet dependence were less likely to access the Internet for academic purposes than were those not meeting this criteria, $\chi^2(4, N = 411) = 16.9$, $p < .01$. In general, those meeting the liberal criteria for Internet abuse (M = 2.7, SD = 1.0; M = 2.1, SD = 1.0; $t[409] = 5.5$, $p < .001$) or dependence (M = 3.0, SD = 0.9; M = 2.3, SD = 1.1; $t[409] = 6.6$, $p < .001$) reported spending more time online each day than did those not meeting criteria, respectively.

Moderate relationships

Large differences

See our analysis

Higher CES-D scores correlated positively with more frequent use of the Internet to meet people, $r(411) = .19$, $p < .001$; socially experiment, $r(411) = .15$, $p < .01$; and chat, $r(411) = .10$, $p < .05$; and with less frequent socialization, $r(411) = .12$, $p < .05$, but not with total time online. Higher ratings on the individual symptoms of Internet

Small r's

abuse and dependence (correlations ranging from .09 to .18, $p < .05$) were positively correlated with higher CES-D scores. People meeting criteria for Internet abuse reported more symptoms of depression than did those not meeting criteria, using both the liberal, $t(409) = 2.9$, $p < .01$ (M = 12.4, SD = 8.7; M = 14.9, SD = 8.9, for those not meeting and meeting criteria, respectively), and conservative, $t(409) = 2.5$, $p < .05$ (M = 13.3, SD = 8.8; M = 15.9, SD = 8.9, respectively), definitions of Internet abuse. Participants who met criteria for Internet dependence using the liberal definition also reported more symptoms of depression than did those not meeting criteria, $t(409) = 2.4$, $p < .05$ (M = 13.2, SD = 8.9; M = 15.6, SD = 8.6, respectively). We could not evaluate the relation between depressive symptoms and Internet dependence under the conservative criteria because of the small number of participants who were Internet dependent ($n = 5$). There were no relations between ratings of sociability and meeting liberal criteria for Internet abuse and dependence; however, those meeting the liberal criteria for Internet abuse (M = 1.5, SD = 0.7; M = 1.3, SD = 0.5; $t[409] = 3.8$, $P < .001$) or dependence (M = 1.4, SD = 0.5; M = 1.2, SD = 0.6; $t[409] = 2.3$, $p < .05$) reported that they socialized less in face-to-face interactions than did those not meeting criteria, respectively.

Small differences See our "Analysis of the Study"

Last, depression also was negatively correlated with the likelihood of using therapy in a face-to-face situation, either individually, $r(411) = -.11$ $p < .05$; in a group, $r(411) = -.18$, $p < .001$; or a workshop $r(411) = -.16$, $p < .01$, and was positively correlated with the likelihood of seeking therapy via e-mail hotline, $r(411) = .15$, $p < .01$, or online with an individual, $r(411) = .13$, $p < .01$.

Small r's

COMMENT

Our study consisted of a sample of frequent Internet users, with 90% of the participants using the Internet daily. The majority (68%) of the participants reported using the Internet between 30 minutes and 4 hours daily. These figures are similar to—if not somewhat higher than—those obtained in previous research.[2,4–6] Men and women did not differ on the mean amount of time accessing the Internet each day; however, as with past research, we found differences between men and women for reasons for accessing the Internet and services used. Past researchers[7,8,12] generally have found that men are more likely than are women to use the Internet for purposes related to entertainment and leisure, whereas women use it primarily for interpersonal communication and educational assistance.[7,8,10,21–24] In our study, men were significantly more likely to use the Internet to meet new people, seek sexual material, and seek illegal or immoral material. In addition, men were significantly more likely than were women to use the Internet to (1) surf the Web, (2) participate in newsgroups, chat rooms, and bulletin boards, and (3) play games (both single- and multiuser games).

Prior research

Small differences (see previous page)

It is interesting to note, however, that men and women in our study, unlike in past studies,[7–8] did not differ on their use of the Internet for educational or academic assistance (eg, library services, course access)—41% of the participants used the Internet daily for academic purposes. These results may have been skewed, however, particularly with regard to male use, because courses on this particular university campus require that students access course materials over the Internet, especially in the course from which we drew this sample. We also found similar rates of Internet use for men and women in shopping and e-mailing. Although several past researchers[7,8] have shown differences between men and women in these activities, Joiner et al,[12] in addition to us, found no differences between men and women in these activities. These results suggest, therefore, that it is likely that as Internet access has become more commonplace, especially on college campuses, there are certain activities (e.g., shopping and e-mailing) that also

Extraneous variable

have become more common. For example, 80% of the participants in our study reported daily use of e-mail.

Most participants (80%) described themselves as sociable, whereas the remaining 20% described themselves as shy but sociable (19%) or as not sociable/loners (1%). Socialization reported by these participants occurred more often face-to-face (74%) or equally face-to-face and on the Internet (23%). A small percentage (3%) stated that they socialized more via the Internet, whereas the remaining 1% seldom socialized. Scherer[4] used such socialization patterns to determine whether dependent Internet users fit the stereotype of the socially introverted computer geek. Our results support her contention (and the results found in other studies) in that those participants meeting the liberal criteria for Internet abuse and dependence had higher depression scores and reported less face-to-face interaction.

Small *r* and ES

Prior researchers[4,5,15] have suggested that between 8% and 13% of all college students meet the criteria for Internet dependence. About half of the students in our study met the liberal criteria for Internet abuse, and one quarter met the liberal Internet dependence criteria (22% and 1.2% using the conservative criteria, respectively). These numbers differ from prior findings likely because most researchers have defined Internet abuse and dependence using the *DSM-IV-TR* criteria for pathological gambling, whereas we used the criteria for substance abuse and dependence and used rating scales rather than yes/no responses. Anderson[5] used substance abuse criteria similar to ours, but with yes/no responses, and found that approximately 9% of students met criteria for dependence. To further investigate the prevalence of Internet abuse and dependence, researchers will need to agree on specific diagnostic criteria and behaviors, as well as how to evaluate the presence, absence, or severity of symptoms. This will help future researchers and clinicians to more fully appreciate the extent to which Internet overuse may interfere with lives and thus constitute a behavioral health problem.

We agree

There was no relation between total time online and depressive symptoms; however, depression was correlated with more frequent use of the Internet to meet people, socially experiment, and participate in chat rooms and with less frequent socialization. In addition, individuals meeting the criteria for Internet abuse and dependence endorsed more depressive symptoms and time online and less face-to-face socialization than did those not meeting the criteria. Although it is tempting to suggest that individuals who are depressed may prefer less face-to-face interaction and thus spend more time online, thereby becoming abusive or dependent on the Internet, these data cannot speak to the directionality of the relations. Understanding such pathways will prove an important research direction and provide guidance to clinicians who may be addressing Internet abuse and dependence in their clientele.

See our analysis

Right

The information we have highlighted has several implications for mental health and student affairs professionals. Mental health professionals should be alert to the problems associated with excessive Internet use, including depression, social withdrawal, a failure to fulfill major responsibilities, and behaviors that resemble the patterns seen in tolerance and withdrawal in substance dependence. As the Internet becomes a more integral component of college life, student affairs professionals may need to expend greater effort alerting students and faculty to the potential difficulties that may arise from significant Internet overuse, including personal difficulties and interference with school-related work and assignments. The modern work environment also is largely computer dependent, making this issue relevant to employee assistance programs. In addition, mental health professionals may need to explore the Internet behaviors of clients, particularly those who are depressed or socially introverted. However, providing therapy

Implications of this study?

resources over the Internet appears to be a somewhat acceptable therapeutic modality, although still less preferred than face-to-face therapy.

Future Directions

As the Internet becomes a more popular method of data collection for research purposes, experts should develop standardized survey instruments, particularly with regard to determining the amount of time an individual spends online, reasons for accessing the Internet, and the services used, so that surveys are more comparable and less idiosyncratic. Investigators also should use available psychometrically sound measures of pathology (e.g., the CES-D) rather than basing constructs on a small number of untested items (e.g., *sociability*, as defined in this and most prior research). Last, if evaluation of Internet abuse and dependence is to be a viable area of clinical research, then experts need to agree on specific criteria (e.g., is Internet abuse more similar to pathological gambling or substance abuse), and use standardized measures (e.g., modifying existing substance abuse measures).

We did not find differences in survey results when participants responded via paper or on the Internet[20]; however, we identified our participants beforehand and assigned them to these conditions. Known respondents on the Internet are likely to produce different results than are unknown respondents who serendipitously come upon the Internet survey site, as seen in several prior studies.[25,26] Thus, researchers will need to clearly define their samples and means of survey access. For clinical research focusing on the potential problem of Internet abuse and dependence, known samples specifically invited to participate in the research would be most appropriate. The increasing availability of Internet courseware on college campuses would make this a practical method of participant recruitment. Because most of the researchers have investigated college student Internet abuse and dependency, future researchers should move to the general population and investigate a wider range of factors that could contribute to abuse and dependency and to determine the extent to which these may constitute a new behavioral health problem.

Good

ACKNOWLEDGMENT

The authors thank Cara O'Connell, Jennifer Guriel, Serena Gibson, Amisha Dean, and Tara Parsons for the time they devoted to the project.

NOTE

Portions of this manuscript were submitted as the master's thesis of the first author. The West Virginia University Department of Psychology Alumni Fund at West Virginia University provided partial funding for this research.

For comments and further information, please address correspondence to Dr Beverly L. Fortson, University of South Carolina–Aiken, 471 University Parkway, Box 2, Aiken, SC 29801 (e-mail; beverlyf@usca.edu).

REFERENCES

1. Perry T, Perry LA, Hosack-Curlin K. Internet use by university students: an interdisciplinary study on three campuses. *Internet Res Electron Netw Appl Policy.* 1998;8:136–141.
2. United States Department of State. College students outpace general US population in Internet use. United States Department of State. Available at: http://usinfo.stae.gov. Accessed November 20, 2002.

3. Attitudes and characteristics of freshmen at 4-year colleges. *Chron Higher Educ.* 2001:48:26.
4. Scherer K. College life online: healthy and unhealthy Internet use. *J Coll Stud Dev.* 1997;38:655–665.
5. Anderson KJ. Internet use among college students: an exploratory study. *J Am Coll Health.* 2001;50:21–26.
6. Rotunda RJ, Kass SJ, Sutton MA, Leon DT. Internet use and misuse: preliminary findings from a new assessment instrument. *Behav Modif.* 2003;27:484–504.
7. Weiser EB. Gender differences in Internet use patterns and Internet application preferences: a two-sample comparison. *Cyberpsychol Behav.* 2000;2:167–177.
8. Odell PM, Korgen KO, Schumacher P, Delucchi M. Internet use among female and male college students. *Cyberpsychol Behav.* 2000;3:855–862.
9. Colley A. Gender differences in adolescent perceptions of the best and worst aspects of computing. *Comput Human Behav.* 2003;19:673–682.
10. Teo TSH, Lim VKG. Gender differences in Internet usage and task preferences. *Behav Inf Technol.* 2000; 19:283–295.
11. Ho SMY, Lee MC. Computer usage and its relationship with adolescent life in Hong Kong. *J Adolesc Health.* 2001;29:258–266.
12. Joiner R, Gavin J, Duffield J, el al. Gender, Internet identification, and Internet anxiety: correlates of Internet use. *Cyberpsychol Behav.* 2005;8:371–378.
13. Kubey RW, Lavin MJ, Barrows JR. Internet use and collegiate academic performance decrements: early findings. *J Commun.* 2001;51:366–382.
14. Young KS, Rogers RC. The relationship between depression and Internet addiction. *Cyberpsychol Behav.* 1998;1:25–28.
15. Morahan-Martin J, Schumacher P. Incidence and correlates of pathological Internet use among college students. *Comput Human Behav.* 2000;16:13–29.
16. American Psychiatric Association. *Diagnostic and Statistical Manual of Mental Disorders.* 4th ed., text rev. Washington, DC: American Psychiatric Association; 2000.
17. DeVellis RF. *Scale Development: Theory and Applications.* Newbury Park, CA: Sage; 1991.
18. Nunnally JC. *Psychometric Theory.* New York, NY: McGraw-Hill; 1978.
19. Radloff LS. The CES-D scale: a self-report depression scale for research in the general population. *Appl Psychol Meas.* 1977;1:385–401.
20. Fortson BL, Scotti JR, Del Ben K, Chen Y. Reliability and validity of an Internet traumatic stress survey with a college student sample. *J Trauma Stress.* 2006;19:709–720.
21. Jackson LA, Ervin KS, Gardner PD, Schmitt N. Gender and the Internet: women communicating and men searching. *Sex Roles.* 2001;44:363–379.
22. Miller LM, Schweingruber H, Bradenberg CL. Middle school student's technological practices and preferences: reexamining gender differences. *J Educ Multimedia Hypermedia.* 2001;10:125–140.
23. Morahan-Martin J. Males, females and the Internet. In: Gackenback J, ed. *Psychology and the Internet.* San Diego, CA: Academic Press; 1999:169–197.
24. Sherman RC, End C, Kraan E, et al. The Internet gender gap among college students: forgotten but not gone? *Cyberpsychol Behav.* 2000;3:885–894.
25. Buchanan T, Smith JL. Using the Internet for psychological research: personality testing on the World Wide Web. *Br J Psychol.* 1999;90:125–144.
26. Joinson A. Social desirability, anonymity, and Internet-based questionnaires. *Behav Res Methods Instrum Comput.* 1999;31:433–434.

Analysis of the Study

PURPOSE

Though stated as the "objective," the purpose is clear—to assess Internet use, abuse, and dependence. Another purpose appears to be adding to a larger study of Internet versus paper completion of surveys. There seem to be no problems of confidentiality or deception. Possible risk was addressed by providing referrals.

JUSTIFICATION/PRIOR RESEARCH

The study justification is embedded in the extensive sections on prior research. It consists of evidence of increasing Internet use by college students and studies suggesting detrimental effects. Presumably, this study was intended to add to and clarify these findings.

DEFINITIONS

Terms are not specifically defined, but we think the primary ones, Internet *abuse* and *dependence* and *depression*, are sufficiently clarified by operational definitions. Many other terms pertaining to demographics and Internet use seem straightforward and are also defined operationally.

HYPOTHESES

None is stated. The principal implied hypothesis appears to be that greater Internet abuse and dependence are causally related to greater depression, a directional hypothesis. Other implied hypotheses are that abuse and dependence are related to amount of Internet use as well as to specific Internet uses and to sex.

SAMPLE

The convenience sample was recruited from introductory psychology classes by offering class credit. The final sample of 411 is satisfactorily large and described as to sex, age, ethnicity, state of origin, and college class, which is helpful in judging generalizability. Data on Internet use collected as part of the study indicate higher usage than an earlier study (90 percent vs. 73 percent).

INSTRUMENTATION

Instrumentation consisted of several sets of questionnaire items using different formats apparently combined into one instrument. The items for sociability, preferred social contexts, and preferred therapy format are provided. Another set of items assessing Internet reasons for use and services used is shown and reported to have internal consistency reliability of .62. We do not agree that this is acceptable for use as a total score; however, data analysis indicates that analysis was done by item as with most of the other preceding sets. A limitation of such analyses is the questionable reliability of single items. Internet abuse and dependence were assessed with a nine-item set of questions based on preexisting criteria for substance abuse and dependence. Rather than a total score, these items were used to divide respondents into abuser–nonabuser and dependent–nondependent. This practice of changing a quantitative into a categorical variable is usually not recommended but seems justified in this case (see text, p. 80).

An existing scale, CES-D was used to measure depression. It is stated to have high internal consistency, moderate retest reliability, and concurrent and construct validity, but no evidence is provided. It should be, especially because the validity of self-report scales is always suspect, especially with such questions.

PROCEDURES/RESULTS AND INTERNAL VALIDITY

Procedures consisted of administering the questionnaire to half the sample on paper, the other half via the Internet per instructions. Separation into groups was based on "the data collection session they attended." It is not clear whether this was done randomly, or how many sessions were involved. The two groups are said to not differ on "key" (unspecified) demographic variables or on time spent on the Internet. They also showed only slight differences on the other variables studied, justifying combining groups for subsequent analyses.

The study used three research methods—survey with respect to descriptive results, causal-comparative, and correlational with respect to relationships among variables. Within the causal-comparative method, three types are evident: type 1 (effects of sex), type 3 (effects of administration type), and a combination of types 1 and 2 (causes and effects of abuse and dependency). These and the correlation analyses raise questions of internal validity of which "subject characteristics" is the most important.

None of the reported correlations is large enough (despite "significance" with such a large sample) to warrant further discussion, even as being of theoretical interest (see text, p. 341).

Of the causal/comparative results, our calculation of Effect Sizes (Δ) shows the only differences between sexes reaching the customary level of .50 (see text, p. 248) indicate males more often using the Internet to access sexual, illegal, or immoral materials, chat rooms, and multigroup games. Although sex can be justified as a predictor of these behaviors for this sample, other possible causes such as differences in child rearing, cannot be ruled out.

With respect to the variables of Internet abuse and dependence the only Effect Sizes over .50 indicate that both groups spent more time on line than nonabusers and nondependents. It would be expected that those dependent on the Internet would spend more time on it, as would the reverse. It seems unlikely that perceived abuse would cause greater use, leading us to tentatively conclude that greater usage leads to more abuse—though other variables may cause both.

Contingency coefficients (see text, pp. 238, 257) calculated from the chi squares provided resulted in moderate correlations (over .44) indicating that abusers were more likely to use the Internet to "maintain relationships," "meet people," "socially experiment," "seek illegal/immoral material," and use chat rooms and play games. Those exhibiting dependence showed similar but not identical results. These relationships are not discussed or interpreted.

DATA ANALYSIS, DISCUSSION, AND INTERPRETATION

The methods used in data analysis are technically appropriate. Our concern is with the all too common reliance on inference techniques in assessing and interpreting data. We think this resulted in making too much of many very small relationships—correlations less than .20 and Effect Sizes under .50. In our opinion, this resulted in too little attention to a stronger and potentially important relationship, (an effect size of .60), indicating that more time on the Internet is likely to result in more perceived Internet abuse, i.e., "failure to fulfill major responsibilities," and "continuing to use the Internet despite recurrent social problems caused or increased by Internet use." We would suggest that future research pursue this finding and, in particular, by using other than the self-report questionnaire (such as in-depth interviews) to study Internet abuse and its causes and effects.

Although we agree with most of the stated implications and suggestions for future research, we do not see that most follow from the results of this study.

Go back to the **INTERACTIVE AND APPLIED LEARNING** feature at the beginning of the chapter for a listing of interactive and applied activities. Go to the **Online Learning Center** at **www.mhhe.com/fraenkel9e** to take quizzes, practice with key terms, and review chapter content.

Main Points

THE NATURE OF CAUSAL-COMPARATIVE RESEARCH

- Causal-comparative research, like correlational research, seeks to identify associations among variables.
- Causal-comparative research attempts to determine the cause or consequences of differences that already exist between or among groups of individuals.
- The basic causal-comparative approach is to begin with a noted difference between two groups and then to look for possible causes for, or consequences of, this difference.
- There are three types of causal-comparative research (exploration of effects, exploration of causes, and exploration of consequences), which differ in their purposes and structure.
- When an experiment would take a considerable length of time and be quite costly to conduct, a causal-comparative study is sometimes used as an alternative.
- As in correlational studies, relationships can be identified in a causal-comparative study, but causation cannot be fully established.

CAUSAL-COMPARATIVE VERSUS CORRELATIONAL RESEARCH

- The basic similarity between causal-comparative and correlational studies is that both seek to explore relationships among variables. When relationships are identified through causal-comparative research (or in correlational research), they often are studied at a later time by means of experimental research.

CAUSAL-COMPARATIVE VERSUS EXPERIMENTAL RESEARCH

- In experimental research, the group membership variable is manipulated; in causal-comparative research, the group differences already exist.

STEPS IN CAUSAL-COMPARATIVE RESEARCH

- The first step in formulating a problem in causal-comparative research is usually to identify and define the particular phenomena of interest and then to consider possible causes for, or consequences of, these phenomena.
- The most important task in selecting a sample for a causal-comparative study is to define carefully the characteristic to be studied and then to select groups that differ in this characteristic.
- There are no limits to the kinds of instruments that can be used in a causal-comparative study.
- The basic causal-comparative design involves selecting two groups that differ on a particular variable of interest and then comparing them on another variable or variables.

THREATS TO INTERNAL VALIDITY IN CAUSAL-COMPARATIVE RESEARCH

- Two weaknesses in causal-comparative research are lack of randomization and inability to manipulate an independent variable.
- A major threat to the internal validity of a causal-comparative study is the possibility of a subject selection bias. The chief procedures that a researcher can use to reduce this threat include matching subjects on a related variable, creating homogeneous subgroups, and using the technique of statistical matching.
- Other threats to internal validity in causal-comparative studies include location, instrumentation, and loss of subjects. In addition, type 3 studies are subject to implementation, history, maturation, attitude of subjects, regression, and testing threats.

DATA ANALYSIS IN CAUSAL-COMPARATIVE STUDIES

- The first step in a data analysis of a causal-comparative study is to construct frequency polygons.
- Means and standard deviations are usually calculated if the variables involved are quantitative.
- The most commonly used test in causal-comparative studies is a *t*-test for differences between means.
- Analysis of covariance is particularly useful in causal-comparative studies.
- The results of causal-comparative studies should always be interpreted with caution, because they do not prove cause and effect.

ASSOCIATIONS BETWEEN CATEGORICAL VARIABLES

- Both crossbreak tables and contingency coefficients can be used to investigate possible associations between categorical variables, although predictions from crossbreak tables are not precise. Fortunately, there are relatively few questions of interest in education that involve two categorical variables.

For Discussion

1. Suppose a researcher was interested in finding out what factors cause delinquent behavior in teenagers. What might be a suitable comparison group for the researcher to use in investigating this question?
2. Could observation be used in a causal-comparative study? If so, how?
3. When, if ever, might a researcher prefer to conduct a causal-comparative study rather than an experimental study? Suggest an example.
4. What sorts of questions might lend themselves better to causal-comparative research than to experimental research? Why?
5. Which do you think would be easier to conduct, causal-comparative or experimental research? Why?
6. Is random assignment possible in causal-comparative research? What about random selection? Explain.
7. Suppose a researcher was interested in the effects of team teaching on student attitudes toward history. Could such a topic be studied by means of causal-comparative research? If so, how?
8. What sorts of variables might it be wise for a researcher to think about controlling for in a causal-comparative study? What sorts of variables, if any, might be irrelevant?
9. Might a researcher ever study the same variables in an experimental study that he or she studied in a causal-comparative study? If so, why?
10. We state in the text that, in general, quantitative variables should not be collapsed into categorical variables because (a) the decision to do so is almost always an arbitrary one and (b) too much information is lost by doing so. Can you suggest any quantitative variables that, for these reasons, should not be collapsed into categorical variables? Can you suggest some quantitative variables that could justifiably be treated as categorical variables?
11. Suppose a researcher reports a higher incidence of childhood sexual abuse in adult women who have eating disorders than in a comparison group of women without eating disorders. Which variable is more likely to be the cause of the other? What other variables could be alternative or contributing causes?
12. Are there any research questions that cannot be studied by the causal-comparative method?
13. A professor at a private women's college wishes to assess the degree of alienation present in undergraduates as compared to graduate students at her institution. She will use an instrument that she has developed.
    a. Which method, causal-comparative or experimental, would you recommend she use in her inquiry? Why?
    b. Would the fact that the researcher plans to use an instrument that she herself developed make any difference in your recommendation?

Reference

1. The interested reader is referred to Miller, G. A., & Chapman, J. P. (2001). Misunderstanding analysis of covariance. *Journal of Abnormal Psychology, 110*(1), 40–48.

17 Survey Research

What Is a Survey?
Why Are Surveys Conducted?
Types of Surveys
Cross-Sectional Surveys
Longitudinal Surveys
Survey Research and Correlational Research
Steps in Survey Research
Defining the Problem
Identifying the Target Population
Choosing the Mode of Data Collection
Selecting the Sample
Preparing the Instrument
Preparing the Cover Letter
Training Interviewers
Using an Interview to Measure Ability
Nonresponse
Total Nonresponse
Item Nonresponse
Problems in the Instrumentation Process in Survey Research
Evaluating Threats to Internal Validity in Survey Research
Data Analysis in Survey Research
An Example of Survey Research
Analysis of the Study
Purpose/Justification
Definitions
Prior Research
Hypotheses
Sample
Instrumentation
Procedures/Internal Validity
Data Analysis/Results/Interpretation

OBJECTIVES **Studying this chapter should enable you to:**

- Explain what a survey is.
- Name three types of surveys conducted in educational research.
- Explain the purpose of surveys.
- Explain the difference between a cross-sectional and a longitudinal survey.
- Describe how survey research differs from other types of research.
- Describe briefly how mail surveys, telephone surveys, and face-to-face interviews differ and state two advantages and disadvantages of each type.
- Describe the most common pitfalls in developing survey questions.
- Explain the difference between a closed-ended and an open-ended question.
- Explain why nonresponse is a problem in survey research and name two ways to improve the rate of response in surveys.
- Name two threats to instrument validity that can affect survey results. Explain how such threats can be controlled.
- Describe possible threats to internal validity in survey research.
- Recognize an example of survey research when you come across it in the educational literature.

INTERACTIVE AND APPLIED LEARNING After, or while, reading this chapter:

Go to the Online Learning Center at www.mhhe.com/fraenkel9e to:

- Learn More About Taking a Census

Go to your online Student Mastery Activities book to do the following activities:

- Activity 17.1: Survey Research Questions
- Activity 17.2: Types of Surveys
- Activity 17.3: Open- vs. Closed-Ended Questions
- Activity 17.4: Conduct a Survey

Tom Martinez, the principal of Grover Creek High School, is meeting with his vice principal, Jesse Sullivan. "I wish I knew how more of the faculty felt about this after-school detention program we've implemented this year," says Tom. "Jose Alcazar stopped me in the hall yesterday to say he thinks it's not working."

"Why?"

"He says many of the faculty think it doesn't do any good, so they don't even bother to send any students there."

"Really?" answers Jesse. "I've heard just the opposite. Just today, at lunch, Becky and Felicia were saying they think it's great!"

"Hmm, that's interesting. It seems we need more data."

A survey is an appropriate way for Tom and Jesse to get such data. How to conduct a survey is what this chapter is about.

What Is a Survey?

Researchers are often interested in the opinions of a large group of people about a particular topic or issue. They ask a number of questions, all related to the issue, to find answers. For example, imagine that the chairperson of the counseling department at a large university is interested in determining how students who are seeking a master's degree feel about the program. She decides to conduct a survey to find out. She selects a sample of 50 students from among those currently enrolled in the master's degree program and constructs questions designed to elicit their attitudes toward the program. She administers the questions to each of the 50 students in the sample in face-to-face interviews over a two-week period. The responses given by each student in the sample are coded into standardized categories for purposes of analysis, and these standardized records are then analyzed to provide descriptions of the students in the sample. The chairperson draws some conclusions about the opinions of the sample, which she then generalizes to the population from which the sample was selected, in this case, all of the graduate students seeking a master's degree in counseling from this university.

This example illustrates the three major characteristics that most surveys possess.

1. Information is collected from a group of people in order to *describe* some aspects or characteristics (such as abilities, opinions, attitudes, beliefs, and/or knowledge) of the population of which that group is a part.
2. The main way in which the information is collected is through *asking questions;* the answers to these questions by the members of the group constitute the data of the study.
3. Information is collected from a *sample* rather than from every member of the population.

Why Are Surveys Conducted?

The major purpose of surveys is to describe the characteristics of a population. In essence, what researchers want to find out is how the members of a population distribute themselves on one or more variables (e.g., age, ethnicity, religious preference, attitudes toward school). As in other types of research, of course, the population as a whole is rarely studied. Instead, a carefully selected sample of respondents is surveyed and a description of the population is inferred from what is found out about the sample.

For example, a researcher might be interested in describing how certain characteristics (age, gender, ethnicity, political involvement, and so on) of teachers in inner-city high schools are distributed within the group. The researcher would select a sample of teachers from inner-city high schools to survey. Generally, in a descriptive survey such as this, researchers are not so much concerned with why the observed distribution exists as with what the distribution *is*.

Types of Surveys

There are two major types of surveys—a cross-sectional survey and a longitudinal survey.

CROSS-SECTIONAL SURVEYS

A **cross-sectional survey** collects information from a sample that has been drawn from a predetermined population. Furthermore, the information is collected at just one point in time, although the time it takes to collect all of the data may take anywhere from a day to a few weeks or more. Thus, a professor of mathematics might collect data from a sample of all the high school mathematics teachers in a particular state about their interests in earning a master's degree in mathematics from his university, or another researcher might take a survey of the kinds of personal problems experienced by students at 10, 13, and 16 years of age. All these groups could be surveyed at approximately the same point in time.

When an entire population is surveyed, it is called a **census**. The prime example is the census conducted by the U.S. Bureau of the Census every 10 years, which attempts to collect data about everyone in the United States.

LONGITUDINAL SURVEYS

In a **longitudinal survey**, on the other hand, information is collected at different points in time to study changes over time. Three longitudinal designs are commonly employed in survey research: trend studies, cohort studies, and panel studies.

In a **trend study**, different samples from a population whose members may change are surveyed at different points in time. For example, a researcher might be interested in the attitudes of high school principals toward the use of flexible scheduling. He would select a sample each year from a current listing of high school principals throughout the state. Although the population would change somewhat and the same individuals would not be sampled each year, if random selection were used to obtain the samples, the responses obtained each year could be considered representative of the population of high school principals. The researcher would then examine and compare responses from year to year to see whether any trends were apparent.

Whereas a trend study samples a population whose members may change over time, a **cohort study** samples a particular population whose members do not change over the course of the survey. Thus, a researcher might want to study growth in teaching effectiveness of all the first-year teachers who had graduated in the past year from San Francisco State University. The names of all of these teachers would be listed, and then a different sample would be selected from this listing at different times.

In a **panel study**, on the other hand, the researcher surveys the *same* sample of individuals at different times during the course of the survey. Because the researcher is studying the same individuals, she can note changes in their characteristics or behavior and explore the reasons for these changes. Thus, the researcher in our previous example might select a sample of last year's graduates from San Francisco State University who are first-year teachers and survey the same individuals several times during the teaching year. Loss of individuals is a frequent problem in panel studies, however, particularly if the study extends over a fairly long period of time.

Following are the titles of some published reports of surveys that have been conducted by educational researchers:

- "What Does It Mean to Be African-American?"[1]
- "Can Teacher Education Make a Difference?"[2]
- "What Makes Professional Development Effective?"[3]
- "The Reading Habits and Literacy Attitudes of In-Service and Prospective Teachers"[4]
- "'You're Only Young Once': Things College Students Report Doing Now Before It Is Too Late"[5]
- "An Investigation into Teacher Turnover in International Schools"[6]
- "Integrating Technology into Preservice Literacy Instruction: A Survey of Elementary Education Students' Attitudes Toward Computers"[7]
- "Reflections on Surveys of Faculty Attitudes Toward Collaboration with Librarians"[8]

Survey Research and Correlational Research

It is not uncommon for researchers to examine the relationship of responses to one question in a survey to another, or of a score based on one set of survey questions to a score based on another set. In such instances, the techniques of correlational research described in Chapter 15 are appropriate.

Suppose a researcher is interested in studying the relationship between attitude toward school of high school students and their outside-of-school interests. A questionnaire containing items dealing with these two variables could be prepared and administered to a sample of high school students, and then relationships could be determined by calculating correlation coefficients or by preparing contingency tables. The researcher may find that students who have a positive attitude toward school also have a lot of outside interests, while those who have a negative attitude toward school have few outside interests.

Steps in Survey Research

DEFINING THE PROBLEM

The problem to be investigated by means of a survey should be sufficiently interesting and important to motivate individuals to respond. Trivial questions usually get what they deserve—they're tossed into the nearest wastebasket. You have probably done this yourself to a survey questionnaire you considered unimportant or found boring.

Researchers need to define clearly their objectives in conducting a survey. Each question should relate to one or more of the survey's objectives. One strategy for defining survey questions is to use a hierarchical approach, beginning with the broadest, most general questions and ending with the most specific. Jaeger[9] gives a detailed example of such a survey on the question of why many public school teachers "burn out" and leave the profession within a few years. He suggests three general factors—economics, working conditions, and perceived social status—around which to structure possible questions for the survey. Here are the questions he developed with regard to economic factors.

I. Do economic factors cause teachers to leave the profession early?
   A. Do teachers leave the profession early because of inadequate yearly income?
      1. Do teachers leave the profession early because their monthly income during the school year is too small?
      2. Do teachers leave the profession early because they are not paid during the summer months?
      3. Do teachers leave the profession early because their salary forces them to hold a second job during the school year?
      4. Do teachers leave the profession early because their lack of income forces them to hold a different job during the summer months?
   B. Do teachers leave the profession early because of the structure of their pay scale?
      1. Do teachers leave the profession early because the upper limit on their pay scale is too low?
      2. Do teachers leave the profession early because their rate of progress on the pay scale is too slow?
   C. Do teachers leave the profession early because of inadequate fringe benefits?
      1. Do teachers leave the profession early because their health insurance benefits are inadequate?
      2. Do teachers leave the profession early because their life insurance benefits are inadequate?
      3. Do teachers leave the profession early because their retirement benefits are inadequate?

A hierarchical set of research questions like this can help researchers identify large categories of issues, suggest more specific issues within each category, and conceive possible questions. By determining whether a proposed question fits the purposes of the intended survey, researchers can eliminate those that do not. This is important, since the length of a survey's questionnaire or interview schedule is a crucial factor in determining the survey's success.

IDENTIFYING THE TARGET POPULATION

Almost anything can be described by means of a survey. That which is studied in a survey is called the **unit of analysis**. Although typically people, units of analysis can also be objects, clubs, companies, classrooms, schools, government agencies, and others. For example, in a survey of faculty opinion about a new discipline policy recently instituted in a particular school district, each faculty member sampled and surveyed would be the unit of analysis. In a survey of urban school districts, the school district would be the unit of analysis.

Survey data are collected from a number of individual units of analysis to describe those units; these descriptions are then summarized to describe the population that the units of analysis represent. In the example given, data collected from a sample of faculty members (the unit of analysis) would be summarized to describe the population that this sample represents (all of the faculty members in that particular school district).

As in other types of research, the group of persons (objects, institutions, and so on) that is the focus of the study is called the *target population.* To make trustworthy statements about the target population, it must be very well defined. In fact, it must be so well defined that it is possible to state with certainty whether or not a particular unit of analysis is a member of this population. Suppose, for example, that the target population is defined as "all of the faculty members in a particular school district." Is this definition sufficiently clear so that one can state with certainty who is or is not a member of this population? At first glance, you may be tempted to say yes. But what about administrators who also teach? What about substitute teachers, or those who teach only part-time? What about student teachers? What about counselors? Unless the target population is defined in sufficient detail so that it is unequivocally clear as to who is, or is not, a member of it, any statements made about this population, based on a survey of a sample of it, may be misleading or incorrect.

CHOOSING THE MODE OF DATA COLLECTION

There are several ways to collect data in a survey: by administering the survey instrument "live" to a group, by telephone, by Internet, by mail, or through face-to-face interviews. Table 17.1 presents a summary of advantages and disadvantages of these methods.

Direct Administration to a Group. This method is used whenever a researcher has access to all (or most) of the members of a particular group in one place. The instrument is administered to all members of the group at the same time and usually in the same place. Examples would include giving questionnaires to students to complete in their classrooms or workers to complete at their job settings. The chief advantage of this approach is the high rate of response—often close to 100 percent (usually in a single setting). Other advantages include a generally low cost factor, plus the fact that the researcher has an opportunity to explain the study and answer any questions that the respondents may have before they complete the questionnaire. The chief disadvantage is that there are not many types of surveys that can use samples of individuals that are collected together as a group.

Telephone Surveys. In a telephone survey the researcher (or his or her assistants) asks questions of the respondents over the telephone. The advantages of telephone surveys are they are cheaper than personal interviews, can be conducted fairly quickly, and lend

TABLE 17.1 *Advantages and Disadvantages of Survey Data Collection Methods*

	Direct Administration	Telephone	Internet or Mail	Interview
Comparative cost	Lowest	Intermediate	Internet=Low; Mail=High	Highest
Facilities needed?	Yes	No	No	Yes
Require training of questioner?	Yes	Yes	No	Yes
Data-collection time	Shortest	Short	Longer	Longest
Response rate	Very high	Good	Poorest	Very high
Group administration possible?	Yes	No	No	Yes
Allow for random sampling?	Possibly	Yes	Yes	Yes
Require literate sample?	Yes	No	Yes	No
Permit follow-up questions?	No	Yes	No	Yes
Encourage response to sensitive topics?	Somewhat	Somewhat	Best	Weak
Standardization of responses	Easy	Somewhat	Easy	Hardest

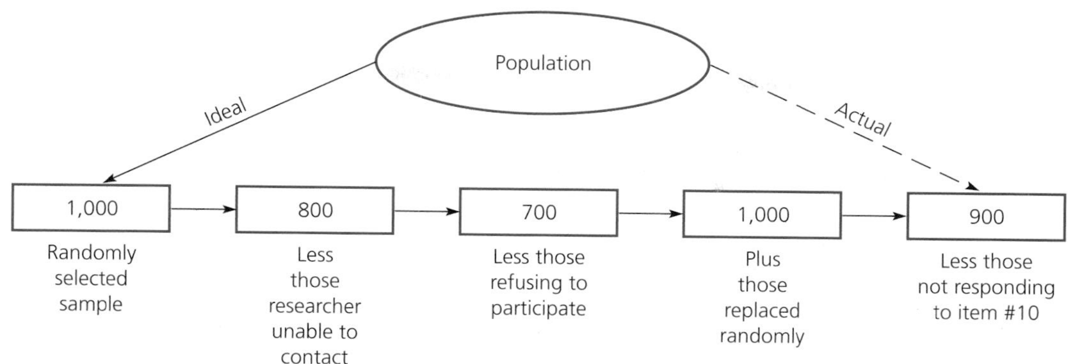

Figure 17.1 *Example of an Ideal Versus an Actual Telephone Sample for a Specific Question*

themselves easily to standardized questioning procedures. They also allow the researcher to assist the respondent (by clarifying questions, asking follow-up questions, encouraging hesitant respondents, and so on), permit a greater amount of follow-up (through several callbacks), and provide better coverage in certain areas where personal interviewers often are reluctant to go.*

The disadvantages of telephone surveys are that access to some samples (obviously, those without telephones and those whose phone numbers are unlisted) is not possible. Telephone interviews also prevent visual observation of respondents and are somewhat less effective in obtaining information about sensitive issues or personal questions. Generally, telephone surveys are reported to result in a 5 percent lower response rate than that obtained by personal interviews.[10] Figure 17.1 illustrates the difficulty sometimes encountered when obtaining a research sample by telephone.

Internet Surveys. Technological advances have made administering surveys on the Internet quite common. Increasingly, researchers and students are turning to Web-based software and services to collect survey data from their target population out of convenience. Other advantages of Web surveys include greater access to distant and hard-to-reach participants, lower costs, faster turnaround, multimedia interface, mobile administration (using portable devices), and reduced data entry. Disadvantages can include lower response rates and invalid data due to speedy entry facilitated by computers. Currently, there are dozens of Internet companies offering Web survey software packages and services. SurveyMonkey and Qualtrics, for example, are popular Web-based survey companies that allow users to design their own basic surveys for free. See Figure 17.2 for an example of an online survey created using SurveyMonkey. Additional services like survey administration and data analysis can be purchased for a nominal fee. Figure 17.3 shows an example of a data analysis report generated from the survey questions in Figure 17.2.

Mail Surveys. When the data in a survey are collected by mail, the questionnaire is sent to each individual in the sample, with a request that it be completed and then returned by a given date. The advantages of this approach are that it is relatively inexpensive and it can be accomplished by the researcher alone (or with only a few assistants). It also allows the researcher to have access to samples that might be hard to reach in person or by telephone (such as the elderly), and it permits the respondents to take sufficient time to give thoughtful answers to the questions asked.

The disadvantages of mail surveys are that there is less opportunity to encourage the cooperation of the respondents (e.g., through building rapport) or to provide assistance (through answering their questions, clarifying

*Computers are being used more in telephone surveys. Typically, an interviewer sits in front of a computer screen. A central computer randomly selects a telephone number and dials it. The interviewer, wearing a headset, hears the respondent answer the phone. On the computer screen appears a typed introduction, such as "Hello, my name is ______," for the interviewer to read, followed by the first question. The interviewer then types the respondent's answer into the computer. The answer is immediately stored inside the central computer. The next question to be asked then appears on the screen, and the interviewer continues the questioning.

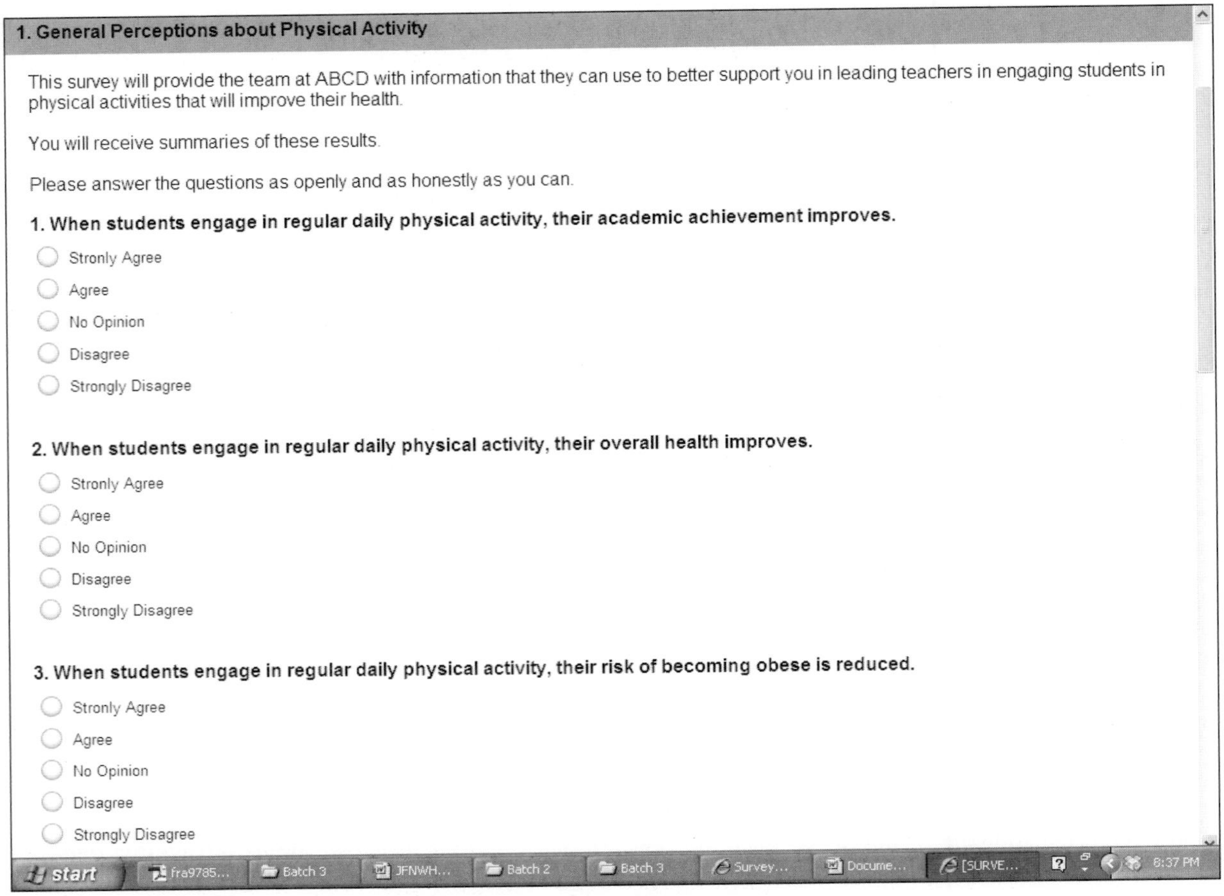

1. General Perceptions about Physical Activity

This survey will provide the team at ABCD with information that they can use to better support you in leading teachers in engaging students in physical activities that will improve their health.

You will receive summaries of these results.

Please answer the questions as openly and as honestly as you can.

1. When students engage in regular daily physical activity, their academic achievement improves.

- Stronly Agree
- Agree
- No Opinion
- Disagree
- Strongly Disagree

2. When students engage in regular daily physical activity, their overall health improves.

- Stronly Agree
- Agree
- No Opinion
- Disagree
- Strongly Disagree

3. When students engage in regular daily physical activity, their risk of becoming obese is reduced.

- Stronly Agree
- Agree
- No Opinion
- Disagree
- Strongly Disagree

start fra9785... Batch 3 JFNWH... Batch 2 Batch 3 Survey... Docume... [SURVE... 8:37 PM

Figure 17.2 *Example of an Internet Survey Created on SurveyMonkey*

instructions, and so on). As a result, mail surveys have a tendency to produce low response rates. Mail surveys also do not lend themselves well to obtaining information from certain types of samples (such as individuals who are illiterate).

Personal Interviews. In a personal interview, the researcher (or trained assistant) conducts a face-to-face interview with the respondent. As a result, this method has many advantages. It is probably the most effective survey method for enlisting the cooperation of the respondents. Rapport can be established, questions can be clarified, unclear or incomplete answers can be followed up, and so on. Face-to-face interviewing also places less of a burden on the reading and writing skills of the respondents and, when necessary, permits spending more time with respondents.

The biggest disadvantage of face-to-face interviews is that they are more costly than direct, mail, or telephone surveys. They also require a trained staff of interviewers, with all that implies in terms of training costs and time. The total data collection time required is also likely to be quite a bit longer than in any of the other three methods. It is possible, too, that the lack of anonymity (the respondent is obviously known to the interviewer, at least temporarily) may result in less valid responses to personally sensitive questions. Last, some types of samples (individuals in high-crime areas, workers in large corporations, students, and so on) are often difficult to contact in sufficient numbers.

SELECTING THE SAMPLE

The subjects to be surveyed should be selected (randomly, if possible) from the population of interest.

Important Findings in Survey Research

Probably the most famous example of survey research was that done by the sociologist Alfred Kinsey and his associates on the sexual behavior of American men (1948)* and women (1953).† While these studies are best known for their shocking (at the time) findings concerning the frequency of various sexual behaviors, they are equally noteworthy for their methodological competence. Using very large (although not random) samples totaling some 12,000 men and 8,000 women, Kinsey and his associates were meticulous in comparing results from different samples (replication) and in examining reliability through retesting and validity through internal cross-checking and comparison with spouses or other partners. One of the more unusual aspects of the basic data-gathering process—individual interviews—was the interview schedule that contained 521 items (although the minimum per respondent was 300). The same information was elicited in several different questions, all asked in rapid-fire succession so as to minimize conscious distortion.

A more recent study came to somewhat different conclusions regarding sexual behavior. The researchers used an interview procedure very similar to that used in the Kinsey studies, but claimed a superior sampling procedure. They selected a random sample of 4,369 adults from a list of nationwide home addresses, with the household respondent also chosen at random. While the final participation rate of 79 percent (sample = 3,500) is high, 79 percent of a random sample is no longer a random sample.‡

*Kinsey, A. C., Pomeroy, W. B., & Martin, C. E. (1948). *Sexual behavior in the human male.* Philadelphia: Saunders.

†Kinsey, A. C., Pomeroy, W. B., Martin, C. E., & Gebhard, P. H. (1953). *Sexual behavior in the human female.* Philadelphia: Saunders.

‡Laumann, E., Michael, R., Michaels, S., & Gagnon, J. (1994). *The social organization of sexuality.* Chicago: University of Chicago Press.

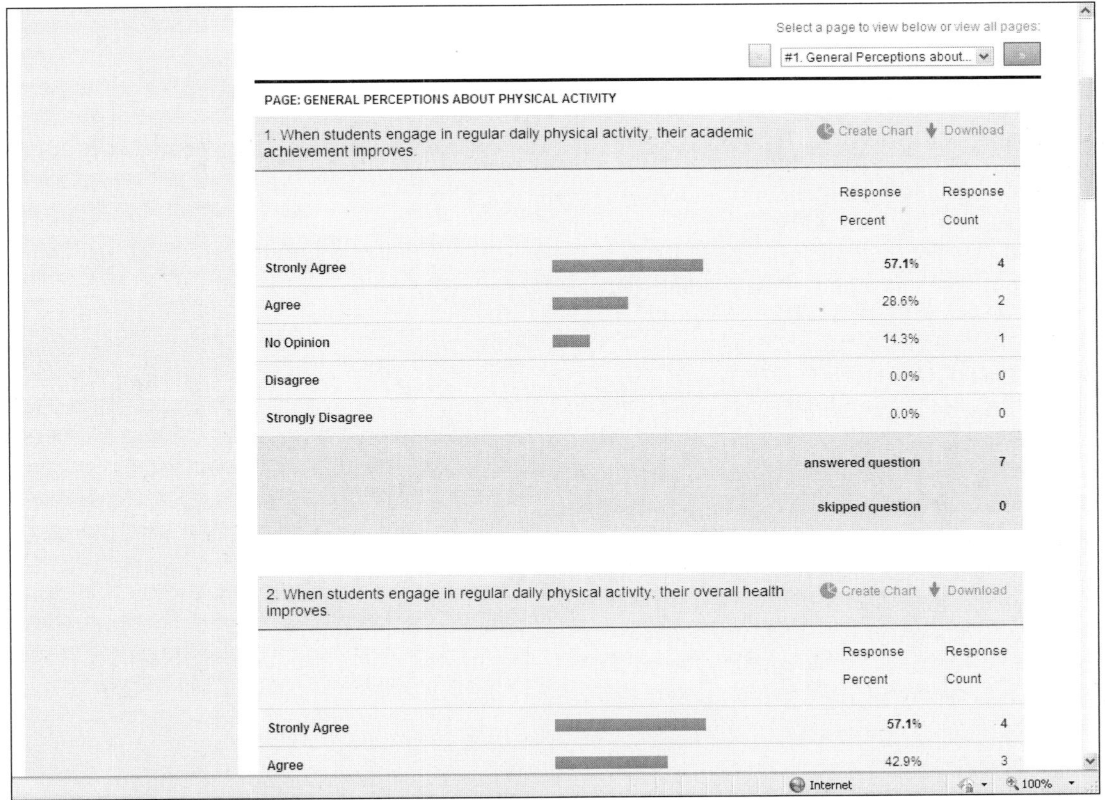

Figure 17.3 *Example of SurveyMonkey Data Results*

Researchers must ensure, however, that the subjects they intend to question possess the desired information and that they will be willing to answer these questions. Individuals who possess the necessary information but who are uninterested in the topic of the survey (or who do not see it as important) are unlikely to respond. Accordingly, it is often a good idea for researchers to conduct a preliminary inquiry among potential respondents to assess their receptivity. Frequently, in school-based surveys, a higher response rate can be obtained if a questionnaire is sent to persons in authority to administer to the potential respondents rather than sending it to the respondents themselves. For example, a researcher might ask classroom teachers to administer a questionnaire to their students rather than asking the students directly.

Some examples of samples that have been surveyed by educational researchers are:

- A sample of all students attending an urban university concerning their views on the adequacy of the general education program at the university.
- A sample of all faculty members in an inner-city high school district as to the changes needed to help "at-risk" students learn more effectively.
- A sample of all such students in the same district concerning their views on the same topic.
- A sample of all women school superintendents in a particular state concerning their views as to the problems they encounter in their administrations.
- A sample of all the counselors in a particular high school district concerning their perceptions as to the adequacy of the school counseling program.

PREPARING THE INSTRUMENT

The most common types of instruments used in survey research are the questionnaire and the **interview schedule** (see Chapter 7).* They are virtually identical, except that the questionnaire is usually self-administered by the respondent, while the interview schedule is administered verbally by the researcher (or trained assistant). In the case of a mailed or self-administered questionnaire, the appearance of the instrument is very important to the overall success of the study. It should be attractive and not too long,† and the questions should be as easy to answer as possible. The questions in a survey, and the way they are asked, are of crucial importance. Fowler points out that there are four practical standards that all survey questions should meet:

1. Is this a question that can be asked exactly the way it is written?
2. Is this a question that will mean the same thing to everyone?
3. Is this a question that people can answer?
4. Is this a question that people will be willing to answer, given the data collection procedures?[11]

The answers to each of the previous questions for every question in a survey should be yes. Any survey question that violates one or more of these standards should be rewritten.

In the case of a personal interview or a telephone survey, the manner of the questioner is of paramount importance. He or she must ask the questions in such a way that the subjects of the study want to respond.

In either case, the audience to whom the questions are to be directed should be clearly identified. Specialized or unusual words should be avoided if possible or, if they must be used, defined clearly in the instructions written on the instrument. The most important thing for researchers to keep in mind, however, is that whatever type of instrument is used, the *same* questions must be asked of all respondents in the sample. Furthermore, the conditions under which the questionnaire is administered or the interview is conducted should be as similar as possible for all respondents.

Types of Questions. The nature of the questions and the way they are asked are extremely important in survey research. Poorly worded questions can doom a survey to failure. Hence, they must be clearly written in a manner that is easily understandable by the respondents.[12]

Most surveys rely on multiple-choice or other forms of what are called **closed-ended questions**. Multiple-choice questions allow a respondent to select his or her answer from a number of options. They may be used to measure opinions, attitudes, or knowledge.

*Tests of various types can also be used in survey research, as when a researcher uses them to describe the reading proficiency of students in a school district. We restrict our discussion here, however, to the description of preferences, opinions, and beliefs.

†This is very important. Long questionnaires discourage people from completing and returning them.

See Chapter 7 for examples of response scales typically used with survey questions.

Closed-ended questions are easy to use, score, and code for analysis on a computer. Because all subjects respond to the same options, standardized data are provided. They are somewhat more difficult to write than open-ended questions, however. They also pose the possibility that an individual's true response is not present among the options given. For this reason, the researcher usually should provide an "other" choice for each item, where the subject can write in a response that the researcher may not have anticipated. Some examples of closed-ended questions are:

1. Which subject do you like *least?*
   a Social studies
   b English
   c Science
   d Mathematics
   e Other (specify)
2. Rate each of the following parts of your master's degree program by circling the number under the phrase that describes how you feel.

	Very dissatisfied	Dissatisfied	Satisfied	Very satisfied
a. Coursework	1	2	3	4
b. Professors	1	2	3	4
c. Advising	1	2	3	4
d. Requirements	1	2	3	4
e. Cost	1	2	3	4
f. Other (specify)	1	2	3	4

Open-ended questions allow for more individualized responses, but they are sometimes difficult to interpret. They are also often hard to score, since so many different kinds of responses are received. Furthermore, respondents sometimes do not like them. Some examples of open-ended questions are:

1. What characteristics of a person would lead you to rate him or her as a good administrator?
2. What do you consider to be the most important problem facing classroom teachers in high schools today?
3. What were the three things about this class you found most useful during the past semester?

Generally, therefore, closed-ended or short-answer questions are preferable, although sometimes researchers find it useful to combine both formats in a single question, as shown in the following example of a question using both open- and closed-ended formats:

1. Please rate and comment on each of the following aspects of this course:

	Very dissatisfied	Dissatisfied	Satisfied	Very satisfied
a. Coursework	1	2	3	4
Comment ______________				
b. Professor	1	2	3	4
Comment ______________				

Table 17.2 presents a brief comparison of the advantages and disadvantages of closed-ended and open-ended questions.

TABLE 17.2 ***Advantages and Disadvantages of Closed-Ended Versus Open-Ended Questions***

Closed-Ended	Open-Ended
Advantages	
• Enhance consistency of response across respondents • Easier and faster to tabulate • More popular with respondents	• Allow more freedom of response • Easier to construct • Permit follow-up by interviewer
Disadvantages	
• May limit breadth of responses • Take more time to construct • Require more questions to cover the research topic	• Tend to produce responses that are inconsistent in length and content across respondents • Both questions and responses subject to misinterpretation • Harder to tabulate and synthesize

Some Suggestions for Improving Closed-Ended Questions. Researchers have found a number of relatively simple tips to be of value in writing good survey questions. A few of the most frequently mentioned ones follow:[13]

1. Be sure the question is *unambiguous*.
   Poor: Do you spend a lot of time studying?
   Better: How much time do you spend each day studying?
   a. More than two hours.
   b. One to two hours.
   c. Thirty minutes to one hour.
   d. Less than 30 minutes.
   e. Other (specify). _______________
2. Keep the focus as simple as possible.
   Poor: Who do you think are more satisfied with teaching in elementary and secondary schools, men or women?
   a. Men are more satisfied.
   b. Women are more satisfied.
   c. Men and women are about equally satisfied.
   d. Don't know.
   Better: Who do you think are more satisfied with teaching in elementary schools, men or women?
   a. Men are more satisfied.
   b. Women are more satisfied.
   c. Men and women are about equally satisfied.
   d. Don't know.
3. Keep the questions short.
   Poor: What part of the district's English curriculum, in your opinion, is of the most importance in terms of the overall development of the students in the program?
   Better: What part of the district's English curriculum is the most important?
4. Use common language.
   Poor: What do you think is the principal reason schools are experiencing increased student absenteeism today?
   a. Problems at home.
   b. Lack of interest in school.
   c. Illness.
   d. Don't know.
   Better: What do you think is the main reason students are absent more this year than previously?
   a. Problems at home.
   b. Lack of interest in school.
   c. Illness.
   d. Don't know.
5. Avoid the use of terms that might bias responses.
   Poor: Do you support the superintendent's "no smoking" policy on campus grounds while school is in session?
   a. I support the policy.
   b. I am opposed to the policy.
   c. I don't care one way or the other about the policy.
   d. I am undecided about the policy.
   Better: Do you support a "no smoking" policy on campus grounds while school is in session?
   a. I support the policy.
   b. I am opposed to the policy.
   c. I don't care one way or the other about the policy.
   d. I am undecided about the policy.
6. Avoid leading questions.
   Poor: What rules do you consider necessary in your classes?
   Better: Circle each of the following that describes a rule you set in your classes.
   a. All homework must be turned in on the date due.
   b. Students are not to interrupt other students during class discussions.
   c. Late homework is not accepted.
   d. Students are counted tardy if they are more than five minutes late to class.
   e. Other (specify). _______________
7. Avoid double negatives.
   Poor: Would you not be opposed to supervising students outside of your classroom?
   a. Yes.
   b. No.
   c. Undecided.
   Better: Would you be willing to supervise students outside of your classroom?
   a. Yes.
   b. No.
   c. Undecided.

"Next question: I believe that life is a constant striving for balance, requiring frequent tradeoffs between morality and necessity, within a cyclic pattern of joy and sadness, forging a trail of bittersweet memories until one slips, inevitably, into the jaws of death. Agree or disagree?"

Pretesting the Questionnaire. Once the questions to be included in the questionnaire or the interview schedule have been written, the researcher is well advised to try them out with a small sample similar to the potential respondents. A "pretest" of the questionnaire or interview schedule can reveal ambiguities, poorly worded questions, questions that are not understood, and unclear choices; it can also indicate whether the instructions to the respondents are clear. For more information on validating survey instruments, see Chapter 7 sections on "Validity, Reliability, and Objectivity" and also "Usability." In addition, see Chapter 8 on "Content-Related Evidence" (of validity).

Overall Format. The format of a questionnaire—how the questions look to the respondents—is very important in encouraging them to respond. Perhaps the most important rule to follow is to ensure that the questions are spread out—that is, uncluttered. No more than one question should be presented on a single line. When respondents have to spend a lot of time reading a question, they quickly become discouraged from continuing.

There are a variety of ways to present the response categories from which respondents are asked to choose. Babbie suggests that boxes, as shown in this question, are the best:[14]

Have you ever taught an advanced placement class?

[ ] Yes
[ ] No

Sometimes, certain questions will apply to only a portion of the subjects in the sample. When this is the case, follow-up questions can be included in the questionnaire. For example, a researcher might ask respondents if they are familiar with a particular activity, and then ask those who say yes to give their opinion of the activity. The follow-up question is called a **contingency question**—it is contingent upon how a respondent answers the first question. If properly used, contingency questions are a valuable survey tool, in that they can make it easier for a respondent to answer a given question and also improve the quality of the data a researcher receives. Although a variety of contingency formats may be used, the easiest to prepare is simply to set off the contingency question by indenting it, enclosing it in a box, and connecting it to the base question by means of an arrow to the appropriate response, as shown here:

Have you ever taught an advanced placement class?

[ ] Yes →
[ ] No

> If yes: Have you ever attended a workshop in which you received special training to teach such classes?
>
> [ ] Yes
> [ ] No

A clear and well-organized presentation of contingency questions is particularly important in interview schedules. An individual who receives a questionnaire in the mail can reread a question if it is unclear the first time through. If an interviewer becomes confused, however, or reads a question poorly or in an unclear manner, the whole interview may become jeopardized. Figure 17.4 illustrates a portion of an interview schedule that includes several contingency questions.

PREPARING THE COVER LETTER

Mailed surveys require something that telephone surveys and face-to-face personal interviews do not—a cover letter explaining the purpose of the questionnaire. Ideally, the cover letter also motivates the members of the sample to respond.

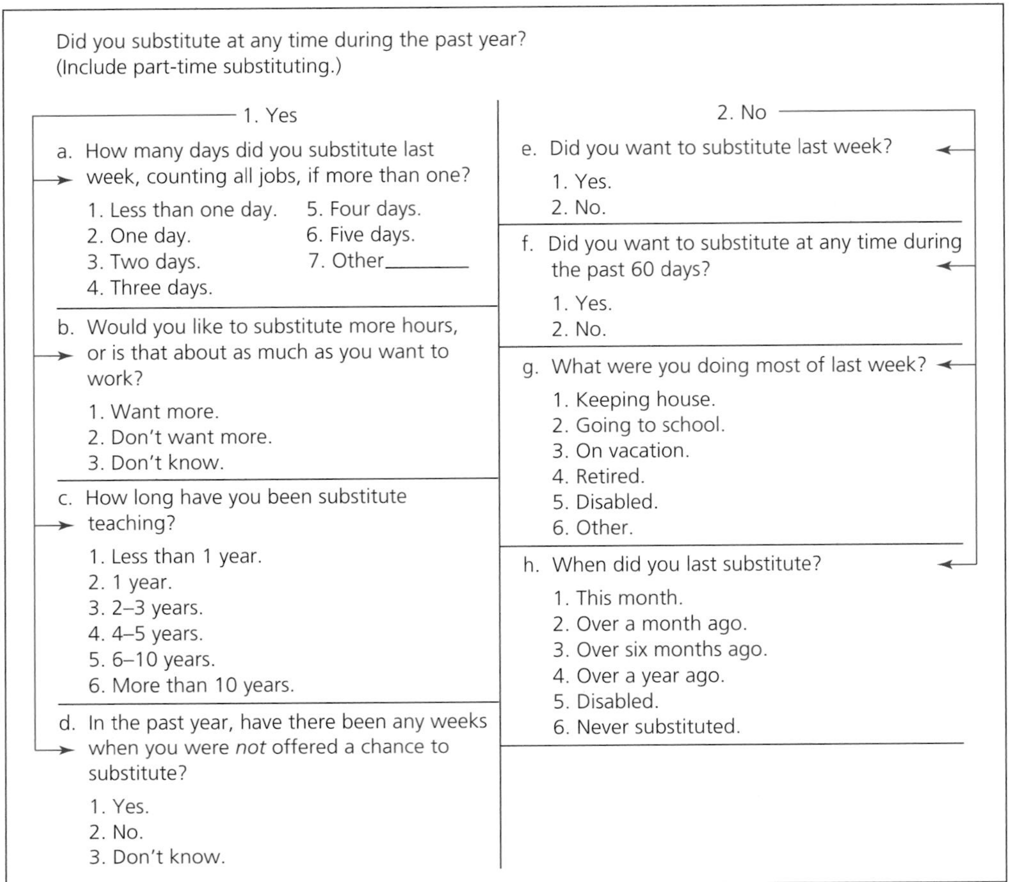

Did you substitute at any time during the past year?
(Include part-time substituting.)

1. Yes

a. How many days did you substitute last week, counting all jobs, if more than one?
1. Less than one day.
2. One day.
3. Two days.
4. Three days.
5. Four days.
6. Five days.
7. Other______

b. Would you like to substitute more hours, or is that about as much as you want to work?
1. Want more.
2. Don't want more.
3. Don't know.

c. How long have you been substitute teaching?
1. Less than 1 year.
2. 1 year.
3. 2–3 years.
4. 4–5 years.
5. 6–10 years.
6. More than 10 years.

d. In the past year, have there been any weeks when you were *not* offered a chance to substitute?
1. Yes.
2. No.
3. Don't know.

2. No

e. Did you want to substitute last week?
1. Yes.
2. No.

f. Did you want to substitute at any time during the past 60 days?
1. Yes.
2. No.

g. What were you doing most of last week?
1. Keeping house.
2. Going to school.
3. On vacation.
4. Retired.
5. Disabled.
6. Other.

h. When did you last substitute?
1. This month.
2. Over a month ago.
3. Over six months ago.
4. Over a year ago.
5. Disabled.
6. Never substituted.

Figure 17.4 *Example of Several Contingency Questions in an Interview Schedule*
Adapted from Babbie, E. S. (1973, p. 149). *Survey research methods.* Belmont, CA: Wadsworth.

The cover letter should be brief and addressed specifically to the individual being asked to respond. It should explain the purpose of the survey, emphasize the importance of the topic of the research, and (it is hoped) engage the respondent's cooperation. If possible, it should indicate the researcher's willingness to share the results of the study once it is completed. Confidentiality and anonymity of the respondents should be assured.* It also helps if the researcher obtains the sponsorship of an institution of some importance that is known to the respondent. The letter should specify the date by which the completed questionnaire is to be returned, and it should be individually signed by the researcher. Every effort should be made to avoid the appearance of a form letter. Finally, the return should be made as easy as possible; hence, enclosing a stamped, self-addressed envelope is always a good idea. Figure 17.5 presents an example of a cover letter.

TRAINING INTERVIEWERS

Both telephone and face-to-face interviewers need to be trained beforehand. Many suggestions have been made in this regard, and we have space to mention only a few of them here.[15] Telephone interviewers need to be shown how to engage their interviewees so that they do not hang up on them before the interview has even begun. They need to know how to explain quickly the purpose of their call and why it is important to obtain

*If done under a university (or other agency) sponsorship, the letter should indicate that the study has been approved by the "Research with Human Subjects" review committee.

COLLEGE OF EDUCATION

San Francisco State University

October 1, 2014

Mr. Robert R. Johnson
Social Studies Department
Oceana High School
Pacifica, California 96321

Dear Mr. Johnson,

The Department of Secondary Education of San Francisco State University prepares over 100 student teachers every year to teach in the public and private schools of California. It is our goal to help our graduates become as well prepared as possible to teach in today's schools. The enclosed questionnaire is designed to obtain your views on how to improve the quality of our training program. Your suggestions will be considered in planning for revisions in the program in the coming academic year. We will also provide you with a copy of the results of our study.

We will greatly appreciate it if you will complete the questionnaire and return it in the enclosed stamped, self-addressed envelope by October 18th. We realize your schedule is a busy one and that your time is valuable, but we are sure that you want to improve the quality of teacher training as much as we do. Your responses will be kept completely confidential; we ask for no identifying information on the questionnaire form. The study has been approved by the University's Research with Human Subjects review committee.

We want to thank you in advance for your cooperation.

William P. Jones
Chair of the Department

Figure 17.5 *Sample Cover Letter for a Mail Survey*

information from the respondent. They need to learn how to ask questions in a way that encourages interviewees to respond honestly.

Face-to-face interviewers need all of the preceding and more. They need to learn how to establish rapport with their interviewees and to put them at ease. If a respondent seems to be resistant to a particular line of questioning, the interviewer needs to know how to move on to a new set of questions and return to the previous questions later. The interviewer needs to know when and how to "follow up" on an unusual answer or one that is ambiguous or unclear. Interviewers also need training in gestures, manner, facial expression, and dress. A frown at the wrong time can discourage a respondent from even attempting to answer a question! In sum, the general topics to be covered in training interviewers should always include at least the following:

1. Procedures for contacting respondents and introducing the study. All interviewers should have a common understanding of the purposes of the study.
2. The conventions that are used in the design of the questionnaire with respect to wording and instructions for skipping questions (if necessary) so that interviewers can ask the questions in a consistent and standardized way.
3. Procedures for probing inadequate answers in a nondirective way. *Probing* refers to following up incomplete answers in ways that do not favor one particular answer over another. Certain kinds of standard probes, such as asking "Anything else?" "Tell me more," or "How do you mean that?" usually will handle most situations.
4. Procedures for recording answers to open-ended and closed-ended questions. This is especially important

with regard to answers to open-ended questions, which interviewers are expected to record verbatim.

5. Rules and guidelines for handling the interpersonal aspects of the interview in a nonbiased way. Of particular importance here is for interviewers to focus on the task at hand and to avoid expressing their views or opinions (verbally or with body language) on any of the questions being asked.[16]

USING AN INTERVIEW TO MEASURE ABILITY

Although the interview has been used primarily to obtain information on variables other than cognitive ability, an important exception can be found in the field of developmental and cognitive psychology. Interviews have been used extensively in this field to study both the content and processes of cognition. The best-known example of such use is to be found in the work of Jean Piaget and his colleagues. They used a semistructured sequence of contingency questions to determine a child's cognitive level of development.

Other psychologists have used interviewing procedures to study thought processes and sequences employed in problem solving. While not used extensively to date in educational research, an illustrative study is that of Freyberg and Osborne, who studied student understanding of basic science concepts. They found frequent and important misconceptions of which teachers were often unaware. Teachers often assumed that students used such terms as *gravity, condensation, conservation of energy,* and *wasteland community* in the same way as they did themselves. Many 10-year-olds and even some older children, for example, believed that condensation on the outside of a water glass was caused by water getting through the glass. One 15-year-old displayed ingenious (although incorrect) thinking as shown in the following excerpt:

> (Jenny, aged 15): Through the glass—the particles of water have gone through the glass, like diffusion through air—well, it hasn't got there any other way. (Researcher): A lot of younger people I have talked to have been worried about this water . . . it troubles them. (Jenny): Yes, because they haven't studied things like we have studied. (Researcher): What have you studied which helps? (Jenny): Things that pass through air, and concentrations and how things diffuse.[17]

Freyberg and Osborne make the argument that teachers and curriculum developers must have such information on student conceptions if they are to teach effectively. They have also shown how such research can improve the content of achievement tests by including items specifically directed at common misconceptions.

Nonresponse

In almost all surveys, some members of the sample will not respond. This is referred to as **nonresponse**. It may be due to a number of reasons (lack of interest in the topic being surveyed, forgetfulness, unwillingness to be surveyed, and so on), but it is a major problem that has been increasing in recent years as more and more people seem (for whatever reason) to be unwilling to participate in surveys.

Why is nonresponse a problem? The chief reason is that those who do not respond will very likely differ from the respondents on answers to the survey questions. Should this be the case, any conclusions drawn on the basis of the respondents' replies will be misleading and not a true indication of the views of the population from which the sample was drawn.

Increasingly, researchers are using incentives to improve survey return rates. For example, in their cover letter to prospective participants, besides describing the purpose of the survey, researchers might also add that respondents may receive gift cards or prizes for returning their surveys. For academic projects where budgets are considerably smaller, student and faculty researchers may offer an executive summary of findings to participants or the promise of a prize; for example, the names of respondents will be entered into a drawing for a gift certificate to the campus bookstore.

TOTAL NONRESPONSE

Kalton points out that total nonresponse can occur in interview surveys for any of the following reasons: Intended respondents can refuse to be interviewed, not be at home when the interviewer calls, be unable to take part in the interview for various reasons (such as illness, deafness, inability to speak the language), or sometimes cannot even be located.[18] Of these, refusals and not-at-homes are the most common.

In mail surveys, a few questionnaires may not be deliverable, and occasionally a few respondents will return their questionnaires unanswered as an indication of their refusal to participate. Generally, however, all that is known about most mail survey nonresponse is that the questionnaire has not been returned. The reason for the lack of return may be any of the ones we have already mentioned.

A variety of techniques are employed by survey researchers to reduce nonresponse. In interview surveys, the interviewers are carefully trained to be courteous, to ask questions pleasantly and sensitively, to dress conservatively, or to return to conduct an interview at a more appropriate time if the situation warrants. Assurances of anonymity and confidentiality are made (this is done in mailed surveys as well). Questions are usually organized to start with fairly simple and nonthreatening questions. Not-at-homes are treated by callbacks (a second, third, or even a fourth visit) on different days and at different times during the day. Sometimes appointments are set up at a convenient time for the respondent. Mailed questionnaires can be followed up with a reminder letter and often a second or sometimes even a third mailing. A frequently overlooked technique is the offering of a tangible reward as an inducement to respond. There is nothing inappropriate about paying (in some manner) respondents for providing information.

Nonresponse is a serious problem in many surveys. Some observers have stated that response rates for uncomplicated face-to-face surveys by nongovernment survey organizations are about 70 to 75 percent. Refusals make up the majority of nonrespondents in face-to-face interviews, with not-at-homes constituting most of the remainder. Telephone surveys generally have somewhat lower response rates than face-to-face surveys (respondents simply hang up). Response rates in mail surveys are quite varied, ranging from as low as 10 percent to as high as 90 percent.[19] Furthermore, nonresponse is not evenly spread out among various subgroups within the United States. Nonresponse rates in face-to-face interview surveys, for example, are much higher in inner cities than in other locations.

A procedure commonly used to handle nonresponse, especially in telephone surveys, is *random replacement,* which is continuing to add randomly selected cases until the desired sample size is reached. This method does not work for the same reason mentioned earlier: Those who are not contacted or who refuse to respond probably would have answered differently than those who do respond. Remember: A random sample requires that the sample actually comprises those who are originally selected.

In addition to doing as much as possible to reduce nonresponse, researchers should obtain, during the survey or in other ways, as much demographic information as they can on respondents. This not only permits a more complete description of the sample, but also may support an argument for representativeness—*if* it turns out that the sample is very similar to the population with regard to those demographics that are pertinent to the study (Figure 17.6). These may include gender, age, ethnicity, family size, and so forth. Needless to say, all such data must be reported, not just those that support the claim of representativeness. Such an argument is always inconclusive since it is impossible to obtain data on all pertinent variables (or even to be sure as to what they all are), but it is an important feature of any survey that has a substantial nonresponse (we would say over 10 percent). A major difficulty with this suggestion is that the needed demographics may not be available for the population. In any case, the nonresponse rate should always be reported.

Figure 17.6 *Demographic Data and Representativeness*

ITEM NONRESPONSE

Partial gaps in the information provided by respondents can also occur for a variety of reasons: The respondent may not know the answer to a particular question; he or she may find certain questions embarrassing or perhaps

CONTROVERSIES IN RESEARCH

Is Low Response Rate Necessarily a Bad Thing?

As pointed out by some researchers, "A basic tenet of survey research is that high response rates are better than low response rates. Indeed, a low rate is one of the few outcomes or features that—taken by itself—is considered to be a major threat to the usefulness of a survey."* Two studies of telephone response rates, however, suggest that this is not necessarily true. In one instance, the authors used an omnibus questionnaire that included demographic, behavioral, attitudinal, and knowledge items. In the other, the researcher used data from the *Index of Consumer Sentiment* (a measure of consumer opinions about the economy). In both studies, a comparison of response rates of 60 to 70 percent to rates substantially lower (i.e., 20 to 40 percent) showed minimal differences in substantive answers.

The implication is that the substantial expense of attaining higher rates may not be worth it. It is pointed out that "observing (the) little effect of nonresponse when comparing response rates of 60 to 70 percent with rates much lower does not mean that the surveys with 60 to 70 percent response rates do not themselves suffer from significant nonresponse bias;"† that is, a 90 percent rate may have given different results from the 60 percent rate. Further, these results should not be generalized to other types of questions or to respondents other than those in these particular surveys.

*Curtin, R. Presser, S., & Singer, E. (2000). The effects of response rate changes on the Index of Consumer Sentiment. *Public Opinion Quarterly, 64,* 413.

†Keeter, S., Miller, C., Kohut, A., Groves, R., & Prosser, S. (2000). Consequences of reducing nonresponse in a large national telephone survey. *Public Opinion Quarterly, 64,* 125–148.

irrelevant; the respondent may be pressed for time, and the interviewer may decide to skip over part of the questions; the interviewer may fail to record an answer. Sometimes during the data analysis phase of a survey, the answers to certain questions are thrown out because they are inconsistent with other answers. Some answers may be unclear or illegible.

Item nonresponse is rarely as high as total nonresponse. Generally it varies according to the nature of the question asked and the mode of data collection. Very simple demographic questions usually have almost no nonresponse. Kalton estimates that items dealing with income and expenditures may experience item nonresponse rates of 10 percent or more, while extremely sensitive or difficult questions may produce nonresponse rates that are much higher.[20]

Listed here is a summary of the more common suggestions for increasing the response rate in surveys:

1. *Administration of the questionnaire or interview schedule:*
   - Make conditions under which the interview is conducted, or the questionnaire administered, as simple and convenient as possible for each individual in the sample.
   - Be sure that the group to be surveyed knows something about the information you want to obtain.
   - Train face-to-face or telephone interviewers in how to ask questions.
   - Train face-to-face interviewers in how to dress.
2. *Format of the questionnaire or interview schedule:*
   - Be sure that sufficient space is provided for respondents (or the interviewer) to fill in the necessary biographical data that is needed (age, gender, grade level, and so on).
   - Specify in precise terms the objectives the questionnaire or interview schedule is intended to achieve—exactly what kind of information is wanted from the respondents?
   - Be sure each item in the questionnaire or interview schedule is related to one of the objectives of the study—that is, it will help obtain information about the objective.
   - Use closed-ended (e.g., multiple-choice) rather than or in addition to open-ended (e.g., free response) questions.
   - Ensure that no psychologically threatening questions are included.
   - Eliminate any leading questions.
   - Check for ambiguity of items with a panel of judges. Revise as needed.
   - Pretest the questionnaire or interview schedule with a small group similar to the sample to be surveyed.

Problems in the Instrumentation Process in Survey Research

Several threats to the validity of the instrumentation process in surveys can cause individuals to respond differently from how they might otherwise respond. Suppose, for example, that a group of individuals is brought together to be interviewed all in one place and an extraneous event (say, a fire drill) occurs during the interview process. The event might upset or otherwise affect various individuals, causing them to respond to the interview questions in a different way from how they would have responded if the event had not occurred.

Whenever researchers do not take care in preparing their questionnaires—if questions are leading or insensitive, for example—it may cause individuals to respond differently. If the conditions under which individuals are questioned in interview studies are somewhat unusual (during the dinner hour; in poorly lit rooms; and so on), they may react in certain ways unrelated to the nature of the questions themselves.

Finally, the characteristics of a data collector (such as garish dress, insensitivity, rudeness, and use of offensive language) can affect how individuals respond, causing them to react in part to the data collector rather than to the questions. There is also the possibility of an unconscious bias on the part of the data collector, as when he or she asks leading questions of some individuals but not others.

Evaluating Threats to Internal Validity in Survey Research

There are four main threats to internal validity in survey research: mortality, location, instrumentation, and instrument decay. A mortality threat arises in longitudinal studies unless all of the data on "lost" subjects are deleted, in which case the problem becomes one of appropriate generalization. A location threat can occur if the collection of data is carried out in places that may affect responses (e.g., a survey of attitudes toward the police conducted in a police station). Instrument decay can occur in interview surveys if the interviewers get tired or are rushed. This, as well as defects in the instruments themselves, not only may reduce the validity of the information obtained but also may introduce a systematic bias.

Data Analysis in Survey Research

After the answers to the survey questions have been recorded, there remains the final task of summarizing the responses in order to draw conclusions from the results. The total size of the sample should be reported, along with the overall percentage of returns. The percentage of the total sample responding for each item should then be reported. Finally, the percentage of respondents who chose each alternative for each question should be given. For example, a reported result might be as follows: "For item 26, regarding the approval of a no-smoking policy while school is in session, 80 percent indicated they were in favor of such a policy, 15 percent indicated they were not in favor, and 5 percent said they were neutral." Items using rating scales should report the mean or median.

With surveys that report results in terms of percentages, it is common to use what is referred to as "the margin of error." An example of such a survey is a *poll* used to track voter opinions and predict political outcomes. The major difference between a poll and other forms of sampling is that the sample statistic we are interested in is usually a percentage (e.g., 37 percent of voters), rather than a mean, (e.g., 165 pounds). Thus, if we find with a large, random sample of Californians that 74 percent are opposed to the death penalty, we would expect that roughly 74 percent of all Californians feel this way. We would still expect some variation from sample to sample in the percentage of 1,000 Californians who are opposed to the death penalty just as we would expect some variation in the mean weight of men if we took different random samples of 1,000 men.

We can estimate the extent that random sample results will deviate from the population by calculating the margin of error—a confidence interval* depending on how confident we want to be about the inferences we make. The formula is that of the standard error, which equals the square root of $p(1 - p)/n$, where p is the proportion of respondents expressing a particular viewpoint, and $1 - p$ is the proportion expressing a different view, and n is the size of the sample. Thus, the standard error gets smaller as n gets larger.

For example, suppose we find in a random poll of 1,000 Californians that 53 percent of Democrats and 45 percent of Republicans intend to vote in an upcoming

*See p. 224.

election with a margin of error equal to ±2 percent. Thus, using the 68-95-99.7 rule, which we discussed in Chapter 10, we can say that in 68 out of 100 times, the poll results will be within one standard error of the population's intentions; that is, between 51 and 55 percent of Democrats and 43 and 48 percent of Republicans intend to vote in the state. However, 32 out of 100 times the results will not be within one standard error of the population outcome. So to be more confident, we can broaden the margin of error to ±4 percent to determine a 95 percent confidence interval of 49 to 57 percent for Democrats and 41 to 49 percent for Republicans. Now we can predict that in only 5 out of 100 times the poll results will not be within two standard errors of the population outcome. Thus, it could happen that the percentage of Democrats and Republicans who will vote would be tied.

An Example of Survey Research

In the remainder of this chapter, we present a published example of survey research, followed by a critique of its strengths and weaknesses. As we did in our critiques of the different types of research studies we analyzed in other chapters, we use several of the concepts introduced in earlier parts of the book in our analysis.

RESEARCH REPORT

From: (2010). *Action in Teacher Education*, by the Association of Teacher Educators. Reprinted by permission of Taylor & Francis Ltd. via Copyright Clearance Center www.tandfco.uk/journals.

Teaching Social Studies in the 21st Century: A Research Study of Secondary Social Studies Teachers' Instructional Methods and Practices

William B. Russell III
University of Central Florida

Abstract

Purpose

Social studies students are inundated with pedagogy in which exposure to factual information is overwhelmingly the paramount means to success. Students are often encouraged to regurgitate facts as a means to demonstrate academic understanding. Passive learning dominates social studies curriculum despite the abundance of research calling for engaged learning. Therefore, the major purpose of this study, as based on a survey research method, was to examine what methods and practices teachers use to teach social studies in the 21st century. In sum, 281 secondary social studies teachers from across the United States completed a 35-question Likert-style survey regarding their teaching practices. Provisional conclusions are reached and discussed.

Research?

Social studies is regarded by many students as boring and dry (Chiodo & Byford, 2004). It evokes images of students stuck in a passive learning environment, which requires good hearing for the lectures and an excellent memory for facts. Are these images accurate? Cuban (1991) concluded that, throughout the 20th century, drilling and memorization of facts dominated the social studies. Cuban also explained that social studies instruction included homework from textbooks, lectures, and seatwork. These methodologies, which according to Cuban dominated the social studies, are considered traditional. Nontraditional methodologies are not common components in the social studies classroom. Many social studies teachers are unable to grasp the notion that how the content is taught is just as important as what is being taught. Teachers tend to have the mentality that covering the content is the same as teaching the content, which is unfortunate. Cuban came to his conclusions about the teaching practices of social studies teachers almost 20 years ago. Is this still the case in 21st-century social studies classrooms?

Research or opinion?

Opinion

Covering the content with the lecture method is a convenient way to disseminate large amounts of content information in a limited time frame. However, the use of only one teaching style, day after day, denies students the opportunity of learning via a variety of teaching techniques (Siler, 1998).

Research?

"Read the chapter and complete the worksheet." How many students have heard this directive or endured a teacher's endless lecture? That social studies must be taught in this way—and in this way only—is an oft-accepted idea. Students are inundated with pedagogy in which exposure of factual information is the paramount means to successful learning. Students are encouraged to regurgitate facts as a means to demonstrate academic understanding—especially with the requirements of No Child Left Behind and adequate yearly progress. According to Pellegrino and Russell (2008), students are aware of the lack of challenging content and mundane methodologies utilized in social studies classes and so desire a more engaging curriculum.

Opinion

Research?

PURPOSE

The purpose of this study was to examine how social studies is being taught in 21st-century social studies classrooms. As such, I attempted to answer the following research questions:

Clear purpose

> How is secondary social studies being taught in the 21st century?
> Has social studies instruction changed since the 20th century?

SOCIAL STUDIES IN THE 21ST CENTURY

On July 17, 2008, the National Council for the Social Studies, in cooperation with the Partnerships for 21st Century Skills, released *The 21st Century Skills and Social Studies Map,* which provides educators with examples of how 21st-century skills can be integrated into classroom instruction and which highlights the critical connections between social studies and 21st-century skills. Moreover, the map demonstrates how the infusion of 21st-century skills into the social studies supports classroom teaching and helps prepare students to become effective and productive citizens in the 21st century (to download map, see Partnership for 21st Century Skills website, http://www.p21.org/documents/ss_map_11_12_08.pdf).

Rationale

Justification

The 21st-century skills outlined in the map include the following: creativity and innovation, critical thinking and problem solving, communication, collaboration, information literacy, media literacy, information and communication technology literacy, flexibility and adaptability, initiative and self-direction, social and cross-cultural skills, productivity and accountability, and leadership and responsibility.

The examples detailed in the map describe activities that engage students and require active participation (e.g., students gather data, create graphs, and present findings) to help ensure that the 21st-century skills are met. Furthermore, all the activities include instructional strategies and methodologies that are typically considered nontraditional. Examples include group discussion, cooperative learning, role playing, games, simulations, media use, analysis of primary/secondary sources, and other activities that require students to participate and think critically. None of the activity examples detailed in the map utilize traditional instructional strategies and methodologies, such as lecture, rote memorization, and reading from textbooks, which are common to social studies (Cuban, 1991).

Twenty-first-century students are unique, especially with regard to technology. Most teachers are considered digital immigrants; however, their students' are digital natives. Bennett, Maton, and Kervin (2008) explained that today's students, or the net generation, are immersed in technology; they have technical skills and learning styles that are not often accommodated with current instructional methodologies.

Research or opinion?

Prior research

Research pertaining to the teaching practices of social studies teachers is limited. The most relevant is that collected by Henke, Chen, and Goldman (1999), who conducted a national study of secondary social studies teachers' instructional practices. They concluded that social studies teachers do not use a variety of instructional methods when teaching—and many fewer than teachers in other subject areas, such as math, science, and English. Specifically, secondary social studies teachers are less likely to use alternative instructional methods to whole-group instruction when compared with other content areas. The majority of social studies teachers implemented answer recall (91%) and talked with students (85%) on a weekly basis; however, only a small portion held student-led discussions (38%) on a weekly basis. In addition, a majority of social studies teachers rely on the textbook for content information, requiring students to read from the book in class (94%) and out (95%). Furthermore, 95% of social studies teachers reported using technology on weekly basis; however, that "technology" was limited to the white board and overhead projector. Note that these data were collected in 1994–1995. Since then, the world has drastically changed, with the Internet and other technological advances, curriculum standards (state and national), standardized testing, and No Child Left Behind.

METHOD

Stratification

The methods and procedures described in this section were designed to parallel the methods outlined by Creswell (2005). To achieve a representative national random sample of secondary public school teachers, the following multistep method was used. Fifty public middle schools (1 from each state) and 50 public high schools (1 from each state) were randomly selected from the National Center for Educational Statistics, which maintains and updates a comprehensive and representative database. Schools were randomly selected with a numbering chart.

Cluster random sample

I then selected all the social studies teachers from each school's faculty listing. In sum, 613 teachers from across the United States were e-mailed a letter of consent asking for their participation in the study. All participants had 1 calendar month to complete the survey. In total, 281 teachers completed the online survey (45.8% return rate). Participants who agreed to participate clicked on a hyperlink embedded in the letter-of-consent e-mail, which redirected participants to an external survey. All surveys were anonymous.

All participants were secondary social studies teachers (Grades 6–12). The participants ranged in teaching experience and educational level (highest degree earned): 102 participants had a bachelor's degree (36.2%); 155 participants, a master's degree (55.1%);

17 participants, a specialist degree (6.0%); and 4 participants, a doctorate (1.4%). Three participants chose not to disclose their educational background. The participants' teaching experience ranged from 1st-year teachers to seasoned veterans: 42 participants reported having 0–3 years of teaching experience (14.9%); 61 participants, 4–9 years (21.7%); 174 participants, 10 or more years (61.9%). Four participants chose not to disclose their teaching experience. Participants taught at schools ranging from small rural to large urban, and they varied in grade level taught (Grades 6–12) and in social science subject matter teaching assignment. Many participants reported teaching multiple social science disciplines (U.S. history, economics, geography). Of the 281 participants, 119 were female, 160 were male, and 2 did not disclose their gender.

Good description

This study utilized a survey method to obtain information regarding social studies teachers' methods of instruction. The instrument consisted of 35 questions (see appendix). Before the instrument was implemented, a pilot study was done to test the instrument's reliability and validity. The pilot study was conducted in a graduate-level social studies education course comprising 20 secondary social studies teachers.

Need more discussion

Need more description of procedures

The questionnaire was designed to measure the frequency with which teachers used various instructional methods and practices when teaching social studies content. The participants' responses were analyzed for percentage per frequency toward each question. The responses were analyzed by numeration toward each Likert-scaled response (1 = *almost all the time or all the time*, 2 = *more than half the time*, 3 = *half the time*, 4 = *less than half the time*, 5 = *very little of the time or never*). The instrument utilized a continuous interval scale similar to the Likert scale, which "provides continuous response options to questions with assumed equal distances between options" (Creswell, 2005, p. 168).

Exactly half? Contradicts "assumed equal distances" statement below

This study used a survey research method, which has limitations. To minimize the limitations, I attempted to align the study with Salant and Dillman's (1994) factors of good survey research. Specifically, I developed an instrument with clear, unambiguous questions and response options; I used a national representative sampling frame to randomly select individuals; I selected as large a sample from the population as possible; and I used appropriate procedures to ensure a decent return rate.

Unclear to us

However, I am aware of possible limitations. As with any survey research study, a larger sample could have possibly uncovered different findings. In addition, this survey required teachers to self-report their teaching practices. Self-reporting can have limitations because participants may not be completely honest. To help prevent this, all surveys were completed anonymously.

Size is adequate

Right

Good

DISCUSSION

The purpose of this study was to examine how social studies is being taught in 21st-century social studies classrooms. The results are troubling. The responses and percentages were tabulated for each question (see Table 1). The bold numerations indicate the mode, or most frequently chosen scale, which corresponds to the higher percentage rate.

Appropriate

The resulting disaggregated data indicate some interesting but disturbing trends from the teachers' responses to the questionnaire. For instance, Statement 27, "listen to teacher lectures," yielded more than a 90% rate in terms of respondents using this method half the time or more. This is a positive, or skewed, trend to the more frequent scale of the survey, illustrating a solid favoritism for teaching using the lecture method. It is also a clear indication that the lecture method is the preferred method for teaching social studies, and these results correspond with the findings of Cuban (1991).

Opinion

Results

Interpretation

No other method or practice was skewed so heavily toward the more frequent scale than the lecture method. However, there were some methods that were heavily

TABLE 1 ***Percentage Responses per Statement***

	1	2	3	4	5
1	0.00	3.55	3.55	**51.24**	40.21
2	0.00	0.00	0.00	2.13	**96.08**
3	1.77	12.45	9.96	**40.21**	31.67
4	0.00	3.91	4.98	32.02	**58.36**
5	4.98	27.04	27.40	**34.87**	4.62
6	1.06	8.89	22.41	30.60	**37.01**
7	2.84	9.25	26.69	29.18	**32.02**
8	0.35	3.55	15.65	32.74	**46.97**
9	4.27	10.32	27.04	**42.34**	15.65
10	0.00	1.77	5.33	30.60	**61.56**
11	1.06	5.33	11.74	**48.39**	32.02
12	4.27	17.43	**55.16**	21.70	1.06
13	2.49	13.16	29.18	**45.90**	9.25
14	28.82	**37.36**	21.35	9.25	3.20
15	10.67	22.77	**41.99**	12.81	11.74
16	24.91	**31.67**	19.92	17.43	6.04
17	9.25	26.33	20.64	**38.79**	4.98
18	9.96	24.91	25.97	**33.80**	4.62
19	12.45	**40.21**	27.75	12.81	6.76
20	1.42	3.20	8.54	31.31	**53.02**
21	1.77	4.27	9.25	**49.46**	34.87
22	3.20	12.09	20.64	**46.26**	17.43
23	2.49	7.11	14.59	**50.53**	24.55
24	0.00	1.06	6.76	20.99	**71.17**
25	2.13	6.40	**60.14**	6.76	24.55
26	10.67	9.96	19.57	**42.34**	17.43
27	14.94	36.29	**39.14**	9.60	0.00
28	0.00	0.71	4.98	26.69	**67.61**
29	4.98	16.72	22.06	**49.11**	7.11
30	3.20	11.03	13.16	**45.90**	26.33
31	4.98	20.99	20.99	**41.99**	11.03
32	9.96	22.06	17.08	**32.02**	18.86
33	13.16	29.18	18.86	**29.53**	9.25
34	0.00	0.00	2.13	10.32	**83.62**
35	3.55	11.74	21.35	**48.04**	14.59

Note. 1 = *almost all the time or all the time,* 2 = *more than half the time,* 3 = *half the time,* 4 = *less than half the time,* 5 = *very little of the time or never.* Bold numerals indicate the mode, or most selected scale response. Because of rounding, total percentages may be slightly more or less than 100%.

Results

skewed toward the more frequent scale. Statement 14, "take notes," showed more than 87% of respondents using this method half the time or more. This is a positive, or skewed, trend to the more frequent scale of the survey, illustrating a solid favoritism for

Interpretation

having students take notes. The results of Statements 27 and 14 can be seen as a common practice because many teachers who utilize the lecture method expect students to take notes on the lecture. Note that the abundant amount of time these methods consume makes neither a best practice.

More than 80% of the respondents reported having students "complete written assignments from the textbook" (Statement 19) half the time or more. Furthermore, over 68% of respondents reported having students "read aloud from the textbook" (Statement 25) half the time or more. Interestingly, just over 38% of respondents reported having students "read silently in the textbook" (Statement 7) half the time or more, indicating that teachers prefer reading aloud over silent reading. Only 40% of respondents reported that they have students "read material other than the textbook" (Statement 26) half the time or more. These results indicate that teachers prefer textbooks as the primary source of information.

As mentioned, 80% of respondents reported having students complete written work from textbooks. However, similar results were found with Statement 16, "complete written assignments not from the textbook," with more than 74% of respondents reporting it as half the time or more. Not only did the respondents report not using the textbook, but more than 75% reported having students "complete worksheets" half the time or more (Statement 15), and more than 60% reported having students "complete written assignments out of class" (Statement 33) half the time or more.

These results demonstrate that the participants use a more traditional style of teaching, by incorporating passive learning methods. Although these methods and practices promote passive learning and are considered inferior to the more authentic methods and practices that encourage active participation, teachers are still using them.

Interpretation

Notably, 0% of respondents reported having students "play educational video games" (Statement 2) half the time or more; only 7% of respondents reported using "movies, films, and/or videos" (Statement 1) half the time or more; and only 8% of respondents reported having students "take virtual tours" (Statement 24) half the time or more. Furthermore, just over 19% of respondents reported having students "utilize the Internet" (Statement 8) half the time or more. However, more than 40% of respondents reported having students "utilize the computer" (Statement 9) half the time or more. This indicates that students are more likely to use the computer but not the Internet. However, if students are not examining videos, taking virtual tours, utilizing the web, and/or playing educational videos on the computer, then what are they doing on the computer? Could they be completing written assignments not from the textbook? This would correspond with idea that computers and all their capabilities are not being fully utilized in social studies classrooms (Cuban, 2001; Russell, 2007).

Interpretation

The utilization of various technologies is discouraging, and sadly, the use of various best practices follows suit. First, 59% of respondents reported having students "participate in cooperative learning groups" (Statement 5) half the time or more. Ideally, social studies educators want to see the social interaction among peers increase. Only 15% of respondents reported having students "participate in role-playing activities" (Statement 21) half the time or more, and only 18% reported having students "participate in simulations (nonelectronic)" (Statement 11) half the time or more. Although the results pertaining to cooperative learning are not encouraging, those pertaining to the discussion method are slightly more optimistic. More than 76% of respondents reported having students "participate in a teacher-led discussions" (Statement 12) half the time or more, but only 44% of respondents reported having students "participate in student-led discussions" (Statement 13) half the time or more. When dealing with controversy, roughly 47% of respondents reported having students "discuss controversial issues" (Statement 31) half the time or more. Only 27%

Interpretation

Interpretation

of respondents reported having students "participate in debates" (Statement 30) half the time or more. If students are not debating or participating in discussions that they lead, how relevant and/or in depth are the discussions? Discussions that teachers lead are oftentimes not as engaging for the majority of students because a few students can monopolize the discussion.

Not only are students not debating one another, but they are also not examining various perspectives. As mentioned previously, only 40% of respondents reported that they have students "read material other than the textbook" (Statement 26) half the time or more. Furthermore, only 32% of respondents reported having students "examine primary sources" (Statement 6) half the time or more. This is another example of the reliance that educators have on textbooks.

We agree

Not clear to us

Results

Misleading see our Analysis of the Study

Opinion

The results of this study continue to demonstrate that teachers are more inclined to encourage passive learning than engaged, active learning. According to some responses, not all students are required to think critically or solve problems. Only 44% of respondents reported having students "participate in critical thinking activities" (Statement 29) half the time or more, and only 36% of respondents reported having students "participate in problem solving activities" (Statement 22) half the time or more. These results illustrate that students do not have to critically think or problem solve the majority of time, which is not productive. Critical thinking and other decision-making skills are essential for successful social studies instruction. According to the Engle (1960/2003), decision making is the heart of social studies education.

CONCLUSION

Opinion

We agree

The first research question attempted to uncover how secondary social studies is being taught in the 21st century, and it was answered in the discussion per the results of the survey. The second research question attempted to uncover if social studies instruction had changed since the 20th century. Unfortunately, the data indicate that social studies instruction has not changed a great deal since the 20th century.

Current theory

The findings of this research study indicate a gap between theory and practice. Because the goal of social studies teachers is to develop students into effective 21st-century citizens through the use of a diverse curriculum and instructional practices, one can conclude that social studies teachers are not maximizing their potential to meet this goal.

Opinion

The lack of engaging and meaningful learning opportunities in the social studies classroom is disheartening. Providing students with an array of learning experiences and ample opportunities to reflect and think critically is an essential element for preparing well-rounded and effective 21st-century citizens who will be able to actively contribute in modern society.

Opinion

We agree

Opinion

Overall, the data from the respondents provide insight and evidence on the methods and practices that social studies teachers utilize. The strong preference for lecturing, note taking, and use of textbooks is troubling. The data indicate that teachers clearly utilize passive and nonengaging methods more frequently than they do methods considered to be active and engaging. The actual classroom teaching practices of social studies teachers do not align with relevant literature supporting more authentic learning strategies, further expanding the gap between theory and research. This widening gap indicates that urgent action needs to be taken to help educators see the importance and value of utilizing various instructional strategies that promote learning and higher-order thinking skills to educate students to become effective 21st-century citizens.

APPENDIX: SURVEY INSTRUMENT

When I teach social studies, I have students . . .	1	2	3	4	5
1. Watch movies, films, and/or videos					
2. Play educational video games					
3. Make PowerPoint presentations					
4. Listen to music					
5. Participate in cooperative learning activities					
6. Examine primary sources					
7. Read silently in the textbook					
8. Utilize the Internet					
9. Utilize the computer					
10. Play educational games (nonelectronic)					
11. Participate in simulations (nonelectronic)					
12. Participate in teacher-led discussions					
13. Participate in student-led discussions					
14. Take notes					
15. Complete worksheets					
16. Complete written assignments not from textbook					
17. Examine visual aids					
18. Read maps, charts, and/or graphs					
19. Complete written assignments from textbook					
20. Participate in service learning					
21. Participate in role-playing activities					
22. Participate in problem solving activities					
23. Make presentations (nonelectronic)					
24. Take virtual tours					
25. Read aloud from the textbook					
26. Read material other than the textbook					
27. Listen to teacher lectures					
28. Listen to guest speakers					
29. Participate in critical thinking activities					
30. Participate in debates					
31. Discuss controversial issues					
32. Utilize graphic organizers					
33. Complete written assignments out of class					
34. Go on field trips					
35. Examine secondary sources					

1 = almost all the time or all the lime, 2 = more than half the time, 3 = half the time, 4 = less than half the time, and 5 = very little of the time or never.

References

Bennett, S., Maton, K., & Kervin, L. (2008). The "digital natives" debate: A critical review of the evidence. *British Journal of Educational Technology, 39*(5), 775–786.

Chiodo, J., & Byford, J. (2004). Do they really dislike social studies? A study of middle school and high school students. *The Journal of Social Studies Research, 28*(1), 16–26.

Cuban, L. (1991). History of teaching in social studies. In J. P. Shaver (Ed.), *Handbook of research on social studies teaching and learning: A project of the National Council for the Social Studies* (pp. 197–209). New York: Macmillan.

Cuban, L. (2001). *Oversold and underused: Computers in the classroom.* Cambridge, MA: Harvard University.

Creswell, J. (2005). *Educational research: Planning, conducting, and evaluating quantitative and qualitative research.* Upper Saddle River, NJ: Pearson Education.

Engle, S. (2003). Decision-making: The heart of social studies instruction. *The Social Studies, 94*(1): 7–10. Reprinted with permission from *Social Education, 27*(4), November 1960, pp. 301–304.

Henke, R., Chen, X., &. Goldman, G. (1999). *What happens in the classroom? Instructional practices in elementary and secondary schools, 1994–95.* Washington, DC: National Center for Education Statistics. (ERIC Reproduction No. ED431735)

Pellegrino, A., & Russell, W. (2008). Constructing meaning from historical content: A research study. *Journal of Social Studies Research, 32*(2), 3–15.

Russell, W. (2007). Teaching the Holocaust with online art: A case study of high school students. *Journal of Social Studies Research, 31(2),* 35–42.

Salant, P., & Dillman, D. A. (1994). *How to conduct you own survey.* New York: Wiley.

Siler, C. R. (1998). *Spatial dynamic: An alternative teaching tool in the social studies.* Bloomington, IN: ERIC Clearinghouse for Social Studies/Social Science Education. (ERIC Reproduction No. ED415179)

Analysis of the Study

PURPOSE/JUSTIFICATION

The purpose is clearly presented. The justification relies on both prior research and professional opinion, in particular, the NCSS Social Studies MAP of 2008 and the Henke et al. study of 1994–95. There appear to be no concerns regarding harm, confidentiality, or deception.

DEFINITIONS

None are provided, however, terminology is straightforward and terms in the questionnaire are common in the field of social studies.

PRIOR RESEARCH

Prior research consists of one directly relevant study (Henke et al.) summarized in detail and several other citations that are unclear as to whether they are research or opinion.

HYPOTHESES

None are stated; two research questions are posed—the first addressed with descriptive data, the second by comparison with prior research and historical opinion.

SAMPLE

The implied population is all teachers of social studies in middle and high schools in the United States. The initial stratified cluster random sample consisted of all social studies teachers in 50 public middle schools (one from each state) and 50 public high schools (one from each state) in the United States (n = 613). The final sample (n = 281) resulted from a return rate of 46 percent. The return rate, though not unusual, is troubling (see text p. 405). This is especially a problem in cluster sampling. With an average of 5.6 teacher responses by state (281/50) some states or regions could be underrepresented. This could be addressed by giving the response number by state. This limitation should be acknowledged.

INSTRUMENTATION

The questionnaire used a well-known format, a Likert Scale with five choices for each of the 35 items. However, use of overlapping categories and one (choice #3) that is actually a point should be defended. A pilot study was conducted; a very good idea but more details as well as data are needed, especially regarding reliability and validity. Assessing reliability with such scales is problematic. It must be done for each item, which rules out split-half and equivalent-forms methods. Test-retest is theoretically possible but likely to strike respondents as silly unless the rationale is explained, and this might defeat the purpose if they remember their earlier responses.

Validity of items would best be assessed by comparison with observations but the cost and effort are usually prohibitive. Principals or co-teachers might be asked to assess the respondents but may feel unprepared to do so. We must assume that content validity was assessed by the pilot group and possibly others. Use of such scales typically relies on the presumed clarity of items. As the author states, such self-report is suspect but not only regarding honesty; it must be assumed that respondents can accurately apportion their behavior.

It is, we think, unfortunate that the author, in the Discussion and Conclusion, uses the terminology "half the time or more." We do not see that "time" can mean "all class time" because this means, for example, that the 90 percent who said they lecture this much had only half (or less) of their class time left to devote to the remaining 34 items, some of which had percents almost as high as 90 percent and for activities that can't be done at the same time as lecturing. Perhaps it means over half of class meetings. In any case, these percentages can be taken as indicating teacher priorities among the methods but not as showing allocation of time.

PROCEDURES/INTERNAL VALIDITY

Procedures are clearly described. Internal Validity is a concern only if responses to one item affect others, which seems unlikely.

DATA ANALYSIS/RESULTS/INTERPRETATION

The results are clearly presented and give a valuable simplification of Table 1. We generally argue for a separation of results and discussion/interpretation so the reader is clear when inferences beyond the data are made. However, in this case, we agree with the format used. The interpretation for each item is legitimate provided the results are taken to show priorities, not actual use of time (see Instrumentation). For example, we agree that it is unfortunate that "critical thinking activities" received 44 percent while "lecturing" received 90 percent. Our experience in schools, however, is such that we would be delighted if 44 percent of social studies teachers devoted half of their class time to "critical thinking."

Go back to the **INTERACTIVE AND APPLIED** Learning feature at the beginning of the chapter for a listing of interactive and applied activities. Go to the **Online Learning Center** at **www.mhhe.com/fraenkel9e** to take quizzes, practice with key terms, and review chapter content.

Main Points

MAJOR CHARACTERISTICS OF SURVEY RESEARCH

- Most surveys possess three basic characteristics: (1) the collection of information (2) from a sample (3) by asking questions to describe some aspects of the population of which the sample is a part.

THE PURPOSE OF SURVEY RESEARCH

- The major purpose of all surveys is to describe the characteristics of a population.
- Rarely is the population as a whole studied, however. Instead, a sample is surveyed and a description of the population is inferred from what the sample reveals.

TYPES OF SURVEYS

- There are two major types of surveys: cross-sectional surveys and longitudinal surveys.
- Three longitudinal designs commonly employed in survey research are trend studies, cohort studies, and panel studies.
- In a trend study, different samples from a population whose members change are surveyed at different points in time.
- In a cohort study, different samples from a population whose members do *not* change are surveyed at different points in time.
- In a panel study, the same sample of individuals is surveyed at different times over the course of the survey.
- Surveys are not suitable for all research topics, especially those that require observation of subjects or the manipulation of variables.

STEPS IN SURVEY RESEARCH

- The focus of study in a survey is called the *unit of analysis.*
- As in other types of research, the group of persons that is the focus of the study is called the *target population.*
- There are four basic ways to collect data in a survey: by direct administration of the survey instrument to a group, by mail, by telephone, or by personal interview. Each method has advantages and disadvantages.
- The sample to be surveyed should be selected randomly if possible.
- The most common types of instruments used in survey research are the questionnaire and the interview schedule.

QUESTIONS ASKED IN SURVEY RESEARCH

- The nature of the questions, and the way they are asked, are extremely important in survey research.
- Most surveys use some form of closed-ended questions.
- The survey instrument should be pretested with a small sample similar to the potential respondents.
- A contingency question is a question whose answer is contingent upon how a respondent answers a prior question to which the contingency question is related. Well-organized and sequenced contingency questions are particularly important in interview schedules.

THE COVER LETTER

- A cover letter is sent to potential respondents in a mail survey explaining the purpose of the survey questionnaire.

INTERVIEWING

- Both telephone and face-to-face interviewers need to be trained before they administer the survey instrument.
- Both total nonresponse and item nonresponse are major problems in survey research that seem to be increasing in recent years. This is a problem because those who do not respond are very likely to differ from respondents in terms of how they would answer the survey questions.

THREATS TO INTERNAL VALIDITY IN SURVEY RESEARCH

- Threats to the internal validity of survey research include location, instrumentation, instrument decay, and mortality.

DATA ANALYSIS IN SURVEY RESEARCH

- The percentage of the total sample responding for each item on a survey questionnaire should be reported, as well as the percentage of the total sample who chose each alternative for each question.

Key Terms

census 392
closed-ended question 398
cohort study 392
contingency question 401
cross-sectional survey 392
interview schedule 398
longitudinal survey 392
nonresponse 404
open-ended question 399
panel study 392
trend study 392
unit of analysis 393

For Discussion

1. For what kinds of topics might a personal interview be superior to a mail or telephone survey? Give an example.
2. When might a telephone survey be preferable to a mail survey? to a personal interview?
3. Give an example of a question a researcher might use to assess each of the following characteristics of the members of a teacher group:
   a. Their income
   b. Their teaching style
   c. Their biggest worry
   d. Their knowledge of teaching methods
   e. Their opinions about homogeneous grouping of students
4. Which mode of data collection—mail, telephone, or personal interview—would be best for each of the following surveys?
   a. The reasons why some students drop out of college before they graduate
   b. The feelings of high school teachers about special classes for the gifted
   c. The attitudes of people about raising taxes to pay for the construction of new schools
   d. The duties of secondary school superintendents in a midwestern state
   e. The reasons why individuals of differing ethnicity did or did not decide to enter the teaching profession
   f. The opinions of teachers about the idea of minimum competency testing before granting permanent tenure
   g. The opinions of parents of students in a private school about the elimination of certain subjects from the curriculum
5. Some researchers argue that conducting a careful cross-sectional survey of the population of the United States would actually be preferable to doing a census of the population every 10 years. What do you think? What might be some arguments for and against this idea?
6. Which do you think would be the hardest type of longitudinal survey to conduct—trend, cohort, or panel? the easiest? Explain your reasoning.

7. Why do you think many people do not respond to survey questionnaires that they receive in the mail?
8. Are there any questions that researchers could not survey people about through the mail? by telephone? personal interview? Explain.
9. When conducting a personal interview, when might it be better to ask a closed-ended rather than an open-ended question? What about the reverse? Suggest some examples.
10. See if you can suggest a question that you believe almost anyone would be sure to answer if asked. Can you think of any they would be sure *not* to answer? Why?
11. What suggestions can you offer, beyond those given in this chapter, for improving the rate of response in surveys?

References

1. Nasir, N. S., et al. (2009). What does it mean to be African-American? Constructions of race and academic identity in an urban public high school. *American Educational Research Journal, 46*(3), 73–114.

2. Brouwer, N., & Korthagen, F. (2005). Can teacher education make a difference? *American Educational Research Journal, 42*(1), 153–224.

3. Penuel, W. R., et al. (2007). What makes professional development effective? Strategies that foster curriculum implementation. *American Educational Research Journal, 44*(12), 921–958.

4. Nathanson, S., et al. (2008). The reading habits and literacy attitudes of in-service and prospective teachers: Results of a questionnaire survey. *Journal of Teacher Education 59*(9), 313–321.

5. Ravert, R. D. (2009). "You're only young once": Things college students report doing now before it is too late. *Journal of Adolescent Research, 24*(5), 376–396.

6. Odland, G., & Ruzicka, M. (2009). An investigation into teacher turnover in international schools. *Journal of Research in International Education, 8*(4), 5–29.

7. Abbott, J., & Faris, S. (2001). Integrating technology into pre-service literacy instruction: A survey of elementary education students' attitudes toward computers. *Journal of Research on Computing in Education, 33*(2), 149–161.

8. Hrycaj, P., & Russo, M. (2007). Reflections on surveys of faculty attitudes toward collaboration with librarians. *Journal of Academic Librarianship, 33*(6), 692–696.

9. Jaeger, R. M. (1988, pp. 308–310). Survey research methods in education. In Richard M. Jaeger (Ed.), *Complementary methods for research in education.* Washington, DC: American Educational Research Association.

10. Grovers, R. M., & Kahn, R. L. (1979). *Surveys by telephone: A national comparison with personal interviews.* New York: Academic Press.

11. Fowler, F. J., Jr. (2009). *Survey research methods* (4th ed., p. 119), Beverly Hills, CA: Sage Publications.

12. The development of survey questions is an art in itself. We can only begin to deal with the topic here. For a more detailed discussion, see Fink, A. (2009). *How to conduct surveys* (4th ed.), Thousand Oaks, CA: Sage.

13. For further suggestions, see Gronlund, N. E. (1988). *How to construct achievement tests.* Englewood Cliffs, NJ: Prentice Hall.

14. Babbie, E. S. (1973, p. 145). *Survey research methods.* Belmont, CA: Wadsworth.

15. For a more detailed discussion, see Fowler, F. J., Jr. (2009). *Survey research methods* (4th ed., chapter 7), Beverly Hills, CA: Sage Publications.

16. Fowler, F. J., Jr. (2009). *Survey research methods* (4th ed., pp. 109–110), Beverly Hills, CA: Sage Publications.

17. Freyberg, P., & Osborne, R. (1981). Who structures the curriculum: Teacher or learner? *Research Information for Teachers,* Number Two. SET, Hamilton, New Zealand.

18. Kalton, G. (1983, p. 64). *Introduction to survey sampling.* Beverly Hills, CA: Sage Publications.

19. Kalton, G. (1983, p. 66). *Introduction to survey sampling.* Beverly Hills, CA: Sage Publications.

20. Kalton, G. (1983, p. 67). *Introduction to survey sampling.* Beverly Hills, CA: Sage Publications.

PART 5

Introduction to Qualitative Research

Part 5 begins our discussion of qualitative research. We devote a separate chapter to the nature of qualitative research and follow it with two chapters on the main techniques that qualitative researchers use to collect and analyze their data. These include observation, interviewing, and content analysis. We provide examples of published studies in which researchers use these techniques, along with our analysis of the strengths and weaknesses of their investigations.

18 The Nature of Qualitative Research

What Is Qualitative Research?

General Characteristics of Qualitative Research

Philosophical Assumptions Underlying Qualitative as Opposed to Quantitative Research

Postmodernism

Steps in Qualitative Research

Approaches to Qualitative Research

Narrative Research

Phenomenology

Grounded Theory

Case Studies

Ethnographic and Historical Research

Sampling in Qualitative Research

Qualitative Data Analysis

Generalization in Qualitative Research

Internal Validity in Qualitative Research

Ethics and Qualitative Research

Qualitative and Quantitative Research Reconsidered

OBJECTIVES **Studying this chapter should enable you to:**

- Explain what is meant by the term "qualitative research."
- Describe five general characteristics that most qualitative studies have in common.
- Describe briefly the philosophical assumptions underlying qualitative and quantitative research.
- Describe briefly some of the steps involved in qualitative research.
- Describe at least three ways that qualitative research differs from quantitative research.
- Describe briefly at least four different approaches to qualitative research.
- Describe the type of samples that are used in qualitative research, and give examples of these types.
- Explain how generalizing differs in qualitative and quantitative research.
- Describe briefly how matters of ethics affect qualitative research.
- Suggest ways that qualitative and quantitative approaches to research might be used together.

INTERACTIVE AND APPLIED LEARNING After, or while, reading this chapter:

Go to the Online Learning Center at www.mhhe.com/fraenkel9e to:

- Learn More About Mixed Designs and Their Limitations

Go to your online Student Mastery Activities book to do the following activities:

- Activity 18.1: Qualitative Research Questions
- Activity 18.2: Qualitative vs. Quantitative Research
- Activity 18.3: Approaches to Qualitative Research

"Hey, Brendan."

"Oh, hi, Melissa. Where've you been?"

"I just came from my research class. We're just starting to learn about qualitative research."

"What's that?"

"Well, sometimes a researcher wants to obtain an in-depth look at a particular individual, say, or a specific situation. Maybe even a particular set of instructional materials."

"Yeah?"

"When they do, they ask some interesting questions. Instead of asking something like 'What do people think about this?' or 'What would happen if I do this?' qualitative researchers ask, 'How do these people act?' or 'How are things done?' or 'How do people give meaning to their lives?'"

"How come?" asks Brendan.

"Because what they want to get at is some idea of the *quality* of the experiences that people have."

"Sounds different. Tell me more."

We shall indeed tell Brendan (and you) more about qualitative research. The nature of qualitative research, and how it differs from quantitative research, is what this chapter is all about.

What Is Qualitative Research?

Most of the questions being asked by researchers who use the methodologies discussed in previous chapters involve the extent to which various learnings, attitudes, or ideas exist, or how well or how accurately they are being developed. Thus, possible avenues of research include comparisons between alternative methods of teaching (as in experimental research); examining research among variables (as in correlational relationships); comparing groups of individuals in terms of existing differences on certain variables (as in causal-comparative research); or surveying different groups of educational professionals, such as teachers, administrators, and counselors (as in survey research). These methods are frequently referred to as *quantitative research.*

As we mentioned in Chapter 1, however, researchers might wish to obtain a more holistic impression of teaching and learning than answers to these questions can provide. A researcher might wish to know more than just "to what extent" or "how well" something is done. He or she might wish to obtain a more complete picture, for example, of what goes on in a particular classroom or school.

Consider the teaching of history in secondary schools. Just how do history teachers teach their subject? What kinds of things do they do as they go about their daily routine? What sorts of things do students do? In what kinds of activities do they engage? What are the explicit and implicit "rules of the game" in history classes that seem to help or hinder the process of learning?

To gain some insight into these concerns, a researcher might try to document or portray the everyday experiences of students (and teachers) in history classrooms. The focus would be on only one classroom (or a small number of them at most). The researcher would observe the classroom on as regular a basis as possible and attempt to describe, as fully and as richly as possible, what he or she sees.

TABLE 18.1 *Quantitative Versus Qualitative Research*

Quantitative Methodologies	Qualitative Methodologies
Preference for precise hypotheses stated at the outset.	Preference for hypotheses that emerge as study develops.
Preference for precise definitions stated at the outset.	Preference for definitions in context or as study progresses.
Data reduced to numerical scores.	Preference for narrative description.
Much attention to assessing and improving reliability of scores obtained from instruments.	Preference for assuming that reliability of inferences is adequate.
Assessment of validity through a variety of procedures with reliance on statistical indices.	Assessment of validity through cross-checking sources of information (triangulation).
Preference for random techniques for obtaining meaningful samples.	Preference for expert informant (purposive) samples.
Preference for precisely describing procedures.	Preference for narrative/literary descriptions of procedures.
Preference for design or statistical control of extraneous variables.	Preference for logical analysis in controlling or accounting for extraneous variables.
Preference for specific design control for procedural bias.	Primary reliance on researcher to deal with procedural bias.
Preference for statistical summary of results.	Preference for narrative summary of results.
Preference for breaking down complex phenomena into specific parts for analysis.	Preference for holistic description of complex phenomena.
Willingness to manipulate aspects, situations, or conditions in studying complex phenomena.	Unwillingness to tamper with naturally occurring phenomena.

The preceding example points to the fact that many researchers are more interested in the *quality* of a particular activity than in how often it occurs or how it would otherwise be evaluated. Research studies that investigate the quality of relationships, activities, situations, or materials are frequently referred to as **qualitative research**. This type of research differs from the methodologies discussed in earlier chapters in that there is a greater emphasis on holistic description—that is, on describing in detail all of what goes on in a particular activity or situation rather than on comparing the effects of a particular treatment (as in experimental research), say, or on describing the attitudes or behaviors of people (as in survey research).

Some actual examples of the kinds of qualitative studies that have been conducted by educational researchers are as follows:

- "Sources of Middle School Students' Self-Efficacy in Mathematics"[1]
- "Shopping Malls: Measuring Interpersonal Distance Under Changing Conditions and Across Cultures"[2]
- "A Framework for Understanding Teaching with the Internet"[3]
- "Go Play in Traffic: Skating, Gender, and Urban Context"[4]
- "Researching Sensitive Topics: Qualitative Research as Emotion Work"[5]

We believe that educational research increasingly is, and should be, a mixture of quantitative and qualitative approaches (we'll discuss this in more detail later in the chapter). However, to assist you in understanding the many types of research that exist, we list the essential differences between quantitative and qualitative research in Table 18.1.

General Characteristics of Qualitative Research

Many different types of qualitative methodologies exist, but there are certain general features that characterize most qualitative research studies. Not all qualitative studies will necessarily display all of these characteristics with equal strength. Nevertheless, taken together, they give a good overall picture of what is involved in this type of research. Bogdan and Biklen describe five such features.[6]

1. *The natural setting is the direct source of data, and the researcher is the key instrument in qualitative research.* Qualitative researchers go directly to the

particular setting of interest to observe and collect their data. They spend a considerable amount of time actually being in a school, sitting in on faculty meetings, attending parent-teacher association meetings, observing teachers in their classrooms and in other locales, and in general directly observing and interviewing individuals as they go about their daily routines.

Sometimes they come equipped only with a pad and a pencil to take notes, but often they use sophisticated audio and video recording equipment. Even when such equipment is used, however, the data are collected right at the scene and supplemented by the researcher's observations and insights about what occurred. As Bogdan and Biklen point out, qualitative researchers go to the particular setting of interest because they are concerned with *context*—they feel that activities can best be understood in the actual settings in which they occur. They also feel that human behavior is vastly influenced by particular settings, and, hence, whenever possible they visit such settings.

2. *Qualitative data are collected in the form of words or pictures rather than numbers.* The kinds of data collected in qualitative research include interview transcripts, field notes, photographs, audio recordings, videotapes, diaries, personal comments, memos, official records, textbook passages, and anything else that can convey the actual words or actions of people. In their search for understanding, qualitative researchers do not usually attempt to reduce their data to numerical symbols,[7] but rather seek to portray what they have observed and recorded in all of its richness. Hence, they do their best not to ignore anything that might lend insight to a situation. Gestures, jokes, conversational gambits, artwork or other decorations in a room—all are noted by qualitative researchers. To a qualitative researcher, no data are trivial or unworthy of notice.
3. *Qualitative researchers are concerned with process as well as product.* Qualitative researchers are especially interested in *how* things occur. Hence, they are likely to observe how people interact with each other; how certain kinds of questions are answered; the meanings that people give to certain words and actions; how people's attitudes are translated into actions; how students seem to be affected by a teacher's manner, gestures, or comments; and the like.
4. *Qualitative researchers tend to analyze their data inductively.* Qualitative researchers do not, usually, formulate a hypothesis beforehand and then seek to test it out. Rather, they tend to "play it as it goes." They spend a considerable amount of time collecting their data (again, primarily through observing and interviewing) before they decide what are the important questions to consider. As Bogdan and Biklen suggest, qualitative researchers are not putting together a puzzle whose picture they already know. They are *constructing* a picture that takes shape as they collect and examine the parts.[8]
5. *How people make sense out of their lives is a major concern to qualitative researchers.* A special interest of qualitative researchers lies in the perspectives of the subjects of a study. Qualitative researchers want to know what the participants in a study are thinking and why they think what they do. Assumptions, motives, reasons, goals, and values—all are of interest and likely to be the focus of the researcher's questions. It also is common for a researcher to show a completed videotape or the contents of his or her notes to a participant to check on the accuracy of the researcher's interpretations. In other words, the researcher does his or her best to capture the thinking of the participants from the *participants'* perspective (as opposed to the researcher merely reporting what he or she thinks) as accurately as possible.

Table 18.2 presents a summary of the main characteristics of qualitative research.

Philosophical Assumptions Underlying Qualitative as Opposed to Quantitative Research

Differences between quantitative and qualitative researchers are often discussed in terms of differing paradigms, or *worldviews*—that is, differences in the basic set of beliefs or assumptions that guide the way they approach their investigations. These assumptions are related to the views they hold concerning the nature of reality, the relationship of the researcher to that which he or she is studying, the role of values in a study, and the process of research itself. Qualitative researchers posit that one's worldview influences the **theoretical framework**, or "theoretical approach," that is used to structure a research study.

The quantitative approach is associated with the philosophy of **positivism**, which emerged in the nineteenth century. Perhaps the person most responsible for the

TABLE 18.2 ***Major Characteristics of Qualitative Research***

1. **Naturalistic inquiry**	Studying real-world situations as they unfold naturally; nonmanipulative, unobtrusive, and noncontrolling; openness to whatever emerges—lack of predetermined constraints on outcomes.
2. **Inductive analysis**	Immersion in the details and specifics of the data to discover important categories, dimensions, and interrelationships; begin by exploring genuinely open questions rather than testing theoretically derived (deductive) hypotheses.
3. **Holistic perspective**	The *whole* phenomenon under study is understood as a complex system that is more than the sum of its parts; focus is on complex interdependencies not meaningfully reduced to a few discrete variables and linear, cause-effect relationships.
4. **Qualitative data**	Detailed, thick description; inquiry in depth; direct quotations capturing people's personal perspectives and experiences.
5. **Personal contact and insight**	The researcher has direct contact with and gets close to the people, situation, and phenomenon under study; researcher's personal experiences and insights are an important part of the inquiry and critical to understanding the phenomenon.
6. **Dynamic systems**	Attention to process; assumes change is constant and ongoing whether the focus is on an individual or an entire culture.
7. **Unique case orientation**	Assumes each case is special and unique; the first level of inquiry is being true to, respecting, and capturing the details of the individual cases being studied; cross-case analysis follows from and depends on the quality of individual case studies.
8. **Context sensitivity**	Places findings in a social, historical, and temporal context; dubious of the possibility or meaningfulness of generalizations across time and space.
9. **Empathic neutrality**	Complete objectivity is impossible; pure subjectivity undermines credibility; the researcher's passion is understanding the world in all its complexity—not proving something, not advocating, not advancing personal agendas, but understanding; the researcher includes personal experience and empathic insight as part of the relevant data, while taking a neutral nonjudgmental stance toward whatever content may emerge.
10. **Design flexibility**	Open to adapting inquiry as understanding deepens and/or situations change; avoids getting locked into rigid designs that eliminate responsiveness; pursues new paths of discovery as they emerge.

Source: Qualitative research and evaluation methods, by Michael Quinn Patton. Copyright © 2008 by Sage Publications Inc. Books. Reproduced with permission of Sage Publications Inc. Books in the textbook format via Copyright Clearance Center.

development and spread of this philosophy was Auguste Comte (1798–1857). In 1824 he wrote, "I believe that I shall succeed in having it recognized . . . that there are laws as well-defined for the development of the human species as for the fall of a stone."[9] Comte argued that the "positive" stage of human knowledge is reached when people begin to rely on empirical data, reason, and the development of scientific laws to explain phenomena. The scientific method, positivists believe, is the surest way to produce effective knowledge.

Although positivism has changed somewhat over the years, a basic premise is that there exists a reality "out there," independent of us, waiting to be discovered, that is driven by stable natural laws. The task of science is to discover the nature of this reality and how it works. A related emphasis is on breaking complex phenomena down into manageable pieces for study and eventual re-assembly into the whole. The researcher's role is that of a "disinterested scientist," standing apart from that which is being studied, with his or her biases and values excluded through experimental design and control.

Challenges to the philosophy of positivism have come from many directions and continue to be debated. In general, qualitative researchers are sympathetic to the issues raised by critical researchers that we described in Chapter 1, and they present their methods as an alternative to the quantitative approach. Many of them advocate a more "artistic," as opposed to a "scientific," approach to research. Further, their goals are often different; this is illustrated by the preference of some for fostering multiple interpretations of events, depending on how they are perceived by the individuals involved. This complicated

TABLE 18.3 *Differing Philosophical Assumptions of Quantitative and Qualitative Researchers*

Assumptions of Quantitative Researchers	Assumptions of Qualitative Researchers
There exists a reality "out there," independent of us, waiting to be known. The task of science is to discover the nature of reality and how it works.	The individuals involved in the research situation construct reality; thus, realities exist in the form of multiple mental constructions.
Research investigations can potentially result in accurate statements about the way the world really is.	Research investigations produce alternative visions of what the world is like.
It is possible for the researcher to remove himself or herself—to stand apart—from that which is being researched.	It is impossible for the researcher to stand apart from the individuals he or she is studying.
Facts stand independent of the knower and can be known in an undistorted way.	Values are an integral part of the research process.
Facts and values are distinct from one another.	Facts and values are inextricably intertwined.
The proper design of research investigations will lead to accurate conclusions about the nature of the world.	The initial ambiguity that occurs in a study is desirable.
The purpose of educational research is to explain and be able to predict relationships. The ultimate goal is the development of laws that make prediction possible.	The purpose of educational research is an *understanding* of what things mean to others. Highly generalizable "laws," as such, can never be found.

perspective is the opposite of what almost all physical scientists (and most social scientists) advocate.

Table 18.3 reveals the basic differences between the two approaches with regard to these philosophical assumptions.

Postmodernism

A number of scholars have begun to question whether research (and educational research in particular) can really contribute to an understanding of human behavior. These scholars, usually referred to as **postmodernists**, criticize the relevance of mainstream research as we have described it in many of the chapters in this text. They present an even more intensive critique of such research, in fact, than do the critical researchers we described in Chapter 1.

Postmodernists offer a number of criticisms of traditional research, but perhaps the most common are these: First, they deny the existence of underlying structures (e.g., meaning, laws) in the domain of social behavior. Foucault, in fact, argues that all knowledge and truth are products of history, power, and social interests and, hence, cannot be "discovered," as positivists, for example, believe.[10] Second, they argue that all naturally occurring (i.e., nonmathematical) languages are inevitably made up of ambiguous terms that change over time and that, therefore, all statements that use these languages cannot be verified.[11] Postmodernism has had an impact on all intellectual disciplines, including an increasing discussion of its implications for educational research.

What do you think? Can "truth" be verified? Or is it "a product of history, power, and social interests" as postmodernists claim?

Steps in Qualitative Research

The steps involved in conducting a qualitative research study are not as distinct as they are in quantitative research; they often overlap and are sometimes even conducted concurrently. Every qualitative study has a distinct starting and ending point, however. It begins when the researcher identifies the phenomenon he or she wishes to study, and it ends when the researcher draws final conclusions.

Although the steps involved in qualitative research are not as distinct as they are in quantitative studies (they aren't even necessarily sequential), several steps can be identified. Let us describe them briefly.

1. *Identification of the phenomenon to be studied.* Before any study can begin, the researcher must identify the particular phenomenon he or she is interested in investigating. Suppose, for example, a researcher wishes to conduct a study to investigate the interaction between minority and nonminority students in

CONTROVERSIES IN RESEARCH

Clarity and Postmodernism

Are the concepts and language that postmodernists use unnecessarily difficult to understand? Such criticisms are frequently made not only by education students but by others as well. Jones, for example, argues that this difficulty results from the fact that most students lack historical exposure to the context of the issues.* Constas believes that proponents of postmodernism in educational research need to provide better clarification† and (as paraphrased by Pillow) that some theorists "exhibit symptoms such as speaking gibberish, while others wander aimlessly (and meaninglessly), and still others are in a state of paralysis."‡ Lather counters that the search for clarity is part of the "humanist romance of knowledge as cure" and that the role of postmodernists is to question "taken-for-granted structures of intelligibility."§ These would include such concepts as "truth," "progress," "rationality," "gender," and "race."

Pillow argues that Constas misses the point. "Why, around questions of postmodernism's influence on educational research, are we still pursuing questions of truth and intelligibility? Perhaps what we need more of are examples of what postmodern research looks like, does, and is committed to. That is, less about attempts to contain what it is, and more working examples of what it may be."‖

*Jones, A. (1997). Teaching post-structuralist feminist theory in education: Student resistances. *Gender and Education, 9*(3), 266–269.
†Constas, M. A. (1998). Deciphering postmodern educational research. *Educational Researcher, 27*(9), 36–42.
‡Pillow, W. S. (2000, June–July). Deciphering attempts to decipher postmodern educational research. *Educational Researcher, 29,* 21–24.
§Lather, P. (1996). Troubling clarity: The politics of accessible language. *Harvard Educational Review 66*(3), 525–554.
‖Pillow, W. S. (2000, June–July). Deciphering attempts to decipher postmodern educational research. *Educational Researcher, 29,* 23.

an inner-city high school. The phenomenon of interest here is student interaction, specifically in an inner-city school. Admittedly, this is a rather general topic, but it does provide a starting point from which the researcher can proceed. Stated as a research question, the researcher might ask: "To what extent and in what ways do minority and nonminority students in an inner-city high school interact?"

Such a question suggests what are known as **foreshadowed problems**. All qualitative studies begin with such problems—they are akin to the overall statement of the problem that we discussed in Chapter 2. They give the researcher something to look for. They should not be considered restrictive or limiting, however, since their purpose is to provide direction, to serve as a guide. For example, as the investigation of the question mentioned proceeds, it may become evident that extracurricular as well as in-school activities need to be looked at, so the kinds of participation by students in such activities would be observed and analyzed. Foreshadowed problems are often reformulated several times during the course of a qualitative study.

2. *Identification of the participants in the study.* The participants in the study constitute the sample of individuals who will be observed (interviewed, etc.)—in other words, the subjects of the study. In almost all qualitative research, the sample is a **purposive sample** (see Chapter 6). Random sampling ordinarily is not feasible, since the researcher wants to ensure that he or she obtains a sample that is uniquely suited to the intent of the study. In the current example, inner-city high school students are the subjects of interest, but not just any group of such students will do. They must be found in a particular inner-city high school or schools.
3. *Generation of hypotheses.* Hypotheses are not usually stated at the beginning of a study as they are in most quantitative studies. The distinctive characteristic of hypotheses in qualitative research is that they are typically formulated *after* the researcher has begun the study; they are grounded in the data and are developed and tested in interaction with them, rather than being prior ideas that are simply tested against the data. It is true that many qualitative researchers explicitly state some of their ideas before they begin a study, but these are usually called "propositions" rather than hypotheses. Propositions differ from hypotheses in that they are flexible, discardable, and replaceable tools intended to help guide qualitative data collection and analysis. Qualitative researchers do not state propositions with the goal of proving or disproving them; rather, propositions are intended to help narrow the myriad foci

Figure 18.1 *How Qualitative and Quantitative Researchers See the World*

that qualitative researchers often face when conducting exploratory research. In the current example, a researcher might explore the proposition that interaction in an inner-city high school between minority and nonminority students, outside of daily class sessions, would be minimal. But as he or she observes the daily goings-on in the school, the researcher may reformulate the proposition to state that interaction between minority and nonminority students may actually occur quite frequently. This hypothesis, in effect, has "emerged" from the data.

4. *Data collection.* There is no "treatment" in a qualitative study, nor is there any "manipulation" of subjects. The participants in a qualitative study are not divided into groups, with one group being exposed to a treatment of some sort and the effects of this treatment then measured in some way. Data are not collected at the "end" of the study. Rather, the collection of data in a qualitative research study is ongoing. The researcher is continually observing people, events, and occurrences, often supplementing his or her observations with in-depth interviews of selected participants and the examination of various documents and records relevant to the phenomenon of interest.
5. *Data analysis.* Analyzing the data in a qualitative study essentially involves analyzing, synthesizing, and reducing the information the researcher obtains from various sources (e.g., observations, interviews, documents) into a coherent description of what he or she has observed or otherwise discovered. Hypotheses are not usually tested by means of inferential statistical procedures, as is the case with experimental or associational research, although some statistics, such as percentages, may be calculated if it appears they can illuminate specific details about the phenomenon under investigation. Data analysis in qualitative research, however, relies heavily on description; even when certain statistics are calculated, they tend to be used in a descriptive rather than an inferential sense (Figure 18.1). We shall discuss the collection and analysis of data in qualitative research in some detail in Chapter 19.
6. *Interpretations and conclusions.* In qualitative research, interpretations are made continuously throughout the course of a study. Whereas quantitative researchers usually leave the drawing of conclusions to the very end of their research, qualitative researchers tend to formulate their interpretations as they go along. As a result, one finds the researcher's conclusions in a qualitative study more or less integrated with other steps in the research process. A qualitative researcher who is observing the ongoing activities of an inner-city classroom, for example, is likely to write up not only what he or she sees each day but also his or her interpretations of those observations.

Approaches to Qualitative Research

One finds a number of approaches to qualitative research. Creswell, for example, has identified five, including narrative research, phenomenology, grounded theory, case studies, and ethnography.[12] Although these five by no means exhaust the variety of approaches that exist, we include them here because: (1) they are frequently seen "in the social, behavioral, and health sciences literature"; and (2) they have "systematic procedures for inquiry." To this list of approaches, we would add historical research. Although it is possible to find two or more variations or combinations of these approaches within a single study, we separate and describe them here as "pure" approaches to research design in order to simplify understanding. Let us present a brief description of each.

NARRATIVE RESEARCH

Narrative research is the study of the life experiences of an individual as told to the researcher or found in documents and archival material. An important aspect of some narrative research is that the participant recalls one or more special events (an "epiphany") in his or her life. The researcher in narrative research describes, in some detail, the setting or context within which the epiphany occurred. Lastly, the researcher is actively present during the study and openly acknowledges that his or her report is an interpretation of the participant's experiences.

Different forms of narrative research exist. "A **biographical study** is a form of narrative study in which the researcher writes and records the experiences of another person's life. **Autobiography** is written and recorded by the individuals who are the subject of the study (Ellis, 2004). A **life history** portrays an individual's entire life, while a personal experience story is a narrative study of an individual's personal experiences found in single or multiple episodes, private situations, or communal folklore (Denzin, 1989a). An **oral history** consists of gathering personal reflections of events and their causes and effects from one individual or several individuals (Plummer, 1983)."[13]

Narrative research is not easy to do, for a number of reasons:

1. The researcher must collect an extensive amount of information about the participant.
2. The researcher must have a clear understanding of the historical period within which the participant lived in order to position the participant accurately within that period.
3. The researcher needs a "sharp eye" to uncover the various aspects of the participant's life.
4. The researcher needs to be reflective about personal and political background, which may shape how the participant's story is told and understood.[14]

In sum, then, the authors of narrative research focus on a single individual, often describe special or important events in the individual's life, place the individual within a historical context, and try to place themselves in the research by acknowledging that the research is their interpretation of the participant's life.

PHENOMENOLOGY

A researcher undertaking a **phenomenological study** investigates various reactions to, or perceptions of, a particular phenomenon (e.g., the experience of teachers in an inner-city high school). The researcher hopes to gain some insight into the world of the participants and to describe their perceptions and reactions (e.g., what it is like to teach in an inner-city high school). Data are usually collected through in-depth interviewing. The researcher then attempts to identify and describe aspects of each individual's perceptions and reactions to his or her experience in some detail.

Phenomenologists generally assume that there is some commonality to how human beings perceive and interpret similar experiences; they seek to identify, understand, and describe these commonalities. This commonality of perception is referred to as the *essence*—the essential characteristic(s)—of the experience. It is the essential structure of a phenomenon that researchers want to identity and describe. They do so by studying multiple perceptions of the phenomenon as experienced by different people, and by then trying to determine what is common to these perceptions and reactions. This searching for the essence of an experience is the cornerstone—the defining characteristic—of phenomenological research.

Here are examples of the kinds of topics that might serve as the focus for a phenomenological study. Researchers might explore the experiences of:

- African-American students in a predominantly white high school

CONTROVERSIES IN RESEARCH

Portraiture: Art, Science, or Both?

Portraiture is a variation on biography. It first appeared in 1983 in a book by Lawrence-Lightfoot entitled *The Good High School: Portraits of Character and Culture.** It won the Outstanding Book Award from the American Educational Research Association in 1984. Its distinctive feature is that the researcher plays an avowedly interactive role with the person being portrayed. In a subsequent book, Lawrence-Lightfoot and her coauthor, Hoffman-Davis, argued that portraiture meets the criteria to be considered a science. They described the process as follows: "They (the portraitist and the person being described) both express their views and together define meaning-making," that is, getting the essence of the subject. Although the portraitist's "soul echoes through the piece," she or he works very hard not to simply produce a self-portrait."†

The controversy in this instance is not about the value of the method in producing powerful and useful results; that was demonstrated in *The Good High School,* but rather, whether the method can be considered "scientific," as its proponents argue. Portraitists cannot, of course, claim generalization beyond the subject(s) portrayed; they can adopt the position only that generalization is left to the reader.

Like all biographers, portraitists can claim only that other researchers would arrive at essentially the same descriptions and conclusions as they have. The nature of the interaction between the portraitist and the individual being portrayed makes triangulation virtually impossible—there is no other source for the portraitist to check his or her descriptions with. English has argued that the "objective of portraiture to capture the 'essence' of the subject is implicitly a quest for a stable truth which, in turn, requires the portraitist to become omniscient." He argues, further, that "the claim that the reader of portraiture can construct his or her own interpretations from 'thick description' ignores the complete dependence of the reader on a finished product from which there can be no independent access to information and alternative explanations" of that which has been described by the portraitist.‡

What do you think? Is portraiture science?

*Lawrence-Lightfoot, S. (1983). *The good high school: Portraits of character and culture.* New York: Basic Books.
†Lawrence-Lightfoot, S., & Hoffman-Davis, J. (1997, pp. 103, 105). *The art and science of portraiture.* San Francisco: Jossey-Bass.

‡English, F. W. (2000). A critical appraisal of Sara Lawrence-Lightfoot's portraiture as a method of educational research. *Educational Researcher, 29,* 7.

- Teachers who have used the inquiry approach in teaching ninth-grade social studies
- Civil rights workers in the South during the 1960s
- Nurses who work in the operating room of a large medical center

Like narrative research, phenomenological studies are not easy to do. The researcher must get the participants in a phenomenological study to relive in their minds the experiences they have had. Often, a number of recorded interview sessions are necessary. Once the interview process is completed, the researcher must search through each participant's statements for those that are especially relevant—those that appear to be particularly meaningful to the participant in describing his or her experience in relation to the phenomenon of interest. The researcher then clusters these statements into *themes,* those aspects of the participants' experiences that they had in common. The researcher then attempts to describe the fundamental features of the experience that have been described by most (ideally, all) of the participants in the study.

In sum, then, researchers who conduct phenomenological studies search for the "essential structure" of a single phenomenon by interviewing, in depth, a number of individuals who have experienced the phenomenon. The researcher extracts what he or she considers to be relevant statements from each participant's description of the phenomenon and then clusters these statements into themes, and then integrates these themes into a narrative description of the phenomenon.

GROUNDED THEORY

In a **grounded theory study**, researchers intend to generate a theory that is "'grounded' in data from participants who have experienced the process (Strauss & Corbin, 1998)."[15] Grounded theories are not generated before a study begins but are formed inductively from the data that are collected during the study itself. In other words, researchers start with the data they have collected and then develop generalizations after they look at the data. Strauss and Corbin put it this way: "One does not begin with a theory, then prove it. Rather one begins with an area of study and what is relevant to that area is allowed to emerge."[16]

Researchers doing a grounded theory study use what is called the *constant comparative method.* There is a continual interplay between the researcher, the data, and the theory that is being developed. Potential categories for grouping items of data are created, tried out, and discarded until a "fit" between theory and data is achieved. Lancy describes the process as follows:

> In a study of parental influence on children's reading of storybooks, Kelly Draper and I videotaped 32 parent-child pairs as they read to each other. We had few if any preconceptions about what we would find, only that we hoped that distinct patterns would emerge and that these would be associated with the children's evident ease/difficulty in learning to read. I spent literally dozens of hours viewing these videotapes, developing, using, and casting aside various categories until I found two clusters of characteristics which I called "reductionist" and "expansionist" that accounted for a large portion of the variation among parents' reading/listening styles. I was, of course, guided in my search for appropriate categories by my [experience] with the setting and by the transcripts of our interview with each parent.[17]

The data in a grounded theory study are collected primarily through one-on-one interviews, focus group interviews, and participant observation by the researcher(s). But it is an ongoing process. Data are collected and analyzed; a theory is suggested; more data are collected; the theory is revised; then more data are collected; the theory is further developed, clarified, revised; and the process continues.

Let us consider a hypothetical example of a grounded research study. Suppose that a researcher is interested in how principals try to maintain and enhance morale among the teachers in their schools. He or she might conduct a series of in-depth interviews with a number of principals in a few large urban high schools. Suppose the researcher finds that these principals utilize a variety of strategies to keep morale high, including having frequent one-on-one "praise sessions" to reward good teaching, acknowledging the efforts of teachers through written and oral commendations at faculty meetings, writing supportive letters and placing them in the teachers' personnel files, providing extra resources, replacing unnecessary meetings with routine information in writing, advising faculty of policy changes in advance and asking for their input and approval beforehand, and so forth.

In addition, the researcher not only observes how the principals interact with their faculties and listen to what they have to say, but also interviews some of their teachers and continually examines and thinks about the data he or she has collected through the interviews and observations. Gradually, the researcher develops a theory about what effective principals do to maintain and enhance morale among their teachers. The theory is then modified over time as the researcher observes and interviews even more principals and teachers. The point to stress here, however, is that the researcher does not go in with a theory ahead of time; rather he or she develops a theory out of the data that are collected—that is, one that is *grounded* in the data. This approach is obviously highly dependent on the insight of the individual researcher.

CASE STUDIES

The study of "cases" has been around for some time. Students in medicine, law, business, and the social sciences often study cases as part of their training. What **case study** researchers have in common is that they call the objects of their research *cases,* and they focus their research on the study of such cases. The case studies of Piaget and Vigotsky, for example, have contributed much to our understanding of cognitive and moral development.[18,19,20]

What is a case? A *case* comprises just one individual, classroom, school, or program. Typical cases are a student who has trouble learning to read, a social studies classroom, a private school, or a national curriculum project. For some researchers, a case is not just an individual or situation that can easily be identified (e.g., a particular individual, classroom, organization, or project); it may be an event (e.g., a campus celebration), an activity (e.g., learning to use a computer), or an ongoing process (e.g., student teaching).

Sometimes much can be learned from studying just one individual, one classroom, one school, or one school district. For example, there are some students who learn a second language rather easily. In hopes of gaining insight into why this is the case, one such student could be observed on a regular basis to see if there are any noticeable patterns or regularities in the student's behavior. The student, as well as his or her teachers, counselors, parents, and friends, might also be interviewed in depth. A similar series of observations (and interviews) might be conducted with a student who finds learning another language very difficult. As much information as possible (study style, attitudes toward the language, approach to the subject, behavior in class, and so on) would be collected. The hope here is that through the study of a somewhat unique individual, insights can be gained that will suggest ways to help other language students in the future.

Similarly, a detailed study might be made of a single school. There might be a particular elementary school in a given school district, for example, that is noteworthy for its success with at-risk students. The researcher might visit the school on a regular basis, observing what goes on in classrooms, during recess periods, in the hallways and lunchroom, during faculty meetings, and so on. Faculty members, administrators, support staff, and counselors could be interviewed. Again, as much information as possible (such as teaching strategies, administrative style, school activities, parental involvement, attitudes of faculty and staff toward students, classroom and other activities) would be collected. Here too, the hope would be that through the study of a single, rather unique case (in this instance not an individual but a school), valuable insights would be gained.

Stake has identified three types of case studies.[21] In an **intrinsic case study**, the researcher is primarily interested in understanding a specific individual or situation. He or she describes, in detail, the particulars of the case to shed light on what is going on. Thus, a researcher might study a particular student to find out why that student is having trouble learning to read. Another researcher might want to understand how a school's student council operates. A third might wish to determine how effectively (or whether) an after-school detention program is working. All three of these examples involve the study of a single case. The researcher's goal in each instance is to understand the case in all its parts, including its inner workings. Intrinsic case studies are often used in exploratory research when researchers seek to learn about some little-known phenomenon by studying it in depth.

In an **instrumental case study**, on the other hand, a researcher is interested in understanding something more than just a particular case; the researcher is interested in studying the particular case only as a means to some larger goal. A researcher might study how Ms. Brown teaches phonics, for example, to learn something about phonics as a method or about the teaching of reading in general. The researcher's goal in such studies is more global and less focused on the particular individual, event, program, or school being studied. Researchers who conduct such studies are more interested in drawing conclusions that apply beyond a particular case than they are in conclusions that apply to just one specific case.

Third, there is the **multiple-** (or **collective**) **case study** in which a researcher studies multiple cases at the same time as part of one overall study. For example, a researcher might choose several cases to study because he or she is interested in the effects of mainstreaming children with disabilities into regular classrooms. Instead of studying the results of such mainstreaming in just a single classroom, the researcher studies its impact in a number of different classrooms.

Which is to be preferred, multiple- or single-case designs? Multiple-case designs have both advantages and disadvantages when compared to single-case designs. The results of multiple-case studies are often considered more compelling, and they are more likely to lend themselves to valid generalization. On the other hand, certain types of cases (the rare case, the critical case for testing a theory, or the case that permits a researcher to observe a phenomenon previously inaccessible to scientific study) require single-case research. Furthermore, multiple-case studies often require extensive resources and time. Any decision to undertake multiple-case studies, therefore, cannot be taken lightly. Yin argues that researchers who do undertake multiple-case studies, therefore, should employ what he calls "replication logic." Here is his rationale:

> Thus, if one has access to only three cases of a rare, clinical syndrome in . . . medical science, the appropriate research design is one in which the same results are predicted for each of the three cases, thereby producing evidence that the three cases did indeed involve the same syndrome. If similar results are obtained from all three cases, replication (of results) is said to have taken place.[22]

ETHNOGRAPHIC AND HISTORICAL RESEARCH

With regard to the remaining two approaches to qualitative research, we shall not describe them here because each is discussed in detail in later chapters. We selected these two to discuss in greater depth because they represent distinctly different approaches. Ethnographic research focuses on the study of culture. Historical research concentrates exclusively on the past. We will discuss them in Chapters 21 and 22.

SAMPLING IN QUALITATIVE RESEARCH

Researchers who engage in some form of qualitative research are likely to select a purposive sample (see Chapter 6)—that is, they select a sample they feel will yield the best understanding of what they are studying. At least nine types of purposive sampling have been identified:[23]

1. **Typical sample**, one that is considered or judged to be typical or representative of that which is being studied (e.g., a class of elementary school pupils selected because they are judged to be typical third-graders).
2. **Critical sample**, one that is considered to be particularly enlightening because it is so unusual or exceptional (e.g., individuals who have attained high achievement despite some serious physical limitations).
3. **Homogeneous sample**, one in which all of the members possess a certain trait or characteristic (e.g., a group of high school students all judged to possess exceptional artistic talent).
4. **Extreme case sample**, one in which all of the members are outliers who do not fit the general pattern or who otherwise display extreme characteristics (e.g., students achieve high grades despite low scores on ability tests and poor home environments).
5. **Theoretical sample**, one that helps the researcher to understand a concept or theory (e.g., selecting a group of tribal elders to assess the relevance of Piagetian theory to the education of Native Americans).
6. **Opportunistic sample**, one chosen during a study to take advantage of new conditions or circumstances that have arisen (e.g., eyewitnesses to a fracas at a high school football game).
7. **Confirming sample**, one that is obtained to validate or disconfirm preliminary findings (e.g., follow-up interviews with students to verify reasons some students drop out).
8. **Maximal variation sample**, one selected to represent a diversity of perspectives or characteristics (e.g., a group of students who possess a wide variety of attitudes toward recent school policies).
9. **Snowball sample**, one selected as need arises during the conduct of a study (e.g., during the interviewing of a group of principals, they recommend others who also should be interviewed because they are particularly knowledgeable about the subject of the research).

Qualitative Data Analysis

Data analysis in qualitative research is an iterative and continuously comparative process that involves reducing and retrieving large amounts of written (and sometimes pictorial) information. Qualitative data are usually obtained from interviews, observations, and focus groups. The technique that qualitative researchers most often use to analyze their data is called **coding** (see Chapter 7 and later discussion in Chapter 20). Strauss and Corbin define coding in qualitative studies "as the analytic process through which data are fractured, conceptualized and integrated to form theory."[24]

In general, codes are tags or labels for assigning meaning to chunks of data. When coding a sentence or paragraph, the coder tries to capture succinctly the major idea brought out by the sentence or paragraph. Qualitative codes can be descriptive or interpretive and are usually generated *a priori* (selective coding) or emerge inductively (open coding) from data. Codes and subcodes are often refined iteratively by qualitative researchers as they strive to make sense of their data through categorization, thematic analysis, and in some cases advanced theory building.

Generalization in Qualitative Research

A **generalization** is usually thought of as a statement or claim of some sort that applies to more than one individual, group, object, or situation. Thus, when a researcher makes a statement, based on a review of the literature, that there is a negative correlation between age and amount of interest in school (older children are less interested in school than younger children), he or she is making a generalization.

The value of a generalization is that it allows us to have expectations (and sometimes to make predictions) about the future. Although a generalization might not be true in every case (e.g., some older children may be more interested in school than some younger children), it describes, more often than not, what we would expect to find. Almost all researchers hope that useful generalizations can be derived from their research. A limitation of qualitative research is that there is seldom methodological justification for generalizing the findings of a particular study. While this limitation also applies to many quantitative studies, it is almost inevitable given the nature of qualitative research. Because of this, **replication** of qualitative studies is even more important than it is in quantitative research.

Eisner points out that not only ideas but also skills and images can be generalized. We generalize a skill when we apply it in a situation different from the one in which we learned the skill. Images also generalize. As Eisner points out, it is this fact—that images generalize—that leads a qualitative researcher to look for certain characteristics in a classroom, certain ways of teaching, that he or she can apply elsewhere. Once a researcher has an image of "excellence" in teaching, for example, he or she can apply this image to a variety of situations. "For qualitative research, this means that the creation of an image—a vivid portrait of excellent teaching, for example—can become a prototype that can be used in the education of teachers or for the appraisal of teaching."[25] In Eisner's words:

> Direct contact with the qualitative world is one of our most important sources of generalization. But . . . we do not need to learn everything first-hand. We listen to storytellers and learn about how things were, and we use what we have been told to make decisions about what will be. We see photos and learn what to expect on our forthcoming trip to Spain. We see the play *On the Waterfront* and learn something about corruption in the shipping industry and, more important, about the conflicts and tensions between two brothers. We see the film *One Flew over the Cuckoo's Nest* and understand a bit more about how people survive in an institution that is hell-bent on their domestication. . . .
>
> Attention to the particular, to the case, is descriptive not only of the case, but of other cases like it. When Sara Lawrence-Lightfoot writes about the Brookline High School or the George Washington Carver High School or the John F. Kennedy High School, she tells us more than just what those particular schools are like; we learn something about what makes a good high school.[26] Do all high schools have to be good in the same way? No. Can some high schools share some of their characteristics? Yes. Can we learn from Lawrence-Lightfoot what to look for? Certainly.[27]

There is little question, we think, that generalization is possible in qualitative research. But it is a type of generalization that differs from what is found in much quantitative research. In many experimental and quasi-experimental studies, the researcher generalizes from the sample under investigation to the population of interest usually with statistics through a process called statistical generalization (see Chapter 6). Note that it is the researcher who does the generalizing.* He or she is likely to suggest to practitioners that the findings are of value and can (sometimes they say *should*) be applied in their situations.

In qualitative studies, on the other hand, the researcher may also generalize, but it is much more likely that any generalizing to be done will be carried out by interested practitioners—by individuals who are in situations similar to the one(s) investigated by the researcher. This is referred to as theoretical generalization using the process of "transferability" that we discuss at the end of this section. It is the practitioner, rather than the researcher, who judges the applicability of the researcher's findings and conclusions, who determines whether the researcher's findings fit his or her situation. Eisner makes this clear:

> The researcher might say something like this: "This is what I did and this is what I think it means. Does it have any bearing on your situation? If it does and if your situation is troublesome or problematic, how did it get that way and what can be done to improve it?"[27]

It is worth noting that not all qualitative researchers look at generalizing in the same way. Some are concerned less "with the question of whether their findings are generalizable, but rather with the question of to *which* other settings and subjects they are generalizable.[28] Bogdan and Biklen give an example:

> In the study of an intensive care unit at a teaching hospital, we studied the ways professional staff and parents communicate about the condition of the children. As we concentrated on the interchanges, we noticed that the professional staff not only diagnosed the infants but sized up the parents as well. These parental evaluations formed the basis for judgments the professionals made about what to say to parents and how to say it. Reflecting about parent-teacher conferences in public schools and other situations where professionals have information about children to which parents might want access, we began to see parallels. . . . One tack we are presently exploring is the extent to which the findings of the intensive care unit are generalizable not to other settings of the same substantive type, but to other settings, such as schools, in which professionals talk to parents.

Qualitative investigators, then, are less definitive, less certain about the conclusions they draw from their research. They tend to view them as ideas to be shared, discussed, and investigated further. Modification in

*Remember that a researcher is entitled to generalize only if the sample has been randomly selected from the population. Many times, such is not the case.

different circumstances and under different conditions will almost always be necessary. These issues are often referred to as *transferability,* defined by Morrow as achieved when "the researcher provides sufficient information about self (the researcher as instrument) and the research context, participants, and the researcher-participant relationship to enable the reader to decide how the findings may transfer."[29] (see discussion in Chapter 23).

Internal Validity in Qualitative Research

To the extent that a qualitative study does not attempt to explore relationships, internal validity is, strictly speaking, not as important as it is in quantitative research. However, because qualitative research is so dependent on the researcher in both collecting and interpreting information, an important consideration, even in purely descriptive studies, is researcher bias. Further, qualitative studies frequently do contain interpretations involving relationships. Examples of this occur in the studies evaluated in Chapters 19 to 24. When this is the case, attention should be given to assessing and, where possible, controlling each of the threats discussed in Chapter 9. Though more difficult in qualitative research, it is sometimes possible, as discussed in the Chapter 20 study critique, to control particular threats. The exception is historical research, wherein control is, we think, virtually impossible.

Ethics and Qualitative Research

Ethical concerns affect qualitative research just as much as they do any of the other kinds of research that we have considered in this book. Nevertheless, a few points bear repeating because of their importance.

First, unless otherwise agreed to, the identities of all who participate in a qualitative study should always be protected; care should be taken to ensure that none of the information collected would embarrass or harm them. If confidentiality cannot be maintained, participants must be so informed and given the opportunity to withdraw from the study.

Second, participants should always be treated with respect. It is especially important in qualitative studies to seek the cooperation of all subjects in the research endeavor. Usually, subjects should be told of the researcher's interests and should give their permission to proceed. Researchers should never lie to subjects nor record any conversations using a hidden recording device or other mechanical apparatus.

Third, researchers should do their best to ensure that no physical or psychological harm will come to anyone who participates in the study. This seems rather obvious, perhaps, but researchers sometimes are placed in a difficult position because they find, inadvertently, that subjects *are* being harmed. Consider the following example. In certain studies in state institutions for the mentally disabled, researchers have witnessed the physical abuse of residents. What is their ethical responsibility in such cases? Here is what two researchers who observed such abuse first-hand had to say:

> In the case of physical abuse, the solution may seem obvious at first: Researcher or not, you should intervene to stop the beatings. In some states, it is illegal not to report abuse. That was our immediate disposition. But, through our research, we came to understand that abuse was a pervasive activity in most such institutions nationally, not only part of this particular setting. Was blowing the whistle on one act a responsible way to address this problem or was it a way of getting the matter off our chests? Intervention may get you kicked out. Might not continuing the research, publishing the results, writing reports exposing national abuse, and providing research for witnesses in court (or being an expert witness) do more to change the conditions than the single act of intervention? Was such thinking a copout, an excuse not to get involved?[30]

What do you think?

As the excerpt reveals, ethical concerns are difficult ones indeed. Two other points deserve mention. Many researchers are concerned that subjects do not get very much in return from participating in a research investigation. After all, the studies that researchers do often lead to the advancement of their careers. They help professors get promoted. Study results are frequently reported in books that bring their authors royalty checks. Researchers get to talk about what they have learned; their work, when well done, helps them gain the respect of their colleagues. But what do subjects get? Participants often (perhaps usually) do not have a chance to reciprocate and/or tell what their lives are like. As a result, subjects sometimes get misrepresented or even demeaned. Accordingly, some researchers have tried to design studies in which researcher and participants are more like partners in an investigation where the subjects definitely have a say.

Furthermore, there is another ethical concern, somewhat related to the preceding, that must be addressed. This occurs when there is the possibility that certain research findings, in the hands of the powerful, may lead to actions that could actually hurt subjects (or people in similar circumstances) and/or lead to public policies or public attitudes that are actually harmful to certain groups. What a researcher might see as "a sympathetic portrayal of people living in a housing project might be read by others as proving prejudices about poor people being irresponsible and prone to violence."[31] The ethical point to stress here, then, is this: While researchers can never be sure how their findings will be received, they must always be sure to think carefully about the implications of their work, who the results of this work may affect, and how.

We offer, then, a number of specific questions that we think all researchers, no matter what kind of research they prefer, should think about before, during, and after the completion of any study they undertake:

- Is the study being contemplated *worth* doing?
- Do the researchers have the necessary *expertise* to carry out a study of good quality?
- Have the participants in the study been given *full information* about what the study will involve?
- Have the participants willingly given their *consent to participate?*
- Who will *gain* from this research?
- Is there a *balance* between gains and costs for both researchers and participants?
- Who, if anyone, might be *harmed* (physically or psychologically) in this study, and to what degree? What is to be done should harmful, illegal, or wrongful behavior be witnessed?
- Will the participants in the study be *deceived* in any way?
- Will *confidentiality* be assured?
- Who *owns the data* that will be collected and analyzed in this study?
- How will the results of the study be *used?* Is there any possibility for misuse? If so, how?

Qualitative and Quantitative Research Reconsidered

Can qualitative and quantitative approaches be used together? Of course. And often they should be. In survey research, for example, it is common not only to prepare a closed-ended (e.g., multiple-choice) questionnaire for people to answer in writing, but also to conduct open-ended personal interviews with a random sample of the respondents. Descriptive statistics are sometimes used to provide quantitative details in an otherwise qualitative study. Many historical studies include a combination of qualitative and quantitative methodologies, and their final reports present both kinds of data.

Nevertheless, it must be admitted that carrying out a sophisticated quantitative study *and* an in-depth qualitative investigation at the same time is difficult to pull off successfully. Indeed, it is *very* difficult. Oftentimes what is produced is a study that is neither a good qualitative nor a good quantitative piece of work.

Which is the better approach—qualitative or quantitative? Although we hear this question a lot, we think it's pretty much a waste of energy. Oftentimes you will hear overly zealous advocates of one or the other approach disparaging the other. They say that theirs is the best (indeed, sometimes the only) method to use if one wants to do really useful research on important questions and that the other is badly flawed and can only lead to spurious or trivial results. But here is what two eminent qualitative researchers have to say:

> By far, the most widely held (view) is that there is no one best method. It all depends on what you are studying and what you want to find out. If you want to find out what the majority of the American people think about a particular issue, survey research which relies heavily on quantitative design in picking your sample, designing and pretesting your instrument, and analyzing the data is best. If you want to know about the process of change in a school and how the various school members experience change, qualitative methods will do a better job. Without a doubt there are certain questions and topics that the qualitative approach will not help you with, and the same is true of quantitative research.[32]

We agree. The important thing is to know what questions can best be answered by which method or combination of methods.

Go back to the **INTERACTIVE AND APPLIED LEARNING** feature at the beginning of the chapter for a listing of interactive and applied activities. Go to the **Online Learning Center** at **www.mhhe.com/fraenkel9e** to take quizzes, practice with key terms, and review chapter content.

Main Points

THE NATURE OF QUALITATIVE RESEARCH

- The term *qualitative research* refers to studies that investigate the *quality* of relationships, activities, situations, or materials.
- The natural setting is a direct source of data, and the researcher is a key part of the instrumentation process in qualitative research.
- Qualitative data are collected mainly in the form of words or pictures and seldom involve numbers. Coding is the primary technique used in data analysis.
- Qualitative researchers are especially interested in how things occur and particularly in the perspectives of the subjects of a study.
- Qualitative researchers do not, usually, formulate a hypothesis beforehand and then seek to test it. Rather, they allow hypotheses to emerge as a study develops.
- Qualitative and quantitative research differ in the philosophical assumptions that underlie the two approaches.

STEPS INVOLVED IN QUALITATIVE RESEARCH

- The steps involved in conducting a qualitative study are not as distinct as they are in quantitative studies. They often overlap and sometimes are even conducted concurrently.
- All qualitative studies begin with a foreshadowed problem, the particular phenomenon the researcher is interested in investigating. Some qualitative researchers state propositions to help their data collection and also analysis.
- Researchers who engage in a qualitative study of some type usually select a purposive sample. Several types of purposive samples exist.
- There is no treatment in a qualitative study, nor is there any manipulation of variables.
- The collection of data in a qualitative study is ongoing.
- Conclusions are drawn continuously throughout the course of a qualitative study.

APPROACHES TO QUALITATIVE RESEARCH

- A biographical study tells the story of the special events in the life of a single individual.
- A researcher studies an individual's reactions to a particular phenomenon in a phenomenological study. He or she attempts to identify the commonalities among different individual perceptions.
- In a grounded theory study, a researcher forms a theory inductively from the data collected as a part of the study.
- A case study is a detailed study of one or (at most) a few individuals or other social units, such as a classroom, a school, or a neighborhood. It can also be a study of an event, an activity, or an ongoing process.

GENERALIZATION IN QUALITATIVE RESEARCH

- Generalizing is possible in qualitative research, but it is of a type different from that found in quantitative studies. Most likely it will be done by interested practitioners.

ETHICS AND QUALITATIVE RESEARCH

- The identities of all participants in a qualitative study should be protected, and they should be treated with respect.

RECONSIDERING QUALITATIVE AND QUANTITATIVE RESEARCH

- Aspects of both qualitative and quantitative research often are used together in a study. Increased attention is being given to such mixed-methods studies.
- Whether qualitative or quantitative research is the most appropriate boils down to what the researcher wants to find out.

Key Terms

autobiography 430
biographical study 430
case study 432
coding 434
confirming sample 434
critical sample 434
extreme case sample 434
foreshadowed problem 428
generalization in qualitative research 434
grounded theory study 431
homogeneous sample 434
instrumental case study 433
intrinsic case study 433
life history 430
maximal variation sample 434
multiple- (collective) case study 433
narrative research 430
opportunistic sample 434
oral history 430
phenomenological study 430
portraiture 431
positivism 425
postmodernist 427
purposive sample 428
qualitative research 424
replication 435
snowball sample 434
theoretical framework 425
theoretical sample 434
typical sample 434

For Discussion

1. What do you see as the greatest strength of qualitative research? the biggest weakness?
2. Are there any topics or questions that could *not* be studied using a qualitative approach? If so, give an example. Is there any type of information that qualitative research cannot provide? If so, what might it be?
3. Qualitative researchers are sometimes accused of being too subjective. What do you think a qualitative researcher might say in response to such an accusation?
4. Qualitative researchers say that "complete" objectivity is impossible. Would you agree? Explain your reasoning.
5. "The essence of all good research is understanding, rather than an attempt to prove something." What does this statement mean?
6. "All researchers are biased to at least some degree. The important thing is to be aware of one's biases!" Is just being "aware" enough? What else might one do?
7. Qualitative researchers often say that "the whole is greater than the sum of its parts." What does this statement mean? What implications does it have for educational research?

8. Would it be possible to use random sampling in qualitative research? Would it be desirable? Explain.
9. In what way is generalization in qualitative research different from generalization in quantitative research—or is it?
10. What do you think is the ethical responsibility of researchers if they witness an instance of physical abuse in a qualitative study they are conducting?

References

1. Usher, E. L. (2009). Sources of middle school students' self-efficacy in mathematics: A qualitative investigation. *American Educational Research Journal, 46*(3), 275–314.

2. Ozdemir, A. (2008). Shopping malls: Measuring interpersonal distance under changing conditions and across cultures. *Field Methods, 20*(8), 226–248.

3. Wallace, R. M. (2004). A framework for understanding teaching with the Internet. *American Educational Research Journal, 41*(1), 447–488.

4. Khan, C. A. (2009). Go play in traffic: Skating, gender, and urban context. *Qualitative Inquiry, 15,* 1084–1102.

5. Dickson-Swift, V., et al. (2009). Researching sensitive topics: Qualitative research as emotion work. *Qualitative Research, 9*(2), 61–79.

6. Bogdan, R. C., & Biklen, S. K. (2007). *Qualitative research for education: An introduction to theory and methods* (5th ed.), Boston: Allyn & Bacon.

7. Some qualitative researchers, however, do use statistical procedures to clarify their data. See, for example, Miles, M. B., & Huberman, A. M. (1994). *Qualitative data analysis (*2nd ed.), Beverly Hills, CA: Sage.

8. Bogdan, R. C., & Biklen, S. K. (2007, p. 6). *Qualitative research for education: An introduction to theory and methods* (5th ed.), Boston: Allyn & Bacon.

9. Bernard, H. R. (2000). *Social research methods: Qualitative and quantitative approaches.* Thousand Oaks, CA: Sage.

10. Foucault, M. (1972). *The archaeology of knowledge.* New York: Harper and Row.

11. Derrida, J. (1972, pp. 242–272). Discussion: Structure, sign, and plot in the discourse of the human sciences. In R. Macksey and E. Donato (Eds.), *The structuralist controversy.* Baltimore: Johns Hopkins University Press.

12. Creswell, J. W. (2007, p. 9). *Qualitative inquiry and research design: Choosing among five approaches.* Thousand Oaks, CA: Sage.

13. Creswell, J. W. (2007, p. 55). *Qualitative inquiry and research design: Choosing among five approaches.* Thousand Oaks, CA: Sage. Citations within the quotation include: Ellis, C. (2004). *The ethnographic it: A methodological novel about autoethnography.* Walnut Creek, CA: AltaMira; Denzin, N. K. (1989a). *Interpretive biography.* Newbury Park, CA: Sage; and Plummer, K. (1983). *Documents of life: An introduction to the problems and literature of a humanistic method.* London: George Allen & Unwin.

14. Creswell, J. W. (2007, p. 57). *Qualitative inquiry and research design: Choosing among five approaches.* Thousand Oaks, CA: Sage.

15. Creswell, J. W. (2007, p. 63). *Qualitative inquiry and research design: Choosing among five approaches.* Thousand Oaks, CA: Sage. Citation within the quotation is: Strauss, A., & Corbin, J. (1998). *Basics of qualitative research: Grounded theory procedures and techniques* (2nd ed.). Newbury Park, CA: Sage.

16. Strauss, A., & Corbin, J. (1994). Grounded theory methodology: An overview. In A. Denzin and Y. Lincoln (Eds.), *Handbook of qualitative research.* Thousand Oaks, CA: Sage.

17. Lancy, D. F. (2001, p. 9). *Studying children in schools: Qualitative research traditions.* Prospect Heights: Waveland Press.

18. Piaget, J. (1936/1963). *The origins of intelligence in the child.* New York: Norton.

19. Piaget, J. (1932/1965). *The moral judgments of the child.* New York: Free Press.

20. Vigotsky, L. S. (1914/1962). *Thought and language.* Cambridge, MA: MIT Press.

21. Stake, R. (1997). *The art of case study research.* Thousand Oaks, CA: Sage.

22. Yin, R. K. (1994). *Case study research: Design and methods.* Thousand Oaks, CA: Sage.

23. Adapted from Creswell, J. W. (2005, pp. 204–207). *Educational research: Planning, conducting, and evaluating quantitative and qualitative research.* Upper Saddle River, NJ: Pearson Merrill Prentice Hall.

24. Strauss, A., & Corbin, J. (1998, p. 3). *Basics of qualitative research: Grounded theory procedures and techniques* (2nd ed.). Newbury Park, CA: Sage.

25. Eisner, E. W. (1991, p. 199). *The enlightened eye: Qualitative inquiry and the enhancement of educational practice.* New York: Macmillan.

26. Lightfoot, S. L. (1983). *The good high school.* New York: Basic Books.

27. Eisner, E. W. (1991, pp. 202–204). *The enlightened eye: Qualitative inquiry and the enhancement of educational practice.* New York: Macmillan.

28. Bogdan, R. C., & Biklen, S. K. (2007). *Qualitative research for education: An introduction to theory and methods* (5th ed., p. 36). Boston: Allyn & Bacon.

29. Morrow, S. (2005). Quality and trustworthiness in qualitative research in counseling psychology. *Journal of Counseling Psychology, 52,* 52.

30. Bogdan, R. C., & Biklen, S. K. (2007). *Qualitative research for education: An introduction to theory and methods* (5th ed., pp. 51–52). Boston: Allyn & Bacon.

31. Bogdan, R. C., & Biklen, S. K. (2007). *Qualitative research for education: An introduction to theory and methods* (5th ed., p. 53). Boston: Allyn & Bacon.

32. Bogdan, R. C., & Biklen, S. K. (2007). *Qualitative research for education: An introduction to theory and methods* (5th ed., p. 53). Boston: Allyn & Bacon.

19 Observation and Interviewing

Observation

Participant Observation
Nonparticipant Observation
Naturalistic Observation
Simulations
Observer Effect
Observer Bias
Coding Observational Data
The Use of Technology

Interviewing

Types of Interviews
Key-Actor Interviews
Types of Interview Questions
Interviewing Behavior
Focus Group Interviews
Recording Interview Data
Ethics in Interviewing: The Necessity for Informed Consent
Data Collection and Analysis in Qualitative Research

Validity and Reliability in Qualitative Research

An Example of Qualitative Research

Analysis of the Study

Purpose/Justification
Definitions
Prior Research
Hypotheses
Sample
Instrumentation
Procedures/Internal Validity
Data Analysis
Result/Interpretation
Conclusions

OBJECTIVES Studying this chapter should enable you to:

- Explain what is meant by the term "observational research."
- Describe at least four different roles an observer can take in a qualitative study.
- Explain what is meant by the term "participant observation."
- Explain what is meant by the term "nonparticipant observation."
- Explain what is meant by the term "naturalistic observation."
- Describe what a simulation is and how it might be used by a researcher.
- Describe what is meant by the term "observer effect."
- Explain what is meant by the term "observer bias."
- Describe the type of sampling that occurs in observational studies.
- Describe briefly four types of interviews qualitative researchers use.
- Explain what a "key actor" is.
- List at least three expectations that exist for all interviews.
- Explain what a focus group interview is.
- Describe briefly why an informed consent form is needed in interview research.
- Give at least four procedures qualitative researchers use to check on or enhance validity and reliability in qualitative studies.

INTERACTIVE AND APPLIED LEARNING After, or while, reading this chapter:

Go to the Online Learning Center at www.mhhe.com/fraenkel9e to:

- Learn More About Interviews and Observations

Go to your online Student Mastery Activities book to do the following activities:

- Activity 19.1: Observer Roles
- Activity 19.2: Types of Interviews
- Activity 19.3: Types of Interview Questions
- Activity 19.4: Do Some Observational Research

"What was it like to be a student teacher?"

"Well, uh, (laughs), it's sort of, uh, hard to describe. I guess I liked it, now that it's all over (laughs). But there were times, uh, . . . I had a lot of trouble at first with discipline. You know, controlling the kids. Couldn't seem to manage them. Especially when they wouldn't sit down and started wandering around the room. Teaching isn't easy, you know, even for the old pros. And there I was, just a beginner. Not even sure I wanted to be a teacher. I was older, too, than most of the other student teachers. Didn't have a lot in common with them, me having been in the military and all. But then, things changed."

"What happened?"

"Well, I sort of got the hang of it. I learned some things. Began to learn my craft, you might say (smiles). I learned to control them better. I, uh, didn't take any guff, you know (laughs). Oh, I wasn't mean or anything like that, just firm. Yeah! You know, uh, uh, they respect it if you're firm. You got to be. They don't like wishy-washy teachers. Took me a while to learn that. But then I got better at explaining things too, and that made it easier to control the kids. And I set up some rules. They had to be in their seats when the bell rang, and they got points if they were. I had an election for a class president who I had sit at the front of the room and whose job was to keep order. That worked great. And then I had a weekly class meeting where we talked about things they liked and things they thought could be improved. And I also . . ."

This conversation is part of an in-depth interview between a qualitative researcher and a 55-year-old retired Air Force Major who has returned to school to get a middle school teaching credential. In-depth interviewing is one of the staples of qualitative research. It is one of the things we shall discuss in some detail in this chapter.

Qualitative researchers use three main techniques to collect and analyze their data: observing people as they go about their daily activities and recording what they do; conducting in-depth interviews with people about their ideas, their opinions, and their experiences; and analyzing documents or other forms of communication (content analysis). Interviews can provide us with information about people's attitudes, their values, and what they think they do. If you want to know what they actually do, however, there is no substitute for watching them or examining documents and other forms of communication that they create. In this chapter, we discuss observation and interviewing in some detail. We will discuss the analysis of documents in Chapter 20.

Observation

Certain kinds of research questions can best be answered by *observing* how people act or how things look. For example, researchers could interview teachers about how their students behave during class discussions of sensitive issues, but a more accurate indication of their activities would probably be obtained by actually observing such discussions while they take place.

The degree of observer participation can vary considerably. There are four different roles that a researcher can take, ranging on a continuum from complete participant to complete observer.

PARTICIPANT OBSERVATION

In **participant observation** studies, researchers actually participate in the situation or setting they are observing.

When a researcher takes on the role of a *complete participant* in a group, his identity is not known to any of the individuals being observed. The researcher interacts with members of the group as naturally as possible and, for all intents and purposes (so far as they are concerned), is one of them. Thus, a researcher might arrange to serve for a year as an actual teacher in an inner-city classroom and carry out all of the duties and responsibilities that are a part of that role, but not reveal that he is also a researcher. Such covert observation is suspect on ethical grounds.

When a researcher chooses the role of *participant-as-observer,* he participates fully in the activities of the group being studied, but also makes it clear that he is doing research. As an example, the researcher just described might tell the faculty that he is a researcher and intends to describe as thoroughly and accurately as he can what goes on in the school over the course of a year's time.

Participant observation can be *overt,* in that the researcher is easily identified and the subjects know that they are being observed; or it can be *covert,* in which case the researcher disguises his or her identity and acts just like any of the other participants. For example, a researcher might ask a ninth-grade geography teacher to allow him to observe one of that teacher's classes over the course of a semester. Both teacher and students would know the researcher's identity. This would be an example of overt observation. Overt participant observation is a key ingredient in ethnographic research, which we will discuss in more detail in Chapter 21.

On the other hand, another researcher might take the trouble to become certified as an elementary school teacher and then spend a period of time actually teaching in an elementary school while observing what is going on. No one would know the researcher's identity (with the possible exception of the district administration, from whom permission would have been obtained beforehand). This would be an example of covert observation. Covert participant observation, although likely to produce more valid observations of what really happens, is often criticized on ethical grounds. Observing people without their knowledge (and/or recording their comments without their permission) seems to some a highly questionable practice.

Is it ethical to observe people without their knowledge? What about so-called passive deception, such as that involved in observing people as they go about their business in public places, like restaurants and airports? Or what about observing children's schoolyard activities from a distance using a telephoto lens? What do you think?

NONPARTICIPANT OBSERVATION

In a **nonparticipant observation** study, researchers do not participate in the activity being observed but rather "sit on the sidelines" and watch; they are not directly involved in the situation they are observing.

When a researcher chooses the role of *observer-as-participant,* she identifies herself as a researcher but makes no pretense of actually being a member of the group she is observing. An example might be a university professor who is interested in what goes on in an inner-city school. The researcher might conduct a series of interviews with teachers in the school, visit classes, attend faculty meetings and collective bargaining negotiations, talk with principals and the superintendent, and talk with students, but she would not attempt to participate in the activities of the group other than superficially. She remains essentially (and does not hide the fact that she is) an interested observer who is doing research.

Finally, the role of *complete observer* is just that—a role at the opposite extreme from the role of complete participant. The researcher observes the activities of a group without in any way participating in those activities. The subjects of the researcher's observations may, or may not, realize they are being observed. An example would be a researcher who observes the daily activities in a school lunchroom.*

Each of the observer roles we have described has both advantages and disadvantages. The complete participant is probably most likely to get the truest picture of a group's activities, and the others less so, but the ethical question involving covert observation remains. The complete observer is probably least likely to affect the actions of the group being studied, the others more so. The participant-as-observer, since he or she is an actual member of the group being studied, will have some (and often an important) effect on what the group does. The participant-as-observer and the observer-as-participant are both likely, in varying degrees, to focus the attention of the group on the activities of the researcher and away from their normal routine, thereby making their activities no longer typical. Figure 19.1 indicates how approaches to observation can vary.

*Note that many of the techniques described in Chapter 7 are also examples of nonparticipant observation frequently used in both qualitative and quantitative studies.

Role of the Observer			
Full-participant observation	Partial participation	Onlooker; observer is an outsider	
How the Observer Is Portrayed to Others			
Participants know that observations are being made and they know who is making them.	Some but not all of the participants know the observer.	Participants do not know that observations are being made or that there is someone observing them.	
How the Purpose of the Observation Is Portrayed to Others			
The purpose of the observation is fully explained to all involved.	The purpose of the observation is explained to some of the participants.	No explanation is given to any of the participants.	False explanations are given; participants are deceived about the purpose of the observation.
Duration of the Observations			
A single observation of limited duration (e.g., 30 minutes).	Multiple observations; long-term duration (e.g., months, even years).		
Focus of the Observations			
Narrow focus: Only a single element or characteristic is observed.	Broad focus: Holistic view of the activity or characteristic being observed and all of its elements sought.		

Figure 19.1 *Variations in Approaches to Observation*

NATURALISTIC OBSERVATION

Naturalistic observation involves observing individuals in their natural settings. The researcher makes no effort whatsoever to manipulate variables or to control the activities of individuals, but simply observes and records what happens as things naturally occur. The activities of students at an athletic event, the interactions between students and teachers on the playground, or the activities of very young children in a nursery, for example, are probably best understood through naturalistic observation.

Much of the work of the famous child psychologist Jean Piaget involved naturalistic observation. Many of his conclusions on cognitive development, which grew out of watching his own children as they developed, have stimulated further research in this area. Insights obtained as a result of naturalistic observation, in fact, often serve as the basis for more formal experiments.

SIMULATIONS

To investigate certain variables, researchers sometimes will *create* a situation and ask subjects to act out, or *simulate,* certain roles. In **simulations**, the researcher, in effect, actually tells the subjects what to do (but not how to do it). This permits a researcher to observe what happens in certain kinds of situations, including those that occur fairly infrequently in schools or other educational settings. For example, individuals might be asked to portray a counselor interacting with a distraught parent, a teacher disciplining a student, or two administrators discussing their views on enhancing teacher morale.

Two main types of role-playing simulations are used by researchers in education: individual role playing and team role playing. In individual role playing, a person is asked to role-play how he or she thinks a particular individual might act in a given situation. The researcher then observes and records what happens. Here is an example:

> You are an elementary school counselor. You have an appointment with a student who is frequently abusive toward his teachers. The student has just arrived for his 9:00 A.M. appointment with you and is sitting before you in your office. What do you say to this student?

In team role playing, a group of individuals is asked to act out a particular situation, with the researcher again observing and recording what goes on. Particular attention is paid to how the members of the group interact. Here is an example:

> You and five of your faculty colleagues have been appointed as a temporary special committee to discuss and come up with solutions to the problem of students cutting classes, which has been increasing this semester. Many of the faculty support a "get tough" policy and have openly advocated suspending students who are frequent cutters. The group's assignment is to come up with other alternatives that the faculty will accept. What do you propose?

The main disadvantage to simulations, as you might have recognized, is their artificiality. Situations are being acted out, and there is no guarantee that what the researcher sees is what would normally occur in a real-life situation. The results of a simulation often serve as hypotheses in other kinds of research investigations.

OBSERVER EFFECT

The presence of an observer can have a considerable impact on the behavior of those being observed and, hence, on the outcomes of a study; this is known as an **observer effect**. Also the **observational data** (that which the observer records) inevitably to some extent reflect the biases and viewpoints of the observer. Let us consider each of these facts a bit further.

There is always the problem of reactivity in observational research. Getting around the reactivity problem involves staying around long enough to get people used to the observer's presence. As Bernard suggests, eventually "people just get plain tired of trying to manage your impression and they act naturally. In [spot sampling] research, the trick is to catch a glimpse of people in their natural activities before they see you coming on the scene—before they have a chance to modify their behavior."[1]

Unless a researcher is concealed, it is quite likely that he or she will have some effect on the behavior of those individuals who are being observed. Two things can happen, particularly if an observer is unexpected. First, the individual is likely to arouse curiosity and result in a lack of attention to the task at hand, thus producing other-than-normal behavior. An inexperienced researcher who records such behavior might easily be misled. It is for this reason that researchers who observe in classrooms, for example, usually alert the teacher beforehand and ask to be introduced. They then may spend four to five days in the classroom before starting to record observations (to enable the students to become accustomed to their presence and go about their usual activities).

The second thing that can happen is that the behavior of those who are being observed might be influenced by the researcher's purpose. For example, suppose a researcher is interested in observing whether social studies teachers ask "high-level questions" during class discussions of controversial issues. If the teachers are aware of what the researcher is looking for, they may tend to ask more questions than normal, thus giving a distorted impression of what really goes on during a typical class discussion. The data obtained by the researcher's observation would not be representative of how the teachers normally behave. It is for this reason that many researchers argue that the participants in a study should not be informed of the study's purposes until after the data have been collected. Instead, the researchers should meet with the participants before the study begins and tell them that they cannot be informed of the purpose of the study since it might affect the study's outcomes. As soon as the data have been collected, however, the researcher should reveal the findings to those who are interested.

OBSERVER BIAS

Observer bias refers to the possibility that certain characteristics or ideas of observers may bias what they "see." Over the years, qualitative researchers have continually had to deal with the charge that it is very easy for their prejudices to bias their data. But this is something with which all researchers must deal. It is probably true that no matter how hard observers try to be impartial, their observations will possess some degree of bias. No one can be totally objective, as we all are influenced to some degree by our past experiences, which in turn affect how we see the world and the people within it. Nevertheless, all researchers should do their best to become aware of, and try to control, their biases.

What qualitative researchers try to do is to study the subjective factors objectively. They do this in a number of ways. They spend a considerable amount of time at the site, getting to know their subjects and the environment (both physical and cultural) in which they live. They collect copious amounts of data and check their perceptions against what the data reveal. Realizing that most situations and settings are very complex, they do their best to collect data from a variety of perspectives, using a variety of formats. Not only do they prepare extremely detailed field notes, but they attempt to reflect on their own subjectivity as a part of these field notes. Often they work in teams so that they can check their observations against another's (Figure 19.2). Although

Figure 19.2 *The Importance of a Second Observer as a Check on One's Conclusions*

they realize (as should all researchers) that one's biases can never be completely eliminated from one's observations, the important thing is to reflect on how one's own attitudes may influence what one perceives.

A related concern here is **observer expectations**. If researchers know they are to observe subjects who have certain characteristics (such as a certain IQ range, ethnicity, or religion), they may "expect" a certain type of behavior, which may not be how the subjects normally behave. It is in this regard that audio and video recordings are so valuable, as they allow researchers to check their observations against the impressions of others.

CODING OBSERVATIONAL DATA

Over the years, quantitative researchers have developed a number of coding schemes to use when they observe. A **coding scheme** is a set of categories (e.g., "gives directions," "asks questions," "praises") that an observer uses to record the frequency of a person's or group's behavior. Coding schemes have been used to measure interactions between parents and adolescent children in a laboratory setting;[2] interactions of college students drinking alcohol in a group setting;[3] doctor-patient interactions in the office of family physicians;[4] and student-teacher interactions in a classroom.[5] One such coding scheme, primarily used in quantitative research, was developed by Amidon and Flanders nearly 50 years ago but is still in use.[6] It is shown in Figure 19.3.

These schemes require the observer to judge and categorize behavior as it occurs. This is in contrast to more qualitative approaches that attempt to describe all or most of what occurs in a given situation. At a later time, these data are coded into categories that emerge as the analysis proceeds. This is particularly true in ethnographic research. We shall give an example of this type of coding in Chapter 20.

THE USE OF TECHNOLOGY

Even with a fixed coding scheme like the one shown in Figure 19.3, however, the observer must still choose from among alternatives when coding the behavior of people. When is someone being "critical," for example, or "encouraging"? Video recording the behavior of people permits the researcher to repeatedly view the behavior of an individual or a group and then decide how to code it at a later, usually more relaxed and convenient time.

Furthermore, a major difficulty in observing people is the fact that much that goes on may be missed by the observer. This is especially true when several behaviors of interest are occurring rapidly in an educational setting. In addition, sometimes a researcher wants to have

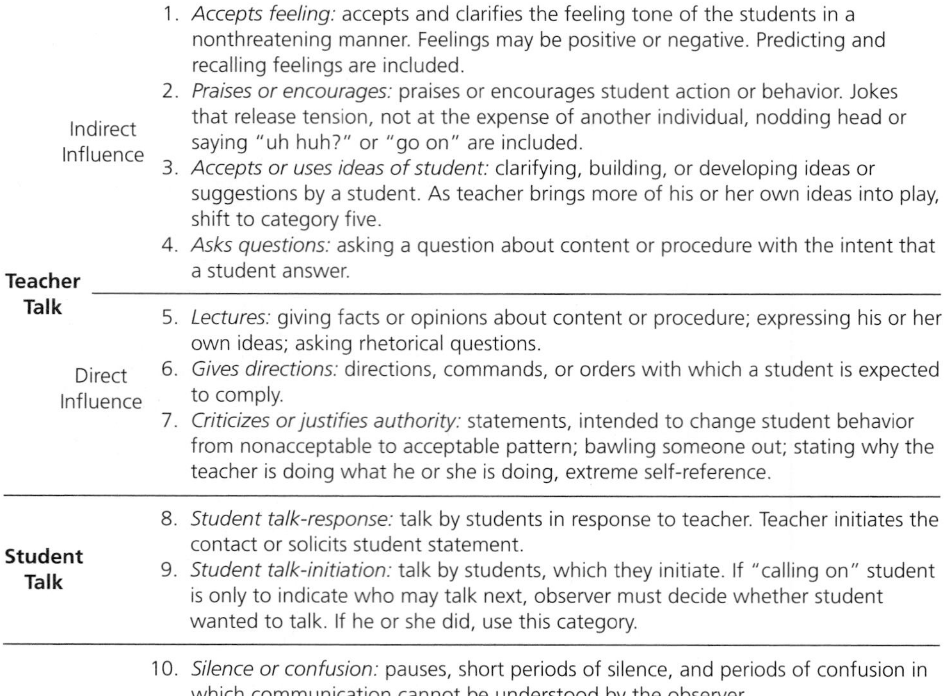

Teacher Talk

Indirect Influence

1. *Accepts feeling:* accepts and clarifies the feeling tone of the students in a nonthreatening manner. Feelings may be positive or negative. Predicting and recalling feelings are included.
2. *Praises or encourages:* praises or encourages student action or behavior. Jokes that release tension, not at the expense of another individual, nodding head or saying "uh huh?" or "go on" are included.
3. *Accepts or uses ideas of student:* clarifying, building, or developing ideas or suggestions by a student. As teacher brings more of his or her own ideas into play, shift to category five.
4. *Asks questions:* asking a question about content or procedure with the intent that a student answer.

Direct Influence

5. *Lectures:* giving facts or opinions about content or procedure; expressing his or her own ideas; asking rhetorical questions.
6. *Gives directions:* directions, commands, or orders with which a student is expected to comply.
7. *Criticizes or justifies authority:* statements, intended to change student behavior from nonacceptable to acceptable pattern; bawling someone out; stating why the teacher is doing what he or she is doing, extreme self-reference.

Student Talk

8. *Student talk-response:* talk by students in response to teacher. Teacher initiates the contact or solicits student statement.
9. *Student talk-initiation:* talk by students, which they initiate. If "calling on" student is only to indicate who may talk next, observer must decide whether student wanted to talk. If he or she did, use this category.

10. *Silence or confusion:* pauses, short periods of silence, and periods of confusion in which communication cannot be understood by the observer.

Figure 19.3 *The Amidon/Flanders Scheme for Coding Categories of Interaction in the Classroom*

Source: Amidon, E. J., & Hough, J. B. (1967). *Interaction analysis: Theory, research, and application.* Reading, MA: Addison-Wesley.

someone else (such as an expert on the topic of interest) offer insights about what is happening. A researcher who observes a number of children's play sessions in a nursery school setting, for example, might want to obtain the ideas of a qualified child psychologist or an experienced teacher of preschool children about what is happening.

To overcome these obstacles, researchers may use recording devices to document their observations. These have several advantages. They may be replayed several times for continued study and analysis. Experts or interested others can also hear and/or see what the researcher observed and offer their insights accordingly. And a permanent record of certain kinds of behaviors is obtained for comparison with later or different samples.

A few disadvantages to such recordings, however, should also be noted. A good video record is not always the easiest to obtain and usually requires training or prior experience by the researcher or technician. Sometimes several microphones must be set up for audio recordings, which can distort the behavior of those being observed. Prolonged recording can be expensive. Audio recordings are somewhat easier to do, but they of course record only verbal behavior. Furthermore, sometimes it is difficult to distinguish specific speakers in a recording of many voices. Noise is difficult to control and often seriously interferes with the understanding of content. Nevertheless, if these difficulties can be overcome, the use of audio and video recording offers considerable promise to researchers as a way to collect, store, and analyze data.

Interviewing

A second method used by qualitative researchers to collect data is to **interview** selected individuals. Interviewing (i.e., the careful asking of relevant questions) is an important way for a researcher to check the accuracy of—to verify or refute—impressions gained through observation. Fetterman, in fact, describes interviewing as the most important data collection technique a qualitative researcher possesses.[7]

The purpose of interviewing people is to find out what is on their minds—what they think or how they feel about something. As Patton has remarked:

> We interview people to find out from them those things we cannot directly observe. The issue is not whether observational data is more desirable, valid, or meaningful than self-report data. The fact of the matter is that we cannot observe everything. We cannot observe feelings, thoughts, and intentions. We cannot observe behaviors that took place at some previous point in time. We cannot observe situations that preclude the presence of an observer. We cannot observe how people have organized the world and the meanings they attach to what goes on in the world. We have to ask people questions about those things.[8]

"How do I feel? I feel that your question is trivial, courts sensationalism, and is designed to appeal to appallingly base instincts. Additionally, it demeans my intelligence. Next question."

TYPES OF INTERVIEWS

There are four types of interviews: structured, semistructured, informal, and retrospective. Although these different types often blend and merge into one another, we shall describe them separately to clarify how they differ.

Structured and **semistructured interviews** are verbal questionnaires. Rather formal, they consist of a series of questions designed to elicit specific answers from respondents. Often they are used to obtain information that can later be compared and contrasted. For example, a researcher interested in how the characteristics of teachers in urban and suburban schools differ might conduct a structured interview (i.e., asking a set of structured questions) with a group of urban high school teachers to obtain background information about them—their education, their qualifications, their previous experience, their out-of-school activities, and so on—in order to compare these data with the same data (i.e., answers to the same questions) obtained from a group of teachers who teach in the suburbs. In qualitative research, structured and semistructured interviews are often best conducted toward the end of a study, as they tend to shape responses to the researcher's perceptions of how things are. They are most useful for obtaining information to test a specific hypothesis that the researcher has in mind.

Informal interviews are much less formal than structured or semistructured interviews. They tend to resemble casual conversations, pursuing the interests of both the researcher and the respondent in turn. They are the most common type of interview in qualitative research. They do not involve any specific type or sequence of questions or any particular form of questioning. The primary intent of an informal interview is to find out what people think and how the views of one individual compare with those of another.

Although at first glance they seem like they would be easy to conduct, informal interviews are probably the most difficult of all interviews to do well. Issues of ethics appear almost immediately. Researchers often need to make some sensitive decisions as an informal interview progresses. When, for example, is a question too personal to pursue? To what extent should the researcher "dig deeper" into how an individual feels about something? When is it more appropriate to refrain from probing further about an individual's response? How, in fact, does a researcher establish a climate of ease and familiarity while at the same time trying to learn in some detail about a respondent's life?

Although informal interviews offer the most natural type of situation for the collection of data, there is always some degree of artificiality present in any type of interview. A skillful interviewer, however, soon learns to begin with nonthreatening questions to put a respondent at ease before he or she poses more personal and (potentially) threatening questions. Always, the researcher must establish an atmosphere of trust, cooperation, and mutual respect if he or she is to obtain accurate information. Planning and asking good questions, while developing and maintaining an atmosphere of mutual trust and respect, is an art that anyone who wishes to do competent qualitative research must learn.

Retrospective interviews can be structured, semi-structured, or informal. A researcher who conducts a retrospective interview tries to get a respondent to recall and then reconstruct from memory something that has happened in the past. A retrospective interview is the least likely of the four interview types to provide accurate, reliable data for the researcher.

Table 19.1 summarizes some of the major interviewing strategies used in educational research. The first three strategies are more likely (although not exclusively) to be utilized in qualitative studies, the fourth more likely (but again, not exclusively) in quantitative studies. The reader is reminded, however, that it is not uncommon to find several of these strategies employed in the same study.

TABLE 19.1 ***Interviewing Strategies Used in Educational Research***

Type of Interview	Characteristics	Strengths	Weaknesses
Informal conversational interview	Questions emerge from the immediate context and are asked in the natural course of things; there is no predetermination of question topics or wording.	Increases the salience and relevance of questions; interviews are built on and emerge from observations; the interview can be matched to individuals and circumstances.	Different information collected from different people with different questions. Less systematic and comprehensive if certain questions do not arise "naturally." Data organization and analysis can be quite difficult.
Interview guide approach	Topics and issues to be covered are specified in advance, in outline form; interviewer decides sequence and wording of questions in the course of the interview.	The outline increases the comprehensiveness of the data and makes data collection somewhat systematic for each respondent. Logical gaps in data can be anticipated and closed. Interviews remain fairly conversational and situational.	Important and salient topics may be inadvertently omitted. Interviewer flexibility in sequencing and wording questions can result in substantially different responses from different perspectives, thus reducing the comparability of responses.
Standardized open-ended interview	The exact wording and sequence of questions are determined in advance. All interviewees are asked the same basic questions in the same order. Questions are worded in a completely open-ended format.	Respondents answer the same questions, thus increasing comparability of responses; data are complete for each person on the topics addressed in the interview. Reduces interviewer effects and bias when several interviewers are used. Permits evaluation users to see and review the instrumentation used in the evaluation. Facilitates organization and analysis of the data.	Little flexibility in relating the interview to particular individuals and circumstances; standardized wording of questions may constrain and limit naturalness and relevance of questions and answers.
Closed, fixed-response interview	Questions and response categories are determined in advance. Responses are fixed; respondent chooses from among these fixed responses.	Data analysis is simple; responses can be directly compared and easily aggregated; many questions can be asked in a short time.	Respondents must fit their experiences and feelings into the researcher's categories; may be perceived as impersonal, irrelevant, and mechanistic. Can distort what respondents really mean or have experienced by so completely limiting their response choices.

Source: Qualitative research and evaluation methods, by Michael Quinn Patton, Copyright © 2008 by Sage Publications Inc. Books. Reproduced with permission of Sage Publications Inc. Books in the textbook format via Copyright Clearance Center.

KEY-ACTOR INTERVIEWS

Some people in any group are more informed about the culture and history of their group, as well as more articulate, than others. Such individuals, traditionally called **key informants**, are especially useful sources of information. Fetterman prefers the term **key actors** to avoid the stigma attached to the term *informant,* as well as the historical roots that underlie the term.[9] Key actors are especially knowledgeable individuals and thus often excellent sources of information. They can often provide detailed information about a group's past and about contemporary happenings and relationships, as well as the everyday nuances—the ordinary details—that others might miss. They offer insights that are often invaluable to a researcher. Fetterman gives an example of a key actor who proved helpful to him in a study of school dropouts.

> James was a long-term janitor in the Detroit dropout program [a program that Fetterman was studying]. He grew up in the local community with many of the students and was extraordinarily perceptive about the differences between the serious and less serious students in the program, as well as between the serious and less serious teachers. I asked him whether he thought the students were obeying the new restrictions against smoking, wearing hats in the building, and wearing sneakers. He said, "You can tell from the butts on the floor that they is still smokin', no matter what dey tell yah. I know, cause I gotta sweep 'em up. . . . It's mostly the new ones, don't yah know, like Kirk, and Dyan, Tina. You can catch 'em almost any ol' time. I seen 'em during class in the hallways, here (in the cafeteria), and afta hours." He provided empirical evidence to support his observations—a pile of cigarette butts he had swept up while we were talking.[10]

Here is another example from Fetterman's research.

> In a study of a gifted and talented education program, my most insightful and helpful key actor was a school district supervisor. He told about the politics of the school district and how to avoid the turf disputes during my study. He drove me around the community to teach me how to identify each of the major neighborhoods and pointed out corresponding socioeconomic differences that proved to have an important impact on the study. He also described the cyclical nature of the charges of elitism raised against the program by certain community members and a former school board member. He confided that his son (who was eligible to enter the program) had decided not to enter. This information opened new doors to my perception of peer pressure in that community.[10]

As you can see, a key actor can be an extremely valuable source of information. Accordingly, researchers need to take the time to seek out and establish a bond of trust with these individuals. The information they provide can serve as a cross-check on data the researcher obtains from other interviews, from observations, and from content analysis. But the musings of a key actor must also be viewed with some caution. Care must be taken to ensure that a key actor is not merely providing information he or she thinks the researcher wants to hear. This is why a researcher needs to seek out multiple sources of information in any study.

TYPES OF INTERVIEW QUESTIONS

Patton has identified six basic types of questions that can be asked of people. Any or all of these questions might be asked during an interview. The six types are background (or demographic) questions, knowledge questions, experience (or behavior) questions, opinion (or values) questions, feelings questions, and sensory questions.[11]

Background (or **demographic**) **questions** are routine sorts of questions about the background characteristics of the respondents. They include questions about education, previous occupations, age, income, and the like.

Knowledge questions pertain to the factual information (as contrasted with opinions, beliefs, and attitudes) respondents possess. Knowledge questions about a school, for example, might concern the kinds of courses available to students, graduation requirements, the sorts of extracurricular activities provided, school rules, enrollment policies, and the like. From a qualitative perspective, what the researcher wants to find out is what the respondents consider to be factual information (as opposed to beliefs or attitudes).

Experience (or **behavior**) **questions** focus on what a respondent is currently doing or has done in the past. Their intent is to elicit descriptions of experience, behaviors, or activities that could have been observed but (for reasons such as the researcher not being present) were not. Examples might include, "If I had been in your class during the past semester, what kinds of things would I have been doing?" or, "If I were to follow you through a typical day here at your school, what experiences would I be likely to see you having?"

Opinion (or **values**) **questions** are aimed at finding out what people *think* about some topic or issue. Answers to such questions call attention to the respondent's goals, beliefs, attitudes, or values. Examples might include such questions as, "What do you think about the principal's new policy concerning absenteeism?" or, "What would you like to see changed in the way things are done in your U.S. history class?"

Feelings questions concern how respondents *feel* about things. They are directed toward people's emotional responses to their experiences. Examples might include such questions as, "How do you feel about the way students behave in this school?" or, "To what extent are you anxious about going to gym class?"

Feelings and opinion questions are often confused. It is important for anyone who wishes to be a skillful interviewer to be able to distinguish between the two types of questions and to know when to ask each. To find out how someone feels about an issue is not the same thing as finding out their opinion about the issue. Thus, the question, "What do you think (what is your opinion) about your teacher's homework policy?" asks for the respondent's *opinion*—what he or she thinks—about the policy. The question, "How do you feel (what do you like or dislike) about your teacher's homework policy?" asks how the respondent *feels* about (his or her attitude toward) the policy. The two, although they appear somewhat similar, ask for decidedly different kinds of information.

Sensory questions focus on what a respondent has seen, heard, tasted, smelled, or touched. Examples might include questions such as, "When you enter your classroom, what do you see?" or, "How would you describe what your class sounds like?" Although this type of question could be considered as a form of experience or behavior question, it is often overlooked by researchers during an interview. Further, such questions are sufficiently distinct to warrant a category of their own.

INTERVIEWING BEHAVIOR

A set of expectations exists for all interviews. Here are some of the most important.

- *Respect the culture of the group being studied.* It would be insensitive, for example, for a researcher to wear expensive clothing while conducting an interview with an impoverished, inner-city high school youth. Of course, a researcher may commit an occasional faux pas inadvertently, which most interviewees will forgive. A constant disregard for a group's traditions and values, however, is bound to impede the researcher's efforts to obtain reliable and valid information.
- *Respect the individual being interviewed.* Those who agree to be interviewed give up time they might spend elsewhere to answer the researcher's questions. An interview, therefore, should not be viewed as an opportunity to criticize or evaluate the interviewee's actions or ideas; rather, it is an opportunity to learn from the interviewee. A classroom teacher, a student, a counselor, a school custodian—all have work to do, and hence every researcher is well reminded not to waste their time. Interviews should start and end at the scheduled times and be conducted courteously. Further, the researcher should pick up on cues given by the interviewee. As Fetterman points out, "repeated glances at a watch are usually a clear signal that the time is up. Glazed eyes, a puzzled look, or an impatient scowl is an interviewee's way of letting the questioner know that something is wrong. The individual is lost, bored, or insulted. Common errors involve spending too much time talking and not enough time listening, failing to make questions clear, and making an inadvertently insensitive comment."[12] (Figure 19.4 illustrates an example of an interviewee who is *not* being respected.)
- *Be natural.* "Acting like an adolescent does not win the confidence of adolescents, it only makes them suspicious."[13] Deception in any form has no place in an interview.
- *Develop an appropriate rapport with the participant.* Here you have to be careful, for dangers lurk. Seidman points out the problem: "Rapport implies getting along with each other, a harmony with, a conformity to, an affinity for one another. The problem is that, carried to an extreme, the desire to build rapport with the participant can transform the interviewing relationship into a full 'We' relationship in which the question of whose experience is being related and whose meaning is being made is critically confounded.[14] He goes on to describe an incident that occurred in a study he conducted in a community college:

> In our community college study, one participant invited my wife and me to his house for dinner after (an) interview . . . I had never had such an invitation from a participant . . . and I did not quite know what to do. I did not want to appear ungracious, so we accepted. My wife and I went to dinner at his home. We had a wonderful California backyard cookout and it was a pleasure to spend time with the participant and his family. But a few days later, when I met him at his faculty office for the third interview, he was so warm and familiar toward me, that I could not retain the distance that I needed to explore his responses. I felt tentative as an interviewer because I did not want to risk violating the spirit of hospitality that he had created by inviting us to his home.[15]

Figure 19.4 *An Interview of Dubious Validity*

- *Ask the same question in different ways during the interview.* This enables the researcher to check his or her understanding of what the interviewee has been saying, and may even shed new light on the topic being discussed.
- *Ask the interviewee to repeat an answer or statement when there is some doubt about the completeness of a remark.* This can stimulate discussion when an interviewee tends to respond with terse, short answers to the researcher's questions.
- *Vary who controls the flow of communication.* In a formal, structured interview, it is often necessary for the researcher to control the asking of questions and the pace of the discussion. In informal interviews, particularly during the exploratory or initial phase of an interview, it is often wise to let the interviewee ramble a bit in order to establish a sense of trust and cooperation.
- *Avoid leading questions.* Leading questions presume an answer, as in questions like "You wanted to do that, of course?" or "Your friends talked you into that, didn't they?" or "How much did that upset you?" Each of these questions leads the participant to respond in a certain way. More appropriate versions of these questions would be "What did you want to do?" and "Why did you do that?" and "How did you feel about that?"

Instead of leading questions, interviewers often ask **open-ended questions**. Open-ended questions indicate an area to be explored without suggesting to the participant how it should be explored. They do not presume an answer. Here are some examples: "What was the meeting like for you?" or "Tell me what your student teaching experience was like?" There are many possibilities for open-ended questions and many ways of asking them. Perhaps none is better than simply asking "What was that like for you?" when an interviewer wants to get at a participant's subjective experience.

- Do not ask **dichotomous questions**, that is, questions that permit a yes-no answer, when you are trying to get a complete picture. Here are some examples: "Were you satisfied with your assignment?" "Have you changed as a result of teaching at Adams School?" "Was that a good experience for you?" "Did you know what to do when you were asked to do that?" And so forth.

The problem with dichotomous questions is that they do not encourage the respondent to talk. Oftentimes, when an interviewer is having trouble getting a participant to talk, it is because he or she is asking a string of dichotomous questions.

Patton presents what is perhaps the classic example of a series of dichotomous questions in the following conversation between a teenager and his parent. The teen has just returned home from a date:

Do you know that you're late?
Yeah.
Did you have a good time?
Yeah.

Did you go to a movie?
Yeah.
Was it a good movie?
Yeah, it was okay.
So, it was worth seeing?
Yeah, it was worth seeing.
I've heard a lot about it. Do you think I would like it?
I don't know. Maybe.
Anything else you'd like to tell me about your evening?
No, I guess that's it.
(Teenager goes upstairs to bed. One parent turns to the other and says: "It sure is hard to get him to talk to us.")[16]

As you can see, the problem with asking dichotomous questions is that they can easily turn an interview into something more like a test or interrogation.

- *Ask only one question at a time.* Asking more than one question is a common error made by novice interviewers, and you sometimes see this on poorly designed questionnaires as well. Rather than asking only a single question and allowing the participant to respond, the interviewer asks several questions one after the other without allowing the interviewee to answer (Figure 19.5). Here is an example:

  What was that like for you? Did you participate? You said you found it difficult. Was it difficult for you or for the other people who were participating as well? And how do you think they felt about it?

- *Listen actively.* Experienced interviewers are patient and listen attentively from beginning to end in order to evaluate if a participant's answer is sufficient. If an answer is incomplete, the seasoned interviewer quickly assesses the possible cause and then asks a follow-up or redirective question to get more precise and complete information.
- *Don't interrupt.* This is perhaps the most important feature of good interviewing. Don't interrupt participants when they are talking. And this is especially true when a participant says something that the interviewer finds particularly interesting. Often it is tempting to interrupt the speaker to pursue this interesting item, but to do so may interrupt the participant's train of thought. It is better to simply jot down a brief note and then follow up on it later, when there is a pause in the conversation.

FOCUS GROUP INTERVIEWS

In a **focus group interview**, the interviewer asks a small group of people (usually four to eight) to think about a series of questions. The participants are seated together

Figure 19.5 *Don't Ask More Than One Question at a Time*

How Not to Interview

Following is a hypothetical situation involving a researcher interviewing a teacher who has just finished using her district's new mathematics curriculum.

Researcher: *This is a very important topic, but don't be nervous. (Fails to establish rapport)*

Teacher: *Okay.*

Researcher: *I assume you had prior experience working with this type of mathematics materials?*

Teacher: *Well, yes, a little.*

Researcher: *That's too bad. I was hoping you would be more experienced. (Indicates desired response)*

Teacher: *Well, actually, now that I think about it, I did use similar materials a year or so ago. (Gives desired response)*

Researcher: *Oh, where was that? (Irrelevant comment)*

Teacher: *In Utah.*

Researcher: *Really? I'm from Utah—how did you like it there? (Loses focus)*

Teacher: *I loved it. Skiing was great!*

Researcher: *I'm a tennis player myself.*

Teacher: *What's this got to do with math?*

in a group and get to hear one another's responses to the questions. Often they offer additional comments beyond what they originally had to say once they hear the other responses. They may agree or disagree; consensus is neither necessary nor desired. The object is to get at what people really think about an issue or issues in a social context where the participants can hear the views of others and consider their own views accordingly.

We should stress, however, that a focus group interview is not a discussion. Neither is it a problem-solving session, nor is it a decision-making group. It is an *interview.*[17]

Focus groups generally last one to two hours, and can cover five to six core questions. There are typically three parts to a focus group discussion guide that are similar to the three parts of an interview. The opening part is when the focus group facilitator or moderator welcomes and introduces members of the group and explains the purpose, context, and rules of the focus group. The middle part is reserved for asking participants to answer the main research questions, and the closing section is typically for thanking and debriefing participants and giving them an opportunity for further input.

Thus, the role of the focus group moderator is critical especially in terms of facilitating interaction between group members, drawing out differing perspectives, and keeping the session focused. In some instances, facilitators will need to challenge participants, especially to tease out differing opinions about a topic. Skilled moderators know when to probe for more details and how to move the discussion forward when it veers off course. Moderators should also be knowledgeable about the project and research in general.

RECORDING INTERVIEW DATA

No matter what kind of interview one conducts, and no matter how carefully one prepares the interview questions, all will be to no avail if the interviewer does not capture what the interviewee actually says. While the interview is going on, therefore, it is essential to record as faithfully as possible what the participant has to say. Some method for recording an interviewee's words exactly is required.

A recording device, therefore, is often considered an indispensable part of any qualitative researcher's equipment. "Tape recorders do not 'tune out' conversations, change what has been said because of interpretation (either conscious or unconscious), or record words more slowly than they are spoken."[18]

Using a recording device, however, does not eliminate the need for taking notes. As Patton points out:

> Notes can serve at least two purposes: (1) Notes taken during the interview can help the interviewer formulate new questions as the interview moves along, particularly where it may be appropriate to check out something that was said earlier; and (2) taking notes about what is said will facilitate later analysis, including locating important quotations from the tape itself . . . the failure to take notes will often indicate to the respondent that nothing of importance is being said.[19]

ETHICS IN INTERVIEWING: THE NECESSITY FOR INFORMED CONSENT

In-depth interviews ask participants to reveal much about their lives. During such interviews, a measure of intimacy can develop between interviewers and participants that can lead participants to share information about events in their lives that, if misused, could leave them very vulnerable. Participants deserve to be protected from such vulnerability. Furthermore, interviewers also need to be protected against any misunderstanding on the part of participants as to the nature and purpose of the interview itself.

Thus, we believe that it is ethically desirable in this instance for interviewers to require participants to sign an informed consent form. We suggest that any such form include points similar to those shown in Figure 4.1.

DATA COLLECTION AND ANALYSIS IN QUALITATIVE RESEARCH

As pointed out in Chapter 18 and described previously, there are important differences between quantitative and qualitative approaches to data collection and analysis. Although qualitative research can, and sometimes does, make use of structured instruments such as those described in Chapter 7, the preference is for less structured, open-ended data collection with structuring taking place later through content analysis or emergent themes (Chapter 20) as the means of data analysis. While other descriptive statistics are often relevant, the most commonly used is reporting of frequencies. As the use of mixed-methods designs continues to increase, we expect to see more use of quantitative analysis in conjunction with more customary qualitative analyses.

Validity and Reliability in Qualitative Research

In Chapter 8, we introduced the concepts of validity and reliability as they apply to the use of instruments in educational research. These two concepts are also very important in qualitative research, only here they apply to the observations researchers make and to the responses they receive to the interview questions. A fundamental concern in qualitative research, in fact, revolves around the degree of confidence researchers can place in what they have seen or heard. In other words, how can researchers be sure that they are not being misled?

You will recall that **validity** refers to the appropriateness, meaningfulness, and usefulness of the inferences researchers make based specifically on the data they collect, while **reliability** refers to the consistency of these inferences over time, location, and circumstances.

Note that qualitative researchers often use the term **credibility** or trustworthiness to encompass not only instrument validity and reliability but internal validity as well.

In a qualitative study, much depends on the perspective of the researcher. All researchers have certain biases. Accordingly, different researchers see some things more clearly than others. Qualitative researchers use a number of techniques, therefore, to check their perceptions to ensure that they are not being misinformed—that they are, in effect, seeing (and hearing) what they think they are. These procedures for checking on or enhancing validity and reliability include:

- *Using a variety of instruments to collect data.* When a conclusion is supported by data collected from a number of different instruments, its validity is thereby enhanced. This kind of checking is often referred to as **triangulation**. (See Figure 21.1 in Chapter 21.)
- *Checking one informant's descriptions of something (a way of doing things or a reason for doing something) against another informant's descriptions of the same thing.* Discrepancies in descriptions may mean the data are invalid.*
- *Learning to understand and, where appropriate, speak the vocabulary of the group being studied.* If researchers do not understand what informants mean when they use certain terms (especially slang) or if they take such terms to mean something that they do not, the recording of invalid data will surely result.
- *Writing down the questions asked (in addition to the answers received).* This helps researchers make sense at a later date out of answers recorded earlier, and helps them reduce distortions owing to selective forgetting.
- *Recording personal thoughts while conducting observations and interviews.* (Also referred to as *researcher reflexivity.*) Responses that seem unusual or incorrect can be noted and checked later against other remarks or observations.
- *Asking one or more participants in the study to review the accuracy of the research report.* This is frequently referred to as **member checking**.
- *Obtaining an individual outside of the study to review and evaluate the report.* This is called an **external audit**, or peer debriefing.
- *Documenting the sources of remarks whenever possible and appropriate.* This helps researchers make

*Not necessarily, of course. It may simply mean a difference in viewpoint or perception.

sense out of comments that otherwise might seem misplaced.

- *Documenting the basis for inferences.*
- *Describing the context in which questions are asked and situations are observed.* Also referred to as *thick description.*
- *Using audio and video recordings when possible and appropriate.*
- *Drawing conclusions based on one's understanding of the situation being observed and then acting on these conclusions.* If these conclusions are invalid, the researcher will soon find out after acting on them.
- *Interviewing individuals more than once.* Inconsistencies over time in what the same individual reports may suggest that this individual is an unreliable informant.
- *Observing the setting or situation of interest over a period of time.* The length of an observation is extremely important in qualitative research. Consistency over time with regard to what researchers are seeing or hearing is a strong indication of reliability. Furthermore, there is much about a group that does not even begin to emerge until some time has passed and the members of the group become familiar with, and willing to trust, the researcher.
- *Analyzing negative cases.* Attempting to eliminate instances that do not fit the pattern by revising that pattern until the instance fits.

Table 19.2 summarizes a number of purposes, research questions, strategies, and data collection techniques used in qualitative research.

TABLE 19.2 ***Qualitative Research Questions, Strategies, and Data Collection Techniques***

Purpose of the Study	Possible Research Questions	Research Strategies	Examples of Data Collection Techniques
Exploratory: • To investigate a little-understood event, situation, or circumstance • To identify or construct important variables • To generate hypotheses for further research	• What is happening in this school? • What are the important themes or patterns in the ways teachers behave in this school? • How are these themes or patterns linked together?	• Case study • Observation • Field study	• Participant observation • Nonparticipant observation • In-depth interviewing • Selected interviewing
Descriptive: • To document an event, situation, or circumstance of interest	• What are the important behaviors, events, attitudes, processes, and/or structures occurring in this school?	• Case study • Field study • Ethnography • Observation	• Participant observation • Nonparticipant observation • In-depth interviewing • Written questionnaire
Explanatory: • To explain the forces causing an event, situation, or circumstance • To identify plausible causal networks shaping an event, situation, or circumstance	• What events, beliefs, attitudes, and/or policies are shaping the nature of this school? • How do these forces interact to shape this school?	• Case study • Field study • Ethnography	• Participant observation • Nonparticipant observation • In-depth interviewing • Written questionnaire
Predictive: • To predict the outcomes of an event, situation, or circumstance • To forecast behaviors or actions that might result from an event, situation, or circumstance	• What is likely to occur in the future as a result of the policies now in place at this school? • Who will be affected, and in what ways?	• Observation • Interview	• In-depth interviewing • Written questionnaire

An Example of Qualitative Research

In the remainder of this chapter, we present a published example of an observational qualitative study, followed by a critique of its strengths and weaknesses. As we did in our critiques of the different types of research studies we analyzed in other chapters, we use concepts introduced in earlier parts of the book in our analysis.

RESEARCH REPORT

From: (2004, Summer). *Adolescence, 39*(154), 373–388. Libra Publishers, Inc. Reprinted with permission.

Walk and Talk: An Intervention for Behaviorally Challenged Youths

Patricia A. Doucette

Abstract

Implied directional hypothesis

This qualitative research explored the question: Do preadolescent and adolescent youths with behavioral challenges benefit from a multimodal intervention of walking outdoors while engaging in counseling? The objective of the Walk and Talk intervention is to help the youth feel better, explore alternative behavioral choices, and learn new coping strategies and life skills by engaging in a counseling process that includes the benefits of mild aerobic exercise, and that nurtures a connection to the outdoors. The intervention utilizes a strong therapeutic alliance based on the Rogerian technique of unconditional positive regard, which is grounded and guided by the principles of attachment theory. For eight weeks, eight students (aged 9 to 13 years) from a middle school in Alberta, Canada, participated weekly in the Walk and Talk intervention. Students' self-reports indicated that they benefited from the intervention. Research triangulation with involved adults supported findings that indicated the students were making prosocial choices in behavior, and were experiencing more feelings of self-efficacy and well-being. Limitations, new research directions, and subsequent longitudinal research possibilities are discussed.

Western societies have seen an increase in violence and antisocial behavior in schools and communities (Pollack, 1998). Juvenile crime rates have increased four times since the early 1970s (Cook & Laub, 1997). After the shock of the Columbine school massacre in the United States and other violent incidents, communities are demanding interventions to help prevent similar occurrences.

Justification

Traditional approaches for various youth behavior challenges have assumed the behavior needs to be controlled and contained by using behavioral and social learning approaches (Moore, Moretti, & Holland, 1998). Many current interventions rely on adaptations of behavior modification strategies to provide structure and control. The tenets of some programs for troubled youth are based on a hierarchy of control, authority, and power. The framework of behavior and behavioral boundaries is directed by coercive control with token economies and earned privileges that are enforced by systems involving revoking social and recreational activities (Moore, Moretti, & Holland, 1998). I question and challenge this type of philosophy. Intrinsic motivation for making positive behavioral choices and taking responsibility and ownership for behavior is unlikely to become the behavioral response when behavior is controlled by others. Research (Deci & Ryan, 1985) suggests intrinsic motivation involves self-determination, self-awareness of one's needs and setting goals to meet those needs. I believe that many behaviorally challenged youths have experienced interactions with key adults that have been punitive, rejecting, and untrustworthy (Moore, Moretti, & Holland, 1998; Staub, 1996). Therefore, many current interventions based on behavioral strategies and coercive control have limited effectiveness (Moore, Moretti, & Holland, 1998; Staub, 1996).

New treatment methods that adopt a therapeutic approach that is grounded and guided by the principles of attachment theory may engage a therapeutic process with the results of youths' prosocial behavioral choices (Centers for Disease Control, 1991; Ferguson, 1999; Holland, Moretti, Verlaan, & Peterson, 1993; Keat, 1990; Moffitt, 1993; Moore, Moretti, & Holland, 1998). By participating in a casual walk outdoors, there can be the physiological advantage of mild aerobic exercise (Franken, 1994; Hays, 1999; Fox, 1997; Baum & Posluszny, 1999; Kolb & Whishaw, 1996, 1998). I believe, as do others (Anderson, 2000; Glaser, 2000; Tkachuk & Martin, 1999; Real Age Newsletter, 2001a), that human beings have a natural bond with the outdoors and other living organisms. By nurturing this bond with a walk outdoors, positive well-being and health can result (Tkachuk & Martin, 1999; Hays, 1999; Orlick, 1993; Real Age Newsletter, 2001b).

Ambiguous

WALK AND TALK INTERVENTION

The Walk and Talk intervention has its fundamental philosophy in Bronfenbrenner's (1979) social ecological theory of behavior, which views the child, family, school, work, peers, neighborhood, and community as interconnected systems. Youths' problem behavior can be attributed to dysfunction between any one or more combinations of these systems (Borduin, 1999). By understanding these dynamics, the Walk and Talk intervention attempts to provide a support network that encourages youths to reconnect with self and the environment through an attachment process, a counseling process, and a physiological response resulting in feelings of self-efficacy.

The Walk and Talk intervention utilizes three components to engage youths. The counseling component of the Walk and Talk intervention borrows seven principles from the Orinoco program used at the Maples Adolescent Centre near Vancouver, British Columbia (Moore, Moretti, & Holland, 1998, pp. 10–18). These principles are driven by an underlying understanding of attachment theory. These principles are as follows:

1. All behavior has meaning. The meaning of the behavior is revealed by understanding the internal working model of the person generating the behavior.
2. Early and repeated experiences with people who care for us set a foundation for our internal working models of relationship with self and others. Our earliest experiences have a profound effect on how we approach relationships, school, work, and play.
3. Biological legacies such as cognitive, emotional, and physical capabilities are an interactive part of our experience and contribute to our working model of relationships with self and others.

4. Internal working models are constantly changing in the context of relationships and expertise. These models are constantly revised based on experience. Experience can be added to but not subtracted.
5. Interpersonal relationships are a process of continuous reciprocal interplay of each person's internal working model with others. It is not possible to hold oneself apart from this interplay.
6. We understand ourselves in relation to others. A sense of self includes our sense of how others view and respond to us.
7. Enduring change in an individual's behavior occurs only when there is change in the internal working model supported by change in the system one lives in and if there is sufficient time, opportunity, and support to integrate the new experience.

The counseling component of the Walk and Talk intervention is interlaced with new strategies for positive life skills and attempts to incorporate solution-focused brief therapy (Riley, 1999). Through counseling, youths discover solutions by way of simple interventions while experiencing positive regard in Rogerian fashion (Rogers, 1980). Focus is kept on the youths' strengths while collaborating for change (Riley, 1999; Orlick, 1993). Identifying highlights is an important element of each walk. Highlights are used to teach youths to think positively so they can reframe their experiences in a way that enhances well-being (Orlick, 1993). By being able to illuminate the good in things that happen in daily life, youths can find inner strength and resilience when experiencing negative events or reactions from others (Orlick, 1993). Youths who have an inner source of reworking setbacks in daily life will be more likely to cope with stress effectively.

The ecopsychology component of the Walk and Talk intervention is tied to the psychological processes that bring people closer to the natural world. Some research suggests that humans have a natural bond with other living organisms, and nurturing that connection may provide a health benefit (Roszak, Gomes, & Kanner, 1995; Real Age Newsletter, 2001a). By walking outdoors, the outdoor connection is nurtured, facilitating youths' awareness of their environment.

Prior research

The physiological component engages the youths in aerobic exercise. Considerable research supports the use of exercise to alleviate many types of mental illness and enhance feelings of well-being (Tkachuk & Martin, 1999). Some research suggests that as little as ten minutes of daily exercise is enough to generate mood-elevating neurochemicals (Real Age Newsletter, 2001b). Recognizing the importance of exercise to well-being is a critical aspect of the Walk and Talk intervention.

Purpose

The intervention for behaviorally challenged youths combines the benefits of a strong therapeutic alliance based on the Rogerian technique of unconditional positive regard (Rogers, 1980), integrated with mild aerobic exercise that occurs outdoors in a place of natural beauty. The research goal is to discover if this combination has a beneficial effect on selected youths and their problem behaviors.

The impetus for this research is to understand the epidemiology and etiology of the problem behaviors while attempting to implement an effective preventative intervention. One objective is to provide fertile ground for the youths to explore and understand alternative behavioral choices. This phenomenological qualitative research approach assumes that the participants are existential individuals and as such, actions, verbalizations, everyday patterns, and ways of interacting can reveal an understanding of human behavior (Addison, 1992). A basic principle of existentialism suggests that each and every expression, even the most insignificant and superficial behavior, reveals and communicates who that individual is (Sartre, 1957). It is hoped that the participants will acquire a stronger self-understanding via a therapeutic alliance, aerobic exercise, experiencing a connection to the outdoors, and be able to choose to make a behavior change.

By understanding and utilizing attachment theory (Ainsworth & Bowlby, 1991; Bowlby, 1969; Centers for Disease Control, 1991; Ferguson, 1999; Holland, Moretti, Verlaan, & Peterson, 1993; Keat, 1990; Moffitt, 1993; Moore, Moretti, & Holland, 1998) and Rogerian (1980) methods to guide the counseling with a walk outdoors, it is hoped that youths' self-esteem will increase as they become connected to another person—myself—and the outdoors.

Why do some young people sabotage themselves with nonproductive behaviors? I believe if an intervention can be introduced and then utilized by youths who have a history of these behaviors, they can be redirected to satisfying, productive lives regardless of their prior personal history. The intervention will help behaviorally troubled youths to feel better and do better by being internally motivated to choose prosocial behavior.

Possible researcher bias

The plasticity, resilience, and remarkable adaptability of youths to their unique selves and situations has been a catalyst for my research. The importance of attachment (as defined by Ainsworth, 2000) and understanding attachment theory (Ainsworth, 2000; Bowlby, 1969) cannot be understated. The Walk and Talk intervention provides a safe place for youths to discover new positive coping strategies that can benefit them throughout life.

METHOD

The middle school principal assigned the student outreach support worker to select appropriate individuals for the Walk and Talk intervention. The assistant superintendent, a licensed psychologist, was selected as a resource and liaison in case crises should arise. A consent form was signed by a school district representative. Further, consent forms were sent to the parents of participants.

Convenience sample

The eight intervention respondents chosen were coded by school assessors as behaviorally challenged and in need of special education. I first met with each of the eight youths for a preintervention interview that allows us to become acquainted and for me to familiarize myself with their understanding of their behavioral challenges. Specifically, the youths' problem behaviors as indicated by school representatives, parents and/or guardians were identified as conduct disorder as described in the *Diagnostic and Statistical Manual of Mental Disorders* (American Psychiatric Association, 1994). Conduct disorders include violating rules, aggressiveness that threatens or causes physical harm to others, bullying, extortion, lack of respect for self and others, suicide attempts, truancy, initiating frequent fights, and various charges by the police such as breaking and entering (DSM-IV, 1994). The problem behaviors were repetitive, resulting in unsuccessful functioning within the school, community, and often family setting.

Ages were 9–13

Good clarification

By utilizing a collaborative, qualitative approach, I disclosed the intentions of the Walk and Talk intervention. I believe this approach facilitated development of alliance, empowerment of the participant, and engagement as the expert (Creswell, 1998; Flick, 1998). My role as researcher was that of an active, interested learner (Creswell, 1998; Flick, 1998). This collaborative, qualitative approach bridges the gap between participant and researcher. A collaborative approach has been preferred for youths since it engages and honors them as their own expert (Axline, 1947/1969; Oaklander, 1978); youths are usually not in control of many decisions that affect them.

Unclear to us

Participant observer

Interviews were conducted before and after the six-week Walk and Talk intervention. The first interview included an introduction by myself and by the youths. They were asked to draw a picture of themselves performing any activity of their choice. Sheets of 8" by 11" white paper and ten assorted gel pens were provided. These pens were chosen because of their popularity with children of all ages. Upon completion of the drawings, the youths

Instrumentation

were asked to make a list of five of their strengths. Next they were asked to list at least five weaknesses. The final activity was to write a short autobiographical incident—about something that had made an impression whether positive or negative. After each activity, discussion was encouraged. A goal of the interview was to start the youths thinking about self, and for me, to learn what they think and feel. At the close of the interview, I prepared them for the week of walking and talking, emphasizing that it would be their opportunity to talk about whatever came to mind and the talks would be confidential—except in extreme situations, for instance, statements about harming themself or others.

Good caution

By conducting the first interview in this manner, it was hoped the youths would start to self-disclose in some or all of the modalities. Also, it provides baseline insight as to how the youths feel at that time. The self-portraits of each youth were examined by a licensed art therapist, Maxine Junge, and myself. Maxine Junge (personal communication, February 18, 2002) provides the caution that what she offered were guesses, hypotheses, and impressions. The autobiographical pieces gave insight into issues considered important by these youths.

The interview was fairly ambitious, but the researcher did not press the youths with the agenda. It was hoped that an alliance would be established wherein trust and respect would be shared. This started the counseling process. It is important to discover what this process is for the youths and report it. It is important to discover the meaning the youths give to events, and resulting actions (Maxwell, 1996). It was the youths' reality that this qualitative approach attempts to understand (Maxwell, 1996). The youths were the focus and their phenomenological experience was explored while psychoeducational interventions were suggested and discussed when appropriate.

It was the counselor's role to help the youths clarify and reframe belief constructs while helping to identify and translate the subconscious into the conscious (Hays, 1999). How youths behave and speak reflects subconscious thoughts and feelings (Hunter, 1987). It was the counselor's role to help the youths identify the connectedness to place and others, identify and verbalize one or more successful survival skills while introducing new conscious approaches that encourage the cognitive strategy of stop, think, do. Introducing young people to the hope of a future that is rewarding and positive and one they can manage and control is a paramount goal. When appropriate, they will be introduced to various life skills that can improve the quality of their life (Orlick, 1993). By learning about positive thinking, positive self-talk, stress management, relaxation skills, imagery, anger physiology, anger management, communication with "I statements," focusing and refocusing, new behavioral choices can be made (Orlick, 1993). Learning one, two, or more key life skills can enhance the youths' lives.

Procedures

I met with each respondent for six consecutive weeks, once a week, for approximately 30–45 minutes per session. Each session entailed a walk on the school grounds. This did not include the pre and post interviews. The eight participants began their first Walk and Talk between December 12, 2001 and January 28, 2002. This wide range of start times was due to the waiting period for parental consents and then arranging appropriate times with the teachers. Also, at the end of December and early January there was a two-week school break which caused a delay in beginning some first sessions. The total Walk and Talk time allotted was 45 minutes, but because of time needed to dress appropriately, actual Walk and Talk time was about 30 minutes. At the start of each walk I asked the youths what they wanted to discuss. If there wasn't anything in particular they wanted to say, I asked them for highlights in their lives since I last saw them a week ago. Highlights are positive events, positive experiences, comments, personal accomplishments or anything that has lifted the quality of the moment for that child (Orlick, 1993, 1998). Next, I asked them about their lowlights. Understanding and verbalizing

Good detail

that life is filled with highs and lows begins the journey of self-discovery and also allows the youth to discuss alternative strategies for dealing with problems.

Throughout the six-week Walk and Talk intervention, I introduced strategies for dealing with stress, identifying what was stressful for the youth, discussing the importance of positive self-talk, mental imagery, visualization techniques, and focusing and refocusing techniques (Orlick, 1993, 1998). Most of the youths chosen for this intervention had anger-management challenges. When appropriate, anger-management techniques, combined with the cognitive strategy of stop, think, do was introduced. Understanding anger cycles and the physiology of anger was discussed. One of the life skills introduced was learning the rules of using assertiveness rather than aggressiveness and utilizing I-statements to convey feelings to others. When appropriate these types of life skills were introduced and practiced in mock situations. Positive life skill techniques were woven into the counseling session during most sessions.

For more detail

Need more detail

The intervention was completed with a post interview. When gathering data from the youths, respondents were informed that the research was intended to help them in the future; therefore, answering honestly is important. Respondents were told there were no right or wrong responses. They were to feel free to talk openly. Similar to the pre intervention interview, youths were asked to draw a picture of themselves in an activity. Next they were asked to write their strengths and weaknesses. At that time, I showed each youth the drawing from their pre intervention interview, and we compared the strengths and weaknesses from before and after the intervention. Together we noted the differences. I asked each youth: What has changed since we started? What did you like about Walk and Talk? What didn't you like about it? What was helpful? What wasn't helpful? What are your concluding comments and remarks? Do you think it would be good for other youths to participate? I asked them what they thought about the art they produced and about the strengths and weaknesses they identified. I assessed self-esteem via the self-portrait they had drawn, comparing pre and post intervention responses. Several methods of communicating with the youths, i.e. art, structured exercise, open-ended questions, and discussion of their experience, made my report of their phenomenological experience more complete.

Good detail

RESULTS AND DISCUSSION

I chose a phenomenological approach because I wanted to capture the essence of the youths' experience as told by them. Did they feel better and do better? The youths' experience was reported as I observed it. I assessed their experience of the Walk and Talk intervention as told to me by them along with collateral observation and/or information given to me by parents, teachers, and other involved school personnel. The ecopsychology aspect of this intervention can be replicated in any safe outdoor environment.

How reported?

The only given variables in this research are the common denominators of age, youths from 9 to 13 years old, and the individual, problematic behaviors, although variations in etiology and epidemiology exist. The factors relating to the causes of the behaviors are individual. The systemic distribution of impacting incidents and contributing components to each youth's behavior vary. By offering a multimodal approach it was hoped that the youths' experience would be positive and result in prosocial behavior.

As the qualitative researcher it was my mandate to utilize rigorous data collection procedures (Creswell, 1998). As a researcher it was also my intent to maintain my distance in order to promote objectivity but still engage them as a counselor. To achieve this result requires walking a fine line. To preserve scientific clarity, conscious effort was required. However, a positive interpersonal relationship was necessary for the success

Good caution

of the research intervention and of the qualitative approach. The characteristics and assumptions of the phenomenological qualitative approach to research necessitates that the participant's view be the entire reality of the study (Creswell, 1998). As such, the reality was purely and subjectively portrayed as an experiential component of the study. To analyze the data, multiple approaches and multiple traditions were included. This was done to provide a fuller, holistic view and richer understanding of the process which occurred during time in the field.

Seven of eight

Combining the three components of counseling, ecopsychology, and physiological enhancement creates a new intervention for behaviorally challenged youths. The youths who completed the intervention stated that it helped them clarify feelings. Overall, I believe the Walk and Talk intervention benefited each youth who completed the intervention. The following discussion provides specifics about the individual participants.

Youth A

What evidence?

Youth A's participation helped him to become more self-aware of his struggles with sister and father. Although strategies were discussed, I do not believe that Youth A assimilated many new life skills. He needed much more individual time and attention to help him cope with the number of problems he faces outside of school. However, his art therapy work showed a definite improvement. The first drawing was very small, not grounded, and "floating," which the art therapist suggested indicated a feeling of smallness, powerlessness, and lack of self-esteem. The final drawing depicted a well-defined boy and girl—Youth A and little sister—in his bedroom with all his prized possessions. Both children were smiling and he looked like a protective big brother. His teacher's comments about Youth A indicated that the Walk and Talk intervention had benefited Youth A at least for the days of each Walk and Talk. The teacher believed Youth A needed more continuous intensive help. Youth A made positive comments about his experience in intervention: He liked talking about his feelings and learning focusing and refocusing skills. His before-and-after strengths ratio was 12/15, indicating that he believed he had more strengths on the completion day of Walk and Talk than on the starting day. His weaknesses ratio was 9/3, indicating that at the start of Walk and Talk he believed he had many more weaknesses than when he finished.

Providing sources of information

Youth B

Good detail

I believe there was a significant improvement with Youth B. Each week he self-disclosed more and more. He was eager to talk about his problems and challenges as time went on. Toward the end of the intervention he was walking with his head held high rather than downcast. He was very pleased to report his new fun relationship with his big brother. His teacher told me throughout the intervention of his improved coping and social skills in the classroom. She gave me detailed accounts of how Youth B avoided confrontations by using newly acquired social skill strategies. In the last discussion with the teacher, on the last day of the intervention, she revealed a violent outburst in his classroom. It was on that day physical abuse charges were reported to social services regarding his mother. Although the teacher could not understand Youth B's incongruent behavior, I knew it all fit.

His before-and-after strengths ratio was 5/8, indicating that he believed he had more strengths on the completion day of Walk and Talk than on the starting day. In addition, three of the strengths mentioned were social skills. His weaknesses ratio was 4/0, indicating that at the start of Walk and Talk he believed he had four weaknesses, and when he finished he had none. Youth B indicated Walk and Talk was a helpful intervention for him.

The art therapist's comments regarding his drawings indicate that he was a boy possibly filled with fear and anger. The drawings denoted a developmental problem, in that they depicted a small and insignificant figure.

Youth C

I think there was a huge improvement with Youth C. He seemed to self-disclose more and more each week. He utilized the life skill techniques we discussed, practiced them throughout the week, and eagerly reported back to me. His self-esteem soared with each new success he experienced. He would retell with enthusiasm his weekly attempts at new life skills, his successes along with some failures. His teacher echoed my sentiments, noticing a remarkable change of attitude in the classroom, his cooperation with peers, and positive choices in behavior. His brother commented on their newly improved relationship.

His before-and-after strengths ratio was 5/5. On completion day of Walk and Talk, three of his five strengths were social skills, whereas on starting day none were social skills. His weaknesses ratio was 5/2, indicating that at the start of Walk and Talk, he had many more weaknesses than when he finished. At the start he indicated that two of his five weaknesses were social skills and at completion, one of his two weaknesses was his temper. I viewed these changes as exemplifying a raised level of self-awareness. Youth C very enthusiastically claimed Walk and Talk was a positive event for him.

"Explaining away"?

The art therapist noted that his first drawing depicted a small, faceless, insignificant boy, and his final drawing was very similar. Sadly, after completion of the intervention, charges of parental child abuse were reported to social services.

Youth D

Youth D was reintegrated into the regular classroom toward the end of the Walk and Talk intervention. I think his participation in the intervention was one of many support efforts that helped him improve his overall success and well-being. During Walk and Talk he talked about his daily challenges. He seemed to develop a self-awareness over time. His teacher reported positive changes: he had started to react appropriately to accept "no" without bursting into tears. He utilized self-chosen time outs and self-talk to help him control his emotions. His teacher indicated that he was more polite and considerate with others. Youth D reported that Walk and Talk had been a great experience for him.

Internal validity

His before-and-after strengths ratio was 7/8. On completion day of Walk and Talk, one of his eight strengths was a social skill. His weaknesses ratio was 5/5. The art therapy assessment for his first drawing suggested an ineffectual, fearful, and avoidant child. His final drawing was grounded, but still revealed a faceless self. Youth D's before-and-after drawings lack depth and involvement.

Youth E

I believe Youth E benefited from his participation in the Walk and Talk intervention, but needed intensive ongoing help. He seemed to have a very low self-image that was controlled by external events. His troubled home life, parents' divorce, and taking a daily drug cocktail for various problems contributed to his need for external support. His teacher agreed. The teacher also said that Youth E had benefited greatly from participating in Walk and Talk. In the classroom he was much calmer and cooperative, thereby experiencing more personal success, something he clearly needed. Youth E said Walk and Talk was good for him because he could get his feelings out.

Questions validity

The art therapist's assessment of his artwork was of a boy with high intelligence, with a good self image. This was contradictory to the boy I knew. Both of his pictures were grounded but showed an avoidant boy who did not know how to handle his impulses.

His before-and-after strengths ratio was 5/8. On completion day of Walk and Talk, seven of his eight strengths were social skills. This was impressive. His weaknesses ratio was 5/1. In his first meeting he identified two social skills weaknesses as being related to being bullied. In our final meeting he admitted that arguing was his weakness. I believe he had acquired more self-awareness over the intervention time and learned new coping strategies.

Youth F

Good detail

Helps to clarify term

Seems to contradict first sentence in paragraph

It was difficult for me to assess whether Youth F, the only female participant, benefited from the intervention. I often wondered what she was learning and what bothered her. However, I found her participation in the ecopsychology aspect remarkable. She became transformed from a girl who threw rocks at birds to one who tried to gently approach them and stroke them. She became increasingly aware of the surrounding trees, an occasional wandering dog, and the variety of birds. She seemed to enjoy the physical aspects of the intervention. I believe she was extremely athletic and often mentioned this to her. Her teacher queried me after the second Walk and Talk to learn what life skills we were concentrating on. The teacher collaborated with me to help the girl control her impulsivity by reminding her when it was appropriate to focus, refocus, stop, think, do, rub her lucky penny, and apply any other life skill strategies I had mentioned. Also, Youth F's mother phoned me to offer collaboration in helping her daughter use life skills at home. Youth F experienced behavioral improvement during the intervention time as reported by all triangulation sources. Youth F told me that Walk and Talk was great.

The art therapist's assessment of her artwork suggested possible organic problems. I agreed. Her before-and-after strengths ratio was 15/7. Her weaknesses ratio was 5/0. I believe Youth F could use ongoing outside support.

Youth G

Unclear to us

"Explaining away"?

Youth G was a total pleasure to have as a participant of Walk and Talk. Although he was mildly developmentally delayed, he was eager to learn new positive life skills. He readily became attached to the outdoor environment, becoming keenly aware of the birds, trees, and sounds. He often made observations that I found remarkable although his kind, gentle spirit was often squelched in his daily struggles with academics and interpersonal relationships, but because of his resilience and willingness to discuss his problems he could find solutions readily. His teachers believed Youth G's success was ongoing after he participated in behavioral program. Youth G's teachers concurred that the Walk and Talk intervention had probably helped to illuminate his positive choices.

Youth G's art assessment denoted his developmental lag. The drawings before-and-after showed him wearing a sport shirt with the number twelve (his lucky number) and playing volleyball. Neither drawing reflected a grounded individual. His before-and-after strengths ratio was 5/5. In his first meeting he identified two social skills as being strengths. In the last meeting he identified three social skills as such. His weaknesses ratio was 1/3. I believe this indicated a keener self awareness. I believe Youth G benefited enormously from his participation in the Walk and Talk intervention.

Youth H

Youth H identified seven strengths and two weaknesses. He liked to talk about playing and watching hockey. His art was not grounded and very simple. The art therapist noted that his drawing was very protected and defensive indicating possible anger and aggression.

Youth H was removed from the intervention after one meeting. At the time of our first meeting the teacher's aide strongly argued against his being a participant in the Walk and Talk intervention. Youth H had been selected by the student outreach worker and his parents had consented to his participation. The new school guidance counselor contacted me with concerns and recommended that he be pulled from the intervention. Due to these objections, Youth H was withdrawn. My advice to future Walk and Talk interventionists is to enlist the support of all people who are in favor of a youth's participation in the program. Otherwise what happened to Youth H could happen to others.

Overall, the research results were positive. From the teachers' perspective, my perspective, and the youths' comments, the intervention seemed to benefit them on many fronts. Introducing alternative life skill strategies was a key counseling component of the intervention. All youths found the focusing and refocusing exercise beneficial and many adopted the technique to everyday life. Focusing and refocusing can facilitate learning to experience life fully. By practicing focusing and refocusing exercises youths can learn to closely observe what is seen, listen intently to what is heard, feel fully and connect completely when interacting with others (Orlick, 1993). The focusing and refocusing technique utilized aspects of the intervention's ecopsychological component by weaving a life skill technique into a closer awareness of self and facets of the outdoors that otherwise would go unnoticed. After applying the technique outdoors it was readily transferable to indoor situations.

What evidence?

It is my belief that to varying degrees, the youths benefited from the experience of counseling outdoors enhanced by the physiological "boost" provided by aerobic exercise. Walking allowed for physical release, something very important for these active youths. Feelings, problems, and sometimes solutions to problems materialized. All respondents found talking about such problems to be beneficial. These respondents were chosen because of their difficulty in managing social situations.

Redundant

Assuming my findings are correct and the intervention can be deemed successful, will the intervention have long-term effects? I can only speculate. Follow-up longitudinal studies are recommended. Suggestions for future research include using control groups with various problem behaviors as well as groups with no problem behaviors, groups with and without the ecopsychological component, groups with and without the walking component. I also advise utilizing quantitative methods to measure success. Possibly my strongest recommendation is to do the Walk and Talk intervention in warm weather.

CONCLUSIONS

A possible limitation of this research could be its subjective nature. Further, my subjectivity presupposes that most people with attachment difficulties respond favorably to Carl Rogers' (1980) therapeutic approach of positive personal regard.

Good caution

Inclement weather could deter respondents from wholehearted participation. Unfortunately, the session times, once established, were not flexible, since they were incorporated into the school day.

This research approached behavioral challenges from an individual vantage point rather than a systemic or societal perspective. Some researchers (e.g., Grossman, 1999) view youths' turmoil and violence as resulting from the ills of society (i.e., television, movies, and video game violence). The present research does not address these types of cultural concerns of society on a macro level.

In sum, I would like to see the Walk and Talk intervention used in middle schools and high schools, and utilized by mental health practitioners. Once youths have completed the intervention, I recommend periodical refreshers on a monthly basis. Walk and Talk refreshers will give the youths a time to reconnect with the outdoors, self, and reinstate positive behaviors and life skills.

References

Addison, R. (1992). Grounded hermeneutic research. In B. F. Crabtree & W. L. Miller (Eds.), *Doing qualitative research* (pp. 110–124). Newbury Park, CA: Sage Publications.

Ainsworth, M. (2000). *Maternal sensitivity scales* (Original work published in 1969). Available at http://www.psy.sunysb.edu/ewaters/senscoop.htm

Ainsworth, M., & Bowlby, J. (1991). An ethological approach to personality development. *American Psychologist, 46,* 333–341.

American Psychiatric Association. (1994). *Diagnostic and statistical manual of mental disorders* (4th ed.). Washington, DC: Author.

Anderson, N. (2000). *Testimony of the Office of the Director of National Institutes of Health, Department of Health and Human Services regarding mind / body interactions and health before the United States Senate, September 22,* 1998. Available at http://www.apa.org/ppo/scitest923.html

Axline, V. (1947/1969). *Play therapy.* New York: Ballantine Books.

Baum, A. & Posluszny, D. (1999). Health psychology: mapping biobehavioral contributions to health and illness. *Annual Review of Psychology, 50,* 137–163.

Borduin, C. (1999). Multisystemic treatment of criminality and violence in adolescents. *Journal of the American Academy of Child and Adolescent Psychiatry, 38*, 242–249.

Bowlby, J. (1969). *Attachment: Attachment and loss* (Vol. 1). New York: Basic Books.

Bronfenbrenner, U. (1979). *The ecology of human development: Experiments by nature and design.* Cambridge, MA: Harvard University Press.

Centers for Disease Control. (1991). Forum on youth violence in minority communities: Setting the agenda for prevention. *Public Health Reports, 106,* 225–253.

Cook, P. J., & Laub, J. H. (1997). The unprecedented epidemic in youth violence. In M. Tonry & M. H. Molore (Eds.), *Crime and justice* (pp. 101–138). Chicago, IL: University of Chicago Press.

Creswell, J. W. (1998). *Qualitative inquiry and research design: Choosing among five traditions.* Thousand Oaks, CA: Sage Publications.

Deci, E., & Ryan, R. (1985). *Intrinsic motivation and self determination in human behavior.* New York: Plenum Press.

Ferguson, G. (1999). *Shouting at the sky: Troubled teens and the promise of the wild.* New York: Thomas Dunne Books.

Flick, U. (1998). *An introduction to qualitative research.* Thousand Oaks, CA: Sage Publications.

Fox, K. (1997). Let's get physical. In K. R. Fox (Ed.), *The physical self: From motivation to well being* (pp. vii–xiii). Champaign, IL; Human Kinetics.

Franken, R. (1994). *Human motivation.* Pacific Grove, CA.: Brooks-Cole Publishers.

Glaser, R. (2000). *Mind-body interactions, immunity, and health.* Available at http://www.apa.org/ppo/mind.html

Grossman, D. (1999). *Stop teaching our kids to kill: A call to action against TV, movie, and video game violence.* New York: Crown Books.

Hays, K. (1999). *Working it out.* Washington, DC: American Psychological Association.

Holland, R., Moretti, M., Verlaan, V., & Peterson, S. (1993). Attachment and conduct disorder: The response program. *Canadian Journal of Psychiatry, 38,* 420–431.

Hunter, M. (1996). *Psych yourself in!* Vancouver, BC: SeaWalk Press.

Keat, D. (1990). *Child multimodal therapy.* Norwood, NJ: Ablex Publishing.

Kolb, B., & Whishaw, I. (1996). *Human neuropsychology.* New York: W. H. Freeman.

Kolb, B., & Whishaw, I. (1998). Brain plasticity and behavior. *Annual Review of Psychology, 49*, 43–64.

Maxwell, J. (1996). *Qualitative research design: An interactive approach.* Thousand Oaks, CA: Sage Publications.

Moffitt, T. (1993). Adolescence—limited and life-course persistent antisocial behavior: A developmental taxonomy. *Psychological Review, 100,* 674–701.

Moore, K., Moretti, M., & Holland, R. (1998). A new perspective on youth care programs: Using attachment theory to guide interventions for troubled youth. *Residential Treatment for Children and Youth, 15*, 1–24.

Oaklander, V. (1978). *Windows to our children: A gestalt therapy approach to children and adolescents.* Moab, UT: Real People Press.

Orlick, T. (1993). *Free to feel great: Teaching children to excel at living.* Carp, Ontario, Canada: Creative Bound.

Orlick, T. (1998). *Feeling great.* Carp, Ontario, Canada: Creative Bound.

Pollack, W. (1998). *Real boys.* New York: Henry Holt & Co.

Real Age Newsletter. (2001a, May 18). *The call of the wild, tip of the day.* Available at http://www.realage.com/

Real Age Newsletter. (2001b, October 9). *Quick mood fix, tip of the day.* Available at http://www.realage.com/

Riley, S. (1999). Brief therapy. An adolescent intervention. *Art Therapy: Journal of the American Art Therapy Association, 16,* 83–86.

Rogers, C. (1980). *A way of being.* Boston: Houghton Mifflin.

Roszak, T., Gomes, M., & Kanner, A. (1995). *Ecopsychology: Restoring the earth, healing the mind.* San Francisco, CA: Sierra Club Books.

Sartre, J. P. (1957). *Existentialism and human emotions.* New York: The Wisdom Library.

Staub, E. (1996). Altruism and aggression in children and youth. In R. Feldman (Ed.), *The psychology of adversity* (pp. 115–144). Amherst, MA: University of Massachusetts Press.

Tkachuk, G. A., & Martin, G. L. (1999). Exercise therapy for patients with psychiatric disorders: Research and clinical implications. *Professional Psychology: Research and Practice, 30,* 275–282.

Analysis of the Study

PURPOSE/JUSTIFICATION

The purpose is found on page 460: "The research goal is to discover if this combination has a beneficial effect on selected youths and their problem behaviors." We would substitute "the Walk and Talk intervention" for "this combination," but the meaning is, we think, nonetheless clear.

The justification is extensive and clear (though somewhat redundant) with respect to both the societal/personal needs the study addresses and the rationale for the intervention. It includes limitations of other interventions and the philosophical and scientific bases of the method.

There appear to be no ethical issues regarding confidentially or deception. Risk to students appears minimal but parental consent forms were obtained and a psychologist was available if needed.

DEFINITIONS

Definitions are not explicit but are made reasonably clear through (sometimes extensive) description of major terms: *"Walk and Talk," beneficial effect,* and *problem behaviors*. The meaning of both these and other terms such as: *counseling component, ecopsychology component, physiological component,* and *collaborative qualitative approach* would be clearer if references and justifications were not mixed in with descriptions.

PRIOR RESEARCH

The author provides extensive references in support of both rationale for the study and the intervention procedures. However, it is often unclear whether the reference is research, theory, or opinion, and whether the reference does, in fact, support the method. For example, on page 459: "There can be the physiological advantage of mild exercise."

HYPOTHESES

No hypotheses are explicitly stated. The research question stated in the Abstract—"Do preadolescent and adolescent youths with behavioral challenges benefit from a multimodal intervention of walking outdoors while engaging in counseling?"—in conjunction with subsequent material clearly implies the directional hypothesis that the students do improve.

SAMPLE

The sample is clearly described as eight students (actually seven because one was withdrawn for reasons not entirely clear), aged 9 to 13 chosen from one school district as having problem behaviors. The method of selection is clear. Each of the students is further described in the section on individual outcomes. Replication of the study would be facilitated by more detail. For example, how many were primarily aggressive, suicidal, or lawbreakers. This convenience sample does not permit generalization, but that is presumably not the intent of the study.

INSTRUMENTATION

Instrumentation included listing of strengths and weaknesses as well as self-drawings by students and interviews by the researcher, all done pre- and post-intervention. It also included researcher observations and interpretations made during each of six intervention periods with each student. Whether a daily log or other recording mechanism was used is not reported; we must assume these are based on researcher recollection. Also included, as we discover in the results section, were comments from teachers and family members.

No discussion of reliability or validity is provided, which is not unusual in qualitative studies. The researcher acknowledges the subjective nature of the study as well as presents the justification for the methodology. Although the report states that "triangulation with involved adults supported findings that indicated the students were making prosocial choices in behavior, and were experiencing more feelings of self-efficacy and well-being," this is not clear to us. As we evaluate the reports on individual students, it appears that the researcher and teacher were in clear agreement on three, perhaps four of the seven students. Comments from family members were rare. There also seems to be a contradiction in one case with the researcher stating, "It was difficult for me to asess whether Youth F . . . benefited from the intervention" but later stating that "Youth F . . . experienced behavioral improvement during the intervention time as reported by all triangulation sources."

PROCEDURES/INTERNAL VALIDITY

The intervention is, in general, well described although more detail would be helpful, especially in replication. Presumably a reader can turn to the Orlick reference on ways of reducing stress, but the anger management, cognitive strategies, and assertiveness strategies need further clarification, as is provided for "life-skills strategies" in the report on Youth F.

The author recognizes the problem of internal validity in discussing Youth D with the statement: "I think his participation in the intervention was one of many support effects that helped him improve." The effect of other variables on outcomes exists for all seven students. Although this type of study cannot effectively control extraneous variables, more discussion is appropriate. It seems to us that it is unlikely that many other threats to internal validity would exist during this particular six-week period, but assessment of such possibilities should be feasible for a researcher who is involved this closely with the schools. One instance of a significant event (physical abuse) and its probable impact is discussed.

DATA ANALYSIS

Statistical analysis is not appropriate for this study. As is usual in studies of this type, the results from various instruments are described, in this case for individual students.

RESULT/INTERPRETATION

The author recognizes the possibilities for bias and subjectivity impacting her reporting and interpreting results. In numerous instances, she gives appropriate cautions. Given this limitation, we find the results impressive, particularly because she is often clear in stating "I believe" so that the reader should realize that this applies to many other statements as well. She also frequently cites sources: for example, "Youth B made positive comments about . . ."; "His teacher told me . . ." and gives behavioral examples such as "She became transformed from a girl who threw rocks at birds to one who tried to gently approach them."

Although we think the totality of evidence and impressions justifies the conclusion that students benefited, we think the amount of benefit is overstated. It appears that the most common positive outcomes were increased self-awareness as perceived by the researcher and the more observable self-disclosure. These are considered desirable in counseling but may have influenced perception of other outcomes.

A problem exists in the interpretation of the pre-post self-listing of strengths and weaknesses. When strengths increased and weaknesses decreased, this is usually interpreted as positive. However, with two students where this is not the case, the result is "explained" as due to greater self-awareness, hence also positive. While this may be true, researchers cannot change their interpretation of data after the fact, at least not without more justification.

CONCLUSIONS

We agree, with the reservation mentioned, that "to varying degrees the youths in this study benefited from the experience." We think the results justify further research, as suggested by the author, and that this research is needed before the intervention is recommended on other than a trial basis.

This study illustrates both the richness of such research and the difficulty of making firm conclusions. It also illustrates a contrast in reporting styles. More "traditional" researchers are likely to prefer, as we do, clearer distinctions among purpose, justification, definition, procedures, results, and interpretations than are found in this report. Others argue that too much attention to such clarity can severely impair the narrative. We agree but believe a middle ground is attainable.

Go back to the **INTERACTIVE AND APPLIED LEARNING** feature at the beginning of the chapter for a listing of interactive and applied activities. Go to the **Online Learning Center** at **www.mhhe.com/fraenkel9e** to take quizzes, practice with key terms, and review chapter content.

Main Points

OBSERVER ROLES

- There are four roles that an observer can play in a qualitative research study, ranging from complete participant, to participant-as-observer, to observer-as-participant, to complete observer. The degree of involvement of the observer in the observed situation diminishes accordingly for each of these roles.

PARTICIPANT VERSUS NONPARTICIPANT OBSERVATION

- In participant observation studies, the researcher actually participates as an active member of the group in the situation or setting he or she is observing.
- In nonparticipant observation studies, the researcher does not participate in an activity or situation but observes "from the sidelines."
- The most common forms of nonparticipant observation studies include naturalistic observation and simulations.
- A simulation is an artificially created situation in which subjects are asked to act out certain roles.

OBSERVATION TECHNIQUES

- A coding scheme is a set of categories an observer uses to record a person's or group's behaviors.
- Even with a fixed coding scheme in mind, an observer must still choose what to observe.
- A major problem in all observational research is that much that goes on may be missed.

OBSERVER EFFECT

- The term *observer effect* refers to either the effect the presence of an observer can have on the behavior of the subjects or observer bias in the data reported. The use of audio and video recordings is especially helpful in guarding against this effect.

- For this reason, many researchers argue that the participants in a study should not be informed of the study's purpose until after the data have been collected.

OBSERVER BIAS

- Observer bias refers to the possibility that certain characteristics or ideas of observers may affect what they observe.

SAMPLING IN OBSERVATIONAL STUDIES

- Researchers who engage in observation usually must choose a purposive sample.

INTERVIEWING

- A major technique commonly used by qualitative researchers is in-depth interviewing.
- One purpose of interviewing the participants in a qualitative study is to find out how they think or feel about something. Another purpose is to provide a check on the researcher's observations.
- Interviews may be structured, semistructured, informal, or retrospective.
- The six types of questions asked by interviewers are background (or demographic) questions, knowledge questions, experience (or behavior) questions, opinion (or values) questions, feelings questions, and sensory questions.
- Respect for the individual being interviewed is a paramount expectation in any proper interview.
- Key actors are people in any group who are more informed about the culture and history of the group and who also are more articulate than others.
- A focus group interview is an interview with a small, fairly homogeneous group of people who respond to a series of questions asked by the interviewer.
- The most effective characteristic of a good interviewer is a strong interest in people and in listening to what they have to say.

RELIABILITY AND VALIDITY IN QUALITATIVE RESEARCH

- An important check on the validity and reliability of the researcher's interpretations in qualitative research is to compare one informant's description of something with another informant's description of the same thing.
- Another, although more difficult, check on reliability/validity is to compare information on the same topic with different information—triangulation.
- Efforts to ensure reliability and validity include use of proper vocabulary, recording questions used as well as personal reactions, describing content, and documenting sources.

Key Terms

background (demographic) question 451
coding scheme 447
credibility 456
dichotomous question 453
experience (behavior) question 451
external audit 456
feelings question 452
focus group interview 454
informal interview 449
interview 448
key actor (informant) 451
knowledge question 451
member checking 456
naturalistic observation 445

nonparticipant observation 444
observational data 446
observer bias 446
observer effect 446
observer expectation 447
open-ended question 453
opinion (values) question 451
participant observation 444
reliability 456
retrospective interview 450
semistructured interview 449
sensory question 452
simulation 445
structured interview 449
triangulation 456
validity 456

For Discussion

1. "Observing people without their knowledge and/or recording their comments without their permission is unethical." Would you agree with this statement? Explain your reasoning.
2. Which method do you think is more likely to produce valid information—participant or nonparticipant observation? Why?
3. Are there any kinds of behaviors that should *not* be observed? Explain your thinking. If so, give an example.
4. What would you say is the biggest advantage of participant observation? The biggest disadvantage?
5. "A major difficulty in observing people is that much that goes on may be missed by the observer." Is this always true? Are there any ways to decrease what is missed during observational research? If so, give an example of what might be done.
6. Is observer effect inevitable? Why or why not?
7. "What qualitative researchers try to do is to study the subjective objectively." What does this mean?
8. Is there any kind of data that cannot be obtained through observation? Through interviews? If so, explain.
9. Of the six types of questions we described on pages 451–452, which do you think interviewees would find the hardest to answer? The easiest? Why?
10. What would you say is the most important quality or characteristic an interviewer should possess? Why?
11. Which do you think would be hardest to master and do well, observing or interviewing? Why?
12. Interviewers are frequently advised to "be natural." What do you think that means? Is it possible? Desirable? Always a good idea or not? Explain your thinking.

References

1. Bernard, H. R. (2000, p. 388). *Social research methods. Qualitative and quantitative approaches.* Thousand Oaks, CA: Sage.

2. Papini, D. R., Datan, N., & McCluskey-Fawcett, K. A. (1988). An observational study of affective and assertive family interactions during adolescence. *Journal of Youth and Adolescence, 17,* 477–492.

3. Lindman, R., Jarvinen, P., & Vidjeskog, J. (1987). Verbal interactions of aggressively and nonaggressively predisposed males in a drinking situation. *Aggressive Behavior, 13,* 187–196.

4. Stewart, M. A. (1984). What is a successful doctor-patient interview? A study of interactions and outcomes. *Social Science and Medicine, 19,* 167–175.

5. Devet, B. (1990). A method for observing and evaluating writing lab tutorials. *Writing Center Journal, 10,* 75–83.

6. Amidon, E. J., & Hough, J. B. (1967). *Interaction analysis: Theory, research, and application.* Reading, MA: Addison-Wesley.

7. Fetterman, M. (1998). *Ethnography: Step by step* (2nd ed.). Thousand Oaks, CA: Sage.

8. Patton, M. Q. (2002). *Qualitative evaluation and research methods* (3rd ed.). Thousand Oaks, CA: Sage.

9. Fetterman, M. (1998). *Ethnography: Step by step* (2nd ed., p. 72). Thousand Oaks, CA: Sage. Fetterman points out that the term *informant* has its roots in anthropological work conducted in colonial settings, specifically in African nations formerly within the British Empire.

10. Fetterman, M. (1998). *Ethnography: Step by step* (2nd ed., p. 73). Thousand Oaks, CA: Sage.

11. Patton, M. Q. (2002). *Qualitative evaluation and research methods* (3rd ed., pp. 348–351). Thousand Oaks, CA: Sage.

12. Fetterman, M. (1998). *Ethnography: Step by step* (2nd ed., p. 70). Thousand Oaks, CA: Sage.

13. Fetterman, M. (1998). *Ethnography: Step by step* (2nd ed., p. 71). Thousand Oaks, CA: Sage.

14. Seidman, I. E. (2006). *Interviewing as qualitative research: A guide for researchers in education and the social sciences* (3rd ed., p. 68). New York: Teacher's College Press.

15. Seidman, I. E. (2006). *Interviewing as qualitative research: A guide for researchers in education and the social sciences* (3rd ed., pp. 73–74). New York: Teacher's College Press.

16. Patton, M. Q. (2002). *Qualitative evaluation and research methods* (3rd ed., pp. 354–355). Thousand Oaks, CA: Sage.

17. Patton, M. Q. (2002). *Qualitative evaluation and research methods* (3rd ed., p. 385). Thousand Oaks, CA: Sage.

18. Patton, M. Q. (2002). *Qualitative evaluation and research methods* (3rd ed., p. 380). Thousand Oaks, CA: Sage.

19. Patton, M. Q. (2002). *Qualitative evaluation and research methods* (3rd ed., p. 383). Thousand Oaks, CA: Sage.

Content Analysis 20

What Is Content Analysis?

Some Applications

Categorization in Content Analysis

Steps Involved in Content Analysis

Determine Objectives

Define Terms

Specify the Unit of Analysis

Locate Relevant Data

Develop a Rationale

Develop a Sampling Plan

Formulate Coding Categories

Check Reliability and Validity

Analyze Data

An Illustration of Content Analysis

Using a Computer in Content Analysis

Advantages of Content Analysis

Disadvantages of Content Analysis

An Example of a Content Analysis Study

Analysis of the Study

Purpose/Justification

Definitions

Prior Research

Hypotheses

Sample

Instrumentation

Internal Validity

Results/Interpretation

OBJECTIVES **Studying this chapter should enable you to:**

- Explain what a content analysis is.
- Explain the purpose of content analysis.
- Name three or four ways content analysis can be used in educational research.
- Explain why a researcher might want to do a content analysis.
- Summarize an example of content analysis.
- Describe the steps involved in doing a content analysis.
- Describe the kinds of sampling that can be done in content analysis.
- Describe the two ways to code descriptive information into categories.
- Describe two advantages and two disadvantages of content analysis research.
- Recognize an example of content analysis research when you come across it in the educational literature.

INTERACTIVE AND APPLIED LEARNING After, or while, reading this chapter:

Go to the Online Learning Center at www.mhhe.com/fraenkel9e to:

- Learn More About Content Analysis

Go to your online Student Mastery Activities book to do the following activities:

- Activity 20.1: Content Analysis Research Questions
- Activity 20.2: Content Analysis Categories
- Activity 20.3: Advantages vs. Disadvantages of Content Analysis
- Activity 20.4: Do a Content Analysis

Darrah Hallowitz, a middle school English teacher, is becoming more and more concerned about the ways that women are presented in the literature anthologies she has been assigned to use in her courses. She worries that her students are getting a limited view of the roles that women can play in today's world. After school one day, she asks Roberta, another English teacher, what she thinks. "Well," says Roberta, "funny you should ask me that. Because I have been kind of worried about the same thing. Why don't we check this out?"

How could they "check this out"? What is called for here is content analysis. Darrah and Roberta need to take a careful look at the ways women are portrayed in the various anthologies they are using. They might find that such studies have been done, or they might do one themselves. That is what this chapter is about.

As we mentioned in Chapter 19, the third method that qualitative researchers use to collect and analyze data is what is customarily referred to as *content analysis,* of which the analysis of documents is a major part.

What Is Content Analysis?

Much of human activity is not directly observable or measurable, nor is it always possible to get information from people who might know of such activity from firsthand experience. **Content analysis** is a technique that enables researchers to study human behavior in an indirect way, through an analysis of their communications.* It is just what its name implies: the analysis of the usually, but not necessarily, written contents of a communication. Textbooks, essays, newspapers, novels, magazine articles, cookbooks, songs, political speeches, advertisements, pictures—in fact, the contents of virtually any type of communication—can be analyzed. A person's or group's conscious and unconscious beliefs, attitudes, values, and ideas often are revealed in their communications.

In today's world, there is a tremendously large number of communications of one sort or another (newspaper editorials, graffiti, musical compositions, magazine articles, advertisements, films, electronic media, etc.). Analysis of such communications can tell us a great deal about how human beings live. To analyze these messages, a researcher needs to organize a large amount of material. How can this be done? By developing appropriate categories, ratings, or scores that the researcher can use for subsequent comparison in order to illuminate what he or she is investigating. This is what content analysis is all about.

By using this technique, a researcher can study (indirectly) anything from trends in child-rearing practices (by comparing them over time or by comparing differences in such practices among various groups of people), to types of heroes people prefer, to the extent of violence on television. Through an analysis of literature, popular magazines, songs, comic strips, cartoons, and movies, the different ways in which sex, crime, religion, education, ethnicity, affection and love, or violence and hatred have been presented at different times can be revealed.

*Many things produced by human beings (e.g., pottery, weapons, songs) were not originally intended as communications but subsequently have been viewed as such. For example, the pottery of the Mayans tells us much about their culture.

A researcher can also note the rise and fall of fads. From such data, researchers can make comparisons about the attitudes and beliefs of various groups of people separated by time, geographic locale, culture, or country.

Content analysis as a methodology is often used in conjunction with other methods, in particular historical and ethnographic research. It can be used in any context in which the researcher desires a means of systematizing and (often) quantifying data. It is extremely valuable in analyzing observation and interview data.

Let us consider an example. In a series of studies during the 1960s and 1970s, Gerbner and his colleagues did a content analysis of the amount of violence on television.[1] They selected for their study all of the dramatic television programs that were broadcast during a single week in the fall of each year (to make comparisons from year to year) and looked for incidents that involved violence.

They videotaped each program and then developed a number of measures used by trained coders to analyze each of the programs. *Prevalence,* for example, referred to the percentage of programs that included one or more incidents of violence; *rate* referred to the number of violent incidents occurring in each program; and *role* referred to the individuals who were involved in the violent incidents. (The individuals who committed the violent act or acts were categorized as "violents," while the individuals against whom the violence was committed were categorized as "victims.")

Gerbner and his associates used these data to report two scores: a *program score,* based on prevalence and rate; and a *character score,* based on role. They then calculated a *violence index* for each program, which was determined by the sum of these two scores. Figure 20.1 shows one of the graphs they presented to describe the violence index for different types of programs between 1967 and 1977. It suggests that violence was higher in children's programs than in other types of programs and that there was little change during the 10-year period.

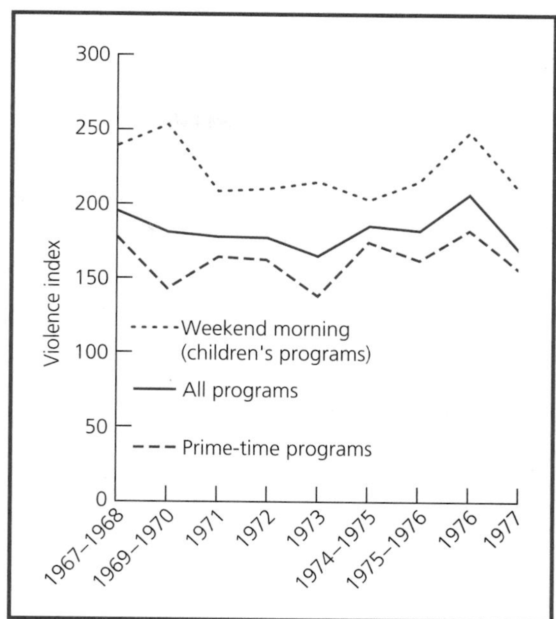

Figure 20.1 *TV Violence and Public Viewing Patterns*

Some Applications

Content analysis is a method that has wide applicability in educational research. For example, it can be used to:

- Describe trends in schooling over time (e.g., the back-to-basics movement) by examining professional and/or general publications.
- Understand organizational patterns (e.g., by examining charts, outlines, etc., prepared by school administrators).
- Show how different schools handle the same phenomena differently (e.g., curricular patterns, school governance).
- Infer attitudes, values, and cultural patterns in different countries (e.g., through an examination of what sorts of courses and activities are—or are not—sponsored and endorsed).
- Compare the myths that people hold about schools with what actually occurs within them (e.g., by comparing the results of polls taken of the general public with literature written by teachers and others working in the schools).
- Gain a sense of how teachers feel about their work (e.g., by examining what they have written about their jobs).
- Gain some idea of how schools are perceived (e.g., by viewing films and television programs depicting same).

Content analysis can also be used to supplement other, more direct methods of research. Attitudes toward women who are working in so-called men's occupations, for example, can be investigated in a variety of ways: questionnaires; in-depth interviews; participant observations; and/or content analysis of social networking sites, magazine articles, television programs, newspapers, films, and autobiographies that touch on the subject.

Lastly, content analysis can be used to give researchers insights into problems or hypotheses that they can then test by more direct methods. A researcher might analyze the content of a student newspaper, for example, to obtain information for devising questionnaires or formulating questions for subsequent in-depth interviews with members of the student body at a particular high school.

Following are the titles of some content analysis studies that have been conducted by educational researchers:

- "Exploring Lesbian, Gay, Bisexual, and Transgender Topics in Foundations of Education Textbooks"[2]
- "An Analysis of Multicultural Teacher Education Coursework Syllabi"[3]
- "Using Alcohol to Sell Cigarettes to Young Adults: A Content Analysis of Cigarette Advertisements"[4]
- "Perceptions of Collaboration: A Content Analysis of Student Journals"[5]
- "Role of Gender in Reviewers' Appraisals of Quality in Political Science Books"[6]
- "A Content Analysis of School Anti-bullying Policies"[7]
- "Teaching Mathematics for Understanding: An Analysis of Lessons Submitted by Teachers Seeking NBPTS Certification"[8]

Categorization in Content Analysis

All procedures that are called *content analysis* have certain characteristics in common. These procedures also vary in some respects, depending on the purpose of the analysis and the type of communication being analyzed.

All must at some point convert (i.e., *code*) descriptive information into *categories*. There are two ways that this might be done:

1. The researcher determines the categories before any analysis begins. These categories are based on previous knowledge, theory, and/or experience. For example, later in this chapter, we use predetermined categories to describe and evaluate a series of journal articles pertaining to social studies education (see p. 485).
2. The researcher becomes very familiar with the descriptive information collected and allows the categories to emerge as the analysis continues (see Figure 20.3 on p. 482).

Steps Involved in Content Analysis

DETERMINE OBJECTIVES

Decide on the specific objectives you want to achieve. There are several reasons why a researcher might want to do a content analysis.

- *To obtain descriptive information about a topic.* Content analysis is a very useful way to obtain information that describes an issue or topic. For example, a content analysis of child-rearing practices in different countries could provide descriptive information that might lead to a consideration of different approaches within a particular society. Similarly, a content analysis of the ways various historical events are described in the history textbooks of different countries might shed some light on why people have different views of history (e.g., Adolf Hitler's role in World War II).
- *To formulate themes (i.e., major ideas) that help to organize and make sense out of large amounts of descriptive information.* **Themes** are typically groupings of codes that emerge either during or after the process of developing codes. An example is shown on page 482.
- *To check other research findings.* Content analysis is helpful in validating the findings of a study or studies using other research methodologies. Statements of textbook publishers concerning what they believe is included in their company's high school biology textbooks (obtained through interviews), for example, could be checked by doing a content analysis of such textbooks. Interviews with college professors as to what they say they teach could be verified by doing a content analysis of their syllabi.
- *To obtain information useful in dealing with educational problems.* Content analysis can help teachers plan activities to help students learn. A content analysis of student compositions, for example, might help teachers pinpoint grammatical or stylistic errors. A content analysis of math assignments might reveal deficiencies in the ways students attempt to solve word problems. While such analyses are similar to grading practices, they differ in that they provide more specific information, such as the relative frequency of different kinds of mistakes.
- *To test hypotheses.* Content analysis can also be used to investigate possible relationships or to test ideas.

MORE ABOUT RESEARCH

Important Findings in Content Analysis Research

One of the classic examples of content analysis was done more than 60 years ago by Whiting and Child.* Their method was to have at least two judges assign ratings on 17 characteristics of child rearing and on the presence or absence of 20 different explanations of illness for 75 "primitive societies" in addition to the United States. Examples of characteristics are: dependence socialization anxiety, age at weaning, and age at toilet training. Ratings were based on ethnographic material on each society (see Chapter 21), available at the Yale Institute of Human Relations, which varied from one printed page to several hundred pages.

Psychoanalytical theory provided the basis for a series of correlational hypotheses. Among the researchers' conclusions was that explanations of illness are related to both early deprivation and severity of training (e.g., societies that weaned earliest were more likely to explain illness as due to eating, drinking, or verbally instigated spells). Another finding was that the U.S. (middle-class) sample was, by comparison, quite severe in its child-rearing practices, beginning both weaning and toilet training earlier than other societies and accompanying both with exceptionally harsh penalties.

*Whiting, M. W., & Child, I. L. (1953). *Child training and personality.* New Haven, CT: Yale University Press.

For example, a researcher might hypothesize that social studies textbooks have changed in the degree to which they emphasize the role of minority individuals in the history of our country. A content analysis of a sample of texts published over the last 20 years would reveal if this is the case.

DEFINE TERMS

As in all research, investigators and/or readers are sure to incur considerable frustration unless important terms, such as *violence, minority individuals,* and *back-to-basics,* are clearly defined, either beforehand or as the study progresses.

SPECIFY THE UNIT OF ANALYSIS

What, exactly, is to be analyzed? Words? Sentences? Phrases? Paintings? The units to be used for conducting and reporting the analysis should be specified before the researcher begins the analysis.

LOCATE RELEVANT DATA

Once the researcher is clear about the objectives and units of analysis, he or she must locate the data (e.g., textbooks, magazines, songs, course outlines, lesson plans) that will be analyzed and that are relevant to the objectives. The relationship between the content to be analyzed and the objectives of the study should be clear. One way to help ensure clarity is to have a specific research question (and possibly a hypothesis) in mind beforehand and then to select a body of material in which the question or hypothesis can be investigated.

DEVELOP A RATIONALE

The researcher needs a conceptual link to explain how the data are related to the objectives. The choice of content should be clear, even to a disinterested observer. Often, the link between question and content is quite obvious. A logical way to study bias in advertisements, for example, is to study the contents of newspaper and magazine advertisements. At other times, the link is not so obvious, however, and needs to be explained. Thus, a researcher who is interested in changes in attitudes toward a particular group (e.g., police officers) over time might decide to look at how they were portrayed in short stories appearing in magazines published at different times. The researcher must assume that changes in how police officers were portrayed in these stories indicate a change in attitudes toward them.

Many content analyses use available material. But it is also common for a researcher to generate his or her own data. Thus, open-ended questionnaires might be administered to a group of students to determine how they feel about a newly introduced curriculum, and then the researcher would analyze their responses. Or a series of open-ended interviews might be held with a group of students to assess their perceptions of the strengths and weaknesses of the school's counseling program, and these interviews would be coded and analyzed.

DEVELOP A SAMPLING PLAN

Once these steps have been accomplished, the researcher develops a sampling plan. Novels, for example, may be sampled at one or any number of levels, such as words, phrases, sentences, paragraphs, chapters, books, or authors. Television programs can be sampled by type, channel, sponsor, producer, or time of day shown. Any form of communication may be sampled at any conceptual level that is appropriate.

One of the *purposive sampling designs* described in Chapter 18 is most commonly used. For example, a researcher might decide to obtain transcribed interviews from several students because all of them are exceptionally talented musicians. Or a researcher might select from among the minutes of school board meetings only those in which specific curriculum changes were recommended.

The sampling techniques discussed in Chapter 6 can also be used in content analysis. For example, a researcher might decide to select a **random sample** of chemistry textbooks, curriculum guides, laws pertaining to education that were passed in the state of California, lesson plans prepared by history teachers in a low-performing high school, or an elementary principal's daily bulletins. Another possibility would be to number all the songs recorded by Madonna and then select a random sample of 50 to analyze.

Stratified sampling also can be used in content analysis. A researcher interested in school board policies in a particular state, for example, might begin by grouping school districts by geographic area and size and then use random or systematic sampling to select particular districts. Stratification ensures that the sample is representative of the state in terms of district size and location. A statement of policies would then be obtained from each district in the sample for analysis.

Cluster sampling can also be used. In the example just described, if the unit of analysis were the minutes of board meetings rather than formal policy statements, the minutes of all meetings during an academic year could be analyzed. Each randomly selected district would thus provide a cluster of meeting minutes. If minutes of only one or two meetings were randomly selected from each district, however, this would be an example of two-stage random sampling (see p. 98).

There are, of course, less desirable ways to select a sample of content to be analyzed. One could easily select a convenience sample of content that would make the analysis virtually meaningless. An example would be assessing the attitudes of American citizens toward free trade by studying articles published only in the *National Review* or *The Progressive.* An improvement over convenience sampling would be, as mentioned earlier, purposive sampling. Rather than relying on simply their own or their colleagues' judgments as to what might be appropriate material for analysis, researchers should, when possible, rely on evidence that the materials they select are, in fact, representative. Thus, deciding to analyze letters to the editor in *Time* magazine to study public attitudes regarding political issues might be justified by previous research showing that the letters in *Time* agreed with polling data, election results, and so on.

FORMULATE CODING CATEGORIES*

After a researcher has defined as precisely as possible what aspects of the content are to be investigated, he or she needs to formulate categories that are relevant to the investigation (Figure 20.2). The categories should be so explicit that another researcher could use them to examine the same material and obtain substantially the same results—that is, find the same frequencies in each category.

Suppose a researcher is interested in the accuracy of the images or concepts presented in high school English texts. She wonders whether the written or visual content in these books is biased in any way, and if it is, how. She decides to do a content analysis to obtain some answers to these questions.

She must first plan how to select and order the content that is available for analysis—in this case, the textbooks. She must develop pertinent categories that will allow her to identify that which she thinks is important.

Let us imagine that the researcher decides to look, in particular, at how women are presented in these texts. She would first select the sample of textbooks to be analyzed—that is, which texts she will read (in this case, perhaps, all of the textbooks used at a certain grade level in a particular school district). She could then formulate categories. How are women described? What traits do they possess? What are their physical, emotional, and social characteristics? These questions suggest categories for analysis that can, in turn, be broken down into even smaller **coding** units such as those shown in Table 20.1.

Another researcher might be interested in investigating whether different attitudes toward intimate human

*An exception to this step occurs when the researcher counts instances of a particular characteristic (e.g., of violence, as in the Gerbner study) or uses a rating system (as was done in the Whiting & Child study—see "Important Findings in Content Analysis Research" on p. 479).

Figure 20.2 *What Categories Should I Use?*

TABLE 20.1 *Coding Categories for Women in Social Studies Textbooks*

Physical Characteristics	Emotional Characteristics	Social Characteristics
Color of hair	Warm	Race
Color of eyes	Aloof	Religion
Height	Stable, secure	Occupation
Weight	Anxious, insecure	Income
Age	Hostile	Housing
Hairstyle	Enthusiastic	Age
etc.	etc.	etc.

relationships are implied in the mass media of the United States, England, France, and Sweden. Films would be an excellent and accessible source for this analysis, although the categories and coding units within each category would be much more difficult to formulate. For instance, three general categories could be formed using Horney's typology of relationships: "going toward," "going away from," and "going against."[9] This would be an example of categories formulated ahead of time. The researcher would then look for instances of these concepts expressed in the films. Other units of behavior, such as hitting someone, expressing a sarcastic remark, kissing or hugging, and refusing a request, are illustrations of other categories that might emerge from familiarity with the data.

Another way to analyze the content of mass media is to use "space" or "time" categories. For example, in the past few years, how many inches of Internet articles have been devoted to student demonstrations on campuses? How many minutes have television news programs devoted to urban riots? How much time has been used for programs that deal with violent topics compared to nonviolent topics?

The process of developing categories that emerge from the data is often complex. An example of coding an interview is shown in Figure 20.3. It is a transcript of an interview with a teacher regarding curriculum change. In this example, both the category codes and the initial themes are identified in the text and annotated in the margins, along with reminders to the researcher.

Manifest Versus Latent Content. In doing a content analysis, a researcher can code either or both the manifest and the latent content of a communication. How do they differ? The **manifest content** of a communication refers to the obvious, surface content—the words,

Codes	Transcript	Themes
	Interviewer: Lucy, what do you perceive as strengths of Greenfield as a community and how that relates to schools?	
Close-knit community Health of community, or community values Change is threatening	**Lucy:** Well, I think Greenfield is a fairly close-knit community. I think people are interested in what goes on. . . . We like to keep track of what our kids are doing, and feel a connection to them because of that. The downside of that perhaps is that kids can feel that we are looking TOO close. . . . you said the health of the community itself is reflected in schools. . . . I think . . . this is a pretty conservative community overall, and look to make sure that what is being talked about in the schools really carries out the community's values. . . . (And I think there might be a tendency to hold back a little bit too much because of that idealization of "you know, we learned the basics, the reading, the writing, and the arithmetic"). So you know, any change is threatening. . . . Sometimes that can get in the way of trying to do different things.	Sense of community
	Interviewer: In terms of looking at leadership strengths in the community, where does Greenfield set in a continuum with planning process, . . . forward thinking, visionary people. . . .	Potential theme: Leaders
Visionary skills of talented people	**Lucy:** I think there are people that have wonderful visionary skills. I would say that the community as a whole . . . would not reflect that . . . I think we have some incredibly talented people who become frustrated when they try to implement what they see as their . . .	

Figure 20.3 *An Example of Coding an Interview*

Source: Creswell, J. W. (2008, p. 253). *Educational research: Planning, conducting, and evaluating qualitative research.* Columbus, OH: Merrill Prentice-Hall.

pictures, images, and so on that are directly accessible to the naked eye or ear. No inferences as to underlying meaning are necessary. To determine, for example, whether a course of study encourages the development of critical thinking skills, a researcher might simply count the number of times the word *thinking* appears in the course objectives listed in the course outline.

The **latent content** of a document, on the other hand, refers to the meaning underlying what is said or shown. To get at the underlying meaning of a course outline, for example, a researcher might read through the entire outline or a sample of pages, particularly those describing the classroom activities and homework assignments to which students will be exposed. The researcher would then make an overall assessment as to the degree to which the course is likely to develop critical thinking. Although the researcher's assessment would surely be influenced by the appearance of the word *thinking* in the document, it would not depend totally on the frequency with which the word (or its synonyms) appeared.

There seems little question that both methods have their advantages and disadvantages. Coding the manifest content of a document has the advantage of ease of coding and *reliability*—another researcher is likely to arrive at the same number of words or phrases counted. It also lets the reader of the report know exactly how the term *thinking* was measured. On the other hand, it would be somewhat suspect in terms of *validity.* Just counting the number of times the word *thinking* appears in the outline for a course would not indicate all the ways in which this skill is to be developed, nor would it necessarily indicate "critical" thinking.

Coding the latent content of a document has the advantage of getting at the underlying meaning of what is written or shown, but it comes at some cost in reliability. It is likely that two researchers would assess differently the degree to which a particular course outline would develop critical thinking. An activity or assignment judged by one researcher as especially likely to encourage critical thinking might be seen by a second researcher as ineffective. A commonly used criterion is 80 percent agreement. But even if a single researcher does all the coding, there is no guarantee that he or she will remain constant in the judgments made or standards used. Furthermore, the reader would probably be uncertain as to exactly how the overall judgment was made.

The best solution, therefore, is to use both methods whenever possible. A given passage or excerpt should receive close to the same description if a researcher's coding of the manifest and latent contents is reasonably reliable and valid. However, if a researcher's (or two or more researchers') assessments, using the two methods, are not fairly close (it is unlikely that there would ever be perfect agreement), the results should probably be discarded and perhaps the overall intent of the analysis reconsidered.

CHECK RELIABILITY AND VALIDITY

Although it is seldom done, we believe that some of the procedures for checking **reliability** and **validity** (see Chapter 8) could at least in some instances be applied to content analysis. In addition to assessing the agreement between two or more categorizers, it would be useful to know how the categorizations by the same researcher agree over a meaningful time period (test-retest method). Furthermore, a kind of equivalent-forms reliability could be done by selecting a second sample of materials or dividing the original sample in half. One would expect, for example, that the data obtained from one sample of editorials would agree with those obtained from a second sample. Another possibility would be to divide each unit of analysis in the sample in half for comparison. Thus, if the unit of analysis is a novel, the number of derogatory statements about foreigners in odd-numbered chapters should agree fairly well with the number in even-numbered chapters.

With respect to validity, we think it should often be possible not only to check manifest against latent content but also to compare either or both with results from different instruments. For example, the relative frequency of derogatory and positive statements about foreigners found in editorials would be expected to correspond with that found in letters to the editor, if both reflected popular opinion.

ANALYZE DATA

Counting is an important characteristic of some content analysis. Each time a unit in a pertinent category is found, it is "counted." Thus, the end product of the coding process must be numbers. It is obvious that counting the frequency of certain words, phrases, symbols, pictures, or other manifest content requires the use of numbers. But even coding the latent content of a document requires the researcher to represent those coding decisions with numbers in each category.

It is also important to record the *base,* or reference point, for the counting. It would not be very informative, for example, merely to state that a newspaper editorial contained 15 anti-Semitic statements without knowing the overall length of the editorial. Knowing the number of speeches a senator makes in which she argues for balancing the budget doesn't tell us very much about how fiscally conservative she is if we don't know how many speeches she has made on economic topics since the counting began.

Let us suppose that we want to do a content analysis of the editorial policies of newspapers in various parts of the United States. Table 20.2 illustrates a portion of a tally sheet that might be used to code such editorials. The first column lists the newspapers by number (each newspaper could be assigned a number to facilitate analysis). The second and third columns list location and circulation, respectively. The fourth column lists the number of editorials coded for each paper. The fifth column shows the subjective assessment by the researcher of each newspaper's editorial policy (these might later be compared with the objective measures obtained). The sixth and seventh columns record the number of certain types of editorials.

The last step, then, is to analyze the data that have been tabulated. As in other methods of research, the descriptive statistical procedures discussed in Chapter 10 are useful to summarize the data and assist the researcher in interpreting what they reveal.

A common way to interpret content analysis data is through the use of frequencies (i.e., the number of specific incidents found in the data) and the percentage and/or proportion of particular occurrences to total occurrences. You will note that we use these statistics in the analysis of social studies research articles that follows (see Tables 20.3, 20.4, and 20.5). In content analysis studies designed to explore relationships, a crossbreak table (see Chapter 10) or chi-square analysis (see Chapter 11) is often used because both are appropriate to the analysis of categorical data.*

Other researchers prefer to use codes and themes as aids in organizing content and arriving at a narrative description of findings.

*In studies in which ratings or scores are used, averages, correlation coefficients, and frequency polygons are appropriate.

TABLE 20.2 *Sample Tally Sheet (Newspaper Editorials)*

Newspaper ID Number	Location	Circulation	Number of Editorials Coded	Subjective Evaluation[a]	Number of Pro-Abortion Editorials	Number of Anti-Abortion Editorials
101	A	3,000,000	29	3	0	1
102	B	675,000	21	3	1	1
103	C	425,000	33	4	2	0
104	D	1,000,000	40	1	0	8
105	E	550,000	34	5	7	0

[a]Categories within the subjective evaluation: 1 = very conservative; 2 = somewhat conservative; 3 = middle-of-the-road; 4 = moderately liberal; 5 = very liberal.

An Illustration of Content Analysis

In 1988, we did a content analysis of all the research studies published in *Theory and Research in Social Education (TRSE)* between the years 1979 and 1986.[10] *TRSE* is a journal devoted to the publication of social studies research. We read 46 studies contained in those issues. The following presents a breakdown by type of study reviewed:

Type of Studies Reviewed	
True experiments	7 (15%)
Quasi-experiments	7 (15%)
Correlational studies	9 (19%)
Questionnaire-type surveys	9 (19%)
Interview-type surveys	6 (13%)
Ethnographies	9 (19%)
	n = 47[a] (100%)

[a]This totals 47 rather than 46 because the researchers in one study used two methodologies.

Both of us read every study that was published during this period that fell into one of these categories. We analyzed the studies using a coding sheet that we jointly prepared. To test our agreement concerning the meaning of the various categories, we each initially read a sample of (the same) six studies, and then met to compare our analyses. We found that we were in substantial agreement concerning what the categories meant, although it soon became apparent that we needed some additional subcategories as well as some totally new categories. Figure 20.4 presents the final set of categories.

We then reread the initial 6 studies using the revised set of categories, as well as the remaining 40 studies. We again met to compare our assessments. Although we had a number of disagreements, the great majority were simple oversights by one or the other of us and were easily resolved.* Tables 20.3 through 20.5 present some of the findings of our research.

TABLE 20.3 *Clarity of Studies*

Category	Number
A. Focus clear?	46 (100%)
B. Variables clear?	
(1) Initially	31 (67%)
(2) Eventually	7 (15%)
(3) Never	8 (17%)
C. Is treatment in intervention studies made explicit?	
(1) Yes	12 (26%)
(2) No	2 (4%)
(3) NA (no treatment)	32 (70%)
D. Is there a hypothesis?	
(1) No	18 (39%)
(2) Explicitly stated	13 (28%)
(3) Clearly implied	15 (33%)

TABLE 20.4 *Type of Sample*

Category	Number
Random selection	2 (4%)
Representation based on argument	6 (13%)
Convenience	29 (62%)
Volunteer	4 (9%)
Can't tell	6 (13%)

Note: One study used more than one type of sample. Percentages are based on n = 46.

*It would have been desirable to compare our analysis with the findings of a second team as a further check on reliability, but this was not feasible.

1. Type of Research

A. Experimental
(1) Pre
(2) True
(3) Quasi
B. Correlational
C. Survey
D. Interview
E. Causal-comparative
F. Ethnographic

2. Justification

A. No mention of justification
B. Explicit argument made with regard to worth of study
C. Worth of study is implied
D. Any ethical considerations overlooked?

3. Clarity

A. Focus clear? (yes or no)
B. Variables clear?
(1) Initially
(2) Eventually
(3) Never
C. Is treatment in intervention studies made explicit? (yes, no, or n.a.)
D. Is there a hypothesis?
(1) No
(2) Yes: explicitly stated
(3) Yes: clearly implied

4. Are Key Terms Defined?

A. No
B. Operationally
C. Constitutively
D. Clear in context of study

5. Sample

A. Type
(1) Random selection
(2) Representation based on argument
(3) Convenience
(4) Volunteer
(5) Can't tell
B. Was sample adequately described? (1 = high; 5 = low)
C. Size of sample (*n*)

6. Internal Validity

A. Possible alternative explanations for outcomes obtained
(1) History
(2) Maturation
(3) Mortality
(4) Selection bias/subject characteristics
(5) Pretest effect
(6) Regression effect
(7) Instrumentation
(8) Attitude of subjects
B. Threats discussed and clarified? (yes or no)
C. Was it clear that the treatment received an adequate trial (in intervention studies)? (yes or no)
D. Was length of time of treatment sufficient? (yes or no)

7. Instrumentation

A. Reliability
(1) Empirical check made? (yes or no)
(2) If yes, was reliability adequate for study?
B. Validity
(1) Empirical check made? (yes or no)
(2) If yes, type:
(a) Content
(b) Concurrent
(c) Construct

8. External Validity

A. Discussion of population generalizability
(1) Appropriate
(a) Explicit reference to defensible target population
(b) Appropriate caution expressed
(2) Inappropriate
(a) No mention of generalizability
(b) Explicit reference to indefensible target population
B. Discussion of ecological generalizability
(1) Appropriate
(a) Explicit reference to defensible settings (subject matter, materials, physical conditions, personnel, etc.)
(b) Appropriate caution expressed
(2) Inappropriate
(a) No mention of generalizability
(b) Explicit reference to indefensible settings

9. Were Results and Interpretations Kept Distinct? (yes or no)

10. Data Analysis

A. Descriptive statistics? (yes or no)
(1) Correct technique? (yes or no)
(2) Correct interpretation? (yes or no)
B. Inferential statistics? (yes or no)
(1) Correct technique? (yes or no)
(2) Correct interpretation? (yes or no)

11. Do Data Justify Conclusions? (yes or no)

12. Were Outcomes of Study Educationally Significant? (yes or no)

13. Relevance of Citations

Figure 20.4 *Categories Used to Evaluate Social Studies Research*

TABLE 20.5 ***Threats to Internal Validity***

Possible Alternative Explanations for Outcomes Obtained	Number
1. History	4 (9%)
2. Maturation	0 (0%)
3. Mortality	10 (22%)
4. Selection bias/subject characteristics	15 (33%)
5. Pretest effect	2 (4%)
6. Regression effect	0 (0%)
7. Instrumentation	21 (46%)
8. Attitude of subjects	7 (15%)

		Threats Discussed and Clarified?	
Type	**Number of Articles**	**Identified by Reviewers**	**Discussed by Authors**
True experiments	7	3 (43%)	2 (29%)
Quasi-experiments	7	7 (100%)	4 (57%)
Correlational studies	9	5 (56%)	3 (33%)
Questionnaire surveys	9	3 (33%)	0 (0%)
Interview-type surveys	6	9 (67%)	1 (17%)
Causal-comparative	0	–	–
Ethnographies	9	9 (100%)	0 (0%)

These tables indicate that the intent of the studies was clear; that the variables were generally clear (82 percent); that the treatment in intervention studies was clear in almost all cases; and that most studies were hypothesis testing, although the latter was not always made clear. Only 17 percent of the studies could claim representative samples, and most of these required argumentation. Mortality, subject characteristics, and instrumentation threats existed in a substantial proportion of the studies. These were acknowledged and discussed by the authors in 9 of the 15 experimental or correlational studies, but rarely by the authors of any of the other types.

Using a Computer in Content Analysis

Computers are now used to offset much of the labor involved in analyzing documents. Various software programs have been a boon to quantitative research, allowing researchers to calculate quite rapidly very complex statistics. Programs to assist qualitative researchers in their analysis, however, now also exist. Many simple word-processing programs can be used for some kinds of data analysis. The "find" command, for example, can locate various passages in a document that contain key words or phrases. Thus, a researcher might ask the computer to search for all passages that contain the words *creative, nonconformist,* or *punishment,* or phrases such as *corporal punishment* or *artistic creativity.*

Notable examples of qualitative computer programs that are currently available include ATLAS.ti, QSR NUD*IST, Nvivo, and HyperResearch. These programs will identify words, phrases, or sentences, tabulate their occurrence, print and graph the tabulations, and sort and regroup words, phrases, or sentences according to how they fit a particular set of categories. Computers, of course, presume that the information of interest is in written form. Optical scanners are available that make it possible for computers to "read" documents and store the contents digitally, thus eliminating the need for data entry by hand. Should you have to do some qualitative data analysis, a few of these programs are worth taking some time to examine.

Advantages of Content Analysis

As we mentioned earlier, much of what we know is obtained not through direct interaction with others but through books, newspapers, and other products of human beings. A major advantage of content analysis is that it is unobtrusive. A researcher can "observe" without being observed, since the contents being analyzed are not influenced by the researcher's presence. Information that might be difficult, or even impossible, to obtain through direct observation or other means can be gained unobtrusively through analysis of textbooks and other communications, without the author or publisher being aware that it is being examined. Another advantage of content analysis is that, as we have illustrated, it is extremely useful as a means of analyzing interview and observational data.

A third advantage of content analysis is that the researcher can delve into records and documents to get some feel for the social life of an earlier time. He or she is not limited by time and space to the study of present events.

A fourth advantage accrues from the fact that the logistics of content analysis are often relatively simple and economical—with regard to both time and resources—as compared to other research methods. This is particularly true if the information is readily accessible, as in newspapers, reports, books, periodicals, and the like.

Lastly, because the data are readily available and almost always can be returned to if necessary or desired, content analysis permits replication of a study by other researchers. Even live television programs can be recorded for repeated analysis at later times.

Disadvantages of Content Analysis

A major disadvantage of content analysis is that it is usually limited to recorded information. The researcher may, of course, arrange the recordings to suit the purposes of the study, as in the use of open-ended questionnaires or projective techniques (see pp. 131–132). However, one would not be likely to use such recordings to study proficiency in calculus, Spanish vocabulary, the frequency of hostile acts, or similar variables, because they require demonstrated behaviors or skills.

The other main disadvantage is in establishing validity. Assuming that different analysts can achieve acceptable agreement in categorizing, the question remains as to the true meaning of the categories themselves. Recall the earlier discussion of this problem under the heading "Manifest Versus Latent Content." A comparison of the results of these two methods provides some evidence of criterion-related validity, although the two measurements obviously are not completely independent. As with any measurement, additional evidence of a criterion or construct nature is important. In the absence of such evidence, the argument for content validity rests on the persuasiveness of the logic connecting each category to its intended meaning. For example, our interpretation of the data on social studies research assumes that what was clear or unclear to us would also be clear or unclear to other researchers or readers. Similarly, it assumes that most, if not all, researchers would agree as to whether definitions and particular threats to internal validity were present in a given article. While we think these are reasonable assumptions, that does not make them so.

With respect to the use of content analysis in historical research, the researcher normally has records only of what has survived or what someone thought was of sufficient importance to write down. Because each generation has a somewhat different perspective on its life and times, what was considered important at a particular time in the past may be viewed as trivial today. Conversely, what is considered important today might not even be available from the past.

Finally, sometimes there is a temptation among researchers to consider that the interpretations gleaned from a particular content analysis indicate the *causes* of a phenomenon rather than being a reflection of it. For example, portrayal of violence in the media may be considered a cause of today's violence in the streets, but a more reasonable conclusion may be that violence in both the media and in the streets reflect the attitudes of people. Certainly much work has to be done to determine the relationship between the media and human behavior. Again, some people think that reading pornographic books and magazines causes moral decay among those who read such materials. Pornography probably does affect some individuals, and it is likely that it affects different people in different ways. It is also quite likely that it does not affect other individuals at all, but exactly how people are affected, and why or why not, is unclear.

An Example of a Content Analysis Study

In the remainder of this chapter, we present a published example of content analysis, followed by a critique of its strengths and weaknesses. As we did in our critiques of other types of research studies, we use concepts introduced in earlier parts of the book in our analysis.

RESEARCH REPORT

From: *Education, 125*, no. 1 (Fall 2004). Reproduced by permission of Project Innovation, Inc.

The "Nuts and Dolts" of Teacher Images in Children's Picture Storybooks: A Content Analysis

Sarah Jo Sandefur
UC Foundation Assistant Professor of Literacy Education, University of Tennessee–Chattanooga

Leeann Moore
Assistant Dean, College of Education and Human Services, Texas A & M University–Commerce

Rationale or conclusion?

Evidence or opinion?

Purpose?

Statement not consistent with results

Children's picture storybooks are rife with contradictory representations of teachers and school. Some of those images are fairly accurate. Some of those images are quite disparate from reality. These representations become subsumed into the collective consciousness of a society and shape expectations and behaviors of both students and teachers. Teachers cannot effectuate positive change in their profession unless and until they are aware of the internal and external influences that define and shape the educational institution. This ethnographic content analysis examines 62 titles and 96 images of teachers to probe the power of stereotypes/clichés. The authors found the following: The teacher in children's picture storybooks is overwhelmingly portrayed as a white, non-Hispanic, woman. The teacher in picture storybooks who is sensitive, competent, and able to manage a classroom effectively is a minority. The negative images outnumbered the positive images. The teacher in children's picture storybooks is static, unchanging, and flat. The teacher is polarized and does not inspire in his or her students the pursuit of critical inquiry.

A recent children's book shares the story of a teacher. Miss Malarkey, home with the flu, narrates her concern about how her elementary students will behave with and be treated by the potential substitutes available to the school. Among the substitutes represented are Mrs. Boba, a 20-something woman who is too busy painting her toenails to attend to Miss Malarkey's students. Mr. Doberman is a drill sergeant of a man who snarls at the children: "So ya think it's time for recess, HUH?" Mr. Lemonjello, drawn as a small, bald, nervous man, is taunted by the students with the class iguana and is subsequently covered in paint at art time (*Miss Malarkey Won't Be in Today,* Finchler, 1998).

In this text, which is representative of many that have been published with teachers as central characters, teachers are portrayed as insensitive; misguided, victimizing, or incompetent. We perceive these invalidating images as worthy of detailed analysis, based on a hypothesis that a propensity of images painting teachers in an unflattering light may have broader consequences on cultural perceptions of teachers and schooling. Our ethnographic content analysis herein examines 96 images of teachers as they are found in 62 picture storybooks from 1965 to present. It is our perspective that these images in part shape and define the idea of "Teacher" in the collective consciousness of a society.

Evidence or opinion

Not research hypothesis in this study

Sample

Those of us in teacher education realize our students come to us with previously constructed images of the profession. What is the origin of those images? When and how are these images formed and elaborated upon? It appears that the popular culture has done much to form or modify those images. Weber and Mitchell (1995) suggest that these multiple, often ambiguous, images are ". . . integral to the form and substance of our self-identities as teachers" (p. 32). They suggest that ". . . by studying images and probing their influence, teachers could play a more conscious and effective role in shaping their own and society's perceptions of teachers and their work" (p. 32). We have supported this "probing of images" by analyzing children's picture storybooks, examining their meanings and metaphors where they intersect with teachers and schooling. It is our intention that by sharing what we have learned about the medium's responses to the profession, we will better serve teachers in playing that "conscious role" in defining their work.

Rationale

We submit that children's picture storybooks are not benign. Although the illustrations of teachers are often cartoon-like and at first glance fairly innocent, when taken as a whole they have power not just in teaching children and their parents about the culture of schooling, but in shaping it, as well. This is of concern particularly when the majority of the images of teachers are negative, mixed, or neutral as we have found in our research and will report herein. Gavriel Salomon, well known for his research in symbolic representations and their impact on children's learning and thinking, has this to say about the power of media:

Rationale/theory

> *Media's symbolic forms of representation are clearly not neutral or indifferent packages that have no effect on the represented information. Being part and parcel of the information itself, they influence the meanings one arrives at, the mental capacities that are called for,* and the ways one comes to view the world. *Perhaps more important, the culture that creates the media and develops their symbolic forms of representation also* opens the door for those forms to act on the minds of the young *in both more and less desirable ways. [italics added] (1997, p. 13)*

Rationale

We see Salomon's work here as foundational to our own in this way: if those images children and parents see of "teacher" are generally negative, then they will create a "world view" of "teacher" based upon stereotype. The many negative images of teachers in children's picture storybooks may be the message to readers that teachers are, at best, kind but uninspiring, and at worst, roadblocks to be torn down in order that children may move forward successfully.

Need definition of "images"

WHY STUDY IMAGES OF TEACHERS FROM POPULAR CULTURE?

Background

As we were preparing to teach a graduate class entitled "Portrayal of Teachers in Children's Literature and in Film," we began gathering a text set of picture storybooks that focused on teachers, teaching, and the school environment. We quickly became aware of the propensity of negative images of teachers, from witch to dragon, drill sergeant to milquetoast, incompetent fool to insensitive clod. We realized early in the graduate course that many teachers had not had the opportunity to critically examine images of their own profession in the popular media. They were unaware of the negative portrayals in existing texts, particularly in children's literature. Teachers may not have considered that the negative images of the teacher "may give the public further justification for a lack of support of education" (Crume, 1989, p. 36).

Research or opinion?

Children's literature is rife with contradictory representations of teachers and school. Some of those images are fairly accurate and some of those images are quite disparate from reality (Farber, Provenso, & Holm, 1994; Joseph & Burnaford, 1994; Knowles, Cole, & Presswood, 1994; Weber & Mitchell, 1995). These representations become subsumed into the collective consciousness of a society and shape expectations and behaviors of both students and teachers. They become a part of the images that children construct when they are invited to "draw a teacher" or "play school," and indeed the images that teachers draw of themselves. Consider, for example, the three-year old boy with no prior schooling experience, who, in playing school, puts the dolls in straight rows, selects a domineering personality for a female teacher, and assigns homework (Weber & Mitchell, 1995).

Rationale

Purpose?

This exploration into teacher images is a critical one at multiple levels of teacher education. Pre-service teachers need to analyze via media images their personal motivations and expectations of the teaching profession and enter into teaching with clear understandings of how the broad culture perceives their work. In-service teachers need to heighten their awareness of how children, parents, and community members perceive them. These perceptions may be in part media-induced and not based on the complex reality of a particular teacher. If information is indeed power, then perhaps those of us in the profession can better understand that popular images contribute to the public's frequent suspicion of our efficacy, and this heightened awareness can support us in addressing the negative images head on.

RESEARCH PERSPECTIVES

Prior research

How do we as teachers, prospective teachers, and teacher educators come to so fully subscribe to the images we have both experienced and imagined? Have those images formed long before adulthood, perhaps even before the child enters school? Weber and Mitchell (1994) contend, "Even before children begin school, they have already been exposed to a myriad of images of teachers, classrooms and schools which have made strong and lasting impressions on them" (p. 2). Some of those images and attitudes form from direct experience with teachers. Barone, Meyerson, and Mallette (1995) explain, "When adults respond to the question of which person had the greatest impact on their lives, other than their immediate family, teachers are frequently mentioned" (p. 257). Those early images are not necessarily positive, often convey traditional teaching styles, and are marked with commonalities across the United States (Joseph & Burnaford, 1994; Weber & Mitchell, 1995).

In addition to the years of "on-the-job" experience with teaching and teachers that one acquires as a student sitting and observing "on the other side of the desk,' a person has also acquired images and stereotypes of teaching and teachers from the person's experiences with literature and media. Lortie calls this "the apprenticeship-of-observation" (1975, p. 67). These forms of print media (literature) and visual media are part of "popular culture," which is inclusive of film, television, magazines, newspapers, music, video, books, cartoons, etc. In the past decade the literature on popular culture has grown dramatically as an increasing number of educators, social scientists, and other critical thinkers have begun to study the field (Daspit & Weaver, 1999; Giroux, 1994; Giroux, 1988; Giroux & Simon, 1989; McLaren, 1994; Trifonas, 2000; Weber & Mitchell, 1995). Weber and Mitchell (1994) explain, "So pervasive are teachers in popular culture that if you simply ask, as we have, schoolchildren and adults to name teachers they remember, not from school but from popular culture, a cast of fictionalized characters emerges that takes on larger than life proportions" (p. 14). These authors challenge us to examine how it is that children—even young children—would hold such strong images and that there be such similarity among the images they hold.

What are the results?

Prior research

Studies of children's literature have previously examined issues of stereotyping (race, gender, ethnicity, age) as well as moral and ethical issues within stories (Dougherty & Engel, 1987; Hurley & Chadwick, 1998; Lamme, 1996). Recently Barone, Meyerson, and Mallette (1995) examined the images of teachers in children's literature. They found a startling paradox: "On one hand, teachers are valued as contributing members of society; on the other hand, teachers are frequently portrayed in the media and literature as inept and not very bright" (p. 257).

Barone, et al. (1995) found two types of teachers portrayed: traditional, non-child centered, and non-traditional, more child-centered. The more prevalent type, the traditional teacher, was not usually liked nor respected by the students in the stories. The non-traditional teacher was seldom portrayed, but when the portrayal was presented, the teacher was shown to be valued and well liked. They contend that the reality of teaching is far too complex to fall into two such simple categories; that the act of teaching is complex. They point out that" . . . the authors of children's books often negate this complexity of teaching and learning, and classify teachers as those who care about students and those who are rigid or less sensitive to students' needs" (p. 260). Their study led to several disturbing conclusions: (a) The ubiquitous portrayal of traditional teachers as mean and strict make schools and schooling appear to be a dreadful experience. (b) The portrayal of teachers is frequently one in which the teacher is shown as having less intelligence than the students have. (c) Teachers are portrayed as having little or no confidence in their students and their abilities. Weber and Mitchell (1995) assert that "the stereotypes that are prevalent in the popular culture and experience of childhood play a formative role in the evolution of a teacher's identity and are part of the enculturation of teachers into their profession" (p. 27). Joseph and Burnaford (1994) address the numerous examples of caricatures or stereotypes as being somewhat different, but ". . . all are negative and all reduce the teacher to an object of scorn, disrespect, and sometimes fear" (p. 15).

Prior research

Research conclusion?

Research results

Based on research?

Research findings?

WHAT RESEARCH FRAMEWORK GUIDED OUR STUDY?

To answer our questions concerning the elements of the children's texts, we required a methodological framework from which we could examine the "character" of the texts. We found that framework in accessing research theories from anthropology and literary criticism which suggested an appropriate approach to content analysis.

Submitting that all research directly or indirectly involves participant observation, David Altheide (1987) finds an ethnographic approach applicable to content analyses, in that the writings or electronic texts are ultimately products of social interaction. Ethnographic content analysis (ECA) requires a reflexive and highly interactive relationship

Justification of method

between researcher and data with the objective of interpreting and verifying the communication of meaning. The meaning in the text message is assumed to be reflected in the multiple elements of form, content, context, and other nuances. The movement between researcher and data throughout the process of concept development, sampling, data collection, data analysis, and interpretation is systematic but not rigid, initially structured but receptive to emerging categories and concepts.

See text, p. 478

As we proceeded through the multiple readings of the picture storybooks, we attempted to foreground three main concepts: (a) To attempt to discover "meaning" is an attempt to include the multiple elements which make up the whole: appearance, language, subject taught, gender issues, racial/ethnic diversity, and other nuances as they became apparent; (b) The multiple readings of the selected sample of children's literature to understand, and to interpret the structures of the texts are not to conform the texts to our analytic notions but to inform them; and (c) In the intimacy of our relationship with the data we are acting on them and changing them, just as the data are changing us and the way we perceive past and present texts. As we encountered new texts, we attempted to consistently return to previous texts and to be receptive to new or revised interpretations that were revealed.

WHAT WAS OUR RESEARCH METHODOLOGY?

Sample

We used Follett Library Resources' database to find titles addressing "teachers" and "schools." This resulted in a list of 62 titles and 96 teacher images published from 1965 to present (Appendix A). No chapter books or *Magic Schoolbus* series books were reviewed, as they did not qualify under the definition of "picture storybook" (Huck, 1997, p. 198). We specifically did not attend to publication dates or "in print/out of print" status, as many of these texts appear on school and public library shelves decades after they have gone out of print. Our approach provided us with the majority of children's picture storybooks available for purchase in the United States or available through public libraries.

How is this known?

To better guide our examinations about the images of teachers, ensure that we reviewed the titles consistently, and in order to record the details of the texts we reviewed, we noted details of each teacher representation in aspects of Appearance, Language, Subject, Approach, and Effectiveness. The specific details we were seeking under each category for each teacher represented in the sample literature are further described below:

Same as image?

Good definitions

Appearance: observable race, gender, approximate age, name, clothing, hairstyle, weight (thin, average, plump)

Language: representative utterances by the teacher represented in the book or as reported by the narrator of the book

Subject: the school subject(s) that the teacher was represented as teaching: reading/language arts, math, geography, history, etc.

Approach: any indicators of a teaching philosophy, including whether children were seated in rows, were working together in learning centers, were reciting memorized material, whether the teacher was shown lecturing, etc.

Effectiveness: indicators included narrator's point of view, images or language about children's learning from that teacher; images or language about children's emotional response to the teacher etc.

We also attempted to note the absence of data as well as the presence of data. For example, we noted the occurrences of a teacher remaining nameless through the book, of a teacher not being represented as teaching any curriculum, or of a teacher failing to inspire any critical thinking in her students.

We entered data in the foregoing categories about each teacher representation onto forms, which we then reviewed in order to group the individually represented teachers into four more specific categories: positive representations, negative representations, mixed review, and neutral. A teacher fitting into the category of "positive teacher" was represented as being sensitive to children's emotional needs, supportive of meaningful learning, compassionate, warm, approachable, able to exercise classroom management skills without resorting to punitive measures or yelling, and was respectful and protective of children. A teacher would be classified as a "negative teacher" if he or she were represented as dictatorial, using harsh language, unable to manage classroom behavior, distant or removed, inattentive, unable to create a learning environment, allowing teasing or taunting among students, or unempathetic to students' diverse backgrounds. A teacher was categorized as "mixed review" if they possessed characteristics that were both positive and negative: for example, if a teacher were otherwise represented as caring and effective in the classroom, but did nothing to halt the teasing of a child. The fourth category for consideration was that of "neutral," in which a teacher was represented in the illustration of a text, but had neither a positive nor a negative effect on the children.

Good definitions

A doctoral student focusing on reading in the elementary school and who is well-versed in children's literature served as an inter-rater for this part of the analysis. After having conferred on the characteristics of each category, she read each text independently of the researchers and categorized each teacher as "positive," negative," "mixed review," and "neutral." We achieved 100% agreement in the category of "positive representations of teachers" and 93% agreement regarding the "negative" images. We had 75% agreement on the "neutral" images and 100% agreement on the category of "mixed" images (two images). Upon further discussion of our qualifications for "neutral," we were able to agree on all 14 images as having neither a positive nor negative impact on the children as represented in the text.

Good reliability check

Who is "we"?

WHAT WERE THE FINDINGS?

Our findings regarding the preponderance of the images are detailed in the following paragraphs.

The teacher in children's picture storybooks is overwhelmingly portrayed as a white, non-Hispanic woman. There were only eight representations of African-American teachers, and only three of them were the protagonists of the books: *The Best Teacher in the World* (Chardiet & Maccarone, 1990); *Show and Tell* (Munsch,1991); and *Will I Have a Friend?* (Cohen, 1967). Two Asians, no Native Americans, and no other persons of color are shown in the 96 teacher images, making the total number of culturally diverse images represented at only 11% of the total.

Good detail

The teacher in picture storybooks who is sensitive, competent, and able to manage a classroom effectively is a minority. The teacher who met the standards we described for a "positive teacher," which include an ability to construct meaningful learning environments, compassion, respect, and management skills for a group of children, exists in only 42% of the teacher images in our sample. This means only 40 images out of a total 96 images were demonstrative of teacher efficacy. Some examples of the "positive teacher" are found in Mr. Slingerland in *Lilly's Purple Plastic Purse* (Henkes, 1996), Mr. Falker in *Thank You, Mr. Falker* (Polacco, 1998), and Arizona Hughes in *My Great-aunt Arizona* (Houston, 1992).

But 42% in each

The negative images outnumbered the positive images. Teachers who were dictatorial, used harsh language with children, were distant or removed, or allowed teasing among students comprised 42% of the total number of 96 teacher representations. Examples of the "negative teacher" are found in the nameless teacher in *John Patrick Norman McHennessy—The Boy Who Was Always Late* (Burningham, 1987), Miss Tyler in *Today Was a Terrible Day* (Giff, 1980), and Miss Landers in *The Art Lesson* (dePaola, 1989). There were only two teachers in the sample who received a "mixed review," which was by definition a generally positive teacher with some negative strategies, approaches, or statements (Mrs. Chud in *Chrysanthemum* [Henkes, 1991] and Mrs. Page in *Miss Alaineus: A Vocabulary Disaster* [Frasier, 2000]). Fourteen teacher images, or 15% of the total number, were represented as "neutral," meaning that the teacher in the text had neither a positive nor a negative impact on the students. The nameless teachers in *Oliver Button Is a Sissy* (de Paola, 1979) and *Amazing Grace* (Hoffman, 1991) are representative of "neutral" teacher images.

The teacher in children's picture storybooks is static, unchanging, and flat. An unexpected finding in this content analysis was that teachers in picture storybooks are never shown as learners themselves, never portrayed as moving from less effective to more effective. Like the nameless teacher in Miriam Cohen's "Welcome to First Grade!" series, if she is a paragon of kindness and patience, she will remain so unfailingly from the beginning of the text to its conclusion. If he is an incompetent novice, like Mr. Lemonjello in *Miss Malarkey Won't Be in Today* (Finchler, 1998), he will not be shown reflecting, learning, and reinventing himself into an informed and effective educator by book's end. Perhaps the evolution from mediocrity to effectiveness holds little in the way of entertainment value, but it could hold great value in the demonstration that teachers are complex human beings with a significant capacity for growth. The potential to paint realistic portraits of teachers is present, but we see little evidence of the medium's desire to construct such an image.

The teacher in children's picture books is polarized. Other researchers have also noted our concerns that we as teachers represented in picture storybooks are "healers or wounders . . . sensitive or callous, imaginative or repressive" (Joseph & Burnaford, 1994, p. 12). Only 15% of the teachers presented in our sample are neutral images, neither positively nor negatively impacting the children in the fictional classroom, and only two images out of the 96 examined qualified as a "mixed review" of mostly positive characteristics with some negative aspects of educational practice. Therefore, approximately 84% of the teachers represented in our sample are either very good or horrid. The teacher paragon in picture books "generally is a woman who never demonstrates the features of commonplace motherhood—impatience, frustration, or possibly interests in the world other than children themselves—demonstrates to children that the teacher is a wonderfully benign creature" (Joseph & Burnaford, 1994, p. 11). Ms. Darcy in *The Best Teacher in the Whole World* (Chardiet & Maccarone, 1990), and Mrs. Beejorgenhoosen in *Rachel Parker, Kindergarten Show-off* (Martin, 1992) fit neatly into the mold of "paragon." They are not represented exhibiting any less-than-perfect, but realistic, characteristics of exhaustion, short-temperedness, or lapses in good judgment.

Disagrees with descriptions that follow

Supported in this study?

But only 2 out of 96

Several texts offer "over the top" representations of bad teachers. The often-reviewed *Black Lagoon* series depicts the teachers in children's imaginations as fire-breathing dragons or huge, green gorillas. The well-known *Miss Nelson* series (Allard) has created substitute teacher Viola Swamp in the likeness of a witch, complete with incredible bulk, large features, warts, and a perpetual bad hair day. The teachers in *The Big Box* (Morrison, 1999) put a child who "just can't handle her freedom" in a big, brown box. Other books offer slightly more subtle; but still alarming, representations of negative

Good examples

teaching practice. Consider Miss Tyler, the heavy-lidded, unsmiling teacher in *Today Was a Terrible Day* (Giff, 1980), who humiliates Ronald five times in the course of the story; or Mrs. Bell, who in *Double Trouble in Walla Walla* (Clements, 1997), takes a child to the principal for her unique language style. Even worse is the nameless teacher who repeatedly (and falsely) accuses a student of lying and threatens to strike him with a stick (*John Patrick Norman McHennessey—The Boy Who Was Always Late,* Burningham, 1987). In less drastic representations but still of concern to those of us who believe that literature informs expectations about reality, teachers are represented as failing to protect children from their peers' taunts. Teachers are shown doing nothing to stop the teasing of children in *Chrysanthemum* (Henkes, 1991), *The Brand New Kid* (Couric, 2000), *Today Was a Terrible Day* (Giff, 1980), and *Miss Alaineus: A Vocabulary Disaster* (Frasier, 2000). If children are learning about teachers and school from the children's books read to them, we propose that there is cause for concern about the unrealistic expectations children could develop from such polarized and unrealistic images.

But horrid? See prior comment

The teacher in children's picture books does not inspire in his or her students the pursuit of critical inquiry. The overwhelming majority of texts which represent teachers in a positive light—and these number in our sample only 42% of the total number of school-related children's literature—show them as kind caregivers who dry tears (Miss Hart in *Ruby the Copycat,* Rathmann, 1991), resolve jealousy between children (Mrs. Beejorgenhoosen in *Rachel Parker, Kindergarten Show-off,* Martin, 1992), restore self-esteem (Mrs. Twinkle in *Chrysanthemum,* Henkes, 1991), teach right from wrong (Ms. Darcy in *The Best Teacher in the Whole World,* Chardiet & Maccarone, 1990). However, few teachers are represented as having a substantial impact on a child's learning. Joseph and Burnaford (1994) found that teachers are not seen "leading students toward intellectual pursuits—toward analyzing and challenging existing conditions of community and society. . . . The 'successful' teacher [in children's literature] . . . does not awaken students' intelligence. Such teachers value order; order is what they strive for, what they are paid for" (p. 16).

Good examples

Our analysis confirms their findings. Examples are common in which teachers actually provide roadblocks to children's success. Tommy in *The Art Lesson* (dePaola, 1989) must wage battle to use his own crayons, use more than just one sheet of paper, and to create art based on his own vision and not the tired model of the art teacher. Miss Kincaid in *The Brand New Kid* (Couric, 2000) actually establishes the opportunity for children to tease the new boy who is an immigrant: "We have a new student . . . His name is a different one, Lazlo S. Gasky." Young Lazlo's mother must help him find his way into the culture of the school and community. In *David Goes to School* (Shannon, 1999), young David is met with negatively framed demands from his nameless and faceless teacher: "No, David!", "You're tardy!", "Keep your hands to yourself!", "Shhhhh!", and "You're staying after school!"

Only six books in our sample represent teachers as intellectually inspiring. Mr. Isobe in *Crow Boy* (Yashima, 1967) is represented as child-centered and appreciative of Chibi's knowledge of agriculture and botany, who values his drawings and stays after school to talk with young Chibi. He is represented as the catalyst for the crow imitations at the school talent show which gain Chibi recognition and a newfound respect among his peers. In *Lilly's Purple Plastic Purse* (Henkes, 1996) Mr. Slingerland is such an effective teacher that he inspires Lilly to want to be a teacher (when she isn't wanting to be "a dancer or a surgeon or an ambulance driver or a diva . . ."). Mr. Cohen in *Creativity* (Steptoe, 1997) uses the arrival of a new immigrant in his class to teach about the history of immigration in this country and to deliver a message about tolerance and shared histories. Mrs. Hughes in *My Great-aunt Arizona* (Houston, 1992) teaches generations of children about "words and numbers and the faraway places they would visit someday."

Six out of 62

Are there differences across time (1965–2005)?

The nameless teacher in *When Will I Read?* (Cohen, 1977) helps young Jim come to the realization that he is a reader, and Mr. Falker in *Thank You, Mr. Falker* (Polacco, 1998), helps fifth-grader Trisha learn to read in three months and cries over her achievement when she reads her first book independently. Although these are excellent examples of how teachers can be represented as dedicated supporters of learning, only six texts out of the 62 in our sample construct images of teacher as an educated professional.

DISCUSSION

Other researchers have found bias, prejudice, and stereotypical presentations of characters in children's books, and our study specifically about images of teachers does not dispute those findings (Barone, Meyerson, & Mallette, 1995; Hurley & Chadwick, 1998; Hurst, 1981). From our extensive 62-book sample of picture storybooks widely available to children, parents, and teachers, we have found a parade of teachers who discourage creativity, ignore teasing, and even threaten to hit children with sticks. We have also found teachers in children's literature who, in great devotion to the human good and the educative process, save children: from boredom, from illiteracy, and from the devastating effects of social isolation. Our deep concern is that the books in which the teacher is demonstrated as intelligent and inspiring (six in our 62 book sample) are dwarfed by the number of books in which the image of Teacher is one of daft incompetence, unreasonable anger, or rigid conformity.

We do not find images of teachers as transformative intellectuals, as educators who "go beyond concern with forms of empowerment that promote individual achievement and traditional forms of academic success" (Giroux, 1989, p. 138). Instead, we find representations of teachers whose negatively metaphoric/derogatory surnames indicate the level of respect for the profession: Mr. Quackerbottom, Mrs. Nutty, Ima Berpur, Miss Bonkers, and Miss Malarkey.

Referring back to the graduate class we taught on representations of teachers in popular culture, we perceived a naiveté in these teachers as to the power of the media, to the power of stereotypes to shape the teaching profession, and the power that teachers have to combat the negative images. An overwhelming majority of our graduate students valued the traditional teacher who maintained order, was nurturing and caring, and whose focus was on the emotional well-being of the child. They failed to notice that it was an extremely rare image in picture storybooks that showed a teacher as an intellectually inspiring force.

Evidence would help here

Teachers cannot effectuate positive change in their profession unless and until they are aware of the internal and external influences that define and shape the educational institution. We want to encourage reflection and conversation about schooling and teaching, careful evaluation of extant images in popular culture in order to develop meaningful dialogue about the accuracy of those images, and to encourage teachers to examine their own memories of teachers and how they form current perceptions.

IMPLICATIONS FOR FUTURE RESEARCH

Our explorations into the representations of teachers in picture storybooks have led to other and further questions regarding images that cultures create of their education professionals.

There is much information to be gleaned from a careful study of the portrayals of school administrators in picture storybooks. How are teachers and administrators represented in basal literature? How often do basal publishers select literature or write their own literature that has school as a setting, and what is the ratio of positive representations to negative ones? Do children's authors in other cultures and countries create similar negative images of educators with the same frequency and ire as they do in the U.S.? How are teachers and administrators portrayed in literature for older children, as in beginning and intermediate chapter books, or young adult novels? How have the images of teachers and administrators evolved over time in our culture? Was there a time in our history that teachers were consistently portrayed in a positive light, and was there perhaps a national event or series of events which caused the images to take on more negative characteristics?

CONCLUSION

Before we began this study we came across a book entitled *Through the Cracks* (Sollman, Emmons, & Paolini, 1994), which we decided not to include in our literature sample as we perceive this text to be more for teachers and teacher educators than children. The text now takes on new importance in light of our findings. It chronicles change on one school campus through the eyes of an elementary-age student, Stella. Early in the story Stella and some of her peers begin to physically shrink and literally fall through the cracks of the classroom floor because of boredom—boredom with both the content and delivery of the school curriculum. The teachers initially are illustrated as lecturing to daydreaming children, running off dittos, and grading papers during class time; one image even shows a teacher sharply reprimanding a child for painting her pig blue instead of the pink anticipated in the teacher's lesson plan. The children have become lost in a kind of academic purgatory under the floorboards. Here they remain until substantial changes are made on their campus. The children at first watch, then come up through the floor to become involved in, a curriculum that has become relevant, child-centered, and integrative of the arts. Teachers are then represented as supporting children's learning through highly integrated explorations of Egypt, the American Revolution, geometry, life in a pond. Their images are shown guiding the children in recreating historical and social events; supporting student inquiry; exploring painting, building, drawing, dancing, and playing music as a way of knowing; cooking; becoming involved in community clean-up projects; interviewing experts; conducting science experiments; and more.

Linda Lamme (1996) concludes that ". . . children's literature is a resource with ample moral and ethical activity, that, when shared sensitively with children, can enhance their moral development and accomplish the lofty goals to which educators in a democracy aspire" (p. 412). Our point in sharing the contents of *Through the Cracks* is this: the picture storybook format has the potential to share with readers the reality of an effective and creative teacher. As opposed to an object of ridicule or scathing humor, a teacher can be represented as an intellectual who inspires children to stretch, grow, and explore previously unknown worlds and communicate that new knowledge through multiple communicative systems. The picture storybook has the potential to encourage a child to anticipate the valuable discoveries that are possible in the school setting; it can also demonstrate to parents how school ought to be and how teachers support children in cognitive and psychosocial ways. Children's literature can also provide positive enculturation for pre-service teachers and validation for in-service teachers of the possibilities inherent in their social contributions. Positive representations of teachers have the potential to empower all the partners in the academic community: the children, their parents, teachers and administrators, and the community at large.

This is not a conclusion from this study

References

Altheide, D. (1987). Ethnographic content analysis. *Qualitative Sociology, 10*(1), 65–76.

Barone, D., Meyerson, M., & Mallette, M. (1995). Images of teachers in children's literature. *The New Advocate, 8*(4), 257–270.

Crume, M. (1989). Images of teachers in films and literature. *Education Week,* October 4, 3.

Daspit, T. & Weaver, J. (1999). *Popular culture and critical pedagogy: Reading, constructing, connecting.* New York: Garland.

Dougherty, W. & Engle, R. (1987). An 80s look for sex equality in Caldecott winners and honor books. *The Reading Teacher, 40,* 394–398.

Farber, P., Provenzo, E. & Holm, G. (1994). *Schooling in the light of popular culture.* Albany, NY: State University of New York Press.

Giroux, H. (1988). *Teachers as intellectuals: Toward a critical pedagogy of learning.* Granby, MA: Bergin and Garvey.

Giroux, H. (1989). Schooling as a form of cultural politics: Toward a pedagogy of and for difference. In Henry A. Giroux & Peter L. McLaren (Eds.), *Critical pedagogy, the state and cultural struggle* (pp. 125–151). Albany, NY: SUNY Press.

Giroux, H. (1994). *Disturbing pleasures.* New York: Routledge.

Giroux, H., & Simon, R. (1989). *Popular culture, schooling and everyday life.* New York: Bergin & Garvey.

Huck, C., Hepler, S., Hickman, J., & Kiefer, B. (1997). *Children's literature in the elementary school* (6th ed.). Boston: McGraw.

Hurley, S., & Chadwick, C. (1998). The images of females, minorities, and the aged in Caldecott Award-winning picture books, 1958–1997. *Journal of Children's Literature, 24*(1), 58–66.

Hurst, J. B. (1981). Images in children's picture books. *Social Education, 45,* 138–143.

Joseph, P. B., & Burnaford, G. E. (1994). *Images of school teachers in Twentieth-Century America.* New York: St. Martin's Press.

Knowles, J. G., & Cole, A. L. (with Presswood, C. S.). (1994). *Through preservice teachers' eyes: Exploring field experiences through narrative and inquiry.* New York: Merrill.

Lamme, L. L. (1996). Digging deeply: Morals and ethics in children's literature. *Journal for a Just and Caring Education, 2*(4), 411–419.

Leitch, V. B. (1988). *American literary criticism from the 30s to the 80s.* New York: Columbia UP.

Lepman, J. (Ed). (1971). *How children see our world.* New York: Avon.

Lortie, D. C. (1975). *Schoolteacher: A sociological study.* Chicago: University of Chicago Press.

McLaren, P. (1994). *Life in schools: An introduction to critical pedagogy in the foundations of education.* White Plains, NY: Longman.

Salomon, G. (1997). Of mind and media: How culture's symbolic forms affect learning and thinking. *Phi Delta Kappan, 78*(5), 375–380.

Sollman, C., Emmons, B., & Paolini, J. (1994). *Through the cracks.* Worcester, MA: Davis Publications.

Trifonas, P. (2000). *Revolutionary pedagogies: Cultural politics, instituting education, and the discourse of theory.* New York: Routledge.

Weber, S. & Mitchell, C. (1995). *'That's funny, you don't look like a teacher': Interrogating images and identity in popular culture.* Washington, DC: The Falmer Press.

Appendix A: Children's Book References

Allard, H. (1977). *Miss Nelson is missing.* Illustrated by James Marshall. Boston: Houghton Mifflin.

Allard, H. (1982). *Miss Nelson is back.* Illustrated by James Marshall. Boston: Houghton Mifflin.

Allard, H. (1985). *Miss Nelson has a field day.* Illustrated by James Marshall. New York: Scholastic.

Burningham, J. (1987). *John Patrick Norman McHennessy—The boy who was always late.* New York: Crown.

Chardiet, B., & Maccarone, G. (1990). *The best teacher in the world.* Illustrated by G. Brian Karas. New York: Scholastic.

Clements, A. (1997). *Double-trouble in Walla-Walla.* Illustrated by Sal Murdocca. Brookfield, CT: Millbrook.

Cohen, M. (1967). *Will I have a friend?* Illustrated by Lillian Hoban. New York: Aladdin.

Cohen, M. (1977). *When will I read?* Illustrated by Lillian Hoban. New York: Bantam.

Couric, K. (2000). *The brand new kid.* Illustrated by Marjorie Priceman. New York: Doubleday.

de Paola, T. (1979). *Oliver Button is a sissy.* San Diego, CA: HBJ.

de Paola, T. (1989). *The art lesson.* New York: Putnam.

Finchler, J. (1995). *Miss Malarkey doesn't live in Room 10.* Illustrated by Kevin O'Malley. New York: Scholastic.

Finchler, J. (1998). *Miss Malarkey won't be in today.* Illustrated by Kevin O'Malley. New York: Walker.

Frasier, D. (2000). *Miss Alaineus: A vocabulary disaster.* San Diego, CA: Harcourt.

Giff, P. R. (1980). *Today was a terrible day.* New York: Puffin.

Hallinan, P. K. (1989). *My teacher's my friend.* Nashville, TN: Ideals.

Henkes, K. (1991). *Chrysanthemum.* New York: Greenwillow.

Henkes, K. (1996). *Lilly's purple plastic purse.* New York: Greenwillow.

Hoffman, M. (1991). *Amazing Grace.* Illustrated by Caroline Binch. New York: Scholastic.

Houston, G. (1992). *My great-aunt Arizona.* Illustrated by Susan Condie Lamb. New York: HarperCollins.

Martin, A. M. (1992). *Rachel Parker, kindergarten show-off.* Illustrated by Nancy Poydar. New York: Holiday House.

McGovern, A. (1993). *Drop everything, it's D.E.A.R. time!* Illustrated by Anna DiVito. New York: Scholastic.

Morrison, T., & Morrison, S. (1999). *The big box.* Illustrated by Giselle Potter. New York: Hyperion.

Munsch, R. (1985). *Thomas' snowsuit.* Illustrated by Michael Martchenko. Toronto, Canada: Annick.

Munsch, R. (1991). *Show and tell.* Illustrated by Michael Martchenko. Toronto, Canada: Annick.

Polacco, P. (1998). *Thank you, Mr. Falker.* New York: Philomel.

Rathmann, P. (1991). *Ruby the copycat.* New York: Scholastic.

Schwartz, A. (1988). *Annabelle Swift, kindergartner.* New York: Orchard.

Seuss, Dr. (1978). *Gerald McBoing Boing.* New York: Random House.

Shannon, D. (1999). *David goes to school.* New York: Scholastic.

Yashima, T. (1965). *Crow Boy.* New York: Scholastic.

Analysis of the Study

PURPOSE/JUSTIFICATION

We do not find a clear statement of purpose. The abstract suggests that it is "to probe the power of stereotypes/clichés," but we do not see that the study does this. It appears to us that the purpose is "to provide further evidence on the way in which teachers are portrayed in children's picture storybooks." An extensive justification for the study is given, including personal experience, theoretical ideas of education writers, and previous studies of children's literature. Although we would prefer clearer distinctions among these, we think the study is adequately justified in terms of importance to children's education and public perception of teachers. We would like to see more on the contribution of this particular study. A justification for the methodology is given.

DEFINITIONS

Clear definitions are provided for the major categories of the content analysis and for the details of teacher representation that were focused on by the reviewers. The term "image" should have been defined because it is prominent throughout and has several possible meanings. Apparently, it refers not to visual images but rather to "portrayals" or "representations" in both pictures and words.

PRIOR RESEARCH

Numerous references are given, often with the implication that they are research studies but sometimes insufficient detail is provided to enable the reader to determine whether the "conclusions" cited are based on a study or on opinion (examples include the references on children's literature and on "popular culture"). One study (Bonnie et al.) is discussed in some detail, but methodology and grade level are unclear.

HYPOTHESES

No hypotheses are stated. The implied hypothesis appears to be that "teacher images in storybooks are generally unrealistic and negative."

SAMPLE

The sample was obtained by locating all picture storybooks addressing "teachers and schools" between 1965 and (presumably) 2005 as identified from a database. The sample consisted of 96 teacher images from 62 books. The authors state that this provided the majority of children's storybooks available in the United States for purchase or available in libraries—presumably the target population. We are unclear as to the basis for this statement. The intended age/grade range for these books is not given, but examples suggest it is "primary" grades.

INSTRUMENTATION

The method of deriving categories is well described. Reliability was asessed through inter-rater agreement; although it is unclear exactly who the "we" refers to (there were presumably three categorizers). The level of agreement is generally good—100% and 93% for the major categories. As is typical of such studies, validity is not discussed. The definitions of major categories seem straightforward, and this is supported by rater agreement. Good examples are given that also support validity. The very small number (two) of "mixed" images is not consistent with our experience with real teachers but supports the author's "hypothesis."

INTERNAL VALIDITY

Because this study does not explicitly focus on relationships, internal validity is not a major issue. However, the definitions of major categories (positive, negative, mixed, and neutral) imply high correlations among the variables (as portrayed) in each category. The small number of "mixed" images provides evidence that this is the case. More serious is the authors' failure to address the effect of possible changes over time—from 1965 to 2005. The question of whether their results are accurate for recent storybooks could have been studied, for example, by dividing images into three time periods.

RESULTS/INTERPRETATION

Results are presented as percentages in each of the four categories. Extensive examples are given that greatly help clarify the findings. In general, we find the interpretation to be consistent with the results. There are, however, important exceptions. Most serious is the statement that there were more negative than positive images. This is not consistent with the data on pages 493–494; both categories contained 42 percent—unless there is a typographical error. We also question the assertion that 84 percent of the teachers represented were either very good or horrid. Only two are cited as "paragons," and among the negative teachers, a number are described as "less drastic" but "still of concern." We also think the authors have sometimes overstated their case. For example, the statement that "we do not find images of teachers as transformative intellectuals" seems inconsistent with the finding that six books did contain such images. We also note that tha author's "conclusion" is not the customary conclusion based on the study but rather an extension into implications from a much broader context.

Go back to the **INTERACTIVE AND APPLIED LEARNING** feature at the beginning of the chapter for a listing of interactive and applied activities. Go to the **Online Learning Center** at **www.mhhe.com/fraenkel9e** to take quizzes, practice with key terms, and review chapter content.

Main Points

WHAT IS CONTENT ANALYSIS?

- Content analysis is an analysis of the contents of a communication.
- Content analysis is a technique that enables researchers to study human behavior in an indirect way by analyzing communications.

APPLICATIONS OF CONTENT ANALYSIS

- Content analysis has wide applicability in educational research.
- Content analysis can give researchers insights into problems that they can test by more direct methods.
- There are several reasons to do a content analysis: to obtain descriptive information of one kind or another; to analyze observational and interview data; to test hypotheses; to check other research findings; and/or to obtain information useful in dealing with educational problems.

CATEGORIZATION IN CONTENT ANALYSIS

- Predetermined categories are sometimes used to code data.
- Sometimes coding is done by using categories that emerge as data is reviewed.

STEPS INVOLVED IN CONTENT ANALYSIS

- In doing a content analysis, researchers should always develop a rationale (a conceptual link) to explain how the data to be collected are related to their objectives.
- Important terms should at some point be defined.
- All of the sampling methods used in other kinds of educational research can be applied to content analysis. Purposive sampling, however, is the most commonly used.
- The unit of analysis—what specifically is to be analyzed—should be specified before the researcher begins an analysis.
- After precisely defining what aspects of the content are to be analyzed, the researcher needs to formulate coding categories.

CODING CATEGORIES

- Developing emergent coding categories requires a high level of familiarity with the content of a communication.
- In doing a content analysis, a researcher can code either the manifest or the latent content of a communication, and sometimes both.
- The manifest content of a communication refers to the specific, clear, surface contents: the words, pictures, images, and such that are easily categorized.
- The latent content of a document refers to the meaning underlying what is contained in a communication.

RELIABILITY AND VALIDITY AS APPLIED TO CONTENT ANALYSIS

- Reliability in content analysis is commonly checked by comparing the results of two independent scorers (categorizers).
- Validity can be checked by comparing data obtained from manifest content to that obtained from latent content.

DATA ANALYSIS

- A common way to interpret content analysis data is by using frequencies (i.e., the number of specific incidents found in the data) and proportion of particular occurrences to total occurrences.
- Another method is to use coding to develop themes to facilitate synthesis.
- Computer analysis is extremely useful in coding data once categories have been determined. It can also be useful at times in developing such categories.

ADVANTAGES AND DISADVANTAGES OF CONTENT ANALYSIS

- Two major advantages of content analysis are that it is unobtrusive and it is comparatively easy to do.
- The major disadvantages of content analysis are that it is limited to the analysis of communications and it is difficult to establish validity.

Key Terms

cluster sampling 480
coding 480
content analysis 476
latent content 482
manifest content 481
random sample 480
reliability 483
stratified sampling 480
theme 478
validity 483

For Discussion

1. When, if ever, might it be more appropriate to do a content analysis than to use some other kind of methodology?
2. When would it be inappropriate to use content analysis?
3. Give an example of some categories a researcher might use to analyze data in each of the following content analyses:
   a. To investigate the amount and types of humor on television
   b. To investigate the kinds of "romantic love" represented in popular songs
   c. To investigate the social implications of impressionistic paintings
   d. To investigate whether civil or criminal law makes the most distinctions between men and women
   e. To describe the assumptions made in elementary school science programs
4. Which do you think would be more difficult to code, the manifest or the latent content of a movie? Why?
5. "*Never* code only the latent content of a document without also coding at least some of the manifest content." Would you agree with this statement? Why or why not?
6. In terms of difficulty, how would you compare a content analysis approach to the study of social bias on television with a survey approach? in terms of useful information?
7. Would it be possible to do a content analysis of Hollywood movies? If so, what might be some categories you would use?
8. Can you think of some things produced by humans that were not originally intended as communications but now are considered to be? Suggest some examples.
9. Content analysis is sometimes said to be extremely valuable in analyzing observational and interview data. If true, how so?
10. The choice of categories in a content analysis study is crucial. Would you agree? If so, explain why.

References

1. Gerbner, G., et al. (1978). Cultural indicators: Violence profile no. 9. *Journal of Communication, 28,* 177–207.

2. Macgillivray, I. K., & Jennings, T. (2008). A content analysis exploring lesbian, gay, bisexual, and transgender topics in foundations of education textbooks. *Journal of Teacher Education 59*(4), 170–188.

3. Gorski, P. C. (2009). What we're teaching teachers: An analysis of multicultural teacher education coursework syllabi. *Teaching and Teacher Education: An International Journal of Research and Studies, 25*(2), 309–318.

4. Belstock, S., et al. (2008). Using alcohol to sell cigarettes to young adults: A content analysis of cigarette advertisements. *Journal of American College Health 56*(4), 383–389.

5. Gallagher, P., et al. (2008, December 1). Perceptions of collaboration: A content analysis of student journals. *Teacher Education and Special Education, 31*(1), 12–21.

6. McGinty, S., & Moore, A. (2008). Role of gender in reviewers' appraisals of quality in political science books: A content analysis. *Journal of Academic Librarianship, 34*(4), 288–294.

7. Smith, P., et al. (2008). A content analysis of school anti-bullying policies: Progress and limitations. *Educational Psychology in Practice, 24*(1), 1–12.

8. Silver, E. A., et al. (2009). Teaching mathematics for understanding: An analysis of lessons submitted by teachers seeking NBPTS certification. *American Educational Research Journal, 46*(6), 501–531.

9. Horney, K. (1945). *Our inner conflicts.* New York: Norton.

10. Fraenkel, J. R., & Wallen, N. E. (1988). *Toward improving research in social studies education.* Boulder, CO: Social Science Consortium.

PART 6

Qualitative Research Methodologies

Part 6 continues the discussion of qualitative research we began in Part 5. We concentrate here on ethnography and historical research. As we did in Parts 4 and 5, we not only discuss each of these methodologies in some detail, but we also provide examples of published studies in which the researchers used these methods. We then provide our analysis of the strengths and weaknesses of these studies.

21 Ethnographic Research

What Is Ethnographic Research?

The Unique Value of Ethnographic Research

Ethnographic Concepts

Topics That Lend Themselves Well to Ethnographic Research

Sampling in Ethnographic Research

Do Ethnographic Researchers Use Hypotheses?

Data Collection in Ethnographic Research

Field Notes

Data Analysis in Ethnographic Research

Roger Harker and His Fifth-Grade Classroom

Advantages and Disadvantages of Ethnographic Research

An Example of Ethnographic Research

Analysis of the Study

Purpose/Justification

Definitions

Hypotheses

Sample

Instrumentation

Procedures/Internal Validity

Data Analysis

Results/Discussion

OBJECTIVES **Studying this chapter should enable you to:**

- Explain what is meant by the term "ethnographic research," and give an example of a research question that might be investigated in an ethnographic study.
- Describe briefly what each of the following concepts mean to ethnographers: "culture," "holistic outlook," "contextualization," and "multiple realities."
- Explain the difference between an "emic" and an "etic" perspective.
- Name at least three topics that would lend themselves well to ethnographic research.
- Describe the characteristics of the kinds of samples used in ethnographic research.
- Explain how ethnographers employ hypotheses in their research.
- Describe the two major data collection techniques used in ethnographic research.
- Explain what is meant by the term "field notes" and how they differ from field jottings, a field diary, and a field log.
- Explain what is meant by the terms "triangulation" and "contextualization."
- Explain what a "key event" is in ethnographic research.
- Describe briefly how statistics are used in ethnographic research.
- Name at least one advantage and one disadvantage of ethnographic research.

INTERACTIVE AND APPLIED LEARNING After, or while, reading this chapter:

Go to the Online Learning Center at www.mhhe.com/fraenkel9e to:

- Learn More About Ethnographic Research

Go to your online Student Mastery Activities book to do the following activities:

- Activity 21.1: Ethnographic Research Questions
- Activity 21.2: True or False?
- Activity 21.3: Do Some Ethnographic Research

"What do you intend to do for your doctoral dissertation, Sam?"

"I'm interested in what it's like to be an elementary school principal day in and day out, so I'm going to do an ethnography of a school principal."

"No kidding! Impressive!"

"I just talked to Elizabeth Rodriguez today—you know, the principal at Roosevelt Elementary. She's agreed to let me follow her around for the next four weeks so that I can see what she does during the day—you know, whom she meets with, where, when, what they talk about, etc."

"You're going to keep a record of this, I assume?"

"You bet! I'll carry a notebook and make notes about what I see and hear. I also have Elizabeth's permission to record our conversations. And I have another idea. During two of these days, I want to video her as she goes about her daily routine, both in school and as she ventures out into the community."

"That's it?"

"Nope. I also intend to take a look at the school's records and the daily log she keeps. I'm planning on doing a lot of interviews, too—talk with her assistant, some of the faculty, the custodial staff, even some students. And, of course, Elizabeth herself. And if she will permit it, the members of her family. I don't plan to do the interviews until after I've finished with my observations, however."

"Boy, that sounds like a lot of work."

"No question, it is. Not to mention writing all this up. But it will be worth it. When I've finished, I think I will be able to paint a pretty accurate picture of what the life of an elementary school principal is like."

Sam's description of what he intends to do is an example *of ethnographic research,* the subject of this chapter.

What Is Ethnographic Research?

Ethnographic research is, in many respects, the most complex of all research methods. A variety of approaches are used in an attempt to obtain as holistic a picture as possible of a particular society, group, institution, setting, or situation. The emphasis in ethnographic research is on documenting or portraying the everyday experiences of individuals by observing and interviewing them and relevant others. The key tools, in fact, in all ethnographic studies are in-depth interviewing and continual, ongoing participant observation of a situation. Researchers try to capture as much of what is going on as they can—the "whole picture," so to speak. Bernard described the process briefly, but well:

> It involves establishing rapport in a new community; learning to act so that people go about their business as usual when you show up; and removing yourself every day from cultural immersion so you can intellectualize what you've learned, put it into perspective, and write about it convincingly. If you are a successful participant observer you will know when to laugh at what your informants think is funny; and when informants laugh at what you say, it will be because you *meant* it to be a joke.[1]

Important Findings in Ethnographic Research

Anthropologist Margaret Mead's ethnography of life in Samoa—in particular her study of the adolescence of girls—is a social science classic. In the 1920s, she spent nine months in Samoa as a participant observer, relying mostly on observation and interviews with selected informants. Her major conclusions were that adolescence in Samoa was not the stressful period it is for adolescents in the United States. She believed that this was largely because Samoans were not faced with the dilemmas that young people in the United States face and because the Samoan culture took a relaxed view toward all forms of behavior. She also concluded that the incidence of emotional disturbance was much lower in Samoa, owing to the diffusion of emotional attachments and the clear-cut rules regarding the forming of relationships.

In the preface to the sixth edition of this report (1973),* Mead pointed out that while neither U.S. nor Samoan culture has remained constant, recent visits had impressed her with the extraordinary persistence of the Samoan culture.

A subsequent ethnography done 10 years later resulted in very different conclusions that anthropologists do not attribute to the passage of time.† This discrepancy illustrates the rich and provocative nature of ethnographic research, as well as the difficulty in arriving at firm conclusions.

*Mead, M. (1973). *Coming of age in Samoa* (6th ed.). New York: Morrow Hill.

†Freeman, D. (1983). *Margaret Mead and Samoa—The making and unmaking of an anthropological myth.* Cambridge, MA: Harvard University Press.

Wolcott has pointed out that ethnographic procedures require three things: a detailed description of the culture-sharing group being studied, an analysis of this group in terms of perceived themes or perspectives, and then some interpretation of the group by the researcher as to meanings and generalizations about the social life of human beings in general.[2] The final product is a *holistic cultural portrait* of the group—a pulling together by the researcher of everything he or she has learned about the group in all its complexity.

Here are some titles of studies that ethnographers have conducted in education:

- "Gang-Related Gun Violence"[3]
- "The Dignity of Job-Seeking Men"[4]
- "Telling the Code of the Street"[5]
- "Streets, Sidewalks, Stores, and Stories"[6]
- "The Power of Names"[7]
- "On Thick Description and Narrative Inquiry in Music Education"[8]
- "Inside High School: The Student's Perspective"[9]

The Unique Value of Ethnographic Research

Ethnographic research has a particular strength that makes it especially appealing to many researchers. It can reveal nuances and subtleties that other methodologies miss. An excellent example is offered by Babbie.

> If you were walking through a public park and you threw down a bunch of trash, you'd discover that your action was unacceptable to those around you. People would glare at you, grumble to each other, and perhaps someone would say something to you about it. Whatever the form, you'd be subjected to definite, negative sanctions for littering. Now here's the irony. If you were walking through that same park, came across a bunch of trash that someone else had dropped, and cleaned it up, it's likely that your action would also be unacceptable to those around you. You'd probably be subject to definite, negative sanctions for cleaning it up.
>
> Most [of my students] felt (this notion) was absurd . . . Although we would be negatively sanctioned for littering, . . . people would be pleased with us for [cleaning up a public place]. Certainly, all my students said *they* would be pleased if someone cleaned up a public place.
>
> To settle the issue, I suggested that my students start fixing the public problems they came across in the course of their everyday activities. . . .
>
> My students picked up litter, fixed street signs, put knocked-over traffic cones back in place, cleaned and decorated communal lounges in their dorms, trimmed trees that blocked visibility at intersections, repaired public playground equipment, cleaned public restrooms, and took care of a hundred other public problems that weren't "their responsibility."
>
> Most reported feeling very uncomfortable doing whatever they did. They felt foolish, goody-goody, conspicuous. . . . In almost every case, their personal feelings of discomfort

> were increased by the reactions of those around them. One student was removing a damaged and long-unused newspaper box from the bus stop where it had been a problem for months when the police arrived, having been summoned by a neighbor. Another student decided to clean out a clogged storm drain on his street and found himself being yelled at by a neighbor who insisted the mess should be left for the street cleaners. Everyone who picked up litter was sneered at, laughed at, and generally put down. One young man was picking up litter scattered around a trashcan when a passerby sneered, "Clumsy!"[10]

The point of this example, we hope, is obvious. What people think and say happens (or is likely to happen) often is not really the case. By going out into the world and observing things as they occur, we are (usually) better able to obtain a more accurate picture. This is what ethnographers try to do—study people in their natural habitat in order to "see" things that otherwise might not even be anticipated. This is a major advantage of the ethnographic approach.

Ethnographic Concepts

A number of concepts guide the work of ethnographers as they go about their research in the field. Some of the most important include culture, a holistic outlook, contextualization, an emic perspective, multiple realities, thick description, member checking, and a nonjudgmental orientation. Let us give a brief description of each.

Culture. The concept of **culture** is typically defined in one of two ways. Those who focus on behavior define it as the sum of a social group's observable patterns of behavior, customs, and ways of life.[11] Those who concentrate on ideas say that it comprises the ideas, beliefs, and knowledge that characterize a particular group of people. However one defines it, culture is the most important of all ethnographic concepts. In Fetterman's words, it

> helps the ethnographer to search for a logical, cohesive pattern in the myriad, often ritualistic behaviors and ideas that characterize a group. This concept becomes immediately meaningful after cross-cultural experience. Everything is new to a student first entering a different culture. Attitudes or habits that natives espouse virtually without thinking are distinct and clear to the stranger. Living in a foreign community for a long period of time enables the fieldworker to see the power of dominant ideas, values, and patterns of behavior in the way people walk, talk, dress, eat, and sleep. The longer an individual stays in a community, building rapport, and the deeper they probe into individual lives, the greater the probability of his or her learning about the sacred subtle elements of the culture: how people pray, how they feel about each other, and how they reinforce their own cultural practices to maintain the integrity of their system.[12]

The interpretation of a group's culture is considered by many researchers to be the primary contribution of ethnographic research. Cultural interpretation refers to the researcher's ability to describe what he or she sees and hears from the point of view of the members of the group. A frequently cited example is that of the difference between a "wink" and a "blink." In one sense, there is no difference between the two. However, "anyone who has ever mistaken a blink for a wink is fully aware of the significance of cultural interpretation."[13]

A Holistic Perspective. Ethnographers try to describe as much as they can about the culture of a group. Thus, they try to gain some idea of the group's history, social structure, politics, religious beliefs, symbols, customs, rituals, and environment. No single study, of course, can ever capture completely an entire culture, but ethnographic researchers do their best to see beyond the immediate scene or event occurring in a classroom, in a neighborhood, on a particular street, or in a location in order to understand the larger picture of which the particular event may be a part. As you can imagine, developing a **holistic perspective** demands that the ethnographer spend a great amount of time out in the field gathering many different kinds of data. Only by doing so is he or she able to develop a picture of the social or cultural whole of that which he or she is studying.

Contextualization. When a researcher **contextualizes** data, he or she places what was seen and heard into a larger perspective. For example, the administrators of a large urban school district in which one of the authors of this text taught were about to terminate an after-school tutoring project because of its low attendance—about 50 percent. It was suggested to them that an attendance rate of 50 percent was actually pretty good when one considered the students involved (the students encouraged to attend the tutoring sessions were those who were doing failing work in most, if not all, of their classes). This suggestion resulted in the district continuing the program, as the administrators were now able to make a more informed decision about the worth of the program. In other words, contextualization helped maintain a worthwhile program that otherwise might have been eliminated.

An Emic Perspective. An **emic perspective**—that is, an "insider's" perspective of reality—is at the heart of ethnographic research. Gaining an emic perspective is essential to understanding—and thus describing accurately—the behaviors and situations an ethnographer sees and hears. An emic perspective requires one to recognize and accept the idea of **multiple realities**. "Documenting multiple perspectives of reality in a given study is crucial to an understanding of why people think and act in the different ways they do."[14]

An **etic perspective**, on the other hand, is the external objective perspective on reality. Most ethnographic researchers try to look at their data from both an emic and etic perspective. They may start collecting data from an emic perspective, doing their best to understand the point of view of those they are studying, and then try to make sense of what they have collected in terms of a more objective, scientific analysis. In short, they try to combine an insightful and sensitive cultural interpretation with a rigorous collection and analysis of what they have seen and heard.

Thick Description. When ethnographers prepare the final report of their research, they engage in what is known as **thick description**. In essence, this involves describing what they have seen and heard—their work in the field—in great detail, frequently using extensive quotations from the participants in their study. The intent is, as mentioned earlier, to "paint a portrait" of the culture they have studied, to make it "come alive" for those who read the report.

Member Checking. As mentioned, a major objective of ethnographic research is to represent as accurately as possible an emic perspective of reality—that is, reality as seen from the point of view of the participants in the study. One way that ethnographic researchers do this is through what is known as **member checking**—by having the participants review what the researchers have written as a check for accuracy and completeness. It is one of the primary strategies used in ethnographic research to validate the accuracy of the researcher's findings.

Critical Colleagues. Another strategy for checking the trustworthiness of the researcher's interpretations of qualitative data involves enlisting others to become part of the researcher's "team" of advisors or "critical colleagues." These people may include students, expert practitioners, and faculty advisors who provide feedback to the researcher on any emerging assumptions about the data.

A Nonjudgmental Orientation. A *nonjudgmental orientation* requires researchers to do their best to refrain from making value judgments about unfamiliar practices. None of us, of course, can be completely neutral. But we can guard against our most obvious biases. How? By doing our best to view another group's behaviors as impartially as we can. Fetterman gives an example of how one of his biases might have been fatal:

> An experience I had with the Bedouin Arabs in the Sinai desert provides a useful example. . . . During my stay with the Bedouins, I tried not to let my bias for Western hygiene practices [show]. [M]y reaction to one of my first acquaintances, a Bedouin with a leathery face and feet, was far from neutral. . . . I admired his ability to survive and adapt in a harsh environment, moving from one water hole to the next throughout the desert. However, my personal reaction to the odor of his garments (particularly after a camel ride) was far from impartial. He shared his jacket with me to protect me from the heat. I thanked him of course, because . . . I did not want to insult him. But I smelled like a camel for the rest of the day in the dry desert heat. I thought I didn't need the jacket because we were only a kilometer or two from our destination. . . . I learned later that without his jacket I would have suffered from sunstroke. The desert heat is so dry that perspiration evaporates almost immediately and an inexperienced traveler does not always notice when the temperature climbs above 130°F. By slowing down the evaporation rate, the jacket helped me retain water. Had I rejected the jacket and, by implication, Bedouin hygiene practices, I would have baked, and I would never have understood how much their lives revolve around water.[15]

The most serious mistake ethnographers can make is to impose their own culture's standards of behavior and values onto those of another culture.

TOPICS THAT LEND THEMSELVES WELL TO ETHNOGRAPHIC RESEARCH

As we have suggested, researchers who undertake an ethnographic study want to obtain as holistic a picture of an educational setting as possible. Indeed, one of the key strengths of ethnographic research is the comprehensiveness of perspective it provides. Because the researcher goes directly to the situation or setting that he or she wishes to study, deeper and more complete understanding becomes possible. As a result, ethnographic research is particularly suitable for topics such as the following:

- Those that by their very nature defy simple quantification (e.g., the interaction of students and teachers in classroom discussions).
- Those that can best be understood in a natural (as opposed to an artificial) setting (e.g., the behavior of students at a school event).
- Those that involve the study of individual or group activities over time (such as the changes that occur in the attitudes of at-risk students as they participate in a specially designed, year-long, reading program).
- Those involving the study of the roles that educators play, and the behaviors associated with those roles (e.g., the behavior of classroom teachers, students, counselors, administrators, coaches, staff, and other school personnel as they fulfill their various roles and how such behavior changes over time).
- Those that involve the study of the activities and behavior of groups as a unit (such as classes, athletic teams, subject matter departments, administrative units, work teams).
- Those involving the study of formal organizations in their totality (e.g., schools, school districts).

Sampling in Ethnographic Research

Since ethnographers attempt to observe everything within the setting or situation they are observing, in a sense they do not sample at all. But as we have mentioned before, no researcher can observe everything. To the extent that what is observed is only a portion of what might be observed, what a researcher observes is, therefore, a de facto sample of all the possible observations that might be made.

Also, the samples of persons studied by ethnographers are typically small (often only a few individuals, or a single class) and do not permit generalization to a larger population. Many ethnographers, in fact, state right at the outset of a study that they have no intention of generalizing the results of their study. What they are after, they point out, is a more complete understanding of a particular situation. The applicability of their findings can best be determined by replication of their work in other settings or situations by other researchers.

Do Ethnographic Researchers Use Hypotheses?

Ethnographic researchers seldom initiate their research with precise hypotheses. Rather, they attempt to understand an ongoing situation or set of activities that cannot be predicted in advance. They observe for a period of time, formulate some initial hypotheses that suggest to them additional kinds of observations that may lead them to revise their initial conclusions, and so on. Ethnographic research, perhaps more so than any other kind of research, relies on both observation and interviewing that is continual and sustained over time.

An example of a question that might be investigated through ethnographic research would be, "What is life like in a rural high school?" The researcher's goal would be to document or portray the daily, ongoing experiences of the teachers, students, administrators, and staff in such a school. The school would be regularly visited over a considerable length of time (a year would not be uncommon). The researcher would observe classrooms on a regular basis and attempt to describe, as fully and as richly as possible, what exists and what happens in those classrooms. He or she would also interview in depth several teachers, students, administrators, and support staff.

Descriptions (a better word might be *portrayals*) might depict the social atmosphere of the school; the intellectual and emotional experiences of students; the manner in which administrators and teachers (and staff and students) act toward and react to others of different ethnic groups, sexes, or abilities; how the "rules" of the school (and the classroom) are learned, modified, and enforced; the kinds of concerns teachers (and students) have; the views students have of the school, and how these compare with the views of the administration and the faculty; and so forth.

The data to be collected might include detailed handwritten prose descriptions by the researcher-observer; audio recordings of pupil-student, administrator-student, and administrator-faculty conferences; video recordings of classroom discussions and faculty meetings; examples of teacher lesson plans and student work; sociograms depicting "power" relationships that exist in a classroom; flowcharts illustrating the direction and frequency of certain types of comments (e.g., the kinds of questions asked by teachers and students of one another, and the responses that different kinds produce);

and anything else the researcher thinks would provide insights into what goes on in this school. Notice that in this instance, hypotheses would not be formulated at the beginning of the study.

In short, then, the goal of researchers engaging in ethnographic research is to "paint a portrait" of a school or a classroom (or any other educational setting) as thoroughly, accurately, and vividly as possible so that others can also truly "see" that school or that classroom and its participants and what they do. In fact, it can be viewed as an attempt to determine how a group gives meaning to its activities. Many believe that the ethnographic approach offers a richness of description that is especially fruitful for understanding education.

Data Collection in Ethnographic Research

The two major means of data collection in ethnographic research are through participant observation and interviewing. Interviewing, in fact, is the most important tool that ethnographers use. Through **interviews**, the researcher is able to put into a larger context that which he or she has seen, heard, or experienced. As we described in Chapter 19, interviews come in many forms: structured, semistructured, informal, and retrospective. We won't expand on the discussion here, except to say that informal interviews are the most common. To the inexperienced, informal interviews may seem to be the easiest to do, as they require neither any particular type of question nor any particular sequence in which questions must be asked. The interviewer can pretty much follow the participant's interests. Often they seem to be no more than a casual conversation. Actually, however, they are quite difficult to do well. The researcher must maintain a comfortable manner and establish a friendly situation, yet still attempt to learn about another individual's life in a fairly systematic fashion. This is not an easy thing to do. Experienced interviewers, therefore, begin with nonthreatening questions posed in a conversational manner before they ask highly personal questions that involve sensitive topics.

The other major technique that ethnographers use is **participant observation**, which we also discussed in some detail in Chapter 19. Participant observation is crucial to effective fieldwork. As Fetterman suggests, participant observation "combines participation in the lives of the people under study with maintenance of a professional distance that allows adequate observation and recording of data."[16] An important aspect of participant observation is that it requires immersion in a culture. Typically, the researcher lives and works in the community of interest for six months to a year or even longer to internalize the basic beliefs, fears, hopes, and expectations of its people. In educational research, participant observation, however, is often noncontinuous and spread out over a long period of time. Fetterman gives an example:

> In two ethnographic studies, of dropouts and gifted children, I visited the programs for only a few weeks every couple of months over a three-year period. The visits were intensive and included classroom observation, nonstop informal interviews, occasional substitute teaching, interaction with community members, and the use of various other research techniques, including long-distance phone calls, dinner with students' families, and time spent hanging out in the hallways and parking lot with students cutting classes.[17]

FIELD NOTES

A major check on the accuracy of an ethnographer's observations lies in the quality of his or her field notes. To place an ethnographic report in perspective, interested readers need to know as much as possible about the ideas and views of the researcher. That is why the researcher's field notes are so important. Unfortunately, this remains a major problem in the reporting of much ethnographic research, in that the readers of ethnographic reports seldom, if ever, have access to the researcher's field notes. Rarely do ethnographers tell us how their information was collected, and hence it often is difficult to determine the reliability of the researcher's observations.

Field notes are just what their name implies—the notes researchers take in the field. In educational research, this usually means the detailed notes researchers take in the educational setting (classroom or school) as they observe what is going on or as they interview their informants. They are the researchers' written account of what they hear, see, experience, and think in the course of collecting and reflecting on their data.[18]

Bernard suggests that field notes be distinguished from three other types of writing: field jottings, a field diary, and a field log.[19]

Field jottings refer to quick notes about something the researcher wants to write more about later. They provide the stimulus to help researchers recall a lot of details they do not have time to write down during an observation or an interview.

A **field diary** is, in effect, a personal statement of the researcher's feelings, opinions, and perceptions about others with whom he or she comes in contact during the course of the work. It provides a place where researchers can relax—an outlet for writing down things that the researcher does not want to become part of the public record. Here is part of a page from such a diary of one of the authors of this book, written during a semester-long observation of a social studies class in a suburban high school.

> *Monday, 11/5.* Cold, very rainy day. Makes me feel sort of depressed. Phil, Felix, Alicia, Robert, and Susan came into classroom early today to discuss yesterday's assignment. Susan is looking more disheveled than usual today—seems preoccupied while others are discussing ways to prepare the group report. She doesn't speak to me, although all others say hello. I regret my failure to support her idea during yesterday's discussion when she asked me to. Hope that it will not result in her refusing to be interviewed.
>
> *Tuesday, 11/13.* Susan and other members of committee supposed to meet me in library before school today for help with their report. Nobody showed. Feel that I've done something to turn these kids off, especially Susan. Makes me angry toward her, as this will now be the third time that she has missed a meeting with me. Only first time for the others. Perhaps she has more influence on them than I thought? I don't feel I am getting anywhere in understanding her, or why she has such influence on so many of the other kids.
>
> *Thursday, 11/29.* Wow! Mrs. R. (teacher) had extremely good discussion today. Seems like entire class participated (note: check discussion tally sheet to corroborate). I think secret is to start off with something that they perceive as interesting. Why is it that sometimes they are so—so good! so involved in ideas and thinking and other times so apathetic? I can't figure it out.

Field work is often an intense, emotionally draining experience, and a diary can serve as a way for the researcher to let out personal feelings, yet still keep them private.

A **field log** is a sort of running account of how researchers plan to spend their time compared to how they actually spend it. It is, in effect, the researcher's plan for collecting data systematically. A field log consists of books of blank, lined paper (or a similar layout on a laptop or electronic tablet). Each day in the field is represented by two pages of the log. On the left page, the researcher lists what he or she plans to do that day—where to go, who to interview, what to observe, and so on. On the right side, the researcher lists what he or she *actually* did that day. As the study progresses, and things come to mind that the researcher wants to know, the log provides a place for them to be scheduled. Bernard gives an example of how such a log is used.

> Suppose you're studying a local educational system. It's April 5 and you are talking with an informant called MJR. She tells you that since the military government took over, children have to study politics for two hours every day, and she doesn't like it. Write a note to yourself in your log to ask other mothers about this issue, and to interview the school principal.
>
> Later on, when you are writing up your notes, you may decide not to interview the principal until after you have accumulated more data about how mothers in the community feel about the new curriculum. On the left-hand page for April 23 you note: "target date for interview with school principal." On the left-hand page of April 10 you note "make appointment for interview on 23rd with school principal." For April 6 you note "need more interviews with mothers about new curriculum."[20]

The value of maintaining a log is that it forces researchers to think hard about the questions they truly want answered, the procedures to be followed, and the data really needed. Taking field notes is an art in itself. We can give only a brief introduction here, but the points presented next should give you some idea of the importance and complexity of the task.

Bogdan and Biklen state that field notes consist of two kinds of materials—descriptive and reflective.[21] **Descriptive field notes** attempt to describe the setting, the people, and what they do according to what the researcher observes. They include:

- Portraits of the subjects—their physical appearance, mannerisms, gestures, how they act, talk, and so on.
- Reconstruction of dialogue—conversations between subjects, as well as what they say to the researcher. Unique or particularly revealing statements should be quoted.
- Description of the physical setting—a quick sketch of the room arrangements, placement of materials, and so on.
- Accounts of particular events—who was involved, when, where, and how.

- Depiction of activities—a detailed description of what happened, along with the order in which it happened.
- The observer's behavior—the researcher's actions, dress, conversations with participants, reactions, and so on.

Reflective field notes present more of what the researcher himself or herself is thinking *about* as he or she observes. These include the following:

- Reflections on analysis—the researcher's speculations about what he or she is learning, ideas that are developing, patterns or connections seen, and so on.
- Reflections on method—procedures and materials the researcher is using in the study, comments about the design of the study, problems that are arising, and so on.
- Reflections on ethical dilemmas and conflicts—such as any concerns that arise over responsibilities to subjects or value conflicts.
- Reflections on the observer's frame of mind—such as on what the researcher is thinking as the study progresses (attitudes, opinions, and beliefs) and how these might be affecting the study.
- Points of clarification—notes to the researcher about things that need to be clarified, checked later, etc.

In no other form of research is the actual doing of the study—the process itself—considered as consciously and deliberately as it is in ethnographic research. The reflective aspect of field notes is the researcher's way of attempting to control for the danger of observer effect that we mentioned in Chapter 19, and to remind us that research, to be done well, requires ongoing evaluation and judgment.

An Example of Field Notes: Marge's Room[22]

Date: March 24, 1980
Joe McCloud
11:00 A.M. to 12:30 P.M.
Westwood High
6th Set of Notes

The Fourth-Period Class in Marge's Room

I arrived at Westwood High at five minutes to eleven, at the time Marge told me her fourth period started. I was dressed as usual: sport shirt, chino pants, and Woolrich parka. The fourth period is the only time during the day when all the students who are in the "neurologically impaired/learning disability" program, better known as "Marge's program," come together. During the other periods, certain students in the program, two or three or four at most, come to her room for help with the work they are getting in other regular high school classes.

It was a warm, fortyish, promise of a spring day. There was a police patrol wagon, the kind that has benches in the back that are used for large busts, parked in the back of the big parking lot that is in front of the school. No one was sitting in it and I never heard its reason for being there. In the circular drive in front of the school was parked a United States Army car. It had insignias on the side and was a khaki color. As I walked from my car, a balding fortyish man in an Army uniform came out of the building and went to the car and sat down. Four boys and a girl also walked out of the school. All were white. They had on old dungarees and colored stenciled t-shirts with spring jackets over them. One of the boys, the tallest of the four, called out, "oink, oink, oink." This was done as he sighted the police vehicle in the back.

> *O.C.:* This was strange to me in that I didn't think that the kids were into "the police as pigs." Somehow I associated that with another time, the early 1970s. I'm going to have to come to grips with the assumptions I have about high school due to my own experience. Sometimes I feel like Westwood is entirely different from my high school and yet this police car incident reminded me of mine.

I walked into Marge's class and she was standing in front of the room with more people than I had ever seen in the room save for her homeroom, which is right after second period. She looked like she was talking to the class or was just about to start. She was dressed as she had been on my other visits—clean, neat, well-dressed but casual. Today she had on a striped blazer, a white blouse and dark slacks. She looked up at me, smiled and said: "Oh, I have a lot more people here now than the last time."

> *O.C.:* This was in reference to my other visits during other periods where there are only a few students. She seems self-conscious about having such a small group of students to be responsible for. Perhaps she compares herself with the regular teachers who have classes of thirty or so.

There were two women in their late twenties sitting in the room. There was only one chair left. Marge said to me something like: "We have two visitors from the central office today. One is a vocational counselor and

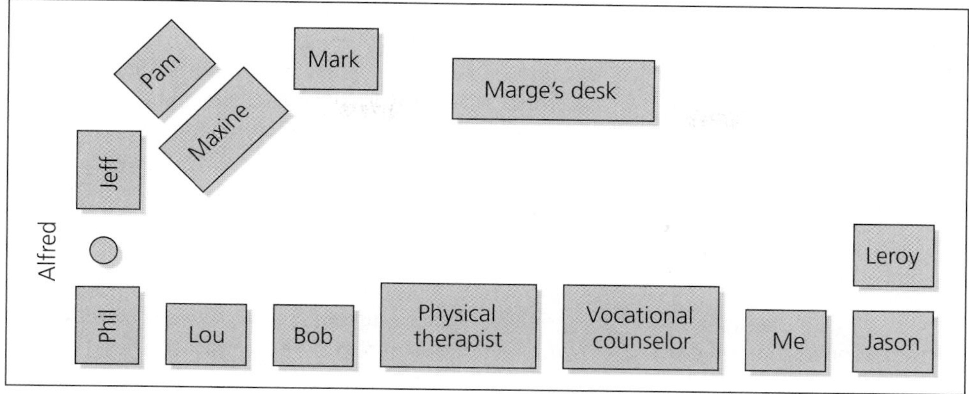

the other is a physical therapist," but I don't remember if those were the words. I felt embarrassed coming in late. I sat down in the only chair available, next to one of the women from the central office. They had on skirts and carried their pocketbooks, much more dressed up than the teachers I've seen. They sat there and observed.

(The class seating arrangement is shown in the diagram.)

. . . Marge walked about near her desk during her talk, which she started by saying to the class: "Now remember, tomorrow is a fieldtrip to the Rollway Company. We all meet in the usual place, by the bus, in front of the main entrance at 8:30. Mrs. Sharp wanted me to tell you that the tour of Rollway is not specifically for you. It's not like the trip to G.M. They took you to places where you were likely to be able to get jobs. Here, it's just a general tour that everybody goes on. Many of the jobs that you will see are not for you. Some are just for people with engineering degrees. You'd better wear comfortable shoes because you may be walking for two or three hours." Maxine and Mark said: "Ooh," in protest to the walking.

She paused and said in a demanding voice: "OK, any questions? You are all going to be there. (Pause) I want you to take a piece of paper and write down some questions so you have things to ask at the plant." She began passing out paper and at this point Jason, who was sitting next to me, made a tutting sound of disgust and said: "We got to do this?" Marge said: "I know this is too easy for you, Jason." This was said in a sarcastic way but not like a strong putdown.

> *O.C.:* It was like sarcasm between two people who know each other well. Marge has known many of these kids for a few years. I have to explore the implications of that for her relations with them.

Marge continued: "OK, what are some of the questions you are going to ask?" Jason yelled out: "Insurance," and Marge said: "I was asking Maxine, not Jason." This was said matter-of-factly without anger toward Jason. Maxine said: "Hours—the hours you work, the wages." Somebody else yelled out: "Benefits." Marge wrote these things on the board. She got to Phil who was sitting there next to Jeff. I believe she skipped over Jeff. Mr. Armstrong was standing right next to Phil. She said: "Have you got one?" Phil said: "I can't think of one." She said: "Honestly, Phil. Wake up." Then she went to Joe, the white boy. Joe and Jeff are the only white boys I've seen in the program. The two girls are white. He said: "I can't think of any."

She got to Jason and asked him if he could think of anything else. He said: "Yeah, you could ask 'em how many of the products they made each year." Marge said: "Yes, you could ask about production. How about Leroy, do you have any ideas, Leroy?" He said: "No." . . . Jason said out loud but not yelling: "How much schooling you need to get it." Marge kept listing them.

> *O.C.:* Marge was quite animated. If I hadn't seen her like this before I would think she was putting on a show for the people from central office. . . .

. . . I looked around the room, noting the dress on some of the students. Maxine had on a black t-shirt that had some iron-on lettering on it. It was a very well-done iron-on and the shirt looked expensive. She had on Levi jeans and Nike jogging sneakers. Mark is about 5′9″ or 5′10″. He had on a long sleeve jersey with an alligator on the front, very stylish but his pants were wrinkled and he had on old muddy black basketball sneakers with both laces broken, one in two places. Pam had on a lilac-colored velour sweater over a button-down striped shirt. Her hair looked very well-kept and looked like she had had it styled at an expensive hair place. Jeff sat next to her in his wheelchair. He had one foot up without a shoe on it as if it were sprained. . . .

Phil had on a beige sweater over a white shirt and dark pants and low-cut basketball sneakers. The sneakers were red and were dirty. He had a dirt ring around the collar. He is the least well-dressed of the crowd. . . .

Jim is probably 5′9″ or 5′10″. He had on a red pullover. Jason had on a black golf cap and a beige spring jacket over a university t-shirt. He had on dark dress pants and a red university t-shirt with a v-neck. It was faded from being washed. Jason's eyes were noticeably red.

> *O.C.:* Two of the kids told me that Westwood High was a fashion show. I have a difficult time figuring out what's in fashion. Jason used that expression. He seems to me to be the most clothes-conscious. . . .

I don't know what got this started but she started talking about the social background of the kids in the class. She said: "Pam lives around here right up there so she's from a professional family. Now, Maxine, that's different. She lives on the east side. She is one of six kids and her father isn't that rich. As a matter of fact, he's in maintenance, taking charge of cleaning crews. Now, Jeff, he lives on Dogwood. He's middle class." I asked about Lou. She said: "Pour Lou, talk about being neurologically impaired. I don't know what to do about that guy. Now he has a sister who graduated two years ago. He worries me more than anybody. I don't know what is going to become of him. He is so slow. I don't know any job that he could do. His father came in and he looks just like him. What are you going to tell him? What is he going to be able to do? What is he going to do? Wash airplanes? I talked to the vocational counselor. She said that there were jobs in airports washing airplanes. I mean, how is he going to wash an airplane? How about sweeping out the hangars? Maybe he could do that. The mother is something else. His mother thinks that Lou is her punishment. Can you imagine an attitude like that? I was just wondering what could she have done to think that she deserved Lou?

"Now Luca Meta, he is upper class all the way. Leroy, there's your low end of the spectrum. I don't know how many kids they have but they have a lot. His mother just had a kidney removed. Everybody knows he is on parole. Matter of fact, whenever there is any stealing in the school, they look at him. He used to go to gym and every time he went, something was stolen. Now they don't let him go to gym anymore. His parole officer was down. He won't be here next year." . . .

. . . She said: "By the way, I was talking and maybe you overheard me about what we need is a competency-based program here. I have already finished a competency-based program if they ever took it. It is silly to have kids spend four years sitting here, when it makes no sense in terms of them. They ought to be out working. If they're not going to graduate, what they ought to have is some living skills like what we did with writing the checks. People aren't going to teach them that out in the world so they could do that. Once they had enough skills, living skills, to make it on their own then they ought to go out. There is no sense to this." . . .

We left the room. Alfred and Marge walked up the empty hall with me. I asked her how the kids felt about being in this class. She said: "Well, it varies. It really bothers Pam. Like she failed history and she has to go to summer school. The reason she failed it was she wouldn't tell them that she was in this program so she didn't get any extra help and then she failed." Marge walked me to the door. Alfred dropped off at the teachers' room.

On the way to the door she said: "Remember that boy I told you about who's going to be in there? The dentist's son, the Swenson boy? Well, I have been hearing stories about him. I come to find out that he is really E.M.H. (Educable Mentally Handicapped) and a hyperactive kid. I really am going to have my hands full with him. If there is twenty in the program next year, I really am going to need another aide." I said good-bye and walked to my car.

Data Analysis in Ethnographic Research

Analysis is one of the most interesting aspects of ethnographic research. It begins from the first moment a researcher selects a problem to study and continues until the final report is written. Many techniques, including content analysis (see Chapter 20) are involved in analyzing ethnographic data. Some of the more important include triangulation, searching for patterns, identifying key events, preparing visual representations, using statistics, and crystallization. What follows is a brief description of each.

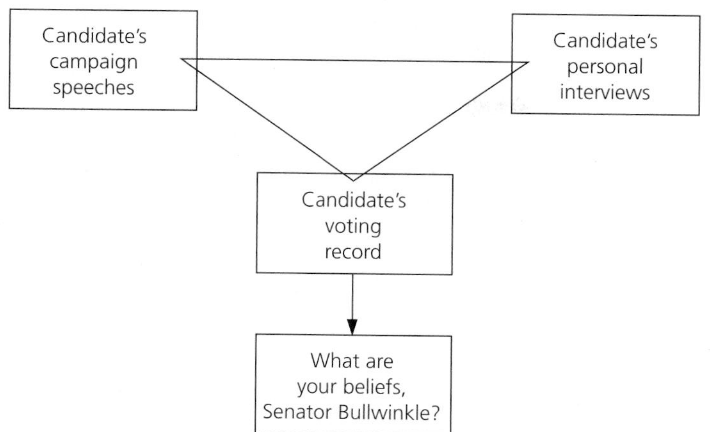

Figure 21.1 *Triangulation and Politics*

Triangulation. **Triangulation** is fundamental in ethnographic research. Essentially, it establishes the validity of an ethnographer's observations. It involves checking what one hears and sees by comparing one's sources of information—do they agree? Here's an example: A researcher might compare a student's oral statements that he was a "good" student with a written transcript of his grades, his teacher's comments in this regard, and, perhaps, some unsolicited remarks from his fellow students. Triangulation here could verify—or not—the student's self-assessment.

Triangulation can work with any subject, in any setting, and at any level (Figure 21.1). It improves the quality of the data that are collected and the accuracy of the researcher's interpretations. It can occur naturally, even in informal conversation. Consider this example:

> A prominent superintendent, managing one of the largest districts in the nation, had just finished explaining why school size made no difference in education. He said that he had one 1500-pupil school and one 5000-pupil school in his district that he was particularly proud of, and that the school size had no effect on school spirit, the educative process, or his ability to manage. He also explained that he had to build two or three new schools next year, either three small schools or one small school and one large one. A colleague interrupted to ask which he preferred. The superintendent replied, "Small ones, of course; they are much easier to handle." He had betrayed himself in one phrase. Although the administrative party line was that size made no difference—management is management no matter how big or small the unit—this superintendent revealed a very different personal opinion in response to a casual question.[23]

Patterns. Those who do ethnographic research look for *patterns* in the ways that people think and behave. They offer a means of checking ethnographic reliability when they reveal consistencies in what people say and what they do. Typically, researchers start with a large mass of undifferentiated information and then, by comparing and contrasting what they collected, sort this information until a discernible line of thought or pattern of behavior emerges. They then observe and listen some more to see whether the new observations correspond to what they saw and heard before. This then requires further sifting and sorting until the researchers are satisfied that what they are describing matches what was observed.

Key Events. **Key events** occur in every social group and provide data that ethnographic researchers can use to describe and analyze an entire culture. They convey a tremendous amount of information. They provide a "lens through which to view a culture."[24] Examples might include the introduction of computers in an elementary school, a fistfight between two girls during a high school basketball game, the response of a group of recovery room nurses to a medical emergency, a fire in a crowded apartment building, the introduction of a new teaching method in a social studies classroom, or the return of a popular professor from sabbatical leave. Such events are especially useful for analysis, as they not only help the researcher understand the group he or she is studying, but they also help the researcher explain the culture of the group to others.

Visual Representations. These include such things as *maps* (e.g., of a classroom or school), *flowcharts* (e.g., of who says what to whom during a classroom discussion), *organizational charts* (e.g., of how a school library is organized), *sociograms* (e.g., of which students receive the most invitations to participate as a member of a classroom research team), *matrices* (e.g., a chart to compare and cross-reference the various categories that exist in a creative arts department in a university, such as music, dance, theater, and painting). The very process of preparing a visual representation often can help a researcher crystallize his or her understanding of an area, a system, a location, or even an interaction. Visual representations are very useful tools in ethnographic research.

Statistics. Although you might not expect it, ethnographers often do use statistics in their work. Usually, however, they use nonparametric techniques (see Chapter 11), such as a chi-square test, more often than parametric ones. Typically, they are more likely to report frequencies than scores. They do use parametric statistics when they have large samples, however.

Nevertheless, the use of statistics in ethnographic research presents a number of problems. Meeting the assumptions that many inferential tests require (e.g., that the sample is random) often is virtually impossible. Typically, ethnographic studies use small samples and purposive samples. On the other hand, descriptive statistics—means and medians—can at times be used to summarize the frequency of actions or events and are increasingly found in ethnographic reports.

Crystallization. Ethnographers try to pull together their thoughts at various stages throughout their research. Sometimes this results in only a summing up of information, but other times it results in a genuine insight. "Every study has classic moments when everything falls into place. After months of thought and immersion in the culture, a special configuration gels. All the subtopics, miniexperiments, layers of triangulated effort, key events, and patterns of behavior form a coherent and often cogent picture of what is happening."[25] Nothing is more exciting to an ethnographer than when this happens.

The important thing to realize about the analysis of ethnographic data is that there is no single stage or time when **crystallization** occurs. Multiple analyses and multiple forms are essential. Often it is cyclical—data are collected, thought about, more data are collected, patterns are looked for, more data are collected, new patterns are looked for, matrices and then more matrices are developed, and on and on. Data analysis in ethnography is ongoing, from start to finish.

Roger Harker and His Fifth-Grade Classroom

Let us look, then, at an example of ethnographic research. What follows is a short description, by the researcher, of an ethnographic study of a fifth-grade classroom.

> I [the researcher] worked in depth with Roger Harker for six months. I did an ethnography of his classroom and the interaction between him and his pupils. This young man had taught for three years in the elementary school. He volunteered for the study in order, he said, "to improve my professional competence."
>
> My collection of data fell into the following categories: (1) personal, autobiographical, and psychological data on the teacher; (2) ratings of him by his principal and other superiors in the superintendent's office; (3) his own self-estimates on the same points; (4) observations of his classroom, emphasizing interaction with children; (5) interviews with each child and the elicitation of ratings of the teacher on many different dimensions, both formally and informally; (6) his ratings and estimates for each child in his classroom, including estimates of popularity with peers, academic performance and capacity, personal adjustment, home background, and liking for him; (7) sociometric data from the children about each other; and (8) interviews with each person (superintendent, principal, supervisors, children) who supplied ratings of him.
>
> I also participated in the life of the school to the extent possible, accompanying the teacher where I could and "melting" into the classroom as much as feasible. I was always there, but I had no authority and assumed none. I became a friend and confidant to the children.
>
> This teacher was regarded by his superiors as most promising—"clear and well-organized," "sensitive to children's needs," "fair and just to all of the children," "knowing his subject areas well." I was not able to elicit with either ratings scales or in interviews any criticisms or

negative evaluations. There were very few suggestions for change—and these were all in the area of subject matter and curriculum.

Roger Harker described himself as "fair and just to all my pupils," as making "fair decisions," and as "playing no favorites." This was a particular point of pride with him.

His classroom was made up of children from a broad social stratum—upper-middle, middle, and lower classes—and the children represented Mexican-American, Anglo-European, and Japanese-American ethnic groups. I was particularly attentive to the relationships between the teacher and children from these various groups.

One could go into much detail, but a few items will suffice since they all point in the same direction, and that direction challenges both his perceptions of his own behavior and those of his superiors. He ranked highest on all dimensions, including personal and academic factors, those children who were most like himself—Anglo, middle to upper-middle social class, and, like him, ambitious (achievement-oriented). He also estimated that these children were the most popular with their peers and were the leaders of the classroom group. His knowledge about the individual children, elicited without recourse to files or notes, was distributed in the same way. He knew significantly more about the children culturally like himself (on items concerned with home background as well as academic performance) and least about those culturally most different.

The children had quite different views of the situation. Some children described him as not always so "fair and just," as "having special pets," as not being easy to go to with their problems. On sociometric "maps" of the classroom showing which children wanted to spend time with other specific children, or work with them, sit near them, invite them to a party or a show, etc., the most popular children were not at all those the teacher rated highest. And his negative ratings proved to be equally inaccurate. Children he rated as isolated or badly adjusted socially, most of whom were non-Anglo or non-middle-class, more often than not turned out to be "stars of attraction" from the point of view of the children.

Observations of his classroom behavior supported the data collected by other means. He most frequently called on, touched, helped, and looked directly at the children culturally like himself. He was never mean or cruel to the other children. It was almost as though they weren't there. His interaction with the children of Anglo-European ethnicity and middle and upper-middle social class background was more frequent than with the other children, and the quality of the interaction appeared to be differentiated in the same way.

This young man, with the best of intentions, was confirming the negative hypotheses and predictions (as well as the positive ones) already made within the social system. He was informing Anglo middle-class children that they were capable, had bright futures, were socially acceptable, and were worth a lot of trouble. He was also informing non-Anglo children that they were less capable, less socially acceptable, less worth the trouble. He was defeating his own declared educational goals.

This young teacher did not know that he was discriminating. He was rated very positively by his superiors on all counts, including being "fair and just to all the children." Apparently they were as blind to his discrimination as he was. The school system supported him and his classroom behavior without questioning or criticizing him. And the dominant social structure of the community supported the school.[26]

Notice several things about this description.

- The study took place in a naturalistic setting—in the classroom and school of Roger Harker.
- The researcher did not try to manipulate the situation in any way.
- There was no comparison of methods or treatments (as is often the case in experimental or causal-comparative research).
- The study involved only a single classroom (an *n* of one).
- The researcher was a participant observer, participating "in the life of the school to the extent possible."
- The researcher used several different kinds of instruments to collect his data.
- The researcher tried to present a holistic description of this teacher's fifth-grade classroom.
- The study revealed much that would have been missed by researchers using other methodologies.
- No attempt was made to generalize the researcher's findings to other settings or situations. The "external validity" of the study, in other words, was very limited, unless similar findings are corroborated in comparable studies. In that case, the transferability of findings (theoretical generalizability) may be possible.
- There is no way, unfortunately, to check the validity of the data or the researcher's interpretations (unless another researcher had independently observed the same classroom).

Advantages and Disadvantages of Ethnographic Research

Ethnographic research has a number of unique strengths but also several weaknesses. A key strength is that it provides the researcher with a much more comprehensive perspective than do other forms of educational research. By observing the actual behavior of individuals in their natural settings, one may gain a much deeper and richer understanding of such behavior. Ethnographic research also lends itself well to research topics that are not easily quantified. The thoughts of teachers and students, ideas, and other nuances of behavior that might escape researchers using other methodologies can often be detected by ethnographic researchers.

Furthermore, ethnographic research is particularly appropriate to behaviors that are best understood by observing them within their natural settings. Other types of research can measure attitudes and behaviors in somewhat artificial settings, but they frequently do not lend themselves well to naturalistic settings. The "dynamics" of a faculty meeting, or the "interaction" between students and teacher in a classroom, for example, can probably best be studied through ethnographic investigation. Finally, ethnographic research is especially suited to studying group behavior over time. Thus, to understand as fully as possible the "life" of an inner-city school over a year-long period, an ethnographic approach may well be the most appropriate methodology for a researcher to use.

Ethnographic research, like all research, however, is not without its limitations. It is highly dependent on the particular researcher's observations and interpretations, and since numerical data are rarely provided, there is usually no way to check the validity of the researcher's conclusions. As a result, observer bias is almost impossible to eliminate. Because usually only a single situation (such as one classroom or one school) is observed, generalizability is almost nonexistent, except when it is possible to replicate the study in other settings or situations by other researchers. Because the researcher usually begins the observations without a specific hypothesis to confirm or deny, terms may not be defined, and hence the specific variables or relationships being investigated (if any) may remain unclear.

Because of the inevitable ambiguity that accompanies this method, preplanning and review by others are much less useful than in quantitative studies. While it is true that no study is ever carried out precisely as planned, potential pitfalls are more easily identified and corrected in other methodologies. For this reason, we believe ethnographic research to be a difficult type of research to do well. It follows that beginning researchers using this method should receive close supervision.

An Example of Ethnographic Research

In the remainder of this chapter, we present a published example of ethnographic research, followed by a critique of its strengths and weaknesses. As we did in our critiques of the different types of research studies we analyzed in other chapters, we use concepts introduced in earlier parts of the book in our analysis.

From: (2006, January). *Middle School Journal, 37*(3), 38–45.

Lessons on Effective Teaching from Middle School ESL Students

This We Believe Characteristics

- *An inviting, supportive, and safe environment*
- *High expectations for every member of the learning community*
- *Students and teachers engaged in active learning*
- *Multiple learning and teaching approaches that respond to their diversity*

Ellen M. Curtin

Jaime loved to read about the Greek gods and complained of being bored a lot in class. He expressed the opinion that he was not challenged academically. Maria loved the Olsen twins (Kate and Ashley) and wanted to be a singer and an actress when she grew up. Rosa wanted to become a doctor, but confessed that she sometimes felt that she was not a good student because she did not make 100% on all her assignments. Angel was reported by his teacher to be the hardest working of all the students, and he told me that he wanted to be an engineer when he grew up. These four students were perceived to be progressing well academically by their mainstream and ESL teachers.

Introduction

Enrique was at risk academically. He was failing many classes and his parents were often called in for conferences. Enrique did not like school and described himself as the person who made the teachers mad because "I just do some jokes to the teachers and they get mad, . . . and they tell my family. . . . Teachers get all this voice and sometimes they kick me out of class." Enrique did not consider himself to be a good student and preferred to earn money with his father on the weekends working on construction sites. Enrique, a seventh grader, skipped classes sometimes, especially science, without the mainstream teacher knowing. Enrique told me that by skipping science he could eat lunch with the eighth graders and be with his friend Jaime who was in the eighth grade.

Lupe was also at risk academically and behaviorally. She was suspended on two occasions during the course of the six-month study. She was very precocious and used a lot of sexual terminology and inappropriate language around other students. She did not like Rosa or Maria. She expressed her love for animals and her desire to be a veterinarian when she grew up.

These six students, all originally from Mexico, presented unique instructional challenges to their mainstream teacher. Children who arrive in a new country by age six or seven do better academically later in middle school and high school than older arrivals (Gibson, 1988). Of course there are exceptions, but in general, the older arrivals (middle school and high school level) are at greater risk of dropping out or of being promoted year by year without ever obtaining the skills in English required to do well academically at the secondary and postsecondary level.

Justification

As immigrant students today are increasingly culturally and linguistically diverse, how teachers accommodate the needs of immigrant students and how these students perceive their own educational experiences are relevant educational issues (Banks, 2001;

Justification

***Ellen M. Curtin** is an assistant professor of early childhood education at Texas Wesleyan University, Fort Worth. E-mail: curtina@txwes.edu*

Nieto, 2000). In this era of accountability and standardized assessment, teachers must be prepared to meet immigrant students' academic needs.

Prior research

In the past 10 years, the number of non-English-speaking students in American schools has increased 95% (National Clearinghouse for English Language Acquisition, 2004). Many of these students are placed with teachers who lack any specialized training in ESL or bilingual education (McKeon, 1994). The increase in non-English-speaking students has resulted in growing pressures on inadequately prepared teachers (Crawford, 1991). Teaching language minority students affects all teachers and can no longer be considered the responsibility of just ESL teachers. "It is a national priority, one that encompasses issues related to instruction, not only for Latino students, but for those speaking a wide range of languages from Hmong to Vietnamese to Russian to Arabic. There is a great demand for information on promising practices" (Gersten, 1996, p. 217).

Prior research

Teachers need to understand that it takes many years for an immigrant student to attain academic proficiency in a second language. Research by Krashen (1996) has demonstrated that it can take from six to twelve years to acquire full cognitive and academic understanding in a second language.

Many teachers are committed to improving instruction, and many also feel the pressure to prepare these students for state mandated standardized tests. For teachers interested in meeting the instructional needs of ESL students, the following accounts from ESL students themselves, may provide some ideas and strategies to consider.

INTRODUCTION TO THE STUDY

Purpose

Limitations

This ethnographic study provides insight into the educational experiences of six Mexican immigrant students in one Texas urban middle school. The students shared their perceptions about the teaching strategies used by their non-ESL teachers. This research was conducted to gain some insight into the world of young adolescents and English as a Second Language (ESL) immigrant youth in the United States today. The perceptions of these immigrant students, though subjective and only from one middle school, provide a valuable perspective for middle school teachers seeking to better understand and plan for the instructional needs of their ESL students.

INTRODUCTION TO THE STUDENTS

Sample

All the students in this study were only in their third year in the United States and, while they were seemingly fluent in English, still struggled a lot with the content and vocabulary required in subjects like social studies, science, and English. All were originally from Mexico and were either in the seventh or eighth grade during the time of this study. These students were preparing to take the state-mandated Texas Assessment of Knowledge and Skills (TAKS) test. All students had spent two years in an English as Second Language classroom and were currently mainstreamed for most or all of the school day with non-ESL trained teachers.

Based on what?

True of these students?

All students liked school in the United States. They found it materially comfortable, and they felt safe, even though they attended an urban school in an economically disadvantaged section of the city. The school was dark, old, and compared to other middle schools in the area, lacked much in the way of resources and amenities. This is consistent with research findings by Ogbu (1992) that immigrants have a "dual frame of reference," which makes them more appreciative of the life and opportunities they have in their new country because they generally came from more impoverished conditions in their countries of origin.

Interactive Model	Didactic Model
Personalized (knew all students by name; greeted students at door; empathized with students; incorporated students' cultural backgrounds; knew backgrounds of students well; communicated with families; used humor well and incorporated classroom interruptions humorously)	Impersonalized (did not know all students by name; did not greet all students at the door; handed out worksheets; blamed students and families for lack of academic progress; did not acknowledge or attempt to address students' cultural diversity; saw students cultural backgrounds as decides)
Used cooperative grouping (students in pairs or grouped regularly)	Individualistic (students in traditional rows and settings; students independently practiced skills; grades called out in front of class)
Child centered (individualized instruction regardless of district or TAKS expectations; individualized testing procedures; planned for different learning styles; forced all students to interact)	Subject centered (all students on same page and skill; subject watered down to lowest common denominator (Gifted and Talented ESL students suffered here and did not feel challenged); heavy emphasis on TAKS and district testing; worksheets; procedures; did not account or plan for different learning styles)
Focus on process of teaching (how to teach)—focuses on improving delivery of instruction; views teaching as fluid and ever changing; teacher circulated around the room	Focus on what to teach (curriculum and content)—focused on blanket coverage and covering content; teacher sat behind desk; heavy emphasis on TAKS skills
Intuition, empathy, nonverbal communication, classroom wittiness (knew what all students were doing); made exceptions to rules for students	Pragmatic, non-empathy, less likely to pick up nonverbal communication of students, little classroom wittiness (students engaged in off-task behaviors without the teacher knowing); rules enforced equally and no exceptions made
Students and teachers active and constantly interacting (more conversation and discussion)	Students and teachers more passive and teacher less active (more silence enforced)
Classroom Discipline Style (Democratic) less emphasis on silence and behaviors	Classroom Discipline Style (Autocratic) more emphasis on silence and behaviors of students

Figure 1 *Teaching Characteristics*

PREFERRED READING STRATEGIES

I spent more than six months interviewing these students and their teachers weekly and observing them in their classrooms. The students in this study verbally shared with me their insights and opinions on the instructional models used by their teachers. After reviewing the literature on effective instructional practices for ESL students, I organized the information into two major categories using Banks's (2001) multicultural teaching behaviors as a model. These categories were the interactive and didactic teaching models (see Figure 1). What emerged from this study was that these ESL students tended to prefer learning from a teacher who exhibited more interactive teaching characteristics.

Procedures

Results

Personalized Classrooms

The students liked the teachers who knew their names, stood at the door to greet them, and who sometimes incorporated their Mexican and Spanish-speaking backgrounds into the lessons. Mrs. O' Reilly was a favorite among these students, including Spanish words

How many?

in her science lesson. Mrs. O' Reilly used humor with these students to keep them on track. Mrs. O' Reilly told me: "They are always telling me about stuff in Mexico. . . . Sometimes I try to infuse culture into my classroom." The students expressed to me that they felt relaxed in her room and offered the opinion that she made a personal effort to get to know them. Miss Monroe, an English teacher who exhibited interactive teaching characteristics, revealed this about her ESL students: "You start picking up, you know, their quirks, and who is a friend with whom. The teasing helps a lot in making sure that sometimes the shy ones will ask questions."

Good specifics

Angel told me that he felt proud to be from Mexico when his science teacher referred to seasons and volcanic activity in Mexico in class. All the students were very proud of being Mexican and appreciated teachers who made references to Mexico in their lessons.

Always?

Research on immigrant and particularly Hispanic students demonstrates that they must like their teacher and need to have a relationship with them to learn and do well in class (Nieto, 2001). Teachers who make a conscious effort to know their students and who positively validate their cultural backgrounds can meet the learning needs of English as a Second Language learners by earning the students' trust and respect (Banks, 2001).

Cooperative Grouping

How many?

The students really liked working in groups and preferred to be able to ask for help from other students without getting in trouble for talking in class.

Data

For Jaime particularly, asking "one of my friends or someone next to me" is how he got further directions when he did not understand something in class. Because sometimes, Jaime told me, "they're [teachers] busy doing other things." All the students in the study clearly stated that some teachers "won't get mad if I ask them" because "I've been with them, like, two years." All the students complained that even if a teacher did not always "get mad" at them for requesting more explanations or examples, teachers sometimes "don't do it in a kind way."

How identified?

These students were reticent to raise their hands in a didactic teacher's classroom. Jaime told me he raised his hand for help in such a classroom only if his friends beside him could not help. But even then Jaime said that he was often "ignored" as often "I raise my hand and she don't come to me."

These students survived the culture of didactic classrooms by taking turns asking their teachers for help so they could all take turns sharing the "unkindness" of teachers. In spite of this strategy, Lupe explained to me that she often got into trouble for talking when she was only asking for help on her assignment. She got upset when she was then moved away from other students and had nobody to help her.

Good example

Students like Lupe often explained to each other in Spanish what the assignment entailed. These students were not engaging in off-task or social behaviors, they were really trying to get help with their assignments. I observed Lupe during science class asking the student beside her in Spanish for help on a graphing assignment. This was done without the knowledge of the teacher. I asked the teacher afterward if he was aware of what Lupe had done. He told me "no" and expressed surprise. I asked him if he encouraged ESL students such as Lupe to ask for help in Spanish, and he said, "no." I asked this of the other didactic teachers and they all responded similarly, stating that they felt it was their responsibility as teachers in the mainstream to help ESL students "transition" to English and that they did not encourage asking for assistance in Spanish from a classmate in class.

When I posed the same question to teachers who were more interactive in their teaching style, I was told that they encouraged the ESL students to help each other in Spanish as needed. My classroom observations in these interactive classrooms substantiated this claim. I saw this happening often, and I saw that the students appeared more at-ease and comfortable doing this in Spanish, knowing they would not get in trouble with the teacher. These same students, however, had figured out that it was not acceptable with their didactic teachers.

Good validation

Student Centered by Planning for Individual Learning Styles

The teachers that the students preferred tended to try many different instructional strategies and made a concerted effort to incorporate multiple intelligence or learning style based teaching strategies. These teachers did not teach to the TAKS tests; they did not have a heavy reliance on worksheets and practice tests. Mrs. O' Reilly, the science teacher, for example, used Reese's Pieces to demonstrate atoms and then had each student create his or her own model. She attended training on multiple intelligences and tried to differentiate her instruction for many different learning styles, truly believing that by doing so she was meeting the needs of all of her ESL students. The students in this study really liked her interactive teaching style and all expressed the view that they learned a lot in her class.

Data

Research on learning styles (Dunn & Dunn, 1993) has substantiated that many ESL students are more global in their orientation to learning. The concept of right brain and left brain teaching techniques was relevant for these students. Teachers who relied heavily on the use of concrete examples provided for these students a more holistic approach to the lesson, and the students were more comfortable with that teaching style. These ESL students liked to see a finished product rather than having to inductively figure out a project or a problem on their own.

These ESL students were not auditory learners and did not like just being told what to do. They preferred a visual support be provided in each lesson, and they all liked concrete examples. In social studies, this might have been a sample of a research paper with the outline provided, or in English it might have been a poem or an essay with vocabulary or ideas brainstormed at the beginning of the lesson and then visually available as a reference for students during their independent practice.

What based on?

These students perceptions of a "good" teacher meant that the teacher used examples, explained a lot, and did not give too many directions at once. The teacher, I observed, spent much more time going over an example to be completed by students. The teacher spent longer explaining, elicited more responses from students, and actually completed an example similar to the one the students had to complete on their own. One teacher verbally and visually walked the students through a particular assignment on prefixes and suffixes. The students had all prefixes and suffixes listed on a chart for reference (they brainstormed these together at the beginning of the lesson), and the teacher constantly asked questions to check for understanding. This explanation process took at least 10 to 15 minutes.

How identified?

In the didactic classrooms, I observed teachers quickly going through one example for a duration of no more than five minutes and then proceeding to let the students practice similar examples independently, without any visual or concrete reference available for students (teachers erased the blackboard or verbally went over a sample from the textbook). *All* the students, particularly Maria and Jaime, stated that the teachers who provided the class with many examples were more effective for their learning needs. The students believed they needed more opportunities to practice and, because

How often?

of this, did not perceive they were being taught as well by teachers who did not use a lot of examples.

Good example

Maria claimed, "Sometimes [teachers] don't give you examples to understand the lesson better, like when you're doing a lesson and you don't understand after you told them to, like, show you an example. [Teachers] should do it by themselves, not by the students telling them" For Maria, this notion of "example" given by the teacher was extremely important in helping her understand and do well in class. She also considered a better teacher to be one who gave lots of examples.

Maria told me, "Ms. Henry, who gives us an example, like, sometimes she gives us homework so we can do maps or something like that, and she has one on the wall so we can see it." In this instance, Maria implied that an example meant a finished product, something that helped her see what she was supposed to be doing.

Follow-up question

For Jaime, a teacher who helped him understand in class gave him examples. He explained, "They, my ESL teachers, usually give us a lot of examples so we can understand. . . . They get us to practice something more than once." When I asked him to tell me more about a teacher who never gave examples, he immediately talked about his social studies teacher, Mr. Bond, who, Jaime told me, did explain the assignment but "never gives examples when he gives us work, he goes over the answers."

For Angel, teachers helped him learn better when "They explain about the things we review." "Homework and more practice" constituted examples for Angel, doing the same things "over and over" again. In this instance, I understood that "example" was akin to repetition and lots of practice to help learning.

Data

I realized that the concept of "example" was somehow connected to how a teacher explained information to students in class. For Lupe, the teacher should explain something "like, two times." Lupe told me, "Not just say one time, you have to do this and this in order" or "I'll no understand what she says." There was a clear connection between explaining more than once and giving examples to help Lupe understand what she was supposed to be doing in class. All students explained to me that they needed to hear something more than once to fully understand.

Data

In response to the question, "What do teachers do to help you learn best?" Maria told me, "I think, like examples. I think the most important to learn is examples." For Maria, an example was something that was done "over and over and over." Maria explained, "Because, you sometimes do something and the next day you forgot it, or she [teacher] doesn't give any more papers like that. So then, like, three months later she give us another paper and she likes 'remember the other day.'" "Examples" was an important concept for these students, as my text search of their interview transcripts counted 57 references made to the word "examples" in the total interview search.

"Examples," as defined by the students I observed, were seldom given by teachers with a didactic teaching style. These teachers never actually completed more than one problem on the chalkboard or overhead projector, and never alerted students to anticipated difficulties they might encounter in a proposed assignment. The students were told what to do and proceeded to do their work silently. After 10 to 15 minutes, the teacher checked in, and, if all students were finished, the teacher simply proceeded to call out the answer or have a student call out the correct answer.

Evidence or opinion?

In middle school, teachers tend to teach to auditory leaners, not realizing that our increasingly diverse students are not auditory in their own learning preference. The reality is that ESL students need a concrete, step-by-step approach. Such concrete teaching styles, which are more prevalent in elementary school, should be incorporated more with ESL middle school students (Dunn & Dunn, 1993).

Focus on Process of Teaching

Teachers who tended to be better at meeting the learning needs of ESL students spent a lot of their time focused on their actual teaching strategies. These teachers had less tendency to blame the students for not learning and were always seeking to try different teaching strategies. These teachers focused on how their students learned, and they had knowledge of multiple intelligence theory and learning style theory. They could tell me about particular students' learning styles, and these teachers all tended to agree that their ESL students preferred a tactile and more kinesthetic mode of learning. These interactive teachers incorporated games into their lessons and used a variety of hands-on approaches to their subjects. Research on how ESL students learn clearly substantiates their tendency to be right brained, more holistic in their learning needs, and prefer to learn in groups (Banks, 2001; Krashen, 1996).

Based on what?

Evidence

Intuitive and Nonverbal Communication

According to these ESL students, the teachers who were successful in meeting their learning needs constantly gauged the reactions of students, constantly walked around the classroom, and sought out students instead of waiting for the students to raise their hands. The students appreciated this and respected those teachers more.

These teachers focused on the faces and relied on nonverbal communication from their students while teaching. They were more in tune to the frustrations of their ESL learners and tended to go to their desks and ask them if they needed help. The students liked this and really believed that an effective teacher would come to them and that they should not have to raise their hand. These teachers used more hands-on approaches to teach science, used flash cards or games to teach English grammar, and used more varied teaching methods to deliver the lessons. The interactive teachers used eye contact well and were constantly asking questions of all students, taking care to call on each student in class.

Effective strategies

The didactic teachers tended to stand at the blackboard or overhead projector and did not walk around the room. After the didactic teachers gave directions, silence ensued and the students were expected to work independently. ESL students who raised their hands for help were often not attended to by the teacher for several minutes and in some classes were totally ignored. The students did not like this kind of teacher and perceived that the teacher was "lazy" because he or she did not come to their desk to offer help.

Contrasting style

ESL students can sometimes appear shy in class and, consequently, their learning needs are sometimes ignored. It is important for teachers to recognize that some students may not ask for help and may prefer the teacher to initiate this at the middle school level.

Perhaps at all levels

Students and Teachers Actively Learning Together

The students liked teachers who used much verbal interaction, questioning for understanding, and conversation, all of which included both student-to-student and teacher-to-student interaction. All the students seemed to enjoy classrooms where there was less silence. In silent classrooms, the ESL students felt more isolated and expressed more fear of the teacher. The need to talk and ask peers questions and to have a teacher take them step-by-step through examples was important for these students.

They liked the teacher who walked them through a math problem or an assignment from beginning to end. They did not like figuring it out on their own. Doing a

How many?

couple of examples together, with the teacher explaining slowly and everyone working at the same pace, was important.

In some classrooms, the teachers had strong didactic teaching styles and did the majority of the talking, without interacting or questioning students. In these classrooms, silence was expected from all students, and there was a heavy reliance on worksheets or completed assignments from either the textbook or overhead projector. The ESL students I observed in these classrooms were often seated in rows, rarely called upon to answer, and worked independently to complete their seatwork. The class period generally consisted of the following formula, regardless of the subject being taught. The teacher gave quick verbal directions on the assigned material at the beginning of the class period; then students worked independently while the teacher sat behind a desk or graded papers. The teacher went over the answers with students who graded each other's papers. The teacher sometimes asked for grades aloud before recording them. Finally, if there was time left in the period, the teacher assigned another activity for the students to work on independently.

Clear

All the students in this study expressed to me that they did not find this didactic instructional practice particularly helpful. They explained to me that they did not like working independently in such silent classrooms where they felt they were unable to ask questions and get help from each other if needed. I observed that these students never raised their hands for help from teachers with a didactic teaching style. The students expressed to me that they were either too shy or afraid to ask questions of such teachers. The ESL students expressed to me that they preferred not to ask for more examples or explanations because the teachers got mad. Other students expressed to me that some teachers never even read or explained the assignments in class. They reported that they were left on their own to figure it out and often, as with Angel, were just referred to the dictionary if they did not understand a word or they asked the person beside them rather than upset a teacher who might be "busy doing something else." For Rosa, the "better" teachers, those who helped her the most, "never get mad at me. If I have trouble with something they help me."

Democratic Classroom Discipline Style

The ESL students preferred a teacher who had a more relaxed discipline style, who incorporated more talk and conversation and had less emphasis on maintaining a silent classroom. These students did not enjoy being in a classroom with a teacher who had discipline management problems. These students appreciated a teacher who had structure, order, and discipline mixed with humor and cooperative grouping. The interactive teachers, most preferred by these students, did not have classroom discipline problems. The students liked teachers who were more democratic, asked for their input, gave them choice in assignments, and "made exceptions" when it was appropriate.

Type

Mr. Bond, the most autocratic and didactic of the teachers in this study, always stood at the door as students entered and silently passed out ditto sheets. He always maintained strict silence in his room and told me, "Some students you may never get to know because they are so quiet, and they just come in and do their work and go home and that is just the way it is." This teacher did not build a relationship with his students, who came to fear him. The ESL students did not like this teacher because they felt that they never learned or were permitted to think in this class because they could never ask for help.

Type

The interactive teachers, like Mrs. O' Reilly, were comfortable with a democratic classroom management style and they promoted more of a classroom family atmosphere. These teachers used appropriate praise in class, conferenced with every student, and used humor to redirect off-task behaviors rather than harsher measures.

CONCLUSION

The picture that emerged was one in which ESL students perceived that interactive instructional models were more congruent with their learning needs than didactic ones. This picture reflects the educational research and literature which showed that many ESL and culturally diverse students prefer styles of inquiry and response different from the standard procedures used in many classrooms. ESL and culturally diverse students often have a global orientation to learning and are receptive to learning that is relational, holistic, and employs thematic approaches (Malloy, 1997). Visual and tactile learning modes are important for culturally and linguistically diverse students as well (Presmeg, 1989). How teachers ask questions is vital, because in many cultures, students are not used to being questioned (Strutchens, 1994). Time and waiting are important when asking questions to ESL students (Callahan, 1994). Use of cooperative work and heterogeneous grouping better suits the learning styles of linguistically and culturally diverse students (Malloy, 1997; Zaslavsky, 1993).

Behaviors?

Overall, a teaching model that incorporates more of the interactive characteristics better suits the learning styles of ESL students. This should be a consideration for principals and teachers as they mainstream ESL students into regular classrooms. Teachers who use more didactic teaching styles might need staff development to help them use more interactive strategies in their classrooms. Teaching should be viewed as a skill that is fluid and should be adapted and refined to meet the needs of students. This is especially important for ESL learners who are striving to practice and use a newly acquired language.

References

Banks, J. (2001). *Cultural diversity and education: Foundations, curriculum, and teaching* (4th ed.). Boston: Allyn & Bacon.

Callahan, W. (1994). Teaching middle school students with diverse cultural backgrounds. *The Mathematics Teacher, 87*, 122–126.

Crawford, J. (1991). *Bilingual education: History, politics, theory, and practice* (2nd ed.). Los Angeles: Bilingual Education Series.

Dunn, R., & Dunn, K. (1993). *Secondary students through their individual learning styles: Practical approaches for grades 7–11.* Boston: Allyn & Bacon.

Gersten, R. (1996). The language-minority student in transition: Contemporary instructional research. *The Elementary School Journal, 6*(3), 217–220.

Gibson, M. A. (1988). *Accommodation without assimilation: Sikh immigrants in an American high school.* Ithaca, NY: Cornell University Press.

Krashen, S. (1996). Is English in trouble? *Multicultural Education, 4*(2), 16–19.

Malloy, C. E. (1997). Including African American students in the mathematics community. In J. Trentacosta & M. J. Kenney (Eds.), *Multicultural and gender equity in the mathematics classroom: The gift of diversity* (pp. 23–33). Reston, VA: National Council of Teachers of Mathematics.

McKeon, D. (1994). When meeting "common" standards is uncommonly difficult. *Educational Leadership, 51*(8), 45–49.

National Clearinghouse for English Language Acquisition (NCELA). (2004). *The growing numbers of limited English proficient students, 1991/92-2001/02,* Retrieved July 6, 2004, from http://www.ncela.gwu.edu/states/stateposter/pdf

Nieto, S. (2000). *Affirming diversity: The sociopolitical context of multicultural education* (3rd ed.). New York: Addison Wesley Longman.

Ogbu, J. (1992). Understanding cultural diversity and learning. *Educational Researcher, 21*(8), 5–24.

Presmeg, N. C. (1989). Visualization in multicultural mathematics classrooms. *Focus on Learning Problems in Mathematics, 11*(1), 17–24.

Strutchens, M. (1994). The conflict between teacher and African American families. In M. M. Atwater, K. Radzik, & M. Strutchens (Eds.), *Muiticultural education: Inclusion of all* (pp: 257–270). Athens, GA: The University of Georgia. Available: SilverPlatter file. ERIC Item: 390–946.

Zaslavsky, C. (1993). Multicultural mathematics: One road to the goal of mathematics for all. In G. Cuevos & M. Driscoll (Eds.), *Reaching all students with mathematics* (pp. 45–55). Reston, VA: National Council of Teachers of Mathematics.

Analysis of the Study

PURPOSE/JUSTIFICATION

The stated purpose is "to gain some insight into the world of young adolescents and English (ESL) immigrant youth in the United States today." The study is clearly focused on perceptions of teacher behaviors.

Justification is based on research into the increasing numbers of ESL students and the need for assistance to their teachers. Citing more recent studies would have strengthened the study. There appear to be no problems of risk or deception. A question of confidentiality arises if student and teacher names were not changed.

DEFINITIONS

"ESL students" is not defined but clearly refers to students having English as a second language. The terms "interactive" and "didactic" teaching strategies are used throughout; they are clarified by extensive description in Figure 1.

HYPOTHESES

No hypotheses are stated, which is customary in ethnographic research. However, one seems to emerge during the study—that ESL students prefer "interactive" teaching behaviors.

SAMPLE

The convenience sample was six Mexican immigrant students, all in their third year in the United States. They were in seventh or eighth grade and described as fluent in English but struggling with content and vocabulary in their social studies, science, and English classes. All had spent two years in an ESL classroom and were currently mainstreamed for all or most of the school day with non-ESL teachers in an urban middle school in Texas. In ethnographic studies we expect more "thick description" (see text, p. 457). In this case, socioeconomic status, ethnicities, and percentage of ESL and free lunch students would have been helpful.

INSTRUMENTATION

Instrumentation consisted of nonparticipant observation and weekly interviews with the students and their teachers. It is evident in the main body of the report that at least one "structured" question was asked of students: "What do teachers do to help you learn best?" There are also examples of structured "follow-up" questions with both students and teachers. Beyond that, it is unclear to what extent structured questions, as opposed to an open-ended, informal approach (see p. 449), were used. More description of how interviews were conducted is needed (e.g., in English, Spanish or both). It appears that observations were done informally without a systematic guide. In one instance—encouraging students to help each other in Spanish—interview information is said to be supported by observations, which is a form of triangulation that lends strength to the results.

PROCEDURES/INTERNAL VALIDITY

No information on the details of data collection is provided. Presumably interviews were conducted in school. Internal validity is less important in a descriptive, exploratory study such as this. However, causal statements are made with respect to the two teaching models, clearly implying that the interactive model causes higher student "liking" and (in conclusion) student learning. Descriptive comments and examples lend plausibility to this, but the study provides no controls over the alternative explanations of other teacher characteristics and data collector bias.

DATA ANALYSIS

As is common in qualitative studies, no statistical data analysis was done. In some instances the terms "all" and "none" provide clarification, but further detail, such as specific counts or percentages, would have been helpful.

RESULTS/DISCUSSION

The results are presented in narrative form supported with examples. The reader must trust that these descriptions accurately reflect what was said and observed, as well as how frequently these occurred. Some assertions, such as "these ESL students were not auditory learners" seem unlikely to have come from interviews or observation.

Although the reference to "interactive" and "didactic" teaching models served to organize the information, their application here implies two recognizable types of teachers among those studied, without evidence that this is so. Perhaps the teachers could have been divided into these two groups, but there is no indication this step was taken. Descriptions of teacher behaviors fit quite well with Banks's model descriptions, but it is likely that individual teachers exhibited behaviors fitting both "types." A more tenable conclusion is that students preferred specific behaviors rather than an overall "type."

We think use of grounded theory (see p. 431) would have avoided this problem and made interpretations clearer. As noted, we think more detail on the school, the instrumentation process, and examples would have greatly strengthened the study. Nevertheless, we think it should alert teachers, particularly those with ESL students, to likely consequences of specific behaviors. The serious limitations of generalizing to other students and teachers are recognized by the author.

Go back to the **INTERACTIVE AND APPLIED LEARNING** feature at the beginning of the chapter for a listing of interactive and applied activities. Go to the **Online Learning Center** at **www.mhhe.com/fraenkel9e** to take quizzes, practice with key terms, and review chapter content.

Main Points

THE NATURE AND VALUE OF ETHNOGRAPHIC RESEARCH

- Ethnographic research is particularly appropriate for behaviors that are best understood by observing them within their natural settings.
- The key techniques in all ethnographic studies are in-depth interviewing and highly detailed, almost continual, ongoing participant observation of a situation.
- A key strength of ethnographic research is that it provides the researcher with a much more comprehensive perspective than do other forms of educational research.

ETHNOGRAPHIC CONCEPTS

- Important concepts in ethnographic research include culture, holistic perspective, thick description, contextualization, a nonjudgmental orientation, emic perspective, etic perspective, member checking, and multiple realities.

TOPICS THAT LEND THEMSELVES WELL TO ETHNOGRAPHIC RESEARCH

- Suitable topics include those that defy simple quantification; those that can best be understood in a natural setting; those that involve studying individual or group activities over time; those that involve studying the roles that individuals play and the behaviors associated with those roles; those that involve studying the activities and behaviors of groups as a unit; and those that involve studying formal organizations in their totality.

SAMPLING IN ETHNOGRAPHIC RESEARCH

- The sample in ethnographic studies is almost always purposive.
- The data obtained from ethnographic research samples rarely, if ever, permit generalization to a population.

THE USE OF HYPOTHESES IN ETHNOGRAPHIC RESEARCH

- Ethnographic researchers seldom formulate precise hypotheses ahead of time. Rather, they develop them as their study emerges.

DATA COLLECTION AND ANALYSIS IN ETHNOGRAPHIC RESEARCH

- The two major means of data collection in ethnographic research are participant observation and detailed interviewing.
- Researchers use a variety of instruments in ethnographic studies to collect data and to check validity. This is frequently referred to as *triangulation.*
- Analysis consists of continual reworking of data with emphasis on patterns, key events, and use of visual representations in addition to interviews and observations.

FIELDWORK

- Field notes are the notes a researcher in an ethnographic study takes in the field. They include both descriptive field notes (what he or she sees and hears) and reflective field notes (what he or she thinks about what has been observed).
- Field jottings refer to quick notes about something the researcher wants to write more about later.
- A field diary is a personal statement of the researcher's feelings and opinions about the people and situations being observed.
- A field log is a sort of running account of how the researcher plans to spend time compared to how he or she actually spends it.

ADVANTAGES AND DISADVANTAGES OF ETHNOGRAPHIC RESEARCH

- A key strength of ethnographic research is that it provides a much more comprehensive perspective than other forms of educational research. It lends itself well to topics that are not easily quantified. Also, it is particularly appropriate for studying behaviors best understood in their natural settings.
- Like all research, ethnographic research also has its limitations. It is highly dependent on the particular researcher's observations. Furthermore, some observer bias is almost impossible to eliminate. Lastly, generalization is practically nonexistent.

Key Terms

contextualization 507
crystallization 516
culture 507
descriptive field notes 511
emic perspective 508
ethnographic research 505
etic perspective 508
field diary 511
field jottings 510
field log 511
field notes 510
holistic perspective 507
interview 510
key event 515
member checking 508
multiple realities/ perspectives 508
participant observation 510
reflective field notes 512
thick description 508
triangulation 515

For Discussion

1. A major criticism of ethnographic research is that there is no way for the researcher to be totally objective about what he or she observes. Would you agree? What might an ethnographer say to rebut this charge?
2. Ethnographic studies are rarely replicated. Why do you suppose this is so? Might they be? If so, how?
3. What would you say is the most difficult aspect of ethnographic research? Why?

4. What do you think is the biggest advantage of ethnographic research? the biggest disadvantage? Explain your thinking.
5. Would you be willing to be a participant in an ethnographic study? Why or why not?
6. Supporters of qualitative research say that it can do something that no other type of research can do. If true, what might this be? Would this be especially true of ethnography?
7. Are there any kinds of information that other types of research can provide *better* than ethnographic research? If so, what might they be?
8. How would you compare ethnographic research to the other types of research we have discussed in this book in terms of difficulty? Explain your reasoning.

References

1. Bernard, H. R. (1994). *Research methods in cultural anthropology* (2nd ed., p. 137). Beverly Hills, CA: Sage.

2. Wolcott, H. F. (1966). Cited in Creswell, J. R. (2008). *Educational research: Planning, conducting, and evaluating qualitative and quantitative research* (3rd ed., p. 480). Columbus, OH: Merrill Prentice-Hall.

3. Stretesky, P. B., & Pogrebin, M. R. (2007). Gang-related gun violence: Socialization, identity, and self. *Contemporary Ethnography, 36*(2), 85–114.

4. Purser, G. (2009). The dignity of job-seeking men: Boundary work among immigrant day laborers. *Contemporary Ethnography, 38*(2), 117–139.

5. Jimerson, J. B., & Oware, M. K. (2006). Telling the code of the street: An ethnomethodological ethnography. *Contemporary Ethnography, 35*(2), 24–50.

6. Simpson, T. A. (2000). Streets, sidewalks, stores, and stories: Narrative and uses of urban space. *Contemporary Ethnography, 29*(12), 682–716.

7. Charmaz, K. (2006). The power of names. *Contemporary Ethnography, 35*(8), 396–399.

8. Jorgensen, E. R. (2009). On thick description and narrative inquiry in music education. *Research Studies in Music Education, 31*(6), 69–81.

9. Cusick, P. A. (1973). *Inside high school: The student's perspective.* New York: Holt, Rinehart & Winston.

10. Babbie, E. (2007). *The practice of social research* (11th ed.). Florence, KY: Wadsworth Cengage.

11. Harris, M. (2000). *The rise of anthropological theory: A history of theories of culture* (updated ed.). Lanham, MD: Altamira Press.

12. Fetterman, D. M. (1989). *Ethnography: Step by step* (2nd ed., p. 39). Thousand Oaks, CA: Sage.

13. Fetterman, D. M. (1989). *Ethnography: Step by step* (2nd ed., p. 40). Thousand Oaks, CA: Sage.

14. Fetterman, D. M. (1989). *Ethnography: Step by step* (2nd ed., p. 42). Thousand Oaks, CA: Sage.

15. Fetterman, D. M. (1989). *Ethnography: Step by step* (2nd ed., p. 44). Thousand Oaks, CA: Sage.

16. Fetterman, D. M. (1989). *Ethnography: Step by step* (2nd ed., p. 56). Thousand Oaks, CA: Sage.

17. Fetterman, D. M. (1989). *Ethnography: Step by step* (2nd ed., pp. 57, 58). Thousand Oaks, CA: Sage.

18. For a good description of field notes, see Bogdan, R. C., & Biklen, S. K. (2007). *Qualitative research in education: An introduction to theory and practice* (5th ed., chapter 4). Boston: Allyn & Bacon.

19. Bernard, H. R. (1994). *Research methods in cultural anthropology* (2nd ed., pp. 181–186). Beverly Hills, CA: Sage.

20. Bernard, H. R. (1994). *Research methods in cultural anthropology* (2nd ed., p. 185). Beverly Hills, CA: Sage.

21. Bogdan, R. C., & Biklen, S. K. (2007). *Qualitative research in education: An introduction to theory and practice* (5th ed., p. 120). Boston: Allyn & Bacon.

22. Bogdan, R. C., & Biklen, S. K. (2007). *Qualitative research in education: An introduction to theory and practice* (5th ed., pp. 260–270). Boston: Allyn & Bacon.

23. Fetterman, D. M. (1989). *Ethnography: Step by step* (2nd ed., pp. 104–105). Thousand Oaks, CA: Sage.

24. Fetterman, D. M. (1989). *Ethnography: Step by step* (2nd ed., p. 106). Thousand Oaks, CA: Sage.

25. Fetterman, D. M. (1989). *Ethnography: Step by step* (2nd ed., p. 112). Thousand Oaks, CA: Sage.

26. Spindler, G. (1982). Doing the ethnography of schooling: Educational anthropology in action. New York: Holt, Rinehart and Winston.

22 Historical Research

What Is Historical Research?

The Purposes of Historical Research

What Kinds of Questions Are Pursued Through Historical Research?

Steps Involved in Historical Research

Defining the Problem

Locating Relevant Sources

Summarizing Information Obtained from Historical Sources

Evaluating Historical Sources

Data Analysis in Historical Research

Generalization in Historical Research

Advantages and Disadvantages of Historical Research

An Example of Historical Research

Analysis of the Study

Purpose/Justification

Definitions

Prior Research

Hypotheses

Sample

Instrumentation

Procedures/Internal Validity

Data Analysis

Results/Discussion

"I'm analyzing early records to determine when men and women first started having disagreements about things."
"Good luck! I assume you're starting with Genesis?"

OBJECTIVES Studying this chapter should enable you to:

- Describe briefly what historical research involves.
- State three purposes of historical research.
- Give examples of the kinds of questions investigated in historical research.
- Name and describe briefly the major steps involved in historical research.
- Give examples of historical sources.
- Distinguish between primary and secondary sources.
- Distinguish between external and internal criticism.
- Discuss when generalization in historical research is appropriate.
- Locate examples of published historical studies and critique some of the strengths and weaknesses of these studies.
- Recognize an example of a historical study when you come across one in the literature.

INTERACTIVE AND APPLIED LEARNING After, or while, reading this chapter:

Go to the Online Learning Center at www.mhhe.com/fraenkel9e to:

- Learn More About Primary vs. Secondary Sources

Go to your online Student Mastery Activities book to do the following activities:

- Activity 22.1: Historical Research Questions
- Activity 22.2: Primary or Secondary Source?
- Activity 22.3: What Kind of Historical Source?
- Activity 22.4: True or False?

"Hey Becky!"

"Hey, Brent, where ya' been?"

"Library. Trying to come up with a topic for my research study."

"How's it going?"

"Pretty good. I think I have an idea. You know, they want to introduce this new reading program—sort of a modified 'look-say' approach—in some of the elementary schools in our district next year, but I sort of have my doubts about it."

"How come?"

"Well, the administration keeps praising it to the skies, but I haven't seen any evidence that it will work any better than the program we now use. Plus it's pretty expensive. I'm on the curriculum advisory council, you know, and I'd like to find out whether it's as effective as they say before we recommend spending a lot of money to buy all of the program materials. So . . ."

"Hey. Sounds like you've found your topic. Some kind of study of the program's past effectiveness (or lack thereof) might be just the ticket, eh?"

"Right! A little historical research is called for here, I think."

We agree. Brent might indeed do a historical study, or perhaps locate one that has already been done. What this involves is what this chapter is about.

What Is Historical Research?

Historical research takes a somewhat different tack from much of the other research we have described. There is, of course, no manipulation or control of variables like there is in experimental research, but more particularly, it is unique in that it focuses primarily on the *past.* As we mentioned in Chapter 1, some aspect of the past is studied by perusing documents of the period, by examining relics, or by interviewing individuals who lived during the time. An attempt is then made to reconstruct what happened during that time as completely and as accurately as possible and (usually) to explain why it happened—although this can never be fully accomplished since information from and about the past is always incomplete. **Historical research**, then, is the systematic collection and evaluation of data to describe, explain, and thereby understand actions or events that occurred sometime in the past.

THE PURPOSES OF HISTORICAL RESEARCH

Educational researchers undertake historical studies for a variety of reasons:

1. To make people aware of what has happened in the past so they may learn from past failures and successes. A researcher might be interested, for example, in investigating why a particular curriculum modification (such as a new inquiry-oriented English curriculum) succeeded in some school districts but not in others.
2. To learn how things were done in the past to see if they might be applicable to present-day problems and concerns. Rather than "reinventing the wheel," for example, it often may be wiser to look to the

past to see if a proposed innovation has been tried before. Sometimes an idea proposed as "a radical innovation" is not all that new. Along this line, the review of literature that we discussed in detail in Chapter 3, which is done as a part of many other kinds of studies, is a kind of historical research. Often a review of the literature will show that what we think is new has been done before (and, surprisingly, many times!).

3. To assist in prediction. If a particular idea or approach has been tried before, even under somewhat different circumstances, past results may offer policy makers some ideas about how present plans may turn out. Thus, if language laboratories have been found effective (or the reverse) in certain school districts in the past, a district contemplating their use would have evidence on which to base its own decisions.
4. To test hypotheses concerning relationships or trends. Many inexperienced researchers tend to think of historical research as purely descriptive in nature. When well designed and carefully executed, however, historical research can lead to the confirmation or rejection of relational hypotheses as well. Here are some examples of hypotheses that would lend themselves to historical research:
   a. In the early 1900s, most female teachers came from the upper middle class, but most male teachers did not.
   b. Curriculum changes that did not involve extensive planning and participation by the teachers involved usually failed.
   c. Nineteenth-century social studies textbooks show increasing reference to the contributions of women to the culture of the United States from 1800 to 1900.
   d. Secondary school teachers have enjoyed greater prestige than elementary school teachers since 1940.

   Many other hypotheses are possible, of course; the ones here are intended to illustrate only that historical research can lend itself to hypothesis-testing studies.
5. To understand present educational practices and policies more fully. Many current practices in education are by no means new. Inquiry teaching, character education, open classrooms, an emphasis on "basics," Socratic teaching, the use of case studies, individualized instruction, team teaching, and teaching "laboratories" are but a few of many ideas that reappear from time to time as "the" salvation for education.

WHAT KINDS OF QUESTIONS ARE PURSUED THROUGH HISTORICAL RESEARCH?

Although historical research focuses on the past, the types of questions that lend themselves to historical research are quite varied. Here are some examples:

- How were students educated in the South during the Civil War?
- How many bills dealing with education were passed during the presidency of Lyndon B. Johnson, and what was the major intent of those bills?
- What was instruction like in a typical fourth-grade classroom 100 years ago?
- How have working conditions for teachers changed since 1900?
- What were the major discipline problems in schools in 1940 as compared to today?
- What educational issues has the general public perceived to be most important during the last 20 years?
- How have the ideas of John Dewey influenced present-day educational practices?
- How have feminists contributed to education?
- How were minorities (or the physically impaired) treated in our public schools during the twentieth century?
- How were the policies and practices of school administrators in the early years of the twentieth century different from those today?
- What has been the role of the federal government in education?

Steps Involved in Historical Research?

Four essential steps are involved in a historical study in education. These include defining the problem or question to be investigated (including the formulation of hypotheses if appropriate), locating relevant sources of historical information, summarizing and evaluating the information obtained from these sources, and presenting and interpreting this information as it relates to the problem or question that originated the study.

DEFINING THE PROBLEM

In the simplest sense, the purpose of a historical study in education is to describe clearly and accurately some aspect of the past as it related to education and/or schooling. As we mentioned previously, however, historical researchers aim to do more than just describe; they want to go beyond description to clarify and explain and sometimes to correct (as when a researcher finds previous accounts of an action or event to be in error).

Historical research problems, therefore, are identified in much the same way as are problems studied through other types of research. Like any research problem, they should be clearly and concisely stated, be manageable, have a defensible rationale, and (if appropriate) investigate a hypothesized relationship among variables. A concern somewhat unique to historical research is that a problem may be selected for study for which insufficient data are available. Often important data of interest (certain kinds of documents, such as diaries or maps from a particular period) simply cannot be located in historical research. This is particularly true the farther back in the past an investigator looks. As a result, it is better to study in depth a well-defined problem that is perhaps more narrow than one would like than to pursue a more broadly stated problem that cannot be sharply defined or fully resolved. As with all research, the nature of the problem or hypothesis guides the study; if it is well defined, the investigator is off to a good start.

Some examples of historical studies that have been published are:

- "Shakespeare Under Different Flags: The Bard in German Classrooms from Hitler to Honecker"[1]
- "A Better Crop of Boys and Girls: The School Gardening Movement, 1890–1920"[2]
- "Making Broad Shoulders: Body-building and Physical Culture in Chicago, 1890–1920"[3]
- "Beyond Civics and the 3 R's: Teaching Economics in the Schools"[4]
- "Education and Marginality: Race and Gender in Higher Education"[5]
- "Science World, High School Girls, and the Prospect of Scientific Careers"[6]
- "Indian Heart/White Man's Head: Native-American Teachers in Indian Schools"[7]
- "The Emergence of the American University: An International Perspective"[8]

LOCATING RELEVANT SOURCES

Categories of Sources. Once a researcher has decided on the problem or question he or she wishes to investigate, the search for sources begins. Just about everything that has been written down in some form or other, and virtually every object imaginable, is a potential source for historical research. In general, however, historical source material can be grouped into four basic categories: documents, numerical records, oral statements and records, and relics.

1. *Documents:* **Documents** are written or printed materials that have been produced in some form or another—annual reports, artwork, bills, books, cartoons, circulars, court records, diaries, diplomas, legal records, newspapers, magazines, notebooks, school yearbooks, memos, tests, and so on. They may be handwritten, printed, typewritten, drawn, or sketched; they may be published or unpublished; they may be intended for private or public consumption; they may be original works or copies. In short, *documents* refers to any kind of information that exists in some type of written or printed form.
2. *Numerical records:* Numerical records can be considered either as a separate type of source in and of themselves or as a subcategory of documents. Such records include any type of numerical data in printed form: test scores, attendance figures, census reports, school budgets, and the like. In recent years, historical researchers are making increasing use of computers to analyze the vast amounts of numerical data that are available to them.
3. *Oral statements:* Another valuable source of information for the historical researcher are the statements people make orally. Stories, myths, tales, legends, chants, songs, and other forms of oral expression have been used by people through the ages to leave a record for future generations. But historians can also conduct *oral interviews* with people who were a part of or witnessed past events. This is a special form of historical research, called *oral history,* which is currently undergoing somewhat of a renaissance.
4. *Relics:* The fourth type of historical source is the relic. A **relic** is any object whose physical or visual characteristics can provide some information about the past. Examples include furniture, artwork, clothing, buildings, monuments, or equipment.

Following are different examples of historical sources.

- A primer used in a seventeenth-century schoolroom
- A diary kept by a woman teacher on the Ohio frontier in the 1800s
- The written arguments for and against a new school bond issue as published in a newspaper at a particular time
- A 1958 junior high school yearbook
- Samples of clothing worn by students in the early nineteenth century in rural Georgia
- High school graduation diplomas from the 1920s
- A written memo from a school superintendent to his faculty
- Attendance records from two different school districts over a 40-year period
- Essays written by elementary school children during the Civil War
- Test scores attained by students in various states at different times
- The architectural plans for a school to be organized around flexible scheduling
- A taped oral interview with a secretary of education who served in the administrations of three different U.S. presidents
- A paid consultant's written evaluation of a new French curriculum adopted in 1985 by a particular school district
- A photograph of an eighth-grade graduating class in 1930
- Letters written between an American student and a Japanese student describing their school experiences during the Korean conflict

Primary Versus Secondary Sources. As in all research, it is important to distinguish between primary and secondary sources. A **primary source** is one prepared by an individual who was a participant in or a direct witness to the event being described. An eyewitness account of the opening of a new school would be an example, as would a researcher's report of the results of his or her own experiment. Other examples of primary source material are:

- A nineteenth-century teacher's account of what it was like to live with a frontier family
- A transcript of an oral interview conducted in the 1960s with the superintendent of a large urban school district concerning the problems his district faces
- Essays written during World War II by students in response to the question, "What do you like most and least about school?"
- Songs composed by members of a high school glee club in the 1930s
- Minutes of a school board meeting in 1878, taken by the secretary of the board

A **secondary source**, on the other hand, is a document prepared by an individual who was not a direct witness to an event but who obtained the description of the event from someone else. They are "one step removed," so to speak, from the event. A newspaper editorial commenting on a recent teachers' strike would be an example. Other examples of secondary source material are:

- An encyclopedia entry describing various types of educational research conducted over a 10-year period
- A magazine article summarizing Aristotle's views on education
- A newspaper account of a school board meeting based on oral interviews with members of the board
- A book describing schooling in the New England colonies during the 1700s
- A parent's description of a conversation (at which she was not present) between her son and his teacher
- A student's report to her counselor of why her teacher said she was being suspended from school
- A textbook (including this one) on educational research

Whenever possible, historians (like other researchers) want to use primary rather than secondary sources. Can you see why?* Unfortunately, primary sources are admittedly more difficult to acquire, especially the further back in time a researcher searches. Secondary sources are of necessity, therefore, used quite extensively in historical research. If it is at all possible, however, the use of primary sources is preferred.

SUMMARIZING INFORMATION OBTAINED FROM HISTORICAL SOURCES

The process of reviewing and extracting data from historical sources is essentially the one described in

*When researchers must rely on secondary data sources, they increase the chance of the data being less detailed and/or less accurate. The accuracy of what is being reported also becomes more difficult to check.

Chapter 3—determining the relevancy of the particular material to the question or problem being investigated; recording the full bibliographic data of the source; organizing the data one collects under categories related to the problem being studied; and summarizing pertinent information (important facts, quotations, and questions) on note cards.

For an example of organizing data, consider a study investigating the daily activities that occurred in nineteenth-century elementary schoolrooms. A researcher might organize the facts under such categories as "subjects taught," "learning activities," "play activities," and "class rules."

Reading and summarizing historical data is rarely, if ever, a neat, orderly sequence of steps to be followed, however. Often reading and writing are interspersed. Edward J. Carr, a noted historian, provides the following description of how historians engage in research:

> [A common] assumption [among lay people] appears to be that the historian divides his work into two sharply distinguishable phases or periods. First, he spends a long preliminary period reading his sources and filling his notebooks with facts; then, when this is over he puts away his sources, takes out his notebooks, and writes his book from beginning to end. This is to me an unconvincing and unplausible picture. For myself, as soon as I have got going on a few of what I take to be the capital sources, the itch becomes too strong and I begin to write—not necessarily at the beginning, but somewhere, anywhere. Thereafter, reading and writing go on simultaneously. The writing is added to, subtracted from, re-shaped, and cancelled, as I go on reading. The reading is guided and directed and made fruitful by the writing; the more I write, the more I know what I am looking for, the better I understand the significance and relevance of what I find.[9]

EVALUATING HISTORICAL SOURCES

Perhaps more so than in any other form of research, the historical researcher must adopt a critical attitude toward any and all sources reviewed. A researcher can never be sure about the genuineness and accuracy of historical sources. A memo may have been written by someone other than the person who signed it. A letter may refer to events that did not occur or that occurred at a different time or in a different place. A document may have been forged or information deliberately falsified. Key questions for any historical researcher are:

- Was this document really written by the supposed author (i.e., is it *genuine*)?
- Is the information contained in this document true (i.e., is it *accurate*)?

The first question refers to what is known as *external criticism,* the second to what is known as *internal criticism.*

External Criticism.

External criticism refers to the genuineness of any and all documents the researcher uses. Researchers engaged in historical research want to know whether or not the documents they find were really prepared by the (supposed) author(s) of the document. Obviously, falsified documents can (and sometimes do) lead to erroneous conclusions. Several questions come to mind in evaluating the genuineness of a historical source.

- *Who* wrote this document? Was the author living at that time? Some historical documents have been shown to be *forgeries.* An article supposedly written by, say, Martin Luther King, Jr., might actually have been prepared by someone wishing to tarnish his reputation.
- *For what purpose* was the document written? For whom was it intended? And why? (Toward whom was a memo from a school superintendent directed? What was the intent of the memo?)
- *When* was the document written? Is the date on the document accurate? Could the details described have actually happened during this time? (Sometimes people write the date of the previous year on correspondence in the first days of a new year.)
- *Where* was the document written? Could the details described have occurred in this location? (A description of an inner-city school supposedly written by a teacher in Fremont, Nebraska, might well be viewed with caution.)
- *Under what conditions* was the document written? Is there any possibility that what was written might have been directly or subtly coerced? (A description of a particular school's curriculum and administration prepared by a committee of nontenured teachers might give quite a different view from one written by those who have tenure.)
- Do *different forms or versions* of the document exist? (Sometimes two versions of a letter are found with

CONTROVERSIES IN RESEARCH

Should Historians Influence Policy?

A recurring controversy in the history of education involves the relationship of history to educational policy. Here is what one scholar recently had to say about the issue: "For historians of education, is political relevance achieved at the expense of academic respectability? Should educational historians involve themselves in discussions of policy and, if so, how?"* David Tyack, a noted historian, replied as follows: "Do historians have anything to contribute to educational policy? Many think not, including some educational historians who fear that 'presentism' will corrupt the disinterestedness of the scholar. That may be, but there is a problem: Everybody uses some kind of history, if only personal memory, in making sense of the world. The question is not whether to use history in policy-making, but whether that history is going to be as accurate as possible. Historians surely do not have policy genes. They do have special knowledge, however, that might prove useful. In educational reform, for example, there is a whole storehouse of experiments to explore for a sense of what works and does not and why. Luckily, it is cheap to learn from those experiments and they don't harm living people."† (We assume this quote refers to naturally occurring "experiments," rather than true experiments.)

What do you think? Should educational historians involve themselves in discussions of policy?

*Mahoney, K. (2000). New times, new questions. *Educational Researcher, 29,* 18–19.

†Tyack, D. (2000). Reflections on histories of U.S. education. *Educational Researcher, 2,* 19–20.

nearly identical wording and only slight differences in handwriting, suggesting that one may be a forgery.)

The important thing to remember with regard to external criticism is that researchers should do their best to ensure that the documents they are using are genuine. The preceding questions (and others like them) are directed toward this end.

Internal Criticism. Once researchers have satisfied themselves that a source document is genuine, they need to determine if the *contents* of the document are *accurate.* This involves what is known as **internal criticism**. Both the accuracy of the information contained in a document and the truthfulness of the author need to be evaluated. Whereas external criticism has to do with the nature or authenticity of the document itself, internal criticism has to do with what the document says. Is it likely that what the author says happened really did happen? Would people at that time have behaved as they are portrayed? Could events have occurred this way? Are the data presented (attendance records, budget figures, test scores, and so on) reasonable? Note, however, that researchers should not dismiss a statement as inaccurate just because it is unlikely—unlikely events do occur. What researchers must determine is whether a particular event *might* have occurred, even if it is unlikely. As with external criticism, several questions need to be asked in attempting to evaluate the accuracy of a document and the truthfulness of its author.

1. *With regard to the author of the document:*
   - Was the author *present* at the event he or she is describing? In other words, is the document a primary or a secondary source? As we mentioned before, primary sources are preferred over secondary sources because they usually (though not always) are considered to be more accurate.
   - Was the author a *participant* in or an *observer* of the event? In general, we might expect an observer to present a more detached and comprehensive view of an event than a participant. Eyewitnesses do differ in their accounts of the same event, however, and hence the statements of an observer are not necessarily more accurate than those of a participant.
   - Was the author *competent* to describe the event? This refers to the qualifications of the author. Was he or she an expert on whatever is being described or discussed? an interested observer? a passerby?
   - Was the author *emotionally involved* in the event? The wife of a fired teacher, for example, might well give a distorted view of the teacher's contributions to the profession.
   - Did the author have any *vested interest* in the outcomes of the event? Might he or she have a grievance, or possibly be biased in some way? A student who continually was in disagreement with his teacher, for example, might tend to describe the teacher more negatively than would the teacher's colleagues.

2. *With regard to the contents of the document:*
   - Do the contents make *sense* (i.e., given the nature of the events described, does it seem reasonable that they could have happened as portrayed)?
   - Could the event described have occurred *at that time?* For example, a researcher might justifiably be suspicious of a document describing a World War II battle that took place in 1946.
   - Would people have behaved as described? A major danger here is what is known as *presentism*—ascribing present-day beliefs, values, and ideas to people who lived at another time. A somewhat related problem is that of *historical hindsight.* Just because we know how an event came out does not mean that people who lived before or during the occurrence of an event believed an outcome would turn out the way it did.
   - Does the language of the document suggest a *bias* of any sort? Is it emotionally charged, intemperate, or otherwise slanted in a particular way? Might the ethnicity, gender, religion, political party, socioeconomic status, or position of the author suggest a particular orientation (Figure 22.1)? For example, a teacher's account of a school board meeting in which a pay raise was voted down might differ from one of the board member's accounts.
   - Do *other versions* of the event exist? Do they present a different description or interpretation of what happened? But note that just because the majority of observers of an event agree about what happened, this does not mean they are necessarily always right. On more than one occasion, a minority view has proved to be correct.

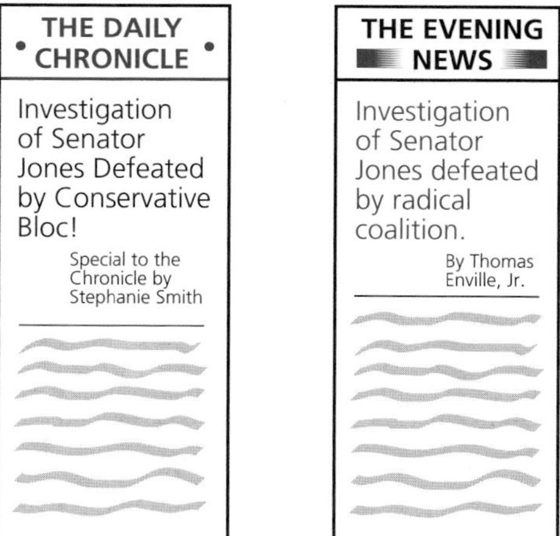

Figure 22.1 *What Really Happened?*

Data Analysis in Historical Research

As is the case with other types of qualitative research, historical researchers must find ways to make sense out of what is usually a very large amount of data and then synthesize it into a meaningful narrative of their own. Some prefer to operate from a theoretical model that helps them organize the information they have collected and may even suggest categories for a content analysis. Others prefer to immerse themselves in their information until patterns or themes suggest themselves. A coding system may be useful in doing so. Some historians have used quantitative data, such as crime and unemployment rates, to validate interpretations derived from documents.[10]

Generalization in Historical Research

Can researchers engaged in historical research generalize from their findings? It depends. As perhaps is obvious to you, historical researchers are rarely, if ever, able to study an entire population of individuals or events. They usually have little choice but to study a sample of the phenomena of interest. And the sample studied is determined by the historical sources that remain from the past. This is a particular problem for the historian, because almost always certain documents, relics, and other sources are missing, have been lost, or otherwise cannot be found. Those sources that are available perhaps are not representative of all the possible sources that did exist.

Suppose, for example, that a researcher is interested in understanding how social studies was taught in high schools in the late 1800s. She is limited to studying whatever sources remain from that time. The researcher may locate several textbooks of the period, plus assignment books, lesson plans, tests, letters and other correspondence written by teachers, and their diaries, all from this period. On the basis of a careful review of this source material, the researcher draws some conclusions about the nature of social studies teaching at that time. The researcher needs to take care to remember, however, that all of these

MORE ABOUT RESEARCH

Important Findings in Historical Research

Perhaps the best-known example of historical research that is pertinent to education is a series of studies begun in 1934 by the German sociologist Max Weber, who offered the theory that religion was a major cause of social behavior and, in particular, of economic capitalism.* A more recent example of such studies is that of Robert N. Bellah, who examined historical documents pertaining to Japanese religion during the late 1800s and early 1900s.† He concluded that several emergent religious beliefs, including the desirability of hard work and the acceptance of being a businessman, heretofore a low-status role, were instrumental in setting the stage for the growth of capitalism in Japan. These conclusions paralleled those of Weber's earlier studies of Calvinism in Europe. Weber also concluded that capitalism failed to develop in the early societies of China, Israel, and India because none of their religious doctrines supported the essential capitalist idea of accumulation and reinvestment of wealth as a sign of worthiness.

*Weber, M. (1958). *The Protestant ethic and the spirit of capitalism.* Translated by T. Parsons. New York: Charles Scribner and Sons.

†Bellah, R.N. (1967). Research chronicle: Tokugawa religion. In P. E. Hammond (Ed.), *Sociologists at work.* Garden City, NY: Anchor Books, pp. 164–185.

are written sources—and they may reflect quite a different view from that held by people who were not inclined to write down their thoughts, ideas, or assignments. What might the researcher do? As with all research, the validity of any generalizations that are drawn can be strengthened by increasing the size and diversity of the sample of data on which the generalizations are based. For those historical studies that involve the study of quantitative records, computers have made it possible, in many instances, for a researcher to draw a representative sample of data from large groups of students, teachers, and others who are represented in school records, test scores, census reports, and other documents.

Advantages and Disadvantages of Historical Research

The principal advantage of historical research is that it permits investigation of topics and questions that can be studied in no other way. It is the only research method that can study evidence from the past in relation to questions such as those presented earlier in the chapter. In addition, historical research can make use of a wider range of evidence than most other methods (with the possible exceptions of ethnographic and case-study research). It thus provides an alternative and perhaps richer source of information on certain topics that can also be studied with other methodologies. A researcher might, for example, wish to investigate the hypothesis that "curriculum changes that did not involve extensive planning and participation by the teachers involved usually fail(ed)" by collecting interview or observational data on groups of teachers who (1) have and (2) have not participated in developing curricular changes (a causal-comparative study), or by arranging for variations in teacher participation (an experimental study). The question might also be studied, however, by examining documents prepared over the past 50 years by disseminators of new curricula (their reports), by teachers (their diaries), and so forth.

A disadvantage of historical research is that the measures used in other methods to control for threats to internal validity are simply not possible in a historical study. Limitations imposed by the nature of the sample of documents and the instrumentation process (content analysis) are likely to be severe. Researchers cannot ensure representativeness of the sample, nor can they (usually) check the reliability and validity of the inferences made from the data available. Depending on the question studied, all or many of the threats to internal validity we discussed in Chapter 9 are likely to exist. The possibility of bias due to researcher characteristics (in data collection and analysis) is always present. The possibility that any observed relationships are due to a threat involving subject characteristics (the individuals on whom information exists), implementation, history, maturation,

Figure 22.2 *Historical Research Is Not as Easy as You May Think!*

attitude, or location also is always present. Although any particular threat depends on the nature of a particular study, methods for its control are unfortunately unavailable to the researcher. Because so much depends on the skill and integrity of the researcher—since methodological controls are unavailable—we believe that historical research is among the most difficult of all types of research to conduct (Figure 22.2).

Doing historical research requires much more than digging up good material; done properly it can demand a broader array of skills than other methods. The historian may find she needs some of the skills of a linguist, chemist, or archaeologist. Further, since history is admittedly highly interpretive in a global sense, knowledge of psychology, anthropology, and other disciplines may also be required.

An Example of Historical Research

In the remainder of this chapter, we present a published example of historical research, followed by a critique of its strengths and weaknesses. As we did in our critiques of the different types of research studies we analyzed in other chapters, we use several of the concepts introduced in earlier parts of the book in our analysis.

From: (2000, Summer). *The Journal of Psychohistory 28*(1), 62–71.

Lydia Ann Stow: Self-Actualization in a Period of Transition

Vivian C. Fox
Worcester State College

This paper is concerned with a crucial period of self-actualization in the life of Lydia Ann Stow (1823–1904), an early nineteenth century Massachusetts woman who illustrates the interactions between adolescent development and the dynamics of reforms in education and feminism. The term "self-actualization" is adopted from Frederic L. Bender, who defines this Marxian concept as "the development of one's talents and abilities and, the pursuit of one's life interests in and through one's work."[1] Although self-actualization appears to be a highly individualized process, it always occurs in a larger social context. It is crucial to emphasize this in Lydia Stow's case since the most relevant context for her self-actualization was highly transitional in two important respects, namely, the development of educational theory and practice, and the evolution in the status of women.

The major source for describing Stow's self-actualization is the set of four Journals which she kept during the period of her training in Massachusetts as a professional teacher at the Lexington Normal School, and for about two years thereafter (July 8, 1839–February 23, 1843).[2]

In this paper I undertake a brief description of the contextual events before proceeding to an analysis of the Journals. I would like to start with school reform.

Definitions

Purpose?

Primary source

SCHOOL REFORM

Independent variable

The process of school reform *that played such an important role* in Lydia's life was itself a reflection of a panoply of post-Revolution concerns. To some, the advent of technology was altering New England's predominantly rural work patterns through the construction of factories and railroads. Cities were growing larger, more varied, and increasingly sinister with vast numbers of immigrant-strangers, prostitutes and salesmen of magical drug products. The new arrivals were, moreover, largely untrained, uneducated and non-Anglo-Saxon men who appeared quickly to acquire political power at the ballot box. In view of these cascading changes, many wondered whether the glorious achievements of the Revolution could be maintained.[3]

To some, the appropriate response to these issues was in the direction of ensuring an educated citizenry. Leaders in this movement emerged in the Northeast, particularly in Massachusetts. Such Massachusetts men as Horace Mann, James G. Carter, Edward Everett, Edmund Dwight, Cyrus Peirce, and Henry Barnard who was from New York, supported the idea that a key to confronting post-Revolutionary challenges was in the field of educational reform.[4]

Background

James G. Carter, for example, while Chairman of the Committee on Education of the Massachusetts House of Representatives, successfully established himself as the architect of an educational renaissance that included creation of a state-wide Board of Education. Horace Mann was appointed in 1837 as the first Secretary of the Board.[5]

Mann immediately launched a crusade, which continued during his twelve years of incumbency, from which his ideas spread throughout the nation. His accomplishments included a proliferation of the common schools, an expansion of their curriculum, and the training of teachers in new approaches to teaching which encompassed a new philosophy of learning and moral discipline.[6]

He accepted the Republican view, moreover, that popular education was necessary for the intellectual and monetary enhancement of citizens which would contribute to the general well-being of the Republic. His beliefs emphasized that the new Republic required a high standard of morality in order to eliminate, as he put it, "the long catalogue of human ills."[7]

Central to achieving educational reform and progress was the provision of professional training for school teachers. Prior to this time, little or no training was required and persons with a minimal amount of education could take charge of classrooms.

Reference needed

Many of the ideas of Mann and his colleagues were obtained from Europe, especially from Prussia. Unlike its European counterparts, however, professional teacher training in what were called the Normal Schools (a title derived from the French École Normale) was open to females. In 1838 Massachusetts adopted a law authorizing the establishment of three Normal Schools. The first appeared in Lexington in 1839, and in accordance with the statute it was open only to females. The other two, in Barre and Bridgewater in 1840, were co-educational. Lydia was a member of the first class to enroll in Lexington.

Speaking for many reformers, Horace Mann emphasized the importance of employing female teachers.

> *Education . . . is woman's work. . . . Let woman, then be educated to the highest practicable point; not only because it is her right, but because it is essential to the world's progress. Let her voice be a familiar voice in the schools and the academies, and in halls of learning and science.*[8]

Primary source

Mann was not, of course, the first to recognize appropriate roles for women in the educational enterprise. By the last part of the eighteenth century, for example, New England clergymen, struck by the greater church attendance of women, intoned that females were purer and more delicate than men, and advocated greater exposure to education for them as caretakers of the very young.[9] From the latter part of the eighteenth century, then, sons as well as daughters came to be under the pedagogy of their mothers, unlike in the prior period when fathers became responsible for the education of boys when they reached the age of seven. The assumption that women had special moral strengths—that they were "angels in the house"—gave them important credentials for both domestic and professional teaching roles.[10]

The call for women's education grew stronger as post-Revolutionary ideology expressed the sentiment that in a Republic, school education must become available to all citizens, both male and female. Boston, for example, allowed girls to be educated in its grammar school in 1789; and Dedham, Lydia's hometown, had already anticipated this as early as the 1750s. In a highly unusual development, one Mary Green was so successful a teacher that she was added to the permanent Dedham teaching staff.[11]

Clearly, when Lydia enrolled at Lexington she was riding the crest of unique educational opportunities. As detailed in the next section, this enhanced status of women as educators of the young was also strongly strengthened by demographic and economic conditions of the time.

We agree

Now I want to discuss the matter of gender reform.

GENDER REFORM

At the same time that Mann and the other reformers were reconstructing the field of education so as to create new opportunities for women, their legal, social and economic circumstances generally were, paradoxically, much against the enhancement of their status. New England continued to follow common law and Christian traditions. These acknowledged the husband to be the head of the household who controlled the landed and personal property of the wife, as well as the wages she might earn. Although white women were legally considered citizens, they were prohibited from most public activities. They could not vote, sit on juries, execute wills, or serve as guardians of their children upon the death of their husbands; and most professions were not open to them.[12]

Secondary source

But there were currents of change as well, and nothing illustrated this better than the opportunities presented to Lydia. In addition to teaching, the newly created New England textile factories welcomed women, as did many of the developing reform movements such as temperance, abolition, and child welfare. Women such as Harriet Beecher Stowe and Louisa May Alcott entered the ranks of professional writers.[13]

Independent variable

Much of this might be explained by demography. From about the end of the eighteenth century, New England generally and Massachusetts in particular experienced an imbalance in the demographic ratio of the sexes in favor of women. This presented the question of how some of these "surplus women," as they were called, would be supported.[14] The problem was further exacerbated by the many new work opportunities for men, such as those that opened in the west and were created by the industrial revolution. An appropriate response to the shortage of male workers was to provide the new opportunities for working class women that have already been noted.[15]

Hypothetical speculation

But there were other less tangible forces at work as well that contributed to the gender evolution that Lydia found herself in. A number of women sensed that they were experiencing a shift in their fortunes. Lucy Larcom, for example, a Massachusetts factory worker during Lydia's time, expressed such a view in her autobiography.

> *[In] the olden times it was seldom said to little girls, as it always has been to boys, that they ought to have some definite plan, while they were children, what to be and do when they were grown up. . . . But when I was growing up, we were often told that it was our duty to develop any talent one might possess, or at least to learn how to do some one thing which the world needed, or which would make it a pleasanter world.*[16]

Primary source

Although when Lydia enrolled at Lexington, legal changes in the status of women were still in the future, the social ecology of women was certainly different from what it had been traditionally. Self-actualization was a possibility.

Interpretation

Dependent variable

LYDIA'S SELF-ACTUALIZATION

I have already mentioned that Lydia's four Journals are the primary source for conclusions concerning self-actualization. The first two of these chronologically were written while she was in residence at Lexington. The latter two were penned after she returned to Dedham having been graduated from Lexington.

The Journals were not a personal indulgence. Keeping them was a daily requirement for all pupils, containing a summary of the day's lectures and reading. Lydia's Journals appear to be unique in their inclusion of personal remarks concerning her responses to the lectures and reading, and evaluations of her own abilities and activities.[17] It was a weekly requirement that the Journals be turned in to the Principal, Cyrus Peirce, who would return them with his comments.

Argues for validity

The four Journals as a whole reveal that the time she spent at Lexington was crucial to the self-actualization Lydia achieved. She came to regard herself as a professional teacher capable of expressing herself fully, able to love her pupils, having the capacity to evaluate teaching performances of herself and others, and contributing to the moral

Interpretation

progress of the larger community. The outward manifestations of this self-actualization included her election as the first woman to the Board of Education of the city of Fall River. It was there that she married, lived with her husband and raised a child. It was also the city where she established a sewing school for young women, to insure that they could earn a wage; where she became a member of the Women's Suffrage League of Fall River; and where she began her work in the anti-slavery movement and the underground railroad, often placing herself at personal risk. Her work in the abolitionist movement led her to entertain such leaders as William Garrison, William Douglas, Sojourner Truth, and Wendell Phillips.[18]

Justification?

One would never expect such accomplishments from a reading of her first two Journals. Significant self-actualization did not appear a promising outcome, especially in the complexities of her family background. There was much to provide an anxiety about accomplishment. Death had been a pervasive presence in her family. Her father died when she was one year old and her mother when she was eleven. With the additional deaths of six siblings, only Lydia and her older sister survived from the nuclear family. After the age of eleven, then, she was dependent upon the care of her kin.[19] It would not be surprising if the pervasiveness of such primary loss surrounded her with uncertainty about any accomplishment, and induced compliant behavior to those willing to become responsible for her well-being. Some of this vulnerability, however, was likely to have been offset by the warmth and support of her kin.

Interpretation

Interpretation

As a child in Dedham, she lived with a grandmother and an aunt. In the same town or nearby vicinity, her last two Journals reveal a rich kin group: it is possible to count two grandmothers, eight aunts, six uncles, and numerous cousins. Among the women there were at least three teachers, one of them her sister, but only Lydia received professional training. In her last two Journals she portrays her family as close, continuously interactive, and as kin who supported one another in illnesses as well as in celebrations. With her aunts and friends she attended lectures and studied French and took singing lessons.[20] Thus, despite the many deaths in her immediate family, the Journals reveal a young woman who did not feel abandoned nor did she act depressed. On the other hand, and most strikingly, while she undertook many challenges during her training at the Normal School, she invariably expressed doubts as to whether she could perform them adequately. The experience at Lexington, however, made all the difference in developing the strengths that were manifested in the rest of her life. It also helped her to assuage her pervasive lack of confidence.

Interpretation

Interpretation

Interpretation

The core of the Lexington experience was Cyrus Peirce.[21] His influence on Lydia was most singular. He belonged to a generation of school reformers who stressed moral development as a central goal of education, a belief that included the fusion of mental discipline and Christian ideals that had already been a key part of Lydia's upbringing.[22] His extraordinary teaching ability attracted the admiration of Horace Mann, who engaged him as Principal and then visited the school in its first weeks of operation. Mann recorded:

Independent variable

> *Highly as I had appreciated his talent, he surpassed the ideas I had formed of his ability to teach, and in the prerequisite of all successful teaching, the power of winning the confidence of his pupils. This surpassed what I had ever seen before in any school. The exercises were conducted in the most thorough manner: the principle being stated, and then applied to various combinations of facts, however different, to find the principle which underlies them all . . .*[23]

Primary source

Peirce's abilities were not lost on Lydia, who developed an emotional and personal response to his work. Her first Journal reveals that her reaction was one of great remorse

Supportive example

whenever she or any of her classmates caused him distress. "There is" she wrote, informing him about her feelings in the Journal he would read, "nothing that more affects my happiness than this . . . to cause him [underlined in original] unhappiness who has been so forbearing and patient with us."[24]

Interpretation

Whenever such episodes happened, Stow increased her effort to improve herself and to be perfect if she could. This was a serious challenge for Lydia, who questioned her performance in almost everything she did as previously mentioned. She complained, for example, that she could not achieve a "balance between impulses and belief"[25] when she would finish eating toffee or something else sweet, or when she chatted with her fellow pupils against the commands of her principal.[26]

Example

Interpretation

More seriously, she questioned her own intelligence, using the language of phrenology, a pseudo-psychological science which demonstrated a person's talent based upon the bumps or organs, or lack thereof, on her head. She expressed her frustration when studying algebra with: "Oh how I wish my organ of calculation was large."[27] Peirce would have none of it. He directly challenged the prevailing view that women were incapable of studying mathematics. Some people, he wrote,

Example

> *have doubted if girls should be taught this branch, and indeed, some have questioned the propriety of educating women for this study! Benevolent spirit indeed. The appropriateness of this study for women, how could it be asked? She fills and ought to fill those stations where this branch is requisite. The discipline of the mind which this branch affords is important to the educator.*[28]

Interpretation

Her self-deprecation and doubts were ubiquitous in the first two Journals. Composition exercises did not escape. "Composition I almost despise [but] I must begin now and do the best I can which is always poor."[29] Peirce's response was simply to write in large capital letters across her Journal, "DESPISE !!". But this expression of disgust was unusual. Normally, he complimented this often anxious and over-critical pupil. These compliments were well deserved; for despite her own doubts, an examination of her Journals in comparison with those of her classmates reveals their superiority in terms of comprehensiveness, understanding and clarity. There may be one exception in the Journals of a Mary Swift, although these were devoid of the personal comments found so often in Lydia's Journals.[30]

Example

Peirce's impact on Lydia may be inferred from a survey of the goals of his interactions with the Lexington pupils. The most prominent of these were (1) to inculcate new teaching methodologies; (2) to challenge the prevailing stereotypes about the nature of women's intelligence; (3) to inspire them in the belief that women, compared to men, possessed at least equal intellectual capabilities and in the case of teaching skills, that they were superior. Peirce also shared Horace Mann's oft-expressed belief in the moral superiority of women.[31]

Interpretation

Given the relationship of affection and respect that existed between Lydia and her mentor, it would not be surprising if many of her initial feelings of inadequacy and inferiority did not begin to be displaced as she entered the practice of professional teaching. Her later Journals reveal a confidence in critically assessing the techniques of fellow teachers, both male and female, whose classrooms she visited. More importantly, she developed an independence from the influence of Peirce, recognizing that some circumstances required a deviation from his teachings. Use of the ferule, for example, she found to be occasionally necessary when confronted by an oversized class of undisciplined young men, even though Peirce had been inexorably opposed to the practice.[32]

Interpretation

Quote would help here

In a later teaching position in Fall River, she found great joy, however, in developing the kind of relationship with her pupils that Peirce had strongly emphasized and she herself wanted to have. She wrote of this achievement: "My scholars are very tractable. I am becoming more attached to them as the weeks glide on and may the love strengthen day by day during our connection."[33] It was in this experience that Lydia fulfilled the promise of the Normal School reform. **Good example**

CONCLUSION

It is possible to conclude that Lydia's self-actualization in the field of professional teaching, and as a concerned and active citizen, flows from diverse sources: those available because of the historical environmental circumstances as well as from her own childhood experiences. Her own efforts to achieve success were of major importance as well, particularly her choice to undertake the new professional training even though members of her own family demonstrated that it was not necessary to becoming a teacher. Even as she doubted her ability to meet the school's standards, she persisted in seeking self-improvement. **Interpretation** At this point fortune joined her fate with the efforts of Cyrus Peirce who was, at a time and at a place that was right for Lydia, crusading for the recruitment of women like Lydia to the teaching profession, and providing inspiration for females to strengthen their capacities to take an active part in the world's affairs. Peirce's mentorship to Lydia, a talented, disciplined, but anxious adolescent, provided her with intellectual tools, a moral and probably emotional guardianship, and an unswerving faith in the abilities of her sex. **Interpretation** It was with these gifts that Lydia Ann Stow underwent the process of self-actualization. She developed her talents, and she pursued her life's interests which were to make moral contributions to her world.

Notes

1. Frederic L. Bender, editor, *Karl Marx, The Communist Manifesto* (New York, 1988): 21. According to Bender, Marx believed this important process could not be achieved under capitalism—where the worker experiences alienation from her work. **Secondary source**

2. See the unpublished four volume *Journal of Lydia Ann Stow* held at Framingham State College at Framington, Massachusetts. Framingham is a successor to the Lexington Normal School. I would like to extend my appreciation to the library staff for their assistance, especially to the archivist Sally Phillips, who was so helpful when I first began my research. **Primary source**

3. Several historians attribute this anxiety to the advance of commerce. See e.g., Charles Sellersk, *The Market Revolution: Jacksonian America, 1815–1840* (New York, 1991). For a more optimistic description of the period, see Daniel Feller, *The Jacksonian Promise: 1815–1846* (Baltimore, 1995). **Secondary source**

4. See, for example, Paul H. Mattingly, *The Classless Profession: American Schoolmen in the Nineteenth Century* (New York: New York University Press, 1975). **Secondary source**

5. Lawrence A. Cremin, *American Education: The National Experience, 1783–1876* (New York, 1980): 136; Arthur O. Norton, *The First Normal School in America: The Journals of Cyrus Peirce and Mary Swift* (Cambridge: Harvard University Press, 1926), Introduction. **Secondary source**

6. Ibid, Cremin.

7. Horace Mann, *Common School Journal*, III (1841) 15, in Cremin, p. 137.

8. Horace Mann, "A Few Thoughts on the Powers and Duties of Women," in *Lectures on Various Subjects* (New York, 1864) in Cremin, p. 143. **Primary source**

9. Winston E. Langley and Vivian C. Fox, *Women's Rights in the United States: A Documentary History,* Parts I and II (Greenwood, 1994); Paula Baker, "The Domestication of Politics: Women and the American Political Society, 1780–1920." *The American Historical Review,* 89:3, June, 1984: 620–647; Nancy Cott, *The Bonds of Womanhood: Woman's Sphere in New England* (New Haven, Yale University Press, 1977). **Secondary source**

10. Ibid, Cott; see also Linda K. Kerber, *Women of the Republic.*

Secondary source — 11. Thomas Woody, *The History of Women's Education in The United States,* Vol. I (New York: The Science Press, 1929); Carlos Slafter, *A Record of Education: The Schools and Teachers of Dedham, Massachusetts, 1644–1904* (Dedham Transcript 1952):45.

Secondary source — 12. See Langley and Fox, *Women's Rights,* especially parts I and II.

Secondary source — 13. Geraldine Jonich Clifford, "Home and School in 19th Century America: Some Personal History Reports From the United States," *History of Education Quarterly,* 18:1 (Spring, 1978): 3–4.

Secondary source — 14. Maris A. Vinovskis, *Fertility in Massachusetts from the Revolution to the Civil War* (New York: Academic Press, 1981): 221. Horace Mann said that in 1839 there were far many more female teachers than male teachers. See Mary Swift's Journals in Norton, *The First Normal School,* footnote 14.

Secondary source — 15. Barbara Myer Wertheimer, *We Were There: The Story of Working Women in America* (New York: Pantheon Books, 1961): Claudi Goldin, "The Economic Status of Women in the Early Republic: Quantitative Evidence," *Journal of Interdisciplinary History,* XVI:3 (Winter, 1986):375–404.

Primary source — 16. Lucy Larcom, *A New England Childhood.*

Primary source — 17. Lydia reveals that it was Professor Newman, principal of Barre Normal School, who introduced her to the high standards of journal-keeping she would maintain. She said, "He gave us some useful tips regarding the importance of writing abstracts of lectures, lessons or anything else we might hear." She recorded this in Volume IV, p. 16 of her Journals. Her summaries of lectures and of the books she read were remarkable especially in contrast to her classmates. Except for Mary Swift, all the other Journals from Lexington do not compare in quality or length with that of Stow's.

Primary source — 18. Most of this information was obtained from her obituary in the *Fall River Evening News* written on Friday, August 16, 1904. Lydia was 81 years old when she died.

Primary source — 19. Don Gleason Hill, editor, *The Record of Baptisms, Marriages and Deaths and Admission to the Church, 1638–1845* (Dedham, 1888):288. This record of the First Parish Church is listed as Dedham Cemetery Epitaphs. In the registry of Probate, Norfolk County, NP 17508, Lydia's father, Timothy Stow, Jr., is listed as a "Hoosewright" or "Housewright." The O.E.D. defines these as housebuilders.

Primary source — 20. These impressions are to be gleaned from her last two Journals when she was living at home. However, while at school Lydia wrote about her feelings regarding her home. "There [meaning home] is the true City of Refuge. Where are we to turn when it is shut from us or changed?" It is interesting to note that Lydia is expressing two feelings: one that she is lucky to have that true refuge, but also, secondly she exhibits an awareness of the plight one would have without it. Probably this is because she is an orphan and probably contemplated what would happen if she were not cared for by her relatives. Journal II, p. 72.

Secondary source — 21. For Peirce's background, see Norton, Introduction, *The First State Normal School.*

Secondary source — 22. For an interesting interpretation of the personality fostered by the Congregationalist religion, see Philip Greven, *The Protestant Temperament: Patterns of Child-Rearing, Religious Experience, and the Self in Early America* (New York, 1977):152–179. Of course reading Lydia's Journals also provides one with the most detailed view of her religious and moral ideas.

Secondary source — 23. See Norton, Introduction, *The First State Normal School.*

24. Stow, Journals, no. 1, p. 25.

25. Ibid., p. 180. See also ibid at 217 and 241 for further examples of this belief.

26. Ibid., p. 217, 241.

27. Ibid., p. 25.

28. Journals vol. II, p. 16.

29. Ibid., p. 56.

Primary source — 30. See Mary Swift's published Journal in Norton, *The First State Normal School.*

Primary source — 31. For Peirce's views see Lydia's Journals and Norton, which contains the Journals of Mary Swift and of Cyrus Peirce. From them it is very clear that Peirce believed women to have many talents including a highly developed moral capacity. For Horace Mann, see his published lectures entitled, *A Few Thoughts on the Powers and Duties of Woman, Two Lectures* (Syracuse, Hall, Mills and Co., 1853).

32. Journals vol. IV, p. 41.

33. Ibid., p. 86.

Analysis of the Study

PURPOSE/JUSTIFICATION

We do not find a clear statement of purpose. In part because of the publication in which the study appears, *The Journal of Psychohistory,* we think the purpose could have been stated as, for example, "to enhance our understanding of the ways in which societal conditions and personal characteristics interact in producing valued qualities such as 'self-actualization.'" The justification implied in the introduction is that the life of Lydia Stow is important to understand; this is elaborated later under "Gender Reform."

There are no problems of risk, deception, or confidentiality.

DEFINITIONS

A clear definition of *self-actualization* is given in the introduction. This is particularly important because not all definitions of this term include "pursuit of one's life interests in and through one's work." Other terms such as *self-improvement* and *concerned and active citizen* are probably clear enough in context.

PRIOR RESEARCH

There is no presentation of previous research, presumably because there is none that is directly relevant. If our interpretation of the author's purpose is correct, it may be that other biographies would be pertinent. There is no mention of other biographies of Stow. If they exist, they might have provided additional evidence.

HYPOTHESES

None is stated. The "interaction" hypothesis is clearly implied; it appears likely that it conceptually preceded the analysis of the information.

SAMPLE

The sampling issue is quite different in historical research as compared with other types of research. There typically is no population of persons to be sampled. It could be argued that a population of events exists, but if so, they are likely to be so different that selection among them makes more sense if done purposefully, in other words, a purposive sample. In this study, a population of persons could have been specified, though it's not clear what its characteristics would be—perhaps "nineteenth-century women who made a significant impact on education." A sample of such women would greatly increase the generalizability of findings but would, presumably, involve major problems in locating suitable source material.

INSTRUMENTATION

There is no instrumentation in the sense that we discuss it in this text. The "instrument" in this case is the researcher's talent for locating, evaluating, and analyzing pertinent sources. The concept of reliability usually has little relevance to historical data, because each item is not meaningfully considered to be a sample across either content or time. In this study, however, comparison of journal statements pertaining to the same topic (e.g., self-confidence) could be made across the early two journals and, again, across the later two. These comparisons would give an indication of the consistency of these statements.

Validity, on the other hand, is paramount. It is addressed by evaluating sources and by comparing different sources regarding the same specifics. In this study, data are from two types of source. Secondary sources are used extensively in the sections on school reform and gender reform. The source of information about Stow is a primary one, her four journals. Some of the secondary sources could, it seems, have been used as cross-checks for validity, but this apparently was not done. The validity of the author's summaries of this information is supported, in some instances, by quotations from the journals and from other primary sources.

External criticism does not appear to be an issue with respect to the journals or, presumably, other references. The question of internal criticism is somewhat difficult to deal with, because the journals must be evaluated in terms of the writer's feelings and perceptions rather than events. Here, we are highly dependent on the researcher's summaries.

PROCEDURES/INTERNAL VALIDITY

There is little to be said about procedures except that some discussion of the plans that the researcher developed and followed for analyzing the documents, particularly the journals, would be useful, especially so that readers could evaluate the presumed selection of content. Historical research is always subject to the allegation that the researcher has selected content based on personal bias. Internal validity concerns are justified regarding this research because of the intent to study the relationships among societal conditions, prior personal qualities, and personal development. In addition to data collector (researcher) bias, other major threats include history (other events) and maturation. There is no way to control for these threats in historical research.

DATA ANALYSIS

Data analysis procedures, as we have explained them in this book, are not used in this study, nor do we see how most of them could be. Use of the content analysis methods in Chapter 20 would serve to organize the information. Category-by-category tabulation of the frequency of similar statements might have clarified interpretations.

RESULTS/DISCUSSION

Though we advocate keeping the results of a study separate from the discussion of them, such separation is extremely difficult in historical research. The question here is whether the information (data) provided justifies the author's interpretations and conclusions. Though not proven, we think the well-documented summaries of school and gender reforms during Stow's young adulthood are persuasive. With respect to changes in Stow over a four-year period (ages 17 to 21), we are very dependent on the author's highly inferential psychological interpretations. Though we find them plausible (e.g., interpretation of Stow's factual family history), more quotations from the journals would strengthen such interpretations, most importantly that her confidence and independence increased greatly during this time. Several are provided from the early journals but none from the later ones.

The assertion that "Even as she doubted her ability to meet the school's standards, she persisted in seeking self-improvement" is reflected in quotations. We must assume, however, that they are typical of both Stow's statements and her feelings. Similarly, the influence of Peirce, in turn reflecting social changes, seems persuasive, but, again, we must assume that the examples are representative. We think there is a clear implication that societal changes, family support, personal persistence, and the influence of Peirce were all necessary to Stow's self-actualization. While this is plausible, it is not demonstrated by the study.

Go back to the **INTERACTIVE AND APPLIED LEARNING** feature at the beginning of the chapter for a listing of interactive and applied activities. Go to the **Online Learning Center** at **www.mhhe.com/fraenkel9e** to take quizzes, practice with key terms, and review chapter content.

Main Points

THE NATURE OF HISTORICAL RESEARCH

- The unique characteristic of historical research is that it focuses exclusively on the past.

PURPOSES OF HISTORICAL RESEARCH

- Educational researchers conduct historical studies for a variety of reasons, but perhaps the most frequently cited is to help people learn from past failures and successes.
- When well designed and carefully executed, historical research may lead to the confirmation or rejection of relational hypotheses.

STEPS IN HISTORICAL RESEARCH

- Four essential steps are involved in a historical study: defining the problem or hypothesis to be investigated; searching for relevant source material; summarizing and evaluating the sources the researcher is able to locate; and interpreting the evidence obtained and then drawing conclusions about the problem or hypothesis.

HISTORICAL SOURCES

- Most historical source material can be grouped into four basic categories: documents, numerical records, oral statements, and relics.
- Documents are written or printed materials that have been produced in one form or another sometime in the past.
- Numerical records include any type of numerical data in printed or handwritten form.
- Oral statements include any form of statement spoken by someone.
- Relics are any objects whose physical or visual characteristics can provide some information about the past.
- A primary source is one prepared by an individual who was a participant in or a direct witness to the event that is being described.
- A secondary source is a document prepared by an individual who was not a direct witness to an event but who obtained his or her description of the event from someone else.

EVALUATION OF HISTORICAL SOURCE MATERIAL

- Content analysis is a primary method of data analysis in historical research.
- External criticism refers to the genuineness of the documents a researcher uses in a historical study.
- Internal criticism refers to the accuracy of the contents of a document. Whereas external criticism has to do with the authenticity of a document, internal criticism has to do with what the document says.

GENERALIZATION IN HISTORICAL RESEARCH

- As in all research, researchers who conduct historical studies should exercise caution in generalizing from small or nonrepresentative samples.

ADVANTAGES AND DISADVANTAGES OF HISTORICAL RESEARCH

- The main advantage of historical research is that it permits the investigation of topics that could be studied in no other way. It is the only research method that can study evidence from the past.
- A disadvantage is that controlling for many of the threats to internal validity is not possible in historical research. Many of the threats to internal validity discussed in Chapter 9 are likely to exist in historical studies.

Key Terms

document 535
external criticism 537
historical research 533
internal criticism 538
primary source 536
relic 535
secondary source 536

For Discussion

1. A researcher wishes to investigate changes in high school graduation requirements since 1900. Pose a possible hypothesis the researcher might investigate. What sources might he or she consult?
2. Why might a researcher be cautious or suspicious about each of the following sources?
   a. A typewriter imprinted with the name "Christopher Columbus"
   b. A letter from Franklin D. Roosevelt endorsing John F. Kennedy for the presidency of the United States
   c. A letter to the editor from an eighth-grade student complaining about the adequacy of the school's advanced mathematics program
   d. A typed report of an interview with a recently fired teacher describing the teacher's complaints against the school district
   e. A 1920 high school diploma indicating a student had graduated from the tenth grade
   f. A high school teacher's attendance book indicating no absences by any member of her class during the entire year of 1942
   g. A photograph of an elementary school classroom in 1800
3. How would you compare historical research to the other methodologies we have discussed in this book—is it harder or easier to do? Why?
4. "Researchers cannot ensure representativeness of the sample" in historical research. Why not?
5. Which of the steps involved in historical research that we have described do you think would be the hardest to complete? the easiest? Why?
6. Can you think of any topic or idea that would *not* be a potential source for historical research? Why not? Suggest an example.
7. Historians usually prefer to use primary rather than secondary sources. Why? Can you think of an instance, however, where the reverse might be true? Discuss.
8. Which do you think is harder to establish—the genuineness or the accuracy of a historical document? Why?

References

1. Korte, B., & Spittel, S. (2009). Shakespeare under different Flags: The bar in German classrooms from Hitler to Honecker. *Journal of Contemporary History, 44,* 267–286.

2. Kohlstedt, S. G. (2008). A better crop of boys and girls: The school gardening movement, 1890–1920. *History of Education Quarterly, 48*(1), 58–93.

3. Churchill, D. S. (2008). Making broad shoulders: Body-building and physical culture in Chicago, 1890–1920. *History of Education Quarterly, 48*(3), 341–370.

4. Yee, A. L. (2008). Beyond civics and the 3 R's: Teaching economics in the schools. *History of Education Quarterly, 48*(3), 397–431.

5. Crocco, M. S., & Waite, C. L. (2007). Education and marginality: Race and gender in higher education. (2007). *History of Education Quarterly, 47*(1), 69–91.

6. Terzian, S. G. (2006). Science world, high school girls, and the prospect of scientific careers. *History of Education Quarterly, 46*(1), 73–99.

7. Gere, A. R. (2005). Indian heart/white man's head: Native-American teachers in Indian schools. *History of Education Quarterly, 45*(1), 38–65.

8. Nelson, A. R. (2005). The emergence of the American university: an international perspective. *History of Education Quarterly, 45*(3), 427–437.

9. Carr, E. J. (1967, pp. 32–33). *What is history?* New York: Random House.

10. Isaac, L., & Griffin, L. (1989). Ahistoricism in time-series analyses of historical process: Critique, redirection, and illustrations from U.S. labor history. *American Sociological Review, 54,* 873–890.

PART 7

Mixed-Methods Studies

Part 7 presents a discussion of mixed-methods studies, which combine quantitative and qualitative methods. Such studies have been receiving increased attention in recent years. Advocates point out the potential for using the strengths of both approaches, whereas critics discuss several limitations including ambiguity regarding the definition of the "method." In Chapter 23, we present pros and cons and conclude with an example of a study that we have annotated and analyzed.

23 Mixed-Methods Research

by Michael K. Gardner,
Department of Educational Psychology,
University of Utah

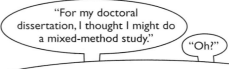

What Is Mixed-Methods Research?
Why Do Mixed-Methods Research?
Drawbacks of Mixed-Methods Studies
A (Very) Brief History
Types of Mixed-Methods Designs
The Exploratory Design
The Explanatory Design
The Triangulation Design
Other Mixed-Methods Research Design Issues
Steps in Conducting a Mixed-Methods Study
Evaluating a Mixed-Methods Study
Ethics in Mixed-Methods Research
Summary
An Example of Mixed-Methods Research
Analysis of the Study
Definitions
Prior Research
Hypotheses and Design
Sample
Instrumentation
Internal Validity/Credibility
Data Analysis
Results/Discussion

OBJECTIVES Studying this chapter should enable you to:

- Explain what a mixed-methods study is.
- Describe how mixed-methods research differs from other types of research.
- Give at least three reasons why a researcher might want to do a mixed-methods study.
- Describe some of the drawbacks to conducting a mixed-methods study.
- Name the three major types of mixed-methods research designs and describe briefly how they differ.
- List some of the steps involved in conducting a mixed-methods study.
- List at least five questions that can be used to evaluate a mixed-methods study.
- Describe briefly how matters of ethics affect mixed-methods research.
- Recognize a mixed-methods study when you come across one in the educational literature.

INTERACTIVE AND APPLIED LEARNING After, or while, reading this chapter:

Go to the Online Learning Center at www.mhhe.com/fraenkel9e to:

- Research in Action

Go to your online Student Mastery Activities book to do the following activities:

- Activity 23.1: Mixed-Methods Research Questions
- Activity 23.2: Identifying Mixed-Methods Designs
- Activity 23.3: Research Questions in Mixed-Methods Designs
- Activity 23.4: Identifying Terms in Mixed-Methods Studies

Alice Ochoa, the superintendent of a large urban school district, is informed by several of her principals that the use of drugs by elementary and middle school students in her district is increasing at an alarming rate. Worried, she asks Alfonso Martinez, a professor at a local university, to investigate the problem. Martinez decides to begin his research by looking into the situation at a nearby middle school where the use of drugs has been reported as being especially high. He begins by obtaining permission from the school principal to investigate the problem and by soliciting informed consent from the students and their parents to participate in his research project. Martinez decides to conduct a mixed-methods study by first collecting some data using a quantitative survey instrument and then following up by interviewing a sample of the students who participated in the survey. He hopes the interviews will provide more details about students' responses to the questionnaire and thereby suggest some ways to combat the drug problem.

What Is Mixed-Methods Research?

Mixed-methods research involves the use of *both quantitative and qualitative methods* in a single study. Those who engage in such research argue that the use of both methods provides a more complete understanding of research problems than does the use of either approach alone.

Although mixed-methods research dates back to the 1950s, only recently has it achieved a significant place in educational research—the first journal devoted to it began publication in 2005. It is not surprising, then, that there are different views as to what it is. For some, the essential feature is that mixed-methods research combines methods of data collection and analysis from both quantitative and qualitative traditions. As we have indicated in earlier parts of this book, the former favors numerical data and statistical analysis, whereas the latter prefers in-depth information, often in narrative form, frequently obtained through the analysis of written communications.

For others, this description is not specific enough. They insist that other features, particularly of qualitative methods, be present. These include developing a holistic picture and analysis of the phenomenon being studied with an emphasis on "thick" rather than "selective" description. We do not expect this matter of definition to be resolved soon; in the meantime, examples of both can be found in the current literature.

It should be noted that the type of instrument used to collect data is not a major difference between quantitative and qualitative methodologies. Observation and interviewing, prominent instruments used in qualitative research, are also commonly found in quantitative studies. It is the manner, context, and sometimes intent that are different (see Chapters 7, 17, 19, and 21).

Some actual examples of the kinds of mixed-methods studies that have been conducted by educational researchers are:

- "Combining Qualitative and Quantitative Methodologies in Research on Teachers' Lives, Work, and Effectiveness"[1]
- "Closed and Open-Ended Question Tools in a Telephone Survey About 'The Good Teacher'"[2]
- "Emotions and Change During Professional Development for Teachers: A Mixed Methods Study"[3]
- "Telling It All: A Story of Women's Social Capital Using a Mixed Methods Approach"[4]

- "The Complexities of Teachers' Commitment to Environmental Education: A Mixed Methods Approach"[5]
- "Dating and Sexual Attitudes in Asian-American Adolescents"[6]

Why Do Mixed-Methods Research?

Mixed-methods research has several strengths. First, it can help to clarify and explain relationships found to exist between variables. For example, correlational data may indicate a slight negative relationship between the time students spend at home using a computer and their grades—that is, as student computer time increased, their grades suffered. The question is raised as to why such a relationship exists. Interviews with students might show that the students fell into two distinct groups: (1) a relatively large group that uses computers primarily for social interaction (e.g., e-mail and instant messaging) and whose members' grades are suffering, and (2) a smaller group that uses computers for gathering school-related information (e.g., through the use of search engines) and whose members' grades are comparatively high. When the two groups were initially combined, the larger number of students in the first group produced the negative relationship found to exist between computer usage and student grades. The subsequent interviews, however, showed that the relationship was somewhat spurious, due more to *the reasons why* students used their computers, not to the use of computers per se.

Second, mixed-methods research allows us to explore relationships between variables in depth. In this situation, qualitative methods may be used to identify the important variables in an area of interest. These variables may then be quantified in an instrument (such as a questionnaire) that is then administered to large numbers of individuals. The variables can then be correlated with other variables. For example, interviews with students might reveal that study problems can be categorized into three areas: (1) too little time spent studying; (2) distractions in the study environment, such as television and radio; and (3) insufficient help given by parents or siblings. These problems could be further investigated by constructing a 12-item questionnaire, with four questions for each of the three study problem areas. After administering this questionnaire to 300 students, researchers could correlate the study problem scores with other variables, such as student grades, standardized test performance, socioeconomic level, and involvement in extracurricular activities, to see if and how any of these other variables are related to particular study problems.

Third, mixed-methods studies can help to confirm or cross-validate relationships discovered between variables, as when quantitative and qualitative methods are compared to see if they converge on a single interpretation of a phenomenon. If they do not converge, the reasons for the lack of convergence can be investigated. For example, a professor specializing in mixed-methods research might be asked to investigate the satisfaction of middle school students with their teachers' grading practices. He or she could prepare a questionnaire designed to determine the attitudes of students and then conduct focus group with various samples of the students. If the survey responses generally reveal satisfaction with the teachers' grading practices, yet the focus group participants indicate a considerable dissatisfaction with them, a possible explanation might be that the students felt that their teachers would see the responses to the surveys (and thus they were reluctant to be critical). However, in the focus groups, with no teachers or other adults present, they could feel free to express their true feelings. Thus, the apparent lack of convergence in this case might be explained by a third variable: whether teachers would have access to the results.

Drawbacks of Mixed-Methods Studies

At this point you might wonder why all research problems are not addressed using mixed-methods designs. Several drawbacks exist. First, mixed-methods studies are often extremely time-consuming and expensive to carry out. Second, many researchers are experienced in only one type of research. To conduct a mixed-methods study properly, one needs expertise in both types of research. Such expertise takes considerable time to develop.

Indeed, the resources, time, and energy required to do a mixed-methods study may be prohibitive for a single researcher to undertake. This drawback can be avoided if multiple researchers, with differing areas of expertise, work as a team. However, if a single researcher does not have sufficient time, resources, and skills, that individual would probably be better off doing a purely quantitative or qualitative study and doing it well.

Nevertheless, mixed-methods research remains a viable option to consider. Increasing numbers of mixed-methods studies are being done, and this type of research should be understood by all who are interested in conducting and designing research.

A (Very) Brief History

Mixed-methods research first came into play in the 1950s when some initial interest developed in using more than one research method in a single study. In 1957, for example, Trow commented as follows:

> Every cobbler thinks that leather is the only thing. Most social scientists . . . have their favorite methods with which they are familiar and have some skill in using. And I suspect we mostly choose to investigate problems that seem vulnerable to attack through these methods. But we should at least try to be less parochial than cobblers. Let us be done with the arguments of "participant observation" *versus* interviewing—as we have largely dispensed with the arguments for psychology *versus* sociology—and get on with the business of attacking our problems with the widest array of conceptual and methodological tools that we possess and they demand.[7]

Campbell and Fiske[8] advocated measuring traits with multiple measures, so that it was possible to separate variance due to the trait from variance due to the method used to measure the trait. They were working strictly in the quantitative domain, but their multitrait-multimethod matrix suggested the importance of separating the phenomenon under study from the tools being used to study it. Denzin[9] and Jick[10] both have been credited with applying the term *triangulation* to research methods. **Triangulation** (or, more precisely, *methodological triangulation*) involves using different methods and/or types of data to study the same research question. If the results are in agreement, they help validate the finding of each. Denzin used triangulation when he utilized multiple data sources to study the same phenomenon. Jick discussed the use of triangulation within a single method (quantitative or qualitative) and across methods (both quantitative and qualitative). He noted how the strengths of one method could offset the weaknesses of another.

In Chapter 18, we pointed out that quantitative and qualitative researchers differ in the set of beliefs or assumptions that guide the way they approach their investigations, and that these assumptions are related to their worldviews—that is, the views they hold concerning, among other things, the nature of reality and the process of research. As we mentioned there, the quantitative approach is associated with the philosophy of **positivism**. Qualitative methodologists, on the other hand, advocate a more "artistic" approach to research, adhering to other worldviews (such as **postmodernism**). (See the Controversies in Research box on p. 428.)

These differences have caused many researchers to believe that quantitative and qualitative research methodologies were a dichotomy: an either-or proposition with no middle ground. During the 1970s and 1980s, in fact, many researchers on both sides of the issue argued strongly that the two methods (often referred to as "paradigms") could not be combined. Many researchers still hold to this view. In 1985, Rossman and Wilson[11] referred to those who stated that paradigms could not be mixed as *purists;* those who could adapt their methods to the particulars of a situation, they called *situationists;* and those who believed that multiple paradigms could be utilized in research, they called *pragmatists*. Although the question of mixing paradigms still exists, more researchers are embracing pragmatism as the best philosophical foundation for mixed-methods research.[12]

Pragmatists proposed that researchers should use whatever works. The most important element in making a decision about which research method or methods to employ should be the research question at hand. Worldviews and preferences about methods should take a back seat, and the researcher should choose the research approach that most readily illuminates the research question. That research approach may be quantitative, qualitative, or a combination of the two.

Consider an example: The superintendent of a large school district hires a consultant to carry out a phone survey to ask respondents a series of questions regarding how much they would be willing to pay in increased taxes for particular expenditures (e.g., such things as smaller class size, pay raises for teachers, or expanded athletics programs). She is disappointed to find an unwillingness on the part of those surveyed to fund any of the options they list at anywhere near the amounts that would be needed. So she decides to have the consultant conduct focus groups to try to find out why. Are these two types of information fundamentally incompatible? By no means. Each type supplies the district superintendent with useful information. The quantitative data tells her *what* the public will accept, while the focus groups tell her *why* they responded as they did, thereby helping to clarify the negative response.

CONTROVERSIES IN RESEARCH

Are Some Methods Incompatible with Others?

Some researchers in education (as well as other disciplines) argue that quantitative methods are incompatible with qualitative methods. They state that the basic assumptions of each method actually prevent the use of the other in the same study. Many qualitative researchers argue that qualitative methods are based on a point of view about the nature of the world—that reality is constructed, not revealed. Since every individual sees the world in his or her own way, there is no single reality "out there" to be discovered; in fact, multiple realities exist. Quantitative researchers, on the other hand, reject this point of view. Still other researchers would argue that this notion of incompatibility has been overblown. Krathwohl, for example, has stated that "quantitative findings compress into summary numbers the trends and tendencies expressed in words in qualitative reports. In many instances, counts of coded qualitative data might have produced data similar to the quantitative summaries . . . Many problems, in fact, actually require more than any one method can deliver; the answer, of course, is a multiple-method approach."*

*Krathwohl, D. R. (1998). *Methods of educational and social science research: An integrated approach* (2nd ed., p. 619), New York: Longman.

Types of Mixed-Methods Designs

While quantitative and qualitative methods may be combined in any way suitable to address a particular research question, certain mixed-methods designs occur with enough frequency for us to look at them in detail. Three major types of mixed-methods design exist: the **exploratory design**, the **explanatory design**, and the **triangulation design**.[13] Each involves a combination of qualitative and quantitative data.

THE EXPLORATORY DESIGN

In this design, researchers first use a qualitative method to discover the important variables underlying a phenomenon of interest and to inform a second, quantitative, method (Figure 23.1). Next, they seek to discover the relationships among these variables. This type of design is often used in the construction of questionnaires or rating scales designed to measure various topics of interest.

In the exploratory design, results of the qualitative phase give direction to the quantitative method, and quantitative results are used to validate or extend the qualitative findings. Data analysis in the exploratory design is separate, corresponding to the first, qualitative, phase of the study and the second, quantitative, phase of the study. The rationale underlying the exploratory design is to explore a phenomenon or to identify important themes. In addition, it is especially useful when one needs to develop and test a particular type of instrument.

The illustration at the beginning of this chapter gives an example of an exploratory design. The student wants to use a qualitative method (ethnography), presumably involving content analysis of in-depth interviews and perhaps other narratives (such as essays), to identify students' reasons for joining a high school gang and to see how gang membership affected them. Subsequently, she would use a causal-comparative design to compare subgroups of students who had different reasons for joining when they were freshmen. To do this, she would have to sort out the subgroups, using her ethnographic data. She would then collect data from them as seniors to see how these groups differ in ways suggested by the ethnography. This will require additional data collection where the preference would be for quantitative information that may require instrument development.

THE EXPLANATORY DESIGN

Sometimes a researcher will do a quantitative study, but will require additional information to flesh out the

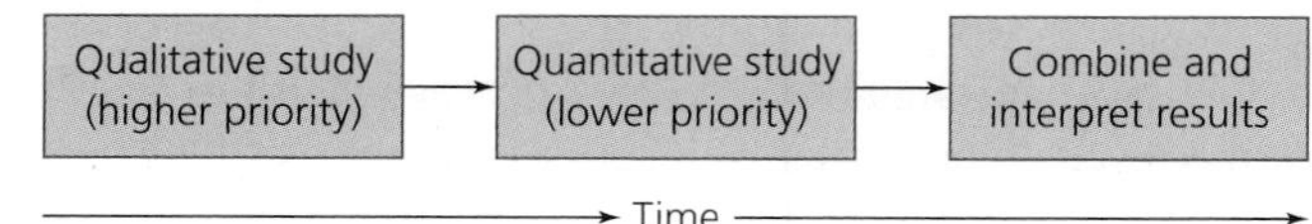

Figure 23.1
Exploratory Design
Source: Adapted from Creswell, J. W., & Plano Clark, V. L. (2006). *Designing and conducting mixed methods research.* Thousand Oaks, CA: Sage.

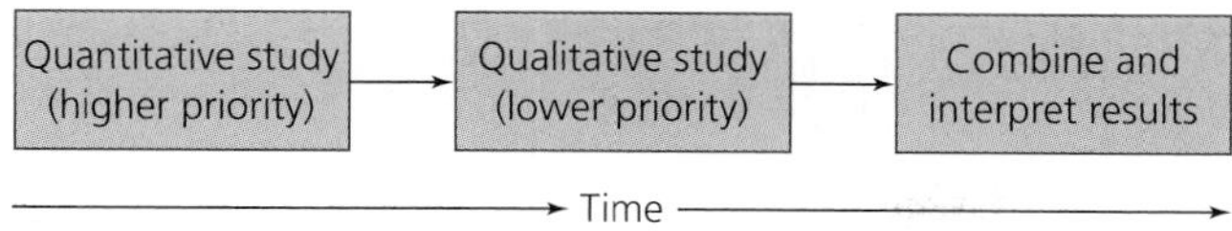

Figure 23.2
Explanatory Design
Source: Adapted from Creswell, J. W., & Plano Clark, V. L. (2006). *Designing and conducting mixed methods research.* Thousand Oaks, CA: Sage.

results. This is the purpose behind the explanatory design. In this design, the researcher first carries out a quantitative method and then uses a qualitative method to follow up and refine the quantitative findings (see Figure 23.2). The two types of data are analyzed separately, with the results of the qualitative analysis used by the researcher to expand upon the results of the quantitative study.

For example, one of the authors was a co-investigator, some years ago, in a study in which four fifth-grade teachers each taught mathematics using ability grouping and non grouping in alternate semesters in a counterbalanced experiment. The study had the unusual feature, in school research, of random assignments of students to teachers. The major finding was that one teacher achieved substantially higher achievement gains with non grouping whereas the other three had greater gains with grouping. A follow-up qualitative study using interviews and narrative description of classroom activities could have tested the informal observation that the one teacher was more adept at individualizing instruction than the three teachers whose students learned more with grouping.[14]

THE TRIANGULATION DESIGN

In the triangulation design, the researcher uses both quantitative and qualitative methods to study the same phenomenon to determine if the two converge upon a single understanding of the research problem being investigated. If they do not, then the researcher must explore why the two methods provide different pictures. Quantitative and qualitative methods are given equal priority, and all data are collected simultaneously (Figure 23.3). The data may be analyzed together or separately. If analyzed together, data from the qualitative study may have to be converted into quantitative data (e.g., assigning numerical codes in a process that is called **quantitizing**) or the quantitative data may have to be converted into qualitative data (e.g., providing narratives in a process that is called **qualitizing**). If the data are analyzed separately, the convergence or divergence of the results would then be discussed. The underlying rationale for the use of the triangulation design is that the strengths of the two methods will complement each other and offset each method's respective weaknesses.

Consider an example. Fraenkel used a modified triangulation design to study four high school social studies teachers identified by their peers as outstanding.[15] He attempted to paint a portrait of what happens on a daily basis in their classrooms and to identify effective teacher techniques and behaviors. To this end, he used several qualitative techniques, including extensive in-class observation using a daily log and interviews with students and teachers. He also used a number of quantitative instruments, including performance checklists, rating scales, and discussion flowcharts. He developed detailed descriptions of each teacher's behaviors, teaching style, and techniques and compared the teachers for similarities and differences. Triangulation was achieved not only by comparing teacher interviews, student interviews and observations, but also by comparing these with the quantitative measures of classroom interaction and achievement.

One illustrative finding was that all four teachers emphasized small-group work, as revealed by observation, teacher interviews, and student ratings. Overall, the study's findings supported frequently recommended teaching strategies, but also suggested some that have not received much attention in the literature. These included extensive personal involvement in the lives of students, promoting social interaction both in and outside of the classroom, and consciously attending to nonverbal cues. Far more information and insight was obtained in this study through the use of both methods than if a purely quantitative or qualitative method had been used.

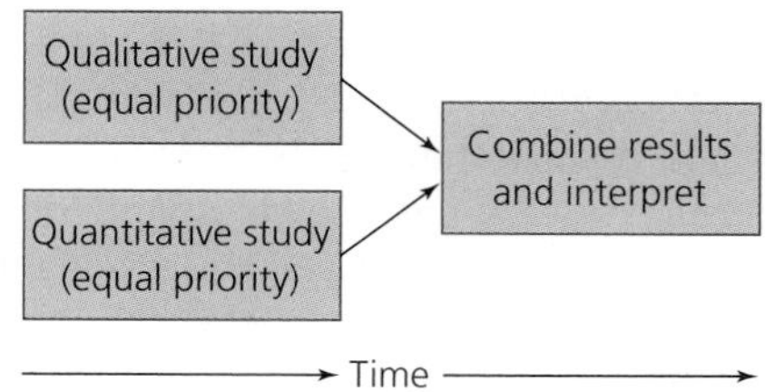

Figure 23.3 *Triangulation Design*
Source: Adapted from Creswell, J. W., & Plano Clark, V. L. (2006). *Designing and conducting mixed methods research.* Thousand Oaks, CA: Sage.

Other Mixed-Methods Research Design Issues[16]

Advocacy Lenses. A factor that can be can be used to categorize mixed-methods designs is the presence or absence of an **advocacy lens**. An advocacy lens occurs when the researcher's worldview implies that the purpose of research is to advocate for the improved treatment of research participants in the world outside research. Examples of worldviews that involve an advocacy lens would be feminist theory, race-based theories, and critical theory. We have discussed the major mixed-methods designs as if there were no advocacy lens present; however, each design can be approached with an explicit advocacy lens. A researcher might, for instance, be interested in triangulating quantitative and qualitative methods concerning student academic performance in elementary school, comparing performance in a primarily white suburban school with that of a primarily black inner-city school. The purpose of the research might be to improve conditions, and academic performance, for black inner-city students.

Sampling. Sampling is as important in mixed methods studies as it is in any other type of research. Qualitative researchers typically use purposive sampling, wherein researchers intentionally select participants who are informed about or have experience with the central concept(s) being investigated. Usually samples are small, the intent being that a comparatively small number of individuals can provide a considerable amount of detailed, in-depth information that large-size samples would not.

Quantitative researchers typically want to choose individuals who are representative of a larger population so that results can be generalized to that population. Generally, random sampling strategies are preferred, but often this is not possible, especially in educational settings. Thus convenience, systematic, or purposive samples must be used, with replication suggested and encouraged. Sample sizes are usually much larger than in qualitative studies.

There are usually multiple samples in mixed-methods studies. For example, a researcher might randomly select two high schools for a mixed-methods study on drug use in suburban schools. First she would administer surveys to all 800 graduating seniors at the two schools, then conduct six focus groups using a purposive sample of students, and conclude by randomly selecting 40 students to interview.

Teddlie and Yu explain that mixed-methods sampling occupies the middle portion of a continuum, with quantitative sampling techniques on one end and qualitative sampling on the other. They argue that mixed-methods researchers should use any and all combinations of random and purposive sampling strategies to address their research questions: "Indeed, the researcher's ability to creatively combine these techniques in answering a study's questions is one of the defining characteristics of mixed-methods research."[17]

Accordingly, researchers must make a number of decisions with regard to sampling before beginning a mixed-methods study, such as the relative size of the two samples involved, whether they are to include the same participants, whether one sample is to be subsumed within the other, or whether the participants should be completely different for the two samples.

Mixed-Model Studies. Tashakkori and Teddlie define mixed-model studies as those that "combine the qualitative and quantitative approaches within several different phases of the research process."[18] In a single study, this might involve an experimental study, followed by qualitative data collection, followed by quantitative analysis of the data after it had been converted to numbers. In mixed-model studies, the quantitative and qualitative approach to research may be addressed during each of three phases of the research process: (1) the type of investigation (confirmatory [typically quantitative] versus exploratory [typically qualitative]); (2) quantitative data collection and operations versus qualitative data collection and operations; (3) statistical analysis and inference versus qualitative analysis and inference. Indeed, Tashakkori and Teddlie use these dimensions to create a classification system for mixed-models research.[19] As may be obvious, this is a more complicated system for classifying research designs, and at least some of the combinations of the three phases of research occur very rarely in practice.

Steps in Conducting a Mixed-Methods Study

Develop a Clear Rationale for Doing a Mixed-Methods Study. A researcher should ask why *both* quantitative and qualitative methods are needed to investigate the problem at hand. If the reasoning is not clear, a mixed-methods study may not be appropriate.

Develop Research Questions for Both the Qualitative and Quantitative Methods. As in all research, the nature of the research question or questions will determine the type of design to be used. Many research questions can be addressed using either or both quantitative and qualitative research techniques. For example, suppose a researcher posed this question: "Why don't Asian-American college students make greater use of college counseling centers?" He or she might begin by interviewing a sample of Asian-American college students about their perceptions of the kinds of students who use these centers. The researcher might then supplement these interviews with survey information provided by these centers about the proportion of students from different ethnic groups who use the centers. The survey data might indicate what degree of underutilization exists, while the interview data might point to student perceptions that produce this underutilization.

In many instances the formation of a general research question can lead to the development of individual research hypotheses, some of which may lend themselves to a quantitative approach and some of which may require a qualitative method. These "lower-level" hypotheses often can suggest specific analyses (either quantitative or qualitative) that will answer specific questions. In the previous example, one such hypothesis might be that Asian-American college students do in fact underutilize college mental health counseling services, which the survey data can address. If the survey results indicate that Asian-American college students utilize such centers less often than do students from other ethnic groups, the reasons can be addressed in the interviews. You will recall that qualitative researchers often prefer that hypotheses emerge as a study progresses. This is much more likely to happen with the exploratory design.

RESEARCH TIPS

What to Do About Contradictory Findings

On occasion, the quantitative and qualitative findings in a mixed-methods study may contradict each other. What does a researcher do if that occurs? There are three possible approaches.

1. Present the two findings in parallel and state that more research is needed.
2. Collect additional data to resolve the contradiction, provided that this is both feasible and timely. This is a less common response insofar as the follow-up study may not get disseminated or published.
3. View the problem as a springboard for new directions of inquiry, which is usually the case for ambiguous research findings.

Decide If a Mixed-Methods Study Is Feasible. Mixed-methods studies, by their very nature, require the researcher or research team to be experienced in both quantitative and qualitative research methods. It is rare that a single individual would have all of the requisite skills necessary to conduct a mixed-methods research study. The key question for anyone contemplating a mixed-method study is this: Do you have the time, energy, and resources necessary to conduct such a study? If not, can you collaborate with others who have the skills and expertise you lack? If you lack the necessary skills or resources, it may indeed be better to re-conceptualize a study as basically a quantitative or qualitative investigation than to begin a mixed-methods study that cannot be completed within the time available.

Determine the Mixed-Methods Design Most Appropriate to the Research Question or Questions. As we mentioned earlier, there are essentially three mixed-methods designs from which a researcher can choose. The triangulation design is appropriate when the researcher is trying to see if quantitative and qualitative methods converge on a single understanding of a phenomenon. The explanatory design is appropriate if one intends to use qualitative data to expand upon the findings of a quantitative study (or vice-versa). The exploratory design is appropriate when one is trying to first identify the relevant variables that may underlie a phenomenon and then later studying the relationships among these variables, or when information is needed to assist in designing quantitative instrumentation.

Collect and Analyze the Data. Data collection and analysis procedures described earlier in this text are applicable and appropriate to all mixed-methods studies, depending on the particular methods used. The difference is that two different types of data are collected and analyzed, sometimes sequentially (as in the exploratory and explanatory designs) and sometimes concurrently (as in the triangulation design).

Triangulation designs may also involve the conversion of one type of data into the other type. As we mentioned earlier, the conversion of qualitative data into quantitative data is referred to as *quantitizing*. For instance, interviews may lead a researcher to believe there are three types of elementary science learners: (1) manipulators, who like to touch and change objects in their environments; (2) memorizers, who attempt to memorize rote facts from textbooks; and (3) cooperative learners, who like to discuss topics with other students in the class. By counting the number of each type of learner in each of a number of science classes, the researcher could convert the qualitative data (the learner types) into quantitative data (the numbers of each type).

Again, as mentioned earlier, the conversion of quantitative data into qualitative data is referred to as *qualitizing*. For instance, individuals who share various quantitative characteristics may be grouped together into types. A researcher might categorize one group of students that is never tardy, always turns in assigned work, and writes long papers as "obsessive students." By way of contrast, the researcher might categorize a second group that is frequently tardy, often fails to turn in assigned work, and writes short papers as "uninterested students."

Write up the Results in a Manner Consistent with the Design Being Used. In writing up the results of a mixed-methods study, the ways in which the data were collected and analyzed are usually integrated in triangulation designs but treated separately for exploratory and explanatory designs.

Evaluating a Mixed-Methods Study

Evaluation is necessary for all research, not just mixed-methods research. However, given that mixed-methods research involves comparing different methods, it is of particular importance here. Due to the fact that mixed-methods studies always involve both quantitative and qualitative data and frequently two different phases of data collection, the evaluation of such studies is often difficult. Nevertheless, each method should be evaluated according to the criteria we have suggested and used with other methods (see Chapter 13).

Ask yourself if both qualitative and quantitative data played a role in the conclusions reached. In good mixed-methods research, these two methods should either complement each other or address different sub-questions related to the larger research question addressed by the study. Sometimes a researcher will collect quantitative or qualitative data, but it will not play a role in answering any of the important research questions. In these cases, the data is just an add-on (perhaps because the researcher "likes" that kind of data), and the project is not truly a mixed-methods approach.

Second, ask yourself if the study contains threats to internal validity (as quantitative researchers refer to it) or credibility (as qualitative researchers refer to it). Are there alternative explanations for the findings, beyond those given by the author? What steps have been taken to ensure that the design is tight and that high levels of internal validity and credibility have been achieved? Some of the appropriate steps have been described elsewhere in this text in discussions of quantitative and qualitative research.

Third, ask yourself about the **generalizability** (as quantitative researchers refer to it) or **transferability** (as qualitative researchers refer to it) of the results. Do the results found in the present study extend beyond the domain studied to other contexts and other individuals? Is the description of the qualitative results sufficient to determine if they would be useful to other researchers in other situations? The answers to these questions are essential because a study without generalizability (external validity) or transferability is of little interest to anyone other than the study's author.

Ethics in Mixed-Methods Research

Ethical concerns and questions affect mixed-methods studies just as much as they do any of the other kinds of research we have described and discussed in this text. Three of the most important are protecting participant identity, treating participants with respect, and protecting participants from both physical and psychological harm. See Chapter 4 and pages 436–437 in Chapter 18 for further discussion.

Summary

In sum, it is apparent that mixed-methods studies are becoming increasingly common in educational research. Their value lies in combining quantitative and qualitative methods in ways that complement each other. The strengths of each approach to a large degree mitigate the weaknesses of the other. While mixed-methods research designs are potentially quite attractive, however, they should be approached with the realization that to carry them out well requires considerable time, energy, and resources. Furthermore, researchers need to be skilled in both quantitative and qualitative methods, or to collaborate with those who possess the skills they lack.

An Example of Mixed-Methods Research

In the remainder of this chapter, we present a published example of mixed-methods research, followed by a critique of its strengths and weaknesses. As we did previously in our critiques of the different types of research studies, we use concepts introduced earlier in the book to perform our analysis.

RESEARCH REPORT

From: (2006). *Journal of Counseling Psychology*, *53*(3), 279–287. Reproduced with permission.

Perceived Family Support, Acculturation, and Life Satisfaction in Mexican American Youth: A Mixed-Methods Exploration

L. M. Edwards
Marquette University

S. J. Lopez
University of Kansas

In this article, the authors describe a mixed-methods study designed to explore perceived family support, acculturation, and life satisfaction among 266 Mexican American adolescents. Specifically, the authors conducted a thematic analysis of open-ended responses to a question about life satisfaction to understand participants' perceptions of factors that contributed to their overall satisfaction with life. The authors also conducted hierarchical regression analyses to investigate the independent and interactive contributions of perceived support from family and Mexican and Anglo acculturation orientations on life satisfaction. Convergence of mixed-methods findings demonstrated that perceived family support and Mexican orientation were significant predictors of life satisfaction in these adolescents. Implications, limitations, and directions for further research are discussed.

Justification

Psychologists have identified and studied a number of challenges faced by Latino youth (e.g., juvenile delinquency, gang activity, school dropout, alcohol and drug abuse), yet little scholarly time and energy have been spent on exploring how these adolescents successfully navigate their development into adulthood or how they experience well-being (Rodriguez & Morrobel, 2004). Researchers have yet to understand the personal characteristics that play a role in Latino adolescents' satisfaction with life or how certain cultural values and/or strengths and resources are related to their well-being. Answers to these questions can begin to provide counseling psychologists with a deeper understanding of how Latino adolescents experience well-being, which can, in turn, hopefully allow researchers to work to improve well-being for those who struggle to find it.

Latino[1] youth are a growing presence in most communities within the United States. The U.S. Census Bureau projects that by the year 2010, 20% of young people between the ages of 10 and 20 years will be of Hispanic origin. Furthermore, it is projected that by the year 2020, one in five children will be Hispanic, and the Hispanic adolescent population will increase by 50% (U.S. Census Bureau, 2000, 2001). Whereas adolescence is a unique developmental period for all youth, Latino adolescents in particular may face additional challenges as a result of their ethnic minority status (Vazquez Garcia, Garcia

[1]In this article, the terms *Latino* and *Hispanic* have been used interchangeably. Specifically, in cases in which research is summarized, the descriptors used by the authors were retained. The participant sample, however, was restricted to adolescents who self-identified as "Mexican" or "Mexican American" and are thus described as such.

Coll, Erkut, Alarcon, & Tropp, 2000). These youth generally have undergone socialization experiences of their Latino culture (known as *enculturation*) and also must learn to *acculturate* to the dominant culture to some degree (Knight, Bernal, Cota, Garza, & Ocampo, 1993). Navigating the demands of these cultural contexts can be challenging, and yet many Latino youth experience well-being and positive outcomes. The increasing numbers of Latino youth, along with the counseling psychology field's imperative to provide culturally competent services, require that professionals continue to understand the full range of psychological functioning for members of this unique population.

Definitions

Counseling psychologists have continually emphasized the importance of well-being and identifying and developing client strengths in theory, research, and practice (Lopez et al., 2006; Walsh, 2003). This commitment to understanding the whole person, including internal and contextual assets and challenges, has been one hallmark of the field (Super, 1955; Tyler, 1973) and has influenced a variety of research about optimal human functioning (see D. W. Sue & Constantine, 2003). More recent discussions in this area have underscored the importance of identifying and nurturing cultural values and strengths in people of color (e.g., family, religious faith, biculturalism), being cautious to acknowledge that strengths are not universal and may differ according to context or cultural background (Lopez et al., 2006; Lopez et al., 2002; D. W. Sue & Constantine, 2003), and may be influenced by certain within-group differences such as acculturation level (Marin & Gamba, 2003; Zane & Mak, 2003).

As scholars respond to the emerging need to explore strengths among Latino youth, the importance of investigating these resources and values within a cultural context is evident. Understanding how Latino adolescents experience well-being from their own perspectives and vantage points is integral, as theories from other cultural worldviews may not be applicable to their lives (Auerbach & Silverstein, 2003; Lopez et al., 2002; D. W. Sue & Constantine, 2003). Furthermore, it is necessary to continue to test propositions about the role of certain Latino cultural values, such as the importance of family, in overall well-being. Given that many Latino adolescents today navigate bicultural contexts and adhere to Latino traditions and customs to differing degrees (Romero & Roberts, 2003), it is likely that the role family plays in adolescent well-being is complex and influenced by individual differences such as acculturation. In this study, we sought to explore the relationships between these variables by focusing specifically on perceived family support, life satisfaction, and acculturation among Mexican American youth.

Justification

Purpose

PERCEIVED FAMILY SUPPORT, ACCULTURATION, AND LIFE SATISFACTION AMONG LATINO YOUTH

The importance of family has been noted as a core Latino cultural value (Castillo, Conoley, & Brossart, 2004; Marin & Gamba, 2003; Paniagua, 1998; Sabogal, Marin, Otero-Sabogal, Marin, & Perez-Stable, 1987). *Familismo* (familism) is the term used to describe the importance of extended family ties in Latino culture as well as the strong identification and attachment of individuals with their families (Triandis, Marin, Betancourt, Lisansky, & Chang, 1982). Familism is not unique to Latino culture and has been noted as an important value for other ethnic groups such as African Americans, Asian Americans, and American Indians (Cooper, 1999; Marin & Gamba, 2003). Nevertheless, it is considered a central aspect of Latino culture, and in some studies, it has been shown to be valued by Latino individuals more than by non-Latino Whites (Gaines et al., 1997; Marin, 1993; Mindel, 1980).

Definition

In a study of *familismo* among Latino adolescents, Vazquez Garcia et al. (2000) found that the length of time youth had been in the United States did not affect their adherence to the value of *familismo*. These results demonstrated that the longer adolescents

Prior research

had been in the United States, the less they endorsed the value of *respeto* (respect), but their endorsement of *familismo* did not change. These findings highlight the central and enduring role that family plays in Latino culture, for both adults and adolescents.

Prior research

Most research about *familismo* has assessed the attitudinal dimension of this construct, which has been hypothesized to include a sense of perceived support from family, family obligations, solidarity, reciprocity, and family as referents (Marin, 1992; Marin & Gamba, 2003; Sabogal et al., 1987). It appears that *perceived family support* may be the key component of this value, as evidenced by research with Latino adults that investigated differences in aspects of *familismo* across acculturation levels. For example, Sabogal et al. found that as acculturation increased, familial obligations and family as referents decreased in respondents. Perceived family support scores, however, did not differ by acculturation level, place of birth or growing up, or generation.

Taken together, research about the importance of family suggests that *familismo* is a core Latino cultural value and that perceived support from family is a crucial component of this value that is not affected by acculturation level in adults (Marin & Gamba, 2003; Sabogal et al., 1987). In addition, research about family with Latino youth has demonstrated a relationship between aspects of familism and a lower risk of substance abuse (Unger et al., 2002), lower juvenile delinquency rates (Pabon, 1998), and other harmful behaviors (Marin, 1993; Moore, 1970; Rodriguez & Kosloski, 1998). Less is known, however, about the relationship between perceived family support and well-being and/or other positive psychological variables. Indeed, findings about family and various negative outcomes cannot be generalized to life satisfaction or well-being because well-being is more than just the absence of pathology or illness (Seligman, 2002). It is important to identify the variables that relate to positive outcomes in youth in addition to those that are related to negative outcomes and pathology (Gilman & Huebner, 2003).

Definition

Life satisfaction, which has been identified as an individual's appraisal of his or her life, is a commonly used indicator of well-being. As the cognitive, judgmental component of subjective well-being (SWB; Diener, Suh, Lucas, & Smith, 1999), life satisfaction can be distinguished from affective components of well-being (e.g., positive and negative affect), and thus transcends the immediate effects of mood states (Diener et al.). Life satisfaction appears to relate to important intra- and interpersonal outcomes (Gilman & Huebner, 2000), and numerous studies with adults suggest that life satisfaction is associated with marital quality, social intimacy, work engagement, positive illusions, self-efficacy, optimism, and goal striving (Diener & Suh, 2000; Myers & Diener, 1995).

In contrast to the large body of literature about life satisfaction in adults, researchers are only beginning to understand life satisfaction among adolescents (Gilman & Huebner, 2000). In a review of existing research, Gilman and Huebner (2003) noted that studies of adolescents have shown significant relationships between life satisfaction and positive and negative life experiences, parent-child conflict, substance use, stress and anxiety, and self-esteem in youth.

Justification

Within minority or Latino youth specifically, less is known about life satisfaction and its correlates. Understanding this variable in the cultural contexts in which Latino adolescents live is important, as life satisfaction can be considered central to decisions that these youth may make about work, education, and relationships (Bradley & Corwyn, 2004; Cooper, 1999; Romero & Roberts, 2003). In addition, understanding the role of acculturation in these relationships also is warranted as the field begins to explore within-group differences in psychological functioning among Latino youth and families (Castañeda, 1994).

Definition

Acculturation has been defined as the process of change that results from continuous contact between two different cultures (Berry, Trimble, & Olmedo, 1986). Several models of acculturation have been proposed and used to guide measures of this construct. Most initial research about acculturation adopted a unidimensional approach, which situated Latino individuals, for example, on a continuum of acculturation between two opposite poles of European American and Latino culture. As individuals assimilated to mainstream culture, this model suggested that they moved toward the European American end of the continuum and away from their Latino culture. A limitation of this approach, however, was that there was no acknowledgment of the possibility that acculturation toward the dominant culture does not necessarily preclude the simultaneous retention of one's culture of origin (LaFromboise, Coleman, & Gerton, 1993; Marin, 1992; Szapocznik & Kurtines, 1993; Zane & Mak, 2003).

One possibility

More recently, conceptualizations of acculturation have allowed for orthogonal, bidimensional measurements, such that acculturation to both Mexican and European American culture can be assessed independently along two axes (e.g., Cuellar, Arnold, & Maldonado, 1995). Some researchers have integrated this approach into their measurement of acculturation (e.g., Cuellar et al., 1995; Marin & Gamba, 1996) and, as such, have provided opportunities to investigate acculturation in a more complex manner and clarify how individuals can identify to differing degrees with both dominant culture and their cultures of origin (S. Sue, 2003). It has been suggested that researchers attend to acculturation as an important variable that can influence a group's values and that investigations of acculturation use more multidimensional conceptualizations in an effort to better understand cultural orientation and functioning (Berry, 2003; Chun & Akutsu, 2003; Kim & Abreu, 2001; Marin & Gamba, 1996). In the case of Latino youth, therefore, an investigation of perceived family support and life satisfaction warrants consideration of acculturation level as a possible factor that influences the relationship of these variables.

Second possibility

THE PRESENT STUDY

The overall purpose of this study was to examine the relationship between perceived family support, acculturation, and life satisfaction in Mexican American adolescents. Specifically, this study was designed to empirically test assumptions about the importance of perceived family support to life satisfaction in Mexican American youth and to address the following research questions: (a) What do Mexican American adolescents describe as variables that contribute to their life satisfaction? (b) How do perceived family support and acculturation relate to life satisfaction? and (c) Does acculturation moderate the relationship between perceived family support and life satisfaction?

Purpose

Implies hypotheses

To address these research questions, we used a mixed-methods approach combining both quantitative and qualitative methodologies. Several researchers have discussed the need for qualitative investigations of multicultural issues within psychology (Choudhuri, 2003; Morrow, Rakhsha, & Castaneda, 2001; Ponterotto, 2002; Umaña-Taylor & Bámaca, 2004), as they can provide an opportunity to better understand new phenomena or understudied populations without assuming that there is "one universal truth to be discovered" (Auerbach & Silverstein, 2003, p. 26). Mixed-methods research may be particularly useful for gaining a more complex understanding of a particular topic while simultaneously testing theoretical models (Hanson, Creswell, Plano Clark, Petska, & Creswell, 2005). Greene, Caracelli, and Graham (1989) suggested that mixed-methods studies can serve several purposes, including triangulation (seeking convergence of results), complementarity (examining overlapping or different facets of a phenomenon), initiation (discovering paradoxes and contradictions), development (using qualitative and quantitative methods sequentially), and expansion (adding breadth or scope to a project).

Mixed methods

Design stated

The present mixed-methods study was conceptualized from a pragmatic theoretical paradigm (Hanson et al., 2005; Tashakkori & Teddlie, 1998). We conceptualized and designed the study as a dominantly quantitative, concurrent design, which is indicated by the following procedural notation (Morse, 1991): QUANT + qual. That is, both quantitative and qualitative data were collected at the same time, and the primary methodology was quantitative, with a lesser emphasis on the qualitative portion (Tashakkori & Teddlie, 1998).

Qualitative and quantitative

For our purposes, qualitative methodology was used to address the first research question, which sought to explore variables that youth described as contributing to their life satisfaction. Open-ended responses provided by participants were analyzed thematically by a collaborative research team, using several strategies from grounded theory methodology (Strauss & Corbin, 1998), including open coding, category/theme generation, and exploring patterns across categories. Themes about factors that participants believed contributed to their life satisfaction were derived and described through this process. Quantitative methodology was used to answer the remaining research questions about the relationship between perceived family support, acculturation, and life satisfaction. We conducted a hierarchical multiple regression of perceived family support and Mexican and Anglo acculturation orientations on life satisfaction. We also added the interactions of perceived family support and both acculturation orientations to see whether these variables significantly predicted life satisfaction beyond the main effects of perceived family support and Mexican and Anglo orientations alone.

Findings from the quantitative and qualitative portions of the study were integrated to reveal areas of convergence as well as areas in which the data suggested discrepant findings or helped to provide a context for the data. Specifically, we sought to understand the relation between life satisfaction and perceived family support by looking for areas of convergence as well as complementarity between our qualitative and quantitative findings (Greene et al., 1989).

METHOD

Participants

By state?

Participants in this study were 309 English-speaking middle and high school students from California, Kansas, and Texas. Because there is research to suggest that grouping Latino adolescents into one collective ethnic group may not appropriately capture the within-group differences of this heterogeneous population (Umaña-Taylor & Fine, 2001), only the participants who self-identified as Mexican American (n = 293) were included in the present study. Furthermore, the small number of middle-school students (n = 27) was removed in order to have a final sample with more homogeneity with respect to age group (e.g., all high school students). Of this final sample of 266 Mexican American high school students, 150 (56%) were girls and 116 (44%) were boys, and they had a mean age of 15.74 years (SD = 1.04, range = 14–18 years). The majority of the sample was Catholic (78%), with 56% reporting that their parents had immigrated to the United States, and 26% reporting that their grandparents had immigrated to the United States.

Procedure

Potential participants were solicited in various ways, including contacting the League of United Latin American Citizens (LULAC) National Educational Service Centers, public and private schools, afterschool programs, and selected Federal TRIO (i.e., Upward Bound, Upward Bound Math/Science, and Educational Talent Search) programs. The primary researcher discussed the project with administrators and other staff to obtain initial approval to solicit participants and provided all the materials for the schools and organizations. In some cases, the primary researcher went to the sites to administer the surveys once parental consent forms were obtained, and in other cases, the site staff administered the surveys and returned them, along with the consent forms, to the researcher via mail. Several sites met with large groups of students on a regular basis (e.g., TRIO programs) and thus were able to monitor the return of informed consents in order to ensure maximum participation by students. For these sites, in addition to those from schools and community programs, the response rate was approximately 65%. At one afterschool program, however, 100 consent forms were given to supervisors to pass out to students, and only 7 were returned. This was surprising considering the relatively high response rate we obtained from other sites, and we are unclear as to what extent the study was actually described to students as was intended at this particular program.

Packets containing two informed consent forms (one for the students/parents to keep and one to return to the investigator), as well as an introductory letter, were distributed to students to take home during school or during their program's activity time. Both consent forms and the letter were translated into Spanish such that all parents received copies in English and Spanish. Parents were asked to send signed consent forms back to school (or the organization) with their children. Once consent was obtained from parents, students who volunteered to participate in the study were asked to complete a student assent form and then were administered a packet of materials during a 45-min period of school or of an afterschool program. Only students whose parents had provided consent and who had themselves completed an assent form were allowed to complete the packet of questionnaires, and the questionnaires were only provided in English. This decision to only sample students who were proficient readers in English was made during the development of the project because there was no existing data regarding the conceptual and functional equivalence of several of the measures for Latino adolescents in particular (American Psychological Association, 2002; Rogler, 1999).

Limits generalizing

Instruments

Demographic questionnaire. A demographic questionnaire was included to obtain participants' age, year in school, gender, race/ethnicity, generational status, and religious affiliation.

Given simultaneously

Open-ended question about well-being. At the bottom of the first page (demographic form) of each packet of measures was the following open-ended question: "What factors do you think contribute to life satisfaction and happiness?" Students were provided with 10 lines on which to write their responses and were encouraged to write on the back of the page if they needed more space.

Qualitative

Perceived social support. The Multidimensional Scale of Perceived Social Support (MSPSS; Zimet, Dahlem, Zimet, & Farley, 1988) is a 12-item scale that measures perceived support from three domains: Family, Friends, and a Significant Other. Participants completing the MSPSS are asked to indicate their agreement with items on a 7-point Likert scale ranging from 1 (*very strongly disagree*) to 7 (*very strongly agree*). A sample item from the Family subscale is "I get the emotional help and support I need from my family." Support for the reliability and validity of the MSPSS has been found with samples of college students, adolescents living abroad, and adolescents on an inpatient psychiatry unit (Canty-Mitchell & Zimet, 2000).

The MSPSS has been used in several studies with young adults and adults in the United States and in Europe (Kazarian & McCabe, 1991; Zimet et al., 1988; Zimet, Powell, Farley, Werkman, & Berkoff, 1990). In a recent study, Canty-Mitchell and Zimet (2000) investigated the MSPSS with a sample of urban adolescents, approximately 75% who were ethnic minority students. Results indicated internal reliability estimates of .93 for the total score, and .91, .89, and .91 for the Family, Friends, and Significant Other subscales. Factor analysis of the MSPSS with this sample confirmed the three-factor structure of the measure. In the present study, the four-item Perceived Support from Family subscale was used, and the internal reliability for this scale was .88.

Operational definition

Operational definition

Life satisfaction. The Multidimensional Students' Life Satisfaction Scale (MSLSS; Huebner, 1994) is a 47-item questionnaire that assesses life satisfaction in youth across six specific domains: Global, Family, Friends, School, Self, and Living Environment. The Global subscale, which comprises seven items, was used in the present study. Respondents were asked to rate items on a 6-point Likert scale ranging from 1 (*strongly disagree*) to 6 (*strongly agree*). A sample item from this subscale is "My life is going well."

Only global scale given?

Support for validity and reliability of the MSLSS has been found with various samples of children, middle- and high school students in the United States and Canada. The MSLSS was found to correlate with other measures of well-being, and its multidimensional factor structure was confirmed (Huebner, 1994; Gilman, Huebner, & Laughlin, 2000). Internal reliability coefficients in various studies with the MSLSS ranged from .77 to .91 across all subscales. In the present study, the internal reliability was .86 for the Global subscale.

Acculturation level. The Acculturation Rating Scale for Mexican Americans-II (ARSMA-II; Cuellar et al., 1995), which comprises 30 items, was used to measure acculturation in this study. Individuals were asked to respond to items about language preference, association, and identification with Mexican and Anglo cultures using a 5-point Likert scale ranging from 1 (*not at all*) to 5 (*extremely often or almost always*). The Mexican and Anglo subscales comprise 17 and 13 items, respectively. Examples of items from the Anglo and Mexican subscales are "I enjoy listening to English language music," and "I associate with Latinos and/or Latin Americans," respectively. In this study, we used Anglo and Mexican orientation subscales independently in order to evaluate their unique contributions to life satisfaction.

Operational definition

Studies with the ARSMA-II (Cuellar et al., 1995) revealed internal consistency estimates for the Anglo Orientation subscale (AOS) and the Mexican Orientation subscale (MOS) as .83 and .88, respectively. Flores and O'Brien (2002) reported reliability coefficients of .77 and .91 for the AOS and MOS with Mexican American adolescent women in particular. Test–retest reliability estimates, over a 2-week period, were .94 for the AOS and .96 for the MOS (Cuellar et al.). Internal reliability estimates of the Mexican and Anglo orientation scales in the present study were .88 and .67, respectively.

RESULTS

Qualitative Analyses

Qualitative analyses were originally conducted with responses from the total sample of both middle- and high school students, and findings were then revised and verified after the removal of the small sample of middle-school students. Of the 266 participants, 260 provided qualitative responses to the open-ended question, "What factors do you think contribute to life satisfaction and happiness?" Responses ranged from one word to short paragraphs of six sentences. In this study, we used several strategies from grounded theory (Strauss & Corbin, 1998) to analyze these responses, including open coding, category/theme generation, and exploring patterns across categories.

Short responses

Several strategies were used throughout the data analysis process to improve the rigor and "trustworthiness" of findings (Strauss & Corbin, 1998). First, a collaborative team, comprising the primary researcher/Lisa M. Edwards (a biethnic Latina/White woman) and two undergraduate Mexican American students, was convened. An external auditor (a female European American graduate student) was asked to review emerging themes and reflect on the analysis process. A second external auditor (a male European American graduate student) was asked to review the findings with the primary researcher after the middle-school students had been removed in order to verify or revise the original themes. Our reviews indicated that the primary themes remained the same.

Trustworthiness discussed

At the outset of data analysis, members of the research team discussed biases and assumptions, noting that they believed family, friends, and religious beliefs would be the most frequent responses reported by participants. Together, the research team then decided how the qualitative data might best be understood. They engaged in "open coding," or breaking down each participant's responses into words, phrases, or sentences that represented meaning units (Strauss & Corbin, 1998). These meaning units were then labeled as *concepts* and were refined and discussed as necessary, eventually leading to a final list of concepts. The final concept list included the following terms: *family, friends, attitude, faith* (e.g., God, spirituality), *love, money, helping others, work, home, education* (e.g., teachers, school), *physical health,* and *goals.* Last, interrelated concepts were grouped together into larger category themes (e.g., descriptive sentences), and the most prominent themes were then selected and reviewed.

Results from this analysis suggested one primary, core theme, as well as two additional, smaller themes. The core theme that emerged from participants' open-ended responses was *Family is important for providing support and love* and included responses that described the significance of family and the ways in which family gives support and love to participants. Specifically, adolescents noted that their families provided unconditional care and encouragement as well as affection and support. Illustrative quotes included the following: "Have a family that will be there for you and inspire you to be a better person in the future"; "Life satisfaction is to have your family be united and have love for one another in the home"; "Above all family, because how you enjoy life is being with those you care about"; "Having your family with you—they are the best that we could have"; "Having a caring family who supports you"; and "Family—especially my father who works hard to put food on the table everyday."

Good clarifying examples

Two prominent additional themes emerged from the data as secondary to the importance of family. The first theme, *Friends provide help and fun*, revealed participants' beliefs that friends contributed to life satisfaction in several ways. Quotes describing the role of friends included "Having friends to talk to and hang around with, who will help you out"; ". . . good friends who can be relied on"; and ". . . kickin' it with my friends—going to school and talking to my homeboys."

The second additional theme that emerged from the qualitative data related to the contribution of a positive approach or attitude toward challenges. We labeled this theme *The importance of a positive attitude toward life and problems.* Illustrative quotes of this theme included "Always be optimistic—there will be ups and downs, but life will still go on"; "Life satisfaction comes when you are satisfied with who you are, but able to change what you can"; and "Do your best—even if you didn't win you could say that you tried your best."

Quantitative Analyses

Assumptions checked

Preliminary analyses included checking the data for outliers, normality, linearity, and homoscedasticity as well as examining potential differences on the basis of the location from which participants were sampled. The scatter plot of the studentized residuals against the predicted values of life satisfaction revealed no violations of assumptions of normality, linearity, and homoscedasticity. Results based on Cook and Weisberg's (1982) distance showed no serious outliers among the study variables (Tabachnick & Fidell, 1996). Missing data points for an item on a subscale, which were found in 14 cases, were handled by substituting participants' subscale or mean scale scores for the missing value.

Incorrect statistics

Independent samples t tests were conducted to see whether there were significant differences in the study variables for respondents who had completed surveys in California and Texas without the lead researcher present during administration ($n = 184$) and those that had completed surveys in Kansas administered by the lead researcher ($n = 82$). Results indicated that there were no significant differences in scores of life satisfaction, $t(262) = -1.65$, $p = .10$; perceived family support, $t(261) = -0.32$, $p = .75$; Mexican orientation, $t(259) = -1.33$, $p = .19$; and Anglo orientation, $t(263) = 0.56$, $p = .58$. Because there were no differences in total scores on the basis of the location of participants, all the data in this sample were analyzed together.

The means, standard deviations, and zero-order correlations for all study variables (perceived family support, Anglo and Mexican orientations, and life satisfaction) are presented in Table 1. As can be seen, life satisfaction was significantly, positively correlated with perceived support from family and Mexican orientation. Thus, as scores of perceived family support and Mexican orientation increased, scores of global life satisfaction increased. Mexican and Anglo orientations also were significantly positively correlated with perceived family support; as scores on each of the acculturation orientations increased, perceived family support increased.

The main and interactive effects of Mexican and Anglo acculturation orientations and perceived family support on life satisfaction were assessed using hierarchical multiple regression procedures described by Cohen, West, and Aiken (2003) and Lubinski and Humphreys (1990). In order to reduce possible multicollinearity, scales were standardized before forming cross-product terms and before running the regression (Dunlap & Kemery, 1987; Jaccard, Wan, & Turrisi, 1990). Lubinski and Humphreys described procedures for the detection of spurious moderator effects, and they argued that moderator effects and quadratic trends are likely to share a large proportion of the variance. In other words, a significant interaction between two variables may be observed only because the effect is correlated substantially with quadratic trends of the component

Descriptive statistics

TABLE 1 ***Means, Standard Deviations, and Correlations Among Variables (N = 266)***

Variable	1	2	3	4
1. Life satisfaction	–	.53***	.07	.22***
2. Perceived family support		–	.15*	.21**
3. Anglo orientation			–	.07
4. Mexican orientation			–	–
M	27.27	47.95	19.88	26.74
SD	8.21	8.40	13.35	16.92

*$p < .05$. **$p < .01$. ***$p < .001$.

TABLE 2 ***Summary of Hierarchical Regression Analysis of Perceived Family Support, Mexican, and Anglo Orientations as Predictors of Life Satisfaction (N = 266)***

Variable	B	SE B	β	t	df	R^2	ΔR^2	ΔF	df
Step 1 (main effects)					254	0.28	0.28	32.17***	3,254
Perceived family support	0.51	0.07	.51	7.01***					
Anglo orientation	0.00	0.06	.00	0.02					
Mexican orientation	0.13	0.06	.13	2.05*					
Step 2 (quadratic effects)					251	0.28	0.00	0.1	3,251
Step 3 (interaction effects)					249	0.29	0.01	1.98	2,249
Perceived family support	0.51	0.07	.51	7.01***					
Anglo orientation	0.00	0.06	.00	0.02					
Mexican orientation	0.13	0.06	.13	2.05*					
Family squared	0.00	0.05	.00	0.02					
Anglo squared	0.04	0.04	.05	0.82					
Mexican squared	0.02	0.05	.03	0.43					
Anglo x Family	−0.07	0.06	−.07	−1.20					
Mexican x Family	−0.11	0.06	−.11	−1.86					

*$p < .05$. **$p < .01$. ***$p < .001$.

Size of R^2

Regression results

variables. Thus, entering quadratic trends into the regression equation reduces the possibility of observing such spurious moderators.

In Lubinski and Humphrey's (1990) recommended procedure, main effects are entered first into the regression equation; after this a priori entry, quadratic trends are entered. In the first step, the main effects of perceived family support, Mexican orientation, and Anglo orientation were entered. Next, quadratic terms of the main effect variables were entered to control for spurious moderator effects. Finally, the two-way interactions of Mexican orientation and perceived family support, and Anglo orientation and perceived family support, were entered.

Table 2 provides the results of the multiple regressions involving our predictor variables. The main effects of perceived family support ($\beta = .50$, $p < .001$) and Mexican orientation ($\beta = .12$, $p < .05$) were significant at Step 1, accounting for 28% of the variance in life satisfaction. Higher scores on the perceived family support and Mexican orientation variables were associated with higher life satisfaction. After controlling for quadratic trends (Step 2), the interactions between Anglo and Mexican orientations and perceived family support were not significant in Step 3, accounting for 1% of the variance in life satisfaction and resulting in a total $R^2 = .29$.

DISCUSSION

Because of the dearth of research examining well-being in Latino youth, the present mixed-methods study was conducted to expand researchers' understanding of the relationship between life satisfaction, acculturation, and perceived family support in Mexican American adolescents. A contribution of this study was that a mixed-method approach was used to obtain qualitative perspectives on life satisfaction as well as quantitative findings about acculturation, perceived family support, and life satisfaction. An additional strength of this study was that acculturation was measured and conceptualized in a bidimensional manner, such that questions about the independent and interactive influences of both Mexican and Anglo orientations and family support on life satisfaction could be investigated (Zane & Mak, 2003). Finally, rather than combining ethnic minority groups or Latino ethnic subgroups, or only sampling adults, we investigated Mexican American adolescents in particular (Castañeda, 1994; Umaña-Taylor & Fine, 2001).

Integration of Mixed-Methods Findings

Convergence discussed

The quantitative and qualitative results converged to provide additional empirical support for the importance of family in the lives of Mexican American adolescents (Marin & Gamba, 2003; Paniagua, 1998; Vazquez Garcia et al., 2000). The qualitative findings suggested that youth identified their family as most important in contributing to their life satisfaction above other factors such as friends, religion, or money. In addition, the qualitative findings suggested that the important role of family was to provide support specifically. These findings also suggest that previous research with adults about perceived support as the critical aspect of *familismo* may also apply to youth (Sabogal et al., 1987).

Two additional themes that emerged from our qualitative data, *Friends provide help and fun* and *The importance of a positive attitude toward life and problems,* suggested aspects of participants' lives that were important to them, though not as critical as family. These additional findings, though not able to be explored by quantitative analyses in this particular study, help to identify additional factors that contribute to life satisfaction from the perspective of Mexican American youth and can be included in future models of life satisfaction.

The quantitative findings about the relationship between perceived family support and acculturation orientations revealed additional information regarding the role of these variables in predicting overall life satisfaction in Mexican American youth. Mexican orientation, but not Anglo orientation, was significantly associated with life satisfaction in this sample, highlighting the importance of investigating acculturation orientations separately (Kim & Abreu, 2001; Marin & Gamba, 2003). As noted by Ruelas, Atkinson, and Ramos-Sanchez (1998) in their study of counselor credibility, unidimensional measures of acculturation may lead to inaccurate inferences about cultural orientation. These authors used the ARSMA-II (Cuellar et al., 1995) and found that Mexican orientation scores were significantly related to credibility of counselors, but not Anglo scores. Although we investigated a different dependent variable, the findings were similar in that Mexican orientation appeared to be the influential acculturation orientation. Future studies about life satisfaction in Mexican American youth should explore why Mexican orientation, in contrast to Anglo orientation, plays this important role.

Limitations, Directions for Future Research, and Implications

Good recognition of limitations

There are several limitations to this study that should be noted. In the qualitative portion of the study, it was not clear whether the open-ended question that was presented to students was understood in the same way by each of the respondents. Furthermore, the question did not ask for an evaluation of participants' life satisfaction. It is possible, therefore, that participants interpreted this question to address factors that contribute to life satisfaction for people in general. The study also was limited in that only English-speaking participants were allowed to participate. By not including Spanish-speaking adolescents, and by recruiting most participants from educational and cultural programs (e.g., TRIO programs and the like), we may have limited the representativeness of the sample across acculturation levels and degree of educational involvement.

One avenue for potential future investigation lies in understanding different types of social support that Latino adolescents use or perceive in their lives. In the present study, only general perceived family support was assessed, and we were unable to measure how specific types of support may contribute to life satisfaction in these youth. A useful conceptualization of social support was proposed by Weiss (1974), who described *provisions* that can result from relationships with others, such as guidance, reliable alliance, attachment reassurance of worth, social integration, and opportunity to provide nurturance. This framework has been used and operationalized by many researchers (Aquino, Russell, Cutrona, & Altmaier, 1996; Cutrona & Russell, 1987) and can provide a beginning structure for researchers to probe more specific types of social support in Latino youth.

In addition, investigating variables such as perceived support from family and acculturation and life satisfaction over time, rather than only focusing on cross-sectional views, also will provide additional information about the changing role of family and its influence on the well-being of Latino youth as they transition into adulthood (Chun & Akutsu, 2003; Marin & Gamba, 2003). The changing demographics of our present society, as well as the demands on the lives of adolescents, require closer investigations of how the function and role of various resources such as family adapt over time and how acculturation (e.g., Mexican orientation) influences this process.

The increasing presence of Mexican American youth in our schools and communities requires that counseling psychologists purposefully work to understand these adolescents' experience of life satisfaction in addition to obstacles that may be hindering their well-being. Low educational attainment as well as problems such as gang involvement, substance abuse, and teenage pregnancy have been identified as significant concerns faced by Latino youth (Chavez & Roney, 1990), and scholars have noted that few mental health professionals are trained to work with Mexican American adolescents (Castañeda, 1994). Investigating within-group variability in the experience of life satisfaction and the role of perceived family support, such as the analyses in the present study, provide a more balanced and detailed portrait of functioning within Latino adolescents (Villarruel & Montero-Sieburth, 2000). Our findings suggest that family and Mexican orientation will be particularly important variables for counseling psychologists to consider when working to promote life satisfaction with Mexican American youth. Future research can continue to elucidate strengths and assets within this important population and contribute to a growing body of knowledge about youth resources.

References

American Psychological Association. (2002). *Guidelines on multicultural education, training, research, practice, and organizational change for psychologists.* Washington DC: Author.

Aquino, J. A., Russell, D., Cutrona, C. E,. & Altmaier, E. M. (1996). Employment status, social support, and life satisfaction among the elderly. *Journal of Counseling Psychology, 43,* 480–489.

Auerbach, C. F., & Silverstein, L. B. (2003). *Qualitative data: An introduction to coding and analysis.* New York: NYU Press.

Berry, J. W. (2003). Conceptual approaches to acculturation. In K. M. Chun, P. B. Organista, & G. Marin (Eds.), *Acculturation: Advances in theory, measurement, and applied research* (pp. 17–37). Washington, DC: American Psychological Association.

Berry, J. W., Trimble, J. E., & Olmedo, E. L. (1986). Assessment of acculturation. In W. J. Lonner & J. W. Berry (Eds.), *Field methods in cross-cultural research* (pp. 291–345). Beverly Hills, CA: Sage.

Bradley, R. H., & Corwyn, R. F. (2004). Life satisfaction among European American, African American, Chinese American, Mexican American, and Dominican American adolescents. *International Journal of Behavioral Development, 28,* 385–400.

Canty-Mitchell, J., & Zimet, G. D. (2000). Psychometric properties of the Multidimensional Scale of Perceived Social Support in urban adolescents. *American Journal of Community Psychology, 28,* 391–400.

Castañeda, D. M. (1994). A research agenda for Mexican-American adolescent mental health. *Adolescence, 29,* 225–240.

Castillo, L. G., Conoley, C. W., & Brossart, D. F. (2004). Acculturation, White marginalization, and family support as predictors of perceived distress in Mexican American female college students. *Journal of Counseling Psychology, 51,* 151–157.

Chavez, J. M., & Roney, C. E. (1990). Psychocultural factors affecting the mental health status of Mexican American adolescents. In A. R. Stiffman & L. E. Davis (Eds.), *Ethnic issues in adolescent mental health* (pp. 73–91). Newbury Park, CA: Sage.

Choudhuri, D. D. (2003). Qualitative research and multicultural counseling competency. In D. B. Pope-Davis, H. L. K. Coleman, W. M. Liu, & R. L. Toporek (Eds.), *Handbook of multicultural competencies in counseling and psychology* (pp. 267–282). Thousand Oaks, CA: Sage.

Chun, K. M., & Akutsu, P. D. (2003). Acculturation among ethnic minority families. In K. M. Chun, P. B. Organista, & G. Marin (Eds.), *Acculturation: Advances in theory, measurement and applied research* (pp. 95–119). Washington, DC: American Psychological Association.

Cohen, J., West, S. G., & Aiken, L. S. (2003). *Applied multiple regression/correlation analysis for the behavioral sciences* (3rd ed.). Mahwah, NJ: Erlbaum.

Cook, R. D., & Weisberg, S. (1982). *Residuals and influence in regression.* New York: Chapman & Hall.

Cooper, G. R. (1999). Multiple selves, multiple worlds: Cultural perspectives on individuality and connectedness in adolescent development. In A. S. Masten (Ed.), *Cultural process in child development* (pp. 25–57). Mahwah, NJ: Erlbaum.

Cuellar, I., Arnold, B., & Maldonado, R. (1995). Acculturation Rating Scale for Mexican Americans-II: A revision of the original ARSMA Scale. *Hispanic Journal of Behavioral Sciences, 17,* 275–304.

Cutrona, C. E., & Russell, D. (1987). The provisions of social relationships and adaptation to stress. In W. H. Jones & D. Perlman (Eds.), *Advances in personal relationships* (Vol. I, pp. 37–68). Greenwich, CT: JAI Press.

Diener, E., & Suh, E. M. (2000). Measuring subjective well-being to compare the quality of life of cultures. In E. Diener & E. M. Suh (Eds.), *Culture aid subjective well-being* (pp. 3–12). Cambridge, MA: MIT Press.

Diener, E., Suh, E. M., Lucas, R., & Smith, H. (1999). Subjective well-being: Three decades of progress. *Psychological Bulletin, 125,* 276–302.

Dunlap, W. P., & Kemery, E. R. (1987). Failure to detect moderating effects. Is multicollinearity the problem? *Psychological Bulletin, 102,* 418–420.

Flores, L. Y., & O'Brien, K. M. (2002). The career development of Mexican American adolescent women: A test of social cognitive career theory. *Journal of Counseling Psychology, 49,* 14–27.

Gaines, S. O., Marelich, W. D., Bledsoe, K. L., Steers, W. N., Henderson, M. C., Granrose, C. S., et al. (1997). Links between race/ethnicity and cultural values as mediated by racial/ethnic identity and moderated by gender. *Journal of Personality and Social Psychology, 72,* 1460–1476.

Gilman, R., & Huebner, E. S. (2000). Review of life satisfaction measures for adolescents. *Behaviour Change, 17,* 178–195.

Gilman, R., & Huebner, E. S. (2003). A review of life satisfaction research with children and adolescents. *School Psychology Quarterly, 18,* 192–205.

Gilman, R., Huebner, E. S., & Laughlin, J. (2000). A first study of the Multidimensional Students' Life Satisfaction Scale with adolescents. *Social Indicators Research, 52,* 135–160.

Greene, J. C., Caracelli, V. J., & Graham, W. F. (1989). Toward a conceptual framework for mixed-method evaluation designs. *Educational Evaluation and Policy Analysis, 11,* 255–274.

Hanson, W. E., Creswell, J. W., Plano Clark, V. L., Petska, K. S., & Creswell, J. D. (2005). Mixed methods research designs in counseling psychology. *Journal of Counseling Psychology, 52,* 224–235.

Huebner, E. S. (1994). Preliminary development and validation of a multidimensional life satisfaction scale for children. *Psychological Assessment, 6,* 149–158.

Jaccard, J., Wan, C. K., & Turrisi, R. (1990). The detection and interpretation of interaction effects between continuous variables in multiple regression. *Multivariate Behavioral Research, 25,* 467–478.

Kazarian, S. S., & McCabe, S. B. (1991). Dimensions of social support in the MSPSS: Factorial structure, reliability, and theoretical implications. *Journal of Community Psychology, 19,* 150–160.

Kim, B. S. K., & Abreu, J. M. (2001). Acculturation measurement. In J. G. Ponterotto, J. M. Casas, L. A. Suzuki, & C. M. Alexander (Eds.), *Handbook of multicultural counseling* (pp. 394–424). Thousand Oaks, CA: Sage.

Knight, G. P., Bernal, M. E., Cota, M. K, Garza, C. A., & Ocampo, K. A. (1993). Family socialization and Mexican American identity and behavior. In M. E. Bernal & G. P. Knight (Eds.), *Ethnic identity* (pp. 105–129). New York: SUNY Press.

LaFromboise, T., Coleman, H., & Gerton, J. (1993). Psychological impact of biculturalism: Evidence and theory. *Psychological Bulletin, 114,* 395–412.

Lopez, S. J., Magyar-Moe, J. L., Petersen, S. E., Ryder, J. A., Krieshok, T. S., O'Byme, K. K, et al. (2006). Contextualizing human strengths: A counseling psychology agenda for increasing the applicability of positive psychology. *The Counseling Psychologist, 34,* 205–227.

Lopez, S. J., Prosser, E. C, Edwards, L. M., Magyar-Moe, J. L., Neufeld, J. E., & Rasmussen, H. N. (2002). Putting positive psychology in a multicultural context. In C. R. Snyder & S. J. Lopez (Eds.), *Handbook of positive psychology* (pp. 700–714). New York: Oxford University Press.

Lubinski, D., & Humphreys, L. G. (1990). Assessing spurious "moderator effects": Illustrated substantively with the hypothesized ("synergistic") relation between spatial and mathematical ability. *Psychological Bulletin, 107,* 385–393.

Marin, G. (1992). Issues in the measurement of acculturation among Hispanics. In K. F. Geisinger (Ed.), *Psychological testing of Hispanics* (pp. 235–251). Washington, DC: American Psychological Association.

Marin, G. (1993). Influence of acculturation on familialism and self-identification among Hispanics. In M. E. Bernal & G. P. Knight (Eds.), *Ethnic identity* (pp. 181–196). New York: SUNY Press.

Marin, G., & Gamba, R. J. (1996). A new measurement of acculturation for Hispanics: The Bidimensional Acculturation Scale for Hispanics (BAS). *Hispanic Journal of Behavioral Sciences, 18,* 297–316.

Marin, G., & Gamba, R. J. (2003). Acculturation and changes in cultural values. In K. M. Chun, P. B. Organista, & G. Marin (Eds.), *Acculturation: Advances In theory, measurement, and applied research* (pp. 83–94). Washington, DC: American Psychological Association.

Mindel, C. H. (1980). Extended familism among urban Mexican Americans, Anglos and Blacks. *Hispanic Journal of Behavioral Sciences, 2,* 21–34.

Moore, J. W. (1970). *Mexican Americans.* Englewood Cliffs, NJ: Prentice Hall.

Morrow, S. L., Rakhsha, G., & Castaneda, C. L. (2001). Qualitative research methods for multicultural counseling. In J. G. Ponterotto, J. M. Casas, L. A. Suzuki, & C. M. Alexander (Eds.), *Handbook of multicultural counseling* (pp. 575–603). Thousand Oaks, CA: Sage.

Morse, J. M. (1991). Approaches to qualitative-quantitative methodological triangulation. *Nursing Research, 40,* 120–123.

Myers, D. G., & Diener, E. (1995). Who is happy? *Psychological Science, 6,* 10–19.

Pabon, E. (1998). Hispanic adolescent delinquency and the family: A discussion of sociocultural influences. *Adolescence, 33,* 941–955.

Paniagua, F. (1998). *Assessing and treating culturally diverse clients: A practical guide.* Thousand Oaks, CA: Sage.

Ponterotto, J. G. (2002). Qualitative research methods: The fifth force in psychology. *The Counseling Psychologist, 30,* 394–406.

Rodriguez, J. M., & Kosloski, K. (1998). The impact of acculturation on attitudinal familism in a community of Puerto Rican Americans. *Hispanic Journal of Behavioral Sciences, 20,* 375–390.

Rodriguez, M. C., & Morrobel, D. (2004). A review of Latino youth development research and a call for an asset orientation. *Hispanic Journal of Behavioral Sciences, 26,* 107–127.

Rogler, L. H. (1999). Methodological sources of cultural insensitivity in mental health research. *American Psychologist, 54,* 424–433.

Romero, A. J., & Roberts, R. E. (2003). Stress within a bicultural context, for adolescents of Mexican descent. *Cultural Diversity & Ethnic Minority Psychology, 9,* 171–184.

Ruelas, S. R., Atkinson, D. R., & Ramos-Sanchez, L. (1998). Counselor helping model and participant ethnicity, locus of control, and perceived counselor credibility. *Journal of Counseling Psychology, 45,* 98–103.

Sabogal, F., Marin, G., Otero-Sabogal, R., Marin, B. V., & Perez-Stable, E. J. (1987). Hispanic familism and acculturation: What changes and what doesn't? *Hispanic Journal of Behavioral Sciences, 9,* 397–412.

Seligman, M. E. P. (2002). Positive psychology, positive prevention, and positive therapy. In C. R. Snyder & S. J. Lopez (Eds.), *Handbook of positive psychology* (pp. 3–9). New York: Oxford University Press.

Strauss, A., & Corbin, J. (1998). *Basics of qualitative research: Techniques and procedures for developing grounded theory* (2nd ed.). Thousand Oaks, CA: Sage.

Sue, D. W., & Constantine, M. G. (2003). Optimal human functioning in people of color in the United States. In B. W. Walsh (Ed.), *Counseling psychology and optimal human functioning* (pp. 151–169). Mahwah, NJ: Erlbaum.

Sue, S. (2003). Foreword. In K. M. Chun, P. B. Organista, & G. Marin (Eds.), *Acculturation: Advances in theory, measurement, and applied research* (pp. xvii–xxi). Washington, DC: American Psychological Association.

Super, D. E. (1955). Transition: From vocational guidance to counseling psychology. *Journal of Counseling Psychology, 2,* 3–9.

Szapocznik, J., & Kurtines, W. (1993). Family psychology and cultural diversity. *American Psychologist, 48,* 400–407.

Tabachnick, B. G., & Fidell, L. S. (1996). *Using multivariate statistics* (3rd ed.). New York: HarperCollins.

Tashakkori, A., & Teddlie, C. (1998). *Mixed methodology.* Thousand Oaks, CA: Sage.

Triandis, H. C., Marin, G., Betancourt, J., Lisansky, J., & Chang, B. (1982). *Dimensions of familism among Hispanic and mainstream Navy recruits.* Chicago: Department of Psychology, University of Illinois.

Tyler, L. E. (1973). Design for a hopeful psychology. *American psychologist, 28,* 1021–1029.

Umaña-Taylor, A. J., & Bámaca, M. Y. (2004). Conducting focus groups with Latino populations: Lessons from the field. *Family Relations, 53,* 261–272.

Umaña-Taylor, A. J., & Fine, M. A. (2001). Methodological implications of grouping Latino adolescents into one collective ethnic group. *Hispanic Journal of Behavioral Sciences, 23,* 347–362.

Unger, J. B., Ritt-Olson, A., Teran, L., Huang, T., Hoffman, B. R., & Palmer, P. (2002). Cultural values and substance use in a multiethnic sample of California adolescents. *Addiction Research & Theory, 10,* 257–279.

U. S. Census Bureau. (2000). *Annual projections of the resident population by age, sex, race, and Hispanic origin: Lowest, middle, highest series and zero international migration series, 1999 to 2100.* Retrieved October 7, 2002, from http://www.census.gov/population/www/projections/natdet-D1A.html

U. S. Census Bureau (2001). The *Hispanic population: Census 2000 brief.* Washington, DC: U.S. Department of Commerce, Economics and Statistical Administration.

Vazquez Garcia, H. A., Garcia Coll, C., Erkut, S., Alarcon, O., & Tropp, L. R. (2000). Family values of Latino adolescents. In M. Montero-Sieburth & F. A. Villarruel (Eds.), *Making invisible Latino adolescents visible* (pp. 239–263). New York: Falmer Press.

Villarruel, F. A., & Montero-Sieburth, M. (2000). Latino youth and America. In M. Montero-Sieburth & F. A. Villarruel (Eds.), *Making invisible Latino adolescents visible* (pp. xiii–xxxii). New York: Falmer Press.

Walsh, W. B. (Ed.). (2003). *Counseling psychology and optimal human functioning.* Mahwah, NJ: Erlbaum.

Weiss, R. S. (1974). The provisions of social relationships. In Z. Rubin (Ed.), *Doing unto others* (pp. 17–26). Englewood Cliffs, NJ: Prentice Hall.

Zane, N., & Mak, W. (2003). Major approaches to the measurement of acculturation among ethnic minority populations: A content analysis and an alternative empirical strategy. In K. M. Chun, P. B. Organista, & G. Marin (Eds.), *Acculturation: Advances in theory, measurement, and applied research* (pp. 39–60). Washington, DC: American Psychological Association.

Zimet, G. D., Dahlem, N. W., Zimet, S. G., & Farley, G. K. (1988). The Multidimensional Scale of Perceived Social Support. *Journal of Personality Assessment, 52,* 30–41.

Zimet, G. D., Powell, S. S., Farley, G. K., Werkman, S., & Berkoff, K. A. (1990). Psychometric characteristics of the Multidimensional Scale of Perceived Social Support. *Journal of Personality Assessment, 55,* 610–617.

Analysis of the Study

The authors do a good job of presenting the variables of interest in this study and clearly stating that this study will employ mixed methods. The justification is somewhat lengthy but can be summarized by saying that there is an increasing population of Latino youth and a need to determine the factors that lead to life satisfaction among this population of adolescents. Notably, the authors attempt to look at the research question from a positive perspective: What are the predictors of life satisfaction, as opposed to what are the predictors of problem behaviors (e.g., dropping out of school or drug usage), among Latino youth?

The authors discuss the importance of family support, or *familismo,* and level of acculturation, or identification and comfort, with both the Latino culture and the Anglo culture, as potential predictors of life satisfaction. While these variables seem quite plausible, we wonder whether other potential predictors might have been chosen in addition to these. It is not completely clear that these are the only (or even the strongest) predictors of life satisfaction among Latino adolescents.

The purpose of the study is clearly stated as follows: "The overall purpose of the study was to examine the relationship between perceived family support, acculturation, and life satisfaction in Mexican American adolescents." Specific questions and the research design follow immediately afterward.

DEFINITIONS

Familismo is defined as the importance of extended family ties in Latino culture as well as the strong identification and attachment of individuals with their families. From this definition the independent variable of family support is derived.

The definition of *acculturation* (also an independent variable) is discussed in terms of its evolution from a unidimensional construct to a pair of independent dimensions. Originally, acculturation was defined as the degree to which one thought of oneself as Latino versus Anglo. Later theories, however, pointed out that it was possible to identify with both cultures rather than with only a single culture. This required measuring identification with the two cultures separately.

The concept of *life satisfaction,* the dependent variable in the study, is defined as an individual's appraisal of his or her life, and is used as an indicator of well-being. In particular, the authors note that life satisfaction involves the cognitive, as opposed to the emotional, components of well-being.

PRIOR RESEARCH

Prior research on the independent and dependent variables is cited extensively throughout the introduction. In some cases the research applies to populations other than Latino youth, which serves as a justification for studying these variables in this population.

HYPOTHESES AND DESIGN

The authors state no hypotheses, but rather three research questions are presented: (1) What do Mexican-American adolescents describe as variables that contribute to their life satisfaction? (2) How do perceived family support and acculturation relate to life satisfaction? (3) Does acculturation moderate the relationship between perceived family support and life satisfaction? The first of these questions is a qualitative one, the other two are quantitative. This demonstrates that the two different types of research methods are tied to specific questions—a good sign in a mixed-methods study, as it makes clear which analyses are intended to answer which questions. We think the latter two questions clearly imply hypotheses, however—that is, that the variables are related.

The authors present an argument for the importance of mixed-methods research and describe the relative importance of the two research method types. Quantitative data is given primary importance. The study uses a triangulation design, and all instruments were given at the same time. That the quantitative variables did not emerge from the qualitative study (as in an exploratory design) is made clear at the outset both in the initial questions and in the choice of quantitative instruments. The qualitative study was intended to elicit variables important to life satisfaction, presumably to support the choice of the quantitative variables—family support and acculturation. The quantitative method was a survey administered in groups followed by regression analysis. The qualitative method was based on grounded theory.

SAMPLE

The target population is presumably all Mexican-American high school students in the United States. The initial sample was a convenience sample of 309 English-speaking middle and high school students from California, Kansas, and Texas recruited from various agencies. The sample was reduced to 266 by only including those students who self-identified as Mexican-American and who were in high school. The number of participants is not listed by state, as probably should have been the case, since this would be a factor in judging the generalizability/transferability of the results. It is unclear when the additional criteria of student volunteering and parental consent were used, but nevertheless they further reduce generalizability.

The authors do a good job of explaining the recruitment procedures, and how consent was sought from the institutions used as recruitment centers, the parents of the participants, and the participants themselves. This explanation addresses certain ethical issues. However, the authors note that one recruitment site had an extremely low percentage of parental consent (7 percent) compared to most others (average of 65 percent). Why did this happen? The authors suggest that inadequate description of the study is the reason. We think differences in consent rate among sites and states should have been reported in addition to the average.

INSTRUMENTATION

The qualitative instrument in the present study was a single question: "What factors do you think contribute to life satisfaction and happiness?" Students were given 10 blank lines on which to respond (with the possibility of using the back of the page). One problem with this type of measure is that some participants may be reluctant to write a long answer, even if they have many things to say. While an interview might have been preferable, it would have been almost impossible to interview 266 participants.

The quantitative variables (perceived family support, life satisfaction, and Anglo and Mexican acculturation) are each operationally defined in terms of scales or subscales of various published instruments. Estimates of reliability are given from the literature, as well as for the current sample. One question did occur to us. Life satisfaction is operationally defined as the Global subscale of the Multidimensional Students' Life Satisfaction Scale. We are unclear whether the entire scale was administered and only the Global subscale used or whether only the questions on the Global subscale were administered (perhaps to shorten the testing time). The latter would raise questions about the validity of results, because changing the context could affect the way items were answered.

INTERNAL VALIDITY/CREDIBILITY

Internal validity/credibility questions involve the soundness of the conclusions reached in the study, based on its design and execution. The quantitative variables seem to have reasonable operational definitions. One should remember, however, that regression analysis is a correlational technique. Therefore, direction of causation cannot be unequivocally determined. While perceived family support and particular levels of acculturation might cause high levels of life satisfaction, it could be that a high degree of life satisfaction causes one to perceive higher levels of support and greater identification with one or both cultures. With regard to credibility, the question arises as to whether respondents might have said more in responding to the short-answer question if they hadn't had to write their responses.

Differences among respondent groups must be considered a possible threat to internal validity. Given the variety of sources students were recruited from, it seems likely that socioeconomic status, for example, is related to both life satisfaction and perceived family support. Comparison of "sources" (e.g., private vs. public schools) could clarify this issue. If such comparisons were made, use of "*t*" tests as was done in some state comparisons would not have been appropriate. Significance tests are appropriate for attempting to generalize, not for assessing equivalence of groups. Important differences can affect outcomes, whether "significant" or not. In the preceding instance, the appropriate index is **effect size** (see p. 248). When computed from data in the article, the largest delta is 0.22, a much better justification for combining groups.

A testing threat may exist. If many students responded to the open-ended question with "family support," it seems likely that they would connect this variable to "life satisfaction" on the questionnaire and, not necessarily intentionally, make their responses consistent.

DATA ANALYSIS

The qualitative results were analyzed using grounded theory, while the quantitative results were analyzed using correlations and hierarchical regression analysis. Both types of data (qualitative and quantitative) were analyzed separately and combined in the discussion section. The analysis of open-ended responses followed recommended procedures, although it seems to us that the use of auditors with closer ties to Mexican-American culture would have been preferable. Examples of responses clarify and support the emergent themes.

RESULTS/DISCUSSION

Three themes emerged from the qualitative data: the importance of family in providing support and love (primary theme), the importance of friends to provide help and fun (a secondary theme), and the importance of a positive attitude toward life (another secondary theme). The authors took the primary theme as support for their implied hypothesis that Mexican-American high school students place high value on perceived family support.

Two additional points require mentioning in regard to the qualitative analysis. As would be expected, responses by students to the single qualitative question were short. Would the results have been different had interviewing (which would not have required the students to write responses) been used? Second, the authors explicitly address the issue of credibility or "trustworthiness" of the qualitative results. It is gratifying to see the steps taken to ensure high-quality qualitative findings.

The authors begin their analysis of the quantitative results by discussing the assumptions underlying regression and demonstrating that the assumptions were met. They address the question of differences in their participants as a function of the state in which they resided. No differences were reported. However, differences between participants from California and Texas should have been specifically examined.

The regression results reveal that perceived family support and Mexican orientation are significant predictors of life satisfaction. Anglo orientation is not a significant predictor. The amount of variance predicted is 28 percent. While this is statistically significant, the high reliability of life satisfaction scores of 0.86 suggests that many other factors appear to determine life satisfaction among Mexican-American high school students. We hope that future research will shed some light on what these other factors may be.

The authors explicitly address the convergence and divergence of the qualitative and quantitative data. Specifically, the primary theme of family support (qualitative data) reinforces the significance of family support in the regression analysis (quantitative data). The role of friends and positive attitude (qualitative data) are not addressed in the regression. These may be some additional factors accounting for life satisfaction that can be studied in the future (quantitatively). The authors are to be commended for acknowledging some, although not all, of the study's limitations.

This article demonstrates how the results of qualitative and quantitative methodology together can provide a more complete understanding of a phenomenon than could be achieved by using only one of the methodologies by itself.

Go back to the **INTERACTIVE AND APPLIED LEARNING** feature at the beginning of the chapter for a listing of interactive and applied activities. Go to the **Online Learning Center** at **www.mhhe.com/fraenkel9e** to take quizzes, practice with key terms, and review chapter content.

Main Points

THE NATURE AND VALUE OF MIXED-METHODS RESEARCH

- Mixed-methods research involves the use of both quantitative and qualitative research methods in a single study. The results of these separate methods are combined to present a more complete picture of the phenomenon under study than either method could produce on its own.
- In mixed-methods research, the respective strengths of qualitative and quantitative methods are seen as compensating for the respective weaknesses of each method.
- Disadvantages of mixed-methods research involve the time, resources, and expertise necessary to conduct this type of research well. With regard to expertise, if the researcher is not proficient in both quantitative and qualitative methods, it is possible to team up with others who have expertise in the methods that the researcher is lacking.

WORLDVIEWS AND MIXED-METHODS RESEARCH

- Quantitative methods are usually associated with positivism.
- Qualitative methods are usually associated with postmodernism.
- Mixed-methods are usually associated with pragmatism.
- Pragmatists believe that one should use whatever methods best answer the research question or questions at hand.

TYPE OF MIXED-METHODS DESIGNS

- The exploratory design involves first conducting a qualitative study to discover important variables underlying a phenomenon and then conducting a quantitative study to discover relationships among the variables. This type of design is often used to develop rating scales in a new area of study.

- The explanatory design involves first conducting a quantitative study and then conducting a qualitative study to expand upon the results of the quantitative study.
- The triangulation design involves conducting both a qualitative study and a quantitative study (usually concurrently) and determining whether the results of the two studies converge on a single understanding of the underlying phenomenon. If the results do not converge, reasons for the lack of convergence need to be explored.
- All three of the mixed-methods designs may be conducted with an advocacy lens. An advocacy lens is present when the researcher's worldview involves advocating for the improvement of conditions of the participants involved in the study.

STEPS IN CONDUCTING MIXED-METHODS RESEARCH

- Develop a clear rationale for the need for mixed-methods in the proposed project.
- Develop research questions that involve both the qualitative and quantitative portions of the study. Although a general research question may have led to the proposed project, sub-questions that involve both qualitative and quantitative issues help show why mixed-methods are appropriate. These sub-questions also help guide data analysis.
- Before conducting a mixed-methods study, one should decide if he or she has the time, resources, and expertise necessary to actually carry out the proposed project, and then decide which mixed-methods research design applies to the proposed project.
- Triangulation designs often involve the conversion of one type of data into the other type. The conversion of qualitative data into quantitative data is referred to as *quantitizing,* while the conversion of quantitative data into qualitative data is referred to as *qualitizing*.
- The results of a mixed-methods study should be written up in a manner consistent with the research design selected.

EVALUATING MIXED-METHODS RESEARCH

- The individual quantitative and qualitative methods used should be evaluated according to the criteria specific to these methods.
- One should check that both quantitative and qualitative data played a role in the conclusions; otherwise, one of the data types may simply be an "add-on."
- Possible threats to the internal validity and/or credibility as well as the external validity or transferability of the study should always be considered.

ETHICS IN MIXED-METHODS RESEARCH

- The basic ethical concerns of protecting participant identity, treating participants with respect, and protecting participants from both physical and psychological harm apply to mixed-methods studies as they do to other types of research.

Key Terms

advocacy lens 560
explanatory design 558
exploratory design 558
generalizability 563
mixed-methods research 555
positivism 557
postmodernism 557
pragmatist 557
qualitizing 559
quantitizing 559
transferability 563
triangulation 557
triangulation design 558

For Discussion

1. What do you see as the greatest strength of mixed-methods research? The greatest weakness?
2. Are there any topics that are particularly suitable to being investigated through a mixed-methods study? If so, give an example.
3. Mixed-methods research involves the collection of both qualitative and quantitative data. Which type of data do you think might be easiest to collect? Hardest? Why?
4. Would it be possible to use random sampling in a mixed-methods study? Why or why not?
5. Is generalization possible in mixed-methods research?
6. "Mixed-methods studies can help a researcher investigate questions that cannot be adequately researched through the use of quantitative or qualitative studies alone." What might be some examples of such questions?
7. Which of the mixed-methods research designs we describe in this chapter might be the easiest to use? The hardest? Explain why.
8. What ethical concerns might possibly arise in doing a mixed-methods study?

References

1. Day, C., et al. (2008). Combining qualitative and quantitative methodologies in research on teachers' lives, work, and effectiveness: From integration to synergy. *Educational Researcher, 37*(8), 330–342.

2. Arnon, S., & Reichel, N. (2009). Closed and open-ended question tools in a telephone survey about "The Good Teacher": An example of a mixed method study. *Journal of Mixed Methods Research, 3*(4), 172–196.

3. Scott, C., & Sutton, R. E. (2009). Emotions and change during professional development for teachers: A mixed methods study. *Journal of Mixed Methods Research, 3*(4), 151–171.

4. Hodgkin, S. (2008). Telling it all: A story of women's social capital using a mixed methods approach. *Journal of Mixed Methods Research, 2*(10), 296–316.

5. Sosu, E. M., et al. (2008). The complexities of teachers' commitment to environmental education: A mixed methods approach. *Journal of Mixed Methods Research, 2*(4), 169–189.

6. Lau, M., et al. (2009). Dating and sexual attitudes in Asian-American adolescents. *Journal of Adolescent Research, 24*(1), 91–113.

7. Trow, M. (1957). Comment of participant observation and interviewing: A comparison. *Human Organization, 16,* 33–35.

8. Campbell, D. T., & Fiske, D. W. (1959). Convergent and discriminant validation by the multitrait-multimethod matrix. *Psychological Bulletin, 54,* 297–312.

9. Denzin, N. K. (1978). The logic of naturalistic inquiry. In Denzin, N. K. (Ed.), *Sociological methods: A sourcebook.* New York: McGraw-Hill.

10. Jick, T. D. (1979). Mixing qualitative and quantitative methods: Triangulation in action. *Administrative Science Quarterly, 24,* 602–611.

11. Rossman, G. B., & Wilson, B. L. (1985). Numbers and words: Combining quantitative and qualitative methods in a single large-scale evaluation study. *Evaluation Review, 9*(5), 627–643.

12. Tashakkori, A., & Teddlie, C. (1998, p. 41). *Mixed methodology: Combining qualitative and quantitative approaches.* Thousand Oaks, CA: Sage; Creswell, J. W., & Plano Clark, V. L. (2006, chapter 2). *Designing and conducting mixed methods research.* Thousand Oaks, CA: Sage.

13. Creswell and Plano Clark also mention what they call an *embedded design*. See Creswell, J. W., & Plano Clark, V. L. (2006, pp. 67–71). *Designing and conducting mixed methods research.* Thousand Oaks, CA: Sage.

14. Wallen, N. E., & Vowles, R. O. (1960). The effects of intra-class ability grouping on arithmetic achievement in the sixth grade. *Journal of Educational Psychology, 51,* 159–163.

15. Fraenkel, J. R. (1994). *A portrait of four social studies teachers and their classes: With special attention paid to identification of teaching techniques and behaviors that contribute to student learning.* In Tierney, D. S. (Ed.), *1994 Yearbook of California Education Research.* San Francisco, CA: Caddo Gap Press.

16. These points were made by Hanson, W. E., Creswell, J. W., Plano Clark, V. L., Petska, K. S., & Creswell, J. D. (2005). Mixed methods research designs in counseling psychology. *Journal of Counseling Psychology, 52*(2), 224–235.

17. Teddlie, C., & Yu, F. (2007). Mixed methods sampling: A typology with examples. *Journal of Mixed Methods Research, 1*(1), 85.

18. Tashakkori, A., & Teddlie, C. (1998, p. 19). *Mixed methodology: Combining qualitative and quantitative approaches.* Thousand Oaks, CA: Sage.

19. Tashakkori A., & Teddlie, C. (1998). *Mixed methodology: Combining qualitative and quantitative approaches.* Thousand Oaks, CA: Sage.

PART 8

Research by Practitioners

Part 8 presents a discussion of action research. Both similar to and different from the more formal methodologies discussed earlier, action research has of late shown increasing popularity. We discuss this methodology in some detail and present several examples of how action research studies might actually be carried out in schools. Lastly, we present a published example of action research, followed by our analysis of its strengths and weaknesses.

24 Action Research

What Is Action Research?

Basic Assumptions Underlying Action Research

Types of Action Research

Practical Action Research

Participatory Action Research

Levels of Participation

Steps in Action Research

Identifying the Research Question

Gathering the Necessary Information

Analyzing and Interpreting the Information

Developing an Action Plan

Similarities and Differences Between Action Research and Formal Quantitative and Qualitative Research

Sampling in Action Research

Internal Validity in Action Research

Action Research and External Validity

The Advantages of Action Research

Hypothetical Examples of Practical Action Research

An Example of Action Research

A Published Example of Action Research

Analysis of the Study

Purpose

Definitions

Hypotheses

Sample

Instrumentation

Procedures/Internal Validity

Data Analysis/Results

OBJECTIVES **Studying this chapter should enable you to:**

- Explain the term "action research."
- Describe the assumptions that underlie action research.
- Explain the purpose of action research.
- Describe the four steps involved in action research.
- Describe some of the advantages of action research.
- Describe some of the similarities and differences between action research and formal quantitative and qualitative research.
- Describe the difference between practical and participatory action research.
- Suggest some ways that other kinds of research methodologies might be used in action research.
- Name some of the threats to internal validity that exist in action research studies.
- Describe the kinds of sampling used in action research.
- Explain why action research studies are weak in external validity.
- Recognize an example of action research when you come across it in the educational literature.

INTERACTIVE AND APPLIED LEARNING After, or while, reading this chapter:

Go to the Online Learning Center at www.mhhe.com/fraenkel9e to:

- Learn More About the Role of the Researcher in Action Research

Go to your online Student Mastery Activities book to do the following activities:

- Activity 24.1: Action Research Questions
- Activity 24.2: True or False?

Robert Jackson is in his second year of teaching at an elementary school in Sarasota, Florida. He has become increasingly bothered by a considerable amount of disruptive behavior in his fifth-grade class. The boys in the class are particularly troublesome. Many take a long time to settle in their seats after the afternoon recess, have trouble paying attention when he is giving instruction, and often punch out at other students for apparently no reason. The girls in the class never seem to stop talking. Robert is becoming very concerned, as a lot of valuable class time is taken up by his so-far-unsuccessful attempts to deal with these problems. Of special concern is that he feels his students are learning only a small amount of what they could were he able to maintain a more orderly class.

What might Robert do in this situation? Action research, the subject of this chapter, is an ideal methodology that he might employ.

What Is Action Research?

Action research is conducted by one or more individuals or groups for the purpose of solving a problem or obtaining information to inform local practice. Those involved in action research generally want to solve some kind of day-to-day immediate problem, such as how to decrease absenteeism or incidents of vandalism among the student body, motivate apathetic students, figure out ways to use technology to improve the teaching of mathematics, or increase funding.

Many kinds of questions lend themselves to action research in schools. What kinds of methods, for example, work best with what kinds of students? How can teachers encourage students to think about important issues? How can content, teaching strategies, and learning activities be varied to help students of differing ages, gender, ethnicity, and ability learn more effectively? How can subject matter be presented so as to maximize understanding? What can teachers and administrators do to increase the interest of students in schooling? What can counselors do? What can other educational professionals do? How can parents become more involved?

Classroom teachers, counselors, supervisors, and administrators can help provide some answers to these (and other) important questions by engaging in action research. Such studies, taken individually, are seriously limited in *generalizability.* If, however, several teachers in different schools within the same district, for example, were to investigate the same question in their classrooms (thereby *replicating* the research of their peers), they could create a base of ideas that could generalize to policy or practice.

Action research often does not require complete knowledge of the major types of research we have described in previous chapters. The steps involved in action research are actually pretty straightforward. The important thing to remember is that such studies are rooted in the interests and needs of practitioners.

Some examples of action research that have been conducted by educational researchers are as follows:

- "Partners in Diabetes: Action Research in a Primary Care Setting"[1]
- "An Understanding of Poverty from Those Who Are Poor"[2]
- "Claiming a Voice on Race"[3]
- "First Graders and Fairy Tales: One Teacher's Action Research of Critical Literacy"[4]
- "Action Research in Teacher Education"[5]
- "Development of a Community of Science Teachers: Participation in a Collaborative Action Research Project"[6]
- "Boys and Reading: An Action Research Project Report"[7]

TABLE 24.1 *Basic Assumptions Underlying Action Research*

Assumption	Example
Teachers and other education professionals have the authority to make decisions.	A team of teachers, after discussions with the school administration, decides to meet weekly to revise the mathematics curriculum to make it more relevant to low-achieving students.
Teachers and other education professionals want to improve their practice.	A group of teachers decides to observe each other on a weekly basis and then discuss ways to improve their teaching.
Teachers and other education professionals are committed to continual professional development.	The entire staff—administration, teachers, counselors, and clerical staff—of an elementary school goes on a retreat to plan ways to improve the attendance and discipline policies for the school.
Teachers and other education professionals will and can engage in systematic research.	Following up on the example just listed, the staff decides to collect data by reviewing the attendance records of chronic absentees over the past year, to interview a random sample of attendees and absentees to determine why they differ, to hold a series of after-school roundtable sessions between discipline-prone students and faculty to identify problems and discuss ways to resolve issues of contention, and to establish a mentoring system in which selected students can serve as counselors to students needing help with their assigned work.

BASIC ASSUMPTIONS UNDERLYING ACTION RESEARCH

A number of assumptions underlie action research. Those who do action research assume that those involved, either singly or in groups, are informed individuals who are capable of identifying problems that need to be solved and of determining how to go about solving them. It is also assumed that those involved are seriously committed to improving their performance and that they want continuously and systematically to reflect on such performance. Further, it is assumed that teachers and others involved in the schools want to engage in research systematically—to identify problems, decide on investigative procedures, determine data collection techniques, analyze and interpret data, and develop plans of action to deal with problems. Lastly, it is assumed that those intending to carry out the research have the authority to undertake the necessary procedures and implement recommendations. These assumptions are described a bit further and exemplified in Table 24.1.

Types of Action Research

Mills has identified two main types of action research, although variations and combinations of the two are possible.[8]

PRACTICAL ACTION RESEARCH

Practical action research is intended to address a specific problem within a classroom, school, or other "community." It can be carried out in a variety of settings, such as educational, social service, or business locations. Its primary purpose is to improve practice in the short term as well as to inform larger issues. It can be carried out by individuals, teams, or even larger groups, provided the focus remains clear and specific. To be maximally successful, practical action research should result in an **action plan** that, ideally, will be implemented and further evaluated.

Teacher Research Using Self-Study. A form of practical action research used by classroom teachers and other education professionals is known as *teacher research*. Teachers engage in systematic research either to address a problem in practice or to improve their own pedagogy by using a reflective process. In the latter case, teachers often use an approach called "self-study," an autobiographical process designed to systematically evaluate and advance educator practice. Although self-study research continues to evolve, critics argue it remains a largely personal, idiosyncratic genre.[9,10] Theorists maintain that while collaborative self-study has the potential to contribute new and generalizable knowledge, the prevailing tendency to minimize discussions of methodology in self-studies limits

Figure 24.1 *Stakeholders*

transferability of findings. Feldman recommended that practitioners increase the internal and external validity of self-study research by explicating their methodology and making it more transparent to readers.[11]

Toward the goal of promoting the validity of self-study research, one of us engaged in a three-year, collaborative self-study project with another colleague to contribute to the gap in the literature.[12] Using a "critical colleague" co-researcher approach, the authors conducted a mixed-methods study that included multiple data sources, validity checks, and triangulation strategies. Ultimately, the authors sought to fully disclose the research process to enhance the truthfulness and transferability of their findings. The research project looked at the authors' work across three years as professors teaching in a new doctoral program. Data were collected using in-depth, semi-structured interviews by the authors at the end of each semester, and content analysis of reflective journals, lecture notes, course syllabi, as well as quantitative data from student course evaluations and dissertation completion rates. The critical colleague relationship that developed between the two authors provided a safe and highly professional space that allowed them to uncover a range of motives and insights within their teaching. Those realizations ultimately led to improvements in their pedagogy, which the authors connect to better student and program-related outcomes.

PARTICIPATORY ACTION RESEARCH

Participatory action research, while sharing the focus on a specific local issue and on using the findings to implement action, differs in important ways from practical action research. The first difference is that it has two additional purposes: to empower individuals and groups to improve their lives and to bring about social change at some level—school, community, or society. Accordingly, it deliberately involves a sizable group of people representing diverse experiences and viewpoints, all of whom are focused on the same problem. The intent is to have intensive involvement of all these **stakeholders**, who function as equal partners (Figure 24.1).

Achieving this goal requires that the stakeholders, although they may not all be involved at the outset, become active early in the process and jointly plan the study. This includes not only clarifying purposes but also agreeing on other aspects, including data collection and analysis, interpretation of data, and resulting actions. For this reason, participatory action research is often referred to as *collaborative research.* In its "pure" form, participatory action research is

> a collaborative approach to research that provides people with the means to take systematic action in an effort to resolve specific problems. [It] encourages consensual, democratic, and participatory strategies to encourage people to examine reflectively problems affecting them . . . . Further, it encourages people to formulate accounts and explanations of their situation, and to develop plans that may resolve these problems.[13]

Sometimes a trained researcher identifies a problem and brings it to the attention of the stakeholders. But

Figure 24.2 *The Role of the "Expert" in Action Research*

it is essential that the researcher realize that the problem to be studied must be a problem that is important *to the stakeholders,* and not simply of interest to the researcher. The researcher and the stakeholders *jointly* formulate the research problem (often through brainstorming or by conducting focus groups). This approach contrasts with many of the more traditional investigations, in which the researchers formulate the problem by themselves (Figure 24.2). Berg describes the trained researcher's role as follows:

> The formally trained researcher stands with and alongside the community or group under study, not outside as an objective observer or external consultant. The researcher contributes expertise when needed as a participant in the process. The researcher collaborates with local practitioners as well as stakeholders in the group or community. Other participants contribute their physical and/or intellectual resources to the research process. The researcher is a partner with the study population; thus, this type of research is considerably more value-laden than other more traditional roles and endeavors.[14]

LEVELS OF PARTICIPATION

In part because of the influence of participatory action research, more attention has been paid in recent years to the role of individuals who participate in research projects. Historically, in most educational and other research, the subjects in a study simply provided data—by being tested, observed, interviewed, and so forth. They received little or no benefit other than a thank-you (and sometimes not even that). The benefits of the study accrued to the researcher and (presumably) to the society as a whole.

Such use of individuals raises questions of ethics, even though there may be no risk, deception, or issues of confidentiality involved. Consequently, more effort has been directed toward at least informing the **participants** in a study as to the purposes of the study. This may, however, create a threat to the internal validity of the study or the validity of the data. Participants may, in some cases, be provided the results of the study and, perhaps, be asked to review them. There is, in fact, a continuum of participation (Figure 24.3). Higher levels of involvement may include helping in instrument development, data collection, and data analysis; participating in data interpretation; making recommendations for further research; actively participating in designing the study; formulating the problem of concern; and even initiating the research effort. In addition to degree of participation, the nature of the participation varies with participant interest and background. It would be unusual, for example, for elementary students to participate at or beyond level three. Similarly, the stakeholders in participatory action research are unlikely to be involved at all levels.

CONTROVERSIES IN RESEARCH

How Much Should Participants Be Involved in Research?

The active involvement of subjects in all aspects of planning and carrying out research has been advocated on the grounds that participants not only have a right to influence the direction and procedures of a study but also that they can make major contributions to the research effort itself. Questions have been raised, however, as to whether participation by individuals with only a limited background in research may result in errors and/or bias in the findings and perhaps be subverted to political ends;* there is additional concern that community participants often could be exploited.†

Sclove contends that policy boards such as the National Science Board should include nonexpert members as a way to democratize science and enhance public support for research—as has been done for years in other countries.‡ Others argue that the active involvement of participants can lead to social change as "community members become self-sufficient researchers and activists."§ Some, however, see a danger in mixing research and activism. Stoecker has explored three major, and controversial, roles that the academic expert might play in participant research: the initiator, the consultant, and the collaborator, each appropriate to different community needs.

What do you think? To what extent should the participants in a study have a say in the planning and execution of the study?

*Bowes, A. (1996). Evaluating an empowering research strategy: Reflections on action research with South Asian women. *Sociological Research Online 1.* Available at http//kennedy.soc .survey.ac.uk.sosresonline/1/1contents.html; Nyoni, S. (1991). People power in Zimbabwe. In O. Fals-Border & M. A. Rahmar (Eds.), *Action and knowledge: Breaking the monopoly with participatory action research (pp. 109–120),* New York: Apex.

†Hall, B. (1992). "From margins to center? The development and purpose of participatory research," *American Sociologist, 23,* 15–28.

‡Sclove, R. E. (1998, February). "Better approaches to science policy." Editorial and Letters, *Science, 279,* 1283.

§Stoecker, R. (1999). Are academics irrelevant? Roles for scholars in participatory research. *American Behavioral Scientist, 42*(5), 840–854.

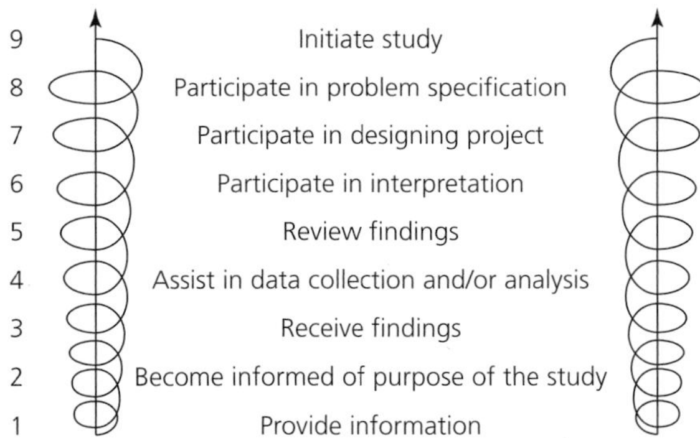

Figure 24.3 *Levels of Participation in Action Research*

Steps in Action Research

Action research involves four basic stages: (1) identifying the research problem or question, (2) obtaining the necessary information to answer the question(s), (3) analyzing and interpreting the information that has been gathered, and (4) developing a plan of action. Let us discuss each of these stages in more detail.

IDENTIFYING THE RESEARCH QUESTION

The first stage in action research is clarifying the problem of concern. An individual or group needs to carefully examine the situation and identify the problem. Action research is most appropriate when teachers or others involved in education wish to make something better, improve their practice, deal with a troublesome issue, or correct something that is not working.

An important thing to remember is that for an action research project to be successful, it must be manageable. Thus, large-scale, complex issues are probably best left to professional researchers. Action research projects are (usually) quite narrow in scope. However, if a group of teachers, students, administrators, and so on have decided to work together on some type of long-term project, the research can be more extensive. Thus, a problem like "What might be a better way to teach fractions?" is more suitable than "Is inquiry teaching more appropriate than more traditional teaching?" While quite important, the latter is too broad for easy resolution with a single classroom or teacher.

GATHERING THE NECESSARY INFORMATION

Once a problem has been identified, the next step is to decide what sorts of data are needed and how to collect them. Any of the methodologies we have described earlier in this book can be used (although usually in a somewhat simplified and less sophisticated form) in action research. Experiments, surveys, causal-comparative studies, observations, interviews, analysis of documents, ethnographies—all are possible methodologies to consider. (We will present some examples of how these might be used later in the chapter.)

Teachers can be either active participants (e.g., observing the computer strategies used by one's students while instructing them in computer usage) or nonparticipants (e.g., observing how students interact with one another during classroom study time). Whichever role is chosen, it is a good idea to record as much as possible during the observations—in short, to take *field notes* to describe what was seen and heard.

In addition to observing, a second major category of data collection involves *interviewing* students or other individuals from whom information is desired. Data collected through observations often can suggest questions to follow up on through interviews or the administration of *questionnaires.* In fact, administering questionnaires and interviewing the participants in a study can be a valid and productive way to assess the accuracy of observations. As is true of other aspects of action research, interviews tend to be less formal and often a bit more unstructured than in more formal research studies.

A third category of data collection involves the examination and *analysis of documents.* This method is perhaps the least time-consuming of the three and the easiest to commence. Attendance records, minutes of faculty meetings, counselor records, school newspaper accounts, student journals, lesson plans, administrative logs, suspension lists, detention records, seating charts, photographs of class and school activities, student portfolios—all are grist for the action researcher's mill.

Action research allows for the use of all of the types of instruments discussed in Chapter 7—questionnaires, interview schedules, checklists, rating scales, attitudinal measures, and so forth. However, often the teachers, administrators, or counselors involved (sometimes even students) develop their own instrument(s) to make them locally appropriate. And they are usually shorter, simpler, and less formal than the instruments used in more traditional research studies.

Some action research uses more than one instrument or other forms of *triangulation* (see pp. 456 and 515). Thus, asking students to respond to carefully prepared interview questions might be supplemented by video recordings; data obtained through the use of observational checklists might be checked against audio recordings of classroom discussions; and so forth. What method(s) to use is dictated, as in any research investigation, by the nature of the research question.

Action researchers must avoid collecting merely anecdotal data—that is, just the opinions of people as to how the problem might be addressed. Although anecdotal data are often valuable, we believe strongly that more substantive evidence of some sort (e.g., audio recordings, video, observations, written replies to questionnaires, and so forth) should be obtained.

ANALYZING AND INTERPRETING THE INFORMATION

This step focuses on analyzing and interpreting the data gathered in step 2. After being collected and summarized, the data need to be analyzed so that the participants can decide what the data reveal. However, analysis of action research data is usually much less complex and detailed than other forms of research.

What is important at this stage is that the data be examined in relation to resolving the research question or problem for which the research was conducted. With regard to participatory action research, Stringer suggests a number of questions that can provide a guiding procedure for analyzing the gathered data.

> The first question, *why,* establishes a general focus for the investigation, reminding everyone what the purpose of the study originally was. The remaining questions—*what, how, who, where,* and *when*—enable participants to identify associated influences. The intent is to better understand the data in context of the setting or situation. *What* and *how* questions help to establish the problems and issues: What is going on that bothers people? How do these problems or issues intrude upon the lives of the people or the group? *Who, where,* and *when* questions focus on specific actions, events, and activities that relate to the problems or issues at hand. The purpose here is not for participants to make quality judgments about these elements; rather, it is to assess the data and clarify information that has been gathered. Additionally, . . . this process provides a means for participants to reflect on things that they have themselves discussed (captured in the data) or that other participants have mentioned.[15]

When analyzing and interpreting data gathered in participatory action research, it is important that the participants try to reflect the perceptions of *all* the stakeholders

Figure 24.4 *Participation in Action Research*

involved in the study. Hence, they should work collaboratively to create descriptions of what the data reveal. Furthermore, the participants must make every effort to keep all of the stakeholders informed of what is going on during the data gathering stage and to provide opportunities for everyone involved to read accounts of what is happening as they are prepared (not simply after the study is completed). This permits all of the stakeholders to give their input continuously as the study progresses (Figure 24.4).

DEVELOPING AN ACTION PLAN

Fulfilling the intent of an action research study requires creating a plan to implement changes based on the findings. While it is desirable that a formal document be prepared, it is not essential; what is essential is that the study, at the very least, indicate clear directions for further work on the original problem or concern.

Similarities and Differences Between Action Research and Formal Quantitative and Qualitative Research

Action research is different in many ways from more formal quantitative and qualitative research, but it also has a number of similarities. Both are shown in Table 24.2.

SAMPLING IN ACTION RESEARCH

Action research problems almost always focus on only a particular group of individuals (a teacher's class, some of a counselor's clients, an administrator's faculty), and hence the sample and population are identical. Random sampling is often difficult in schools, but this is not as critical as it would be in more traditional research endeavors, because generalizing is not necessarily likely nor desired.

INTERNAL VALIDITY IN ACTION RESEARCH

Action research studies are subject to all of the threats to internal validity we described in Chapter 9, although in differing degrees. Such studies suffer particularly from the possibility of data collector bias, because the data collector is well aware of the intent of the study. This individual must take care not to overlook results or responses he or she does not want to see. Implementation and attitudinal effects are also a strong possibility, as either implementers or data collectors can, unwittingly, distort the results of a study.

ACTION RESEARCH AND EXTERNAL VALIDITY

As is true of single-subject experimental studies, action research studies are weak when it comes to external validity (generalizability). One cannot recommend using a practice found to be effective in only one classroom!

TABLE 24.2 ***Similarities and Differences Between Action Research and Formal Quantitative and Qualitative Research***

Action Research	Formal Research
Systematic inquiry.	Systematic inquiry.
Goal is to solve problems of local concern.	Goal is to develop and test theories and to produce knowledge generalizable to wide population.
Little formal training required to conduct such studies.	Considerable training required to conduct such studies.
Intent is to identify and correct problems of local concern.	Intent is to investigate larger issues.
Carried out by teacher or other local education professional.	Carried out by researcher who is not usually involved in local situation.
Uses primarily teacher-developed instruments.	Uses primarily professionally developed instruments.
Less rigorous.	More rigorous.
Usually value-based.	Frequently value-neutral.
Purposive samples selected.	Random samples (if possible) preferred.
Selective opinions of researcher often considered as data.	Selective opinions of researcher never considered as data.
Generalizability is very limited.	Generalizability often appropriate.

Thus, action research studies that show a particular practice to be effective, that reveal certain types of attitudes, or that encourage particular kinds of changes need to be replicated if their results are to be generalized to other individuals, settings, and situations.

The Advantages of Action Research

We can think of at least five advantages of doing action research. First, it can be done by almost any professional, in any type of school, at any grade level, to investigate just about any kind of problem. It can be carried out by an individual teacher in his or her classroom. It can be done by a group of teachers and/or parents, by a school principal or counselor, or by a school administrator at the district level.

Second, action research can improve educational practice. It helps teachers, counselors, and administrators become more competent professionals. Not only can it help them to become more competent and effective in what they do, but it can also help them be better able to understand and apply the research findings of others. By doing action research *themselves,* teachers and other education professionals not only can improve their skills, they can also improve their ability to read, interpret, and critique more formal research when appropriate.

Third, when teachers or other professionals design and carry out their own action research, they can develop more effective ways to practice their craft. This can lead them to read formal research reports about similar practices with greater understanding as to how the results of such studies might apply to their own situations. More importantly, such research can serve as a rich source of ideas about how to modify and perhaps enrich one's own strategies and techniques.

Fourth, action research can help teachers identify problems and issues systematically. Learning how to do action research requires that individuals define a problem precisely (often operationally), identify and try out alternative ways to deal with the problem, evaluate these ways, and then share what they have learned with their peers. In effect, action research "shows practitioners that it is possible to break out of the rut of institutionalized, taken-for-granted routines and to develop hope that seemingly intractable problems in the workplace can be solved."[16]

Fifth, action research can build up a small community of research-oriented individuals within the school itself. Action research, when systematically undertaken, can involve several individuals working together to solve a problem or issue of mutual concern. This can help reduce the feeling of isolation that many teachers, counselors, and administrators experience as they go about their daily tasks within the school. One of the current authors, before becoming a university professor, taught high school social studies. During his first year of teaching, he was assigned a class of particularly difficult

MORE ABOUT RESEARCH

An Important Example of Action Research

The early 1990s provide an example of effective participatory action research. When a new powerhouse for the Bonneville Dam was to be built in the center of the town of North Bonneville, Washington, all 470 residents faced eviction, relocation, and the probable demise of their town. Citizens rallied around the goal of relocating as an existing town where they chose. To do so, they had to oppose the U.S. Army Corps of Engineers. With help from faculty and students at the University of Washington and Evergreen State College, a broad-based citizen group undertook research to inform themselves in detail about the assets and characteristics of their town as well as the details of community planning and the political process. College students lived and worked in the town as they gathered data through documents, informal discussions, and workshops accompanied by ongoing feedback and discussion with all sectors of the community. The town council provided financial and logistical support. Citizens became increasingly involved in providing information and in carrying out political action. In the end, they not only attained their goal but succeeded in having their design for their "new" town replace the one proposed by the Corps of Engineers.*

*Fischer, F. (2000, pp. 268–272). *Citizens, experts and the environment: The politics of local knowledge.* Durham and London: Duke University Press.

students. Some of the other teachers in the school had been working systematically as part of an action research project to test and evaluate various strategies for dealing with such students. They shared what they had learned (through their own action research). Their support and sharing of information proved invaluable to a somewhat overwhelmed beginner.

Hypothetical Examples of Practical Action Research

Almost all of the methodologies described in the other chapters in this book can be adapted (in a less formal and sophisticated form) by teachers and other education professionals in the schools to investigate problems and questions of interest. Although we use school-based settings for the examples that follow, it takes only a little imagination to conceptualize how action research can be used elsewhere (e.g., mental health institutions, volunteer organizations, community service agencies). We now present some examples of what could be done.

Investigating the Teaching of Science Concepts by Means of a Comparison-Group Experiment. Ms. Gonzales, a fifth-grade teacher, is interested in the following question:

- Does using drama improve fifth-graders' understanding of basic science concepts?

How might Ms. Gonzales proceed?

Although it could be investigated in a number of ways, this question lends itself particularly well to a comparison-group experiment (see Chapter 13). Ms. Gonzales could randomly assign students to classes in which some teachers use dramatics and some teachers do not. She could compare the effects of these contrasting methods by testing the students in these classes at specified intervals with an instrument designed to measure conceptual understanding. The average score of the different classes on the test (the dependent variable) would give Ms. Gonzales some idea of the effectiveness of the methods being compared.

Of course, Ms. Gonzales wants to have as much control as possible over the assignment of individuals to the various treatment groups. In most schools, the random assignment of students to treatment groups (classes) would be very difficult to accomplish. Should this be the case, comparison still would be possible using a quasi-experimental design. Ms. Gonzales might, for example, compare student achievement in two or more *intact* classes in which some teachers agree to use the drama approach. Because the students in these classes would not have been assigned randomly, the design could not be considered a true experiment; but if the differences between the classes in terms of what is being measured are quite large, and if students have been matched on pertinent variables (including a pretest of conceptual understanding), the results could still be useful in showing how the two methods compare.

We would be concerned that the classes might differ with regard to important variables that could affect the outcome of the study. If Ms. Gonzales is the data collector, she could unintentionally favor one group when she administers the instrument(s).

Ms. Gonzales should attempt to control for all extraneous variables (student ability level, age, instructional time, teacher characteristics, and so on) that might affect the outcome under investigation. Several control procedures were described in Chapter 9: teaching during the same or closely connected periods of time, using equally experienced teachers for both methods, matching students on ability and gender, having someone else administer the instrument(s), and so forth.

Ms. Gonzales might decide to use the causal-comparative method if some classes are *already* being taught by teachers using the drama approach.

Studying the Effects of Time-Out on a Student's Disruptive Behavior by Means of a Single-Subject Experiment. Ms. Wong, a third-grade teacher, finds her class continually interrupted by a student who can't seem to keep quiet. Distressed, she asks herself what she can do to control this student and wonders if some kind of time-out activity might work. Accordingly, she asks:

- Would brief periods of removal from the class decrease the frequency of this student's disruptive behavior?

What might Ms. Wong do to get an answer to her question?

This sort of question can best be answered by means of a single-subject A-B-A-B design (see Chapter 14). First, Ms. Wong needs to establish a baseline of the student's disruptive behavior. Hence, she should observe the student carefully over a period of several days, charting the frequency of the disruptive behavior. Once she has recognized a stable pattern in the student's behavior, she should introduce the treatment—in this instance, time-out, or placing the student outside the classroom for a brief period of time—for several days and observe the frequency of the student's disruptive behavior after the treatment periods. She then should repeat the cycle. Ideally, the student's disruptive behavior will decrease and Ms. Wong will no longer need to use a time-out period with this student.

The main problem for Ms. Wong is being able to observe and chart the student's behavior during the time-out period and still teach the other students in her class. She may also have difficulty making sure the treatment (time-out) works as intended (e.g., that the student is not wandering the halls). Both of these problems would be greatly diminished if she had a teacher's aide to assist with these concerns.

Determining What Students Like About School by Means of a Survey. Mr. Abramson, a high school guidance counselor, is not interested in comparing instructional methods. He is interested in how students feel about school in general. Accordingly, he asks the following questions:

- What do students like about their classes? What do they dislike? Why?
- What types of subjects do they like the best or least?
- How do the feelings of students of different ages, sexes, and ethnicities in our school compare?

What might Mr. Abramson do to get some answers?

These sorts of questions can best be answered by a survey that measures student attitudes toward their classes (see Chapter 17). Mr. Abramson will need to prepare a questionnaire, taking time to ensure that the questions are directed toward the information he wants to obtain. Next, he should have some other members of the faculty look over the questions and identify any they feel will be misleading or ambiguous.

Such a survey presents two difficulties. First, Mr. Abramson must ensure that the questions are clear and not misleading. He can accomplish this, to an extent, by using objective or closed-ended questions, ensuring that they all pertain to the topic under investigation, and then further eliminating ambiguity by pilot-testing a draft of the questionnaire with a small group of students. Second, Mr. Abramson must be sure that a sufficient number of questionnaires are completed and returned so that he can make meaningful analyses. He can improve the rate of return by giving the questionnaire to students to complete when they are all in one place. Once he collects the completed questionnaires, he should tally the responses and see what he's got.

The big advantage of questionnaire research is that it has the potential to provide a lot of information from quite a large sample of individuals. If more details about particular questions are desired, Mr. Abramson can also conduct personal interviews with students. As we have mentioned before, the advantage here is that

Mr. Abramson can ask open-ended questions (those giving the respondent maximum freedom of response) with more confidence and pursue particular questions of special interest or value in depth. He would also be able to ask follow-up questions and explain any items that students find unclear.

One problem here may be that some students may not understand the questions, or they may not return their questionnaire. Mr. Abramson has an advantage over many survey researchers in that he can probably ensure a high rate of return by administering his questionnaire directly to students in their classrooms. He must be careful to give directions that facilitate honest and serious answers and to ensure the anonymity of the respondents. Although it is difficult, he also should try to get data on both reliability (perhaps by giving the questionnaire to a subsample a second time after an appropriate time interval—say, two weeks) and validity (perhaps by selecting a subsample to interview immediately after they individually fill out the questionnaire). Checking reliability and validity requires sacrificing anonymity for those students in the subsample, since he must be able to identify individual questionnaires.

Checking for Bias in English Anthologies by Means of a Content Analysis. Ms. Hallowitz, an eighth-grade English teacher, is concerned about the accuracy of the images or concepts that are presented to her students in their literature anthologies. She asks the following questions.

- Is the content presented in the literature anthologies in our district biased in any way? If so, how?

What might Ms. Hallowitz do to get answers?

To investigate these questions, content analysis is called for (see Chapter 20). Ms. Hallowitz decides to look particularly at the images of heroes that are presented in the literature anthologies used in the district. First, she needs to select the sample of anthologies to be analyzed—that is, to determine which texts she will peruse. (She restricts herself to only the current texts available for use in the district.) She then needs to think about the specific categories she wants to look at. Let us assume she decides to analyze the physical, emotional, social, and mental characteristics of heroes that are presented. She could then break these categories down into smaller coding units such as those shown here.

Physical	Emotional	Social	Mental
Weight	Friendly	Ethnicity	Wise
Height	Aloof	Dress	Funny
Age	Hostile	Occupation	Intelligent
Body type	Uninvolved	Status	Superhuman
.	.	.	.
.	.	.	.
.	.	.	.

Ms. Hallowitz can prepare a coding sheet to tally the data in each of the categories that she identifies in each anthology she studies. She can also readily compare among categories to determine, for example, whether white men are portrayed as white-collar workers and nonwhite people are portrayed as blue-collar workers.

A major advantage of content analysis is that it is unobtrusive. Ms. Hallowitz can "observe" without being observed, since the contents being analyzed are not influenced by her presence. Information that she might find difficult or even impossible to obtain through direct observation or other means can be gained through a content analysis of the sort sketched here.

A second advantage is that content analysis is fairly easy for others to replicate. Lastly, the information obtained through content analysis can be very helpful in planning for further instruction. Data of the type sought by Ms. Hallowitz can suggest additional information that may help students to gain a more accurate and complete picture of the world they live in, the factors and forces that exist within it, and how these factors and forces impinge on people's lives.

Ms. Hallowitz's major problem lies in being able to specify clearly the categories that will suit her questions. If, for example, nonwhite males are less often portrayed as professionals, does this indicate bias in the materials, or does it reflect reality (or both)? She should try to identify all the anthologies being used in her district and then either analyze each one or select a random sample.

Ms. Hallowitz could, of course, survey teacher and/or student opinions about bias, but that would answer a different question.

Predicting which Kinds of Students are Likely to have Trouble Learning Algebra by Means of a Correlational Study. Let us turn to mathematics for our next example. Mr. Thompson, an algebra teacher, is bothered by the fact that some of

RESEARCH TIPS

Things to Consider When Doing In-School Research

- Check the clarity of purpose and definitions with others.
- Give attention to obtaining and describing your sample in a way that is clear to others and, it is hoped, permits generalization of results.
- If appropriate, use existing instruments; if it is necessary to develop your own, remember the guidelines presented in Chapter 7.
- Make an effort to check the reliability and validity of your measures.
- Give thought to each of the threats to internal validity. Take steps to reduce these threats as much as possible.
- Use statistics where appropriate to clarify data. Use inferential statistics only when justified—or as rough guides.
- Be clear about the population to which you are entitled to generalize. It may be only those you actually include in your study (i.e., your sample). It may be that you can provide a rationale for broader generalization.
- Make sure to get permission from appropriate administrators at the school site to conduct your study. Keep in mind the school district may have its own IRB from which you will need to get permission before gathering any data at the school.

his students have difficulty learning algebra while other students learn it with ease. As a result, he asks:

- How can I predict which sorts of individuals are likely to have trouble learning algebra?

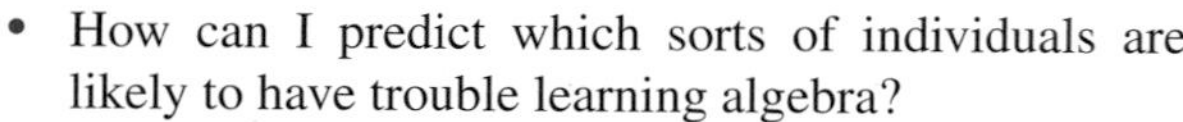

What might Mr. Thompson do to investigate this question?

If Mr. Thompson could make fairly accurate predictions in this regard, he might be able to suggest some corrective measures that he or other teachers in his school could use to help students so that large numbers of "math haters" are not produced. In this instance, correlational analysis would be appropriate (see Chapter 15). Mr. Thompson could use a variety of measures to collect different sorts of data on his students: their performance on a number of "readiness" tasks related to algebra learning (e.g., calculating, story problems); other variables that might be related to success in algebra (anxiety about math, critical thinking ability); familiarity with specific concepts ("constant," "variable," "distributed"); and any other variables that might conceivably point out how those students who do better in algebra differ from those who do more poorly.

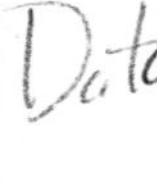

The information obtained from such research can help Mr. Thompson predict more accurately which students will have learning difficulties in algebra and should suggest some techniques to help students learn.

The main problem for Mr. Thompson is likely to be getting adequate measurements on the different variables he wishes to study. Some information should be available from school records; other variables will probably require special instrumentation. (He must remember that this information must apply to students *before* they take the algebra class, not during or after.)

Mr. Thompson must, of course, have an adequately reliable and valid way to measure proficiency in algebra. He must also try to avoid incomplete data (i.e., missing scores for some students on some measures).

Comparing two Ways of Teaching Chemistry by Means of a Causal-Comparative Study. Ms. Perea, a first-year chemistry teacher, is interested in discovering whether students in past classes achieved more in and felt better about chemistry when they were taught by a teacher who used "inquiry science" materials. Accordingly, she asks the following question:

- How has the achievement of those students who have been taught with inquiry science materials compared with that of students who have been taught with traditional materials?

What might Ms. Perea do to get some answers to her question?

If this question were to be investigated experimentally, two groups of students would have to be formed and then each group taught differently by the teachers involved (one teacher using a standard text, let's say, and the other using the inquiry-oriented materials). The achievement and attitude of the two groups could then be compared by means of one or more assessment devices.

To test this question using a causal-comparative design (see Chapter 16), however, Ms. Perea must find a group of students who *already* have been exposed to the inquiry science materials and then compare their achievement with that of another group taught with the standard text. Do the two groups differ in their achievement and attitude toward chemistry? Suppose they do. Can Ms. Perea then conclude with confidence that the difference in materials produced the difference in achievement and/or attitude? Alas, no, for other variables may be the cause. To the extent that she can rule out such alternative explanations, she can have some confidence that the inquiry materials are at least one factor in causing the difference between groups.

Ms. Perea's main problems are in getting a good measure of achievement and in controlling extraneous variables. The latter is likely to be difficult, since she needs to have access to prior classes to get the relevant information (such as student ability and teacher experience). She might locate classes that were as similar as possible with regard to extraneous variables that might affect results.

Unless she has a special reason for wanting to study previous classes, Ms. Perea might be advised to compare methods that are being used currently. She might be able to use a quasi-experimental approach (by assigning teachers to methods and controlling the way in which the methods are carried out; see Chapter 13). If not, her causal-comparative approach would permit easier control of extraneous variables if current classes were used.

Finding Out How Music Teachers Teach by Means of an Ethnographic Study. Mr. Adams, the director of curriculum in an elementary school district, is interested in knowing more about how the district's music teachers teach their subject. Accordingly, he asks:

- What do our music teachers do as they go about their daily routine—in what kinds of activities do they engage?
- What are the explicit and implicit rules of the game in music classes that seem to help or hinder the process of learning?

What can Mr. Adams do to get some answers?

To gain some insight into these questions, Mr. Adams could choose to carry out an ethnography (see Chapter 21). He could try to document or portray the activities that go on in a music teacher's classes as the teacher goes about his or her daily routine. Ideally, Mr. Adams should focus on only one classroom (or a small number of them at most) and plan to observe the teacher and students in that classroom on as regular a basis as possible (perhaps once a week for one semester). He should attempt to describe, as fully and as richly as possible, what he sees going on.

The data to be collected might include interviews with the teacher and students, detailed prose descriptions of classroom routines, audio recordings of teacher-student conferences, video of classroom discussions, examples of teacher lesson plans and student work, and flowcharts that illustrate the direction and frequency of certain types of comments (e.g., the kinds of questions that teacher and students ask of one another and the responses that different kinds of questions produce).

Ethnographic research can lend itself well to a detailed study of individuals as well as classrooms. Sometimes much can be learned from studying just one individual. For example, some students learn how to play a musical instrument very easily. In hopes of gaining insight into why this is the case, Mr. Adams might observe and interview one such student on a regular basis to see if there are any noticeable patterns or regularities in the student's behavior. Teachers and counselors, as well as the student, might be interviewed in depth. Mr. Adams might also conduct a similar series of observations and interviews with a student who finds learning how to play an instrument very difficult, to see what differences can be identified. As in the study of a whole classroom, as much information as possible (study style, attitudes toward music, approach to the subject, behavior in class) would be collected. The hope here is that through the study of an individual, insights can be gained that will help the teacher with similar students in the future.

In short, then, Mr. Adams's goal should be to "paint a portrait" of a music classroom (or an individual teacher or student in such a classroom) in as thorough and accurate a manner as possible so that others can also "see" that classroom and its participants, and what they do.*

One of the difficulties in conducting an ethnographic study is that relatively little advice can be

*Although it may appear that ethnographic research is relatively easy to do, it is, in fact, extremely difficult to do well. If you wish to learn more about this method, consult one or more of the following references: Bernard, H. B. (2000). *Social research methods.* Thousand Oaks, CA: Sage Publications; Goetz, J. P., & LeCompte, M. D. (1993). *Ethnography and qualitative design in educational research* (2nd ed.). San Diego, CA: Academic Press; Lincoln, Y. S., & Guba, E. G. (1985). *Naturalistic inquiry.* Newbury Park, CA: Sage Publications; Lancy, D. F. (2001). *Studying children and schools: Qualitative research traditions.* Prospect Heights, IL: Waveland Press; Fetterman, D. M. (1989). *Ethnography: Step by step.* Thousand Oaks, CA: Sage; Bogdan, R. C., & Biklen, S. K. (2007). *Qualitative research in education: An introduction to theory and methods* (5th ed.). Boston: Allyn & Bacon.

given beforehand. The primary pitfall is allowing personal views to influence the information obtained and its interpretation.

Mr. Adams could elect to use a more structured observation system and a structured interview. This would reduce the subjectivity of his data, but it might also detract from the richness of what he reports. We believe that an ethnographic study should be done only under the guidance of someone with prior training and experience in using this methodology.

An Example of Action Research

At this point, we want to present a real-life example of how even one of the most difficult types of research to do in schools (a quasi-experiment) can be carried out in the context of ongoing school activities and responsibilities. The following study was done by one of our students, Darlene DeMaria, in her special class for learning-disabled students in a public elementary school near San Francisco, California.[17] Ms. DeMaria hypothesized that male learning-disabled students in elementary schools who receive a systematic program of relaxation exercises would show a greater reduction in off-task behaviors than students who do not receive such a program of exercise.

Using an adaptation of an existing instrument, Ms. DeMaria selected 25 items (behaviors) from a 60-item scale previously designed to assess attention deficit. The 25 items selected were those most directly related to off-task behavior. Each item was rated from 0 to 4 on the basis of prior observation of the student, with a rating of 0 indicating that the behavior had never been observed and a rating of 4 indicating that the behavior had been observed so frequently as to seriously interfere with learning.

Three weeks after school began, Ms. DeMaria and her aide independently filled out the rating scale for each of the 18 students. The scores provided the basis for assessing improvement and for matching two groups prior to intervention.

Because the students were assigned to the "resource room" (where Ms. DeMaria taught) approximately one hour a day in groups of two to four and their schedules had been set previously, random assignment was not possible. It was, however, possible to match students across groups on grade level and (roughly) on initial ratings of off-task behavior. The class included students in grades 1 through 6. Students selected to be in the experimental group received the relaxation program on a daily basis for four weeks (Phase I), after which both Ms. DeMaria and her aide again independently rated all 18 students. Comparison of the groups at this time provided the first test of the hypothesis. Next, the relaxation program was continued for the original experimental group and *begun* for the comparison group for another four weeks (Phase II), permitting additional comparison of groups and resolving the ethical question of excluding one group from a potentially beneficial experience. At the end of this time, all students were again rated independently by Ms. DeMaria and her aide. The experimental design is shown in Figure 24.5.

			Phase I		**Phase II**	
Group I	*O*	*M*	X_1	*O*	X_1	*O*
Group II	*O*	*M*		*O*	X_1	*O*

Figure 24.5 *Experimental Design for the DeMaria Study*

The results showed that after Phase I, the experimental group showed deterioration (*more* off-task behavior—contrary to the hypothesis), whereas the comparison group showed little change. At the end of Phase II, the scores for both groups remained about the same as at the end of Phase I. Further analysis of the various subgroups (each instructed during a different time period) showed little change in the groups that received only four weeks of training. Of the three subgroups that received eight weeks of training, two showed a substantial *decrease* in off-task behavior, and one showed a marked *increase.* The explanation for the latter appears clear. One student who was placed in the resource-room program just prior to the onset of relaxation training had an increasingly disruptive effect on the other members of his subgroup, an influence that the training was not powerful enough to counteract.

This study demonstrates how research on important questions can be conducted in real-life situations in schools and can lead to useful, although tentative, implications for practice.

Like any study, this one has several limitations. The first is that agreement between Ms. DeMaria and her aide on the pretest was insufficient and required further discussion and reconciliation of differences, thus making the pretest scores somewhat suspect. Agreement, however, was satisfactory (an *r* above .80) for the posttests.

A second limitation is that the comparison groups could not be precisely matched on the pretest, since the control group had more students at both extremes. Although neither group initially showed more off-task behavior overall, this difference, as well as other uncontrolled differences in subject characteristics, could conceivably explain the different outcomes for the two groups. Further, the fact that the implementer (Ms. DeMaria) was one of the raters could certainly have influenced the ratings. That this did not happen is suggested by the fact that Ms. DeMaria's Phase II scores for the original experimental group were in fact higher (contrary to her hypothesis) than in Phase I. Evidence of retest reliability of scores could not be obtained during the time available for the study. Evidence for validity rests on the agreement between independent judges. Generalization beyond this one group of students and one teacher (Ms. DeMaria) clearly is not justified. The analysis of subgroups, although enlightening, is after the fact, and hence the results are highly tentative.

Despite these limitations, the study does suggest that the relaxation program may have value for at least some students if it is carried out long enough. One or more other teachers should be encouraged to replicate the study. An additional benefit was that the study clarified, for the teacher, the dynamics of each of the subgroups in her class.

Classroom teachers and other professionals can (and should, we would argue) conduct studies like the one we have summarized. As mentioned earlier, there is much in education about which we know little. Many questions remain unanswered; much information is needed. Classroom teachers, counselors, and administrators can help to provide this information. We hope you will be one of those who do.

A Published Example of Action Research

To conclude this chapter, we present a published example of action research, followed by a critique of its strengths and weaknesses. As we did in our critiques of other types of research studies, we use concepts introduced in earlier parts of the book in our analysis.

RESEARCH REPORT

From: (2008). *Journal of Social Studies Research, 32*(1), 22–27.

An Action Research Exploration Integrating Student Choice and Arts Activities in a Sixth Grade Social Studies Classroom

Courtney Kosky
West Virginia University

Reagan Curtis
West Virginia University

Abstract

We report on an action research study undertaken to explore how integrating the Arts in social studies education can increase student participation and motivation, and impact student achievement through that increased motivation and participation. Initial lesson plans addressed multiple intelligences while integrating Arts activities and were

Purpose

adjusted based on the teacher's reflective notes and student feedback. Although not anticipated, we found that giving students' choice in what type of activities to complete had the greatest perceived impact on their motivation and participation. Many students' social studies grades increased in response to the integration of Arts activities and student choice.

Introduction

Prior research

With national literacy and math standards becoming stricter and more time consuming, subjects such as social studies are being squeezed into smaller time allotments (e.g., Burstein, Hutton, & Curtis, 2006).

Opinion

Sixth grade students do not always see the importance of social studies because teachers are focusing primarily on math and literacy. Social studies content is important because it is many students' only link to the world outside of their community in every aspect from language and culture to landscape and climate. How does one plan to teach a unit about World War II if the students have no spatial concept of where Europe is? Diversity is becoming such a big issue in school curricula, yet helping students understand diversity through the study of other cultures, "Social Studies", is overshadowed by a focus on subjects for which standardized testing is required.

We integrated the Arts into a sixth grade Social Studies classroom in hopes of boosting student participation and motivation, thereby impacting student achievement.

Research question

Our guiding questions were, "Does integrating the Arts into a social studies classroom increase student participation and motivation?" and, "Does increased participation and motivation lead to greater academic achievement?"

Result

Along the way, as this action research exploration unfolded, we found that providing students' choice about what they did in the classroom had an important effect on their motivation and participation.

Prior research

Arts integration in the classroom has been spreading through the United States for many years. For example, in a study of 2000 fourth through eighth grade public school children, Burton, Horowitz, and Abeles (2000) found significant relationships between rich in-school Arts programs and creative, cognitive, and personal competencies needed for academic success. Oddleifson (1995) reported that high school students at an integrative Arts-based school in Montreal achieved at a rate 20–25 percent higher on average than their counterparts in other Montreal high schools, even though students enrolled in that school because they were at risk academically. Oddleifson also described an Arts-based school in South Carolina that rated second in academic achievement statewide, exceeded only by a school for the academically gifted. That school's test scores were 30 to 40 percent higher than county and state averages even though the school served a low SES community and a third of the students had learning disabilities.

Prior research

"The research shows Arts integrated learning goes well beyond the basics and test scores. Students become better thinkers, develop higher order skills, and deepen their inclination to learn," (Rabkin & Redmond, as cited in Cornett, 2003, p. 41). In an interview with EducationWorld.com, Redmond stated that "students invest emotionally in Arts integrated classrooms because the curriculum often connects the lessons to their own experiences, raising their emotional connection to what they learn and build a community of learners in classrooms where students used to learn alone." (Delisio, 2005, p. 6). Students need to have the opportunity to be actively involved in what and how they learn. *Social Studies for the Elementary and Middle School Grades: A Constructivist Approach* emphasized using art and artifacts as well as role play and simulations to enhance history lessons (Haas & Sunal, 2005, pp. 154, 306).

Rationale

With Arts integration, students have the chance to play a more active role in their learning, which sets up the classroom to be a more positive learning experience.

In the 1990's, the Chicago Arts Partnership in Education (CAPE) program was put into place in low achieving schools that were below other schools in every aspect from academics and professional development to classroom environment and parent involvement (DeMoss, 2002). The students involved in CAPE improved greatly when Arts integration was introduced into subjects such as reading and math. Students also developed more independence in their work, and were actually learning content more deeply, not just memorizing facts. By the time students reached ninth grade, they were reading above grade level and scores on the ITBS and the Illinois State IGAP tests rose significantly.

In a study involving teachers from 75 third, fourth, and fifth grade classrooms in Pennsylvania, Purnell and Gray (2004) found that 100% of the participants reported that integrating the Arts in other core subjects improved or greatly improved the teacher's ability to meet their students' multiple learning styles and 96% believed that Arts integration improved or greatly improved the teacher's ability to work with special needs or at risk students. Maintaining student motivation and engagement can be a challenge with sixth grade students. "Active engagement is a key to academic success. The participative nature of the Arts counters the passive habits that television and computers have developed in Americans" (Cornett, 2003, p. 9). Introducing the Arts into everyday classroom work may provide the extra push students need to gain or maintain a desire to learn.

Prior research

The Action Research Context

This action research study was undertaken in a sixth grade classroom in a professional development school associated with the Benedum Five Year Teacher Education Program. This teacher education program immerses students in over 1000 hours of clinical practice within the Benedum Collaborative. Established in 1990, the Collaborative is one of the oldest and most successful school-university partnerships in the United States. With a strong commitment to the tenets of simultaneous renewal, it is a collaborative effort between 28 public schools, five school districts, and West Virginia University's College of Human Resources and Education and the Eberly College of Arts and Science. The first author of this article was an intern conducting her student teaching while completing this study collaboratively with her host teacher and the second author, who served as her university mentor.

Sample

The school where our teaching and action research took place served about 650 students, grades six through eight, with 40 full time faculty and staff. The student population was approximately 95% White, and about 22% of the students received a free or reduced lunch. The school was meeting all Academic Yearly Progress (AYP) regulations with standardized test scores. The school building was fairly new and provided each grade level a dedicated computer lab, which was used regularly in delivering instruction during this action research project. The first author taught four periods of social studies and implemented Arts integrative lessons and action research with all four classes. One period in the schedule served as an inclusion classroom, which contained seven special needs students. Each class was taught the same lesson, with appropriate modifications based on the special needs of each specific classroom.

Good description

Our main goal for this project was to get students more actively involved in their learning. We used a variety of methods that incorporated Multiple Intelligence theory (e.g., Gardner & Moran, 2006). For example, when learning about ancient civilization, the students worked with their visual intelligence to create maps, kinesthetic intelligence to act out a Mayan fable, verbal intelligence to tell stories, read and write using glyphs, and logical intelligence to solve problems that ancient

Purpose of project

peoples may have faced as they settled. The main focus was to get students involved using the Arts, but every concept was covered in ways informed by Multiple Intelligence theory.

Because the student teacher's teaching style was different from that of her host teacher, it took the students about a week to get used to new expectations. Students were forced to think for themselves, encouraged to ask questions, and encouraged to participate fully in class discussions. The student teacher wanted to hear how they related what they were studying to themselves or prior experiences. Students quickly learned that once they got through background information on a new topic, they would get into truly engaging activities, which led to their being more focused and motivated to learn throughout.

Opinion?

Opinion?

A typical lesson consisted of students copying vocabulary terms into their notebooks, a classroom read of background information, and a follow-up Arts integrative activity corresponding to the new information. Because the student teacher was obligated to finish workbook pages as assigned by the host teacher, these were often assigned as homework. The student teacher felt that the activities and classroom discussions were more meaningful to the students than were completing workbook pages. Once students recognized the trade-off and found that they enjoyed the new teaching style, they stopped complaining about homework assignments.

Good description

Data Sources and Analysis

Various sources of data were used throughout this project. The student teacher spoke daily with students regarding how they felt about the lessons and what changes were going on in the classroom. She kept a reflective teaching journal to record these conversations, including daily notes on how each activity went and if any modifications should be made for future lessons. This journal also served to *note student participation* levels for each lesson and activity. An informal online Multiple Intelligence evaluation was given to students at the start of the study in order to understand students' interests and current areas of strength. Results from the Multiple Intelligence evaluations were used as a guide to create diverse and engaging lesson plans. Students completed *attitude surveys* at the beginning and end of the Action Research project. These surveys gave us insight into how students felt about social studies before and after Arts integration was implemented. At the end of each lesson, students would complete a "Rate this Lesson" card using a 1–10 scale and including written feedback regarding their least and most favorite aspects of that lesson or activity. The students' ratings and feedback were incorporated into subsequent lessons.

Instruments

Operational definition

Initial assessment

Need more detail here

Students' term grades were based on a wide variety of assessment types. Three big projects (where students had choice as to how to represent their learning) were graded using rubrics specific to the type of project turned in. Tests, quizzes, workbook pages, and graphic organizers allowed students to earn points, as did participation in classroom activities and discussion.

Operational definition of achievement

Data analysis was an ongoing process throughout the study. The student teacher reflected daily on lessons taught and data collected, using those reflections to plan subsequent lessons. Student input was highly valued as a guide to develop lessons that would be born engaging and meaningful to the students. Based on "Rate this Lesson" scores and students' written comments, lessons that received the highest ratings were grouped to find common threads. If most students did not like a particular activity or assignment and participation was low on that day, that activity was removed from subsequent lesson plans.

Procedures

Results and Discussion

Multiple Intelligence scores provided an outline of students' interests and learning strengths. A majority of the students had strengths in bodily/kinesthetic or verbal/linguistic intelligence. Because of this, the student teacher used open discussion as much as possible in the classroom. She also gave the students many opportunities to handle materials and utilize their kinesthetic intelligence as they were given *choice* in how they would represent information they were studying. For example, during our study of the Mayan civilization, we read Mayan fables in class. Students were given a long term project to choose a fable, and represent it in one of about twelve different choices that were offered. Students were given a list of activities to choose from, or they could have their own ideas approved by the student teacher. Examples of choices included: (a) draw an illustration, (b) draw a comic strip, (c) write a fable and illustrate it in a book, (d) write a fable as a screenplay or script, (e) create a computer generated picture, (f) prepare a scene from a fable, (g) build a costume for a fable, (h) write a fable as a song or poem, (i) create a PowerPoint about a fable, and (j) create a diorama that depicts a scene from a fable. Whenever activities with student choice were assigned, at least one way of representing the material drawing on each of the Multiple Intelligences was included.

Description of sample

Clarifying "choice"

Many students represented the fables with artwork, a few were able to create a song or poem about the fable, and a few students planned, rehearsed, and acted out a scene from their fable. For another example, during our study of the Aztec civilization, another big project required students to create something that would tell about their beliefs, family, culture, architecture, or way of life. Some students created artwork, such as pottery, paintings, soap carvings, portraits, or dioramas; while others wrote songs, poems, or stories.

We kept track of how students rated the lessons, as well as which strategies or intelligences were used for each. Figure 1 shows how student lesson ratings varied across the 20 lessons given during this action research study. The darker columns signify lessons that integrated the use of the Arts, whereas the lighter columns represent lessons that followed more traditional social studies pedagogy. Notice that all of the lessons that integrated Arts were rated higher than any of the lessons that did not Lessons or activities that were more traditional (e.g., book work, worksheets, readings, or lectures) were rated lower; with an average at a 5.83 out of a possible 10 compared to 9.29 for those lessons that incorporated the Arts (e.g., pictures, music, or drama). The figure clearly shows that students rated the lessons that integrated the Arts higher than those that did not. (See Figure 1.)

Results

Data

Student participation was also noted in the student teacher's reflective journal. She noticed from the start that student participation was very high on days where the Arts were integrated into the content. Student participation was recorded as "low", "average", or "high" and later assigned a number value of 1 for low, 2 for average, and 3 for high. Low participation was mentioned if students did not seem motivated or interested

Instrument

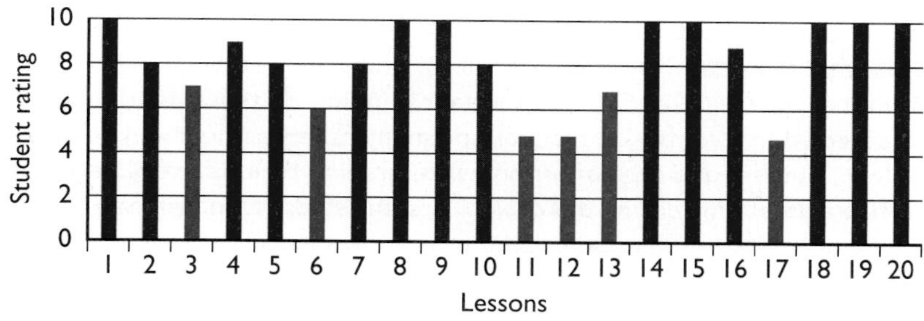

Figure 1 *Student Lesson Ratings*

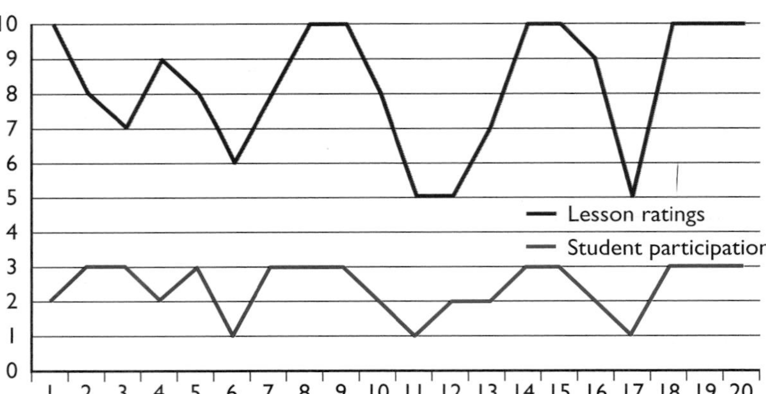

Figure 2 *Student Participation Compared to Lesson Ratings*

in what was going on in class that day (e.g., not volunteering information, asking questions, or offering discussion). An average rating was given when students discussed and

Ambiguous terms

answered questions, but were not fully engaged in and excited about the activity for that day. Students were rated as having high participation on days that they were fully involved in the classroom activities. On these days, students were obviously *motivated* and interested in the content or activity. Students were willing to discuss and ask questions, as well as provide personal connections with the content.

Results

The results of student participation can be seen in the lower portion of Figure 2. Students were extremely participative on days that they were assigned the long term projects, as well as when the projects were shared in class. Other lessons that students received a high participation rating during included: lesson two, watching a video; lesson three, examining ancient art and artifacts from the Maya; lesson five, introducing Mayan glyphs and writing; lesson seven, introducing Mayan literature; and lesson eighteen, playing a review game.

Results

The data showed that students were more participative in class and rated lessons higher when lessons included activities that they were not normally exposed to or that incorporated Multiple Intelligences. In addition to student participation, Figure 2 displays the relation between student lesson ratings and levels of participation. Notice how student participation mirrored their ratings of the lessons: most lessons with high ratings also had high participation and vice versa. The three big projects took place during lessons 8, 14, and 19; with projects being shared with the class during lessons 9, 15, and 20.

Not clear to us

The figure shows that the highest lesson ratings and highest participation scores were when students worked on and shared big projects where they had a choice in what was to be created. (See Figure 2.)

It seems reasonable that if students were enjoying what they were doing in the classroom more, they might learn more as well. Our results show that student grades were higher during implementation of this action research.

Small differences

While the overall student average before and after this study were 90.6% and 89.0%, respectively, that same figure during the study was 92.4%.

Threats to internal validity

It is important to point out that this achievement data was not collected in a controlled manner and many other factors should be taken into account (e.g., number and type of assignments, grading by a different instructor). The students had a great time during this project, and the student teacher enjoyed the experience as well. This study had results similar to what was found in Chicago's CAPE schools in the 1990's (DeMoss, 2002), however, because this study took place in a middle school and data was collected in only one subject, we are unsure whether integration had any impact on these students' performance in other content areas.

Conclusion

Completing action research in this classroom proved to be a great experience for the student teacher. Through her research and teaching practice, she gained a variety of skills and knowledge that she could not have learned in a classroom lecture setting. She found that offering students choice and mobility in classroom activities was a great way to get students involved in the learning process. Why should students have to sit and listen all day? Why not give them the opportunities they deserve to be active participants in their own learning? Students were much more involved in activities that were different from what they saw as "regular classroom activities." Just because the students were having fun in their learning, did not mean that the activities were not meaningful. More often than not, students actually took more away from hands on activities that got them up out of their seats and where discussion was used as opposed to a lecture format We feel that an extremely effective learning environment was provided for these students, and they clearly felt very comfortable discussing the lesson content with their peers and teacher. This study allowed the student teacher to try out many creative ideas designed to increase student engagement, ideas that she expects to use in her future classrooms.

Evidence?

Data?

We recommend integrating the Arts into every classroom no matter what the content or grade level. When done appropriately, Arts integrative activities are a great way to get students actively involved in their learning. However, the teacher must be able to effectively integrate the Arts into the content and still meet state and national standards and learning objectives. Also, the teacher must be flexible and willing to take risks. The most important aspect of our study was the relationship and communication between teacher and students. Students knew exactly what the student teacher would be doing and what she expected from them. If they did not like a lesson or activity, she expected them to tell her. If the students had any ideas or suggestions about classroom activities or assignments, they knew their teacher would listen and usually find a way to incorporate that input into their classroom activities.

Too strong a generalization based on just this one sample?

Evidence?

How?

References

Burstein, J., Hutton, L., & Curtis, R. (2006). The state of elementary social studies teaching in one urban district. *Journal of Social Studies Research, 30*(1), 15–20.

Burton, J., Horowitz, R., & Abeles, H. (2000). Learning in and through the arts: The question of transfer. *Studies in Art Education, 41*(3), 228.

Cornett, C. E. (2003). *Creating meaning through literature and the arts: An integration resource for classroom teachers*. Upper Saddle River, NJ: Merrill, Prentice Hall.

Delisio, E. R. (2005). Putting the arts in the (everyday) picture: Wire side chat. Retrieved February 3, 2006, from http://www.education-world.com/a_issues/chat/chat129.shtml

DeMoss, K. (2002). How arts integration supports student learning: Students shed light on the connections. Retrieved from http://www.capeweb.org/demoss.pdf

Gardner, H., & Moran, S. (2006). The science of Multiple Intelligences Theory: A response to Lynn Waterhouse. *Educational Psychologist, 41*(4), 227–232.

Haas, M. E., & Sunal, C. S. (2005). *Social studies for the elementary and middle grades: A constructivist approach.* New York: Pearson Education, Inc.

Oddleifson, E. (1995, May 18). Boston Public Schools as arts-integrated learning organizations: An address to the Council of Elementary Principals meeting. Retrieved April 9, 2006, from http://www.newhorizons.org/strategies/arts/cabc/oddleifson3.htm

Purnell, P., & Gray, D. (2004). Teaching artist journal. [Electronic Version] *A Place for the Arts: The Past Present and Teacher Perceptions, 2*(3), 153–161.

Wiles, J., & Bondi, J. (2000). *The new American middle school: Educating preadolescents in an era of change.* Merrill, Prentice Hall, 3rd edition.

Analysis of the Study

PURPOSE

The purpose was to "explore how integrating the Arts in social studies education can increase student participation and motivation, and impact student achievement." Justification consists of a rationale combining research findings and author opinion, the distinction not always made clear. Identified as "action research" by the authors, the study had a broader purpose of getting students "more actively involved in their learning." Reference to its placement in "a professional development school" and "a collaborative effort" implies the intention to improve practice within this setting. There appear to be no problems regarding risk, confidentiality, or deception.

DEFINITIONS

Terms are not explicitly defined. "Student participation" is operationally defined as ratings made by the student teacher based on observations during each of 20 lessons. The explanation of these is weakened by the ambiguous terms "fully engaged" and "obviously motivated." Student achievement was operationally defined as term grades. "Choice" is clarified under "Results and Discussion" as selecting from topics previously covered and then selecting and producing a means of representation either on their own or from a list of suggested options. "Art activities" is not clarified except with the examples of "pictures, music or drama."

HYPOTHESES

None is stated, but it is clearly implied that art-integrating activities will result in higher participation, motivation, and achievement—a directional hypothesis.

SAMPLE

The sample comprised four sixth-grade social studies classes taught by the same teacher. The number of students is not given. School and some student demographics *are* given.

INSTRUMENTATION

Participation was assessed by student teacher (lesson teacher) ratings after each of 20 lessons given to each of four classes. Additional information derived from observations and conversations with students was recorded in a reflective teaching journal and was used to modify subsequent lessons. There is no identified measure of motivation; we do not agree that "liking for a lesson" measures motivation (if that was the intent). Each student rated each of the lessons on a 10-point scale. It appears that the rating was on "liking" of the lesson. Achievement was assessed by term grades based on a "variety of assessment types." A student survey of attitudes toward social studies is mentioned but not referred to thereafter.

No reliability or validity evidence is included. It seems that class participation could have been independently observed by the regular teacher, providing data on observer agreement. Judging the "content" validity of the participation measure is hindered by the lack of clarity of definitions.

PROCEDURES/INTERNAL VALIDITY

Procedures for data collection are well described. The study design compares the 14 "Arts" lessons with six "traditional" lessons, both types described in some detail. "Subject characteristics" is not a threat, because each student should have received both "Art" and "non-Art" lessons "loss of subjects" for particular lessons should not have introduced a bias. Location, instrumentation, history, maturation, and regression are well controlled by the design. Data collector bias is possible because the (only) data collector for "participation" clearly knew which type of lesson she was observing. An implementation threat is possible if the teacher behaved differently during the "Arts" lessons in ways not integral to the enrichment, such as being more enthusiastic or accessible.

DATA ANALYSIS/RESULTS

Data analysis used appropriate descriptive statistics. The results show quite clearly that students liked the "Arts" lessons better and that this was accompanied by higher levels of rated participation. This conclusion would be more persuasive if there had been more than six "traditional" lessons. The differences in student grades seems to us, in the absence of standard deviations, to be too small to be of importance. A number of other "results" are discussed, but without specific evidence.

Whether these results support the hypothesis depends on the validity of the measures. Although we wish for greater clarity, it appears that the participation ratings would measure participation. We are bothered by the statement (p. 606) that students rated as having high participation were "obviously motivated," which appears to mix both intended outcomes in the same rating. More information should have been provided to enable the reader to judge the validity of inferences from the daily log and conversations with students.

We do not think the data presented justify the emphasis given to student "choice." It appears that all "Arts" lessons included choice, in which case it can't be separated out. If some Art lessons did not involve choice, these could have been compared with those that did. If this emphasis is based on other information such as student comments, this information should have been included.

It is clear that the student teacher/researcher found the study rewarding in several ways. It seems likely that both she and the regular teacher (and perhaps other colleagues) will incorporate the findings and methods into their future teaching—a goal of action research. We think many of the conclusions, although agreeable to us, are not supported by the findings of this study. Recommendations for generalizing are not justified from this study alone.

Go back to the **INTERACTIVE AND APPLIED LEARNING** feature at the beginning of the chapter for a listing of interactive and applied activities. Go to the **Online Learning Center** at **www.mhhe.com/fraenkel9e** to take quizzes, practice with key terms, and review chapter content.

Main Points

THE NATURE OF ACTION RESEARCH

- Action research is conducted by a teacher, administrator, or other education professional to solve a problem at the local level.
- Each of the specific methods of research can be used in action research studies, although on a smaller scale.
- A given research question may often be investigated by any one of several methods.
- Some methods are more appropriate to a particular research question and/or setting than other methods.

ASSUMPTIONS UNDERLYING ACTION RESEARCH

- Several assumptions underlie action research studies. These are that the participants have the authority to make decisions, want to improve their practice, are committed to continual professional development, and will engage in systematic inquiry.

TYPES OF ACTION RESEARCH

- Practical action research addresses a specific local problem.
- Participatory action research, while also focused on addressing a specific local problem, attempts to empower participants or bring about social change.

LEVEL OF PARTICIPATION IN ACTION RESEARCH

- Participation can range from giving information to increasingly greater involvement in the various aspects of the study.

STEPS IN ACTION RESEARCH

- Action research involves four steps: identifying the research question or problem, gathering the necessary data, analyzing and interpreting the data and sharing the results with the participants, and developing an action plan.
- In participatory research, every effort is made to involve all those who have a vested interest in the outcomes of the study—the stakeholders.

ADVANTAGES OF ACTION RESEARCH

- There are at least five advantages to action research. It can be done by just about anyone, in any type of school or other institution, to investigate just about any kind of problem or issue. It can help to improve educational practice. It can help education and other professionals to improve their craft. It can help them learn to identify problems systematically. Finally, it can build up a small community of research-oriented individuals at the local level.
- Action research has both similarities to and differences from formal quantitative and qualitative research.

SAMPLING IN ACTION RESEARCH

- Action researchers are most likely to choose a purposive sample.

THREATS TO THE INTERNAL VALIDITY OF ACTION RESEARCH

- Action research studies suffer especially from the possibility of data collector bias, implementation, and attitudinal threats. Most others can be controlled to a considerable degree.

EXTERNAL VALIDITY AND ACTION RESEARCH

- Action research studies are weak in external validity. Replication is, therefore, essential in these studies.

Key Terms

action plan 588
action research 587
participant 590
participatory action research 589
practical action research 588
stakeholder 589

For Discussion

1. Are there any kinds of questions that could *not* be investigated by means of an action research study? If you think so, give an example.
2. Do you think the assumptions that underlie action research are true? Explain your reasoning. Are any of them questionable?
3. Which of the four stages of action research would be the hardest to carry out? Why?
4. "The important thing in action research is *not* to rely on collecting merely anecdotal data." Would you agree? Why would this be insuffícent (if it would be)?
5. All of the participants—the stakeholders—in an action research study must be involved in the entire research process. Why not also require this in formal qualitative and quantitative studies?
6. What do you think is the major advantage of action research? the major disadvantage?

7. Which methodologies, other than the ones discussed, might be used in each of the hypothetical examples in this chapter?
8. What other methods might have been used in the DeMaria study? Which, if any, would you recommend? Why?

References

1. Mendenhall, T. J., & Doherty, W. J. (2007). Partners in diabetes: Action research in a primary care setting. *Action Research, 5*(12), 378–406.
2. Collins, S. B. (2005). An understanding of poverty from those who are poor. *Action Research, 3*(3), 9–31.
3. Foldy, E. G. (2005). Claiming a voice on race. *Action Research, 3*(93), 33–54.
4. Bourke, R. (2008). First graders and fairy tales: One teacher's action research of critical literacy. *The Reading Teacher; 62*(4), 304–312.
5. Kitchen, J., & Stevens, D. (2008). Action research in teacher education: Two teacher-educators practice action research as they introduce action research to pre-service teachers. *Action Research, 6*(3), 7–28.
6. Fazio, X. (2009). Development of a community of science teachers: Participation in a collaborative action research project. *School Science and Mathematics, 109*(2), 95.
7. Kwok, J. (2009). Boys and reading: An action research project report. *Library Media Connection, 27*(4), 20.
8. Mills, G. E. (2000). *Action research: A guide for the teacher researcher.* Upper Saddle River, NJ: Merrill.
9. Louie, B. Y., Drevdahl, D. J., Purdy, J. M., & Stackman, R. W. (2003). Advancing the scholarship of teaching through collaborative self-study. *The Journal of Higher Education, 74*(2), 150–171.
10. Zeichner, K. (1999). The new scholarship in teacher education. *Educational Researcher, 28*(9), 4–15.
11. Feldman, A. (2003). Validity and quality in self-study. *Educational Researcher, 32*(3), 26–28.
12. Henderson, B., & Hyun, H. (2013). Doctoral andragogy: A three-year study on developing highly effective teaching practices for a new professional doctorate program in education. Paper presented at the American Educational Research Association Annual Meeting, San Francisco, CA, May 1, 2013.
13. Mills, G. E. (2000, p. 6). *Action research: A guide for the teacher researcher.* Upper Saddle River, NJ: Merrill.
14. Berg, B. L. (2001, p. 180). *Qualitative methods for the social sciences.* Boston: Allyn & Bacon.
15. Stringer, E. T. (1999). *Action research* (2nd ed.). Thousand Oaks, CA: Sage. Cited in Berg, B. L. (2001, p. 183). *Qualitative methods for the social sciences.* Boston: Allyn & Bacon.
16. Berg, B. L. (2001, p. 182). *Qualitative methods for the social sciences.* Boston: Allyn & Bacon.
17. DeMaria, D. (1990). *A study of the effect of relaxation exercises on a class of learning-disabled students.* Master's thesis. San Francisco State University, San Francisco, CA.

PART 9

Writing Research Proposals and Reports

Part 9 discusses how to prepare a research proposal or report. We describe the major sections of such proposals and reports and then describe sections that are unique to reports. We conclude with an example of a student's research proposal, followed by our analysis of it.

25 Preparing Research Proposals and Reports

The Research Proposal

The Major Sections of a Research Proposal or Report

Problem to Be Investigated

Background and Review of Related Literature

Procedures

Budget

General Comments

Sections Unique to Research Reports

General Rules to Consider

Format

A Few Comments About Qualitative Research Reports

An Outline of a Research Report

A Sample Research Proposal

OBJECTIVES Studying this chapter should enable you to:

- Describe briefly the main sections of a research proposal and a research report.
- Describe the major difference between a research proposal and a research report.
- Write a research proposal.
- Understand and critique a typical research report or proposal.

INTERACTIVE AND APPLIED LEARNING After, or while, reading this chapter:

Go to the Online Learning Center at www.mhhe.com/fraenkel9e to:

- Review the Guide to Electronic Research

Go to your online Student Mastery Activities book to do the following activity:

- Activity 25.1: Put Them in Order

By now we hope you have learned many of the concepts and procedures involved in educational research. You may, in fact, have done considerable thinking about a research study of your own. To help you further, we discuss in this chapter the major components involved in proposal and report writing. A research proposal is nothing more than a written plan for conducting a research study. It is a generally accepted and commonly required prerequisite for carrying out a research investigation.

Research proposals and research reports are similar in many respects, the main difference being that a **research proposal** is generated *before* a study begins, whereas a **research report** is prepared *after* a study has been completed. In this chapter, we describe and illustrate what is expected and usually included in each section of these documents. We also discuss what is appropriate to include in the two sections that are unique to research reports—those involving the results of the study and the subsequent discussion of those results. We will highlight what we have found to be the most common mistakes made by beginning researchers in preparing research proposals. Finally, we will present an example of a research proposal prepared by one of our students and comment on its strengths and weaknesses.

The Research Proposal

A research proposal is nothing more than a written plan for conducting a research study. It is a generally accepted and commonly required prerequisite for carrying out a research investigation. It communicates a researcher's intentions, makes clear the purpose of the intended study and its justification, and provides a step-by-step plan for conducting the study. The research proposal identifies problems, states questions or hypotheses, identifies variables, and defines terms. The subjects to be included in the sample, the instrument(s) to be used, the research design chosen, the procedures to be followed, how the data will be analyzed—all are spelled out in some detail, and at least a partial review of previous related research is included.

A research proposal, then, is a written plan of a study. It spells out in detail what the researcher intends to do. It permits others to learn about the intended research and to offer suggestions for improving the study. It helps the researcher clarify what needs to be done and helps him or her avoid unintentional pitfalls or unknown problems. Such a written plan is highly desirable, since it allows interested others to evaluate the worth of a proposed study and to make suggestions for improvement.

Let us begin, then, by describing and illustrating the major components that make up the research proposal.

The Major Sections of a Research Proposal or Report

PROBLEM TO BE INVESTIGATED

The section describing the problem to be investigated usually addresses four topics: (1) the purpose of the study, including the researcher's assumptions; (2) the justification for the study; (3) the research question and/or hypotheses, including the variables to be investigated; and (4) the definition of terms.

Purpose of the Study. Usually the first topic in the proposal or report, the **purpose** states succinctly what the researcher proposes to investigate. The purpose should be a concise statement, providing a framework to which details are added later. Generally speaking, any study should seek to clarify some aspect of the field of interest that is considered important, thereby contributing both to overall knowledge and to current practice. Here are examples of statements of purpose in research reports taken from the literature:

- "The purpose of this study was to identify and describe the bedtime routines and self-reported nocturnal sleep patterns of women over age 65 and to determine the differences and relationships between these routines and patterns according to whether or not the subject was institutionalized."[1]
- "The purpose of this study was to explore how young adolescents portray the ideal person in drawing and in response to a survey."[2]
- "This study attempts to identify some of the processes mediating self-fulfilling prophecies in the classroom."[3]

The researcher should articulate any *assumptions* that are basic to the study. For example:

- It is assumed that, if found effective, the methods studied could be adopted by many teachers without special training.
- It is assumed that the descriptive information on family interaction that is provided by this study, if disseminated, will have an influence on family functioning.
- It is assumed that predictive information from this study would be used by counselors in advising students.

Justification for the Study. In the **justification**, researchers must make clear why this particular subject is important to investigate. They must present an argument for the "worth" of the study, so to speak. For example, if a researcher intends to study a particular method for modifying student attitudes toward government, he or she must make the case that such a study is important—that people are, or should be, concerned about it. The researcher must also make clear why he or she chooses to investigate the particular method. In many such proposals, there is the implication that current methods are not good enough; this should be made explicit, however.

A good justification should also include any specific implications that follow if relationships are identified. In an intervention study, for example, if the method being studied appears to be successful, changes in pre-service or in-service training for teachers may be necessary; money may need to be spent in different ways; materials and other resources may need to be used differently, and so on. In survey studies, strong opinions on certain issues (such as peer opinions about drug use) may have implications for teachers, counselors, parents, and others. Relationships found in correlational or causal-comparative studies may justify predictive uses. Also, results of correlational or ethnographic studies may suggest possibilities for subsequent experimental studies. These should be discussed.

Here is an example of a justification. It is taken from a report of a study investigating the relationship between narrative and historical understanding in a literature-based sixth-grade history program.

> Recent research on the development of historical understanding has focused on secondary students. For several decades research has rested on the premise that historical understanding is demonstrated in the ability to analyze and interpret passages of history—or at least passages containing historical names, dates, and events. The results have indicated that if historical understanding develops at all, it does not appear until late adolescence (Hallam, 1970, 1979; Peel, 1967). From the perspective of those who work with younger children, however, this approach reflects an incomplete view of historical understanding.
>
> The inference often drawn from the research is that young children cannot understand history; therefore history should not be part of their curriculum. Certainly, surveys have shown that young children do not indicate much interest in history as a school subject. Yet teachers and parents know that children evince interest in the old days, in historical events or characters, and in descriptions of everyday life in historic times, such as Laura Ingalls Wilder's *Little House* books (e.g., 1953). Children respond to history long before they are capable of handling current tests of historical understanding. The research, however, has not taken historical response into account in the development of mature understanding.
>
> The research on children's response to literature provides some guidelines for examining historical response. Research by Applebee (1978), Favat (1977), and Schlager (1975) suggests that aspects of response are developmental. Other scholars (Britton, 1978; Egan, 1983; Rosenblatt, 1938) extend that suggestion to historical understanding, arguing that early, personal responses to history—especially history embedded in narrative—are precursors to more mature and objective historical understanding.
>
> Little has been done to study the form of such early historical response. Kennedy's (1983) study examined the relationship between information-processing capacity and historical understanding, but concentrated on adolescents.

Reviews of research on historical understanding also fail to uncover studies of early response. There is nothing describing how children respond to historical material in a regular classroom setting. How do children respond on their own, or in contact with peers? What forms of history elicit the strongest responses? How do children express interest in historical material? Does the classroom context influence responses? What teacher behaviors inhibit or encourage response?

These are important questions for the elementary teacher faced with a social studies curriculum that continues to emphasize history, as well as for the theorist interested in the development of historical understanding. Yet these questions cannot easily be answered by traditional empirical models. Research needs to be extended to include focus on the range of evidence available through naturalistic inquiry. . . .

Classroom observation suggests that narrative is a potent spur to historical interest. Teachers note the interest exhibited by students in such historical stories as *The Diary of Anne Frank* (Frank, 1952) and *Little House on the Prairie* (Wilder, 1953) and in the oral tradition of family history (Huck, 1981). Research in discourse analysis and schema theory suggests that narrative may help children make sense of history. White and Gagne (1976), for instance, found that connected discourse leads to better memory for meaning. Such discourse provides a framework that improves recall and helps children recognize important features in a text (Kintsch, Kozminsky, Streby, McKoon, & Keenan, 1975). DeVilliers (1974) and Levin (1970) found that readers processed words in connected discourse more deeply than when the same words appeared in sentences or lists. Cullinan, Harwood, and Galda (1983) suggest that readers may be better able to remember things in narratives where the "connected discourse allows the reader to organize and interrelate elements in the text" (p. 31).

One way to help children understand history, then, may be to use the connected discourse of literature. Such an approach also allows the researcher to focus on response as the ongoing construction of meaning as children encounter history in literature. The following study investigated children's responses to a literature-based approach to history.[4]

Key Questions to Ask Yourself at This Point:

1. Have I identified the specific research problem I wish to investigate?
2. Have I indicated what I intend to do about this problem?
3. Have I put forth an argument as to why this problem is worthy of investigation?
4. Have I made my assumptions explicit?

Research Questions or Hypothesis. The particular question to be investigated should be stated next. This is usually, but not always, a more specific form of the problem in question form. As you will recall, we, along with many other researchers, favor **hypotheses** for reasons of clarity and as a research strategy. If a researcher has a hypothesis in mind, it should be stated as clearly and as concisely as possible. It is unnecessarily frustrating for a reader to have to infer what a researcher's hypothesis or hypotheses might be. (See Chapter 2 for several examples of typical research questions and hypotheses in education.) Similarly, qualitative research proposals often include a statement positing one or several propositions (tentative or mini-hypotheses) that are used to help guide data collection and sometimes also analysis.

Key Questions to Ask Yourself at This Point:

5. Have I asked the specific research question I wish to pursue?
6. Do I have a hypothesis in mind? If so, have I expressed it?
7. Do I intend to investigate a relationship? If so, have I indicated the variables I think may be related?

Definitions. All key terms should be defined. In a hypothesis-testing study, these are primarily the terms that describe the variables of the study. The researcher's task is to make his or her definitions as clear as possible. If previous definitions found in the literature are clear to all concerned, well and good. Often, however, they need to be modified to fit the present study. It is often helpful to formulate operational definitions as a way of clarifying terms or phrases. While it is probably impossible to eliminate all ambiguity from definitions, the clearer the terms are—to both the researcher and others—the fewer difficulties will be encountered in subsequent planning and conducting of the study.

Here are examples of definitions taken from the literature. The first three are taken from a study investigating the relationship between peer experiences and social self-perceptions among Canadian students from a variety of socioeconomic backgrounds in 10 elementary schools:

- *Social preference* was assessed by asking each child to name three other children they would like most and like least for playing together, inviting to a birthday party, and sitting next to each other on a bus.

- *Victimization by peers* was measured by asking each child to nominate up to five other students who could be described as being made fun of, being called names, and getting hit and pushed by other kids.
- *Loneliness* was measured with a 16-item questionnaire with higher scores indicating greater loneliness.[5]

This next definition is taken from a study in which the researcher investigated why students of color were not entering teaching:

- *Minority teacher* was defined as "Latino/Hispanic, African-American/Black, Asian American, or Native American."[6]

This last definition comes from a study investigating how people see their work:

- *People who have jobs* was defined as being "only interested in the material benefits from work and do not seek or receive any other type of reward from it." *People who have careers* was defined as having "a deeper personal investment in their work and mark their achievements not only through monetary gain, but through advancement within the occupational structure." *People who have callings* was defined as people who "find their work is inseparable from their life. A person with a Calling works not for financial gain or Career advancement, but instead for the fulfillment that doing the work brings to the individual."[7]

Key Question to Ask Yourself at This Point:

8. Have I defined all key terms clearly (and, if possible, operationally)?

BACKGROUND AND REVIEW OF RELATED LITERATURE

In a research report, the **literature review** may be a lengthy section, especially in a master's thesis or a doctoral dissertation. In a research proposal, it is a partial summary of previous work related to the hypothesis or focus of the study. The researcher is trying to show here that he or she is familiar with the major trends in previous research and opinion on the topic and understands their relevance to the study being planned. This review may include theoretical conceptions, directly related studies, and studies that provide additional perspectives on the research question. In our experience, the major weakness of many literature reviews is that they cite references (often many references) without indicating their relevance or implications for the planned study. (See Chapter 3 for details on literature reviews.) A portion of a literature review follows. It is taken from a study investigating the relationship between kindergarten teachers' theoretical orientation toward reading and student outcomes of children with different initial reading abilities.

> The *whole language* approach to teaching reading has captured the attention of many teachers and teacher educators over the past 20 years. It . . . asserts that children learn language most effectively at their own developmental pace through social interaction in language-rich environments and through exposure to quality literature. This approach is often contrasted with a phonics-oriented strategy in which children receive formal instruction emphasizing sound-symbol correspondence. . . . Stahl and Miller (1989) and Stahl, McKenna, and Pagnucco (1994) conducted meta-analyses of studies conducted in kindergarten and first-grade classrooms comparing the relative impact of whole language and traditional approaches to reading instruction. Both meta-analyses yielded the general conclusion that the overall impact of the two approaches was "essentially similar" (Stahl et al., 1994, p. 175), a position disputed by Schickedanz (1990) and McGee and Lomaz (1990).
>
> In reviewing the whole language/phonics debate, and the inability of researchers to reach similar conclusions after reviewing the same studies, several problematic areas emerge. First, the meaning of the term *whole language* and a set of distinctive classroom practices representing its operationalization are difficult to specify (Stahl & Miller, 1989). This is exacerbated by the fact that some proponents conceive of whole language as a philosophy rather than an explicitly defined instructional methodology (Edelsky, 1990; Goodman, 1986; McKenna, Robinson, & Miller, 1990; Newman, 1985; Rich, 1985). Second, many—if not most—teachers are eclectic in their approach to reading instruction, and pure contrasts between whole language- and phonics-oriented instruction are generally difficult to find in naturally occurring, unmanipulated classroom environments (Slaughter, 1988). Third, with the exception of Fisher and Hiebert (1990), relatively little research has documented differences in the instructional behavior and practices of teachers subscribing to whole language versus traditional approaches to early reading instruction (Feng & Etheridge, 1993; Lehman, Allen, & Freeman, 1990; Stahl et al., 1994). Finally, "relatively few studies" (Stahl et al., 1994, p. 175) comparing whole language and traditional reading instruction have used standardized achievement measures or included large numbers of students (e.g., Watson, Crenshaw, & King, 1984). . . .

A number of researchers have examined the impact of whole language approaches to reading development for students considered educationally at risk. Stahl and Miller (1989) concluded that "whole language/language experience approaches . . . produce weaker effects with populations labeled specifically as disadvantaged" (p. 87). This conclusion is supported by the research of Gersten, Darch, and Gleason (1988), who reported positive effects for at-risk (economically disadvantaged) children of a direct instruction kindergarten classroom, based largely on traditional, phonics-oriented principles. However, a number of recent studies (Milligan & Berg, 1992; Otto, 1993; Pinnell, Lyons, DeFord, Bryk, & Seltzer, 1994; Sulzby, Branz, & Buhle, 1993) present evidence consistent with Kasten and Clarke's (1989) argument that whole language-based reading instruction should be especially beneficial for disadvantaged children. . . .

Otto (1993) and Sulzby et al. (1993) presented evidence suggesting that storybook reading, generally associated with developmentally sensitive, whole language approaches to reading instruction, was helpful in increasing the emergent reading ability of inner-city kindergartners (Otto, 1993; Sulzby et al., 1993) and first graders (Sulzby et al., 1993). However, neither of these studies used control groups, either of children not seen as at-risk or of children receiving more traditional instruction in the same schools. Purcell-Gates, McIntyre, and Freppon (1995) reported that children in well-implemented whole language classes showed significantly greater growth in their knowledge of written language and more extensive breadth of knowledge of written linguistic features than their peers in skills-based kindergarten classes. Putnam (1990) found that inner-city kindergarten students in a "Literate Environment" classroom gained more in vocabulary and syntactic complexity than students in "Traditional" or "IBM Write to Read" classrooms.

Finally, research by Pinnell et al. (1994) found that "Reading Recovery," a tutoring program for educationally disadvantaged children, was more effective in improving the reading efficacy of high-risk first graders than a similar program (called "Reading Success") provided by teachers who were more traditional (phonics- or skills-oriented) compared to the "Reading Recovery" teachers. However, given that the "Reading Recovery" and the "Reading Success" teachers also differed in a number of other ways (previous experience and training, training time schedule, training activities), it is impossible to tease out the effects of the teachers' theoretical orientations toward reading.[8]

Key Questions to Ask Yourself at This Point:

9. Have I surveyed and described relevant studies related to the problem?
10. Have I surveyed existing expert opinion on the problem?
11. Have I summarized the existing state of opinion and research on the problem?

PROCEDURES

The **procedures** section includes discussions of: (1) the research design, (2) the sample, (3) instrumentation, (4) the procedural details, (5) internal validity, and (6) data analysis.

Research Design. In experimental or correlational studies, the **research design** can be described using the symbols presented in Chapters 13 or 15. In causal-comparative studies, the research design should be described using the symbols presented in Chapter 16. The particular research design to be used in the study and its application to the study should be identified. In most studies, the basic design is fairly clear-cut and fits one of the models we presented in Chapters 13 to 17 and in Chapters 20 to 22.

Sample. In a proposal, a researcher should indicate in considerable detail how he or she will obtain the subjects—the **sample**—for the study. If generalization is intended, a *random sample* should be used. If a *convenience sample* must be used, relevant *demographics* (gender, ethnicity, occupation, IQ, and so on) of the sample should be described. Lastly, the legitimate population to which the results of the study may be generalized should be indicated. (See Chapter 6 for details on sampling.)

Here is an example of a description of a convenience sample. It was taken from the report of a study designed to investigate the effects of behavior modification on the classroom behavior of first- and third-graders.

> Thirty grade 1 (mean age = 7 years, 1 month) and 25 grade 3 children (mean age = 9 years, 3 months) were identified by their classroom teachers as exhibiting inappropriate classroom behavior, receiving no special services, and having intelligence quotients between 85 and 115. These children represented 23% of the grade 1 children in a large elementary school in the southeastern United States and 21% of the grade 3 children in the same school. All participants were from regular classrooms;

none were receiving special educational services. Fifteen grade 1 subjects were assigned randomly to the experimental treatment and 15 to the control condition; 25 grade 3 subjects were assigned randomly to each of the two conditions, with the experimental treatment receiving 13 and control, 12. The experimental group included 22 boys, 6 girls; 11 black children, 17 white children; 14 of low socioeconomic status, 14 of middle to high socioeconomic status. The control group was composed of 15 boys, 12 girls; 15 black children, 12 white children; 7 of low socioeconomic status, 20 of middle to high socioeconomic status. No attrition occurred during this study.[9]

Key Questions to Ask Yourself at This Point:

12. Have I described my sampling plan?
13. Have I described the relevant characteristics of my sample in detail?
14. Have I identified the population to which the results of the study may legitimately be generalized?

Instrumentation. Whenever possible, existing instruments should be used in a study, since construction of even the most straightforward test or questionnaire is often a time-consuming and difficult task. The use of an existing instrument, however, is not justified unless sufficiently reliable and valid results can be obtained for the researcher's purpose. Too many studies are done with instruments that are merely convenient or well known. Usage is a poor criterion of quality, as shown by the continuing popularity of some widely used achievement tests despite years of scathing professional criticism. (See Chapter 7 for examples of the many types of instruments that educational researchers can use.)

In the event that appropriate ready-made instruments are not available, the procedures followed in developing the instruments should be described with attention to how validity and reliability will (presumably) be enhanced. At least some sample items from the instruments should be included in the proposal.

Even with instruments for which reliability and validity of scores are supported by impressive evidence, there is no guarantee that these instruments will function in the same way in the study itself. Differences in subjects and conditions may make previous estimates of validity and reliability inapplicable to the current context. Further, validity always depends on the intent and interpretation of the researcher. For all these reasons, the reliability and validity of the scores obtained from all instruments should be checked as a part of every study, preferably before the study begins.

It is almost always feasible to check internal consistency reliability since no additional data are required. Checking reliability of scores over time *(stability)* is more difficult, since an additional administration of the instrument is required. Even when feasible, repetition of exactly the same instrument may be questionable, since individuals may alter their responses as a result of taking the instrument the first time.* Asking respondents to reply to a questionnaire or an interview a second time is often difficult, since it seems rather foolish to them. Nonetheless, ingenuity and the effort required to develop a parallel form of the instrument(s) can often overcome these obstacles.†

The most straightforward way to check validity is to use a second instrument to measure the same variable. Often, this is not as difficult as it may seem, given the variety of instruments that are available (see Chapter 7). Frequently, the judgment of knowledgeable persons (teachers, counselors, parents, and friends, for instance), expressed as ratings or as a ranking of the members of a group, can serve as the second instrument. Sometimes a useful means of validating the responses to attitude, opinion, or personality (such as self-esteem) scales filled out by subjects is to have a person who knows each subject well fill out the same scale (as it applies to the subject) and then check to see how well the ratings correspond. A final point is that reliability and validity data need not be obtained for the entire sample, although this is preferable. It is better to obtain such data for only a portion of the sample (or even for a separate, although comparable, sample) than to obtain no data at all. (For a more detailed discussion of reliability and validity, see Chapter 8.)

In some studies, especially historical and qualitative ones, there may be no formal instrument like a test or a rating scale involved. In such studies, the researcher is often the "instrument" for obtaining data. Even so, ways of maximizing and checking on validity and reliability should be set forth in the proposal and described later in the report.

Here are examples of instruments taken from the literature:

- *Social class:* "Socioeconomic status (SES) was determined on the basis of parental occupation of father or mother, whomever was higher. Occupations were

*For example, they may look up the answers.

†A compromise is to divide the existing instrument into two halves (as in the split-half procedure) and administer each half with a time interval between administrations.

indexed according to the Warner Revised Occupational Rating Scale. . . . The Warner Scale consists of seven occupational categories with assigned values ranging from 1 to 7, based on the skill requirements and social prestige of the job." Higher scores indicated higher social class standing.[10]

- *Self-esteem:* "We used the Coopersmith Self-Esteem Inventory . . . , a 50-item scale, to measure global self-esteem. Adequate assessments of construct, concurrent, and predictive validity are reported in the manual. Higher scores indicate higher self-esteem."[11]
- *Psychological distress:* "The Symptom Checklist-90-Revised . . . , a 90-item self-report inventory, was used to assess psychological symptoms."[11]

Key Questions to Ask Yourself at This Point:

15. Have I described the instruments to be used?
16. Have I indicated their relevance to the present study?
17. Have I stated how I will check the reliability of scores obtained from all instruments?
18. Have I stated how I will check the validity of scores obtained from all instrument(s)?

Procedural Details. Next, the procedures to be followed in the study—what will be done, as well as when, where, and how—should be described in detail. In intervention studies in particular, additional details are usually needed on the nature of the intervention and on the means of introducing the method or treatment. Keep in mind that the goal here is to make it possible to replicate the study; another researcher should, on the basis of the information provided in this section, be able to repeat the study in exactly the same way as the original researcher. Certain procedures may change as the study is carried out, it is true, but a proposal should nonetheless have this level of clarity as its goal.

The researcher should also make clear how the information collected will be used to answer the original question or to test the original hypothesis.

Here are some examples of procedural details taken from the literature:

- (From a study investigating why students of color are not entering teaching): "Over a two-year period, I conducted face-to-face, semi-structured interviews with 140 teachers of color in Cincinnati, Ohio; Seattle, Washington; and Long Beach, California. Semi-structured, face-to-face interviewing was selected as the most appropriate research strategy because of the intense and critical nature of the topic under scrutiny and the informants involved."[6]
- (From a descriptive study of eleventh-grade U.S. History classes): "Four 11th-grade United States history classes, located in a large urban high school (grades 9–12) on the west coast of the United States, were observed unobtrusively at least three times a week for six weeks during January and February of 1993. In addition, each of the teachers of those classes were interviewed at length."[12]

Key Question to Ask Yourself at This Point:

19. Have I fully described the procedures to be followed in the study—what will be done, where, when, and how?

Internal Validity. At this point, the essential planning for a study should be nearly completed. It is now necessary for the researcher to examine the proposed methodology for the presence of any feasible alternative explanations for the results should the study's hypothesis be supported (or should nonhypothesized relationships be identified). We suggest that each of the threats to internal validity discussed in Chapter 9 be reviewed to see if any might apply to the proposed study. Should any troublesome areas be found, they should be mentioned and their likelihood discussed. The researcher should describe what he or she would do to eliminate or minimize them. Such an analysis often results in substantial changes in or additions to the methodology of the study; if this occurs, realize that it is better to become aware of the need for such changes at this stage than after the study is completed.

Key Questions to Ask Yourself at This Point:

20. Have I discussed any feasible alternative explanations that might exist for the results of the study?
21. Have I discussed how I will deal with these alternative explanations?

Data Analysis. The researcher then should indicate how the data to be collected will be organized (see Chapter 7) and analyzed (see Chapters 10, 11, and 12).

Key Questions to Ask Yourself at This Point:

22. Have I described how I will organize the data I will collect?
23. Have I described how I will analyze the data, including statistical procedures that will be used and why these procedures are appropriate?

RESEARCH TIPS

Questions to Ask When Evaluating a Research Report

- Is the literature review sufficiently comprehensive? Does it include studies that might be relevant to the problem under investigation?
- Was each of the variables in the study clearly defined?
- Was the sample representative of an identifiable population? If not, were limitations discussed?
- Was the methodology the researchers used appropriate and understandable so that other researchers could replicate the study if they wished?
- Was each of the instruments sufficiently valid and reliable for its intended purpose?
- Were the statistical techniques, if used, appropriate and correct?
- Did the report include a thick description that revealed how individuals responded (if appropriate)?
- Was the researchers' conclusions supported by the data?
- Did the researchers draw reasonable implications for theory and/or practice from their findings?

BUDGET

Research proposals are often submitted to government or private funding institutions in hopes of obtaining financial support. Such institutions almost always require submission of a tentative budget along with the proposal. Needless to say, the amount of money involved in a research proposal can have a considerable impact on whether or not it is funded. Thus, great care should be given to preparing the budget. Budgets usually include such items as salaries, materials, equipment costs, administrative and other assistance, expenses (such as travel and postage), and overhead.

GENERAL COMMENTS

One other comment may not seem necessary, but in our experience it is. Remember that all sections of a proposal must be consistent. It is not uncommon to read a proposal in which each section by itself is quite acceptable but some sections contradict others. The terms used in a study, for example, must be used throughout as originally defined. Any hypotheses must be consistent with the research question. Instrumentation must be consistent with or appropriate for the research question, the hypotheses, and the procedures for data collection. The method of obtaining the sample must be appropriate for the instruments that will be used and for the means of dealing with alternative explanations for the results, and so forth. Finally, for proposals that involve two or more researchers who will contribute to the final report, it is always a good idea to discuss the order of authorship before starting the project.

Sections Unique to Research Reports

Once researchers have conducted and completed their study, they must write a report of their procedures and findings. The unique features of a report describe what was done in the study, how it was done, what results were obtained, and what they mean. Although the details of a quantitative study may differ somewhat from those of a qualitative study, the emphasis in both should be on accurate description so that the reader is quite clear about what happened. The old standbys—what, why, where, when, and how—are, as always, good guides to follow.

GENERAL RULES TO CONSIDER

A research report should be written as clearly and concisely as possible. If at all possible, jargon is to be avoided. Research reports are always written in the past tense. As might be expected, spelling, punctuation, and grammar must be correct. (The spelling and grammar checks on a computer are a big help here!)

A style manual should be consulted before beginning the report. A good source, recommended by most journal editors and used by many researchers when preparing their research reports, is the *Publication Manual of the American Psychological Association* (APA), 6th ed. (2010). Although various manuals emphasize different rules, all have certain ones in common. The use of abbreviations and contractions, for example, is usually discouraged, the only exceptions being those that are

TABLE 25.1 *References APA Style*

Type of Reference	Format
Book	Fraenkel, J. R., Wallen, N. E., & Hyun, H. (2012). *How to design and evaluate research in education* (8th ed.). San Francisco: McGraw-Hill.
Edited book	Jacoby, R., & Glauberman, N. (Eds.). (1995). *The bell curve debate: History, documents, opinions.* New York, NY: Random House.
Chapter in a book	Gould, S. J. (1995). Mismeasure by any measure. In R. Jacoby & N. Glauberman (Eds.), *The bell curve debate: History, documents, opinions* (pp. 3–13). New York, NY: Random House.
Journal article	Clarke, A. T., & Kurtz-Costes, B. (1997, May/June). Television viewing, educational quality of the home environment, and school readiness. *The Journal of Educational Research, 90*(5), 279–285.
Dissertation (unpublished)	Spitzer, S. L. (2001). *No words necessary: An ethnography of daily activities with young children who don't talk.* Unpublished doctoral dissertation, University of Southern California.
Book review	Liss, A. (2004). Whose America? Culture wars in the public schools [Review of the book *Whose America? Culture wars in the public schools*]. *Social Education, 68,* 238.
Electronic source	Learnframe. (2000, August). *Facts, figures, and forces behind e-learning.* Retrieved from http://www.learnframe.com/aboutlearning/
ERIC reference	Mead, J. V. (1992). *Looking at old photographs: Investigating the teacher tales that novice teachers bring with them.* Retrieved from ERIC database. (ED346082)

commonly used and understood (such as *IQ*) or those that are repeated frequently in the report. Authors of references cited in the report are usually referred to by last name only (first name and middle initials are given only in the bibliography; Table 25.1). Honorifics (e.g., Dr., Professor) are not given.

Once a report is completed, it is a good idea to have someone who is knowledgeable about the topic review the report for clarity and errors. Reading the report aloud also can help check for mistakes in grammar as well as identify unclearly written passages. Computers make it easy to rearrange words and sentences, check spelling and grammar, and number pages automatically.

FORMAT

The format of a report is the way it is organized. Research reports generally follow a format that reflects the steps involved in the study itself; they also have many of the same components included in research proposals. Figure 25.1 illustrates the organization of a typical research report. Let us address those components we have not yet discussed.

Abstract. The **abstract** is a brief summary of the entire research report. It is usually no longer than a paragraph or two and is typed on a separate page with the word *Abstract* centered at the top of the page. Usually, an abstract contains a brief statement of the research problem, the hypothesis, a description of the sample, followed by a brief summary of the procedures, including a description of the instrument(s) used, how the data were collected, the results of the study, and the researcher's conclusions.

Results/Findings. As discussed previously, the **results** of a study can be presented only in a research report; ordinarily there are no results in a proposal (unless results of some exploratory research or a pilot study are included as part of the background of the proposal). A report of the results, sometimes called the **findings**, is included near the end of the report. The findings of the study constitute the results of the researcher's analysis of his or her data—that is, what the collected data reveal. In comparison-group studies, the means and standard deviation for each group on the posttest measure(s) usually are reported. In correlational studies, correlation coefficients and scatterplots are reported. In survey studies, percentages of responses to the questions asked, crossbreak tables, contingency coefficients, and so forth, are given.

The results section should describe any statistical techniques that were applied to the data and the results that

Figure 25.1
Organization of a Research Report

Introductory section
- Title Page
- Table of Contents
- List of Figures
- List of Tables

Main Body

I. Problem to be investigated
   - A. Purpose of the study (including assumptions)
   - B. Justification of the study
   - C. Research question, hypotheses, and propositions
   - D. Definition of terms
   - E. Brief overview of study

II. Background and review of related literature
   - A. Theoretical framework, if appropriate
   - B. Studies directly related
   - C. Studies tangentially related

III. Procedures
   - A. Description of the research design
   - B. Description of the sample
   - C. Description of instruments used (scoring procedures; reliability; validity)
   - D. Explanation of the procedures followed (the what, when, where, and how of the study)
   - E. Discussion of internal validity
   - F. Discussion of external validity
   - G. Description and justification of the data analysis methods (e.g., statistical techniques for quantitative studies and data reduction strategies for qualitative studies)

IV. Findings
   Description of findings pertinent to each of the research questions, hypotheses, and propositions stated

V. Summary and conclusions
   - A. Brief summary of the research question being investigated, the procedures employed, and the results obtained
   - B. Discussion of the implications of the findings—their meaning and significance
   - C. Limitations—unresolved problems and weaknesses
   - D. Suggestions for further research

References (Bibliography)

Appendixes

were obtained. Each result should be discussed in relation to the topic studied. The results of any statistical tests of significance should be reported. Qualitative data analysis should present clear descriptions (and sometimes quotations) to support and/or illustrate results obtained through observations and/or interviews. Tables and figures should present clear summaries of the data analysis.

It is particularly important in the results section of a research report that the data collection procedures be clearly described, including what kinds of analyses were done. Here are two examples taken from the literature:

- (From a study investigating the effects of cooperative learning among Hispanic students in elementary social studies): "Means and standard deviations of raw scores for the social studies achievement pretests and posttests, as well as the adjusted means for the social studies achievement posttest, are reported. Results of the ANCOVA revealed a statistically significant main effect for treatment, $F(1,93) = 25.72, p <$ .001, favoring cooperative learning over traditional instruction; however, no statistically significant effects were found for gender or for an interaction between treatment and gender on social studies achievement. The correlation r between the pretest and the posttest was .67 ($p = .001$)."[13]

- (From a study investigating the relationship between time to completion and achievement on multiple-choice items): "The relationship between time to completion and examination achievement was explored separately for mid-semester and final examinations. The resultant correlation coefficients were low and not statistically significant ($p > .05$). Although the range of coefficients extended from +.27 (+.02) to −.30, the coefficients of determination for these values suggest that 0.04% to 9% of variance in examination performance could be explained by differences in time to completion variables."[14]

Discussion. The **discussion** section of a report presents the author's interpretation of what the results imply for theory and/or practice. This includes, in hypothesis-testing studies, an assessment of the extent to which the hypothesis was supported.

In the discussion section, researchers place their results in a broader context. Here they recapitulate any difficulties that were encountered, make note of the limitations of the study, and suggest further, related studies that might be done.

To the extent possible, we believe the results and discussion sections of a study should be kept distinct from each other. A discussion section will typically go considerably beyond the data in attempting to place the findings in a broader perspective. It is important that the reader not be misled into thinking that the investigator has obtained evidence for something that is only speculation. To put it differently, there should be no room for disagreement regarding the statements in the results section of the report. The statements should follow clearly and directly from the data that were obtained. There may be much argumentation and disagreement about the broader interpretation of these results, however.

Let us consider the results of a study on teacher personality and classroom behavior. As hypothesized in that study, correlations of .40 to .50 were found between a test of control need on the part of the teacher and (1) the extent of controlling behavior in the classroom as observed and (2) ratings by interviewers as "less comfortable with self" and "having more rigid attitudes of right and wrong." These were the results of the study and should clearly be identified as such in a report. In the discussion section, however, these findings might be placed in a variety of controversial perspectives. Thus, one investigator might propose that the study provides support for selection of prospective teachers, arguing that anyone scoring high in control need should be excluded from a training program on the grounds that this characteristic and the classroom behavior it appears to predict are undesirable in teachers. In contrast, another investigator might interpret the results to support the desirability of attracting people with higher control need into teaching. This investigator might argue that, at least in inner-city schools, teachers scoring higher in control need are likely to have more orderly classrooms.

Clearly, both of these interpretations go far beyond the results of the particular study. There is no reason the investigator should not make such an interpretation, provided that it is clearly identified as such and does not give the impression that the results of the study provide direct evidence in support of the interpretation. Many times a researcher will sharply differentiate between results and interpretation by placing them in different sections of a report and labeling them accordingly. At other times a researcher may intermix the two, making it difficult for the reader to distinguish the results of the study from the researcher's interpretations. (For examples of discussions, see any of the published research reports presented in Chapters 13 through 17 and 19 through 24.)

Suggestions for Further Research. Normally, this is the final section of a report. Based on the findings of the present study, the researcher suggests some related and follow-up studies that might be conducted in the future to advance knowledge in the field.

References. Finally, the references (bibliography) should list all sources that were used in the writing of the report. Every (yes, every!) source cited in the report must be included in the references, and every (yes, every!) report cited there must appear in the body of the report. The reference section should begin on a new page. Usually a hanging-indent format is used, with all sources listed alphabetically by authors' last names.

Footnotes. Footnotes are numbered consecutively, using a superscript Arabic numeral, in the order in which they appear in the text of the report.

Figures. Figures consist of drawings, graphs, charts, even photographs or pictures. All figures should be numbered consecutively and referred to in the text of the report. They should be included in a report only when they can convey information better or more clearly than the text itself or when they can summarize information that would require an extremely long explanation. Each figure should be accompanied by a caption that captures the essence of the information illustrated.

Tables. Tables also should be used only when they can summarize or convey information better, more simply, or more clearly than the text alone. Tables (and figures) should always be viewed as supplements to text, never as providing new information meant to stand alone. They should always, however, be referred to in the text. Like figures, each table should have a brief title that captures the essence of the information contained in the table. It is a good idea to consult the APA *Publication Manual* for specifics regarding the presentation of figures and tables in a research report.

A FEW COMMENTS ABOUT QUALITATIVE RESEARCH REPORTS

Much of the information that needs to be included in a qualitative research report is similar to that included in a quantitative research report. At present, however, there is no commonly agreed-on format for a qualitative research report. One currently finds a variety of formats, with researchers often including such things as poems, stories, diaries, photographs, essays, even song lyrics and drawings in their reports.

Two noticeable characteristics of qualitative reports that are rarely found in quantitative reports are that (1) qualitative researchers often write their reports in the first person (e.g., using the pronouns *I* or *we* rather than *the researcher* or *the author*), and (2) they often use the active rather than the passive voice ("We observed classroom *X*," rather than "Classroom X was observed by the researcher.")*

Furthermore, the issue of confidentiality is of greater concern in qualitative than quantitative reports. Often a considerable amount of information, much of it extremely private, is obtained from the participants in a qualitative study. Because of this and also because the sample size is usually much smaller than in quantitative studies, a simple guarantee of confidentiality may be insufficient to protect identity. Therefore, fictitious names should generally be used. If a researcher is conducting a series of interviews in a high school over a period of weeks, for example, readers who are familiar with the high school might be able to recognize who he or she interviewed. The use of pseudonyms, therefore, is further protection of their identity.

AN OUTLINE OF A RESEARCH REPORT

Figure 25.1 shows an outline of a research report. Although the topics listed are generally agreed to within the research community, the particular sequence may vary in different studies. This is partly because of different preferences among researchers and partly because the headings and organization of the outline will be somewhat different for different research methodologies. This outline may also be used for a research proposal, in which case sections IV and V would be omitted (and the future tense used throughout). Also, a budget might be added.

A Sample Research Proposal

The research proposal that follows was prepared by a student in one of our classes and is a good example of a beginning effort. Such a proposal will normally go through further revision based on the comments of faculty and others, but this will give you some idea of what a completed proposal by a student looks like. We comment on both its strengths and weaknesses in the margins.

Note that this proposal does not follow the organization recommended in Figure 25.1 exactly. It does, however, contain all of the major components previously discussed. It also includes a report of a **pilot study**—a small-scale trial of the proposed procedures. Its purpose is to detect any problems so that they can be remedied before the study proper is carried out.

*The APA *Publication Manual* recommends such practice even for quantitative reports.

THE EFFECTS OF INDIVIDUALIZED READING
UPON STUDENT MOTIVATION IN GRADE FOUR

Nadine DeLuca*

1. The Problem to be Investigated

The purpose of this study is to evaluate the effectiveness of individualized reading programs

Purpose

The general purpose of this research is to add to the existing knowledge about reading methods. Many educators have become dissatisfied with general reading programs in which teacher-directed group instruction means boredom and delay for quick students and embarrassment and lack of motivation for others. Although there has been a great deal of writing in favor of an individualized reading approach which is supposedly a highly-motivating method of teaching reading, sufficient data has not been presented to make the argument for or against individualized reading programs decisive. With the data supplied by this study (and future ones), soon schools will be free to make the choice between implementing an individualized reading program or retaining a basal reading method.

Requires documentation

Demonstrates importance of study

Indicates implications if hypothesis is supported

Replace with "better able"

Res. Q. and Hypothesis (from p. 3)

Hypothesis?

Definitions

Motivation: Motivation is inciting and sustaining action in an organism. The motivation to learn could be thought of as being derived from a combination of several more basic needs such as the need to achieve, to explore, to satisfy curiosity.

Individualization: Individualization is characteristic of an individualized reading program. Individualized reading has as its basis the concepts of seeking, self-selection, and pacing. An individualized reading program has the following characteristics:

Could be more specific to this study

An operational definition would help.

"Motivation to read" is really the variable.

You should delete this sentence.

1. Literature books for children predominate.
2. Each child makes personal choices with regard to his reading materials.
3. Each child reads at his own rate and sets his own pace of accomplishment.
4. Each child confers with the teacher about what he has read and the progress he has made.
5. Each child carries his reading into some form of summarizing activity.
6. Some kind of record is kept by the teacher and/or the student.

Good—clear and specific

*Used by permission of the author.

7. Children work in groups for an immediate learning purpose and leave group when the purpose is accomplished.
8. Word recognition and related skills are taught and vocabulary is accumulated in a natural way at the point of each child's need.

2. LIT Review

Prior Research

Abbott, J. L., "Fifteen Reasons Why Personalized Reading Instruction Doesn't Work." Elementary English (January, 1972), *44:*33–36.

This article refutes many of the usual arguments against individualized reading instruction. It lists those customary arguments then proceeds to explain why the objections are not valid ones.

Helpful descriptions

It explains how such a program can be implemented by an ordinary classroom teacher in order to show the fallacy in the complaint that individualizing is impractical. Another fallacy involves the argument that unless a traditional basal reading program is used, children do not gain all the necessary reading skills.

OK

Barbe, Walter B., Educator's Guide to Personalized Reading Instruction. Englewood Cliffs, New Jersey: Prentice-Hall, Inc., 1961.

Mr. Barbe outlines a complete individualized reading program. He explains the necessity of keeping records of children's reading. The book includes samples of book-summarizing activities as well as many checklists to ensure proper and complete skill development for reading.

OK

Hunt, Lyman C., Jr., "Effect of Self-selection, Interest, and Motivation upon Independent, Instructional and Frustrational Levels." Reading Teacher (November, 1970), *24:*146–151.

Dr. Hunt explains how self-selection, interest, and motivation (some of the basic principles behind individualized reading), when used in a reading program, result in greater reading achievement.

Miel, Alice, Ed., Individualizing Reading Practices. New York: Bureau of Publications, Teachers College, Columbia University, 1959.

Veatch, Jeanette, Reading in the Elementary School. New York, NY: The Roland Press Co., 1966.

This is not really a literature review, although it is a good beginning at preparing one. Additional material needs to be added and summarized to justify the study.

West, Roland, Individualized Reading Instruction. Port Washington, New York, NY: Kennikat Press, 1964.

The three books listed above all provide examples of various individualized reading programs actually being used by different teachers. (The definitions and items on the rating scale were derived from these three books.)

Good—shows relevance to present study

Res. Q.: Do individualized reading programs have a positive impact on student motivation?

Hypothesis

The greater the degree of individualization in a reading program, the higher will be the students' motivation.

Variables are clear and hypothesis is directional

3. PROCEDURES: — Method used!

Population

Right

An ideal population would be all fourth graders in the United States. Because of different teacher-qualification requirements, different laws, and different teaching programs, though, such a generalization may not be justifiable. One that might be justifiable would be a population of all fourth-grade classrooms in the San Francisco-Bay Area.

Good distinction!

Sampling

Good sampling plan

The study will be conducted in fourth-grade classrooms in the San Francisco-Bay Area, including inner-city, rural, and suburban schools. The sample will include at least one hundred classrooms. Ideally, the sampling will be done randomly by identifying all fourth-grade classrooms for the population described and using random numbers to select the sample classrooms. As this would require excessive amounts of time, this sampling might need to be modified by taking a sample of schools in the area, identifying all fourth-grade classrooms in these schools only, then taking a random sample from these classrooms.

Add "random"!

Two-stage sampling

Instrumentation

Rating scale (Individualization)

Appears to have good content validity: items are consistent with definition

Instrumentation will include a rating scale to be used to rate the degree of individualization in the reading program in each classroom. A sample rating scale is shown below. Those items on the left indicate characteristics of classrooms with little individualization.

Reliability: The ratings of the two observers who are observing separately but at the same time in the same room will be compared to see how closely the ratings agree. The rating scale will be ~~repeated for~~ each classroom on at least three different days.

Should state how data on different days will be used; it can be used to check stability

Three days may not be sufficient to get reliable scores.

Validity: Certain items on the student questionnaire (to be discussed in the next section) will be compared with the ratings on the rating scale to determine if there is a correlation between the degree of individualization apparently observed and the degree indicated by students' responses. In the same manner, responses to questions asked of teachers and parents can be used to indicate whether the rating scale is a true measure of the degree of individualization.

Would parents be qualified to judge this?

Good

Another means of instrumentation to be used is a student questionnaire. A sample questionnaire is included. The following questions have as their purpose to determine the degree of motivation by asking how many books read and how the child indicates what he feels about reading: questions numbered 1, 4, 5, 6, 7, 9, 10, 11, 12, and 13. Questions 2, 3, 4, and 8 have as their purpose to help determine the validity of the items on the rating scale. Questions 14 and 15 are included to determine the students' attitudes toward the questionnaire to help determine if their attitudes are possible sources of bias for the study. Questions 8 and 9 have an additional purpose which is to add knowledge about the novelty of the reading situation in which the child now finds himself. This may be used to determine if there is a relationship between the novelty of the situation and the degree of motivation.

Can't use the same item for both variables

Good idea, but may be too few items to give a reliable index

Most items appear to have logical validity, but the lack of definition of motivation to read makes it difficult to judge.

Good idea, but may not be enough items to give a reliable index

But why? to control novelty as an extraneous variable?

RATING SCALE

1. Basal readers or programmed readers predominate in room.	1	2	3	4	5	There is an obvious center in the room containing at least five library books per child.
2. Teacher teaches class as a group.	1	2	3	4	5	Teacher works with individuals or small groups.
3. Children are all reading from the same book series.	1	2	3	4	5	Children are reading various materials at different levels.
4. Teacher initiates activities.	1	2	3	4	5	Student initiates activities.
5. No reading records are in evidence.	1	2	3	4	5	Children or teacher are observed to be making notes or keeping records of books read.

	RATING SCALE	
6. There is no evidence of book summarizing activities in the room.	1 2 3 4 5	There is evidence of book summarizing activities around room (e.g., student-made book jackets, paintings, drawings, models of scenes or characters from books, class list of books read, bulletin board displays about books read . . .).
7. Classroom is arranged with desks in rows and no provision for a special reading area.	1 2 3 4 5	Classroom is arranged with a reading area so that children have opportunities to find quiet places to read silently.
8. There is no conference area in the room for the teacher to work with children individually.	1 2 3 4 5	There is a conference area set apart from the rest of the class where the teacher works with children individually.
9. Children are doing the same activities at the same time.	1 2 3 4 5	Children are doing different activities from their classmates.
10. Teacher tells children what they are to read during class.	1 2 3 4 5	Children choose their own reading materials.
11. Children read aloud in turn to teacher as part of a group using the same reading textbook.	1 2 3 4 5	Children read silently at their desks or in a reading area or orally to the teacher on an individual basis.

Student Questionnaire

Age ________ Grade ________ Father's work ________________________

Mother's work ________________________

Is your intent here to get at socioeconomic level?

Appears valid 1. How many books have you read in the last month? ___________

2. Do you choose the books you read by yourself? ______________

Appears valid If not, who does choose them for you? ______________________

Some indication of the scoring system should be given. Open-ended questions must rely on logical analysis of responses. You could use examples from your pilot study.

Comment	Item
Appears valid	3. Do you keep a record of what books you have read? ______ Does your teacher? ______
Appears valid	4. What different kinds of reading materials have you read this year?
Question-able validity	5. Do you feel you are learning very much in reading this year? ______ Why or why not? ______
How scored?	6. Complete these sentences: Books ______ Reading ______
Appears valid	7. Do you enjoy reading time? ______
Appear valid as indications of novelty; generally not a good idea to have one item (9) dependent on another item (8)	8. Have you ever been taught reading a different way? ______ When? ______ How was it different? ______ 9. Which way of learning to read do you like better? ______ ______ Why? ______
Appears valid	10. If you couldn't come to reading class for some reason, would you be disappointed? ______ Why? ______
Appears valid	11. Is this classroom a happy place for you during reading time? ______
Questionable validity	12. Do most of the children in your classroom enjoy reading? ______
Appears valid	13. How much of your spare time at home do you spend reading just for fun? ______
Good idea	14. Did you like answering these questions or would you have preferred not to? ______ 15. Were any of the questions confusing? ______ If so, which ones? ______ How were they confusing? ______

Student Questionnaire:

Reliability: An attempt will be made to control item reliability by asking the same question in different ways and comparing the answers.

Which items will be compared?

Validity: Validity may be questionable to some degree since school children may be reluctant to report anything bad about their teachers or the school. Observers will be reminded to establish rapport with children as much as possible before administering questionnaires and to assure them that the purpose of the questions does not affect them or their school in any way.

Good point

Good idea

A teacher questionnaire

Why do you want this information?

A teacher questionnaire will also be administered. A sample questionnaire is included. Some of the questions are intended to indicate if the approach being used by the teacher is new to her and what her attitude is toward the method. These questions are numbered 1, 2, 3, and 4. Question 5 is supposed to indicate how available reading materials are so that this can be compared to the degree of student motivation. Questions 6 and 8 will provide validity checks for the rating scale. Question 7 will help in determining a relationship between socioeconomic levels and student motivation.

Why? How is this related to your hypothesis?

Good

May be too few items to give reliable index

Reliability: Reliability should not be too great a problem with this instrument since most questions are of a factual nature. ??

Incorrect. It is the reliability of information that counts. Persons may or may not be consistent in giving factual information. It does seem likely that these questions would provide reliable data.

Validity: There may be a question as to validity depending upon how the questions are asked (if they are used in a structured interview). The way they are asked may affect the answers. An attempt has been made to state the questions so that the teacher does not realize what the purposes of this study are and so prejudice her answers.

Good

Why include? as a means of controlling "experience"?

Teacher Questionnaire

1. How long have you been teaching? ____________________

Why? to assess novelty?

2. How long have you taught using the reading approach you are now using? ____________________

Why?

3. What other approaches have you used? ____________________

Why?

4. If you could use any reading approach you liked, which would you use?

____

Why? ____________________

Under procedures, you explain that items 1–5 and 7 are intended as attempts to control extraneous variables. This is a very good idea, but the purpose should be made clear earlier (in this section).

Why?

5. In what manner do you obtain reading materials? ______________

   Where did you get most of those you now use? ______________

Appears valid for individualization

6. How often are the children grouped for reading? ______________

To assess socioeconomic status

7. From what neighborhood or area do most of the children in this class come?

Appears valid for individualization

8. How do you decide when and how word recognition skills and vocabulary are taught to each child? ______________

Good idea; parents should be able to judge "motivation to read."

If it were feasible, an excellent instrument would be a parent questionnaire. The purpose of it would be to determine how much the child reads at home, his general attitude toward reading, and any changes in his attitude the parent has noticed.

Parent Questionnaire?

Procedures

Identify the research method to be used.

Since the sample of one hundred classrooms is large and each classroom will need to be visited at least three times for thirty minutes to one hour during each visit on different weeks, quite a large team of observers—probably around twenty—will be needed. They will work in pairs observing independently. They will spend about one-half hour each visit on the rating scale. The visits should take place between Monday and Thursday, since activities and attitudes are often different on Fridays. The investigation will not begin until after school has been in session for at least six weeks so that all programs have had sufficient time to function smoothly.

Sampling

Good idea

Control of extraneous variables: Sources of extraneous variables might include that teachers using individualized reading might be the more skillful and innovative teachers. Also, in cases where the individualized reading program is a new one, teacher enthusiasm for the new program might carry over to students. In this case it might be the novelty of the approach and teacher enthusiasm rather than the program itself that is motivating. An attempt will be made to

Good

Good

Extraneous variables

This section does a good job of identifying and attempting to control variables likely to be detrimental to internal validity.

determine if there is a relationship between novelty and teacher enthusiasm and student motivation by correlating the results of the teacher questionnaire (showing newness of program and teacher preference of program), indications from questions on student questionnaire, and statistics on motivation in a scatterplot. The influence of student socioeconomic levels on motivation will be determined by comparing the answers to the question on the teacher questionnaire concerning what area or neighborhood children live in, the question on parental occupations on the student questionnaire with student motivation. The amount and availability of materials may influence motivation also. This influence will be determined by the answers of teachers concerning where and how they get materials.

The presence of observers in the classroom may cause distraction and influence the degree of motivation. By having observers repeat procedures three or more times, later observations may prove to be nearly without this procedure bias. By keeping observers in the dark about the purpose of the study, it is hopeful that will control as much bias in their observations and question-asking as possible.

Good

OK but could be clearer

Better to use term "relationship," since we aren't sure about causality, which is implied by the word "influence"

Good

You should delete this.

Good, but how will information be scored?

"relate to"

Isn't it likely that all classrooms would be affected the same? Further, it seems unlikely that your second variable (individualization) would be affected. If so, it's no problem so far as internal validity is concerned.

Will you use all of the observations?

Good idea. However, since they both observe (individualization) and administer your questionnaire (motivation) they may well figure out the hypothesis. If there is concern that this "awareness" could influence their ratings and/or administration of the questionnaire, it would be preferable to have each instrument administered by different persons.

Data Analysis

Observations on the rating scale and answers on the questionnaires will be given number ratings according to the degree of individualization and amount of motivation respectively. The average of the total ratings will then be averaged for the two observers on the rating scale, and the average of the total ratings will be averaged for the questionnaires in each classroom to be used on a scatterplot to show the relationship between motivation and individualization in each classroom. Results of the teacher questionnaire will be compared similarly with motivation on the scatterplot. The correlation will be used to further indicate relationships.

Delete. This is incorrect. Do you see why? Ratings converted to # Correlation analysis

But teacher questions lack content validity as indicators of "motivation." Items 6 and 8 can check "individualization," however.

PILOT STUDY

Procedure

The pilot study was conducted in three primary grade schools in San Francisco. The principals of each school were contacted and were asked if one or two reading classes could be observed by the investigator for an hour or less. The principals chose the classrooms observed. About forty-five minutes was spent in each of four third-grade classrooms. No fourth grades were available in these schools.

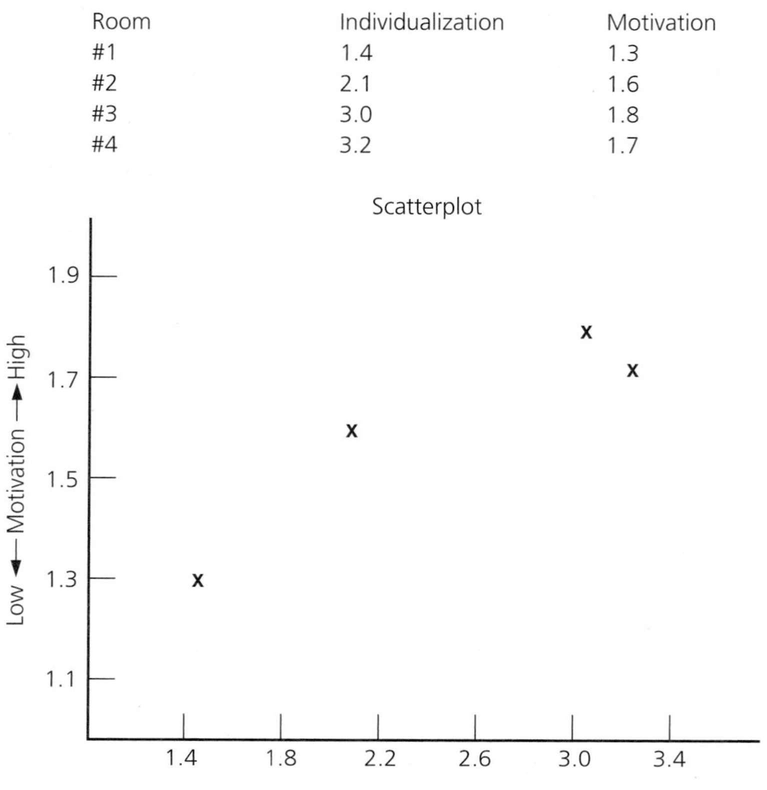

Room	Individualization	Motivation
#1	1.4	1.3
#2	2.1	1.6
#3	3.0	1.8
#4	3.2	1.7

The instruments administered were the student questionnaire and the rating scale.

Both the questionnaire and rating scale were coded by school and by classroom so that the variables for each classroom might be compared. The ratings on the rating scale for each classroom were added together then averaged. Answers on items for the questionnaire were rated "1" for answers indicating low motivation and "2" for answers indicating high motivation. (Note: Some items had as their purpose to test validity of rating scale or to provide data concerning possible biases, so these items were not rated.) Determining whether answers indicated high or low motivation created no problem except on Item #1. It was decided that fewer than eight books (two books per week) read in the past month indicated low motivation, while more indicated high motivation. The ratings for these questions were then added and averaged. Then these averaged numbers for all the questionnaires in each classroom were averaged. The results were as follows:

Problem questions

Although this pilot study could not possibly be said to uphold or disprove the hypothesis, we might venture to say that if the actual study were to yield results similar to those shown on the graph, there would be a strong correlation (estimate: r = .90) between individualization and motivation. This correlation is much too high to be attributed to chance with a random sample of 100 classrooms. If these were the results of the study described in the research proposal, the hypothesis would seem to be upheld.

Indications

Unfortunately, I was unable to conduct the pilot study in any fourth-grade classrooms which immediately throws doubt upon the validity of the results. In administering the student questionnaire, I discovered that many of the third-graders had difficulty understanding the questions. Therefore, the questioning took the form of individual structured interviews. Whether or not this difficulty would hold for fourth-graders, too, would need to be determined by conducting a more extensive pilot study in fourth-grade classrooms.

Good observation

Pilot sample limited to 3rd graders

Right

It was also discovered that Item #7 in the rating scale was difficult to rate. Perhaps it should be divided into two separate items—one concerning desk arrangement and one on the presence of a reading area—and worded more clearly.

Right

Item #8 on the student questionnaire seemed to provide some problems for children. Third-graders, at least, didn't seem to understand the intent of the question. There is also some uncertainty as to whether the answers on Item #15 reflected the students' true feelings. Since it was administered orally, students were probably reluctant to answer negatively about the test to the administrator of the test. Again, a more extensive pilot study would be helpful in determining if these indications are typical.

Right

Although the results of the pilot study are not very valid due to its size and the circumstances, its value lies in the knowledge gained concerning specific items in the instruments and problems that can be anticipated for observers or participants in similar studies.

Go back to the **INTERACTIVE AND APPLIED LEARNING** feature at the beginning of the chapter for a listing of interactive and applied activities. Go to the **Online Learning Center** at **www.mhhe.com/fraenkel9e** to take quizzes, practice with key terms, and review chapter content.

Main Points

RESEARCH PROPOSAL VERSUS RESEARCH REPORT

- A research proposal communicates a researcher's plan for a study.
- A research report communicates what was actually done in a study and what resulted.

MAJOR SECTIONS OF A RESEARCH PROPOSAL OR REPORT

- The main body is the largest section of a proposal or a report and generally includes the problem to be investigated (including the statement of the problem or question, the research hypotheses and variables, and the definition of terms); the review of the literature; the procedures (including a description of the sample, the instruments to be used, the research design, and the procedures to be followed; an identification of threats to internal validity; a description and a justification of the statistical procedures used); and (in a proposal) a budget of expected costs.
- All sections of a research proposal or a research report should be consistent with one another.

SECTIONS UNIQUE TO RESEARCH REPORTS

- The essential difference between a research proposal and a research report is that a research report states what was done rather than what will be done and includes the actual results of the study. Thus, in a report, a description of the findings pertinent to each of the research hypotheses or questions is presented, along with a discussion of what the findings of the study imply for overall knowledge and current practice.
- Normally, the final section of a report offers suggestions for further research.

For Review

1. Review the problem sheets that you have completed to see how they correspond to the suggestions made in this chapter.
2. Review any or all of the critiques of studies included in the chapters on quantitative and qualitative research to see how they correspond to the suggestions made in this chapter.

Key Terms

abstract 623
discussion 625
findings 623
hypothesis 617
justification (of a study) 616
literature review 618
pilot study 626
procedures 619
purpose (of a study) 615
research design 619
research proposal 615
research report 615
results (of a study) 623
sample 619

For Discussion

1. To what extent should a researcher allow his or her personal writing style to influence the headings and organizational sequence in a research proposal (assuming that there is no mandatory format prescribed by, e.g., a funding agency)?
2. To what common function do the problem statement, the research question, and the hypotheses all contribute? In what ways are they different?
3. When instructors of introductory research courses evaluate research proposals of students, they sometimes find logical inconsistencies among the various parts. What do you think are the most commonly found inconsistencies?
4. Why is it especially important in a study involving a convenience sample to provide a detailed description of the characteristics of the sample in the research report? Would this be necessary for a random sample as well? Explain.
5. Why is it important for a researcher to discuss threats to internal validity in (*a*) a research proposal and (*b*) a research report?
6. Often researchers do *not* describe their samples in detail in research reports. Why do you suppose this is so?

References

1. Johnson, J. E. (1988). Bedtime routines: Do they influence the sleep of elderly women? *Journal of Applied Gerontology, 7,* 97–110.

2. Stiles, D. A., Gibbons, J. L., & Schnellman, J. (1987). The smiling sunbather and the chivalrous football player: Young adolescents' images of the ideal woman and man. *Journal of Early Adolescence, 7,* 411–427.

3. Coleman, L. M., Jussim, L., & Abraham, J. (1987). Students' reactions to teachers' evaluations: The unique impact of negative feedback. *Journal of Applied Social Psychology, 17,* 1051–1070.

4. Levstik, L. S. (1986). The relationship between historical response and narrative in a sixth-grade classroom. *Theory and Research in Social Education, 14*(1), 1–19. Reprinted with permission of the National Council for the Social Studies and the author.

5. Boivin, M., & Hymel, S. (1997). Peer experiences and social self-perceptions: A sequential model. *Developmental Psychology, 33,* 135–143.

6. Gordon, J. A. (1994). Why students of color are not entering teaching: Reflections from minority teachers. *Journal of Teacher Education, 45,* 220–227.

7. Wrzesniewski, A., et al. (1997). Jobs, careers, and callings: People's relations to their work. *Journal of Research in Personality, 31*(1), 21–31.

8. Sacks, C. H., & Mergendoller, J. R. (1997, Winter). The relationship between teachers' theoretical orientation toward reading and student outcomes in kindergarten children with different initial reading abilities. *American Educational Research Journal, 34*(4), 722–723.

9. Manning, B. H. (1988). Application of cognitive behavior modification: First and third graders' self-management of classroom behaviors. *American Educational Research Journal, 25*(2), 194.

10. Norman, A. D., et al. (1998). Moral reasoning and religious belief: Does content influence structure. *Journal of Moral Reasoning, 27*(1), 140–149.

11. Bee-Gates, D., et al. (1996). Help-seeking behavior of Native American Indian high school students. *Professional Psychology: Research and Practice, 27,* 495–499.

12. Fraenkel, J. R. (1994). A portrait of four social studies teachers and their classes. In D. S. Tierney (Ed.), *1994 yearbook of California education research* (pp. 89–115). San Francisco: Caddo Gap Press.

13. Lampe, J. R., Rooze, G. R., & Tallent-Runnels, M. (1996). Effects of cooperative learning among Hispanic students in elementary social studies. *Journal of Educational Research, 89,* 187–191.

14. Herman, W. E. (1997). The relationship between time to completion and achievement on multiple-choice items. *Journal of Research and Development in Education, 30*(2), 113–117.

Appendixes

APPENDIX A Portion of a Table of Random Numbers **A-2**

APPENDIX B Selected Values from a Normal Curve Table **A-3**

APPENDIX C Chi-Square Distribution **A-4**

APPENDIX D Using Microsoft Excel **A-5**

APPENDIX A

Portion of a Table of Random Numbers

(a)	(b)	(c)	(d)	(e)	(f)	(g)	(h)	(i)
83579	52978	49372	01577	62244	99947	76797	83365	01172
51262	63969	56664	09946	78523	11984	54415	37641	07889
05033	82862	53894	93440	24273	51621	04425	69084	54671
02490	75667	67349	68029	00816	38027	91829	22524	68403
51921	92986	09541	58867	09215	97495	04766	06763	86341
31822	36187	57320	31877	91945	05078	76579	36364	59326
40052	03394	79705	51593	29666	35193	85349	32757	04243
35787	11263	95893	90361	89136	44024	92018	48831	82072
10454	43051	22114	54648	40380	72727	06963	14497	11506
09985	08854	74599	79240	80442	59447	83938	23467	40413
57228	04256	76666	95735	40823	82351	95202	87848	85275
04688	70407	89116	52789	47972	89447	15473	04439	18255
30583	58010	55623	94680	16836	63488	36535	67533	12972
73148	81884	16675	01089	81893	24114	30561	02549	64618
72280	99756	57467	20870	16403	43892	10905	57466	39194
78687	43717	38608	31741	07852	69138	58506	73982	30791
86888	98939	58315	39570	73566	24282	48561	60536	35885
29997	40384	81495	70526	28454	43466	81123	06094	30429
21117	13086	01433	86098	13543	33601	09775	13204	70934
50925	78963	28625	89395	81208	90784	73141	67076	58986
63196	86512	67980	97084	36547	99414	39246	68880	79787
54769	30950	75436	59398	77292	17629	21087	08223	97794
69625	49952	65892	02302	50086	48199	21762	84309	53808
94464	86584	34365	83368	87733	93495	50205	94569	29484
52308	20863	05546	81939	96643	07580	28322	22357	59502

APPENDIX B

Selected Values from a Normal Curve Table

Column A lists the z-score values. Column B provides the proportion of area between the mean and the z-score value. Column C provides the proportion of area beyond the z score.

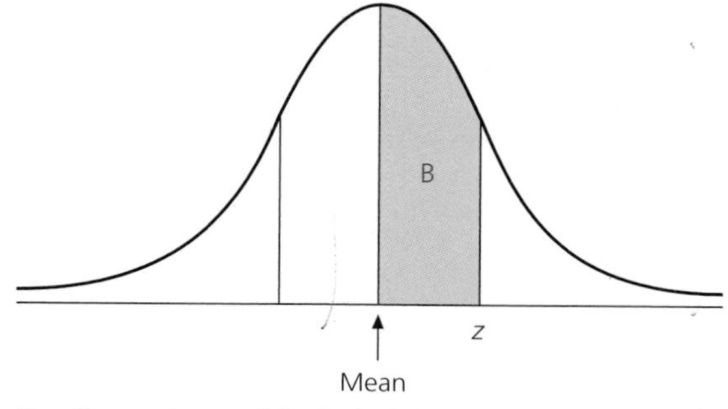

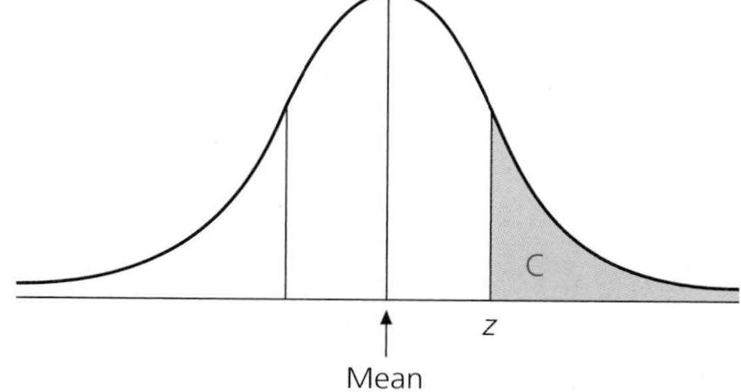

Note: Because the normal distribution is symmetrical, areas for negative z scores are the same as those for positive z scores.

(A) z	(B) Area Between Mean and z	(C) Area Beyond z	(A) z	(B) Area Between Mean and z	(C) Area Beyond z
0.00	.0000	.5000	2.10	.4821	.0179
0.10	.0398	.4602	2.20	.4861	.0139
0.20	.0793	.4207	2.30	.4893	.0107
0.30	.1179	.3821	2.40	.4918	.0082
0.40	.1554	.3446	2.50	.4938	.0062
0.50	.1915	.3085	2.58	.4951	.0049
0.60	.2257	.2743	2.60	.4953	.0047
0.70	.2580	.2420	2.70	.4965	.0035
0.80	.2881	.2119	2.80	.4974	.0026
0.90	.3159	.1841	2.90	.4981	.0019
1.00	.3413	.1587	3.00	.4987	.0013
1.10	.3643	.1357	3.10	.4990	.0010
1.20	.3849	.1151	3.20	.4993	.0007
1.30	.4032	.0968	3.30	.4995	.0005
1.40	.4192	.0808	3.40	.4997	.0003
1.50	.4332	.0668	3.50	.4998	.0002
1.65	.4505	.0495	3.60	.4998	.0002
1.70	.4554	.0446	3.70	.4999	.0001
1.80	.4641	.0359	3.80	.49993	.00007
1.90	.4713	.0287	3.90	.49995	.00005
1.96	.4750	.0250	4.00	.49997	.00003
2.00	.4772	.0228			

From Table II of Fisher, R. A. & Yates, F. *Statistical tables for biological, agricultural, and medical research*. London: Longman Group Ltd. (previously published by Oliver & Boyd Ltd., Edinburgh). Reprinted by permission of the authors and publishers.

APPENDIX C

Chi-Square Distribution

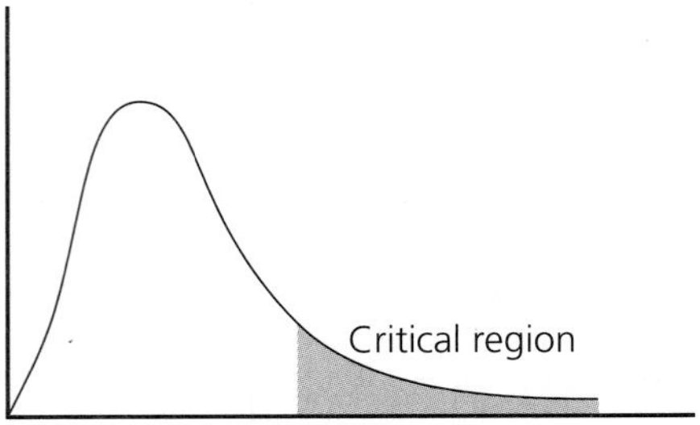

The table entries are critical values of χ^2.

Degrees of Freedom (*df*)	Proportion in Critical Region				
	0.10	0.05	0.025	0.01	0.005
1	2.71	3.84	5.02	6.63	7.88
2	4.61	5.99	7.38	9.21	10.60
3	6.25	7.81	9.35	11.34	12.84
4	7.78	9.49	11.14	13.28	14.86
5	9.24	11.07	12.83	15.09	16.75
6	10.64	12.59	14.45	16.81	18.55
7	12.02	14.07	16.01	18.48	20.28
8	13.36	15.51	17.53	20.09	21.96
9	14.68	16.92	19.02	21.67	23.59
10	15.99	18.31	20.48	23.21	25.19
11	17.28	19.68	21.92	24.72	26.76
12	18.55	21.03	23.34	26.22	28.30
13	19.81	22.36	24.74	27.69	29.82
14	21.06	23.68	26.12	29.14	31.32
15	22.31	25.00	27.49	30.58	32.80
16	23.54	26.30	28.85	32.00	34.27
17	24.77	27.59	30.19	33.41	35.72
18	25.99	28.87	31.53	34.81	37.16
19	27.20	30.14	32.85	36.19	38.58
20	28.41	31.41	34.17	37.57	40.00
21	29.62	32.67	35.48	38.93	41.40
22	30.81	33.92	36.78	40.29	42.80
23	32.01	35.17	38.08	41.64	44.18
24	33.20	36.42	39.36	42.98	45.56
25	34.38	37.65	40.65	44.31	46.93
26	35.56	38.89	41.92	45.64	48.29
27	36.74	40.11	43.19	46.96	49.64
28	37.92	41.34	44.46	48.28	50.99
29	39.09	42.56	45.72	49.59	52.34
30	40.26	43.77	46.98	50.89	53.67
40	51.81	55.76	59.34	63.69	66.77
50	63.17	67.50	71.42	76.15	79.49
60	74.40	79.08	83.30	88.38	91.95
70	85.53	90.53	95.02	100.42	104.22
80	96.58	101.88	106.63	112.33	116.32
90	107.56	113.14	118.14	124.12	128.30
100	118.50	124.34	129.56	135.81	140.17

From Table VII (abridged) of Fisher, R. A., & Yates, F. *Statistical tables for biological, agricultural, and medical research*. London: Longman Group Ltd. (previously published by Oliver & Boyd Ltd., Edinburgh). Reprinted by permission of the authors and publishers.

APPENDIX D

Using Microsoft Excel*

INTRODUCTION

Excel is a powerful spreadsheet program that can be used to perform a variety of statistical procedures. Like any such program, there are a number of techniques that you need to learn to use the program correctly and efficiently, but they are not difficult to learn. In this appendix, we provide you with a few worked-out, step-by-step examples that will enable you to see how the program works and, in turn, use the program yourself. You will learn not only how to run basic analyses but also to understand and interpret the output generated by the program. For all examples and illustrations we use Excel for Windows, but there is also a version of Excel that is compatible with Macintosh computers.

*Please note that because the screen interface differs, Mac users should consult the Microsoft website (www.microsoft.com) for help on how to use Excel for Mac.

LOADING THE ANALYSIS TOOLPAK FOR MICROSOFT OFFICE EXCEL

The default installation of Excel does not normally include the Analysis ToolPak (a set of data analysis tools) necessary to complete most statistical functions. If you do not see a box labeled "Data Analysis" under the Data tab (as shown in Figure D.1), then use the following

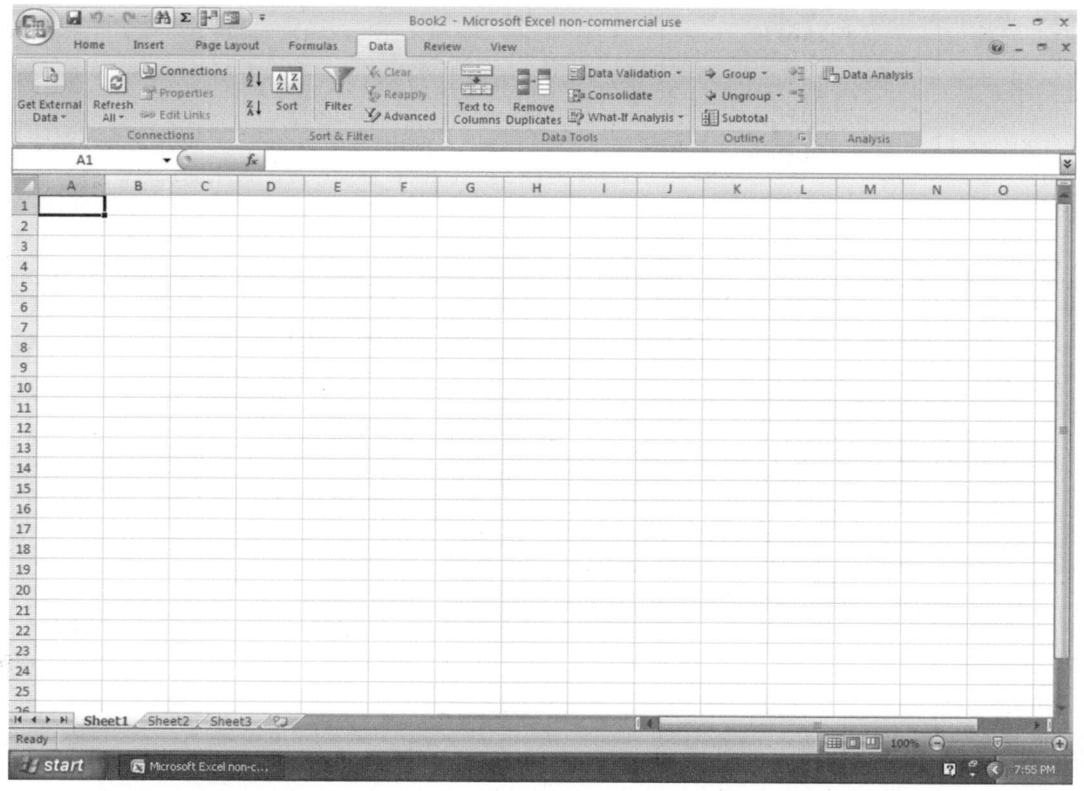

Figure D.1 *Data Window*

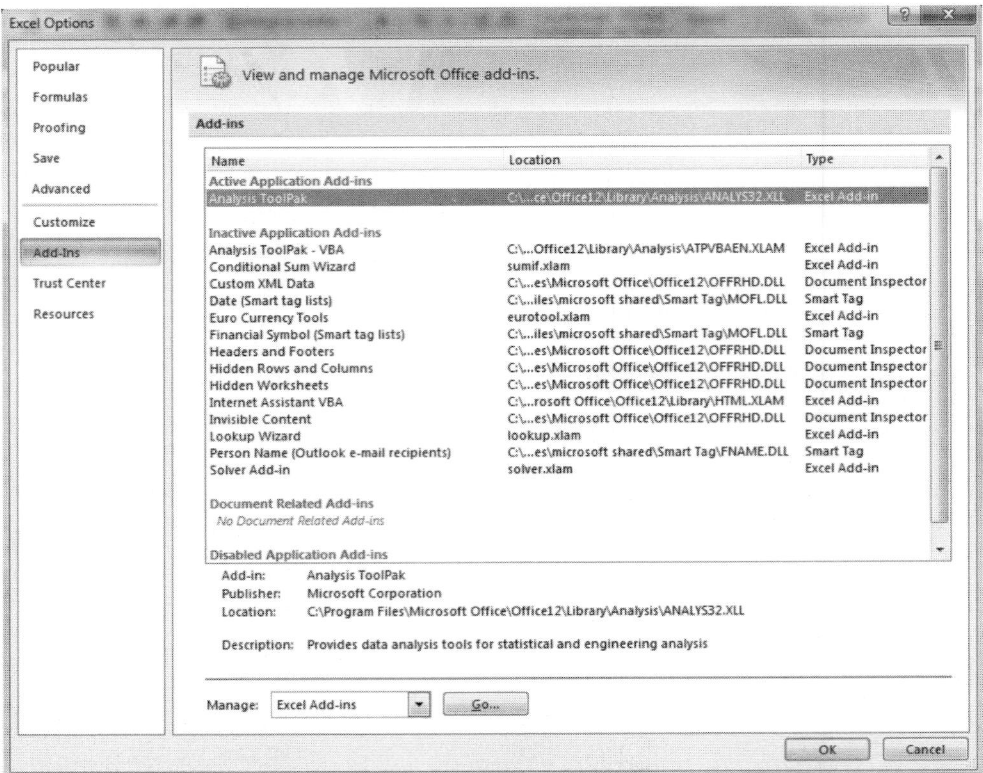

Figure D.2 *Manage Box*

instructions to load the Analysis ToolPak:

1. Click the **Microsoft Office Button** at the top left of the menu bar, and then click **Excel Options**.
2. Click **Add-Ins**, and then in the **Manage** box, select **Excel** Add-ins (Figure D.2).
3. Click **Go**.
4. In the **Add-Ins available** box, select the **Analysis ToolPak** check box, *make sure you check the box*, and then click **OK** (Figure D.3).

Tips: If **Analysis ToolPak** is not listed in the **Add-Ins available** box, click **Browse** to locate it. If you get prompted that the Analysis ToolPak is not currently installed on your computer, click **Yes** to install it, and follow the preceding instructions on how to load it.

After you load the Analysis ToolPak, the **Data Analysis** command should be visible on the far right in the **Analysis** group on the **Data** tab.

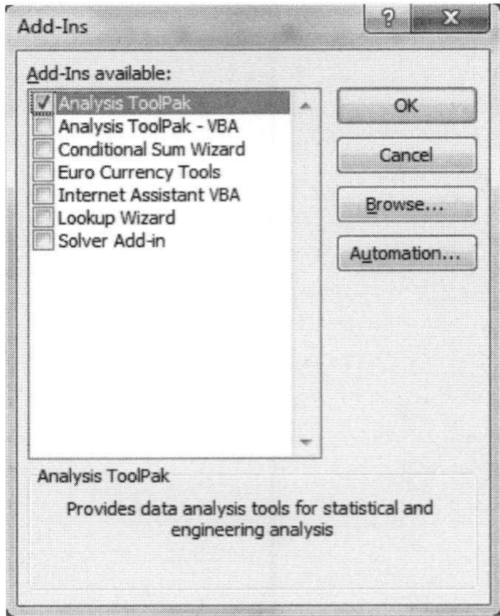

Figure D.3 *Analysis ToolPak Check Box*

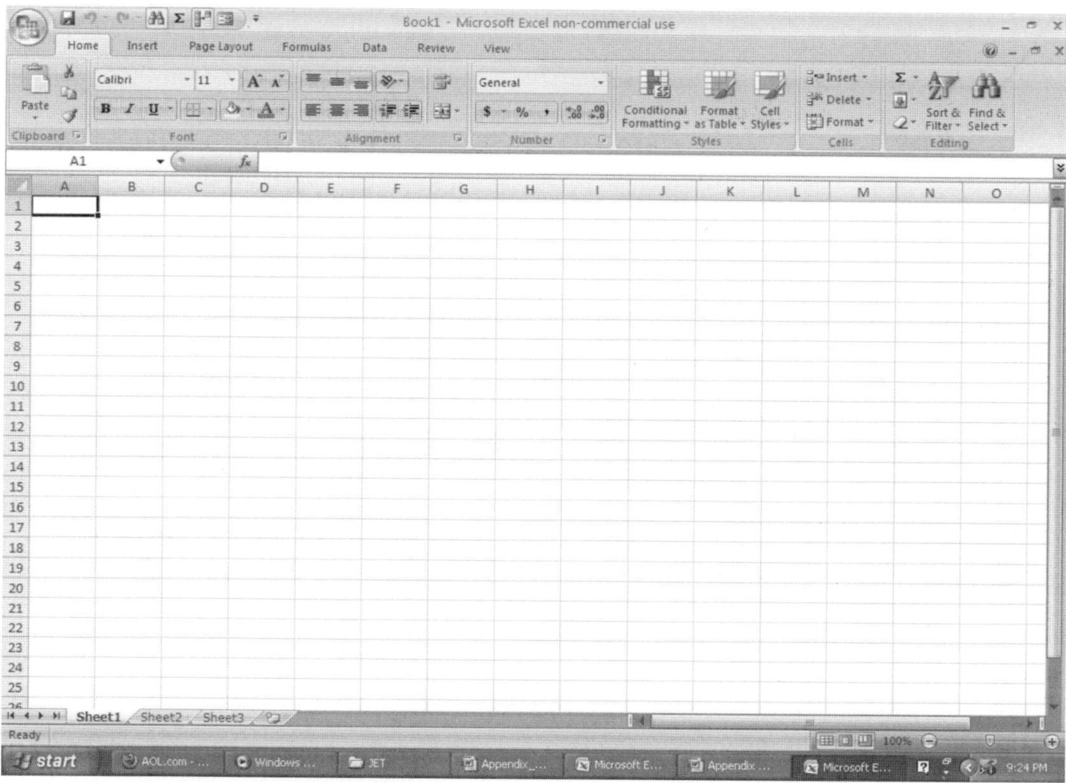

Figure D.4 *Data Window*

STARTING EXCEL

Excel start-up procedures differ slightly, depending on how the program was installed. On most computers, the program is started by clicking on the Excel icon or by choosing it from a menu of options. The program should then open automatically with a blank data window that looks like Figure D.4. Along the top of the screen, you will see the words **Home, Insert, Page Layout**, and so forth (this line is called the *menu bar*). Clicking on any of the words will produce additional features that you can choose to perform certain tasks (we will show you some examples a bit later). Most of the screen, however, is taken up by several cells for entering data or displaying results.

ENTERING DATA

Data are entered into a matrix containing *rows* that are identified by numbers and *columns that are identified by letters.* Each cell is identified by its row and column address; for example, the upper leftmost cell's address is A1.

Here is an example to illustrate how to enter data. Imagine that we have collected the following quiz scores for five students:

Student Gender Quiz Score

1 1 88 2 1 94 3 1 79 4 2 85 5 2 91 (see Table 1)

Entering the data is quite simple. Highlight the upper-left cell (i.e., row 1, column A) by clicking on it, and then type the column heading "Student." Then press the right arrow key or tab key. The word "Student" will appear inside the cell A1. Next, type the second column heading "Gender." Press the right arrow key or the tab key and type the last column heading "Quiz Score." Using the arrow keys or the mouse, click cell A2 and type in a **"1"** to represent the first student's identification number. Then press the right arrow key or the tab key. The numeral **"1"** will appear inside cell A2. Next, move one cell to the right with the arrow or tab key

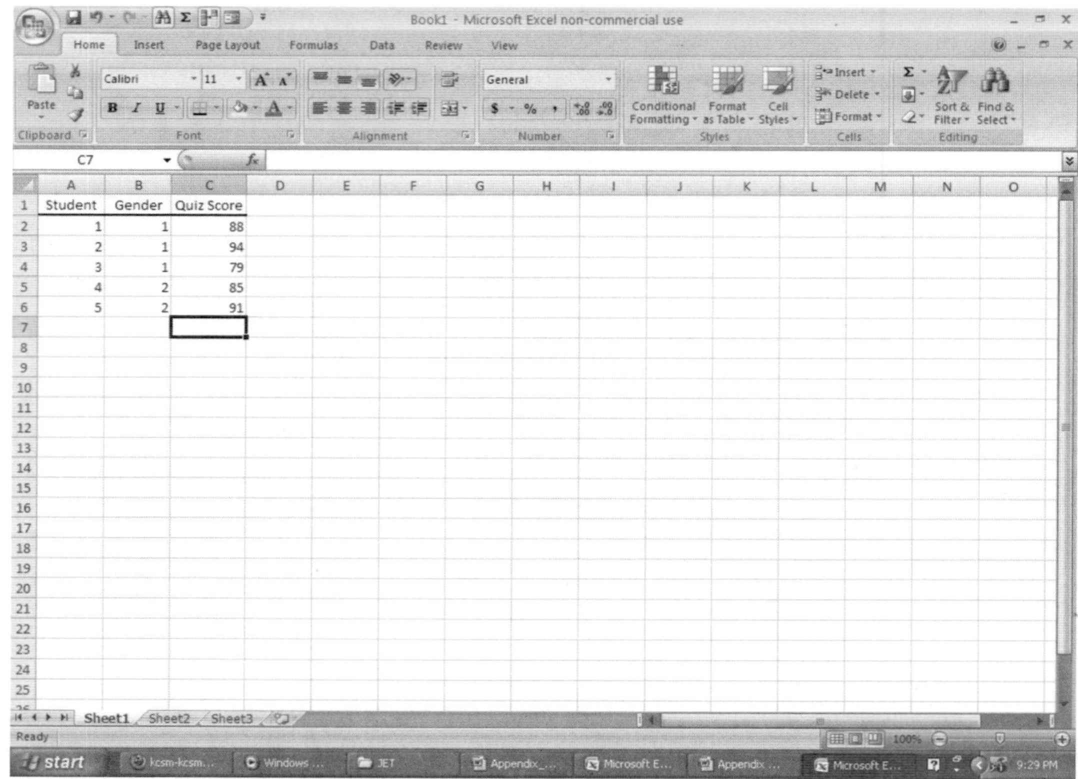

Figure D.5 *Data Window with Scores*

and click on it, and type **"1"** again (which represents the student's gender). Then, move right one cell again with the arrow or tab key, and enter into this cell the student's quiz score **(88).** This completes the first row of data entry.

Now, move to the third row of cells and enter the values for the second student in the appropriate columns just as you did for the first student. Repeat this procedure until the data for all five students are entered. When you have finished, the screen should look like that in Figure D.5.

SPECIFYING ANALYSES

Once the data have been entered into the spreadsheet, you are ready to tell Excel what you want the program to do—that is, what type of statistical analysis you want Excel to conduct. The procedure is really quite easy.

First, click on **Data** on the menu bar. Various features will appear. On the far right, click **Data Analysis** and a new window appears that lists several analysis options, including **Correlation**, **Covariance**, **Descriptive Statistics**, **Histogram**, **Regression**, and **T-Test.** Clicking on any of these options will produce another window of options. For example, clicking on **Descriptive Statistics** will produce a window of options, one of which is **Summary statistics.** Checking the box next to **Summary statistics** and defining a row or column of data using the **Input Range** box enables calculation of a data sample's mean, standard error, median, mode, standard deviation, in addition to other quantities. Once these choices have been made, click OK and Excel will do the rest for you. That's all there is to it. So, let's look at some examples.

OBTAINING A FREQUENCY DISTRIBUTION AND SOME DESCRIPTIVE STATISTICS

Table 1 shows the scores for a random sample of 30 students chosen (from all of the statistics students at a large university) to take a specially designed

TABLE 1 *Data for 30 Students Taking a Specially Designed Statistics Examination*

Student	Gender	Score	Student	Gender	Score
1	1	88	16	2	88
2	1	94	17	2	92
3	1	79	18	2	74
4	2	85	19	2	64
5	2	91	20	2	81
6	1	84	21	1	95
7	1	68	22	1	89
8	1	73	23	1	73
9	1	69	24	2	63
10	1	71	25	2	94
11	1	77	26	1	75
12	2	83	27	1	82
13	2	70	28	1	87
14	2	65	29	1	86
15	2	80	30	1	91

statistics exam, along with their student identification number and gender (1 = male, 2 = female). Let us obtain some descriptive statistics for the variables *gender* and *score.*

First, enter the data into the first three columns of the spreadsheet and label the column headings *student, gender,* and *score.* In a fourth column to the right of score, type the heading *bin* and enter the numbers 60 through 100. These numbers represent the intervals that you want the Histogram tool to use for measuring the input data, *score* in this case, in the data analysis. Next, click on **Data** on the menu bar. On the far right, click on **Data Analysis.** This will produce the **Data Analysis** window. Click on **Histogram** and click **OK.** This will produce yet another window that looks like Figure D.6.

Click the **Collapse Dialog** button located to the right of the box entitled **Input Range.** Highlight with the cursor the column of data under the heading *score,* and again press the **Collapse Dialog** button. Be sure to include in the highlighting the cell containing the word *score.* Next, click the **Collapse Dialog** button located to the right of the box entitled **Bin Range**, and highlight the column of data under the heading *bin.* Again, remember to include in the highlighting the cell containing the word *bin.* Click the check box next to **Chart Output** in the lower left, and select among the output option buttons to specify your choice for the format of the analysis results. This is shown in Figure D.7. Click **OK** and Excel will run the analysis, create a frequency distribution table, and print a frequency distribution bar graph (histogram). Table 2 shows the result in tabular form, and Figure D.8 shows the bar graph form. Repeat the foregoing for the variable *gender* to analyze the *gender* data.

Descriptive Statistics. To obtain descriptive statistics, click on **Data** on the menu bar, then click **Data Analysis** at the far right. When the **Data Analysis** window appears, click on **Descriptive Statistics** and then click **OK.** Click the **Collapse Dialog** button located to the right of the box entitled **Input Range.** Highlight with the cursor the column of data under the heading *score,* and again press the **Collapse Dialog** button. In this case do not highlight the cell containing the word *score.* Select among the output option buttons to specify your choice for the format of the analysis results, and click the check box next to **Summary statistics**. Click **OK** and Excel will compute various descriptive statistics, including mean, standard error, median, mode, standard deviation, and so forth. Table 2 shows the result. Repeat the foregoing for the variable *gender* to analyze the *gender* data.

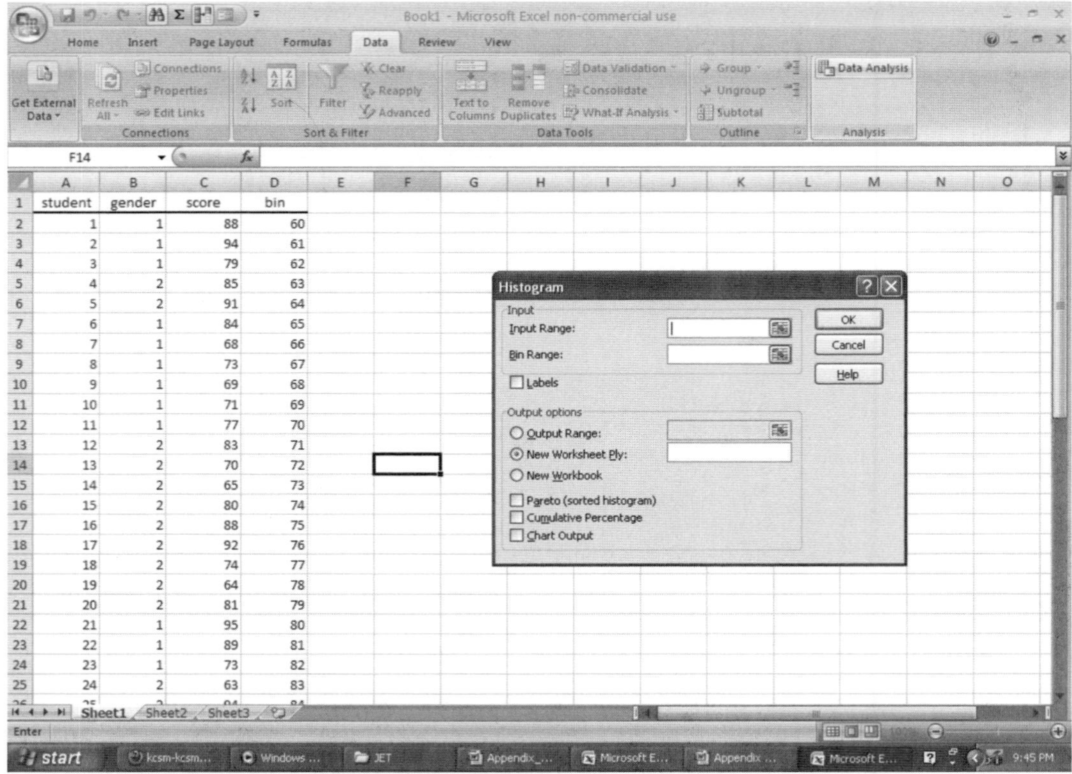

Figure D.6 *Data Analysis Window for Histogram*

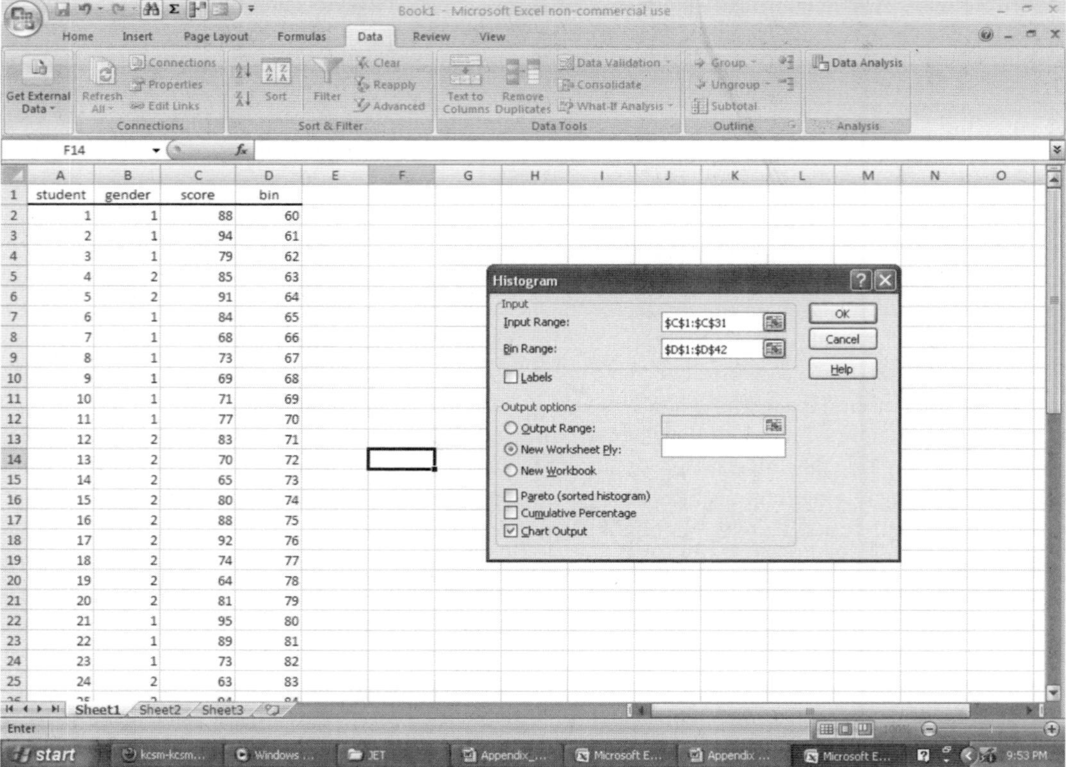

Figure D.7 *Data Analysis Window: Histogram*

TABLE 2

Frequencies

Statistics

		Gender	Score
N	Valid	30	30
	Missing	0	0
Mean		1.4333	80.37667
Std. Error of Mean		.09202	1.77238
Median		1.0000	81.5000
Mode		1.00	73.00(a)
Std. Deviation		.50401	9.70774
Variance		.254	94.240
Range		1.00	32.00
Minimum		1.00	63.00
Maximum		2.00	95.00
Sum		43.00	2411.00

a. Multiple modes exists. The smallest value is shown

Frequency Table

Gender

		Frequency	Percent	Valid Percent	Cumulative Percent
Valid	1.00	17	56.7	56.7	56.7
	2.00	13	43.3	43.3	100.0
	Total	30	100.0	100.0	

Frequency Table

Score

		Frequency	Percent	Valid Percent	Cumulative Percent
Valid	63.00	1	3.3	3.3	3.3
	64.00	1	3.3	3.3	6.7
	65.00	1	3.3	3.3	10.0
	68.00	1	3.3	3.3	13.3
	69.00	1	3.3	3.3	16.7
	70.00	1	3.3	3.3	20.0
	71.00	1	3.3	3.3	23.3
	73.00	2	6.7	6.7	30.0
	74.00	1	3.3	3.3	33.3
	75.00	1	3.3	3.3	36.7
	77.00	1	3.3	3.3	40.0
	79.00	1	3.3	3.3	43.3
	80.00	1	3.3	3.3	46.7

(continued)

TABLE 2 *Continued*

Frequency Table

Score				
	Frequency	**Percent**	**Valid Percent**	**Cumulative Percent**
81.00	1	3.3	3.3	50.0
82.00	1	3.3	3.3	53.3
83.00	1	3.3	3.3	56.7
84.00	1	3.3	3.3	60.0
85.00	1	3.3	3.3	63.3
86.00	1	3.3	3.3	66.7
87.00	1	3.3	3.3	70.0
88.00	2	6.7	6.7	76.7
89.00	1	3.3	3.3	80.0
91.00	2	6.7	6.7	86.7
92.00	1	3.3	3.3	90.0
94.00	2	3.3	3.3	96.7
95.00	1	6.7	6.7	100.0
Total	30	100.0	100.0	

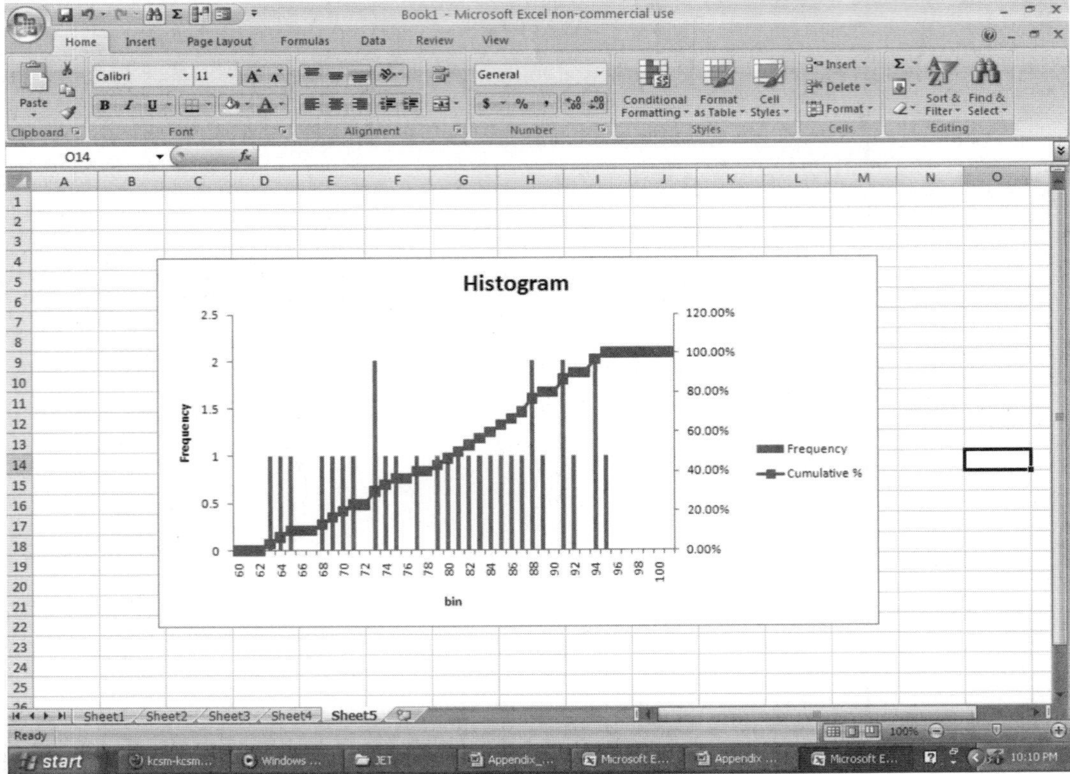

Figure D.8 *Excel Bar Graph*

CONDUCTING AN INDEPENDENT SAMPLES *t*-TEST

Let us now conduct an independent samples *t*-test on the same group of students shown in Table 1. Let us imagine that the instructor of this class hypothesizes that the female students in the class (who are indicated by the numeral **"2"**) will perform differently on the specially designed statistics examination from the male students (who are indicated by the numeral **"1"**). We want to test the null hypothesis that there is no difference in student performance between the female and male students—that is, that the mean difference in the population of students from which this sample is drawn is zero. The research hypothesis is that the population means for the two groups of students are not equal.

Analysis. Separate the 30 entries under the *score* column into to two columns, one column for males and a second for females, then label the columns *males score* and *females score.* Then we click on **Data** on the menu bar, and then select Data Analysis. When the **Data Analysis** window appears, we select **t-Test: Two-Sample Assuming Equal Variances**. This gives us a window that looks like Figure D.9.

Click the **Collapse Dialog** button located to the right of the box entitled **Variable 1 Range**. Highlight with the cursor the column of data under the heading *Males Scores,* and again press the **Collapse Dialog** button. Repeat same by entering the data under *Females Scores* in the **Variable 2 Range** box. Enter zero (0) in the box entitled **Hypothesized Mean Difference.** Enter 0.05 in the box entitled **Alpha**, which is the confidence level for the test that is related to the probability of having a type I error (rejecting a true hypothesis). This gives us a window that looks like Figure D.10. Select among the output option buttons to specify your choice for the format of the analysis results, click **OK**, and Excel will run the analysis. The output produced by Excel is shown in Figure D.11.

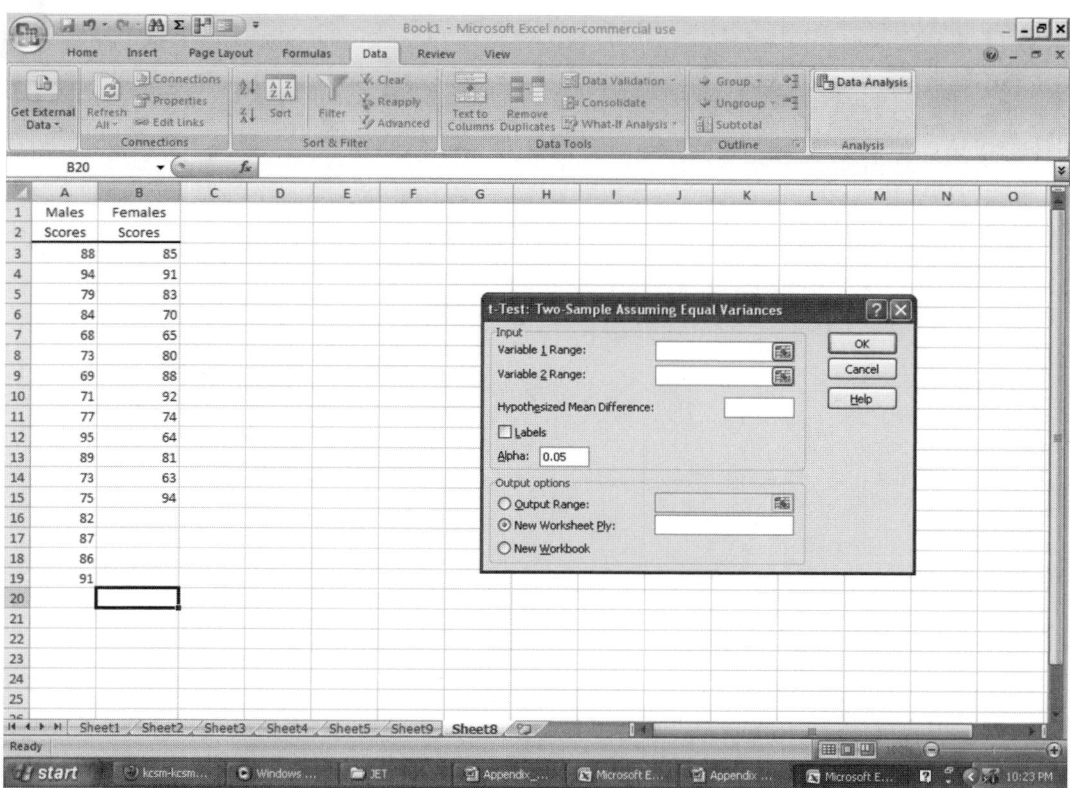

Figure D.9 *Data Analysis Window: Independent Samples t-test*

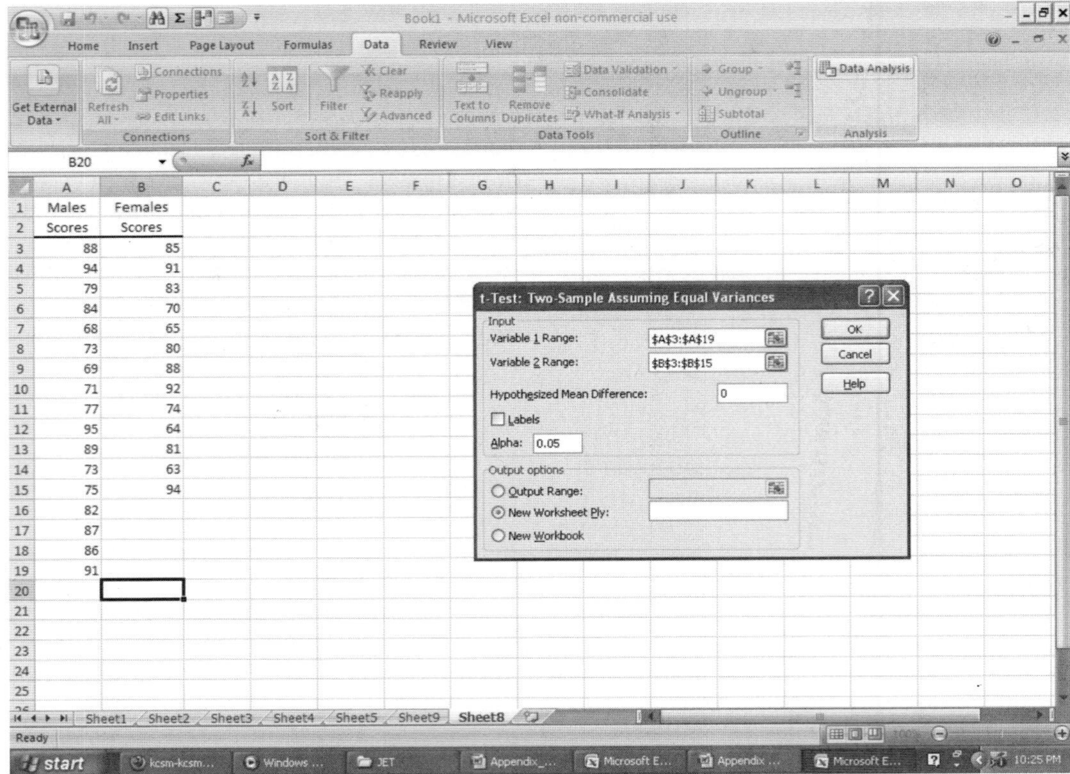

Figure D.10 *Data Analysis Window: Independent Samples t-test*

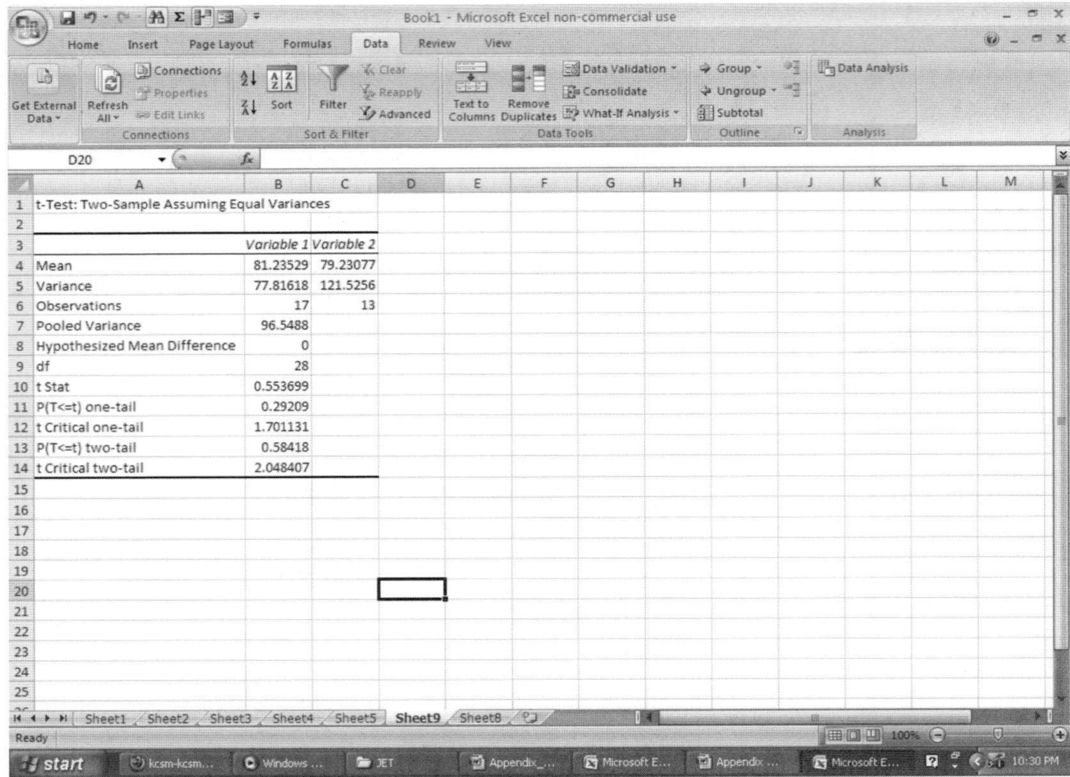

Figure D.11 *Results of Independent Samples t-test*

Excel creates a table labeled **t-Test: Two-Sample Assuming Equal Variances** that reveals the results of the *t*-test. If the process is repeated by clicking on **Data** on the menu bar, selecting **Data Analysis**, then selecting **t-Test: Two-Sample Assuming Unequal Variances**, Excel produces another table labeled **t-Test: Two-Sample Assuming Unequal Variances.** Notice that there are two tables of information here, one labeled **Equal variances assumed** and one labeled **Equal variances not assumed.** To know which table we should use, we must turn to the column labeled **Levene's Test for Equality of Variances.** One of the assumptions of the *t*-test is that the population variances from the two groups we are comparing are equal. Levene's Test is a test of this assumption. The specifics of this test are beyond the scope of this text, but in brief, a statistically significant Levene's Test indicates that we have violated this assumption and that the population variances are not equal. By looking at the column labeled **Sig.,** you can see that the significance level for the Levene's Test is **.350,** which is considerably greater than **.05,** and hence not statistically significant. We can conclude, therefore, that the population variances of the two groups do *not* differ significantly and that we should look only at the first row labeled **Equal variances assumed.**

You can see that Excel reports the observed *t*-value, the degrees of freedom ("df"), and the two-tailed *p*-value ("Sig. (2-tailed)"). Also reported on this line are the differences between the means, the standard error of the difference, and the 95 percent confidence interval for the difference between population means. The observed *t*-value is .554, which results in a probability of .584, with degrees of freedom = 28. Since this is much greater than the value required at .05, the result is considered to be NOT statistically significant at the .05 level.

CALCULATING A CORRELATION

Let us suppose that a psychology instructor is interested in seeing if there is any relationship between a student's achievement on her quizzes and the student's anxiety level. Accordingly, she recruits a random sample of 30 students to participate in a study. She measures the anxiety level of each student in the sample (using a specially designed "anxiety test" she has developed) as well as their achievement scores on her midsemester examination. The data are shown in Table 3.

As before, she enters the data into the first three columns of the spreadsheet and labels the columns *student, anxiety,* and *score.* She is interested in calculating the Pearson product-moment correlation between the two variables, *anxiety* and *score.* In addition, she wants to test the null hypothesis that the correlation between the variables in the population from which the sample was drawn equals zero.

TABLE 3

	Student	Anxiety	Score		Student	Anxiety	Score
1	1	24	88	16	16	34	88
2	2	36	94	17	17	39	92
3	3	40	79	18	18	35	74
4	4	31	85	19	19	38	64
5	5	50	91	20	20	40	81
6	6	32	84	21	21	35	95
7	7	30	68	22	22	39	89
8	8	28	73	23	23	22	73
9	9	36	69	24	24	20	63
10	10	34	71	25	25	37	94
11	11	18	77	26	26	35	75
12	12	36	83	27	27	29	82
13	13	21	70	28	28	20	87
14	14	30	65	29	29	40	96
15	15	40	80	30	30	30	91

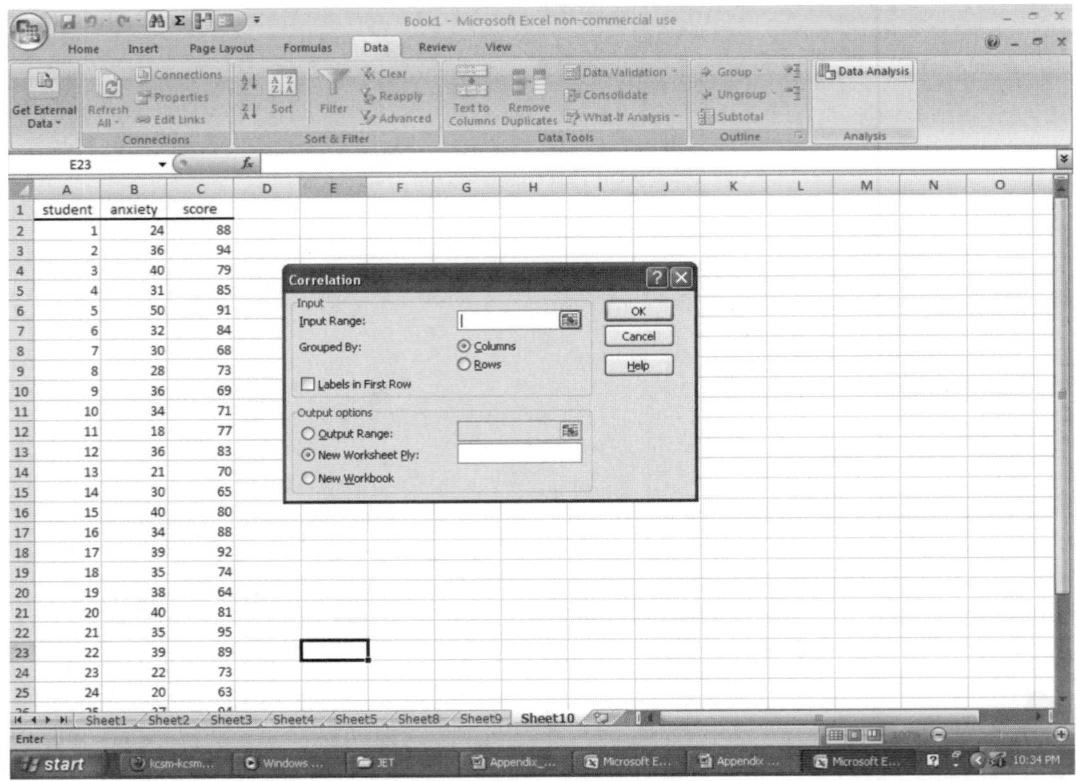

Figure D.12 *Data Analysis Window-Correlation*

Analysis. The instructor clicks on **Data** on the menu bar, clicks **Data Analysis** at the far right, and then selects **Correlation** on the **Data Analysis** window that appears. This produces another window labeled Correlation, as shown in Figure D.12. She clicks the **Collapse Dialog** button located to the right of the box entitled **Input Range,** highlights with the cursor *both* columns of data under the headings *anxiety* and *score,* and again presses the **Collapse Dialog** button. She selects among the output option buttons to choose the format of the analysis results output, and clicks **OK.** Excel runs the analysis to determine the correlation between *anxiety* and *score,* producing the results shown in Table 4. As you can see, the correlation between "anxiety" and "score" for this sample of 30 students is **.364**

The examples we have presented here only begin to show you the power of Excel. We have not even looked at the many graphing capabilities Excel possesses. Nevertheless, this should give you an idea of what Excel can do. We urge you to try out Excel for yourself so that you can discover the many types of analyses the program can deliver, as well as the many graphs it can create.

TABLE 4

Correlations

		Anxiety	**Score**
Anxiety	Pearson Correlation	1	.364*
	Sig. (2-tailed)		.048
	N	30	30
Score	Pearson Correlation	.364*	1
	Sig. (2-tailed)	.048	
	N	30	30

*Correlation is significant at the 0.05 level (2-tailed).

GLOSSARY

A-B design A single-subject experimental design in which measurements are repeatedly made until stability is presumably established (baseline), after which treatment is introduced and an appropriate number of measurements are made.
A-B-A design Same as an A-B design, except that a second baseline is added.
A-B-A-B design Same as an A-B-A design, except that a second treatment is added.
A-B-C-B design Same as an A-B-A-B design, except that the second baseline phase is replaced by a modified treatment phase.
abstract A summary of a study that describes its most important aspects, including major results and conclusions.
accessible population The population from which the researcher can realistically select subjects for a sample, and to which the researcher is entitled to generalize findings.
achievement test An instrument used to measure the proficiency level of individuals in given areas of knowledge or skill.
action plan A plan to implement change as a result of an action research study.
action research A type of research focused on a specific local problem and resulting in an action plan to address the problem.
advocacy lens Exists when the researcher indicates or implies that the purpose of the research is to improve conditions of the participant population.
age-equivalent score A score that indicates the age level for which a particular performance (score) is typical.
alpha coefficient See **Cronbach alpha.**
analysis of covariance (ANCOVA) A statistical technique for equating groups on one or more variables when testing for statistical significance; it adjusts scores on a dependent variable for initial differences on other variables, such as pretest performance or IQ.
analysis of variance (ANOVA) A statistical technique for determining the statistical significance of differences among means; it can be used with two or more groups and one independent variable.
applied research Research that seeks to solve practical problems (compare to *basic research*).
aptitude test An ability test used to predict performance in a future situation.
associational research A general type of research in which a researcher looks for relationships having predictive and/or explanatory power. Both correlational and causal-comparative studies are examples.
assumption Any important assertion presumed to be true but not actually verified; major assumptions should be described in one of the first sections of a research proposal or report.
autobiography A narrative by those who are the subjects of the study.
average A number representing the typical score attained by a group of subjects. See **measures of central tendency.**

B-A-B design The same as an A-B-A-B design, except that the initial baseline phase is omitted.
background question Question asked by an interviewer or on a questionnaire to obtain information about a respondent's background (age, occupation, etc.).
bar graph A graphic way of illustrating differences.
baseline The graphic record of measurements taken prior to introducing an intervention in a time-series design.
basic research Research that seeks to produce new knowledge or theory (compare to *applied research*).
behavior question See **experience question.**
bias Occurs when the design of a study systematically favors certain outcomes.
biographical study A form of qualitative research in which the researcher works with the individual to clarify important life experiences.
boxplot A graphic summary of statistical data based on the minimum, first quartile, median, third quartile, and maximum.

case study A form of qualitative research in which a single individual or example is studied through extensive data collection.
categorical variable Data (variable) that differ only in kind, not in amount or degree.
causal-comparative research Research to explore the cause for, or consequences of, existing differences in groups of individuals; also referred to as *ex post facto research.*
census An attempt to acquire data from every member of a population.
chaos theory A theory and methodology of science that emphasizes the rarity of general laws, the need for very large data bases, and the importance of studying exceptions to overall patterns.
chi-square test A nonparametric test of statistical significance appropriate when the data are in the form of frequency counts; it compares frequencies actually observed in a study with expected frequencies to see whether they are significantly different.
closed-ended question A question and a list of alternative responses from which the respondent selects; also referred to as a *closed-form item.*
cluster sampling/cluster random sampling The selection of groups of individuals, called *clusters,* rather than single individuals. All individuals in a cluster are included in the sample; the clusters are preferably selected randomly from the larger population of clusters.
coding In qualitative research, the process of assigning meaning to chunks or segments of data.

coding scheme A set of categories an observer uses to record the frequency of behaviors.

coefficient of determination The square of the correlation coefficient. It indicates the proportion of variance common to two variables.

coefficient of multiple correlation A numerical index describing the relationship between predicted and actual scores using multiple regression. The correlation between a criterion and the "best combination" of predictors.

cohort study A design (in survey research) in which a particular population is studied over time by taking different random samples at various points in time. The population remains conceptually the same, but individuals change (e.g., graduates of San Francisco State University surveyed 10, 20, and 30 years after graduation).

comparison group The group in a research study that receives a different treatment from that of the experimental group.

concurrent validity The degree to which the scores on an instrument are related to the scores on another instrument administered at the same time, or to some other criterion available at the same time.

confidence interval An interval used to estimate a parameter that is constructed in such a way that the interval has a predetermined probability of including the parameter.

confirming sample In qualitative research, a sample selected to validate or extend previous findings.

constant A characteristic that has the same value for all individuals.

constitutive definition The explanation of the meaning of a term by using other words to describe what is meant.

construct-related validity The degree to which an instrument measures an intended hypothetical psychological construct, or nonobservable trait.

content analysis A method of studying human behavior indirectly by analyzing communications, usually through a process of categorization.

content-related validity The degree to which an instrument logically appears to measure an intended variable; it is determined by expert judgment.

contextualization Placing information/data into a larger perspective, especially in ethnography.

contingency coefficient An index of relationship derived from a crossbreak table.

contingency question A question whose answer depends on the answer to a prior question.

contingency table See **crossbreak table.**

control Efforts on the part of the researcher to remove the effects of any variable other than the independent variable that might affect performance on a dependent variable.

control group The group in a research study that is treated "as usual."

convenience sample/sampling A sample that is easily accessible.

correlational research Research that involves collecting data in order to determine the degree to which a relationship exists between two or more variables.

correlation coefficient A decimal number between .00 and ±1.00 that indicates the degree to which two quantitative variables are related.

counterbalanced design An experimental design in which all groups receive all treatments. Each group receives the treatments in a different order, and all groups are posttested after each treatment.

credibility In qualitative research encompasses instrument reliability and validity, as well as internal validity.

criterion A second measurement used to evaluate instrument validity.

criterion-referenced instrument An instrument that specifies a particular goal, or criterion, for students to achieve.

criterion-related validity The degree to which performance on an instrument is related to performance on other instruments intended to measure the same variable, or to other variables logically related to the variable being measured.

criterion variable The variable that is predicted in a prediction study; also any variable used to assess the criterion-related validity of an instrument.

critical researchers Researchers who raise philosophical and ethical questions about the way educational research is conducted.

critical sample In qualitative research, a sample considered to be enlightening because it is unusual.

Cronbach alpha An internal consistency or reliability coefficient for an instrument requiring only one test administration.

crossbreak table A table that shows all combinations of two or more categorical variables and portrays the relationship (if any) between the variables. Also known as a contingency table.

cross-sectional survey A survey in which data are collected at one point in time from a predetermined population or populations.

crystallization Occasions, especially in ethnography, when different kinds of data "fall into place" to make a coherent picture.

culture The sum of a social group's observable patterns of behavior and/or their customs, beliefs, and knowledge.

curvilinear relationship A relationship shown in a scatterplot in which the line that best fits the points is not straight.

data Any information obtained about a sample or a population.

data analysis The process of simplifying data to make it comprehensible.

data collector bias Unintentional bias on the part of data collectors that may create a threat to the internal validity of a study.

degrees of freedom (df) A number indicating how many instances out of a given number of instances are "free to vary"—that is, not predetermined.

demographic questions See **background questions.**

dependent variable A variable affected or expected to be affected by the independent variable; also called *criterion* or *outcome variable.*

derived score A score obtained from a raw score in order to aid in interpretation. Derived scores provide a quantitative measure of each student's performance relative to a comparison group.

descriptive field notes The researchers' attempt to record what they observe completely and objectively.

descriptive study Research to describe existing conditions without analyzing relationships among variables.

descriptive statistics Data analysis techniques that enable the researcher to meaningfully describe data with numerical indices or in graphic form.

descriptor Term used to locate sources during a computer search of the literature.

design See **research design.**
dichotomous question Question that permits only a yes or no answer.
directional hypothesis A relational hypothesis stated in such a manner that a direction, often indicated by "greater than" or "less than," is hypothesized for the results.
discriminant function analysis A statistical procedure for predicting group membership (a categorical variable) from two or more quantitative variables.
discussion (of a study) A review of the results including limitations of a study, placing the findings in a broader perspective.
distribution curve The real or theoretical frequency distribution of a set of scores.
document Any written or printed material.

ecological generalizability The degree to which results can be generalized to environments and conditions outside the research setting.
effect size (ES) An index used to indicate the magnitude of an obtained result or relationship.
emic perspective The view of reality of a cultural "insider," especially in ethnography.
empirical Based on observable evidence.
equivalent-forms method Two tests identical in every way except for the actual items included.
errors of measurement Inconsistency of individual scores on the same instrument.
eta (η) An index that indicates the degree of a curvilinear relationship.
ethnographic study/research The collection of data on many variables over an extended period of time in a naturalistic setting, usually using observation and interviews.
etic perspective The "outsider" or "objective" view of a culture's reality, especially in ethnography.
evaluation research A systematic attempt to assess the quality or effectiveness of an evaluation object.
expectancy table A chart comparing predictor categories with criterion categories in order to evaluate instrument validity.
experience question Question a researcher asks to find out what sorts of things an individual is doing or has done.
experiment A research study in which one or more independent variables is/are systematically varied by the researcher to determine the effects of this variation.
experimental group The group in a research study that receives the treatment (or method) of special interest in the study.
experimental research Research in which at least one independent variable is manipulated, other relevant variables are controlled, and the effect on one or more dependent variables is observed.
experimental variable The variable that is manipulated (systematically altered) in an intervention study by the researcher.
explanatory (mixed-methods) design A study in which quantitative data are collected first and further clarified with qualitative data.
exploratory (mixed-methods) design A study in which qualitative data are collected first and findings are tested with subsequent quantitative data.
external audit A review of the methods and interpretations of a qualitative study by an individual outside the study.
external criticism Evaluation of the genuineness of a document in historical research.
external validity The degree to which results are generalizable, or applicable, to groups and environments outside the research setting.
extraneous variable A variable that makes possible an alternative explanation of results; an uncontrolled variable.
extreme case example Study of an atypical group.

factor analysis A statistical method for reducing a set of variables to a smaller number of factors.
factorial design An experimental design that involves two or more independent variables (at least one of which is manipulated) in order to study the effects of the variables individually, and in interaction with each other, upon a dependent variable.
feelings question Question researchers ask to find out how people feel about things.
field diary A personal statement of a researcher's opinions about people and events he or she comes in contact with during research.
field jottings Quick notes taken by an ethnographer.
field log A running account of how an ethnographer plans to, and actually does, spend time in the field.
field notes The notes researchers take about what they observe and think about in the field.
findings See **results (of a study).**
five-number summary A means of describing a skewed frequency distribution giving the lowest, first quartile, median, third quartile, and highest score.
focus group interview An interview conducted with a group in which respondents hear the views of each other.
foreshadowed problem The problem or topic that serves, in a general way, as the focus for a qualitative inquiry.
formative evaluation An evaluation intended to improve the object being assessed.
frequency distribution A tabular method of showing all of the scores obtained by a group of individuals.
frequency polygon A graphic method of showing all of the scores obtained by a group of individuals.
Friedman two-way analysis of variance A nonparametric inferential statistic used to compare two or more groups that are not independent.

gain score The difference between the pretest and posttest scores of a measure.
generalizing/generalizability See **ecological generalizability; population generalizability.**
general reference tool Source that researchers use to identify more specific references (e.g., indexes, abstracts).
grade-equivalent score A score that indicates the grade level for which a particular performance (score) is typical.
grounded theory study A form of qualitative research that derives interpretations inductively from raw data with continual interplay between data and emerging interpretations.
grouped frequency distribution A frequency distribution in which scores are grouped into equal intervals.

Hawthorne effect A positive effect of an intervention resulting from the subjects' knowledge that they are involved in a study or their feeling that they are in some way receiving "special" attention.

histogram A graphic representation, consisting of rectangles, of the scores in a distribution; the height of each rectangle indicates the frequency of each score or group of scores.

historical research The systematic collection and objective evaluation of data related to past occurrences to examine causes, effects, or trends of those events that may help explain present events and anticipate future events.

history threat The possibility that results are due to an event that is not part of an intervention but that may affect performance on the dependent variable, thereby affecting internal validity.

holistic perspective The attempt to incorporate all aspects of a culture into an ethnographic interpretation.

homogeneous sample In qualitative research, a sample selected in which all members are similar with respect to one or more characteristics.

hypothesis A tentative, testable assertion regarding the occurrence of certain behaviors, phenomena, or events; a prediction of study outcomes.

implementation threat The possibility that results are due to variations in the implementation of the treatment in an intervention study, thereby affecting internal validity.

independent variable A variable that affects (or is presumed to affect) the dependent variable under study and is included in the research design so that its effect can be determined; sometimes called the *experimental* or *treatment variable.*

index A general reference that gives the author, title, and place of publication of a published work.

inferential statistics Data analysis techniques for determining how likely it is that results based on a sample or samples are similar to results that would have been obtained for the entire population.

informal interview Less-structured form of interview, usually conducted by qualitative researchers. It does not involve any specific type or sequence of questioning, but resembles more the give-and-take of a casual conversation.

informed consent Requiring subjects (or their guardians) to formally agree in writing that they willingly consent to serve as a participant in research.

institutional review board (IRB) A research review board required of all institutions receiving federal research funds.

instrument Any device for systematically collecting data, such as a test, a questionnaire, or an interview schedule.

instrumental case study Study that focuses on a particular individual or situation with little effort to generalize.

instrumentation Instruments and procedures used in collecting data in a study.

instrument decay Changes in instrumentation over time that may affect the internal validity of a study.

interaction An effect created by unique combinations of two or more independent variables; systematically evaluated in a factorial design.

interlibrary loan A service whereby a library user can borrow books or documents owned by another library.

internal-consistency method Procedure for estimating reliability of scores using only one administration of the instrument.

internal criticism Determining whether the contents of a document are accurate.

internal validity The degree to which observed differences on the dependent variable are directly related to the independent variable, not to some other (uncontrolled) variable.

interval scale A measurement scale that, in addition to ordering scores from high to low, also establishes a uniform unit in the scale so that any equal distance between two scores is of equal magnitude.

intervention study A general type of research in which variables are manipulated in order to study the effect on one or more dependent variables.

interview A form of data collection in which individuals or groups are questioned orally.

interview protocol A data-gathering instrument or tool used in an interview.

interview schedule A set of questions to be asked by an interviewer.

intrinsic case study A study that attempts to generalize beyond the particular case.

justification (of a study) A rationale statement in which a researcher indicates why the study is important to conduct; includes implications for theory and/or practice.

key actor See **key informant.**

key event Event that provides unusually valuable data in an ethnographic study.

key informant Individual identified as expert source of information, especially in qualitative research.

knowledge question Question interviewers ask to find out what factual information a respondent possesses about a particular topic.

Kruskal-Wallis one-way analysis of variance A nonparametric inferential statistic used to compare two or more independent groups for statistical significance of differences.

Kuder-Richardson approach Procedure for determining an estimate of the internal consistency reliability of a test or other instrument from a single administration of the test without splitting the test into halves.

latent content The underlying meaning of a communication.

level of significance The probability that a discrepancy between a sample statistic and a specified population parameter is due to sampling error, or chance. Commonly used significance levels in educational research are .05 and .01.

life history A portrayal of a person's entire life.

Likert scale A self-reporting instrument in which an individual responds to a series of statements by indicating the extent of agreement. Each choice is given a numerical value, and the total score is presumed to indicate the attitude or belief in question.

linear relationship A relationship in which an increase (or decrease) in one variable is associated with a corresponding increase (or decrease) in another variable.

literature review The systematic identification, location, and analysis of documents containing information related to a research problem.

location threat The possibility that results are due to characteristics of the setting or location in which a study is conducted, thereby producing a threat to internal validity.
longitudinal survey A study in which information is collected at different points in time to study changes over time (usually of considerable length, such as several months or years).

manifest content The obvious meaning of a communication.
manipulated variable See **experimental variable.**
Mann-Whitney *U* test A nonparametric inferential statistic used to determine whether two uncorrelated groups differ significantly.
matching design A technique for equating groups on one or more variables, resulting in each member of one group having a direct counterpart in another group.
maturation threat The possibility that results are due to changes that occur in subjects as a direct result of the passage of time and that may affect their performance on the dependent variable, thereby affecting internal validity.
maximal variation sample In qualitative research, a sample selected to represent diversity in one or more characteristics.
mean/arithmetic mean ($\overline{X}$) The sum of the scores in a distribution divided by the number of scores in the distribution; the most commonly used measure of central tendency.
measures of central tendency Indices representing the average or typical score attained by a group of subjects; the most commonly used in educational research are the *mean* and the *median.*
mechanical matching A process of pairing two persons whose scores on one or more variables are similar.
median That point in a distribution having 50 percent of the scores above it and 50 percent of the scores below it.
mediator variable A variable that attempts to explain the relationship between two other variables.
member checking Procedure that involves asking participants in a qualitative study to check the accuracy of the research report.
meta-analysis A statistical procedure for combining the results of several studies on the same topic.
mixed-methods (design) research A study combining quantitative and qualitative methods.
mode The score that occurs most frequently in a distribution of scores.
moderator variable A variable that may or may not be controlled but has an effect on the research situation.
mortality threat The possibility that results are due to the fact that subjects who are for whatever reason "lost" to a study may differ from those who remain so that their absence has an important effect on the results of the study.
multiple-baseline design A single-subject experimental design in which baseline data are collected on several behaviors for one subject, after which the treatment is applied sequentially over a period of time to each behavior one at a time until all behaviors are under treatment. Also used to collect data on different subjects with regard to a single behavior, or to assess a subject's behavior in different settings.
multiple (collective) case study A study of multiple cases at the same time.
multiple realities/perspectives The recognition and acceptance of multiple views of reality, especially in ethnography.
multiple regression A technique using a prediction equation with two or more variables in combination to predict a criterion ($y = a + b_1 X_1 + b_2 X_2 + b_3 X_3 \ldots$).
multivariate analysis of covariance (MANCOVA) An extension of analysis of covariance that incorporates two or more dependent variables in the same analysis.
multivariate analysis of variance (MANOVA) An extension of analysis of variance that incorporates two or more dependent variables in the same analysis.

narrative research Study of the life experiences of an individual as told to the researcher or found in documents and archival material.
naturalistic observation Observation in which the observer controls or manipulates nothing and tries not to affect the observed situation in any way.
negatively skewed A distribution in which there are more scores at the upper end than at the lower end.
nominal scale A measurement scale that classifies elements into two or more categories, the numbers indicating that the elements are different, but not according to order or magnitude.
nondirectional hypothesis A prediction that a relationship exists without specifying its exact nature.
nonequivalent control group design An experimental design involving at least two groups, both of which may be pretested; one group receives the experimental treatment, and both groups are posttested. Individuals are not randomly assigned to treatments.
nonparametric technique A test of statistical significance appropriate when the data represent an ordinal or nominal scale, or when assumptions required for parametric tests cannot be met.
nonparticipant observation Observation in which the observer is not directly involved in the situation to be observed.
nonrandom sample/sampling The selection of a sample in which every member of the population does not have an equal chance of being selected.
nonresponse Lack of response to some or all items on a survey.
normal curve A graphic illustration of a normal distribution. See **normal distribution.**
normal distribution A theoretical "bell-shaped" distribution having a wide application to both descriptive and inferential statistics. It is known or thought to portray many human characteristics in "typical" populations.
norm group The sample group used to develop norms for a norm-referenced instrument.
norm-referenced instrument An instrument that permits comparison of an individual score to the scores of a group of individuals on that same instrument.
null hypothesis A statement that any difference between obtained sample statistics and specified population parameters is due to sampling error, or chance.

objectivity A lack of bias or prejudice.
observational data Data obtained through direct observation.
observer bias The possibility that an observer does not observe objectively and accurately, thus producing invalid observations and a threat to the internal validity of a study.
observer effect The impact of an observer's presence on the behavior observed.

observer expectation The effect that an observer's prior information can have on observational data.

one-group pretest-posttest design A weak experimental design involving one group that is pretested, exposed to a treatment, then posttested.

one-shot case study design A weak experimental design involving one group that is exposed to a treatment and then posttested.

one-tailed test The use of only one tail of the sampling distribution of a statistic—used when a directional hypothesis is stated.

open-ended question A question giving the responder complete freedom of response.

operational definition Defining a term by stating the actions, processes, or operations used to measure or identify examples of it.

opinion question Question a researcher asks to find out what people think about a topic.

opportunistic sample In qualitative research, a sample chosen to take advantage of conditions that arise during a study.

oral history Personal reflections of events and their causes gathered from one or more individuals.

ordinal scale A measurement scale that ranks individuals in terms of the degree to which they possess a characteristic of interest.

outcome variable See **dependent variable.**

outlier Score or other observation that deviates or falls considerably outside most of the other scores or observations in a distribution or pattern.

panel study A longitudinal design (in survey research) in which the same random sample is measured at different points in time.

parameter A numerical index describing a characteristic of a population.

parametric technique A test of significance appropriate when the data represent an interval or ratio scale of measurement and other specific assumptions have been met.

partial correlation A method of controlling the subject characteristics threat in correlational research by statistically holding one or more variables constant.

participant observation Observation in which the observer actually becomes a participant in the situation to be observed.

participant Individual whose involvement in a study can range from providing data to initiating and designing the study.

participatory action research Action research intended not only to address a local problem but also to empower individuals and to bring about social change.

path analysis A type of sophisticated analysis investigating causal connections among correlated variables.

Pearson product-moment coefficient (Pearson *r*) An index of correlation appropriate when the data represent either interval or ratio scales; it takes into account each pair of scores and produces a coefficient between 0.00 and either ± 1.00.

percentile The score below which a given percent of a known group scores, for example, the 60th percentile is a score of 120.

percentile rank An index of relative position indicating the percentage of scores that fall at or below a given score.

performance instrument An instrument designed to measure ability to follow procedures or produce a product.

phenomenological study A form of qualitative research in which the researcher attempts to identify commonalities in the perceptions of several individuals regarding a particular phenomenon.

pie chart A graphic method of displaying the breakdown of data into categories.

pilot study A small-scale study administered before conducting an actual study—its purpose is to reveal defects in the research plan.

plagiarism Misrepresenting another's work as one's own.

population The group to which the researcher would like the results of a study to be generalizable; it includes all individuals with certain specified characteristics.

population generalizability The extent to which the results obtained from a sample are generalizable to a larger group.

portraiture A form of qualitative research in which the researcher and the individual being portrayed work together to define meaning.

positively skewed A distribution in which there are more scores at the lower end than at the higher end.

positivism A philosophic viewpoint emphasizing an "objective" reality that includes universal laws governing all things including human behavior.

postmodernism/postmodernist An intensive criticism of scientific research.

power of a statistical test The probability that the null hypothesis will be rejected when there is a difference in the populations; the ability of a test to avoid a Type II error.

practical action research Action research intended to address a specific local problem.

practical significance A difference large enough to have some practical effect. Contrast with *statistical significance,* which may be so small as to have no practical consequences.

pragmatist A methodologist who proposes using whatever research methods work or will shed light on a problem. Pragmatists believe that quantitative and qualitative methods can be "mixed" in a research endeavor and might be more informative than using only a single method.

prediction The estimation of scores on one variable from information about one or more other variables.

prediction equation A mathematical equation used in a prediction study.

prediction study An attempt to determine variables that are related to a criterion variable.

predictive validity The degree to which scores on an instrument predict characteristics of individuals in a future situation.

predictor variable(s) The variable(s) from which projections are made in a prediction study.

pretest treatment interaction The possibility that subjects may respond or react differently to a treatment because they have been pretested, thereby creating a threat to internal validity.

primary source Firsthand information, such as the testimony of an eyewitness, an original document, a relic, or a description of a study written by the person who conducted it.

probability The relative frequency with which a particular event occurs among all events of interest.

problem statement A statement that indicates the specific purpose of the research, the variables of interest to the researcher, and any specific relationship between those variables that is to be, or was, investigated; includes description of background and rationale (justification) for the study.

procedures A detailed description by the researcher of what was (or will be) done in carrying out a study.

projective device An instrument that includes vague stimuli that subjects are asked to interpret. There are no correct answers or replies.

proposition A tentative, flexible hypothesis used by qualitative researchers to guide their data collection and analysis.

purpose (of a study) A specific statement by a researcher of what he or she intends to accomplish.

purposive sample/sampling A nonrandom sample selected because prior knowledge suggests it is representative, or because those selected have the needed information.

qualitative research Research in which the investigator attempts to study naturally occurring phenomena in all their complexity.

qualitizing The process of converting quantitative data into qualitative data.

quantitative data Data that differ in amount or degree along a continuum from less to more.

quantitative research Research in which the investigator attempts to clarify phenomena through carefully designed and controlled data collection and analysis.

quantitative variable A variable that is conceptualized and analyzed along a continuum. It differs in amount or degree.

quantitizing The process of converting qualitative data into quantitative data.

quasi-experimental design A type of experimental design in which the researcher does not use random assignment of subjects to groups.

questionnaire A form for written or marked answers to questions.

random assignment The process of assigning individuals or groups randomly to different treatment conditions.

randomized posttest-only control group design An experimental design with subjects randomly assigned to treatment and control groups.

randomized pretest-posttest control group design A randomized posttest-only control group design with pretest added.

random sample/sampling A sample selected in such a way that every member of the population has an equal chance of being selected.

random selection The process of selecting a random sample.

randomized Solomon four-group design An experimental design that involves random assignment of subjects to each of four groups. Two groups are pretested, two are not, one of the pretested groups and one of the unpretested groups receive the experimental treatment, and all four groups are posttested.

range The difference between the highest and lowest scores in a distribution; measure of variability.

ratio scale A measurement scale that, in addition to being an interval scale, also has an absolute zero in the scale.

raw score The score attained by an individual on the items on a test or other instrument.

reflective field notes A record of the observer's thoughts and reflections during and after observation.

regressed gain score A score indicating amount of change that is determined by the correlation between scores on a posttest and a pretest (and/or other scores). It provides more stable information than a simple posttest-pretest difference.

regression line The line of best fit for a set of scores plotted on coordinate axes (on a scatterplot).

regression threat The possibility that results are due to a tendency for groups, selected on the basis of extreme scores, to regress toward a more average score on subsequent measurements, regardless of the experimental treatment.

reliability The degree to which scores obtained with an instrument are consistent measures of whatever the instrument measures.

reliability coefficient An index of the consistency of scores on the same instrument. There are several methods of computing a reliability coefficient, depending on the type of consistency and characteristics of the instrument.

relic Any object whose physical characteristics provide information about the past.

replication Refers to conducting a study again; the second study may be a repetition of the original study, using different subjects, or specified aspects of the study may be changed.

representativeness The extent to which a sample is identical (in all characteristics) to the intended population.

research The formal, systematic application of scholarship, disciplined inquiry, and most often the scientific method to the study of problems.

research design The overall plan for collecting data to answer the research question. Also the specific data analysis techniques or methods that the researcher intends to use.

research hypothesis A prediction of study outcomes. Often a statement of the expected relationship between two or more variables.

research proposal A detailed description of a proposed study designed to investigate a given problem.

research report A description of how a study was conducted, including results and conclusions.

researcher reflexivity Recording personal thoughts while conducting observations or interviews for later cross-checking.

results (of a study) A statement that explains what is shown by analysis of the data collected; includes tables and graphs when appropriate.

retrospective interview A form of interview in which the researcher tries to get a respondent to reconstruct past experiences.

sample The group on which information is obtained.

sampling The process of selecting a number of individuals (a sample) from a population, preferably in such a way that the individuals are representative of the larger group from which they were selected.

sampling distribution The theoretical distribution of all possible values of a statistic from all possible samples of a given size selected from a population.

sampling error Expected, chance variation in sample statistics that occurs when successive samples are selected from a population.

sampling interval The distance in a list between individuals chosen when sampling systematically.

sampling ratio The proportion of individuals in the population who are selected for the sample in systematic sampling.

scatterplot The plot of points determined by the cross-tabulation of scores on coordinate axes; used to represent and illustrate the relationship between two quantitative variables.

scientific method A way of knowing that is characterized by the public nature of its procedures and conclusions and by rigorous testing of conclusions.

scoring agreement The percentage agreement among different scorers or observers.

search engine A comprehensive computer system for locating references to specific topics.

search term See **descriptor.**

secondary source Secondhand information, such as a description of historical events by someone not present when the event occurred.

semantic differential An attitude scale using pairs of opposites such as hot-cold.

semistructured interview A structured interview, combined with open-ended questions.

sensory question Question asked by a researcher to find out what a person has seen, heard, or experienced through his or her senses.

sign test A nonparametric inferential statistic used to compare two groups that are not independent.

simple random sample See **random sample/sampling.**

simulation Research in which an "artificial" situation is created and participants are told what activities they are to engage in.

single-subject design/research Design applied when the sample size is one; used to study the behavior change that an individual exhibits as a result of some intervention or treatment.

snowball sample A nonrandom sampling technique used to recruit future study participants through referrals from current participants.

split-half procedure A method of estimating the internal-consistency reliability of an instrument; it is obtained by giving an instrument once but scoring it twice—for each of two equivalent "half tests." These scores are then correlated.

stakeholder A person who has a vested interest in the outcomes of a study.

standard deviation The most stable measure of variability; it takes into account each score in a distribution.

standard error of the difference (SED) The standard deviation of a distribution of differences between sample means.

standard error of estimate An estimate of the size of the error to be expected in predicting a criterion score.

standard error of the mean (SEM) The standard deviation of sample means that indicates by how much the sample means can be expected to differ if other samples from the same population are used.

standard error of measurement (SEMeas) An estimate of the size of the error that one can expect in an individual's score.

standard score See ***z* score.**

static-group comparison design A weak experimental design that involves at least two nonequivalent groups; one receives a treatment and both are posttested.

static-group pretest-posttest design The same as the static-group comparison design, except that both groups are pretested.

statistic A numerical index describing a characteristic of a sample.

statistical equating See **statistical matching.**

statistical generalization Generalizing from a sample to a population, usually using statistical methods.

statistical matching A means of equating groups using statistical prediction.

statistical significance The conclusion that results are unlikely to have occurred due to sampling error or "chance"; an observed correlation or difference probably exists in the population.

stem-leaf plot A method for showing individual scores in a grouped frequency distribution.

stratified sampling/stratified random sampling The process of selecting a sample in such a way that identified subgroups in the population are represented in the sample in the same proportion as they exist in the population.

structured interview A formal type of interview, in which the researcher asks, in order, a set of predetermined questions.

subject characteristics threat The possibility that characteristics of the subjects in a study may account for observed relationships, thereby producing a threat to internal validity.

subjects Individuals whose participation in a study is limited to providing information.

summative evaluation An evaluation that seeks to determine the overall effectiveness or usefulness of an evaluation object.

survey research An attempt to obtain data from members of a population (or a sample) to determine the current status of that population with respect to one or more variables.

systematic sampling A selection procedure in which all sample elements are determined after the selection of the first element, since each element on a selected list is separated from the first element by a multiple of the selection interval; for example, every tenth element may be selected.

table of random numbers A table of numbers that provides the best means of random selection or random assignment.

tally sheet A form for recording observed instances of behavior.

target population The population to which the researcher, ideally, would like to generalize results.

testing threat A threat to internal validity that refers to improved scores on a posttest that are a result of subjects having taken a pretest.

test-retest method A procedure for determining the extent to which scores from an instrument are reliable over time by correlating the scores from two administrations of the same instrument to the same individuals.

theme A means of organizing and interpreting data in a content analysis by grouping codes as the interpretation progresses.

theoretical framework The theoretical approach used to structure a research study.

theoretical generalization Generalizing from a sample by practitioners based on judged applicability.

theoretical sample In qualitative research, a sample that helps the researcher understand or formulate a concept or interpretation.

thick description In ethnography, the provision of great detail on the basic data/information.

threat to internal validity An alternative explanation for research results, that is, that an observed relationship is an artifact of another variable.

time-series design An experimental design involving one group that is repeatedly pretested, exposed to an experimental treatment, and repeatedly posttested.

transferability In qualitative research, the degree to which an individual can expect the results of a particular study to apply in a new situation or with new people. Transferability, in the qualitative domain, is similar to generalizability in the quantitative domain.

treatment variable See **experimental variable.**

trend study A longitudinal design (in survey research) in which the same population (conceptually but not literally) is studied over time by taking different random samples.

triangulation Cross-checking of data using multiple data sources or multiple data-collection procedures.

triangulation (mixed-methods) design A study in which quantitative and qualitative data are collected simultaneously and used to validate and clarify findings.

***T* score** A standard score derived from a *z* score by multiplying the *z* score by 10 and adding 50.

***t*-test for correlated means** A parametric test of statistical significance used to determine whether there is a statistically significant difference between the means of two matched, or nonindependent, samples. It is also used for pre-post comparisons.

***t*-test for correlated proportions** A parametric test of statistical significance used to determine whether there is a statistically significant difference between two proportions based on the same sample or otherwise nonindependent groups.

***t*-test for independent means** A parametric test of significance used to determine whether there is a statistically significant difference between the means of two independent samples.

***t*-test for independent proportions** A parametric test of statistical significance used to determine whether there is a statistically significant difference between two independent proportions.

t*-test for *r This test is used to see whether a correlation coefficient calculated on sample data is statistically significant.

two-stage random sampling A combination of individual random sampling and cluster random sampling.

two-tailed test Use of both tails of a sampling distribution of a statistic—when a nondirectional hypothesis is stated.

Type I error The rejection by the researcher of a null hypothesis that is actually true; also called an *alpha error.*

Type II error The failure of a researcher to reject a null hypothesis that is really false; also called a *beta error.*

typical sample In qualitative research, a sample judged to be representative of the population of interest.

unit of analysis The unit that is used in data analysis (individuals, objects, groups, classrooms, etc.).

unobtrusive measures Measures obtained without subjects being aware that they are being observed or measured, or by examining inanimate objects (such as school suspension lists) in order to obtain desired information.

validity The degree to which correct inferences can be made based on results from an instrument; depends not only on the instrument itself but also on the instrumentation process and the characteristics of the group studied.

validity coefficient An index of the validity of scores; a special application of the correlation coefficient.

values question See **opinion question.**

variability The extent to which scores differ from one another.

variable A characteristic that can assume any one of several values, for example, cognitive ability, height, aptitude, teaching method.

variance The square of the standard deviation; a measure of variability.

Web browser A computer program providing access to the World Wide Web.

Wilk's lambda The numerical index calculated when carrying out MANOVA or MANCOVA.

World Wide Web (WWW) An Internet reservoir of information used in searching literature.

written-response instrument An instrument requiring written or marked responses.

***z* score** The most basic standard score that expresses how far a score is from a mean in terms of standard deviation units.

CREDITS

p. 9, Photos 1.1, 1.2: Heinz-Otto Peitgen and Peter H. Richter (1986) *The beauty of fractals*. Berlin: Springer-Verlag.

p. 30, un. fig.: The New Yorker Cartoon: It all depends on how you define "chop"; © Tom Cheney/The New Yorker Collection/ www.cartoonbank.com

pp. 42, 43, 45 & 47, Figs. 3.1, 3.2, 3.4 & 3.6: © 2013 EBSCO Information Services. All rights reserved.

p. 44, Fig. 3.3: Image published with permission of ProQuest LLC. Further reproduction is prohibited without permission.

p. 52, Fig. 3.8: Fredricks, J.A., Blumenfeld, P.C., & Paris, A.M. (2004). School engagement: Potential of the concept, state of the evidence. Review of Educational Research, 74(1), 59–109. Reprinted by Permission of SAGE Publications.

pp. 116, 117, & 118, Figs. 7.1, 7.2 & 7.3: From ERIC (Educator Resources Information Center). Reprinted by permission of the US Department of Education, operated by Computer Sciences Corporation. www.eric.ed.gov

p. 120, Fig. 7.6: Handwriting scale used in the California Achievement Tests Form W (1957), CTB/McGraw-Hill, Monterey, CA © 1957 by McGraw-Hill.

p. 124, Fig. 7.11: Adapted from Enoch I. Sawin. Evaluation and the work of the teacher. Belmont, Cal.: Wadsworth, 1969, p. 179. Reprinted by Permission of SAGE Publications.

p. 125, Fig. 7.12: Copyright 1930 from Educational Research Bulletin (1922–61) by R.W. Tyler. Reproduced by permission of Taylor & Francis Group, LLC. (http://www.tandfonline.com)

p. 126, Fig. 7.13: Republished with permission from ASCD, from "Problem Identification" (pp. 60–61), by Hilda Taba, from *Research for Curriculum Improvement—ASCD 1957 Yearbook*, Alexandria, VA: ASCD, © 1957 by ASCD; permission conveyed through Copyright Clearance Center, Inc.

p. 132, Fig. 7.22: Example from the Blum Sewing Machine Test, M. Blum (1943) Selection of sewing machine operators. *Journal of Applied Psychology*, Vol. 27 (1) p. 35–40.

p. 133, Fig. 7.23: N.T. Rowan (1967). The relationship of teacher interaction in classroom situations to teacher personality variables. Unpublished doctoral dissertation. Salt Lake City: University of Utah, p. 68.

p. 153, un. fig.: The New Yorker Cartoon: He looks very promising—but let's see how he does on the written test." © Sidney Harris/The New Yorker Collection/www.cartoonbank.com

p. 248, un. fig.: The New Yorker cartoon: That's the gist of what I want to say . . . © Joseph Mirachi/The New Yorker Collection/ www.cartoonbank.com

p. 286, Research Report: Cognitive Effects of Chess Instruction on Students at Risk for Academic Failure by the Center for Human Development and Research. From the *International Journal of Special Education*, Vol. 22, 1986. pp. 89–96.

p. 315, Research Report: Implementation of the Guided Teaching Approach with Elementary School Deaf Students by Schirmer & Schaffer from American Annals of the Deaf, 155(3), pp. 377–385 (2010). Reproduced with permission from Gallaudet University Press.

p. 348, Research Report: Physical Education in Urban High School Class Settings by Zeng, Wenhao & Hirscher from The Physical Educator by Matthews, David O.; Phi Epsilon Kappa, Copyright 2009. Reproduced with permission of Phi Epsilon Kappa Fraternity in the format Republish in a textbook via Copyright Clearance Center.

p. 374, Research Report: Journal of American College Health, Vol. 56, No. 2, pp. 137–144. Reprinted by permission of the publisher (Taylor & Francis Ltd, http://www.tandf.co.uk/journals) via Copyright Clearance Center.

p. 401, un. fig.: The New Yorker Cartoon: Next questions: I believe that life is a constant striving for balance; © George Price/The New Yorker Collection/www.cartoonbank.com

p. 408, Research Report: Teaching Social Studies in the 21st Century by Wm. B. Russell; Vol. 32(1) pp. 65–72; from Action in Teacher Education by the Association of Teacher Educators. Reprinted by permission of Taylor & Francis Ltd. via Copyright Clearance Center http;/www.tandfco.uk/journals.

pp. 426, 450, Table 18.2 & Table 19.1: Qualitative evaluation and research methods by PATTON, MICHAEL Q. Reproduced with permission of SAGE PUBLICATIONS, INCORPORATED in the format Republish in a book via Copyright Clearance Center.

p. 448, Fig. 19.3: The Amidon/Flanders Scheme for Coding Categories of Interaction in the Classroom, Amidon & Hough (1967) Interaction Analysis: Theory, research and application. Addison-Wesley.

p. 449, un. fig.: The New Yorker Cartoon: How Do I Feel? © Edward Koren/The New Yorker Collection/www.cartoonbank.com

p. 458, Research Report: Walk and Talk: An Intervention for Behaviorally Challenged Youths by Doucette from Adolescence 2004, Vol. 39, No. 154, pp. 373–388.

p. 488, Research Report: From: *Education*, Vol. 125, No. 1, Fall 2004. Reproduced by permission of Project Innovation, Inc.

p. 519, Research Report: Ethnographic Research by Ellen M. Curtin. Lessons on effective teaching from middle school ESL students (2006.) Middle School Journal, January, 2006, pp. 38–45. Reprinted with permission from National Middle School Association.

p. 542, Research Report: From: *Journal of Psychohistory*, 28, no. 1 (Summer 2000): 62–71.

pp. 558–559, Figs. 23.1, 23.2 & 23.3: Designing and conducting mixed methods research by CRESWELL, PLANO-CLARK. Reproduced with permission of SAGE PUBLICATIONS INC in the format Republish in a book via Copyright Clearance Center.

p. 564, Research Report: Copyright © 2006 by the American Psychological Association. Reproduced with permission. No further reproduction or distribution is permitted without written permission from the American Psychological Association. Perceived Family Support, Acculturation, and Life Satisfaction in Mexican American Young: A Mixed-Methods Exploration by Edwards & Lopez in *Journal of Counseling Psychology* 2006, V 53, N 3, pp. 279–287.

p. 601, Research Report: Journal of social studies research by UNIVERSITY OF GEORGIA Copyright 1977, Kosky & Curtis pp. 22–27. Reproduced with permission of ELSEVIER SCIENCE & TECHNOLOGY JOURNALS in the format Textbook via Copyright Clearance Center.

INDEX

Note: Boldface page numbers indicate terms in the text; italicized f indicates a figure, italicized n indicates a footnote, and italicized t indicates a table.

A-B design, **304***f*, 305
A-B-A design, **305***f*
A-B-A-B design, **305,** 306*f*
A-B-A-C-A design, 314
A-B-C-B design, **307,** 308*f*
A-B-C-B-C design, 314
ability, measuring with interviews, 404
ability test. *See* achievement tests
abscissa, 303
abstracts, **38,** 39
  from ERIC database, 118*f*
  of research reports, **623**
academic cheating, 72
Academic Search Premier, 56
accessible population, **93**–94
achievement tests, **128**–29, 130*f*
action plan, 593
action research, **14,** 585, 586–611
  advantages of, 594–95
  assumptions underlying, 588*t*
  considerations when doing school research, 598
  defined, **587**
  examples of, 595–609
  participant involvement in, 591
  similarities and differences between qualitative and quantitative research, and, 593–94
  steps in, 591–93
  types of, 588–91
adjusted disruptive behavior score, 342
administration of data-collection instruments, 114, 117–36
advocacy lenses, **560**
AERA. *See* American Educational Research Association (AERA)
age-equivalent scores, **189**
agreement with others as way of knowing, 4
alpha coefficient, 158–**59**
alternate forms. *See* equivalent-forms method
alternating-treatments design, 314
A Manual for Writers of Term Papers, Theses, and Dissertations (Turabian), 53
American Educational Research Association (AERA), 40, 149*n*
American Psychological Association (APA), 39, 41, 149*n*
  ethics committee, 61–62
  style guide, 53, 622, 623*t*
American Psychological Association Task Force on Statistical Inference, 249
Amidon/Flanders Scheme for coding data, 447, 448*f*
"An Action Research Exploration Integrating Student Choice and Arts Activities in a Sixth Grade Social Studies Classroom" (Kosky, Curtis), 601–7
  analysis of, 608–9
analysis of covariance (ANCOVA), **236,** 239*t*
  in causal-comparative research, 371
  in experimental research, 268
analysis of variance (ANOVA), **236,** 239*t*. *See also* variance
ANCOVA. *See* analysis of covariance (ANCOVA)
anecdotal records, 114, 124–26
annotated bibliography, 42
annotated table, 52*f*
ANOVA. *See* analysis of variance (ANOVA)
APA. *See* American Psychological Association (APA)
APA PsycNET, 41
applied behavior analysis, 303
applied research, defined, **7**
aptitude tests, **129**–30, 131*f*
arithmetic mean, 196*n*
assessments acquired from ERIC, 115, 116*f*, 117*f*
associational research, **16**
  causal-comparative and, 364–66
  correlational and, 332–33
assumption(s), **17**
  in action research, 588*t*
  critical analysis and unstated, 17, 18*f*, 19
  mixed-methods research and, 557
  in parametric *vs.* nonparametric techniques, 233
  in qualitative *vs.* quantitative research, 425–26, 427*t*
  in research proposals and reports, 616
attitude as threat. *See* subject attitude threat
attitude scales, 127, 128*f*, 129*f*, 130*f*
autobiography, **430**
averages, **195**–97*f*
  mean, 196*t*, 197*t*
  median, 196*t*
  mode, 195, 196*t*

B-A-B design, **306,** 307*f*
background (demographics) questions, **451**
bar graphs, **211***f*
  constructing, with Excel, 192
baseline (single-subject designs), 303, **304**
  designs with multiple, 307, 308*f*, 309*f*, 310*f*
  number of, 313
  return to levels, 312, 313*f*
  variations in stability of, 311*f*
baseline period, 304
basic research, defined, **7**
B-C-B design, 314
behavior(s), independence of, in single-subject designs, 312
behavior modification, 303
behavior (experience) questions, **451**
behavior rating scales, 119*f*, 120*n*
bias, **85**
  in convenience sampling, 100–101
  data collector, 171–72 (*see also* data collector bias)
  hypotheses and, 85
  implementation and, 177–78
  observer, 446–47*f*
  selection, 168
  in survey interviews, 400, 404
  in systematic sampling, 100
bibliography
  annotated, 42
  in research reports, 625
bimodal distribution, 196
biographical study, **430**
  portraiture as, 431
biography, 13
Blum Sewing Machine Test, 132*f*
Books in Print, 40
Boolean operators, **46***f*
boundaries (confidence intervals), 224, 225
box-and-whiskers diagrams, 198*n*
boxplots, **198***f*
Boyle's law, 213
Buckley Amendment, 70
budget in research proposals and reports, 622
Buros Institute, 116
Buros Test Review Locator, 117

California Achievement Test, 128
California Department of Education, 55–56
California Test of Mental Maturity (CTMM), 131
case, 432
case study, 13–14, 187, **432**–33
  instrumental, 433
  interviews, 432–33
  intrinsic, 433
  multiple (collective), 433
  observations, 432–33
  questions in, 28
categorical data, **188**–89
  in causal-comparative research, 365, 366, 372, 373
  coding of, 141–42
  comparing groups using, 255–57
  in content analysis, 478, 480–83, 484*t*, 485*t*
  interpreting, 256–57
  quantitative *vs.,* 78, 79, 80–81, 138
  relating variables within groups using, 257, 258*t*
  tabulating of, 141–42
  techniques for summarizing (*see* categorical data techniques)
categorical data techniques, 209–14
  bar graphs and pie charts, 211*f*, 212*f*
  chi-square test, 238, 516
  commonly used, 257, 258*t*
  for comparing groups, 255–56
  contingency coefficient, 214, 238*t*
  crossbreak table, 211–14, 255–27
  frequency table, 209–11
  parametric and nonparametric techniques for analyzing, 237–38, 239*t*
categorical variable(s), **78.** *See also* variable(s)
  in causal-comparative research, 373–74
  quantitative variables *vs.*, 78, 79*f*, 80–81, 138, 337
categorization in content analysis, 478, 480–83, 484*t*, 485*t*
causal-comparative research, **12,** 363–89
  categorical variables, associations between, 373–74
  correlational research and, 365–66
  data analysis in, 371–73
  defined, and types of, 364–66
  design, 368*f*
  ethics and, 364
  example of, 374–85
  experimental research and, 366
  instrumentation, 368
  limitations of, 365
  practical action research using, 598–600
  predictions in, 373–74
  problem formulation, 367
  questions in, 27
  sample, 103, 367–68
  significant findings in, 373
  steps in, 367–68
  threats to internal validity of, 365, 368–70
  threats to internal validity of, evaluation of, 370–71
causation
  causal-comparative research and, 364, 365, 366
  correlational research and, 333–34, 339
cause-and-effect relationships, 265
census, 103, **392**
change, degree and speed of, in single-subject designs, 311, 312*f*
chaos theory, **8,** 9*f*
character inventories, 128, 130*f*
charts. *See* pie charts
cheating, academic, 72
checklists, self, 127*f*
children
  ethical research with, 67–68
  semantic differential scales used with, 128, 129*f*
chi-square distribution, A4
chi-square test, **238,** 516
CIJE. See Current Index to Journals in Education (CIJE)
circle diagrams, 344*f*, 347*f*
citation documentation, 48
CITI. *See* Collaborative Institutional Training Initiative (CITI)
clarification by example, **31**

clarity
postmodernism and, 428
of research questions, 28, 29–33
of studies, 484*t*
clinical trials, ethical controversies surrounding, 63
closed-ended questions, **398**–99
improving, 400
in interviews, 398–99, 400
in surveys, 398–401, 402*f*
cluster random sampling, 96, **97,** 98*f,* 99*f,* 102
cluster sampling, **480**
coding, **434**
in content analysis, 478, 480–83
of data, for analysis, 141–42, 434, 447–48
of interviews, 482*f*
of observational data, 447, 448*f*
selective *vs.* open, 434
coding scheme, **447**
coefficient of determination (r^2), 336–37
coefficient of multiple correlation (*R*), **336*f***
"Cognitive Effects of Chess Instruction on Students at Risk for Academic Failure" (Hong, Bar), 286–94
analysis of, 294–95
cohort study, **392**
Collaborative Institutional Training Initiative (CITI), 69
collaborative research, 589
collective (multiple) case study, **433**
Committee on Scientific and Professional Ethics, American Psychological Association, 61–62
communication(s)
content analysis of, 476–77
critical analysis and question of, 17, 19
privileged, 72
comparison(s)
commonly used techniques for group, 247–51, 255–57
derived scores and, 189–90
effect size and, 248
of groups, in experimental research, 266
of groups, using categorical data, 255–57
of groups, using quantitative data, 247–51
inferential statistics and, 248–51
of samples, 226–27
comparison group(s), **266**
ethical research and, 67
handling internal validity threats in, 281, 282*f*
practical action research using, 595–96
Comprehensive Tests of Basic Skills, 128
computerized literature search, 39, 43, 44–51. *See also* Web (World Wide Web)
problem definition for, 44–45
sample ERIC search, 44–48
computer technology. *See also* Microsoft Excel
chaos theory and, 8
for content analysis, 486–87
for qualitative research, 486
for telephone surveys, 395*n*
Comte, Auguste, 425
conclusions, logic and, 5
concurrent validity, **153**–54
condition(s) of data collection, 113, 304
condition length, as threat to internal validity of single-subject research, 309–10, 311*f*
condition lines, 304
confidence intervals, **224**–25*f,* 226*f,* 227*f*
probability and, 226
confidentiality of research data, 64, 66, 67, 626
confirming sample, **434**
connections, 78. *See also* relationships
consent form, 64*f,* 68*f,* 456. *See also* informed consent
consequential validity, concept usefulness, 161
constant(s), **78**
constant comparative method, 432
constitutive definitions, **30**
construct-related evidence of validity, 149, 150*f,* **154**–55
content, manifest *vs.* latent, 481–83
content analysis, 475–502
advantages of, 487
applications of, 477–78
categorization in, 478, 480–83, 484*t*, 485*t*
computer software used in, 486–87
defined, **476**–77
disadvantages of, 487–88
example of, 488–500
illustration of, 484–86
important findings in, 479
practical action research using, 597
steps in, 478–83
content-related evidence of validity, 149, 150*f,* **151**–53, 159*t*
context, qualitative research and, 425
contextualization in ethnographic research, **507**–8
contingency coefficient, **238**
crossbreak tables and, 214, 238*t*, 256, 257
contingency questions, **401,** 402*f*
contingency table, **211,** 393. *See also* crossbreak table
control, **268**
in group experimental research, 268
of threats to internal validity in single-subject research, 314
control group, **266**
convenience sampling, **100*f*,** 101, 102*f,* 103, 619
bias in, 100–101
in mixed-methods research, 560
correlation(s), 204–9
computing with Excel, 205
correlation coefficients, scatterplots, and, 207–8, 209*f,* 341, 342
eta and, 208, 210*f*
in everyday life, 213
inferential statistics and, 228
partial, 342, 344*f*
Pearson product-moment coefficient and, 208
positive *vs.* negative, 208, 210*f*
quantitative *vs.* categorical data and, 337*f*
scatterplots and, 205, 206*f,* 207–8, 209*f,* 333*f,* 342, 343*f,* 347*f*
correlated means, *t*-test for, 236
correlational research, 12, 331–62
basic steps in, 339–41
correlation coefficients and, 332, 341
data analysis and interpretation, 341
data collection, 340–41, 344
design and procedures, 340*t*
example of, 347–60
important findings in, 334
instruments, 340, 344–45
nature of, 332–33
practical action research using, 597–98
problem selection in, 339
purposes of, 333–39
questions in, 27
research reports of, 623
samples for, 103, 339
survey research and, 393
threats to external validity in, 345
threats to internal validity in, 341–45
threats to internal validity in, evaluation of, 345
correlation coefficient, 49, **153, 207, 251,** 332, **341**
correlational research and, 341
hypothesis testing and, 228
inferential statistics and, 228
in relating variables, 208*n*, 251–55
scatterplots and, 207–8
in survey research, 393
validity and, 153
correlation matrix for variables, 338*f*
counterbalanced designs, **275,** 276*f*
covariate, 236
cover letter for mail survey, 401–2, 403*f*
credibility, **456**
criterion, **153**
predictor *vs.*, 334
criterion-referenced instruments, **137**–38
criterion-related evidence of validity, 149, 150*f,* **153**–54, 159*t*
predictive, and concurrent, 153
criterion variable, **265, 334, 337**
critical analysis of historical sources, 537–39
critical colleague
in ethnographic research, 508
self-study, 589
critical researchers, **17**
critical sample, **434**
Cronbach alpha, **159**
crossbreak table, **211**–14. *See also* contingency table
comparing groups using categorical data and, 255–57
contingency coefficient and, 214, 238*t*, 256, 257
expected frequencies and, 212, 213*t*
cross-sectional surveys, **392**
crystallization, **516**
CTMM. *See* California Test of Mental Maturity (CTMM)
culture, ethnographic research and concept of, **507**
Current Index to Journals in Education (CIJE), 39, 40
curvilinear relationship, 208, 210*f,* 251

data, **112**–14
categorical, 188–89 (*see also* categorical data)
collection of (*see* data collection)
contextualization of, 507–8
deciding who provides, 114
ensuring confidentiality of, 64, 66, 67
key questions about, 112–13
locating relevant, in content analysis, 479
numerical, types of, 187–89
observational, 446, 447–48
preparing, for analysis, 141–42
qualitative (*see* qualitative data)
quantitative, 188 (*see also* quantitative data)
data analysis, **21**
in action research, 592–93
in causal-comparative research, 371–73
in content analysis, 483, 484*t*
in correlational research, 341
in ethnographic research, 514–16
grounded theory and, 431–32
in historical research, 539
in mixed-methods research, 562
in qualitative research, 425, 429, 434, 456
research proposals/reports and, 621
scoring, 141
in survey research, 407
tabulating and coding, 141*t*, 142
databases, on-line, 39
searching, 43, 44–51, 53–56
data collection
for action research, 592
classifying instruments of, 114–17
in correlational research, 340–41, 344
in ethnographic research, 509, 510–14
examples of instruments for, 117–36
in experimental design, 279, 280*t*
grounded theory and, 431–32
instruments for (*see* instrument(s); instrumentation)
key questions in, 112–13
location of, 170
location threat to validity of, 170
in mixed-methods research, 555, 562
in qualitative research, 429, 443, 448, 456, 457*t* (*see also* content analysis; interview(s); observation)
research proposals/reports and, 620
in survey research, 394*t*–97
data collector bias, 171, **172**
in action research, 593
in causal-comparative research, 344–45, 369, 371
in correlational research, 344–45, 346
in experimental design, 279, 280*t*, 283
in single-subject design, 314
in survey research, 407
data collector characteristics
in causal-comparative research, 369, 371
in correlational research, 344, 346
in experimental design, 279, 280*t*
in single-subject design, 314
in survey research, 407
as threat to internal validity, 171, 283, 346
data points, 304
deception of research subjects, 64–65, 67

definition(s)
constitutive, 30
of key research terms, 20*f*, 27, 31
operational, 31
of question terms, 30–33
in research proposals and reports, 617–18
degrees of freedom (df), **234**–35
demographic (background) questions, 451
demographics, 619
demoralization effect, 280
dependent variable, **81, 265**
in experimental research, 11
independent variable *vs.*, 81–82*f*, 84*n*
in single-subject design, 303–8
derived scores, **189**–90
description(s), 13
ethnographic researchers and, 509
surveys and, 391
descriptive field notes, **511**–12
descriptive research, 15–16, 332. *See also* correlational research
questions, 77
sample size and, 103
descriptive statistics, **187**–218
categorical data and, 188–89, 209–14
in causal-comparative research, 371
in content analysis, 483
Microsoft Excel for, 188, 192, 202, 205, 207
qualitative research and, 434, 437
quantitative data and, 188, 190–208
recommendations on research and, 259
scores in, 189–90
statistics *vs.* parameters and, 187
techniques summary, 258*t*
types of numerical data, 187–89
descriptive studies, **15**–16. *See also* descriptive research
descriptive surveys, 13
descriptors, ERIC, **43,** 45–46
design of experiments, **268.** *See also* research design
deviation, standard, 198, 200–201
dichotomous questions, **453**
dictionary approach, 30
direct administration of surveys to groups, 394*t*
directional hypothesis, **86,** 87*f*, 230
direct observation. *See* observation
discriminant function analysis, **337***f*
discussion section of research report, **625**
discussion-analysis tally sheet, 123*f*
dissertations used in literature reviews, 42, 44*f*, 56
distribution. *See also* frequency distribution; mean(s); median
bimodal, 196
calculating mean, median and standard deviation of, with Excel, 202
example of mode, median, and mean in, 196*t*
normal (*see* normal distribution)
spreads and, 197–201
distribution curve, **195**
distribution of sample means, 222, 223*f*, 224*f*

documents, **535**
action research and analysis of, 592
content analysis and, 476–77, 487
external criticism of, 537–39
internal criticism of, 538–39
for historical research, 535, 537–39
latent *vs.* manifest content of, 481–83
double-blind experiments, 280

EBSCO, search results, 47*f*
ECER. *See* Exceptional Child Education Resources (ECER)
ecological generalizability, **106***f*
educational concerns, examples of, 3
educational research. *See* research
Education Full Text, 45*f*, **56**
Education Index, 41
Education Research Complete, 56
Education Resources Information Center. *See* ERIC (Education Resources Information Center)
effect size (ES), 49, 178, **248.** *See also* group(s)
indexes of, 248
meta-analysis and, 178
Einstein, Albert, 84
emic perspective in ethnographic research, **508**
empirical referents, **28**
Encyclopedia of Educational Research, 40
equivalent-forms method, **157**
ERIC (Education Resources Information Center), 39, 41, 56
abstracts from, 118*f*
descriptors in, 43, 45–46
excerpts from, 42*f*, 43*f*
searching, 44–51
tests and assessments from, 115, 116*f*, 117*f*
ERIC Clearinghouse on Assessment and Evaluation, The, 116
ERIC Document Reproduction Service, 115
ERIC/ETS Test Collection Test File, 116
error, margin of, 407
errors of measurement, 155, **156***f*
essay questions, 136
essence, 430
eta (η), **208,** 210*f*, 251
ethical research, 60–75
academic cheating, plagiarism, and, 72
deception of subjects and, 64–65, 67
defined, **61**
ensuring confidentiality of research data, 64, 66, 67
examples of unethical research, 61, 66*f*
examples with ethical concerns, 65, 66*f*, 67, 70
protecting participants from harm and, 63, **64,** 66, 67, 436–37
questions and, 28
regulation of research and, 69–72
research with children and, 67–68
statement of ethical principles, 61–63
ethics, 61. *See also* ethical research
in action research, 590
causal-comparative research and, 366

examples of problems with, 65, 66*f*, 67, 70
in interviewing, 455–56
manipulated variables, 364
in mixed-methods research, 563
in observation studies, 65–66, 444
in qualitative research, 436–37
ethnographic research, 13–14, 433
advantages and disadvantages of, 518
concepts in, 507–9
content analysis and, 477
data analysis in, 514–16
data collection in, 510–14
defined, **505**–6
example of, 518, 519–27
example of, in Roger Harker's fifth-grade classroom, 516–17
hypotheses and, 509–10
important findings in, 506
observation and interviewing in, 444, 509
overt participant observation in, 444
sampling in, 509
topics good for, 508–9
unique value of, 506–7
ethnographic study, **13,** 187. *See also* ethnographic research
etic perspective, **508**
evaluation(s)
formative, and summative, 14
of historical sources, 537–39
of mixed-methods study, 563
of research reports, 622
evaluation research, **14**
evaluative statements, 124
evidence of validity, 149, 150*f*
construct-related, 149, 150*f*, 154–55
content-related, 149, 150*f*–53
criterion-related, 149, 150*f*, 153–54
example, clarification by, **31**
Excel. *See* Microsoft Excel
Exceptional Child Education Resources (ECER), 41
expectancy table, **154***t*
expectations
for interviews, 452–54
observer, 447
expected frequencies, 212, 213*t*
experience (behavior) questions, **451**
experiment, **266**
experimental group, **266**
experimental research, **11**–12, 264, **265**–300
causal-comparative research compared to, 366
control of experimental treatments in, 284–85
control of extraneous variables in, 268
control of threats to internal validity, 279, 280*t*, 281
essential characteristics of, 266–67
evaluating likelihood of threat to internal validity in, 281–84
examples of, 11*f*, 285–94
group designs in (*see* group designs in experimental research)
placebos and, 281
questions in, 27
sample size, 103
significant findings in, 283

single-subject (*see* single-subject research)
uniqueness of, **265**–66
experimental research validity threats
control of, 279, 280*t*, 281
likelihood of, 281–84
experimental variable, **81, 265**
expert opinion, 4–5
explanatory design, **558,** 559*f*, 562
explanatory studies, 333, 334*f*
exploratory design, **558***f*, 562
ex post facto studies. *See also* causal-comparative research
external audit, **456**
external criticism, **537**–38
external validity, **104**
in action research, 593
in correlational research, 345
generalizability and, 104–6
in single-subject research, **314**
extraneous variables, **83***f*, 84*n*, **267**
control of, 268
in intervention studies, 370
extreme case sample, **434**

face-to-face interviews, 396, 405
factor analysis, **338**
factorial designs, **277**–79*f*
Family Privacy Act (1974), 70
feasibility
of mixed-methods research, 562
of research questions, 28, 29
Federal Drug Administration (FDA), 65
feelings questions, **452**
field diary, **511**
field jottings, **510**–11
field log, **511**–12
field notes, 114, **510**–12
action research and, 592
example of, 512–14
figures in research reports, 626
findings, research report, **623**
first principles, chaos theory and, 8
first quartile (Q), 198
five-number summary, **198**
flowcharts, 123, 124*f*, 516
focus group interviews, **454**–55
footnotes in research reports, 626
foreshadowed problems, **428**
format(s), 48. *See also* style(s)
of literature review reports, 53
of research reports, 623–26
formative evaluations, **14**
formula(s)
KR 20, KR21, 157–58
percentile rank, 189
split-half, 157
standard error of measurement, 160
frequency(ies), 191*n*
content analysis, 483
expected, 212, 213
frequency distribution, **190,** 191*t*
averages *vs.* spreads in, 197–98
constructing with Excel, 192
grouped, 190, 191*t*
variability in, 198 (*see also* spreads)
frequency polygon(s), **190**–91, 192*f*
comparing groups using, 192, 193*f*
constructing, 191, 192
frequency distribution and, 190, 191*t*
gain scores and, 250*f*
skewed, 191–94
frequency tables, 209–11

Friedman two-way analysis of variance, **237**–38
F value, 236

gain scores, 250*t*, 250*f*, **275**
regressed, 275
generalizability, 104. *See also* external validity; replication
action research and, 587
ecological, 106*f*
in experimental research, 435
in grounded theory, 431–32
in historical research, 539–40
meta-analysis and, **563**
in mixed-methods research, 560, 563
mortality threat and, 168–69
of populations, 104–5, 106*f*
in quantitative *vs.* qualitative research, 427, 433, 434–36
of samples, 104–6
in single-subject research, 314
in survey research, 407
generalization, **434**–36
generalized statements, 124, 125
generalizing, **104.** *See also* generalizability
general reference tools, **38**–44
searching using, 44
selecting appropriate, 41, 42*f*, 43*f*
Google Scholar, 54, 56
grade-equivalent scores, **189**
Graduate Record Examination (GRE), 128–29
graphic rating scales, 119*f*
graphic techniques. *See* bar graphs; crossbreak table; pie charts
graphs. *See also* bar graphs
boxplot, 198*f*
frequency polygon (*see* frequency polygon(s))
for single-subject designs, 303*f*, 304*f*, 305*f*, 306*f*, 307*f*, 308*f*, 309*f*, 310*f*, 311*f*, 312*f*, 313*f*
GRE. *See* Graduate Record Examination (GRE)
grounded theory study, **431**–32
group(s). *See also* comparison group(s)
causal-comparative research and, 364–66
comparing, in experimental research, 266
comparing, using categorical data, 255–57
comparing, using quantitative data, 247–51
control, 266
control of extraneous variables in, 268
ethnographic procedures and descriptions of, 506
frequency polygons used to compare, 192, 193*f*
homogeneous subgroups, 369
known, 247–48
norm, 137
random assignment of subjects to, 267
relating variables within, using categorical data, 257, 258*t*
relating variables within, using quantitative data, 251–55
single-subject research *vs.*, 302
group designs in experimental research, 268–79
counterbalanced, **275**–76
factorial, **277,** 278*f*, 279*f*
group comparisons in, 266
manipulation of independent variables in, 267
matching-only, **275**
nonequivalent control group, **270**
one-group pretest-posttest, **269***f*–70
one-shot case study, **269***f*
one static group comparison, 270
poor, 269–70
quasi-, **275**–77
random assignment with matching, 272–75
randomization in, 267, 268
randomized posttest-only control group, **271***f*
randomized pretest-posttest control group, **271,** 272*f*
randomized Solomon four-group, **272,** 273*f*
static-group comparison, **270***f*
static-group pretest-posttest, **270**
time-series, **276**–77*f*
true, 270–75
grouped frequency distribution, **190,** 191*t*
group play, 132, 135*f*
group tests, 130–31

Handbook of Research on Teaching, 40
Hawthorne effect, **175**
HHS. *See* U.S. Department of Health and Human Services (HHS)
high-stakes testing, 151
histograms, **194***f*–95. *See also* bar graphs
constructing with Excel, 192
historical research, 13, **14,** 532–52
advantages and disadvantages of, 540–41
content analysis and, 477, 487
data analysis in, 539
defined, **533**
example research report, 541–50
generalization in, 539–40
important findings in, 540
influence of historians on public policy and, 538
kinds of questions pursued through, 534
purposes of, 533–34
steps in, 534–39
history threat, **173**–74, 180*t*
in experimental design, 277, 283
in single-subject design, 270*n*, 314
in time-series design, 277
holistic perspective in ethnographic research, **507**
homogeneous sample, 369, **434**
hypothesis, 6, **20, 84,** 85*f*, 86–88
advantages of stating, 84
in causal-comparative research, 367
defined, **84**
directional *vs.* nondirectional, 86–87 (*see also* directional hypothesis)
disadvantages of stating, 85–86
in ethnographic research, 509–10
important, 86
in mixed-methods study, 561
null, 228, 229*f*, 230*f* (*see also* null hypothesis)
propositions *vs.*, 87–88, 428
qualitative research and, 87–88
relationships and, 78, 86, 87, 228
research, 228, 229*f*
in research proposals and reports, **617,** 622
stating research problem as, 20
testing (*see* hypothesis testing)
hypothesis testing, 228–29, 625
in causal-comparative research, 367, 372
in content analysis, 478–79
experimental research for, 265
historical research and, 534
null hypothesis and, 232–33
one-tailed test in, 230, 231*f*, 232*f*
two-tailed test in, 232*f*

"Implementation of the Guided Reading Approach With Elementary School Deaf Students" (Schirmer, Schaffer), 315–26
analysis of, 327–28
implementation threat, **177**–78, 180*t*
in action research, 593
in experimental design, 283–84
in single-subject design, 314
independent variable, **81, 265**
dependent variable *vs.*, 81–82*f*, 84*n*
in experimental research, 11, **265,** 267
inability to manipulate, in causal-comparative studies, 368
manipulation of, 267
moderator variable interaction with, 277
in single-subject design, 303–8
indexes, 38, 39, **53**–54
of effect size, 248
validity of, 140
inferences. *See also* inferential statistics
about populations, 220–21
validity and, 148–45 (*see also* validity)
inference techniques, 233–41, 248
comparing groups using, 249–51, 252*t*
nonparametric, for categorical data, 238
nonparametric, for quantitative data, 237
parametric, for categorical data, 237–38
parametric, for quantitative data, 233–37
power of statistical test, 239–41
summary, 238, 239*t*
inferential statistics, 219–44, **248**
comparing groups using, 248–51
defined, **220**–21
Excel and, 235
hypothesis testing and, 228–29, 230*f*
inference techniques and, 233–41
logic of, 221–27
practical *vs.* statistical significance and, 230–33
recommendations on research and, 259
techniques summary, 258*t*
informal interviews, **449**
informants, **114**
key, 451
information. *See also* data; data collection
sources of, 114, 535–39
summarizing, for historical research, 536–37
validity and meaning of, 149
information overload, 6
informed consent, **63,** 64*f*, 456. *See also* consent form
inquiry method, 278
Institute of Education Sciences, 39
institutional review boards (IRBs), **69**–70
criteria for approval by, 69*t*
instrument(s), research, **20, 117–36.** *See also* data collection; instrumentation
acquisition of, 114–17
administering, 117–18
for causal-comparative research, 368, 371
for correlational research, 340, 344–45
decay of, 171 (*see also* instrument decay)
informant, 114
means of classifying data-collection, 114–17
norm-referenced *vs.* criterion-referenced, 137–38
objectivity of, 113
reliability of, 113, 148, 155–62 (*see also* reliability)
researcher-completed, 114, 118, 119–26
subject-completed, 114, 118, 126–36
for survey research, 398–401
tips on developing, 115
usability of, 113–14
validity of, 113, 148–55 (*see also* validity)
written-response *vs.* performance, 117
instrumental case study, **433**
instrumentation, 111–46. *See also* data collection; instrument(s)
in causal-comparative research, 368, 371
in correlational research, 340, 346
data fundamentals and, 112–14
data preparation for analysis and, 131–42
defined, **112**–13
examples of data-collection, 117–36
means of classifying data-collection, 114–17
measurement scales and, 138–41
norm-referenced *vs.* criterion-referenced, 137–38
reliability of, 148, 155 (*see also* reliability)
research proposals/reports and, reports, 620–21
in survey research, 398–401, 407
as threat to internal validity (*see* instrumentation threats)
validity of, 148 (*see also* validity)
written-response *vs.* performance, 117
instrumentation threats, 170–72, 180*t*
in correlational research, 344–45, 346
to experimental group designs, 277, 283
in survey research, 407

instrument decay, **171**
  in causal-comparative research, 369, 371
  in correlational research, 344, 346
  in experimental design, 279, 280t, 283
  in single-subject design, 314
  in survey research, 407
instrument validity. *See* validity
intelligence (aptitude) tests, 129–30, 131f. *See also* IQ tests
  quick and easy, 160f
interactions of variables in factorial designs, **277**
interlibrary loan, **49**
internal-consistency methods, **157**–59t
internal criticism, **538**–39
internal validity, 166–83
  in action research, 593
  in comparison group studies, 281, 282f
  defined, **167**–68
  minimizing threats to, 180–81
  in qualitative research, 436
  research proposals/reports and, 621
  in single-subject research, 305, 309
  threats to, 168–80 (*see also* threats to internal validity)
Internet. *See also* Web (World Wide Web)
  advantages/disadvantages of searching, 54–55
  instrumentation and, 116–17
  plagiarism and, 72
  surveys administered on, 15, 394t–95f
"Internet Use, Abuse, and Dependence Among Students at a Southeastern Regional University" (Fortson, et. al), 374–85
  analysis of, 386–87
interpretation
  in action research, 589, 590, 600
  of categorical data for comparing groups, 256
  of categorical data for relating variables within group, 251
  in causal-comparative research, 372, 387
  confidence levels and, 255f
  in content analysis, 487
  contingency coefficient and, 256
  correlational coefficients and, 253
  in correlational research, 241
  crossbreak tables and, 256–57
  effect size and, 248
  generalizability and, 249, 253, 256, 259
  inferential statistics for, 248–51
  known groups and, 247–48
  parametric/nonparametric techniques and, 259
  percentages and, 255, 256t
  probabilities and, 248, 249, 251, 255, 257, 258
  in qualitative research, 425, 426–27, 429, 430, 431
  of quantitative data for comparing groups, 247–51
  of quantitative data for relating variables within group, 251–55
  of scatterplots, 207
  statistics, 258
interpretive exercises, 133–35
interpretive statements, 124, 125
interval scales, **139,** 140t
intervention studies, **16**
  in causal-comparative research, 370
  procedural details, 621
interview(s), 13, 187, 443, **448**–56
  in action research, 592
  behavior of interviewer, expectations for, 452–54
  for case studies, 432–33
  coding of, 481, 482f
  content analysis and, 477, 481, 482f, 487
  data collection and analysis and, 455, 456
  ethics in conducting, 455–56
  in ethnographic research, 509, 510
  expectations for, 452
  face-to-face, 396, 405
  focus group, 454–55
  in grounded theory, 431–32
  informal, 449
  key-actor, 451
  for measuring ability, 404
  in mixed-methods research, 555
  oral, 535
  personal survey, 396
  in phenomenological studies, 431
  protocols for (*see* interview protocol)
  questions for, 28, 451–52, 453
  questions for survey, 398–402f
  recording data from, 455
  retrospective, 450
  strategies for, 450t
  structured/semi-structured, 449
  training for, 492–94
  types of, 449, 450t
  what to avoid in, 455
interviewers, training for, 402–4
interview protocol, **120,** 121f, 122f
interview schedule, 114, 121f, **398**–401
  contingency questions in, 401, 402f
  nonresponse and, 404–6
  for surveys, 398–400
intrinsic case study, **433**
Iowa Tests of Basic Skills, 128
IPAT Anxiety Scale, 128
IQ tests, 159. *See also* intelligence (aptitude) test
IRBs. *See* institutional review boards (IRBs)
item formats, 132–36

jigsaw technique, 283
journal(s), use of in literature reviews, 39, 48
  peer-reviewed, 39
  summary of articles in, 50
Journal of Educational Research, 39
Journal of Research in Science Teaching, 39
JSTOR, 56
justification for research studies, **616**

key actors, **451**
key events in ethnographic research, **515**
key informants, **451**
keywords, searching with, 55
knowing, ways of, 4–7, 10f
knowledge. *See* knowing, ways of
knowledge questions, **451**
known groups, 247–48
Kruskal-Wallis one-way analysis of variance, **237**
Kuder Preference Record, 128
Kuder-Richardson approach, **157**–58

landmark studies, 49
latent content, 481, **482,** 483
leading questions, 400, 406, 407, 453
"Lessons on Effective Teaching from Middle School ESL Students" (Curtin), 519–27
  analysis of, 528–29
level in independent variables, 81
level of significance, **228**
Librarians' Index, 54
life history, **430**
Likert scale, **127**, 128f
linear (straight-line) relationship, **251**
line graphs, for single-subject designs, 303f, 304f, 305f, 306f, 307f, 308f, 309f, 310f, 311f, 312f, 313f
literature review, **20,** 37–59
  computerized searches, 44–51
  definition and value of, **38**
  general reference tools in, 38–39, 40, 41–42, 43f, 44
  meta-analysis for, 49–50
  primary *vs.* secondary sources for, 39 (*see also* primary sources; secondary sources)
  research proposals/reports and, **618**–19
  search terms for, 42–44
  steps involved in searching, 39–44
  types of sources, 38–39
  writing report on, 51–56
location threat, **170**f, 180t
  in causal-comparative research, 369, 371
  in correlational research, 342, 344, 346
  in experimental design, 279, 282
  in single-subject design, 314
  in survey research, 407
logic, as way of knowing, 5
longitudinal survey, **392**
long-term studies, 8
"Lydia Ann Stow: Self-Actualization in a Period of Transition" (Fox), 542–48
  analysis of, 549–50

mail surveys, 394t, 395–96
  cover letter for, 401–2, 403f
  nonresponse to, 404–5
major premise, 5
Mandlebrot Bug, 8, 9f
manifest content, **481**–83
manipulated variables, **81,** 265, 266, 267
  in causal-comparative research, 364, 365, 366, 368, 370, 372
  ethics and, 364
Mann-Whitney *U* test, **237**
MANOVA. *See* multivariate analysis of variance (MANOVA)
maps, 516
margin of error, 407
matching
  mechanical, 274f, 275
  statistical, 274–75, 369
  subject, 268, 369
matching designs, **272,** 273, 274f
matching groups, 236, 237, 367–68, 369
matching items, 133
matching-only designs, 273, 274f, **275,** 276f
matching variables, 268, 367
mathematics, chaos theory and, 8

matrices, 518
maturation threat, **174**–75, 180t
  in causal-comparative research, 369–70
  in experimental design, 270n, 283
  in single-subject design, 314
  in time-series design, 279
maximal variation sample, **434**
mean(s), **196**t–97t
  calculating with Excel, 202
  difference between sample, 226f, 227
  distribution of sample, 222, 223f, 224f
  estimating standard error of, 224
  probability areas between *z* scores and, 203f
  standard deviation, variance and, 198
  standard error of (SEM), 223–24
  standard error of the difference between samples (SED), 227f
  t-tests for, 233–36, 371
  types of, 196n
  as *z* scores, 224
measurement errors, 155–56
  standard (SEMeas), 159f–60
measurement scales, 138–41
  characteristics of four types of, 140t
  interval, 139
  nominal, 138f, 139
  ordinal, 139f
  ratio, 139–40
  reconsideration of, 140–41
measures of central tendency (averages), **195**–97
  spreads *vs.*, 197–98
mechanical matching, **274**f, 275
median, **196**t
  calculating with Excel, 202
mediator variables, **82**–84
member checking in ethnographic research, **456**
Mental Measurements Yearbooks, The, 116
meta-analysis, **16, 49**
  literature review and, 49–50
  reducing internal validity threats using, 178
metaphysical questions, 28
methodological triangulation, 557. *See also* triangulation
Metropolitan Achievement Test, 128
Microsoft Excel, A5–A16
  calculating mean, median, and standard deviation of distributions using, 202
  calculating correlations, 205, A15–A16
  conducting independent samples *t*-test, A13–A15
  entering data, A7–A8
  frequency distribution and histographs or bar graphs constructed with, 192
  introduction to, A5
  loading analysis toolpak, A5–A6
  obtaining frequency distribution and descriptive statistics, A8–A12
  performing statistical calculations using, 188
  random sampling with, 235
  scatterplots with, 207
  specifying analysis, A8
  starting, A7

Minnesota Multiphasic Personality Inventory, 128
minor premise, 5
mixed-methods research, **11,** 553, 554–84
 brief history of, 557
 contradictory findings in, 562
 data collection and analysis, 562
 defined, **555**–56
 designs for, 558–59, 562
 designs issues, 560–61
 drawbacks of 556–57
 ethics in, 563
 evaluation of studies by, 563
 example of research study, 563–78
 feasibility of, 562
 incompatibility of some, 558
 questions in, 27, 28
 results, 562
 steps in, 561–62
 strengths of, 556
mixed-model studies, 561
MLA Handbook for Writers of Research Papers, 53
mode, **195,** 196*t*
moderator variables, **82, 277**–78
mortality threat, **168,** 169*f,* 170, 180*t*
 in causal-comparative research, 371
 in correlational research, 345, 346
 in experimental design, 279, 280*t*, 282
 in single-subject design, 314
 in survey research, 407
multiple-baseline designs, **307,** 308*f,* 309*f,* 310*f*
multiple (collective) case study, **433**
multiple-choice items, 133
multiple correlation, coefficient of, 336*f*
multiple realities, **508**
multiple regression, **335**–36
multiprobe design, 314
multi-treatment designs, 314
multivariate analysis of covariance (MANCOVA), **237,** 239*t*
multivariate analysis of variance (MANOVA), **237**

narrative description, 13–14, 187–88
narrative research, **430**
National Center for Education Statistics (NCES), 55
National Council on Measurement in Education, 149*n*
National Institutes of Health (NIH), 69
National Research Act (1974), 69
National Society for the Study of Education (NSSE) Yearbooks, 40
naturalistic observation, **445**
natural sciences, chaos theory and, 8
natural settings, 424–25, 518
NCES. *See* National Center for Education Statistics (NCES)
negatively-skewed polygons, **191,** 193*f*
nominal scales, **138***f,* 139, 140*t*
nondirectional hypothesis, **86,** 87*f,* 230
nonequivalent control group design, **270**
nonjudgmental orientation in ethnographic research, 508
nonintervention studies, 269
nonlinear/curvilinear relationships, 208, 210*f,* 251
nonparametric techniques, **233**
 for categorical data, 238, 239*t*
 ethnographic research and, 516
 interpretation and, 259
 for quantitative data, 237, 239*t*
nonparticipant observation, **444**
nonrandom sampling
 methods of, 98–101, 102*f*
 random sampling *vs.*, 94–95
nonrepresentative samples, 94*f*
nonresponse to surveys, **404**–6
 to items, 405–6
 low response and, 406
 total, 404–5
normal curve, **195***f. See also* normal distribution
 probabilities under, 203*f*
 standard scores and, 201–4
 z scores and, 204
normal curve table values, A3
normal distribution, **195.** *See also* normal curve
 calculating mean, median, and standard deviation of, using Excel, 202
 standard deviation in, 200*f,* 201
norm group, **137**
norm-referenced instruments, **137**
null hypothesis, **228,** 229*f*
 power of statistical test and, 239*f*
 rejection of, 230*f*
numbers, table of random, **95,** 96*t*, A2
numerical rating scales, 119
numerical records, 535

objective(s), of content analysis, 478–79
objectivity, **113**
observation, 443–48
 in action research, 592
 coding data from, 447, 448*f*
 content analysis and, 477, 487
 ethics in, 65–66
 in ethnographic research, 444, 509, 510
 example of research based on, 458–69
 grounded theory and, 431–32
 in mixed-methods research, 555
 naturalistic, 445
 nonparticipant, 444
 observer bias in, 446–47*f,* 518
 observer effect in, 446
 overt *vs.* covert, 444
 participant, 444
 ratings *vs.*, 119
 reactivity and, 446
 simulations and, 445–46
 technology used in, 447–48
 variations in approaches to, 445*f*
observational data, **446**
 coding, 447, 448*f*
observation forms, 122*f*
observation schedules, 122
observer-as-participant, 444
observer bias, **446**–47*f,* 518
observer effect, **446**
observer expectations, **447**
one-group pretest-posttest design, **269***f,* 270
one-shot case study, **269***f*
one-tailed test, **231***f,* 232*f*
open-ended questions, **399, 453**
operant conditioning, 303
operational definitions, **31,** 32*f*
opinion(s)
 expert, 4–5
 of others, 4
opinion (values) questions, **451**–52
opportunistic sample, **434**
oral history, **430,** 535
oral interviews, 535
oral statements, 535
ordinal scales, **139***f,* 140*t*
ordinate, 303
organizational charts, 516
Otis-Lennon test, 131
outcome patterns, 276, 277*f*
outcome variable, **82, 265**
outliers, **207,** 207*f*

panel study, **392**
paradigms, 27, 557
parameters, statistics *vs.*, **187**
parametric techniques, **233**–38, 239*t*
 for analyzing categorical data, 237–38
 for analyzing quantitative data, 233–37
 interpretation, 259
partial correlation, **342,** 344*f*
participant(s), **590.** *See also* subject(s)
 in action research, 14, 590, 591*f*
 ensuring confidentiality of data of, 64, 66, 67
 identifying, for qualitative research, 428
 member checking of, 508
 protecting from harm, 63, **64,** 66, 67, 436–37
participant-as-observer, 444
participant observation, **444**
 ethics of, 65–66, 444
 in ethnographic research, **510**
participation, levels of, in action research, 590, 591*f*
participatory action research, **589**–90
passive deception, 444
path analysis, **338,** 339*f*
patterns, 78, 187, 207
 chaos theory and, 8
 in ethnographic research, 515
 hypotheses and, 78
 outcome, 276, 277*f*
 systematic sampling and, 99
PDF (Portable Document Format), 48
Pearson product moment coefficient (Pearson *r*), **208,** 237, 251, 336
Pearson *r*. *See* Pearson product moment coefficient
peer debriefing, 456
"Perceived Family Support, Acculturation, and Life Satisfaction in Mexican American Youth: A Mixed-Methods Exploration" (Edwards, Lopez), 564–78
 analysis of, 578–81
percentages, 188, 189, 198, 200*f,* 201
 interpretation and, 255, 256*t*
 probability and, 202–3
 in qualitative research, 429
percentile(s), 189, **198**
percentile ranks, **189,** 190*f*
perceptions, 4, 13, 17, 430
performance assessments
 ethics and, 67
 written response *vs.*, 117
performance checklists, 123–24, 125*f,* 131
performance instruments, **117**
 checklists, 123–24, 125*f*
performance rating scale, 131
performance tests, 131, 132*f*
periodicity, **99**
personal interviews, 396
personality inventories, 128, 130*f*
phenomenological study, **430**–31
"Physical Education in Urban High School Class Settings: Features and Correlations between Teaching Behaviors and Learning Activities" (Zeng, Leung, Liu, Hipscher), 347–57
 analysis of, 358–60
Piaget, Jean, 404, 445
pictorial attitude test, 129*f*
Picture Situation Inventory, 132, 133*f*
pie charts, **211,** 212*f*
Piers-Harris Children's Self-Concept Scale, 128
pilot study, 623, **626**
placebo effect, 281
plagiarism, **72**
 avoiding unintentional, 51
planned ignorance, 172
point biserial coefficient, 214
poll, 407
population(s), **20, 92**
 accessible, 93–94
 boundaries of (confidence intervals), 224–25
 census of, 103, 392
 cohort studies of, 392
 defining, 93
 inferences about, 220–21 (*see also* inferential statistics)
 random *vs.* nonrandom sampling and, 94*f*–95 (*see also* nonrandom sampling; random sampling)
 relevance, 104
 samples from, 92–93, 221, 619
 sampling of (*see* sampling)
 survey research and characteristics of, 391–92
 target, 93–94, 393–94
population generalizability, **104**–5, 106*f*
portraiture, **431**
portrayals, 13, 509
positive correlations, 208, 213
positively skewed polygons, **191,** 193*f*
positivism, **425**–27, **557**
post hoc analysis, 236
postmodernism/postmodernists, **427, 557**
 clarity and, 428
posttest, 266
 in one-group pretest-posttest design, 269–70
 in static-group pretest-posttest design, 270
power curve, 240*f*
power of a statistical test, **239**–41
practical action research, **588**–90
 hypothetical examples of, 595–600
practical significance, **230**
 statistical significance *vs.*, 230–33

pragmatists, **557**
precoding, 121
prediction(s), **334.** *See also* prediction studies
  chaos theory and, 8
  role of historical research in making, 534
  using scatterplots for, 334*f,* 335*t*
prediction equation, **335, 337**
prediction studies, **334**
  in causal-comparative research, 373–74
  correlational studies and, 334–35, 340, 341
  validity and, 153–54
predictive validity, **153**–54
predictor, 153, 154
predictor variable, **334,** 335–36
presentism, 538, 539
pretest, 173
  in one-group pretest-posttest design, 269–70
  regressed gain scores and, 275
  sign test and, 237
  in static-group pretest-posttest design, 270
  as threat to internal validity, 172–73
pretest treatment interaction, **272**
primary sources, **39, 536**
  evaluating, 50, 51*f*
  locating, 49
  secondary sources *vs.,* 536
prior experience, 247, 256
probability, **202, 226**
  confidence intervals and, 226
  under normal curve, 203*f*
  z scores and, 202, 203*f*
probability sampling, 105
probes/probing questions, 121, 122*f,* 403
problem(s). *See also* research problem
  defining, 39–40, 44–45
  foreshadowed, 428
problem statement, **20**
procedure(s), **20.** S*ee also* research procedures
  correlational research, 340
  for data collection, 113, 117
  research proposals/reports and, **619**–21
process. *See* research process
product(s), 117
product rating scales, 119–20*f*
program evaluation, 138*n*
projective devices, **131**–32, 133*f*
proportions, *t*-tests for, 237–38
propositions, **87**
  hypotheses *vs.,* 87–88, 428
  in qualitative research, 428–29
ProQuest, 42, 44*f,* 56
ProQuest Education Journals, 56
prototypes, 435
Psychological Abstracts, 39
PsycINFO, 39, 41, 48
Publication Manual of the American Psychological Association (APA Style Manual), 53, 622, 623*t*
public policies
  historical research and, 538
  qualitative research and, 437
purists, 557
purpose, research proposals and reports and statement of, **615**–16
purposive sampling, **101,** 102*f,* 103, **428**
  in content analysis, 480
  generalization from, 105
  meta-analysis and, 178
  in mixed-methods research, 460
  in qualitative research, 428

qualitative data
  analysis of, 425, 429, 434, 456
  collection of, 118
  techniques for summarizing, 209–14
qualitative research, **7**–11, 421–41, 457*t. See also* qualitative research methodologies
  action research and, 593, 594*t*
  approaches to, 430–34
  characteristics of, 424–25, 426*t*
  combined with quantitative research, 437 (*see also* mixed-methods research)
  data analysis, 425, 429, 434, 456
  data collection, 456, 457*t* (*see also* interview(s); observation)
  defined, 423, **424**
  design of, 10
  ethics and, 70–71, 436–37
  example of, 458–71
  generalization in, 434–36
  hypotheses and, 87–88, 428–29
  philosophical assumptions of, 425–26, 427*t*
  portraiture and, 431
  postmodernism and, 427, 428
  quantitative research *vs.,* 423, 424*t,* 425–26, 427*t*
  research reports unique to, 626
  steps in, 427–29
  validity and reliability in, 162, 436, 456–57
qualitative research methodologies
  content analysis, 443 (*see also* content analysis)
  ethnographic research as, 433 (*see also* ethnographic research)
  historical research as, 433 (*see also* historical research)
  interviews, 432–33, 448–56
  observation, 432–33, 443–48
qualitizing, **562**
quantitative data, **188,** 189. *See also* quantitative data techniques
  categorical *vs.,* 78, 79, 80–81, 138
  causal-comparative research and, 366, 371
  comparing groups using, 247–51
  for comparing more than one sample, 226–27
  correlational research and, 332, 337, 340
  in mixed-methods research, 555, 557, 558
  for relating variables within groups, 251–55
  sample size, 104
quantitative data techniques
  nonparametric techniques for analyzing, 237, 239*t*
  parametric techniques for analyzing, 233–37, 239*t*
  for summarizing, 190–208
quantitative research, **7**–11
  action research and, 593, 594*t*
  combined with qualitative research, 437 (*see also* mixed-methods research)
  design, 10–11
  ethics and, 70
  methodologies of (*see* quantitative research methodologies)
  philosophical assumptions underlying, 425–26, 427*t*
  questions in, 27, 28
  qualitative *vs.,* 423, 424*t,* 425–26, 427*t*
  variables (*see* quantitative variable(s))
quantitative research methodologies, 263
  causal-comparative, 363–89
  classification of, 366
  correlational, 331–62
  experimental, 264–300
  single-subject, 301–30
  survey, 390–420
quantitative variable(s), **78, 337**
  categorical variables *vs.,* 78, 79*f,* 80–81, 138, 337
quantitizing, **562**
quartiles, 198
quasi-experimental designs, **275**–77
  counter-balanced design, 275–76*f*
  example of, 600–601
  matching-only design, 275
  time-series design, 276–77*f*
question(s), 27–34. *See also* research question(s)
  characteristics of good, 28–34
  closed-ended, 398–99, 400
  contingency, 401, 402*f*
  empirical referents in, 28
  essay, 136
  in interviews, 451–52
  key, in data collection, 112–13
  leading, 400, 406, 407, 453
  matching, 117, 127
  metaphysical, 28
  multiple-choice, 133
  open-ended (*See* open-ended questions)
  probing, 121, 122*f,* 403
  researchable, *vs.* nonresearchable, 29*f*
  short-answer, 117, 127, 136, 399, 400
  in surveys, 391, 398–400
  true-false, 133
  value and, 28
questionnaires, **114,** 398–401. *See also* interview schedule; question(s)
  in action research, 592
  in content analysis, 477, 478, 479, 484, 487
  contingency questions on, 401, 402*f*
  ethics and, 72
  format of, 401
  interviews and, 120–22
  mortality threat to validity of, 168
  nonresponse to, 404–6
  pretesting, 401
  as subject-completed instruments, 126–27
  survey, 398–401

RAND Education, 56
random assignment, **267**
random assignment with matching designs, 272–75
randomization, 267, 268
randomized posttest-only control group design, **271***f*
randomized posttest-only control group with matching subjects design, 273, 274*f*
randomized pretest-posttest control group design, **271,** 272*f*
randomized pretest-posttest control group design using matched subjects, 273–74
randomized Solomon four-group design, **272,** 273*f*
random numbers, table of, **95,** 96*t,* A2
random replacement, 405
random sampling, **94,** 95–98, 99, **480,** 593, 619
  in causal-comparative research, 368
  cluster, 96, 97, 98*f,* 99, 102
  in content analysis, 480
  with Excel, 235
  feasibility of, 105
  inferential statistics and, 221, 234, 238
  methods of, 95, 96, 97*f,* 98
  in mixed-methods research, 560
  nonrandom sampling *vs.,* 94–95 (*see also* nonrandom sampling)
  sample size and, 230, 234
  simple, 95, 96, 99*f,* 101
  stratified, 96, 97*f,* 99*f*
  in survey research, 407
  two-stage, 98, 99*f,* 102
random selection, **267**
random start, **99**
range, **198**
rating(s), observations *vs.,* 119
rating scale(s), 119–20, 131
  behavior, 119*f,* 120*n*
  product rating, 119, 120*f*
rationale
  developing content analysis, 479
  developing mixed-method research, 561
ratio scales, **139,** 140*t*
raw scores, **189**
  comparison of *z* scores and, 202*t*
reality
  critical analysis and question of, 17, 18–19
  single, *vs.* multiple, 7–10
references in research reports, 625
reference tools for literature reviews, **38**–44
reflective field notes, **512**
regressed gain score, **275**
regression line, **334**–35
regression threat, **176,** 177*f,* 180*t*
  in experimental design, 270, 280–81, 283
  in single-subject design, 314
relationships, 5, 51, 52*f,* 77, 78, 167. *See also* correlation(s)
  associational studies and, 332–33, 365–66
  in causal-comparative research, 365, 366, 372, 373
  cause-and-effect, 265
  circle diagrams of, 347*f*
  in content analysis, 479, 483
  correlations and, 12, 204–5
  descriptive studies and, 10, 16
  example of important, 80
  factors reducing likelihood of finding, 179–80

relationships—*Cont.*
hypotheses and, 84–85, 228
importance of studying, 77–78
important, clarified by educational research, 80
between independent and dependent variables, 82*f*
index of strength of, 213–14
linear/straight-line, 251
mixed-methods research and variable, 556
nonlinear/curvilinear, 208, 210*f*, 251
in qualitative research, 534, 535
research questions and, 34*f*
in survey research, 393
relativity, theory of, 84
relevance of populations, 104
reliability, **113,** 148, **155**–62, **456, 483**
in content analysis, 482, 483
correlation coefficient and, 156, 341
equivalent-forms method and, 157
errors of measurement and, 155–56
internal consistency methods, 157–59, 159*t*
importance of, 148
instrument, 113
methods of checking, 158, 159*t*
in qualitative research, 162, 456–57
reliability coefficient and, 156, 341
research proposals/reports and instrument, 620
scoring agreement and, 160–62
standard error of measurement and, 159–60
test-retest method for, 156–57, 159*t*
validity *vs.*, 155, 156*f*
worksheet for, 161*f*
reliability coefficient, **156,** 341. *See also* correlation coefficient
relics, **535**
replication, **105.** *See also* external validity; generalizability
in action research, 587, 594, 597, 601
in content analysis, 487
in convenience sampling, 101
in mixed-methods research, 560
in qualitative research, **435**
random sampling and, 105
of scientific research, 6
in single-subject research, 314
reports. *See also* research report(s)
as primary sources, 48–49
writing literature review, 51–56
representativeness, **104**
representative sample, 94*f*, 95
research, 2–24. *See also* research design
action, 14 (*see also* action research)
approaches to, 246, 247*f*
basic, *vs.* applied, 7
causal-comparative, 12
chaos theory and, 8
controversies in, 15, 63, 70, 103, 140, 151, 161, 240, 281, 366, 406, 558
correlational, 12
critical analysis of, 16–19
defined, **7**
in digital age, 15
ethics and (*see* ethical research)
ethnographic, 13–14
evaluation, 14
examples of educational concerns and, 3
experimental, 11–12
external validity of (*see* external validity)
federal regulations for, 69–72
general categories of, 15–16
historical, 14
instruments for (*see* instrument(s); instrumentation)
mixed-methods, 11
philosophical and theoretical framework of, 425–26, 427*t*
problems addressed by (*see* research problems)
procedures, 20–21, 117
process of, overview, 19–21 (*see also* research process)
qualitative, 7–11 (*see also* qualitative research)
quantitative, 7–11 (*see also* quantitative research)
rationale for, 33
recommendations on doing, 259
reliability of (*see* reliability)
in schools, 598
study of relationships, 77–78
suggestions for further, 625
survey, 12–13
types of, 7–15
validity of (*see* validity)
value of, 4, 15, 33–34
ways of knowing and, 4–7, 10*f*
Web-based, 15, 395
research design
causal-comparative research, 368*f*
correlational research, 340*t*
experimental research, 268–79
explanatory, 558–59*f*
exploratory, 558*f*
factorial, 277–79
qualitative research, 10
quantitative research, 10–11
reliability of (*see* reliability)
research proposals/reports and, **619**
single-subject, 303–8*f*, 309*f*, 310*f*
triangulation, 559*f*
validity of (*see* validity)
researcher-completed instruments, 114, 118, 119–26
anecdotal records, 124–25
flowcharts, 123, 124*f*
interview protocol, 120, 121*f*, 122*f*
observation forms, 122*f*
performance checklists, 123–24, 125*f*
rating scales, 119*f*–20*f*
tally sheets, 122*f*–23
time and motion logs, 125, 126*f*
research hypothesis, **228,** 229*f*. *See also* hypothesis; hypothesis testing
research literature. *See* literature review
research problem, 20, 26–36
for causal-comparative studies, 367
for correlational studies, 339
defining, for historical research, 535
defining, for literature reviews, 39–40, 44–45
defining, for survey research, 393
definition, 27
identifying, for qualitative research, 427–28
qualitative research and, 428
research proposals/reports and, 615–18
research questions and, 27–34
research procedures, **20*f***–21, 113, **619**–21
research process, 19, 20*f*, 21
definitions of terms, 20
design (*see* research design)
hypothesis, 20
instrumentation, 20
literature review, 20
qualitative research and, 425
research problem statement and, 20, 26–36
samples, 20
research proposals, 613, 614–40
defined, **615**
IRB board classification of, 70
major sections of, 615–22
sample, 626–37
research question(s), 27–34. *See also* question(s)
action research and identification of, 591
advantages of restating, as hypotheses, 84
in case study research, 28
characteristics of good, 28–34
in experimental research, 27
in interview research, 28, 451–52
in mixed-methods studies, 27, 28, 561, 562
in qualitative research, 28
in quantitative research, 27, 28
relationships and, 77–78 (*see also* relationships)
in research proposals and reports, 617
survey research and, 28, 398–401
research report(s), 613, 614–26
action research example, 601–9
causal-comparative example, 374–87
content analysis example, 488–500
correlational research example, 348–57
defined, **615**
ethnographic research example, 518–27
evaluating, 622
experimental design example, 285–95
historical research example, 542–50
mixed-methods research example, 563–78
outline of, 624*f*, 626
qualitative design example, 458–69
sections of, major, 615–22
sections of, unique, 622–26
single-subject design example, 314–26
survey research example, 408–17
Resources in Education (RIE), 39, 40
results
mixed-methods research, 562
in research reports, **623**–25
statistically significant research report, 228
retrospective interviews, **450**
reversal designs, 305
Review of Educational Research, 40
Review of Research in Education (RRE), 40
reward to induce survey response, 405
RIE. See Resources in Education (RIE)
role playing, 445–46
Rorschach Ink Blot Test, 132
RRE. See Review of Research in Education (RRE)

sample(s), **20,** 91–95. *See also* sampling
causal-comparative, 367–68
census or, 103
comparing more than one, 226*f*, 227
content analysis, 480
correlational, 339
defined, **92**
generalizing from, 104–6
means and standard deviation of, 222
nonrandom, 94–95, 98–101, 102*f*
populations and, 92–94, 221
random, 94–95, 235, 407
representative *vs.* nonrepresentative, **94**
research proposals/reports and, 619–20
standard error of the difference between means of, 227
survey, 391, 397–98
types of qualitative research, 434
sample size, 103–4
in correlational research, 339
in mixed-methods design, 560–61
statistical significance and, 234
sampling, 91–110. *See also* sample(s); sample size
in action research, 593
in causal-comparative research, 367–68
census *vs.*, 103
cluster, 96, 97, 99*f*, 102
in content analysis, 480
controversies in, 103
convenience, 100*f*, 101, 102*f*, 103, 619
in correlational research, 339
in ethnographic research, 509
external validity and generalizing from, 104–6
methods review, 101–3
in mixed-methods research, 560–61
nonrandom, 94–95, 98–101, 102–3 (*see also* nonrandom sampling)
poll, 407
probability and, 105
purposive (*see* purposive sampling)
in qualitative research, 434
random methods of, 95–98, 101–2 (*see also* random sampling)
random *vs.* nonrandom, 94–95
representative *vs.* nonrepresentative, **94**
review of methods of, 101–3
samples, populations, and, 91–94
sample size and, 103–4
stratified, 96–98, 102
systematic, 98–100, 102*f*, 103
two-stage, 98, 99*f*, 102

sampling distribution, **222**–23
of means, 223*f*
sampling error, **221,** 222*f*
sampling interval, 99
sampling ratio, **99**
scales, measurement, 138–41
scatterplots, **205**–7, **251**
construction of, 205, 206, 207
correlation coefficients and, 207–8, 209*f,* 332*f*
drawing, with Excel, 207
interpreting, 207
outliers in, 207, 208*f*
prediction using, 334*f,* 335*t*
in relating variables within a group, 251, 253*f,* 255*f*
science, 5
scientific method, **5**–7
score(s), 189
age-equivalent, 189
averages of, 195–97
derived, 189–90, 201
gain (*see* gain scores)
grade-equivalent, 189
percentile ranks, 189, 190*t*
raw, 189, 190*t*, 201
scatterplots used to predict, 334–35
spreads, 197–201
standard, 190, 201–4 (*see also* standard scores)
T (*see T* scores)
z (*see z* scores)
scoring, 189. *See also* score(s)
choosing method of, 190
data, 142
scoring agreement, 159*t*, **160**–62
search engines, **54**
search terms for literature reviews, **42**–44, 45–46
secondary sources, **39, 536**
most commonly-used educational, 40
locating primary sources using, 49
primary *vs.,* 536
SED. *See* standard error of the difference (SED)
selected variable, 81
selection items, 132, 133–35
self-checklists, 127*f*
self-study, teacher research using, 588–89
SEM. *See* standard error of the mean (SEM)
semantic differential, **128,** 129*f*
SEMeas. *See* standard error of measurement (SEMeas)
semistructured interviews, **449**
sensory data/experience, as way of knowing, 4
sensory questions, **452**
Sequential Tests of Educational Progress (STEP), 128
significance of research questions, 28, 33–34
sign test, **237**
simple random sampling, **95,** 96, 99*f,* 101
simulations, **445**–46
single-subject design, **302,** 303–8. *See also* baselines (single-subject design)
A-B design, 304*f*–5
A-B-A design, 305*f*
A-B-A-B design, 305, 306*f*
A-B-C-B design, 303, 308*f*
B-A-B design, 306, 307*f*
graphing of, 303*f,* 304
multiple baseline designs, 307, 308*f,* 309*f,* 310*f,* 312
other types of, 314
practical action research example and, 596
single-subject research, **12,** 301–30
characteristics of, 302–3
designs for, 303–8*f,* 309*f,* 310*f,* 314
example of, 314–28
external validity of, 314
important findings in, 303
questions in, 27
threats to internal validity of, 309–14
situationists, 557
68-95-99.7 rule, **200***f,* 201
skewed polygons, 191–94
snowball sample, **434**
Social Science Citation Index (SSCI), 41–42
social sciences, chaos theory and, 8
social studies research
categories used to evaluate, 485*f*
content analysis of, 484–86
example of, 408–17
societal consequences, critical analysis and, 18, 19
sociogram, 132, 134*f,* 518
sociometric devices, **132,** 134*f,* 135*f*
software for content analysis, 486–87
sources of information
categories of, for historical research, 535–36
evaluating historical, 537–39
primary *vs.* secondary, 536
summarizing information from historical, 536–37
Spearman-Brown prophecy formula, 157
specific/concrete statements, 124, 125
spiders, Web, 54
split-half procedure, **157**
spreads, 197–201
averages *vs.,* 197, 198*f*
boxplots and, 198
quartiles, five-number summary, and, 198
range and, 198
standard deviation and, 198, 199*f,* 200*f,* 201
SSCI. *See* Social Science Citation Index (SSCI)
stakeholders, 14, **589,** 590, 592–93
standard deviation (SD), **198**–99, 200*f*
calculation of, 199*t*
calculation of mean, median, and, using Excel, 202
of normal distribution, 200–201
of sampling distribution, 222
standard error of estimate, **335**
standard error of measurement (SEMeas), **159***f*–60
standard error of the difference (SED), **227***f*
standard error of the mean (SEM), **223**–24
estimating, 224
standard scores, **190**
examples of, 204*f*
normal curve and, 201–4
T scores, 190, 203–4 (*see also T* scores)
z scores, 190, 201, 202*t*, 203, 204 (*see also z* scores)
Stanford Achievement Test, 128
Stanford-Binet Intelligence Scale, 131
static-group comparison design, **270***f*
static-group pretest-posttest design, **270**
statistical equating, **274***n*
statistical inference tests, 249. *See also* statistical significance
statistical index, validity of, 140
statistical matching, **274**–75, 369
statistical power analysis, 240
statistical significance, 228, **230**
level of, 228
null hypothesis as evaluation, 232–33
one-tailed and two-tailed test of, 230–32
practical significance *vs.,* 230–33
sample size and, 234
statistics, 185, **187,** 245–61
approaches to research including, 246–47*f*
categorical data and techniques of, 255–58
comparing groups using categorical data and, 255–57
comparing groups using quantitative data and, 247–51
descriptive (*see* descriptive statistics)
in ethnographic research, 516
inferential (*see* inferential statistics)
interpreting, 258
meta-analysis and, 49–50
parameters *vs.,* 187
quantitative data and techniques of, 247–55
recommendations on research and, 259
relating variables within a group using categorical data, 257
relating variables within a group using quantitative data, 251–55
summary of commonly used statistical techniques, 258*t*
status quo, investigations of, 18
stem-leaf plot, **194**–95
STEP. *See* Sequential Tests of Educational Progress (STEP)
straight-line (linear) relationship, **251**
stratified random sampling, **96,** 97*f,* 99, 102
stratified sampling, **480**
structural modeling, 339
structured interviews, 449
style(s), 48, 53. *See also* format(s)
style manual, 53, 622, 623*t*
subject(s), **20.** *See also* participant(s)
in action research, 14
characteristics of, 168
ensuring confidentiality of data from, 64, 66, 67
ethics and deception of, 64–65, 67
loss of (mortality), 168, 169*f,* 170, 180*t*
matching, 268, 273–75, 369
as own controls, 268
protecting from harm, 63, **64,** 66, 67
qualitative research and perspective of, 425
random assignment of, to groups, 267
regulations on research with, 71
subject attitude threat, **175**–76, 180*t*
in causal-comparative design, 370
in experimental design, 280, 283
in single-subject design, 314
subject characteristics threat, 168, 180*t*
in causal-comparative research, 368, 369*f,* 370–71
in correlational research, 342, 343*f,* 344*f,* 345–46
in group experimental studies, 268, 281–82
in single-subject studies, 314
subject-completed instruments, 114, 118, 126–36
achievement tests, 128–29, 130*f*
aptitude tests, 129–30, 131*f*
attitude scales, 127, 128*f,* 129*f,* 130*f*
item formats, 132–36
performance tests, 131, 132*f*
projective devices, 131–32, 133*f*
questionnaires, 126–27
self-checklists, 127*f*
sociometric devices, 132, 134*f,* 135*f*
Subject Guide to Books in Print, 40
subject headings, **43**
subject instruments, 114
subject terms, **43**
summative evaluations, **14**
supply items, 132, 136
survey(s)
characteristics of, 391
cross-sectional, 392
descriptive, 13, 15–16, 391
increasing response to, 406–7
interviews, 13 (*see also* interview(s))
survey research, 12–**13,** 390–420. *See also* interview(s); questionnaires
correlational research and, 393
data analysis in, 407
data collection for, 394–97
defined, **391**
example of, 408–17
important findings in, 397
instrumentation problems in, 407
low response to, 406
nonresponse to, 404–6
practical action research example using, 596–97
questions in, 28, 398–401, 402*f*
reasons for conducting, 391–92
steps in, 393–404
threats to internal validity of, 407
types of, 392
Web-based, 15, 394*t*–95*f*
syllogism, logic, 5
systematic sampling, **98**–100, 102, 103

Taba, Hilda, 126
table(s)
annotated, 52*f*
of random numbers, 95, 96*t*, A2
in research reports, 626
tabulating data, 141–42
tally sheet, **114,** 122, 123*f,* 484*t*
target population, **93**–94, 393–94
teacher(s), involvement in action research, 588–89, 592, 594
teacher research, 588–89
Teachers College, Columbia University, 40

"Teaching Social Studies in the 21st Century: A Research Study of Secondary Social Studies Teachers' Instructional Methods and Practices" (Russell), 408–17
analysis of, 416–17
team role playing, 445–46
telephone surveys, 394–95, 397*f*, 405
terms
defining, in content analysis, 479
defining, in questions, 30–33
defining key research, 20, 27
test(s). *See also* testing threat
achievement, 128–29, 130*f*
acquired from ERIC, 115, 116*f*, 117*f*
aptitude, 129–30, 131*f*
chi-square, 238, 516
high-stakes, 151
IQ, 159
Mann Whitney *U*, 237
performance, 131, 132*f*
questions on (*see* questions)
sign, 237
statistical inference, 249
in survey research, 398*n*
t-tests, 233–38, 239*t*, 371
testing, high stakes, 151
testing threat, **171,** 172, 180*t*
in correlational research, 345, 346
in experimental design, 270, 279, 280*t*, 283
in single-subject design, 314
test-retest method, **156**–57, 159*t*
Tests in Print, 116
textbooks, 39
"The 'Nuts and Dolts' of Teacher Images in Children's Picture Storybooks: A Content Analysis" (Sandefur, Moore), 488–99
analysis of, 499–500
theoretical framework, **425**–26, 427*t*
theoretical sample, **434**
theses used in literature reviews, 42, 44*f*, 56
thick description in ethnographic research, **508**
third quartile (Q_3), 198
threats to external validity
in correlational research, 345
threats to internal validity, **168**–80, 180*t*
in action research, 593
in causal-comparative research, 365, 368–71
commonly held beliefs and, 176
in correlational research, 341–45
data collector bias, 171–72, 283, 344, 369
data collector characteristics, 171, 283, 344, 346, 369
examples of, in everyday life, 176
experimental designs and control of (summary), 279, 280*t*, 281
experimental designs and evaluating likelihood of, 281–84
factors reducing likelihood of finding relationship, 179–80
history, 173–74
implementation, 177–78, 283–84
instrumentation, 170–72
instrument decay, 171, 344
location, 170
maturation, 174–75
meta-analysis and, 178
minimizing, 180–81
regression, 176, 177*f*
in single-subject research, 309–14
subject attitude, 175–76
subject characteristics, 168
subject loss (mortality), 168–70 (*see also* mortality)
summary of, 179*f*, 180*t*
in survey research, 407
testing, 172–73
time-and-motion logs, 125, 126*f*
time-series designs, **276,** 277*f*
transferability, 105, 435, 436, 563
treatment variable, **81, 265**
control of experimental, 284–85
trend study, **392**
triangulation, **456, 515, 557**
in action research, 592
in ethnographic research, 515*f*
in mixed-methods research, 557, 559*f*
triangulation design, **558,** 559*f*, 562
true-false items, 133
T scores, 190, **203**–4
t-test(s), 239*t*
in causal-comparative research, 371
for correlated means, 236
for correlated proportions, 238
for difference in proportions, 237
for independent proportions, 238
for means, 233–36
for *r*, 237
t-test for a difference in proportions, **237**–38, 239*t*
t-test for correlated means, **236,** 239*t*
t-test for correlated proportions, **238**
t-test for independent means, **234,** 239*t*
t-test for independent proportions, **238**
t-test for *r*, **237,** 239*t*
two-stage random sampling, **98,** 99*f*, 102
two-tailed test, **232***f*, 233*f*
Type I error, **232,** 233*f*
Type II error, **232,** 233*f*
typical sample, **434**

U.S. Bureau of the Census, 103, 392
U.S. Department of Education, 15, 39
U.S. Department of Health and Human Services (HHS), 69, 70
revised regulations for research with human subjects, 71
U.S. Job Corps program, 70
unit of analysis, **393**–94
in content analysis, 479
University of Chicago Manual of Style, 53
unobtrusive measures, **136**
Urban Institute, 56
usability, instrument, 113
validity, **113,** 148–55, **456, 483**
in action research, 589
checking (example), 158
concurrent, 153–54
consequential, 161
construct-related evidence of, 149, 150, 154–55, 159*t*
in content analysis, 483, 487
content-related evidence of, 149, 150*f*, 150–53, 159*t*
correlation coefficients and, 153, 341
criterion-related evidence of, 149, 150*f*, 153–54, 159*t*
defined, **13, 149**
evidence and, 149, 150*f*
external (*see* external validity)
importance of, 148
of indexes, 140
instrument, 113, 148
internal (*see* internal validity)
methods of checking, 158, 159*t*
predictive, 153–55
in qualitative research, 162, 456–57
quantitative *vs.* categorical, 78, 79*f*, 80–81, 138
reliability *vs.*, 155, 156*f*
research proposals/reports and instrument, 620
of self-study, 589
validity coefficient, **153,** 341
value(s),
critical analysis and question of, 17, 19
of literature reviews, 38
questions based on, 28
value of research, 4, 33–34
values (opinion) questions, **451**–52
variability, **197,** 198*f*
range and, 198
standard deviation and, 198–99
variable(s), **20, 78**–84
associations between categorical, 373–74
circle diagrams showing relationships among, 347*f*
correlational research and relationships among, 332, 333*t*
correlation coefficients and, degree of relationship between, 208*n*
correlation matrix for, 338*f*
criterion, 265, 334
defined, 78
dependent, 265
dependent *vs.* independent, 11, 81–82*f*, 84*n*
experimental, 81, 265
in experimental research, 265–66
extraneous, 83*f*–84*n*, 267, 268
interactions between, in factorial designs, 277
internal validity and, 347*f*
manipulated, 81
matching, 268, 367
measurement scales and, 138–41
mediator, 82–83
mixed-methods research and relationships among, 556
moderator, 82, 277
outcome, 82, 265
predictor, 334, 335–36
quantitative *vs.* categorical, 78, 79, 80–81, 138, 337
relating, within a group using categorical data, 257, 258*t*
relating, within groups using quantitative data, 251–55
reliability and, 155–62
scatterplots for combinations of, 343*f*
selected, 81
in single-subject design, 311
treatment, 81, 265, 284–85
validity and (*see* validity)
variable interest, 78
variance, 198
Friedman two-way analysis of, 237
Kruskal-Wallis one-way analysis of, 237
Venn diagrams, Boolean operators and, 46*f*
visual representation in ethnographic research, 516

WAIS-III. *See* Wechsler Adult Intelligence Scale (WAIS-III)
"Walk and Talk: An Intervention for Behaviorally Challenged Youths" (Doucette), 458–69
analysis of, 469–71
Warner Revised Occupational Rating, 621
ways of knowing, 4–7, 10*f*
Web (World Wide Web), **53.** *See also* Internet
instrumentation and, 116–17
searching databases on, 39, 43, 44–51, 53–55
surveys administered on, 15, 394–95*f*
Web browser, **53**
Web crawlers, 54
Web of Science, 56
Wechsler Adult Intelligence Scale (WAIS-III), 131
Wechsler Intelligence Scale for Children (WISC-III), 131
Wilk's lambda, **237**
WISC-III. *See* Wechsler Intelligence Scale for Children (WISC-III)
World Wide Web (WWW), **53.** *See also* Web (World Wide Web)
worldviews, research and, 425
written-response instruments, **117**
WWW. *See* Web (World Wide Web)

z scores, 190, **201**–2
comparison of raw scores and, 202*t*
importance of normal curve and, 204
means expressed as, 224
negative, 203
probability and, 202–3